OXFORD

The world's most trusted dictionaries

LEARNER'S
FRENCH
Dictionary

Project Management
Nicholas Rollin • Joanna Rubery

Editors
Isabelle Stables-Lemoine • Mary O'Neill
Pat Bulhosen • Alain Nogaret • Gabrielle Goldet
Amanda Leigh

Consultants
Danièle Bourdais • Sue Finnie

OXFORD
UNIVERSITY PRESS

Great Clarendon Street, Oxford OX2 6DP

Oxford University Press is a department of the University of Oxford.
It furthers the University's objective of excellence in research,
scholarship, and education by publishing worldwide in

Oxford   New York

Auckland   Cape Town   Dar es Salaam   Hong Kong   Karachi
Kuala Lumpur   Madrid   Melbourne   Mexico City   Nairobi
New Delhi   Shanghai   Taipei   Toronto

With offices in

Argentina   Austria   Brazil   Chile   Czech Republic   France   Greece
Guatemala   Hungary   Italy   Japan   Poland   Portugal   Singapore
South Korea   Switzerland   Thailand   Turkey   Ukraine   Vietnam

Oxford is a registered trade mark of Oxford University Press
in the UK and in certain other countries

Illustrations © El primo Ramón (Borja Ramón López Cotelo)

Photocredits: Car mechanic and goalkeeper©wavebreakmedia/Shutterstock • Eating out
©Monkey Business Images/Shutterstock • Cinema©Nestor Rizhniak/Shutterstock.com
• Wind turbines©Ferenc Cegledi/Shutterstock • Glastonbury Festival©antb/Shutterstock

First published 2006
Second edition 2012
This edition 2017

British Library Cataloguing in Pub
Data available

ISBN: 978-0-19-840798-0

10 9 8 7 6 5 4 3 2

Printed in China by Golden Cup

Contents

Introduction

This bilingual dictionary has been specifically written for
students of French – from those just starting out all the way up
to those preparing for exams. It presents essential information
in a format designed to be clear and easy to consult. There are
two main sections: **FRENCH – ENGLISH** and **ENGLISH – FRENCH**.
These sections are divided by a central, '**Using your French**'
section in full colour.

TIP *To help you find words quickly, the first word on each page is
printed top left and the last word on the page is printed top right.*

FRENCH – ENGLISH

Look up French words – listed alphabetically – to find their
meaning in English. When a word has more than one meaning,
make sure you choose the one that is most relevant.

TIP *Look at the number after a verb you look up and find that
number in the verb table: it shows the endings for that verb.*

ENGLISH – FRENCH

Look up English words – listed alphabetically – to find out how
to say them in French. When you find the French word, the
entry will tell you whether it is masculine *(MASC)* or feminine
(FEM). To choose the right word and use it properly, make sure
you read through the examples provided.

TIP *To find out more about the French translation that you are
given, look it up on the **FRENCH – ENGLISH** side of the dictionary
afterwards.*

'Using your French' colour section

In the colour section you will find: verb tables for regular verbs
and most common irregular verbs, and key vocabulary to
help you prepare for your exams. There are useful phrases for
role play and sample questions and answers for photo card
activities. These will help you to build your own answers using
them as a guide.

Get to know your dictionary

User-friendly layout

- **Two-colour layout**
  In this dictionary, all the French words are in blue and all the English words are in **black** for easy identification.

- **Easy to navigate**
  The alphabet runs down the side of each page indicating what letter you are looking at, and whether you are on the **FRENCH – ENGLISH** or **ENGLISH – FRENCH** side of the dictionary:

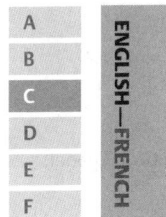

- **Symbols explained**
  The key symbols and être symbols are explained along the bottom of every other page.

  ℘ indicates key words

  ◍ means the verb takes être to form the perfect

Clear entries

- **Word classes written out in full**
  NOUN, VERB, ADJECTIVE, ADVERB, CONJUNCTION, PREPOSITION, DETERMINER or *PRONOUN* are all written out clearly after the headword:

  calmement *ADVERB*
  calmly

- **Gender of nouns doubly clear**
  Both the definite (or if appropriate, the indefinite) article and the abbreviations *MASC* and *FEM* are used on both sides of the dictionary to make it clear whether a word is masculine or feminine.

  ℘ **balcony** *NOUN*　　　　　℘ le **balcon** *MASC NOUN*
  　le **balcon** *MASC*

  Other abbreviations used are:

PL	plural	*ADV*	adverb
ADJ	adjective	*PREP*	preposition
PRON	pronoun		

- **All variations shown**

  Both the masculine and feminine singular, and the masculine and feminine plural forms of adjectives are usually shown:

  central MASC ADJECTIVE, **centrale** FEM,
  centraux MASC PL, **centrales** FEM PL

  ♂ **beautiful** ADJECTIVE
  beau MASC, bel MASC, belle FEM, beaux MASC
  PL, belles FEM PL

- **Pointers to other word classes**

  Where a word can do more than one job (be a noun *and* a verb, for example), a helpful pointer reminds students to check other word classes:

  ♂ **back** ADJECTIVE ▶ SEE **back** ADVERB, VERB, NOUN

Extra help with verbs

- **Heavy-duty verbs**

  Common verbs are given special treatment in tinted panels:

  > ♂ **aller** VERB ◉ [7]
  > ▶ SEE **aller** NOUN
  > **1 to go**
  > Je vais à Paris. I'm going to Paris.
  > Je vais chez le boulanger. I'm going to the baker's.

- **Verb tables in centre section**

  The centre section contains full conjugations for regular -er, -ir and -re verbs plus the most common irregular verbs.

- **Links to verb tables**

  On both sides of the dictionary, each French verb is followed by a number linking it to the central verb tables:

  to **baptize** VERB   **chatouiller** VERB [1]
  baptiser [1]   to tickle

- **Use of 'to' before a verb**

  On the **ENGLISH – FRENCH** side of the dictionary, English verbs are preceded by 'to' *(see above)*.

- **Conjugations with être**

  A symbol ◉ reminds you that this particular verb is conjugated with être in the perfect tense:

  se **cacher** REFLEXIVE VERB ◉
  to hide

- **Irregular forms of verbs**

  If you look up past participles and non-infinitive forms of a verb, you are cross-referenced to the relevant headword:

  a VERB ▶ SEE **avoir**

Extra help with difficult points of French

• Help with grammar and spelling

'Word tips' give extra help with tricky grammatical points and reminders on how French spelling is different from English:

WORD TIP Adjectives never have capitals in French, even for nationality or regional origin.

• Typical problematic areas

Extra help is given with traditionally problematic areas, such as agreement in French:

℗ **by** *PREPOSITION*

5 *(with myself, yourself, etc)* **tout seul** *MASC,*
toute seule *FEM*
by yourself tout seul *(boy, man),* toute
seule *(girl, woman)*
I was by myself. J'étais tout seul *(boy
speaking),* J'étais toute seule *(girl speaking).*
She did it by herself. Elle l'a fait toute seule.

• False friends

False friends are shown on the **FRENCH – ENGLISH** side of the dictionary:

WORD TIP actuel does not mean **actual** in English; for the meaning of **actual** ▸ SEE **vrai**

Language in context – example sentences

• Thousands of example sentences

Thousands of examples of 'real language' at an appropriate level for the age group, progressing from simpler to more complex sentences:

℗ to **phone** *VERB* ▸ SEE **phone** *NOUN*
1 téléphoner [1]
while I was phoning pendant que je
téléphonais
It's quicker to phone. Ça va plus vite de
téléphoner.
Phone up and ask for information.
Téléphone et demande-leur des
renseignements.

• Correctly punctuated

All example sentences are correctly punctuated with capital letters and full stops *(see above).*

Additional features

• Core vocabulary highlighted

All the key curriculum words secondary school pupils need are highlighted with a key to help you prepare for your exams.

ℓ le **manteau** *MASC NOUN*, les **manteaux** *PLURAL*
    coat

• Using your French colour section

The full-colour centre section will help you communicate in both written and spoken French.

• Mini-infos

Boxed notes provide interesting cultural information throughout the alphabetical entries:

> **⬤ CYCLING**
>
> The Tour de France cycle race takes place in France every summer. The 4,000 kilometre route changes every year but always finishes in Paris. The previous day's winner wears a special yellow jersey.

> **⬤ POSTE**
>
> Les boîtes aux lettres de la Poste sont rectangulaires et jaunes.

• Language functions covered

Exam syllabus language functions, such as requests and demands, are covered within example sentences:

ℓ le **café** *MASC NOUN*
  1 coffee
    prendre un café to have a coffee
    Vous prendrez un café? Would you like a coffee? *(formal)*
    Tu veux prendre un café? Do you want a coffee? *(informal)*
  2 cafe
    aller au café to go to the cafe
    Leila va au café tous les midis. Leila goes to the cafe every lunchtime.
  • le café au lait
    white coffee
  • le café-crème
    white coffee
  • le café en grains
    coffee beans
  • le café instantané
    instant coffee
  • le café moulu
    ground coffee
  • le café soluble
    instant coffee
  • le café-tabac
    cafe *(where you can buy cigarettes and stamps)*

Aa

a *VERB* ▸ SEE **avoir**

ℓ **à** *PREPOSITION*

1 at
à la maison at home
à l'école at school
au marché at the market
à deux heures at two o'clock
À quelle heure? At what time?

2 in
à Londres in London
à la campagne in the country
au printemps in the spring
assis au soleil sitting in the sun

3 to
aller à Paris to go to Paris
aller aux États-Unis to go to the United States
Donnez l'argent à Julie. Give the money to Julie.

4 *(showing how)* à vélo by bike
Tu viens à vélo? Are you coming by bike?
aller à pied to go on foot

5 with
une fille aux yeux bleus a girl with blue eyes
le garçon aux lunettes the boy with glasses

6 *(in distances)* à trois kilomètres d'ici three kilometres from here
à quelques mètres de la route a few metres from the road
à 100 kilomètres de Paris 100 kilometres from Paris

7 *(showing ownership)* Ce bracelet est à Natalie. This bracelet belongs to Natalie.
À qui est ce portable? Whose is this mobile?
C'est à moi. It's mine.

8 *(showing where)* à côté de beside
à droite on the right
à gauche on the left
à l'étranger abroad

9 *(in notices, etc)* 'À vendre' 'For sale'
'Vélos à louer' 'Bicycles for hire'

> **WORD TIP** à + le gives au; à + les gives aux.

abandonner *VERB* [1]

1 to give up
Elle a abandonné les maths. She has given up maths.

2 to abandon
un enfant abandonné an abandoned child

un **abat-jour** *MASC NOUN*
lampshade

un **abattoir** *MASC NOUN*
slaughterhouse

abattre *VERB* [21]

1 to shoot down *(a person)*
2 to slaughter *(an animal)*
3 to demolish *(a building)*
4 to cut down *(a tree)*

une **abbaye** *FEM NOUN*
abbey
l'abbaye de Westminster Westminster Abbey

un **abbé** *MASC NOUN*
priest

une **abeille** *FEM NOUN*
bee

abîmer *VERB* [1]

1 to damage
2 to ruin
La grêle a abîmé les raisins. The hail has ruined the grapes.

s'**abîmer** *REFLEXIVE VERB* ◎

1 to get damaged
2 to go bad *(fruit, meat, etc)*

abolir *VERB* [2]
to abolish

abominable *MASC & FEM ADJECTIVE*
abominable

une **abondance** *FEM NOUN*
Il y a des fruits en abondance. There's plenty of fruit.

un **abonné** *MASC NOUN*, une **abonnée** *FEM* ▸ SEE
abonné *ADJECTIVE*

1 season ticket holder *(for bus, train, etc)*
2 subscriber *(to a magazine)*

abonné *MASC ADJECTIVE*, **abonnée** *FEM* ▸ SEE
abonné *NOUN*

1 être abonné to have a season ticket
2 être abonné to have a subscription

un **abonnement** *MASC NOUN*

1 subscription
2 season ticket

s'**abonner** *REFLEXIVE VERB* ◎ [1]
s'abonner à quelque chose to subscribe to something
Je m'abonne à un magazine de musique rock. I subscribe to a rock music magazine.

abord *MASC NOUN*

1 ▸ SEE **d'abord**
2 les abords the surrounding area

abordable *MASC & FEM ADJECTIVE*

1 affordable *(prices)*
2 approachable *(person)*

aborder *VERB* [1]

1 to tackle *(a problem)*
2 to approach *(a person)*

aboutir *VERB* [2]
1 aboutir à quelque chose to lead to something
2 aboutir à to end up in
Nous avons abouti à Rennes. We ended up in Rennes.

aboyer *VERB* [39]
to bark

abrégé *MASC ADJECTIVE*, **abrégée** *FEM*
abridged
la version abrégée the abridged version

une **abréviation** *FEM NOUN*
abbreviation

un **abri** *MASC NOUN*
1 shelter
trouver un abri to take shelter
2 shed
3 être à l'abri de quelque chose to be sheltered from something
Nous étions à l'abri du vent. We were sheltered from the wind.

ℓ un **abricot** *MASC NOUN*
apricot

un **abricotier** *MASC NOUN*
apricot tree

abriter *VERB* [1]
to shelter
s'**abriter** *REFLEXIVE VERB* ●
to take shelter

abrupt *MASC ADJECTIVE*, **abrupte** *FEM*
1 steep *(slope, path, etc)*
2 abrupt *(in manner, tone)*

abrutir *VERB* [2]
1 to deafen
2 to stupefy *(from work, heat, etc)*

une **absence** *FEM NOUN*
absence
pendant mon absence while I was away

ℓ **absent** *MASC ADJECTIVE*, **absente** *FEM*
1 être absent to be out, to be away
Je serai absent pendant une heure. I'll be out for an hour.
2 absent *(from school, work)*
Elle était absente hier. She was absent yesterday.

s'**absenter** *REFLEXIVE VERB* ● [1]
to go away
Elle s'est absentée pendant deux jours. She was away for two days.

absolu *MASC ADJECTIVE*, **absolue** *FEM*
absolute

ℓ **absolument** *ADVERB*
absolutely

absorbant *MASC ADJECTIVE*, **absorbante** *FEM*
1 absorbing *(book, story)*
2 absorbent *(cloth)*

absorber *VERB* [1]
1 to absorb
2 to take *(food, drink)*

absurde *MASC & FEM ADJECTIVE*
absurd

l'**absurdité** *FEM NOUN*
1 absurdity *(of a situation)*
2 des absurdités nonsense
Il dit des absurdités. He's talking nonsense.

l'**abus** *MASC NOUN*
abuse
l'abus d'alcool alcohol abuse

abuser *VERB* [1]
1 abuser de quelque chose to misuse
abuser de l'alcool to drink too much *(regularly)*
2 abuser de ta gentillesse to take advantage of your kindness

abusif *MASC ADJECTIVE*, **abusive** *FEM*
1 excessive
2 unfair

l'**acajou** *MASC NOUN*
mahogany

accablant *MASC ADJECTIVE*, **accablante** *FEM*
overwhelming

un **accélérateur** *MASC NOUN*
accelerator

l'**accélération** *FEM NOUN*
acceleration

accélérer *VERB* [24]
1 to speed up *(a process)*
2 to accelerate *(in a car)*

ℓ un **accent** *MASC NOUN*
1 accent
un accent étranger a foreign accent
2 accent *(in French spelling)*
Ça s'écrit avec ou sans accent? Is it spelt with or without an accent?
• un accent aigu
acute accent *(as in é)*
• un accent grave
grave accent *(as in è)*
• un accent circonflexe
circumflex *(as in ê)*

accentuer *VERB* [1]
to stress

accepter *VERB* [1]
1 to accept
J'ai accepté son invitation. I accepted her invitation.

2 accepter de faire quelque chose to agree to do something
Elle a accepté de m'aider. She agreed to help me.

un **accès** MASC NOUN
1 access
'Accès interdit' 'No entry'
2 outburst
un accès de colère an outburst of rage

accessible MASC & FEM ADJECTIVE
1 accessible (place)
C'est un livre accessible. It's an easy book to read.
2 affordable
des prix accessibles affordable prices

un **accessoire** MASC NOUN
accessory
• les accessoires
fashion accessories

♟ un **accident** MASC NOUN
1 accident
un accident de la route a road accident
avoir un accident to have an accident
2 hitch
Il y a eu un petit accident. There's been a slight hitch.

accidenté MASC ADJECTIVE, **accidentée** FEM
1 injured
2 damaged
3 uneven
'Chaussée accidentée' 'Uneven road surface'

un **accompagnateur** MASC NOUN, une
accompagnatrice FEM
1 tourist guide
2 courier (for package holidays)
3 accompanying adult (with a child)
4 accompanist (for a singer)

♟ **accompagner** VERB [1]
1 to accompany
Je t'accompagne. I'll go with you., I'll come with you.
Je t'accompagne jusqu'à chez toi. I'll see you home.
2 accompagné de quelqu'un accompanied by somebody
Elle est partie accompagnée de son frère. She left accompanied by her brother.
3 to accompany (on the piano)

accomplir VERB [2]
to carry out (a task, a project)

♟ un **accord** MASC NOUN
1 agreement
2 d'accord all right
Je suis d'accord. I agree.
Je ne suis pas d'accord avec Odile. I don't

agree with Odile.
être d'accord pour faire quelque chose to agree to do something
Paul est d'accord pour venir avec nous. Paul's agreed to come with us.
se mettre d'accord to come to an agreement
Ils se sont mis d'accord sur le prix. They agreed on the price.

un **accordéon** MASC NOUN
accordeon

accorder VERB [1]
1 to grant (permission)
2 to tune (an instrument)
s'**accorder** REFLEXIVE VERB ◉
to agree
Nous nous sommes accordés sur le prix. We agreed on the price.

un **accotement** MASC NOUN
verge (beside a road)

accoucher VERB [1]
to give birth

accoutumé MASC ADJECTIVE, **accoutumée** FEM
1 usual
2 être accoutumé à quelque chose to be accustomed to something

s'**accoutumer** REFLEXIVE VERB ◉ [1]
s'accoutumer à faire quelque chose to get used to doing something
On s'accoutume à se lever tôt. You get used to getting up early.

accro MASC & FEM ADJECTIVE
(informal) être accro de quelque chose to be hooked on something
Il est complètement accro de la télé. He's completely hooked on the telly.

un **accroc** MASC NOUN
1 tear (in clothes)
2 hitch
sans accrocs without a hitch

accrocher VERB [1]
to hang
accrocher un tableau au mur to hang a picture on the wall
s'**accrocher** REFLEXIVE VERB ◉ [1]
s'accrocher à quelque chose to hold on to something

s'**accroupir** REFLEXIVE VERB ◉ [2]
to crouch (down), to squat

un **accueil** MASC NOUN
1 welcome
un accueil chaleureux a warm welcome
2 reception desk
Madame Martin est priée de se présenter à l'accueil. Would Mrs Martin please go to the

reception desk.

accueillir VERB [35]
1 **to welcome**
être bien accueilli to be given a warm welcome
être accueilli par quelque chose to be greeted with something
Ils sont accueillis par des acclamations. They are greeted with cheers.
2 **to receive** (guests, visitors)

accumuler VERB [1]
to collect

s'**accumuler** REFLEXIVE VERB ⬆
to pile up (leaves, problems, etc)

une **accusation** FEM NOUN
accusation

un **accusé de réception** MASC NOUN
recorded delivery
envoyer une lettre avec accusé de réception to send a letter by recorded delivery

accuser VERB [1]
to accuse
accuser quelqu'un d'avoir fait quelque chose to accuse somebody of doing something
Il m'a accusé d'avoir volé son stylo. He accused me of stealing his pen.

s'**acharner** REFLEXIVE VERB ⬆ [1]
s'acharner à faire quelque chose to keep on doing something
Ils s'acharnent à la taquiner. They keep on teasing her.

♟ un **achat** MASC NOUN
purchase
j'ai fait plusieurs achats I've bought several things

♟ **acheter** VERB [16]
1 **to buy**
Je vais acheter du pain. I'm going to buy some bread.
2 acheter quelque chose pour quelqu'un to buy somebody something
Il m'a acheté un cadeau. He bought me a present.
Qu'est-ce que tu lui achètes? What are you buying for him?
3 acheter quelque chose à quelqu'un to buy something from somebody
C'est Lisa qui m'a acheté le portable. Lisa bought my mobile from me.

un **acheteur** MASC NOUN, une **acheteuse** FEM
buyer

achever VERB [50]
1 **to finish** (an assignment)

2 **to finish off** (to kill)

acide MASC & FEM ADJECTIVE ▸ SEE **acide** NOUN
sharp, **sour** (taste)

un **acide** MASC NOUN ▸ SEE **acide** ADJECTIVE
acid

l'**acier** MASC NOUN
steel

l'**acné** FEM NOUN
acne

une **acoustique** FEM NOUN
acoustics

acquérir VERB [17]
to acquire

un & une **acrobate** MASC & FEM NOUN
acrobat

l'**acrobatie** FEM NOUN
acrobatics

un **acte** MASC NOUN
1 **act**
2 **deed** (legal document)

♟ un **acteur** MASC NOUN
actor

actif MASC ADJECTIVE, **active** FEM
active
la vie active working life

une **action** FEM NOUN
1 **action**
un film d'action an action film
une bonne action a good deed
2 **effect**

activement ADVERB
actively

activer VERB [1]
to speed up (a process, work)

s'**activer** REFLEXIVE VERB ⬆
to hurry up
Il faudrait s'activer là! We'd better hurry up!

♟ une **activité** FEM NOUN
activity
• une activité professionelle
occupation

♟ un **actrice** FEM NOUN
actress

♟ l'**actualité** FEM NOUN
1 les actualités news
regarder les actualités à la télévision to watch the news on television
2 **current affairs**
s'intéresser à l'actualité to be interested in current affairs

actuel MASC ADJECTIVE, **actuelle** FEM
present

⬆ means the verb takes être to form the perfect

la situation actuelle the present situation
le monde actuel today's world

WORD TIP actuel does not mean **actual** in
English; for the meaning of **actual** ▸ SEE **vrai**.

actuellement ADVERB
at present

WORD TIP actuellement does not mean **actually**
in English; for the meaning of **actually** ▸ SEE **fait**
ADVERB.

adapté MASC ADJECTIVE, **adaptée** FEM
1 **suitable**
des vêtements adaptés aux climats chauds
clothes suitable for a warm climate
2 **adjusted**
une élève bien adaptée a well-adjusted
student
3 **adapted** (for the cinema, TV, theatre)

adapter VERB [1]
to adapt
s'**adapter** REFLEXIVE VERB ◎
s'adapter à quelque chose to get used to
something
Nous nous sommes adaptés à la situation.
We've got used to the situation.

un **additif** MASC NOUN
additive

ℙ une **addition** FEM NOUN
1 **bill** (in a restaurant)
L'addition, s'il vous plaît. Can I have the bill
please?
2 **addition** (in arithmetic)

additionner VERB [1]
to add up

adhésif MASC ADJECTIVE, **adhésive** FEM
adhesive (tape, etc)

un **adieu** MASC NOUN, les **adieux** PL
goodbye, farewell (for ever)

un **adjectif** MASC NOUN
(Grammar) adjective

un **adjoint** MASC NOUN, une **adjointe** FEM
1 **assistant**
2 **deputy**

admettre VERB [11]
1 **to admit**
Il faut admettre qu'ils ont raison. You have
to admit that they're right.
2 **to allow in** (dogs, children, etc)
Les chiens ne sont pas admis. Dogs are not
allowed in.
3 **to suppose**
Admettons que la France gagne. Let's
suppose that France wins.

une **administration** FEM NOUN
administration

l'**admiration** FEM NOUN
admiration

admirer VERB [1]
to admire

un & une **ado** MASC & FEM NOUN
(informal) teenager, adolescent

une **adolescence** FEM NOUN
adolescence

ℙ un **adolescent** MASC NOUN, une **adolescente**
FEM ▸ SEE **adolescent** ADJECTIVE
teenager, adolescent

ℙ **adolescent** MASC ADJECTIVE, **adolescente** FEM
▸ SEE **adolescent** NOUN
teenage, adolescent

adopter VERB [1]
to adopt

adoptif MASC ADJECTIVE, **adoptive** FEM
adopted
un enfant adoptif an adopted child

une **adoption** FEM NOUN
adoption

adorable MASC & FEM ADJECTIVE
adorable

adorer VERB [1]
to love, to adore

ℙ une **adresse** FEM NOUN
1 **address**
Quelle est ton adresse? What's your
address?
Vous vous êtes trompé d'adresse. You've
got the wrong address.
2 **skill**
Elle fait ça avec beaucoup d'adresse. She
does that very skilfully.
3 **speech**
• une adresse électronique, une adresse
email
email address

adresser VERB [1]
1 adresser une lettre to address a letter
2 adresser une lettre à quelqu'un to send
somebody a letter
3 adresser la parole à quelqu'un to speak to
somebody
Elle ne m'adresse jamais la parole. She
never speaks to me.
s'**adresser** REFLEXIVE VERB ◎
1 s'adresser à to enquire at
Adressez-vous à la réception. Enquire at
reception.
2 s'adresser à quelqu'un to be aimed at
somebody

Le film s'adresse aux adolescents. The film is aimed at teenagers.

adroit *MASC ADJECTIVE*, **adroite** *FEM*
skilful

ℓ **adulte** *MASC & FEM ADJECTIVE* ▸ SEE **adulte** *NOUN*
adult

ℓ un **adulte** *MASC & FEM NOUN* ▸ SEE **adulte** *ADJECTIVE*
adult

un **adverbe** *MASC NOUN*
(Grammar) adverb

un & une **adversaire** *MASC & FEM NOUN*
opponent

adverse *MASC & FEM ADJECTIVE*
opposing

l'**aération** *FEM NOUN*
ventilation

l'**aérobic** *MASC NOUN*
aerobics
faire de l'aérobic to do aerobics

une **aérogare** *FEM NOUN*
terminal *(in an airport)*

l'**aéroglisseur** *MASC NOUN*
hovercraft

l'**aéronautique** *FEM NOUN*
aeronautics

ℓ un **aéroport** *MASC NOUN*
airport
à l'aéroport at the airport, to the airport

un **aérosol** *MASC NOUN*
aerosol

une **affaire** *FEM NOUN* ▸ SEE **affaires**
1 business
une sale affaire a nasty business
2 matter
C'est une autre affaire. That's another matter.
3 affair *(scandal)*
4 bargain
Ça, c'est une affaire! That's a real bargain!

ℓ les **affaires** *PLURAL FEM NOUN* ▸ SEE **affaire**
1 business
les affaires business
un homme d'affaires a businessman
une femme d'affaires a businesswoman
un voyage d'affaires a business trip
2 business *(personal information)*
Occupe-toi de tes affaires! Mind your own business!
3 belongings
Tu peux laisser tes affaires dans la chambre. You can leave your things in the bedroom.

affamé *MASC ADJECTIVE*, **affamée** *FEM*
starving

affamer *VERB* [1]
to starve

affecter *VERB* [1]
to affect

l'**affection** *FEM NOUN*
affection

affectueusement *ADVERB*
affectionately

affectueux *MASC ADJECTIVE*, **affectueuse** *FEM*
affectionate

ℓ une **affiche** *FEM NOUN*
1 poster
mettre des affiches to put posters up
2 notice

afficher *VERB* [1]
1 to put up *(posters, pictures)*
'Défense d'afficher' 'Stick no bills'
2 to display *(on a computer screen)*

affligeant *MASC ADJECTIVE*, **affligeante** *FEM*
distressing, pathetic

affliger *VERB* [52]
to distress

une **affluence** *FEM NOUN*
crowds *(at busy times in shops, streets)*
aux heures d'affluence at peak times

affoler *VERB* [1]
affoler quelqu'un to send somebody into a panic
s'**affoler** *REFLEXIVE VERB* ◉
to panic
Ne t'affole pas. Don't panic.

ℓ **affreux** *MASC ADJECTIVE*, **affreuse** *FEM*
1 dreadful
un accident affreux a dreadful accident
Le temps était affreux. The weather was dreadful.
2 hideous
une couleur affreuse a hideous colour

afin *PREPOSITION*
1 afin de faire quelque chose in order to do something
afin de travailler ensemble in order to work together
2 afin que ... so that ...
Je lui ai écrit afin qu'il ne se sente pas abandonné. I wrote to him so that he wouldn't feel so neglected.

africain *MASC ADJECTIVE*, **africaine** *FEM* ▸ SEE
Africain
African

◉ means the verb takes être to form the perfect

un **Africain** MASC NOUN, une **Africaine** FEM ▶SEE
africain
African

l'**Afrique** FEM NOUN
Africa

agaçant MASC ADJECTIVE, **agaçante** FEM
annoying

agacer VERB [61]
to annoy
Ça m'agace! That gets on my nerves!

ℓ un **âge** MASC NOUN
age
à l'âge de cinq ans at the age of five
Quel âge as-tu? How old are you?
Il a l'âge de mon père. He's the same age as
my father.
Elle a l'âge de voyager seule. She's old
enough to travel on her own.

ℓ **âgé** MASC ADJECTIVE, **âgée** FEM
1 old
les personnes âgées old people
Audrey est deux ans plus âgée que moi.
Audrey is two years older than me.
2 **âgé de** aged
une femme âgée de trente ans a woman
aged thirty

ℓ une **agence** FEM NOUN
1 agency
2 branch (of a bank)
• une agence de voyages
travel agent's
• une agence immobilière
estate agent's

un **agenda** MASC NOUN
diary

ℓ un **agent** MASC NOUN
1 official
2 agent
• un agent commercial
sales rep

ℓ un **agent de police** MASC NOUN, une **agente
de police** FEM
police officer

aggraver VERB [1]
to make worse
aggraver la situation to make things worse
s'**aggraver** REFLEXIVE VERB ◎
to get worse
La situation s'aggrave. Things are getting
worse.

agir VERB [2]
1 to act, to take action
Il faut agir. We've got to act.
2 to behave
agir comme un idiot to behave like an idiot

s'**agir** REFLEXIVE VERB ◎
s'agir de quelque chose to be about
something
De quoi s'agit-il? What's it about?
Il s'agit de ton frère. It's about your brother.

l'**agitation** FEM NOUN
1 hustle and bustle
2 unrest
3 restlessness

agité MASC ADJECTIVE, **agitée** FEM
1 restless
2 rough (sea)
3 bustling (street)

agiter VERB [1]
to shake
agiter la main to wave your hand

ℓ un **agneau** MASC NOUN, les **agneaux** PL
lamb

une **agrafe** FEM NOUN
1 staple
2 hook (in clothes)

agrafer VERB [1]
1 to staple
2 to fasten

une **agrafeuse** FEM NOUN
stapler

agrandir VERB [2]
1 to enlarge (a photo)
2 to extend (a house)

un **agrandissement** MASC NOUN
1 enlargement (of a photo)
2 extension (of a house)

ℓ **agréable** MASC & FEM ADJECTIVE
pleasant, nice

agréer VERB [32]
1 to agree to
2 Veuillez agréer l'expression de mes
sentiments respectueux. Yours faithfully,
Yours sincerely,

WORD TIP A typical ending for a formal letter.

agresser VERB [1]
1 to attack
2 to mug
Il a été agressé dans le parking. He was
mugged in the car park.
se faire agresser to get mugged

un **agresseur** MASC NOUN
attacker

agressif MASC ADJECTIVE, **agressive** FEM
aggressive

une **agression** FEM NOUN
1 attack

2 mugging

l'**agressivité** *FEM NOUN*
  aggressiveness

agricole *MASC & FEM ADJECTIVE*
  agricultural

♂ un **agriculteur** *MASC NOUN*, une **agricultrice**
  FEM
  farmer

ai *VERB* ▸ SEE **avoir**

une **aide** *FEM NOUN* ▸ SEE **aide** *NOUN*
1 help
  avec l'aide de Claire with Claire's help
  à l'aide de quelque chose with the help of
  something
  à l'aide d'un ordinateur with the help of a
  computer
  venir à l'aide de quelqu'un to help
  somebody
2 aid *(to a person, country)*

un & une **aide** *MASC & FEM NOUN* ▸ SEE **aide** *NOUN*
1 assistant
2 helper

♂ **aider** *VERB* [1]
1 to help
  Est-ce que je peux t'aider? Would you like
  some help?
  Aide-moi. Help me.
  aider quelqu'un à faire quelque chose to
  help somebody to do something
  Il m'a aidé à faire mes devoirs. He helped
  me do my homework.
2 to give aid to *(a person, a country)*

aie, **aies**, **ait**, **aient** *VERB* ▸ SEE **avoir**

un **aigle** *MASC & FEM NOUN*
  eagle

un **aiglefin** *MASC NOUN*
  haddock

aigre *MASC & FEM ADJECTIVE*
1 sour *(taste)*
2 sharp *(tone)*

aigu *MASC ADJECTIVE*, **aiguë** *FEM*
1 high-pitched *(sound)*
2 acute *(very bad)*
  une douleur aiguë acute pain

une **aiguille** *FEM NOUN*
1 needle
2 hand *(on a watch)*
  dans le sens des aiguilles d'une montre
  clockwise

un **aiguilleur du ciel** *MASC NOUN*, une
  aiguilleuse du ciel *FEM*
  air traffic controller

un **ail** *MASC NOUN*
  garlic
  à l'ail with garlic

une **aile** *FEM NOUN*
  wing

ailleurs *ADVERB*
1 somewhere else
  partout ailleurs everywhere else
  nulle part ailleurs nowhere else
2 d'ailleurs besides

♂ **aimable** *MASC & FEM ADJECTIVE*
  kind, **nice**
  Vous êtes très aimable. That's very kind
  of you.
  Ils ne sont pas du tout aimables. They're
  really not very nice.

un **aimant** *MASC NOUN*
  magnet

♂ **aimer** *VERB* [1]
1 to like
  Est-ce que tu aimes les fraises? Do you like
  strawberries?
  J'aime le poisson. I like fish.
  J'aime ça! I like it!
  aimer faire quelque chose to like doing
  something
  Elle aime aller au cinéma. She likes going to
  the cinema.
  Elle aimerait aller au cinéma. She'd like to
  go to the cinema.
  J'ai toujours aimé aller à la plage. I've
  always liked going to the beach.
2 aimer mieux to prefer
  J'aime mieux les fraises que les framboises.
  I prefer strawberries to raspberries
  J'aimerais mieux aller au cinéma. I'd rather
  go to the cinema.
3 to love
  Je t'aime. I love you.
4 aimer bien to like
  J'aime bien les frites. I like chips.
  On aime bien faire du camping. We like
  going camping.
  Elle aimerait bien un portable. She would
  like a mobile phone.
  J'aimerais bien savoir. I'd like to know.

---

s'**aimer** *REFLEXIVE VERB* ⏺
1 to love each other
2 to like each other
  Ils ne s'aiment pas beaucoup. They don't
  like each other much.

♂ **aîné** *MASC ADJECTIVE*, **aînée** *FEM* ▸ SEE **aîné** *NOUN*
1 elder, **older** *(of two)*
  leur fils aîné their elder son
2 eldest, **oldest** *(of more than two)*

⏺ means the verb takes être to form the perfect

ma sœur aînée my eldest sister

ℱ un **aîné** MASC NOUN, une **aînée** FEM ► SEE **aîné**
ADJECTIVE
l'aîné the eldest, the oldest *(boy)*
l'aînée the eldest, the oldest *(girl)*

ainsi ADVERB
1 so, thus
C'est ainsi que l'on fait. That's the way you
do it.
2 in this way
3 ainsi que as well as, along with

un **aïoli** MASC NOUN
garlic mayonnaise

ℱ un **air** MASC NOUN
1 air
en plein air in the open air
2 avoir l'air ... to look ...
Le gâteau a l'air bon. The cake looks
good.
Chloë a l'air très fatiguée. Chloë looks very
tired.
3 avoir l'air de to look like
Il a l'air d'un policier. He looks like a
policeman.
4 avoir l'air de faire quelque chose to look as
if you are doing something
Il a l'air de comprendre. He looks as if he
understands.
5 *(saying how)* d'un air ..., d'un air méfiant
suspiciously
Elle souriait d'un air heureux. She was
smiling happily
6 tune
l'air d'une chanson the tune of a
song

un **air bag** MASC NOUN
airbag *(in a car)*

une **aire** FEM NOUN
area *(for an activity)*
• une aire de jeux
playground
• une aire de pique-nique
picnic area
• une aire de repos
motorway rest area
• une aire de services
motorway service station

l'**aise** FEM NOUN
1 être à l'aise to be at ease
être à l'aise avex tout le monde to be at
ease with everybody
2 être mal à l'aise to feel uneasy
J'étais vraiment mal à l'aise. I felt really
uneasy.

une **aisselle** FEM NOUN
armpit

ajouter VERB [1]
to add
Ajoutez un œuf. Add an egg.
Ajoutez du sucre. Add some sugar.

une **alarme** FEM NOUN
alarm
sonner l'alarme to sound the alarm

un **album** MASC NOUN
album
• un album de bandes dessinées
comic book
• un album de photos
photograph album
• un album de timbres
stamp album

l'**alcool** MASC NOUN
alcohol

alcoolique MASC & FEM NOUN
alcoholic
C'est un alcoolique. He's an alcoholic.

alcoolisé MASC ADJECTIVE, **alcoolisée** FEM
une boisson alcoolisée an alcoholic drink
une boisson non alcoolisée a soft drink

un **alcootest** MASC NOUN
breathalyzer

les **alentours** PLURAL MASC NOUN
1 surrounding area
2 aux alentours de Paris in the area around
Paris

l'**algèbre** FEM NOUN
algebra

l'**Algérie** FEM NOUN
Algeria

algérien MASC ADJECTIVE, **algérienne** FEM ► SEE
Algérien
Algerian

un **Algérien** MASC NOUN, une **Algérienne** FEM
► SEE **algérien**
Algerian *(person)*

les **algues** PLURAL FEM NOUN
seaweed

un **aliment** MASC NOUN
food

alimentaire MASC & FEM ADJECTIVE
des produits alimentaires food products
l'industrie alimentaire the food industry

ℱ l'**alimentation** FEM NOUN
1 groceries
2 diet

une **allée** FEM NOUN
path, drive

l'**Allemagne** *FEM NOUN*
  Germany

allemand *MASC ADJECTIVE*, **allemande** *FEM* ▸ SEE
Allemand
  German

un **Allemand** *MASC NOUN*, une **Allemande** *FEM*
  ▸ SEE **allemand**
1 German *(person)*
2 l'allemand *MASC* German *(the language)*

 ℰ **aller** *VERB* ◎ [7]
  ▸ SEE **aller** *NOUN*
1 **to go**
  Je vais à Paris. I'm going to Paris.
  Je vais chez le boulanger. I'm going to the
  baker's.
  Elle n'est pas allée à l'école jeudi. She
  didn't go to school on Thursday.
  Hier nous sommes allés au cinéma.
  Yesterday we went to the cinema.
  Où vas-tu? Where are you going?
  Où va-t-elle demain? Where is she going
  tomorrow?
  Ne va pas si vite. Don't go so fast.
  Allons en ville. Let's go into town.
  Allons-y! Let's go!
  Vas-y, demande au professeur. Go on, ask
  the teacher.
2 *(to say how you are, etc)* Comment ça va?,
  Ça va? How are you?
  Ça va bien. I'm fine.
  Ça ne va pas du tout. I'm really not well.
  Ça mieux. I feel better.
  Comment va ta mère? How's your
  mother?
  Elle va bien. She's fine.
  Tout va bien. Everything's fine.
  Qu'est-ce qui ne va pas? What's wrong?
3 *(to say something will happen)* Je vais
  sortir avec Julien ce soir. I'm going out
  with Julien this evening.
  Il va chercher le balai. He's going to get the
  brush.
  Elle ne va pas oublier. She's not going to
  forget.
4 **to suit**
  Cette robe te va bien. That dress suits you.
  Est-ce que jeudi te va? Does Thursday suit
  you?

s'**en aller** *REFLEXIVE VERB* ◎
  to leave
  Je m'en vais! I'm off!
  Va-t-en! Go away! *(to one person)*
  Allez-vous-en Go away! *(to two or more
  people)*

 ℰ un **aller** *MASC NOUN* ▸ SEE **aller** *VERB*
1 **outward journey**

2 **away match**

allergique *MASC & FEM ADJECTIVE*
  être allergique à quelque chose to be
  allergic to something
  Elle est allergique aux chats. She's allergic
  to cats.

 ℰ un **aller-retour** *MASC NOUN*
  return ticket
  Un aller-retour pour Tours, s'il vous plaît. A
  return ticket to Tours, please.

 ℰ un **aller simple** *MASC NOUN*
  single ticket
  Avignon aller simple, s'il vous plaît. A
  single to Avignon, please.

une **alliance** *FEM NOUN*
1 **wedding ring**
2 **alliance**

un **allié** *MASC NOUN*, une **alliée** *FEM*
  ally

 ℰ **allô** *EXCLAMATION*
  hello *(when answering a phone)*

une **allocation** *FEM NOUN*
  benefit
  • l'allocation chômage
    unemployment benefit
  • les allocations familiales
    family allowance

allonger *VERB* [52]
1 **to lengthen** *(a dress)*
2 **to extend** *(a holiday, a journey)*
s'**allonger** *REFLEXIVE VERB* ◎
  to lie down

 ℰ **allumer** *VERB* [1]
1 **to light**
  allumer le feu to light the fire
2 **to switch on**
  allumer la télé to switch on the TV
3 **to switch on the lights**

 ℰ une **allumette** *FEM NOUN*
  match

une **allure** *FEM NOUN*
1 **speed**
  à toute allure at top speed
2 **appearance** *(of a person)*

 ℰ **alors** *ADVERB*
1 **so**
  Alors, comment ça va? So how are you?
  Je suis en retard. Et alors? I'm late. So
  what?
2 alors que while
  alors qu'elle faisait ses devoirs while she
  was doing her homework
3 **then, at that time**
  Elle travaillait alors à Paris. She was

working in Paris then.

une **alouette** *FEM NOUN*
skylark

Alpes *PLURAL FEM NOUN*
les Alpes the Alps

ℓ un **alphabet** *MASC NOUN*
alphabet

alphabétique *MASC & FEM ADJECTIVE*
alphabetical
par ordre alphabétique in alphabetical
order

ℓ l'**alpinisme** *MASC NOUN*
mountaineering

alsacien *MASC ADJECTIVE*, **alsacienne** *FEM* ▸ SEE
Alsacien
from Alsace, Alsatian

> **WORD TIP** Adjectives never have capitals in
> French, even for nationality or regional origin.

un **Alsacien** *MASC NOUN*, une **Alsacienne** *FEM*
▸ SEE **alsacien**
Alsatian *(person from Alsace)*

alternatif *MASC ADJECTIVE*, **alternative** *FEM*
alternative

une **altitude** *FEM NOUN*
altitude

l'**aluminium** *MASC NOUN*
aluminium

une **amande** *FEM NOUN*
1 almond
2 kernel *(stone of a fruit)*

un **amant** *MASC NOUN*
lover

amateur *MASC & FEM ADJECTIVE* ▸ SEE **amateur**
NOUN
amateur
C'est une photographe amateur. She's an
amateur photographer.

un **amateur** *MASC NOUN* ▸ SEE **amateur** *ADJECTIVE*
enthusiast
un amateur de musique a music lover

une **ambassade** *FEM NOUN*
embassy
l'ambassade de France the French Embassy

un **ambassadeur** *MASC NOUN*
ambassador

une **ambiance** *FEM NOUN*
atmosphere
une bonne ambiance a good atmosphere

ambitieux *MASC ADJECTIVE*, **ambitieuse** *FEM*
ambitious

ℓ une **ambition** *FEM NOUN*
ambition

ℓ une **ambulance** *FEM NOUN*
ambulance

un **ambulancier** *MASC NOUN*, une
ambulancière *FEM*
ambulance driver

une **amélioration** *FEM NOUN*
improvement

améliorer *VERB* [1]
to improve

s'**améliorer** *REFLEXIVE VERB*
to get better, to improve

aménagé *MASC ADJECTIVE*, **aménagée** *FEM*
1 equipped *(kitchen, etc)*
2 converted *(attic, loft)*

aménager *VERB* [52]
1 to convert, to do up *(a building, a room)*
2 to develop *(an area)*
3 to improve *(a road, a road system)*

une **amende** *FEM NOUN*
fine
une amende de 500 euros a 500-euro fine

amener *VERB* [50]
1 to bring
Elle a amené son cousin. She brought her
cousin.
Tu amènes ton frère? Are you bringing your
brother?
2 to take
amener un enfant à l'école to take a child
to school

amer *MASC ADJECTIVE*, **amère** *FEM*
bitter

américain *MASC ADJECTIVE*, **américaine** *FEM*
▸ SEE **Américain**
American

> **WORD TIP** Adjectives never have capitals in
> French, even for nationality or regional origin.

un **Américain** *MASC NOUN*, une **Américaine**
FEM ▸ SEE **américain**
1 American *(person)*
2 l'américain American English

l'**Amérique** *FEM NOUN*
America
l'Amérique du nord North America
l'Amérique du sud South America

> **WORD TIP** Countries and regions in French take
> le, la or les.

l'**ameublement** *MASC NOUN*
furniture

ℓ indicates key words

♪ un **ami** MASC NOUN, une **amie** FEM
  friend
  un ami à moi a friend of mine
  une amie à Lisa a friend of Lisa's
  se faire des amis to make friends
  Je me suis fait quelques amis. I've made
  some friends.

amical MASC ADJECTIVE, **amicale** FEM, **amicaux**
MASC PL, **amicales** FEM PL ▸ SEE **amicale**
  friendly

une **amicale** FEM NOUN ▸ SEE **amical**
  association

amicalement ADVERB
  1 in a friendly way
  2 Amicalement, Odile Best wishes, Odile
    (informal letter ending)

l'**amitié** FEM NOUN
  1 friendship
  2 Amitiés, Hélène Love, Hélène (informal
    letter ending)

♪ l'**amour** MASC NOUN
  love
  • l'amour-propre
    self-esteem

amoureux MASC ADJECTIVE, **amoureuse** FEM
  in love
  être amoureux de quelqu'un to be in love
  with somebody
  Elle était amoureuse de lui. She was in love
  with him.
  Il est amoureux d'elle. He is in love with her.

un **amphithéâtre** MASC NOUN
  1 amphitheatre
  2 lecture theatre (in a university)

ample MASC & FEM ADJECTIVE
  1 loose-fitting (clothes)
  2 ample (amount)

une **ampleur** FEM NOUN
  1 size (of a problem)
  2 scope (of a project)

un **ampli** MASC NOUN
  (informal) amplifier

un **amplificateur** MASC NOUN
  amplifier

une **ampoule** FEM NOUN
  1 light bulb
  2 blister
  J'ai une ampoule au pied. I've got a blister
  on my foot.

♪ **amusant** MASC ADJECTIVE, **amusante** FEM
  1 funny
  2 entertaining

un **amuse-gueule** MASC NOUN
  des amuse-gueule nibbles (crisps, nuts, etc)

amuser VERB [1]
  1 to amuse
    Ça l'amuse de faire des grimaces. He enjoys
    pulling faces.
  2 to entertain
    amuser les gens dans la rue to entertain
    people in the street

s'**amuser** REFLEXIVE VERB ☺
  1 to play
    Ils s'amusent dans le jardin. They're playing
    in the garden.
  2 to have a good time
    On s'est bien amusé. We had a really good
    time.
    Amuse-toi bien! Have fun! (to one person)
    Amusez-vous bien! Have fun! (to two or
    more people)

♪ un **an** MASC NOUN
  year
  Elle a dix ans. She's ten (years old).
  le Nouvel An the New Year
  le jour de l'an New Year's Day
  tous les ans every year

un **analgésique** MASC NOUN
  analgesic, painkiller

une **analyse** FEM NOUN
  analysis
  • une analyse de sang
    blood test

♪ un **ananas** MASC NOUN
  pineapple

l'**anatomie** FEM NOUN
  anatomy

un & une **ancêtre** MASC & FEM NOUN
  ancestor

un **anchois** MASC NOUN
  anchovy

♪ **ancien** MASC ADJECTIVE, **ancienne** FEM
  1 old
    une maison ancienne an old house
    une table ancienne an antique table
  2 former
    l'ancien président the former president
    mon ancienne école my old school

> **WORD TIP** ancien, after a noun, means old or
> ancient. ancien, before a noun, means former.

une **ancre** FEM NOUN
  anchor

un **âne** MASC NOUN
  donkey

un **ange** MASC NOUN
  angel

une **angine** FEM NOUN
  throat infection
  avoir une angine to have a throat infection

ℱ **anglais** MASC ADJECTIVE, **anglaise** FEM ▶SEE
Anglais
  English
  un mot anglais an English word
  la cuisine anglaise English cooking

> **WORD TIP** Adjectives never have capitals in French, even for nationality or regional origin.

ℱ un **Anglais** MASC NOUN, une **Anglaise** FEM ▶SEE
anglais
1 **Englishman, Englishwoman**
  les Anglais the English
2 l'anglais MASC **English** (the language)

> **WORD TIP** Languages never have capitals in French.

un **angle** MASC NOUN
1 **angle**
2 **corner**
  à l'angle de la rue at the corner of the street
• un angle droit
  right angle

ℱ l'**Angleterre** FEM NOUN
  England
  en Angleterre in England
  aller en Angleterre to go to England

> **WORD TIP** Countries and regions in French take le, la or les.

Anglo-Normande MASC & FEM ADJECTIVE
  les îles Anglo-Normandes the Channel Islands

anglophone MASC & FEM ADJECTIVE
  English-speaking

une **angoisse** FEM NOUN
  anxiety

angoissé MASC ADJECTIVE, **angoissée** FEM
  anxious

une **anguille** FEM NOUN
  eel

anguleux MASC ADJECTIVE, **anguleuse** FEM
  bony

un **animal** MASC NOUN, les **animaux** PL
  animal
• un animal domestique
  pet

un **animateur** MASC NOUN, une **animatrice** FEM
1 **group leader**
2 **organizer** (of a festival, conference)
3 **presenter** (in radio, TV)

l'**animation** FEM NOUN
1 **liveliness, life**
  Il y a beaucoup d'animation dans le quartier le soir. There's a lot going on in the area at night.
2 **organization** (of a group, a programme)

animé MASC ADJECTIVE, **animée** FEM
1 **lively** (person, discussion)
2 **busy** (street, market)
  des rues animées busy streets

animer VERB [1]
1 **to run** (a course)
2 **to lead** (a group)
3 **to present** (a programme)
4 **to liven up** (a party)
s'**animer** REFLEXIVE VERB ◎
1 **to liven up**
2 **to come to life**
  Le quartier s'anime dès huit heures. The area comes to life after eight o'clock.

l'**anis** MASC NOUN
  aniseed

un **anneau** MASC NOUN, les **anneaux** PL
  ring

ℱ une **année** FEM NOUN
  year
  l'année prochaine next year
  l'année dernière last year
  les années 90 the nineties
  une année bissextile a leap year
  une année scolaire a school year
  Bonne année! Happy New Year!

une **annexe** FEM NOUN
1 **appendix** (of a book)
2 **annexe** (of a building)

ℱ un **anniversaire** MASC NOUN
1 **birthday**
  fêter son anniversaire to celebrate your birthday
  Bon anniversaire!, Joyeux anniversaire! Happy Birthday!
2 **anniversary**
• un anniversaire de mariage
  wedding anniversary

une **annonce** FEM NOUN
1 **advertisement**
  les petites annonces the small ads (in a newspaper)
2 **announcement** (of results, an event)
3 **sign**

annoncer VERB [61]
1 **to announce**
2 **to forecast**
  Ils annoncent de la neige pour demain. Snow is forecast for tomorrow.

ℱ indicates key words

ƒ un **annuaire** *MASC NOUN*
directory
- un annuaire téléphonique
telephone directory

annuel *MASC ADJECTIVE*, **annuelle** *FEM*
yearly

annuler *VERB* [1]
to cancel
Le match a été annulé. The match has been
cancelled.

anonyme *MASC & FEM ADJECTIVE*
anonymous

un **anorak** *MASC NOUN*
anorak

l'**anorexie** *FEM NOUN*
anorexia

l'**Antarctique** *MASC NOUN*
the Antarctic

une **antenne** *FEM NOUN*
1 aerial *(for a radio, TV)*
2 antenna *(of an insect, radio mast)*
- une antenne parabolique
satellite dish

un **antibiotique** *MASC NOUN*
antibiotic
prendre des antibiotiques to be on
antibiotics

anticiper *VERB* [1]
to foresee *(a change)*

un **antidépresseur** *MASC NOUN*
antidepressant

l'**antigel** *MASC NOUN*
antifreeze

antillais *MASC ADJECTIVE*, **antillaise** *FEM* ▶SEE
Antillais
West Indian

un **Antillais** *MASC NOUN*, une **Antillaise** *FEM*
▶SEE **antillais**
West Indian *(person)*

les **Antilles** *PLURAL FEM NOUN*
the West Indies

une **antilope** *FEM NOUN*
antelope

antiquaire *MASC & FEM NOUN*
antique dealer

une **antiquité** *FEM NOUN*
antique

antiseptique *MASC & FEM ADJECTIVE* ▶SEE
antiseptique *NOUN*
antiseptic

un **antiseptique** *MASC NOUN* ▶SEE **antiseptique**
ADJECTIVE
antiseptic

antiterroriste *MASC & FEM ADJECTIVE*
antiterrorist

un **antivol** *MASC NOUN*
1 lock *(on a bike, motorcycle)*
2 steering lock *(in a car)*

anxieux *MASC ADJECTIVE*, **anxieuse** *FEM*
anxious

ƒ **août** *MASC NOUN*
August
en août, au mois d'août in August

> **WORD TIP** Months of the year and days of the
> week start with small letters in French.

apercevoir *VERB* [66]
to catch sight of

s'**apercevoir** *REFLEXIVE VERB* ⊘
s'apercevoir de quelque chose to notice
something
Elle s'est aperçue de mon absence. She
noticed my absence.
s'apercevoir que ... to notice that ...
Je m'aperçois que la clé est sur la porte. I
notice that the key is in the door.

un **aperçu** *MASC NOUN*
1 insight
2 glimpse

un **apéritif** *MASC NOUN*
drink *(usually alcoholic, before a meal)*

aplatir *VERB* [2]
1 to flatten
2 to smooth out

une **apostrophe** *FEM NOUN*
apostrophe

apparaître *VERB* [57]
1 to appear
2 to seem

ƒ un **appareil** *MASC NOUN*
1 device, appliance
2 telephone
Qui est à l'appareil? Who's calling, please?
C'est Paul à l'appareil. It's Paul speaking.
- un appareil (dentaire)
brace *(for teeth)*
- un appareil photo
camera
- un appareil photo numérique
digital camera

apparemment *ADVERB*
apparently

une **apparence** *FEM NOUN*
appearance *(seen from outside)*

⊘ means the verb takes être to form the perfect

se fier aux apparences to judge by appearances

apparent *MASC ADJECTIVE*, **apparente** *FEM*
1 **obvious**
2 **apparent**
   sans raison apparente for no apparent reason

une **apparition** *FEM NOUN*
   appearance *(when something or somebody becomes visible)*
   l'apparition des boutons the appearance of spots
   Il a fait son apparition très tard. He turned up very late.

un **appartement** *MASC NOUN*
   flat, **apartment**

appartenir *VERB* [81]
   appartenir à quelqu'un to belong to somebody
   Ces chaussures m'appartiennent. These shoes belong to me.
   Est-ce que ce stylo t'appartient? Is this pen yours?

un **appel** *MASC NOUN*
1 **call**, **appeal**
   un appel d'aide a call for help
   Ils ont lancé un appel à la radio. They made an appeal on the radio.
2 faire appel à quelqu'un to appeal to somebody
3 faire l'appel to take the register *(in class)*
• un appel (téléphonique) telephone call

ℒ **appeler** *VERB* [18]
1 **to call**
   Ils l'ont appelé Hassan. They called him Hassan.
2 **to phone**
   Appelle-moi ce soir. Phone me this evening.
3 **to call**
   appeler un taxi to call a taxi
s'**appeler** *REFLEXIVE VERB* ◎
   to be called
   Il s'appelle Romain. He's called Romain.
   Comment t'appelles-tu?, Tu t'appelles comment? What's your name?
   Je m'appelle Marie. My name is Marie.

un **appendice** *MASC NOUN*
   appendix *(part of the body)*

l'**appendicite** *FEM NOUN*
   appendicitis

appétissant *MASC ADJECTIVE*, **appétissante** *FEM*
   appetizing

un **appétit** *MASC NOUN*
   appetite

Bon appétit! Enjoy your meal. *(said to others at table)*

applaudir *VERB* [2]
   to applaud

les **applaudissements** *PLURAL MASC NOUN*
   applause

l'**application** *FEM NOUN*
1 **care and attention**
   Elle a écrit la lettre avec beaucoup d'application. She wrote the letter with great care.
2 **application** *(of a law, rule)*

appliquer *VERB* [1]
   to apply
s'**appliquer** *REFLEXIVE VERB* ◎
1 **to apply yourself**
   Il s'applique mieux cette année. He's applying himself more this year.
2 s'appliquer à quelqu'un to apply to somebody
   Le règlement ne s'applique pas à vous. The rule doesn't apply to you.

ℒ **apporter** *VERB* [1]
   to bring
   Apporte-moi mon cahier. Bring me my note book.

ℒ **apprécier** *VERB* [1]
1 **to appreciate** *(food, music, help)*
   Il a apprécié la blague. He liked the joke.
2 **to like** *(a person)*

appréhender *VERB* [1]
1 **to arrest**
2 **to dread**

un **apprenant** *MASC NOUN*, une **apprenante** *FEM*
   learner

ℒ **apprendre** *VERB* [64]
1 **to learn**
   apprendre à parler français to learn to speak French
2 **to hear**
   J'ai appris que tu vas partir. I hear you're leaving.
3 **to teach**
   apprendre quelque chose à quelqu'un to teach somebody something
   Elle leur apprend le français. She's teaching them French.
   apprendre à faire quelque chose à quelqu'un to teach somebody something
   Elle leur apprend à conduire. She's teaching them to drive.

un **apprenti** *MASC NOUN*, une **apprentie** *FEM*
   apprentice

ℒ indicates key words

un **apprentissage** *MASC NOUN*
  apprenticeship
  Il va en apprentissage. He's going to do an
  apprenticeship.

une **approche** *FEM NOUN*
  approach

approcher *VERB* [1]
1 to approach
  Les vacances approchent. The holidays are
  approaching.
  Nous approchons de Rouen. We're
  approaching Rouen.
2 approcher quelqu'un to go up to somebody
3 to move (something) closer
  approcher quelque chose de quelque
  chose to move something closer to
  something
  Approche ta chaise de la table. Move your
  chair closer to the table.

s'**approcher** *REFLEXIVE VERB* ◯
  to get close
  Je m'approche un peu pour mieux voir. I'm
  getting closer to see better.
  s'approcher de quelque chose to get close
  to something
  Ne t'approche pas de ce chien, il mord.
  Don't go near that dog, he bites.

approuver *VERB* [1]
1 to approve of
2 to give approval to (officially)

un **appui** *MASC NOUN*
  support

appuyer *VERB* [41]
1 appuyer sur quelque chose to press
  something
  Appuie sur le bouton. Press the button.
2 to lean
  appuyer quelque chose contre quelque
  chose to lean something against something

♀ **après** *ADVERB* ▶ SEE **après** *PREPOSITION*
  afterwards, later
  peu après shortly afterwards
  une heure après an hour later
  longtemps après a long time later

♀ **après** *PREPOSITION* ▶ SEE **après** *ADVERB*
1 after
  après dix heures after ten o'clock
  après l'école after school
2 après avoir fait quelque chose after doing
  something
  Après avoir mangé, j'ai écouté des CD.
  After eating, I listened to some CDs.
  Après être rentrée, elle s'est couchée. After
  she got home, she went to bed.

♀ **après-demain** *ADVERB*
  the day after tomorrow

♀ un & une **après-midi** *MASC & FEM NOUN*
  afternoon
  cet après-midi this afternoon
  demain après-midi tomorrow afternoon
  hier après-midi yesterday afternoon
  tous les après-midi every afternoon
  à une heure de l'après-midi at one o'clock
  in the afternoon

♀ un **après-rasage** *MASC NOUN*
  aftershave

une **aptitude** *FEM NOUN*
  aptitude

l'**aquarelle** *FEM NOUN*
  watercolours (method of painting)
  une aquarelle a watercolour (painting)

un **aquarium** *MASC NOUN*
1 fish tank
2 aquarium

arabe *MASC & FEM ADJECTIVE* ▶ SEE **Arabe**
1 Arab
2 Arabic (numeral, text)

un & une **Arabe** *MASC & FEM NOUN* ▶ SEE **arabe**
1 Arab (a person)
2 l'arabe *MASC* Arabic (the language)

une **araignée** *FEM NOUN*
  spider

un **arbitre** *MASC NOUN*
  referee

♀ un **arbre** *MASC NOUN*
  tree
  • un arbre généalogique
    family tree

un **arbuste** *MASC NOUN*
  bush

un **arc** *MASC NOUN*
1 arch
2 bow (for arrows)
  • un arc-en-ciel
    rainbow

l'**archéologie** *FEM NOUN*
  archeology

un & une **archéologue** *MASC & FEM NOUN*
  archeologist

un **archevêque** *MASC NOUN*
  archbishop

un & une **architecte** *MASC & FEM NOUN*
  architect

l'**Arctique** *MASC NOUN*
  the Arctic

une **ardoise** *FEM NOUN*
  slate

◯ means the verb takes être to form the perfect

une **arène** *FEM NOUN*
1 **arena**
2 **bullring**

une **arête** *FEM NOUN*
fishbone

ℒ l'**argent** *MASC NOUN*
1 **money**
dépenser de l'argent to spend money
retirer de l'argent à la banque to take
money out of the bank
2 **silver**
une chaîne en argent a silver chain
• l'argent de poche
pocket money

l'**argile** *FEM NOUN*
clay

l'**argot** *MASC NOUN*
slang

l'**arithmétique** *FEM NOUN*
arithmetic

une **arme** *FEM NOUN*
weapon
• une arme à feu
firearm

une **armée** *FEM NOUN*
army
• l'armée de l'air
air force
• l'armée de terre
army

ℒ une **armoire** *FEM NOUN*
1 **wardrobe**
2 **cupboard**

une **arobase** *FEM NOUN*
at @ *(in email addresses)*
jean-point-dupont-arobase-mondecom-
point-com jean-dot-dupont-at-mondecom-
dot-com

les **aromates** *PLURAL MASC NOUN*
herbs and spices

l'**aromathérapie** *FEM NOUN*
aromatherapy

aromatisé *MASC ADJECTIVE*, **aromatisée** *FEM*
flavoured

un **arôme** *MASC NOUN*
1 **flavouring, flavour**
arôme fraise strawberry flavour
à l'arôme de vanille vanilla-flavoured
2 **aroma** *(smell)*

arracher *VERB* [1]
1 arracher quelque chose à quelqu'un to
snatch something from somebody
Elle m'a arraché mon porte-monnaie. She

snatched my purse from me.
2 **to rip out**
J'ai arraché les pages de mon journal. I
ripped the pages out of my diary.
3 **to pull up** *(weeds, vegetables)*

un **arrangement** *MASC NOUN*
arrangement

arranger *VERB* [52]
1 **to arrange** *(flowers)*
2 **to sort out** *(a problem)*
Cela ne va pas arranger les choses. That's
not going to help things.
3 **to repair** *(a watch)*
4 **to suit**
Si ça t'arrange, on peut partir d'ici. If it
suits you better, we can leave from here.
s'**arranger** *REFLEXIVE VERB* ☺
1 **to get better** *(weather, situation)*
Ça va s'arranger. It'll sort itself out.
2 s'arranger avec quelqu'un to sort it out
with somebody
Tu t'arranges avec Jean. Sort it out with
Jean.
s'arranger avec quelqu'un pour faire
quelque chose to arrange with somebody
to do something
Elle s'est arrangée avec Julie pour aller en
ville. She's arranged with Julie to go into
town.

une **arrestation** *FEM NOUN*
arrest

ℒ un **arrêt** *MASC NOUN*
1 **stop**
au prochain arrêt at the next stop
2 sans arrêt non-stop
Ils bavardent sans arrêt. They chat away
non-stop.
• un arrêt de bus
bus stop

ℒ **arrêter** *VERB* [1]
1 **to arrest** *(a suspect)*
2 **to stop**
arrêter la voiture to stop the car
3 **to switch off** *(an engine, a machine)*
4 arrêter de faire quelque chose to stop
doing something
Il a arrêté de fumer. He's stopped smoking.
Elle n'arrête pas de travailler. She doesn't
stop working.
s'**arrêter** *REFLEXIVE VERB* ☺
to stop
On va s'arrêter à la boulangerie. We'll stop
at the baker's.

les **arrhes** *PLURAL FEM NOUN*
deposit

ℒ **indicates key words**

arrière *MASC & FEM ADJECTIVE* ▸ SEE **arrière** *NOUN*
  back
  la porte arrière the back door
un **arrière** *MASC NOUN* ▸ SEE **arrière** *ADJECTIVE*
  back
  à l'arrière in the back *(of a car)*
  regarder en arrière to look back
  rester en arrière to stay back
• un **arrière-goût**
  after-taste
• une **arrière-grand-mère**
  great-grandmother
• un **arrière-grand-père**
  great-grandfather
• les **arrière-grands-parents**
  great-grandparents
• les **arrière-petits-enfants**
  great-grandchildren

une **arrivée** *FEM NOUN*
  arrival

♪ **arriver** *VERB* ⬤ [1]
1 to arrive
  arriver à Londres to arrive in London
  Je suis arrivé à cinq heures. I arrived at five
  o'clock.
  Ils arrivent à quelle heure? What time do
  they arrive?
  J'arrive! I'm coming!
2 to happen
  L'accident est arrivé hier. The accident
  happened yesterday.
  Qu'est-ce qui arrive? What's happening?
  Ça m'est arrivé aussi. That happened to
  me too.
3 arriver à faire quelque chose to be able to
  do something
  Est-ce que tu arrives à voir? Can you see?
  Je n'arrive pas à tourner la clef. I can't turn
  the key.

arrogant *MASC ADJECTIVE*, **arrogante** *FEM*
  arrogant

un **arrondissement** *MASC NOUN*
  arrondissement *(a numbered area of a
  large French-speaking city)*
  dans le neuvième arrondissement in the
  ninth arrondissement

arroser *VERB* [1]
1 to water
  arroser les plantes to water the plants
2 to celebrate *(with drinks)*
  On va arroser l'anniversaire de mon
  frère. We're going to have a few drinks to
  celebrate my brother's birthday.

un **arrosoir** *MASC NOUN*
  watering can

l'**art** *MASC NOUN*
  art
• l'art dramatique
  dramatic art
• les arts martiaux
  martial arts
• les arts ménagers
  home economics

une **artère** *FEM NOUN*
1 artery
2 arterial road
3 main road

un **artichaut** *MASC NOUN*
  artichoke

♪ un **article** *MASC NOUN*
1 article *(in a newspaper)*
2 item *(on sale)*
  les articles de sport sports equipment
  les articles de toilette toiletries
3 article *(in grammar: un, une; le, la, les)*
• l'article défini
  definite article *(le, la, les)*
• l'article indéfini
  indefinite article *(un, une)*

une **articulation** *FEM NOUN*
  joint *(of elbow, knee)*

artificiel *MASC ADJECTIVE*, **artificielle** *FEM*
  artificial

un **artisan** *MASC NOUN*
  craftsman

artisanal *MASC ADJECTIVE*, **artisanale** *FEM*,
artisanaux *MASC PL*, **artisanales** *FEM PL*
1 traditional *(skill, craft)*
  une foire artisanale a craft fair
  de fabrication artisanale made by
  traditional methods
2 home-made *(food)*
  biscuits artisanaux home-made biscuits

un & une **artiste** *MASC & FEM NOUN*
1 artist
2 performer

un **as** *MASC NOUN* ▸ SEE **as** *VERB*
  ace

as *VERB* ▸ SEE **as** *NOUN* ▸ SEE **avoir**

♪ un **ascenseur** *MASC NOUN*
  lift
  prendre l'ascenseur to take the lift

asiatique *MASC & FEM ADJECTIVE*
  Asian

l'**Asie** *FEM NOUN*
  Asia
  aller en Asie to go to Asia

un **asile** *MASC NOUN*
1 refuge

⬤ means the verb takes être to form the perfect

2 asylum
l'asile politique political asylum
le droit d'asile the right of asylum

un **aspect** *MASC NOUN*
1 aspect *(of a problem)*
2 appearance *(of a person, thing)*
3 side

les **asperges** *PLURAL FEM NOUN*
asparagus

ℒ un **aspirateur** *MASC NOUN*
vacuum cleaner
passer l'aspirateur to do the vacuuming

ℒ une **aspirine** *FEM NOUN*
aspirin

assaisonner *VERB* [1]
to season

un **assassin** *MASC NOUN*, une **assassine** *FEM*
murderer

l'**assassinat** *MASC NOUN*
murder

assassiner *VERB* [1]
to murder

une **assemblée** *FEM NOUN*
1 meeting
2 assembly *(in politics)*

assembler *VERB* [1]
to assemble *(a kit, a machine)*

s'**assembler** *REFLEXIVE VERB* ◯
to gather *(people, crowds)*

s'**asseoir** *REFLEXIVE VERB* ◯ [20]
to sit down
s'asseoir sur une chaise to sit down on a
chair
Assieds-toi. Take a seat.
Asseyez-vous. Do sit down. *(polite form)*
▶ SEE **assis**

ℒ **assez** *ADVERB*
1 enough
Elle ne mange pas assez. She doesn't eat
enough.
Est-ce que tu dors assez? Are you getting
enough sleep?
2 assez de enough *(of something)*
assez de pain enough bread
Il y a assez de verres. There are enough
glasses.
Il n'y a pas assez d'argent. There isn't
enough money.
3 enough
Est-ce que l'eau est assez chaude? Is the
water hot enough?
Il n'est pas assez fort pour porter la
valise. He's not strong enough to carry the
suitcase.

4 quite
assez joli quite pretty
Je la vois assez souvent. I see her quite
often.
5 *(informal)* J'en ai assez! I've had enough!

ℒ une **assiette** *FEM NOUN*
plate
• une assiette plate
dinner plate
• une assiette creuse
soup plate
• une assiette à soupe
soup plate

ℒ **assis** *MASC ADJECTIVE*, **assise** *FEM*
être assis to be sitting
Elle était assise dans un fauteuil. She was
sitting in an armchair.

une **assistance** *FEM NOUN*
1 audience
2 assistance *(help)*

un **assistant** *MASC NOUN*, une **assistante** *FEM*
assistant

assister *VERB* [1]
1 assister à quelque chose to attend
something, to be at *(an event)*
J'ai assisté à leur mariage. I was at their
wedding.
2 to help
3 to aid *(a country, etc)*

une **association** *FEM NOUN*
association

un **associé** *MASC NOUN*, une **associée** *FEM*
associate, partner

s'**associer** *REFLEXIVE VERB* ◯
1 s'associer à un groupe to join a group
2 s'associer pour faire quelque chose to join
forces to do something

assommer *VERB* [1]
1 assommer quelqu'un to knock somebody
out
2 *(informal)* assommer quelqu'un to bore
somebody stiff
Ça m'assomme de rester ici! I'm bored stiff
staying here!

assorti *MASC ADJECTIVE*, **assortie** *FEM*
1 matching
2 assorted *(chocolates, etc)*

un **assortiment** *MASC NOUN*
assortment, selection

assumer *VERB* [1]
assumer la responsabilité de quelque
chose to take responsibility for something
assumer une fonction to hold a position

ℒ indicates key words

l'**assurance** FEM NOUN
1 confidence
prendre de l'assurance to gain confidence
avec assurance confidently
2 insurance
• une assurance maladie
health insurance
• une assurance voyage
travel insurance

assuré MASC ADJECTIVE, **assurée** FEM
1 confident
2 insured

assurer VERB [1]
1 to assure
Je vous assure que c'est vrai. I assure you
it's true.
2 to insure
3 to provide (a service)
4 to carry out (a task)
s'**assurer** REFLEXIVE VERB ⊙
to make sure

un **astérisque** MASC NOUN
asterisk

asthmatique MASC & FEM ADJECTIVE
asthmatic

un **asthme** MASC NOUN
asthma

un **asticot** MASC NOUN
maggot

l'**astrologie** FEM NOUN
astrology

un & une **astrologue** MASC & FEM NOUN
astrologer

un & une **astronome** MASC & FEM NOUN
astronomer

l'**astronomie** FEM NOUN
astronomy

l'**astuce** FEM NOUN
1 cleverness
2 craftiness, shrewdness
3 une astuce a trick (for getting something)

astucieux MASC ADJECTIVE, **astucieuse** FEM
1 clever
2 crafty

un **atelier** MASC NOUN
1 workshop
2 studio (of an artist, sculptor)
3 work group

un & une **athée** MASC & FEM NOUN
atheist

Athènes NOUN
Athens

un & une **athlète** MASC & FEM NOUN
athlete

♂ l'**athlétisme** MASC NOUN
athletics
faire de l'athlétisme to do athletics

l'**Atlantique** MASC NOUN
l'Atlantique the Atlantic

un **atlas** MASC NOUN
atlas

l'**atmosphère** FEM NOUN
atmosphere

atomique MASC & FEM ADJECTIVE
atomic

un **atout** MASC NOUN
1 advantage
2 trump card
C'est atout pique. Spades are trumps.

atroce MASC & FEM ADJECTIVE
dreadful, terrible

une **atrocité** FEM NOUN
atrocity

attachant MASC ADJECTIVE, **attachante** FEM
lovable

une **attache** FEM NOUN
1 tie
2 attaches familiales family ties
3 string
4 strap

♂ **attacher** VERB [1]
to tie
attacher ses cheveux to tie your hair back
Attachez vos ceintures. Fasten your
seatbelts.
s'**attacher** REFLEXIVE VERB ⊙
to stick (to a pot, a table)
La sauce s'attache à la poêle. The sauce is
sticking to the pan.

une **attaque** FEM NOUN
attack

♂ **attaquer** VERB [1]
to attack

atteindre VERB [60]
1 to reach, to get to
La temperature atteint 35° à midi. The
temperature reaches 35° at midday.
2 to achieve (an aim, a goal)

atteint MASC ADJECTIVE, **atteinte** FEM
être atteint par quelque chose to be
affected by something
les pays atteints par le désastre the
countries affected by the disaster

⊙ means the verb takes être to form the perfect

attendant *IN PHRASE*
en attendant meanwhile, in the meantime

ℓ **attendre** *VERB* [3]
1 **to wait for**
J'attends le bus. I'm waiting for the bus.
Je t'attends dehors. I'll wait for you outside.
2 **to expect**
attendre un bébé to be expecting a baby
J'attends le médecin. I'm expecting the
doctor.
3 **to wait**
Tu peux attendre deux minutes? Can you
wait two minutes?

s'**attendre** *REFLEXIVE VERB* ◯
s'attendre à quelque chose to expect
something
Je ne m'attendais pas aux cadeaux. I wasn't
expecting the presents.

WORD TIP attendre does not mean attend in
English; for the meaning of **attend** ▸ SEE **assister**.

un **attentat** *MASC NOUN*
1 **attack**
un attentat à la bombe a bomb attack
2 **assassination attempt**

une **attente** *FEM NOUN*
wait
une attente de vingt minutes a twenty-
minute wait

attentif *MASC ADJECTIVE*, **attentive** *FEM*
1 **attentive**
2 **careful**

ℓ l'**attention** *FEM NOUN*
1 **attention**
Attention! Watch out!
Attention au chien! Beware of the dog!
à l'attention de for the attention of
faire attention to pay attention
Fais attention à l'annonce. Pay attention to
the announcement.
Ne fais pas attention à Pierre. Don't take
any notice of Pierre.
2 faire attention à quelque chose to watch
out for something
Faites attention aux pickpockets! Watch
out for pickpockets!

atterrir *VERB* [2]
to land

un **atterrissage** *MASC NOUN*
landing
• un atterrissage en catastrophe
crash landing

attirant *MASC ADJECTIVE*, **attirante** *FEM*
attractive

attirer *VERB* [1]
to attract
Il a essayé d'attirer mon attention. He tried
to attract my attention.

s'**attirer** *REFLEXIVE VERB* ◯
s'attirer des ennuis to make trouble for
yourself

une **attitude** *FEM NOUN*
attitude

une **attraction** *FEM NOUN*
attraction
les attractions touristiques the tourist
attractions

attraper *VERB* [1]
to catch (a ball, a cold)

attrayant *MASC ADJECTIVE*, **attrayante** *FEM*
attractive

attrister *VERB* [1]
to sadden

au
▸ SEE **à**

l'**aube** *FEM NOUN*
dawn
à l'aube at dawn

ℓ une **auberge** *FEM NOUN*
inn
• une auberge de jeunesse
youth hostel

une **aubergine** *FEM NOUN*
aubergine

aucun *MASC ADJECTIVE*, **aucune** *FEM* ▸ SEE **aucun**
PRONOUN
no
en aucun cas under no circumstances
sans aucun doute without any doubt
Elle n'a aucun talent. She has no talent.
Je n'ai eu aucune nouvelle de Laura. I
haven't had any news from Laura.

WORD TIP ne or n' is used with aucun or aucune
when there is a verb.

aucun, aucune *PRONOUN* ▸ SEE **aucun** *ADJECTIVE*
1 (for a masc noun) **none**
Aucun d'entre eux n'est venu. None of
them came.
Aucun des deux n'est venu. Neither of the
two came.
Je ne connais aucun de tes amis. I don't
know any of your friends.
2 (for a fem noun) **none**
Aucune d'entre elles n'est venue. None of
them came.
Aucune des cartes n'est pour moi. None of
the cards is for me.
Je ne connais aucune de tes amies. I don't

know any of your friends.

WORD TIP ne or n' is used with aucun or aucune when there is a verb.

ℰ **au-delà de** *PREPOSITION*
beyond
au-delà de cette limite beyond that limit

ℰ **au-dessous** *ADVERB*
1 underneath
2 below
Il habite l'étage au-dessous. He lives on the floor below.
3 au-dessous de underneath, below
au-dessous de la table underneath the table
Elle habite l'étage au-dessous de chez nous. She lives on the floor below us.

ℰ **au-dessus** *ADVERB*
1 above
à l'étagère au-dessus on the shelf above.
2 au-dessus de above
au-dessus de ma tête above my head

audiovisuel *MASC ADJECTIVE,* **audiovisuelle** *FEM*
audiovisual

un **auditeur** *MASC NOUN,* une **auditrice** *FEM*
listener *(to radio)*

une **augmentation** *FEM NOUN*
increase
l'augmentation des prix the increase in prices

augmenter *VERB* [1]
1 to raise
2 to go up

ℰ **aujourd'hui** *ADVERB*
today
Nous sommes lundi aujourd'hui. Today is Monday.

auparavant *ADVERB*
1 before
2 previously

auprès de *PREPOSITION*
1 beside, next to
2 to *(when talking to someone)*
se plaindre auprès du professeur to complain to the teacher

auquel *PRONOUN*
to whom
le garçon auquel je parle the boy I'm talking to, the boy to whom I'm talking

WORD TIP auquel becomes à laquelle for a fem singular noun, auxquels for a masc plural noun, and auxquelles for a fem plural noun.

aura, aurai, auras, aurez, aurons, auront *VERB* ▸ SEE avoir

aurais, aurait, auraient *VERB* ▸ SEE avoir

ℰ **au revoir** *EXCLAMATION*
goodbye

aurions, auriez *VERB* ▸ SEE avoir

ℰ **aussi** *ADVERB*
1 also, too
Moi aussi. Me too.
J'ai aussi invité ton frère. I also invited your brother.
2 *(in comparisons)* aussi ... que as ... as
Mon panier est aussi lourd que le tien. My basket is as heavy as yours.
3 aussi bien que as well as
les enfants aussi bien que les adultes children as well as adults

aussitôt *ADVERB*
immediately
aussitôt que possible as soon as possible

l'**Australie** *FEM NOUN*
Australia
être en Australie to be in Australia
aller en Australie to go to Australia

WORD TIP Countries and regions in French take le, la or les.

australien *MASC ADJECTIVE,* **australienne** *FEM*
▸ SEE Australien
Australian

WORD TIP Adjectives never have capitals in French, even for nationality or regional origin.

un **Australien** *MASC NOUN,* une **Australienne** *FEM* ▸ SEE australien
Australian

autant *ADVERB*
1 as much, so much
Je n'ai jamais mangé autant. I've never eaten so much.
2 autant que as much as, as many as
Tu en as autant que moi. You have as much as I have., You have as many as I have.
3 autant de ... que as much ... as, as many ... as
Elle a autant d'argent que toi. She has as much money as you do.
Tu as autant de problèmes que moi. You have as many problems as I do.

ℰ un **auteur** *MASC NOUN*
author

ℰ une **auto** *FEM NOUN*
car

ℰ un **autobus** *MASC NOUN*
bus

⬤ means the verb takes être to form the perfect

_ℓ_ un **autocar** MASC NOUN
coach

autocollant MASC ADJECTIVE, **autocollante** FEM
self-adhesive

une **auto-école** FEM NOUN
driving school

un **automate** MASC NOUN
robot

automatique MASC & FEM ADJECTIVE
automatic

l'**automne** MASC NOUN
autumn
en automne in autumn

automobile MASC & FEM ADJECTIVE ▸ SEE
automobile NOUN
l'industrie automobile the car industry

_ℓ_ une **automobile** FEM NOUN ▸ SEE **automobile**
ADJECTIVE
car

automobiliste MASC & FEM NOUN
motorist

un **autoradio** MASC NOUN
car radio

une **autorisation** FEM NOUN
1 permission
avoir l'autorisation de faire quelque chose
to have permission to do something
2 permit

autoriser VERB [1]
1 to authorize
2 autoriser quelqu'un à faire quelque chose
to allow somebody to do something
Mes parents m'autorisent à sortir le
week-end. My parents allow me to go out
at weekends.

autoritaire ADJECTIVE
strict

une **autorité** FEM NOUN
authority

_ℓ_ une **autoroute** FEM NOUN
motorway
• une autoroute à péage
toll motorway

_ℓ_ l'**auto-stop** MASC NOUN
hitchhiking
faire de l'auto-stop to hitchhike

un **auto-stoppeur** MASC NOUN, une **auto-
stoppeuse** FEM
hitchhiker

_ℓ_ **autour** ADVERB
1 around
un lac avec des arbres tout autour a lake

with trees all around it
2 autour de round, around
Nous étions assis autour de la table. We
were sitting around the table.

_ℓ_ **autre** MASC & FEM ADJECTIVE ▸ SEE **autre** PRONOUN
1 other
l'autre jour the other day
2 un autre, une autre another
un autre film another film
3 quelqu'un d'autre somebody else
personne d'autre nobody else

_ℓ_ **autre** PRONOUN ▸ SEE **autre** ADJECTIVE
1 un autre, une autre another one
Donne-moi un autre. Give me another one.
2 les autres the others
Où sont les autres? Where are the others?

_ℓ_ **autrefois** ADVERB
in the past
Autrefois là il y avait une épicerie. In the
past there was a grocer's shop there.

autre part ADVERB
somewhere else

l'**Autriche** FEM NOUN
Austria

autrichien MASC ADJECTIVE, **autrichienne** FEM
▸ SEE **Autrichien**
Austrian

un **Autrichien** MASC NOUN, une **Autrichienne**
FEM ▸ SEE **autrichien**
Austrian

une **autruche** FEM NOUN
ostrich

aux PREPOSITION

> **WORD TIP** aux is formed by à + les ▸ SEE **à**

auxquelles PRONOUN
to whom
les filles auxquelles je parlais the girls I was
talking to, the girls to whom I was talking

auxquels PRONOUN
to whom
les garçons auxquels je parlais the boys
I was talking to, the boys to whom I was
talking

avais, **avait**, **avaient** VERB ▸ SEE **avoir**

une **avalanche** FEM NOUN
avalanche

avaler VERB [1]
1 to swallow
2 to inhale

une **avance** FEM NOUN
1 advance
2 lead

A
B
C
D
E
F
G
H
I
J
K
L
M
N
O
P
Q
R
S
T
U
V
W
X
Y
Z

_ℓ_ indicates key words

avoir deux buts d'avance to have a two-goal lead

3 en avance early
Je suis arrivé dix minutes en avance. I arrived ten minutes early.

4 à l'avance in advance
Il faut réserver à l'avance. You must book in advance.

avancer VERB [61]

1 to move forward

2 avancer quelque chose to bring something forward
Ils ont avancé le match. They brought the match forward.

3 to be fast (watches, clocks)
Ma montre avance de cinq minutes. My watch is five minutes fast.

♟ **avant** MASC & FEM ADJECTIVE ▸ SEE **avant** ADVERB, NOUN, PREPOSITION
front (set, wheel)

♟ **avant** ADVERB ▸ SEE **avant** ADJECTIVE, NOUN, PREPOSITION

1 before
longtemps avant a long time before
la semaine d'avant the week before

2 en avant forward

♟ l'**avant** MASC NOUN ▸ SEE **avant** ADJECTIVE, ADVERB, PREPOSITION

1 front
à l'avant in the front (of a car)

2 forward (in football, etc)

♟ **avant** PREPOSITION ▸ SEE **avant** ADJ, ADV, NOUN

1 before
avant Noël before Christmas
avant six heures before six o'clock

2 avant de faire quelque chose before doing something
Je vais lui téléphoner avant de partir. I'll phone her before I leave.

un **avantage** MASC NOUN
advantage

avantageux MASC ADJECTIVE, **avantageuse** FEM
advantageous

avant-dernier MASC ADJECTIVE, **avant-dernière** FEM
last but one

♟ **avant-hier** ADVERB
the day before yesterday
Nous sommes arrivés avant-hier. We arrived the day before yesterday.

♟ **avec** PREPOSITION
with
avec Chloé with Chloé

avec un couteau with a knife
Avec ça? Anything else? (in a shop)

l'**avenir** MASC NOUN
future
à l'avenir in the future

une **aventure** FEM NOUN
adventure

aventureux MASC ADJECTIVE, **aventureuse** FEM

1 adventurous
une vie aventureuse an adventurous life

2 risky
une idée aventureuse a risky idea

♟ une **avenue** FEM NOUN
avenue

♟ une **averse** FEM NOUN
shower
Des averses sont à craindre en soirée. Showers are to be expected in the evening.

avertir VERB [2]

1 to inform

2 to warn

un **avertissement** MASC NOUN
warning

aveugle MASC & FEM ADJECTIVE
blind

avez VERB ▸ SEE **avoir**

l'**aviation** FEM NOUN

1 aviation

2 air force

♟ un **avion** MASC NOUN
aeroplane
par avion by airmail
aller à Paris en avion to fly to Paris, to go to Paris by air

un **aviron** MASC NOUN

1 rowing
faire de l'aviron to row

2 oar

un **avis** MASC NOUN

1 opinion
à mon avis in my opinion
changer d'avis to change your mind
Elle a changé d'avis. She's changed her mind.

2 notice

un **avocat** MASC NOUN, une **avocate** FEM

1 lawyer

⬤ means the verb takes être to form the perfect

2 **avocado** *(fruit)*

l'**avoine** *FEM NOUN*
   oats

ℓ **avoir** *VERB* [5]
1 **to have, to have got**
   Elle a un vélo. She has a bike., She's got a bike.
   Je n'ai pas d'argent. I don't have any money.
   Nous avons un chien. We have a dog.
   As-tu des frères et sœurs? Do you have brothers and sisters?
2 *(talking about age)* **to be**
   Élodie a douze ans. Élodie's twelve.
   Quel âge a Pierre? How old is Pierre?
   quand j'avais cinq ans when I was five
3 *(to say you're cold, hot, etc)* **to be**
   J'ai chaud. I'm hot.
   J'ai froid. I'm cold.
   Ils ont très froid. They're very cold.
   J'ai mal. It hurts.
   avoir mal à la tête to have a headache
4 *(to say you're hungry, thirsty, etc)* **to be**
   Est-ce que tu as faim? Are you hungry?
   Je n'ai pas faim. I'm not hungry.
   J'ai vraiment soif. I'm really thirsty.
5 **il y a** **there is, there are**
   Il y a une femme à la porte. There's a woman at the door.
   Il y avait trois livres sur la table. There were three books on the table.
   Il n'y a pas de temps. There's no time.
   Qu'est-ce qu'il y a? What's the matter?

WORD TIP However many there are, French always uses il y + a, il y + avait, etc.

6 *(to say ago)* il y a un an a year ago
   il y a huit jours a week ago
7 *(Used with the past participle (usually ending -é, -i or -u) to form the* **have** *and* **had** *tenses.)*
   J'ai perdu mon stylo. I have lost my pen.
   J'ai vu ta mère hier. I saw your mother yesterday.
   Ils avaient déjà parlé avec le prof. They had already spoken to the teacher.

WORD TIP You will find phrases using avoir at entries like besoin, envie, lieu, raison and tort.

avons *VERB* ▸SEE **avoir**

un **avortement** *MASC NOUN*
   abortion

ℓ **avril** *MASC NOUN*
   April
   en avril, au mois d'avril in April

WORD TIP Months of the year and days of the week start with small letters in French.

🔘 **AVRIL**

Le Premier avril, à l'école, on colle des poissons en papier dans le dos des profs ! On fait des farces. On dit: « Poisson d'avril ! » Les médias aussi font des farces.

ayons, **ayez** *VERB* ▸SEE **avoir**

Bb

le **baby-foot** *MASC NOUN*
   table football
   une partie de baby-foot a game of table football

baby-sitting *MASC NOUN*
   baby-sitting
   faire du baby-sitting to baby-sit

ℓ le **bac** *MASC NOUN*
1 *(informal)* **baccalaureate**
   ▸SEE **baccalauréat**
2 **tub**
• le bac blanc
   mock baccalaureate
• le bac à glace
   ice tray

ℓ le **baccalauréat** *MASC NOUN*
   baccalaureate *(exam taken by French secondary school students at 17-18, which leads to higher education)*
   réussir au baccalauréat to pass the baccalaureate
   être reçu au baccalauréat to pass the baccalaureate
   Je vais passer le baccalauréat. I'm going to sit the baccalaureate.
   Il a échoué au baccalauréat. He failed the baccalaureate.

le **badaud** *MASC NOUN*, la **badaude** *FEM*
1 **passerby**
2 **onlooker** *(watching out of curiosity)*

le **baffle** *MASC NOUN*
   speaker *(on a music system)*

ℓ le **bagage** *MASC NOUN*
   un bagage a piece of luggage
   des bagages luggage
   Où sont tes bagages? Where's your luggage?
   Je dois faire mes bagages. I've got to pack.

- le bagage à main
  hand luggage

la **bagarre** *FEM NOUN*
  fight

se **bagarrer** *REFLEXIVE VERB* ⊜ [1]
  to fight
  Ils se bagarrent toujours. They're always
  fighting.

la **bagnole** *FEM NOUN*
  (informal) car

la **bague** *FEM NOUN*
  ring

♟la **baguette** *FEM NOUN*
  1 baguette (French bread stick)
  2 stick (of wood)
  3 drumstick
  4 chopstick
  - la baguette magique
    magic wand

les **Bahamas** *PLURAL FEM NOUN*
  les îles Bahamas the Bahamas, the Bahama
  Islands

la **baie** *FEM NOUN*
  1 bay (on the coast)
  2 berry

la **baignade** *FEM NOUN*
  swimming
  'Baignade interdite' 'No swimming'

♟se **baigner** *REFLEXIVE VERB* ⊜ [1]
  to go for a swim
  Je suis allé me baigner. I went for a swim.
  Allons nous baigner! Let's go for a swim!

♟la **baignoire** *FEM NOUN*
  bath

bâiller *VERB* [1]
  to yawn

♟le **bain** *MASC NOUN*
  1 bath
    un bain moussant a bubble bath
    prendre un bain to have a bath
  2 (in swimming)
    le grand bain the main pool
    le petit bain the learners' pool

le **baiser** *MASC NOUN*
  kiss
  Bons baisers Love and kisses (letter ending)

la **baisse** *FEM NOUN*
  fall
  être en baisse to be falling
  La température est en baisse. The
  temperature is falling.

baisser *VERB* [1]
  to lower

baisser le store to lower the blind
baisser les prix to reduce prices
Tu peux baisser la lumière? Can you turn
down the lights?

se **baisser** *REFLEXIVE VERB* ⊜
  to bend down

♟le **bal** *MASC NOUN*
  1 dance
    un bal populaire a dance (or disco)
    Il y aura un bal populaire le 14 juillet. There
    will be a dance on July 14.
  2 ball (a formal dance)

la **balade** *FEM NOUN*
  1 walk
  2 cycle ride
  3 drive
    faire une balade à la campagne to go for a
    drive in the country

se **balader** *REFLEXIVE VERB* ⊜ [1]
  1 to go for a walk
    Je vais me balader au bord du lac. I'm going
    for a walk by the lake.
  2 to go for a cycle ride
  3 to go for a drive
    Ils se baladent en Écosse. They're driving
    round Scotland.

le **baladeur** *MASC NOUN*
  personal stereo

le **balai** *MASC NOUN*
  brush (for sweeping)
  passer le balai to sweep the floor

la **balance** *FEM NOUN* ▶SEE **Balance**
  scales
  - la balance de cuisine
    kitchen scales

la **Balance** *FEM NOUN* ▶SEE **balance**
  Libra
  Emilie est Balance. Emilie is a Libra.

  WORD TIP Signs of the zodiac do not take an
  article: un or une.

balancer *VERB* [61]
  1 to swing (your arms, legs, etc)
  2 (informal) to chuck, to throw
    Arrête de balancer des cailloux! Stop
    throwing stones!
  3 (informal) to throw out
    J'ai balancé mes vieux vêtements. I threw
    out my old clothes.

la **balançoire** *FEM NOUN*
  1 swing
  2 seesaw

balayer *VERB* [59]
  1 to sweep
    balayer la cuisine to sweep the kitchen

⊜ means the verb takes être to form the perfect

2 to sweep up
balayer les miettes to sweep up the crumbs

la **balayeuse** *FEM NOUN*
roadsweeper *(a machine)*

balbutier *VERB* [1]
to mumble

ℓ le **balcon** *MASC NOUN*
1 balcony
Le balcon donne sur la rue. The balcony looks onto the street.
2 circle *(in a theatre)*

la **baleine** *FEM NOUN*
whale

ℓ la **balle** *FEM NOUN*
1 ball
une balle de tennis a tennis ball
jouer à la balle to play ball
2 bullet

la **ballerine** *FEM NOUN*
ballerina

le **ballet** *MASC NOUN*
ballet

ℓ le **ballon** *MASC NOUN*
1 ball
un ballon de football a football
jouer au ballon to play ball
2 balloon *(for parties, decoration)*
3 *(informal)* **breathalyzer**

le **ball-trap** *MASC NOUN*
clay pigeon shooting

balnéaire *MASC & FEM ADJECTIVE*
seaside

le **bambou** *MASC NOUN*
bamboo

banal *MASC ADJECTIVE*, **banale** *FEM*, **banals** *MASC PL*, **banales** *FEM PL*
ordinary
une histoire peu banale an unusual story

ℓ la **banane** *FEM NOUN*
1 banana
un kilo de bananes a kilo of bananas
2 bumbag

le **banc** *MASC NOUN*
bench

la **bande** *FEM NOUN*
1 group
une bande de jeunes a group of young people
2 gang
une bande de criminels a gang of criminals
3 strip *(of fabric, paper)*
4 tape *(for recordings)*
On va faire une bande démo. We're going

to make a demo tape.
5 bandage
• la bande-annonce
trailer *(for a film)*
• la bande d'arrêt d'urgence
hard shoulder *(on motorway)*

le **bandeau** *MASC NOUN*, les **bandeaux** *PL*
1 headband
2 blindfold

la **bande dessinée** *FEM NOUN*
1 comic strip
2 comic book

ℹ BANDE DESSINÉE
La bande dessinée (BD) a son musée et son festival à Angoulême.

la **bande rugueuse** *FEM NOUN*
rumble strip *(on motorway)*

la **bande sonore** *FEM NOUN*
1 rumble strip *(on motorway)*
2 soundtrack *(of film)*

le **bandit** *MASC NOUN*
bandit

le **banditisme** *MASC NOUN*
crime *(as an activity)*

ℓ la **banlieue** *FEM NOUN*
1 la banlieue the suburbs
2 une banlieue a suburb
un train de banlieue a commuter train
J'habite dans la banlieue de Leeds. I live in the suburbs of Leeds.

ℓ la **banque** *FEM NOUN*
1 bank
aller à la banque to go to the bank
Elle a 950 euros sur son compte en banque. She has 950 euros in the bank.
2 banking
Je voudrais travailler dans une banque. I'd like to work in banking.

le **banquet** *MASC NOUN*
banquet

la **banquette** *FEM NOUN*
1 wall seat *(in a cafe, restaurant)*
2 seat *(in a car, bus, train)*

le **banquier** *MASC NOUN*, la **banquière** *FEM*
banker

le **baptême** *MASC NOUN*
christening

baptiser *VERB* [1]
1 to christen
2 to name
3 to nickname

♀ le **bar** MASC NOUN
1 **bar** (place for drinking)
le bar au coin de la rue the bar on the
corner
2 **bar** (the counter)
On va prendre un pot au bar. We're going
to have a drink at the bar.

la **baraque** FEM NOUN
(informal) **house**

la **Barbade** FEM NOUN
Barbados
à la Barbade in Barbados
aller à la Barbade to go to Barbados

barbadien MASC ADJECTIVE, **barbadienne** FEM
▶ SEE **Barbadien**
Barbadian

le **Barbadien** MASC NOUN, la **Barbadienne** FEM
▶ SEE **barbadien**
Barbadian

barbant MASC ADJECTIVE, **barbante** FEM ADJECTIVE
boring
C'est barbant, les maths. Maths is a drag.

la **barbe** FEM NOUN
1 **beard**
Mon père porte une barbe. My dad has a
beard.
2 **drag**
Quelle barbe! What a drag!
• la barbe à papa
candyfloss

le **barbecue** MASC NOUN
barbecue
On va faire un barbecue ce soir. We're
going to have a barbecue this evening.

barbouiller VERB [1]
1 **to smear**
J'avais la figure barbouillée de chocolat. I
had chocolate all over my face.
2 **to daub**
un mur barbouillé de slogans a wall daubed
with slogans

barbu MASC ADJECTIVE, **barbue** FEM ▶ SEE **barbu**
NOUN
bearded

le **barbu** MASC NOUN ▶ SEE **barbu** ADJECTIVE
un barbu a bearded man

la **barmaid** FEM NOUN
barmaid

le **barman** MASC NOUN
barman

le **baromètre** MASC NOUN
barometer

la **barque** FEM NOUN
rowing boat

faire une promenade en barque to go for
a boat ride

la **barquette** FEM NOUN
tub, **container**
une barquette de frites a portion of chips
(sold in a plastic container)
une barquette de fraises a punnet of
strawberries

le **barrage** MASC NOUN
1 **dam**
2 **roadblock**

la **barre** FEM NOUN
bar
une barre de fer an iron bar
une barre de chocolat a chocolate bar

le **barreau** MASC NOUN, les **barreaux** PL
bar
Il y a des barreaux sur les fenêtres. There
are bars on the windows.

barrer VERB [1]
1 **to block**
'Route barrée' 'Road closed'
2 **to cross out**
barrer trois mots to cross out three words

se **barrer** REFLEXIVE VERB ☺
to push off, **to leave**
Je me barre! I'm off!

la **barrette** FEM NOUN
hairslide

la **barrière** FEM NOUN
1 **fence**
2 **gate**

le **bar-tabac** MASC NOUN, les **bars-tabac** PL
cafe (selling cigarettes, tobacco, stamps)

♀ **bas** MASC ADJECTIVE, **basse** FEM ▶ SEE **bas** ADV, NOUN
low
un prix bas a low price
une température basse a low temperature
Ils vendent des CD à bas prix. They sell CDs
at a low price.

♀ **bas** ADVERB ▶ SEE **bas** ADJECTIVE, NOUN MASC
1 **low**
plus bas lower down
2 en bas **downstairs**
La salle de bains est en bas. The bathroom
is downstairs.
3 en bas **at the bottom**
Les notes sont marquées en bas de la page.
The marks are written at the bottom of the
page.

♀ le **bas** NOUN MASC ▶ SEE **bas** ADJ, ADV
1 **bottom** (the lowest part of something)
le bas de la liste the bottom of the list
au bas de l'escalier at the bottom of the
stairs

☺ means the verb takes être to form the perfect

2 les bas stockings

le **bas-côté** *MASC NOUN*
verge *(on the roadside)*

la **bascule** *FEM NOUN*
1 weighing machine
2 seesaw
3 rocker
un fauteuil à bascule a rocking chair

basculer *VERB* [1]
to topple over
faire basculer quelqu'un to knock
somebody off balance

la **base** *FEM NOUN*
1 basis
une bonne base pour faire quelque chose a
good basis for doing something
2 base
un plat à base de riz a rice-based dish
3 de base basic
les ingrédients de base the basic
ingredients
• la base de données
database

le **base-ball** *MASC NOUN*
baseball
jouer au base-ball to play baseball

baser *VERB* [1]
to base
être basé sur quelque chose to be based on
something

le **basilic** *MASC NOUN*
basil

le **basket** *MASC NOUN*
1 basketball
jouer au basket to play basketball
2 trainer
acheter des baskets to buy some trainers

le **basketteur** *MASC NOUN*, la **basketteuse** *FEM*
basketball player

basque *MASC & FEM ADJECTIVE* ▶ SEE **Basque**
Basque
le Pays basque the Basque Country

un & une **Basque** *MASC & FEM NOUN* ▶ SEE **basque**
1 Basque *(person)*
2 le basque Basque *(the language)*

basse *FEM ADJECTIVE* ▶ SEE **basse** *NOUN* ▶ SEE **bas**
la **basse** *FEM NOUN* ▶ SEE **basse** *ADJECTIVE*
bass *(in music)*

ℒ le **bassin** *MASC NOUN*
1 pond
2 pelvis

la **bassine** *FEM NOUN*
bowl

le & la **bassiste** *MASC & FEM NOUN*
bassist

la **bataille** *FEM NOUN*
1 battle
la bataille de Normandie the Battle of
Normandie *(in 1944)*
2 a card game *(like beggar-my-neighbour)*
3 en bataille in a mess
Elle a les cheveux en bataille. Her hair is in
a mess.

ℒ le **bateau** *MASC NOUN*, les **bateaux** *PL*
boat, ship
faire du bateau to go boating
Je vais faire du bateau en Corse. I'm going
sailing in Corsica.
Nous y allons en bateau. We're going there
by boat.
• le bateau à moteur
motorboat
• le bateau de plaisance
pleasure boat
• le bateau-mouche
sight-seeing boat
• le bateau pneumatique
rubber dinghy
• le bateau à voile
sailing boat

bâti *MASC ADJECTIVE*, **bâtie** *FEM*
built
un homme bien bâti a well-built man

ℒ le **bâtiment** *MASC NOUN*
1 un bâtiment a building
les vieux bâtiments du centre-ville the old
buildings in the town centre
2 le bâtiment the building trade
Son père travaille dans le bâtiment. His
father works in the building trade.

bâtir *VERB* [2]
to build

la **bâtisse** *FEM NOUN*
building

le **bâton** *MASC NOUN*
stick
• le bâton de ski
ski pole

le **bâtonnet** *MASC NOUN*
stick *(small in size)*
• le bâtonnet de poisson
fish finger

la **batte** *FEM NOUN*
bat *(for cricket, baseball)*

la **batterie** *FEM NOUN*
1 battery *(for a car)*
2 drum kit
être à la batterie to be on drums *(in a band)*

- la batterie de cuisine
  pots and pans

le **batteur** MASC NOUN
1 drummer
2 whisk
- le batteur électrique
  (electric) mixer

battre VERB [21]
1 to beat (in a competition)
  Nous allons les battre. We're going to beat them.
  Nicole m'a battu au tennis. Nicole beat me at tennis.
2 to beat (causing pain)
  battre quelqu'un to beat somebody
3 to beat (in cooking)
  battre les œufs to beat the eggs
  battre la crème to whip the cream
4 to clap
  battre des mains to clap your hands
5 to beat
  Mon cœur battait fort. My heart was beating like mad.
6 to bang
  La porte bat. The door's banging.

se **battre** REFLEXIVE VERB ◯
  to fight
  Ils n'arrêtent pas de se battre. They're always fighting.
  Je me suis battu avec mon frère. I fought with my brother.

bavard MASC ADJECTIVE, **bavarde** FEM
  talkative
  Paul est trop bavard. Paul talks too much.

♪ **bavarder** VERB [1]
  to chat
  J'aime bavarder avec mes copains. I like chatting with my friends.
  Arrêtez de bavarder. Stop chattering.

la **bavure** FEM NOUN
1 smudge (of ink, paint)
2 blunder

le **bazar** MASC NOUN
1 general store
2 (informal) mess
  C'est le bazar dans ma chambre! My bedroom's a complete mess!

BCBG ABBREVIATION
  (= bon chic, bon genre) chic and stylish

la **B.D.** INVARIABLE FEM NOUN
  (= bande dessinée) comic book
  ma collection de B.D. my comic book collection
  lire les B.D. to read comic books
  bande dessinée

♪ **beau** MASC ADJECTIVE, **bel** MASC, **belle** FEM,
    beaux MASC PL, **belles** FEM PL
1 beautiful, lovely
  un beau bébé a beautiful baby
  une belle maison a beautiful house
  un bel instrument a beautiful instrument
  un bel homme a handsome man
  de beaux vêtements lovely clothes
2 (talking of the weather) Il fait beau. It's a lovely day.
  Il fait moins beau qu'hier. It's not as nice as yesterday.

WORD TIP bel is used before words beginning with a, e, i, o, u and silent h.

♪ **beaucoup** ADVERB
1 a lot
  Je lis beaucoup. I read a lot.
  20 euros, c'est beaucoup. 20 euros, that's a lot.
  J'aime beaucoup les jeux d'ordinateur. I like computer games a lot.
  J'ai beaucoup aimé le film. I enjoyed the film a lot.
2 (when you use ne ... pas, etc) not ... much
  Camille ne parle pas beaucoup. Camille doesn't talk much.
  Il n'aime pas beaucoup la viande. He doesn't like meat very much.
3 beaucoup de a lot of
  beaucoup de jeux a lot of games
  Il a beaucoup d'argent. He has a lot of money.
  Il y avait beaucoup de gens au cinéma. There were a lot of people at the cinema.
  J'ai beaucoup de choses à faire. I've got a lot of things to do.
  Il n'a pas beaucoup d'amis. He doesn't have many friends.
  Est-ce que tu as beaucoup de devoirs à faire? Do you have a lot of homework to do?
  Non, je n'en ai pas beaucoup. No, I don't have much.
4 (expressions with beaucoup)
  beaucoup plus much more
  beaucoup moins much less
  beaucoup trop far too much
  beaucoup trop court far too short
  beaucoup plus rapide much faster
  beaucoup mieux much better
  Yasmina va beaucoup mieux. Yasmina is feeling much better.

le **beau-fils** MASC NOUN, les **beaux-fils** PL
1 son-in-law
2 stepson

le **beau-frère** MASC NOUN, les **beaux-frères** PL
  brother-in-law

◯ means the verb takes être to form the perfect

ℱ le **beau-père** *MASC NOUN*, les **beaux-pères** *PL*
1 father-in-law
2 stepfather

la **beauté** *FEM NOUN*
beauty

les **beaux-arts** *PLURAL MASC NOUN*
fine arts *(a subject to study)*
l'école des beaux-arts art school

les **beaux-parents** *PLURAL MASC NOUN*
parents-in-law

ℱ le **bébé** *MASC NOUN*
baby
s'occuper du bébé to look after the baby

le **bec** *MASC NOUN*
beak

la **bêche** *FEM NOUN*
spade

bégayer *VERB* [59]
to stammer

beige *MASC & FEM ADJECTIVE*
beige

le **beignet** *MASC NOUN*
1 fritter
2 doughnut

bel *MASC ADJECTIVE* ▸ SEE **beau**

la **belette** *FEM NOUN*
weasel

ℱ **belge** *MASC & FEM ADJECTIVE* ▸ SEE **Belge**
Belgian

> **WORD TIP** Adjectives never have capitals in French, even for nationality or regional origin.

ℱ un & une **Belge** *MASC & FEM NOUN* ▸ SEE **belge**
Belgian *(person)*
les Belges the Belgians

la **Belgique** *FEM NOUN*
Belgium
en Belgique in Belgium
aller en Belgique to go to Belgium

> **WORD TIP** Countries or regions in French take le, la or les.

le **bélier** *MASC NOUN* ▸ SEE **Bélier**
ram

Bélier *MASC NOUN* ▸ SEE **bélier**
Aries
Je suis Bélier. I'm an Aries.

> **WORD TIP** Signs of the zodiac do not take an article: un or une.

belle *FEM ADJECTIVE* ▸ SEE **beau**
la **belle** *FEM NOUN*
ma belle darling *(said to a girl)*

la **belle-famille** *FEM NOUN*
in-laws

la **belle-fille** *FEM NOUN*, les **belles-filles** *PL*
1 daughter-in-law
2 stepdaughter

ℱ la **belle-mère** *FEM NOUN*, les **belles-mères** *PL*
1 mother-in-law
2 stepmother

la **belle-sœur** *FEM NOUN*, les **belles-sœurs** *PL*
sister-in-law

le **bénéfice** *MASC NOUN*
profit
faire un bénéfice de 10 000 euros to make a
profit of 10,000 euros

bénéficier *VERB* [1]
bénéficier de quelque chose to get
something, to profit from something
J'ai bénéficié d'une remise de 10 pour cent.
I got a 10 per cent discount.

bénévole *MASC & FEM ADJECTIVE* ▸ SEE **bénévole**
NOUN
voluntary, unpaid
le & la **bénévole** *MASC & FEM NOUN* ▸ SEE
bénévole *ADJECTIVE*
voluntary worker

bénévolement *ADVERB*
voluntarily, for nothing

la **benne** *FEM NOUN*
skip *(for rubbish)*

la **béquille** *FEM NOUN*
crutch
marcher avec des béquilles to walk on
crutches

le **berceau** *MASC NOUN*, les **berceaux** *PL*
cradle

bercer *VERB* [61]
to rock *(a baby)*

le **béret** *MASC NOUN*
beret

la **berge** *FEM NOUN*
bank *(of a river, canal)*

le **berger** *MASC NOUN*, **bergère** *FEM*
shepherd
• le berger allemand
German shepherd

ℱ le **besoin** *MASC NOUN*
need
avoir besoin de quelque chose to need
something
J'ai besoin de 10 euros. I need 10 euros.
avoir besoin de faire quelque chose to need
to do something
J'ai besoin de faire une pause. I need to

A
B
C
D
E
F
G
H
I
J
K
L
M
N
O
P
Q
R
S
T
U
V
W
X
Y
Z

take a break.
Tu n'as pas besoin de téléphoner. You don't
need to phone.

le **bétail** MASC NOUN
1 livestock *(farm animals)*
2 cattle

bête MASC & FEM ADJECTIVE ▸ SEE **bête** NOUN
stupid

♀ la **bête** FEM NOUN ▸ SEE **bête** ADJECTIVE
animal

la **bêtise** FEM NOUN
1 faire une bêtise to do something stupid
Il fait toujours des bêtises. He's always
doing stupid things.
2 la bêtise stupidity

le **béton** MASC NOUN
concrete

la **bétonnière** FEM NOUN
cement mixer

la **betterave** la **betterave rouge** FEM NOUN
beetroot

le & la **beur** MASC & FEM NOUN
young person of North African origin

♀ le **beurre** MASC NOUN
butter
une tartine de beurre et de confiture a slice
of bread and butter with jam

beurrer VERB [1]
to butter

le **bibelot** MASC NOUN
ornament

le **biberon** MASC NOUN
baby's bottle

la **Bible** FEM NOUN
(Religion) the Bible

le & la **bibliothécaire** MASC & FEM NOUN
librarian

♀ la **bibliothèque** FEM NOUN
1 library
emprunter des livres à la bibliothèque to
borrow books from the library
2 bookcase

le **bic**® MASC NOUN
un stylo bic® a Biro®

la **biche** FEM NOUN
doe

♀ la **bicyclette** FEM NOUN
bicycle
faire de la bicyclette to cycle, to go cycling

♀ le **bidet** MASC NOUN
bidet *(part of a bathroom suite)*

bidon INVARIABLE ADJECTIVE ▸ SEE **bidon** NOUN
(informal) false, phoney
une adresse bidon a false address
Son histoire est bidon! His story's rubbish!

le **bidon** MASC NOUN ▸ SEE **bidon** INVARIABLE
ADJECTIVE
1 can *(for paint, petrol)*
2 drum *(larger, for oil)*

le **bidonville** MASC NOUN
shanty town

le **bidule** MASC NOUN
(informal) whatsit, thingamajig

♀ **bien** INVARIABLE ADJECTIVE ▸ SEE **bien** ADV, NOUN
1 good, nice
des gens bien nice people
C'est bien! That's good!
Ce sera bien de revoir mes copains. It'll be
nice to see my friends again.
2 well
Je me sens vraiment bien ce matin. I feel
really good this morning.
Pauline ne se sent pas très bien. Pauline
isn't feeling very well.
3 nice, comfortable
On est bien ici. It's very comfortable here.
On est très bien dans ce fauteuil. This
chair's really comfortable.

♀ **bien** ADVERB ▸ SEE **bien** ADJ, NOUN
1 well
Elle chante bien. She sings well.
Ce travail est bien payé. This job is well
paid.
Bien joué! Well done!
J'aime mon bifteck bien cuit. I like my steak
well done.
Elle est bien habillée. She is well dressed.
2 aller bien to be well
Tu vas bien? Are you well?
Je vais très bien, merci. I'm very well,
thanks.
3 aller bien à quelqu'un to suit somebody
Ça me va? Does it suit me?
Le blouson te va bien. The jacket suits you.
4 bien se passer to go well
Ça se passe bien. Things are going well.
Alors, la fête s'est bien passée? So, did the
party go well?
5 bien vouloir quelque chose not to mind
something
Je voudrais bien de la confiture. I wouldn't
mind some jam.
Tu veux de l'eau? Oui, je veux bien. Would
you like some water? Yes please.
6 bien vouloir faire quelque chose to be
happy to do something
Il veut bien t'aider. He's happy to help you.
Je veux bien le faire. I'm happy to do it.
7 very, really

○ means the verb takes être to form the perfect

bien triste very sad
J'espère bien! I really hope so!
8 at least
Il a bien 20 ans. He's at least 20.
Ça vaut bien 100 euros. It's worth 100
euros at least.
9 much *(with a following adjective)*
bien mieux much better
bien plus chaud much hotter
10 bien de many, a great deal of
bien des gens many people
Elle s'est donnée bien du mal. She went to a
great deal of trouble.

le **bien** *MASC NOUN* ▶ SEE **bien** *ADJ, ADV*
1 good
le bien et le mal good and evil
Ça te fera du bien. That'll do you good.
2 possession
tous leurs biens all their possessions
• **bien entendu**
of course
• le **bien-être**
well-being

bien que *CONJUNCTION*
although
Bien qu'il soit petit, il est assez fort.
Although he is small, he is quite strong.

WORD TIP bien que is followed by a verb in the
subjunctive.

bien sûr *ADVERB*
of course
Bien sûr que oui! Of course!
Bien sûr que je viens! Of course I'm coming!

ℓ **bientôt** *ADVERB*
soon
À bientôt! See you soon! *(when saying
goodbye, in a letter, etc)*

ℓ le **bienvenu** *NOUN MASC*, la **bienvenue** *FEM* ▶ SEE
bienvenue *FEM*
welcome
Soyez le bienvenu! Welcome! *(to a boy)*
Soyez la bienvenue! Welcome! *(to a girl)*

ℓ la **bienvenue** *FEM NOUN* ▶ SEE **bienvenu** *MASC*
welcome
Bienvenue! Welcome!
souhaiter la bienvenue à quelqu'un to
welcome somebody
Allons leur souhaiter la bienvenue. Let's go
and welcome them.

ℓ la **bière** *FEM NOUN*
beer
boire de la bière to drink beer
Trois bières, s'il vous plaît! Three beers,
please!
• la **bière blonde**
lager

• la **bière brune**
brown ale

ℓ le **bifteck** *MASC NOUN*
steak

la **bifurcation** *FEM NOUN*
fork *(in a road)*

le **bijou** *MASC NOUN*, les **bijoux** *PL*
un bijou a piece of jewellery
des bijoux jewellery

la **bijouterie** *FEM NOUN*
jeweller's (shop)

le **bijoutier** *MASC NOUN*, la **bijoutière** *FEM*
jeweller

le **bilan** *MASC NOUN*
1 balance sheet *(in accounts)*
2 faire le bilan de quelque chose to assess
something
'Tremblement de terre, bilan: 1 000 morts'
'1,000 dead in earthquake' *(in a headline)*

bilingue *MASC & FEM ADJECTIVE*
bilingual

le **billard** *MASC NOUN*
1 billiards
jouer au billard to play billiards
2 billiard table
• le **billard américain**
pool
• le **billard anglais**
snooker

la **bille** *FEM NOUN*
1 marble
jouer aux billes to play marbles
2 billiard ball

ℓ le **billet** *MASC NOUN*
1 note
un billet de banque a banknote
un billet de cent euros a hundred-euro
note
2 ticket
un billet de train a train ticket

le **billion** *MASC NOUN*
billion

bio *INVARIABLE ADJECTIVE*
(informal) **organic**
les produits bio organic produce

la **biochimie** *FEM NOUN*
biochemistry

la **biographie** *FEM NOUN*
biography

ℓ la **biologie** *FEM NOUN*
biology

biologique *MASC & FEM ADJECTIVE*
1 biological

ℓ **indicates key words**

2 organic (agriculture, food)

le & la **biologiste** MASC & FEM NOUN
biologist

le **bip** MASC NOUN
beep
Parlez après le bip sonore. Speak after the
tone (on an answering machine)

la **biscotte** FEM NOUN
crispbread

♀ le **biscuit** MASC NOUN
biscuit

la **bise** FEM NOUN
1 (informal) **kiss**
faire la bise à quelqu'un to kiss somebody
on the cheek (when saying hello, goodbye)
Fais-moi la bise! Give me a kiss!
Grosses bises Lots of love (in an informal
letter)
2 north wind (a cold wind)

🔵 BISE

Pour dire bonjour ou au revoir à la famille et aux
amis, les Français font des bises : une, deux, trois
ou quatre, ça dépend des gens et des régions!

♀ le **bistro, bistrot** MASC NOUN
bistro, cafe

bizarre MASC & FEM ADJECTIVE
strange
C'est vraiment bizarre. It's really strange.

la **blague** FEM NOUN
1 (informal) **joke**
Sans blague! No joking!
2 (informal) **trick**
Je lui ai fait une blague. I played a trick on
him/her.

blaguer VERB [1]
(informal) **to joke**

le **blaireau** MASC NOUN, les **blaireaux** PL
1 badger
2 shaving brush

blâmer VERB [1]
1 to criticize
2 to blame

♀ **blanc** MASC ADJECTIVE, **blanche** FEM ▸ SEE **blanc**,
Blanc NOUN
1 white
des chaussures blanches white shoes
2 blank
une feuille blanche a blank sheet of paper

♀ le **blanc** MASC NOUN ▸ SEE **blanc** ADJECTIVE,
Blanc NOUN
1 white
peint en blanc painted white

2 blank space
laisser un blanc to leave a blank space
3 breast (of chicken, etc)
un blanc de poulet a chicken breast
• le blanc d'œuf
egg white

un **Blanc** MASC NOUN ▸ SEE **blanc** ADJ, NOUN
white man
les Blancs white people

WORD TIP Names of peoples take a capital in
French.

blanche FEM ADJECTIVE ▸ SEE **blanc** MASC ADJECTIVE

une **Blanche** FEM NOUN
white woman
▸ SEE **Blanc**

blanchir VERB [2]
to whiten

la **blanchisserie** FEM NOUN
laundry

le **blé** MASC NOUN
wheat

blessé MASC ADJECTIVE, **blessée** FEM ▸ SEE **blessé**
NOUN
injured

le **blessé** MASC NOUN, la **blessée** FEM ▸ SEE **blessé**
ADJECTIVE
injured person

♀ **blesser** VERB [1]
to injure
Elle a été blessée dans l'accident. She was
injured in the accident.

se **blesser** REFLEXIVE VERB 🔵
to hurt yourself
Il s'est blessé. He hurt himself.
Elle s'est blessée à la main. She hurt her hand.

la **blessure** FEM NOUN
1 injury
2 wound

♀ **bleu** MASC ADJECTIVE, **bleue** FEM ▸ SEE **bleu** NOUN
blue
bleu clair light blue
bleu foncé dark blue
peint en bleu painted blue
une veste bleu marine a navy blue jacket

♀ le **bleu** MASC NOUN ▸ SEE **bleu** ADJECTIVE
1 blue
Le bleu est ma couleur préférée. Blue is my
favourite colour.
2 bruise
J'ai un bleu sur le bras. I've got a bruise on
my arm.

le **bloc** MASC NOUN
1 block (of concrete, etc)

🔵 means the verb takes être to form the perfect

2 pad (for notes, letters)
un bloc de papier à lettres a writing pad
- les **bloc-notes**
notepad
- le **bloc sanitaire**
toilet block (in a campsite)

le **blog** MASC NOUN
blog

le **blogueur** MASC NOUN, **blogueuse** FEM
blogger

ℒ **blond** MASC ADJECTIVE, **blonde** FEM
fair-haired
la fille blonde the fair-haired girl
J'ai les cheveux blonds. I've got fair hair.

bloqué MASC ADJECTIVE, **bloquée** FEM
1 blocked (road)
2 jammed (mechanism)
3 stuck (car)

bloquer VERB [1]
1 to block (a road)
2 to jam (a mechanism)

la **blouse** FEM NOUN
overall (to protect clothes)

ℒ le **blouson** MASC NOUN
jacket
un blouson en jean a denim jacket
un blouson en cuir a leather jacket

le **blue-jean** MASC NOUN
jeans
J'ai acheté un blue-jean. I bought a pair of
jeans.

la **bobine** FEM NOUN
reel

le **bocal** MASC NOUN, les **bocaux** PL
jar

ℒ le **bœuf** MASC NOUN
1 beef
Est-ce que tu aimes le bœuf? Do you like
beef?
2 bullock

bof EXCLAMATION
(informal)
'C'était bien hier?' – 'Bof!' 'Did you have a
good time yesterday?' – 'Nothing special.'

le **bohémien** MASC NOUN, la **bohémienne** FEM
gypsy

ℒ **boire** VERB [22]
to drink
Vous voulez boire quelque chose? Would
you like something to drink?
Je boirais bien un jus d'orange. I'd really like
an orange juice.

ℒ le **bois** MASC NOUN
1 wood (the material)
une table en bois a wooden table
2 wood (of trees)
se promener dans les bois to take a walk in
the woods

ℒ la **boisson** FEM NOUN
drink
une boisson fraîche a cold drink
Et comme boisson? What would you like to
drink? (in a restaurant)

ℒ la **boîte** FEM NOUN
1 tin
une boîte de sardines a tin of sardines
2 box
une boîte d'allumettes a box of matches
3 (informal) **club**
aller en boîte to go out to a club
On va en boîte ce soir. We're going out to a
club tonight.
- la **boîte de conserve**
tin, can
- la **boîte de dialogue**
dialog box (on the computer screen)
- la **boîte d'envoi**
outbox (in email)
- la **boîte aux lettres**
post box
- la **boîte de nuit**
nightclub
- la **boîte de réception**
intray (in email)
- la **boîte de vitesses**
gearbox

ℒ le **bol** MASC NOUN
1 bowl
un bol de riz a bowl of rice
2 en avoir ras le bol (informal) to be fed up

bombarder VERB [1]
1 to bombard
2 to bomb

la **bombe** FEM NOUN
1 bomb
2 spray (aerosol)
une bombe de peinture paint spray

ℒ **bon** MASC ADJECTIVE, **bonne** FEM ▶SEE **bon** ADV,
EXCL, NOUN
1 good
un bon repas a good meal
J'ai de bonnes copines. I've got good
friends.
C'est bon pour la santé. It's good for your
health.
être bon en quelque chose to be good at
something
Max est bon en français. Max is good at
French.

ℒ indicates key words

2 right
le bon numéro the right number
la bonne adresse the right address
C'est bon. It's OK, It's fine.

3 valid
Mon ticket est bon. My ticket is valid.

ℰ **bon** ADVERB ▸ SEE **bon** ADJ, EXCL, NOUN
sentir bon to smell good
Ça sent bon! That smells good!
Il fait bon aujourd'hui. It's a nice day today.
Il fait bon chez moi. It's lovely and warm at
my house.

ℰ **bon** EXCLAMATION ▸ SEE **bon** ADJ, ADV, NOUN

1 Bon! Right!
Bon, on y va? Right, shall we go?
Ah bon? Really?

2 (in greetings and wishes) Bonne année!
Happy New Year!
Bon anniversaire! Happy birthday!
Bon appétit! Enjoy your meal!
Bonne chance! Good luck!
Bonne journée! Have a nice day!
Bonne nuit! Good night!
Bon retour! Safe journey back!
Bon voyage! Have a nice trip!

ℰ le **bon** NOUN MASC ▸ SEE **bon** ADJ, ADV, EXCL

1 voucher

2 pour de bon for good
partir pour de bon to go away for good

ℰ le **bonbon** MASC NOUN
sweet
un bonbon à la menthe a mint

la **bonbonne** FEM NOUN
une bonbonne de gaz a gas cylinder

le **bond** MASC NOUN
jump
se lever d'un bond to jump to your feet

bondé MASC ADJECTIVE, **bondée** FEM
crowded
un bus bondé d'étudiants a bus packed
with students

bondir VERB [2]
to jump
bondir de joie to jump for joy

le **bonheur** MASC NOUN

1 happiness
Je vous souhaite beaucoup de bonheur. I
wish you every happiness.

2 pleasure
avoir le bonheur de faire quelque chose to
have the pleasure of doing something

le **bonhomme de neige** MASC NOUN, les
bonshommes de neige PL
snowman

ℰ **bonjour** GREETING

1 hello

2 good morning

3 good afternoon

> **WORD TIP** You can use bonjour at most times
> of the day.

bon marché INVARIABLE ADJECTIVE
cheap
des vêtements bon marché cheap clothes

bonne FEM ADJECTIVE ▸ SEE **bon**

bonne heure IN PHRASE
de bonne heure early
Demain, il faudra se lever de bonne heure.
Tomorrow we'll have to get up early.

le **bonnet** MASC NOUN
(woolly) hat

le **bon sens** MASC NOUN
common sense

ℰ **bonsoir** GREETING

1 good evening

2 good night

la **bonté** FEM NOUN
kindness

le **boom** MASC NOUN
boom (a time of prosperity)

ℰ le **bord** MASC NOUN

1 edge (of a table, cliff)

2 rim (of a glass, cup, vase)

3 side (of a road)
au bord de la route at the side of the road

4 au bord de la mer at the seaside

5 bank (of a lake, river, stream)
les bords de la Loire the banks of the Loire

6 à bord on board
Il y a 300 passagers à bord de l'avion. There
are 300 passengers on board the plane.
Bienvenue à bord! Welcome aboard!

bordeaux INVARIABLE ADJECTIVE
maroon
une jupe bordeaux a maroon skirt

border VERB [1]
to edge
une route bordée d'arbres a tree-lined road
un mouchoir bordé de dentelle a
handkerchief edged with lace

la **bordure** FEM NOUN

1 border (of fabric, flowers)

2 edge (of a road, a path)

3 en bordure de on the edge of

la **borne** FEM NOUN

1 kilometre marker (like a milestone)

2 bollard

◉ means the verb takes être to form the perfect

la **bosse** FEM NOUN
bump

bosser VERB [1]
(informal) **to work**
Elle bosse tard le soir. She works late into the evening.

botanique MASC & FEM ADJECTIVE ▸ SEE **botanique** NOUN
les jardins botaniques the botanic gardens
la **botanique** FEM NOUN ▸ SEE **botanique** ADJECTIVE
botany

ℰ la **botte** FEM NOUN
1 **boot** (shoe)
des bottes de cuir leather boots
2 **bale** (of hay, straw)
3 **bunch** (of carrots, radishes)

la **bottine** FEM NOUN
ankle boot

le **bouc** MASC NOUN
billy goat

ℰ la **bouche** FEM NOUN
mouth
• le bouche-à-bouche
mouth-to-mouth resuscitation
• la bouche d'égout
manhole

la **bouchée** FEM NOUN
mouthful

boucher VERB [1]
▸ SEE **boucher** NOUN
1 **to cork** (a bottle)
2 **to fill** (a hole, a gap, a crack, etc)
se **boucher** REFLEXIVE VERB ◉
to get blocked up
se boucher le nez to hold your nose

ℰ le **boucher** MASC NOUN, la **bouchère** FEM ▸ SEE **boucher** VERB
butcher
aller chez le boucher to go to the butcher's

la **boucherie** FEM NOUN
butcher's (shop)

le **bouchon** MASC NOUN
1 **cork** (for a wine bottle)
2 **screw-cap** (for a bottle of water)
3 **traffic jam**
un bouchon sur la A-10 a traffic jam on the A-10 motorway

la **boucle** FEM NOUN
1 **buckle** (of a belt)
2 **curl** (in your hair)

bouclé MASC ADJECTIVE, **bouclée** FEM
curly
Elle a les cheveux bouclés. She has curly hair.

la **boucle d'oreille** FEM NOUN
earring
porter des boucles d'oreille to wear earrings

le **Bouddha** MASC NOUN
Buddha

le **bouddhisme** MASC NOUN
Buddhism

> **WORD TIP** Use a small letter for names of religions in French.

bouder VERB [1]
to sulk

le **boudin** MASC NOUN
black pudding

la **boue** FEM NOUN
mud

la **bouée** FEM NOUN
1 **rubber ring**
2 **buoy**
• la bouée de sauvetage
lifebelt

boueux MASC ADJECTIVE, **boueuse** FEM
muddy

la **bouffe** FEM NOUN
(informal) **food, grub**

la **bouffée** FEM NOUN
une bouffée d'air frais a breath of fresh air

le **bougeoir** MASC NOUN
candlestick

bouger VERB [52]
to move
Ne bougez plus! Stay still! (to people when taking a photo)

la **bougie** FEM NOUN
1 **candle** (on a cake)
2 **spark plug** (in a car engine)

la **bouillabaisse** FEM NOUN
Mediterranean fish soup (made with fish and vegetables)

bouillant MASC ADJECTIVE, **bouillante** FEM
boiling
faire cuire à l'eau bouillante cook in boiling water

bouillir VERB [23]
1 **to boil** (in cooking)
faire bouillir le lait to boil the milk
2 (to get angry) Ça me fait bouillir! It makes me mad!

la **bouilloire** FEM NOUN
kettle

ℰ indicates key words

le **bouillon** *MASC NOUN*
stock *(made with meat, fish, or vegetables)*
- le bouillon-cube
stock cube

la **bouillotte** *FEM NOUN*
hot-water bottle

♪ le **boulanger** *MASC NOUN*, la **boulangère** *FEM*
baker

la **boulangerie** *FEM NOUN*
bakery
acheter du pain à la boulangerie to buy
bread at the baker's

la **boulangerie-pâtisserie** *FEM NOUN*
bakery *(selling bread, pastries, cakes, etc)*

la **boule** *FEM NOUN*
1 boule
jouer aux boules to play boules
2 scoop *(of ice cream)*
Vous voulez combien de boules? How
many scoops would you like?
- la boule de neige
snowball

le **bouleau** *MASC NOUN*, les **bouleaux** *PL*
birch tree

la **boulette** *FEM NOUN*
pellet
- la boulette de viande
meatball

♪ le **boulevard** *MASC NOUN*
boulevard
- le boulevard périphérique
ring road

bouleverser *VERB* [1]
1 to shatter, to overwhelm
être bouleversé par une mauvaise nouvelle
to be shattered by bad news
2 to disrupt *(a schedule, plans)*

le **boulot** *MASC NOUN*
1 *(informal)* work
C'est un boulot immense. It's a huge
amount of work.
2 *(informal)* job
Elle a un nouveau boulot. She has a new
job.

le **bouquet** *MASC NOUN*
bunch *(of flowers or herbs)*

le **bouquin** *MASC NOUN*
(informal) book

le **bourdon** *MASC NOUN*
bumblebee

le **bourg** *MASC NOUN*
1 market town
2 village

bourgeois *MASC ADJECTIVE*, **bourgeoise** *FEM*
▸ SEE **bourgeois** *NOUN*
middle-class

le **bourgeois** *MASC NOUN*, la **bourgeoise** *FEM*
▸ SEE **bourgeois** *ADJECTIVE*
middle-class person

le **bourgeon** *MASC NOUN*
bud *(on a tree)*

la **Bourgogne** *FEM NOUN*
Burgundy

WORD TIP Countries or regions in French take
le, la or les.

bourré *MASC ADJECTIVE*, **bourrée** *FEM*
1 bourré de crammed with
bourré de monde packed *(with people)*
2 *(informal)* drunk

bourrer *VERB* [1]
to cram

la **bourse** *FEM NOUN*
1 purse
2 grant *(for studies)*
3 la Bourse the stock exchange

bousculer *VERB* [1]
1 to bump into
Quelqu'un m'a bousculé. Someone bumped
into me.
2 to rush

la **boussole** *FEM NOUN*
compass

♪ le **bout** *MASC NOUN*
1 end
Il est resté jusqu'au bout. He stayed until
the end.
au bout de at the end of
Julien habite tout au bout de la rue. Julien
lives right at the end of the street.
2 tip *(of nose, finger, tongue)*
3 piece
un bout de pain a piece of bread
un petit bout de fromage a little bit of
cheese
des bouts de papier scraps of paper
4 au bout de after
au bout d'une demi-heure after half an
hour

♪ la **bouteille** *FEM NOUN*
bottle
une bouteille de lait a milk bottle
de l'eau en bouteille bottled water
- la bouteille d'oxygène
oxygen cylinder

♪ la **boutique** *FEM NOUN*
shop
une boutique hors taxes a duty-free shop

ℓ le **bouton** MASC NOUN
1 **button** (on clothes, machines)
Appuie sur le bouton! Press the button!
2 **spot** (on your skin)
Ça me donne des boutons. It brings me out in spots.
3 **bud** (of a flower)
• le bouton d'or
buttercup

la **boxe** FEM NOUN
boxing

le **boxeur** MASC NOUN
boxer

le **bracelet** MASC NOUN
1 **bracelet**
2 **bangle**
• le bracelet-montre
wristwatch

le **brancard** MASC NOUN
stretcher

la **branche** FEM NOUN
branch (of a tree)

branché MASC ADJECTIVE, **branchée** FEM
(informal) **trendy**

brancher VERB [1]
1 **to plug in** (an iron, a television)
2 **to connect** (electricity, telephone, computer)

ℓ le **bras** MASC NOUN
arm
• le bras de fer
arm wrestling

la **brasse** FEM NOUN
breaststroke
• la brasse papillon
butterfly (stroke)
• la brasse coulée
racing breaststroke

la **brasserie** FEM NOUN
1 **brasserie**
2 **brewery**

brave MASC & FEM ADJECTIVE
1 **nice**
Ce sont de braves gens. They're nice people.
2 **brave**

bravo EXCLAMATION
bravo, **well done**
Bravo, tes notes sont excellentes! Well done, your marks are excellent!

le **break** MASC NOUN
estate car

la **brebis** FEM NOUN
ewe

bref MASC ADJECTIVE, **brève** FEM
1 **short** (vowel, sound)
en bref in short
2 **brief** (story, visit)
dans les plus brefs délais as soon as possible

le **Brésil** MASC NOUN
Brazil

brésilien MASC ADJECTIVE, **brésilienne** FEM ▸ SEE
Brésilien
Brazilian

le **Brésilien** MASC NOUN, la **Brésilienne** FEM ▸ SEE
brésilien
1 **Brazilian**
2 le brésilien Brazilian Portuguese (the language)

la **Bretagne** FEM NOUN
Brittany

WORD TIP Countries or regions in French take le, la or les.

la **bretelle** FEM NOUN
1 **strap** (of a dress, a swimsuit)
2 des bretelles braces
3 **slip road** (of a motorway)

breton MASC ADJECTIVE, **bretonne** FEM ▸ SEE
Breton
Breton

WORD TIP Adjectives never have capitals in French, even for nationality or regional origin.

le **Breton** MASC NOUN, la **Bretonne** FEM ▸ SEE
breton
1 **Breton** (person from Brittany)
2 le breton Breton (language)

le **brevet** MASC NOUN
certificate
• le brevet des collèges
certificate of general education (taken at around 15 at the end of study in a collège)
• le brevet de secourisme
first aid certificate

ℓ le **bricolage** MASC NOUN
DIY

bricoler VERB [1]
to do DIY

le **bricoleur** MASC NOUN, la **bricoleuse** FEM
DIY enthusiast

brièvement ADVERB
briefly

brillamment ADVERB
brilliantly

brillant MASC ADJECTIVE, **brillante** FEM
1 **shiny** (hair, shoes)

2 **bright** *(eyes)*
3 **brilliant** *(pupil, result)*

ℰ **briller** *VERB* [1]
    to shine
    faire briller ses chaussures to polish your
    shoes

la **brindille** *FEM NOUN*
    twig

la **brioche** *FEM NOUN*
    brioche

la **brique** *FEM NOUN*
1 **brick**
2 **carton** *(of fruit juice, milk)*

le **briquet** *MASC NOUN*
    lighter

la **brise** *FEM NOUN*
    breeze

briser *VERB* [1]
    to break

ℰ **britannique** *MASC & FEM ADJECTIVE* ▶SEE
    Britannique
    British

> **WORD TIP** Adjectives never have capitals in
> French, even for nationality or regional origin.

ℰ le & la **Britannique** *MASC & FEM NOUN* ▶SEE
    britannique
    Briton
    les Britanniques the British

la **brocante** *FEM NOUN*
1 **second-hand shop**
2 **flea market**

la **broche** *FEM NOUN*
1 **brooch**
2 **spit** *(for roasting)*
    faire cuire un poulet à la broche to spit-
    roast a chicken

la **brochette** *FEM NOUN*
1 **skewer**
2 **kebab**
    une brochette de viande a meat kebab

ℰ la **brochure** *FEM NOUN*
1 **booklet**
2 **brochure**

les **brocolis** *PLURAL*
    broccoli

broder *VERB* [1]
    to embroider

la **broderie** *FEM NOUN*
    embroidery
    des broderies embroidery

la **bronchite** *FEM NOUN*
    bronchitis
    avoir une bronchite to have bronchitis

le **bronzage** *MASC NOUN*
    suntan

ℰ **bronzer** *VERB* [1]
1 **to tan**
    Je bronze facilement. I tan easily.
2 **to sunbathe**

ℰ la **brosse** *FEM NOUN*
    brush
    • la **brosse à cheveux**
      hairbrush
    • la **brosse à dents**
      toothbrush

brosser *VERB* [1]
    to brush

se **brosser** *REFLEXIVE VERB* ⌃
    se brosser les dents to brush your teeth

la **brouette** *FEM NOUN*
    wheelbarrow

ℰ le **brouillard** *MASC NOUN*
    fog
    Il y a du brouillard ce matin. It's foggy this
    morning.

le **brouillon** *MASC NOUN*
    draft *(of a letter, a document, etc)*

la **bru** *FEM NOUN*
    daughter-in-law

le **brugnon** *MASC NOUN*
    nectarine

ℰ le **bruit** *MASC NOUN*
1 **noise**
    entendre un bruit to hear a noise
    le bruit de la circulation the noise of the
    traffic
    Vous faites trop de bruit. You're making
    too much noise.
2 **rumour**
    Le bruit court qu'elle a un petit copain.
    They say she's got a boyfriend.

brûlant *MASC ADJECTIVE*, **brûlante** *FEM*
1 **boiling hot** *(tea, coffee)*
2 **burning hot** *(oven, sand)*

le **brûlé** *MASC NOUN*
    un goût de brûlé a burnt taste
    Ça sent le brûlé. There's a smell of burning.

brûler *VERB* [1]
    to burn
    Attention, ça brûle! Careful, it's very hot!

se **brûler** *REFLEXIVE VERB* ⌃
    to burn yourself
    Pierre s'est brûlé. Pierre burnt himself.
    Elle s'est brûlée. She's burnt herself.

Je me suis brûlé la main. I burnt my hand.

la **brûlure** *FEM NOUN*
burn

la **brume** *FEM NOUN*
mist
la brume matinale early morning mist

brumeux *MASC ADJECTIVE*, **brumeuse** *FEM*
misty

ℓ **brun** *MASC ADJECTIVE*, **brune** *FEM*
1 **dark** *(hair)*
2 **dark-haired**
Moi, je suis brune et Sylvie est blonde. I'm dark-haired and Sylvie is blonde.
3 **brown** *(eyes, skin, fur)*
J'ai les yeux bruns. I've got brown eyes.

le **brushing** *MASC NOUN*
blow-dry
se faire un brushing to have a blow-dry.

brut *MASC ADJECTIVE*, **brute** *FEM*
1 **raw** *(material)*
2 **crude** *(oil)*
3 **gross** *(income)*
4 **dry** *(champagne, cider)*

brutal *MASC ADJECTIVE*, **brutale** *FEM*, **brutaux** *MASC PL*, **brutales** *FEM PL*
1 **sudden** *(pain, death)*
2 **violent** *(shock, attack)*
3 **brutal** *(words)*

Bruxelles *NOUN*
Brussels *(capital of Belgium)*

bruyant *MASC ADJECTIVE*, **bruyante** *FEM*
1 **noisy**
2 **loud** *(music)*

la **bruyère** *FEM NOUN*
heather

bu *VERB* ▸ SEE **boire**

la **bûche** *FEM NOUN*
log
• la bûche de Noël
Yuletide log

le **budget** *MASC NOUN*
budget

ℓ le **buffet** *MASC NOUN*
1 **sideboard**
2 **buffet** *(food)*

le **buisson** *MASC NOUN*
bush

buissonnière *FEM ADJECTIVE*
faire l'école buissonnière to play truant

la **Bulgarie** *FEM NOUN*
Bulgaria

la **bulle** *FEM NOUN*
bubble

ℓ le **bulletin** *MASC NOUN*
1 **bulletin**
un bulletin d'information a news bulletin
2 **report**
un bulletin scolaire a school report
3 **certificate**
un bulletin de naissance a birth certificate
• le bulletin de notes
school report

ℓ le **bureau** *MASC NOUN*, les **bureaux** *PL*
1 **desk**
Elle est à son bureau. She's at her desk.
2 **office**
aller au bureau to go to the office
Ma mère travaille dans un bureau. My mother works in an office.
3 **study** *(at home)*
L'ordinateur se trouve dans le bureau. The computer is in the study.
• le bureau de change
bureau de change
• le bureau d'accueil
reception
• le bureau des objets trouvés
lost property office
• le bureau de poste
post office
• le bureau de tabac
tobacconist's
• le bureau de tourisme
tourist information office

la **bureaucratie** *FEM NOUN*
bureaucracy

ℓ le **bus** *MASC NOUN*
bus
prendre le bus to take the bus
Allons-y en bus. Let's go there by bus.

la **buse** *FEM NOUN*
buzzard

le **buste** *MASC NOUN*
bust

le **but** *MASC NOUN*
1 **aim** *(objective)*
2 **goal** *(in football, hockey)*
marquer un but to score a goal

buvable *MASC & FEM ADJECTIVE*
drinkable

le **buvard** *MASC NOUN*
blotter
du papier buvard blotting paper

la **buvette** *FEM NOUN*
bar *(at a dance, village fair, etc)*

A
B
C
D
E
F
G
H
I
J
K
L
M
N
O
P
Q
R
S
T
U
V
W
X
Y
Z

buvez, buvons VERB ▸ SEE **boire**

Cc

c' ABBREVIATION: CE

> **WORD TIP** ce becomes c' before a word beginning with e- or é- ▸ SEE **ce**

ℓ **ça** PRONOUN ▸ SEE **ça** ADV
1 Ça va? How are you?
    Comment ça va? How are you?
    Ça va bien, merci. I'm fine, thanks.
2 that
    Donne-moi ça! Give me that!
    Je n'aime pas ça! I don't like that!
    Ça, c'est un moineau. That's a sparrow.
    C'est ça. That's right.
    Ça y est, j'ai terminé mes devoirs! That's it, I've finished my homework!
3 it
    Ça ne fait rien. It doesn't matter.
    Ça dépend. It depends.
    Ça me fait mal. It hurts.
    Ça me va! It fits me.
    Dix heures, ça me va. 10 o'clock suits me.

> **WORD TIP** ça is the informal version of cela.

ℓ **çà** ADVERB ▸ SEE **ça**
    çà et là here and there

la **cabane** FEM NOUN
    hut
    une cabane dans le jardin a hut in the garden

le **cabillaud** MASC NOUN
    cod

ℓ la **cabine** FEM NOUN
1 cabin (on a ship)
2 cab (on a lorry)
3 cubicle, changing room (at the swimming pool)
• la cabine de douche
    shower cubicle
• la cabine d'essayage
    fitting room
• la cabine téléphonique
    telephone box

le **cabinet** MASC NOUN ▸ SEE **cabinets** PL MASC NOUN
1 office (solicitor's)
2 surgery (doctor's, dentist's)
• le cabinet médical
    medical practice
• le cabinet de travail
    study

les **cabinets** PLURAL MASC NOUN ▸ SEE **cabinet**
    toilet

ℓ le **câble** MASC NOUN
1 cable
    un câble électrique an electric cable
2 cable TV
    J'aimerais avoir le câble. I'd like to have cable TV.

câblé MASC ADJECTIVE, **câblée** FEM
    être câblé to have cable TV
    Nous sommes câblés. We have cable TV.

cabosser VERB [1]
    to dent

la **cacahuète** FEM NOUN
    peanut
• les cacahuètes grillées
    roasted peanuts

le **cacao** MASC NOUN
    cocoa

caché MASC ADJECTIVE, **cachée** FEM
    hidden

cache-cache INVARIABLE MASC NOUN
    jouer à cache-cache to play hide and seek

le **cachemire** MASC NOUN
    cashmere

le **cache-nez** INVARIABLE MASC NOUN
    (thick) scarf

le **cache-pot** INVARIABLE MASC NOUN
    flowerpot holder

cacher VERB [1]
    to hide
    cacher quelque chose to hide something
    J'ai caché mon journal intime. I hid my diary.

se **cacher** REFLEXIVE VERB ◯
    to hide
    Elle s'est cachée dans le cagibi. She hid in the store cupboard.

le **cachet** MASC NOUN
    tablet
• le cachet d'aspirine
    aspirin
• le cachet de la poste
    postmark

la **cachette** FEM NOUN
1 hiding place
2 en cachette secretly
    Il lui téléphone en cachette. He phones her secretly.

le **cachot** MASC NOUN
    dungeon

le **cactus** MASC NOUN
    cactus

◯ means the verb takes être to form the perfect

le **cadavre** *MASC NOUN*
  corpse, body

le **caddie®** *MASC NOUN*
  shopping trolley

ℰ le **cadeau** *MASC NOUN*, les **cadeaux** *PL*
1 present
  un cadeau d'anniversaire a birthday
  present
  les cadeaux de Noël Christmas presents
  faire un cadeau à quelqu'un to give
  somebody a present
  J'ai fait un cadeau au professeur. I gave a
  present to the teacher.
  faire cadeau de quelque chose à quelqu'un
  to give somebody something
  Il m'a fait cadeau de son portable. He gave
  me his mobile.
2 du papier cadeau wrapping paper
  Je vous fais un paquet-cadeau? Shall I gift-
  wrap it for you?

le **cadenas** *MASC NOUN*
  padlock

la **cadence** *FEM NOUN*
  rhythm

ℰ **cadet** *MASC ADJECTIVE,* **cadette** *FEM* ▸ SEE **cadet**
    NOUN
1 younger
  mon frère cadet my younger brother
2 youngest
  ma sœur cadette my youngest sister

ℰ le **cadet** *MASC NOUN,* la **cadette** *FEM* ▸ SEE **cadet**
    ADJECTIVE
  younger child, youngest child
  Le cadet, c'est Antoine. Antoine's the
  youngest.

le **cadran** *MASC NOUN*
1 face *(of a watch, a clock)*
2 dial *(on a speedometer)*
• le cadran solaire
  sundial

le **cadre** *MASC NOUN*
1 frame *(of a picture, a window, a bicycle)*
2 surroundings *(of a place)*
3 executive *(in business)*
  un cadre supérieur à la banque a senior
  executive at the bank

le **cafard** *MASC NOUN*
1 cockroach
2 depression
  avoir le cafard to be down in the dumps
  J'ai un peu le cafard aujourd'hui. I'm a bit
  down in the dumps today.
  donner le cafard à quelqu'un to get
  somebody down
  Cette pluie me donne le cafard! This rain is
  getting me down!

ℰ le **café** *MASC NOUN*
1 coffee
  prendre un café to have a coffee
  Vous prendrez un café? Would you like a
  coffee? *(formal)*
  Tu veux prendre un café? Do you want a
  coffee? *(informal)*
2 cafe
  aller au café to go to the cafe
  Leila va au café tous les midis. Leila goes to
  the cafe every lunchtime.
• le café au lait
  white coffee
• le café-crème
  white coffee
• le café en grains
  coffee beans
• le café instantané
  instant coffee
• le café moulu
  ground coffee
• le café soluble
  instant coffee
• le café-tabac
  cafe *(where you can buy cigarettes and
  stamps)*

la **caféine** *FEM NOUN*
  caffeine

la **cafétéria** *FEM NOUN*
  cafeteria

ℰ la **cafetière** *FEM NOUN*
1 coffee pot
2 coffee maker
  une cafetière électrique a coffee machine

la **cage** *FEM NOUN*
  cage

le **cageot** *MASC NOUN*
  crate

le **cagibi** *MASC NOUN*
  store cupboard

la **cagnotte** *FEM NOUN*
1 kitty *(of money)*
2 jackpot *(in a lottery)*

la **cagoule** *FEM NOUN*
  balaclava *(winter hat for children)*

ℰ le **cahier** *MASC NOUN*
  notebook
• le cahier d'appel
  register
• le cahier de brouillon
  roughbook
• le cahier de correspondance
  school diary *(recording marks for parent-
  teacher meetings)*
• le cahier d'exercices
  exercise book

A B C D E F G H I J K L M N O P Q R S T U V W X Y Z

- le **cahier de textes**
  homework diary

la **caille** *FEM NOUN*
  quail *(a small game bird)*

cailler *VERB* [1]
1 to curdle *(milk)*
2 *(informal)* to be freezing
  Ça caille ici! It's freezing here!

le **caillou** *MASC NOUN*, les **cailloux** *PL*
  stone
  jeter des cailloux to throw stones

♪ la **caisse** *FEM NOUN*
1 till, cash register
2 checkout
  Je dois passer à la caisse. I've got to go to
  the checkout.
3 crate *(for fruit, vegetables)*
- la **caisse à outils**
  toolbox
- la **caisse d'épargne**
  savings bank

le **caissier** *MASC NOUN*, la **caissière** *FEM*
  checkout assistant

le **cake** *MASC NOUN*
  fruit cake

la **calamité** *FEM NOUN*
  disaster

calcaire *MASC & FEM ADJECTIVE* ▸ SEE **calcaire** *NOUN*
  eau calcaire hard water
  L'eau ici est très calcaire. The water here is
  very hard.

le **calcaire** *MASC NOUN* ▸ SEE **calcaire** *ADJECTIVE*
1 limestone *(the rock)*
2 fur *(inside a kettle)*

le **calcium** *MASC NOUN*
  calcium

le **calcul** *MASC NOUN*
1 arithmetic
  Elle est bonne en calcul. She's good at
  arithmetic.
2 calculation
  faire des calculs to do some calculations
  J'ai fait des calculs avant d'acheter la robe.
  I did some calculations before I bought the
  dress.
- le **calcul mental**
  mental arithmetic

la **calculatrice** *FEM NOUN*
  pocket calculator

calculer *VERB* [1]
  to calculate

la **calculette** *FEM NOUN*
  pocket calculator

calé *MASC ADJECTIVE*, **calée** *FEM*
  (informal) **clever**
  Elle est calée en maths. She's clever at
  maths.

le **caleçon** *MASC NOUN*
1 boxer shorts
2 leggings

le **calembour** *MASC NOUN*
  pun, play on words

le **calendrier** *MASC NOUN*
  calendar

caler *VERB* [1]
1 caler quelque chose to wedge something
  in place
2 to stall
  La voiture a calé. The car stalled.

le **calibre** *MASC NOUN*
1 grade *(of eggs, fruit, vegetables)*
2 calibre *(of a gun)*

câlin *MASC ADJECTIVE*, **câline** *FEM* ▸ SEE **câlin** *NOUN*
  affectionate

le **câlin** *MASC NOUN* ▸ SEE **câlin** *ADJECTIVE*
  cuddle
  faire un câlin à quelqu'un to give somebody
  a cuddle
  Fais un câlin à ta grand-mère! Give your
  gran a cuddle!
  Fais-moi un câlin! Give me a cuddle! *(said to
  a child, friend or family member)*

câliner *VERB* [1]
  to cuddle

calmant *MASC ADJECTIVE*, **calmante** *FEM* ▸ SEE
  calmant *NOUN*
  soothing

le **calmant** *MASC NOUN* ▸ SEE **calmant** *ADJECTIVE*
  sedative

le **calmar** *MASC NOUN*
  squid

♪ **calme** *MASC & FEM ADJECTIVE* ▸ SEE **calme** *NOUN*
  calm, quiet
  D'habitude, Chloë est assez calme. Chloë is
  usually quite calm.

♪ le **calme** *MASC NOUN* ▸ SEE **calme** *ADJECTIVE*
  peace and quiet

calmement *ADVERB*
  calmly

calmer *VERB* [1]
1 calmer quelqu'un to calm somebody down
  Va te promener. Ça va te calmer. Go for a
  walk. That will calm you down.
2 to ease
  L'aspirine a calmé la douleur. The aspirin
  eased the pain.

⊙ means the verb takes être to form the perfect

se **calmer** *REFLEXIVE VERB* ◌
  to calm down
  Calme-toi! Calm down!

la **calorie** *FEM NOUN*
  calorie

le **calque** *MASC NOUN*
  un calque a tracing
  du papier-calque tracing paper

le **calvados** *MASC NOUN*
  calvados *(apple brandy made in Normandy)*

℘ le & la **camarade** *MASC & FEM NOUN*
  friend
  mes camarades de classe my classmates

℘ le **cambriolage** *MASC NOUN*
  burglary
  Il y a eu un cambriolage. There's been a
  burglary.

cambrioler *VERB* [1]
  être cambriolé to be burgled
  La maison a été cambriolée hier soir. The
  house was burgled last night.
  se faire cambrioler to be burgled
  Les voisins se sont fait cambrioler. The
  neighbours were burgled.

le **cambrioleur** *MASC NOUN*, la **cambrioleuse**
  FEM
  burglar

la **caméra** *FEM NOUN*
  cine-camera

le **caméscope** *MASC NOUN*
  camcorder

℘ le **camion** *MASC NOUN*
  truck, **lorry**

le **camion-citerne** *MASC NOUN*
  tanker lorry

la **camionnette** *FEM NOUN*
  van

le **camionneur** *MASC NOUN*
  lorry driver, **truck driver**

le **camp** *MASC NOUN*
  camp

campagnard *MASC ADJECTIVE*, **campagnarde**
  FEM
  country
  les fêtes campagnardes country fairs

℘ la **campagne** *FEM NOUN*
  1 **country**
    vivre à la campagne to live in the country
    J'aimerais vivre à la campagne. I'd like to
    live in the country.
    La campagne est jolie par ici. The
    countryside round here is pretty.

  2 **campaign** *(for a war, an election)*
    La campagne électorale a commencé. The
    election campaign has started.

℘ **camper** *VERB* [1]
  to camp

℘ le **campeur** *MASC NOUN*, la **campeuse** *FEM*
  camper

℘ le **camping** *MASC NOUN*
  1 **camping**
    faire du camping to go camping
    Nous faisons du camping en Bretagne.
    We're camping in Brittany.

  2 **campsite**
    Nous cherchons le camping. We're looking
    for the campsite.
    Le camping était complet. The campsite
    was full.
  • le camping-car
    camper van
  • le camping-gaz®
    camping stove

le **Canada** *MASC NOUN*
  Canada
  habiter au Canada to live in Canada
  Marie va au Canada. Marie's going to
  Canada.

  WORD TIP Countries and regions in French take
  le, la or les.

canadien *MASC ADJECTIVE*, **canadienne** *FEM* ▶ SEE
  Canadien
  Canadian
  Julie est canadienne. Julie is Canadian.

  WORD TIP Adjectives never have capitals in
  French, even for nationality or regional origin.

le **Canadien** *MASC NOUN*, la **Canadienne** *FEM*
  ▶ SEE **canadien**
  Canadian

le **canal** *MASC NOUN*, les **canaux** *PL*
  canal

℘ le **canapé** *MASC NOUN*
  sofa

le **canapé-lit** *MASC NOUN*, les **canapés-lits** *PL*
  sofa bed

℘ le **canard** *MASC NOUN*
  duck

le **canari** *MASC NOUN*
  canary

le **cancer** *MASC NOUN* ▶ SEE **Cancer**
  cancer
  avoir un cancer to have cancer
  Elle a un cancer du sein. She has breast
  cancer.

le **Cancer** *MASC NOUN* ▶ SEE **cancer**
Cancer
Lucien est Cancer. Lucien's a Cancer.

WORD TIP Signs of the zodiac do not take an article: un or une.

le **candidat** *MASC NOUN*, la **candidate** *FEM*
1 candidate *(in an election, an exam)*
les candidats à l'examen the exam candidates
2 applicant *(for a job)*
se porter candidat à un poste to apply for a post
3 contestant
J'étais candidate à un jeu-concours à la télévision. I was a contestant in a TV gameshow.

la **candidature** *FEM NOUN*
application *(for a job)*
poser sa candidature à un poste to apply for a job
J'ai posé ma candidature pour un emploi de vacances. I've applied for a summer job.

le **caneton** *MASC NOUN*
duckling

la **canette** *FEM NOUN*
1 une canette de bière a small bottle of beer
2 can *(of beer, soft drink)*

le **canevas** *MASC NOUN*
tapestry work

le **caniche** *MASC NOUN*
poodle

la **canicule** *FEM NOUN*
1 scorching heat
sortir en pleine canicule to go out in the scorching heat
2 heatwave

le **canif** *MASC NOUN*
penknife

le **caniveau** *MASC NOUN*, les **caniveaux** *PL*
gutter

la **canne** *FEM NOUN*
walking stick
• la canne à pêche
fishing rod
• la canne à sucre
sugar cane

la **cannelle** *FEM NOUN*
cinnamon

la **cannette** *FEM NOUN*
can *(for drinks)*

le **canoë** *MASC NOUN*
1 canoe
2 faire du canoë to go canoeing

J'ai fait du canoë sur la rivière. I went canoeing on the river.

le **canoë-kayak** *MASC NOUN*
kayak

le **canon** *MASC NOUN*
1 gun
2 barrel *(of a gun)*
3 cannon
On peut voir les vieux canons au musée. You can see the old cannons in the museum.

le **canot** *MASC NOUN*
small boat, dinghy
• le canot pneumatique
inflatable dinghy
• le canot de sauvetage
lifeboat

la **cantatrice** *FEM NOUN*
opera singer

la **cantine** *FEM NOUN*
canteen
manger à la cantine to have school dinners
Je déteste manger à la cantine. I hate school dinners.
Nous mangeons à la cantine tous les jours. We have school dinners every day.

le **caoutchouc** *MASC NOUN*
rubber
des gants en caoutchouc rubber gloves
des bottes en caoutchouc wellington boots

le **cap** *MASC NOUN*
1 cape *(a headland)*
le cap Horn Cape Horn
2 course *(of a ship)*
changer le cap to change course
mettre le cap sur l'ouest to head west

capable *MASC & FEM ADJECTIVE*
capable
être capable de faire quelque chose to be capable of doing something
Je suis bien capable de courir un marathon. I'm quite capable of running a marathon.

la **capacité** *FEM NOUN*
1 ability
2 capacity
la capacité de mémoire d'un ordinateur the memory capacity of a computer

la **cape** *FEM NOUN*
cape, cloak
un film de cape et d'épée a swashbuckler

le **capitaine** *MASC NOUN*
captain
le capitaine des pompiers the chief fire officer

◠ means the verb takes être to form the perfect

capital *MASC ADJECTIVE*, **capitale** *FEM*, **capitaux** *MASC PL*, **capitales** *FEM PL* ▶ SEE **capital** *NOUN*
1 **major**
Cette information est d'une importance capitale. This piece of information is of major importance.
2 **key**
un chapitre capital du roman a key chapter in the novel
3 la peine capitale capital punishment

le **capital** *MASC NOUN*, les **capitaux** *PL* ▶ SEE **capital** *ADJECTIVE*
capital *(in finance)*

la **capitale** *FEM NOUN*
capital city
Paris est la capitale de la France. Paris is the capital of France.

le **capot** *MASC NOUN*
bonnet *(of a car)*

la **câpre** *FEM NOUN*
caper
une sauce aux câpres a caper sauce

le **caprice** *MASC NOUN*
1 **whim**
2 **tantrum**
faire un caprice to throw a tantrum
Elle fait souvent des caprices. She often throws tantrums.

le **Capricorne** *MASC NOUN*
Capricorn
Daniel est Capricorne. Daniel's a Capricorn.

> **WORD TIP** Signs of the zodiac do not take an article: un or une.

la **capsule** *FEM NOUN*
1 **cap, top** *(of a bottle)*
2 **capsule**
une capsule spatiale a space capsule

capter *VERB* [1]
1 **to receive** *(TV channel, programme)*
On capte combien de chaînes ici? How many channels can you receive here?
2 capter l'attention de quelqu'un to catch somebody's attention
Il essaie de capter l'attention des filles. He's trying to catch the girls' attention.

le **captif** *MASC NOUN*, la **captive** *FEM*
captive

captivant *MASC ADJECTIVE*, **captivante** *FEM*
1 **fascinating** *(person)*
2 **gripping** *(book, film, story)*

la **captivité** *FEM NOUN*
captivity
en captivité in captivity
Ce lion a été né en captivité. This lion was born in captivity.

capturer *VERB* [1]
to capture

la **capuche** *FEM NOUN*
hood *(on a jacket)*

le **capuchon** *MASC NOUN*
top, cap *(of a pen)*

la **capucine** *FEM NOUN*
nasturtium

ℓ **car** *CONJUNCTION* ▶ SEE **car** *NOUN*
because

ℓ le **car** *MASC NOUN* ▶ SEE **car** *CONJUNCTION*
coach, bus
en car by coach
Nous allons voyager en car. We're going to travel by coach.
• le car de ramassage scolaire school bus

la **carabine** *FEM NOUN*
rifle

le **caractère** *MASC NOUN*
1 **nature**
avoir bon caractère to be good-natured
avoir mauvais caractère to be bad-tempered
Ce cheval a mauvais caractère. This horse is bad-tempered.
2 **character**
Leur maison a beaucoup de caractère. Their house has a lot of character.
3 **character** *(in print)*
écrit en gros caractères written in large print

caractéristique *MASC & FEM ADJECTIVE* ▶ SEE **caractéristique** *NOUN*
characteristic

la **caractéristique** *FEM NOUN* ▶ SEE **caractéristique** *ADJECTIVE*
characteristic

ℓ la **carafe** *FEM NOUN*
carafe, jug *(for wine, water)*

les **Caraïbes** *PLURAL FEM NOUN*
les îles Caraïbes the Caribbean Islands
habiter aux Caraïbes. to live in the Caribbean.
Je vais aux Caraïbes. I'm going to the Caribbean.

le **carambolage** *MASC NOUN*
pile-up
Il y a eu un carambolage sur l'autoroute. There was a pile-up on the motorway.

le **caramel** *MASC NOUN*
1 **caramel** *(in ice cream, cakes)*
du caramel caramel

ℓ indicates key words

un dessert au caramel a toffee-flavoured dessert

2 toffee *(a sweet)*
un caramel a toffee

ℓ la **caravane** *FEM NOUN*
caravan

le **carbone** *MASC NOUN*
1 carbon
2 carbon paper

carbonisé *MASC ADJECTIVE*, **carbonisée** *FEM*
burnt *(to cinders)*

le **carburant** *MASC NOUN*
fuel

le **carburateur** *MASC NOUN*
carburettor *(in an engine)*

la **carcasse** *FEM NOUN*
carcass

cardiaque *MASC & FEM ADJECTIVE*
une crise cardiaque a heart attack
Il est cardiaque. He has a heart condition.

le **cardinal** *MASC NOUN*, les **cardinaux** *PL*
1 *(Religion)* cardinal
2 cardinal number

le **carême** *MASC NOUN*
(Religion) Lent

caresser *VERB* [1]
to stroke *(an animal)*
Je peux le caresser? Can I stroke him?

la **cargaison** *FEM NOUN*
cargo

la **caricature** *FEM NOUN*
caricature

le & la **caricaturiste** *MASC & FEM NOUN*
cartoonist

la **carie** *FEM NOUN*
1 la carie dentaire tooth decay
2 hole *(in a tooth)*
J'ai une carie. I've got a hole in my tooth.

le **carillon** *MASC NOUN*
1 bell *(of a church)*
2 chimes *(of a clock, a door)*

caritatif *MASC ADJECTIVE*, **caritative** *FEM*
charitable
une association caritative a charity

le **carnaval** *MASC NOUN*
carnival
le carnaval de Nice the Nice carnival
On se déguise pour le carnaval. We dress up for the carnival.

ℓ le **carnet** *MASC NOUN*
1 notebook
2 book *(of tickets, stamps)*

- le carnet de chèques
  chequebook
- le carnet de correspondance
  school diary
- le carnet de notes
  school report
- le carnet de timbres
  book of stamps

> **CARNET (DE CORRESPONDANCE)**
>
> Les élèves ont un carnet de correspondance pour les communications école-parents. Il y a des informations générales sur l'école. On note les absences, les retards, les problèmes, les rendez-vous, etc.

ℓ la **carotte** *FEM NOUN*
carrot
les carottes râpées grated carrots

la **carpe** *FEM NOUN*
carp *(fish)*

ℓ **carré** *MASC ADJECTIVE*, **carrée** *FEM* ▸ SEE **carré** *NOUN*
square
un écran carré a square screen
un mètre carré a square metre

ℓ le **carré** *MASC NOUN* ▸ SEE **carré** *ADJECTIVE*
square
- le carré d'agneau
  rack of lamb
- le carré de chocolat
  piece of chocolat

le **carreau** *MASC NOUN*, les **carreaux** *PL*
1 floor tile
2 wall tile
3 window pane
faire les carreaux to clean the windows
4 une chemise à carreaux a checked shirt
du tissu à carreaux checked fabric
du papier à carreaux squared paper
5 diamonds *(in cards)*
la reine de carreau the queen of diamonds

ℓ le **carrefour** *MASC NOUN*
crossroads, junction
Au carrefour, tournez à droite. Turn right at the crossroads.

le **carrelage** *MASC NOUN*
tiled floor
Le carrelage est sale. The floor is dirty.
Il y a du carrelage dans la salle de bains.
There are tiles in the bathroom.

le **carrelet** *MASC NOUN*
plaice

carrément *ADVERB*
completely
être carrément fou to be completely mad
C'est carrément malhonnête. It's

⊜ means the verb takes être to form the perfect

downright dishonest.

la **carrière** *FEM NOUN*
1 career
une carrière de médecin a career as a doctor
faire carrière to make a career
J'aimerais faire carrière dans le journalisme. I'd like to make a career in journalism.
2 quarry

la **carrosserie** *FEM NOUN*
bodywork *(of a car)*
un atelier de carrosserie a body repair workshop

le **cartable** *MASC NOUN*
schoolbag, satchel
J'ai oublié mon cartable. I forgot my schoolbag.

℘ la **carte** *FEM NOUN*
1 card *(for greetings)*
Il m'a envoyé une carte. He sent me a card.
2 playing card
un jeu de cartes a pack of cards
J'ai horreur des jeux de cartes. I hate card games.
Nous jouons aux cartes. We're playing cards.
3 map
Regardons la carte. Let's look at the map.
4 menu *(with dishes priced separately)*
manger à la carte to eat à la carte
Nous mangeons toujours à la carte. We always eat à la carte.
    ►SEE **menu**
• la carte d'abonnement
  season ticket
• la carte d'adhérent
  membership card
• la carte d'anniversaire
  birthday card
• la carte bancaire
  bank card
• la carte bleue
  credit card *(used only in France)*
• la carte de crédit
  credit card
• la carte d'embarquement
  boarding card
• la carte grise
  logbook *(for a car)*
• la carte de fidelité
  loyalty card
• la carte d'identité
  identity card
• la carte à jouer
  playing card
• la carte mémoire
  smart card

• la carte postale
  postcard
• la carte à puce
  chip and pin card
• la carte routière
  roadmap
• la carte de séjour
  resident's permit
• la carte SIM
  SIM card
• la carte de téléphone
  phonecard
• la carte des vins
  wine list
• la carte de visite
  business card
• la carte de vœux
  greetings card

le **carton** *MASC NOUN*
1 cardboard
une chemise en carton a cardboard folder
2 cardboard box
Il faut beaucoup de cartons quand on déménage. You need a lot of cardboard boxes when you move house.

la **cartouche** *FEM NOUN*
cartridge
une cartouche d'encre an ink cartridge

le **cas** *MASC NOUN*
1 case
trois cas de rougeole three cases of measles
en tout cas in any case, at any rate
En tout cas, ce n'était pas moi! In any case, it wasn't me!
2 en aucun cas on no account
3 au cas où just in case.
Je prends mon manteau, au cas où. I'm taking my coat, just in case.

la **cascade** *FEM NOUN*
1 waterfall
2 stunt *(in a film)*

le **cascadeur** *MASC NOUN*, la **cascadeuse** *FEM*
1 stuntman
2 stuntwoman

cascher *INVARIABLE MASC & FEM ADJECTIVE*
(Religion) kosher

la **case** *FEM NOUN*
1 square *(on a board game)*
2 box *(in a form)*
Cochez la bonne case. Tick the correct box.
3 hut *(for living in)*

casier *MASC NOUN*
1 pigeonhole *(for post)*
2 locker *(for belongings)*
3 rack *(for storage)*
un casier à bouteilles a bottle rack

le **casino** MASC NOUN
casino

le **casque** MASC NOUN
1 crash helmet
2 headphones

la **casquette** FEM NOUN
cap
• la casquette de base-ball
baseball cap

le **casse-croûte** INVARIABLE MASC NOUN
snack

le **casse-noisettes** INVARIABLE MASC NOUN
nutcracker

casse-pieds INVARIABLE MASC & FEM ADJECTIVE
être casse-pieds (informal) to be a pain in
the neck
Elle est un peu casse-pieds! She's a bit of
a pain!

𝄞 **casser** VERB [1]
to break
Qui a cassé la tasse? Who broke the cup?
C'est Pierre qui l'a cassée. Pierre broke it.

se **casser** REFLEXIVE VERB ◯
to break
Tout d'un coup, la branche s'est cassée. All
of a sudden, the branch broke.
se casser la jambe to break your leg
Elle s'est cassé la jambe au ski. She broke
her leg skiing.

𝄞 la **casserole** FEM NOUN
saucepan

le **casse-tête** INVARIABLE MASC NOUN
brainteaser

𝄞 la **cassette** FEM NOUN
cassette, tape
• la cassette vidéo
video cassette

𝄞 le **cassis** MASC NOUN
blackcurrant

le **cassoulet** MASC NOUN
oven-baked beans (with meat and sausage)

le **castor** MASC NOUN
beaver

le **catalogue** MASC NOUN
catalogue

la **catastrophe** FEM NOUN
disaster, catastrophe

le **catch** MASC NOUN
wrestling

le **catcheur** MASC NOUN, la **catcheuse** FEM
wrestler

la **catégorie** FEM NOUN
category

𝄞 la **cathédrale** FEM NOUN
cathedral
la cathédrale de Chartres Chartres
Cathedral

le **catholicisme** MASC NOUN
(Roman) Catholicism

catholique MASC & FEM ADJECTIVE ▶ SEE
catholique NOUN
(Roman) Catholic

le & la **catholique** MASC & FEM NOUN ▶ SEE
catholique ADJECTIVE
(Roman) Catholic

le **cauchemar** MASC NOUN
nightmare
Quel cauchemar! What a nightmare!
faire un cauchemar to have a nightmare
J'ai fait un cauchemar cette nuit. I had a
nightmare last night.

la **cause** FEM NOUN
1 cause
la cause de l'accident the cause of the
accident
2 à cause de because of
Nous avons perdu à cause de lui. We lost
because of him.
3 reason
la cause de la réunion the reason for the
meeting
4 cause
une bonne cause a good cause

causer VERB [1]
1 to cause
causer un accident to cause an accident
La canicule a causé une centaine de morts.
The heatwave caused about a hundred
deaths.
2 (informal) to talk, to chat

la **caution** FEM NOUN
1 deposit
verser une caution to pay a deposit
Il faut verser une caution pour louer un
vélo. You have to pay a deposit to hire a
bicycle.
2 bail
libéré sous caution released on bail

le **cavalier** MASC NOUN, la **cavalière** FEM
rider

𝄞 la **cave** FEM NOUN
cellar
Il y a une cave au sous-sol. There is a cellar
in the basement.

le **caveau** MASC NOUN, les **caveaux** PL
vault (of a church)

◯ means the verb takes être to form the perfect

la **caverne** *FEM NOUN*
cave

le **CD** *MASC NOUN*, les **CD** *PLURAL*
CD

le **CDD** *MASC NOUN*
(= *contrat à durée déterminée*) **temporary contract**

le **CDI** *MASC NOUN*
1 (= *centre de documentation et d'information*) **school library**
2 (= *contrat à durée indéterminée*) **permanent contract**

ℓ **ce** *MASC ADJECTIVE*, **cet** *MASC*, **cette** *FEM*, **ces** *MASC & FEM PL* ▸ SEE **ce** *PRONOUN*
1 this
ce magasin this shop
cet acteur this actor
cet hôpital this hospital
ce couteau-ci this knife (*right here*)
Ce stylo ne marche pas. This pen doesn't work.
2 this
cette semaine this week
cette actrice this actress
Je n'aime pas cette image. I don't like that picture.
3 that
Ce DVD est cassé. That DVD's broken.
Passe-moi cette assiette-là. Pass me that plate (*over there*).
4 cette nuit last night, tonight
J'ai mal dormi cette nuit. I didn't sleep well last night.
Tu vas bien dormir cette nuit. You'll sleep well tonight.

> **WORD TIP** ce is used before masc nouns in the singular. cet is used before masc nouns beginning with a, e, i, o, u or silent h. cette is used with fem nouns in the singular ▸ SEE **ces**

ℓ **ce**, **c'** *PRONOUN* ▸ SEE **ce** *ADJECTIVE*
1 it, that, this
C'est vrai? Is that true?
Non, ce n'est pas vrai. No, it's not true.
Ce n'était pas une bonne idée. That wasn't a good idea.
Qui est-ce? Who is it?
C'est moi. It's me.
Qu'est-ce que c'est? What is it?
C'est un MP3. It's an MP3.
C'est la première maison à gauche. It's the first house on the left.
2 he, she, they
C'est un médecin. He's a doctor.
C'est une infirmière. She's a nurse.
Ce sont mes copains. They're my friends.
3 ce qui what
Mange ce qui reste. Eat what's left.

C'est ce qui énerve Laura. That's what annoys Laura.
4 ce que, ce qu' what
Prends ce que tu veux. Take what you want.
Je ne sais pas ce qu'on dit en français. I don't know what they say in French.
5 C'est tout ce qui reste. That's all that's left.
Prends tout ce que tu veux. Take whatever you want.

> **WORD TIP** ce becomes c' before a word beginning with e-. ce que becomes ce qu' before a, e, i, o, u. ce qui never changes. ▸ SEE **cet**, **cette**

ceci *PRONOUN*
this
Ceci n'est pas à moi. This is not mine.

la **cécité** *FEM NOUN*
blindness

céder *VERB* [24]
1 to give in
Mes parents n'ont pas cédé. My parents didn't give in.
céder à quelqu'un to give in to somebody
Ils cèdent toujours à mon petit frère. They always give in to my little brother.
2 to give up (*a seat, a share*)
Il a cédé sa place. He gave up his seat.
'Cédez le passage' 'Give way' (*road sign*)

ℓ le **cédérom** *MASC NOUN*
CD-ROM

la **cédille** *FEM NOUN*
cedilla (*the letter* ç)

le **cèdre** *MASC NOUN*
cedar

ℓ la **ceinture** *FEM NOUN*
1 belt
J'aime mieux la ceinture rouge. I like the red belt better.
Elle est ceinture noire de judo. She's got a black belt in judo.
2 waist
J'avais de l'eau jusqu'à la ceinture. I was up to my waist in water.
• la ceinture de sauvetage
lifebelt

la **ceinture de sécurité** *FEM NOUN*
seatbelt
Attachez vos ceintures de sécurité. Fasten your seatbelts.

cela *PRONOUN*
that, this, it
Cela change tout. That changes everything.
Cela ne fait rien. It doesn't matter.
Cela ne me concerne pas. That doesn't concern me.

Il y a un an de cela. That was one year ago.

WORD TIP cela is the formal form of ça.

la **célébration** *FEM NOUN*
celebration

ℰ **célèbre** *MASC & FEM ADJECTIVE*
famous
quelques personnages célèbres some
famous people

célébrer *VERB* [24]
to celebrate

la **célébrité**
1 fame
2 celebrity

le **céleri** *MASC NOUN*
celery
• le céleri-rémoulade
grated celeriac in a mayonnaise dressing

ℰ **célibataire** *MASC & FEM ADJECTIVE* ▸ SEE
célibataire *NOUN*
single, unmarried
Il est toujours célibataire. He's still single.

ℰ le & la **célibataire** *MASC & FEM NOUN* ▸ SEE
célibataire *ADJECTIVE*
1 bachelor
2 single woman

celle *PRONOUN*

WORD TIP This is the fem form of celui.

celle-ci *PRONOUN*

WORD TIP This is the fem form of celui-ci.

celle-là *PRONOUN*

WORD TIP This is the fem form of celui-là.

celles *PRONOUN*

WORD TIP This is the fem form of ceux.

celles-ci *PRONOUN*

WORD TIP This is the fem form of ceux-ci.

celles-là *PRONOUN*

WORD TIP This is the fem form of ceux-là.

la **cellule** *FEM NOUN*
1 (prison) cell
2 cell *(in biology and medicine)*

celui, **celle** *PRONOUN*
1 *(for a masc singular noun)* **the one**
Quel portable? Celui qui est sur la table.
Which mobile ? The one on the table.
2 *(for a fem singular noun)* **the one**
Quelle bague? Celle qui est dans la vitrine.
Which ring? The one in the shop window.

ℰ **celui-ci**, **celle-ci** *PRONOUN*
1 *(for a masc singular noun)* **this one**
Quelle robe? Prends celui-ci. Which dress?
Take this one.
2 *(for a fem singular noun)* **this one**
Quelle veste? Prends celle-ci. Which jacket?
Take this one.

celui-là, **celle-là** *PRONOUN*
1 *(for a masc singular noun)* **that one**
Quel pull? Je préfère celui-là. Which
sweater? I prefer that one.
2 *(for a fem singular noun)* **that one**
Quelle jupe? Je préfère celle-là. Which
skirt? I prefer that one.

la **cendre** *FEM NOUN*
ash

le **cendrier** *MASC NOUN*
ashtray

Cendrillon *FEM NOUN*
Cinderella

censé *MASC ADJECTIVE*, **censée** *FEM*
être censé faire quelque chose to be
supposed to do something
Je suis censé rentrer après le cours. I'm
supposed to go home after the class.
Nous sommes censés faire nos devoirs.
We're supposed to do our homework.

ℰ **cent** *NUMBER* ▸ SEE **cent** *NOUN*
a hundred, one hundred
trois cents personnes three hundred people
deux cent cinquante personnes two
hundred and fifty people

WORD TIP cent does not take -s when it is
followed by another number.

ℰ le **cent** *MASC NOUN* ▸ SEE **cent** *NUMBER*
cent *(in euros and dollars)*

la **centaine** *FEM NOUN*
une centaine de personnes about a
hundred people
plusieurs centaines de personnes several
hundred people
des centaines de lettres hundreds of letters

le **centenaire** *MASC NOUN*
centenary

le & la **centième** *NUMBER*
hundredth

le **centilitre** *MASC NOUN*
centilitre

ℰ le **centime** *MASC NOUN*
1 cent *(one hundredth of a euro)*
2 centime *(one hundredth of the former
French currency, the franc)*

ℱ le **centimètre** *MASC NOUN*
1 **centimetre**
un centimètre carré a square centimetre
un centimètre cube a cubic centimetre
2 **tape measure**

central *MASC ADJECTIVE*, **centrale** *FEM*,
centraux *MASC PL*, **centrales** *FEM PL* ▶ SEE
central, centrale *NOUN*
central
le **central** *MASC NOUN*, les **centraux** *PL* ▶ SEE
central *ADJECTIVE*
• le central téléphonique
telephone exchange

la **centrale** *FEM NOUN* ▶ SEE **central** *NOUN*
power station
une centrale nucléaire a nuclear power
station

centraliser *VERB* [1]
to centralize

le **centre** *MASC NOUN*
centre
au centre de in the centre of
un marché au centre du village a market in
the centre of the village
• le centre aéré
day centre *(for children)*
• le centre commercial
shopping centre, mall
• le centre de documentation et
d'information
school library
• le centre de formation
training centre
• le centre de loisirs
leisure centre
• le centre de recyclage
recycling centre
• le centre sportif
sports centre

ℱ le **centre-ville** *MASC NOUN*
town centre, city centre
Le 46 va au centre-ville. The number 46 bus
goes to the town centre.
Julien habite au centre-ville. Julien lives in
the town centre.

cependant *ADVERB*
however

le **cercle** *MASC NOUN*
circle
en cercle in a circle

le **cercueil** *MASC NOUN*
coffin

la **céréale** *FEM NOUN*
1 **cereal, grain**
2 des céréales cereal

Je mange des céréales au petit déjeuner. I
have cereal for breakfast.

la **cérémonie** *FEM NOUN*
ceremony

le **cerf** *MASC NOUN*
stag

le **cerf-volant** *MASC NOUN*
kite
jouer au cerf-volant to fly a kite

ℱ la **cerise** *FEM NOUN*
cherry
J'adore la confiture aux cerises. I love
cherry jam.

le **cerisier** *MASC NOUN*
cherry tree

ℱ **certain** *MASC ADJECTIVE*, **certaine** *FEM* ▶ SEE
certains *PRON*
1 **certain**
un certain nombre d'élèves a certain
number of students
une certaine personne a certain person
2 **some**
dans certains pays in some countries
certaines personnes some people
3 **certain, sure**
être certain que ... to be certain that ...
Il est certain que c'était Sophie. He's
certain it was Sophie.
être certain d'avoir fait quelque chose to
be sure that you've done something
Est-ce que tu es certaine d'avoir fermé
la fenêtre? Are you sure you closed the
window?
Oui, j'en suis certaine. Yes, I'm sure I did.

certainement *ADVERB*
1 **most probably**
Nicolas arrivera certainement en retard.
Nicolas will most probably be late.
2 **certainly**
Je n'irai certainement pas! I certainly won't
be going!
3 **of course**
Je peux t'emprunter ton stylo? Mais
certainement! May I borrow your pen? Of
course!

ℱ **certains**, **certaines** *PRONOUN* ▶ SEE **certain**
some
certains de mes copains some of my friends
certaines de mes copines some of my
girlfriends

certes *ADVERB*
admittedly

le **certificat** *MASC NOUN*
certificate
un certificat médical a medical certificate

ℱ indicates key words

certifier VERB [1]
to certify

le **cerveau** MASC NOUN, les **cerveaux** PL
brain
C'est le cerveau de la classe! He's the brains of the class.

₽ **ces** PLURAL MASC DETERMINER
1 these
Léa m'a acheté ces fleurs. Léa bought me these flowers.
2 those
Ces livres que je t'ai prêtés, où sont-ils? Those books I lent you, where are they?

₽ le **CES** MASC NOUN
(= Collège d'enseignement secondaire)
secondary school

cesse FEM NOUN
sans cesse all the time
Antoine sourit sans cesse. Antoine smiles all the time.

cesser VERB [1]
to stop
Francine a cessé le piano. Francine has stopped her piano lessons.
cesser de faire quelque chose to stop doing something
Elle a cessé de fumer. She's stopped smoking.

le **cessez-le-feu** INVARIABLE MASC NOUN
ceasefire

₽ **c'est-à-dire** PHRASE
1 that is ..., that's to say ... (when you want to make something clearer)
Mes amis, c'est-à-dire Pierre, Anita, Julie, Rashid ... My friends, that's Pierre, Anita, Julie, Rashid, ...
Elle est rédactrice, c'est-à-dire qu'elle écrit des articles pour un journal. She's an editor, that's to say she writes articles for a newspaper.
2 well, actually
'Tu n'en veux pas?' – 'C'est-à-dire que je suis au régime.' 'You don't want any?' – 'Well, actually I'm on a diet.'

cet MASC DETERMINER

> **WORD TIP** ce becomes cet before a word beginning with a, e, i, o, u or silent h. ▸ SEE ce
> ADJECTIVE

cette FEM DETERMINER

> **WORD TIP** ce becomes cette before a fem singular word. ▸ SEE ce

ceux, **celles** PRONOUN
the ones
'Quels DVD?' – 'Ceux qui sont sur la table.'

'Which DVDs?' – 'The ones on the table.'
(DVD is masc plural, so replaced by ceux)
'Quelles vidéos?' – 'Celles que tu m'as montrées hier.' 'Which videos?' – 'The ones you showed me yesterday.' (vidéos is fem plural, so replaced by celles)
▸ SEE **celui**

ceux-ci, **celles-ci** PRONOUN
these ones

ceux-là, **celles-là** PRONOUN
those ones

le **chacal** MASC NOUN
jackal

₽ **chacun**, **chacune** PRONOUN
1 (for masc nouns in the singular) each
Ils ont chacun un billet. They each have a ticket.
2 (for fem nouns in the singular) each
Elles ont chacune un maillot de bain. They each have a swimsuit.
3 everyone
comme chacun sait ... as everyone knows ...
Chacun son tour! Wait your turn!

le **chagrin** MASC NOUN
grief

₽ la **chaîne** FEM NOUN
1 chain
2 channel (on TV)
C'est sur quelle chaîne? What channel is it on?
• la chaîne hi-fi
hi-fi system
• la chaîne laser
CD player
• la chaîne stéréo
stereo system

la **chair** FEM NOUN
1 flesh (of fruit, fish)
2 meat (of chicken)
• la chair de poule
goose pimples
• la chair à saucisses
sausage meat

₽ la **chaise** FEM NOUN
chair
Il n'y a pas assez de chaises. There aren't enough chairs.

le **châle** MASC NOUN
shawl

le **chalet** MASC NOUN
chalet

la **chaleur** FEM NOUN
heat, warmth
Quelle chaleur! It's sweltering!

◔ means the verb takes être to form the perfect

chaleureux *MASC ADJECTIVE*, **chaleureuse** *FEM*
warm *(hospitable, friendly)*
un accueil chaleureux a warm welcome

ℰ la **chambre** *FEM NOUN*
1 **bedroom**
Je reste dans ma chambre. I'm staying in
my bedroom.
2 **room** *(in a hotel, etc)*
une chambre pour une personne a single
room
une chambre pour deux personnes a
double room
une chambre à deux lits a twin room
une chambre de famille a family room
Il ne reste plus de chambres. There are no
rooms left.
• la chambre d'amis
spare bedroom
• la chambre de commerce
chamber of commerce
• la chambre à deux lits
twin room
• la chambre d'hôte
bed and breakfast

le **chameau** *MASC NOUN*, les **chameaux** *PL*
camel

ℰ le **champ** *MASC NOUN*
field
se promener dans les champs to go for a
walk in the fields
• le champ de bataille
battlefield
• le champ de courses
racetrack

le **champagne** *MASC NOUN*
champagne *(the drink)*

la **Champagne** *MASC NOUN*
the Champagne region *(in north-east
France)*

WORD TIP Countries and regions in French take
le, la or les.

ℰ le **champignon** *MASC NOUN*
1 **mushroom**
Je n'aime pas les champignons. I don't like
mushrooms.
2 **fungus** *(skin infection)*
• le champignon de Paris
button mushroom

ℰ le **champion** *MASC NOUN*, la **championne** *FEM*
champion
le champion d'Europe the European
champion
une championne de ski a skiing champion

le **championnat** *MASC NOUN*
championship

ℰ la **chance** *FEM NOUN*
luck
un coup de chance a stroke of luck
Bonne chance! Good luck!
Pas de chance! Bad luck!
avoir de la chance to be lucky
Tu as de la chance de vivre ici! You're lucky
to live here!
J'ai eu la chance de les voir en concert. I
was lucky enough to be able to see them in
concert.
ne pas avoir de chance to be unlucky
Elle n'a pas eu de chance. She was unlucky.

le **chancelier** *MASC NOUN*
chancellor

le **chandail** *MASC NOUN*
jumper *(woolly and thick)*

le **chandelier** *MASC NOUN*
1 **candlestick**
2 **candelabra** *(for several candles)*

le **change** *MASC NOUN*
exchange rate
See ▸ SEE **bureau de change**

changeant *MASC ADJECTIVE*, **changeante** *FEM*
changeable

le **changement** *MASC NOUN*
change
• le changement climatique
climate change

ℰ **changer** *VERB* [52]
1 **to change**
Tu n'as pas changé. You haven't changed.
J'ai beaucoup changé. I've changed a lot.
2 **to change** *(money)*
On peut changer jusqu'à 1 000 euros. You
can change up to 1,000 euros.
Je voudrais changer 100 livres sterling en
euros. I'd like to change 100 pounds into
euros.
3 **changer quelque chose to change
something**
Ils n'ont pas changé les draps. They haven't
changed the sheets.
Tu sais changer un bébé? Can you change a
baby's nappy?
4 **changer quelque chose pour to exchange
something for** *(something else)*
J'ai changé les bottes pour une paire de
chaussures. I've exchanged the boots for a
pair of shoes.
5 **changer quelque chose, quelqu'un en ... to
turn something, somebody into a ...**
Harry l'a changé en rat. Harry turned him
into a rat.
6 **changer de to change** *(by switching)*
Je dois changer de chaussures. I've got to

ℰ indicates key words

change my shoes.

Elle a changé de place avec Nicole. She changed places with Nicole.

Il faut changer de train. You have to change trains.

changer d'avis to change your mind

J'ai changé d'avis. I've changed my mind.

changer d'adresse to change address

Nous avons changé d'adresse. We've changed our address.

se **changer** REFLEXIVE VERB ⬅
to get changed

Va te changer. Go and get changed.

Nous nous sommes changés après le match. We got changed after the match.

℘ la **chanson** FEM NOUN
song

ma chanson préférée my favourite song

une chanson populaire a popular song

une chanson pour enfants a children's song

C'est une vedette de la chanson. She's a singing star.

Je voudrais faire carrière dans la chanson. I'd like to have a career as a singer.

le **chant** MASC NOUN
1 **singing**
une leçon de chant a singing lesson
2 **song** (of a bird, an instrument)
• le chant choral
choral singing
• le chant de Noël
Christmas carol

le **chantage** MASC NOUN
blackmail

℘ **chanter** VERB [1]
to sing

chanter juste to sing in tune

chanter quelque chose à quelqu'un to sing something for somebody

Tu me chantes quelque chose? Will you sing something for me?

Non, j'ai peur de chanter faux. No, I'm afraid I'll sing out of tune.

℘ le **chanteur** MASC NOUN, la **chanteuse** FEM
singer

le **chantier** MASC NOUN
1 **building site**
2 (informal) **mess**
Quel chantier! What a mess!

chantonner VERB [1]
to hum

le **chaos** MASC NOUN
chaos

chaotique MASC & FEM ADJECTIVE
chaotic

℘ le **chapeau** MASC NOUN, les **chapeaux** PL
1 **hat**
2 (informal) Chapeau! Well done!
• le chapeau melon
bowler hat
• le chapeau de paille
straw hat

la **chapelle** FEM NOUN
chapel

le **chapiteau** MASC NOUN, les **chapiteaux** PL
1 **marquee**
2 **big top** (in a circus)

le **chapitre** MASC NOUN
chapter

℘ **chaque** MASC & FEM DETERMINER
each, **every**

Chaque été, nous allons à la plage. Every summer we go to the beach.

Chaque candidat porte un numéro. Each candidate has a number.

À chaque fois, c'est la même chose! It's the same thing every time!

le **char** MASC NOUN
1 **tank** (for battle)
2 **carnival float**

la **charade** FEM NOUN
riddle

le **charbon** MASC NOUN
coal
• le charbon de bois
charcoal

℘ la **charcuterie** FEM NOUN
1 **pork butcher's** (selling pork, ham, sausages and bacon as well as salads and prepared dishes)
le rayon charcuterie the delicatessen counter (at a supermarket)
J'ai acheté le rôti de porc à la charcuterie. I bought the pork joint at the delicatessen.
2 **pork products** (ham, salami, pâté, etc)
une assiette de charcuterie a plate of assorted cold pork meats

le **charcutier** MASC NOUN, la **charcutière** FEM
pork butcher

le **chardon** MASC NOUN
thistle

la **charge** FEM NOUN
1 **load** (a burden)
2 **responsibility**
avoir la charge de faire quelque chose to be responsible for doing something
J'avais la charge de distribuer les livres. I was responsible for giving out the books.

⬅ means the verb takes être to form the perfect

ℱ **charger** VERB [52]
1 **to load** (goods, luggage)
   charger quelque chose dans quelque chose
   to load something into something
   J'ai chargé le programme dans
   l'ordinateur. I loaded the program into the
   computer.
2 charger quelqu'un de faire quelque
   chose to give somebody the job of doing
   something
   Il m'a chargé d'acheter les pizzas. He gave
   me the job of buying the pizzas.
   Nous sommes chargés de faire l'enquête.
   Our job is to do the survey.
3 **to charge** (a battery)

ℱ le **chariot** MASC NOUN
1 **trolley** (in a supermarket)
2 **wagon** (horse-drawn)

la **charité** FEM NOUN
   charity

ℱ **charmant** MASC ADJECTIVE, **charmante** FEM
   charming
   un endroit charmant au bord de la mer a
   charming place by the sea
   C'est une petite fille charmante. She's a
   delightful little girl.
   Ils sont partis sans nous? C'est charmant!
   They've left without us? How charming!

le **charme** MASC NOUN
1 **charm**
   Odile a beaucoup de charme. Odile has lots
   of charm.
   faire du charme to turn on the charm
   Regarde, Jean-Marie fait du charme! Look,
   Jean-Marie's turning on the charm!
2 **spell**
   tomber sous le charme de quelqu'un to fall
   under somebody's spell
   Pierre est tombé sous le charme d'Élodie.
   Pierre's fallen under Élodie's spell.

charmer VERB [1]
   to charm

la **charnière** FEM NOUN
   hinge

le **charpentier** MASC NOUN
   carpenter

la **charrette** FEM NOUN
   cart

la **charrue** FEM NOUN
   plough

la **charte** FEM NOUN
   charter

charter INVARIABLE MASC & FEM ADJECTIVE
   un vol charter a charter flight

la **chasse** FEM NOUN
   hunting, **shooting** (with a gun)
   une manifestation contre la chasse a
   demonstration against hunting
• la chasse au trésor
   treasure hunt

la **chasse d'eau** FEM NOUN
   (toilet) flush
   tirer la chasse to flush the toilet

le **chasse-neige** INVARIABLE MASC NOUN
   snowplough

chasser VERB [1]
1 **to hunt**, **to shoot** (with a gun)
2 chasser quelqu'un to chase somebody away
   Le chien nous a chassés. The dog chased
   us away.
   chasser quelqu'un de quelque part to drive
   somebody out of somewhere
   On a chassé les musiciens du métro.
   They've driven the buskers out of the
   underground.

le **chasseur** MASC NOUN
   hunter

ℱ le **chat** MASC NOUN
1 **cat**
   Je n'ai pas de chat. I don't have a cat.
2 **tom cat**
3 jouer à chat to play tag
   Les petits jouent à chat pendant la
   récréation. The little children play tag at
   break.
   C'est toi le chat! You're it!
4 (Internet, mobile phones) **chat** (pronounced
   as in English)

la **châtaigne** FEM NOUN
   sweet chestnut

le **châtaignier** MASC NOUN
   sweet chestnut tree

ℱ **châtain** MASC & FEM ADJECTIVE
   brown (hair)
   Il est châtain. He has brown hair.
   Elle a les cheveux châtains. She has brown
   hair.

   WORD TIP châtain has no feminine form.

ℱ **château** MASC NOUN, les **châteaux** PL
1 **castle**
   le château de Warwick Warwick Castle
2 **manor** (large country house)
3 **palace**
   le château de Versailles the palace of
   Versailles
   les châteaux de la Loire the châteaux of the
   Loire Valley
• le château d'eau
   water tower

ℱ indicates key words

chatouiller *VERB* [1]
to tickle

le **chatroom** *MASC NOUN*
chatroom

la **chatte** *FEM NOUN*
female cat

♀ **chaud** *MASC ADJECTIVE*, **chaude** *FEM*
1 **hot**, **warm**
du lait chaud hot milk
des chaussettes chaudes warm socks
2 **avoir chaud** to be hot
J'ai chaud. I'm hot.
Elle a trop chaud. She's too hot.
3 **faire chaud** to be hot
Il fait chaud ici. It's hot here.
Il ne fait pas très chaud. It's not very warm.
4 **tenir chaud à quelqu'un** to keep somebody
warm
Ce pull me tient chaud. This jumper's
keeping me warm.

la **chaudière** *FEM NOUN*
boiler

♀ le **chauffage** *MASC NOUN*
heating
mettre le chauffage to put on the heating
• le **chauffage central**
central heating

le **chauffe-eau** *INVARIABLE MASC NOUN*
water heater

chauffer *VERB* [1]
1 **to heat**, **to heat up**
être bien chauffé to be well heated
La maison n'est pas bien chauffée. The
house isn't well heated.
faire chauffer quelque chose to heat
something up
Je fais chauffer la sauce. I'm heating the
sauce up.
2 **to warm**
chauffer les assiettes to warm the plates

♀ le **chauffeur** *MASC NOUN*
1 **driver**
Mon frère est chauffeur de taxi. My brother
is a taxi driver.
2 **chauffeur** *(of a limousine)*

la **chaumière** *FEM NOUN*
thatched cottage

la **chaussée** *FEM NOUN*
roadway

♀ la **chaussette** *FEM NOUN*
sock
des chaussettes blanches white socks

le **chausson** *MASC NOUN*
slipper

• le **chausson aux pommes**
apple turnover
• le **chausson de danse**
ballet shoe

♀ la **chaussure** *FEM NOUN*
shoe
faire les magasins de chaussures to go
around the shoe shops

chauve *MASC & FEM ADJECTIVE*
bald

la **chauve-souris** *FEM NOUN*, les **chauves-
souris** *PL*
bat

chavirer *VERB* [1]
to capsize
faire chavirer un bateau to capsize a boat

♀ le **chef** *MASC NOUN*
1 **leader** *(of a group, a political party)*
2 **head** *(of a company)*
3 **boss**
C'est le chef. He's the boss.
• le **chef de classe**
class monitor
• le **chef de cuisine**
chef
• le **chef-d'œuvre**
masterpiece
• le **chef d'orchestre**
conductor

♀ le **chemin** *MASC NOUN*
1 **country lane**, **path**
2 **way**
en chemin on the way
sur le chemin du collège on the way to the
school
sur le chemin du retour on the way back
demander son chemin à quelqu'un to ask
somebody the way
Demandons notre chemin au policier! Let's
ask the policeman the way!
indiquer le chemin à quelqu'un to tell
somebody the way
Pourriez-vous m'indiquer le chemin de
la gare, s'il vous plaît? Could you tell me
the way to the train station, please? *(polite
form.)*
perdre son chemin to lose your way
Nous avons perdu notre chemin. We lost
our way.
se tromper de chemin to go the wrong way
Je me suis trompé de chemin. I went the
wrong way.
• le **chemin de fer**
railway

la **cheminée** *FEM NOUN*
1 **chimney**
2 **fireplace**

⊙ means the verb takes être to form the perfect

3 mantlepiece

le **cheminot** *MASC NOUN*
  railway worker

ℱ la **chemise** *FEM NOUN*
1 shirt
  une chemise à manches courtes a short-sleeved shirt
2 folder *(for homework, papers)*
  une chemise en plastique a plastic folder
• la chemise de nuit
  nightdress

ℱ le **chemisier** *MASC NOUN*
  blouse

le **chêne** *MASC NOUN*
1 oak tree
2 oak
  une table en chêne massif a solid oak table

le **chenil** *MASC NOUN*
1 dog kennel *(for one dog)*
2 kennels *(for housing dogs)*

la **chenille** *FEM NOUN*
  caterpillar

ℱ le **chèque** *MASC NOUN*
  cheque
  un chèque à l'ordre de M. Dubois a cheque payable to M. Dubois
  faire un chèque to write a cheque
  Je vous fais un chèque de 100 euros. I'll write you a cheque for 100 euros.
• le chèque de voyage
  traveller's cheque

le **chéquier** *MASC NOUN*
  chequebook

ℱ **cher** *MASC ADJECTIVE,* **chère** *FEM* ▶ SEE **cher** *ADVERB*
1 dear
  Chère Anne Dear Anne *(informally to a girl)*
  Cher Monsieur Dear Sir *(formally to a man)*
2 expensive
  C'est trop cher. It's too expensive.
  Un euro pour un sandwich, ce n'est pas cher! A sandwich for one euro! That's really reasonable.
  À Londres la vie est plus chère. In London the cost of living is higher.

cher *ADVERB* ▶ SEE **cher** *ADJECTIVE*
  coûter cher to be expensive
  Les jeux électroniques coûtent cher. Computer games are expensive.

ℱ **chercher** *VERB* [1]
1 chercher quelque chose to look for something
  Qu'est-ce que tu cherches? What are you looking for?
  Je cherche mes lunettes. I'm looking for my glasses.

Vous cherchez quelqu'un? Are you looking for someone?
Je cherchais le professeur. I was looking for the teacher.
2 chercher quelque chose dans to look something up in *(a dictionary, the phone book)*
  J'ai cherché le nom dans l'annuaire. I looked the name up in the phone book.
  Cherchez le mot dans le dictionnaire. Look up the word in the dictionary.
3 aller chercher to go and get *(somebody or something)*
  Va chercher le médecin! Go and get the doctor!
  Je vais chercher des verres. I'll fetch some glasses.
4 to pick up
  Il est venu nous chercher à l'école. He came and picked us up from school.
  On vient me chercher. I'm being picked up.
5 chercher à faire quelque chose to try to do something
  Je cherche à comprendre, c'est tout. I'm just trying to understand, that's all.

le **chercheur** *MASC NOUN,* la **chercheuse** *FEM*
  researcher
  Elle est chercheuse dans un laboratoire. She's a researcher in a laboratory.

le **chéri** *MASC NOUN,* la **chérie** *FEM*
  darling

chérir *VERB* [2]
  to cherish

ℱ le **cheval** *MASC NOUN,* les **chevaux** *PL*
1 horse
  un garçon à cheval a boy on horseback
  monter à cheval to ride a horse
  J'aime monter à cheval. I love riding horses.
2 horseriding
  faire du cheval to go horseriding
  Elle fait du cheval tous les dimanches. She goes horseriding every Sunday.
• le cheval à bascule
  rocking horse
• le cheval de trait
  carthorse

le **chevet** *MASC NOUN*
1 bedhead
  une lampe de chevet a bedside lamp
  L'infirmière est restée à mon chevet. The nurse stayed at my bedside.
2 bedside table

ℱ le **cheveu** *MASC NOUN,* les **cheveux** *PL*
1 un cheveu a hair
2 les cheveux hair
  Il a les cheveux blonds. He has blond hair.
  Elle s'est fait couper les cheveux. She's had

her hair cut.

3 Adrien a un cheveu sur la langue. Adrien has a lisp.

la **cheville** *FEM NOUN*
ankle
J'ai une entorse à la cheville. I've got a sprained ankle.

la **chèvre** *FEM NOUN* ▸ SEE **chèvre** *NOUN*
goat

le **chèvre** *MASC NOUN* ▸ SEE **chèvre** *NOUN*
goat's cheese

le **chèvrefeuille** *MASC NOUN*
honeysuckle

le **chevreuil** *MASC NOUN*
1 roe deer
2 venison

♪ **chez** *PREPOSITION*
1 at
être chez quelqu'un to be at somebody's (house)
Camille est chez sa grand-mère. Camille is at her grandmother's.
Je suis chez moi. I'm at home.
Il sera chez lui. He'll be at home.
Elle est chez le coiffeur. She's at the hairdresser's.
Chez Maxipop, on trouve des CD bon marché. At Maxipop's, you can get cheap CDs.
Fais comme chez toi. Make yourself at home.
2 to
aller chez quelqu'un to go to somebody's (place)
Viens chez moi. Come round to my place.
Je vais chez Léa ce soir. I'm going to Léa's this evening.
Je rentre chez moi. I'm going home.
Elle est rentrée chez elle. She's gone home.
aller chez Harrods to go to Harrods
Va chez le boulanger. Go to the baker's.
Je dois aller chez le dentiste demain. I've got to go to the dentist's tomorrow.
3 chez moi in my family
Chez eux, on dîne à six heures. In their family, they eat at six o'clock.

♪ **chic** *INVARIABLE MASC & FEM ADJECTIVE*
1 chic, well-dressed
Marine est toujours très chic. Marine is always very chic.
2 nice
C'est chic de ta part. It's really nice of you.
3 Chic alors! *(informal)* Cool!

la **chicorée** *FEM NOUN*
1 curly endive *(for salads)*
2 chicory powder *(in hot drinks or added to coffee)*

♪ le **chien** *MASC NOUN*
dog
J'ai toujours voulu un chien. I've always wanted a dog.
'Chien Méchant!' 'Beware of the Dog!'
• le chien d'aveugle
guide dog
• le chien de berger
sheepdog
• le chien de garde
guard dog

la **chienne** *FEM NOUN*
bitch

le **chiffon** *MASC NOUN*
1 rag
une poupée de chiffons a rag doll
2 duster
un chiffon humide a damp cloth

♪ le **chiffre** *MASC NOUN*
figure
un numéro à cinq chiffres a five-figure number
Donne-moi un chiffre entre zéro et neuf! Give me a number between zero and nine!
• le chiffre arabe
Arabic numeral
• le chiffre romain
Roman numeral

le **chignon** *MASC NOUN*
bun
Elle a un chignon. She wears her hair in a bun.

♪ la **chimie** *FEM NOUN*
chemistry
Alice est bonne en chimie. Alice is good at chemistry.
La chimie est ma matière préférée. Chemistry is my favourite subject.

chimique *MASC & FEM ADJECTIVE*
chemical

le **chimpanzé** *MASC NOUN*
chimpanzee

la **Chine** *FEM NOUN*
China

chinois *MASC ADJECTIVE*, **chinoise** *FEM* ▸ SEE
Chinois
Chinese

le **Chinois** *MASC NOUN*, la **Chinoise** *FEM* ▸ SEE
chinois
1 Chinese man, Chinese woman
les Chinois the Chinese
2 le chinois *MASC* Chinese *(the language)*

☺ means the verb takes être to form the perfect

le **chiot** *MASC NOUN*
puppy

ℐ les **chips** *PLURAL FEM NOUN*
crisp
un paquet de chips a packet of crisps

chirurgical *MASC ADJECTIVE*, **chirurgicale** *FEM*,
chirurgicaux *MASC PL*, **chirurgicales** *FEM PL*
surgical
une intervention chirurgicale an operation

la **chirurgie** *FEM NOUN*
surgery
• la chirurgie au laser
laser surgery

le **chirurgien** *MASC NOUN*, la **chirurgienne** *FEM*
surgeon
• le chirurgien-dentiste
dental surgeon

le **choc** *MASC NOUN*
shock
Ça m'a fait un choc. It gave me a shock.

ℐ le **chocolat** *MASC NOUN*
chocolate
un gâteau au chocolat a chocolate cake
une tablette de chocolat a bar of chocolate
une boîte de chocolats a box of chocolates
Au petit déjeuner, les enfants prennent un
bol de chocolat. For breakfast children have
a bowl of hot chocolate.
• le chocolat blanc
white chocolate
• le chocolat chaud
hot chocolate
• le chocolat à croquer
plain chocolate
• le chocolat au lait
milk chocolate
• le chocolat noir
plain chocolate
• le chocolat en poudre
drinking chocolate

le **chœur** *MASC NOUN*
1 **choir** *(professional)*
2 **chorus** *(in an opera, a piece of music)*
chanter en chœur to sing in a chorus

ℐ **choisir** *VERB* [2]
to choose
Choisis une couleur! Choose a colour!
choisir de faire quelque chose to choose to
do something
Nous avons choisi de manger chinois. We
chose to eat Chinese.
choisir quelqu'un comme to choose
somebody as
J'ai choisi Romain comme partenaire. I
chose Romain as my partner.
Pizza ou pâtes - c'est à toi de choisir. Pizza

or pasta - it's up to you.

ℐ le **choix** *MASC NOUN*
1 **choice**
Il y a un grand choix de DVD. There's a wide
choice of DVDs.
C'est un bon choix. It's a good choice.
'Fromage ou dessert au choix' 'A choice of
cheese or dessert' *(on a menu)*
2 de choix choice *(high quality)*
des produits de premier choix top quality
products

ℐ le **chômage** *MASC NOUN*
unemployment
le chômage des jeunes youth
unemployment
être au chômage to be unemployed
Il est au chômage depuis janvier. He's been
unemployed since January.
mettre quelqu'un au chômage to make
somebody redundant
L'usine a mis 500 ouvriers au chômage. The
factory made 500 workers redundant.

le **chômeur** *MASC NOUN*, la **chômeuse** *FEM*
unemployed person
On doit aider les chômeurs. We must help
the unemployed.

la **chope** *FEM NOUN*
beer mug

choquer *VERB* [1]
to shock
Ça m'a vraiment choqué. I was really
shocked by that.

la **chorale** *FEM NOUN*
choir *(amateur)*

le & la **choriste** *MASC & FEM NOUN*
1 **choir member, chorister**
les choristes the choir
2 **member of a chorus** *(in an opera)*
les choristes the chorus

ℐ la **chose** *FEM NOUN*
thing
les choses qui m'intéressent the things that
interest me
J'ai plusieurs choses à te dire. I've got
several things to tell you.
Je prends la même chose. I'll have the
same.
Tiens, j'ai pensé à une chose. Hang on, I've
just thought of something.
Parlons d'autre chose! Let's talk about
something else.
Ce sont des choses qui arrivent. These
things happen.

ℐ le **chou** *MASC NOUN*, les **choux** *PL*
cabbage

ℐ *indicates key words*

- le **chou de Bruxelles**
  Brussels sprout
- le **chou à la crème**
  cream puff

le **chouchou** *MASC NOUN*, la **chouchoute** *FEM*
▸SEE **chouchou** NOUN
  teacher's pet
  Cédric est le chouchou de la prof. Cédric is
  the teacher's pet.

chouchou *MASC NOUN* ▸SEE **chouchou** NOUN
  scrunchie

la **choucroute** *FEM NOUN*
  sauerkraut *(pickled cabbage served with
  different types of sausage, ham and bacon)*

♪ **chouette** *MASC & FEM ADJECTIVE, EXCLAMATION* ▸SEE
  chouette NOUN
1 *(informal)* **great**
  Chouette! Great!
  C'est chouette! That's great!
  Leur maison est très chouette. Their house
  is really lovely.
2 *(informal)* **nice** *(person)*
  C'est vraiment chouette de ta part! It's
  really nice of you!
  Il est chouette avec nous. He's nice to us.

♪ la **chouette** *FEM NOUN* ▸SEE **chouette** ADJ, EXCL
  owl

le **chou-fleur** *MASC NOUN*, les **choux-fleurs** *PL*
  cauliflower

chrétien *MASC ADJECTIVE*, **chrétienne** *FEM* ▸SEE
  chrétien NOUN
  Christian

le **chrétien** *MASC NOUN*, la **chrétienne** *FEM* ▸SEE
  chrétien ADJECTIVE
  Christian

WORD TIP Adjectives and nouns of religion start
with a small letter in French.

le **christianisme** *MASC NOUN*
  Christianity

WORD TIP Use le or la before the name of a
religion in French.

le **chrome** *MASC NOUN*
  chromium

chronique *MASC & FEM ADJECTIVE* ▸SEE **chronique**
  NOUN
  chronic

la **chronique** *FEM NOUN* ▸SEE **chronique**
  ADJECTIVE
1 **column** *(by a journalist in a newspaper)*
2 **(radio) programme**

le **chronomètre** *MASC NOUN*
  stopwatch

le **chrysanthème** *MASC NOUN*
  chrysanthemum

chuchoter *VERB* [1]
  to whisper
  chuchoter quelque chose à l'oreille
  de quelqu'un to whisper something in
  somebody's ear
  Elle m'a chuchoté quelques mots à l'oreille.
  She whispered a few words in my ear.

chut *EXCLAMATION*
  shh!

la **chute** *FEM NOUN*
1 **fall**
  Il a fait une chute de cinq mètres. He fell
  five metres.
2 **fall, drop** *(in price, value, temperature)*
  Il y aura une chute de température. There
  will be a drop in temperature.
- la chute de neige
  snowfall
- la chute de pluie
  rainfall

chuter *VERB* [1]
  to fall, to drop

Chypre *FEM NOUN*
  Cyprus
  Anita va à Chypre. Anita's going to Cyprus.

WORD TIP Unlike the names of most other
countries, Chypre does not take le or la.

♪ **-ci** *SUFFIX*
  ce côté-ci this side
  ce mois-ci this month
  ces timbres-ci these stamps
  ces jours-ci these last few days

WORD TIP -ci is attached to a noun for emphasis.
Compare with -là.

la **cible** *FEM NOUN*
  target

la **ciboulette** *FEM NOUN*
  de la ciboulette chives

la **cicatrice** *FEM NOUN*
  scar

ci-contre *ADVERB*
  opposite

ci-dessous *ADVERB*
  below

ci-dessus *ADVERB*
  above

♪ le **cidre** *MASC NOUN*
  cider

♪ le **ciel** *MASC NOUN*, les **cieux** *PL*
1 **sky**

◉ means the verb takes être to form the perfect

dans le ciel in the sky
2 heaven
au ciel in heaven

la **cigale** FEM NOUN
cicada (type of insect)

le **cigare** MASC NOUN
cigar

ℱ la **cigarette** FEM NOUN
cigarette

la **cigogne** FEM NOUN
stork

ci-inclus MASC ADJECTIVE, **ci-incluse** FEM ▸ SEE
ci-joint ADJECTIVE

ci-joint MASC ADJECTIVE, **ci-jointe** FEM ▸ SEE **ci-joint** ADVERB
enclosed (in a letter), **attached** (to an email)
la facture ci-jointe the enclosed invoice

ci-joint ADVERB ▸ SEE **ci-joint** ADJECTIVE
enclosed, attached
Veuillez trouver ci-joint une facture. Please find enclosed an invoice.

le **cil** MASC NOUN
eyelash

le **ciment** MASC NOUN
cement

le **cimetière** MASC NOUN
1 cemetery
2 churchyard, graveyard
• le cimetière de voitures
  scrapyard

le & la **cinéaste** MASC & FEM NOUN
film director

le **ciné-club** MASC NOUN
film club

ℱ le **cinéma** MASC NOUN
1 cinema
aller au cinéma to go to the cinema
Je vais au cinéma avec mes copains. I go to the cinema with my friends.
2 (informal) **play-acting**
Arrête ton cinéma! Stop that nonsense!

🔵 **CINÉMA**

Deux Français, les frères Lumière, ont inventé le 'cinématographe' en 1895.

le & la **cinéphile** MASC & FEM NOUN
cinema enthusiast

cinglé MASC ADJECTIVE, **cinglée** FEM
(informal) **crazy**

cinq NUMBER
five
Lucie a cinq ans. Lucie's five.
À cinq heures, je pars. I'm leaving at five

o'clock.
Le cinq avril, c'est mon anniversaire. The fifth of April is my birthday.
Ça fait cinq euros. That's five euros.

la **cinquantaine** FEM NOUN
une cinquantaine about fifty
une cinquantaine de personnes about fifty people
Elle a la cinquantaine. She is about fifty.

cinquante NUMBER
fifty

cinquantième NUMBER
fiftieth

cinquième MASC & FEM ADJECTIVE ▸ SEE **cinquième** MASC NOUN, FEM NOUN
fifth
C'est la cinquième fois qu'elle gagne. It's the fifth time she's won.

le **cinquième** MASC NOUN ▸ SEE **cinquième** ADJECTIVE, NOUN
fifth (in a series)
J'habite au cinquième. I live on the fifth floor.

la **cinquième** FEM NOUN ▸ SEE **cinquième** ADJECTIVE, NOUN
the equivalent of Year 8 (in a French collège)
Aurélie est en cinquième. Aurélie is in year 8.

le **cintre** MASC NOUN
(clothes) hanger

le **cirage** MASC NOUN
shoe polish

la **circonférence** FEM NOUN
circumference

le **circonflexe** MASC NOUN
un accent circonflexe a circumflex accent (as on â, ê, î, ô, û)

la **circonstance** FEM NOUN
circumstance

le **circuit** MASC NOUN
1 circuit (on an athletics track)
2 tour (in tourism)
3 un circuit électrique an electrical circuit

circulaire MASC & FEM ADJECTIVE ▸ SEE **circulaire** NOUN
circular

la **circulaire** FEM NOUN ▸ SEE **circulaire** ADJECTIVE
circular (leaflet)

ℱ la **circulation** FEM NOUN
1 traffic
Il y a beaucoup de circulation ce soir. There's a lot of traffic this evening.
2 circulation

la circulation du sang blood circulation

circuler VERB [1]
1 **to run** (providing a transport service)
  Ce train ne circule pas le dimanche. That train doesn't run on Sundays.
2 **to get around**
  Elle circule à vélo. She gets around by bike.
  Circulez, s'il vous plaît! Move along please!
3 **to circulate** (blood, air)

la **cire** FEM NOUN
  wax
  les personnages en cire the wax models

cirer VERB [1]
  to polish

♂ le **cirque** MASC NOUN
  circus
  Les enfants adorent aller au cirque. Children love going to the circus.

les **ciseaux** PLURAL MASC NOUN
  scissors
  une paire de ciseaux a pair of scissors

le **citadin** MASC NOUN, la **citadine** FEM
  city dweller

la **citation** FEM NOUN
  quotation

la **cité** FEM NOUN
1 **city**, **town**
2 **housing estate**
  les cités de banlieue suburban housing estates (typically tower blocks)
  une cité universitaire a university hall of residence

citer VERB [1]
  to quote

la **citerne** FEM NOUN
  tank

le **citoyen** MASC NOUN, la **citoyenne** FEM
  citizen

♂ le **citron** MASC NOUN
  lemon
  du jus de citron lemon juice
  une tarte au citron a lemon tart
  • le citron givré
    lemon sorbet (served inside a lemon)
  • un citron pressée
    freshly squeezed lemon juice
  • le citron vert
    lime

la **citronnade** FEM NOUN
  lemonade (not fizzy)

le **citronnier** MASC NOUN
  lemon tree

la **citrouille** FEM NOUN
  pumpkin

le **civet** MASC NOUN
  stew

civil MASC ADJECTIVE, **civile** FEM ▸ SEE **civil** NOUN
1 **civilian** (life, authorities, clothes)
2 **civil** a civil wedding (as opposed to a church wedding)

le **civil** MASC NOUN ▸ SEE **civil** ADJECTIVE
  civilian
  un soldat en civil a soldier in civilian clothes
  un policier en civil a plain-clothes policeman
  Que fait-il dans le civil? What does he do in civilian life?

la **civilisation** FEM NOUN
  civilization

civique MASC & FEM ADJECTIVE
  civic
  l'éducation civique civics (equivalent to PHSE)

clair MASC ADJECTIVE, **claire** FEM ▸ SEE **clair** ADVERB
1 **light**
  bleu clair light blue
  J'aimerais mieux une couleur plus claire. I'd prefer a lighter colour.
  La chambre est très claire. The bedroom is very light.
2 **clear** (sky, water, idea)
  Le temps est clair aujourd'hui. It's a clear day today.
  Elle a été très claire sur ce point. She was very clear on this point.

♂ **clair** ADVERB ▸ SEE **clair** ADJECTIVE
1 **clearly**
  Je n'arrive pas à voir clair. I can't see clearly.
2 **faire clair** to get light
  Il fait clair très tôt. It gets light very early.

le **clair de lune** MASC NOUN
  moonlight

clairement ADVERB
  clearly

le **clapier** MASC NOUN
  rabbit hutch

la **claque** FEM NOUN
  slap

claqué MASC ADJECTIVE, **claquée** FEM
  (informal) **exhausted**, **whacked out**

claquer VERB [1]
1 **to slam**
  Il a claqué la porte. He slammed the door.
2 (informal) **to spend**, **to blow**
  J'ai claqué mon argent de poche en jeux électronique. I blew all my pocket money

◉ means the verb takes être to form the perfect

on computer games.

clarifier *VERB* [1]
to clarify

la **clarinette** *FEM NOUN*
clarinet
Jean-Marc joue de la clarinette. Jean-Marc plays the clarinet.

la **clarté** *FEM NOUN*
1 **light** *(in a room)*
2 **clarity** *(of water, speech)*

ℱ la **classe** *FEM NOUN*
1 **class** *(the year, the form)*
en classe in class
Elle est dans ma classe à l'école. She's in my class (or year) at school.
Tu es dans quelle classe cette année? What form are you in this year?
Je redouble ma classe. I'm repeating the year.
Denise est la première de la classe. Denise is top of the class.
2 **school, lesson**
le soir après la classe in the evening after school
aller en classe to go to school
Je ne suis pas allé en classe hier. I didn't go to school yesterday.
avoir classe to have school
Nous n'avons pas classe demain. We don't have school tomorrow.
Il n'y aura pas classe ce matin. There'll be no lesson this morning.
faire classe to teach
C'est Mme Petit qui fera classe. Mme Petit will be teaching.
3 **classroom**
Notre classe est située près du laboratoire. Our classroom is next to the laboratory.
4 **class** *(category)*
voyager en première classe to travel first class
voyager en classe touriste to travel in economy class
5 les classes sociales the social classes
• la classe de mer
school trip to the seaside
• la classe de neige
school skiing trip
• la classe verte
school field trip

le **classement** *MASC NOUN*
1 **classification** *(of objects, books, animals)*
2 **ranking** *(in sports)*
le classement par équipe team ranking
3 **grading** *(of students, employees)*
4 **filing** *(of documents)*

classer *VERB* [1]
1 **to classify** *(objects, books, animals)*
2 **to grade** *(students, employees)*
3 **to file** *(documents, archives)*

le **classeur** *MASC NOUN*
1 **ring binder, folder**
2 **filing cabinet**

classique *MASC & FEM ADJECTIVE*
1 **classical**
Je préfère la musique classique. I prefer classical music.
2 **classic**
La question classique - Qu'est-ce que tu veux faire plus tard? The classic question - What do you want to be when you grow up? C'est classique! That's typical!

ℱ le **clavier** *MASC NOUN*
keyboard
• le clavier numérique
keypad *(on a telephone)*

ℱ la **clé** *FEM NOUN*
1 **key**
fermer quelque chose à clé to lock something
Je ferme toujours la porte de ma chambre à clé. I always lock my bedroom door.
2 **spanner**
3 **clef** *(in music)*
la clé de sol the treble clef
la clé de fa the bass clef

la **clef**

▶SEE **clé**

la **clémentine** *FEM NOUN*
clementine

le **clic** *MASC NOUN*
click *(of a mouse)*
en un seul clic with a click *(of the mouse)*
Tu peux fermer le programme en un seul clic. You can close the program with one click.

ℱ le **client** *MASC NOUN*, la **cliente** *FEM*
1 **customer**
2 **client**
3 **guest** *(of a hotel)*

la **clientèle** *FEM NOUN*
customers

cligner *VERB* [1]
1 **cligner des yeux** to blink
Le soleil m'a fait cligner des yeux. The sunshine made me blink.
2 **cligner de l'œil** to wink
Il n'arrête pas de me cligner de l'œil! He keeps winking at me!

ℱ indicates key words

le **clignotant** *MASC NOUN*
   indicator *(on a vehicle)*
   mettre le clignotant to indicate *(when driving)*

clignoter *VERB* [1]
   to flash

♪ le **climat** *MASC NOUN*
   climate
   un climat doux a mild climate
   J'adore le climat chaud de Provence. I love the hot climate of Provence.

la **climatisation** *FEM NOUN*
   air-conditioning

climatisé *MASC ADJECTIVE*, **climatisée** *FEM*
   air-conditioned

le **clin d'œil** *MASC NOUN*
1   **wink**
    faire un clin d'œil à quelqu'un to wink at somebody
    Son copain m'a fait un clin d'œil. His friend winked at me.
2   en un clin d'œil in a flash
    Ils ont disparu en un clin d'œil. They disappeared in a flash.

la **clinique** *FEM NOUN*
   private hospital
   • la clinique vétérinaire
     veterinary clinic

le **clip** *MASC NOUN*
1   **pop video**
2   **clip-on** (earring)

cliquer *VERB* [1]
   cliquer sur quelque chose to click on something *(using the mouse)*
   Clique deux fois sur l'icône. Double-click on the icon.
   Il faut cliquer sur l'image en appuyant sur le bouton droit de la souris. You have to right-click on the image.

cliqueter *VERB* [48]
1   **to jingle** *(coins, keys)*
2   **to rattle** *(chains)*

le **clochard** *MASC NOUN*, la **clocharde** *FEM*
1   **tramp**
2   **bag lady**

la **cloche** *FEM NOUN*
1   **bell**
2   *(informal)* **idiot**
    Quelle cloche! What an idiot!

le **clocher** *MASC NOUN* ▶ SEE **clocher** *VERB*
1   **church tower**
2   **steeple**

clocher *VERB* [1]
   ▶ SEE **clocher** *NOUN*
   (informal)
   Ça cloche! It's not quite right.
   Il y a quelque chose qui cloche. There's something wrong.

la **cloison** *FEM NOUN*
1   **partition wall**
2   **movable screen**

le **cloître** *MASC NOUN*
   cloister

le **clonage** *MASC NOUN*
   cloning

le **clone** *MASC NOUN*
   clone

clos *MASC ADJECTIVE*, **close** *FEM*
   closed

la **clôture** *FEM NOUN*
1   **fence** *(around a field)*
2   **closing** *(of shops, offices)*

le **clou** *MASC NOUN*
1   **nail** *(for attaching, hanging)*
2   les clous **pedestrian crossing** *(once marked by studs in the street)*
    traverser la rue dans les clous to cross at the pedestrian crossing
   • le clou de girofle
     clove

clouer *VERB* [1]
   clouer quelque chose to nail something down
   Il cloue le couvercle sur la caisse. He's nailing down the lid of the crate.
   clouer quelqu'un au sol to pin somebody down
   Le catcheur a cloué son adversaire au sol. The wrestler pinned his opponent down.

le **clown** *MASC NOUN*
   clown
   faire le clown to clown about
   Omar n'arrête pas de faire le clown en classe. Omar's always clowning about in class.

♪ le **club** *MASC NOUN*
   club
   un club de foot a football club
   un club des jeunes a youth club
   Je fais partie d'un club sportif. I'm in a sports club.

le **cobaye** *MASC NOUN*
   guinea pig

♪ le **coca** *MASC NOUN*
   Coke® *(short for Coca-Cola®)*
   Tu veux du coca? Would you like some

⊙ means the verb takes être to form the perfect

Coke® ?
Je voudrais un coca, s'il vous plaît. I'd like a Coke® please.

la **cocaïne** *FEM NOUN*
  cocaine

la **coccinelle** *FEM NOUN*
  ladybird

cocher *VERB* [1]
  to tick
  Cochez la bonne case. Tick the correct box.

ℓ**cochon** *MASC ADJECTIVE*, **cochonne** *FEM* ▶SEE
  cochon *NOUN*
  (informal) **dirty** *(joke, story)*

ℓle **cochon** *MASC NOUN* ▶SEE **cochon** *ADJECTIVE*
  pig
  • le cochon d'Inde
    guinea pig

le **cocktail** *MASC NOUN*
  1 **cocktail**
  2 **cocktail party**

le **cocorico** *MASC NOUN*
  cock-a-doodle-do

la **cocotte** *FEM NOUN*
  1 **casserole**
    du bœuf à la cocotte beef casserole
  2 **hen** *(in baby talk)*
  3 ma cocotte **sweetheart** *(said with affection to someone)*
  4 une cocotte en chocolat **chocolate hen** *(eaten at Easter)*
  • la cocotte-minute®
    pressure cooker

ℓle **code** *MASC NOUN*
  code
  en code in code
  des messages en code coded messages
  J'ai déchiffré le code. I cracked the code.
  • le code confidentiel (d'identification)
    PIN number
  • le code postal
    postcode
  • le code de la route
    the highway code

les **codes** *PLURAL MASC NOUN*
  dipped headlights

le **cœur** *MASC NOUN*
  1 **heart**
    avoir mal au cœur to feel sick
    J'ai souvent mal au cœur en voiture. I often feel car sick.
  2 par cœur by heart
    apprendre quelque chose par cœur to learn something by heart
    Il faut apprendre ces paroles par cœur. You've got to learn these words by heart.

savoir quelque chose par cœur to know something by heart
Je le savais par cœur. I knew it by heart.
  3 **hearts** *(in card games)*
    le roi de cœur the king of hearts

ℓle **coffre** *MASC NOUN*
  1 **chest**
    un coffre au trésor a treasure chest
    un coffre à jouets a toy box
  2 **safe** *(for valuables)*
  3 **boot**
    Mettez les valises dans le coffre. Put the suitcases in the boot.
  • le coffre-fort
    safe *(for valuables)*

cogner *VERB* [1]
  1 **to knock, to bang**
    On a cogné à la porte. Somebody banged on the door.
    Il cognait du poing sur la table. He was banging his fist on the table.
  2 *(informal)* **to hit**
    Ce boxeur cogne dur. This boxer hits hard.

se **cogner** *REFLEXIVE VERB* ☺
  to bump into something, to bang something
  Il s'est cogné contre le mur. He bumped into the wall.
  Elle s'est cognée contre le mur. She bumped into the wall.
  Je me suis cogné au genou. I got a bang on my knee.
  Annie s'est cogné la tête contre la table. Annie bumped her head on the table.

coiffé *MASC ADJECTIVE*, **coiffée** *FEM*
  Tu es bien coiffée aujourd'hui. Your hair looks really nice today.
  Je suis vraiment mal coiffé. My hair's really untidy.

coiffer *VERB* [1]
  coiffer quelqu'un to do somebody's hair
  C'est toujours Pauline qui me coiffe. Pauline always does my hair. *(at hair stylist's)*

se **coiffer** *REFLEXIVE VERB* ☺
  to do your hair
  Je n'ai pas eu le temps de me coiffer. I didn't have time to do my hair.

se **faire coiffer** *REFLEXIVE VERB* ☺
  to get your hair done

ℓle **coiffeur** *MASC NOUN*, la **coiffeuse** *FEM* ▶SEE
  coiffeuse
  hairdresser
  Je déteste aller chez le coiffeur. I hate going to the hairdresser's.

ℓla **coiffeuse** *FEM NOUN* ▶SEE **coiffeur**
  dressing table

ℓ indicates key words

la **coiffure** *FEM NOUN*
1 **hairdressing**
apprendre la coiffure to train to be a hairdresser
2 **hairstyle**
Tu as changé de coiffure. You've changed your hairstyle.

♀ le **coin** *MASC NOUN*
1 **corner**
un coin de table a corner of the table
le coin de la rue the corner of the street
au coin in the corner
Ça se trouve au coin de la rue. It's on the corner of the street.
Allons nous asseoir au coin du feu! Let's sit down by the fire!
Il étudie dans son coin. He's working in his own little corner.
2 **area** *(a district)*
Tu habites dans le coin? Do you live in the area?
Je vais au café du coin. I go to the local cafe.
Les gens du coin sont sympas. The locals are nice.

coincé *MASC ADJECTIVE*, **coincée** *FEM*
stuck
Le tiroir est coincé. The drawer is stuck.
J'étais coincé dans un embouteillage. I was stuck in a traffic jam.

coincer *VERB* [61]
1 **to wedge** *(a door)*
Trouve quelque chose pour coincer la porte! Find something to wedge the door!
2 **to jam** *(a drawer, a zip, a key)*
J'ai coincé la clé dans la serrure. I jammed the key in the lock.

se **coincer** *REFLEXIVE VERB* ◉
1 **to get stuck**
Ma fermeture s'est coincée. My zip's got stuck.
2 Estelle s'est coincé le doigt dans la porte. Estelle jammed her finger in the door.

la **coïncidence** *FEM NOUN*
coincidence

le **col** *MASC NOUN*
1 **collar** *(of a shirt)*
2 **neck** *(of a vase, bottle)*
3 **pass** *(in the mountains)*

la **colère** *FEM NOUN*
anger
être en colère contre quelqu'un to be angry with somebody
Il est très en colère contre toi. He's very angry with you.
mettre quelqu'un en colère to make somebody angry
Ça me met toujours en colère. That always

makes me angry.
se mettre en colère to get angry
Il se met en colère quand on bavarde en cours. He gets angry when people chat in class.

le **colin** *MASC NOUN*
hake

la **colique** *FEM NOUN*
diarrhoea

le **colis** *MASC NOUN*
parcel

collant *MASC ADJECTIVE*, **collante** *FEM* ▶ SEE **collant** *NOUN*
sticky

♀ le **collant** *MASC NOUN* ▶ SEE **collant** *ADJECTIVE*
un collant a pair of tights
un collant noir a pair of black tights

la **colle** *FEM NOUN*
1 **glue**
2 **detention** *(at school)*
une heure de colle an hour's detention

la **collecte** *FEM NOUN*
collection *(of money)*

la **collection** *FEM NOUN*
collection

collectionner *VERB* [1]
to collect *(comics, stamps, cards, etc)*

le **collectionneur** *MASC NOUN*, la **collectionneuse** *FEM*
collector

♀ le **collège** *MASC NOUN*
secondary school *(French students spend their first 4 years of secondary education in the CES. There, la sixième, la cinquième, la quatrième and la troisième are the equivalent of years 7, 8, 9 and 10 of the British system. Students then go on to le lycée for 3 years: la seconde, la première and la terminale at the end of which they sit le baccalauréat.)*

le **collégien** *MASC NOUN*, la **collégienne** *FEM*
schoolboy *(at secondary school)*, **schoolgirl** *(at secondary school)*

le & la **collègue** *MASC & FEM NOUN*
colleague

coller *VERB* [1]
1 **to stick** *(a photo, a stamp)*
Ils ont collé des affiches sur les murs. They stuck posters on the walls.
J'ai collé la photo dans mon cahier. I stuck the photo in my exercise book.
2 **to glue** *(paper, wood)*
3 **to be sticky**

◉ means the verb takes être to form the perfect

J'ai les doigts qui collent. I have sticky fingers.
4 **to press**
Il collait son nez contre la vitre. He was pressing his nose against the window.
5 coller quelqu'un to give somebody detention
On m'a collé pour bavardage. I got detention for talking in class.
6 (informal) se faire coller to fail (an exam)
Il s'est fait coller en chimie. He failed chemistry.

le **collier** MASC NOUN
1 **necklace**
2 **collar** (for a pet)

ℱ la **colline** FEM NOUN
hill

la **collision** FEM NOUN
collision

la **colo** FEM NOUN
(informal) **holiday camp** (for children)
aller en colo to go to a holiday camp

la **colombe** FEM NOUN
dove

le **colonel** MASC NOUN
colonel

ℱ la **colonie** FEM NOUN
colony
• la colonie de vacances
holiday camp (for children)

la **colonne** FEM NOUN
column
• la colonne vertébrale
spine

le **colorant** MASC NOUN
colouring (for hair, food)

coloré MASC ADJECTIVE, **colorée** FEM
1 **coloured**
des dessins très colorés brightly-coloured drawings
2 **colourful** (crowd, life)

colorer VERB [1]
to colour

colorier VERB [1]
to colour in

le **coloris** MASC NOUN
colour (within a range of clothes on sale)
Existe en plusieurs coloris. Available in several colours.

le **combat** MASC NOUN
fighting
• un combat de boxe
a boxing match

le **combattant** MASC NOUN, la **combattante** FEM
un ancien combattant a war veteran

combattre VERB [21]
to fight

ℱ **combien** ADVERB ▸ SEE **combien** INVARIABLE MASC & FEM NOUN
1 **how much?**
C'est combien? How much is it?
Ça coûte combien? How much does it cost?
Je vous dois combien? How much do I owe you?
Tu pèses combien? How much do you weigh?
Tu en veux combien? How much do you want?
2 **how many?**
Tu en veux combien? How many do you want?
Combien sont-elles? How many of them are there?
3 combien de how much, how many
Combien de fois dois-je le répéter? How many times do I have to repeat it?
Combien de chaises faut-il? How many chairs do we need?
Tu as besoin de combien d'argent? How much money do you need?
4 combien de temps how long
Tu as mis combien de temps? How long did it take you?
5 combien de kilomètres how far
C'est à combien de kilomètres d'ici? How far is it from here?

ℱ le & la **combien** INVARIABLE MASC & FEM NOUN ▸ SEE **combien** ADVERB
1 (about dates) Nous sommes le combien aujourd'hui? What's the date today?
Vous arrivez le combien? What date are you coming?
2 (about shoe sizes) Tu chausses du combien? What shoe size do you take?
3 (about positions in a race, a class) Elle est la combien en classe? Where is she in the class?
Vous êtes arrivés les combien à la course? Where did you come in the race?

la **combinaison** FEM NOUN
1 **combination** (of a padlock, safe)
2 **overalls**
3 **petticoat**
• la combinaison de ski
ski suit
• la combinaison de plongée
wetsuit

le **combiné** MASC NOUN
receiver (of a telephone)

le **comble** MASC NOUN
1 le comble de the height of
   le comble du luxe the height of luxury
2 Ça c'est le comble! That's the last straw!

la **comédie** FEM NOUN
1 comedy
2 (informal) to-do
   Quelle comédie! What a to-do!
• la comédie dramatique
   comedy drama
• la comédie musicale
   musical

le **comédien** MASC NOUN, la **comédienne** FEM
1 actor
2 actress

comestible MASC & FEM ADJECTIVE
   edible

comique MASC & FEM ADJECTIVE ▶ SEE **comique**
   NOUN
   funny

le **comique** MASC NOUN ▶ SEE **comique** ADJECTIVE
   comic, comedian

le **comité** MASC NOUN
   committee

le **commandant** MASC NOUN
1 major (in the army)
2 squadron leader (in the air force)
• le commandant en chef
   commander-in-chief

la **commande** FEM NOUN
1 order
   sur commande to order
2 command (on the computer)

ℰ **commander** VERB [1]
1 to order (at the restaurant, cafe)
   Avez-vous commandé? Have you ordered?
   Nous n'avons pas encore commandé. We
   haven't ordered yet.
   J'ai commandé un steak-frites. I've ordered
   steak and chips.
2 to be in charge
   Ce n'est pas toi qui commandes. You're not
   in charge.

ℰ **comme** CONJUNCTION ▶ SEE **comme** ADVERB
1 like
   J'ai une montre comme la tienne. I have a
   watch like yours.
   Marion est comme moi, elle adore les
   chevaux. Marion's like me, she loves horses.
   Tiens-le comme ça! Hold it like this!
   Je n'ai jamais vu un château comme celui-
   là. I've never seen a castle like that.
2 as
   Comme tu veux! As you wish!
   Je ferai comme toi. I'll do as you do.

Comme d'habitude, ils sont en retard. As
usual, they're late.
3 as (at the time when)
   Comme je fermais la porte, j'ai glissé. As I
   was closing the door, I slipped.
4 as, since
   Comme je suis malade, je dois rester au lit.
   As I'm ill, I've got to stay in bed.
   Comme il fait beau, on va se promener. As
   it's nice, we're going for a walk.
5 as a
   Adam travaille comme serveur. Adam
   works as a waiter.
   Qu'est-ce qu'il y a comme dessert? What's
   for dessert?
6 comme si as if
   Fais comme si tu ne l'as pas vue. Act as if
   you haven't seen her.
7 comme il faut properly, correctly
   faire quelque chose comme il faut to do
   something properly
   Elle s'habille comme il faut. She dresses
   properly.
8 comme ci comme ça so-so, not bad

comme ADVERB ▶ SEE **comme** CONJUNCTION
   Comme il est gentil! He's so nice!
   Comme c'est gentil! That's so kind of you!
   Comme c'est beau! It's so beautiful!
   Comme il fait chaud! It's so hot!
   Comme tu as grandi! You've grown so
   much!

le **commencement** MASC NOUN
   beginning, start

ℰ **commencer** VERB [61]
1 to begin, to start
   Le film a déjà commencé. The film has
   already started.
2 commencer à faire quelque chose to start
   to do something
   Elle a commencé à faire ses devoirs. She's
   started to do her homework.
   Je commence à comprendre. I'm beginning
   to understand.
   Il commence à pleuvoir. It's starting to rain.

ℰ **comment** ADVERB
1 how
   Comment vas-tu? How are you?
   Comment va ta mère? How's your mother?
   Comment as-tu fait ce gâteau? How did you
   make this cake?
   Je ne sais pas comment le faire. I don't
   know how to do it.
   Comment ça va? How are things?
2 what
   Elle est comment leur maison? What's their
   house like?
   Comment t'appelles-tu? What's your
   name?

means the verb takes être to form the perfect

Il s'appelle comment, ton frère? What's your brother's name?

3 pardon?, excuse me?
Comment? Pouvez-vous répéter, s'il vous plaît? Pardon? Could you repeat please?

le **commentaire** *MASC NOUN*
1 comment
faire des commentaires désagréables to make nasty comments
2 commentary *(on TV, radio)*

commenter *VERB* [1]
commenter quelque chose to comment on something *(on a poem, a text)*

ℓ le **commerçant** *MASC NOUN*, la **commerçante** *FEM*
shopkeeper

le **commerce** *MASC NOUN*
1 shop
Il y a beaucoup de commerces par ici. There are a lot of shops around here.
2 business
un commerce d'import-export an import-export business
Je fais des études de commerce. I'm doing business studies.
3 trade
le commerce équitable fair trade
le commerce mondial world trade

commercial *MASC ADJECTIVE*, **commerciale** *FEM*, **commerciaux** *MASC PL*, **commerciales** *FEM PL*
commercial
• le centre commercial
shopping centre

commettre *VERB* [11]
1 commettre une erreur to make a mistake
J'ai commis une erreur. I made a mistake.
2 commettre un crime to commit a crime
Il a commis un crime. He committed a crime.

ℓ le **commissariat de police** *MASC NOUN*
police station

la **commission** *FEM NOUN*
1 committee
2 commission *(money paid for a service)*
3 errand
faire une commission pour quelqu'un to run an errand for somebody
4 les commissions the shopping
faire les commissions to do the shopping
Qui fait les commissions? Who's doing the shopping?

ℓ **commode** *MASC & FEM ADJECTIVE* ▶SEE **commode** *NOUN*
1 convenient
La télécommande, c'est bien commode.

The remote control is very convenient.
2 easy
L'étagère est commode à monter. The bookshelf is easy to assemble.
Pour aller chez toi, ce n'est pas commode. It's not easy to get to your house.
3 easy-going *(person)*
Le professeur est assez commode. The teacher's quite easy-going.

ℓ la **commode** *FEM NOUN* ▶SEE **commode** *ADJECTIVE*
chest of drawers

commun *MASC ADJECTIVE*, **commune** *FEM*
1 common
Nous avons des amis communs. We have friends in common.
C'est une faute commune. It's a common mistake.
2 shared
La piscine est commune aux deux hôtels. The pool is shared by both hotels.
3 en commun jointly, together
les transports en commun public transport
faire quelque chose en commun to do something together
Nous faisons un exposé en commun. We're doing a presentation together.
avoir quelque chose en commun to have something in common
Ils n'ont rien en commun. They have nothing in common.

la **communauté** *FEM NOUN*
community

la **communication** *FEM NOUN*
communication
• la communication téléphonique
telephone call

la **communion** *FEM NOUN*
communion

communiquer *VERB* [1]
1 to communicate
2 communiquer quelque chose à quelqu'un to pass something on to somebody
Je lui ai communiqué la nouvelle. I passed the news on to him.

le **communisme** *MASC NOUN*
communism

communiste *MASC & FEM ADJECTIVE* ▶SEE **communiste** *NOUN*
communist
le & la **communiste** *MASC & FEM NOUN* ▶SEE **communiste** *ADJECTIVE*
communist

compact *MASC ADJECTIVE*, **compacte** *FEM*
1 dense *(fog)*
2 compact *(soil)*

ℓ **indicates key words**

un disque compact a compact disc, a CD
J'ai acheté deux disques compacts. I
bought two compact discs.

la **compagnie** *FEM NOUN*
1 company, firm
une compagnie d'assurances an insurance
company
2 company
tenir compagnie à quelqu'un to keep
somebody company
Tiens-moi compagnie! Keep me company!
Elle m'a tenu compagnie. She kept me
company.
• la compagnie aérienne
airline

le **compagnon** *MASC NOUN*
companion

comparable *MASC & FEM ADJECTIVE*
comparable

la **comparaison** *FEM NOUN*
comparison
faire la comparaison to compare
si on fait la comparaison if you compare
them

comparatif *MASC ADJECTIVE*, **comparative** *FEM*
comparative

comparé *MASC ADJECTIVE*, **comparée** *FEM*
comparé à compared to
Comparé à mes copains, je n'ai pas
beaucoup grandi. Compared to my friends,
I haven't grown very much.

comparer *VERB* [1]
to compare
Tu me compares toujours à mes copines.
You're always comparing me with my
friends.

ℓ le **compartiment** *MASC NOUN*
compartment
le compartiment non fumeurs the non-
smoking compartment

le **compas** *MASC NOUN*
compass

compatir *VERB* [2]
to sympathize

la **compensation** *FEM NOUN*
compensation

compenser *VERB* [1]
to compensate for

la **compétence** *FEM NOUN*
1 ability
2 skill, competence
Il a de bonnes compétences en
informatique. He has good computing
skills.

compétent *MASC ADJECTIVE*, **compétente** *FEM*
competent
une cavalière compétente a competent
horse rider
être compétent en quelque chose to be
competent at something
Il est compétent en calcul mental. He's
competent at mental arithmetics.

compétitif *MASC ADJECTIVE*, **compétitive** *FEM*
competitive

la **compétition** *FEM NOUN*
competition
Je participe à une compétition de natation.
I'm taking part in a swimming competition.

complémentaire *MASC & FEM ADJECTIVE*
further
pour toute information complémentaire
for further information

ℓ **complet** *MASC ADJECTIVE*, **complète** *FEM* ▶ SEE
complet *NOUN*
1 complete (silence, success, revision, list)
Elle a la série complète des Tintins. She's
got the complete series of Tintin books.
2 comprehensive
un guide complet sur le MP3 a
comprehensive guide to the MP3
3 full (camp site, train, car park)
'Complet' 'No Vacancies'
Toutes les chambres d'hôtes sont
complètes. All the B&Bs are full.
4 wholemeal (bread, flour, pasta)
le pain complet wholemeal bread

ℓ le **complet** *MASC NOUN* ▶ SEE **complet** *ADJECTIVE*
suit

ℓ **complètement** *ADVERB*
completely

compléter *VERB* [24]
1 to complete
2 to fill in (a form)

complexe *MASC & FEM ADJECTIVE* ▶ SEE **complexe**
NOUN
complex

le **complexe** *MASC NOUN* ▶ SEE **complexe**
ADJECTIVE
complex
Ça me donne un complexe. I'm getting a
complex about it.

la **complication** *FEM NOUN*
complication

le & la **complice** *MASC & FEM NOUN*
accomplice

le **compliment** *MASC NOUN*
compliment
faire des compliments à quelqu'un to
compliment somebody

⊜ means the verb takes être to form the perfect

On m'a fait des compliments sur ma robe.
People complimented me on my dress.

compliqué *MASC ADJECTIVE*, **compliquée** *FEM*
  complicated
  Ça devient compliqué! It's getting
  complicated!

compliquer *VERB* [1]
  to complicate

le **complot** *MASC NOUN*
  plot

le **comportement** *MASC NOUN*
  behaviour

comporter *VERB* [1]
1 **to include** *(notes, bibliography)*
2 **to be made up of**
   Le mot de passe comporte des chiffres et
   des lettres. The password is made up of
   numbers and letters.

se **comporter** *REFLEXIVE VERB* ◯
  to behave
  Il se comporte comme un enfant. He's
  behaving like a child.

composé *MASC ADJECTIVE*, **composée** *FEM*
1 être composé de to be made up of
   L'équipe est composée de filles et de
   garçons. The team is made up of boys and
   girls.
2 une salade composée a mixed salad

composer *VERB* [1]
1 **to make up**
   les gaz qui composent l'air the gases that
   make up the air
2 **to put together** *(a menu, a programme)*
   Eric a composé des pages web. Eric has put
   together some web pages.
3 **to compose** *(music)*
4 composer un numéro (de téléphone) to
   dial a (telephone) number
   Composez le 00 44 pour le Royaume Uni.
   Dial 00 44 for the United Kingdom.

se **composer** *REFLEXIVE VERB* ◯
  se composer de to be made up of
  Le comité se compose de cinq personnes.
  The committee is made up of five people.

le **compositeur** *MASC NOUN*, la **compositrice**
  FEM
  composer

la **composition** *FEM NOUN*
  composition

composter *VERB* [1]
  to punch *(a ticket)*
  N'oubliez pas de composter votre billet.
  Remember to punch your ticket. *(at the
  machines in train stations and on buses in
  France. It is an offence not to.)*

la **compote** *FEM NOUN*
  stewed fruit
• la compote de pommes
  apple puree

compréhensible *MASC & FEM ADJECTIVE*
  understandable

compréhensif *MASC ADJECTIVE*,
  compréhensive *FEM*
  understanding *(sympathetic)*

la **compréhension** *FEM NOUN*
  comprehension
  un test de compréhension a
  comprehension test

♪ **comprendre** *VERB* [64]
1 **to understand**
   Est-ce que tu comprends l'allemand? Do
   you understand German?
   Je ne comprends pas la question. I don't
   understand the question.
   Elle n'a rien compris. She didn't understand
   anything.
   Je comprends ce que tu veux dire. I know
   what you mean.
   J'ai mal compris. I misunderstood.
2 **to include**
   Le prix du billet comprend une boisson. A
   drink is included in the price of the ticket.

se **comprendre** *REFLEXIVE VERB* ◯
1 **to understand each other**
   Ils se comprennent bien. They understand
   each other well.
2 **to be understandable**
   Ça se comprend. That's understandable.

♪ le **comprimé** *MASC NOUN*
  tablet

♪ **compris** *MASC ADJECTIVE*, **comprise** *FEM*
1 **included**
   service compris service included
   non compris not included
   Les boissons ne sont pas comprises. Drinks
   are not included.
2 tout compris all inclusive
   un séjour au ski tout compris an all-
   inclusive ski holiday
   Ça fait 100 euros tout compris. It's 100
   euros all in.
3 y compris including
   tout le monde y compris les enfants
   everybody including the children

le **compromis** *MASC NOUN*
  compromise

la **comptabilité** *FEM NOUN*
1 **accountancy**
   Elle fait des études de comptabilité. She's
   studying accountancy.
2 **accounting**

♪ indicates key words

Mon père travaille dans la comptabilité.
My father works in accounting.
3 accounts *(of a business)*

le & la **comptable** *MASC & FEM NOUN*
accountant

le **compte** *MASC NOUN*
1 count *(a calculation)*
faire le compte de quelque chose to count
up something *(things, people)*
On a fait le compte de nos CD. We counted
up our CDs.
2 amount *(of money)*
Le compte est bon. That's the right amount.
3 account *(in a bank)*
ouvrir un compte to open an account
J'ai cent livres sur mon compte. I have a
hundred pounds in my account.
4 tenir compte de quelque chose to take
something into account
Il faut tenir compte de ces conseils. We
need to take this advice into account.
5 se rendre compte de quelque chose to
realize something
Il ne se rend pas compte du danger. He
doesn't realize the danger.
Je me suis rendu compte que j'avais oublié
mes clés. I realized that I had forgotten my
keys.
6 en fin de compte in the end, all things
considered
En fin de compte, il avait raison. In the end,
he was right.
• le compte bancaire
bank account
• le compte d'épargne
savings account
• le compte rendu
report

ℓ **compter** *VERB* [1]
1 to count
Compte les visiteurs. Count the visitors.
2 to count *(to be valid)*
Est-ce que ça compte? Does that count?
Ça ne compte pas. That doesn't count.
3 compter faire quelque chose to intend to
do something
Je compte acheter un lecteur DVD. I intend
to buy a DVD player.
4 compter sur quelqu'un to count on
somebody
Elle compte sur moi pour l'aider. She's
counting on me to help her.

le **compteur** *MASC NOUN*
meter *(to measure gas, water, speed)*
• le compteur de vitesse
speedometer

la **comptine** *FEM NOUN*
nursery rhyme

le **comptoir** *MASC NOUN*
1 bar *(in a cafe)*
2 counter *(in a shop)*

concentré *MASC ADJECTIVE*, **concentrée** *FEM*
concentrated
• le concentré de tomate
tomato puree

se **concentrer** *REFLEXIVE VERB* ◯ [1]
to concentrate
Concentre-toi. Concentrate.
Je me concentre sur le film. I'm
concentrating on the film.

la **conception** *FEM NOUN*
design *(of a product)*

concernant *PREPOSITION*
1 concerning
des informations concernant l'école some
information concerning the school
2 as regards, with regard to
Concernant la sortie de demain, il n'y a
pas de changements. There are no changes
with regard to tomorrow's trip.

concerner *VERB* [1]
to concern
Cela ne me concerne pas. This doesn't
concern me.
En ce qui me concerne, je préfère rester ici.
As far as I'm concerned, I'd rather stay here.

ℓ le **concert** *MASC NOUN*
concert
Je suis allé à un concert de reggae hier soir.
I went to a reggae concert last night.
Le groupe est en concert le 25 juin à Bercy.
The band is playing at Bercy on June 25.
• le concert de rock
rock concert

le & la **concessionnaire** *MASC & FEM NOUN*
agent, dealer *(for motor vehicles)*

ℓ le & la **concierge** *MASC & FEM NOUN*
caretaker
Je laisserai la clé chez la concierge. I'll leave
the key with the caretaker.

conclure *VERB* [25]
to conclude

la **conclusion** *FEM NOUN*
conclusion

le **concombre** *MASC NOUN*
cucumber

le **concours** *MASC NOUN*
1 competition
un concours de gymnastique a gymnastics
competition

◯ means the verb takes **être** to form the perfect

Je l'ai gagné à un concours sur le net. I won it in an Internet competition.

2 competitive examination *(for a school place, job)*
Il faut passer un concours. You have to sit an exam.

concret *MASC ADJECTIVE*, **concrète** *FEM*
1 concrete *(real)*
2 practical *(person, mind)*

la **concurrence** *FEM NOUN*
competition *(between people)*
Il y a beaucoup de concurrence. There's a lot of competition.

le **concurrent** *MASC NOUN*, la **concurrente** *FEM*
competitor

condamner *VERB* [1]
to sentence *(a criminal)*

la **condition** *FEM NOUN*
1 condition
Le VTT est en bonne condition. The mountain bike is in good condition
Il est en bonne condition physique. He's fit.
conditions de travail working conditions
2 à condition que provided that
Tu peux sortir à condition que tu me préviennes d'abord. You can go out provided you tell me beforehand.
à condition de provided that
Tu peux emprunter mon vélo à condition de me le rendre. You can borrow my bike provided you give it back to me.
3 à une condition on one condition
Il veut bien aider, mais à une condition ... He's happy to help but on one condition ...

le **conditionnel** *MASC NOUN*
conditional tense

conditionner *VERB* [1]
1 to package *(products, goods)*
2 to condition *(a person, an animal)*

le **conducteur** *MASC NOUN*, la **conductrice** *FEM*
driver

ℓ **conduire** *VERB* [26]
1 to drive *(a vehicle)*
J'apprends à conduire. I'm learning to drive.
Il m'a conduit à la gare. He drove me to the station.
2 to take *(a person)*
Je vous conduis à votre chambre. I'll take you to your room.
se **conduire** *REFLEXIVE VERB* ☻
to behave
Elle s'est bien conduite à l'enterrement. She handled herself well at the funeral.

la **conduite** *FEM NOUN*
1 behaviour

une mauvaise conduite bad behaviour
2 driving
En France, la conduite à droite est obligatoire. In France, you must drive on the right.
3 riding *(on motorbike)*
4 driving test
Demain, je passe la conduite. Tomorrow I'm taking my driving test.
• la conduite accompagnée
driving *(accompanied by a qualified driver)*

la **confection** *FEM NOUN*
clothing industry

la **conférence** *FEM NOUN*
1 lecture
2 conference

se **confesser** *REFLEXIVE VERB* ☻ [1]
to go to confession

la **confiance** *FEM NOUN*
1 trust
faire confiance à quelqu'un to trust somebody
Fais-moi confiance! Trust me!
Je te fais confiance. I trust you.
Je n'ai pas trop confiance en lui. I don't really trust him.
2 confidence *(in your ability)*
la confiance en soi self-confidence
avoir confiance en soi to be self-confident
Elle a beaucoup de confiance en elle. She is very self-confident.

confiant *MASC ADJECTIVE*, **confiante** *FEM*
confident

la **confidence** *FEM NOUN*
secret
faire des confidences à quelqu'un to confide in somebody
Je lui ai fait des confidences. I confided in her.
Elle me fait souvent des confidences sur Paul. She often confides in me about Paul.

confier *VERB* [1]
confier quelque chose à quelqu'un to entrust something to somebody
Je peux te confier mon portable? Can I leave my mobile with you?
se **confier** *REFLEXIVE VERB* ☻
se confier à quelqu'un to confide in somebody
Il s'est confié à son ami. He confided in his friend.

la **confirmation** *FEM NOUN*
confirmation

confirmer *VERB* [1]
to confirm

ℓ indicates key words

♀ la **confiserie** *FEM NOUN*
1 sweet shop
2 confectionery

confisquer *VERB* [1]
to confiscate
On a confisqué mon portable. My mobile was confiscated.

confit *MASC ADJECTIVE*, **confite** *FEM*
les fruits confits crystallized fruits

♀ la **confiture** *FEM NOUN*
jam
• la confiture d'abricots
apricot jam
• la confiture d'oranges
marmalade

le **conflit** *MASC NOUN*
conflict

confondre *VERB* [69]
1 confondre quelque chose to get something mixed up
confondre 'malle' et 'mâle' to confuse 'malle' with 'mâle'
Je confonds toujours les noms. I always get the names mixed up.
2 confondre quelqu'un avec quelqu'un to mistake somebody for somebody
On me confond souvent avec ma jumelle. People often mistake me for my twin sister.

le **confort** *MASC NOUN*
comfort
un appartement tout confort a flat with all mod cons
aimer son confort to like your home comforts

♀ **confortable** *MASC & FEM ADJECTIVE*
comfortable
Le canapé n'est pas confortable. The sofa is uncomfortable.

la **confrontation** *FEM NOUN*
confrontation

confus *MASC ADJECTIVE*, **confuse** *FEM*
1 confused (muddled)
2 embarrassed

la **confusion** *FEM NOUN*
1 confusion (disorder)
2 embarrassment
être rouge de confusion to be blushing with embarrassment

♀ le **congé** *MASC NOUN*
1 holiday (from work)
son jour de congé his/her day off
Elle est en congé aujourd'hui. She's on holiday today.
Mes parents prennent une semaine de congé. My parents are taking a week's

holiday.
2 leave
en congé de maladie on sick leave

♀ le **congélateur** *MASC NOUN*
freezer

congeler *VERB* [45]
to freeze

la **congestion** *FEM NOUN*
congestion

le **congrès** *MASC NOUN*
conference

le **conifère** *MASC NOUN*
conifer

le **conjoint** *MASC NOUN*, la **conjointe** *FEM*
spouse (husband or wife)

la **conjonctivite** *FEM NOUN*
conjunctivitis

la **conjugaison** *FEM NOUN*
conjugation

la **connaissance** *FEM NOUN*
1 knowledge
tes connaissances en français your knowledge of French
2 acquaintance
une nouvelle connaissance a new acquaintance
faire la connaissance de quelqu'un to meet somebody
J'ai fait sa connaissance à Paris. I met him/her in Paris.
Nous avons déjà fait connaissance. We've already met.
3 consciousness
perdre connaissance to lose consciousness
J'ai failli perdre connaissance. I almost lost consciousness.

♀ **connaître** *VERB* [27]
1 to know
connaître quelqu'un to know somebody
Est-ce que tu connais Emma? Do you know Emma?
Je la connais depuis trois ans. I've known her for three years.
Je ne connais pas Londres. I don't know London.
C'est une actrice très connue. She's a very well-known actor.
2 to meet
Il a connu ma tante à Jersey. He met my aunt in Jersey.

WORD TIP Compare with savoir which means to know facts and to know how to do something.

♀ se **connaître** *REFLEXIVE VERB* ◔
1 to know each other

◔ means the verb takes être to form the perfect

On se connaît. We know each other.
2 **to meet**
Nous nous sommes connus en vacances.
We met on holiday.
3 s'y connaître en quelque chose to know all
about something
Tu t'y connais en informatique? Do you
know anything about computers?
Je ne m'y connais pas du tout. I know
absolutely nothing about them.

connecter *VERB* [1]
  to connect
  être connecté to be on line *(on a computer)*
se **connecter** *REFLEXIVE VERB* ◐
  to get on line *(on a computer)*
  Je me connecte à Internet et j'écoute de la
  musique. I get on line and listen to music.

la **connexion** *FEM NOUN*
  connection

connu *MASC ADJECTIVE*, **connue** *FEM*
  well-known
  une chanteuse très connue a very well-
  known singer

consacrer *VERB* [1]
  to devote
  Elle consacre tout son temps libre à la
  lecture. She devotes all her spare time to
  reading.

consciemment *ADVERB*
  consciously

la **conscience** *FEM NOUN*
1 **conscience**
  avoir mauvaise conscience to have a guilty
  conscience
  J'ai un peu mauvaise conscience. I have a
  slightly guilty conscience.
2 avoir conscience de quelque chose to be
  aware of something
  Il n'a pas conscience du danger. He's not
  aware of the danger.

consciencieux *MASC ADJECTIVE*,
  consciencieuse *FEM*
  conscientious

conscient *MASC ADJECTIVE*, **consciente** *FEM*
1 **aware**
  être conscient de quelque chose to be
  aware of something
  Je suis consciente du problème. I'm aware
  of the problem.
2 **conscious** *(lucid)*
  rester conscient to remain conscious

le **conseil** *MASC NOUN*
1 **advice**
  un conseil a piece of advice
  donner un conseil à quelqu'un to give
  someone a piece of advice

Je te donne un conseil. Ne dis rien. I'd
advise you to say nothing.
2 des conseils advice
  suivre les conseils de quelqu'un to follow
  somebody's advice
  Je n'ai pas suivi tes conseils. I didn't follow
  your advice.
3 **council** *(a gathering of people)*
  • le conseil de classe
    staff meeting *(for staff teaching a particular
    class)*
  • le conseil de famille
    family meeting *(to discuss a subject,
    problem)*

le **conseiller** *MASC NOUN*, la **conseillère** *FEM*
  ▶ SEE **conseiller** *VERB*
  adviser
  • le conseiller d'éducation
    supervisor *(with a disciplinary role in French
    schools)*
  • le conseiller d'orientation
    careers adviser

conseiller *VERB* [1]
  ▶ SEE **conseiller** *NOUN*
1 **to advise**
  conseiller à quelqu'un de faire quelque
  chose to advise somebody to do something
  Je te conseille de parler au professeur. I
  advise you to talk to the teacher.
2 **to recommend**
  Pouvez-vous me conseiller un dentiste?
  Could you recommend a dentist for me?

le **consentement** *MASC NOUN*
  consent *(agreement)*

consentir *VERB* [58]
  consentir à faire quelque chose to agree to
  do something
  Ils consentent à partir demain. They agree
  to leave tomorrow.

la **conséquence** *FEM NOUN*
1 **consequence**
2 en conséquence consequently

conséquent *MASC ADJECTIVE*, **conséquente** *FEM*
1 **substantial**
  une somme d'argent conséquente a
  substantial amount of money
2 par conséquent therefore, consequently

le **conservateur** *MASC NOUN*, la **conservatrice**
  FEM ▶ SEE **conservateur** *NOUN*
1 **conservative**
  un parti politique conservateur a
  conservative political party
2 **curator** *(in a museum)*

conservateur *MASC NOUN* ▶ SEE **conservateur**
  NOUN
  (food) preservative

A
B
C
D
E
F
G
H
I
J
K
L
M
N
O
P
Q
R
S
T
U
V
W
X
Y
Z

la **conservation** FEM NOUN
1   **conservation** (of wildlife, heritage)
2   **lait longue conservation** long-life milk

la **conserve** FEM NOUN
1   **les conserves** canned food
    les légumes en conserve canned
    vegetables.
2   **preserve** (home-made jam, pickle)
    des conserves de tomates tomato
    preserves

conserver VERB [1]
    to keep
    J'ai conservé tous mes vieux cahiers. I've
    kept all my old copybooks.
    'À conserver au frais' 'Keep in a cool place'

se **conserver** REFLEXIVE VERB ⬤
    to keep
    Ce fromage se conserve bien. This cheese
    keeps well.

considérable MASC & FEM ADJECTIVE
    considerable

considérablement ADVERB
    considerably

la **considération** FEM NOUN
    consideration

considérer VERB [24]
    to consider
    considérer quelqu'un comme to consider
    somebody to be
    Je l'ai considéré comme un frère. I
    considered him to be like a brother.

♪ la **consigne** FEM NOUN
1   **left luggage office**
    On a laissé les sacs à dos à la consigne. We
    left the rucksacks at the left luggage office.
2   **deposit** (on a returnable bottle)
3   **instructions**
    les consignes à suivre en cas d'incendie
    what to do in the event of a fire
•   **la consigne automatique**
    left-luggage lockers

consistant MASC ADJECTIVE, **consistante** FEM
    substantial
    un repas consistant a substantial meal

consister VERB [1]
    consister en to consist of, to consist in
    Le village consiste en quelques maisons
    et une église. The village consists of a few
    houses and a church.

la **console** FEM NOUN
    console
    J'aime jouer sur une console. I like playing
    on a console.
•   **la console de jeux**
    games console

le **consommateur** MASC NOUN, la
consommatrice FEM
1   **consumer**
2   **customer** (in a cafe)

la **consommation** FEM NOUN
1   **consumption** (of fuel, electricity)
2   **drink** (at a cafe, bar)
    regler les consommations to pay for the
    drinks
    pousser à la consommation to encourage
    people to drink more (negative sense)

consommer VERB [1]
1   **to use** (fuel)
2   **to eat** (meat, fish)
    Ils ne consomment pas de viande. They
    don't eat meat.
3   **to have a drink** (in a cafe)

la **consonne** FEM NOUN
    consonant (any letter except a, e, i, o, u)

la **conspiration** FEM NOUN
    conspiracy

conspirer VERB [1]
    to conspire, **to plot**

constamment ADVERB
    constantly

constant MASC ADJECTIVE, **constante** FEM
    constant

constater VERB [1]
    to notice

constipé MASC ADJECTIVE, **constipée** FEM
    constipated

la **construction** FEM NOUN
    construction
    Le gymnase est en construction. The sports
    hall is under construction.

construire VERB [26]
    to build
    Il adore construire des maquettes. He loves
    building models.
    faire construire quelque chose to have
    something built
    Ils font construire une maison de vacances.
    They're having a holiday home built.

le **consul** MASC NOUN
    consul

le **consulat** MASC NOUN
    consulate

la **consultation** FEM NOUN
1   **consultation** (with a doctor, an expert)
2   **surgery hours**
    Elle est actuellement en consultation. She's
    with a patient at the moment.

⬤ means the verb takes être to form the perfect

consulter *VERB* [1]
1 **to consult** *(a doctor, an expert)*
2 **to check**
   Allez consulter l'horaire. Go and check the timetable.
3 **to hold surgery** *(doctors)*

le **contact** *MASC NOUN*
1 **contact**
   prendre contact avec quelqu'un to contact somebody
   Je prendrai contact avec Mélanie. I'll contact Melanie.
   rester en contact avec quelqu'un to keep in touch with somebody
   Je ne suis pas restée en contact avec elle. I didn't keep in touch with her.
   Restons en contact. Let's stay in touch.
2 mettre le contact to switch on the ignition
   couper le contact to switch off the ignition

contacter *VERB* [1]
   to contact

contagieux *MASC ADJECTIVE*, **contagieuse** *FEM*
   infectious

la **contamination** *FEM NOUN*
   contamination

contaminer *VERB* [1]
   to contaminate

le **conte** *MASC NOUN*
   tale, **story**
• le conte de fées
   fairy tale

contempler *VERB* [1]
1 **to look at** *(a picture)*
2 **to contemplate** *(a scene)*

contemporain *MASC ADJECTIVE*,
   contemporaine *FEM*
   contemporary

le **conteneur** *MASC NOUN*
   container

contenir *VERB* [77]
1 **to contain**
   'Ne contient pas de sucre' 'Does not contain sugar'
2 **to hold** *(a certain amount)*
   La boîte contient jusqu'à cent stylo-feutre. The box holds up to one hundred felt-tips.

ℙ **content** *MASC ADJECTIVE*, **contente** *FEM*
   pleased, **glad**, **happy**
   Il n'est pas content. He's not happy.
   être content de quelque chose to be pleased with something
   Je suis très contente de ma nouvelle chambre. I'm very pleased with my new room.
   Ils étaient contents de me voir. They were

pleased to see me.

contenter *VERB* [1]
   to satisfy
se **contenter** *REFLEXIVE VERB* ◎
   se contenter de faire quelque chose to content yourself with doing something
   Je dois me contenter de rester à la maison. I've got to content myself with staying at home.

le **contenu** *MASC NOUN*
   contents
   Le contenu de la caisse pèse 20 kg. The contents of the crate weigh 20kg.

contesté *MASC ADJECTIVE*, **contestée** *FEM*
   controversial

contester *VERB* [1]
1 **to challenge** *(an authority)*
2 **to question** *(a need, a decision)*

le **contexte** *MASC NOUN*
   context

le **continent** *MASC NOUN*
   continent

continu *MASC ADJECTIVE*, **continue** *FEM*
   continuous

la **continuation** *FEM NOUN*
   continuation

ℙ **continuer** *VERB* [1]
   to continue, **to go on with**
   Je peux continuer mon histoire? Can I go on with my story?
   Continue! Go on!
   continuer à faire, de faire quelque chose to go on doing something
   Elle a continué à parler. She went on talking.
   Je vais continuer de faire du dessin. I'm going to continue drawing.

le **contour** *MASC NOUN*
   outline

contourner *VERB* [1]
   to go round *(an obstacle)*

le **contraceptif** *MASC NOUN*
   contraceptive

la **contraception** *FEM NOUN*
   contraception

le **contractuel** *MASC NOUN*, la **contractuelle** *FEM*
   traffic warden

la **contradiction** *FEM NOUN*
   contradiction

contradictoire *MASC & FEM ADJECTIVE*
   contradictory

contraindre *VERB* [31]
  to force

contraire *MASC & FEM ADJECTIVE* ▶ SEE **contraire**
  NOUN
  opposite
  Il est allé dans le sens contraire. He went in
  the opposite direction.

le **contraire** *MASC NOUN* ▶ SEE **contraire** *ADJECTIVE*
  1 the opposite
    C'est le contraire de ce que je pensais. It's
    the opposite of what I thought.
  2 au contraire on the contrary

contrairement *ADVERB*
  1 contrary to
    Contrairement à ce qu'il nous a dit …
    Contrary to what he told us …
  2 unlike
    Contrairement à Raphaël, j'aime la techno.
    Unlike Raphaël, I like techno music.

contrariant *MASC ADJECTIVE*, **contrariante** *FEM*
  annoying

contrarier *VERB* [1]
  1 to upset
    Je suis contrarié parce que j'ai perdu mon
    appareil photo. I'm upset because I've lost
    my camera.
  2 to annoy
    C'est ce qui me contrarie. That's what
    annoys me.

le **contraste** *MASC NOUN*
  contrast

contraster *VERB* [1]
  to contrast

le **contrat** *MASC NOUN*
  contract

la **contravention** *FEM NOUN*
  1 parking ticket
  2 speeding ticket

ℓ **contre** *PREPOSITION* ▶ SEE **contre** *ADVERB, NOUN*
  1 against
    contre le mur against the wall
    être contre quelque chose to be against
    something
    Je suis tout à fait contre cette idée. I'm
    totally against this idea.
    jouer contre quelqu'un to play against
    somebody
    Dimanche, on joue contre Valbonne. On
    Sunday we play against Valbonne.
  2 versus
    C'est Lyon contre Marseille. It's Lyons
    versus Marseilles.
  3 échanger quelque chose contre to
    exchange something for (something else)
    J'ai échangé ma console de jeux contre

un lecteur DVD. I exchanged my games
console for a DVD player.
  4 par contre on the other hand
    Il ne téléphone pas, par contre il envoie
    des textos. He doesn't phone. On the other
    hand, he sends text messages.

ℓ **contre** *ADVERB* ▶ SEE **contre** *NOUN, PREPOSITION*
  'Que penses-tu de l'idée?' – 'Je suis contre.'
  'What do you think of the idea?' – 'I'm
  against it.'
  Moi, je n'ai rien contre. I have nothing
  against it.

ℓ le **contre** *MASC NOUN* ▶ SEE **contre** *ADVERB,*
  PREPOSITION
  le pour et le contre the pros and cons
  (points for and against)

la **contrebande** *FEM NOUN*
  1 smuggling
  2 smuggled goods

la **contrebasse** *FEM NOUN*
  double bass

contredire *VERB* [47]
  to contradict

la **contrefaçon** *FEM NOUN*
  1 forgery (a signature, banknote, painting)
    Méfiez-vous des contrefaçons! Beware of
    forgeries!
  2 counterfeit (money)
  3 pirated copy (of DVD)

le **contremaître** *MASC NOUN*
  foreman

la **contremaîtresse** *FEM NOUN*
  supervisor

le **contreplaqué** *MASC NOUN*
  plywood

le & la **contribuable** *MASC & FEM NOUN*
  taxpayer

contribuer *VERB* [1]
  contribuer à quelque chose to contribute
  to something
  Natalie contribue au débat. Natalie
  contributes to the discussion.

la **contribution** *FEM NOUN*
  contribution
  apporter sa contribution à quelque chose
  to make your contribution to something
  Chacun peut apporter sa contribution
  à la tâche. Everyone can make their
  contribution to the task.

le **contrôle** *MASC NOUN*
  1 control
  2 test (at school)
    J'ai un contrôle de français lundi. I've got a
    French test on Monday.

ⓐ means the verb takes être to form the perfect

- le contrôle des billets
  ticket inspection
- le contrôle continu
  continuous assessment
- le contrôle d'identité
  identity check
- le contrôle des naissances
  birth control
- le contrôle des passeports
  passport control
- le contrôle de police
  police check

contrôler *VERB* [1]
1 **to control** *(a country, an organization)*
2 **to check** *(a ticket, somebody's identity)*

ℰ le **contrôleur** *MASC NOUN*, la **contrôleuse** *FEM*
ticket inspector
- le contrôleur aérien
  air traffic controller

controversé *MASC ADJECTIVE*, **controversée**
FEM
controversial
une décision controversée a controversial
decision

convaincant *MASC ADJECTIVE*, **convaincante**
FEM
convincing

convaincre *VERB* [79]
1 **to convince**
Elle n'est pas convaincue. She's not
convinced.
2 **to persuade**
Je les ai convaincus d'acheter un
ordinateur. I persuaded them to buy a
computer.

convenable *MASC & FEM ADJECTIVE*
1 **suitable** *(place, clothes)*
2 **decent** *(salary, housing, meal)*
3 **proper** *(behaviour)*

convenir *VERB* [81]
1 convenir à to suit, to be suitable for
Est-ce que dix heures te convient? Does ten
o'clock suit you?
Ça me convient mieux. That suits me
better.
Le film ne convient pas aux enfants. The
film isn't suitable for children.
2 convenir de faire quelque chose to agree to
do something
Nous avons convenu de travailler
ensemble. We agreed to work together.

la **convention** *FEM NOUN*
1 **agreement**
2 **convention**

la **conversation** *FEM NOUN*
conversation

faire de la conversation to make
conversation

convertir *VERB* [2]
to convert

la **conviction** *FEM NOUN*
conviction
avoir la conviction que... to be convinced
that...
J'ai la conviction que Leila va gagner. I am
convinced that Leila will win.

le & la **convive** *MASC & FEM NOUN*
guest *(at a meal, a party)*

convivial *MASC ADJECTIVE*, **conviviale** *FEM*,
conviviaux *MASC PL*, **conviviales** *FEM PL*
1 **friendly**
une atmosphère conviviale a friendly
atmosphere
2 **user-friendly**
un jeu d'ordinateur très convivial a user-
friendly computer game

le **convoi** *MASC NOUN*
convoy
'Convoi Exceptionnel' 'Abnormal Load' *(on
truck)*

convoquer *VERB* [1]
1 **to invite** *(to a meeting)*
2 **to summon, to call**
J'ai été convoqué au bureau du directeur. I
was called to the headmaster's office.

coopératif *MASC ADJECTIVE*, **coopérative** *FEM*
cooperative

la **coopération** *FEM NOUN*
cooperation

la **coopérative** *FEM NOUN*
cooperative *(a business)*

coopérer *VERB* [24]
to cooperate

les **coordonnées** *PLURAL FEM NOUN*
address and telephone number
Je te donnerai mes coordonnées. I'll give
you my address and telephone number.

coordonner *VERB* [1]
to coordinate

ℰ le **copain** *MASC NOUN*
1 **mate, friend**
Je sors avec les copains. I'm going out with
my mates.
2 **boyfriend**
Elle est partie en vacances avec son copain.
She's gone on holiday with her boyfriend.

la **copie** *FEM NOUN*
1 **copy** *(of something)*
Tu peux me faire une copie de ce logiciel?

ℰ indicates key words

Can you make me a copy of this software?
Ce serait une copie pirate! That would be a
pirate copy!

2 image (of somebody)
C'est la copie conforme de son père. He's
the spitting image of his father.

3 paper (an exam script or written exercise)
Elle ramasse les copies déjà. She's already
collecting the papers.
J'ai rendu une copie blanche. I handed in a
blank sheet of paper.
Elle aura un tas de copies à corriger. She's
going to have a pile of marking to do.

copier VERB [1]
to copy

copier-coller VERB [1]
to cut and paste
Copiez-collez la liste! Cut and paste the list!

copieux MASC ADJECTIVE, **copieuse** FEM
hearty
un petit déjeuner copieux a hearty
breakfast

la **copine** FEM NOUN
1 mate, friend (female)
Je sors avec les copines. I'm going out with
my mates.
2 girlfriend
Il est parti en vacances avec sa copine. He's
gone on holiday with his girlfriend.

le **coq** MASC NOUN
cockerel

la **coque** FEM NOUN
1 hull (of a boat)
2 shell (of a nut)
3 un œuf à la coque a soft-boiled egg

le **coquelicot** MASC NOUN
poppy

la **coqueluche** FEM NOUN
whooping-cough

coquet MASC ADJECTIVE, **coquette** FEM
1 être coquet to like to look good
Paul est coquet. Paul likes to look good.
C'est une petite fille coquette. She likes to
look pretty.
2 pretty (village, house)
un petit coin coquet de la Bretagne a
pretty little spot in Brittany

le **coquetier** MASC NOUN
eggcup

le **coquillage** MASC NOUN
1 shellfish
À la mer, on mange des coquillages. At the
seaside, we eat shellfish.
2 seashell
J'aime ramasser des coquillages. I like

collecting seashells.

la **coquille** FEM NOUN
1 shell (of an egg, a nut, a shellfish)
2 misprint
• la coquille Saint-Jacques
scallop

coquin MASC ADJECTIVE, **coquine** FEM
cheeky (child)

le **cor** MASC NOUN
horn (musical instrument)

le **corail** MASC NOUN, **coraux** PL
coral

le **Coran** MASC NOUN
(Religion) le Coran the Koran

le **corbeau** MASC NOUN, les **corbeaux** PL
crow

la **corbeille** FEM NOUN
basket
• la corbeille à papier
wastepaper basket
• la corbeille à linge
linen basket

le **corbillard** MASC NOUN
hearse

la **corde** FEM NOUN
1 rope
2 string (of a racket, bow, guitar)
• la corde à linge
clothes line
• la corde à sauter
skipping rope

cordial MASC ADJECTIVE, **cordiale** FEM,
cordiaux MASC PL, **cordiales** FEM PL
warm, cordial

cordialement ADVERB
1 warmly
2 Cordialement à vous Yours sincerely
(formal ending to a letter)

la **cordonnerie** FEM NOUN
shoe repair shop

le **cordonnier** MASC NOUN
shoe repairer
aller chez le cordonnier to go to the shoe
repair shop

la **corne** FEM NOUN
horn

la **cornemuse** FEM NOUN
bagpipes
jouer de la cornemuse to play the bagpipes

le **cornet** MASC NOUN
cone (for ice cream)
une glace en cornet an ice-cream cone

- le cornet de frites
  a box of chips *(in cardboard box)*

la **corniche** *FEM NOUN*
1 **cornice** *(on a building)*
2 la (route de) corniche the coastal road

le **cornichon** *MASC NOUN*
  gherkin

la **Cornouailles** *FEM NOUN*
  Cornwall
  en Cornouailles in Cornwall

> **WORD TIP** Countries and regions in French take le, la or les.

ℱ le **corps** *MASC NOUN*
  body
  le corps humain the human body

correct *MASC ADJECTIVE*, **correcte** *FEM*
1 **correct**
  La réponse est correcte. The answer is correct.
2 **reasonable**
  à un prix correct at a reasonable price
  Le repas était tout à fait correct. The meal was quite good.
3 **proper** *(behaviour)*

correctement *ADVERB*
1 **correctly**
  Il faut remplir le formulaire correctement. You have to fill in the form correctly.
2 **properly**
  savoir se conduire correctement to know how to behave properly
3 **reasonably well**
  manger correctement to eat reasonably well

le **correcteur orthographique** *MASC NOUN*
  spell checker

la **correction** *FEM NOUN*
1 **correction**
  J'ai quelques corrections à faire dans ma dissertation. I've got some corrections to make to my essay.
2 **marking** *(of an exam paper)*
  La prof n'a pas fini ses corrections. The teacher hasn't finished marking the papers.
3 **good manners**
  manquer de correction to have no manners
4 **hiding**
  recevoir une bonne correction to get a good hiding

ℱ la **correspondance** *FEM NOUN*
1 **letters, correspondence**
  Elle a fini sa correspondance pour aujourd'hui. She's finished writing letters for today.
  Je fais signer mon carnet de

correspondance tous les jours. I get my school diary signed every day.
2 **mail order**
  acheter quelque chose par correspondance to buy something by mail order
  Quelquefois, j'achète des vêtements par correspondance. I sometimes buy clothes by mail order.
3 **connection** *(in air, rail travel)*
  les vols en correspondance connecting flights
  J'ai raté ma correspondance. I missed my connection.

ℱ le **correspondant** *MASC NOUN*, la **correspondante** *FEM*
  penfriend
  Ma correspondante habite à Nice. My penfriend lives in Nice.

correspondre *VERB* [3]
  to correspond

la **corrida** *FEM NOUN*
  bullfight

corriger *VERB* [52]
1 **to correct** *(a mistake)*
2 **to mark** *(school work, exam papers)*
  Elle est en train de corriger ses copies. She's doing her marking.

corse *MASC & FEM ADJECTIVE* ▶ SEE **Corse**
  Corsican

> **WORD TIP** Adjectives never have capitals in French, even for nationality or regional origin.

la **Corse** *FEM NOUN* ▶ SEE **corse**
1 **Corsica**
  Nous allons en Corse. We're going to Corsica.
2 le & la Corse **Corsican** *(person from Corsica)*

> **WORD TIP** Countries and regions in French take le, la or les.

la **corvée** *FEM NOUN*
1 **chore**
2 C'est la corvée! It's a real drag!

les **cosmétiques** *PLURAL MASC NOUN*
  cosmetics

costaud *MASC ADJECTIVE*, **costaude** *FEM*
  strong, sturdy

ℱ le **costume** *MASC NOUN*
1 **suit**
  Il a mis un costume cravate. He wore a suit and tie.
2 **costume** *(for dressing up, in film)*
  Les costumes d'époque sont superbes. The period costumes are superb.

la côte *FEM NOUN*

1 **coast**

2 **hill, slope**
Il faut monter la côte à vélo. We have to cycle up the hill.

3 **rib**
Elle s'est cassé une côte. She broke a rib.

4 **chop**
des côtes de porc grillées grilled pork chops

5 côte à côte side by side
Ils galopaient côte à côte. They were cantering side by side.

• la côte d'agneau
lamb chop

• la Côte d'Azur
French Riviera

• la côte de bœuf
rib of beef

le côté *MASC NOUN*

1 **side**
Mettez ça de l'autre côté. Put that on the other side.
de l'autre côté de on the other side of
de chaque côté de on each side of
Ils habitent de l'autre côté de la rue. They live on the other side of the street.

2 **way** *(direction)*
De quel côté vas-tu? Which way are you going?

3 d'un côté on the one hand
d'un autre côté on the other hand
D'un côté j'aime le ski ... On the one hand I love skiing ...
... d'un autre côté je déteste le froid. ... on the other hand I hate the cold.

4 à côté nearby
Mon frère habite à côté. My brother lives nearby.

5 à côté de next to, beside
Mets-toi à côté de Romain. Go and sit beside Romain.
Elle était assise à côté de moi. She was sitting next to me.

6 mettre quelque chose de côté to put something aside
J'ai mis de l'argent de côté pour m'acheter ce blouson. I put some money aside to buy that jacket.

la côtelette *FEM NOUN*
chop

• la côtelette de porc
pork chop

la cotisation *FEM NOUN*
subscription *(to an association, a club)*

♪ **le coton** *MASC NOUN*

1 **cotton**
un pull en coton a cotton jumper

2 **cotton wool**

du coton some cotton wool
Passe-moi un coton. Give me a piece of cotton wool.

3 *(informal)*
une question plutôt coton a rather tricky question

♪ **le cou** *MASC NOUN*
neck

le couchage *MASC NOUN*
sleeping arrangements
une villa avec couchage pour douze a villa sleeping twelve people

• le sac de couchage
sleeping bag

couchant *MASC ADJECTIVE*
le soleil couchant the setting sun
au soleil couchant at sunset

la couche *FEM NOUN*

1 **layer**

2 **coat** *(of paint)*

3 **nappy**

• la couche d'ozone
ozone layer

♪ **coucher** *VERB* [1]

1 **to sleep**
Nous allons toutes coucher chez Sophie. We're all sleeping at Sophie's house.

2 coucher un enfant to put a child to bed
J'arrive à 7 heures et je couche les enfants. I arrive at 7 and I put the children to bed.

se **coucher** *REFLEXIVE VERB* ◯

1 **to go to bed**
Elle s'est couchée tôt. She went to bed early.
Je ne me couche jamais avant dix heures. I never go to bed before ten o'clock.

2 **to lie down**
Il va se coucher dans son panier. He goes and lies down in his basket.

• le coucher de soleil
sunset

♪ **la couchette** *FEM NOUN*
berth *(on a train or boat)*
une cabine avec deux couchettes a two-berth cabin

le coucou *MASC NOUN*

1 **cuckoo**

2 **cowslip**

♪ **le coude** *MASC NOUN*
elbow

coudre *VERB* [28]
to sew
J'ai cousu un bouton à ma chemise. I sewed a button onto my shirt.

◯ **means the verb takes être to form the perfect**

la **couette** *FEM NOUN*
1 duvet, continental quilt
2 des couettes bunches *(hairstyle)*

couler *VERB* [1]
1 to flow
2 J'ai le nez qui coule. I've got a runny nose.
Il va faire couler un bain. He's going to run a bath.
3 to sink *(a boat)*

ℓ la **couleur** *FEM NOUN*
colour
De quelle couleur sont ses yeux? What colour are his eyes?
une couleur peu commune an unusual colour

la **couleuvre** *FEM NOUN*
grass snake

les **coulisses** *PLURAL FEM NOUN*
wings *(in a theatre)*

le **couloir** *MASC NOUN*
corridor
• le couloir d'autobus
bus lane

ℓ le **coup** *MASC NOUN*
1 blow, knock
un coup à la tête a blow to the head
J'ai entendu un coup à la porte. I heard a knock on the door.
Il a reçu un coup dans l'estomac. He was hit in the stomach.
2 time
à tous les coups every time
Elle me dit ça à tous les coups. She says that to me every time.
Ce coup-ci, je ne le raterai pas. This time I won't miss it.
Il a eu son permis du premier coup. He passed his driving test first time.
Il a bu son verre d'un seul coup. He emptied his glass in one go.
3 tenir le coup to hold out *(keep going)*
Je ne tiens plus le coup! I can't go on any longer!
4 *(informal)* boire un coup to have a drink
On va boire un coup. We're going to have a drink.
5 donner un coup de balai to sweep the floor
Il donne un coup de balai à la cuisine. He's sweeping the kitchen floor.
6 sur le coup at first
Sur le coup, il a été très surpris. At first, he was very surprised.
7 tout d'un coup, tout à coup all of a sudden
Tout d'un coup, l'alarme a sonné. All of a sudden, the bell rang.
• le coup de chance
stroke of luck

• le coup de feu
(gun)shot

le & la **coupable** *MASC & FEM NOUN* ▶SEE
coupable *ADJECTIVE*
culprit

coupable *MASC & FEM ADJECTIVE* ▶SEE **coupable** *NOUN*
guilty

le **coup de fil** *MASC NOUN*
phone call
passer un coup de fil to make a phone call
passer un coup de fil à quelqu'un to phone somebody
Je te passe un coup de fil demain. I'll phone you tomorrow.

le **coup de main** *MASC NOUN*
donner un coup de main à quelqu'un to give somebody a hand
Tu peux me donner un coup de main? Can you give me a hand?
Je te donne un coup de main pour ranger. I'll give you a hand tidying up.

le **coup de peinture** *MASC NOUN*
lick of paint

ℓ le **coup de pied** *MASC NOUN*
kick
donner un coup de pied à quelqu'un to kick somebody
Il lui a donné un coup de pied. He kicked her.

le **coup de poing** *MASC NOUN*
punch
donner un coup de poing à quelqu'un to punch somebody

ℓ le **coup de soleil** *MASC NOUN*
attraper un coup de soleil to get sunburnt
J'ai attrapé un coup de soleil à la plage. I got sunburnt on the beach.

ℓ le **coup de téléphone** *MASC NOUN*
phone call
Je peux faire un coup de téléphone? Can I make a phone call?

le **coup de tonnerre** *MASC NOUN*
clap of thunder
J'ai entendu des coups de tonnerre. I heard thunder.

le **coup de vent** *MASC NOUN*
gust of wind

le **coup d'œil** *MASC NOUN*
glance
jeter un coup d'œil à quelque chose to have a quick look at something
Je peux jeter un coup d'œil à tes photos? Can I have a quick look at your pictures?

ℓ indicates key words

la **coupe** *FEM NOUN*
1 **cup** *(a trophy)*
2 **haircut**
• la Coupe du Monde
World Cup

🔊 **couper** *VERB* [1]
1 **to cut**
J'ai coupé le tissu en trois morceaux. I've cut the material into three pieces.
2 **to cut down**
Cet arbre est trop haut. Il faut le couper. The tree is too high. It must be cut down.
3 **to turn off** *(the gas, the electricity)*
Ils ont coupé l'électricité pour faire des réparations. They turned off the electricity in order to carry out repairs.
4 **to cut off** *(a telephone line)*
On a coupé le téléphone. The phone's been cut off.
5 couper l'appétit à quelqu'un to spoil somebody's appetite
Ça m'a coupé l'appétit. It spoilt my appetite.
6 couper la parole à quelqu'un to interrupt somebody
Excuse-moi, je t'ai coupé la parole. Sorry, I interrupted you.

se **couper** *REFLEXIVE VERB* ⊘
1 **to cut yourself**
Elle s'est coupée. She cut herself.
Elle s'est coupé le doigt. She cut her finger.
2 se faire couper les cheveux to have your hair cut
Elle s'est fait couper les cheveux. Have you had your hair cut?
Demain je me fais couper les cheveux. Tomorrow I'm having my hair cut.

le **coup franc** *MASC NOUN*
free kick *(in football)*

le **couple** *MASC NOUN*
couple

le **couplet** *MASC NOUN*
verse *(of song)*

la **coupure** *FEM NOUN*
cut
J'ai eu une coupure au menton. I got a cut on my chin.
• la coupure de courant
power cut

la **cour** *FEM NOUN*
1 **school playground**
2 **inner courtyard** *(of an apartment block)*
3 **court** *(of a king, queen)*
4 **law court**
• la cour de récréation
school playground

le **courage** *MASC NOUN*
1 **courage, bravery**
2 **energy**
avoir le courage de faire quelque chose to have the energy to do something
Je n'ai pas le courage de travailler tard. I haven't got the energy to work late.
3 Allons, courage! Come on, don't lose heart! Bon courage! Good luck!

courageux *MASC ADJECTIVE*, **courageuse** *FEM*
brave

couramment *ADVERB*
fluently
Il parle couramment le français. He speaks fluent French.

courant *MASC ADJECTIVE*, **courante** *FEM* ▶ SEE **courant** *NOUN*
1 **common** *(word, activity)*
C'est devenu très courant chez les jeunes. It's become very common among young people.
C'est un problème courant. It's a common problem.
2 le français courant standard French

le **courant** *MASC NOUN* ▶ SEE **courant** *ADJECTIVE*
1 **current** *(in sea, river)*
2 **electricity**
On a coupé le courant. The electricity has been cut off.
Il y a une panne de courant. There's a power cut.
3 être au courant de quelque chose to know about something
Est-ce que ta sœur est au courant? Does your sister know?
Elle n'est pas encore au courant. She doesn't know yet.
Tiens-moi au courant. Keep me posted.
• le courant d'air
draught

la **courbe** *FEM NOUN*
curve

courber *VERB* [1]
to bend

le **coureur** *MASC NOUN*, la **coureuse** *FEM*
runner *(athlete)*

la **courge** *FEM NOUN*
marrow *(the vegetable)*

la **courgette** *FEM NOUN*
courgette

🔊 **courir** *VERB* [29]
1 **to run**
Estelle court vite. Estelle runs fast.
J'ai traversé la rue en courant. I ran across the street.

⊘ means the verb takes être to form the perfect

2 courir un risque to run a risk
Nous courons un gros risque. We're running a big risk.
C'est un risque à courir. It's a risk you have to take.

la **couronne** FEM NOUN
crown

ʒ le **courriel** MASC NOUN
email

ʒ le **courrier** MASC NOUN
1 post, mail
Je n'ai pas eu de courrier. I didn't get any post.
Le courrier est en retard ce matin. The post is late this morning.
2 letter
un courrier de confirmation a letter of confirmation
• le courrier électronique
electronic mail, email

le **cours** MASC NOUN
1 class, lesson
le cours de français the French lesson
Je vais suivre des cours d'espagnol. I'm going to go to Spanish classes.
Nous n'avons pas cours le mercredi après-midi. We don't have lessons on Wednesday afternoons.
2 course (of events)
au cours de in the course of
au cours de l'été during the summer
• le cours particulier
private lesson

ʒ la **course** FEM NOUN
1 race
On fait la course? Shall we have a race?
2 running (in athletics)
3 une course à faire an errand
J'ai une course à faire. I've got to get something.

ʒ les **courses** PLURAL FEM NOUN
shopping
faire des courses to go shopping
On fait les courses le samedi. We do the shopping on Saturdays.
• les courses hippiques
horse-racing

ʒ **court** MASC ADJECTIVE, **courte** FEM ▸ SEE **court** NOUN
short
une jupe très courte a very short skirt
Ce chemin-là est plus court. That way is shorter.
• le court-circuit
short-circuit
• le court-métrage
short film

ʒ le **court** MASC NOUN ▸ SEE **court** ADJECTIVE
court (for tennis, squash, etc)
• le court de tennis
tennis court

couru VERB ▸ SEE **courir**

ʒ le **cousin** MASC NOUN, la **cousine** FEM
cousin
mon cousin germain my first cousin
C'est ma cousine préférée. She's my favourite cousin.

le **coussin** MASC NOUN
cushion

le **coût** MASC NOUN
cost
• le coût de la vie
cost of living

ʒ le **couteau** MASC NOUN, les **couteaux** PL
knife
• le couteau à pain
breadknife

ʒ **coûter** VERB [1]
to cost
Ça coûte combien? How much is it?, How much does it cost?
Ça coûte dix euros. It's ten euros.
Cette voiture nous a coûté mille livres. This car cost us a thousand pounds.
coûte que coûte at all costs
coûter cher to be expensive
Est-ce que ça t'a coûté cher? Was it expensive?
Ça ne m'a pas coûté cher. It wasn't expensive.

la **coutume** FEM NOUN
custom
une coutume très ancienne a very old custom

la **couture** FEM NOUN
1 dressmaking
2 sewing (activity, piece of sewing)
faire de la couture to sew
J'ai de la couture à faire. I have some sewing to do.
3 seam
La couture se défait. The seam is coming apart.

le **couturier** MASC NOUN
fashion designer

la **couturière** FEM NOUN
dressmaker

le **couvent** MASC NOUN
convent

le **couvercle** MASC NOUN
1 lid

ʒ indicates key words

2 **screwtop**

couvert *MASC ADJECTIVE*, **couverte** *FEM* ▸ SEE **couvert** *NOUN*

1 **covered**
un marché couvert a covered market
la piscine couverte the indoor swimming-pool

2 **couvert de quelque chose** covered with something
Le sommet de la montagne est couvert de neige. The summit is covered with snow.

3 **overcast, cloudy**
Le temps est couvert. The weather is overcast.

le couvert *MASC NOUN* ▸ SEE **couvert** *ADJECTIVE*

1 **place setting**
un repas de 10 couverts a meal for 10
Mets le couvert, s'il te plaît. Lay the table please.

2 **les couverts** the cutlery
Il manque les couverts. The knives and forks aren't on the table.

la couverture *FEM NOUN*

1 **blanket**
2 **cover** (of a book)

le couvre-lit *MASC*, **les couvre-lits** *PL*
bedspread

couvrir *VERB* [30]
to cover

se couvrir *REFLEXIVE VERB* ◐

1 **to wrap up**
Couvre-toi bien, il fait très froid! Wrap up well, it's freezing!

2 **to cloud over**
Ça s'est couvert dans l'après-midi. It clouded over in the afternoon.

3 **se couvrir de quelque chose** to be covered with something
L'arbre se couvre de fleurs. The tree is covered with blooms.

4 **se couvrir de ridicule** to make a laughing stock of yourself

le crabe *MASC NOUN*
crab

cracher *VERB* [1]
to spit

le crachin *MASC NOUN*
drizzle

la craie *FEM NOUN*
chalk

craindre *VERB* [31]
to be afraid of

la crainte *FEM NOUN*
fear

la crampe *FEM NOUN*
cramp
une crampe à la jambe a cramp in your leg

le crâne *MASC NOUN*
skull
J'ai mal au crâne. (informal) I've got a headache.

crâner *VERB* [1]
(informal) **to show off**

le crapaud *MASC NOUN*
toad

le craquement *MASC NOUN*
creak

craquer *VERB* [1]

1 **to split**
Ma jupe a craqué. My skirt split at the seams.

2 **to creak**
Le plancher craque. The floor creaks.

3 (informal) **to crack up** (because of pressure)
Je vais craquer! I'm going to crack up!
J'ai craqué, alors je l'ai acheté. I just couldn't resist it, so I bought it.

4 **craquer pour quelqu'un** to fall in love with somebody
Elle a craqué pour lui. She fell in love with him.

la crasse *FEM NOUN*
filth

la cravate *FEM NOUN*
tie

le crawl *MASC NOUN*
crawl
Je sais bien nager le crawl. I can do the crawl well.

le crayon *MASC NOUN*
pencil

créatif *MASC ADJECTIVE*, **créative** *FEM*
creative

la création *FEM NOUN*
creation

la créativité *FEM NOUN*
creativity

la crèche *FEM NOUN*

1 **crèche, day nursery**
2 **nativity scene** (as a Christmas decoration)

le crédit *MASC NOUN*

1 **credit**
2 **funds**
• **le crédit immobilier**
mortgage

créer *VERB* [32]
to create

◐ means the verb takes être to form the perfect

_ₚ_ la **crème** _FEM NOUN_
cream
- la crème anglaise
custard
- la crème caramel
crème caramel
- la crème Chantilly
whipped cream
- la crème solaire
sun cream

la **crémerie** _FEM NOUN_
shop selling dairy products

crémeux _MASC ADJECTIVE_, **crémeuse** _FEM_
creamy

_ₚ_ la **crêpe** _FEM NOUN_
pancake
Ils font sauter des crêpes. They're tossing pancakes.

la **crêperie** _MASC NOUN_
shop or stall sellingcrêpes

le **crépon** _MASC NOUN_
crêpe paper

le **crépuscule** _MASC NOUN_
twilight

le **cresson** _MASC NOUN_
watercress

creuser _VERB_ [1]
to dig (a hole)

se **creuser** _REFLEXIVE VERB_ ☁
1 to widen (of a gap, differences between people)
2 (informal)
se creuser la cervelle to rack your brains
Je me suis creusé la cervelle pour trouver une solution. I've been racking my brains to find a solution.

creux _MASC ADJECTIVE_, **creuse** _FEM_ ▸ SEE **creux** _NOUN_
1 hollow
2 une assiette creuse a soup plate

le **creux** _MASC NOUN_ ▸ SEE **creux** _ADJECTIVE_
1 hollow, dip
2 (informal)
J'ai un petit creux. I've got the munchies.

la **crevaison** _FEM NOUN_
puncture

crevant _MASC ADJECTIVE_, **crevante** _FEM_
(informal) exhausting
Mélanie a eu une journée crevante.
Mélanie's had an exhausting day.

_ₚ_ **crevé** _MASC ADJECTIVE_, **crevée** _FEM_
1 burst
un pneu crevé a burst tyre, a puncture
2 (informal) knackered

crever _VERB_ [50]
1 to burst (a bubble, balloon)
Le paquet de chips a crevé. The bag of crisps burst open.
2 to get a puncture
Nous avons crevé en route. We got a puncture on the way.
3 (informal) to die
Je crève de faim! I'm starving!
Elle crève de chaud. She's boiling hot.

la **crevette** _FEM NOUN_
prawn

le **cri** _MASC NOUN_
cry, shout

criard _MASC ADJECTIVE_, **criarde** _FEM_
garish (colour)

le **cric** _MASC NOUN_
(car) jack

le **cricket** _MASC NOUN_
cricket
Il joue au cricket le dimanche. He plays cricket on Sundays.

_ₚ_ **crier** _VERB_ [1]
to shout
Ne crie pas! Don't shout!
Ils crient de joie. They're shouting for joy.
J'ai crié de douleur. I cried out in pain.
Ce n'est pas la peine de crier. There's no point in shouting.

le **crime** _MASC NOUN_
1 crime
2 murder

criminel _MASC ADJECTIVE_, **criminelle** _FEM_ ▸ SEE **criminel** _NOUN_
criminal
des activités criminelles criminal activities

le **criminel** _MASC NOUN_, la **criminelle** _FEM_ ▸ SEE **criminel** _ADJECTIVE_
1 criminal
2 murderer

la **crinière** _FEM NOUN_
mane

le **criquet** _MASC NOUN_
grasshopper

la **crise** _FEM NOUN_
1 crisis
2 attack (of an illness)
3 (informal) fit (of rage)
piquer une crise to have a fit
Mes parents ont failli piquer une crise. My parents nearly had a fit.
- la crise cardiaque
heart attack
- la crise de foie
indigestion

_ₚ_ indicates key words

- la crise de nerfs
hysterics

le **cristal** MASC NOUN, les **cristaux** PL
crystal

le **critère** MASC NOUN
criterion (for assessing, judging)
les critères criteria

critique MASC & FEM ADJECTIVE ▸ SEE **critique** NOUN
critical

la **critique** FEM NOUN ▸ SEE **critique** ADJECTIVE
criticism

critiquer VERB [1]
to criticize

la **Croatie** FEM NOUN
Croatia

le **croche-pied** MASC NOUN, les **croche-pieds**
PL
faire un croche-pied à quelqu'un (informal)
to trip somebody up
Quelqu'un m'a fait un croche-pied.
Someone tripped me up.

le **crochet** MASC NOUN
1 **hook** (for hanging up)
2 **detour**
J'ai fait un crochet par la boulangerie. I
made a detour via the bakery.
3 **crochet** (way of knitting)
Elle se fait un poncho au crochet. She's
crocheting a poncho for herself.

le **crocodile** MASC NOUN
crocodile

♪ **croire** VERB [33]
1 **to think**
croire que ... to think that ...
Je crois qu'il est parti. I think he's left.
Tu crois que c'est trop tard? Do you think
it's too late?
Je ne crois pas. I don't think so.
Je crois que oui. I think so.
2 **to believe**
Je ne peux pas le croire. I can't believe it.
3 croire à quelque chose to believe in
something
Kevin croit aux fantômes. Kevin believes
in ghosts.
Je n'y crois pas. I don't believe in them.
4 croire en to believe in
Je n'en croyais pas mes yeux! I couldn't
believe my eyes!

croiser VERB [1]
1 **to cross** (arms, legs)
Elle s'asseoit les jambes croisées. She's
sitting with her legs crossed.
Ne croisez pas les bras. Don't fold your
arms.

Je croise les doigts! I'll keep my fingers
crossed!
2 croiser quelqu'un to bump into somebody
J'ai croisé Odile devant la banque. I
bumped into Odile outside the bank.

se **croiser** REFLEXIVE VERB ◙
to cross
Nos lettres se sont croisées. Our letters
crossed in the post.
Les routes se croisent dans un kilomètre.
The roads cross a kilometre from here.

la **croisière** FEM NOUN
cruise

la **croissance** FEM NOUN
growth

♪ le **croissant** MASC NOUN
croissant
On mange des croissants au beurre pour
le petit déjeuner. We have croissants for
breakfast.
- le croissant aux amandes
almond croissant

croître VERB [34]
to grow

la **croix** FEM NOUN
cross
- la Croix-Rouge
Red Cross

croquant MASC ADJECTIVE, **croquante** FEM
crunchy

le **croque-monsieur** INVARIABLE MASC NOUN
toasted ham and cheese sandwich

le **croque-mort** MASC NOUN
(informal) **undertaker**

croquer VERB [1]
to crunch (an apple)
un biscuit qui croque a crunchy biscuit
J'ai croqué dans la pomme. I took a bite of
the apple.

le **croquis** MASC NOUN
sketch (a drawing)

la **crotte** FEM NOUN
dropping
des crottes de souris mouse droppings
des crottes de chien dog mess

croustillant MASC ADJECTIVE, **croustillante** FEM
crispy

la **croûte** FEM NOUN
1 **crust** (of bread)
2 **rind** (of cheese)
3 **scab** (on a cut)

le **croûton** MASC NOUN
crouton (for salads, soups)

la **croyance** *FEM NOUN*
   belief

cru *VERB* ▸ SEE **cru** *ADJECTIVE* ▸ SEE **croire**

cru *MASC ADJECTIVE*, **crue** *FEM* ▸ SEE **cru** *VERB*
1 raw *(meat, vegetables)*
2 uncooked *(pastry)*
3 crude *(language)*

la **cruauté** *FEM NOUN*
   cruelty
   Ils ont été traités avec beaucoup de
   cruauté. They were cruelly treated.

la **cruche** *FEM NOUN*
   (large) jug

ℓ les **crudités** *PLURAL FEM NOUN*
   raw vegetables and salads *(served as a
   starter)*

cruel *MASC ADJECTIVE*, **cruelle** *FEM*
   cruel

le **crustacé** *MASC NOUN*
   shellfish

la **crypte** *FEM NOUN*
   crypt

Cuba *FEM NOUN*
   Cuba

> **WORD TIP** Unlike the names of most other
> countries, Cuba does not take le or la.

cubain *MASC ADJECTIVE*, **cubaine** *FEM* ▸ SEE
   Cubain
   Cuban

le **Cubain** *MASC NOUN*, la **Cubaine** *FEM* ▸ SEE
   cubain
   Cuban

cube *MASC & FEM ADJECTIVE* ▸ SEE **cube** *NOUN*
   cubic
   un mètre cube a cubic metre

le **cube** *MASC NOUN* ▸ SEE **cube** *ADJECTIVE*
   cube

cueillir *VERB* [35]
   to pick *(fruit, flowers)*
   On va cueillir des fraises. We're going
   strawberry-picking.

ℓ la **cuiller** *FEM NOUN*
1 spoon
2 spoonful

la **cuillère** *FEM NOUN* ▸ SEE **cuiller**

la **cuillerée** *FEM NOUN*
   spoonful

ℓ le **cuir** *MASC NOUN*
   leather
   une blouson en cuir a leather jacket
 • le cuir chevelu
   scalp

cuire *VERB* [36]
1 to cook
   Ça cuit. It's cooking.
   faire cuire du riz to cook some rice
   Faire cuire les légumes à la poêle. Fry the
   vegetables.
2 to bake *(bread)*
   On cuit les pommes de terre au four. You
   bake the potatoes in the oven.
3 to roast *(meat)*

ℓ la **cuisine** *FEM NOUN*
1 kitchen
2 cooking
   faire la cuisine to cook, to do the cooking
   Mon père aime faire la cuisine. My dad likes
   cooking.
   C'est moi qui fait la cuisine ce soir. I'm
   doing the cooking tonight.
3 food
   Je n'aime pas la cuisine chinoise. I don't like
   Chinese food.

cuisiner *VERB* [1]
   to cook

le **cuisinier** *MASC NOUN*, la **cuisinière** *FEM* ▸ SEE
   cuisinière
   cook
   Elle est cuisinière. She's a cook.

ℓ la **cuisinière** *FEM NOUN* ▸ SEE **cuisinier**
   cooker
 • la cuisinière à gaz
   gas cooker
 • la cuisinière électrique
   electric cooker

la **cuisse** *FEM NOUN*
   thigh
 • la cuisse de grenouille
   frog's leg
 • la cuisse de poulet
   chicken leg

ℓ **cuit** *MASC ADJECTIVE*, **cuite** *FEM*
   cooked
   bien cuit well done *(meat)* trop cuit
   overcooked
   pas assez cuit undercooked

le **cuivre** *MASC NOUN*
   copper
 • le cuivre jaune
   brass

le **culot** *MASC NOUN*
   (informal) cheek
   Elle a du culot! She's got a nerve!

la **culotte** *FEM NOUN*
   une (petite) culotte knickers

la **culpabilité** *FEM NOUN*
   guilt

le **cultivateur** MASC, la **cultivatrice** FEM
farmer

cultivé MASC ADJECTIVE, **cultivée** FEM
cultivated (well educated)

cultiver VERB [1]
1 to grow (plants, vegetables)
2 to cultivate (a field)
se **cultiver** REFLEXIVE VERB ⬤
to broaden your general knowledge

la **culture** FEM NOUN
1 farming
une région de grande culture a large-scale
farming region
2 growing (of crops)
la culture du blé wheat growing
de culture biologique organically produced
3 crop (the harvest)
4 culture (of a society, country)
5 general knowledge
Il a une bonne culture générale. His general
knowledge is good.

culturel MASC ADJECTIVE, **culturelle** FEM
cultural

le **culturisme** MASC NOUN
bodybuilding

la **cure** FEM NOUN
course of treatment

le **curé** MASC NOUN
parish priest

le **cure-dent** INVARIABLE MASC NOUN
toothpick

se **curer** REFLEXIVE VERB ⬤ [1]
se curer les ongles to clean your nails
Arrête de te curer le nez! Stop picking your
nose!

curieux MASC ADJECTIVE, **curieuse** FEM
1 strange, odd
par une curieuse coïncidence by a strange
coincidence
C'est curieux, je pensais avoir éteint la télé.
That's odd, I thought I switched the TV off.
2 curious
Je suis curieux de voir leur réaction. I'm
curious to see their reaction.
Il est trop curieux. He's nosy.
Elle est curieuse d'apprendre tout sur les
animaux. She's keen to learn everything
about animals.

la **curiosité** FEM NOUN
curiosity

♪ le **curseur** MASC NOUN
cursor

la **cuve** FEM NOUN
vat, tank

la **cuvette** FEM NOUN
bowl
la cuvette des wc the toilet bowl

le **CV** MASC NOUN
CV, curriculum vitae

le **cybercafé** MASC NOUN
Internet cafe
Où est-ce qu'il y a un cybercafé? Where can
I find an Internet cafe?

le **cyberharcèlement** MASC NOUN
cyberbullying

le & la **cybernaute** MASC & FEM NOUN
web surfer, cybernaut

cyclable MASC & FEM ADJECTIVE
une piste cyclable a cycle track

le **cycle** MASC NOUN
cycle

♪ le **cyclisme** MASC NOUN
cycling
faire du cyclisme to go cycling

♪ le & la **cycliste** MASC & FEM NOUN
cyclist
un short de cycliste cycling shorts

le **cyclone** MASC NOUN
hurricane

le **cygne** MASC NOUN
swan

le **cylindre** MASC NOUN
cylinder

cynique MASC & FEM ADJECTIVE
cynical

le **cyprès** MASC NOUN
cypress (tree)

Dd

d' ABBREVIATION: **de**

> **WORD TIP** de becomes d' before a word
> beginning with a, e, i, o, u, y or silent h. ▶ SEE **de**
> DETERMINER, PREPOSITION

♪ **d'abord** ADVERB
1 first
Je vais d'abord faire du café. I'll make some
coffee first.
tout d'abord first of all
2 at first
J'ai d'abord cru qu'il était français. I
thought at first that he was French.

♪ **d'accord** ADVERB
'D'accord!' 'All right!'

⬤ means the verb takes être to form the perfect

être d'accord to agree
Je suis d'accord avec toi. I agree with you.

le daim *MASC NOUN*
1 suede
  des chaussures en daim suede shoes
2 fallow deer

la dalle *FEM NOUN*
1 paving slab
2 J'ai la dalle! I'm starving!

daltonien *MASC ADJECTIVE*, **daltonienne** *FEM*
colour-blind

ℓ **la dame** *FEM NOUN* ▶ SEE **dames** PL
1 lady
  la vieille dame the old lady
2 queen *(in cards, chess)*

les dames *PLURAL FEM NOUN* ▶ SEE **dame**
draughts
On joue aux dames? Shall we play
draughts?

le Danemark *MASC NOUN*
Denmark

le danger *MASC NOUN*
danger
en danger in danger

ℓ **dangereux** *MASC ADJECTIVE*, **dangereuse** *FEM*
1 dangerous
  'Baignade dangereuse' 'Caution: no
swimming'
2 hazardous

danois *MASC ADJECTIVE*, **danoise** *FEM* ▶ SEE
Danois
Danish

le Danois *MASC NOUN*, la **Danoise** *FEM* ▶ SEE
danois
1 Dane *(person)*
2 le danois Danish *(the language)*

ℓ **dans** *PREPOSITION*
1 in
  Mon sac est dans la voiture. My bag is in
the car.
  J'arrive dans cinq minutes. I'm coming in
five minutes.
2 into
  Il a sauté dans la piscine. He jumped into
the swimming pool.
3 on *(the plane, train)*
  Monte vite dans le train! Quickly get on
the train!
4 out of
  Prends 10 euros dans mon porte-monnaie!
Take 10 euros out of my purse!

la danse *FEM NOUN*
1 dance
2 dancing

• la danse classique
ballet

ℓ **danser** *VERB* [1]
to dance

le danseur *MASC NOUN*, la **danseuse** *FEM*
dancer

d'après *PREPOSITION*
1 according to
  d'après le ministre according to the
minister
  d'après moi in my opinion
2 based on
  un film d'après le roman de Flaubert a film
based on the novel by Flaubert
3 in the style of
  un tableau d'après Degas a painting in the
style of Degas

ℓ **la date** *FEM NOUN*
date
  la date d'aujourd'hui today's date
  date et lieu de naissance date and place
of birth
  C'est quelle date? What's today's date?
  À quelle date pars-tu en vacances? When
do you go on holiday?
• la date limite de vente
sell-by date
• la date de naissance
date of birth

la datte *FEM NOUN*
date *(fruit)*

le dauphin *MASC NOUN*
dolphin

davantage *ADVERB*
1 more
  Puis-je avoir davantage d'argent de poche?
May I have more pocket money?
2 longer
  Alice peut rester davantage. Alice can stay
longer.

ℓ **de d', du, des** *PREPOSITION* ▶ SEE **de** *DETERMINER*
1 *(For expressions such as de bonne heure, de
la part de, de rien, de temps en temps etc, see
the entries for heure, part, rien, temps etc.)*
2 of
  un verre de limonade a glass of lemonade
  une boîte d'allumettes a box of matches
3 *(talking about who something belongs to)*
  le nom du chat the cat's name
  le père de Marie Marie's father
  la porte de la classe the classroom door
4 from
  Isabelle vient de Paris. Isabelle comes from
Paris.
  Elle rentre du bureau à six heures. She
comes home from the office at six o'clock.

5 de … à … from … to …
  de Paris à Lourdes from Paris to Lourdes
  du 2 au 8 mai from 2 to 8 May
6 by
  Ce livre est de Jeanne Bourrin. This book is
  by Jeanne Bourrin.
7 with
  Daniel écrit de la main gauche. Daniel
  writes with his left hand.
8 *(with quantity, duration, age, etc)*
  un livre de 250 pages a 250-page book
  un stage de 2 mois a 2-month training
  course
  Elle a une fille de 9 ans. She has a nine-year-
  old daughter.
9 made from
  une table de bois a wooden table
10 about
  Ils parlent de football. They are talking
  about football.

> **WORD TIP** de becomes d' before a, e, i, o, u, y or
> silent h; de + le becomes du; de + les becomes
> des.

♀ **de, de la, du, des** *DETERMINER* ▸ SEE **de**
  PREPOSITION
1 some
  du chocolat (some) chocolate
  Veux-tu de l'eau? Would you like some
  water?
2 any
  Je n'ai pas de chocolat. I don't have any
  chocolate.
  Il n'a pas de gants. He hasn't got any gloves.
  Est-ce qu'il y a du lait? Is there any milk?
3 Nous avons des pommes et des oranges.
  We have apples and oranges.
  Annie et Martin sont des amis à moi. Annie
  and Martin are friends of mine.
  Elle ne boit jamais de vin. She never drinks
  wine.

> **WORD TIP** de + le becomes du; de + les becomes
> des.

le **dé** *MASC NOUN*
  dice
  Lance le dé! Throw the dice!

déballer *VERB* [1]
  to unpack

le **débardeur** *MASC NOUN*
  vest top

débarquer *VERB* [1]
1 to disembark *(passengers)*
2 to land *(soldiers)*
3 *(informal)* to turn up
  Elle a débarqué chez moi. She turned up at
  my place.

le **débarras** *MASC NOUN*
1 junk room
2 *(informal)*
  'Annick est partie.' – 'Bon débarras!'
  'Annick has gone.' – 'Good riddance!'

débarrasser *VERB* [1]
1 to clear *(the table)*
2 to clear out *(a room)*
se **débarrasser** *REFLEXIVE VERB* ⊙
  se débarrasser de quelque chose to get rid
  of something

le **débat** *MASC NOUN*
  debate

débattre *VERB* [21]
1 to discuss *(an issue)*
2 to negotiate *(a price)*
  'Prix à débattre' 'Price negotiable'
se **débattre** *REFLEXIVE VERB* ⊙
  to struggle *(in a fight)*

débile *MASC & FEM ADJECTIVE* *(informal)*
1 stupid
  Tu es débile ou quoi? Are you stupid or
  something?
2 crazy
  C'est complètement débile! That's
  completely crazy!

déblayer *VERB* [59]
  to clear *(a road)*

le **déboisement** *MASC NOUN*
  deforestation

débordé *MASC ADJECTIVE*, **débordée** *FEM*
  être débordé to be up to your eyes in work

le **débordement** *MASC NOUN*
1 overflowing *(of a river)*
2 flood *(of insults)*

déborder *VERB* [1]
1 to overflow *(river)*
2 déborder de quelque chose to overflow
  with something
  Ses yeux débordaient de larmes. His eyes
  were overflowing with tears.

le **débouché** *MASC NOUN*
  job opportunity

déboucher *VERB* [1]
1 to uncork *(a bottle)*
2 to unblock *(a drain, a pipe)*
3 déboucher sur quelque chose to lead onto
  something *(a street)*

déboussoler *VERB* [1]
  (informal) to confuse

debout *ADVERB*
1 standing
  les personnes debout the people standing
  Je suis resté debout toute la journée. I've

⊙ means the verb takes être to form the perfect

been on my feet all day.
être, se tenir debout to stand
Tiens-toi debout près de la porte! Stand next to the door!
se mettre debout to stand up
Tout le monde s'est mis debout. Everybody stood up.
2 upright
Mets le verre debout! Stand the glass upright!
3 up *(out of bed)*
Je suis debout à six heures tous les jours. I'm up at six every day.

débrancher *VERB* [1]
1 to unplug *(an iron, a television set)*
2 to disconnect *(the electricity, gas, water, telephone)*

le **débris** *MASC NOUN*
1 fragment *(of glass)*
2 piece of wreckage
dans les débris de sa voiture in the wreckage of her car

se **débrouiller** *REFLEXIVE VERB* ⊘ [1]
to manage
Je peux me débrouiller tout seul. I can manage by myself.
Je me débrouille en français. I can get by in French.
Débrouille-toi! Get on with it!

le **début** *MASC NOUN*
beginning, start
le début des vacances the beginning of the holidays
au début to start with, at first
Au début, je n'aimais pas la prof. At first I didn't like the teacher.
du début jusqu'à la fin from start to finish
On commencera début mars. We'll start at the beginning of March.

le **débutant** *MASC NOUN*, la **débutante** *FEM*
beginner

débuter *VERB* [1]
to begin, to start

décaféiné *MASC ADJECTIVE*, **décaféinée** *FEM*
decaffeinated

le **décalage horaire** *MASC NOUN*
time difference *(between time zones)*
À son retour, il a mal supporté le décalage horaire. When he came back, he suffered from jet-lag.

décaler *VERB* [1]
to move *(forward or back)*

décapotable *MASC & FEM ADJECTIVE*
une voiture décapotable a convertible (car)

le **décapsuleur** *MASC NOUN*
bottle opener

décéder *VERB* [24]
to die
Jean-Paul est décédé en novembre. Jean-Paul died in November.
Marie-Thérèse est décédée en novembre. Marie-Thérèse died in November.

ℰ **décembre** *MASC NOUN*
December
en décembre, au mois de décembre in December

WORD TIP Months of the year and days of the week start with small letters in French.

la **décennie** *FEM NOUN*
decade

décent *MASC ADJECTIVE*, **décente** *FEM*
decent

la **déception** *FEM NOUN*
disappointment

le **décès** *MASC NOUN*
death

décevant *MASC ADJECTIVE*, **décevante** *FEM*
disappointing

décevoir *VERB* [66]
to disappoint

WORD TIP décevoir does not mean **deceive** in English; for the meaning of **deceive** ▸ SEE **tromper**.

la **décharge** *FEM NOUN*
(public) rubbish tip

décharger *VERB* [52]
to unload

se **déchausser** *REFLEXIVE VERB* ⊘ [1]
to take your shoes off

les **déchets** *PLURAL MASC NOUN*
waste
• les déchets nucléaires
nuclear waste

déchiffrer *VERB* [1]
to decipher

déchirant *MASC ADJECTIVE*, **déchirante** *FEM*
heart-rending *(cry, story)*

déchirer *VERB* [1]
1 to tear
2 to tear up *(a cheque, a piece of work)*
3 to tear out *(pages)*
4 to tear off *(wrapping paper)*
se **déchirer** *REFLEXIVE VERB* ⊘
to tear, to rip
Morgane s'est déchiré un muscle en tombant. Morgane tore a muscle when

A
B
C
D
E
F
G
H
I
J
K
L
M
N
O
P
Q
R
S
T
U
V
W
X
Y
Z

she fell.

décidé *MASC ADJECTIVE*, **décidée** *FEM*
1 **determined** (person)
Laurie est décidée à gagner. Laurie is determined to win.
2 **settled** (decision)
C'est décidé, je l'achète. It's settled, I'm buying it.

décidément *ADVERB*
really
Décidément, il n'a pas de chance! He really is unlucky!

♂ **décider** *VERB* [1]
to decide
décider de faire quelque chose to decide to do something

se **décider** *REFLEXIVE VERB* ☁
to make up your mind
se décider à faire quelque chose to decide to do something

la **décimale** *FEM NOUN*
decimal

la **décision** *FEM NOUN*
decision
Il est temps de prendre une décision. It's time to make a decision.

la **déclaration** *FEM NOUN*
1 **statement** (to the press)
2 **declaration** (of love, war)

déclarer *VERB* [1]
to declare

déclencher *VERB* [1]
1 **to cause** (an explosion, a reaction)
2 **to set off** (an alarm)

le **déclic** *MASC NOUN*
click (of a camera)

décliner *VERB* [1]
to decline (an invitation)

le **décollage** *MASC NOUN*
take-off (of a plane)

décoller *VERB* [1]
1 **to take off** (planes)
2 **to peel off** (stickers)

se **décoller** *REFLEXIVE VERB* ☁
to peel off

le **décolleté** *MASC NOUN*
neckline (of a sweater, a dress)

se **décolorer** *REFLEXIVE VERB* ☁ [1]
to bleach (hair, material)
se faire décolorer les cheveux to have your hair bleached
Magali s'est fait décolorer les cheveux. Magali had her hair bleached.

les **décombres** *PLURAL MASC NOUN*
rubble

décongeler *VERB* [45]
to defrost

déconseillé *MASC ADJECTIVE*, **déconseillée** *FEM*
not recommended
'Déconseillé pour les enfants' 'Not recommended for children'

déconseiller *VERB* [1]
déconseiller à quelqu'un de faire quelque chose to advise somebody not to do something

décontracté *MASC ADJECTIVE*, **décontractée** *FEM*
1 **relaxed** (person, body)
2 **laid-back** (person, attitude)
3 **casual** (clothes)

se **décontracter** *REFLEXIVE VERB* ☁ [1]
to relax
Essaie de te décontracter! Try to relax!

le **décor** *MASC NOUN*
1 **decor** (of a room)
2 **setting** (the surroundings outside)
3 **set** (at the theatre)

le **décorateur** *MASC NOUN*, la **décoratrice** *FEM*
interior designer

décoratif *MASC ADJECTIVE*, **décorative** *FEM*
1 **ornamental**
2 **decorative**

la **décoration** *FEM NOUN*
1 **decoration**
2 **interior design**

décorer *VERB* [1]
to decorate

découper *VERB* [1]
1 **to cut out** (a picture, an article)
2 **to carve** (meat)

décourager *VERB* [52]
to discourage

la **découverte** *FEM NOUN*
discovery

découvrir *VERB* [30]
to discover

♂ **décrire** *VERB* [38]
to describe

♂ **décrocher** *VERB* [1]
1 **to pick up the receiver** (of a telephone)
2 **to take down** (a picture, curtains)

♂ **déçu** *MASC ADJECTIVE*, **déçue** *FEM*
disappointed
Nous sommes tous très déçus. We're all very disappointed.

☁ means the verb takes être to form the perfect

dedans ADVERB
  inside

déduire VERB [26]
1 to deduce (a consequence)
2 to deduct (a sum of money)
  Tu peux déduire 10 euros du prix total. You may deduct 10 euros from the total price.

la **déesse** FEM NOUN
  goddess

défaire VERB [10]
1 to undo (a tie, a belt, a parcel)
2 to untie (laces, shoes)
3 to unpack (a suitcase)

la **défaite** FEM NOUN
  defeat

le **défaut** MASC NOUN
1 fault (of a person)
2 defect (in a product)

défavorisé MASC ADJECTIVE, **défavorisée** FEM
  underprivileged

défectueux MASC ADJECTIVE, **défectueuse** FEM
  faulty
  une prise défectueuse a faulty plug

défendre VERB [3]
1 to forbid
  défendre à quelqu'un de faire quelque chose to forbid somebody to do something
2 to defend
se **défendre** REFLEXIVE VERB ◯
  to defend oneself
  Ne te laisse pas insulter, défends-toi! Don't let them abuse you, stand up for yourself!

℘ **défendu** MASC ADJECTIVE, **défendue** FEM
  forbidden
  Il est défendu de boire de l'alcool. It is forbidden to drink alcohol.

℘ la **défense** FEM NOUN
1 defence (against an aggressor)
2 protection
  la défense de l'environnement the protection of the environment
3 (in signs) 'Défense de fumer' 'No smoking' 'Défense d'entrer' 'No entry'
4 tusk (of an elephant)

le **défi** MASC NOUN
  challenge
  lancer un défi à quelqu'un to challenge somebody

le **défilé** MASC NOUN
1 parade (in a fête, a carnival)
2 march (of demonstrators)
3 stream (of visitors)
• le défilé de mode
  fashion show

défiler VERB [1]
1 to parade
2 to march (demonstrators, soldiers)
3 to scroll down (the text on a computer screen)

définir VERB [2]
  to define

la **définition** FEM NOUN
  definition

définitivement ADVERB
  for good
  Vanessa est définitivement éliminée. Vanessa is eliminated for good.

défoncer VERB [61]
  to smash in (a door)

déformer VERB [1]
1 to bend out of shape (a piece of metal)
2 to stretch (a garment, shoes)
3 to distort (a picture)

se **défouler** REFLEXIVE VERB ◯ [1]
1 to let off steam
  Il se défoule sur son vélo. He lets off steam riding his bike.
2 to unwind
  La télé, ça me défoule. The TV helps me to unwind.
3 se défouler sur quelqu'un to take it out on somebody
  Il se défoule toujours sur sa petite sœur. He always takes it out on his little sister.

dégagé MASC ADJECTIVE, **dégagée** FEM
1 clear (sky, view, way)
2 casual (attitude)

dégager VERB [52]
1 to free (something trapped)
2 to clear (a desk, the road, the way)

les **dégâts** PLURAL MASC NOUN
  damage
  faire des dégâts to cause damage

dégeler VERB [45]
  to thaw

dégénérer VERB [24]
1 to degenerate
2 to get out of hand

dégivrer VERB [1]
1 to defrost (a fridge)
2 to de-ice (a windscreen, a lock)

dégonfler VERB [1]
  to let down (a tyre, an airbed)

dégouliner VERB [1]
  to trickle

dégourdi MASC ADJECTIVE, **dégourdie** FEM
  smart

℘ indicates key words

C'est un gamin dégourdi. He's a smart kid.

P **dégoûtant** *MASC ADJECTIVE*, **dégoûtante** *FEM*
► SEE **dégoûté**

1 **filthy**
Tes mains sont dégoûtantes. Your hands
are filthy.

2 **disgusting**
Cette histoire est dégoûtante. This story is
disgusting.

dégoûté *MASC ADJECTIVE*, **dégoûtée** *FEM* ► SEE
dégoûtant
disgusted
être dégoûté de quelque chose to have had
enough of something

dégoûter *VERB* [1]

1 **to disgust**

2 dégoûter quelqu'un de quelque chose to
put somebody off something
Ça m'a dégoûté du poisson. That put me
off fish.

dégrader *VERB* [1]
to damage *(a site, a monument)*

se **dégrader** *REFLEXIVE VERB* ☁
to deteriorate

dégraisser *VERB* [1]
to dry-clean

P le **degré** *MASC NOUN*
degree
Il fait 20 degrés aujourd'hui. It's 20 degrees
today.

dégringoler *VERB* [1]
(informal) **to tumble down**

déguisé *MASC ADJECTIVE*, **déguisée** *FEM*

1 **in fancy dress**

2 Valentin est déguisé en punk. Valentin is
dressed up as a punk.
une soirée déguisée a fancy-dress party

3 **disguised** *(in order to deceive)*

déguiser *VERB* [1]
to disguise

se **déguiser** *REFLEXIVE VERB* ☁
to dress up
Il s'est déguisé en Père Noël. He dressed up
as Father Christmas.

la **dégustation** *FEM NOUN*
tasting

déguster *VERB* [1]

1 **to savour, to enjoy**

2 **to taste** *(wine, cheese)*

P **dehors** *ADVERB*

1 **outside**
Je t'attends dehors. I'll wait for you outside.

2 en dehors de apart from
En dehors de la salade, tout est prêt.

Everything's ready apart from the salad.

3 Dehors! Get out!

P **déjà** *ADVERB*

1 **already**
Tu pars déjà? Are you leaving already?
Il a déjà fini ses devoirs. He's already
finished his homework.

2 **before**
Tu es déjà venu ici? Have you been here
before?
Je t'ai déjà dit de ne pas faire ça! I told you
before not to do that!

P le **déjeuner** *MASC NOUN* ► SEE **déjeuner** *VERB*
lunch
la pause du déjeuner lunch break
C'est l'heure du déjeuner. It's lunchtime.
Après déjeuner, je vais à la piscine. After
lunch I'm going swimming.

P **déjeuner** *VERB* [1]
► SEE **déjeuner** *NOUN*

1 **to have lunch**
Nous déjeunons à une heure. We have
lunch at one o'clock.

2 **to have breakfast**

délacer *VERB* [61]
to undo *(shoes)*

le **délai** *MASC NOUN*

1 **period of time allowed**
Tu as un délai de deux jours pour me
rendre mon vélo. You have two days to
return my bicycle.

2 **wait**
dans les plus brefs délais as soon as
possible
Il y a deux semaines de délai pour la
livraison d'un ordinateur. There is a two-
week wait for the delivery of a computer.

3 **extra time**
J'ai besoin d'un délai, je ne peux pas payer
maintenant. I need extra time, I can't pay
now.

WORD TIP délai does not mean delay in English;
for the meaning of **delay** ► SEE **retard**.

se **délecter** *REFLEXIVE VERB* ☁ [1]
se délecter de quelque chose to enjoy
something thoroughly

le **délégué** *MASC NOUN*, la **déléguée** *FEM*
delegate *(at a conference)*
• le délégué de classe
student representative

délibéré *MASC ADJECTIVE*, **délibérée** *FEM*
deliberate

délibérer *VERB* [24]
to discuss

☁ means the verb takes être to form the perfect

délicat MASC ADJECTIVE, **délicate** FEM
1 delicate
2 thoughtful (person, gesture)

le **délice** MASC NOUN, les **délices** PL
delight
C'est un vrai délice! It's absolutely delicious!

ℱ **délicieux** MASC ADJECTIVE, **délicieuse** FEM
delicious

la **délinquance** FEM NOUN
crime (illegal activities)

le **délinquant** MASC NOUN, la **délinquante** FEM
offender

délirant MASC ADJECTIVE, **délirante** FEM
(informal) crazy

le **délire** MASC NOUN
1 (informal) madness
2 frenzy

délirer VERB [1]
(informal) to be crazy

le **délit** MASC NOUN
crime, criminal offence

délivrer VERB [1]
to free

déloyal MASC ADJECTIVE, **déloyale** FEM,
déloyaux MASC PL, **déloyales** FEM PL
disloyal

le **deltaplane** MASC NOUN
hang-glider
faire du deltaplane to go hang-gliding

le **déluge** MASC NOUN
downpour

ℱ **demain** ADVERB
tomorrow
À demain! See you tomorrow!
Elle arrive après-demain. She's coming the day after tomorrow.
Nous partirons demain en huit. We'll be leaving a week tomorrow.

la **demande** FEM NOUN
1 request
à la demande générale by popular request
2 demand
l'offre et la demande supply and demand
3 application
J'ai fait une demande d'inscription à l'université de Bristol. I've applied for a place at Bristol university.
une demande d'emploi a job application
'Demandes d'emplois' 'Situations wanted'

demandé MASC ADJECTIVE, **demandée** FEM
très demandé very popular

ℱ **demander** VERB [1]
1 to ask for
Il faut demander de l'aide. We need to ask for help.
demander quelque chose à quelqu'un to ask somebody (for) something
Demande de l'argent à ton père! Ask your father for some money!
Il m'a demandé ton adresse. He asked me for your address.
2 demander à quelqu'un de faire quelque chose to ask somebody to do something
Elle m'a demandé de mettre la table. She asked me to lay the table.

se **demander** REFLEXIVE VERB ◉
to wonder
Je me demande ce qu'elle est en train de faire. I wonder what she's doing.

le **demandeur** MASC NOUN, la **demandeuse** FEM
applicant
• le demandeur d'asile asylum-seeker
• le demandeur d'emploi job-seeker

la **démangeaison** FEM NOUN
itch

démanger VERB [52]
Ça me démange. It's itchy.

le **démaquillant** MASC NOUN
make-up remover

la **démarche** FEM NOUN
1 walk (the way you walk)
Il a une démarche bizarre. He has a funny walk.
2 step
faire des démarches to take steps
Nous avons fait des démarches pour obtenir une classe plus grande. We took steps to obtain a larger classroom.

démarrer VERB [1]
1 to start
La voiture ne veut pas démarrer. The car won't start.
2 to drive off (driver)
3 to start up (a project)

le **démarreur** MASC NOUN
starter (in a car)

démêler VERB [1]
to untangle

le **déménagement** MASC NOUN
1 house move
C'est mon premier déménagement. It's my first house move.
2 removal

ℱ indicates key words

une société de déménagement a removals firm

déménager VERB [52]
1 to move (house)
Bernard déménage à Rennes. Bernard is moving to Rennes.
2 to move out
Nous déménageons la semaine prochaine. We're moving out next week.

le **déménageur** MASC NOUN, la **déménageuse** FEM
removal man, removal woman

la **déménageuse** FEM NOUN
removal van

dément MASC ADJECTIVE, **démente** FEM
crazy

démentir VERB [53]
to deny (an accusation, information)

démesuré MASC ADJECTIVE, **démesurée** FEM
excessive

la **demeure** FEM NOUN
residence

demeurer VERB [1]
to reside
Hugo demeure 9 avenue Manet. Hugo resides at 9 avenue Manet.

♀ **demi** MASC ADJECTIVE, **demie** FEM ▸ SEE **demi** NOUN
▸ SEE **demie**
1 half
2 une demi-pomme half an apple
une demi-bouteille half a bottle
3 et demi, et demie and a half
un mètre et demi one and a half metres
deux millions et demi de personnes two and a half million people
une heure et demie an hour and a half
Elle a trois ans et demi. She's three and a half.
Il est trois heures et demie It's half past three.
• le demi-frère
half-brother
• la demi-sœur
half-sister

♀ le **demi** MASC NOUN ▸ SEE **demi** ADJECTIVE
▸ SEE **demie**
half (litre, of beer)

le **demi-cercle** MASC NOUN
semicircle

la **demi-douzaine** FEM NOUN
half a dozen

la **demie** FEM NOUN ▸ SEE **demi** NOUN,
half-hour

à la demie on the half-hour

demi-écrémé MASC ADJECTIVE, **demi-écrémée** FEM
semi-skimmed

la **demi-finale** FEM NOUN
semifinal

le **demi-frère** MASC NOUN
half brother

la **demi-heure** FEM NOUN
une demi-heure half an hour
toutes les demi-heures every half hour

la **demi-journée** FEM NOUN
half a day

le **demi-litre** MASC NOUN
half a litre

la **demi-pension** FEM NOUN
half board

le & la **demi-pensionnaire** MASC & FEM NOUN
pupil who eats school lunches

demi-sel INVARIABLE ADJECTIVE
slightly salted

la **demi-sœur** FEM NOUN
half-sister

la **démission** FEM NOUN
resignation

démissionner VERB [1]
to resign

demi-tarif INVARIABLE ADJECTIVE
half-price
un billet demi-tarif a half-price ticket

le **demi-tour** MASC NOUN
a U-turn
Il faut faire demi-tour. We have to turn back.

le & la **démocrate** MASC & FEM NOUN ▸ SEE **démocrate** ADJECTIVE
democrat

démocrate MASC & FEM ADJECTIVE ▸ SEE **démocrate** NOUN
democratic

la **démocratie** FEM NOUN
democracy

démocratique MASC & FEM ADJECTIVE
democratic

démodé MASC ADJECTIVE, **démodée** FEM
old-fashioned

la **demoiselle** FEM NOUN
young lady
• la demoiselle d'honneur
bridesmaid

⬤ means the verb takes être to form the perfect

démolir *VERB* [2]
   to demolish

la **démolition** *FEM NOUN*
   demolition

le **démon** *MASC NOUN*
   demon

la **démonstration** *FEM NOUN*
1 **demonstration** (of a product, appliance)
2 **display** (of strength, courage)

démonter *VERB* [1]
1 **to take apart** (a piece of furniture, a model)
2 **to take down** (a tent)

démontrer *VERB* [1]
   to demonstrate

dénoncer *VERB* [61]
   to denounce

se **dénoncer** *REFLEXIVE VERB* ◐
   to give yourself up (culprit)

le **dénouement** *NOUN*
   ending, dénouement (of a film, book)

dénouer *VERB* [1]
   to undo

dense *MASC & FEM ADJECTIVE*
   dense

la **densité** *FEM NOUN*
   density

ℓ la **dent** *FEM NOUN*
   tooth
   avoir mal aux dents to have toothache
   Kevin a mal aux dents. Kevin has toothache.
 • la dent de lait
   milk tooth
 • la dent de sagesse
   wisdom tooth

dentaire *MASC & FEM ADJECTIVE*
   dental

dentelé *MASC ADJECTIVE*, **dentelée** *FEM*
1 **indented** (coast)
2 **serrated** (paper, blade)
3 **perforated** (stamp)

la **dentelle** *FEM NOUN*
   lace

le **dentier** *MASC NOUN*
   dentures
   Ma grand-mère a un dentier. My
   grandmother has dentures.

ℓ le **dentifrice** *MASC NOUN*
   toothpaste

ℓ le & la **dentiste** *MASC & FEM NOUN*
   dentist
   Jérémy est chez le dentiste. Jérémy is at the
   dentist's.

le **déodorant** *MASC NOUN*
   deodorant

le **dépannage** *MASC NOUN*
   repair
   le service de dépannage the breakdown
   service
   un véhicule de dépannage a breakdown
   vehicle

dépanner *VERB* [1]
1 **to repair**
2 dépanner quelqu'un to repair somebody's
   car
3 (informal)
   dépanner quelqu'un to help somebody out

la **dépanneuse** *FEM NOUN*
   breakdown truck

ℓ le **départ** *MASC NOUN*
1 **departure**
   Je t'appellerai avant mon départ. I'll phone
   you before I leave.
2 **start** (of a race)
3 au départ at first, to start with
   Au départ, j'ai eu peur. At first I was scared.

ℓ le **département** *MASC NOUN*
   department
 • les départements et territoires d'outre-mer
   DOM-TOM
   French overseas departments and
   territories

> 🔵 **DÉPARTEMENT**
>
> La France a 101 départements, numérotés
> par ordre alphabétique (excepté autour de
> Paris). Il y a aussi cinq départements loin de la
> France : la Guadeloupe, la Martinique, Mayotte,
> la Guyane et la Réunion.

dépassé *MASC ADJECTIVE*, **dépassée** *FEM*
1 **outdated** (style)
2 **overwhelmed** (person)

dépasser *VERB* [1]
1 **to overtake** (a vehicle, a competitor)
2 **to exceed** (a weight, a temperature)
3 **to go past** (a place)
4 Ça me dépasse! It's beyond me!

ℓ se **dépêcher** *REFLEXIVE VERB* ◐ [50]
   to hurry up
   Dépêche-toi! Hurry up!

la **dépendance** *FEM NOUN*
1 **dependence** (of a country, a person)
2 **outbuilding**

dépendre *VERB* [3]
1 dépendre de quelque chose to depend on
   something
   Ça dépend (de l'heure). It depends (on the
   time).
2 dépendre de quelqu'un to be dependent

A B C D E F G H I J K L M N O P Q R S T U V W X Y Z

101

on somebody

dépenser *VERB* [1]
to spend

les **dépenses** *PLURAL FEM NOUN*
1 expenses
2 spending

dépensier *MASC ADJECTIVE*, **dépensière** *FEM*
extravagant

dépilatoire *MASC & FEM ADJECTIVE*
une crème dépilatoire a hair-removing
cream

le **dépit** *MASC NOUN*
en dépit de in spite of

déplacé *MASC ADJECTIVE*, **déplacée** *FEM*
out of place

le **déplacement** *MASC NOUN*
trip
les frais de déplacement travel expenses

déplacer *VERB* [61]
to move

se **déplacer** *REFLEXIVE VERB* ⬤
to travel

déplaire *VERB* [62]
Le film lui a déplu. He didn't like the film.
Ça ne me déplairait pas de visiter la Chine. I
wouldn't mind visiting China.

déplaisant *MASC ADJECTIVE*, **déplaisante** *FEM*
unpleasant

le **dépliant** *MASC NOUN*
leaflet

déplier *VERB* [1]
to unfold

déposer *VERB* [1]
1 to put down *(luggage)*
2 to dump *(rubbish)*
3 to drop off
4 déposer un chèque to pay in a cheque

le **dépôt** *MASC NOUN*
1 warehouse
2 deposit *(of money)*
• le dépôt d'ordures
rubbish tip

la **dépression** *FEM NOUN*
depression
Sa sœur fait de la dépression. Her sister
suffers from depression.
• la dépression nerveuse
nervous breakdown

déprimant *MASC ADJECTIVE*, **déprimante** *FEM*
depressing

déprimer *VERB* [1]
1 to depress

2 to be depressed

depuis *ADVERB* ▶ SEE **depuis** *PREPOSITION*
since
Je n'ai pas revu Frédéric depuis. I haven't
seen Frédéric since.

depuis *PREPOSITION* ▶ SEE **depuis** *ADVERB*
1 since
depuis vendredi since Friday
Je suis à Paris depuis le 2 janvier. I've been
in Paris since 2 January.
J'habite à Londres depuis avril. I've been
living in London since April.
Depuis leur dispute, ils ne se parlent plus.
Since they had an argument, they haven't
spoken to each other.
2 for
Elle habite à Londres depuis cinq ans. She's
lived in London for five years.
Je le connais depuis longtemps. I've known
him for a long time.
3 Depuis quand... ?, Depuis combien de
temps... ? How long... ?
Depuis quand es-tu à Paris? How long have
you been in Paris?
Tu es là depuis combien de temps? How
long have you been here?

WORD TIP In French, depuis refers to a state
which is still going on, so use the present tense
rather than the perfect tense.

le **député** *MASC NOUN*
deputy *(the French equivalent of a member
of Parliament)*

déranger *VERB* [52]
to disturb
'Ne pas déranger' 'Do not disturb'
Excusez-moi de vous déranger! Sorry to
bother you!
Est-ce que cela vous dérange si j'ouvre la
fenêtre? Do you mind if I open the window?
Cela ne me dérange pas du tout. I don't
mind at all.

déraper *VERB* [1]
1 to skid *(car, motorbike)*
2 to get out of control *(discussion)*

dérisoire *MASC & FEM ADJECTIVE*
trivial
Je l'ai acheté pour une somme dérisoire. I
bought it for next to nothing.

le **dériveur** *MASC NOUN*
sailing dinghy

le & la **dermatologue** *MASC & FEM NOUN*
dermatologist

dernier *MASC ADJECTIVE*, **dernière** *FEM* ▶ SEE
dernier *NOUN*
1 last

⬤ means the verb takes **être** to form the perfect

jeudi dernier last Thursday
la semaine dernière last week
l'année dernière last year
Le dernier train part à minuit. The last train leaves at midnight.
2 latest
leur dernier album their latest album
les dernières nouvelles the latest news
ces derniers temps recently
3 en dernier last
Il est arrivé en dernier. He arrived last.

ℓ le **dernier** *MASC NOUN*, la **dernière** *FEM NOUN*
▶ SEE **dernier** *ADJECTIVE*
last
C'est le dernier qui me reste. It's my last one.
Martin est le dernier de la classe. Martin is bottom of the class.
Angeline est la petite dernière. Angeline is the youngest child.

dernièrement *ADVERB*
recently

dérouler *VERB* [1]
to unroll
se **dérouler** *REFLEXIVE VERB* ⚪
to take place
L'histoire se déroule au dix-huitième siècle. The story takes place in the eighteenth century.
Ça s'est très bien déroulé. It went very well.

déroutant *MASC ADJECTIVE*, **déroutante** *FEM*
puzzling

ℓ **derrière** *ADVERB* ▶ SEE **derrière** *NOUN*, *PREPOSITION*
behind
Le prof est juste derrière. The teacher is just behind.
Ne poussez pas derrière! Stop pushing at the back!

ℓ le **derrière** *MASC NOUN* ▶ SEE **derrière** *ADVERB*, *PREPOSITION*
1 back *(of an object, a house)*
2 *(informal)* **bottom, backside**

ℓ **derrière** *PREPOSITION* ▶ SEE **derrière** *ADVERB*, *NOUN*
behind
derrière la porte behind the door

des *DETERMINER*
some, any

WORD TIP des is formed by de + les. ▶ SEE **de** *DETERMINER, PREPOSITION*

dès *PREPOSITION*
1 from
dès l'âge de cinq ans from the age of five
2 dès que as soon as
Dès que j'arrive, je t'envoie un SMS. As soon as I arrive, I'll send you a text.

désagréable *MASC & FEM ADJECTIVE*
unpleasant

le **désastre** *MASC NOUN*
disaster

le **désavantage** *MASC NOUN*
disadvantage

désavantager *VERB* [52]
to penalize, to put at a disadvantage
Cette loi désavantage les jeunes. This law penalizes young people.

ℓ **descendre** *VERB* [3]
1 ⚪ **to come down** *(from upstairs)*
Je descends dans une seconde! I'll be down in a second!
2 ⚪ **to get out** *(of a bus, train)*
Il est descendu à Dijon. He got off at Dijon.
3 descendre de quelque chose ⚪ **to come from something**
Clara descend d'une famille d'émigrés italiens. Clara comes from a family of Italian emigrants.
4 to get down *(an object from storage)*
Elle a descendu ma valise. She got my case down.
5 to take, bring downstairs *(an object)*
Je vais descendre mes bagages. I'm going to bring down my luggage.
6 to go down *(the stairs)*
Il a descendu l'escalier. He went down the stairs.

WORD TIP When you say what you get down, take down, go down etc, use avoir in the perfect tense in French.

la **descente** *FEM NOUN*
descent
À la descente du bus... When you get off the bus...

descriptif *MASC ADJECTIVE*, **descriptive** *FEM*
descriptive

ℓ la **description** *FEM NOUN*
description
faire une description de quelque chose to give a description of something
Faites une description de ta maison. Give a description of your home.

le **désert** *MASC NOUN* ▶ SEE **désert** *ADJECTIVE*
desert
désert *MASC ADJECTIVE*, **déserte** *FEM* ▶ SEE **désert** *NOUN*
deserted
une île déserte a desert island

désespéré *MASC ADJECTIVE*, **désespérée** *FEM*
1 desperate *(attempt)*
2 in despair *(a person)*
3 hopeless *(situation)*

désespérer VERB [24]
to despair, to give up hope
Ne vous désespérez pas! Don't give up hope!
Ils désespèrent de l'avenir. They despair of the future.

le **désespoir** MASC NOUN
despair

℘ **déshabiller** VERB [1]
to undress (a child, a doll)

se **déshabiller** REFLEXIVE VERB ◯
1 to get undressed
2 to take your coat off

le **déshérité** MASC NOUN, la **déshéritée** FEM
les déshérités the underprivileged

déshydraté MASC ADJECTIVE, **déshydratée** FEM
dehydrated

désigner VERB [1]
1 to refer to
2 to choose

le **désinfectant** MASC NOUN
disinfectant

désintoxiquer VERB [1]
1 to treat for alcohol addiction
2 to treat for drug addiction

le **désir** MASC NOUN
wish, desire

℘ **désirer** VERB [1]
to want
Que désirez-vous? What would you like?

désobéir VERB [2]
1 to be disobedient
2 désobéir à quelqu'un to disobey somebody

désobéissant MASC ADJECTIVE, **désobéissante** FEM
disobedient

désobligeant MASC ADJECTIVE, **désobligeante** FEM
unpleasant

le **désodorisant** MASC NOUN
air freshener

℘ **désolé** MASC ADJECTIVE, **désolée** FEM
sorry
Désolé, c'est fermé! Sorry, we're closed!
Je suis désolé de te déranger. I'm sorry to bother you.

désopilant MASC ADJECTIVE, **désopilante** FEM
hilarious

désordonné MASC ADJECTIVE, **désordonnée** FEM
untidy

le **désordre** MASC NOUN
1 mess
être en désordre to be in a mess (room)
2 disorder

désorganisé MASC ADJECTIVE, **désorganisée** FEM
disorganized

désorienté MASC ADJECTIVE, **désorientée** FEM
confused

désormais ADVERB
from now on

desquels, **desquelles** PRONOUN
of which
Les vacances ont duré dix jours au cours desquels nous avons fait du kayak. The holidays lasted ten days during which we went canoeing.

WORD TIP de + lesquels becomes desquels; de + lesquelles becomes desquelles.

---

dessécher VERB [24]
to dry out
Le froid dessèche la peau. The cold dries your skin out.

se **dessécher** REFLEXIVE VERB ◯
to dry out
J'ai des cheveux fins qui se dessèchent facilement. My hair is fine and dries out easily.

desserrer VERB [1]
to loosen

℘ le **dessert** MASC NOUN
dessert, pudding
Comme dessert Estelle a pris une glace. For dessert Estelle had an ice cream.

desservir VERB [58]
1 to call at (trains)
2 to clear (the table)

℘ le **dessin** MASC NOUN
1 drawing, art
un dessin a drawing
Marie fait du dessin. Marie is drawing.
2 design
le dessin de la voiture the design of the car
• le dessin animé
cartoon (on TV)
• le dessin humoristique
cartoon (in newspaper)

le **dessinateur** MASC NOUN, la **dessinatrice** FEM
designer
un dessinateur de mode a fashion designer

℘ **dessiner** VERB [1]
to draw
Nous dessinons au crayon. We are drawing in pencil.

◯ means the verb takes être to form the perfect

dessous ADVERB ▶ SEE **dessous** NOUN
underneath
Soulève la pierre, la clé est dessous. Lift the stone, the key is underneath.

le **dessous** MASC NOUN ▶ SEE **dessous** ADVERB
1 **underside**
le dessous du pied the sole of the foot
2 **les voisins du dessous** the neighbours below
3 **les dessous** underwear
4 **en dessous** underneath
Mets-le en dessous. Put it underneath.
Il me faut la taille en dessous. I need the next size down.
5 **en dessous de** below
30 degrés en dessous de zéro 30 degrees below zero
• le **dessous-de-plat**
table mat (for a dish)

dessus ADVERB ▶ SEE **dessus** NOUN
on top
un gâteau avec des fraises dessus a cake with strawberries on top
Prends celui du dessus. Take the top one.

le **dessus** MASC NOUN ▶ SEE **dessus** ADVERB
1 **top**
le dessus du carton the top of the box
2 **les voisins du dessus** the neighbours above
3 **en dessus** above
• le **dessus-de-lit**
bedspread

le **destin** MASC NOUN
fate, destiny

le & la **destinataire** MASC & FEM NOUN
addressee

ℱ la **destination** FEM NOUN
destination
le train à destination de Nice the train for Nice

destiner VERB [1]
être destiné à quelque chose to be intended for something

le **détachant** MASC NOUN
stain remover

détacher VERB [1]
1 **to untie** (a horse)
2 **to undo** (a knot)
3 **to tear off** (a cheque)
4 **to remove**
5 **to remove the stains from** (clothes)
se **détacher** REFLEXIVE VERB ◎
1 **to break loose** (horse)
2 **to come out**

le **détail** MASC NOUN
1 **detail**
en détail in detail

2 **retail**
Il achète au détail. He buys retail.

détecter VERB [1]
to detect

le **détective** MASC NOUN
detective

déteindre VERB [60]
1 **to fade**
2 **to run** (in the wash)

détendre VERB [3]
1 **to be relaxing**
2 **to calm**
se **détendre** REFLEXIVE VERB ◎
to relax

détendu MASC ADJECTIVE, **détendue** FEM
relaxed

détenir VERB [81]
1 **to keep** (objects)
2 **to detain** (a criminal)

la **détente** FEM NOUN
relaxation

le **détenu** MASC NOUN, la **détenue** FEM
prisoner

le **détergent** MASC NOUN
detergent

se **détériorer** REFLEXIVE VERB ◎ [1]
to deteriorate

le **déterminant** MASC NOUN
(Grammar) **determiner**

> **WORD TIP** In French these are un, une, des and le, la, les. In English they are a, an and the.

la **détermination** FEM NOUN
determination

détestable MASC & FEM ADJECTIVE
appalling

ℱ **détester** VERB [1]
to hate
Karine déteste faire la vaisselle. Karine hates doing the dishes.

le **détour** MASC NOUN
detour
Nous allons faire un détour par Lille. We'll make a detour via Lille.

le **détournement** MASC NOUN
un détournement d'avion a hijacking

détourner VERB [1]
1 **to divert** (somebody's attention, the traffic)
2 Leila essaie de détourner la conversation. Leila is trying to change the subject.
3 **to hijack**
4 **to look away**

ℱ indicates key words

les **détritus** *PLURAL MASC NOUN*
rubbish

détruire *VERB* [26]
to destroy

la **dette** *FEM NOUN*
debt

le **deuil** *MASC NOUN*
1 bereavement
2 mourning
Yasmina est en deuil de sa grand-
mère. Yasmina is in mourning for her
grandmother.

ℐ **deux** *NUMBER*
1 two
deux enfants two children
Elle a deux ans. She's two.
Il est deux heures. It's two o'clock.
2 deux fois twice
une fois sur deux fifty percent of the time
Laurie s'entraîne un jour sur deux. Laurie
trains every other day.
3 second
(in dates) le deux juin the second of June
4 both
les deux frères both brothers
tous les deux, toutes les deux both
Ils sont malades tous les deux. They're both
ill *(males or mixed group)*.
Toutes les deux sont malades. They're both
ill *(females only)*.
• le deux-points
(Grammar) colon

ℐ **deuxième** *MASC & FEM ADJECTIVE*
second
une deuxième fois a second time
Nelly habite au deuxième (étage). Nelly
lives on the second floor.

ℐ **deuxièmement** *ADVERB*
secondly

dévaliser *VERB* [1]
1 to rob *(a bank)*
2 to raid *(the fridge)*

ℐ **devant** *ADVERB* ▸ SEE **devant** *NOUN, PREPOSITION*
Assieds-toi devant! Sit in the front! *(in a car)*
Si tu cherches le cinéma, tu te trouves
juste devant. If you're looking for the
cinema, you're standing just in front of it.
Tu es trop lent, je passe devant. You're too
slow, I'll go ahead of you.

ℐ le **devant** *MASC NOUN* ▸ SEE **devant** *ADVERB,*
PREPOSITION
front
Regarde ton T-shirt, il y a une tache sur le
devant. Look at your T-shirt, there is a stain
on the front.

ℐ **devant** *PREPOSITION* ▸ SEE **devant** *ADVERB, NOUN*
1 in front of
Elle était devant moi dans la queue. She
was in front of me in the queue.
Il l'a dit devant ses parents. He said it in
front of his parents.
2 outside
Je t'attendrai devant la bibliothèque. I will
wait for you outside the library.
3 ahead of
Julien est loin devant nous. Julien is a long
way ahead of us.

le **développement** *MASC NOUN*
development
les pays en voie de développement
developing countries

développer *VERB* [1]
to develop

se **développer** *REFLEXIVE VERB* ◯
1 to expand
2 to become widespread

devenir *VERB* [81]
to become
Il est devenu célèbre. He's become famous.
Philippe voudrait devenir avocat. Philippe
would like to be a lawyer.
Elle est devenue infirmière. She went into
nursing.
Elle est devenue toute pâle. She went really
pale.

déverser *VERB* [1]
1 to pour *(liquid)*
2 to dump *(rubbish, chemicals)*

ℐ la **déviation** *FEM NOUN*
diversion

deviner *VERB* [1]
to guess
Devine qui vient nous voir? Guess who's
coming to see us?

la **devinette** *FEM NOUN*
riddle

le **devis** *MASC NOUN* ▸ SEE **devises** *PL NOUN*
quote, estimate

les **devises** *PLURAL FEM NOUN* ▸ SEE **devis**
(foreign) currency

dévisser *VERB* [1]
to unscrew

le **devoir** *MASC NOUN* ▸ SEE **devoir** *VERB*
1 test
On a un devoir de physique la semaine
prochaine. We have a physics test next
week.
2 homework
Je fais mes devoirs. I'm doing my
homework.

◯ means the verb takes être to form the perfect

As-tu fini ton devoir de maths? Have you finished your maths homework?

3 **duty**

_ℓ_ **devoir** VERB [8]
▸ SEE **devoir** NOUN

1 **to owe**
Alexandre me doit vingt euros. Alexandre owes me twenty euros.
Je vous dois combien? How much do I owe you?

2 **to have to, must**
Je dois partir à dix heures. I have to leave at ten o'clock.

3 **must** (in guessing)
Tu dois être fatigué. You must be tired.
Elle doit avoir quarante ans. She must be forty.
Yves a dû oublier. Yves must have forgotten.

4 (in recommendations) Tu devrais reviser davantage. You ought to revise more.
Malaurie aurait dû partir. Malaurie should have left.

5 **to be supposed to**
Éric doit le voir demain. Éric is supposed to see him tomorrow.

dévoué MASC ADJECTIVE, **dévouée** FEM
devoted

se **dévouer** REFLEXIVE VERB ◉ [1]
se dévouer à quelque chose to devote oneself to something

_ℓ_ **d'habitude** ADVERB
usually
D'habitude Chloë va au lit à 8 heures du soir. Usually Chloë goes to bed at 8 p.m.

le **diabète** MASC NOUN
diabetes

diabétique MASC & FEM ADJECTIVE
diabetic

le **diable** MASC NOUN
devil

le **diabolo** MASC NOUN
fruit cordial and lemonade
un diabolo menthe a mint cordial and lemonade

le **diagnostic** MASC NOUN
diagnosis

diagnostiquer VERB [1]
to diagnose

diagonal MASC ADJECTIVE, **diagonale** FEM, **diagonaux** MASC PL, **diagonales** FEM PL ▸ SEE **diagonale**
diagonal

la **diagonale** FEM NOUN ▸ SEE **diagonal**
diagonal
en diagonale diagonally

le **diagramme** MASC NOUN
graph

le **dialogue** MASC NOUN
dialogue

le **diamant** MASC NOUN
diamond

le **diamètre** MASC NOUN
diameter

la **diapositive** FEM NOUN
slide (in photography)

la **diarrhée** FEM NOUN
diarrhoea

le **dico** MASC NOUN
(informal) **dictionary**
short for ▸ SEE **dictionnaire**

le **dictateur** MASC NOUN
dictator

la **dictature** FEM NOUN
dictatorship

dicter VERB [1]
to dictate

le **dictionnaire** MASC NOUN
dictionary

le **dicton** MASC NOUN
saying

le **diesel** MASC NOUN
diesel

diététique MASC & FEM ADJECTIVE ▸ SEE **diététique** NOUN
dietary
des produits diététiques health food

la **diététique** FEM NOUN ▸ SEE **diététique** ADJECTIVE
un magasin de diététique a health-food shop

le **dieu** MASC NOUN, les **dieux** PL ▸ SEE **Dieu**
god

Dieu MASC NOUN ▸ SEE **dieu**
God

_ℓ_ la **différence** FEM NOUN

1 **difference**
Vois-tu la différence? Can you see the difference?

2 à la différence de unlike

_ℓ_ indicates key words

À la différence de Louis, Maxime aime la musique classique. Unlike Louis, Maxime likes classical music.

le **différend** MASC NOUN
disagreement

♂ **différent** MASC ADJECTIVE, **différente** FEM
1 **different**
Ce mot a des sens différents. This word has different senses.
Elle est vraiment différente de sa sœur. She's really different from her sister.
2 **various, different**
différentes personnes various people, different people

♂ **difficile** MASC & FEM ADJECTIVE
1 **difficult, hard**
difficile à faire difficult to do
Leur maison est difficile à trouver. Their house is difficult to find.
C'est difficile à imaginer. It's hard to imagine.
2 **hard to please**
Je me demande si Éliza va aimer mon cadeau, elle est si difficile. I wonder if Éliza will like my present, she's so hard to please.

difficilement ADVERB
with difficulty

la **difficulté** FEM NOUN
difficulty
avoir de la difficulté à faire quelque chose to have difficulty in doing something
faire des difficultés to raise objections

diffuser VERB [1]
1 **to broadcast** (a programme)
2 **to distribute** (a magazine)

digérer VERB [24]
to digest

le **digestif** MASC NOUN
(after-dinner) liqueur

la **digestion** FEM NOUN
digestion

digital MASC ADJECTIVE, **digitale** FEM, **digitaux** MASC PL, **digitales** FEM PL
digital

digne MASC & FEM ADJECTIVE
1 **dignified** (person, silence)
2 **worthy**
digne de confiance trustworthy

la **dignité** FEM NOUN
dignity

la **digue** FEM NOUN
sea wall

le **dilemme** MASC NOUN
dilemma

diligent MASC ADJECTIVE, **diligente** FEM
diligent

diluer VERB [1]
1 **to dilute**
2 **to thin** (paint)

♂ le **dimanche** MASC NOUN
1 **Sunday**
Nous sommes dimanche aujourd'hui. It's Sunday today.
dimanche dernier last Sunday
dimanche prochain next Sunday
2 **on Sunday**
Je t'appellerai dimanche soir. I'll ring you on Sunday evening.
3 le dimanche on Sundays
fermé le dimanche closed on Sundays
4 tous les dimanches every Sunday

WORD TIP Months of the year and days of the week start with small letters in French.

la **dimension** FEM NOUN
1 **dimension**
un objet à trois dimensions a three-dimensional object
prendre les dimensions de quelque chose to measure something
2 **size**
Cette glace existe en plusieurs dimensions. This mirror comes in several sizes.

diminuer VERB [1]
1 **to reduce** (a quantity, the cost, the duration)
2 **to decrease**
3 **to go down** (candle, fever)

la **dinde** FEM NOUN
turkey (the female bird, the meat)

le **dindon** MASC NOUN
turkey (the male bird)

♂ le **dîner** MASC NOUN ▸ SEE **dîner** VERB
dinner
C'est l'heure du dîner. It's dinner time.
Qu'est-ce qu'on mange pour dîner? What's for dinner?
Elle prépare le dîner. She's getting dinner ready.
Nous prenons le dîner à 19 h 30. We have dinner at 7.30 p.m.

dîner VERB [1]
▸ SEE **dîner** NOUN
to have dinner
Viens dîner chez nous ce soir. Come to dinner with us this evening.

dingue MASC & FEM ADJECTIVE
(informal) **crazy**

le **dinosaure** MASC NOUN
dinosaur

le & la **diplomate** MASC & FEM NOUN
diplomat

ℰ le **diplôme** MASC NOUN
1 qualification, diploma
Quels diplômes faut-il pour devenir
vétérinaire? Which qualifications do you
need to be a vet?
2 (university) degree
Marine a un diplôme d'architecte. Marine
has a degree in architecture.
3 certificate
un diplôme de secouriste a first aid
certificate

diplômé MASC ADJECTIVE, **diplômée** FEM
qualified
une infirmière diplômée a qualified nurse
Anthony est diplômé en droit. Anthony has
a degree in law.

ℰ **dire** VERB [9]
1 to say
Qu'est-ce qu'elle a dit? What did she say?
Comment dit-on 'gourmand' en anglais?
How do you say 'gourmand' in English?
2 to tell
dire quelque chose à quelqu'un to tell
somebody something
J'ai dit à Anne que tu l'appellerais. I told
Anne you'd ring her.
dire à quelqu'un de faire quelque chose
to tell somebody to do something
Je leur ai dit de venir à cinq heures. I told
them to come at five o'clock.
dire la vérité to tell the truth
dire des mensonges to tell lies
dire l'heure to tell the time
3 to think
Qu'en dis-tu? What do you think?
On dirait que Léa me déteste. You'd think
that Léa hated me.
On dirait qu'il va pleuvoir. It looks like
rain.
4 Ça ne me dit rien. I don't feel like it.
5 vouloir dire quelque chose to mean
something
Qu'est-ce que ça veut dire? What does it
mean?
6 à vrai dire actually
À vrai dire, je préfère ne pas y aller.
Actually, I prefer not to go.

se **dire** REFLEXIVE VERB ◯
1 to tell oneself
Je me dis souvent ... I often tell myself ...
2 to claim to be

3 to say
Ça se dit comment 'l'ordinateur' en
allemand? How do you say 'the computer'
in German?
Ça ne se dit pas. You can't say that.

ℰ **direct** MASC ADJECTIVE, **directe** FEM
1 direct
un vol direct a direct flight
2 (in broadcasting) en direct de ... live from ...

directement ADVERB
1 straight
Je rentre directement à la maison. I'm
going straight home.
2 directly

ℰ le **directeur** MASC NOUN, la **directrice** FEM
1 director
2 manager
3 head (of a school)

le **directeur général** MASC NOUN, la
directrice générale FEM
managing director

ℰ la **direction** FEM NOUN
1 direction
en direction de towards, in the direction of
Nous sommes dans la bonne direction. We
are heading the right way.
Fahrid s'est trompé de direction. Fahrid
went in the wrong direction.
Demande la direction de la gare! Ask for
directions to the station!
Pouvez-vous m'indiquer la direction du
musée, s'il vous plaît? Could you please tell
me the way to the museum?
2 management
'Changement de direction' 'Under new
management'
3 steering (of a vehicle)

le **dirigeant** MASC NOUN, la **dirigeante** FEM
leader

diriger VERB [52]
1 to manage
2 to direct (an operation)
3 to steer (a vehicle)
4 to conduct (an orchestra)

se **diriger** REFLEXIVE VERB ◯
se diriger vers quelque chose to make for
something
Flore s'est dirigée vers la porte. Flore made
for the door.

discerner VERB [1]
to make out (a shape, an object)

la **discipline** FEM NOUN
1 discipline
2 subject (of study)

A B C D E F G H I J K L M N O P Q R S T U V W X Y Z

discipliner VERB [1]
to control

le **disco** MASC NOUN
disco music

♀ la **discothèque** FEM NOUN
1 club, disco
Samedi soir, nous allons à la discothèque. On Saturday evening we are going clubbing.
2 music library

le **discours** MASC NOUN
speech

discret MASC ADJECTIVE, **discrète** FEM
1 discreet
2 subtle

la **discrimination** FEM NOUN
discrimination

la **discussion** FEM NOUN
discussion

discutable MASC & FEM ADJECTIVE
questionable

♀ **discuter** VERB [1]
1 to talk
On peut discuter tranquillement chez moi. We can talk in peace at my house.
2 discuter de quelque chose to discuss something
Nous allons discuter du pour et du contre. We are going to discuss the pros and cons.
On va en discuter demain. We'll discuss it tomorrow.
3 discuter avec quelqu'un to talk to somebody
Mes parents ont discuté avec la directrice. My parents talked to the headmistress.
4 to argue
Ça se discute. It's arguable.

disparaître VERB [27]
1 to disappear
Mes clés ont encore disparu. My keys have disappeared again.
Disparaissez! Out of my sight!
2 to go
Ma douleur à l'épaule a disparu. My shoulder pain has gone.
3 to come out (stain)
4 faire disparaître quelque chose to remove something
5 to die
6 to die out (traditions, customs)

la **disparition** FEM NOUN
1 disappearance
2 une espèce en voie de disparition an endangered species

disparu MASC ADJECTIVE, **disparue** FEM ▸ SEE **disparu** NOUN
1 missing
la petite fille disparue depuis deux semaines the little girl who has been missing for two weeks
2 lost
la civilisation disparue des Mayas the lost civilisation of the Mayas
3 dead
mille personnes disparues en mer one thousand people lost at sea
4 extinct
une espèce disparue an extinct species

le **disparu** MASC NOUN, la **disparue** FEM ▸ SEE **disparu** ADJECTIVE
1 missing person
2 les disparus the dead

dispenser VERB [1]
1 to give
2 dispenser quelqu'un de quelque chose to excuse somebody from something
Amélie est dispensée de gym. Amélie is excused from gymnastics.

disperser VERB [1]
1 to scatter
2 to break up (a crowd, a demonstration)
se **disperser** REFLEXIVE VERB ◐
to break up
La foule s'est dispersée. The crowd broke up.

disponible MASC & FEM ADJECTIVE
available

disposé MASC ADJECTIVE, **disposée** FEM
1 arranged
2 être disposé à faire quelque chose to be willing to do something

disposer VERB [1]
1 to arrange
Le prof a disposé les tables en cercle. The teacher arranged the tables in a circle.
2 disposer de quelque chose to have something (at your disposal)
L'école dispose d'une piscine. The school has a swimming pool at its disposal.

le **dispositif** MASC NOUN
device

la **disposition** FEM NOUN
1 arrangement
la disposition de l'appartement the layout of the flat
2 disposal
à votre disposition at your disposal

la **dispute** FEM NOUN
argument

◐ means the verb takes être to form the perfect

disputé *MASC ADJECTIVE*, **disputée** *FEM*
1 contested
2 controversial

disputer *REFLEXIVE VERB* ◎ [1]
se faire disputer *(informal)* to get told off
Mon père me dispute pour tout. My father
tells me off all the time.

se **disputer** *REFLEXIVE VERB* ◎
1 to argue
Ils se sont disputés. They had an argument.
2 se disputer quelque chose to fight over
something
Les deux chiens se disputaient le jouet. The
two dogs were fighting over the toy.

disqualifier *VERB* [1]
to disqualify

♪ le **disque** *MASC NOUN*
1 record
passer un disque to play a record
2 (computer) disk
3 discus
le lancer du disque the discus
• le disque compact
compact disc, CD
• le disque dur
hard disk *(of a computer)*

♪ la **disquette** *FEM NOUN*
diskette, floppy disk

la **dissertation** *FEM NOUN*
essay

dissimuler *VERB* [1]
to conceal

dissocier *VERB* [1]
to separate

le **dissolvant** *MASC NOUN*
1 nail polish remover
2 solvent

dissoudre *VERB* [67]
to dissolve

dissuader *VERB* [1]
1 dissuader quelqu'un de faire quelque
chose to put somebody off doing
something
La pluie l'a dissuadée de sortir. The rain put
her off going out.
2 to deter
pour dissuader les voleurs in order to deter
thieves

♪ la **distance** *FEM NOUN*
1 distance
une distance de cinq kilomètres a distance
of five kilometres
C'est à quelle distance d'ici? How far is it
from here?
l'enseignement à distance distance

learning
2 gap
Elles sont nées à deux mois de distance.
They were born two months apart.

distant *MASC ADJECTIVE*, **distante** *FEM*
distant
distant de far away from
un village distant de trois kilomètres a
village three kilometres away

la **distillerie** *FEM NOUN*
distillery

distinct *MASC ADJECTIVE*, **distincte** *FEM*
1 distinct
2 clear *(voice)*
Il s'exprime de façon distincte. He speaks
clearly.

la **distinction** *FEM NOUN*
distinction

distingué *MASC ADJECTIVE*, **distinguée** *FEM*
distinguished

distinguer *VERB* [1]
1 to distinguish between
J'ai du mal à distinguer les jumeaux. I find
it hard to tell the twins apart.
2 to distinguish
Ce qui distingue Laura de Claire, c'est ...
What distinguishes Laura from Claire is ...
3 to make out
Nous distinguons un bateau à l'horizon.
We can make out a boat on the horizon.

la **distraction** *FEM NOUN*
1 entertainment, leisure
On a besoin d'un peu de distraction. We
need a bit of entertainment.
Ma distraction favorite est le jeu vidéo. My
favourite way of relaxing is to play video
games.
Il n'y a pas beaucoup de distractions ici.
There isn't much to do for entertainment
around here.
2 absent-mindedness

distraire *VERB* [78]
1 to entertain
2 to distract
se **distraire** *REFLEXIVE VERB* ◎
to enjoy yourself

distrait *MASC ADJECTIVE*, **distraite** *FEM*
absent-minded

distribuer *VERB* [1]
1 to distribute, to give out
Maeva distribue les cahiers. Maeva is
distributing the exercise books.
distribuer les cartes to deal (the cards)
2 to deliver *(the mail)*
3 to award *(the prizes)*

le **distributeur** MASC NOUN
distributor
- le distributeur d'argent
cashpoint
- le distributeur automatique
vending machine
- le distributeur de billets
cashpoint
- le distributeur de tickets
ticket machine

la **distribution** FEM NOUN
1 distribution
2 delivery (of mail)
3 cast (of a play)
- la distribution des prix
prizegiving

divers MASC ADJECTIVE, **diverse** FEM
various

divertir VERB [2]
to entertain

se **divertir** REFLEXIVE VERB ⊘
to enjoy oneself
Nous nous sommes bien divertis. We really
enjoyed ourselves.

divertissant MASC ADJECTIVE, **divertissante**
FEM
amusing, entertaining

le **divertissement** MASC NOUN
entertainment
Le cinéma est notre divertissement
préféré. Cinema is our favourite leisure
activity.
Je regarde surtout des émissions
de divertissement. I mostly watch
entertainment programmes.

diviser VERB [1]
to divide

la **division** FEM NOUN
division

le **divorce** MASC NOUN
divorce

ℒ **divorcé** MASC ADJECTIVE, **divorcée** FEM
divorced
Mes parents sont divorcés. My parents are
divorced.

divorcer VERB [61]
to get divorced
Ses parents ont divorcé. Her parents got
divorced.

ℒ **dix** NUMBER
ten
Elle a dix ans. She's ten.
Il est dix heures. It's ten o'clock.
le dix juillet the tenth of July

ℒ **dix-huit** NUMBER
eighteen
Il a dix-huit ans. He's eighteen.
à dix-huit heures at six p.m.
On a un rendez-vous le dix-huit. We have
an appointment on the eighteenth.

ℒ **dixième** MASC & FEM ADJECTIVE
tenth

ℒ **dix-neuf** NUMBER
nineteen
Elle a dix-neuf ans. She's nineteen.
à dix-neuf heures at seven p.m.

ℒ **dix-sept** NUMBER
seventeen
Elle a dix-sept ans. She's seventeen.
à dix-sept heures at five p.m.

ℒ la **dizaine** FEM NOUN
ten
une dizaine de personnes about ten people

ℒ **d'occasion** ADVERB
secondhand
Je l'ai acheté d'occasion. I bought it
secondhand.
C'est une voiture d'occasion. It's a
secondhand car.

ℒ le **docteur** MASC NOUN
doctor

le **document** MASC NOUN
document

le **documentaire** MASC NOUN
documentary

le & la **documentaliste** MASC & FEM NOUN
(school) librarian

la **documentation** FEM NOUN
1 information, material
Voici une documentation sur la région.
Here is some information about the area.
2 research

se **documenter** REFLEXIVE VERB ⊘ [1]
se documenter sur quelque chose to gather
information on something

le **dodo** MASC NOUN
(baby talk)
Fais dodo! Go to sleep!
Au dodo! Off to bed!

ℒ le **doigt** MASC NOUN
finger
Levez le doigt! Put your hand up!
le bout des doigts the fingertips
se couper le doigt to cut your finger
Clara s'est coupé le doigt. Clara cut her
finger.
- le doigt de pied
toe

⊘ means the verb takes être to form the perfect

les **DOM** *MASC PL NOUN*
(= *départements d'outre-mer*) **French overseas departments**

le **domaine** *MASC NOUN*
1 **estate** (area of land)
2 **field** (area of interest)

le **dôme** *MASC NOUN*
dome

le & la **domestique** *MASC & FEM NOUN*
servant

℘ le **domicile** *MASC NOUN*
place of residence
à domicile **at home**
livraison à domicile **home delivery**
Elle travaille à domicile. **She works from home.**
Ils ont changé de domicile. **They moved.**

dominant *MASC ADJECTIVE*, **dominante** *FEM*
1 **dominant** (colour, character)
2 **main** (idea, theme)

dominer *VERB* [1]
1 **to dominate**
2 **to rule**
3 **to be in the lead**
se **dominer** *VERB REFLEXIVE* ◌
to control oneself

dominicain *MASC ADJECTIVE*, **dominicaine** *FEM*
Dominican
la République dominicaine **the Dominican Republic**

le **domino** *MASC NOUN*
domino
jouer aux dominos **to play dominoes**

℘ le **dommage** *MASC NOUN*
1 Quel dommage! **What a pity!**
C'est dommage qu'elle n'y soit pas allée. **It's a pity she didn't go.**
2 les dommages **damage**
causer des dommages à quelque chose **to damage something**

dompter *VERB* [1]
to tame

le **don** *MASC NOUN*
1 **donation**
2 **gift**, **talent**
Elle a un don pour les langues. **She has a gift for languages.**
avoir le don de faire quelque chose **to have a talent for doing something**

℘ **donc** *CONJUNCTION*
so, **therefore**
La voiture est tombée en panne, ils ont donc pris le train. **The car broke down so they took the train.**

donné *MASC ADJECTIVE*, **donnée** *FEM* ▶ SEE **donnée**
1 **given**
à un endroit donné **in a given place**
Deux euros, c'est donné! **Two euros, it's a bargain!**
2 étant donné **given**
Étant donné les circonstances … **Given the circumstances …**
Étant donné qu'il pleut, je ne crois pas qu'il viendra. **Given that it's raining, I don't think he'll come.**

la **donnée** *FEM NOUN* ▶ SEE **donné**
1 **fact**
2 les données **data**
les données informatiques **computer data**

℘ **donner** *VERB* [1]
1 **to give**
donner quelque chose à quelqu'un **to give somebody something**
Elle m'a donné dix euros. **She gave me ten euros.**
Donne-moi ton adresse. **Give me your address.**
2 donner à boire à quelqu'un **to give somebody something to drink**
Tu me donnes à boire, s'il te plaît, j'ai soif. **Give me something to drink please, I'm thirsty.**
3 **to give away**
Il a donné tous ses livres. **He gave away all his books.**
4 donner sur quelque chose **to overlook something**
Ma chambre donne sur la mer. **My bedroom overlooks the sea.**
se **donner** *REFLEXIVE VERB* ◌
se donner à quelque chose **to devote yourself to something**
Perrine se donne toute entière à la peinture. **Perrine is devoting herself entirely to her painting.**

℘ **dont** *RELATIVE PRONOUN*
1 **whose**
la fille dont la mère est française **the girl whose mother is French**
une personne dont j'ai oublié le nom **a person whose name I've forgotten**
2 **of which**
six verres dont l'un est cassé **six glasses, one of which is broken**
3 **of whom**
dix élèves, dont cinq ont moins de dix ans **ten pupils, of whom five are under ten**
4 la maison dont je parle **the house I'm talking about**
le bébé dont je m'occupe **the baby I look after**

℘ **indicates key words**

doré MASC ADJECTIVE, **dorée** FEM
golden

dorénavant ADVERB
from now on

♪ **dormir** VERB [37]
to sleep
Elle dort. She's asleep.
Tu as bien dormi? Did you sleep well?
Cindy va dormir chez moi. Cindy's going to spend the night at my house.
Clément a envie de dormir. Clément is sleepy.

♪ le **dortoir** MASC NOUN
dormitory

♪ le **dos** MASC NOUN
back
Elle me tournait le dos. She had her back to me.
Signe au dos du chèque. Sign on the back of the cheque.
avoir mal au dos to have backache
Lucile a mal au dos. Lucile has backache.

le **dosage** MASC NOUN
amount

la **dose** FEM NOUN
1 dose
2 measure

le **dossier** MASC NOUN
1 file
2 application form
3 project (at school)
4 back (of a chair)
• le dossier médical
medical records

♪ la **douane** FEM NOUN
la douane customs
Il faut passer à la douane. We need to go through customs.

♪ le **douanier** MASC NOUN, la **douanière** FEM NOUN
customs officer

double MASC & FEM ADJECTIVE ▸ SEE **double** NOUN
double
une chambre double a double room
une rue à double sens a two-way street
en double exemplaire in duplicate
Camille a la double nationalité. Camille has dual nationality.

le **double** MASC NOUN ▸ SEE **double** ADJECTIVE
1 double
le double (de) twice as much, twice as many
Arnaud gagne le double de moi. Arnaud earns twice as much as I do.
Leur jardin fait le double du nôtre. Their garden is twice as big as ours.

100 est le double de 50. 100 is twice 50.
2 copy
Tu envoies l'original et tu gardes le double. You send the original and you keep the copy.

doublé MASC ADJECTIVE, **doublée** FEM
1 lined (coat)
2 dubbed (film)

♪ **doubler** VERB [1]
1 to double
2 to overtake
3 to line (a coat)
4 to dub (a film)

la **doublure** FEM NOUN
1 lining (of a coat)
2 double (of an actor)

douce FEM ADJECTIVE ▸ SEE **doux**

♪ **doucement** ADVERB
1 gently
Doucement, tu me fais mal! Gently please, you're hurting me!
2 slowly
La vieille dame marche doucement. The old lady walks slowly.
3 quietly
Ferme la porte tout doucement! Shut the door very quietly!

la **douceur** FEM NOUN
1 softness
2 gentleness
3 mildness (of weather)

♪ la **douche** FEM NOUN
shower
Nelly prend une douche. Nelly is having a shower.
Djamila est sous la douche. Djamila is in the shower.

se **doucher** REFLEXIVE VERB ◯ [1]
to have a shower
Delphine se douche. Delphine is having a shower.

doué MASC ADJECTIVE, **douée** FEM
gifted, talented
être doué en quelque chose to have a talent for something
Raphaël est doué en musique. Raphaël has a talent for music
être doué pour quelque chose to have a gift for something
Gwenaëlle est douée pour la danse classique. Gwenaëlle has a gift for ballet.

douillet MASC ADJECTIVE, **douillette** FEM
1 soft (person)
2 cosy (bed, apartment)

◯ means the verb takes être to form the perfect

la **douleur** *FEM NOUN*
1 **pain**
J'ai une douleur dans le coude. I've got a pain in my elbow.
un médicament contre la douleur a painkiller
2 **grief**

douloureux *MASC ADJECTIVE*, **douloureuse** *FEM*
painful

le **doute** *MASC NOUN*
1 **doubt**
J'ai des doutes. I have my doubts.
2 **sans doute** probably

douter *VERB* [1]
to doubt
douter de quelque chose to have doubts about something
Il doutait de son amitié. He had doubts about his friendship.
se **douter** *REFLEXIVE VERB* ◌
1 se douter de quelque chose to think you know something
Je me doute de sa réponse. I think I know his reply.
Je m'en doutais. I thought as much.
2 se douter que ... to suspect that ...
Il se doutait bien que ce serait difficile à faire. He suspected that it would be hard to do.

douteux *MASC ADJECTIVE*, **douteuse** *FEM*
1 **doubtful**
2 **dubious** (taste, piece of information)

Douvres *NOUN*
Dover

ℓ **doux** *MASC ADJECTIVE*, **douce** *FEM*
1 **soft**
Elle a la peau douce. She has soft skin.
2 **gentle** (person, expression)
3 **mild** (weather)
4 **sweet** (cider)

ℓ la **douzaine** *FEM NOUN*
dozen
une douzaine d'œufs a dozen eggs

ℓ **douze** *NUMBER*
twelve
Elle a douze ans. She's twelve.
le douze juillet the twelfth of July

ℓ **douzième** *MASC & FEM ADJECTIVE*
twelfth

la **dragée** *FEM NOUN*
sugared almond

draguer *VERB* [1]
(informal)
draguer quelqu'un to chat somebody up
se faire draguer to get chatted up

dramatique *MASC & FEM ADJECTIVE*
1 **tragic**
Ce n'est pas dramatique si ... It's not the end of the world if ...
2 **dramatic**
l'art dramatique drama

le **drame** *MASC NOUN*
1 **tragedy**
un drame de famille a family tragedy
2 **drama**
un drame en trois actes a three-act play

ℓ le **drap** *MASC NOUN*
sheet
• le drap de bain
bath towel

le **drapeau** *MASC NOUN*, les **drapeaux** *PL*
flag

dresser *VERB* [1]
1 **to train** (an animal)
2 **to put up** (a tent)
3 **to draw up** (a list)
se **dresser** *REFLEXIVE VERB* ◌
to stand up

ℓ la **drogue** *FEM NOUN*
drug
la drogue drugs
• les drogues douces
soft drugs
• les drogues dures
hard drugs

droguer *VERB* [1]
to drug
se **droguer** *REFLEXIVE VERB* ◌
to take drugs

la **droguerie** *FEM NOUN*
hardware shop

droit *MASC ADJECTIVE*, **droite** *FEM* ▶ SEE **droit**
ADVERB, *NOUN*
1 **straight**
une ligne droite a straight line
2 **right**
ma main droite my right hand
3 un angle droit a right angle
droit *ADVERB* ▶ SEE **droit** *ADJECTIVE*, *NOUN*
straight
droit devant straight ahead
Continuez tout droit. Carry straight on.

ℓ le **droit** *MASC NOUN* ▶ SEE **droit** *ADJECTIVE*, *ADVERB*
1 **right**
Je connais mes droits. I know my rights.
les droits de l'homme human rights
2 avoir le droit de faire quelque chose to be allowed to do something
Je n'ai pas le droit de sortir ce soir. I'm not allowed to go out tonight.

3 avoir le droit de faire quelque chose to have the right to do something
   J'ai le droit de savoir. I have a right to know.
4 avoir droit à quelque chose to be entitled to something
   Vous avez droit à une boisson chacun. You're allowed one drink each.
5 le droit law
   un étudiant en droit a law student
6 fee
   les droits d'inscription the enrolment fees

la **droite** *FEM NOUN*
1 right
   à droite on the right
   l'élève de droite the pupil on the right
   tourner à droite to turn right
   En France, on roule à droite. In France, you drive on the right.
   à ta droite, sur ta droite on your right
2 la droite the right *(in politics)*
3 une droite a straight line *(in maths)*

droitier *MASC ADJECTIVE*, **droitière** *FEM*
   right-handed

♪ **drôle** *MASC & FEM ADJECTIVE*
1 funny
   une histoire drôle a funny story
2 odd
   un drôle de film an odd film
   C'est drôle qu'elle n'ait pas appelé. It's odd she hasn't phoned.

drôlement *ADVERB*
   (informal) **really**
   C'était drôlement bon! It was really good!

du *DETERMINER* ▸ SEE **dû**
   some, any

WORD TIP de + le becomes du. ▸ SEE de

dû, **due**, **dus** *VERB* ▸ SEE **devoir**

le **duc** *MASC NOUN*
   duke

la **duchesse** *FEM NOUN*
   duchess

la **dune** *FEM NOUN*
   dune

le **duo** *MASC NOUN*
   duet

le **duplex** *MASC NOUN*
   maisonette

duquel *PRONOUN*
   le mur au-dessus duquel il a sauté the wall over which he jumped
   18 ans, c'est l'âge à partir duquel on peut

voter. You can vote from the age of 18.

WORD TIP de + lequel becomes duquel. duquel becomes de laquelle when it is used for a fem singular noun, desquels when it is used for a masc plural noun, and desquelles when it is used for a fem plural noun. ▸ SEE **dont**

♪ **dur** *MASC ADJECTIVE*, **dure** *FEM* ▸ SEE **dur** *ADVERB*
1 hard
   Cette boîte est dure à ouvrir. This box is hard to open.
2 tough *(meat)*
   La viande est un peu dure. The meat is a bit tough.
3 difficult, hard
   L'exercice de maths est vraiment dur. The maths exercise is really hard.
4 harsh *(criticism, voice, climate)*
   Ses parents ont été durs avec elle. Her parents were harsh with her.

♪ **dur** *ADVERB* ▸ SEE **dur** *ADJECTIVE*
   hard
   Marc travaille dur. Marc works hard.

durant *PREPOSITION*
1 for
   des années durant for years
2 during
   durant la partie during the game
   durant les deux derniers mois during the last two months

durcir *VERB* [2]
1 to harden
   Le beurre durcit au frigidaire. The butter hardens in the fridge.
2 to set
   La colle n'a pas encore durci. The glue hasn't set yet.

se **durcir** *REFLEXIVE VERB* ☺
1 to harden
2 to become harsher

la **durée** *FEM NOUN*
   length
   La durée du spectacle est de trois heures. The length of the show is three hours.
   pendant toute la durée des vacances for the duration of the holidays

durement *ADVERB*
   harshly

♪ **durer** *VERB* [1]
1 to last
   Ça ne durera pas. It won't last.
   La grève a duré deux semaines. The strike lasted two weeks.
2 to go on
   durer pendant trois mois to go on for three months
   Cela fait dix ans que ça dure. It's been

☺ means the verb takes être to form the perfect

going on for ten years.

3 to run
L'exposition dure du 2 au 20 juin. The exhibition runs from the 2nd to the 20th of June.

la **dureté** *FEM NOUN*
1 hardness
2 toughness
3 difficulty

le **duvet** *MASC NOUN*
sleeping bag

♪ le **DVD** *INVARIABLE MASC NOUN*
DVD
J'ai une centaine de DVD. I've got about a hundred DVDs.

dynamique *MASC & FEM ADJECTIVE*
dynamic

dyslexique *MASC & FEM ADJECTIVE*
dyslexic

Ee

♪ l'**eau** *FEM NOUN*
water
un verre d'eau a glass of water
de l'eau du robinet some tap water
'Eau potable' 'Drinking water'
'Eau non potable' 'Not drinking water'
- l'eau de Javel
bleach
- l'eau de toilette
eau de toilette (perfume)
- l'eau douce
fresh water
- l'eau gazeuse
sparkling mineral water
- l'eau minérale
mineral water
- l'eau plate
still mineral water
- l'eau salée
salt water

ébaucher *VERB* [1]
1 to sketch
2 to outline

un & une **ébéniste** *MASC & FEM NOUN*
cabinet maker

éblouir *VERB* [2]
to dazzle

éblouissant *MASC ADJECTIVE*, **éblouissante** *FEM*
dazzling

un **éboueur** *MASC NOUN*
refuse collector

ébouillanter *VERB* [1]
to scald

ébranler *VERB* [1]
to shake, to rattle

l'**ébullition** *FEM NOUN*
boiling point

une **écaille** *FEM NOUN*
1 scale (of a fish, a reptile)
2 tortoiseshell

s'**écailler** *REFLEXIVE VERB* ◐ [1]
to flake

un **écart** *MASC NOUN*
1 gap
un écart de 10 mètres a 10-metre gap
2 swerve
faire un écart to swerve
3 difference (in prices, temperatures)
4 à l'écart de away from
5 lapse
faire des écarts to allow oneself the occasional treat

écarté *MASC ADJECTIVE*, **écartée** *FEM*
1 remote
un village écarté a remote village
2 les jambes écartées with legs apart
3 les bras écartés with arms outstretched

écarter *VERB* [1]
1 to move apart
écarter les rideaux to open the curtains
2 to move aside (things or people in the way)
s'**écarter** *REFLEXIVE VERB* ◐
to move back, to move out of the way

un **échafaudage** *MASC NOUN*
scaffolding

une **échalote** *FEM NOUN*
shallot

♪ un **échange** *MASC NOUN*
exchange
faire un échange en France to go to France on an exchange
en échange (de) in exchange (for), in return (for)

échanger *VERB* [52]
to exchange, to swap

un **échangeur** *MASC NOUN*
(motorway) interchange

un **échantillon** *MASC NOUN*
sample

échapper *VERB* [1]
échapper à quelque chose, quelqu'un to escape from something, somebody
Ils ont réussi à échapper à la police. They managed to escape from the police.

♪ indicates key words

s'**échapper** REFLEXIVE VERB ⬤
to escape
Ils se sont échappés. They escaped.

une **écharde** FEM NOUN
splinter

une **écharpe** FEM NOUN
scarf

une **échasse** FEM NOUN
stilt

un **échec** MASC NOUN
failure

� les **échecs** PLURAL MASC NOUN
chess
jouer aux échecs to play chess

une **échelle** FEM NOUN
1 ladder
monter à une échelle to climb up a ladder
2 scale (of a map, a scale model)

un **échelon** MASC NOUN
1 rung (of a ladder)
2 grade (in a company, an organization)

un **échiquier** MASC NOUN
chessboard

un **écho** MASC NOUN
1 echo
2 des échos rumours

une **échographie** FEM NOUN
(medical) scan
passer une échographie to have a scan

� **échouer** VERB [1]
1 to fail
échouer à quelque chose to fail something
2 to run aground

éclabousser VERB [1]
to splash, to spatter

� un **éclair** MASC NOUN
flash of lightning
Il y a des éclairs. There is lightning.
• un éclair au chocolat
chocolate eclair

l'**éclairage** MASC NOUN
lighting

un & une **éclairagiste** MASC & FEM NOUN
lighting engineer

� une **éclaircie** FEM NOUN
sunny interval

éclaircir VERB [2]
to clear up (mystery, puzzle)

s' **éclaircir** REFLEXIVE VERB ⬤
to clear up (weather)

éclairer VERB [1]
to light (up)

un **éclat** MASC NOUN
1 splinter of glass
2 brightness, sparkle
3 splendour
• un éclat de rire
roar of laughter

éclatant MASC ADJECTIVE, **éclatante** FEM
brilliant (colours)

éclater VERB [1]
1 to burst (balloons, tyres)
2 to shatter (bottles, bulbs)
3 to break out (war, fighting)
4 (with emotions) éclater de rire to burst out
laughing
éclater en sanglots to burst into tears

une **éclipse** FEM NOUN
eclipse

une **écluse** FEM NOUN
lock (on a canal, a river)

écœurant MASC ADJECTIVE, **écœurante** FEM
1 sickly
2 revolting

écœurer VERB [1]
to make (somebody) feel sick

� une **école** FEM NOUN
school
aller à l'école to go to school
• une école de conduite
driving school
• une école de langues
language school
• une école maternelle
(state) nursery school (age 2 to 6)
• une école primaire
primary school (age 6 to 11)
• une école privée
private school
• une école publique
state school

un **écolier** MASC NOUN, une **écolière** FEM
schoolchild

l'**écologie** FEM NOUN
ecology

écologique MASC & FEM ADJECTIVE
1 ecological
2 environmentally friendly

un & une **écologiste** MASC & FEM NOUN
ecologist

un **économe** MASC NOUN ▶ SEE **économe**
ADJECTIVE
vegetable peeler

⬤ means the verb takes être to form the perfect

économe *MASC & FEM ADJECTIVE* ▶ SEE **économe**
NOUN
economical

l'**économie** *FEM NOUN*
1 economy
2 economics
faire des études d'économie to study
economics
3 les économies savings
Je vais faire des économies. I'm going to
save up.

économique *MASC & FEM ADJECTIVE*
1 economical
2 economic

économiser *VERB* [1]
to save
économiser l'énergie to save energy

un & une **économiste** *MASC & FEM NOUN*
economist

l'**écorce** *FEM NOUN*
1 bark *(of a tree)*
2 peel *(of an orange, a lemon)*

s'**écorcher** *REFLEXIVE VERB* ⊘ [1]
to graze yourself
Chloë s'est écorché la main. Chloë grazed
her hand.

une **écorchure** *FEM NOUN*
graze

ℓ **écossais** *MASC ADJECTIVE*, **écossaise** *FEM* ▶ SEE
écossais *NOUN*
▶ SEE **Écossais** *MASC & FEM NOUN*
1 Scottish
2 tartan

> **WORD TIP** Adjectives never have capitals in
> French, even for nationality or regional origin.

un **écossais** *MASC NOUN* ▶ SEE **écossais** *ADJECTIVE*
▶ SEE **Écossais**
tartan *(the cloth)*

ℓ un **Écossais** *MASC NOUN*, une **Écossaise** *FEM* ▶ SEE
écossais *MASC NOUN, ADJ*
Scotsman, Scotswoman, Scot
les Écossais the Scots

ℓ l'**Écosse** *FEM NOUN*
Scotland
habiter en Écosse to live in Scotland
aller en Écosse to go to Scotland

> **WORD TIP** Countries and regions in French take
> le, la or les.

écourter *VERB* [1]
to shorten

ℓ **écouter** *VERB* [1]
to listen to
Dans la voiture, j'écoute la radio. In the car,

I listen to the radio.
Écoute-moi. Listen to me.
Je vous écoute. I'm listening.

un **écouteur** *MASC NOUN*
1 receiver *(on a telephone)*
2 headphones

ℓ un **écran** *MASC NOUN*
screen
• l' écran tactile
touchscreen

écrasant *MASC ADJECTIVE*, **écrasante** *FEM*
1 crushing, overwhelming
2 sweltering

écraser *VERB* [1]
1 to crush
2 to squash
3 écraser une cigarette to stub out a
cigarette
4 se faire écraser to get run over
Mon chien s'est fait écraser. My dog got
run over.

s'**écraser** *REFLEXIVE VERB* ⊘
to crash

écrémé *MASC ADJECTIVE*, **écrémée** *FEM*
skimmed
le lait écrémé skimmed milk
le lait demi-écrémé semi-skimmed milk

une **écrevisse** *FEM NOUN*
crayfish

ℓ **écrire** *VERB* [38]
to write
Elle m'a écrit une lettre. She wrote me a
letter.
J'écris mes cartes postales. I'm writing my
postcards.

s'**écrire** *REFLEXIVE VERB* ⊘
1 to write to each other
Ils s'écrivent tous les jours. They write to
each other every day.
2 to be spelled
Le mot s'écrit avec un accent. The word is
spelled with an accent.
Comment ça s'écrit? How do you spell it?

écrit *MASC ADJECTIVE*, **écrite** *FEM* ▶ SEE **écrit** *NOUN*
written

un **écrit** *MASC NOUN* ▶ SEE **écrit** *ADJECTIVE*
1 (piece of) writing
2 written paper *(of an exam)*
3 à l'écrit, par écrit in writing

une **écriture** *FEM NOUN*
1 handwriting
2 writing *(on a page)*

un **écrivain** *MASC NOUN*
writer

> **WORD TIP** A female writer is also un écrivain.

ℓ indicates key words

un **écrou** MASC NOUN
nut (screwed onto a bolt)

s'**écrouler** REFLEXIVE VERB ◉ [1]
to collapse
s'écrouler de rire (informal) to be doubled
up laughing

l'**écume** FEM NOUN
1 **foam, froth**
2 **scum** (on a liquid)

un **écureuil** MASC NOUN
squirrel

une **écurie** FEM NOUN
stable

l'**eczéma** MASC NOUN
eczema

EDF FEM NOUN
(= Électricité de France) (French electricity
company)

Édimbourg NOUN
Edinburgh

éditer VERB [1]
to publish

un **éditeur** MASC NOUN, une **éditrice** FEM
publisher

l'**édition** FEM NOUN
1 **l'édition publishing**
2 **edition**
• une édition de poche
paperback edition

l'**édredon** MASC NOUN
eiderdown

un **éducateur** MASC NOUN, une **éducatrice** FEM
teacher, youth worker

éducatif MASC ADJECTIVE, **éducative** FEM
educational

l'**éducation** FEM NOUN
education
• l'éducation physique
physical education, PE

éduquer VERB [1]
1 **to educate**
2 **to bring up** (a child)

effacer VERB [61]
to rub out, to erase

un **effaceur** MASC NOUN
correction pen

effarant MASC ADJECTIVE, **effarante** FEM
amazing, alarming

effarer VERB [1]
to alarm

effectivement ADVERB
indeed (showing agreement)
'Tu as oublié ton maillot.' – 'Ah oui,
effectivement!' 'You've left your swimsuit
behind.' – 'Oh yes, so I have!'

effectuer VERB [1]
to carry out (a change, repairs)

un **effet** MASC NOUN
1 **effect**
Ça n'a aucun effet. It has no effect.
2 **en effet indeed** (showing agreement)
'Il fait très froid.' – 'Oui, en effet.' 'It's very
cold.' – 'Yes, it is, isn't it?'

efficace MASC & FEM ADJECTIVE
1 **efficient**
Elle est très efficace. She's very efficient.
2 **effective**
C'est un remède très efficace. It's a very
effective remedy.

l'**efficacité** FEM NOUN
1 **efficiency**
Il est connu pour son efficacité. He's known
for his efficiency.
2 **effectiveness**

s'**effondrer** REFLEXIVE VERB ◉ [1]
to collapse

s'**efforcer** REFLEXIVE VERB ◉ [61]
s'efforcer de faire quelque chose to try
hard to do something

un **effort** MASC NOUN
effort
faire l'effort de faire quelque chose to
make the effort to do something
J'ai fait l'effort d'y aller. I made the effort
to go.

effrayant MASC ADJECTIVE, **effrayante** FEM
frightening

effrayer VERB [59]
to frighten

l'**effroi** MASC NOUN
terror

effronté MASC ADJECTIVE, **effrontée** FEM
cheeky

effroyable MASC & FEM ADJECTIVE
dreadful

égal MASC ADJECTIVE, **égale** FEM, **égaux** MASC PL,
égales FEM PL ▸SEE **égal** NOUN
1 **equal**
une distance égale an equal distance
des quantités égales equal quantities
être égal à to be equal to
2 être égal à quelqu'un to be all the same to
somebody
Ça m'est égal. I don't mind., I don't care.

◉ means the verb takes être to form the perfect

'Tu veux aller au cinéma?' – 'Ça m'est égal.' 'Do you want to go to the cinema?' – 'I don't mind.'

un **égal** MASC NOUN, une **égale** FEM les **égaux** MASC PL les **égales** FEM PL ▶ SEE **égal** ADJECTIVE
equal

également ADVERB
also

égaler VERB [1]
to equal
Trois plus cinq égalent huit. Three plus five equals eight.

égaliser VERB [1]
to equalize

l'**égalité** FEM NOUN
equality

l'**égard** MASC NOUN
1 à l'égard de towards, regarding
à mon égard towards me
2 à cet égard in this respect

égaré MASC ADJECTIVE, **égarée** FEM
stray, lost

égarer VERB [1]
to mislay
s'**égarer** REFLEXIVE VERB ⊙
to get lost

égayer VERB [59]
1 to brighten up
2 to cheer up

℘ une **église** FEM NOUN
church
aller à l'église to go to church

l'**égoïsme** MASC NOUN
selfishness

égoïste MASC & FEM ADJECTIVE
selfish

un **égout** MASC NOUN
sewer

égoutter VERB [1]
1 to drain (vegetables)
2 to strain (pasta)
3 to drip

une **égratignure** FEM NOUN
scratch

l'**Égypte** FEM NOUN
Egypt

℘ **eh bien** EXCLAMATION
well
Eh bien, ça me fait plaisir de te revoir. Well, it's nice to see you again.

s'**élancer** REFLEXIVE VERB ⊙ [61]
to dash

élargir VERB [2]
to widen

élastique MASC & FEM ADJECTIVE ▶ SEE **élastique** NOUN
1 elastic
2 elasticated

un **élastique** MASC NOUN ▶ SEE **élastique** ADJECTIVE
1 rubber band
2 elastic

un **électeur** MASC NOUN, une **électrice** FEM
voter

℘ une **élection** FEM NOUN
election

un **électricien** MASC NOUN, une **électricienne** FEM
electrician

℘ l'**électricité** FEM NOUN
electricity

électrique MASC & FEM ADJECTIVE
1 electric
2 electrical

l'**électroménager** MASC NOUN
domestic appliances

électronique MASC & FEM ADJECTIVE ▶ SEE **électronique** NOUN
electronic

l'**électronique** FEM NOUN ▶ SEE **électronique** ADJECTIVE
electronics

℘ **élégant** MASC ADJECTIVE, **élégante** FEM
elegant

un **élément** MASC NOUN
1 element
2 part, section (to be assembled)

élémentaire MASC & FEM ADJECTIVE
basic, elementary

un **éléphant** MASC NOUN
elephant

l'**élevage** MASC NOUN
1 farming (of cattle, pigs, sheep)
2 farm

℘ un & une **élève** MASC & FEM NOUN
student, pupil

élevé MASC ADJECTIVE, **élevée** FEM
high
une note élevée a high mark

élever VERB [50]
1 élever un enfant to bring up a child
2 to breed (animals)
3 élever la voix to raise one's voice

℘ indicates key words

s'**élever** REFLEXIVE VERB ⬆
1 to rise (temperatures)
2 s'élever à quelque chose to amount to
   something
   La facture s'élève à cinq cents euros. The
   bill amounts to five hundred euros.

un **éleveur** MASC NOUN, une **éleveuse** FEM
   breeder

éliminer VERB [1]
1 to eliminate, to get rid of
2 to eliminate, to knock out
3 to rule out (a possibility, an option)

élire VERB [51]
   to elect

⚲ **elle** PRONOUN
1 (as the subject of the verb) she
   Elle parle bien français. She speaks French
   well.
2 (for a fem singular noun) it
   'Où est ma tasse?' – 'Elle est sur la table.'
   'Where's my cup?' – 'It's on the table.'
3 her (as opposed to anybody else)
   C'est elle. It's her.
   chez elle at her house
   Je pense à elle. I'm thinking of her.
4 (for emphasis) she
   C'est elle qui me l'a dit. She's the one who
   told me.
   Elle et moi sommes très copines. She and I
   are good friends.
   Elle, elle n'est jamais contente! She's never
   happy!
5 (after prepositions like avec or sans and in
   comparisons) her
   Paul est avec elle. Paul's with her.
   Je suis plus grande qu'elle. I'm taller than
   her.
6 à elle hers (belonging to her)
   Ce sont des amis à elle. They're friends of
   hers.

elle-même PRONOUN
1 herself
   Elle a tout fait elle-même. She did
   everything herself.
   'Madame Dubois?' – 'Elle-même.' 'Madame
   Dubois?' – 'Speaking.'
2 (for fem things) itself
   La chanson elle-même est bien mais je
   n'aime pas ce groupe. The song itself is
   good but I don't like that group.

⚲ **elles** FEM PLURAL PRONOUN
1 (for female people and things as the subject)
   they
   Elles habitent tout près. They live near
   here.
   Mes chaussures! Elles sont ruinées! My
   shoes! They're ruined!

2 (after prepositions like avec or sans and in
   comparisons) them
   Je reste avec elles. I'm staying with them.
   Tu es plus sympa qu'elles. You're nicer than
   them.
3 à elles theirs (belonging to them)
   Le voiture rouge est à elles. The red car is
   theirs.
4 chez elles at their house

elles-mêmes PRONOUN
   (for female people and objects) themselves

éloigné MASC ADJECTIVE, **éloignée** FEM
   distant
   éloigné du centre-ville far from the town
   centre
   la maison la plus éloignée the house
   furthest away

s'**éloigner** REFLEXIVE VERB ⬆ [1]
   to move away
   Ne t'éloigne pas trop. Don't go too far
   away.
   s'éloigner de quelque chose to move away
   from something
   Le ferry s'éloignait de la côte. The ferry was
   moving away from the coast.

l'**Élysée** MASC NOUN
   the Élysée Palace (the official residence of
   the French President)

l'**email**, **e-mail** MASC NOUN
   email

l'**émail** MASC NOUN
   enamel

   WORD TIP émail does not mean email in
   English; for the meaning of email ▸ SEE courrier
   électronique, courriel, email.

l'**emballage** MASC NOUN
   wrapping

emballer VERB [1]
1 to wrap, to pack
2 (informal)
   emballer quelqu'un to fill somebody with
   enthusiasm
   Le film ne m'emballe pas. I'm not keen on
   the film.

s'**emballer** REFLEXIVE VERB ⬆ [1]
1 to bolt (horses)
2 (informal)
   s'emballer pour quelque chose to become
   enthusiastic about something
   Ne t'emballe pas! Don't get carried away!

l'**embarquement** MASC NOUN
   boarding

embarquer VERB [1]
1 to board
2 (informal) to go off with

⬆ means the verb takes être to form the perfect

Qui a embarqué la télécommande? Who's gone off with the remote?

s'**embarquer** REFLEXIVE VERB ◎
s'embarquer pour l'Amérique to set sail for America

un **embarras** MASC NOUN
1 embarrassment
2 dilemma
être dans l'embarras to have money problems
3 avoir l'embarras du choix to be spoilt for choice

embarrassé MASC ADJECTIVE, **embarrassée** FEM
1 embarrassed
2 cluttered

embarrasser VERB [1]
1 to embarrass
2 to clutter up

embaucher VERB [1]
to take on (an employee)

embêtant MASC ADJECTIVE, **embêtante** FEM
annoying

embêter VERB [1]
to annoy

s'**embêter** REFLEXIVE VERB ◎
1 to be bored
On ne s'embête pas ici. There's plenty going on here.
2 to worry
Ne t'embête pas pour ça. Don't worry about it.
3 to bother
Est-ce que ça t'embête? Does it bother you?

ℒ un **embouteillage** MASC NOUN
traffic jam

embrasser VERB [1]
1 to kiss
2 (in greetings) Je t'embrasse. Lots of love. (in letters)
Salut, je t'embrasse. Take care, bye. (in phone calls)

un **embrayage** MASC NOUN
clutch (in a vehicle)

une **émeraude** FEM NOUN
emerald

émerger VERB [52]
to emerge

une **émeute** FEM NOUN
riot

ℒ une **émission** FEM NOUN
programme
On a regardé une émission à la télé. We watched a programme on TV.
Qu'est-ce qu'il y a comme émission? What

programmes are on?

emménager VERB [52]
to move in (to a flat, a house)

emmener VERB [50]
to take
Il m'emmène au cinéma. He's taking me to the cinema.
Tu veux que je t'emmène? Would you like a lift?

émotif MASC ADJECTIVE, **émotive** FEM
emotional

une **émotion** FEM NOUN
emotion

émouvant MASC ADJECTIVE, **émouvante** FEM
moving

s'**emparer** REFLEXIVE VERB ◎ [1]
s'emparer de quelque chose to seize something

empêcher VERB [1]
1 to prevent, to stop
empêcher quelqu'un de faire quelque chose to stop somebody from doing something
Rien ne t'empêche d'essayer. There's nothing to stop you trying.
2 Elle n'a pas pu s'empêcher de rire. She couldn't help laughing.

un **empereur** MASC NOUN
emperor

empiler VERB [1]
to pile up

empirer VERB [1]
to get worse

ℒ un **emplacement** MASC NOUN
1 pitch (for a tent)
Est-ce qu'il reste des emplacements? Are there any pitches left?
2 site (for a building)

ℒ un **emploi** MASC NOUN
1 job
Il cherche un emploi. He's looking for a job.
Après mes examens, je vais trouver un emploi. After my exams, I'm going to find a job.
2 use
le mode d'emploi instructions for use
• un emploi du temps
timetable (at school)

ℒ un **employé** MASC NOUN, une **employée** FEM
employee

employer VERB [39]
1 to employ
2 to use

ℒ indicates key words

un **employeur** *MASC NOUN*, une **employeuse** *FEM*
employer

empoisonné *MASC ADJECTIVE*, **empoisonnée** *FEM*
poisoned

empoisonner *VERB* [1]
to poison

emporter *VERB* [1]
1 **to take away**
Ils ont emporté le vieux frigo. They took away the old fridge.
'Plats à emporter' 'Takeaway meals'
2 se laisser emporter **to get carried away**
Je me suis laissé emporter. I got carried away.
3 **to sweep away**
Ils ont été emportés par le courant. They were swept away by the current.

une **empreinte** *FEM NOUN*
footprint
• une empreinte digitale
fingerprint

emprisonner *VERB* [1]
to imprison

un **emprunt** *MASC NOUN*
loan
• un emprunt-logement
mortgage

emprunter *VERB* [1]
to borrow
emprunter de l'argent to borrow money
emprunter quelque chose à quelqu'un to borrow something from somebody
Je peux t'emprunter ta montre? Can I borrow your watch?

l'**EMT** *NOUN FEM*
(= Éducation manuelle et technique) **Design and Technology, DT**

ému *MASC ADJECTIVE*, **émue** *FEM*
moved

♪ **en** *PREPOSITION* ▸ SEE **en** *PRONOUN*
1 **in**
en été in summer
en avril in April
une chanson en français a song in French
habillé en noir dressed in black
J'étais en pyjama. I was in my pyjamas.
Elle habite en Écosse. She lives in Scotland.
2 **into**
aller en ville to go into town
traduire en anglais to translate into English
3 **to**
aller en Italie to go to Italy
rentrer en Angleterre to return to England

4 **by**
en avion by plane
5 **made of**
une table en bois a wooden table
une jupe en jean a denim skirt
6 en vacances on holiday
en voyage d'affaires on a business trip
7 Elle s'est brûlée en repassant sa chemise.
She burned herself (while) ironing her shirt.

WORD TIP en followed by any verb ending in -ant shows one action taking place at the same time as another.

♪ **en** *PRONOUN* ▸ SEE **en** *PREPOSITION*
1 (in general statements) **some**
Tu veux des pièces d'un euro? J'en ai. You want 1 euro coins? I've got some.
Du beurre? Il y en a dans le frigo. Butter? There's some in the fridge.
Des biscuits? Je crois qu'il en reste. Biscuits? I think there are some left.
2 (in negative statements and in simple questions) **any**
Je n'en veux pas. I don't want any.
Est-ce que tu en as? Do you have any?
Est-ce qu'il en reste? Is there any left?
3 **of it, of them** (en is often not translated)
Tu en as combien? How much (of it) do you have?, How many (of them) do you have?
Elle en a quatre. She's got four.
'Qui a un stylo?' – 'J'en ai un.' 'Who's got a pen?' – 'I've got one.'
4 **it, about it** (referring to something known about)
Elle m'en a parlé. She told me about it.
Ne m'en parle pas! Don't even talk to me about it!
Je m'en souviens très bien. I remember it very well.
Est-ce que tu en as besoin? Do you need it?

un **encadrement** *MASC NOUN*
1 **frame**
2 **framing**

encadrer *VERB* [1]
to frame

enceinte *FEM ADJECTIVE* ▸ SEE **enceinte** *NOUN*
pregnant
Elle est enceinte de six mois. She's six months pregnant.

une **enceinte** *FEM NOUN* ▸ SEE **enceinte** *ADJECTIVE*
1 **surrounding wall**
2 **compound**
3 **loudspeaker**

l'**encens** *MASC NOUN*
incense

encercler *VERB* [1]
1 **to surround**

2 to circle *(when filling in a questionnaire)*

ℰ **enchanté** *MASC ADJECTIVE*, **enchantée** *FEM*
1 **delighted**
2 *(in introductions)* Enchanté. Pleased to meet you *(boy speaking)*.
Enchantée. Pleased to meet you *(girl speaking)*.
'Anaïs, je te présente mes parents.' – 'Enchantée.' 'Anaïs, this is my Mum and Dad.' – 'Pleased to meet you.'
3 **enchanted**

une **enchère** *FEM NOUN*
bid *(in an auction)*
une vente aux enchères an auction

encombrant *MASC ADJECTIVE*, **encombrante** *FEM*
cumbersome

encombrer *VERB* [1]
1 **to clutter up**
2 **to obstruct**

ℰ **encore** *ADVERB*
1 **still**
Elle est encore au supermarché. She's still at the supermarket.
Il reste encore du poulet. There's still some chicken left.
2 **pas encore** not yet
Ce n'est pas encore prêt. It's not ready yet.
Il n'est pas encore rentré. He hasn't come home yet.
3 **again**
Je l'ai encore oublié. I've forgotten it again.
C'est encore moi! It's me again!
4 **more**
encore un peu a little more
encore une fois one more time
attendre encore une semaine to wait for another week
5 **even**
encore mieux even better
encore pire even worse

encourageant *MASC ADJECTIVE*,
encourageante *FEM*
encouraging

l'**encouragement** *MASC NOUN*
encouragement

encourager *VERB* [52]
1 **to encourage**
2 **to cheer on** *(a team)*

l'**encre** *FEM NOUN*
ink

l'**encyclopédie** *FEM NOUN*
encyclopedia

l'**endive** *FEM NOUN*
chicory

endommager *VERB* [52]
to damage

endormi *MASC ADJECTIVE*, **endormie** *FEM*
asleep
J'étais à moitié endormi. I was half asleep.

endormir *VERB* [37]
endormir quelqu'un to send somebody to sleep *(literally)*
s'**endormir** *REFLEXIVE VERB* ◯
to fall asleep, to go to sleep
Je n'arrive pas à m'endormir. I can't get to sleep.

ℰ un **endroit** *MASC NOUN*
1 **place**
un drôle d'endroit a strange place
2 **the right side** *(of a garment)*
3 à l'endroit the right way up *(for parcels, crates)*

l'**énergie** *FEM NOUN*
energy
• l'énergie renouvelable
renewable energy
• l'énergie solaire
solar energy

énergique *MASC & FEM ADJECTIVE*
energetic

énervé *MASC ADJECTIVE*, **énervée** *FEM*
irritated, **annoyed**

énerver *VERB* [1]
to irritate, to annoy
Ça m'énerve! This is getting on my nerves!
s'**énerver** *REFLEXIVE VERB* ◯
to get annoyed
Ne t'énerve pas! Calm down!

l'**enfance** *FEM NOUN*
childhood

ℰ un & une **enfant** *MASC & FEM NOUN*
child
• un & une enfant unique
only child

enfantin *MASC ADJECTIVE*, **enfantine** *FEM*
1 **easy**
2 **childish**

l'**enfer** *MASC NOUN*
hell

enfermer *VERB* [1]
1 **to shut up**
2 **to lock up** *(your property, valuables)*
s'**enfermer** *REFLEXIVE VERB* ◯
to shut yourself up

enfiler *VERB* [1]
1 **to put on** *(clothes)*
2 enfiler une aiguille to thread a needle

ℰ **indicates key words**

ℓ **enfin** *ADVERB*
 1 **at last**
    J'ai enfin fini. I've finished at last.
 2 **finally**
    Elle a enfin réussi. She finally succeeded.
 3 **for heaven's sake**
    Mais enfin, qu'est-ce qui se passe? Oh for
    heaven's sake, what's happening?

enflé *MASC ADJECTIVE*, **enflée** *FEM*
    swollen

une **enflure** *FEM NOUN*
    swelling

enfoncer *VERB* [61]
 1 **to push in** (a nail, a pin)
 2 **to break down** (a door)
s'**enfoncer** *REFLEXIVE VERB* ◯
    s'enfoncer dans quelque chose to sink into
    something
    Mes pieds s'enfoncent dans la neige. My
    feet are sinking into the snow.

enfreindre *VERB* [2]
    to disobey

un **engagement** *MASC NOUN*
    commitment

engager *VERB* [52]
 1 **to take on** (an employee)
 2 engager la conversation to strike up a
    conversation
s'**engager** *REFLEXIVE VERB* ◯
    s'engager à faire quelque chose to promise
    to do something

une **engelure** *FEM NOUN*
    chilblain

un **engin** *MASC NOUN*
    device

engourdi *MASC ADJECTIVE*, **engourdie** *FEM*
    numb

s'**engourdir** *REFLEXIVE VERB* ◯ [2]
    to go numb

l'**engrais** *MASC NOUN*
    fertilizer

engueuler *VERB* [1]
    (informal) **to tell off**
    Elle nous engueule tout le temps. She's
    always telling us off.
    se faire engueuler to get a telling off
    Je me suis fait engueuler. I got a telling off.
s'**engueuler** *REFLEXIVE VERB* ◯ [1]
    to have a row
    Je me suis engueulée avec ma copine. I've
    had a row with my friend.

énième *MASC & FEM ADJECTIVE*
    umpteenth

pour la énième fois for the umpteenth time

une **énigme** *FEM NOUN*
    riddle

enivrer *VERB* [1]
    enivrer quelqu'un to make somebody
    drunk
s'**enivrer** *REFLEXIVE VERB* ◯
    to get drunk

un **enlèvement** *MASC NOUN*
    kidnapping

enlever *VERB* [50]
 1 **to take off** (a garment)
    Enlève tes baskets. Take your trainers off.
 2 **to remove, to take away**
    enlever une tache to remove a stain
    Tu peux enlever les assiettes. You can take
    away the plates.
 3 **to kidnap**

enneigé *MASC ADJECTIVE*, **enneigée** *FEM*
 1 **snowy**
 2 **snow-covered**
    une route enneigée a snow-covered road

un **ennemi** *MASC NOUN*, une **ennemie** *FEM*
    enemy

l'**ennui** *MASC NOUN*
 1 **boredom**
 2 **problem**
    avoir des ennuis to have problems

ennuyé *MASC ADJECTIVE*, **ennuyée** *FEM*
 1 **bored**
 2 **embarrassed**

ennuyer *VERB* [41]
 1 **to bore**
    Le film m'a vraiment ennuyé. I found the
    film really boring.
 2 **to bother**
    Je t'ennuie? Am I bothering you?
s'**ennuyer** *REFLEXIVE VERB* ◯
    to be bored, to get bored
    s'ennuyer à mourir to be bored stiff
    On s'ennuie ici. It's boring here.
    On ne s'ennuie pas! We're having fun!

ℓ **ennuyeux** *MASC ADJECTIVE*, **ennuyeuse** *FEM*
 1 **boring**
    une émission ennuyeuse a boring
    programme
 2 **annoying**
    Ça, c'est vraiment ennuyeux. That's a real
    nuisance.

énorme *MASC & FEM ADJECTIVE*
    huge

énormément *ADVERB*
 1 **tremendously**
 2 énormément de quelque chose masses of

◯ means the verb takes être to form the perfect

something
J'ai énormément de choses à faire. I've got masses of things to do.

une **enquête** *FEM NOUN*
1 **investigation**
2 **inquiry**
3 **survey**

un **enregistrement** *MASC NOUN*
1 **recording**
2 **check-in** *(at an airport)*

℘ **enregistrer** *VERB* [1]
1 **to record**
2 **to register**
3 **to check in** *(at an airport)*
enregistrer ses bagages to check in your luggage
s'**enregistrer** *REFLEXIVE VERB* ⊘ [1]
to record oneself *(on an audio tape)*

enregistreur DVD *MASC NOUN*
DVD recorder

enrhumer *VERB* [1]
être enrhumé to have a cold
s'**enrhumer** *REFLEXIVE VERB* ⊘
to catch a cold
Je me suis enrhumé. I caught a cold.

enrichir *VERB* [2]
1 **to make rich**
2 **to enrich**

enrichissant *MASC ADJECTIVE*, **enrichissante** *FEM*
rewarding

enrouler *VERB* [1]
to wind

℘ un **enseignant** *MASC NOUN*, une **enseignante** *FEM*
teacher

une **enseigne** *FEM NOUN*
sign
• une enseigne lumineuse
neon sign

l'**enseignement** *MASC NOUN*
1 **teaching**
2 **education**

enseigner *VERB* [1]
to teach

℘ **ensemble** *ADVERB* ▶SEE **ensemble** *NOUN*
together
Ils sont toujours ensemble. They're still together.
un **ensemble** *MASC NOUN* ▶SEE **ensemble** *ADVERB*
1 **outfit**
2 l'ensemble de the whole of
l'ensemble des élèves dans la classe all the students in the class

3 dans l'ensemble on the whole

℘ **ensoleillé** *MASC ADJECTIVE*, **ensoleillée** *FEM*
sunny

ensommeillé *MASC ADJECTIVE*, **ensommeillée** *FEM*
sleepy

℘ **ensuite** *ADVERB*
then

entamer *VERB* [1]
to start *(when eating, drinking or opening something)*
On entame le dessert? Shall we start eating dessert?

entasser *VERB* [1]
to pile up

℘ **entendre** *VERB* [3]
1 **to hear**
Je n'entends rien. I can't hear a thing.
2 J'ai entendu dire que … I've heard that …
s'**entendre** *REFLEXIVE VERB* ⊘
s'entendre bien to get on well
Je m'entends très bien avec eux. I get on very well with them.
Je ne m'entends pas avec mon frère. I don't get on with my brother.

entendu *EXCLAMATION*
1 **okay**, **fine**
2 bien entendu of course

une **entente** *FEM NOUN*
1 **understanding**
2 **agreement**

un **enterrement** *MASC NOUN*
funeral, **burial**

enterrer *VERB* [1]
to bury

entêté *MASC ADJECTIVE*, **entêtée** *FEM*
stubborn

s'**entêter** *REFLEXIVE VERB* ⊘ [1]
to be stubborn

l'**enthousiasme** *MASC NOUN*
enthusiasm

s'**enthousiasmer** *REFLEXIVE VERB* ⊘ [1]
to get enthusiastic

enthousiaste *MASC & FEM ADJECTIVE*
enthusiastic

entier *MASC ADJECTIVE*, **entière** *FEM*
1 **whole**
le monde entier the whole world
2 Je n'ai pas lu sa lettre en entier. I haven't read his letter right through.
3 le lait entier full-fat milk

℘ indicates key words

entièrement ADVERB
completely, totally
entièrement gratuit completely free of charge
Je suis entièrement d'accord avec vous. I totally agree with you.

une **entorse** FEM NOUN
sprain

♀ **entouré** MASC ADJECTIVE, **entourée** FEM
1 entouré de surrounded by
Elle est entourée d'amis. She's surrounded by friends.
2 être bien entouré to be well looked after

entourer VERB [1]
to surround
les vignobles qui entourent le village the vineyards surrounding the village
entourer de to surround with
entourer d'un cercle la bonne réponse to circle the correct answer

un **entracte** MASC NOUN
interval (at the theatre)

l'**entraînement** MASC NOUN
1 **training** (in sport)
2 **practice**

entraîner VERB [1]
1 to lead to
2 to take
3 to train
4 to drag along
s'**entraîner** REFLEXIVE VERB ⬤
to train

♀ **entre** PREPOSITION
1 **between**
entre la porte et la fenêtre between the door and the window
un match entre la France et l'Italie a match between France and Italy
2 **among**
entre eux among themselves
3 l'un d'entre eux, l'une d'entre elles one of them
L'une d'entre elles monte à cheval. One of them goes horse-riding.

♀ une **entrecôte** FEM NOUN
steak

une **entrée** FEM NOUN
1 **entrance**
billets à l'entrée tickets at the door
2 **hall(way)**
3 **admission**
entrée gratuite free admission
4 **starter, first course**
Qu'est-ce que tu prends en entrée? What are you having as a starter?

un **entremets** MASC NOUN
flan, cream dessert

un **entrepôt** MASC NOUN
warehouse

entreprendre VERB [64]
1 to undertake (work)
2 to start (a task)

une **entreprise** FEM NOUN
firm, business

♀ **entrer** VERB [1]
1 **to go in**
entrer dans un magasin to go into a shop
entrer à l'hôpital to go into hospital
2 **to come in**
entrer dans une pièce to come into a room
Entrez! Come in!

entre-temps ADVERB
meanwhile

entretenir VERB [81]
1 to maintain (a building, a car)
2 to look after (plants, clothes)
3 to support (a family)

un **entretien** MASC NOUN
1 **interview**
L'entretien s'est bien passé. The interview went well.
2 **discussion**
avoir un entretien avec le professeur to have a discussion with the teacher
3 **upkeep**
l'entretien de la maison the upkeep of the house

une **entrevue** FEM NOUN
interview

entrouvert MASC ADJECTIVE, **entrouverte** FEM
ajar, half-open

envahir VERB [2]
to invade

une **enveloppe** FEM NOUN
envelope
• une enveloppe matelassée
padded envelope

envelopper VERB [1]
to wrap up

l'**envers** MASC NOUN ▶ SEE **envers** PREPOSITION
1 **wrong side** (of fabric, of knitting)
2 à l'envers upside down, inside out, back to front

envers PREPOSITION ▶ SEE **envers** NOUN
towards, to

♀ l'**envie** FEM NOUN
1 **urge**
avoir envie de faire quelque chose to

⬤ means the verb takes être to form the perfect

want to do something, to feel like doing
something
Tu as envie d'aller au cinéma? Do you feel
like going to the cinema?
2   avoir envie de quelque chose to feel like
something
J'ai envie d'une glace. I feel like an ice
cream.
3   envy
Tu me fais envie. You're making me
envious.

envier VERB [1]
to envy

envieux MASC ADJECTIVE, **envieuse** FEM
envious

℘ **environ** ADVERB
about
environ trente personnes about thirty
people

l'**environnement** MASC NOUN
environment

les **environs** PLURAL MASC NOUN
surroundings
J'habite aux environs de Londres. I live near
London.

envisager VERB [52]
envisager de faire quelque chose to plan to
do something
Qu'est-ce que vous envisagez de faire?
What are you planning to do?

un **envoi** MASC NOUN
1   dispatch
2   consignment

s'**envoler** REFLEXIVE VERB ◯ [1]
to fly away

℘ **envoyer** VERB [40]
to send
envoyer quelque chose à quelqu'un to send
somebody something
Elle m'a envoyé une carte. She sent me a
card.
Elle m'a envoyé chercher les verres. She
sent me to get the glasses.

℘ **épais** MASC ADJECTIVE, **épaisse** FEM
thick
une tranche épaisse a thick slice

l'**épaisseur** FEM NOUN
thickness

l'**épargne** FEM NOUN
savings
un compte d'épargne a savings account

épatant MASC ADJECTIVE, **épatante** FEM
(informal) great
C'était vraiment épatant! It was really

great!

℘ une **épaule** FEM NOUN
shoulder

une **épaulette** FEM NOUN
1   shoulder strap
2   shoulder pad

une **épave** FEM NOUN
wreck

une **épée** FEM NOUN
sword

épeler VERB [18]
to spell

un **épi** MASC NOUN
ear (of corn)
● un épi de maïs
corn cob

une **épice** FEM NOUN
spice

épicé MASC ADJECTIVE, **épicée** FEM
spicy, hot

une **épicerie** FEM NOUN
grocer's (shop)

℘ un **épicier** MASC NOUN, une **épicière** FEM
grocer

une **épidémie** FEM NOUN
epidemic

l'**épilepsie** FEM NOUN
epilepsy

épiler VERB [1]
une pince à épiler tweezers
s'**épiler** REFLEXIVE VERB ◯
s'épiler les sourcils to pluck your eyebrows
s'épiler les jambes to shave your legs (or use
wax or cream to remove hair)

les **épinards** PLURAL MASC NOUN
spinach

une **épine** FEM NOUN
thorn

épineux MASC ADJECTIVE, **épineuse** FEM
prickly

une **épingle** FEM NOUN
pin
● une épingle de sûreté
safety pin

épingler VERB [1]
to pin

éplucher VERB [1]
to peel

une **éponge** FEM NOUN
1   sponge
2   towelling

éponger VERB [52]
1 to mop up
2 to sponge

une **époque** FEM NOUN
time
à cette époque-là at that time

♀ une **épouse** FEM NOUN
wife

épouser VERB [1]
to marry

épouvantable MASC & FEM ADJECTIVE
dreadful

un **épouvantail** MASC NOUN
scarecrow

l'**épouvante** FEM NOUN
terror
un film d'épouvante a horror film

épouvanter VERB [1]
to terrify

♀ un **époux** MASC NOUN
husband

une **épreuve** FEM NOUN
1 test
2 exam
l'épreuve de français the French exam
3 event (in athletics)
4 ordeal

éprouver VERB [1]
to feel, to experience

une **éprouvette** FEM NOUN
test tube

l'**EPS** FEM NOUN
(= Éducation physique et sportive) PE

épuisant MASC ADJECTIVE, **épuisante** FEM
exhausting

épuisé MASC ADJECTIVE, **épuisée** FEM
1 exhausted, worn out
Je suis épuisé. I'm worn out.
2 out of stock

épuiser VERB [1]
to wear out

l'**équateur** MASC NOUN
equator

équestre MASC & FEM ADJECTIVE
un centre équestre a riding school

l'**équilibre** MASC NOUN
balance
perdre l'équilibre to lose your balance

équilibré MASC ADJECTIVE, **équilibrée** FEM
balanced
une alimentation équilibrée a balanced diet

un **équipage** MASC NOUN
crew

♀ une **équipe** FEM NOUN
team
Je voudrais faire partie de l'équipe. I'd like
to join the team.

équipé MASC ADJECTIVE, **équipée** FEM
1 equipped
Il est bien équipé pour le voyage. He's well
equipped for the journey.
mal équipé ill equipped
2 une cuisine équipée a fitted kitchen

un **équipement** MASC NOUN
equipment

les **équipements** PLURAL MASC NOUN
facilities
• les équipements sportifs
sports facilities

♀ l'**équitation** FEM NOUN
(horse-)riding
faire de l'équitation to go horse-riding

équivalent MASC ADJECTIVE, **équivalente** FEM
equivalent

un **érable** MASC NOUN
maple tree
le sirop d'érable maple syrup

errer VERB [1]
to wander, to roam

une **erreur** FEM NOUN
mistake
par erreur by mistake

es VERB ▸ SEE **être**

un **escabeau** MASC NOUN
stepladder

l'**escalade** FEM NOUN
rock-climbing

♀ un **escalier** MASC NOUN
1 stairs
dans l'escalier on the stairs
2 staircase
• un escalier de secours
emergency staircase
• un escalier mécanique
escalator
• un escalier roulant
escalator

♀ un **escargot** MASC NOUN
snail

l'**esclavage** MASC NOUN
slavery

un & une **esclave** MASC & FEM NOUN
slave

● means the verb takes être to form the perfect

l'**escrime** *FEM NOUN*
fencing
faire de l'escrime to do fencing

un **escroc** *MASC NOUN*
crook, swindler

escroquer *VERB* [1]
to swindle

l'**escroquerie** *FEM NOUN*
swindle

un **espace** *MASC NOUN*
1 space
2 (outer) space
• un espace de loisirs
leisure complex
• les espaces verts
open spaces (in cities)

espacer *VERB* [61]
to space out

un **espadon** *MASC NOUN*
swordfish

l'**Espagne** *FEM NOUN*
Spain

espagnol *MASC ADJECTIVE*, **espagnole** *FEM* ▶ SEE
Espagnol
Spanish

un **Espagnol** *MASC NOUN*, une **Espagnole** *FEM*
▶ SEE **espagnol**
1 Spaniard (person)
les Espagnols the Spanish
2 l'espagnol Spanish (the language)

une **espèce** *FEM NOUN*
1 sort
une espèce de sauce épicée a sort of spicy sauce
2 species
une espèce très rare a very rare species
3 en espèces in cash
4 (showing annoyance) Espèce d'idiot! You idiot!

ℙ **espérer** *VERB* [24]
to hope
J'espère que tu vas mieux. I hope you're feeling better.
espérer faire quelque chose to hope to do something
Ils espèrent pouvoir venir. They're hoping to be able to come.
J'espère qu'elle n'a pas oublié. I hope she hasn't forgotten.
J'espère bien! I certainly hope so!
J'espère que non! I hope not!

espiègle *MASC & FEM ADJECTIVE*
mischievous

un **espion** *MASC NOUN*, une **espionne** *FEM NOUN*
spy

l'**espionnage** *MASC NOUN*
spying, espionage

espionner *VERB* [1]
to spy on

un **espoir** *MASC NOUN*
hope

l'**esprit** *MASC NOUN*
1 mind
Ça ne m'est pas venu à l'esprit. It didn't cross my mind.
2 wit
avoir de l'esprit to be witty
• l'esprit d'équipe
team spirit

un **Esquimau** *MASC NOUN*, les **Esquimaux** *PL*
Eskimo, Inuit

un **esquimau**® *MASC NOUN*, les **esquimaux** *PL*
ice lolly

une **esquisse** *FEM NOUN*
sketch (in drawing)

esquisser *VERB* [1]
to sketch

un **essai** *MASC NOUN*
1 trial (of a new model of car, plane)
2 test (in a laboratory)
3 attempt

un **essaim** *MASC NOUN*
swarm

ℙ **essayer** *VERB* [59]
1 to try
Tiens, est-ce que tu veux essayer? Here, do you want to try?
essayer de faire quelque chose to try to do something
J'ai essayé de t'appeler. I tried to phone you.
Essaie de la convaincre. Try to persuade her.
2 to try on
essayer une robe to try on a dress
3 to test

ℙ l'**essence** *FEM NOUN*
1 petrol
2 essential oil
• l'essence sans plomb
unleaded petrol

essentiel *MASC ADJECTIVE*, **essentielle** *FEM* ▶ SEE
essentiel *NOUN*
essential

l'**essentiel** *MASC NOUN* ▶ SEE **essentiel** *ADJECTIVE*
main thing
L'essentiel, c'est de participer. The main

thing is to take part.

essentiellement *ADVERB*
1 mainly
2 essentially

l'**essorage** *MASC NOUN*
spin-dry

essorer *VERB* [1]
to spin-dry

une **essoreuse** *FEM NOUN*
spin-drier

essoufflé *MASC ADJECTIVE*, **essoufflée** *FEM*
out of breath

un **essuie-glace** *MASC NOUN*
windscreen wiper

un **essuie-tout** *MASC NOUN*
(paper) kitchen towel

⚑ **essuyer** *VERB* [41]
to wipe
essuyer le plancher to wipe the floor
J'ai essuyé la vaisselle. I did the drying-up.

s'**essuyer** *REFLEXIVE VERB* ●
s'essuyer les mains to dry your hands

est *ADJECTIVE* ▶ SEE **est** *NOUN, VERB*
1 east
2 eastern

⚑ l'**est** *MASC NOUN* ▶ SEE **est** *ADJECTIVE, VERB*
east
l'est de Paris the east of Paris
dans l'est de la France in the east of France
l'Europe de l'Est Eastern Europe

⚑ **est** *VERB* ▶ SEE **est** *ADJECTIVE, NOUN* ▶ SEE **être** *NOUN*

⚑ **est-ce que** *PHRASE*
Est-ce qu'il pleut? Is it raining?
Est-ce que Julie est partie? Has Julie left?
Où est-ce qu'il habite? Where does he live?

une **esthéticienne** *FEM NOUN*
beautician

l'**estime** *FEM NOUN*
respect

estimer *VERB* [1]
1 to think
J'estime qu'ils ont raison. I think that
they're right.
2 to think highly of (a person)
3 to value
faire estimer un tableau to have a painting
valued

estival *MASC ADJECTIVE*, **estivale** *FEM*, **estivaux**
MASC PL, **estivales** *FEM PL*
summer

un **estivant** *MASC NOUN*, une **estivante** *FEM*
summer visitor

⚑ l'**estomac** *MASC NOUN*
stomach
avoir mal à l'estomac to have stomachache

l'**Estonie** *FEM NOUN*
Estonia

une **estrade** *FEM NOUN*
platform

l'**estragon** *MASC NOUN*
tarragon (the herb)

et *CONJUNCTION*
and

établir *VERB* [2]
1 to establish
2 to draw up (a plan, a document)
s'**établir** *REFLEXIVE VERB* ●
to settle
Ils se sont établis en France. They settled
in France.

un **établissement** *MASC NOUN*
1 institution
2 organization

⚑ un **étage** *MASC NOUN*
floor
au premier étage on the first floor
au dernier étage on the top floor
à l'étage upstairs

une **étagère** *FEM NOUN*
1 shelf
2 set of shelves

l'**étain** *MASC NOUN*
1 tin
2 pewter

étais, **était**, **étaient** *VERB* ▶ SEE **être**

étaler *VERB* [1]
1 to spread
2 to spread out
3 to roll out (pastry)

étanche *MASC & FEM ADJECTIVE*
1 watertight
2 waterproof

un **étang** *MASC NOUN*
pond

⚑ une **étape** *FEM NOUN*
1 stage
la dernière étape de la course the last stage
of the race
2 stopping place
faire étape to stop off
On a fait étape à Rouen. We stopped off in
Rouen.

⚑ l'**état** *MASC NOUN* ▶ SEE **état** *NOUN*
1 state (of an object)
en mauvais état in a bad state

● means the verb takes être to form the perfect

en bon état in good condition
en état de marche in working order
2 state *(of a person)*
être dans tous ses états to be in a state
être en état de faire quelque chose to be in
a fit state to do something
Elle n'est pas en état de passer l'examen.
She's not in a fit state to take the exam.

ℓ un **état** *MASC NOUN* ▸ SEE **état** *NOUN*
state, State

les **États-Unis** *PLURAL MASC NOUN*
les États-Unis the United States
aux États-Unis in the United States, to the
United States

WORD TIP Countries and regions in French take
le, la or les.

l'**été** *MASC NOUN* ▸ SEE **été** *VERB*
summer
en été in summer
l'été dernier last summer
l'été prochain next summer
été *VERB* ▸ SEE **été** *NOUN* ▸ SEE **être** *VERB*

éteindre *VERB* [60]
1 to turn off, to switch off *(the lights, the TV)*
2 to put out *(a fire, a cigarette)*
s'**éteindre** *REFLEXIVE VERB* ◎
to go out

éteint *MASC ADJECTIVE*, **éteinte** *FEM*
extinct *(volcano)*

étendre *VERB* [3]
1 to stretch out *(your arms or legs)*
Étendez les bras. Stretch out your arms.
2 to spread out
J'ai étendu ma serviette. I spread my towel
out.
3 étendre le linge to hang out the washing
s'**étendre** *REFLEXIVE VERB* ◎
1 s'étendre sur le canapé to stretch out on
the sofa
2 to stretch
3 to spread, to expand

éternel *MASC ADJECTIVE*, **éternelle** *FEM*
eternal

l'**éternité** *FEM NOUN*
eternity

un **éternuement** *MASC NOUN*
sneeze

éternuer *VERB* [1]
to sneeze

êtes *VERB* ▸ SEE **être**

une **ethnie** *FEM NOUN*
ethnic group

ethnique *MASC & FEM ADJECTIVE*
ethnic

étinceler *VERB* [18]
to sparkle, to twinkle

une **étincelle** *FEM NOUN*
spark

étions, **étiez** *VERB* ▸ SEE **être**

une **étiquette** *FEM NOUN*
1 label
2 l'étiquette etiquette

étirer *VERB* [1]
to stretch

une **étoffe** *FEM NOUN*
fabric

ℓ une **étoile** *FEM NOUN*
star
un hôtel trois étoiles a three-star hotel
dormir à la belle étoile to sleep out in the
open
• une étoile filante
shooting star

étoilé *MASC ADJECTIVE*, **étoilée** *FEM*
starry

ℓ **étonnant** *MASC ADJECTIVE*, **étonnante** *FEM*
1 surprising
2 astonishing

l'**étonnement** *MASC NOUN*
1 surprise
2 astonishment

étonner *VERB* [1]
to surprise
étonner Ça ne m'étonne pas du tout. That
doesn't surprise me at all.
s'**étonner** *REFLEXIVE VERB* ◎
to be surprised

étouffant *MASC ADJECTIVE*, **étouffante** *FEM*
stifling

étouffer *VERB* [1]
1 to stifle
2 to suffocate
s'**étouffer** *REFLEXIVE VERB* ◎
to choke
s'étouffer de rire to be choking with
laughter

l'**étourderie** *FEM NOUN*
1 absent-mindedness
2 une étourderie a careless mistake

étourdi *MASC ADJECTIVE*, **étourdie** *FEM* ▸ SEE
étourdi *NOUN*
scatterbrained, absent-minded
un **étourdi** *MASC NOUN*, une **étourdie** *FEM* ▸ SEE
étourdi *ADJECTIVE*
scatterbrain

étourdir VERB [2]
to daze, to stun

un **étourneau** MASC NOUN
starling

étrange MASC & FEM ADJECTIVE
strange

♂ **étranger** MASC ADJECTIVE, **étrangère** FEM ▶ SEE
étranger NOUNS
foreign
un pays étranger a foreign country
les mœurs étrangères foreign customs

un **étranger** MASC NOUN, une **étrangère** FEM
▶ SEE **étranger** ADJECTIVE, NOUN
1 foreigner
2 stranger

♂ l'**étranger** MASC NOUN ▶ SEE **étranger** ADJECTIVE,
NOUN
à l'étranger abroad
aller à l'étranger to go abroad

étrangler VERB [1]
1 to strangle
2 to choke

♂ un **être** MASC NOUN ▶ SEE **être** VERB
being
• un être humain
human being

♂ **être** VERB [6]
▶ SEE **être** NOUN
1 to be
Je suis le frère de Jean. I'm Jean's brother.
Nous sommes dans la cuisine. We're in the
kitchen.
Elle est malade. She's ill.
Le jardin n'est pas grand. The garden isn't
big.
Qui est-ce? Who is it?
Où sont-ils? Where are they?
C'est moi. It's me.
2 to be (talking about what you do for a
living)
être professeur to be a teacher
Elle est infirmière. She's a nurse.
3 être à quelqu'un to belong to somebody,
to be somebody's
Ce livre est à Paul. This book is Paul's.
Ce livre est à moi. This book is mine.
Le stylo n'est pas à elle. The pen isn't hers.
4 to be (telling the time)
Il est 6 heures. It's 6 o'clock.
Il était tard. It was late.
Il n'est même pas midi. It's not even
midday.
5 to be (talking about the date)
Nous sommes le 7 mars. It's the 7th of

March (today).
Quelle date sommes-nous? What's the
date today?
6 (used with some verbs to form past tenses:
for a list of these, see the centre pages)
Je suis allé à Paris. I went to Paris.
Elle est tombée dans l'escalier. She fell
down the stairs.
Nous sommes rentrés à 7 heures. We got
home at 7 o'clock.
7 (used to form the passive)
Ses robes sont faites par sa mère. Her
dresses are made by her mother.
8 ▶ SEE **est-ce que**

étroit MASC ADJECTIVE, **étroite** FEM
1 narrow
une veste aux manches étroites a jacket
with narrow sleeves
2 close

étroitement ADVERB
closely

l'**étude** FEM NOUN
1 study
L'étude a été réalisée par notre classe. Our
class carried out the study.
2 les études studies
les études universitaires university studies
faire des études to be a student
faire des études de médecine to study
medicine
3 study period
J'ai une heure d'étude. I've got an hour's
study period.

un **étudiant** MASC NOUN, une **étudiante** FEM
student (at university)

♂ **étudier** VERB [1]
to study

un **étui** MASC NOUN
case (for spectacles, small items)

eu VERB ▶ SEE **avoir**

un **euro** MASC NOUN
euro
L'euro est divisé en cents. The euro is
divided into cents.

l'**Europe** FEM NOUN
Europe
en Europe in Europe, to Europe
les pays de l'Europe the countries of Europe

WORD TIP Countries and regions in French take
le, la or les.

⬤ means the verb takes être to form the perfect

européen *MASC*, **européenne** *FEM*
European

> **WORD TIP** Adjectives never have capitals in French, even for nationality or regional origin.

l'**euthanasie** *FEM NOUN*
euthanasia

eux *PRONOUN*
1 *(for males after prepositions like avec or sans and in comparisons)* **them**
Je suis parti sans eux. I left without them.
Tu es plus grand qu'eux. You're taller than them.
2 à eux theirs *(belonging to them)*
Jean et Paul sont des amis à eux. Jean and Paul are friends of theirs.
La voiture n'est pas à eux. The car isn't theirs.
3 *(for emphasis)* **they**
Eux, ils sont parfaitement contents. They are perfectly happy.
Ce sont eux qui me l'ont dit. They're the ones who told me.
4 chez eux at their house

eux-mêmes *PRONOUN*
(for males and male objects) **themselves**

évacuer *VERB* [1]
to evacuate

s'**évader** *REFLEXIVE VERB* ☁ [1]
to escape

évaluer *VERB* [1]
to assess

s'**évanouir** *REFLEXIVE VERB* ☁ [2]
to faint
Je me suis évanoui. I fainted.

s'**évaporer** *REFLEXIVE VERB* ☁ [1]
to evaporate

l'**évasion** *FEM NOUN*
escape
une tentative d'évasion an attempt to escape

éveillé *MASC ADJECTIVE*, **éveillée** *FEM*
1 **awake**
rester éveillé to stay awake
2 **alert**

éveiller *VERB* [1]
1 **to arouse** *(somebody's curiosity, suspicion)*
2 **to awaken** *(somebody's interest)*

ℱ un **événement** *MASC NOUN*
event
C'est l'événement de l'année. It's the big event of the year.

un **éventail** *MASC NOUN*
fan *(for staying cool)*

une **éventualité** *FEM NOUN*
possibility

éventuel *MASC ADJECTIVE*, **éventuelle** *FEM*
possible

éventuellement *ADVERB*
1 **possibly**
David vient et Manon aussi éventuellement. David's coming and possibly Manon too.
2 **if necessary**
Éventuellement, on contacte les parents. If necessary, we contact the parents.

> **WORD TIP** éventuellement does not mean eventually in English; for the meaning of eventually ▶ SEE **finalement**.

un **évêque** *MASC NOUN*
bishop

évidemment *ADVERB*
of course
Elle est arrivée en retard, évidemment. She arrived late, of course.
'Tu vois, je suis au courant.' – 'Évidemment!' 'You see, I know all about it.' – 'So I see!'

l'**évidence** *FEM NOUN*
1 être en évidence to be clearly visible
Ne laisse pas tes affaires en évidence comme ça. Don't leave your things around like that for people to see.
2 de toute évidence clearly
De toute évidence il a oublié de venir. He's clearly forgotten to come.

évident *MASC ADJECTIVE*, **évidente** *FEM*
obvious
C'est évident. It's obvious.
Ce n'est pas évident. *(informal)* It's not that easy.

ℱ un **évier** *MASC NOUN*
sink

éviter *VERB* [1]
1 **to avoid**
Il m'évite, j'en suis sûr. He's avoiding me, I'm sure of it.
éviter de faire quelque chose to avoid doing something
J'évite de manger tard le soir. I avoid eating late at night.
2 éviter à quelqu'un de faire quelque chose to save somebody having to do something
Ça t'évitera de sortir. That'll save you having to go out.

évolué *MASC ADJECTIVE*, **évoluée** *FEM*
advanced

évoluer *VERB* [1]
1 **to develop**

Nous ne savons pas comment la situation va évoluer. We do not know how the situation will develop.
2 to progress
L'informatique évolue très rapidement. Computer science progresses very rapidly.
3 to change
Les choses ont évolué depuis. Things have changed since.

l'évolution *FEM NOUN*
1 development
2 progress
3 evolution

exact *MASC ADJECTIVE*, **exacte** *FEM*
1 correct
C'est exact. That's absolutely right.
2 exact, precise
le chiffre exact the exact figure

exactement *ADVERB*
exactly

exagéré *MASC ADJECTIVE*, **exagérée** *FEM*
1 exaggerated
2 excessive

exagérer *VERB* [24]
1 to exaggerate
2 to go too far
Là, tu exagères! You're going too far now!

ℒ un **examen** *MASC NOUN*
exam
passer un examen to sit an exam
réussir à un examen to pass an exam
échouer à un examen to fail an exam
• un examen blanc
mock exam
• un examen final
final exam
• un examen médical
medical examination

un **examinateur** *MASC NOUN*, une **examinatrice** *FEM*
examiner

examiner *VERB* [1]
to examine

exaspérant *MASC ADJECTIVE*, **exaspérante** *FEM*
exasperating

exaspérer *VERB* [24]
to exasperate

l'excellence *FEM NOUN*
excellence

ℒ **excellent** *MASC ADJECTIVE*, **excellente** *FEM*
excellent

un & une **excentrique** *MASC & FEM NOUN*
eccentric

excepté *PREPOSITION*
except

une **exception** *FEM NOUN*
1 exception
faire une exception to make an exception
2 à l'exception de except for
tout le monde, à l'exception des parents
everybody, except for the parents

exceptionnel *MASC ADJECTIVE*, **exceptionnelle** *FEM*
1 exceptional
2 special

exceptionnellement *ADVERB*
exceptionally

l'excès *MASC NOUN*
excess
• l'excès de vitesse
speeding

excessif *MASC ADJECTIVE*, **excessive** *FEM*
excessive

excessivement *ADVERB*
excessively
Il est excessivement timide. He's incredibly shy.

excitant *MASC ADJECTIVE*, **excitante** *FEM* ▸ SEE **excitant** *NOUN*
exciting

un **excitant** *MASC NOUN* ▸ SEE **excitant** *ADJECTIVE*
stimulant

l'excitation *FEM NOUN*
excitement

excité *MASC ADJECTIVE*, **excitée** *FEM*
1 frenzied
2 over-excited
3 thrilled

s'**exciter** *REFLEXIVE VERB* ⊘ [1]
1 to get excited
2 to get wound up

une **exclamation** *FEM NOUN*
exclamation

s'**exclamer** *REFLEXIVE VERB* ⊘ [1]
to exclaim

exclu *MASC ADJECTIVE*, **exclue** *FEM*
excluded
se sentir exclu to feel left out
Elle se sent exclue. She feels left out.

exclusif *MASC ADJECTIVE*, **exclusive** *FEM*
exclusive

ℒ une **excursion** *FEM NOUN*
excursion, trip
faire une excursion to go on an outing
une excursion scolaire a school trip

⊘ means the verb takes être to form the perfect

une **excuse** *FEM NOUN*
1 des excuses an apology
Je vous dois des excuses. I owe you an apology.
2 excuse
Ce n'est pas une excuse. That's no excuse.

ℓ **excuser** *VERB* [1]
to forgive
Excusez-moi! Sorry!
Excusez-moi de vous déranger. Sorry to disturb you.

s'**excuser** *REFLEXIVE VERB* ○
to apologize
Je m'excuse. I'm sorry.
Je m'excuse d'être en retard. Sorry I'm late.

exécuter *VERB* [1]
1 to execute
2 to carry out (a task, work)

un **exemplaire** *MASC NOUN*
copy

ℓ un **exemple** *MASC NOUN*
example
par exemple for example
donner l'exemple to set an example
J'ai suivi l'exemple de Julien. I followed Julien's example.

exercer *VERB* [61]
1 to exercise (a right)
2 to practise (an art, a profession)
3 to exert (authority, pressure)

s'**exercer** *REFLEXIVE VERB* ○
1 to practise (as a musician)
2 to train (as an athlete)

l'**exercice** *MASC NOUN*
exercise
faire de l'exercice to get some exercise

exhiber *VERB* [1]
1 to show off (possessions, wealth etc)
2 to display

un **exhibitionniste** *MASC NOUN*
flasher

exigeant *MASC ADJECTIVE*, **exigeante** *FEM*
demanding

exiger *VERB* [52]
1 to demand
2 to require

l'**exil** *MASC NOUN*
exile (far from home)

un **exilé** *MASC NOUN*, une **exilée** *FEM*
exile (a person)

l'**existence** *FEM NOUN*
existence

exister *VERB* [1]
to exist

exotique *MASC & FEM ADJECTIVE*
exotic

l'**expansion** *FEM NOUN*
1 expansion
2 growth

expédier *VERB* [1]
to send (off)

un **expéditeur** *MASC NOUN*, une **expéditrice** *FEM*
sender

une **expédition** *FEM NOUN*
expedition

une **expérience** *FEM NOUN*
1 experience
avoir de l'expérience to be experienced
2 experiment
faire une expérience to carry out an experiment

expérimenté *MASC ADJECTIVE*, **expérimentée** *FEM*
experienced

expérimenter *VERB* [1]
1 to test out (a method, a product)
2 to experiment

un **expert** *MASC NOUN*
expert

> **WORD TIP** A female expert is also un expert.

ℓ une **explication** *FEM NOUN*
explanation
demander des explications to ask for an explanation

explicite *MASC & FEM ADJECTIVE*
explicit

ℓ **expliquer** *VERB* [1]
to explain
Explique-moi comment faire. Explain to me how it's done.
J'ai du mal à expliquer. I find it hard to explain.
expliquer quelque chose à quelqu'un to explain something to somebody
Elle ne m'a rien expliqué. She didn't explain anything to me.

un **exploit** *MASC NOUN*
1 achievement
2 feat

exploiter *VERB* [1]
1 to exploit (a person)
2 to use, to make use of (resources, talents)

137

explorer VERB [1]
   to explore

exploser VERB [1]
   to explode, to blow up
   faire exploser un bâtiment to blow up a
   building

explosif MASC ADJECTIVE, **explosive** FEM
   explosive

une **explosion** FEM NOUN
1 explosion
2 boom

un **export** MASC NOUN
   export

un **exportateur** MASC NOUN, une
   exportatrice FEM
   exporter

l'**exportation** FEM NOUN
   export

exporter VERB [1]
   to export

exposé MASC ADJECTIVE, **exposée** FEM ▸ SEE
   exposé NOUN
1 exposed
2 on display

un **exposé** MASC NOUN ▸ SEE **exposé** ADJECTIVE
   talk, presentation

exposer VERB [1]
1 to exhibit
2 to expose
3 to explain

une **exposition** FEM NOUN
   exhibition

exprès ADJECTIVE ▸ SEE **exprès** ADVERB
   special delivery
   envoyer un paquet en exprès to send a
   package special delivery

exprès ADVERB ▸ SEE **exprès** ADJECTIVE
1 deliberately
   faire quelque chose exprès to do
   something deliberately
   Tu l'as fait exprès. You did it on purpose.
   Je ne l'ai pas fait exprès. I didn't mean to
   do it.
2 specially
   Je suis venu exprès pour te voir. I've come
   specially to see you.

un **express** MASC NOUN
1 fast train
2 espresso coffee

une **expression** FEM NOUN
   expression

exprimer VERB [1]
   to express

s'**exprimer** REFLEXIVE VERB ◉
   to express yourself
   Je m'exprime mal. I'm expressing myself
   badly.

expulser VERB [1]
1 to evict
2 to expel

exquis MASC ADJECTIVE, **exquise** FEM
   exquisite, delightful

l'**extase** FEM NOUN
   ecstasy

extensif MASC ADJECTIVE, **extensive** FEM
   extensive

une **extension** FEM NOUN
   extension

extérieur MASC ADJECTIVE, **extérieure** FEM ▸ SEE
   extérieur NOUN
1 outside
2 outer

l'**extérieur** MASC NOUN ▸ SEE **extérieur** ADJECTIVE
1 outside
   à l'extérieur outside
2 exterior

un **externat** MASC NOUN
   day school

un & une **externe** MASC & FEM NOUN
   day pupil

un **extincteur** MASC NOUN
   fire extinguisher

l'**extinction** FEM NOUN
   extinction
   en voie d'extinction in danger of extinction

extra ADJECTIVE
   (informal) **great, fantastic**

l'**extraction** FEM NOUN
1 extraction
2 mining

extraire VERB [78]
1 to extract
2 to mine

un **extrait** MASC NOUN
   extract

♂ **extraordinaire** MASC & FEM ADJECTIVE
   extraordinary, amazing

un & une **extra-terrestre** MASC & FEM NOUN
   alien, extra-terrestrial

extravagant MASC ADJECTIVE, **extravagante**
   FEM
1 eccentric
2 extravagant

◉ means the verb takes être to form the perfect

un **extrême** *MASC NOUN*
extreme

extrêmement *ADVERB*
extremely

l'**Extrême-Orient** *MASC NOUN*
l'Extrême-Orient the Far East

une **extrémité** *FEM NOUN*
1 **end** *(of a line, a road)*
2 **tip** *(of your finger, a stick)*
3 **edge** *(of a town or an area in general)*

Ff

F *ABBREVIATION*
(= *franc*) franc *(the currency of Switzerland)*

le **fabricant** *MASC NOUN*
manufacturer

la **fabrication** *FEM NOUN*
manufacture
une voiture de fabrication française a car
made in France

fabriquer *VERB* [1]
1 **to make**
des meubles fabriqués en France furniture
made in France
André fabrique une boîte en bois. André is
making a wooden box.
2 *(informal)* **to do**
Qu'est-ce que tu fabriques? What are you
doing?

fabuleux *MASC ADJECTIVE*, **fabuleuse** *FEM*
1 **fabulous**
une fortune fabuleuse a fabulous fortune
2 **mythical**
La licorne est un animal fabuleux. The
unicorn is a mythical animal.

la **fac** *FEM NOUN*
(informal) **uni**, **university**
Rémy ira en fac l'année prochaine. Rémy
will go to university next year.
Audrey est en fac d'anglais. Audrey is doing
a degree in English.

ℱ la **face** *FEM NOUN*
1 **face**
face à face face to face
Il est tombé face contre terre. He fell flat
on his face.
2 **side**
la face d'un disque the side of a record
Examinons la question sous toutes ses
faces. Let's examine the issue from all
angles.
3 **en face** opposite

en face de l'école opposite the school
la maison d'en face the house opposite
le magasin en face de chez nous the shop
opposite our house
Quentin est assis en face d'Elsa. Quentin is
sitting opposite Elsa.
4 **face à** facing
face à la mer facing the sea
Mon bureau est face à la porte. My desk is
facing the door.
Face aux nombreuses difficultés, il
abandonne son projet. Faced with many
difficulties, he's giving up his project.
5 *(when you toss a coin)* Pile ou face? Heads
or tails?

ℱ **fâché** *MASC ADJECTIVE*, **fâchée** *FEM*
angry, **upset**
Est-ce que tu es fâché? Are you angry? *(to
a boy)*
Est-ce que tu es fâchée? Are you angry? *(to
a girl)*
Elle est fâchée contre moi. She's angry
with me.

se **fâcher** *REFLEXIVE VERB* ☉ [1]
1 **to get angry**
Ne te fâche pas, je vais le recoller! Don't
get angry, I'll glue it back on.
se fâcher contre quelqu'un to get angry
with somebody
Elle s'est fâchée contre moi. She got angry
with me.
2 se fâcher avec quelqu'un to fall out with
somebody
Olivier s'est fâché avec Pierre. Olivier has
fallen out with Pierre.

ℱ **facile** *ADJECTIVE*
1 **easy**
C'est facile. It's easy.
C'est facile à comprendre. It's easy to
understand.
2 **easy-going**
Amandine a un caractère facile. Amandine
is easy-going.

facilement *ADVERB*
easily

la **facilité** *FEM NOUN*
easiness

faciliter *VERB* [1]
to make things easier
Ton aide va nous faciliter les choses. Your
help will make things easier for us.

la **façon** *FEM NOUN*
1 **way**
d'une façon extraordinaire in an
extraordinary way
Il y a plusieurs façons de le faire. There are
several ways of doing it.

De quelle façon est-il tombé? How did he
fall?
En voilà une façon d'étudier! What a way
to study!
Je n'aime pas la façon dont il me parle. I
don't like the way he speaks to me.
2 de toute façon anyway
De toute façon, ce n'est pas mon
problème. Anyway, it isn't my problem.
3 des façons manners, behaviour
Je n'aime pas ses façons. I don't like his
manners.
En voilà des façons! That's no way to
behave!
faire des façons to stand on ceremony
Ne fais pas tant de façons! Don't stand on
ceremony!
Non merci, sans façons! No thank you,
really!

façonner VERB [1]
1 to make
Il façonne des objets en bois. He makes
things in wood.
2 to shape (clay, stone)

♀ le **facteur** MASC NOUN, la **factrice** FEM
1 postman
Est-ce que le facteur est passé? Has the
postman been?
2 postwoman

la **facture** FEM NOUN
bill
la facture d'électricité the electricity bill

facultatif MASC ADJECTIVE, **facultative** FEM
optional

la **faculté** FEM NOUN
faculty

la **fade** MASC & FEM ADJECTIVE
bland
La sauce est un peu fade. The sauce is a bit
bland.

♀ **faible** MASC & FEM ADJECTIVE ▸ SEE **faible** NOUN
weak, faint
une voix faible a faint voice
une classe très faible a very weak class
des résultats faibles en maths poor results
in maths
Élisa est faible en chimie. Élisa is weak in
chemistry.
Elle est encore très faible après son
opération. She's still very weak after her
operation.

un **faible** MASC NOUN ▸ SEE **faible** ADJECTIVE
avoir un faible pour quelqu'un to have a
soft spot for someone
Elle a un faible pour le prof d'anglais. She
has a soft spot for the English teacher.

avoir un faible pour quelque chose to have
a weakness for something
J'ai un faible pour le chocolat. I have a
weakness for chocolate.

la **faiblesse** FEM NOUN
weakness

faiblir VERB [2]
to weaken

la **faïence** FEM NOUN
earthenware
une tasse en faïence an earthenware cup

faillir VERB [42]
faillir faire (to say something nearly
happened)
J'ai failli tomber. I nearly fell.
Elle a failli gagner. She nearly won.
Il a failli rater le train. He nearly missed the
train.

la **faillite** FEM NOUN
bankruptcy
faire faillite to go bankrupt
La société Dupont a fait faillite. The Dupont
company went bankrupt.

♀ la **faim** FEM NOUN
hunger
Je meurs de faim! I'm dying of hunger.
Ces gâteaux me donnent faim. Those cakes
make me feel hungry.
avoir faim to be hungry
Les enfants ont très faim. The children are
very hungry.
Elle n'a plus faim. She's had enough to eat.

fainéant MASC ADJECTIVE, **fainéante** FEM
lazy

♀ **faire** VERB [10]
1 to make
faire un gâteau to make a cake
faire du bruit to make a noise
faire une erreur to make a mistake
faire son lit to make your bed
Faites comme chez vous! Make yourselves
at home!
2 to do
Il fait ses devoirs. He's doing his
homework.
Qu'est-ce que tu fais? What are you
doing?
Fais comme tu veux! Do as you like!
Je fais de mon mieux. I'm doing my best.
faire du français to do French
Ils font du français. They do French.
3 to play (sports, music, an instrument)
Camille fait du piano. Camille plays the
piano.

⬤ means the verb takes être to form the perfect

Sophie et Inès font de la clarinette.
Sophie and Inès play the clarinet.
Oscar fait du football. Oscar plays
football.

4 to dial, to press
Appelez le numéro suivant et puis faire
le 2. Call the following number and then
press 2.

5 *(in sums, measurements)* 2 plus 2 font 4.
2 plus 2 make 4.
Ça fait 10 euros. That's 10 euros.
Elle fait 1,65 m. She's 1.65m tall.

6 *(talking about the weather)* Il fait beau. It's
a nice day.
Quel temps fait-il? What's the weather
like?
Il fait froid. It's cold.
Il fait chaud. It's hot.
Il fait beau en été ici. The weather's nice
here in summer.

7 *(saying how long something takes)* Ça fait
10 minutes. That's 10 minutes.
Ça fait une heure que j'attends. I've been
waiting for an hour.

8 *(talking about distances, journeys)* On a
fait 10 kilomètres à pied. We walked 10
kilometres.
Ils ont fait le Maroc à cheval. They
travelled around Morocco on horseback.
Cette année nous faisons les châteaux de la
Loire. This year we are visiting the châteaux
along the Loire.

9 *(to imitate)* faire le clown to act the clown
Mon chien fait le mort. My dog's
pretending to be dead.

10 to look
Ça fait joli. It looks pretty.
Il fait vieux. He looks old.

11 *(to cause)* L'accident a fait 10 morts. 10
people died in the accident.
Ça ne fait rien. It doesn't matter.

12 *(asking what's happened to something)*
Qu'as-tu fait de mes clés? What have you
done with my keys?

13 faire faire quelque chose to have
something done
Elle a fait réparer son vélo. She had her bike
repaired.
J'ai fait tondre le chien. I've had the dog
clipped.

14 faire + infinitive
Je fais bouillir de l'eau pour le café. I'm
boiling some water for the coffee.

Elle fait cuire des frites. She's cooking chips.

WORD TIP faire is used with many nouns to
say 'to do' an activity, e.g. faire du bricolage,
faire du camping, faire la cuisine. You can
work out the translation from the meaning of
the noun. These examples give: to do DIY, to go
camping, to cook.

---

se **faire** *REFLEXIVE VERB* ◎

1 to make
se faire des amis to make friends
se faire un thé to make yourself a cup of tea

2 to do
Ça ne se fait pas. You don't do that.

3 se faire faire quelque chose to have
something done
se faire couper les cheveux to have one's
hair cut
Il s'est fait faire des mèches. He's had
highlights done.
Anne s'est fait voler son sac. Anne had her
bag stolen.

4 se faire + infinitive to be + past participle
Luc se fait gronder. Luc is being scolded.
Le chat s'est fait écraser. The cat's been
run over.

5 s'en faire to worry
Ne t'en fais pas pour moi! Don't worry
about me!

6 se faire à quelque chose, quelqu'un to get
used to something, somebody
Claire se fait bien à son nouveau maître.
Claire is getting used to her new teacher.
Je ne m'y fais pas. I can't get used to it.

le **faire-part** *INVARIABLE MASC NOUN*
announcement *(of a birth, a wedding, etc)*

fais *VERB* ▸ SEE **faire**

le **faisan** *MASC NOUN*
pheasant

faisons *VERB* ▸ SEE **faire**

le **fait** *MASC NOUN* ▸ SEE **fait** *VERB*

1 fact
C'est un fait. It's a fact.
Le fait est que ça ne marche pas. The fact is
that it doesn't work.

2 en fait actually
En fait je l'ai vu hier. In fact I saw him
yesterday.

3 au fait by the way
Au fait, as-tu fermé la porte à clé? By the
way, did you lock the door?

4 event
des faits réels real-life events

5 point
Il est allé droit au fait. He went straight to
the point.

ℓ indicates key words

6 tout à fait absolutely
C'est tout à fait vrai. It's absolutely true.
- le **fait d'actualité**
news item
- le **fait divers**
small news item

fait *VERB* ▸ SEE **fait** *NOUN*
(*in expressions*) un travail bien fait a job
well done
un fromage bien fait a ripe cheese
un gâteau fait maison a home-made cake
C'est mal fait. It's badly designed.
'Il a été puni.' – 'C'est bien fait, je l'avais
prévenu.' 'He's been punished.' – 'Serves
him right, I warned him.'

faites *VERB* ▸ SEE **faire**

la **falaise** *FEM NOUN*
cliff

fallait *VERB* ▸ SEE **falloir**

falloir *IMPERSONAL VERB* [43]
1 (*to say something must be done*) Il faut le
faire. You must do it., It has to be done.
Il ne faut pas faire ça. You mustn't do that.
Il ne fallait pas faire ça. You shouldn't have
done that.
Il faudra partir à six heures. We'll have to
leave at six o'clock.
Il faudrait téléphoner à ta grand-mère. You
should phone your grandmother.
2 (*to say something is needed*) Il me faut un
stylo. I need a pen.
Il leur faut une voiture. They need a car.
Il nous faut 100 euros. We need 100 euros.
Il faut 100 grammes de beurre pour cette
recette. We need 100 grams of butter for
this recipe.
Qu'est-ce qu'il te faut? What do you need?
3 (*to say the time needed to do something*) Il
faut une heure pour aller de Tours à Blois.
It takes an hour to go from Tours to Blois.
Il nous a fallu deux ans pour finir la maison.
It took two years to finish the house.
4 il faut que... + subjunctive I, you, she, he,
etc, must, ought to ...
Il faut que tu viennes. You must come., You
have to come., You ought to come.
5 comme il faut properly
Il le fait comme il faut. He does it properly.
Marche comme il faut! Walk properly

WORD TIP falloir is only used with il.

famé *MASC ADJECTIVE*, **famée** *FEM*
un quartier mal famé a rough area

fameux *MASC ADJECTIVE*, **fameuse** *FEM*
1 excellent
Ton rôti était fameux. Your roast was
excellent.

2 famous
les fameuses grottes de Lascaux the
famous caves at Lascaux

familial *MASC ADJECTIVE*, **familiale** *FEM*,
familiaux *MASC PL*, **familiales** *FEM PL*
family
la vie familiale family life

se **familiariser** *REFLEXIVE VERB* ◯ [1]
se familiariser avec quelque chose to
become familiar with something
Je me suis familiarisé avec mon nouvel
ordinateur. I've become familiar with my
new computer.
Les filles se sont familiarisées avec leur
nouvelle école. The girls have got used to
their new school.

la **familiarité** *FEM NOUN*
familiarity

familier *MASC ADJECTIVE*, **familière** *FEM*
familiar
un endroit familier a familiar place

la **famille** *FEM NOUN*
1 family
la famille Leprêtre the Leprêtre family
un déjeuner en famille a family lunch
une famille nombreuse a large family
une famille monoparentale a single-parent
family
2 relatives
J'ai de la famille à Dijon. I have relatives in
Dijon.
Elle rentre dans sa famille tous les weekends. She goes home every weekend.

la **famine** *FEM NOUN*
famine

le & la **fana** *MASC & FEM NOUN*
(*informal*) fan

fanatique *MASC & FEM NOUN*
fanatic

fané *MASC ADJECTIVE*, **fanée** *FEM*
withered

la **fanfare** *FEM NOUN*
brass band

la **fantaisie** *FEM NOUN*
1 imagination
un enfant plein de fantaisie a child full of
original ideas
2 des bijoux fantaisie costume jewellery

fantastique *MASC & FEM ADJECTIVE*
fantastic

le **fantôme** *MASC NOUN*
ghost

◯ means the verb takes être to form the perfect

la **farce** *FEM NOUN*
1 **practical joke**
Elle a fait une farce à son oncle. She played a practical joke on her uncle.
2 **stuffing** *(for a chicken, a turkey)*

farci *MASC ADJECTIVE*, **farcie** *FEM*
stuffed *(in cooking)*
des tomates farcies stuffed tomatoes

farcir *VERB* [2]
to stuff *(a chicken, a turkey)*

le **fard à paupières** *MASC NOUN*
eye shadow

le **fardeau** *MASC NOUN*, les **fardeaux** *PLURAL*
burden

farfelu *MASC ADJECTIVE*, **farfelue** *FEM*
bizarre, weird
C'est un type farfelu. He's a bizarre bloke.
Elle a toujours des idées farfelues. She always has weird ideas.

la **farine** *FEM NOUN*
flour

fascinant *MASC ADJECTIVE*, **fascinante** *FEM*
fascinating
Son histoire était fascinante. His story was fascinating.

la **fascination** *FEM NOUN*
fascination

fasciner *VERB* [1]
to fascinate
Ça me fascine. I find that fascinating.

le **fascisme** *MASC NOUN*
fascism

le **fast-food** *MASC NOUN*
1 **fast food restaurant**
Antoine connaît tous les fast-foods du coin. Antoine knows all the local fast food restaurants.
2 **fast food**
Tatiana est une peu ronde car elle ne mange que du fast-food. Tatiana is a bit plump because she only eats fast food.

fastidieux *MASC ADJECTIVE*, **fastidieuse** *FEM*
tedious
un travail fastidieux tedious work

fatal *MASC ADJECTIVE*, **fatale** *FEM*
1 **inevitable**
Un accident était fatal. An accident was bound to happen.
2 **fatal**
des coups fatals fatal blows

la **fatalité** *FEM NOUN*
fate

fatigant *MASC ADJECTIVE*, **fatigante** *FEM*
1 **tiring**
un travail fatigant a tiring job
2 **tiresome**
Arrête, tu es fatigante! Stop it, you're so tiresome!
3 **boring**
Il est fatigant avec ses histoires. He's boring with his stories.

la **fatigue** *FEM NOUN*
tiredness

ℱ **fatigué** *MASC ADJECTIVE*, **fatiguée** *FEM*
tired
Je suis fatigué. I'm tired *(boy speaking)*.
Je suis fatiguée. I'm tired *(girl speaking)*.
Tu as l'air fatigué. You look tired.

fatiguer *VERB* [1]
1 **to tire (somebody) out**
La promenade m'a fatigué. The walk tired me out.
2 **to strain** *(your eyes)*
se **fatiguer** *REFLEXIVE VERB* ◎
to get tired
Elle se fatigue vite. She gets tired quickly .

le **faubourg** *MASC NOUN*
suburb
les faubourgs de Marseille the suburbs of Marseilles

fauché *MASC ADJECTIVE*, **fauchée** *FEM*
(informal) **broke**
Je suis fauché, je ne peux pas aller au cinéma. I'm broke, I can't go to the cinema.

faucher *VERB* [1]
1 **to mow** *(hay)*
2 *(informal)* **to pinch**
On m'a fauché mon vélo. Somebody's pinched my bike.

le **faucon** *MASC NOUN*
falcon

faudra, **faudrait** *VERB* ▶ SEE **falloir**

se **faufiler** *REFLEXIVE VERB* ◎ [1]
Diane se faufile entre deux spectateurs. Diane is squeezing between two spectators.

la **faune** *FEM NOUN*
wildlife
• la faune marine
marine life

fausse *FEM ADJECTIVE* ▶ SEE **faux**

faussement *ADVERB*
wrongly

fausser *VERB* [1]
1 **to distort**
2 **to bend**

ℱ **indicates key words**

faut VERB ▶SEE **falloir**

♀ la **faute** FEM NOUN
1 mistake, error
une faute d'orthographe a spelling mistake
J'ai fait deux fautes dans la dictée. I made
two mistakes in the dictation.
2 fault
C'est ma faute. It's my fault.
C'est de ma faute. It's my fault.
C'est la faute de Sophie. It's Sophie's fault.
C'est de la faute de Jacques. It's Jacques'
fault.
3 sans faute without fail
À demain, sans faute. See you tomorrow,
without fail.
4 faute de for lack of
Le projet n'a pas abouti, faute de temps.
The project didn't come off for lack of time.
Faute de mieux, je le prendrai. For want of
anything better, I'll take it.

♀ le **fauteuil** MASC NOUN
1 armchair
2 seat (in a cinema, a theatre)
• le fauteuil à bascule
rocking chair
• le fauteuil roulant
wheelchair

fautif MASC ADJECTIVE, **fautive** FEM
guilty
C'est son frère qui est fautif. Her brother
is guilty.

fauve MASC & FEM ADJECTIVE ▶SEE **fauve** NOUN
tawny

le **fauve** MASC NOUN ▶SEE **fauve** ADJECTIVE
1 wild animal
2 big cat

♀ **faux** ADVERB ▶SEE **faux** ADJ, NOUN
out of tune
Nicolas chante faux. Nicolas sings out of
tune.

♀ le **faux** MASC NOUN ▶SEE **faux** ADJ, ADV
fake, forgery
Ce billet de 50 euros est un faux. This 50-
euro note is a forgery.

♀ **faux** MASC ADJECTIVE, **fausse** FEM ▶SEE **faux** ADV,
NOUN
1 wrong
Ton résultat est faux. Your result's wrong.
2 untrue
C'est faux, ça ne s'est pas passé ainsi. That's
not true, it didn't happen like that.
3 false
une fausse barbe a false beard
4 imitation
C'est un faux diamant. It's an imitation
diamond.

• le faux ami
false friend (A French word, spelt the same in
English, but with a different meaning.)
• le faux-filet
sirloin

la **faveur** FEM NOUN
favour

favorable MASC & FEM ADJECTIVE
favourable

♀ **favori** MASC ADJECTIVE, **favorite** FEM
favourite
C'est mon groupe favori. It's my favourite
pop band.

favoriser VERB [1]
to favour

♀ le **fax** MASC NOUN
1 fax
Je vous envoie un fax. I'm sending you a fax.
2 fax machine
L'imprimante est aussi un fax. The printer is
also a fax machine.

fédéral MASC ADJECTIVE, **fédérale** FEM,
fédéraux MASC PL, **fédérales** FEM PL
federal

la **fédération** FEM NOUN
federation

la **fée** FEM NOUN
fairy

féerique MASC & FEM ADJECTIVE
magical

feignant MASC ADJECTIVE, **feignante** FEM
(informal) lazy

fêler VERB [1]
to crack

se **fêler** REFLEXIVE VERB ◎
to crack

♀ les **félicitations** PLURAL FEM NOUN
congratulations
Tu as eu ton bac. Félicitations! You passed
your baccalaureat. Congratulations!

féliciter VERB [1]
to congratulate

la **fêlure** FEM NOUN
crack

la **femelle** FEM NOUN
female (of a species)
La femelle du merle est brune. The female
blackbird is brown.

féminin MASC ADJECTIVE, **féminine** FEM ▶SEE
féminin NOUN
1 female
le sexe féminin the female sex

◎ means the verb takes être to form the perfect

2 feminine
Elle est très féminine. She's very feminine.
Cet ensemble est très féminin. This outfit is
very feminine.

3 women's
la presse féminine women's magazines
les questions féminines women's issues

le **féminin** *MASC NOUN* ▸ SEE **féminin** *ADJECTIVE*
(Grammar) **feminine**
au féminin in the feminine
'Boulangère' est le féminin de 'boulanger.'
'Boulangère' is the feminine for 'boulanger.'

le & la **féministe** *MASC & FEM NOUN*
feminist

ℓ la **femme** *FEM NOUN*
1 woman
C'est une femme très cultivée. She's a very
educated woman

2 wife
la femme de David David's wife
- la femme d'affaires
businesswoman
- la femme au foyer
housewife
- la femme de ménage
cleaning lady

fendre *VERB* [3]
1 to chop
Il fend du bois pour faire du feu. He's
chopping wood to make a fire.
2 to crack (a wall, a vase)
3 fendre le cœur à quelqu'un to break
somebody's heart
Ses pleurs me fendent le cœur. Her tears
break my heart.

ℓ la **fenêtre** *FEM NOUN*
window
Ouvre la fenêtre! Open the window!
Il regarde par la fenêtre. He's looking out of
the window.

la **fente** *FEM NOUN*
1 slit
une jupe avec une fente a skirt with a slit
2 slot
Mets une pièce d'un euro dans la fente. Put
a one-euro coin in the slot.
3 crack
Il y a une fente dans le mur. There is a crack
in the wall.

le **fer** *MASC NOUN*
iron
- le fer à cheval
horseshoe
- le fer forgé
wrought iron
- le fer à repasser
iron (for clothes)

ℓ **férié** *MASC ADJECTIVE*, **fériée** *FEM*
un jour férié a public holiday
Demain c'est férié. Tomorrow is a public
holiday.

ferme *MASC & FEM ADJECTIVE* ▸ SEE **ferme** *NOUN*
firm
un matelas ferme a firm mattress
une voix ferme a firm voice

ℓ la **ferme** *FEM NOUN* ▸ SEE **ferme** *ADJECTIVE*
1 farm
Pendant les vacances je travaille dans une
ferme. During the holidays I work on a farm.
2 farmhouse
Nous passons nos vacances dans une ferme
du Limousin. We spend our holidays in a
farmhouse in the Limousin.
- la ferme éolienne
windfarm

ℓ **fermé** *MASC ADJECTIVE*, **fermée** *FEM*
closed
Le magasin est fermé le dimanche. The
shop is closed on Sundays.
Les volets sont fermés. The shutters are
closed.
Le robinet est mal fermé. The tap is not
properly turned off.

fermenter *VERB* [1]
to ferment

ℓ **fermer** *VERB* [1]
1 to close, to shut
Il ferme la porte. He shuts the door.
Il a fermé les yeux. He closed his eyes.
Je ferme la porte à clé. I lock the door.
2 to turn off (the tap, the water, etc)
N'oublie pas de fermer le gaz. Don't forget
to turn off the gas.
3 to do up (clothes, shoes)
Ferme ton manteau, il fait froid! Do your
coat up, it's cold!
4 to close down
On a fermé l'usine. They closed down the
factory.
se **fermer** *REFLEXIVE VERB* ☺
to close (by itself)
La porte s'est fermée. The door closed.

ℓ la **fermeture** *FEM NOUN*
1 closing
les heures de fermeture closing times
2 fastening (on a garment)
- la fermeture annuelle
annual close-down (of businesses for
holidays)
- la fermeture éclair®
zip

ℓ indicates key words

A B C D E F G H I J K L M N O P Q R S T U V W X Y Z

fermier MASC ADJECTIVE, **fermière** FEM ▶SEE
    fermier NOUN
    farm, farm-produced
    des produits fermiers farm produce
    un poulet fermier a free-range chicken

ℰ le **fermier** MASC NOUN, la **fermière** FEM ▶SEE
    fermier ADJECTIVE
1   farmer
    Mon oncle et ma tante sont fermiers en
    Normandie. My uncle and aunt are farmers
    in Normandy.
2   la fermière the farmer's wife

le **fermoir** MASC NOUN
    clasp

féroce MASC & FEM ADJECTIVE
    fierce
    un examinateur féroce a fierce examiner
    une bête féroce a fierce animal
    un appétit féroce a terrific appetite

la **ferraille** FEM NOUN
    scrap metal

ferroviaire MASC & FEM ADJECTIVE
    rail, railway
    le réseau ferroviaire the rail network

fertile MASC & FEM ADJECTIVE
    fertile

la **fertilité** FEM NOUN
    fertility

la **fesse** FEM NOUN
    buttock
    les fesses your bottom

le **festin** MASC NOUN
    feast
    Nous avons fait un festin. We had a feast.

le **festival** MASC NOUN
    festival
    un festival de folk a folk music festival

ℰ la **fête** FEM NOUN
1   public holiday
    les fêtes de Pâques Easter
    sauf dimanches et fêtes except Sundays
    and public holidays
    un jour de fête a public holiday
    les fêtes de fin d'année the end-of-year
    festive season
2   party
    Estelle fait une fête pour son anniversaire.
    Estelle is having a party for her birthday.
    faire la fête to party
    Ils ont fait la fête tout le week-end. The've
    been partying all weekend.
3   fête, fair
    Il y a la fête au village. There's a fair in the
    village.
    une fête de la musique a music festival

4   saint's name day (In France every day has a
    saint and many people celebrate their saint's
    day.)
    La fête de Sophie est le 23 mai. Sophie's
    saint's day is 23 May.
•   la fête foraine
    funfair
•   la fête des Mères
    Mother's Day (in France on the last Sunday
    in May)
•   la fête nationale
    Bastille Day (14 July)
•   la fête des Pères
    Father's Day

fêter VERB [1]
    to celebrate
    Elle vient de fêter ses 18 ans. She's just
    celebrated her eighteenth birthday.

ℰ le **feu** MASC NOUN, les **feux** PLURAL
1   fire
    Il jette les vieux cartons au feu. He's
    throwing the old boxes onto the fire.
    faire du feu to light a fire
    Faisons du feu dans la cheminée. Let's light
    a fire in the fireplace.
    prendre feu to catch fire
    La poêle a pris feu. The frying pan caught
    fire.
    éteindre le feu to put the fire out
    Les pompiers ont éteint le feu. The firemen
    have put the fire out.
    mettre le feu à quelque chose to set fire to
    something
    Ils ont mis le feu à la grange. They set fire
    to the barn.
2   (as a warning) Au feu! Fire!
3   light (in road signals)
    le feu rouge red light
    le feu vert green light
    les feux de signalisation the traffic lights
4   heat (when cooking)
    Faites cuire à feu doux. Cook on a gentle
    heat.

le **feu d'artifice** MASC NOUN
1   firework
2   firework display
    le feu d'artifice du 14 juillet the firework
    display on 14 July

le **feuillage** MASC NOUN
    foliage

la **feuille** FEM NOUN
1   leaf
2   une feuille de papier a sheet of paper
    une feuille double a double sheet of paper

feuilleté MASC ADJECTIVE, **feuilletée** FEM ▶SEE
    feuilleté NOUN
    la pâte feuilletée puff pastry

⊙ means the verb takes être to form the perfect

le **feuilleté** *MASC NOUN* ▸ SEE **feuilleté** *ADJECTIVE*
  savoury pasty

feuilleter *VERB* [48]
  to leaf through
  Elle feuillette des magazines en attendant.
  She's leafing through magazines as she
  waits.

ℒ le **feuilleton** *MASC NOUN*
1 **serial**
2 **soap opera** *(on television)*

le **feutre** *MASC NOUN*
1 **felt**
2 un feutre a felt-tip pen

la **fève** *FEM NOUN*
1 **broad bean**
2 **small figurine** *(in a Twelfth Night cake)*
  galette des Rois

ℒ **février** *MASC NOUN*
  February
  en février, au mois de février in February
  Fin février nous allons au ski. In late
  February we're going skiing.

> **WORD TIP** Months of the year and days of the
> week start with small letters in French.

fiable *MASC & FEM ADJECTIVE*
  reliable

les **fiançailles** *PLURAL FEM NOUN*
  engagement *(to be married)*
  la bague de fiançailles the engagement ring
  Les fiançailles d'Aurélie et Boris auront lieu
  le 2 juin. Aurélie's and Boris's engagement
  will take place on 2 June.

ℒ le **fiancé** *MASC NOUN*, la **fiancée** *FEM*
1 **fiancé** *(man)*
2 **fiancée** *(woman)*

se **fiancer** *REFLEXIVE VERB* ◉ [61]
  to get engaged
  Arthur et Joséphine se sont fiancés
  hier. Arthur and Joséphine got engaged
  yesterday.

la **fibre** *FEM NOUN*
  fibre

ficeler *VERB* [18]
  to tie up

la **ficelle** *FEM NOUN*
1 **string**
2 **thin baguette** *(French bread)*

ℒ la **fiche** *FEM NOUN*
1 **form**
  remplir une fiche to fill in a form
2 **index card**
  Pour mes révisions, je fais des fiches. When
  I revise, I fill in index cards.

- la fiche d'inscription
  registration form
- la fiche de travail
  worksheet

ficher *VERB* [1]
1 ficher quelqu'un to open a file on
  somebody
  Le cambrioleur est fiché à la police. The
  burglar is on the police files.
2 *(informal)* **to do**
  Qu'est-ce que tu fiches? What on earth are
  you doing?
3 *(informal)* **to put**
  Fiche ce vieux pull à la poubelle! Put this
  old jumper in the bin!
4 ficher la paix à quelqu'un to leave
  somebody alone
  Fiche-moi la paix! Leave me alone!

se **ficher** *REFLEXIVE VERB* ◉
  (informal)
  se ficher de quelqu'un to make fun of
  somebody
  Ne te fiche pas de lui! Don't make fun of
  him!
  Je m'en fiche! I don't care!
  se ficher de ce que quelqu'un fait not to
  care less about what somebody does
  Elle se fiche bien de ce qu'il pense. She
  couldn't care less what he thinks.

le **fichier** *MASC NOUN*
  file *(for documents)*

fichu *MASC ADJECTIVE*, **fichue** *FEM*
  (informal) **done for**
  Ma voiture est fichue. My car's done for.
  S'il me pose des questions, je suis fichu. If
  he asks me any questions, I'm done for.

la **fiction** *FEM NOUN*
  fiction

fidèle *MASC & FEM ADJECTIVE*
1 **faithful**
  Malgré tout, elle est restée fidèle à son
  mari. In spite of everything she stayed
  faithful to her husband.
2 **loyal**
  un consommateur fidèle à une marque a
  customer loyal to a brand

fier *MASC ADJECTIVE*, **fière** *FEM*
  proud
se **fier** *REFLEXIVE VERB* ◉ [1]
  se fier à to trust
  Je me fie à Thomas pour nous montrer le
  chemin. I trust Thomas to show us the way.

la **fierté** *FEM NOUN*
  pride

la **fièvre** *FEM NOUN*
  fever

ℒ indicates key words

avoir de la fièvre to have a temperature

la **figue** *FEM NOUN*
fig

le **figuier** *MASC NOUN*
fig tree

la **figure** *FEM NOUN*
1 face
2 figure *(in maths)*
une figure géométrique geometric figure

figurer *VERB* [1]
to be, to appear
Ton nom ne figure pas sur la liste. Your name isn't on the list.

se **figurer** *REFLEXIVE VERB* ◌
to imagine
Tu te figures que je vais payer. And you imagine I'm going to pay.
Figure-toi qu'il a eu son permis de conduire! He passed his driving test, can you imagine!

le **fil** *MASC NOUN*
1 thread
du fil à coudre sewing thread
2 wire, flex *(of a telephone, an electrical appliance)*
• le fil de fer
wire
• le fil de fer barbelé
barbed wire

la **file** *FEM NOUN*
1 queue
Il y a une longue file devant le cinéma. There's a long queue in front of the cinema.
2 lane *(on a road)*
Reste dans la file de gauche! Stay in the left-hand lane!
3 à la file in a row
Ils ont regardé trois films à la file. They watched three films in a row.
• la file d'attente
queue
• la file indienne
single file

filer *VERB* [1]
1 to speed along
2 *(informal)* to pass on
Elle m'a filé deux robes. She passed on two dresses to me.

le **filet** *MASC NOUN*
1 net
un filet de pêche a fishing net
2 fillet
un filet de poisson a fish fillet

ℱ la **fille** *FEM NOUN*
1 girl
une petite fille a little girl

une jeune fille a young woman
2 daughter
C'est la fille du directeur. She's the headmaster's daughter.

la **fillette** *FEM NOUN*
little girl

le **filleul** *MASC NOUN*
godson

la **filleule** *FEM NOUN*
goddaughter

ℱ le **film** *MASC NOUN*
film
• le film d'animation
cartoon
• le film d'aventure
adventure film
• le film d'épouvante
horror film
• le film de fantaisie
fantasy film
• le film de guerre
war film
• le film policier
detective film
• le film romantique
romantic film

filmer *VERB* [1]
to film

ℱ le **fils** *MASC NOUN*
son

le **filtre** *MASC NOUN*
filter

filtrer *VERB* [1]
to filter

ℱ **fin** *MASC ADJECTIVE*, **fine** *FEM* ▸ SEE **fin** *NOUN*
1 fine
du sable fin fine sand
2 thin
une tranche fine a thin slice
3 slender
Elle a la taille fine. She has a slender waist.

ℱ la **fin** *FEM NOUN* ▸ SEE **fin** *ADJECTIVE*
end
à la fin in the end
à la fin du film at the end of the film
en fin de journée at the end of the day
la fin de semaine the weekend
sans fin endless
Je commence fin juillet. I'm starting at the end of July.

final *MASC ADJECTIVE*, **finale** *FEM*, **finaux** *MASC PL*, **finales** *FEM PL* ▸ SEE **finale**
final

◌ means the verb takes être to form the perfect

la **finale** *FEM NOUN* ▶ SEE **final**
final *(in a competition)*

finalement *ADVERB*
1 **in the end, finally**
Finalement nous avons choisi la rouge. In the end we chose the red one.
2 **after all**
Finalement c'est une bonne idée. After all, it's a good idea.

la **finance** *FEM NOUN*
finance

financer *VERB* [61]
to finance

les **fines herbes** *PLURAL FEM NOUN*
mixed herbs

ℱ **finir** *VERB* [2]
1 **to finish, to end**
Le film finit à dix heures. The film finishes at ten o'clock.
2 **finir quelque chose** to finish something
J'ai fini le roman. I've finished the novel.
As-tu fini tes devoirs? Have you finished your homework?
Qui veut finir le gâteau? Who wants to finish the cake?
J'ai fini le sucre. I've used up the sugar.
3 **finir de faire quelque chose** to finish doing something
J'ai fini de faire ma valise. I've finished packing.
4 **finir par faire quelque chose** to end up doing something
Il a fini par aller à Paris. He ended up going to Paris.

---

finlandais *MASC ADJECTIVE*, **finlandaise** *FEM* ▶ SEE
Finlandais
Finnish

le **Finlandais** *MASC NOUN*, la **Finlandaise** *FEM*
▶ SEE **finlandais**
Finn

la **Finlande** *FEM NOUN*
Finland

le **finnois** *MASC NOUN*
Finnish *(the language)*

la **firme** *FEM NOUN*
firm

le **fisc** *MASC NOUN*
tax office

la **fissure** *FEM NOUN*
crack

fixe *MASC & FEM ADJECTIVE*
1 **fixed**

une idée fixe a fixed idea
un menu à prix fixe a fixed-price menu
Nous mangeons à heures fixes. We eat at set times.
2 **permanent**
un emploi fixe a permanent job

fixer *VERB* [1]
1 **to fix** *(to attach)*
Il fixe un cadre au mur. He's fixing a frame on the wall.
2 **to set** *(a date, a price)*
Il a fixé la date de la rencontre au samedi 2 mai. He's set the date for the match for Saturday 2 May.
3 **to stare at**
Pourquoi me fixe-t-il ainsi? Why is he staring at me like that?

le **flacon** *MASC NOUN*
(small) bottle

flamand *MASC ADJECTIVE*, **flamande** *FEM* ▶ SEE
Flamand
Flemish

> **WORD TIP** Adjectives never have capitals in French, even for nationality or regional origin.

le **Flamand** *MASC NOUN*, la **Flamande** *FEM* ▶ SEE
flamand
1 **Fleming** *(Dutch-speaking Belgian)*
2 le flamand Flemish *(the language)*

le **flamant** *MASC NOUN*
flamingo

flamber *VERB* [1]
1 **to blaze** *(fires)*
2 **to rocket** *(prices)*

la **flamme** *FEM NOUN*
flame

le **flan** *MASC NOUN*
custard tart

> **WORD TIP** flan does not mean flan in English; for the meaning of flan ▶ SEE **tarte**.

le **flanc** *MASC NOUN*
side *(of a person, an animal)*

flâner *VERB* [1]
to stroll

la **flaque** *FEM NOUN*
une flaque d'eau a puddle

le **flash** *MASC NOUN*
1 **flash** *(on a camera)*
2 **news headlines**
le flash de midi the news headlines at midday *(on the radio)*

flatter *VERB* [1]
to flatter

ℱ indicates key words

flatteur *MASC ADJECTIVE*, **flatteuse** *FEM*
   flattering

la **flèche** *FEM NOUN*
1 arrow
2 road sign, arrow
   Suivez la flèche. Follow the arrow.
3 spire
   les flèches de la cathédrale de Chartres the
   spires of Chartres cathedral

la **fléchette** *FEM NOUN*
   dart
   une partie de fléchettes a game of darts

fléchir *VERB* [2]
1 to bend
   Fléchis les genoux! Bend your knees!
2 to weaken
   Sa détermination fléchit. His determination
   is weakening.

♀ la **fleur** *FEM NOUN*
   flower
   un tissu à fleurs a flower-patterned fabric
   un cerisier en fleur a cherry-tree in blossom

fleuri *MASC ADJECTIVE*, **fleurie** *FEM*
1 flowery, with lots of flowers
   du tissu fleuri flowery material
2 Ton jardin est très fleuri. You've got lots of
   flowers in your garden.

fleurir *VERB* [2]
1 to flower
   Le rosier fleurit. The rose is flowering.
   Le pommier fleurit. The apple tree is
   coming into blossom.
2 to flourish
   Le commerce fleurit. Business is flourishing.

le & la **fleuriste** *MASC & FEM NOUN*
   florist

le **fleuve** *MASC NOUN*
   river (that reaches the sea, e.g. la Seine, la
   Loire, etc)

flexible *MASC & FEM ADJECTIVE*
   flexible

♀ le **flic** *MASC NOUN*
   (informal) policeman, cop

le **flipper** *MASC NOUN*
   pinball machine

flirter *VERB* [1]
   to flirt

le **flocon** *MASC NOUN*
   flake
• le flocon de neige
   snowflake
• les flocons d'avoine
   porridge oats

floral *MASC ADJECTIVE*, **florale** *FEM*, **floraux** *MASC
PL*, **florales** *FEM PL*
   floral

la **flotte** *FEM NOUN*
   fleet (of ships)

flotter *VERB* [1]
1 to float
   Une bouteille flotte à la surface du lac. A
   bottle is floating on the lake.
2 to fly
   Le drapeau flotte au vent. The flag is flying
   in the wind.
3 (informal) to rain
   Et voilà, il flotte! There you are, it's raining!

flou *MASC ADJECTIVE*, **floue** *FEM*
1 blurred
   une image floue a blurred image
2 vague
   Ses projets sont un peu flous. Her plans are
   a bit vague.

fluide *MASC & FEM ADJECTIVE*
   fluid

fluo *INVARIABLE MASC & FEM ADJECTIVE*
   (informal) **fluorescent**
   du vert fluo fluorescent green

le **fluor** *MASC NOUN*
   fluorine
   du dentifrice au fluor fluoride toothpaste

fluorescent *MASC ADJECTIVE*, **fluorescente** *FEM*
   fluorescent

la **flûte** *FEM NOUN*
   flute
   Elle joue de la flûte. She plays the flute.
• la flûte à bec
   recorder
• la flûte à champagne
   flute
• la flûte traversière
   flute

focaliser *VERB* [1]
   to focus

la **foi** *FEM NOUN*
   faith

le **foie** *MASC NOUN*
   liver
   pâté de foie gras foie gras (goose liver pâté)
   une crise de foie a bout of indigestion
   J'ai une crise de foie. I have indigestion.

le **foin** *MASC NOUN*
   hay

la **foire** *FEM NOUN*
   fair

♀ **means the verb takes être to form the perfect**

ℓ la **fois** *FEM NOUN*

1 time
  une fois once
  deux fois twice
  trois fois three times
  plusieurs fois several times
  la première fois the first time
  trois fois plus grand three times as big
  Trois fois dix font trente. Tree times ten is thirty.

2 à la fois at the same time, at once
  trois à la fois three at a time

3 une fois que once
  Une fois que j'aurai pris une douche ... Once I've had a shower ...
  Une fois j'ai vu ... I once saw...

4 à chaque fois whenever, each time
  À chaque fois que nous sortons, nous fermons la porte à clé. Whenever we go out, we lock the door.

5 *(to begin stories)* Il était une fois... Once upon a time...

la **folie** *FEM NOUN*
  madness
  C'est de la folie! It's madness!

le **folk** *MASC NOUN*
  folk music

la **folle** *FEM NOUN, ADJECTIVE* ▶SEE **fou**

ℓ **foncé** *MASC ADJECTIVE*, **foncée** *FEM*
  dark
  des couleurs foncées dark colours
  le bleu foncé dark blue
  J'ai les cheveux bruns foncés. I have dark brown hair.

foncer *VERB* [61]
  (informal) **to rush**
  Ils ont foncé vers la porte. They rushed for the door.

la **fonction** *FEM NOUN*

1 function

2 post, **job**
  une voiture de fonction a company car
  Le nouveau directeur prend ses fonctions en septembre. The new head is taking up his post in September.

• la fonction publique
  civil service

fonctionnaire *MASC & FEM NOUN*
  civil servant

le **fonctionnement** *MASC NOUN*
  working
  Je ne comprends pas le fonctionnement de cette machine. I don't understand how this machine works.

fonctionner *VERB* [1]
  to work

ℓ le **fond** *MASC NOUN*

1 bottom
  au fond du lac at the bottom of the lake
  au fond de la bouteille at the bottom of the bottle

2 back
  au fond du tiroir at the back of the drawer
  au fond de la classe at the back of the classroom

3 end
  au fond du couloir at the end of the corridor

4 background
  sur fond blanc on a white background
  de la musique de fond background music

5 au fond, dans le fond in fact
  Au fond, c'est assez simple. In fact it's quite easy.

• le fond de teint
  foundation *(make-up)*

fondamental *MASC ADJECTIVE*, **fondamentale** *FEM*, **fondamentaux** *MASC PL*, **fondamentales** *FEM PL*
  basic, **fundamental**

le **fondateur** *MASC NOUN*, la **fondatrice** *FEM*
  founder

la **fondation** *FEM NOUN*

1 founding *(of a hospital, a college, etc)*

2 les fondations the foundations *(of a building)*

fonder *VERB* [1]

1 to found
  Mon oncle a fondé une association. My uncle has founded an association.

2 to base
  Ses conclusions sont fondées sur des faits. His conclusions are based on facts.

fondre *VERB* [3]

1 to melt
  Le beurre fond au soleil. The butter is melting in the sun.

2 to dissolve
  Le sucre fond dans l'eau. Sugar dissolves in water.

3 fondre en larmes to burst into tears
  L'histoire était si triste qu'elle fondit en larmes. The story was so sad that she burst into tears.

fondu *MASC ADJECTIVE*, **fondue** *FEM*
  melted

font *VERB* ▶SEE **faire**

la **fontaine** *FEM NOUN*
  fountain
  Alice boit à la fontaine. Alice is drinking from the fountain.

la **fonte** *FEM NOUN*

1 cast iron

une poêle en fonte a cast-iron frying pan
2 melting (of metal, ice)
3 thaw (of ice, snow)

le **foot** MASC NOUN
football
un match de foot a football match
Ludivine joue au foot. Ludivine plays
football.

♪ le **football** MASC NOUN
football
Je joue au football après l'école. I play
football after school.
Il aime regarder le football à la télé. He
likes watching football on TV.

le **footballeur** MASC NOUN, la **footballeuse** FEM
footballer

le **footing** MASC NOUN
jogging
Je fais du footing tous les matins. I go
jogging every morning.

forain MASC ADJECTIVE, **foraine** FEM
un marchand forain a stallkeeper
une fête foraine a funfair

la **force** FEM NOUN
1 strength
la force de caractère strength of character
Il reprend des forces après sa maladie. He's
getting his strength back after his illness.
Suzanne est à bout de forces. Suzanne is
feeling drained.
avoir de la force to be strong
Tu as assez de force pour le faire. You're
strong enough to do it.
avoir la force de faire quelque chose to
have the strength to do something
Je n'ai pas la force de sortir ce soir. I haven't
got the strength to go out tonight.
2 force
de force by force
Ils sont entrés de force dans la maison.
They entered the house by force.
3 à force de faire quelque chose by doing
something
À force d'économiser, elle a pu s'acheter
son portable. By saving very hard, she was
able to buy her mobile.
4 les forces de l'ordre the police
les forces armées the armed forces

forcément ADVERB
1 inevitably
Il y a forcément une solution. There has to
be a solution.
2 pas forcément not necessarily

forcer VERB [61]
to force
Les cambrioleurs ont forcé la porte. The

burglars forced the door.
forcer quelqu'un à faire quelque chose to
force somebody to do something
Sa mère le force à manger des épinards.
His mother forces him to eat spinach.

se **forcer** REFLEXIVE VERB ◯
to force yourself
se forcer à faire quelque chose to make
yourself do something
Je me force à boire un litre d'eau tous les
jours. I make myself drink one litre of water
a day.

♪ la **forêt** FEM NOUN
forest

le **forfait** MASC NOUN
1 fixed price
Il est payé au forfait. He's paid a fixed rate.
2 package
un forfait tout compris an all-inclusive
package
3 withdrawal (of a player, a team in a
competition)
déclarer forfait to withdraw
Notre équipe a déclaré forfait. Our team
withdrew.
4 (serious) crime
Il a été condamné à 25 ans de prison pour
son forfait. He was sentenced to 25 years'
prison for his crime.

le **forgeron** MASC NOUN
blacksmith

la **formalité** FEM NOUN
formality

le **format** MASC NOUN
1 format (of a disquette, a newspaper)
2 size (of a sheet of paper, a photo)

♪ la **formation** FEM NOUN
training
Elle a une formation d'infirmière. She's a
trained nurse.
• la formation continue
continuing education
• la formation professionnelle
vocational training

la **forme** FEM NOUN
1 shape
une sucette en forme de lapin a lolly in the
shape of a rabbit
2 form
dans sa forme actuelle in its present form
J'aime la musique sous toutes ses formes. I
like all kinds of music.
3 en forme in form
David est en forme. David's on form.
Tu as l'air en pleine forme. You're looking in
great shape.

◯ means the verb takes être to form the perfect

formel *MASC ADJECTIVE*, **formelle** *FEM*
1 **formal**
2 **categorical**
   un refus formel a categorical refusal
   Elle a dit 100 euros, je suis formel. She said
   100 euros, I'm positive about it.
3 **strict**
   un ordre formel a strict order

formellement *ADVERB*
   strictly
   formellement interdit strictly forbidden

former *VERB* [1]
1 **to form**
   Formez un cercle! Form a circle!
   Ils ont formé une deuxième équipe. They
   formed a second team.
   Nous formons une famille très unie. We are
   a close-knit family.
2 **to train**
   Ici on forme des programmeurs. They train
   programmers here.

ℓ formidable *MASC & FEM ADJECTIVE*
   (informal) **great**, **fantastic**
   Le film était formidable. The film was
   fantastic.
   Le baby-sitter est formidable avec mon
   petit frère. The babysitter's wonderful with
   my little brother.

le formulaire *MASC NOUN*
   form
   Nous devons remplir un formulaire pour
   nous inscrire. We have to fill in a form to
   enrol.

la formule *FEM NOUN*
1 **formula**
   la formule un Formula One *(in car racing)*
2 **expression** *(in language)*
   une formule toute faite a set expression

ℓ fort *MASC ADJECTIVE*, **forte** *FEM* ▸ SEE **fort** *ADVERB*
1 **strong**
   Nadia est très forte. Nadia's very strong.
   Ton café est trop fort. Your coffee's too
   strong.
2 **être fort en quelque chose** to be good at
   something
   Olivier est fort en maths. Olivier's good at
   maths.
3 **stout**
   une jeune fille un peu forte a girl on the
   stout side

fort *ADVERB* ▸ SEE **fort** *ADJECTIVE*
1 **extremely**
   C'était fort bon. It was extremely good.
2 **hard**
   Ce boxeur frappe fort. This boxer hits hard.
3 **loudly**
   Il chante fort. He sings loudly.

Parle plus fort! Speak louder!

la forteresse *FEM NOUN*
   fortress

le fortifiant *MASC NOUN*
   tonic

fortifier *VERB* [1]
1 **to strengthen**
   Ce shampooing fortifie les cheveux. This
   shampoo strengthens your hair.
   Le sport, ça fortifie. Sport makes you
   strong.
2 **to fortify** *(a city, a port, etc)*

fortuit *MASC ADJECTIVE*, **fortuite** *FEM*
   accidental

la fortune *FEM NOUN*
1 **fortune**
   les grandes fortunes big fortunes
   Ce tableau vaut une fortune. This painting
   is worth a fortune.
   faire fortune to make a fortune
   Il a fait fortune au Japon. He made his
   fortune in Japan.
2 **de fortune** makeshift
   un lit de fortune a makeshift bed

le fossé *MASC NOUN*
1 **ditch**
   Sa voiture est allée dans le fossé. His car
   went into the ditch.
2 **moat** *(around a castle)*
3 **gap**
   le fossé qui sépare les riches et les pauvres
   the gap between the rich and the poor

la fossette *FEM NOUN*
   dimple

ℓ fou *MASC ADJECTIVE*, **folle** *FEM* ▸ SEE **fou** *NOUN*
1 **mad**
   Il devient fou. He's going mad.
2 **crazy**, **amazing**
   On a passé une soirée folle. We had an
   amazing evening.
3 **huge**
   Ils ont un succès fou. They're having a huge
   success.
   Il y a un monde fou. There are masses of
   people.
4 **être fou de quelque chose** to be mad about
   something
   Il est fou de musique ska. He's mad about
   ska music.

le fou *MASC NOUN*, **la folle** *FEM* ▸ SEE **fou** *ADJECTIVE*
   madman, **madwoman**
   Un fou m'a doublé dans un virage. A
   madman overtook me on a bend.
   Elle travaille comme une folle. She works
   like mad.

ℓ indicates key words

la **foudre** FEM NOUN
  lightning
  un arbre frappé par la foudre a tree struck
  by lightning

le **fouet** MASC NOUN
1 whip
2 whisk (for eggs, cream, etc)
  un fouet électrique an electric whisk

fouetter VERB [1]
1 to whip
2 to whisk (eggs, cream)
  Pour faire une omelette, fouette trois
  œufs. To make an omelette, whisk three
  eggs.
  la crème fouettée whipped cream

la **fougère** FEM NOUN
1 fern
2 bracken
  Le chevreuil disparut dans les fougères.
  The deer disappeared in the bracken.

la **fouille** FEM NOUN
  search

fouiller VERB [1]
1 to search
  La police a fouillé la maison. The police
  searched the house.
  J'ai été fouillé à l'aéroport. I was searched
  at the airport.
2 fouiller dans quelque chose to rummage
  through something
  Tu as fouillé dans mon sac à main. You've
  rummaged through my handbag.

le **fouillis** MASC NOUN
  mess (in a room)
  ranger le fouillis dans la cuisine to tidy up
  the mess in the kitchen

le **foulard** MASC NOUN
  scarf
• le foulard islamique
  Muslim headscarf

la **foule** FEM NOUN
1 crowd
  Anaïs s'est perdue dans la foule. Anaïs got
  lost in the crowd.
  venir en foule to flock to
  Les fans sont venus en foule au concert.
  The fans flocked to the concert.
2 une foule de quelque chose lots of
  something
  Il m'a posé une foule de questions. He
  asked me lots of questions.

le **four** MASC NOUN
  oven
  à four moyen in a medium oven
  un poulet au four a roast chicken
  des légumes cuits au four baked vegetables

  mettre quelque chose au four to put
  something in the oven
  Mamie a mis le gâteau au four. Granny put
  the cake in the oven.
• le four à micro-ondes
  microwave oven

la **fourche** FEM NOUN
  fork

la **fourchette** FEM NOUN
  fork

le **fourgon** MASC NOUN
  van

la **fourgonnette** FEM NOUN
  (small) van

la **fourmi** FEM NOUN
1 ant
  Il y a des fourmis partout. There are ants
  everywhere.
2 avoir des fourmis to have pins and needles
  Je suis restée assise trop longtemps,
  maintenant j'ai des fourmis dans les
  jambes. I've been sitting down too long,
  now I've got pins and needles in my legs.

fourmiller VERB [1]
  fourmiller de quelque chose to be
  swarming with something
  La ville fourmille de touristes. The town is
  swarming with tourists.

le **fourneau** MASC NOUN, les **fourneaux** PLURAL
  stove

la **fournée** FEM NOUN
  batch (of cakes, bread)

fournir VERB [2]
  to supply
  fournir quelqu'un en quelque chose to
  supply somebody with something
  Mes voisins me fournissent en légumes
  frais. My neighbours supply me with fresh
  vegetables.

le **fournisseur** MASC NOUN
  supplier

les **fournitures** PLURAL FEM NOUN
  stationery
• les fournitures de bureau
  office stationery
• les fournitures scolaires
  school stationery

WORD TIP fournitures does not mean furniture
in English; for the meaning of furniture ► SEE
meuble.

fourré MASC ADJECTIVE, **fourrée** FEM
1 filled
  un gâteau fourré au chocolat a cake with a
  chocolate filling

⊜ means the verb takes être to form the perfect

2 fur-lined
des bottes fourrées fur-lined boots

la **fourrure** FEM NOUN
1 fur
un manteau de fourrure a fur coat
de la fausse fourrure imitation fur
2 coat (of animals)

ℓ le **foyer** MASC NOUN
1 home
rester au foyer to stay at home
une femme au foyer a housewife
2 household
La majorité des foyers disposent d'un
micro-ordinateur. The majority of
households have a PC.
3 hostel
un foyer d'étudiants a student's hostel
4 club
un foyer de jeunes a youth club
5 fireplace

le **fracas** MASC NOUN
crash (noise)

fracasser VERB [1]
to smash, to break to pieces

la **fraction** FEM NOUN
fraction

la **fracture** FEM NOUN
fracture
une fracture de la cheville a fractured ankle

fracturer VERB [1]
1 to fracture
un os fracturé a fractured bone
2 to break
Les voleurs ont fracturé le coffre-fort. The
thieves broke open the safe.

ℓ **fragile** MASC & FEM ADJECTIVE
1 fragile
Ne touche pas, c'est fragile! Don't touch,
it's fragile!
2 frail, delicate
une vieille dame fragile a frail old lady
Il a l'estomac fragile. He has a delicate
stomach.
Mon oncle a le cœur fragile. My uncle has a
weak heart.
Il a une santé fragile. He has poor health.

le **fragment** MASC NOUN
fragment

fraîche FEM ▸ SEE **frais**

la **fraîcheur** FEM NOUN
1 coolness
la fraîcheur de la cave the coolness of the
cellar
2 freshness (of food)

ℓ **frais** MASC ADJECTIVE, **fraîche** FEM ▸ SEE **frais** ADV,
NOUN
1 cool, cold
un matin frais a chilly morning
2 cool
une boisson fraîche a cool drink
3 fresh
du pain frais fresh bread
des nouvelles fraîches fresh news
'Peinture Fraîche' 'Wet Paint'

ℓ **frais** ADVERB ▸ SEE **frais** ADJ, NOUN
Il fait frais ce soir. It's cool tonight.
'Servir frais' 'Serve chilled'

ℓ le **frais** MASC NOUN ▸ SEE **frais** ADJ, ADV
1 (about food) À conserver au frais. Keep in a
cool place.
J'ai mis du jus d'orange au frais. I put some
orange juice to cool.
2 prendre le frais to get some fresh air
Il y a trop de fumée ici, je vais prendre le
frais. It's too smoky in here, I'm going to get
some fresh air.
3 les frais expenses, costs
les frais de déplacement travelling
expenses
les frais de publicité advertising costs

ℓ la **fraise** FEM NOUN
strawberry
une glace à la fraise a strawberry ice cream
• la fraise des bois
wild strawberry

ℓ la **framboise** FEM NOUN
raspberry
un yaourt à la framboise a raspberry
yoghurt

franc MASC ADJECTIVE, **franche** FEM ▸ SEE **franc**
NOUN
frank

le **franc** MASC NOUN ▸ SEE **franc** ADJECTIVE
franc (the currency of Switzerland; name of
the currencies used in France, Belgium and
Luxembourg until replaced by the euro; 100
French francs = 15.24 euros)
L'euro a remplacé le franc en 2002. The
euro replaced the franc in 2002.

ℓ **français** MASC ADJECTIVE, **française** FEM ▸ SEE
Français
French
un film français a French film
la cuisine française French cooking

WORD TIP Adjectives never have capitals in
French, even for nationality or regional origin.

ℓ le **Français** MASC NOUN, la **Française** FEM ▸ SEE
français
1 Frenchman
2 Frenchwoman

3 les Français the French
4 le français French *(language)*
J'apprends le français. I'm learning French.
Laura parle très bien français. Laura speaks
very good French.

WORD TIP Languages never have capitals in
French.

♀ la **France** *FEM NOUN*
France
Mon amie habite en France. My friend lives
in France.
Nous allons en France pour nos vacances.
We go to France for our holidays.

WORD TIP Countries and regions in French take
le, la or les.

franche *FEM* ▶ SEE **franc**

franchement *ADVERB*
1 frankly
Franchement, je ne le crois pas. Frankly, I
don't believe him.
2 really
Le film était franchement nul. The film was
really awful.

franchir *VERB* [2]
to cross
Le coureur franchit la ligne d'arrivée. The
runner is crossing the finishing line.
Le cheval a franchi l'obstacle. The horse has
cleared the fence.

la **franchise** *FEM NOUN*
1 frankness
en toute franchise quite frankly
2 franchise
un magasin en franchise a franchise *(shop,
business, etc)*

francophone *MASC & FEM ADJECTIVE*
French-speaking
les pays francophones French-speaking
countries

la **frange** *FEM NOUN*
fringe

le **frangin** *MASC NOUN*, la **frangine** *FEM*
(informal)
1 brother
2 sister

la **frangipane** *FEM NOUN*
almond cream

le **franglais** *MASC NOUN*
Franglais *(a mixture of French and English,
eg footing = jogging)*

♀ **frapper** *VERB* [1]
1 to hit
Il a frappé son chien. He hit his dog.

une région frappée par le chômage an area
hit by unemployment
La Louisiane a été frappée par un terrible
ouragan. Louisiana was hit by a terrible
hurricane.
2 to knock
frapper à la porte to knock at the door
On a frappé. There was a knock on the door.
frapper dans ses mains to clap your hands
3 être frappé par quelque chose to be struck
by something
J'ai été frappé par sa timidité. I was struck
by his shyness.
Ça m'a beaucoup frappé. That made a big
impression on me.
4 to chill *(wine)*

la **fraude** *FEM NOUN*
1 fraud
la fraude informatique computer fraud
2 cheating *(in an exam)*

fredonner *VERB* [1]
to hum

le **freezer** *MASC NOUN*
freezer compartment *(in a fridge)*

WORD TIP freezer does not mean freezer
in English; for the meaning of freezer ▶ SEE
congélateur.

le **frein** *MASC NOUN*
brake
les freins the brakes
le frein à main the handbrake

♀ **freiner** *VERB* [1]
1 to brake
La voiture a freiné trop tard. The car
braked too late.
2 to slow down *(on skis, skates)*
Freine un peu ou tu vas tomber! Slow down
a bit or you'll fall over!

frêle *MASC & FEM ADJECTIVE*
frail

le **frelon** *MASC NOUN*
hornet

frémir *VERB* [2]
1 to shudder
Cette idée me fait frémir. This idea makes
me shudder.
2 to simmer
Laisser frémir pendant 5 minutes. Simmer
for 5 minutes.

le **frêne** *MASC NOUN*
ash tree

fréquemment *ADVERB*
frequently, often

⊙ means the verb takes être to form the perfect

la **fréquence** *FEM NOUN*
  frequency

fréquenté *MASC ADJECTIVE*, **fréquentée** *FEM*
1 popular
  un café très fréquenté a very popular cafe
2 un quartier mal fréquenté a rough area

fréquenter *VERB* [1]
1 to see *(people)*
  Nous fréquentons beaucoup les Tournier.
  We see the Tourniers a lot.
2 to go often to *(a beach, a cafe, a restaurant)*
  Didier fréquente le restaurant du coin.
  Didier often goes to the local restaurant.
3 to go to *(a school, a church)*
  Elle fréquente l'école Sainte Marie. She
  goes to Saint Mary's (school).

ℙ le **frère** *MASC NOUN*
  brother
  C'est mon petit frère. He's my little brother.

les **friandises** *PLURAL FEM NOUN*
  sweet things
  À ma fête d'anniversaire, on a mangé
  beaucoup de friandises. At my birthday
  party we ate a lot of sweet things.

le **fric** *MASC NOUN*
  (informal) money

frictionner *VERB* [1]
  to rub

le **frigidaire**® *MASC NOUN*
  fridge

ℙ le **frigo** *MASC NOUN*
  (informal) fridge
  La soupe est au frigo. The soup is in the
  fridge.

frileux *MASC ADJECTIVE*, **frileuse** *FEM*
  être frileux to feel the cold
  Je ne suis pas frileuse. I don't feel the cold.

la **frime** *FEM NOUN*
  (informal)
  C'est de la frime! It's all show!

frimer *VERB* [1]
  (informal) to show off

le **frimeur** *MASC NOUN*, la **frimeuse** *FEM*
  (informal) show-off
  C'est un vrai frimeur. He's a real show-off.

les **fringues** *PLURAL FEM NOUN*
  (informal) clothes

fripé *MASC ADJECTIVE*, **fripée** *FEM*
  crumpled
  Ma jupe est toute fripée. My skirt is all
  crumpled.

frire *VERB* [74]
  faire frire quelque chose to fry something
  Il faut d'abord faire frire les oignons. First
  you've got to fry the onions.

frisé *MASC ADJECTIVE*, **frisée** *FEM* ▸ SEE **frisée**
1 curly
  des cheveux frisés curly hair
2 curly-haired
  un petit garçon frisé a curly-haired little
  boy

la **frisée** *FEM NOUN* ▸ SEE **frisé**
  curly endive, frisée *(a type of lettuce)*

friser *VERB* [1]
  to curl

le **frisson** *MASC NOUN*
  shiver
  avoir des frissons to shiver
  J'ai froid, j'ai des frissons. I'm cold, I'm
  shivering.

frissonner *VERB* [1]
1 to shiver
  Elle a beaucoup de fièvre et elle frissonne.
  She's got a high temperature and she's
  shivering.
2 to shudder
  Il frissonnait d'horreur. He was shuddering
  with horror.

frit *MASC ADJECTIVE*, **frite** *FEM*
  fried
  du poisson frit fried fish

ℙ la **frite** *FEM NOUN*
  chip, French fry
  un steak frites steak and chips

la **friture** *FEM NOUN*
1 frying
2 une friture de poissons fried fish, whitebait

ℙ **froid** *MASC ADJECTIVE*, **froide** *FEM* ▸ SEE **froid** *NOUN*
1 cold
  de l'eau froide cold water
2 cold, cool
  La maîtresse est très froide avec les
  parents. The teacher is very cold towards
  the parents.
  Nous avons eu un accueil froid. We had a
  cool welcome.

ℙ le **froid** *MASC NOUN* ▸ SEE **froid** *ADJECTIVE*
1 cold
  Je n'aime pas le froid. I don't like the cold.
  avoir froid to be cold *(person)*
  Elle a froid. She's cold.
  J'ai froid aux mains. My hands are cold.
2 faire froid to be cold *(weather)*
  Il fait froid aujourd'hui. It's cold today.

ℙ indicates key words

3 prendre froid to catch a chill
Il a pris froid au parc. He caught a chill at
the park.

froidement ADVERB
coldly

la **froideur** FEM NOUN
coldness

froisser VERB [1]
1 to crease
Il a froissé son pantalon. He creased his
trousers.
2 to hurt (upset)
Ta plaisanterie l'a froissé. Your joke hurt
him.

se **froisser** REFLEXIVE VERB ◎
1 to crease
La soie se froisse facilement. Silk creases
easily.
2 to take offence
Ne te froisse pas, c'était seulement pour
rire! Don't take offence, it was only a joke!
3 to strain (a muscle)

frôler VERB [1]
to brush against

♂ le **fromage** MASC NOUN
cheese

> 🔵 **FROMAGE**
>
> Les Français mangent le plus de fromage au
> monde: environ 26 kg par personne par an !

la **fromagerie** FEM NOUN
1 cheese shop
le rayon fromagerie du supermarché the
supermarket's cheese counter
2 dairy
Pendant les vacances je travaille à la
fromagerie. During the holidays I work at
the dairy.

le **froment** MASC NOUN
wheat

froncer VERB [61]
froncer les sourcils to frown

le **front** MASC NOUN
1 forehead
2 faire front à quelque chose to face up to
something
Il fait front à ses problèmes. He's facing up
to his problems.

3 faire front contre quelque chose to make a
stand against something
Nous faisons front contre le racisme. We're
making a stand against racism.

la **frontière** FEM NOUN
border
passer la frontière to cross the border
Nous avons passé la frontière à Bâle. We
crossed the border at Basle.

frotter VERB [1]
1 to rub
Frotte-moi le dos! Rub my back!
2 to scrub
Elle frotte le plancher. She's scrubbing the
floor.

se **frotter** REFLEXIVE VERB ◎
to rub
Estelle se frotte les yeux. Estelle is rubbing
her eyes.
Le chat aime se frotter contre mes jambes.
The cat likes rubbing against my legs.

♂ le **fruit** MASC NOUN
les fruits fruit
Il faut acheter des fruits. We need to buy
some fruit.
un fruit a piece of fruit
Veux-tu un fruit? Would you like some
fruit?
• les fruits de mer
seafood

fruité MASC ADJECTIVE, **fruitée** AJECTIVE FEM
fruity

frustrant MASC ADJECTIVE, **frustrante** FEM
frustrating

frustré MASC ADJECTIVE, **frustrée** FEM
frustrated

la **fugue** FEM NOUN
1 une adolescente en fugue a runaway
teenager
faire une fugue to run away
Juliette a fait une fugue. Juliette has run
away.
2 (Music) fugue
une fugue de Bach a fugue by Bach

fuir VERB [44]
1 to run away, to flee
2 fuir quelque chose, quelqu'un to run away
from something, somebody
La vedette a voulu fuir les journalistes. The
star tried to run away from the journalists.

◎ means the verb takes être to form the perfect

3 to leak
La bouilloire fuit. The kettle's leaking.

la **fuite** *FEM NOUN*
1 flight
la fuite du fugitif the escape of the fugitive
la fuite des cerveaux the brain drain
2 prendre la fuite to flee
L'automobiliste a pris la fuite après
l'accident. The motorist fled after the
accident.
3 leak
une fuite de gaz a gas leak
Il y a une fuite dans le tuyau. There is a leak
in the hosepipe.

fulgurant *MASC ADJECTIVE*, **fulgurante** *FEM*
dazzling

fumé *MASC ADJECTIVE*, **fumée** *FEM* ▸ SEE **fumée**
smoked
du saumon fumé smoked salmon

la **fumée** *FEM NOUN* ▸ SEE **fumé**
smoke

ℰ **fumer** *VERB* [1]
1 to smoke
Je ne fume pas. I don't smoke.
2 fumer une cigarette to smoke a cigarette
Elle fume la cigarette. She smokes.
Mon père fume la pipe. My father smokes
a pipe.

WORD TIP Use la pipe, la cigarette to say what
kind of smoker a person is.

le **fumeur** *MASC NOUN*, la **fumeuse** *FEM*
smoker
un zone non-fumeurs a no-smoking area

le **fumier** *MASC NOUN*
manure

le & la **funambule** *MASC & FEM NOUN*
tightrope walker

funèbre *MASC & FEM ADJECTIVE*
1 funeral
les pompes funèbres the undertaker's
2 gloomy
une voix funèbre a gloomy voice

les **funérailles** *PLURAL FEM NOUN*
funeral

le **funiculaire** *MASC NOUN*
funicular

le **furet** *MASC NOUN*
ferret

fur et à mesure *ADVERB*
1 au fur et à mesure as you go along
Je corrige les erreurs au fur et à mesure.
I correct the mistakes as I go along.
2 au fur et à mesure que as
Au fur et à mesure que les années
passent, Nicolas devient plus tolérant. As
the years go by, Nicolas's becoming more
tolerant.

la **fureur** *FEM NOUN*
1 rage, fury
un accès de fureur an outburst of rage
la fureur des combats the fury of the
fighting
2 frenzy
avec fureur frenziedly
3 faire fureur to be all the rage
Cette chanson fait fureur en ce moment.
This song is all the rage at the moment.

furibond *MASC ADJECTIVE*, **furibonde** *FEM*
furious

furieusement *ADVERB*
furiously

furieux *MASC ADJECTIVE*, **furieuse** *FEM*
furious
être furieux contre quelqu'un to be furious
with somebody
Elle est furieuse contre son copain. She's
furious with her boyfriend.

le **fusain** *MASC NOUN*
charcoal *(for drawing)*

le **fuseau** *MASC NOUN*, les **fuseaux** *PL*
ski pants
• le fuseau horaire
time zone

la **fusée** *FEM NOUN*
rocket

le **fusible** *MASC NOUN*
fuse

le **fusil** *MASC NOUN*
gun, rifle
un coup de fusil a gun shot

fusiller *VERB* [1]
to shoot *(to execute)*

fusionner *VERB* [1]
to merge

le **fût** *MASC NOUN*
cask, barrel
un fût de vin a cask of wine

ℰ indicates key words

futé MASC ADJECTIVE, **futée** FEM
1 **crafty**
   Émilie est une petite fille futée. Émilie is a crafty little girl.
2 **clever**
   Il n'est pas très futé. He isn't very clever.

futur MASC ADJECTIVE, **future** FEM ▸ SEE **futur** NOUN
   future
   le futur président the future president
   son futur mari her husband-to-be

le **futur** MASC NOUN ▸ SEE **futur** ADJECTIVE
   future
   dans un futur proche in the near future
   Ce sont nos projets pour le futur. These are our future plans.

Gg

gâcher VERB [1]
1 **to waste** (food)
2 **to spoil** (fun)

la **gaffe** FEM NOUN (informal)
1 **blunder**
   Aurore a fait une gaffe. Aurore has done something stupid.
2 **faire gaffe** to watch out

le **gagnant** MASC NOUN, la **gagnante** FEM
   winner

ℰ **gagner** VERB [1]
1 **to win**
   Il a gagné! He's won!
   Elles ont gagné le match. They won the match.
2 **to earn**
   Elle gagne bien sa vie. She makes a good living.
3 **gagner du temps** to save time

gai MASC ADJECTIVE, **gaie** FEM
   cheerful

la **galerie** FEM NOUN
   gallery
• la galerie d'art
   art gallery
• la galerie marchande
   shopping arcade

le **galet** MASC NOUN
   pebble

la **galette** FEM NOUN
1 **biscuit**
2 **pancake** (savoury)
3 **round flat cake or loaf**

• la galette des Rois
   Twelfth Night cake

ⓘ **GALETTE**

Le 6 janvier, c'est l'Épiphanie. On mange une galette des Rois, un gâteau rond et plat avec une fève. Si on a la fève, on est roi ou reine. On met une couronne en papier !

ℰ **Galles** NOUN
   le pays de Galles Wales

   WORD TIP Countries and regions in French take le, la or les.

ℰ **gallois** MASC ADJECTIVE, **galloise** FEM ▸ SEE **Gallois**
   Welsh

   WORD TIP Adjectives never have capitals in French, even for nationality or regional origin.

ℰ le **Gallois** MASC NOUN, la **Galloise** FEM ▸ SEE **gallois**
1 **Welshman, Welshwoman**
   les Gallois the Welsh
2 le gallois **Welsh** (the language)
   Je parle gallois. I speak Welsh.

   WORD TIP Languages never have capitals in French.

galoper VERB [1]
1 **to canter** (horses)
2 **to gallop** (horses)
3 **to dash around** (people)

le **gamin** MASC NOUN, la **gamine** FEM
   (informal) **kid**

la **gamme** FEM NOUN
1 **range** (of products)
2 **scale** (in music)

ℰ le **gant** MASC NOUN
   glove

ℰ le **garage** MASC NOUN
   garage

ℰ le & la **garagiste** MASC & FEM NOUN
1 **garage owner**
2 **motor mechanic**

la **garantie** FEM NOUN
   guarantee

garantir VERB [2]
   to guarantee

ℰ le **garçon** MASC NOUN
1 **boy**
2 **young man**
3 **bachelor**
4 **waiter**

le & la **garde** MASC & FEM NOUN
1 **guard**
2 **nurse**

ⓐ means the verb takes être to form the perfect

3 être de garde to be on duty
la pharmacie de garde the duty chemist's
4 mettre quelqu'un en garde to warn somebody
prendre garde to be careful

ℰ **garder** *VERB* [1]
1 **to keep**
Est-ce que tu peux garder mon sac? Can you keep my bag for me?
Il t'a gardé une place. He's kept you a seat.
Pour garder la forme ... To keep healthy...
2 **to keep on**
Elle a gardé son manteau. She kept her coat on.
3 **to look after**
Audrey garde les enfants ce soir. Audrey is looking after the children this evening.
4 **to guard**
Le chien garde la maison. The dog guards the house.
se **garder** *REFLEXIVE VERB* ◯
to keep *(food)*

la **garderie** *FEM NOUN*
day nursery

la **garde-robe** *FEM NOUN*
wardrobe

le **gardien** *MASC NOUN*, la **gardienne** *FEM*
1 **security guard**
2 **caretaker** *(in a hotel)*
3 **attendant** *(in a museum)*
4 **warder** *(in a prison)*
• le gardien de but
goalkeeper
• le gardien de la paix
policeman

ℰ la **gare** *FEM NOUN*
(railway) station
• la gare routière
coach station

garer *VERB* [1]
to park *(a car)*
se **garer** *REFLEXIVE VERB* ◯
to park

garnir *VERB* [2]
1 **to decorate** *(a cake)*
2 **to garnish** *(meat)*
3 **to stock** *(shelves)*

la **garniture** *FEM NOUN*
1 **side dish**
2 **filling** *(for a sandwich)*
3 **topping** *(for a pizza)*
4 **trimming** *(for clothes)*

le **gars** *MASC NOUN*
(informal) **guy**

la **Gascogne** *FEM NOUN*
Gascony

> **WORD TIP** Countries and regions in French take le, la or les.

le **gasoil** *MASC NOUN*
diesel (oil)

gaspiller *VERB* [1]
to waste

ℰ le **gâteau** *MASC NOUN*, les **gâteaux** *PLURAL*
cake
un gâteau au chocolat a chocolate cake
un petit gâteau a biscuit

gâter *VERB* [1]
to spoil
se **gâter** *REFLEXIVE VERB* ◯
to go bad

ℰ **gauche** *MASC & FEM ADJECTIVE* ▶ SEE **gauche** *NOUN*
left
sa main gauche his left hand

ℰ la **gauche** *FEM NOUN* ▶ SEE **gauche** *ADJECTIVE*
1 **left**
à gauche on the left
tournez à gauche turn left
à ma gauche, sur ma gauche on my left
2 la gauche the Left *(in politics)*

gaucher *MASC ADJECTIVE*, **gauchère** *FEM*
left-handed

la **gaufre** *FEM NOUN*
waffle

le **gaz** *INVARIABLE MASC NOUN*
gas
le chauffage au gaz gas central heating
• le gaz carbonique
carbon dioxide
• le gaz d'échappement
exhaust fumes

gazeux *MASC ADJECTIVE*, **gazeuse** *FEM*
fizzy
eau gazeuse sparkling mineral water

le **gazole** *MASC NOUN*
diesel (oil)

le **gazon** *MASC NOUN*
lawn

le **géant** *MASC NOUN*, **géante** *FEM*
giant

le **gel** *MASC NOUN*
1 **frost**
2 **gel**

gelé *MASC ADJECTIVE*, **gelée** *FEM* ▶ SEE **gelée**
frozen

la **gelée** *FEM NOUN* ▶ SEE **gelé**
1 **jelly**

ℰ **indicates key words**

2 frost

ℰ **geler** *VERB* [45]
to freeze
Il gèle dehors. It's freezing outside.

les **Gémeaux** *PLURAL MASC NOUN*
Gemini *(sign of the Zodiac)*
Yasmina est Gémeaux. Yasmina is a Gemini.

WORD TIP Signs of the zodiac do not take an
article: un or une.

gémir *VERB* [2]
to moan

gênant *MASC ADJECTIVE,* **gênante** *FEM*
1 annoying *(noise, person)*
2 awkward *(situation)*

la **gencive** *FEM NOUN*
gum *(part of your mouth)*

ℰ le **gendarme** *MASC NOUN*
policeman

la **gendarmerie** *FEM NOUN*
police station
• la gendarmerie nationale
(French) national police force

le **gendre** *MASC NOUN*
son-in-law

la **gêne** *FEM NOUN*
1 embarrassment
sans aucune gêne without a hint of
embarrassment
2 discomfort *(physical)*
3 inconvenience

gêné *MASC ADJECTIVE,* **gênée** *FEM*
embarrassed

gêner *VERB* [1]
1 to bother
Ça te gêne si je mets la radio? Do you mind
if I put the radio on?
2 to embarrass
Ça me gêne. It's embarrassing.
3 to block *(traffic)*

général *MASC ADJECTIVE,* **générale** *FEM,*
généraux *MASC PL,* **générales** *FEM PL* ▸SEE
général *NOUN*
general
en général in general, generally

le **général** *MASC NOUN,* les **généraux** *PLURAL*
▸SEE **général** *ADJECTIVE*
general
le général Dubois General Dubois

généralement *ADVERB*
generally

la **génération** *FEM NOUN*
generation

généreux *MASC ADJECTIVE,* **généreuse** *FEM*
generous

la **générosité** *FEM NOUN*
generosity

la **génétique** *FEM NOUN*
genetics

Genève *NOUN*
Geneva

génial *MASC ADJECTIVE,* **géniale** *FEM,* **géniaux**
MASC PL, **géniales** *FEM PL*
brilliant

le **génie** *MASC NOUN*
1 genius
2 engineering

ℰ le **genou** *MASC NOUN,* les **genoux** *PLURAL*
knee
être à genoux to be kneeling
Elle est à genoux. She's kneeling.
se mettre à genoux to kneel down
Mettez-vous à genoux! Kneel down!

le **genre** *MASC NOUN*
kind
Quel genre de livre aimes-tu lire? What
kind of book do you like to read?
• le genre humain
mankind

ℰ les **gens** *PLURAL MASC NOUN*
people
beaucoup de gens a lot of people

ℰ **gentil** *MASC ADJECTIVE,* **gentille** *FEM*
1 kind, nice
Elle est très gentille. She's really nice.
C'est très gentil de ta part. It's very kind
of you.
2 good
Sois gentil! Be good!

la **gentillesse** *FEM NOUN*
kindness

gentiment *ADVERB*
1 nicely
2 kindly

ℰ la **géographie** *FEM NOUN*
geography

la **géologie** *FEM NOUN*
geology

le **gérant** *MASC NOUN,* la **gérante** *FEM*
manager, manageress

gérer *VERB* [24]
1 to manage
2 to run *(a country)*
3 to handle *(a problem)*

⬥ **means the verb takes être to form the perfect**

germain *MASC ADJECTIVE*, **germaine** *FEM*
  un cousin germain a first cousin

le **geste** *MASC NOUN*
  gesture

la **gestion** *FEM NOUN*
  management

la **gifle** *FEM NOUN*
  slap

gifler *VERB* [1]
  to slap

gigantesque *MASC & FEM ADJECTIVE*
  gigantic

le **gigaoctet** *MASC NOUN*
  gigabyte

le **gigot** *MASC NOUN*
  leg of lamb

le **gilet** *MASC NOUN*
1 cardigan
2 waistcoat
  • le gilet de sauvetage
    life-jacket

le **gingembre** *MASC NOUN*
  ginger

la **girafe** *FEM NOUN*
  giraffe

le **gitan** *MASC NOUN*, la **gitane** *FEM*
  gipsy

ℐ le **gîte**, **gîte rural** *MASC NOUN*
  self-catering cottage

ℐ la **glace** *FEM NOUN*
1 ice cream
2 ice
3 mirror
  se regarder dans la glace to look at yourself
  in the mirror
4 window *(in a car)*
  Peux-tu baisser ta glace? Can you open
  your window?

glacé *MASC ADJECTIVE*, **glacée** *FEM*
1 icy cold
2 du thé glacé iced tea

le **glaçon** *MASC NOUN*
  ice cube

glissant *MASC ADJECTIVE*, **glissante** *FEM*
  slippery

ℐ **glisser** *VERB* [1]
1 to slip
  Attention, ça glisse! Be careful, it's slippery!
2 to slide
  Il a glissé une lettre sous la porte. He slid a
  letter under the door.

global *MASC ADJECTIVE*, **globale** *FEM*, **globaux**
MASC PL, **globales** *FEM PL*
  total

la **gloire** *FEM NOUN*
  glory

glorieux *MASC ADJECTIVE*, **glorieuse** *FEM*
  glorious

gluant *MASC ADJECTIVE*, **gluante** *FEM*
1 sticky *(pasta, rice)*
2 slimy *(fish)*

le **goal** *MASC NOUN*
  goalkeeper

le **gobelet** *MASC NOUN*
  cup

la **godasse** *FEM NOUN*
  (informal) shoe

gogo *ADVERB*
  (informal) à gogo as much as you like
  pizza à gogo as much pizza as you can eat

le **golf** *MASC NOUN*
1 golf
  jouer au golf to play golf
2 golf course

la **gomme** *FEM NOUN*
  rubber

gommer *VERB* [1]
  to rub out

gonfler *VERB* [1]
1 to pump up *(tyres)*
2 to blow up *(a balloon)*

ℐ la **gorge** *FEM NOUN*
1 throat
  J'ai mal à la gorge. I've got a sore throat.
2 gorge

la **gorgée** *FEM NOUN*
  sip

le **gorille** *MASC NOUN*
  gorilla

ℐ le & la **gosse** *MASC & FEM NOUN*
  (informal) kid

le **goudron** *MASC NOUN*
  tar

la **gourde** *FEM NOUN*
  bottle *(made of plastic, metal)*

gourmand *MASC ADJECTIVE*, **gourmande** *FEM*
1 greedy
  Il est gourmand. He loves his food.
2 un repas gourmand a gourmet meal

la **gourmandise** *FEM NOUN*
  greed

ℐ indicates key words

la **gousse d'ail** *FEM NOUN*
clove of garlic

le **goût** *MASC NOUN*
1 taste
Cette eau a un goût de citron. The water
tastes of lemon.
de bon goût in good taste
chacun ses goûts each to their own
2 flavour
un yaourt au goût vanille a vanilla-
flavoured yoghurt
3 liking
à mon goût for my liking

ℓ le **goûter** *MASC NOUN* ▸ SEE **goûter** *VERB*
1 afternoon snack
2 children's party
le goûter d'anniversaire de Camille
Camille's birthday party

goûter *VERB* [1]
▸ SEE **goûter** *NOUN*
1 to taste, to try
Je peux goûter? May I taste it?
2 goûter à to taste, to try
Il n'a même pas goûté au foie gras. He
didn't even try the foie gras.
3 to have a mid-afternoon snack
Aujourd'hui les enfants ont goûté au parc.
Today the children had their mid-afternoon
snack in the park.

goûteux *MASC ADJECTIVE*, **goûteuse** *FEM*
tasty

la **goutte** *FEM NOUN*
drop
goutte à goutte drop by drop

le **gouvernement** *MASC NOUN*
government

gouverner *VERB* [1]
to rule

la **goyave** *FEM NOUN*
guava

la **grâce** *FEM NOUN*
1 grace
2 grâce à thanks to

gracieux *MASC ADJECTIVE*, **gracieuse** *FEM*
graceful

le **grade** *MASC NOUN*
rank

les **gradins** *PLURAL MASC NOUN*
terraces *(in a stadium)*

graduel *MASC ADJECTIVE*, **graduelle** *FEM*
gradual

le **grain** *MASC NOUN*
1 grain, corn
2 du poivre en grains peppercorns

du café en grains coffee beans
• le grain de raisin
grape
• le grain de sable
grain of sand

la **graine** *FEM NOUN*
seed

la **graisse** *FEM NOUN*
fat

la **grammaire** *FEM NOUN*
grammar

ℓ le **gramme** *MASC NOUN*
gramme

ℓ **grand** *ADVERB* ▸ SEE **grand** *ADJECTIVE*
wide
La porte était grande ouverte. The door
was wide open.
Ouvre grand la bouche! Open your mouth
wide!
Ouvre grand tes oreilles! Listen carefully!

ℓ **grand** *MASC ADJECTIVE*, **grande** *FEM* ▸ SEE **grand**
ADVERB
1 big
une grande maison a big house
C'est ma grande sœur. She's my big sister.
2 tall
un grand arbre a tall tree
Ton frère est très grand. Your brother's
very tall.
Elle est plus grande que moi. She's taller
than me.
3 long
un grand voyage a long journey
4 great
un grand artiste a great artist
un grand ami a great friend
5 old
Manon est assez grande pour sortir seule.
Manon is old enough to go out on her own.
6 main
les grandes lignes main (railway) lines
• la grande personne
grown-up
• la grande surface
hypermarket

ℓ **grand-chose** *PRONOUN*
much
pas grand-chose not much
Il ne reste pas grand-chose. There's not
much left.

ℓ la **Grande-Bretagne** *FEM NOUN*
Great Britain

WORD TIP Countries and regions in French take
le, la or les.

means the verb takes être to form the perfect

la **grandeur** FEM NOUN
size
grandeur nature life-size

grandir VERB [2]
to grow, to grow up

ℓ la **grand-mère** FEM NOUN, les **grands-mères** PLURAL
grandmother

ℓ le **grand-père** MASC NOUN, les **grands-pères** PLURAL
grandfather

la **grand-rue** FEM NOUN
main street

ℓ les **grands-parents** PLURAL MASC NOUN
grandparents

la **grange** FEM NOUN
barn

le & la **graphiste** MASC & FEM NOUN
graphic designer

la **grappe** FEM NOUN
bunch
• la grappe de raisin
bunch of grapes

ℓ **gras** MASC ADJECTIVE, **grasse** FEM ▶ SEE **gras** NOUN
1 fatty
40% de matières grasses 40% fat (on cheese or yoghurt label)
2 oily, greasy
une peau grasse oily skin

ℓ le **gras** MASC NOUN ▶ SEE **gras** ADJECTIVE
1 fat
2 grease

le **gratte-ciel** INVARIABLE MASC NOUN
skyscraper

gratter VERB [1]
1 to scratch
Est-ce que tu peux me gratter le dos? Can you scratch my back?
2 to itch
Ça me gratte partout. I'm itching all over.
se **gratter** REFLEXIVE VERB ◔
to scratch

ℓ **gratuit** MASC ADJECTIVE, **gratuite** FEM
free
Le concert est gratuit. The concert's free.
'Entrée gratuite' 'Admission free'

gratuitement ADVERB
1 free
2 for nothing (without payment)

grave MASC & FEM ADJECTIVE
1 serious
un grave accident a serious accident
un blessé grave a seriously injured person

Ce n'est pas grave. It doesn't matter.
2 deep
une voix grave a deep voice

gravement ADVERB
seriously
Elle est gravement malade. She's seriously ill.

le **gré** MASC NOUN
contre son gré against his will
de plein gré willingly
de bon gré gladly

grec MASC ADJECTIVE, **grecque** FEM ▶ SEE **Grec**
Greek

le **Grec** MASC NOUN, la **Grecque** FEM ▶ SEE **grec**
1 Greek (person)
2 le grec Greek (the language)

la **Grèce** FEM NOUN
Greece

la **grêle** FEM NOUN
hail

grêler VERB [1]
to hail
Il grêle. It's hailing.

grelotter VERB [1]
to shiver

la **grenade** FEM NOUN
1 grenade
2 pomegranate

la **grenadine** FEM NOUN
grenadine (pomegranate cordial)

le **grenier** MASC NOUN
attic
au grenier in the attic

la **grenouille** FEM NOUN
frog
les cuisses de grenouille frogs' legs

la **grève** FEM NOUN
1 strike
une grève des trains a train strike
Le métro est en grève. The underground's on strike.
faire grève to strike
2 shore

le & la **gréviste** MASC & FEM NOUN
striker

grièvement ADVERB
seriously
grièvement blessé seriously injured

la **griffe** FEM NOUN
claw

griffonner VERB [1]
to scribble

ℓ indicates key words

la **grillade** *FEM NOUN*
grilled meat
une grillade de porc a pork steak

le **grillage** *MASC NOUN*
wire netting

la **grille** *FEM NOUN*
1 metal gate
2 railings

♂ **grillé** *MASC ADJECTIVE*, **grillée** *FEM*
1 grilled
2 toasted
du pain grillé toast
3 roasted *(nuts)*
des cacahuètes grillées roasted peanuts

le **grille-pain** *INVARIABLE MASC NOUN*
toaster

griller *VERB* [1]
1 to grill
2 to toast

la **grimace** *FEM NOUN*
grimace
faire des grimaces à quelqu'un to make
faces at somebody

grimper *VERB* [1]
to climb
Elle aime grimper aux arbres. She likes
climbing trees.

grincer *VERB* [61]
to creak
La porte grince. The door creaks.

grincheux *MASC ADJECTIVE*, **grincheuse** *FEM*
grumpy

♂ la **grippe** *FEM NOUN*
flu
avoir la grippe to have flu
Aurélie a la grippe. Aurélie has flu.
• la grippe aviaire
bird flu

♂ **gris** *MASC ADJECTIVE*, **grise** *FEM*
grey

la **grisaille** *FEM NOUN*
dull overcast weather

grogner *VERB* [1]
1 to grumble
2 to growl *(dog)*

gronder *VERB* [1]
1 to tell off
Ses parents l'ont grondé. His parents told
him off.
se faire gronder to get a telling-off
Brice s'est fait gronder. Brice got told off.
2 to rumble *(thunder, cannons)*

♂ **gros** *MASC ADJECTIVE*, **grosse** *FEM*
1 big
un gros problème a big problem
des grosses larmes big tears
2 fat
un gros monsieur a fat man
3 bad
un gros rhume a bad cold
4 heavy
un gros fumeur a heavy smoker
5 en gros roughly
En gros, nous sommes une vingtaine.
Roughly there are about twenty of us.
• le gros lot
jackpot
• le gros mot
swear word

la **groseille** *FEM NOUN*
redcurrant
• la groseille à maquereau
gooseberry

grosse *FEM ADJECTIVE* ▶ SEE **gros**

la **grossesse** *FEM NOUN*
pregnancy

la **grosseur** *FEM NOUN*
1 size
deux oranges de la même grosseur two
oranges of the same size
2 lump
Il a une grosseur dans le cou. He has a lump
in his neck.

grossier *MASC ADJECTIVE*, **grossière** *FEM*
1 rude
David est grossier. David is rude.
2 crude
un travail grossier a crude piece of work
une erreur grossière a bad mistake

grossir *VERB* [2]
1 to enlarge *(photo)*
2 to put on weight
Annie a grossi de dix kilos. Annie put on
ten kilos.

grosso modo *ADVERB*
roughly

grotesque *MASC & FEM ADJECTIVE*
ridiculous

la **grotte** *FEM NOUN*
cave

♂ le **groupe** *MASC NOUN*
group
un groupe de lycéens a group of secondary
school students
un groupe scolaire a school group
un groupe theâtral a drama group
en groupe in a group

⬥ means the verb takes être to form the perfect

travailler en groupes de deux to work in pairs
- le groupe sanguin
  blood group

grouper VERB [1]
to group

se **grouper** REFLEXIVE VERB ⊚
1 to gather
2 to form a group

la **grue** FEM NOUN
crane

le **guépard** MASC NOUN
cheetah

la **guêpe** FEM NOUN
wasp

guère ADVERB
ne ... guère ... hardly
Je ne l'ai guère vu depuis Noël. I've hardly seen him since Christmas.

guérir VERB [2]
1 to cure
Le médecin l'a guéri. The doctor cured him.
2 to get better
J'espère que tu vas vite guérir. I hope you'll get better soon.

la **guérison** FEM NOUN
recovery (from an illness, an injury)

Guernesey FEM NOUN
Guernsey (in the Channel Islands)

> **WORD TIP** Unlike the names of most other islands, Guernesey does not take le or la.

la **guerre** FEM NOUN
war
en guerre at war
la Deuxième Guerre mondiale the Second World War

guetter VERB [1]
to watch out for

la **gueule** FEM NOUN
1 mouth (of an animal) (considered rude if used for a person)
2 (informal)
faire la gueule to sulk
Elle fait la gueule. She's sulking.

gueuler VERB [1]
(informal) to yell

ℱ le **guichet** MASC NOUN
1 ticket office (in a station)
2 box office (in a theatre)
3 counter, window (in a bank)
- le guichet automatique
  cashpoint

ℱ le **guide** MASC NOUN
guide

guider VERB [1]
to guide

le **guidon** MASC NOUN
handlebars

les **guillemets** PLURAL MASC NOUN
quotations marks
entre guillemets in quotation marks
(usually « ... » in French)

la **guirlande** FEM NOUN
1 garland
2 tinsel
- la guirlande électrique
  fairy lights
- la guirlande en papier
  paper chain

la **guitare** FEM NOUN
guitar
jouer de la guitare to play the guitar

le & la **guitariste** MASC & FEM NOUN
guitarist

guyanais MASC ADJECTIVE, **guyanaise** FEM ▶ SEE
Guyanais
Guianese

le **Guyanais** MASC NOUN, la **Guyanaise** FEM ▶ SEE
guyanais
Guianese (person)

la **Guyane** FEM NOUN
French Guiana
Je vais en Guyane. I'm going to French Guiana.

la **gym** FEM NOUN
gymnastics, PE

ℱ le **gymnase** MASC NOUN
gym

la **gymnastique** FEM NOUN
1 gymnastics
2 exercises

Hh

habile MASC & FEM ADJECTIVE
clever
Elle est habile de ses mains. She's clever with her hands.

habillé MASC ADJECTIVE, **habillée** FEM
1 dressed
2 smart (dress, suit)

habiller VERB [1]
to dress (a child)

ℱ indicates key words

s'**habiller** *REFLEXIVE VERB* ⬭
  to get dressed
  Habille-toi vite! Get dressed quick!

un **habitant** *MASC NOUN*, une **habitante** *FEM*
  inhabitant

une **habitation** *FEM NOUN*
  house
• une habitation à loyer modéré HLM
  council flat

♀ **habiter** *VERB* [1]
  to live
  Ils habitent Paris., Ils habitent à Paris. They
  live in Paris.
  Nous habitons en Angleterre. We live in
  England.

♀ une **habitude** *FEM NOUN*
1 habit
  une mauvaise habitude a bad habit
2 d'habitude usually
3 comme d'habitude as usual
4 avoir l'habitude de faire quelque chose to
  be used to doing something
  J'ai l'habitude de travailler le soir. I tend to
  work in the evening.

habitué *MASC ADJECTIVE*, **habituée** *FEM*
  être habitué à quelque chose to be used to
  something
  Nous sommes habitués aux bruits de la
  rue. We are used to the noise from the
  street.

habituel *MASC ADJECTIVE*, **habituelle** *FEM*
  usual

s'**habituer** *REFLEXIVE VERB* ⬭ [1]
  s'habituer à quelque chose to get used to
  something
  Il s'est habitué à sa nouvelle école. He got
  used to his new school.

haché *MASC ADJECTIVE*, **hachée** *FEM*
1 chopped
2 minced
  un bifteck haché a burger *(without the bun)*

le **hachis Parmentier** *MASC NOUN*
  shepherd's pie

le **haddock** *MASC NOUN*
  smoked haddock

la **haie** *FEM NOUN*
  hedge

la **haine** *FEM NOUN*
  hatred

haïr *VERB* [46]
  to hate

Haïti *MASC NOUN*
  Haiti

en Haïti in Haiti

WORD TIP Unlike the names of most other
countries, Haiti does not take le or la.

haïtien *MASC ADJECTIVE*, **haïtienne** *FEM* ▸ SEE
Haïtien
  Haitian

le **Haïtien** *MASC NOUN*, la **Haïtienne** *FEM* ▸ SEE
haïtien
  Haitian

l'**haleine** *FEM NOUN*
  breath
  hors d'haleine out of breath

le **hall** *MASC NOUN*
  entrance hall

les **halles** *PLURAL FEM NOUN*
  covered market

la **halte** *FEM NOUN*
  stop
  Halte! Stop!

l'**haltérophilie** *FEM NOUN*
  weightlifting

le **hamster** *MASC NOUN*
  hamster

la **hanche** *FEM NOUN*
  hip

le **handball** *MASC NOUN*
  handball
  jouer au handball to play handball

le **handicap** *MASC NOUN*
  handicap

un **handicapé** *MASC NOUN*, une **handicapée**
  FEM
  disabled person
  les handicapés the disabled

le **harcèlement** *MASC NOUN*
1 harassment
2 bullying

harceler *VERB* [45]
1 to harass
2 to bully

le **hareng** *MASC NOUN*
  herring
• le hareng saur
  smoked herring

♀ le **haricot** *MASC NOUN*
  bean
• le haricot blanc
  haricot bean
• le haricot vert
  French bean

⬭ means the verb takes être to form the perfect

une **harmonie** FEM NOUN
　harmony

la **harpe** FEM NOUN
　harp

le **hasard** MASC NOUN
1 chance
　par hasard by chance
2 au hasard at random
3 à tout hasard just in case

la **hâte** FEM NOUN
　haste
　à la hâte hastily

la **hausse** FEM NOUN
　increase, rise
　une hausse des prix a rise in prices

hausser VERB [1]
1 to raise
2 hausser les épaules to shrug your shoulders

ℯ **haut** MASC ADJECTIVE, **haute** FEM ▸ SEE **haut**
　ADVERB, NOUN
　high
　un immeuble haut de 50 étages a block of
　flats 50 storeys high

ℯ **haut** ADVERB ▸ SEE **haut** ADJECTIVE, NOUN
　high
　Voir plus haut. See above (in a book).

ℯ le **haut** MASC NOUN ▸ SEE **haut** ADJECTIVE, ADVERB
1 top
　le haut du mur the top of the wall
　J'ai acheté un haut. I bought a top.
2 L'arbre fait 10 mètres de haut. The tree is
　10 metres high.
3 en haut upstairs
4 en haut de at the top of

le **hautbois** MASC NOUN
　oboe
　Luc joue du hautbois. Luc plays the oboe.

la **hauteur** FEM NOUN
1 height
　Quelle est la hauteur de la porte? How high
　is the door?
2 le saut en hauteur high jump (the sport)
3 hill

le **haut-parleur** MASC NOUN
　loudspeaker

un **hebdomadaire** MASC NOUN
　weekly magazine

ℯ un **hébergement** MASC NOUN
1 accommodation
2 hosting
　l'hébergement de site Internet website
　hosting

héberger VERB [52]
1 to put up (a guest for the night)
2 to host (a website)

hein EXCLAMATION
　(informal) what?, eh?

hélas EXCLAMATION
　unfortunately

ℯ l'**herbe** FEM NOUN
1 grass
2 herb
　• les herbes de Provence
　　mixed herbs

le **hérisson** MASC NOUN
　hedgehog

un **héritage** MASC NOUN
　inheritance

hériter VERB [1]
　to inherit
　hériter de quelque chose to inherit
　something

hermétique MASC & FEM ADJECTIVE
　airtight

l'**héroïne** FEM NOUN
1 heroine
2 heroin (the drug)

le **héros** MASC NOUN
　hero

une **hésitation** FEM NOUN
　hesitation

hésiter VERB [1]
　to hesitate
　Nous hésitons entre … We can't decide
　between …

ℯ une **heure** FEM NOUN
1 hour
　une demi-heure half an hour
　une heure et demie an hour and a half
　toutes les heures every hour
　à l'heure per hour
2 time
　Quelle heure est-il? What time is it?
　C'est l'heure de… It's time for…
　à huit heures du matin at eight o'clock in
　the morning
　à six heures et demie at half past six
　à deux heures moins le quart at quarter
　to two
　À quelle heure te lèves-tu demain? What
　time are you getting up tomorrow?
3 à l'heure on time
4 de bonne heure early
5 tout à l'heure (in a while) later (a moment
　ago), earlier
　À tout à l'heure! See you later!

169

heureusement *ADVERB*
fortunately

♪ **heureux** *MASC ADJECTIVE*, **heureuse** *FEM*
1 **happy**
Elle est heureuse d'être ici. She's happy to be here.
2 **pleased**
Je suis heureux que Grégory soit guéri
I am pleased that Grégory is better *(boy speaking)*.
Je suis heureuse que Grégory soit guéri
I am pleased that Grégory is better *(girl speaking)*.
3 **lucky**
un heureux gagnant a lucky winner

heurter *VERB* [1]
to hit

un **hexagone** *MASC NOUN*
1 **hexagon**
2 l'Hexagone France *(French journalists often refer to France as l'Hexagone as it has a six-sided shape on the map)*

le **hibou** *MASC NOUN*, les **hiboux** *PLURAL*
owl

♪ **hier** *ADVERB*
yesterday
hier matin yesterday morning
hier soir last night
avant-hier the day before yesterday

la **hi-fi** *INVARIABLE FEM NOUN*
hi-fi

hippique *MASC & FEM ADJECTIVE*
equestrian
un club hippique a riding school

une **hirondelle** *FEM NOUN*
swallow

♪ une **histoire** *FEM NOUN*
1 **history**
l'histoire de France French history
2 **story**
une histoire d'espionnage a spy story
l'histoire de ma vie the story of my life
3 **matter**
une histoire de famille a family matter
4 faire des histoires to make a fuss
Il fait toujours des histoires. He's always making a fuss.
• l'histoire-géo
history and geography *(school subject)*

historique *MASC & FEM ADJECTIVE*
historic

le **hit-parade** *MASC NOUN*
charts *(in pop music)*

l'**hiver** *MASC NOUN*
winter
en hiver in winter

♪ un **HLM** *INVARIABLE MASC & FEM NOUN*
(= *habitation à loyer modéré*) un logement
HLM a council flat
les HLM council housing

hocher *VERB* [1]
1 hocher la tête to shake your head *(in disagreement)*
2 hocher la tête to nod *(in agreement)*

le **hockey** *MASC NOUN*
hockey
jouer au hockey to play hockey
• le hockey sur glace
ice hockey

hollandais *MASC ADJECTIVE*, **hollandaise** *FEM*
▸ SEE **Hollandais**
Dutch

le **Hollandais** *MASC NOUN*, la **Hollandaise** *FEM*
▸ SEE **hollandais**
1 **Dutchman, Dutchwoman**
les Hollandais the Dutch
2 l'hollandais Dutch *(the language)*

la **Hollande** *FEM NOUN*
Holland

le **homard** *MASC NOUN*
lobster

homéopathique *MASC & FEM ADJECTIVE*
homeopathic

un **hommage** *MASC NOUN*
tribute

♪ un **homme** *MASC NOUN*
1 **mankind**
2 **human being**
3 **man**
l'homme de la rue the man in the street

homosexuel *MASC ADJECTIVE*, **homosexuelle** *FEM*
homosexual

la **Hongrie** *FEM NOUN*
Hungary

hongrois *MASC ADJECTIVE*, **hongroise** *FEM* ▸ SEE **Hongrois**
Hungarian

le **Hongrois** *MASC NOUN*, la **Hongroise** *FEM NOUN* ▸ SEE **hongrois**
1 **Hungarian** *(person)*
2 l'hongrois Hungarian *(the language)*

♪ **honnête** *MASC & FEM ADJECTIVE*
honest

170

honnêtement *ADVERB*
  honestly

l'**honnêteté** *FEM NOUN*
  honesty

un **honneur** *MASC NOUN*
  honour

honorer *VERB* [1]
  to honour

la **honte** *FEM NOUN*
1 shame
  avoir honte de quelque chose to be ashamed of something
2 disgrace

honteux *MASC ADJECTIVE*, **honteuse** *FEM*
  disgraceful

ℓ un **hôpital** *MASC NOUN*
  hospital
  être à l'hôpital to be in hospital

le **hoquet** *MASC NOUN*
  hiccup
  avoir le hoquet to have hiccups

ℓ un **horaire** *MASC NOUN*
1 timetable
  les horaires de train the train timetable
2 hours
  les horaires du travail the working hours

un **horizon** *MASC NOUN*
  horizon

horizontal *MASC ADJECTIVE*, **horizontale** *FEM*, **horizontaux** *MASC PL*, **horizontales** *FEM PL*
  horizontal

une **horloge** *FEM NOUN*
  clock

une **horreur** *FEM NOUN*
1 horror
  Quelle horreur! How awful!
2 avoir horreur de quelque chose to hate something
  Nina a horreur des épinards. Nina hates spinach.

horrifier *VERB* [1]
  to horrify

ℓ **hors** *PREPOSITION*
  hors de outside
  Hors d'ici! Get out of here!
  les boutiques hors taxes the duty-free shops
• le hors-d'œuvre
  starter *(to a meal)*
• hors-jeu
  offside *(in sports)*
• hors service
  out of order

hospitalier *MASC ADJECTIVE*, **hospitalière** *FEM*
  un centre hospitalier a hospital

l'**hospitalité** *FEM NOUN*
  hospitality

l'**hostilité** *FEM NOUN*
  hostility

un **hôte** *MASC NOUN* ▸ SEE **hôte** *NOUN*
  host

un & une **hôte** *MASC & FEM NOUN* ▸ SEE **hôte** *NOUN*
  guest
• un hôte payant
  paying guest

ℓ un **hôtel** *MASC NOUN*
  hotel
  Nous passons deux nuits à l'hôtel. We are spending two nights in a hotel.
• un hôtel de ville
  town hall

ℓ une **hôtesse** *FEM NOUN*
1 hostess
2 receptionist
• une hôtesse de l'air
  flight attendant

la **housse** *FEM NOUN*
  cover *(for a chair)*
• la housse de couette
  duvet cover

le **houx** *MASC NOUN*
  holly

ℓ un **hovercraft** *MASC NOUN*
  hovercraft

ℓ une **huile** *FEM NOUN*
  oil
  des sardines à l'huile sardines in vegetable oil
• l'huile d'olive
  olive oil

ℓ **huit** *NUMBER*
1 eight
  Paul a huit ans. Paul's eight.
  le huit juillet the eighth of July
2 huit jours a week

huitième *MASC & FEM ADJECTIVE*
  eighth

une **huître** *FEM NOUN*
  oyster

humain *MASC ADJECTIVE*, **humaine** *FEM*
1 human
2 humane

une **humeur** *FEM NOUN*
  mood
  Il est de bonne humeur. He's in a good mood.

Elle est de mauvaise humeur. She's in a bad mood.

être d'humeur à faire quelque chose to be in the mood to do something

humide MASC & FEM ADJECTIVE
damp

l'**humidité** FEM NOUN
1 damp
2 humidity (of climate)

humoristique MASC & FEM ADJECTIVE
humorous
un dessin humoristique a cartoon

l'**humour** MASC NOUN
humour
avec humour humorously
avoir de l'humour to have a sense of humour

hurler VERB [1]
1 to yell
2 to howl
3 hurler de rire to roar with laughter

la **hutte** FEM NOUN
hut

hydratant MASC ADJECTIVE, **hydratante** FEM
moisturizing

l'**hygiène** FEM NOUN
hygiene
une bonne hygiène de vie a healthy lifestyle

hygiénique MASC & FEM ADJECTIVE
hygienic

un **hymne** MASC NOUN
hymn
• un hymne national
national anthem

ℰ un **hypermarché** MASC NOUN
hypermarket

Ii

un **iceberg** MASC NOUN
iceberg

ℰ **ici** ADVERB
1 here
Il y a trop de monde ici. There are too many people here.
Suivez-moi, c'est par ici. Follow me, it's this way.
2 jusqu'ici so far, as far as this
Jusqu'ici, il a fait beau. So far the weather's been good.
Les bus ne viennent pas jusqu'ici. The buses don't come this far.

une **icône** FEM NOUN
icon

idéal MASC ADJECTIVE, **idéale** FEM, **idéaux** MASC PL, **idéales** FEM PL
ideal

ℰ une **idée** FEM NOUN
idea
Quelle bonne idée! What a good idea!
Je n'ai aucune idée. I've got no idea.

identifier VERB [1]
to identify

identique MASC & FEM ADJECTIVE
identical

une **identité** FEM NOUN
identity

ℰ **idiot** MASC ADJECTIVE, **idiote** FEM ▸ SEE **idiot** NOUN
stupid
C'est vraiment idiot! It's really stupid!

ℰ un **idiot** MASC NOUN, une **idiote** FEM ▸ SEE **idiot**
ADJECTIVE
idiot
Ne fais pas l'idiot! Don't fool around!

l'**igname** FEM NOUN
yam

l'**ignorance** FEM NOUN
ignorance

ignorant MASC ADJECTIVE, **ignorante** FEM
ignorant

ignorer VERB [1]
1 not to know
J'ignore leur adresse. I don't know their address.
2 to ignore
Ils l'ont ignorée. They ignored her.

ℰ **il** PRONOUN
1 (as the subject of the verb) he
'Où est Robert?' – 'Il est dans la cuisine.'
'Where's Robert?' – 'He's in the kitchen.'
Il parle bien français. He speaks French well.
2 (for masc things) it
'Où est mon sac?' – 'Il est sur la chaise.'
'Where's my bag?' – 'It's on the chair.'
3 (to talk about weather, time, and with verbs like **pleuvoir**, **falloir**) it
Il pleut. It's raining.
Il faut attendre. We must wait.
Il fait beau. It's sunny.
▸ SEE **il y a**

une **île** FEM NOUN
island
les îles Anglo-normandes the Channel Islands
l'île Maurice Mauritius

⬆ means the verb takes être to form the perfect

illégal *MASC ADJECTIVE*, **illégale** *FEM*, **illégaux** *MASC PL*, **illégales** *FEM PL*
  illegal

illimité *MASC ADJECTIVE*, **illimitée** *FEM*
  unlimited

illisible *MASC & FEM ADJECTIVE*
  illegible

l'**illumination** *FEM NOUN*
  floodlighting
- les illuminations de Noël
  Christmas lights

illuminer *VERB* [1]
  to floodlight

une **illusion** *FEM NOUN*
  illusion
  Elle se fait des illusions. She's fooling
  herself.

une **illustration** *FEM NOUN*
  illustration

illustré *MASC ADJECTIVE*, **illustrée** *FEM* ▶ SEE
  illustré *ADJECTIVE*
  illustrated

un **illustré** *MASC NOUN* ▶ SEE **illustré** *ADJECTIVE*
  comic (magazine)

illustrer *VERB* [1]
  to illustrate

℘**ils** *PRONOUN*
  (for male people and things as the subject)
  they
  Ils sont en vacances. They're on holiday.
  Mes baskets! Ils sont ruinés! My trainers!
  They're ruined!

  WORD TIP ils is used for people when you talk
  about males and females together.

℘**il y a** *PHRASE*
  there is, there are
  Il y a une fête ce soir. There's a party
  tonight.
  Il y a beaucoup de gens. There are lots of
  people.
    ▶ SEE **avoir**

℘une **image** *FEM NOUN*
  picture
  une vraie image a true picture

imaginaire *MASC & FEM ADJECTIVE*
  imaginary

l'**imagination** *FEM NOUN*
  imagination
  avoir de l'imagination to be imaginative

imaginer *VERB* [1]
1 **to imagine**
  Je n'arrive pas à l'imaginer. I can't imagine
  it.

2 **to suppose**
  Elle va appeler, j'imagine. I suppose she'll
  phone.

imbattable *MASC & FEM ADJECTIVE*
  unbeatable

imbécile *MASC & FEM ADJECTIVE* ▶ SEE **imbécile**
  NOUN
  idiotic

un & une **imbécile** *MASC & FEM NOUN* ▶ SEE
  imbécile *ADJECTIVE*
  fool

une **imitation** *FEM NOUN*
  imitation

imiter *VERB* [1]
  to imitate

immangeable *MASC & FEM ADJECTIVE*
  inedible

l'**immatriculation** *FEM NOUN*
  registration (of a car)

immédiat *MASC ADJECTIVE*, **immédiate** *FEM*
  immediate
  dans l'immédiat for the time being

℘**immédiatement** *ADVERB*
  immediately

immense *MASC & FEM ADJECTIVE*
  huge

℘un **immeuble** *MASC NOUN*
1 **block of flats**
2 **building**
  un immeuble de six étages a six-storey
  building
- un immeuble de bureaux
  office block

l'**immigration** *FEM NOUN*
  immigration

un **immigré** *MASC NOUN*, une **immigrée** *FEM*
  immigrant

immobile *MASC & FEM ADJECTIVE*
  motionless

immobilier *MASC ADJECTIVE*, **immobilière** *FEM*
  un agent immobilier an estate agent

immobiliser *VERB* [1]
  to immobilize

immoral *MASC ADJECTIVE*, **immorale** *FEM*,
immoraux *MASC PL*, **immorales** *FEM PL*
  immoral

immuniser *VERB* [1]
  to immunize

un **impact** *MASC NOUN*
  impact

℘ indicates key words

impair MASC ADJECTIVE, **impaire** FEM
  odd
  un nombre impair an odd number

imparfait MASC ADJECTIVE, **imparfaite** FEM ▸ SEE
  imparfait NOUN
  imperfect

l'**imparfait** MASC NOUN ▸ SEE **imparfait** ADJECTIVE
  (Grammar) imperfect
  à l'imparfait in the imperfect

une **impasse** FEM NOUN
  dead end

l'**impatience** FEM NOUN
  impatience

impatient MASC ADJECTIVE, **impatiente** FEM
  impatient

s'**impatienter** REFLEXIVE VERB ⊙ [1]
  to lose patience
  Ils commencent à s'impatienter. They're
  getting impatient.

impeccable MASC & FEM ADJECTIVE
1 perfect
2 spotless
  L'appartement est impeccable. The flat's
  spotless.
3 brilliant
  'On a rendez-vous au café à midi.' –
  'Impeccable!' 'We're meeting in the cafe at
  twelve.' – 'Brilliant!'

un **imper** MASC NOUN (informal)
  raincoat, mac

l'**impératif** MASC NOUN
  (Grammar) imperative
  à l'impératif in the imperative

une **impératrice** FEM NOUN
  empress

une **imperfection** FEM NOUN
  defect

ℓ un **imperméable** MASC NOUN
  raincoat

impertinent MASC ADJECTIVE, **impertinente**
  FEM
  cheeky

impliquer VERB [1]
1 to mean
  Cela implique que ... This means that ...
2 être impliqué dans quelque chose to be
  involved in something

impoli MASC ADJECTIVE, **impolie** FEM
  rude

l'**importance** FEM NOUN
  importance
  Ça n'a pas d'importance. It doesn't matter.

ℓ **important** MASC ADJECTIVE, **importante** FEM
1 important
  des événements importants important
  events
  Ce n'est pas important. It's not important.
  Il est important de savoir que ... It's
  important to know that ...
2 considerable
  un nombre important d'élèves a
  considerable number of students
  Il y aura des retards importants. There will
  be considerable delays.
3 sizeable
  C'est une ville importante. It's a sizeable
  city.

les **importations** PLURAL FEM NOUN
  imports

importer VERB [1]
1 to import (goods)
2 to matter
  'Lequel veux-tu?' - 'N'importe!' 'Which one
  do you want?' - 'It doesn't matter!'
  ▸ SEE **n'importe**

imposer VERB [1]
1 to impose
2 imposer à quelqu'un de faire quelque
  chose to make somebody do something

ℓ **impossible** MASC & FEM ADJECTIVE ▸ SEE
  impossible NOUN
  impossible

ℓ l'**impossible** MASC NOUN ▸ SEE **impossible**
  ADJECTIVE
  faire l'impossible to do your utmost
  Nous ferons l'impossible pour les
  contacter. We'll do our utmost to contact
  them.

un **impôt** MASC NOUN
  tax

imprécis MASC ADJECTIVE, **imprécise** FEM
  vague

une **impression** FEM NOUN
  impression
  ma première impression my first
  impression
  Elle a fait très bonne impression. She made
  a very good impression.

impressionnant MASC ADJECTIVE,
  impressionante FEM
  impressive

impressionner VERB [1]
  to impress

imprévisible MASC & FEM ADJECTIVE
  unpredictable

⊙ means the verb takes être to form the perfect

imprévu *MASC ADJECTIVE*, **imprévue** *FEM*
  unexpected

ℱ une **imprimante** *FEM NOUN*
  printer *(for a computer)*
• une imprimante laser
  laser printer

imprimé *MASC ADJECTIVE*, **imprimée** *FEM* ▸ SEE
  imprimé *NOUN*
  printed *(fabrics, letters)*
un **imprimé** *MASC NOUN* ▸ SEE **imprimé** *ADJECTIVE*
  form *(to be filled in)*

imprimer *VERB* [1]
  to print

improviser *VERB* [1]
  to improvise

l'**improviste** *MASC NOUN*
  à l'improviste unexpectedly

imprudent *MASC ADJECTIVE*, **imprudente** *FEM*
1 careless
  un conducteur imprudent a careless driver
2 rash

impuissant *MASC ADJECTIVE*, **impuissante** *FEM*
  helpless

impulsif *MASC ADJECTIVE*, **impulsive** *FEM*
  impulsive

inacceptable *MASC & FEM ADJECTIVE*
  unacceptable

inaccessible *MASC & FEM ADJECTIVE*
  inaccessible

inachevé *MASC ADJECTIVE*, **inachevée** *FEM*
  unfinished

inadapté *MASC ADJECTIVE*, **inadaptée** *FEM*
  unsuitable

inaperçu *MASC ADJECTIVE*, **inaperçue** *FEM*
  passer inaperçu to go unnoticed

inattendu *MASC ADJECTIVE*, **inattendue** *FEM*
  unexpected
  une visite inattendue an unexpected visit

l'**inattention** *FEM NOUN*
  lack of attention
  une faute d'inattention a careless mistake

inaugurer *VERB* [1]
1 to open *(an exhibition, a new building)*
2 to unveil *(a monument)*

incassable *MASC & FEM ADJECTIVE*
  unbreakable

un & une **incendiaire** *MASC & FEM NOUN*
  arsonist

ℱ une **incendie** *MASC NOUN*
  fire
  L'incendie a détruit l'église. The fire
  destroyed the church.

incertain *MASC ADJECTIVE*, **incertaine** *FEM*
1 uncertain
  Le résultat est toujours incertain. The
  result is still uncertain.
2 unsettled *(weather)*

un **incident** *MASC NOUN*
  incident

inciter *VERB* [1]
1 to encourage
  inciter quelqu'un à faire quelque chose to
  encourage somebody to do something
2 inciter à la haine to stir up hatred

les **incivilités** *PLURAL FEM NOUN*
  antisocial behaviour

inclure *VERB* [25]
1 to include
2 to enclose

inclus *MASC ADJECTIVE*, **incluse** *FEM*
  including
  jusqu'à samedi inclus up to and including
  Saturday
  Il y aura trente invités, enfants inclus.
  There will be thirty guests, including
  children.

incollable *MASC & FEM ADJECTIVE*
  le riz incollable easy-cook rice

incolore *MASC & FEM ADJECTIVE*
  colourless

incommode *MASC & FEM ADJECTIVE*
1 awkward
2 uncomfortable

incompétent *MASC ADJECTIVE*, **incompétente**
  FEM
  incompetent

incompréhensible *MASC & FEM ADJECTIVE*
  incomprehensible

l'**inconditionnel** *MASC NOUN*,
  l'**inconditionnelle** *FEM*
  devotee, fan
  C'est un inconditionnel du jazz. He's a real
  jazz fan.

inconfortable *MASC & FEM ADJECTIVE*
  uncomfortable

inconnu *MASC ADJECTIVE*, **inconnue** *FEM* ▸ SEE
  inconnu *NOUN*
  unknown
  Elle m'est inconnue. I don't know her.
un **inconnu** *MASC NOUN*, une **inconnue** *FEM* ▸ SEE
  inconnu *ADJECTIVE*
  stranger

inconsciemment *ADVERB*
  unconsciously

inconscient *MASC ADJECTIVE*, **inconsciente** *FEM*
1 **unthinking**
2 **unconscious** *(in a faint)*

incontournable *MASC & FEM ADJECTIVE*
unavoidable
C'est un fait incontournable. It's an undeniable fact.

un **inconvénient** *MASC NOUN*
drawback
Il y a plusieurs inconvénients. There are several drawbacks.

incorporer *VERB* [1]
to blend in *(ingredients)*
Incorporez les œufs au mélange. Blend the eggs into the mixture.

incorrect *MASC ADJECTIVE*, **incorrecte** *FEM*
1 **incorrect**
2 **rude**, **impolite**

incroyable *MASC & FEM ADJECTIVE*
incredible
une coïncidence incroyable an incredible coincidence

inculper *VERB* [1]
inculper quelqu'un de quelque chose to charge somebody with something
Elle a été inculpée de vol. She was charged with theft.

l'**Inde** *FEM NOUN*
India

indécis *MASC ADJECTIVE*, **indécise** *FEM*
1 **undecided**
2 **indecisive**

indemne *MASC & FEM ADJECTIVE*
unharmed
sortir indemne to escape unharmed

l'**indemnisation** *FEM NOUN*
compensation

indemniser *VERB* [1]
to compensate
demander à être indemnisé to demand compensation

indépendamment *ADVERB*
independently

l'**indépendance** *FEM NOUN*
independence

indépendant *MASC ADJECTIVE*, **indépendante** *FEM*
1 **independent**
2 **separate** *(kitchen, bathroom)*

un **index** *MASC NOUN*
1 **index**
2 **forefinger**

un **indicateur** *MASC NOUN*
1 **timetable** *(for trains, coaches)*
2 **street directory**
3 un panneau indicateur a road sign
• un indicateur de pression pressure gauge
• un indicateur des départs departures board

un **indicatif** *MASC NOUN*
1 **dialling code**
Quel est l'indicatif pour l'Angleterre? What's the dialling code for England?
L'indicatif pour la Grande Bretagne est 44. The dialling code for Britain is 44.
2 **theme tune**
3 *(Grammar)* **indicative**

les **indications** *PLURAL FEM NOUN*
directions

un **indice** *MASC NOUN*
clue

indien *MASC ADJECTIVE*, **indienne** *FEM* ▸ SEE **Indien**
Indian

Indien *MASC NOUN*, **Indienne** *FEM* ▸ SEE **indien**
Indian

indifférent *MASC ADJECTIVE*, **indifférente** *FEM*
indifferent

un & une **indigène** *MASC & FEM NOUN*
native
les indigènes the locals

une **indigestion** *FEM NOUN*
indigestion

indigne *MASC & FEM ADJECTIVE*
1 **unworthy**
2 **disgraceful**

s'**indigner** *REFLEXIVE VERB* ◉ [1]
to be outraged

indiqué *MASC ADJECTIVE*, **indiquée** *FEM*
recommended
Ce n'est pas très indiqué. It's not a very good idea.

indiquer *VERB* [1]
to point out, **to show**
Pouvez-vous m'indiquer la gare? Can you show me the way to the station?

indirect *MASC ADJECTIVE*, **indirecte** *FEM*
indirect

indiscret *MASC ADJECTIVE*, **indiscrète** *FEM*
1 **indiscreet**
2 **nosy**

indispensable *MASC & FEM ADJECTIVE*
essential
les vêtements indispensables essential

◉ **means the verb takes être to form the perfect**

clothing

indisposé *MASC ADJECTIVE*, **indisposée** *FEM*
unwell

un **individu** *MASC NOUN*
individual
C'est un drôle d'individu. He's strange.

individuel *MASC ADJECTIVE*, **individuelle** *FEM*
1 individual
2 separate
une chambre individuelle a single room

indolore *MASC & FEM ADJECTIVE*
painless

indulgent *MASC ADJECTIVE*, **indulgente** *FEM*
lenient

industrialisé *MASC ADJECTIVE*, **industrialisée**
FEM
les pays industrialisés the industrialized
countries

ℓ une **industrie** *FEM NOUN*
industry
l'industrie du spectacle the entertainment
industry

industriel *MASC ADJECTIVE*, **industrielle** *FEM*
industrial

inédit *MASC ADJECTIVE*, **inédite** *FEM*
1 unpublished
2 new
un spectacle inédit a totally new show

inefficace *MASC & FEM ADJECTIVE*
1 inefficient *(worker)*
2 ineffective *(cure)*

inégal *MASC ADJECTIVE*, **inégale** *FEM*, **inégaux**
MASC PL, **inégales** *FEM PL*
1 uneven
2 unequal

inévitable *MASC & FEM ADJECTIVE*
1 inevitable
2 unavoidable
C'était inévitable. It was bound to happen.

inexact *MASC ADJECTIVE*, **inexacte** *FEM*
1 incorrect
2 inaccurate

inexpérimenté *MASC ADJECTIVE*,
inexpérimentée *FEM*
inexperienced

un **infarctus** *MASC NOUN*
heart attack

infect *MASC ADJECTIVE*, **infecte** *FEM*
revolting
Le repas était infect! The meal was
revolting!

infecter *VERB* [1]
to infect

s'**infecter** *REFLEXIVE VERB* ⊚
to go septic

une **infection** *FEM NOUN*
infection

inférieur *MASC ADJECTIVE*, **inférieure** *FEM*
1 lower
des prix inférieurs à la moyenne lower-
than-average prices
2 smaller
la taille inférieure the smaller size
3 inferior, worse
des produits de qualité inférieure poorer-
quality products

infernal *MASC ADJECTIVE*, **infernale** *FEM*,
infernaux *MASC PL*, **infernales** *FEM PL*
frightful, dreadful

infini *MASC ADJECTIVE*, **infinie** *FEM*
infinite

l'**infinitif** *MASC NOUN*
(Grammar) infinitive

infirme *MASC & FEM ADJECTIVE* ▸SEE **infirme** *NOUN*
disabled
Est-il infirme? Does he have a disability?

un & une **infirme** *MASC & FEM NOUN* ▸SEE **infirme**
ADJECTIVE
disabled person

une **infirmerie** *FEM NOUN*
medical room *(in a school)*

ℓ un **infirmier** *MASC NOUN*, une **infirmière** *FEM*
nurse

l'**infirmité** *FEM NOUN*
disability

inflammable *MASC & FEM ADJECTIVE*
flammable

l'**inflation** *FEM NOUN*
inflation

une **influence** *FEM NOUN*
influence

influencer *VERB* [61]
to influence

un **informaticien** *MASC NOUN*, une
informaticienne *FEM*
computer scientist

ℓ les **informations** *PLURAL FEM NOUN*
the news
les informations de midi the mid-day news

ℓ **informatique** *MASC & FEM ADJECTIVE* ▸SEE
informatique *NOUN*
computer
un système informatique a computer

system

ρ l'**informatique** FEM NOUN ▸SEE **informatique**
ADJECTIVE
computer science, IT

informatiser VERB [1]
to computerize

informer VERB [1]
to inform

s'**informer** REFLEXIVE VERB ◯
to find out
Je peux m'informer si tu veux. I can find out
if you like.

les **infos** PLURAL FEM NOUN
the news (on TV or radio)

une **infusion** FEM NOUN
herbal tea

l'**ingénierie** FEM NOUN
engineering

ρ un & une **ingénieur** MASC NOUN
engineer
faire des études d'ingénieur to study
engineering

ingénieux MASC ADJECTIVE, **ingénieuse** FEM
ingenious

ingrat MASC ADJECTIVE, **ingrate** FEM
ungrateful

un **ingrédient** MASC NOUN
ingredient

inhabité MASC ADJECTIVE, **inhabitée** FEM
uninhabited

inhabituel MASC ADJECTIVE, **inhabituelle** FEM
unusual

un **inhalateur** MASC NOUN
inhaler

inhumain MASC ADJECTIVE, **inhumaine** FEM
inhuman

une **initiale** FEM NOUN
initial (for your name)

une **initiation** FEM NOUN
introduction (to a new place, skill)
une initiation à la salsa an introduction to
salsa dancing
une journée d'initiation an introductory
day (on a course)

une **initiative** FEM NOUN
initiative

initier VERB [1]
1 initier quelqu'un à quelque chose to
introduce somebody to something (a new
skill)
2 to initiate (a plan, an idea, a change)

s'**initier** REFLEXIVE VERB ◯
s'initier à quelque chose to learn about
something
Elle s'initie à la photo. She's starting to
learn photography.

injecter VERB [1]
to inject

une **injection** FEM NOUN
injection

une **injure** FEM NOUN
insult

injurier VERB [1]
injurier quelqu'un to swear at somebody
Il m'a injurié. He swore at me.

injuste MASC & FEM ADJECTIVE
unfair

innocent MASC ADJECTIVE, **innocente** FEM
innocent

innombrable MASC & FEM ADJECTIVE
countless

innover VERB [1]
to break new ground

inoccupé MASC ADJECTIVE, **inoccupée** FEM
empty

une **inondation** FEM NOUN
flood
des inondations flooding

inonder VERB [1]
to flood

inoubliable MASC & FEM ADJECTIVE
unforgettable

inouï MASC ADJECTIVE, **inouïe** FEM
incredible

l'**inox** MASC NOUN
stainless steel
une casserole en inox a stainless steel sauce
pan

inoxydable MASC & FEM ADJECTIVE
l'acier inoxydable stainless steel

ρ **inquiet** MASC ADJECTIVE, **inquiète** FEM
anxious, worried
Nous étions inquiets pour toi. We were
worried about you.

inquiétant MASC ADJECTIVE, **inquiétante** FEM
worrying

ρ **inquiéter** VERB [24]
to worry
Ça m'inquiète un peu. It worries me.

s'**inquiéter** REFLEXIVE VERB ◯
to worry, to be worried
Elle va s'inquiéter si nous sommes en

178

◯ means the verb takes être to form the perfect

retard. She'll worry if we're late.
Ne t'inquiète pas! Don't worry!

une **inquiétude** *FEM NOUN*
anxiety

insatisfait *MASC ADJECTIVE*, **insatisfaite** *FEM*
dissatisfied

une **inscription** *FEM NOUN*
enrolment *(for a course, in a school)*

inscrire *VERB* [38]
1 to enrol *(someone for a course, school)*
Elle m'a inscrit pour l'examen. She's
entered me for the exam.
2 to register *(someone for university)*
s'**inscrire** *REFLEXIVE VERB* ○
to enrol
s'inscrire au club de foot to join the football
club
Je me suis inscrit au cours de poterie. I've
enrolled on the pottery course.

♪ un **insecte** *MASC NOUN*
insect

insérer *VERB* [24]
1 to insert
2 to integrate *(into a community)*

l'**insertion** *FEM NOUN*
1 insertion *(of an advertisement in a paper)*
2 integration *(into a new community)*
l'insertion des jeunes dans la société the
integration of young people into society

insignifiant *MASC ADJECTIVE*, **insignifiante** *FEM*
insignificant

insister *VERB* [1]
to insist *(on doing something)*
Elle insiste pour être vue. She insists on
being seen.
Il faut insister. Keep on trying.

une **insolation** *FEM NOUN*
sunstroke
attraper une insolation to get sunstroke

insoutenable *MASC & FEM ADJECTIVE*
unbearable

inspecter *VERB* [1]
to inspect

un **inspecteur** *MASC NOUN*, une **inspectrice**
FEM
inspector

une **inspection** *FEM NOUN*
inspection
• l'inspection académique
the local education authority

l'**inspiration** *FEM NOUN*
inspiration

inspirer *VERB* [1]
1 to inspire
2 Ça ne m'inspire pas. That doesn't appeal
to me.
3 to breathe in
Inspire fort! Breathe in deeply!
s'**inspirer** *REFLEXIVE VERB* ○
s'inspirer de quelqu'un, quelque chose to
be inspired by somebody, something
Il s'est inspiré de Picasso. He was inspired
by Picasso.

instable *MASC & FEM ADJECTIVE*
unstable
Il fait un temps instable. The weather's
unsettled.

l'**installation** *FEM NOUN*
1 installation *(of central heating, a washing
machine, etc)*
2 move *(to a house, a town)*
avant son installation à Paris before he
moved to Paris
• les installations sportives
sports facilities

installer *VERB* [1]
1 to install *(central heating, a dishwasher)*
2 to connect up *(gas, electricity, a phone)*
s'**installer** *REFLEXIVE VERB* ○
to settle, to settle in
Je me suis installée dans ma nouvelle
maison. I settled into my new house.
On va s'installer au soleil. We're going to
sit in the sun.
Installez-vous. Please sit down.

un **instant** *MASC NOUN*
moment
dans un instant in a moment
pour l'instant for the moment

instantané *MASC ADJECTIVE*, **instantanée** *FEM*
instant
une réaction instantanée an instant
reaction

l'**instinct** *MASC NOUN*
instinct

un **institut** *MASC NOUN*
institute
• l'institut de beauté
beautician's

♪ un **instituteur** *MASC NOUN*, une **institutrice**
FEM
primary school teacher

une **institution** *FEM NOUN*
1 institution
2 private school

une **institutrice** *FEM NOUN* ▸ SEE **instituteur**

un **instructeur** *MASC NOUN*, une **instructrice**
FEM
instructor

l'**instruction** *FEM NOUN*
education
• l'instruction civique
civics, citizenship studies

ℓ les **instructions** *PLURAL FEM NOUN*
instructions
suivre les instructions to follow the
instructions
• les instructions de lavage
washing instructions

instruire *VERB* [26]
to teach, to train

s'**instruire** *REFLEXIVE VERB* ⬥
to learn

instruit *MASC ADJECTIVE*, **instruite** *FEM*
educated

ℓ un **instrument** *MASC NOUN*
1 instrument
un instrument de mesure a measuring
instrument
2 jouer d'un instrument to play an
instrument
• un instrument de musique
musical instrument
• les instruments de bord
controls (on a plane)

une **insuffisance** *FEM NOUN*
shortage

insuffisant *MASC ADJECTIVE*, **insuffisante** *FEM*
1 insufficient
2 inadequate
C'est insuffisant. It's not good enough.

insultant *MASC ADJECTIVE*, **insultante** *FEM*
insulting

une **insulte** *FEM NOUN*
insult

insulter *VERB* [1]
to insult

insupportable *MASC & FEM ADJECTIVE*
unbearable
Je la trouve insupportable. I can't stand her.

intact *MASC ADJECTIVE*, **intacte** *FEM*
intact

intégral *MASC ADJECTIVE*, **intégrale** *FEM*,
intégraux *MASC PL*, **intégrales** *FEM PL* ▸ SEE
intégrale
complete (unedited, uncut)

l'**intégrale** *FEM NOUN* ▸ SEE **intégral**
complete works (usually music)

l'intégrale des Beatles the complete
Beatles' collection

intellectuel *MASC ADJECTIVE*, **intellectuelle** *FEM*
▸ SEE **intellectuel** *NOUN*
intellectual

un **intellectuel** *MASC NOUN*, une **intellectuelle**
FEM ▸ SEE **intellectuel** *ADJECTIVE*
intellectual

l'**intelligence** *FEM NOUN*
intelligence

ℓ **intelligent** *MASC ADJECTIVE*, **intelligente** *FEM*
clever, intelligent

l'**intendance** *FEM NOUN*
administration (in a school)

intense *MASC & FEM ADJECTIVE*
intense

intensif *MASC ADJECTIVE*, **intensive** *FEM*
intensive

une **intention** *FEM NOUN*
intention
avoir l'intention de faire quelque chose to
mean to do something
J'avais l'intention d'y aller mais ... I meant
to go but ...

une **interdiction** *FEM NOUN*
ban
'Interdiction de fumer' 'No smoking'

interdire *VERB* [47]
to forbid
interdire à quelqu'un de faire quelque
chose to forbid somebody to do something
On nous a interdit de quitter la cour. We
were not allowed to leave the playground.

ℓ **interdit** *MASC ADJECTIVE*, **interdite** *FEM*
1 forbidden
'Entrée interdite' 'No entry'
'Stationnement interdit' 'No parking'
Le film est interdit aux moins de 18 ans.
The film has got an 18 certificate.
2 banned (by censor)

ℓ **intéressant** *MASC ADJECTIVE*, **intéressante** *FEM*
▸ SEE **intéressant** *NOUN*
1 interesting
une ville très intéressante a very
interesting town
2 attractive (financially)
une offre intéressante an attractive offer
à un prix intéressant at a good price

l'**intéressant** *MASC NOUN*, l'**intéressante** *FEM*
▸ SEE **intéressant** *ADJECTIVE*
faire l'intéressant to show off

ℓ **intéressé** *MASC ADJECTIVE*, **intéressée** *FEM* ▸ SEE
intéressé *NOUN*
1 interested

⬥ means the verb takes être to form the perfect

être intéressé par quelque chose to be interested in something
J'ai toujours été intéressé par les animaux. I've always been interested in animals.
2 attentive
Ils étaient peu intéressés. They weren't very attentive.

ℰ un **intéressé** *MASC NOUN*, une **intéressée** *FEM*
▸SEE **intéressé** *ADJECTIVE*
person concerned

ℰ **intéresser** *VERB* [1]
to interest
Tout les intéresse à cet âge. Everything interests them at that age.
s'**intéresser** *REFLEXIVE VERB* ◉
s'intéresser à quelque chose to be interested in something
Elle s'intéresse beaucoup à l'informatique. She's very interested in computing.

l'**intérêt** *MASC NOUN*
1 interest
2 avoir intérêt à faire quelque chose to had better do something
Tu as intérêt à le dire à Faiza. You'd better tell Faiza.

intérieur *MASC ADJECTIVE*, **intérieure** *FEM* ▸SEE **intérieur** *NOUN*
inside, internal
le côté intérieur the inside

ℰ un **intérieur** *MASC NOUN* ▸SEE **intérieur** *ADJECTIVE*
inside, interior
l'intérieur du placard the inside of the cupboard
'Où est-elle?' - 'À l'intérieur' 'Where is she?' – 'Inside.' *(in the house)*

intermédiaire *MASC & FEM ADJECTIVE* ▸SEE
intermédiaire *NOUN*
intermediate
Avez-vous la taille intermédiaire? Do you have the size in between?
un & une **intermédiaire** *MASC & FEM NOUN* ▸SEE
intermédiaire *ADJECTIVE*
go-between

un **internat** *MASC NOUN*
boarding school

ℰ **international** *MASC ADJECTIVE*, **internationale** *FEM*, **internationaux** *MASC PL*, **internationales** *FEM PL*
international
un concours international an international competition

l'**internaute** *MASC & FEM NOUN*
Internet user

interne *MASC & FEM ADJECTIVE* ▸SEE **interne** *NOUN*
internal

un & une **interne** *MASC & FEM NOUN* ▸SEE **interne** *ADJECTIVE*
boarder *(in a school)*

l'**Internet** *MASC NOUN*
l'Internet the Internet
sur Internet on the Internet

⊙ **INTERNET**
Les sites Internet français finissent par « .fr » (point f r).

interpeller *VERB* [1]
1 to call out to
2 to question *(by police)*

un **interphone** *MASC NOUN*
entry phone

un & une **interprète** *MASC & FEM NOUN*
1 actor *(in the theatre)*
2 performer, soloist *(in music)*
3 interpreter

interpréter *VERB* [24]
1 to perform *(a theatre role, a piece of music)*
2 to sing *(a song)*
3 to interpret *(a language, a remark)*
Il l'a mal interprété. He took it the wrong way.

l'**interrogatif** *MASC NOUN*
(Grammar) **interrogative**
à l'interrogatif in the interrogative

une **interrogation** *FEM NOUN*
1 test *(at school)*
2 questioning

interroger *VERB* [52]
1 to question
interroger quelqu'un sur quelque chose to ask somebody about something
Il m'a interrogé sur mon séjour en France. He asked me about my stay in France.
2 to test *(at school)*

interrompre *VERB* [69]
to interrupt
interrompre quelqu'un to interrupt somebody

un **interrupteur** *MASC NOUN*
switch

une **interruption** *FEM NOUN*
1 interruption
2 sans interruption without stopping

une **intersection** *FEM NOUN*
intersection, junction

un **intervalle** *MASC NOUN*
1 interval *(a gap between things, events)*
2 dans l'intervalle in the meantime

ℰ indicates key words

intervenir *VERB* [81]
  to intervene

une **intervention** *FEM NOUN*
  1 intervention *(by the police, army)*
  2 operation *(by a surgeon)*

♀ une **interview** *FEM NOUN*
  interview *(on TV, radio, for a magazine)*

un **intestin** *MASC NOUN*
  intestine

intime *MASC & FEM ADJECTIVE*
  intimate
  un journal intime personal diary

intimider *VERB* [1]
  to intimidate

l'**intimité** *FEM NOUN*
  intimacy
  dans l'intimité in private

intolérable *MASC & FEM ADJECTIVE*
  intolerable

intolérant *MASC ADJECTIVE*, **intolérante** *FEM*
  intolerant

l'**intoxication** *FEM NOUN*
  poisoning
  • l'intoxication alimentaire
    food poisoning

intoxiquer *VERB* [1]
  to poison

une **intrigue** *FEM NOUN*
  plot *(of a play, a novel)*

une **introduction** *FEM NOUN*
  introduction

introduire *VERB* [26]
  to introduce

s'**introduire** *REFLEXIVE VERB* ⬆
  s'introduire dans quelque chose to get into
  something
  Un cambrioleur s'est introduit dans
  l'appartement. A burglar got into the flat.

un **intrus** *MASC NOUN*, une **intruse** *FEM*
  intruder

l'**intuition** *FEM NOUN*
  intuition

inusable *MASC & FEM ADJECTIVE*
  hard-wearing

> **WORD TIP** inusable does not mean unusable
> in English; for the meaning of **unusable** ▶ SEE
> **inutilisable**.

♀ **inutile** *MASC & FEM ADJECTIVE*
  pointless
  Il est inutile de l'appeler. There's no point
  phoning him.

Inutile de dire que ... Needless to say ...

inutilisable *MASC & FEM ADJECTIVE*
  unusable

un & une **invalide** *MASC & FEM NOUN*
  disabled person

une **invasion** *FEM NOUN*
  invasion

inventer *VERB* [1]
  to invent

une **invention** *FEM NOUN*
  invention

inverse *MASC & FEM ADJECTIVE* ▶ SEE **inverse** *NOUN*
  opposite
  en sens inverse in the opposite direction
  dans l'ordre inverse in reverse order

l'**inverse** *MASC NOUN* ▶ SEE **inverse** *ADJECTIVE*
  l'inverse the opposite
  L'inverse est vrai. The opposite is true.

une **investigation** *FEM NOUN*
  investigation

un **investissement** *MASC NOUN*
  investment

invisible *MASC & FEM ADJECTIVE*
  invisible

une **invitation** *FEM NOUN*
  invitation

un **invité** *MASC NOUN*, une **invitée** *FEM*
  guest
  Nous avons des invités ce soir. We've got
  visitors this evening.

♀ **inviter** *VERB* [1]
  to invite
  Ils l'ont invité à dîner. They invited him to
  dinner.
  On a été invités chez eux. They invited us
  home.

involontaire *MASC & FEM ADJECTIVE*
  unintentional

invraisemblable *MASC & FEM ADJECTIVE*
  unlikely
  une explication invraisemblable an unlikely
  explanation

ira, **irai**, **iraient**, **irais**, **irait**, **iras** *VERB* ▶ SEE
  aller *VERB*

♀ **irlandais** *MASC ADJECTIVE*, **irlandaise** *FEM* ▶ SEE
  Irlandais
  Irish

> **WORD TIP** Adjectives never have capitals in
> French, even for nationality or regional origin.

⬆ means the verb takes être to form the perfect

ℓ un **Irlandais** *MASC NOUN*, une **Irlandaise** *FEM*
  ▶ SEE **irlandais**
1 Irishman, Irishwoman
  les Irlandais the Irish
2 l'irlandais Irish *(the language)*

WORD TIP Languages never have capitals in French.

ℓ l'**Irlande** *FEM NOUN*
  Ireland
  en Irlande in Ireland
  aller en Irlande to go to Ireland
• l'Irlande du Nord
  Northern Ireland

WORD TIP Countries and regions in French take le, la or les.

l'**ironie** *FEM NOUN*
  irony

ironique *MASC & FEM ADJECTIVE*
  ironic

irons, iront *VERB* ▶ SEE **aller** *VERB*

irréel *MASC ADJECTIVE*, **irréelle** *FEM*
  unreal

irrégulier *MASC ADJECTIVE*, **irrégulière** *FEM*
  irregular

irrésistible *MASC & FEM ADJECTIVE*
  irresistible

irresponsable *MASC & FEM ADJECTIVE*
  irresponsible

irritable *MASC & FEM ADJECTIVE*
  irritable

l'**irritation** *FEM NOUN*
  irritation

irriter *VERB* [1]
  to irritate
  Cela m'irrite. That makes me cross.

islamique *MASC & FEM ADJECTIVE*
  Islamic

WORD TIP Adjectives and nouns of religion start with a small letter in French.

l'**isolation** *FEM NOUN*
  insulation
• l'isolation acoustique
  soundproofing

isolé *MASC ADJECTIVE*, **isolée** *FEM*
  remote *(place)*

isoler *VERB* [1]
1 to insulate *(a room, a building)*
2 to isolate *(a sick person, a prisoner)*

l'**Israël** *MASC NOUN*
  Israel

israélien *MASC ADJECTIVE*, **israélienne** *FEM* ▶ SEE
  Israélien
  Israeli

Israélien *MASC NOUN*, **Israélienne** *FEM* ▶ SEE
  israélien
  Israeli

une **issue** *FEM NOUN*
  exit
• une issue de secours
  emergency exit

l'**Italie** *FEM NOUN*
  Italy

italien *MASC ADJECTIVE*, **italienne** *FEM* ▶ SEE
  Italien
  Italian

un **Italien** *MASC NOUN*, une **Italienne** *FEM* ▶ SEE
  italien
1 Italian *(person)*
2 l'italien Italian *(the language)*

un **itinéraire** *MASC NOUN*
  route *(of a journey)*

itinérant *MASC ADJECTIVE*, **itinérante** *FEM*
  travelling

l'**ivoire** *MASC NOUN*
  ivory

ivre *MASC & FEM ADJECTIVE*
  drunk

l'**ivresse** *FEM NOUN*
  drunkenness

un & une **ivrogne** *MASC & FEM NOUN*
  drunkard

Jj

j' *ABBREVIATION: JE* ▶ SEE **je**

WORD TIP je becomes j' before a word beginning with a, e, i, o, u or silent h.

la **jacinthe** *FEM NOUN*
  hyacinth

la **jalousie** *FEM NOUN*
  jealousy

jaloux *MASC ADJECTIVE*, **jalouse** *FEM*
  jealous
  Elle est jalouse de mes résultats d'examen.
  She's jealous of my exam results.

jamaïquain *MASC ADJECTIVE*, **jamaïquaine** *FEM*
  ▶ SEE **Jamaïquain**
  Jamaican

un **Jamaïquain** *MASC NOUN*, une **Jamaïquaine** *FEM* ▶SEE **jamaïquain**
Jamaican *(person)*

la **Jamaïque** *FEM NOUN*
Jamaica

♀ **jamais** *ADVERB*
1 **never**
Elle ne fume jamais. She never smokes.
On ne sait jamais. You never know.
Jamais plus! Never again!
▶SEE **ne**
2 **ever**
plus grand que jamais bigger than ever
si jamais il pleut if by any chance it rains
Si jamais tu viens à Londres, passe me voir.
If you're ever in London, come and see me.
à jamais forever

♀ la **jambe** *FEM NOUN*
leg
Sandrine s'est cassé la jambe à la patinoire.
Sandrine broke her leg at the ice rink.

♀ le **jambon** *MASC NOUN*
ham
un jambon beurre a ham sandwich *(with
buttered bread)*
• le jambon blanc
cooked ham
• le jambon de pays
cured raw ham

♀ **janvier** *MASC NOUN*
January
en janvier, au mois de janvier in January
un mois de janvier pluvieux a rainy January

WORD TIP Months of the year and days of the
week start with small letters in French.

le **Japon** *MASC NOUN*
Japan

japonais *MASC ADJECTIVE*, **japonaise** *FEM* ▶ SEE
Japonais
Japanese

un **Japonais** *MASC NOUN*, une **Japonaise** *FEM*
▶SEE **japonais**
1 **Japanese** *(person)*
les Japonais the Japanese
2 le japonais Japanese *(language)*

♀ le **jardin** *MASC NOUN*
garden
Patrick est dans le jardin. Patrick's in the
garden.
une chaise de jardin a garden chair
• le jardin anglais
landscape garden
• le jardin d'enfants
kindergarten

• le jardin à la française
formal garden
• le jardin potager
vegetable garden
• le jardin public
park
• le jardin zoologique
zoo

le **jardinage** *MASC NOUN*
gardening
Mon grand-père fait le jardinage. My
grandpa does the gardening.

le **jardinier** *MASC NOUN*, la **jardinière** *FEM*
gardener

la **jardinière** *FEM NOUN*
(large) plant pot
• la jardinière de légumes
mixed vegetables

le **jaune** *MASC NOUN* ▶ SEE **jaune** *ADJECTIVE*
yellow
• le jaune d'œuf
egg-yolk

♀ **jaune** *MASC & FEM ADJECTIVE* ▶ SEE **jaune** *NOUN*
yellow
une robe jaune a yellow dress

la **jaunisse** *FEM NOUN*
jaundice

Javel *NOUN*
l'eau de Javel bleach

le **jazz** *MASC NOUN*
jazz
J'aime le jazz. I like jazz.

je, **j'** *PRONOUN*
I
Je me lève à huit heures. I get up at eight.
J'habite à Lyon. I live in Lyons.

WORD TIP je becomes j' before a, e, i, o, u or
silent h.

le **jean** *MASC NOUN*
1 **(pair of) jeans**
J'ai acheté un jean. I've bought a pair of
jeans.
2 **denim**
une jupe en jean a denim skirt

le **jet** *MASC NOUN*
jet *(of water, steam)*
les jets d'eau de Versailles the fountains at
Versailles

jetable *MASC & FEM ADJECTIVE*
disposable
Je me sers d'un appareil photo jetable. I
use a disposable camera.

la **jetée** FEM NOUN
   jetty

ℰ **jeter** VERB [48]
   1 to throw
      Ne jette pas de cailloux! Do not throw
      stones!
   2 to throw away
      J'ai jeté ces vieilles chaussures. I've thrown
      away those old shoes.
   3 jeter un coup d'œil to have a look
      Est-ce que tu peux jeter un coup d'œil à ce
      blog? Can you have a look at this blog?

le **jeton** MASC NOUN
   1 counter (for a board game)
   2 token (for a machine)

le **jeu** MASC NOUN, les **jeux** PLURAL
   1 le jeu play
      Les enfants apprennent par le jeu. Children
      learn through play.
   2 un jeu a game
      On va faire un jeu! Let's play a game!
      gagner par trois jeux à deux to win by
      three games to two
      les Jeux Olympiques the Olympic Games
      un jeu télévisé a game show
   3 set (collection of similar things)
      un jeu d'échecs a chess set
   4 gambling
   5 acting
   • le jeu-concours
      competition
   • le jeu de société
      board game

le **jeu de cartes** MASC NOUN
   1 pack of cards
   2 game of cards

ℰ le **jeudi** MASC NOUN
   1 Thursday
      Nous sommes jeudi aujourd'hui. It's
      Thursday today.
      jeudi prochain next Thursday
      jeudi dernier last Thursday
   2 on Thursday
      Je l'ai vu jeudi soir. I saw him on Thursday
      evening.
   3 le jeudi on Thursdays
      'Fermé le jeudi' 'Closed on Thursdays'
   4 tous les jeudis every Thursday

   WORD TIP Months of the year and days of the
   week start with small letters in French.

le **jeu électronique** MASC NOUN
   computer game

ℰ le & la **jeune** MASC & FEM NOUN ▸ SEE **jeune**
      ADJECTIVE
   young person
   une émission destinée aux jeunes a

programme aimed at young people

ℰ **jeune** MASC & FEM ADJECTIVE ▸ SEE **jeune** NOUN
   1 young
      un jeune homme a young man
      une jeune femme a young woman
      une jeune fille a girl
   2 younger
      ma jeune sur my younger sister
   3 new
      un jeune diplômé a new graduate
      une jeune avocate a newly-qualified lawyer
      les jeunes mariés the newly-weds

la **jeunesse** FEM NOUN
   1 young people
      la jeunesse d'aujourd'hui young people
      today
   2 youth
      dans ma jeunesse in my youth

le **jeu vidéo** MASC NOUN
   video game

un **job** MASC NOUN
   job
      J'ai un job (d'été). I have a summer job.

le **jogging** MASC NOUN
   1 faire du jogging to go jogging
      Il fait du jogging pour se maintenir en
      forme. He goes jogging to keep fit.
   2 un jogging a track-suit

la **joie** FEM NOUN
   joy

joindre VERB [49]
   1 to get hold of
      Je n'ai pas pu la joindre. I wasn't able to get
      hold of her.
   2 to enclose (in a letter, a parcel)
   3 to put together
      les pieds joints feet together
se **joindre** REFLEXIVE VERB ◎
   se joindre à quelqu'un to join somebody
   Tout le monde se joint à moi pour te
   souhaiter un bon anniversaire. Everybody
   joins me in wishing you happy birthday.

ℰ **joli** MASC ADJECTIVE, **jolie** FEM
   pretty

jongler VERB [1]
   to juggle

le **jongleur** MASC NOUN, la **jongleuse** FEM
   juggler

la **jonquille** FEM NOUN
   daffodil

la **joue** FEM NOUN
   cheek

ℰ **jouer** VERB [1]
   1 to play

ℰ indicates key words

Elle joue avec le chien. She's playing with the dog.
À toi de jouer! Your go!
Bien joué! Well done!

2 jouer à quelque chose to play something *(a sport, a game)*
On va jouer au foot. We're going to play football.

3 jouer de quelque chose to play something *(an instrument)*
Sophie joue du cor d'harmonie. Sophie plays the French horn.
Il joue du Chopin. He's playing some Chopin.

4 *(in a film, play)* Elle joue mal. She can't act.
Il joue bien dans ce film. He's really good in this film.
Il joue le rôle d'Octave. He plays the part of Octave.
Maxime joue dans 'Othello.' Maxime is performing in 'Othello.'
On joue 'Le Parrain' au cinéma du coin. The local cinema is showing 'The Godfather.'
Au Théâtre de la Ville on joue 'Le Tartuffe.' The Théâtre de la Ville is putting on 'Tartuffe.'

5 to gamble
Il joue au casino. He gambles at the casino.
Mon oncle joue aux courses. My uncle bets on horses at the races.

♪ le **jouet** *MASC NOUN*
toy

♪ le **joueur** *MASC NOUN*, la **joueuse** *FEM* ▶ SEE **joueur** *ADJECTIVE*
player

♪ **joueur** *MASC ADJECTIVE*, **joueuse** *FEM* ▶ SEE **joueur** *NOUN*
playful
Les chiots sont joueurs. Puppies are playful.

♪ le **jour** *MASC NOUN*

1 day
les jours de la semaine the days of the week
trois jours plus tard three days later
tous les jours every day
le jour où the day when
un de ces jours one of these days
dans huit jours in a week
dans quinze jours in two weeks
au jour le jour one day at a time
Quel jour on est? What day is it today?

2 être à jour to be up to date
Le calendrier n'est pas à jour. The schedule is not up to date.
mettre quelque chose à jour to bring something up to date
Elle doit mettre à jour son journal intime. She must bring her diary up to date.

3 de nos jours nowadays

De nos jours, ils sont assez fréquents. Nowadays they are quite common.

4 daylight
Il fait jour. It's daylight.
en plein jour in broad daylight
jour et nuit night and day

• le jour de l'an
New Year's Day

• le jour férié
public holiday

• le jour ouvrable
working day

♪ le **journal** *MASC NOUN*, les **journaux** *PLURAL*

1 newspaper
Mon père lit le journal tous les jours. My father reads the newspaper every day.
Le matin, je distribue les journaux. In the mornings I do a paper round.
le journal du soir the evening paper

2 news
le journal de vingt heures the eight o'clock news *(on TV, radio)*

• le journal intime
diary

• le journal télévisé
news *(on television)*

le **journalisme** *MASC NOUN*
journalism

♪ le & la **journaliste** *MASC & FEM NOUN*
journalist

♪ la **journée** *FEM NOUN*
day
toute la journée all day, the whole day
Il est payé à la journée. He's paid by the day.
une journée de repos a rest day, a day off
une journée scolaire a school day

♪ **joyeux** *MASC ADJECTIVE*, **joyeuse** *FEM*
happy
Joyeux Anniversaire Happy Birthday
Joyeux Noël Merry Christmas

le **judaïsme** *MASC NOUN*
Judaism

> **WORD TIP** Adjectives and nouns of religion start with a small letter in French.

judicieux *MASC ADJECTIVE*, **judicieuse** *FEM*
sensible
un choix judicieux a wise choice

le **judo** *MASC NOUN*
judo

le **juge** *MASC NOUN*
judge

• le juge d'instruction
examining magistrate

• le juge de ligne
line judge *(in tennis)*

⬤ means the verb takes être to form the perfect

- le **juge de touche**
  linesman *(in football, rugby)*

le **jugement** *MASC NOUN*
  judgement

juger *VERB* [52]
1 **to judge**
  Il ne faut pas juger sur les apparences. You mustn't judge by appearances.
2 **to consider**
  Ils ont jugé l'exercice trop difficile. They considered the exercise too difficult.
  Elle a jugé bon de partir tôt. She considered it a good idea to leave early.

le **juif** *MASC NOUN*, la **juive** *FEM* ▸ SEE **juif** *ADJECTIVE*
  Jew

> **WORD TIP** Adjectives and nouns of religion start with a small letter in French.

juif *MASC ADJECTIVE*, **juive** *FEM* ▸ SEE **juif** *NOUN*
  Jewish

ℓ **juillet** *MASC NOUN*
  July
  en juillet, au mois de juillet in July
  le quatorze juillet Bastille Day

> **WORD TIP** Months of the year and days of the week start with small letters in French.

🔵 **JUILLET**

Le 14 Juillet est la fête nationale en France. C'est l'anniversaire de la Révolution française en 1789. Il y a des défilés militaires, des bals et des feux d'artifice.

ℓ **juin** *MASC NOUN*
  June
  en juin, au mois de juin in June
  J'aime le mois de juin. I like June.

> **WORD TIP** Months of the year and days of the week start with small letters in French.

ℓ le **jumeau** *MASC NOUN*, la **jumelle** *FEM* les **jumeaux** *PLURAL*
  twin
  des vrais jumeaux identical twins
  des faux jumeaux non-identical twins
  Elsa a des frères jumeaux. Elsa has twin brothers.

ℓ **jumeler** *VERB* [18]
  to twin *(towns)*
  Oxford est jumelé avec Grenoble. Oxford is twinned with Grenoble.

ℓ la **jumelle** *FEM NOUN* jumeau

les **jumelles** *PLURAL FEM NOUN*
  binoculars

la **jument** *FEM NOUN*
  mare

la **jungle** *FEM NOUN*
  jungle

ℓ la **jupe** *FEM NOUN*
  skirt

le **jupon** *MASC NOUN*
  petticoat

jurer *VERB* [1]
  to swear

juridique *MASC & FEM ADJECTIVE*
  legal
  le système juridique the legal system

le **jury** *MASC NOUN*
1 **jury**
2 **board of examiners**

ℓ le **jus** *MASC NOUN*
1 **juice**
  un jus d'orange an orange juice
2 **juices**
  le jus de viande the meat juices
- le **jus de fruit**
  fruit juice

ℓ **jusque** *PREPOSITION*
1 **as far as** *(a place)*
  Ce train va jusqu'à Paris. This train goes as far as Paris.
  Nous avons marché jusqu'au lac. We walked as far as the lake.
  Il m'a accompagné jusque chez moi. He took me all the way home.
  Jusqu'où va le train? How far does the train go?
2 **until**
  Elle reste jusqu'en avril. She's staying until April.
  Jusqu'à quand reste-t-il? How long is he staying for?
  jusqu'à présent, jusqu'ici until now
3 **jusqu'à ce que until**
  On peut aller jouer jusqu'à ce qu'on nous appelle pour le dîner. We can go and play until we are called for dinner.

juste *MASC & FEM ADJECTIVE* ▸ SEE **juste** *ADVERB*
1 **fair**
  Ce n'est pas juste! It's not fair!
2 **right**
  le mot juste the right word
  Ce que tu dis est juste. What you say is right.
  J'ai tout juste. I've got everything right.
3 **correct**
  Mon calcul est juste. My sum is correct.
  As-tu l'heure juste? Have you got the correct time?
4 **in tune**
  Ton piano est juste. Your piano's in tune.
5 **tight**

Mon T-shirt est trop juste. My T-shirt's too tight.
Une heure pour visiter le château, c'est un peu juste. An hour to visit the château is a bit tight.
6 valid
Ta remarque est juste. Your comment is valid.
Il dit des choses justes. He's making some valid points.

juste ADVERB ▸ SEE **juste** ADJECTIVE
1 just
juste à temps just in time
Il vient tout juste d'arriver. He's only just arrived.
La poste est juste après la boulangerie. The post office is just after the bakery.
C'est juste ce qui me faut. That's just what I need.
2 in tune
Elle chante juste. She sings in tune.

justement ADVERB
1 precisely
C'est justement ce qu'il faut faire. That's precisely what you should do.
2 just
Je parlais justement de toi. I was just talking about you.
3 correctly
Comme elle a dit très justement… As she so rightly said…

la **justesse** FEM NOUN
1 correctness
avec justesse correctly
2 de justesse only just
Il a eu son avion, mais de justesse. He caught his plane but only just.
J'ai eu mon examen de justesse. I passed my exam but only just.

la **justice** FEM NOUN
justice

justifier VERB [1]
to justify

juteux MASC ADJECTIVE, **juteuse** FEM
juicy

juvénile MASC & FEM ADJECTIVE
youthful

Kk

kaki INVARIABLE ADJECTIVE
khaki
une casquette kaki a khaki cap

le **kangourou** MASC NOUN
kangaroo

le **karaté** MASC NOUN
karate

le **karting** MASC NOUN
go-karting
On va faire du karting. We're going go-karting.

kascher INVARIABLE ADJECTIVE
kosher

le **képi** MASC NOUN
cap (with a flat top, worn by police and military)

la **kermesse** FEM NOUN
fête
La kermesse de l'école a lieu le 22 juin. The school fête will take place on 22 June.

le **ketchup** MASC NOUN
ketchup

kidnapper VERB [1]
to kidnap

le **kidnappeur** MASC NOUN, la **kidnappeuse** FEM
kidnapper

♪ le **kilo** MASC NOUN
kilo
deux kilos de pommes two kilos of apples
J'ai pris trois kilos. I've put on three kilos.
C'est trois euros le kilo. It's three euros a kilo.

le **kilogramme** MASC NOUN
kilogram

le **kilométrage** MASC NOUN
mileage

le **kilomètre** MASC NOUN
kilometre
à dix kilomètres d'ici ten kilometres from here
Paris est à combien de kilomètres de Dijon? How many kilometres is it from Paris to Dijon?
Elle a combien de kilomètres votre voiture? What's the mileage on your car?

le & la **kinésithérapeute** MASC & FEM NOUN
physiotherapist

la **kinésithérapie** FEM NOUN
physiotherapy

♪ le **kiosque** MASC NOUN
kiosk
• le kiosque à journaux newspaper kiosk

⬤ means the verb takes être to form the perfect

le **kiwi** *MASC NOUN*
kiwi *(the bird and the fruit)*

le **klaxon**® *MASC NOUN*
horn *(on a car)*

klaxonner *VERB* **[1]**
to beep the horn *(in a car)*

le **kleenex**® *MASC NOUN*
tissue

km *ABBREVIATION*
short for **kilomètre**
km/h **kph** *(kilometres per hour)*

KO *INVARIABLE ADJECTIVE*
1 mettre quelqu'un KO **to knock somebody out**
Youssef a mis Arnaud KO. **Youssef knocked Arnaud out.**
2 Je suis KO. **I'm whacked.** *(informal)*

le **koala** *MASC NOUN*
koala bear

le **kraft** *MASC NOUN*
le papier kraft **brown paper**

le **K-way**® *MASC NOUN*
windcheater

Ll

l' *ABBREVIATION: LE OR LA* ▸ SEE **le, la** *DETERMINER, PRONOUN*

> **WORD TIP** le or la becomes l' before a word beginning with a, e, i, o, u or silent h.

⟋ **la, l'** *FEM DETERMINER* ▸ SEE **la** *PRONOUN*
1 *(with singular fem nouns)* **the**
la voiture **the car**
l'école **the school**
l'habitude **the habit**
2 *(with parts of the body la is translated by my, your, his, her, etc)* Je lui ai serré la main. **I shook his hand.**
Le chien s'est cassé la patte. **The dog broke its leg.**
3 *(la is often not translated)* la lutte pour la justice **the fight for justice.**
J'adore la glace. **I love ice cream.**
C'est la maison d'Annie. **That's Annie's house.**

> **WORD TIP** la becomes l' before a, e, i, o, u or silent h. ▸ SEE **le, les**

⟋ **la, l'** *PRONOUN* ▸ SEE **la** *FEM DETERMINER*
1 *(as direct object for a female)* **her**
Je la connais bien. **I know her well.**
Je l'ai aidé. **I helped her.**

2 *(for a fem direct object)* **it**
Attention à la tasse! Tu vas la casser. **Mind the cup! You'll break it!**

> **WORD TIP** la becomes l' before a, e, i, o, u or silent h. ▸ SEE **le, les**

⟋ **là** *ADVERB*
1 **here**
Danielle n'est pas là. **Danielle's not here.**
2 **there**
Est-ce que Paul est là? **Is Paul there?**
3 **when**
C'est là que j'ai pensé à toi. **That's when I thought of you.**
4 **where**
C'est là que nous habitons. **That's where we live.**
5 **then**
Et là, elle s'est mise à hurler. **And then, she started screaming.**
6 *(for emphasis)* cette maison-là **that house**
ces gens-là **those people**
à ce moment-là **at that moment**
dans ce cas-là **in that case**

> **WORD TIP** -là is attached to a noun for emphasis. Compare with -ci, meaning **this** or **these**.

⟋ **là-bas** *ADVERB*
1 **there**
Qu'est-ce que vous avez fait là-bas? **What did you do there?**
2 **over there**
Notre maison est là-bas. **Our house is over there.**

le **labo** *MASC NOUN*
(informal) **lab**

le **laboratoire** *MASC NOUN*
laboratory
• le laboratoire de langues
language laboratory

⟋ le **lac** *MASC NOUN*
lake
le lac Léman **Lake Geneva**

lacer *VERB* **[61]**
lacer ses chaussures **to do up your shoes**

le **lacet** *MASC NOUN*
lace
des chaussures à lacets **lace-up shoes**

lâche *MASC & FEM ADJECTIVE*
1 **cowardly**
Samuel est lâche. **Samuel's a coward.**
2 **loose** *(belt, rope, knot)*

lâcher *VERB* **[1]**
1 lâcher quelqu'un **to let go of somebody**
Lâche-moi! **Let go of me!**
2 **to drop**

⟋ **indicates key words**

Elle a lâché son sac. She dropped her bag.

la **lâcheté** *FEM NOUN*
  cowardliness

là-dedans *ADVERB*
  in there, in here
  Qu'est-ce qu'il y a là-dedans? What's in
  there?
  Je mettrai l'argent là-dedans. I'll put the
  money in here.
  Il n'y a rien là-dedans. There's nothing in
  there.

là-dessous *ADVERB*
  under here, under there
  Viens voir là-dessous! Come and look under
  here!
  Les chaussures sont là-dessous. The shoes
  are under there.

là-dessus *ADVERB*
1 on here, on there
  Monte là-dessus! Climb on here!
  Ne laisse pas tes livres là-dessus, c'est
  mouillé. Don't leave your books on there,
  it's wet.
2 about it, on it
  Ils sont d'accord là-dessus. They agree
  about it.
  Est-ce qu'il a dit quelque chose là-dessus?
  Did he say anything about it?
  J'ai un livre là-dessus. I've got a book about
  it.

là-haut *ADVERB*
1 up there, up here
  Il est là-haut dans l'arbre. He's up there in
  the tree.
  Viens là-haut, il fait plus frais. Come up
  here, it's cooler.
2 upstairs
  Nathalie est là-haut. Nathalie's upstairs.

♪ **laid** *MASC ADJECTIVE*, **laide** *FEM*
  ugly

la **laideur** *FEM NOUN*
  ugliness

♪ la **laine** *FEM NOUN*
  wool
  un pull en laine a woollen jumper
  acheter de la laine to buy some wool
  • la laine vierge
    pure new wool

laïque *MASC & FEM ADJECTIVE*
  non-denominational

la **laisse** *FEM NOUN*
  lead

♪ **laisser** *VERB* [1]
1 to leave
  J'ai laissé mon portable chez toi. I've left

my mobile at your house.
  Tu peux laisser ta valise ici. You can leave
  your case here.
  Bon, je vous laisse. Right, I must go.
2 laisser quelqu'un faire quelque chose to let
  somebody do something
  Laisse-le parler! Let him speak!
  Laisse-moi t'aider. Let me help you.
3 to leave *(till later)*
  J'ai laissé mes devoirs pour demain. I've left
  my homework till tomorrow.

se **laisser** *REFLEXIVE VERB* ☻
  to put up with
  Il se laisse insulter. He puts up with being
  insulted.

le **laisser-aller** *INVARIABLE MASC NOUN*
  carelessness

♪ le **lait** *MASC NOUN*
  milk
  un café au lait a white coffee
  • le lait demi-écrémé
    semi-skimmed milk
  • le lait écrémé
    skimmed milk
  • le lait entier
    whole milk

laitier *MASC ADJECTIVE*, **laitière** *FEM*
  les produits laitiers dairy products

la **laitue** *FEM NOUN*
  lettuce

la **lame** *FEM NOUN*
  blade
  • la lame de rasoir
    razor blade

lamentable *MASC & FEM ADJECTIVE*
  awful

le **lampadaire** *MASC NOUN*
1 standard lamp
2 street lamp

♪ la **lampe** *FEM NOUN*
  lamp
  • la lampe de chevet
    bedside lamp
  • la lampe de poche
    torch

la **lance** *FEM NOUN*
  spear

le **lancement** *MASC NOUN*
  launch *(of a film, a product, a spacecraft)*

lancer *VERB* [61]
1 to throw
  Arrêtez de lancer des cailloux! Stop
  throwing stones!
  lancer quelque chose à quelqu'un to throw
  something to somebody

☻ means the verb takes être to form the perfect

Il m'a lancé le ballon. He threw the ball to me.
2 **to launch** *(a product, a spacecraft)*

le **landau** *MASC NOUN*
pram

la **lande** *FEM NOUN*
moor

WORD TIP lande does not mean land in English; for the meaning of land ▸ SEE **terre, terrain**.

le **langage** *MASC NOUN*
language
• le langage de programmation
programming language

la **langouste** *FEM NOUN*
crayfish

ℰ la **langue** *FEM NOUN*
1 **tongue**
Il m'a tiré la langue. He stuck his tongue out at me.
2 **language**
les pays de langue française French-speaking countries
• la langue étrangère
foreign language
• les langues vivantes
modern languages

la **lanière** *FEM NOUN*
strap

ℰ le **lapin** *MASC NOUN*
1 **rabbit**
2 **sweetheart**
Ça va mon petit lapin? Are you all right, sweetheart?

la **laque** *FEM NOUN*
hairspray

laquelle *PRONOUN* ▸ SEE **lequel**

le **lard** *MASC NOUN*
streaky bacon

les **lardons** *PLURAL MASC NOUN*
diced bacon

La Réunion *FEM NOUN*
Réunion, Réunion island

ℰ **large** *MASC & FEM ADJECTIVE* ▸ SEE **large** NOUN
wide
un large couloir a wide corridor
Le fleuve est large de cinquante mètres. The river is fifty metres wide.
avoir les idées larges to be broadminded

WORD TIP large does not mean large in English; for the meaning of large ▸ SEE **grand**.

le **large** *MASC NOUN* ▸ SEE **large** ADJECTIVE
1 **faire un mètre de large** to be a metre wide

Ça fait dix mètres de large. It's ten metres wide.
2 **open sea**

largement *ADVERB*
C'est largement suffisant. That's more than enough.
J'ai largement le temps. I've got plenty of time.

la **largeur** *FEM NOUN*
width
Le ruban fait deux centimètres de largeur. The ribbon is two centimetres wide.

la **larme** *FEM NOUN*
tear
en larmes in tears
Elle avait les larmes aux yeux. She had tears in her eyes.
fondre en larmes to burst into tears

la **laryngite** *FEM NOUN*
laryngitis

les **lasagnes** *PLURAL FEM NOUN*
lasagna

le **laser** *MASC NOUN*
laser
un spectacle laser a laser show

se **lasser** *REFLEXIVE VERB* [1]
se lasser de quelque chose to get tired of something
Je me lasse de cette musique. I'm getting tired of this musique.

la **lassitude** *FEM NOUN*
tiredness

le **latin** *MASC NOUN*
Latin *(language)*

le **lauréat** *MASC NOUN*, la **lauréate** *FEM*
winner
un lauréat du prix Nobel a Nobel Prize winner

le **laurier** *MASC NOUN*
laurel

lavable *MASC & FEM ADJECTIVE*
washable
lavable en machine machine-washable

ℰ le **lavabo** *MASC NOUN*
washbasin

le **lavage** *MASC NOUN*
1 **washing** *(of floor, clothes)*
2 **wash programme** *(on a washing-machine)*

la **lavande** *FEM NOUN*
lavender

le **lave-linge** *INVARIABLE MASC NOUN*
washing machine

ℰ **indicates key words**

laver VERB [1]
to wash, to clean
Il lave la voiture. He's washing the car.
J'ai lavé le carrelage. I cleaned the floor.

se **laver** REFLEXIVE VERB ◎
to wash
Je vais me laver. I'm going to have a wash.
Elle se lave la tête. She's washing her hair.

la **laverie** FEM NOUN
launderette

ℓ le **lave-vaisselle** INVARIABLE MASC NOUN
dishwasher

WORD TIP lave-vaisselle never changes in the plural.

ℓ **le** MASC DETERMINER, **l'** ▸ SEE **le** PRONOUN
1 (with singular masc nouns) **the**
le chat the cat
l'homme the man
2 (with parts of the body le is translated by **my, your, his, her,** etc)
Je me suis brûlé le doigt. I burnt my finger.
3 (le is often not translated) J'aime le chocolat.
I love chocolate.
pendant le déjeuner during lunch
le vélo d'Isabelle Isabelle's bicycle
4 **a, an**
cinq euros le kilo five euros a kilo

WORD TIP le becomes l' before a, e, i, o, u or silent h. ▸ SEE **le, les**

ℓ **le, l'** PRONOUN ▸ SEE **le** DETERMINER
1 (as direct object for a male) **him**
Je le connais. I know him.
Je l'ai vu hier soir. I saw him last night.
2 (for a masc direct object) **it**
Tu vois le couteau? Donne-le-moi. Do you see that knife? Give it to me.
Mon vélo? Il l'a déjà emprunté. My bike? He's already borrowed it.
3 (le is often not translated)
Je le sais. I know.
Il me l'a dit. He told me.

WORD TIP le becomes l' before a, e, i, o, u or silent h. ▸ SEE **la, les**

lécher VERB [24]
to lick
se lécher les doigts to lick your fingers

le **lèche-vitrines** INVARIABLE MASC NOUN
faire du lèche-vitrines to go window-shopping

la **leçon** FEM NOUN
lesson

le **lecteur** MASC NOUN, la **lectrice** FEM
1 **reader**
2 **foreign language assistant** (at a school, university)
• le lecteur DVD
DVD player
• le lecteur laser
CD player
• le lecteur mp3
mp3 player

ℓ la **lecture** FEM NOUN
reading
J'aime la lecture. I like reading.

WORD TIP lecture does not mean **lecture** in English; for the meaning of **lecture** ▸ SEE **conférence**.

légal MASC ADJECTIVE, **légale** FEM, **légaux** MASC PL, **légales** FEM PL
legal

la **légende** FEM NOUN
1 **legend**
2 **caption** (for a picture)
3 **key** (to a map)

ℓ **léger** MASC ADJECTIVE, **légère** FEM
1 **light**
une veste légère a light jacket
2 **weak**
un café léger a weak coffee
3 **slight**
un léger retard a slight delay
une légère différence a slight difference

légèrement ADVERB
1 **lightly**
légèrement parfumé lightly perfumed
2 **slightly**
Il est légèrement blessé. He's slightly hurt.

la **légèreté** FEM NOUN
lightness

les **législatives** PLURAL FEM NOUN
general election

ℓ le **légume** MASC NOUN
vegetable
• les légumes secs
pulses (beans, peas, lentils)
• les légumes verts
green vegetables

ℓ le **lendemain** MASC NOUN
le lendemain the next day
le lendemain matin the next morning
Marc est arrivé le lendemain. Marc arrived the next day.
C'était le lendemain de l'accident. It was the day after the accident.

◎ means the verb takes être to form the perfect

_ℓ_ **lent** MASC ADJECTIVE, **lente** FEM
  slow
  Ce film est trop lent. This film is too slow.

lentement ADVERB
  slowly

la **lenteur** FEM NOUN
  slowness

la **lentille** FEM NOUN
1 **lens**
  Elle porte des lentilles. She wears contact lenses.
2 **lentil**
  la soupe aux lentilles lentil soup
• les lentilles de contact
  contact lenses

le **léopard** MASC NOUN
  leopard

lequel MASC PRONOUN, **laquelle** FEM, **lesquels** MASC PL, **lesquelles** FEM PL
1 (in questions) **which one**
  'J'adore cette veste!' – 'Laquelle?' 'I just love that jacket!' – 'Which one?'
  'Passe-moi les verres.' – 'Lesquels?' 'Pass me the glasses.' – 'Which ones?'
  Lequel des deux chevaux préfères-tu? Which of the two horses do you prefer?
2 (after prepositions like avec, dans) **which**, **whom**
  l'immeuble dans lequel ils habitaient the block of flats which they were living in
  les gens chez lesquels je passe mes vacances the people with whom I spend my holidays
  la dame avec laquelle je discutais the lady I was talking to

_ℓ_ **les** DETERMINER ▸ SEE **les** PRONOUN
1 (with plural nouns) **the**
  les enfants the children
2 (with parts of the body les is translated by my, your, his, her, etc)
  Elle se lave les cheveux. She's washing her hair.
3 (les is often not translated) les cousins d'Amélie Amélie's cousins
  J'aime bien les nouilles. I like noodles.
  Les Français roulent à droite. The French drive on the right .
  ▸ SEE **la** and **le**

_ℓ_ **les** PRONOUN ▸ SEE **les** DETERMINER
1 (as direct object for people) **them**
  Je les connais bien. I know them well.
  Aide-les! Help them!
  Mes parents les ont aidés. My parents helped them.

2 (for a plural direct object) **them**
  Les billets – où est-ce que tu les as mis? The tickets – where did you put them?
  Donne-les-moi. Give them to me.
  ▸ SEE **le** PRONOUN and **la** PRONOUN

lesquels, lesquelles PRONOUN ▸ SEE **lequel**

la **lessive** FEM NOUN
1 **washing**
  mettre la lessive à sécher to put the washing out to dry
2 **washing powder, washing liquid**
  Je n'ai plus de lessive. I've run out of washing powder.

_ℓ_ la **lettre** FEM NOUN
1 **letter** (postal)
  J'ai écrit une lettre à ma correspondante. I wrote a letter to my penpal.
2 **letter** (in the alphabet)
  en lettres majuscules in capital letters
3 les lettres arts (at university)
• la lettre de candidature
  job application letter
• la lettre majuscule
  capital letter
• la lettre minuscule
  small letter, lower-case letter
• la lettre de motivation
  covering letter

_ℓ_ **leur** MASC & FEM ADJECTIVE, **leurs** PL ▸ SEE **leur** PRONOUN
  their
  C'est leur nouvelle maison. It's their new house.
  Leurs voisins sont sympathiques. Their neighbours are nice.

WORD TIP leur, adjective, takes -s with plural nouns.

_ℓ_ **leur** PRONOUN ▸ SEE **leur** ADJECTIVE
1 (as indirect object) **(to) them**
  Elle leur a expliqué le problème. She explained the problem to them.
  Nous leur envoyons de l'argent. We send money to them.
  Donne-leur un coup de main. Give them a hand.

WORD TIP leur, pronoun, never changes.

2 le leur, la leur, les leurs theirs
  C'est notre jardin, et ça, c'est le leur. That's our garden, and that's theirs.
  Ça, c'est votre maison, et ça, c'est la leur. That's your house and that's theirs.
  Nous avons appelé nos parents et ils ont appelé les leurs. We phoned our parents

_ℓ_ indicates key words

and they phoned theirs.

> **WORD TIP** Choose le leur, la leur, les leurs
> according to whether the noun referred to is
> masc, fem, plural.

ℓ **lever** *VERB* [50]
▶ SEE **lever** *NOUN*
to raise
lever les bras to raise your arms *(in gym)*
lever la main to put your hand up *(in class)*
lever les yeux to look up
Il a levé les yeux. He looked up.

se **lever** *REFLEXIVE VERB* ◎
1 to get up
Je me lève à sept heures. I get up at seven
o'clock.
Nous nous sommes levés tôt. We got up
early.
2 to stand up
Levez-vous! Stand up!
3 to rise
Le soleil va se lever. The sun is about to rise.

le **lever** *MASC NOUN* ▶ SEE **lever** *VERB*
au lever du soleil at sunrise

le **levier** *MASC NOUN*
lever

la **lèvre** *FEM NOUN*
lip

le **lévrier** *MASC NOUN*
greyhound

le **lexique** *MASC NOUN*
word list

le **lézard** *MASC NOUN*
lizard

la **liaison** *FEM NOUN*
1 love affair
2 link
une liaison aérienne an air link
3 contact
une liaison radio a radio contact
4 connection *(on telephone)*
La liaison est mauvaise. It's a bad line.
• la liaison satellite
satellite link

la **libellule** *FEM NOUN*
dragonfly

la **libération** *FEM NOUN*
1 release
la libération des otages the release of the
hostages
2 liberation
la libération de la ville the liberation of the
city
• la Libération
the Liberation *(the end of the German
occupation in 1944)*

• la libération des femmes
women's liberation

libérer *VERB* [24]
1 to set free *(a prisoner, a hostage)*
2 to vacate *(a hotel room, a flat)*

se **libérer** *REFLEXIVE VERB* ◎
to free yourself
Le renard s'est libéré du piège. The fox
freed itself from the trap.
Je ne peux pas me libérer ce week-end. I
can't get away this weekend.

la **liberté** *FEM NOUN*
freedom, liberty
la Statue de la liberté the Statue of Liberty
être en liberté to be free

le & la **libraire** *MASC & FEM NOUN*
bookseller

ℓ la **librairie** *FEM NOUN*
bookshop

> **WORD TIP** librairie does not mean library
> in English; for the meaning of library ▶ SEE
> bibliothèque.

• la librairie-papeterie
bookseller's and stationer's shop

ℓ **libre** *MASC & FEM ADJECTIVE*
1 free
Est-ce que cette place est libre? Is this seat
free?
Il n'y a plus de places libres. There are no
free seats left.
Je suis libre le week-end prochain. I'm free
next weekend.
2 available
Avez-vous une chambre libre? Do you have
a room available?

librement *ADVERB*
freely

ℓ le **libre-service** *MASC NOUN*
self-service *(shop, restaurant)*

la **licence** *FEM NOUN*
degree
une licence de chimie a chemistry degree

> **WORD TIP** licence does not mean licence in
> English; for the meaning of licence ▶ SEE permis.

licencier *VERB* [1]
licencier quelqu'un to make somebody
redundant
Ils licencient du personnel. They are
making staff redundant.

le **lien** *MASC NOUN*
1 link
établir des liens avec des villes françaises
to create links with French towns
2 link

◎ means the verb takes être to form the perfect

suivre les liens follow the links

le **lierre** *MASC NOUN*
ivy

ℱ le **lieu** *MASC NOUN*, les **lieux** *PLURAL*
1 **place**
un lieu public a public place
le lieu de travail the workplace
2 **en premier lieu** in the first place
En premier lieu, je n'ai pas d'argent et en plus … In the first place, I've got no money and what's more …
3 **avoir lieu** to take place
Le festival aura lieu en juin. The festival will take place in June.
4 **au lieu de faire quelque chose** instead of doing something
Au lieu de prendre le bus, il est parti à pied. Instead of taking the bus, he went off on foot.
5 **les lieux** the premises

le **lieutenant** *MASC NOUN*
lieutenant

le **lièvre** *MASC NOUN*
hare

le **lifting** *MASC NOUN*
face-lift

ℱ la **ligne** *FEM NOUN*
1 **line**
une ligne droite a straight line
2 **line**
la ligne Paris-Dijon the Paris-Dijon line
3 **cable**
une ligne électrique an electric cable
4 **(telephone) line**
Restez en ligne, s'il vous plaît! Hold the line please!
5 **figure**
pour garder la ligne to keep your figure, to stay slim
6 **fishing line**
7 *(Computers)* **en ligne** online
Cara a mis les photos en ligne. Cara posted the photos online.
Je l'ai commandé en ligne. I ordered it online.
• la ligne d'arrivée
finishing line

la **ligue** *FEM NOUN*
league

le **lilas** *INVARIABLE MASC NOUN*
lilac

la **limace** *FEM NOUN*
slug

la **lime** *FEM NOUN*
file *(for metal, wood)*

> **WORD TIP** lime does not mean lime in English; for the meaning of **lime** ▸ SEE **citron vert**.

• la lime à ongles
nail file

la **limitation de vitesse** *FEM NOUN*
speed limit

la **limite** *FEM NOUN*
1 **border** *(between countries)*
2 **boundary** *(of a village, town)*
3 **limit**
Sa patience a des limites. There are limits to his, her patience.
4 **sans limites** endless
Ils ont une énergie sans limites. They have endless energy.
5 **dans la limite de quelque chose** within the limits of something
dans la limite du possible as far as possible
6 **maximum**
la vitesse limite the maximum speed
• la limite d'âge
age limit

limiter *VERB* [1]
to limit
limiter une recherche to limit a computer search

se **limiter** *REFLEXIVE VERB* ◉
to limit yourself

ℱ la **limonade** *FEM NOUN*
lemonade

le **lin** *MASC NOUN*
linen

ℱ le **linge** *MASC NOUN*
1 **linen**
du linge sale dirty linen
le linge de maison household linen
2 **washing**
J'ai du linge à laver. I've got some washing to do.
3 **underwear**
changer de linge to change your underwear
• le linge de corps
underwear
• le linge de lit
bed linen

la **lingerie** *FEM NOUN*
lingerie

le **lion** *MASC NOUN* ▸ SEE **Lion**
lion

le **Lion** *MASC NOUN* ▸ SEE **lion**
Leo
Nicolas est Lion. Nicolas is a Leo.
Les Lions sont généreux. Leos are

A B C D E F G H I J K L M N O P Q R S T U V W X Y Z

generous.

WORD TIP Signs of the zodiac do not take an article: un or une.

la **lionne** *FEM NOUN*
lioness

la **liqueur** *FEM NOUN*
liqueur

la **liquidation** *FEM NOUN*
clearance sale *(in a shop)*
'Liquidation totale' 'Everything must go'

liquide *MASC & FEM ADJECTIVE* ▸ SEE **liquide** *NOUN*
liquid

le **liquide** *MASC NOUN* ▸ SEE **liquide** *ADJECTIVE*
1 liquid
2 cash
payer en liquide to pay cash

ℓ **lire** *VERB* [51]
to read
Lis le texte. Read the text.
Elle sait lire en français. She can read French.
Elle nous lisait des histoires. She used to read us stories.

lis *VERB* ▸ SEE **lire**

lisible *MASC & FEM ADJECTIVE*
legible

lisse *MASC & FEM ADJECTIVE*
smooth

la **liste** *FEM NOUN*
list
la liste des courses the shopping list
une liste des prix a price list
faire une liste to make a list
faire la liste de quelque chose to make a list of something
J'ai fait la liste des invités. I've made a guest list.
• la liste d'attente
waiting list

ℓ le **lit** *MASC NOUN* ▸ SEE **lit** *VERB*
bed
une chambre à deux lits a twin room
Je vais au lit à 20 heures. I go to bed at 10 p.m.
Tu n'as pas encore fait ton lit. You haven't made your bed yet.
• le lit à une place
single bed
• le lit à deux places
double bed

ℓ **lit** *VERB* ▸ SEE **lit** *NOUN* ▸ SEE **lire**

la **literie** *FEM NOUN*
bedding

la **litière** *FEM NOUN*
litter
• la litière pour chat
cat litter

ℓ le **litre** *MASC NOUN*
litre
un litre de jus d'orange a litre of orange juice

littéralement *ADVERB*
literally

la **littérature** *FEM NOUN*
literature

la **livraison** *FEM NOUN*
delivery
Ils font des livraisons à domicile. They do home deliveries.

ℓ le **livre** *MASC NOUN* ▸ SEE **livre** *NOUN*
book
un livre pour enfants a children's book
• le livre de cuisine
cookery book
• le livre de poche
paperback
• le livre scolaire
school book

ℓ la **livre** *FEM NOUN* ▸ SEE **livre** *NOUN*
1 pound
la livre sterling the pound sterling
Ça coûte une livre. It costs a pound.
Il a gagné mille livres. He won a thousand pounds.
2 half a kilo *(half a kilo or 500 grammes)*
une livre de cerises half a kilo of cherries

livrer *VERB* [1]
1 to deliver
livrer quelque chose à quelqu'un to deliver something to somebody
Le facteur nous a livré un colis. The postman delivered a parcel to us.
2 to hand over
Il a été livré à la police. He was handed over to the police.

se **livrer** *REFLEXIVE VERB* ◎
to surrender

le **livret** *MASC NOUN*
booklet
• le livret de famille
family record book *(with dates of births, marriages and deaths)*
• le livret scolaire
school report book

local *MASC ADJECTIVE*, **locale** *FEM*, **locaux** *MASC PL*, **locales** *FEM PL* ▸ SEE **local** *NOUN*
local
un journal local a local newspaper

◎ means the verb takes être to form the perfect

à minuit heure locale at midnight, local time

le **local** MASC NOUN, les **locaux** PLURAL ▸ SEE local
ADJECTIVE
place *(usually a building)*
des locaux commerciaux business premises
dans les locaux du lycée on school premises

localement ADVERB
locally

le & la **locataire** MASC & FEM NOUN
1 tenant
2 lodger

ℓ la **location** FEM NOUN
1 renting
un appartement de location a rented flat
être en location to live in rented accommodation
2 hire, rental
la location de voitures car hire
C'est une voiture de location. It's a hire car.
3 reservation *(of theatre seats)*

WORD TIP location does not mean location in English; for the meaning of location ▸ SEE endroit.

la **locomotive** FEM NOUN
engine, locomotive

la **loge** FEM NOUN
1 (caretaker's) lodge *(in a block of flats)*
2 dressing-room *(for actors)*
3 box *(for theatregoers)*

le **logement** MASC NOUN
1 accommodation
chercher un logement to look for accommodation
2 flat
un logement au deuxième étage a flat on the second floor
3 housing
la crise du logement the housing crisis

ℓ **loger** VERB [52]
to stay
Nous logeons à l'auberge de jeunesse. We're staying at the youth hostel.
loger chez quelqu'un to stay at somebody's house
Pour l'instant, elle loge chez nous. For the moment, she's staying at our house.

le **logiciel** MASC NOUN
1 software
2 (computer) program
• le logiciel antivirus
antivirus software
• le logiciel de jeux
games program

logique MASC & FEM ADJECTIVE
logical

la **loi** FEM NOUN
law
enfreindre la loi to break the law

ℓ **loin** ADVERB
1 far
C'est un peu loin. It's a bit far.
Ce n'est pas loin d'ici. It's not far from here.
10 kilomètres, c'est loin! 10 kilometres is a long way!
Elle habite trop loin de chez moi. She lives too far away from me.
Le cinéma est plus loin. The cinema is further on.
2 far off *(in time)*
Mon anniversaire n'est pas très loin. My birthday isn't far off.
Les vacances sont encore loin. The holidays are still a long way off.
Il n'est pas loin de midi. It's almost midday.
3 de loin by far
C'est de loin le plus cher. It's by far the most expensive.
4 au loin in the distance
On voit la mer tout au loin. You can see the sea far away in the distance.
5 de loin from a long way off

lointain MASC ADJECTIVE, **lointaine** FEM
distant

ℓ les **loisirs** PLURAL MASC NOUN
1 spare time
Pendant mes loisirs je vais en ville avec mes copines. In my spare time I go to town with my (girl) friends.
2 leisure activities
Le club propose de nombreux loisirs. The club offers lots of leisure activities.

le **Londonien** MASC NOUN, la **Londonienne** FEM
Londoner

Londres NOUN
London

ℓ **long** MASC ADJECTIVE, **longue** FEM ▸ SEE long NOUN
long
un long silence a long silence
une longue vie a long life
la rue la plus longue de Paris the longest street in Paris
une chemise à manches longues a long-sleeved shirt
être long d'un mètre to be a metre long
La pièce est longue de quatre mètres. The room is four metres long.

ℓ le **long** MASC NOUN ▸ SEE long ADJECTIVE
1 faire un mètre de long to be a metre long
Ça fait cinq mètres de long. It's five metres long.
2 le long de quelque chose along something

Il marche le long de la route. He's walking along the road.

3 tout le long de quelque chose all the way through something

tout le long du voyage all the way through the journey

Elle a dormi tout le long du film. She slept all the way through the film.

ρ **longtemps** ADVERB
(for) a long time

Ça va prendre longtemps. It will take a long time.

Elle travaille ici depuis longtemps. She's been working here for a long time.

Ils ne se sont pas vus depuis longtemps. They haven't seen each other for ages.

Ça fait longtemps qu'on ne s'est pas téléphoné! It's ages since we've phoned each other!

Il y a longtemps que j'y suis allé. I went there a long time ago.

Tu peux le garder plus longtemps. You can keep it for longer.

longtemps après a long time afterwards

longuement ADVERB
for a long time

la **longueur** FEM NOUN
1 **length**

De quelle longueur est le bateau? How long is the boat?

faire des longueurs to swim lengths

le saut en longueur the long jump

2 traîner en longueur to go on forever

Le film traîne en longueur. The film goes on forever.

Il y a des longueurs dans le film. The film tends to drag.

lorsque, **lorsqu'** CONJUNCTION
when

Lorsque j'étais petite … When I was a little girl…

Lorsqu'il est arrivé … When he arrived…

WORD TIP lorsque becomes lorsqu' before a, e, i, o, u or silent h.

le **lot** MASC NOUN
1 **batch**

un lot de trente cahiers a batch of thirty exercise books

un lot de trois boîtes a pack of three cans

2 **prize**

le gros lot the jackpot

WORD TIP lot does not mean lot in English; for the meaning of a lot of ▸ SEE **beaucoup**.

la **loterie** FEM NOUN
1 **lottery**
2 **raffle**

la **lotion** FEM NOUN
lotion

le **lotissement** MASC NOUN
housing estate

le **loto** MASC NOUN
lottery

la **lotte** FEM NOUN
monkfish

la **louche** FEM NOUN ▸ SEE **louche** ADJECTIVE
ladle

louche MASC & FEM ADJECTIVE ▸ SEE **louche** NOUN
fishy, odd

un type louche a fishy-looking guy

ρ **louer** VERB [1]
1 **to let** (a house, a flat)

Ils louent leur maison. They let their house.

'À louer' 'To let', 'To rent'

2 **to rent**

Nous avons loué un appartement à la plage. We rented a flat by the beach.

3 **to hire** (a car, a bike, a boat)

Peut-on louer des vélos? Is it possible to hire bicycles?

4 **to praise**

Le professeur a loué toute la classe. The teacher praised the whole class.

le **loup** MASC NOUN
wolf

la **loupe** FEM NOUN
magnifying glass

louper VERB [1]
1 (informal) **to miss** (a train, an opportunity, a person)
2 (informal) **to fail** (an exam, a test)

ρ **lourd** MASC ADJECTIVE, **lourde** FEM
1 **heavy**

Ta valise est très lourde. Your case is very heavy.

Le repas était un peu lourd. The meal was a bit heavy.

2 **muggy**

Il fait lourd aujourd'hui. It's muggy today.

3 **serious**

une lourde erreur a serious mistake

4 **annoying**

Tu es vraiment lourd! You're a real pest!

la **loutre** FEM NOUN
otter

loyal MASC ADJECTIVE, **loyale** FEM, **loyaux** MASC PL, **loyales** FEM PL
faithful

la **loyauté** FEM NOUN
loyalty

⬤ means the verb takes être to form the perfect

le **loyer** *MASC NOUN*
rent
Le loyer est de 700 euros par mois. The rent is 700 euros a month.

lu *VERB* ▶ SEE **lire**

la **lucarne** *FEM NOUN*
skylight

la **luge** *FEM NOUN*
sledge

lugubre *MASC & FEM ADJECTIVE*
gloomy

ℒ **lui** *PRONOUN*
1 **him** *(as opposed to anybody else)*
C'est lui. It's him.
chez lui at his house
Elle pense à lui. She's thinking of him.
2 *(as indirect object for a male)* **(to) him**
Pierre est vexé, qu'est-ce que tu lui as dit? Pierre's upset, what did you say to him?
Je lui ai envoyé un texto. I sent him a text message.
Où est le livre que je lui ai prêté? Where's the book I lent him?
Donne-lui quelque chose à boire! Give him something to drink!
3 *(as indirect object for a female)* **(to) her**
Nadine est vexée, qu'est-ce que tu lui as dit? Nadine's upset, what did you say to her?
Je lui ai envoyé un e-mail. I sent her an email.
Donne-lui un pull! Give her a jumper!
4 *(as indirect object for animals)* **(to) it**
Ce chat a peur. Qu'est-ce que tu lui as fait? That cat's afraid. What did you do to it?
Donne-lui de l'eau! Give it some water!
5 *(for emphasis)* **he**
C'est lui qui me l'a dit. He's the one who told me.
Lui et moi sommes très copains. He and I are good friends.
Elle aime le cinéma mais lui préfère le théâtre. She likes the cinema but he prefers the theatre.
Lui, il n'est jamais content! He's never happy!
6 *(after prepositions like avec or sans and in comparisons)* **him**
Daniel joue avec lui. Daniel plays with him.
Oscar est plus grand que lui. Oscar is taller than him.
7 à lui **his** *(belonging to him)*
Ce sont des amis à lui. They're friends of his.

lui-même *PRONOUN*
1 **himself**
Il l'a fait lui-même. He did it himself.
'Monsieur Dubois?' - 'Lui-même.' 'Monsieur

Dubois?' – 'Speaking.'
2 *(for masc things)* **itself**
Le tableau lui-même ne vaut rien. The painting itself is worth nothing.

la **lumière** *FEM NOUN*
light

lumineux *MASC ADJECTIVE*, **lumineuse** *FEM*
luminous
un panneau lumineux an electronic display board

le **lunch** *MASC NOUN*
buffet *(lunch, supper)*

ℒ le **lundi** *MASC NOUN*
1 **Monday**
lundi dernier last Monday
lundi prochain next Monday
On est lundi aujourd'hui. It's Monday today.
2 **on Monday**
Appelle-moi lundi. Ring me on Monday.
À lundi! See you on Monday!
3 le lundi **on Mondays**
La boulangerie est fermée le lundi. The bakery is closed on Mondays.
4 tous les lundis **every Monday**
Tous les lundis, j'ai un cours de danse. Every Monday I have a dance class.

WORD TIP Months of the year and days of the week start with small letters in French.

la **lune** *FEM NOUN*
moon
• la lune de miel
honeymoon

ℒ les **lunettes** *PLURAL FEM NOUN*
glasses
mettre ses lunettes to put on your glasses
porter des lunettes to wear glasses
• les lunettes de natation
swimming goggles
• les lunettes de soleil
sunglasses

la **lutte** *FEM NOUN*
1 **fight**
la lutte contre la drogue the fight against drugs
la lutte pour la justice the fight for justice
2 **wrestling**

lutter *VERB* [1]
to fight

le **luxe** *MASC NOUN*
luxury
une voiture de luxe a luxury car

le **Luxembourg** *MASC NOUN*
Luxembourg

ℒ indicates key words

au Luxembourg in Luxembourg

WORD TIP Countries and regions in French take: le, la or les.

luxueux MASC ADJECTIVE, **luxueuse** FEM
luxurious

♀ le **lycée** MASC NOUN
secondary school (for students aged 15-18, leading to the baccalauréat exam)
• le lycée professionnel
vocational school

le **lycéen** MASC NOUN, la **lycéenne** FEM
secondary school student

Mm

m' ABBREVIATION: ME ►SEE **me**

WORD TIP me becomes m' before a word beginning with a, e, i, o, u or silent h.

M. ABBREVIATION
(= Monsieur) **Mister**
M. Dupont Mr Dupont
►SEE **Monsieur**

♀ **ma** FEM ADJECTIVE
my
►SEE **mon**

les **macaronis** PLURAL MASC NOUN
macaroni

mâcher VERB [1]
to chew

le **machin** MASC NOUN
(informal) **thing, whatsit**
Qu'est-ce que c'est que ce machin? What's this thing?

la **machine** FEM NOUN
machine
Mon T-shirt se lave en machine. My T-shirt is machine-washable.
• la machine à écrire
typewriter
• la machine à laver
washing machine
• la machine à sous
fruit machine

la **mâchoire** FEM NOUN
jaw

mâchonner VERB [1]
to chew

le **maçon** MASC NOUN
1 builder
2 bricklayer

♀ **madame** FEM NOUN, **mesdames** PLURAL
1 Madame Jones Ms Jones, Mrs Jones
2 Madame, ... Dear Madam, ... (in a letter)
3 Bonsoir, madame. Good evening. (When greeting a woman you don't know well, add 'Madame' or 'Mademoiselle' to the greeting.)

♀ **mademoiselle** FEM NOUN, **mesdemoiselles**
PLURAL
Miss, Ms
►SEE **Madame**

♀ le **magasin** MASC NOUN
shop
un magasin de chaussures a shoe shop
un grand magasin a department store
faire les magasins to go shopping
Sara travaille dans un magasin. Sara works in a shop.

♀ le **magazine** MASC NOUN
magazine

maghrébin MASC ADJECTIVE, **maghrébine** FEM
►SEE **Maghrébin**
North African

un **Maghrébin** MASC NOUN, une **Maghrébine**
FEM ►SEE **maghrébin**
North African (person)

le **magicien** MASC NOUN, la **magicienne** FEM
magician

la **magie** FEM NOUN
magic

magique MASC & FEM ADJECTIVE
1 magic
2 magical

magistral MASC ADJECTIVE, **magistrale** FEM,
magistraux MASC PL, **magistrales** FEM PL
un cours magistral a lecture (at university)

magnétique MASC & FEM ADJECTIVE
magnetic

♀ le **magnétophone** MASC NOUN
tape recorder

♀ le **magnétoscope** MASC NOUN
video recorder

♀ **magnifique** MASC & FEM ADJECTIVE
splendid

♀ **mai** MASC NOUN
May
en mai, au mois de mai in May
le premier mai May Day
fin mai late May

WORD TIP Months of the year and days of the week start with small letters in French.

♀ **maigre** MASC & FEM ADJECTIVE
1 thin, skinny

⊙ means the verb takes être to form the perfect

2 lean *(meat)*
3 low-fat *(cheese)*

maigrir *VERB* [2]
  to lose weight
  Lisa a maigri de deux kilos. Lisa's lost two kilos.

le **mail** *MASC NOUN*
  email
  Audrey m'a envoyé un mail. Audrey sent me an email.

ℓ le **maillot** *MASC NOUN*
1 shirt *(in football, rugby)*
2 jersey *(in cycling)*
  le maillot jaune the yellow jersey *(worn by the leader in the Tour de France)*
• le maillot de bain
  swimsuit, swimming trunks
• le maillot de corps
  vest

ℓ la **main** *FEM NOUN*
  hand
  avoir quelque chose à la main to have something in your hand
  Qu'est-ce que tu as à la main? What have you got in your hand?
  serrer la main à quelqu'un to shake hands with somebody
  Le gagnant sert la main du perdant. The winner shakes hands with the loser.
  se serrer la main to shake hands
  Nous nous sommes serré la main. We shook hands.
  se donner la main to hold hands
  Anna et Djamel se donnaient la main. Anna and Djamel were holding hands.
  donner un coup de main à quelqu'un to give somebody a hand
  Tu veux un coup de main? Do you want a hand?
  fait à la main, fait main handmade
• la main-d'œuvre
  labour

ℓ **maintenant** *ADVERB*
1 now
  à partir de maintenant from now on
2 nowadays
  Maintenant presque tout le monde a un portable. Nowadays nearly everybody has a mobile phone.

maintenir *VERB* [81]
1 to maintain
2 to keep
3 to stand by
  Je maintiens ce que j'ai dit. I stand by what I said.

le **maire** *MASC NOUN*
  mayor

la **mairesse** *FEM NOUN*
  mayoress

ℓ la **mairie** *FEM NOUN*
1 town hall
2 town council, city council *(the administration)*

ℓ **mais** *CONJUNCTION*
  but
  Mais oui. Yes of course.
  Mais non. Of course not.

le **maïs** *MASC NOUN*
1 maize
2 sweetcorn
3 un épi de maïs corn on the cob

ℓ la **maison** *FEM NOUN*
1 house *(building)*
  une maison individuelle a detached house
2 home *(where you live)*
  rester à la maison to stay at home
  Il pleut, je reste à la maison. It's raining, I'm staying at home.
  rentrer à la maison to go home
  C'est l'heure de rentrer à la maison. It's time to go home.
• la maison de retraite
  old people's home
• la maison des jeunes
  youth club
• la maison des jeunes et de la culture
  community youth club and arts centre

le **maître** *MASC NOUN*, la **maîtresse** *FEM NOUN*
  teacher *(in a primary school)*
  Maîtresse! Please, miss!
• le maître-nageur
  swimming instructor, pool attendant

la **maîtresse** *FEM NOUN*
  lover
  ►SEE **maître**

la **maîtrise** *FEM NOUN*
1 skill
  la maîtrise du pianiste the pianist's skill
2 command
  une bonne maîtrise de la langue française a good command of the French language
3 master's degree
  une maîtrise de langues modernes a master's in modern languages
• la maîtrise de soi
• self-control

maîtriser *VERB* [1]
1 to control
  Les pompiers ont maîtrisé les flammes. The firefighters brought the flames under control.
2 to master
  Il a maîtrisé la langue française. He's

mastered the French language.

se **maîtriser** *REFLEXIVE VERB* ⊘
to have self-control

majestueux *MASC ADJECTIVE*, **majestueuse** *FEM*
majestic

majeur *MASC ADJECTIVE*, **majeure** *FEM* ▶ SEE
majeur *NOUN*
1 major
la majeure partie des Français the majority
of French people
2 être majeur to be over 18

majeur *MASC NOUN* ▶ SEE **majeur** *ADJECTIVE*
middle finger

la **majorité** *FEM NOUN*
majority

la **majuscule** *FEM NOUN*
capital (letter)
en majuscules in capital letters
une R majuscule a capital R

ℙ le **mal** *MASC NOUN*, les **maux** *PLURAL* ▶ SEE **mal**
ADJ, ADV
1 pain, ache
Luc a mal à la tête. Luc has a headache.
faire mal to hurt
Ça fait mal. It hurts.
faire mal à quelqu'un to hurt somebody
Aïe! Tu me fais mal! Ouch! you're hurting
me!
se faire mal to hurt yourself
Benoît s'est fait mal. Benoît hurt himself.
2 avoir du mal à faire quelque chose to have
difficulty in doing something
J'ai du mal à comprendre ce qu'il dit. I have
difficulty in understanding what he says.
se donner du mal pour faire quelque chose
to go to a lot of trouble to do something
Elle s'est donné beaucoup de mal pour
contacter tout le monde. She went to a lot
of trouble to contact everybody.
3 harm
Il n'y a pas de mal. No harm done.
4 evil
le bien et le mal good and evil
• le mal de dents
toothache
• le mal de mer
seasickness
• le mal de tête
headache
• le mal des transports
motion sickness
• le mal du pays
homesickness

ℙ **mal** *INVARIABLE ADJECTIVE* ▶ SEE **mal** *ADV, NOUN*
1 wrong
2 pas mal not bad
3 pas mal de quite a lot of

On a pas mal de devoirs. We've got quite a
lot of homework.

WORD TIP mal never changes.

ℙ **mal** *ADVERB* ▶ SEE **mal** *ADJ, NOUN*
badly
Nina chante plus mal que moi. Nina sings
worse than me.
Ça va mal. It's going badly.
C'est un enfant mal élevé. He's a badly
brought up child.
Je t'entends mal. I can't hear you very well.
Je me sens mal. I don't feel well.
Cette machine fonctionne mal. This
machine doesn't work.

ℙ le & la **malade** *MASC & FEM NOUN* ▶ SEE **malade**
ADJECTIVE
patient

ℙ **malade** *MASC & FEM ADJECTIVE* ▶ SEE **malade** *NOUN*
1 ill, sick
tomber malade to fall ill
Marie est tombée malade. Marie has fallen
ill.
2 crazy
Tu es malade! Ne fais pas ça! You're crazy!
Don't do that!

la **maladie** *FEM NOUN*
1 illness
2 disease

la **maladresse** *FEM NOUN*
1 clumsiness
2 blunder

maladroit *MASC ADJECTIVE*, **maladroite** *FEM*
clumsy

le **malaise** *MASC NOUN*
1 feeling of faintness
avoir un malaise to feel faint, to pass out
2 créer un malaise to make people feel
uncomfortable

la **malchance** *FEM NOUN*
bad luck

le **mâle** *MASC NOUN* ▶ SEE **mâle** *ADJECTIVE*
male

mâle *MASC & FEM ADJECTIVE* ▶ SEE **mâle** *NOUN*
male

la **malédiction** *FEM NOUN*
curse

le **malentendu** *MASC NOUN*
misunderstanding

le **malfaiteur** *MASC NOUN*
criminal

malgré *PREPOSITION*
1 in spite of
malgré le froid in spite of the cold

⊘ means the verb takes être to form the perfect

2 malgré tout all the same
Mais malgré tout nous avons décidé d'y
aller. But we decided to go all the same.

le **malheur** MASC NOUN
misfortune
porter malheur to be bad luck
Ne passe pas là-dessous, ça porte malheur!
Don't walk under there, it's bad luck!

ℒ **malheureusement** ADVERB
unfortunately

ℒ le **malheureux** MASC NOUN, la **malheureuse**
FEM ▸ SEE **malheureux** ADJECTIVE
Le malheureux, il a tout perdu. Poor man,
he lost everything.
La malheureuse, elle a beaucoup souffert.
Poor woman, she suffered a lot.

ℒ **malheureux** MASC ADJECTIVE, **malheureuse**
FEM ▸ SEE **malheureux** NOUN
1 unhappy (feeling)
avoir l'air malheureux to look unhappy
Cet enfant a l'air malheureux. This child
looks unhappy.
2 unfortunate (choice, decision)
un choix malheureux an unfortunate choice

malhonnête MASC & FEM ADJECTIVE
dishonest

la **malice** FEM NOUN
mischief

> **WORD TIP** malice does not mean **malice**
> in English; for the meaning of malice ▸ SEE
> **malveillance**.

malicieux MASC ADJECTIVE, **malicieuse** FEM
mischievous

> **WORD TIP** malicieux does not mean **malicious**
> in English; for the meaning of malicious ▸ SEE
> **malveillant**.

malin MASC ADJECTIVE, **maligne** FEM
1 clever (person)
Ce n'était pas très malin. That wasn't very
clever.
2 malignant (tumour)

la **malle** FEM NOUN
trunk

malodorant MASC ADJECTIVE, **malodorante**
FEM
smelly

malpoli MASC ADJECTIVE, **malpolie** FEM
rude

malpropre MASC & FEM ADJECTIVE
dirty

malsain MASC ADJECTIVE, **malsaine** FEM
unhealthy

maltraiter VERB [1]
to ill-treat
les enfants maltraités battered children

la **malveillance** FEM NOUN
malice

malveillant MASC ADJECTIVE, **malveillante** FEM
malicious

ℒ la **maman** FEM NOUN
mum, mummy

la **mamie** FEM NOUN
grandma, granny

le **mammifère** MASC NOUN
mammal

la **mamy** FEM NOUN
grandma, granny

manager VERB [52]
to manage

le **manageur** MASC NOUN
manager

le **manche** MASC NOUN ▸ SEE **manche** NOUN
handle (of a tool)

la **manche** FEM NOUN ▸ SEE **manche** NOUN
1 sleeve
à manches courtes short-sleeved
sans manches sleeveless
2 round (of a game)
3 leg (of a football match)

ℒ la **Manche** FEM NOUN
la Manche the Channel
le tunnel sous la Manche the Channel
Tunnel

la **mandarine** FEM NOUN
mandarin orange

le **manège** MASC NOUN
1 merry-go-round
2 riding school

la **manette** FEM NOUN
lever
• la manette de jeu
joystick

mangeable MASC & FEM ADJECTIVE
edible

ℒ **manger** VERB [52]
to eat
Qu'est-ce qu'on va manger? What shall we
have to eat?
J'ai déjà mangé. I've already eaten.
J'ai assez mangé. I've had enough.
Ce soir, on mange chinois. Tonight we'll
have a Chinese meal.
donner à manger à quelqu'un to feed
someone
As-tu donné à manger au chien? Have you

fed the dog?
faire à manger to cook
Qu'est-ce que tu fais à manger pour midi?
What are you cooking for lunch?
manger au restaurant to go out for a meal
Il a invité son père à manger au restaurant.
He invited his father out for a meal.

la **mangue** FEM NOUN
mango

le & la **maniaque** MASC & FEM NOUN ▶ SEE
maniaque ADJECTIVE
1 fusspot
2 (informal) fanatic
Valérian est un maniaque du foot. Valérian
is football mad.

maniaque MASC & FEM ADJECTIVE ▶ SEE **maniaque**
NOUN
fussy

la **manie** FEM NOUN
1 habit
2 mania

manier VERB [1]
to handle

la **manière** FEM NOUN
1 way
à ma manière my way
une manière plus facile an easier way
de cette manière like this, like that
d'une autre manière in another way
d'une certaine manière in a way
2 de toute manière in any case
3 les manières manners
les bonnes manières good manners

le **manifestant** MASC NOUN, la **manifestante**
FEM
demonstrator

la **manifestation** FEM NOUN
demonstration
une manifestation contre le racisme a
demonstration against racism

manifester VERB [1]
to demonstrate, to take part in a
demonstration

le **manioc** MASC NOUN
cassava

manipuler VERB [1]
1 to handle
2 to manipulate

le **mannequin** MASC NOUN
1 fashion model
2 dummy (in a shop window)

le **manque** MASC NOUN
le manque de the lack of, the shortage of

manqué MASC ADJECTIVE, **manquée** FEM
1 failed
un acteur manqué a failed actor
2 missed
une occasion manquée a missed
opportunity

♗ **manquer** VERB [1]
1 to be missing
Il manque trois fourchettes. There are
three forks missing.
manquer de quelque chose to lack
something
Il manque d'ambition. He lacks ambition.
2 (a person, a place you like) manquer à
quelqu'un to miss somebody or something
Tu me manques. I miss you.
Londres leur manque. They miss London.
3 (a train, a bus, etc) manquer quelque chose
to miss something
Elle a manqué son train. She missed her
train.
J'ai manqué le début. I missed the
beginning.
4 manquer de faire quelque chose manquer
faire quelque chose to almost do
something
Il a manqué de tomber dans la piscine. He
almost fell into the pool.
Ella a manqué se faire écraser par un bus.
Ella almost got run over by a bus.

♗ le **manteau** MASC NOUN, les **manteaux** PLURAL
coat

le **manuel** MASC NOUN ▶ SEE **manuel** ADJECTIVE
1 manual
2 textbook
• le manuel scolaire
school book

manuel MASC ADJECTIVE, **manuelle** FEM ▶ SEE
manuel NOUN
manual

la **manufacture** FEM NOUN
factory

le **manuscrit** MASC NOUN ▶ SEE **manuscrit**
ADJECTIVE
manuscript

manuscrit MASC ADJECTIVE, **manuscrite** FEM
▶ SEE **manuscrit** NOUN
handwritten

le **maquereau** MASC NOUN, les **maquereaux**
PLURAL
mackerel

la **maquette** FEM NOUN
scale model
une maquette d'avion a model aeroplane

♗ le **maquillage** MASC NOUN
make-up

◔ **means the verb takes être to form the perfect**

se **maquiller** REFLEXIVE VERB ◐ [1]
1 **to put make-up on**
Attends-moi, je me maquille. Wait for me, I'm just putting some make-up on.
2 **to wear make-up**
Aurélie n'a pas le droit de se maquiller. Aurélie is not allowed to wear make-up.

le **marais** MASC NOUN
marsh

le **marathon** MASC NOUN
marathon

le **marbre** MASC NOUN
marble
une cheminée en marbre a marble fireplace

ℓ le **marchand** MASC NOUN, la **marchande** FEM
1 **shopkeeper**
2 **stallholder** (on a market)
3 **merchant**
• le marchand de fruits et légumes
greengrocer
• le marchand de journaux
newsagent

marchander VERB [1]
to haggle (over)

la **marchandise** FEM NOUN
goods

la **marche** FEM NOUN
1 **walking** (for exercise, to get from one place to another)
la marche à pied walking
faire de la marche to go walking
2 **march** (in the army)
une marche pour la paix a peace march
3 **step** (on a staircase, ladder, bus, train)
Attention à la marche! Mind the step!
4 en marche **running** (an engine), **on** (TV sets, radios)
Le moteur est en marche. The engine is running.
La télévision est en marche. The TV is on.
mettre en marche quelque chose to start something
Peux-tu mettre la machine à laver en marche? Can you start the washing-machine?
en état de marche in working order

ℓ le **marché** MASC NOUN
1 **market**
le marché aux fleurs the flower market
aller au marché to go to market
Je vais au marché tous les dimanches matin. I go to market every Sunday morning.
2 **deal**
3 bon marché **cheap**
Elle l'a acheté bon marché. She bought it

cheap.
• le marché aux puces
flea market
• le marché de l'emploi
job market

la **marche arrière** MASC NOUN
reverse

le **marchepied** MASC NOUN
step (on a train)

ℓ **marcher** VERB [1]
1 **to walk**
On va marcher jusqu'au parc. We'll walk as far as the park.
marcher sur quelque chose to tread on something
Tu as marché sur mes lunettes. You trod on my glasses.
2 **to march** (in the army)
3 **to work** (machines)
Le lecteur DVD ne marche pas. The DVD player doesn't work.
4 (informal)
Et ton boulot, ça marche? And how's the job going?
5 (informal) **to fall for it**
Tu vas voir, elle marche à tous les coups. You'll see, she falls for it every time.
faire marcher quelqu'un to pull somebody's leg
Je te faisais marcher. I was pulling your leg.

ℓ le **mardi** MASC NOUN
1 **Tuesday**
On est mardi aujourd'hui. It's Tuesday today.
mardi prochain next Tuesday
mardi dernier last Tuesday
2 **on Tuesday**
3 le mardi **on Tuesdays**
C'est fermé le mardi. It's closed on Tuesdays.
4 tous les mardis **every Tuesday**
• le mardi gras
Shrove Tuesday

WORD TIP Months of the year and days of the week start with small letters in French.

la **mare** FEM NOUN
pond

WORD TIP mare does not mean mare (female horse) in English; for the meaning of mare ▸ SEE **jument**.

le **marécage** MASC NOUN
swamp

ℓ la **marée** FEM NOUN
tide
à marée haute at high tide

A B C D E F G H I J K L **M** N O P Q R S T U V W X Y Z

à marée basse at low tide
La marée monte. The tide's coming in.
La marée descend. The tide's going out.
• la marée noire
oil slick

la **margarine** FEM NOUN
margarine

la **marge** FEM NOUN
1 margin
2 en marge de on the fringe of
Il vit en marge de la société. He lives on the
fringes of society.

♂ le **mari** MASC NOUN
husband

♂ le **mariage** MASC NOUN
1 marriage
2 wedding
le jour de leur mariage their wedding day

Marianne FEM NOUN
Marianne (a female figure representing the
French Republic in statues, paintings and on
the standard French stamp)

♂ le **marié** MASC NOUN, la **mariée** FEM ▸ SEE **marié**
ADJECTIVE
1 bridegroom
2 bride
3 les mariés the bride and groom
les jeunes mariés the newly-weds

marié MASC ADJECTIVE, **mariée** FEM ▸ SEE **marié**
NOUN
married

marier VERB [1]
to marry somebody (person who carries
out ceremony)
le prêtre qui les a mariés the priest who
married them

se **marier** REFLEXIVE VERB ⊙
to get married (bride and groom)
Ils se sont mariés à Londres. They got
married in London.
se marier avec quelqu'un to marry
somebody
Frank s'est marié avec Rita. Frank married
Rita.
Rita s'est mariée avec Frank. Rita married
Frank.

le **marin** MASC NOUN ▸ SEE **marin** ADJECTIVE
sailor

marin MASC ADJECTIVE, **marine** FEM ▸ SEE **marin**
NOUN
sea
l'air marin the sea air

marine INVARIABLE ADJECTIVE ▸ SEE **marine** NOUN
bleu marine navy blue

marine FEM NOUN ▸ SEE **marine** INVARIABLE
ADJECTIVE
navy

la **marionnette** FEM NOUN
puppet

la **marmelade** FEM NOUN
la marmelade d'oranges amères orange
marmalade

la **marmite** FEM NOUN
cooking pot

marmonner VERB [1]
to mutter, to mumble

le **Maroc** MASC NOUN
Morocco

marocain MASC ADJECTIVE, **marocaine** FEM ▸ SEE
Marocain
Moroccan

un **Marocain** MASC NOUN, une **Marocaine** FEM
▸ SEE **marocain**
Moroccan (person)

la **maroquinerie** FEM NOUN
1 leather shop
2 leather goods

marquant MASC ADJECTIVE, **marquante** FEM
memorable

♂ la **marque** FEM NOUN
1 brand (of a product)
une marque de nourriture pour chats a
brand of cat food
2 make (of appliances, cars, etc)
C'est une marque de voiture bien connue.
It's a well-known make of sports car.
3 mark
une marque sur le mur a mark on the wall
• la marque déposée
registered trademark

marquer VERB [1]
1 to write down
J'ai marqué ton nom sur la liste. I've
written down your name on the list.
2 to score
Il a marqué deux buts. He scored two goals.
3 to be significant
Le 14 juillet 1789 est une date qui a marqué
dans l'histoire de France. July 14th 1789 is a
significant date in French history.

le **marqueur** MASC NOUN
marker pen

la **marraine** FEM NOUN
godmother

marrant MASC ADJECTIVE, **marrante** FEM
(informal) funny

⊙ means the verb takes être to form the perfect

marre *ADVERB*
en avoir marre *(informal)* to be fed up
J'en ai marre. I'm fed up.

se **marrer** *REFLEXIVE VERB* ☁ [1] *(informal)*
1 **to have a great time**
On s'est bien marrés chez Jonathan. We had a great time at Jonathan's.
2 **to have a good laugh**
Pourquoi tu te marres? Why are you laughing?

ℓ le **marron** *MASC NOUN* ▸ SEE **marron** *INVARIABLE ADJECTIVE*
1 **(sweet) chestnut**
2 **(horse) chestnut**

ℓ **marron** *INVARIABLE ADJECTIVE* ▸ SEE **marron** *NOUN*
brown
des chaussures marron brown shoes
marron clair light brown
marron foncé dark brown

> **WORD TIP** marron never changes.

le **marronnier** *MASC NOUN*
chestnut tree

ℓ **mars** *MASC NOUN*
March
en mars, au mois de mars in March

> **WORD TIP** Months of the year and days of the week start with small letters in French.

la **Marseillaise** *FEM NOUN*
the Marseillaise *(the French national anthem)*

le **marteau** *MASC NOUN*, les **marteaux** *PLURAL*
1 **hammer**
2 **doorknocker**

martyrisé *MASC ADJECTIVE*, **martyrisée** *FEM*
un enfant martyrisé a battered child

la **mascotte** *FEM NOUN*
mascot

le **masculin** *MASC NOUN* ▸ SEE **masculin** *ADJECTIVE*
(Grammar) **masculine**
au masculin in the masculine

masculin *MASC ADJECTIVE*, **masculine** *FEM* ▸ SEE **masculin** *NOUN*
1 **male**
2 **men's**
3 **masculine**

le **masque** *MASC NOUN*
mask

le **massacre** *MASC NOUN*
1 **massacre**
2 *(informal)* **botch**

massacrer *VERB* [1]
to massacre

le **massage** *MASC NOUN*
massage

la **masse** *FEM NOUN*
1 **mass**
2 une masse de *(informal)* a lot of
J'ai une masse de choses à faire. I've got a lot of things to do.
(informal) 'Tu as aimé ce film?' – 'Pas des masses!' 'Did you like the film?' – 'Not much!'

masser *VERB* [1]
to massage

se **masser** *REFLEXIVE VERB* ☁
to assemble

massif *MASC ADJECTIVE*, **massive** *FEM*
1 **solid**
2 **massive**

le **Massif central** *MASC NOUN*
Massif Central *(mountainous region of southern France)*

les **mass media** *PLURAL MASC NOUN*
the mass media

mastiquer *VERB* [1]
1 **to chew**
2 **to putty** *(a window)*
3 **to fill** *(a crack)*

mat *MASC ADJECTIVE*, **mate** *FEM*
matt
le papier mat matt paper

le **mât** *MASC NOUN*
1 **mast**
2 **pole**

ℓ le **match** *MASC NOUN*
match
un match de foot a football match
un match nul a draw
faire match nul to draw
Levallois a fait match nul contre Bourg-la-Reine. Levallois drew against Bourg-la-Reine.
• le match aller
first leg
• le match amical
friendly match
• le match à domicile
home match
• le match à l'extérieur
away match

le **matelas** *MASC NOUN*
mattress
• le matelas pneumatique
air bed

matelassé *MASC ADJECTIVE*, **matelassée** *FEM*
quilted

ℓ **indicates key words**

le **matelot** MASC NOUN
sailor

les **matériaux** PLURAL MASC NOUN
materials

le **matériel** MASC NOUN
equipment
le matériel de sport sports equipment

maternel MASC ADJECTIVE, **maternelle** FEM ▸ SEE
maternelle
1 motherly
2 maternal
mon grand-père maternel my grandfather
on my mother's side of the family

la **maternelle** FEM NOUN ▸ SEE **maternelle** ADJ
(state) nursery school (for French children
aged between 2 and 6)

la **maternité** FEM NOUN
1 motherhood
2 pregnancy
le congé de maternité maternity leave
3 maternity unit

♀les **mathématiques** PLURAL FEM NOUN
mathematics

le **matheux** MASC NOUN, la **matheuse** FEM
(informal) maths genius

les **maths** PLURAL FEM NOUN
maths

♀la **matière** FEM NOUN
1 subject
Ma matière préférée, c'est l'histoire. My
favourite subject is history.
2 material
• les matières grasses
fat (in food)
• la matière première
raw material

♀le **matin** MASC NOUN
morning
À quelle heure te lèves-tu le matin? What
time do you get up in the morning?
lundi matin Monday morning
à six heures du matin at six o'clock in the
morning
du matin au soir from morning till night
de bon matin early in the morning

matinal MASC ADJECTIVE, **matinale** FEM,
matinaux MASC PL, **matinales** FEM PL
1 morning
mon jogging matinal my morning jog
2 être matinal to be an early riser

la **matinée** FEM NOUN
1 morning
au cours de la matinée during the morning
2 matinée

Nous allons voir la pièce en matinée. We're
going to see a matinée.
3 faire la grasse matinée to have a lie-in
Le week-end mes parents font la grasse
matinée. At the weekend my parents have
a lie-in.

le **matou** MASC NOUN
tomcat

matrimonial MASC ADJECTIVE, **matrimoniale**
FEM, **matrimoniaux** MASC PL,
matrimoniales FEM PL
une agence matrimoniale a marriage
bureau

la **maturité** FEM NOUN
maturity

maudire VERB [9]
to curse

maussade MASC & FEM ADJECTIVE
1 sullen
2 dull

♀**mauvais** MASC ADJECTIVE, **mauvaise** FEM ▸ SEE
mauvais ADVERB
1 bad
une mauvaise expérience a bad experience
Le temps est mauvais. The weather is bad.
Rosie est mauvaise en physique. Rosie is
bad at physics.
2 wrong (not correct)
le mauvais numéro the wrong number
3 poor
une mauvaise éducation a poor education
de mauvais résultats poor results
4 nasty (vicious)
un mauvais rhume a nasty cold
5 not well, unwell
Elle a mauvaise mine. She doesn't look well.
• la mauvaise herbe
weed

♀**mauvais** ADVERB ▸ SEE **mauvais** ADJECTIVE
1 sentir mauvais to smell
Ce chien sent mauvais. This dog smells.
2 Il fait mauvais. The weather is bad.

les **maux** PLURAL MASC NOUN ▸ SEE **mal**

le **maximum** MASC NOUN ▸ SEE **maximum**
ADJECTIVE
maximum
faire le maximum to do your utmost
maximum MASC & FEM ADJECTIVE ▸ SEE **maximum**
NOUN
maximum

la **mayonnaise** FEM NOUN
mayonnaise

le **mazout** MASC NOUN
fuel oil

● means the verb takes être to form the perfect

me, **m'** *PRONOUN*
1 *(as a direct object)* **me**
Elle me déteste. She hates me.
Il m'a vu. He saw me.
2 *(as an indirect object)* **(to) me**
Elle ne me parle jamais. She never speaks to me.
Il va m'expliquer tout ça. He's going to explain all that to me.
Elle m'a donné son adresse. She gave me her address.
Il me l'a donné. He gave it to me.
3 *(with reflexive verbs)* **myself**
Je me lève à sept heures. I get up at seven o'clock.
Je me brosse les dents. I brush my teeth.
Je me suis blessé. I hurt myself.
4 *(with reflexive verbs)* **(for) myself**
Je me fais une salade. I'm making a salad for myself.
Je me suis acheté un cadeau. I bought myself a present.

> **WORD TIP** me becomes m' before a, e, i, o, u or silent h.

le **mec** *MASC NOUN*
(informal) **guy**

ℱ le **mécanicien** *MASC NOUN*, la **mécanicienne** *FEM*
1 **mechanic**
2 **train driver**

la **mécanique** *FEM NOUN* ▶ SEE **mécanique** *ADJECTIVE*
mechanics
mécanique *MASC & FEM ADJECTIVE* ▶ SEE **mécanique** *NOUN*
1 **mechanical**
2 **clockwork**

> **WORD TIP** mécanique does not mean mechanic in English; for the meaning of mechanic ▶ SEE mécanicien.

le **mécanisme** *MASC NOUN*
mechanism

méchamment *ADVERB*
nastily

la **méchanceté** *FEM NOUN*
nastiness

ℱ **méchant** *MASC ADJECTIVE*, **méchante** *FEM*
1 **nasty**
2 **spiteful**
3 **vicious**
'Chien méchant' 'Beware of the dog'

la **mèche** *FEM NOUN*
1 **lock** *(of hair)*
2 **wick** *(of a candle)*

méconnaissable *MASC & FEM ADJECTIVE*
unrecognizable

mécontent *MASC ADJECTIVE*, **mécontente** *FEM*
dissatisfied

le **mécontentement** *MASC NOUN*
1 **dissatisfaction**
2 **displeasure**

la **médaille** *FEM NOUN*
1 **medal**
2 **medallion**
3 **name tag**

ℱ le **médecin** *MASC NOUN*
doctor
aller chez le médecin to go to the doctor's
Je dois aller chez le médecin. I must go to the doctor's.
• le médecin généraliste
general practitioner

ℱ la **médecine** *FEM NOUN*
medicine
faire des études de médecine to go to medical school
• les médecines douces
alternative medicine

les **médias** *PLURAL MASC NOUN*
the media

la **médiathèque** *FEM NOUN*
multimedia library

médical *MASC ADJECTIVE*, **médicale** *FEM*, **médicaux** *MASC PL*, **médicales** *FEM PL*
medical

ℱ le **médicament** *MASC NOUN*
drug, **medicine**

médiéval *MASC ADJECTIVE*, **médiévale** *FEM*, **médiévaux** *MASC PL*, **médiévales** *FEM PL*
medieval

médiocre *MASC & FEM ADJECTIVE*
second-rate, **poor**

médire *VERB* [9]
to criticize

la **méditation** *FEM NOUN*
meditation

méditer *VERB* [1]
to meditate

la **Méditerranée** *FEM NOUN*
the Mediterranean

méditerranéen *MASC ADJECTIVE*, **méditerranéenne** *FEM*
Mediterranean

la **méduse** *FEM NOUN*
jellyfish

le **méfait** MASC NOUN
  crime

la **méfiance** FEM NOUN
  suspicion

méfiant MASC ADJECTIVE, **méfiante** FEM
  suspicious

se **méfier** REFLEXIVE VERB ◎ [1]
  Méfie-toi! Watch out!
  se méfier de quelqu'un not to trust
  somebody
  Tu dois te méfier de lui. You mustn't trust
  him.

le **mégaoctet** MASC NOUN
  megabyte

le **mégot** MASC NOUN
  cigarette end

ℓ le **meilleur** MASC NOUN ▸ SEE **meilleur** ADJECTIVE
  best
  le meilleur des deux the better of the two
  C'est le meilleur. It's the best one.

ℓ **meilleur** MASC ADJECTIVE, **meilleure** FEM ▸ SEE
  meilleur NOUN
1 better
  Le climat est bien meilleur au sud. The
  climate's much better in the south.
  meilleur que better than
  Ton gâteau est meilleur que le mien. Your
  cake's better than mine.
2 best
  C'est ma meilleure amie. She's my best
  friend.
  André est le meilleur nageur de la classe.
  André is the best swimmer in the class.
  meilleurs vœux best wishes

ℓ le **mél** MASC NOUN
  email address

le **mélange** MASC NOUN
  mixture

mélanger VERB [52]
1 to mix
  Mélange le sucre et le beurre. Mix the
  sugar and the butter.
2 to mix up
  J'ai mélangé les dates. I got the dates mixed
  up.

la **mêlée** FEM NOUN
  scrum

mêler VERB [1]
  to mix

se **mêler** REFLEXIVE VERB ◎
1 se mêler à quelque chose to get mixed up
  with something
  Il s'est mêlé à une affaire douteuse. He got
  mixed up in some shady business.

se mêler à quelqu'un to mingle with
  somebody
  Elle s'est mêlée aux invités. She mingled
  with the guests.
2 se mêler de quelque chose to meddle in
  something
  Mêle-toi de tes affaires! Mind your own
  business!

la **mélodie** FEM NOUN
  melody

ℓ le **melon** MASC NOUN
  melon

le **membre** MASC NOUN
1 member
2 limb

même MASC & FEM ADJECTIVE ▸ SEE **même** ADVERB
1 same
  Inès a le même anniversaire que toi. Inès
  has the same birthday as you.
  en même temps at the same time
2 tout de même, quand même all the same
  Tout de même tu pourrais faire un effort.
  All the same you could try harder.

même ADVERB ▸ SEE **même** ADJECTIVE
  even
  Il n'a même pas demandé. He didn't even
  ask.
  Je la vois souvent même si je ne lui parle
  pas. I see her often although I don't talk
  to her.

la **mémé** FEM NOUN
  grandma, granny

la **mémoire** FEM NOUN
  memory
  Rosalie a de la mémoire. Rosalie has a good
  memory.
  Mon ordinateur a une mémoire de 3
  gigaoctets. My computer has a 3-gigabyte
  memory.

mémoriser VERB [1]
  to memorize

la **menace** FEM NOUN
  threat

menacer VERB [61]
  to threaten

ℓ le **ménage** MASC NOUN
  housework
  faire le ménage to do the cleaning
  Marie fait le ménage tous les lundis. Marie
  does the cleaning every Monday.
  une femme de ménage a cleaning lady

ménager VERB [52]
  ▸ SEE **ménager** ADJECTIVE
  ménager quelqu'un to treat somebody
  gently

◎ means the verb takes être to form the perfect

Il ménage son vieux grand-père. He's treating his old grandfather gently.
ménager quelque chose to be careful with something
Ménage ma vieille voiture! Be careful with my old car!

se **ménager** *REFLEXIVE VERB* ◉
to take it easy
Elle doit se ménager après son opération. She must take it easy after her surgery.

ménager *MASC ADJECTIVE*, **ménagère** *FEM* ▶SEE **ménager** *VERB*
household
les travaux ménagers housework

la **ménagère** *FEM NOUN*
house-wife

le **mendiant** *MASC NOUN*, la **mendiante** *FEM*
beggar

mendier *VERB* [1]
to beg

mener *VERB* [50]
1 to lead
Elle mène son cheval par la bride. She's leading her horse by the reins.
mener à quelque chose to lead to something
Les disputes ne mènent à rien. Arguments don't lead anywhere.
2 to run
Il mène une société. He runs a company.

la **méningite** *FEM NOUN*
meningitis

les **menottes** *PLURAL FEM NOUN*
handcuffs

le **mensonge** *MASC NOUN*
lie
dire des mensonges to tell lies
Vincent adore dire des mensonges. Vincent loves telling lies.

la **mensualité** *FEM NOUN*
monthly payment

mensuel *MASC ADJECTIVE*, **mensuelle** *FEM*
monthly

mental *ADJECTIVE MASC*, **mentale** *FEM*, **mentaux** *MASC PL*, **mentales** *FEM PL*
mental

la **mentalité** *FEM NOUN*
mentality

le **menteur** *MASC NOUN*, la **menteuse** *FEM* ▶SEE **menteur** *ADJECTIVE*
liar

menteur *MASC ADJECTIVE*, **menteuse** *FEM* ▶SEE **menteur** *NOUN*
untruthful

la **menthe** *FEM NOUN*
mint
un bonbon à la menthe a mint

la **mention** *FEM NOUN*
1 mention (in conversation)
2 grade (in exams, a degree)
Elle a eu son bac avec mention bien. She got a grade B plus in her baccalaureate.

mentionner *VERB* [1]
to mention

mentir *VERB* [53]
to lie
mentir à quelqu'un to lie to somebody
Il ne faut pas me mentir. You musn't lie to me.

ℓ le **menton** *MASC NOUN*
chin

ℓ le **menu** *MASC NOUN* ▶SEE **menu** *ADJECTIVE*
menu
le menu du jour today's menu
un menu à prix fixe a set menu
Qu'est-ce qu'il y a au menu? What's on the menu?
Je prends le menu à 20 euros. I'll have the 20 euro menu.

⏺ MENU

Les restaurants français ont une carte et des menus à prix fixe, avec entrée, plat principal et dessert. Avant le dessert, on mange souvent une salade verte et du fromage.

ℓ **menu** *MASC ADJECTIVE*, **menue** *FEM* ▶SEE **menu** *NOUN*
1 slight (person)
2 tiny (feet, steps)

la **menuiserie** *FEM NOUN*
joinery

le **menuisier** *MASC NOUN*
joiner

le **mépris** *MASC NOUN*
contempt

mépriser *VERB* [1]
to despise

ℓ la **mer** *FEM NOUN*
sea
au bord de la mer at the seaside
aller à la mer to go to the seaside
Ce week-end, nous allons à la mer. This weekend we're going to the seaside.
• la mer du Nord
the North Sea
• la mer des Antilles
the Caribbean (Sea)

la **mercerie** *FEM NOUN*
haberdashery

♪ **merci** *EXCLAMATION*
  thank you, thanks
  merci beaucoup, merci bien thank you very
  much
  non, merci no, thank you
  Merci de m'avoir rappelé. Thank you for
  calling me back.

♪ le **mercredi** *MASC NOUN*
  1 Wednesday
  On est mercredi aujourd'hui. It's
  Wednesday today.
  mercredi prochain next Wednesday
  mercredi dernier last Wednesday
  2 on Wednesday
  3 le mercredi on Wednesdays
  C'est fermé le mercredi. It's closed on
  Wednesdays.
  tous les mercredis every Wednesday
  • le mercredi des Cendres
  Ash Wednesday

  WORD TIP Months of the year and days of the
  week start with small letters in French.

♪ la **mère** *FEM NOUN*
  mother
  la mère de Sophie Sophie's mother
  une mère célibataire a single mother

  🔵 **MÈRE**
  En France, la fête des Mères est le dernier
  dimanche de mai.

la **merguez** *INVARIABLE FEM NOUN*
  spiced beef sausage

méridional *ADJECTIVE MASC*, **méridionale**
  FEM, **méridionaux** *MASC PL*, **méridionales**
  FEM PL
  southern

la **meringue** *FEM NOUN*
  meringue

la **mérite** *FEM NOUN*
  merit

mériter *VERB* [1]
  to deserve

le **merlan** *MASC NOUN*
  whiting

le **merle** *MASC NOUN*
  blackbird

la **merveille** *FEM NOUN*
  1 wonder
  Ton gâteau est une vraie merveille. Your
  cake's absolutely wonderful.
  2 à merveille wonderfully
  Tout a marché à merveille. Everything went
  like a dream.
  se porter à merveille to be in excellent

  health
  Mamie se porte à merveille. Granny is in
  excellent health.

♪ **merveilleux** *MASC ADJECTIVE*, **merveilleuse**
  FEM
  marvellous

mes *MASC & FEM PLURAL ADJECTIVE* ▶ SEE **mon**

♪ **mesdames** *PLURAL FEM NOUN* ▶ SEE **madame**

mesdemoiselles *PLURAL FEM NOUN* ▶ SEE
  mademoiselle

mesquin *MASC ADJECTIVE*, **mesquine** *FEM*
  petty

le **message** *MASC NOUN*
  message

le **messager** *MASC NOUN*, la **messagère** *FEM*
  messenger

la **messagerie vocale** *FEM NOUN*
  voicemail

la **messe** *FEM NOUN*
  mass (religious service)

♪ **messieurs** *PLURAL MASC NOUN* ▶ SEE **monsieur**

la **mesure** *FEM NOUN*
  1 measurement
  un costume fait sur mesure a made-to-
  measure suit
  2 measure
  prendre des mesures pour faire quelque
  chose to take measures to do something
  3 être en mesure de faire quelque chose to
  be in a position to do something
  Nous ne sommes pas en mesure de vous
  aider. We are not in a position to help you.

mesurer *VERB* [1]
  to measure

met *VERB: PRESENT TENSE* ▶ SEE **mettre**

le **métal** *MASC NOUN*, les **métaux** *PLURAL*
  metal

métallique *MASC & FEM ADJECTIVE*
  metallic

métallisé *MASC ADJECTIVE*, **métallisée** *FEM*
  metallic
  bleu métallisé metallic blue

♪ la **météo** *FEM NOUN*
  weather forecast

la **méthode** *FEM NOUN*
  1 method
  2 manual, tutor
  une méthode de clarinette a clarinet tutor

le **métier** *MASC NOUN*
  job
  Pour moi, le métier idéal, c'est journaliste.

  ◎ **means the verb takes être to form the perfect**

My ideal job is a journalist.

ℓ le **mètre** *MASC NOUN*
1 **metre**
Ça fait deux mètres. This is two metres long.
2 **metre rule**
Passe-moi le mètre! Pass me the metre rule!

métrique *MASC & FEM ADJECTIVE*
metric

ℓ le **métro** *MASC NOUN*
underground
une station de métro an underground station

mets *VERB* ▶SEE **mettre**

le **metteur en scène** *MASC NOUN*
director

ℓ **mettre** *VERB* [11]
1 **to put**
Il met les pieds sur la table. He puts his feet on the table.
Où as-tu mis le sel? Where have you put the salt?
2 **to put on**
Je mets mon manteau. I'm putting my coat on.
3 **to wear**
Mon père ne met jamais de cravate. My father never wears a tie.
4 **to turn on** (the radio, the television, the heating)
J'ai mis le chauffage. I've turned the heating on.
5 mettre le couvert to lay the table
J'ai mis le couvert dans la cuisine. I've laid the table in the kitchen.
6 mettre quelqu'un en colère to make somebody angry
Elle met souvent sa mère en colère. She often makes her mother angry.
7 **to take**
J'ai mis trois heures pour le faire. It took me three hours to do it.

se **mettre** *REFLEXIVE VERB* ◎
1 **to put yourself** (standing or sitting)
Mets-toi devant la fenêtre! Go over to the window!
se mettre debout to stand up
Nous nous mettons debout quand elle arrive. We stand up when she arrives.
2 se mettre à faire quelque chose to start to do something
Estelle s'est mise à chanter. Estelle started to sing.

ℓ le **meuble** *MASC NOUN*
piece of furniture
des meubles furniture

ℓ **meublé** *MASC ADJECTIVE*, **meublée** *FEM*
furnished

le **meurtre** *MASC NOUN*
murder

le **meurtrier** *MASC NOUN*, la **meurtrière** *FEM*
▶SEE **meurtrier** *ADJECTIVE*
murderer

meurtrier *MASC ADJECTIVE*, **meurtrière** *FEM*
▶SEE **meurtrier** *NOUN*
deadly

mexicain *MASC ADJECTIVE*, **mexicaine** *FEM* ▶SEE
Mexicain
Mexican

un **Mexicain** *MASC NOUN*, une **Mexicaine** *FEM*
▶SEE **mexicain**
Mexican (person)

Mexico *NOUN*
Mexico City

le **Mexique** *MASC NOUN*
Mexico

mi- *PREFIX*
1 **half-**
mi-anglais, mi-français half-English, half-French
2 **mid-**
à la mi-février in mid-February

le **mi-bas** *INVARIABLE MASC NOUN*
knee sock

le **micro** *MASC NOUN*
microphone

le **microbe** *MASC NOUN*
germ

le **micro-ondes** *INVARIABLE MASC NOUN*
microwave

ℓ le **micro-ordinateur** *MASC NOUN*
microcomputer

le **microscope** *MASC NOUN*
microscope

ℓ le **midi** *MASC NOUN* ▶SEE **Midi**
1 **midday, noon**
Il est midi vingt. It's twenty past twelve.
2 **lunchtime**
Je fais mes courses à midi. I do my shopping in my lunch hour.

le **Midi** *MASC NOUN* ▶SEE **midi**
le Midi the South of France

le **miel** *MASC NOUN*
honey

213

ℓ indicates key words

le **mien** *MASC PRONOUN*, la **mienne** *FEM* les
miens *MASC PL* les **miennes** *FEM PL*
mine
Tu n'as pas ta moto? On va prendre la
mienne. You don't have your motorbike?
We'll take mine.
'À qui sont ces chaussures?' – 'Ce sont les
miennes.' 'Whose shoes are these?'
– 'They're mine.'
Puis-je t'emprunter ton vélo? Le mien est
chez moi. Can I borrow your bike? Mine's
at home.
'Est-ce que ces chaussures sont à Natalie?'
– 'Non, ce sont les miennes.' 'Are these
shoes Natalie's?' – 'No, they're mine.'

WORD TIP The article and pronoun change in
French when they refer to fem and plural nouns.

la **miette** *FEM NOUN*
crumb

♪ **mieux** *INVARIABLE ADJECTIVE* ▸ SEE **mieux** *ADV, NOUN*
1 better
C'est mieux comme ça. It's better like that.
de mieux en mieux better and better
2 best
C'est le rouge que j'aime le mieux. I like the
red one best., I prefer the red one.

WORD TIP mieux never changes.

♪ **mieux** *ADVERB* ▸ SEE **mieux** *ADJ, NOUN*
better
Tu la connais mieux que moi. You know her
better than I do.
Je me sens mieux. I feel better.
Mon père va mieux maintenant. My
father's better now.

♪ le **mieux** *MASC NOUN* ▸ SEE **mieux** *ADJ, ADV*
Le mieux est de revenir. The best thing is to
come back.
au mieux at best, at least
Fais de ton mieux! Do your best!

♪ **mignon** *MASC ADJECTIVE*, **mignonne** *FEM*
sweet

la **migraine** *FEM NOUN*
migraine

mijoter *VERB* [1]
to simmer

♪ le **milieu** *MASC NOUN*, les **milieux** *PLURAL*
1 middle
au milieu de la journée in the middle of
the day
au beau milieu du déjeuner right in the
middle of lunch
2 environment
le milieu familial the home environment
en milieu urbain in a town

en milieu rural in the country
3 background
Il vient d'un milieu pauvre. He comes from
a poor background.

le **militaire** *MASC NOUN* ▸ SEE **militaire** *ADJECTIVE*
serviceman

militaire *MASC & FEM ADJECTIVE* ▸ SEE **militaire**
NOUN
military
le service militaire military service

♪ **mille** *NUMBER*
a thousand
mille personnes a thousand people
deux mille personnes two thousand people

le **millefeuille** *MASC NOUN*
millefeuille *(small layered cake made of puff
pastry filled with custard and cream)*

le **millénaire** *MASC NOUN*
millennium

le **mille-pattes** *INVARIABLE MASC NOUN*
centipede

le **milliard** *MASC NOUN*
billion

le & la **milliardaire** *MASC & FEM NOUN*
multimillionaire

le **millier** *MASC NOUN*
thousand
des milliers d'euros thousands of euros

le **milligramme** *MASC NOUN*
milligramme

le **millimètre** *MASC NOUN*
millimetre

♪ le **million** *MASC NOUN*
million
deux millions d'euros two million euros

le & la **millionnaire** *MASC & FEM NOUN*
millionaire

mi-long *MASC ADJECTIVE*, **mi-longue** *FEM*
mid-length

le & la **mime** *MASC & FEM NOUN*
mime artist

mimer *VERB* [1]
1 to mime
2 to mimic

minable *MASC & FEM ADJECTIVE (informal)*
1 pathetic
Ses plaisanteries sont minables. Her jokes
are pathetic.
2 crummy
un film minable a crummy film

♪ **mince** *MASC & FEM ADJECTIVE*
1 thin

☁ means the verb takes être to form the perfect

une mince tranche de viande a thin slice
of meat
2 **slim**
Elle est mince. She's slim.
3 (informal)
Mince alors! Oh bother!

la **minceur** FEM NOUN
1 **thinness**
2 **slimness**

la **mine** FEM NOUN
1 **appearance**
Elle a bonne mine. She looks well.
Tu as mauvaise mine. You don't look well.
2 **expression**
Il a une mine réjouie. He has a cheerful
expression.
Pourquoi fais-tu cette mine? Why are you
pulling that face?
3 **mine** (for coal, diamonds, etc)
4 **pencil lead**

minéral MASC ADJECTIVE, **minérale** FEM,
minéraux MASC PL, **minérales** FEM PL ▶ SEE
minéral NOUN
mineral
eau minérale mineral water
le **minéral** MASC NOUN, les **minéraux** PLURAL
▶ SEE **minéral** ADJECTIVE
mineral

mineur MASC ADJECTIVE, **mineure** FEM ▶ SEE
mineur NOUN
1 **under 18**
Elle est mineure. She's under 18.
2 **minor**
un problème mineur a minor problem
le **mineur** MASC NOUN, la **mineure** FEM ▶ SEE
mineur ADJECTIVE
1 **person under 18, minor**
2 **miner** (working in a mine)

la **minijupe** FEM NOUN
mini-skirt

minimal MASC ADJECTIVE, **minimale** FEM,
minimaux MASC PL, **minimales** FEM PL
minimal

minimiser VERB [1]
to minimize

le **minimum** MASC NOUN ▶ SEE **minimum**
ADJECTIVE
minimum
au minimum at the very least
minimum MASC & FEM ADJECTIVE ▶ SEE **minimum**
NOUN
minimum
l'âge minimum the minimum age

le **ministère** MASC NOUN
ministry

> **WORD TIP** ministère does not mean minister
> in English; for the meaning of minister ▶ SEE
> ministre.

le **ministre** MASC NOUN
minister

le **Minitel**® MASC NOUN
Minitel is an online data service; users
can access many kinds of information,
including telephone directories

la **minorité** FEM NOUN
minority

le **minou** MASC NOUN
pussycat

ℰ **minuit** MASC NOUN
midnight
à minuit at midnight

> **WORD TIP** minuit doesn't take the determiner
> le.

minuscule MASC & FEM ADJECTIVE ▶ SEE **minuscule**
NOUN
tiny
la **minuscule** FEM NOUN ▶ SEE **minuscule**
ADJECTIVE
small letter (not a capital letter)
en miniscules in small letters
une T miniscule a small T

ℰ la **minute** FEM NOUN
minute
dans dix minutes in ten minutes
Attends une minute! Wait a minute!

minutieux MASC ADJECTIVE, **minutieuse** FEM
1 **meticulous**
un travail minutieux a meticulous work
2 **detailed**
une étude minutieuse a detailed study

la **mirabelle** FEM NOUN
small yellow plum

le **miracle** MASC NOUN
miracle
par miracle miraculously

miraculeux MASC ADJECTIVE, **miraculeuse** FEM
miraculous

ℰ le **miroir** MASC NOUN
mirror

mis VERB: PAST PARTICIPLE ▶ SEE **mettre**

miser VERB [1]
to bet

misérable *MASC & FEM ADJECTIVE*
poor

> **WORD TIP** misérable does not mean miserable in English; for the meaning of miserable ▸ SEE **malheureux**.

la **misère** *FEM NOUN*
extreme poverty

> **WORD TIP** misère does not mean misery in English; for the meaning of misery ▸ SEE **souffrance**.

le **missile** *MASC NOUN*
missile

le & la **missionnaire** *MASC & FEM NOUN*
missionary

le **mistral** *MASC NOUN*
mistral *(a strong cold north wind which blows down the Rhône valley to the Mediterranean)*

♂ le **mi-temps** *INVARIABLE MASC NOUN* ▸ SEE **mi-temps** *FEM NOUN*
part-time job
travailler à mi-temps to work part-time
La prof de gym travaille à mi-temps. The PE teacher works part-time.

> **WORD TIP** mi-temps never changes.

♀ la **mi-temps** *INVARIABLE FEM NOUN* ▸ SEE **mi-temps** *MASC NOUN*
half-time *(in a match)*
à la mi-temps at half-time

> **WORD TIP** mi-temps never changes.

miteux *MASC ADJECTIVE*, **miteuse** *FEM*
1 **seedy**
2 **shabby**

la **mitraillette** *FEM NOUN*
submachine gun

le **mi-trimestre** *MASC NOUN*
half term

mixer *VERB* [1]
to mix

♂ **mixte** *MASC & FEM ADJECTIVE*
1 **coeducational**
une école mixte a coeducational school
2 **mixed**
une équipe mixte a mixed team

MJC *FEM NOUN*
(= maison des jeunes et de la culture)
community youth club and arts centre

Mlle *ABBREVIATION*
(= Mademoiselle) **Miss**
Mlle Dupont Miss Dupont
▸ SEE **Mademoiselle**

Mme *ABBREVIATION*
(= Madame) **Ms, Mrs**
Mme Dupont Mrs Dupont, Ms Dupont
▸ SEE **Madame**

mobile *MASC & FEM ADJECTIVE* ▸ SEE **mobile** *NOUN*
1 **mobile**
2 **loose** *(pages, etc)*

le **mobile** *MASC NOUN* ▸ SEE **mobile** *ADJECTIVE*
1 **motive**
le mobile du crime the motive for the crime
2 **mobile**

le **mobilier** *MASC NOUN*
furniture

la **mobylette** *FEM NOUN*
moped

♂ **moche** *MASC & FEM ADJECTIVE*
1 *(informal)* **ugly**
Ce nouvel immeuble est vraiment moche. This new block of flats is really ugly.
2 *(informal)* **awful**, **nasty** .
Le temps est moche ce matin. The weather is awful this morning.
C'est moche de dire ça! That's a nasty thing to say!

la **mode** *FEM NOUN* ▸ SEE **mode** *NOUN*
fashion
être à la mode to be fashionable
La mini-jupe est à la mode. The miniskirt is fashionable.

le **mode** *MASC NOUN* ▸ SEE **mode** *NOUN*
way, mode
un mode de paiement a method of payment
le mode de vie the way of life
• le mode d'emploi
instructions for use

le **modèle** *MASC NOUN*
1 **example**
2 **model, size**
3 **style** *(of clothing)*
Ce modèle existe en plusieurs coloris. This style is available in several colours.

modéré *MASC ADJECTIVE*, **modérée** *FEM*
moderate

♂ **moderne** *MASC & FEM ADJECTIVE*
modern

moderniser *VERB* [1]
to modernize

modeste *MASC & FEM ADJECTIVE*
1 **modest** *(person, house)*
2 **humble** *(family, origin)*

la **modestie** *FEM NOUN*
modesty

⊙ means the verb takes être to form the perfect

modifier *VERB* [1]
  to change

la **moelle** *FEM NOUN*
  marrow *(of bone)*

moelleux *MASC ADJECTIVE*, **moelleuse** *FEM*
1 soft *(towel, bed)*
2 mellow *(wine)*

les **mœurs** *PLURAL FEM NOUN*
1 customs
2 morals

⚟ **moi** *PRONOUN*
1 me *(as opposed to anybody else)*
  Âllo, c'est moi. Hello, it's me.
  'J'ai froid.' – 'Moi pas.' 'I'm cold.' – 'I'm not.'
  Elle pense à moi. She's thinking of me.
  chez moi at my house
2 *(after prepositions like avec or sans and in comparisons)* me
  Tu viens avec moi? Are you coming with me?
  C'est pour moi. It's for me.
  Elle est plus grande que moi. She's taller than me.
  Camille travaille plus que moi. Camille works harder than me.
3 à moi mine *(belonging to me)*
  C'est à moi, ça? Is that mine?
  C'est un ami à moi. He's a friend of mine.
  Ce DVD n'est pas à moi. This DVD is not mine.
4 I *(for emphasis)*
  Moi, je reste ici. I'm staying here.
  Alex et moi, nous partons en vacance. Alex and I are going on holiday.
  C'est moi qui ai payé. I'm the one who paid.
  C'est à moi de jouer. It's my turn to play.

moi-même *PRONOUN*
  myself
  Je l'ai fait moi-même. I did it myself.

moindre *MASC & FEM ADJECTIVE*
  slightest
  Je n'en ai pas la moindre idée. I haven't the slightest idea.

le **moine** *MASC NOUN*
  monk

le **moineau** *MASC NOUN*, les **moineaux** *PLURAL*
  sparrow

⚟ **moins** *PREPOSITION* ▶ SEE **moins** *ADVERB*
1 minus
  Sept moins deux égale cinq. Seven minus two equals five.
2 Il est dix heures moins cinq. It's five to ten.

⚟ **moins** *ADVERB* ▶ SEE **moins** *PREPOSITION*
1 less
  de moins en moins less and less

Tu as moins d'argent que moi. You've got less money than I have.
Il est moins grand que son frère. He's shorter than his brother.
2 le moins the least
  C'est le parfum caramel que j'aime le moins. I like the caramel flavour the least.
3 le moins, la moins, les moins the least
  le moins difficile the least difficult
  la moins jolie the least pretty
  le moins gros the smallest
  les jeunes et les moins jeunes the young and the not so young
4 de moins less, fewer
  Le voyage dure deux heures de moins en voiture. The journey takes two hours less by car.
  Il y a 100 candidats de moins. There are 100 fewer candidates.
5 moins de less, fewer
  moins de beurre less butter
  moins de voitures fewer cars
6 moins... moins... the less... the less
  Moins on travaille, moins on a envie de travailler. The less you work, the less you feel like working.
7 au moins at least
  Au moins, il s'est excusé. At least he apologized.
8 du moins at least
  Du moins, c'est ce qu'il m'a dit. At least, that's what he told me.
9 à moins que unless
  à moins qu'elle soit malade unless she's ill

⚟ le **mois** *MASC NOUN*
  month
  au mois de mai in May
  le mois dernier last month
  le mois prochain next month
  Il reçoit 100¤ d'argent de poche par mois. He gets ¤100 pocket money a month.

le **moisi** *MASC NOUN* ▶ SEE **moisi** *ADJECTIVE*
  mould

moisi *MASC ADJECTIVE*, **moisie** *FEM* ▶ SEE **moisi** *NOUN*
  mouldy

moisir *VERB* [2]
  to go mouldy

la **moisson** *FEM NOUN*
  harvest

moite *MASC & FEM ADJECTIVE*
1 sweaty
  J'ai les mains moites. I've got sweaty hands.
2 muggy
  Il y a une chaleur moite. It's muggy.

⚟ la **moitié** *FEM NOUN*
1 half

⚟ indicates key words

la moitié d'une pomme half an apple
la moitié d'entre eux half of them
2 à moitié half
à moitié vide half empty

moitié-moitié ADVERB
half-and-half
On partage moitié-moitié. We go halves.

la **molaire** FEM NOUN
molar

molle FEM ADJECTIVE ▶ SEE **mou**

le **mollet** MASC NOUN
calf (of the leg)

le & la **môme** MASC & FEM NOUN
(informal) kid

♀ le **moment** MASC NOUN
1 moment
Un moment, s'il vous plaît. Just a moment,
please.
en ce moment at the moment
pour le moment for the moment
2 time
Elle a attendu un bon moment. She waited
for some time.
par moments at times
3 À ce moment-là, on a frappé à la porte. Just
then, there was a knock on the door.
au moment où... just when...

mon MASC ADJECTIVE, **ma** FEM, **mes** MASC & FEM
PLURAL
my
mon frère my brother
ma sœur my sister
mes amis my friends
mes yeux my eyes

♀ la **monarchie** FEM NOUN
monarchy

le **monastère** MASC NOUN
monastery

le **monde** MASC NOUN
1 world
2 people
Il y a beaucoup de monde. There are a lot
of people.
peu de monde not many people
tout le monde everybody

mondial MASC ADJECTIVE, **mondiale** FEM,
mondiaux MASC PL, **mondiales** FEM PL
1 world
la Seconde Guerre mondiale the Second
World War
2 worldwide
un problème mondial a worldwide issue

la **monétique** FEM NOUN
electronic banking

le **moniteur** MASC NOUN, la **monitrice** FEM
1 instructor (in sports, driving)
un moniteur de ski a ski instructor
2 group leader (at a camp)
3 (Computers) monitor

♀ la **monnaie** FEM NOUN
1 currency
La monnaie de l'Angleterre est la livre
sterling. The English currency is the pound
sterling.
2 une pièce de monnaie a coin
3 change
Je n'ai pas de monnaie. I don't have any
change.

monotone MASC & FEM ADJECTIVE
monotonous

♀ **monsieur** MASC NOUN, **messieurs** PLURAL
1 Monsieur Leprêtre Mr Leprêtre
Bonjour monsieur. Good morning. (When
greeting a man you don't know well, add
'Monsieur' to the greeting.)
2 Monsieur, ... Dear Sir, ... (in a letter)
3 man
un grand monsieur a tall man

le **monstre** MASC NOUN
monster

monstrueux MASC ADJECTIVE, **monstrueuse**
FEM
monstrous

le **mont** MASC NOUN
mountain
le mont Blanc Mont Blanc

♀ la **montagne** FEM NOUN
1 mountain
la montagne the mountains
à la montagne in the mountains
2 une montagne de a mountain of
Il y a une montagne de formulaires à
remplir. There is a mountain of forms to
fill in.
• les montagnes russes
roller coaster

montagneux MASC ADJECTIVE, **montagneuse**
FEM
mountainous

le **montant** MASC NOUN ▶ SEE **montant** ADJECTIVE
sum

montant MASC ADJECTIVE, **montante** FEM ▶ SEE
montant NOUN
1 rising
la marée montante the rising tide
2 des chaussures montantes ankle boots

la **montée** FEM NOUN
1 way up, ascent
la montée de la côte the way up the hill

⬛ means the verb takes être to form the perfect

2 hill
Elle habite en haut de la montée. She lives at the top of the hill.

3 rise
la montée des prix du pétrole the rise in oil prices

ℐ **monter** *VERB* [1]

1 to go up, to come up
monter l'escalier to go or come up the stairs
monter la colline to go up the hill

2 monter quelque chose to take something up *(from downstairs)*
Je vais monter ta valise. I'll take your case up.

3 to assemble *(a kit)*

4 to put up *(a tent)*

5 monter dans quelque chose ◌ to get on something *(a bus, a train, etc)*
Il est monté dans le train. He got on the train.

6 monter sur quelque chose ◌ to get on something *(a bike, a horse)*
Monte sur ton vélo! Get on your bicycle!
Elle est monté sur le tabouret. She climbed onto the stool.

7 ◌ **to rise** *(prices)*
Les prix ont monté. Prices have risen.

8 monter à cheval to ride a horse
Arnaud apprend à monter à cheval. Arnaud is learning to ride a horse.

WORD TIP When you say what you go up, take up, assemble, put up etc, use avoir in the perfect tense.

la **montgolfière** *FEM NOUN*
hot-air balloon

la **montre** *FEM NOUN*
watch

montrer *VERB* [1]
to show

la **monture** *FEM NOUN*
frames *(of glasses)*

ℐ le **monument** *MASC NOUN*

1 monument

2 historic building

• le monument aux morts
war memorial

se **moquer** *REFLEXIVE VERB* ◌ [1]

1 se moquer de quelqu'un to make fun of somebody
Tout le monde s'est moqué de moi. Everybody made fun of me.

2 se moquer de quelque chose not to care about something
Je m'en moque. I couldn't care less.

la **moquette** *FEM NOUN*
fitted carpet

moqueur *MASC ADJECTIVE*, **moqueuse** *FEM*
mocking

moral *MASC ADJECTIVE*, **morale** *FEM*, **moraux** *MASC PL*, **morales** *FEM PL* ▸ SEE **moral** *NOUN*

1 moral

2 mental

le **moral** *MASC NOUN* ▸ SEE **moral** *ADJECTIVE*
morale
Les élèves ont mauvais moral. The pupils' morale is low.
Je n'ai pas le moral. I'm feeling really down.

la **morale** *FEM NOUN*

1 moral
la morale de la fable the moral of the fable
La prof lui a fait la morale. The teacher gave him a lecture.

2 morality

la **moralité** *FEM NOUN*
moral
Je n'ai pas travaillé mes maths. Moralité: j'ai eu une mauvaise note au contrôle. I didn't work on my maths. The moral is: I got a bad mark in the test.

le **morceau** *MASC NOUN*, les **morceaux** *PL*
piece, **bit**
un morceau de sucre a sugar lump
un morceau de piano a piano piece

mordre *VERB* [3]
to bite

mordu *MASC ADJECTIVE*, **mordue** *FEM* ▸ SEE **mordu** *NOUN*
être mordu de quelque chose to be mad about something
Olivier est mordu de snowboard. Olivier is mad about snowboarding.

le **mordu** *MASC NOUN*, LA, **mordue** *FEM* ▸ SEE **mordu** *ADJECTIVE*
(informal) **fanatic**

morne *MASC & FEM ADJECTIVE*

1 gloomy

2 dismal, **dreary**

la **morsure** *FEM NOUN*
bite

ℐ **mort** *MASC ADJECTIVE*, **morte** *FEM* ▸ SEE **mort** *MASC & FEM NOUNS*
dead

ℐ le **mort** *MASC NOUN*, la **morte** *FEM* ▸ SEE **mort** *ADJ, FEM NOUN*

1 dead man

2 dead woman

3 les morts the dead

ℐ indicates key words

la **mort** FEM NOUN ▸ SEE **mort** ADJ, MASC NOUN
  death
  • la mort-aux-rats
    rat poison

mortel MASC ADJECTIVE, **mortelle** FEM
  1 **deadly**
    un champignon mortel a deadly poisonous
    mushroom
  2 **fatal**
    un coup mortel a fatal blow
  3 **deadly boring**
    Cette soirée est mortelle. This party is
    deadly boring.

la **morue** FEM NOUN
  1 **cod**
  2 **salt cod**

la **mosaïque** FEM NOUN
  mosaic

Moscou NOUN
  Moscow

la **mosquée** FEM NOUN
  mosque

le **mot** MASC NOUN
  1 **word**
    mot à mot word for word
    en quelques mots in a few words
    Nous ne parlons pas un mot d'italien. We
    don't speak a word of Italian.
    dire un mot à quelqu'un to have a word
    with somebody
    Attends une minute, j'ai un mot à te dire.
    Wait a minute, I'd like a word with you.
  2 **note**
    Il a laissé un mot sur la table. He left a note
    on the table.
  • le mot de passe
    password
  • les mots croisés
    crossword

le **motard** MASC NOUN, la **motarde** FEM
  (informal) **motorcyclist**

le **moteur** MASC NOUN
  engine

le **motif** MASC NOUN
  1 **motive**
  2 **pattern**
    un tissu à motifs géométriques a material
    with a geometric pattern

motiver VERB [1]
  to motivate

la **moto** FEM NOUN
  motorbike
  Je suis venu à moto. I came by motorbike.

le & la **motocycliste** MASC & FEM NOUN
  motorcyclist

la **motte** FEM NOUN
  1 **lump**
  2 **slab**

mou MASC ADJECTIVE, **molle** FEM
  1 **soft**
  2 **listless**

la **mouche** FEM NOUN
  fly

se **moucher** REFLEXIVE VERB ☻ [1]
  to blow your nose
  Mouche-toi et arrête de renifler! Blow your
  nose and stop sniffing!

le **moucheron** MASC NOUN
  midge

le **mouchoir** MASC NOUN
  handkerchief
  • le mouchoir en papier
    tissue

la **moue** FEM NOUN
  pout
  faire la moue to pout

la **mouette** FEM NOUN
  seagull

la **moufle** FEM NOUN
  mitten

mouillé MASC ADJECTIVE, **mouillée** FEM
  wet

mouiller VERB [1]
  to wet
se **mouiller** REFLEXIVE VERB ☻
  to get wet

moulant MASC ADJECTIVE, **moulante** FEM
  tight-fitting
  un jean moulant tight-fitting jeans

le **moule** MASC NOUN ▸ SEE **moule** NOUN
  1 **mould** (for modelling)
  2 **tin** (for baking)
  • le moule à cake
    loaf tin
  • le moule à gâteau
    cake tin
  • le moule à tarte
    flan dish

la **moule** FEM NOUN ▸ SEE **moule** NOUN
  mussel

mouler VERB [1]
  to mould

le **moulin** MASC NOUN
  mill

☻ means the verb takes être to form the perfect

- le **moulin à poivre**
  pepper mill
- le **moulin à vent**
  windmill

mourir *VERB* ⊘ [54]
  to die
  Elle est morte en février. She died in February.
  mourir de quelque chose to die of something
  Mon grand-père est mort d'un cancer. My grandfather died of cancer.
  Je meurs de faim! I'm starving!

moussant *MASC ADJECTIVE*, **moussante** *FEM*
  foaming

la **mousse** *FEM NOUN*
1 **foam** *(in the bath)*, **lather** *(on soap)*, **froth** *(on milk, coffee)*
2 **foam** *(for mattresses, etc)*
   un matelas de mousse a foam mattress
3 **moss**
4 **mousse** *(food)*
- la mousse au chocolat
  chocolate mousse
- la mousse à raser
  shaving foam

mousser *VERB* [1]
  to foam

mousseux *MASC ADJECTIVE*, **mousseuse** *FEM*
  du vin mousseux sparkling wine

la **moustache** *FEM NOUN*
  moustache

le **moustique** *MASC NOUN*
  mosquito

ℓ la **moutarde** *FEM NOUN*
  mustard

ℓ le **mouton** *MASC NOUN*
1 **sheep**
2 **mutton**
   un ragoût de mouton a mutton stew

le **mouvement** *MASC NOUN*
1 **movement**
2 **bustle**
3 **impulse**, **reaction**
   Mon premier mouvement a été de refuser. My first impulse was to refuse.
4 **action**
   un mouvement de grève industrial action

mouvementé *MASC ADJECTIVE*, **mouvementée** *FEM*
  hectic, **eventful**
  J'ai eu une semaine mouvementée. I've had a hectic week.

ℓ le **moyen** *MASC NOUN* ►SEE **moyen** *ADJECTIVE*
1 **means**, **way**
   un moyen de transport a means of transport
2 les moyens the means *(enough money)*
   Je n'ai pas les moyens de m'acheter un ordinateur. I can't afford to buy a computer.

ℓ **moyen** *MASC ADJECTIVE*, **moyenne** *FEM* ►SEE **moyen** *NOUN*
1 **medium**
   un poids moyen a medium weight
2 **medium-sized**
   une école de taille moyenne a medium-sized school
3 **average**
   la température moyenne the average temperature
- le Moyen Âge
  Middle Ages

la **moyenne** *FEM NOUN*
1 **average**
   en moyenne on average
2 **half marks**, **50%**
   J'ai eu la moyenne à mon devoir de maths. I got 50% for my maths test.

le **Moyen-Orient** *MASC NOUN*
  Middle East

muet *MASC ADJECTIVE*, **muette** *FEM*
1 **dumb**
   Sasha est sourd et muet. Sasha is deaf and dumb.
2 **silent**
   le cinéma muet silent movies

multiculturel *MASC ADJECTIVE*, **multiculturelle** *FEM*
  multicultural

multiple *MASC & FEM ADJECTIVE*
  multiple

la **multiplication** *FEM NOUN*
1 **multiplication**
2 **increase**

multiplier *VERB* [1]
1 **to multiply**
   Dix multiplié par cinq égale cinquante. Ten multiplied by five equals fifty.
2 **to increase**
   Le club multiplie le nombre de ses adhérents. The club is increasing the number of its members.

se **multiplier** *REFLEXIVER VERB* ⊘
  to increase
  Les accidents se multiplient. The accidents are on the increase.

municipal *MASC ADJECTIVE*, **municipale** *FEM*, **municipaux** *MASC PL*, **municipales** *FEM PL*
1 local, town
le conseil municipal the town council
les élections municipales the local elections
2 municipal
la bibliothèque municipale the municipal library

la **municipalité** *FEM NOUN*
1 municipality
2 town council

les **munitions** *PLURAL FEM NOUN*
ammunition

ℰ le **mur** *MASC NOUN*
wall

mûr *MASC ADJECTIVE*, **mûre** *FEM*
1 ripe
2 mature
l'âge mûr middle age

la **muraille** *FEM NOUN*
wall
la Grande Muraille de Chine the Great Wall of China

la **mûre** *FEM NOUN*
blackberry

mûrir *VERB* [2]
1 to ripen
2 to mature (people, wines)

le **murmure** *MASC NOUN*
murmur

murmurer *VERB* [1]
to murmur

la **muscade** *FEM NOUN*
nutmeg

le **muscle** *MASC NOUN*
muscle

musclé *MASC ADJECTIVE*, **musclée** *FEM*
muscular

la **musculation** *FEM NOUN*
bodybuilding

le **museau** *MASC NOUN*, les **museaux** *PLURAL*
muzzle (of a dog)

ℰ le **musée** *MASC NOUN*
1 museum
le musée des sciences the science museum
2 art gallery
un musée d'art contemporain a modern art gallery

musical *ADJECTIVE MASC*, **musicale** *FEM*, **musicaux** *MASC PL*, **musicales** *FEM PL*
musical

ℰ le **musicien** *MASC NOUN*, la **musicienne** *FEM*
musician

ℰ la **musique** *FEM NOUN*
music
la musique pop pop music
J'aime la musique classique. I like classical music.
mettre de la musique to put some music on
Lorsque j'étudie, je mets de la musique. When I study, I put some music on.

musulman *MASC ADJECTIVE*, **musulmane** *FEM*
▶ SEE **musulman** *NOUN*
Muslim

le **musulman** *MASC NOUN*, la **musulmane** *FEM*
▶ SEE **musulman** *ADJECTIVE*
Muslim (person)

WORD TIP Adjectives and nouns of religion start with a small letter in French.

mutuel *MASC ADJECTIVE*, **mutuelle** *FEM*
mutual

myope *MASC & FEM ADJECTIVE*
short-sighted

le **mystère** *MASC NOUN*
mystery

ℰ **mystérieux** *MASC ADJECTIVE*, **mystérieuse** *FEM*
mysterious

mystifier *VERB* [1]
to fool

mystique *MASC & FEM ADJECTIVE*
mystical

le **mythe** *MASC NOUN*
myth

Nn

la **nage** *FEM NOUN*
swimming
Ils ont traversé la fleuve à la nage. They swam across the river.

ℰ **nager** *VERB* [52]
to swim
Je sais nager. I can swim.

le **nageur** *MASC NOUN*, la **nageuse** *FEM*
swimmer

naïf *MASC ADJECTIVE*, **naïve** *FEM*
naïve

le **nain** *MASC NOUN*, la **naine** *FEM*
dwarf

ℰ la **naissance** *FEM NOUN*
birth

⬥ means the verb takes être to form the perfect

lieu de naissance place of birth

_ℓ_ **naître** _VERB_ ◯ [55]
to be born
Je suis né à Londres en 1990. I was born in London in 1990 _(boy speaking)_.
Je suis née en Écosse le 11 mars. I was born in Scotland on 11th March _(girl speaking)_.

la **nana** _FEM NOUN_
(informal) **girl**

_ℓ_ la **nappe** _FEM NOUN_
tablecloth

la **narine** _FEM NOUN_
nostril

natal _MASC ADJECTIVE_, **natale** _FEM_
native
ma ville natale my home town

la **natalité** _FEM NOUN_
le taux de natalité the birth rate

_ℓ_ la **natation** _FEM NOUN_
swimming
faire de la natation to go swimming
• une leçon de natation
a swimming lesson

natif _MASC ADJECTIVE_, **native** _FEM_
native

la **nation** _FEM NOUN_
nation
les Nations unies the United Nations

national _MASC ADJECTIVE_, **nationale** _FEM_, **nationaux** _MASC PL_, **nationales** _FEM PL_
national
une route nationale a main road

nationaliser _VERB_ [1]
to nationalize

la **nationalité** _FEM NOUN_
nationality
la double nationalité dual nationality
acquérir la nationalité française to become a French citizen

la **nativité** _FEM NOUN_
Nativity

la **natte** _FEM NOUN_
1 **plait** _(of hair)_
2 **mat**

nature _INVARIABLE ADJECTIVE_ ▶ SEE **nature** _NOUN_
plain
yaourt nature plain yoghurt
un thé nature tea without milk or sugar

la **nature** _FEM NOUN_ ▶ SEE **nature** _INVARIABLE ADJECTIVE_
nature

naturel _MASC ADJECTIVE_, **naturelle** _FEM_ ▶ SEE **naturel** _NOUN_
natural

_ℓ_ **naturel** _MASC NOUN_ ▶ SEE **naturel** _ADJECTIVE_
1 **nature** _(of a person)_
2 au naturel **plain** _(food)_
riz au naturel plain rice

naturellement _ADVERB_
1 **of course**
Naturellement, il a oublié. Of course, he forgot.
2 **naturally**
Ses cheveux bouclent naturellement. Her hair is naturally curly.

la **nausée** _FEM NOUN_
nausea
avoir[5]la nausée to feel sick
J'ai la nausée. I feel sick.

nautique _MASC & FEM ADJECTIVE_
faire du ski nautique to go water-skiing
Club Nautique de la Baule la Baule Sailing Club

le **navet** _MASC NOUN_
1 **turnip**
2 **flop** _(film, event, etc)_

la **navette** _FEM NOUN_
shuttle _(bus)_
faire la navette to commute

le **navigateur** _MASC NOUN_
(Computers) **browser**

naviguer _VERB_ [1]
1 **to sail** _(in a boat)_
2 _(Computers)_ **to surf**
naviguer sur le Web to surf the Web

le **navire** _MASC NOUN_
ship
• le navire-citerne
oil tanker

navré _MASC ADJECTIVE_, **navrée** _FEM_
sorry
Je suis vraiment navré. I'm very sorry.

_ℓ_ **ne, n'** _ADVERB_
1 ne … pas **not**
Je ne veux pas le faire. I don't want to do it.
Je n'aime pas le lait. I don't like milk.
2 ne … jamais **never**
Je ne vais jamais au marché. I never go to the market.
3 ne … que **only**
Je n'ai que dix euros. I only have ten euros.
4 ne … plus **no longer**
Elle n'habite plus à Cardiff. She no longer lives in Cardiff.
5 ne … rien **not … anything, nothing**
Il ne mange rien. He doesn't eat anything.

Elle ne s'intéresse à rien. She's not interested in anything.

6 ne ... personne not ... anybody, nobody
Il n'y a personne. There's nobody there.
Personne n'a compris. Nobody understood.

> **WORD TIP** ne becomes n' before a, e, i, o, u or silent h. ne goes before the verb, and pas, que, jamais etc come after it.

♪ **né** *MASC ADJECTIVE*, **née** *FEM*
born

néanmoins *ADVERB*
nevertheless
Il est néanmoins vrai que ... Nevertheless, it's true that ...

♪ **nécessaire** *MASC & FEM ADJECTIVE*
necessary
Est-ce qu'il est nécessaire de réserver? Is it necessary to book?

la **nécessité** *FEM NOUN*
necessity
Le téléphone mobile est devenu une nécessité. A mobile phone has become a necessity.

la **nectarine** *FEM NOUN*
nectarine

néerlandais *MASC ADJECTIVE*, **néerlandaise** *FEM*
▶ SEE **Néerlandais**
Dutch

un **Néerlandais** *MASC NOUN*, une **Néerlandaise** *FEM* ▶ SEE **néerlandais**
1 Dutch *(person)*
2 le néerlandais Dutch *(language)*

négatif *MASC ADJECTIVE*, **négative** *FEM* ▶ SEE **négatif** *NOUN*
negative

le **négatif** *MASC NOUN* ▶ SEE **négatif** *ADJECTIVE*
negative *(of a photo)*

négligé *MASC ADJECTIVE*, **négligée** *FEM*
scruffy

négligent *MASC ADJECTIVE*, **négligente** *FEM*
careless

négliger *VERB* [52]
to neglect
Il a négligé de le faire. He didn't bother to do it.

le **négociant** *MASC NOUN*, la **négociante** *FEM*
merchant

négocier *VERB* [1]
négocier avec quelqu'un to negotiate with someone

la **neige** *FEM NOUN*
snow

♪ **neiger** *VERB* [52]
to snow
Il neige. It's snowing.

le **néon** *MASC NOUN*
neon

néo-zélandais *MASC ADJECTIVE*, **néo-zélandaise** *FEM* ▶ SEE **Néo-Zélandais**
fromorof New Zealand

> **WORD TIP** Adjectives never have capitals in French, even for nationality or regional origin.

un **Néo-Zélandais** *MASC NOUN*, une **Néo-Zélandaise** *FEM* ▶ SEE **néo-zélandais**
New Zealander

le **nerf** *MASC NOUN*
nerve
Elle me tape sur les nerfs! She's getting on my nerves!

nerveux *MASC ADJECTIVE*, **nerveuse** *FEM*
nervous

♪ **n'est-ce pas?** *ADVERB*
Il fait froid ce soir, n'est-ce pas? It's cold this evening, isn't it?
Il habite à Paris, n'est-ce pas? He lives in Paris, doesn't he?
Tu as déjà mangé, n'est-ce pas? You've already eaten, haven't you?

> **WORD TIP** n'est-ce pas is translated by isn't it, don't you, haven't you etc depending on the subject of the sentence that comes before it.

net *MASC ADJECTIVE*, **nette** *FEM*
1 clear *(picture, etc)*
2 net *(in weights, prices, etc)*
3 distinct *(improvement)*

nettement *ADVERB*
much
C'est nettement meilleur. It's much better.

le **nettoyage** *MASC NOUN*
cleaning
• le nettoyage à sec
dry cleaning

♪ **nettoyer** *VERB* [39]
to clean

♪ **neuf** *MASC ADJECTIVE*, **neuve** *FEM* ▶ SEE **neuf** *NUMBER*
new
C'est tout neuf. It's brand new.
une voiture toute neuve a brand new car

> **WORD TIP** neuf always means just bought, just made etc.

♪ **neuf** *NUMBER* ▶ SEE **neuf** *ADJECTIVE*
nine
Il est neuf heures du matin. It's nine o'clock

⬤ means the verb takes être to form the perfect

in the morning.
Julie a neuf ans. Julie's nine.
le neuf juillet the ninth of July

neutre *MASC & FEM ADJECTIVE*
neutral

neuvième *MASC & FEM ADJECTIVE* ▸ SEE **neuvième**
NOUN
ninth
au neuvième étage on the ninth floor

la **neuvième** *FEM NOUN* ▸ SEE **neuvième** *ADJECTIVE*
year 4
Pierre est en neuvième. Pierre is in year 4.

ℱ le **neveu** *MASC NOUN*, **neveux** *PL*
nephew

ℱ le **nez** *MASC NOUN*
nose
J'ai le nez bouché. I have a blocked nose.
Tu saignes du nez. Your nose is bleeding.

ni *CONJUNCTION*
ni ... ni ... neither ... nor
ni lui ni son frère neither he nor his brother
Ni Françoise ni Andrée ne le sait. Neither
Françoise nor Andrée knows.

la **niche** *FEM NOUN*
1 **kennel** *(for a dog)*
2 **niche** *(for a statue, etc)*

le **nid** *MASC NOUN*
nest

ℱ la **nièce** *FEM NOUN*
niece

nier *VERB* [1]
to deny

n'importe *ADVERB*
1 **either, it doesn't matter**
'Tu veux une aile ou une cuisse?' –
'N'importe.' 'Do you want a wing or a leg?'
– 'Either will do.'
2 **n'importe qui anybody**
N'importe qui peut le faire. Anybody can
do it.
On ne peut pas demander à n'importe qui.
We can't ask just anybody.
3 **n'importe quoi anything**
Je ferai n'importe quoi pour t'aider. I'll do
anything to help you.
4 **n'importe quand any time**
Tu peux m'appeler n'importe quand. You
can ring me any time.
5 **n'importe comment any how**
Tu peux les ranger n'importe comment.
You can put them away any old how.
6 **n'importe où anywhere (you like)**
Asseyez-vous n'importe où. Sit down
anywhere you like.

le **niveau** *MASC NOUN*, **niveaux** *PLURAL*
level
au même niveau at the same level
• le niveau de vie
standard of living

les **noces** *PLURAL FEM NOUN*
wedding
• les noces d'argent
silver wedding anniversary
• les noces d'or
golden wedding anniversary

nocif *MASC ADJECTIVE*, **nocive** *FEM*
harmful

nocturne *MASC & FEM ADJECTIVE* ▸ SEE **nocturne**
NOUN
nocturnal

la **nocturne** *FEM NOUN* ▸ SEE **nocturne** *ADJECTIVE*
late-night opening *(of shops)*

ℱ le **Noël** *MASC NOUN*
Christmas
à Noël at Christmas
Joyeux Noël! Merry Christmas!

le **nœud** *MASC NOUN*
knot
faire un nœud to tie a knot

ℱ **noir** *MASC ADJECTIVE*, **noire** *FEM* ▸ SEE **noir** *NOUN*
1 **black**
un chapeau noir a black hat
2 **dark**
Il fait noir. It's dark.

ℱ le **noir** *MASC NOUN* ▸ SEE **noir** *ADJECTIVE*
1 **black**
Elle s'habille toujours en noir. She always
wears black.
2 **dark**
J'ai peur du noir. I'm scared of the dark.

ℱ un **Noir** *MASC NOUN*, une **Noire** *FEM*
1 **black man**
2 **black woman**
3 les Noirs black people

> **WORD TIP** Names of peoples take a capital in
> French.

noircir *VERB* [2]
to blacken

la **noisette** *FEM NOUN*
hazelnut

la **noix** *FEM NOUN*
1 **walnut**
2 **small amount**
une noix de beurre a knob of butter
• la noix de cajou
cashew nut
• la noix de coco
coconut

♟ le **nom** MASC NOUN
1 **name**
2 **au nom de** on behalf of
   au nom de la famille Dupont on behalf of
   the Dupont family
 • le nom de famille
   surname
 • le nom de jeune fille
   maiden name

le **nombre** MASC NOUN
   number
   un bon nombre de a good many
   Le nombre de victimes s'élève à 13. The
   number of dead is 13.

nombreux MASC ADJECTIVE, **nombreuse** FEM
   many
   de nombreuses personnes many people
   Ils étaient nombreux. There were a lot of
   them.
   Une famille nombreuse a big family

le **nombril** MASC NOUN
   navel

nommer VERB [1]
1 **to name**
   On l'a nommé Alex. They named him Alex.
2 **to appoint** (to a job)

♟ **non** ADVERB
1 **no**
   Elle a dit non. She said no.
2 **non seulement** not only
3 **non loin de** not far from
4 **non plus** neither
   moi non plus me neither
5 (with nouns, adjectives) un non-fumeur a
   non-smoker
   eau non potable water not suitable for
   drinking

♟ **nord** INVARIABLE ADJECTIVE ▸ SEE **nord** NOUN
1 **north**
   le côté nord the north side
2 **northern**
   la région nord the northern area

   WORD TIP nord never changes.

♟ le **nord** MASC NOUN ▸ SEE **nord** INVARIABLE ADJECTIVE
   north
   le nord de la France northern France
   le vent du nord the north wind
   Je suis du nord. I'm from the north.
   J'habite dans le nord (de l'Ecosse). I live in
   the north (of Scotland).
   La Belgique est au nord de la France.
   Belgium is to the north of France.

nord-américain MASC ADJECTIVE, **nord-
américaine** FEM ▸ SEE **Nord-américain** NOUN
   North American

le **Nord-Américain** MASC NOUN, la **Nord-
Américaine** FEM ▸ SEE **nord-américain**
   North American

le **nord-est** MASC NOUN
   north-east
   le nord-est de l'Angleterre north-east
   England

le **nord-ouest** MASC NOUN
   north-west
   le nord-ouest du Pays de Galles north-west
   Wales

♟ **normal** MASC ADJECTIVE, **normale** FEM,
normaux MASC PL, **normales** FEM PL
   normal
   un enfant normal a normal child
   C'est normal. There's nothing unusual
   about it.

normalement ADVERB
1 **normally**
   Normalement, je la vois tous les jours.
   Normally, I see her every day.
2 **according to plan**
   Normalement, elle doît être à Newcastle.
   If things have gone according to plan, she
   should be in Newcastle.

normand MASC ADJECTIVE, **normande** FEM ▸ SEE
Normand
   of or **from Normandy**
   la côte normande the Normandy coast

   WORD TIP Adjectives never have capitals in
   French, even for nationality or regional origin.

un **Normand** MASC NOUN, une **Normande** FEM
▸ SEE **normand**
   a person from Normandy

la **Normandie** FEM NOUN
   Normandy
   en Normandie in Normandy

   WORD TIP Countries and regions in French take
   le, la or les.

la **Norvège** FEM NOUN
   Norway

norvégien MASC ADJECTIVE, **norvégienne** FEM
▸ SEE **Norvégien**
   Norwegian

un **Norvégien** MASC NOUN, une **Norvégienne**
FEM ▸ SEE **norvégien**
   Norwegian

♟ **nos** PLURAL MASC & FEM ADJECTIVE
   our
   nos amis français our French friends
   nos idées our ideas

   WORD TIP Use nos for our with plural French
   nouns. ▸ SEE **notre**

◔ means the verb takes être to form the perfect

le **notaire** MASC NOUN
　lawyer, notary (dealing with property sales, wills, etc)

notamment ADVERB
　especially

ℱ la **note** FEM NOUN
　1 bill
　　La note, s'il vous plaît. Can I have the bill please?
　2 mark
　　J'ai eu une bonne note en allemand. I got a good mark in German.
　3 note
　　prendre des notes to take notes

noter VERB [1]
　1 to write down
　　C'est bien noté? Have you got that?
　2 to notice (something unusual)

la **notion** FEM NOUN
　idea
　　des notions basic knowledge
　　J'ai des notions d'espagnol. I have a basic knowledge of Spanish.

ℱ **notre** MASC & FEM ADJECTIVE, **nos** PL
　our
　　notre professeur our teacher
　　notre voiture our car

　WORD TIP Use notre for our with singular French nouns. ▸ SEE **nos**

ℱ le **nôtre** MASC PRONOUN, la **nôtre** FEM les **nôtres** PL
　ours
　　un pays comme le nôtre a country like ours
　　Cette voiture, c'est la nôtre. This car is ours.
　　'Ces photos sont à vous?' – 'Oui, ce sont les nôtres.' 'Are these photos yours?' – 'Yes, they're ours.'

　WORD TIP The article and pronoun change in French when they refer to fem and plural nouns.

nouer VERB
　to tie
　　nouer ses cheveux to tie one's hair back

les **nouilles** PLURAL FEM NOUN
　noodles

la **nourrice** FEM NOUN
　1 childminder
　2 babysitter

nourrir VERB [2]
　nourrir de quelque chose to feed on something
　　bien nourri well-fed
　　mal nourri undernourished

la **nourriture** FEM NOUN
　food
　　la nourriture et la boisson food and drink

ℱ **nous** PRONOUN
　1 (as the subject of the verb) we
　　Nous apprenons le français. We're learning French.
　　Nous allons au cinéma ce soir. We're going to the cinema tonight.
　　▸ SEE **on**
　2 (after prepositions like avec, contre and in comparisons) us
　　Viens avec nous. Come with us.
　　Ils sont plus âgés que nous. They're older than us.
　3 (as a direct object) us
　　Elle nous aide. She helps us.
　　Elle nous a aidés. She helped us.
　4 (as an indirect object) to us, us
　　Elle nous a parlé longtemps. She spoke to us for a long time.
　　Elle nous a donné son adresse. She gave us her address.
　　Elle nous achète des cadeaux. She buys us presents.
　5 à nous ours
　　Ce sont des amis à nous. They're friends of ours.
　　La voiture n'est pas à nous. The car is not ours.
　6 (with reflexive verbs) Nous nous levons à sept heures. We get up at seven o'clock.
　7 for ourselves, ourselves
　　Nous nous ferons quelque chose à manger. We'll make ourselves something to eat.
　8 chez nous at our house

nous-mêmes PRONOUN
　ourselves
　　Nous l'avons fait nous-mêmes. We did it ourselves.

ℱ **nouveau** MASC ADJECTIVE, **nouveaux** MASC PL, **nouvel** MASC SING, **nouvelle** FEM, **nouvelles** FEM
　1 new (new or different to the speaker)
　　mon nouveau sac my new bag
　　mon nouvel appartement my new flat
　2 à nouveau, de nouveau again
　　Elle l'a fait à nouveau. She did it again

　WORD TIP Masculine nouveau becomes nouvel before a vowel or silent h.

la **nouveauté** FEM NOUN
　1 novelty (something new)
　2 new release (single, album, etc)

le **Nouvel An** *MASC NOUN*
New Year
fêter le Nouvel An to celebrate New Year

♀ une **nouvelle** *FEM NOUN*
1 une nouvelle a piece of news
J'ai une bonne nouvelle! I've got good news!
2 **short story**
une nouvelle de Sagan a Sagan short story
3 les nouvelles the news *(on TV, radio)*
4 des nouvelles news
As-tu des nouvelles de lui? Have you any news of him?
Nous n'avons pas de nouvelles pour l'instant. We have no news for the moment.

la **Nouvelle-Calédonie** *FEM NOUN*
New Caledonia *(French island territory in the Pacific)*

la **Nouvelle-Zélande** *FEM NOUN*
New Zealand

WORD TIP Countries and regions in French take le, la or les.

♀ le **novembre** *MASC NOUN*
November
en novembre, au mois de novembre in November

WORD TIP Months of the year and days of the week start with small letters in French.

🔘 **NOVEMBRE**

Le 1er novembre, c'est la Toussaint, la fête des morts. Les Français ne travaillent pas. Beaucoup vont au cimetière en famille. Ils mettent des chrysanthèmes sur les tombes familiales.

le **noyau** *MASC NOUN*, **noyaux** *PL*
1 **stone** *(in fruit)*
2 **nucleus** *(in an atom)*

le **noyer** *MASC NOUN* ▶ SEE **noyer** *VERB*
walnut tree

♀ **noyer** *VERB* [39]
▶ SEE **noyer** *NOUN*
to drown

se **noyer** *REFLEXIVE VERB* 🔵
to drown
Il s'est noyé. He drowned.

nu *MASC ADJECTIVE*, **nue** *FEM*
1 **naked**
2 **bare** *(feet, walls)*

♀ le **nuage** *MASC NOUN*
cloud

nuageux *MASC ADJECTIVE*, **nuageuse** *FEM*
cloudy
un ciel nuageux a cloudy sky

nucléaire *MASC & FEM ADJECTIVE*
nuclear
l'énergie nucléaire nuclear power
une centrale nucléaire a nuclear power station

nuisible *MASC & FEM ADJECTIVE*
harmful

♀ la **nuit** *FEM NOUN*
1 **night**
cette nuit last night, tonight
dans la nuit in the night
toute la nuit all night
toutes les nuits every night
2 **dark**
Il fait nuit. It's getting dark.
La nuit tombe à sept heures. It gets dark at seven o'clock.

nul *MASC ADJECTIVE*, **nulle** *FEM*
1 *(informal)* **awful**
Le film était nul. The film was awful.
Je suis nul en histoire. I'm hopeless at history.
2 *(Sport)* un match nul a draw

nulle part *ADVERB*
nowhere
Je ne trouve nulle part mon portable. I can't find my mobile anywhere.

numérique *MASC & FEM ADJECTIVE*
digital

♀ le **numéro** *MASC NOUN*
number
Ils habitent au numéro cinq. They live at number five.

le **nu-pied** *MASC NOUN*
open sandal

nutritif *MASC ADJECTIVE*, **nutritive** *FEM*
nutritious
valeur nutritive nutritional value

♀ le **nylon** *MASC NOUN*
nylon

🔵 means the verb takes être to form the perfect

Oo

une **oasis** *INVARIABLE FEM NOUN*
oasis

obéir *VERB* [2]
Manon, tu dois obéir. Manon, you must do as you're told.
obéir à quelqu'un to obey somebody

obéissant *MASC ADJECTIVE*, **obéissante** *FEM ADJ*
obedient

obèse *MASC & FEM ADJECTIVE*
obese

l'**obésité** *FEM NOUN*
obesity

un **objectif** *MASC NOUN*
objective

une **objection** *FEM NOUN*
objection

un **objet** *MASC NOUN*
1 object
un objet volant non identifié an unidentified flying object
2 subject (of a debate, criticism, inquiry)
• les objets trouvés
lost property

♪ **obligatoire** *MASC & FEM ADJECTIVE*
compulsory

obligé *MASC ADJECTIVE*, **obligée** *FEM*
être obligé de faire quelque chose to have to do something
Léa est obligée de rester. Léa must stay.

obliger *VERB* [52]
obliger quelqu'un à faire quelque chose to force somebody to do something
La grève m'a obligé à rester chez moi. The strike forced me to stay at home.

obscur *MASC ADJECTIVE*, **obscure** *FEM*
dark
une pièce obscure a dark room

l'**obscurité** *FEM NOUN*
darkness
dans l'obscurité in the dark
Il a peur de l'obscurité. He's afraid of the dark.

obséder *VERB* [24]
to obsess
être obsédé par quelque chose to be obsessed by something
Elle est obsédée par son travail. She's obsessed by her work.

les **obsèques** *PLURAL FEM NOUN*
funeral

une **observation** *FEM NOUN*
comment
faire des observations sur quelque chose to make comments on something
Ils ont fait des observations sur mon exposé. They made comments on my talk.

observer *VERB* [1]
1 to watch
Elle nous observait de loin. She was watching us from a distance.
2 to observe (rules)
observer le règlement de l'école to observe the school rules

une **obsession** *FEM NOUN*
obsession

un **obstacle** *MASC NOUN*
obstacle

obstiné *MASC ADJECTIVE*, **obstinée** *FEM*
stubborn

obtenir *VERB* [77]
to get

occasionner *VERB* [1]
to cause (an accident)

l'**occident** *MASC NOUN*
l'Occident the West (Europe & America, etc)

occidental *MASC ADJECTIVE*, **occidentale** *FEM*,
occidentaux *MASC PL*, **occidentales** *FEM PL*
western

une **occupation** *FEM NOUN*
1 occupation
Mon occupation préférée c'est la causette. My favourite occupation is chatting on the Internet.
2 l'Occupation the Occupation (France 1940-1944)

♪ **occupé** *MASC ADJECTIVE*, **occupée** *FEM*
1 busy
Elle est occupée en ce moment. She's busy at the moment.
2 engaged (telephones, toilets)
Ça sonne occupé. It's engaged.
3 taken
Cette place est occupée. This seat is taken.
4 occupied (by an army)

occuper *VERB* [1]
1 to take up
L'armoire occupe trop de place. The wardrobe takes up too much room.
2 to occupy
Les grévistes occupent les locaux. The strikers are occupying the premises.
Il occupe la troisième place du classement. He's third in the ranking.
3 to keep busy
Ses maquettes d'avion l'occupent tout le

week-end. His model aeroplanes keep him
busy all weekend.

s'occuper REFLEXIVE VERB ⊙

1 s'occuper de quelque chose to deal with
something, to see to something
Je vais m'occuper du dîner. I'll go and see
to dinner.
Je m'en occupe. I'll see to it.

2 s'occuper de quelqu'un to look after
somebody
Ce soir, je m'occupe de ma petite sœur. The
evening I am looking after my little sister.
Est-ce qu'on s'occupe de vous? Are you
being served? (in shops)

un **océan** MASC NOUN
ocean

• l'océan Atlantique
the Atlantic Ocean

• l'océan Pacifique
the Pacific Ocean

un **octet** MASC NOUN
(Computers) byte

octobre MASC NOUN
October
en octobre, au mois d'octobre in October

WORD TIP Months of the year and days of the
week start with small letters in French.

un & une **oculiste** MASC & FEM NOUN
eye specialist

une **odeur** FEM NOUN

1 smell
une bonne odeur a nice smell
des odeurs de cuisine cooking smells

2 scent (of flowers, etc)

♀ un **œil** MASC NOUN, les **yeux** PLURAL
eye
Il a les yeux bleus. He has blue eyes.

♀ un **œuf** MASC NOUN
egg
un œuf à la coque a boiled egg
un œuf dur a hard-boiled egg
un œuf mollet a soft-boiled egg
un œuf au plat, un œuf sur le plat a fried
egg
des œufs brouillés scrambled eggs
une œuf de Pâques Easter egg

une **œuvre** FEM NOUN
work
les œuvres complètes de Flaubert the
complete works of Flaubert

• une œuvre d'art
a work of art

offenser VERB [1]
to offend

s'offenser REFLEXIVE VERB ⊙
to take offence

un **office** MASC NOUN

1 office

2 un office religieux a religious service

• l'office de tourisme
tourist information office

officiel MASC ADJECTIVE, **officielle** FEM
official

un **officier** MASC NOUN
officer

une **offre** FEM NOUN
offer
une offre d'emploi a job offer
'Offres d'emploi' 'Situations Vacant' (in the
small ads)

offrir VERB [56]

1 to offer
offrir quelque chose à quelqu'un to offer
somebody something
Il nous a offert à boire. He offered us a
drink.
Elle a offert de nous aider. She offered to
help us.

2 to give
Elle m'a offert une montre. She gave me a
watch.

3 to buy
Je t'offre un DVD. I'll buy you a DVD.

s'offrir REFLEXIVE VERB ⊙
s'offrir quelque chose to treat yourself to
something
Je vais m'offrir un nouveau jeu
électronique. I'm going to treat myself to a
new computer game.

une **oie** FEM NOUN
goose

♀ un **oignon** MASC NOUN

1 onion
une soupe à l'oignon an onion soup

2 bulb
un oignon de tulipe a tulip bulb

♀ un **oiseau** MASC NOUN, les **oiseaux** PLURAL
bird

• un oiseau de proie
bird of prey

une **olive** FEM NOUN
olive
l'huile d'olive olive oil

un **olivier** MASC NOUN
olive tree

olympique MASC & FEM ADJECTIVE
Olympic

⊙ means the verb takes être to form the perfect

ombragé *MASC ADJECTIVE*, **ombragée** *FEM*
  shaded *(from the sun)*

une **ombre** *FEM NOUN*
1 shade
  à l'ombre in the shade
2 shadow
• une ombre à paupières
  eyeshadow

une **ombrelle** *FEM NOUN*
  sun umbrella

une **omelette** *FEM NOUN*
  omelette
  une omelette aux champignons a
  mushroom omelette

omettre *VERB* [11]
  to omit, to leave out
  Il n'omet aucun détail. He leaves nothing
  out.
  omettre de faire quelque chose to fail to do
  something
  Elle a omis de saluer la directrice. She failed
  to greet the headmistress.

on *PRONOUN*
1 we *(more informal than nous)*
  On va au cinéma. We're going to the
  cinema.
2 you
  De la terrasse, on voit la mer. From the
  terrace you can see the sea.
3 *(when you don't say exactly who)* On
  t'appelle. Someone's calling you.
  On m'a dit que … I've been told that …
  On a volé leur voiture. Their car's been
  stolen.
  En France, on aime beaucoup le fromage.
  In France people love cheese.

ℐ un **oncle** *MASC NOUN*
  uncle
  Oncle Didier est prof de tennis. Uncle
  Didier is a tennis coach.

une **onde** *FEM NOUN*
  radio wave

une **ondée** *FEM NOUN*
  shower *(of rain)*

ondulé *MASC ADJECTIVE*, **ondulée** *FEM*
  wavy *(hair)*

un **ongle** *MASC NOUN*
  nail
  se faire les ongles to do your nails
  Je me suis coupé les ongles. I've cut my
  nails.
• un ongle de pied
  toenail

ont *VERB* ▸SEE **avoir**

l'**ONU** *NOUN FEM*
  (= Organisation des Nations unies) **UN**,
  United Nations

onze *NUMBER*
  eleven
  Mélanie a onze ans. Mélanie is eleven.
  le onze mai the eleventh of May

> **WORD TIP** Use the definite article le in front of
> onze, rather than l'.

onzième *MASC & FEM ADJECTIVE*
  eleventh
  au onzième étage on the eleventh floor
  la onzième fois the eleventh time

un **opéra** *MASC NOUN*
  opera

un **opérateur** *MASC NOUN*, une **opératrice** *FEM*
  operator

une **opération** *FEM NOUN*
1 operation
2 calculation *(in maths)*

opérer *VERB* [24]
  to operate on
  opérer quelqu'un to operate on somebody
  On l'a opéré d'un cancer à la gorge. He was
  operated on for throat cancer.
  se faire opérer to have an operation
  Il s'est fait opérer du foie. He's had a liver
  operation.

ℐ une **opinion** *FEM NOUN*
  opinion

opposé *MASC ADJECTIVE*, **opposée** *FEM*
1 opposite
  dans le sens opposé in the opposite
  direction
2 opposed
  être opposé à quelque chose to be opposed
  to something
  Nous sommes opposés à cette idée. We are
  opposed to this idea.

opposer *VERB* [1]
  Le match de samedi oppose les Anglais et
  les Français. The Saturday match brings the
  English and the French head to head.

s'**opposer** *REFLEXIVE VERB* ◎
  s'opposer à quelque chose to oppose
  something
  Ils s'opposent à tous les changements.
  They oppose all the changes.

une **opposition** *FEM NOUN*
  opposition

opter *VERB* [1]
  to opt

ℐ indicates key words

🔎 un **opticien** *MASC NOUN*, une **opticienne** *FEM*
optician
Elle est opticienne. She's an optician.

optimiste *MASC & FEM ADJECTIVE*
optimistic
de façon optimiste optimistically

une **option** *FEM NOUN*
option
Elle a pris l'option informatique pour son examen. She took computing as an optional subject for her exam.

l'**or** *MASC NOUN* ▶SEE **or** *CONJUNCTION*
gold
une montre en or a gold watch
des cheveux d'or golden hair
une occasion en or a golden opportunity

or *CONJUNCTION* ▶SEE **or** *NOUN*
and yet
Tu m'as dit que tu étais là or personne ne t'a vu. You told me you were there, and yet nobody saw you.

🔎 un **orage** *MASC NOUN*
storm, thunderstorm
Il fait de l'orage. It's stormy.

orageux *MASC ADJECTIVE*, **orageuse** *FEM*
stormy

oral *MASC ADJECTIVE*, **orale** *FEM*, **oraux** *MASC PL*, **orales** *FEM PL* ▶SEE **oral** *NOUN*
1 **oral**
une épreuve orale an oral exam
2 administrer par voie orale to be taken orally *(medicine)*

un **oral** *MASC NOUN*, les **oraux** *PLURAL* ▶SEE **oral** *ADJECTIVE*
oral (exam)
l'oral de français the French oral
• un oral de rattrapage
a resit oral *(taken when a written exam is failed)*

🔎 **orange** *INVARIABLE MASC & FEM ADJECTIVE* ▶SEE **orange** *NOUN*
orange
des cubes orange orange cubes

WORD TIP orange never changes.

une **orange** *FEM NOUN* ▶SEE **orange** *INVARIABLE MASC & FEM ADJECTIVE*
orange
• une orange givrée
orange sorbet
• une orange pressée
freshly squeezed orange juice

un **orchestre** *MASC NOUN*
1 **orchestra**
un orchestre de chambre a chamber orchestra

2 **band**
un orchestre de jazz a jazz band

🔎 **ordinaire** *MASC & FEM ADJECTIVE* ▶SEE **ordinaire** *NOUN*
1 **ordinary**
une journée ordinaire an ordinary day
un repas ordinaire an average meal
2 **usual**
sa gentillesse ordinaire her usual kindness

🔎 l'**ordinaire** *MASC NOUN* ▶SEE **ordinaire** *ADJECTIVE*
sortir de l'ordinaire to be out of the ordinary
Ce film sort de l'ordinaire. This film is out of the ordinary.

🔎 un **ordinateur** *MASC NOUN*
computer

une **ordonnance** *FEM NOUN*
prescription

ordonné *MASC ADJECTIVE*, **ordonnée** *FEM*
tidy

ordonner *VERB* [1]
to order
ordonner à quelqu'un de faire quelque chose to order somebody to do something
Le prof nous a ordonné de nous taire. The teacher ordered us to keep quiet.

un **ordre** *MASC NOUN*
1 **order, command**
2 **order**
par ordre alphabétique in alphabetical order
mettre de l'ordre to tidy up
Je dois mettre de l'ordre dans mon atelier. I must tidy up my workshop.

les **ordures** *PLURAL FEM NOUN*
rubbish
les ordures ménagères household rubbish
mettre quelque chose aux ordures to put something in the bin

🔎 une **oreille** *FEM NOUN*
ear

un **oreiller** *MASC NOUN*
pillow

les **oreillons** *PLURAL MASC NOUN*
mumps

un **organe** *MASC NOUN*
organ *(of the body)*

organique *MASC & FEM ADJECTIVE*
organic

un **organisateur** *MASC NOUN*, une **organisatrice** *FEM*
organizer

⊙ means the verb takes être to form the perfect

une **organisation** *FEM NOUN*
  organization

organiser *VERB* [1]
  to organize

s'**organiser** *REFLEXIVE VERB* ⊜
  to get organized

un & une **organiste** *MASC & FEM NOUN*
  organist

l'**orge** *FEM NOUN*
  barley

un **orgue** *MASC NOUN*
  organ
  Il joue de l'orgue. He plays the organ.

orgueilleux *MASC ADJECTIVE*, **orgueilleuse** *FEM*
  proud

l'**Orient** *MASC NOUN*
  l'Orient the East *(Asia, etc)*

oriental *MASC ADJECTIVE*, **orientale** *FEM*,
orientaux *MASC PL*, **orientales** *FEM PL*
1 eastern
  la côte orientale the eastern coast
2 oriental
  les langues orientales oriental languages

l'**orientation** *FEM NOUN*
1 le sens de l'orientation a good sense of
  direction
2 l'orientation professionnelle careers advice
  (for students)
3 orienteering *(the sport)*

s'**orienter** *REFLEXIVE VERB* ⊜ [1]
1 to get one's bearings
2 s'orienter vers quelque chose to turn
  towards something
  Mathis s'oriente vers les langues. Mathis is
  going in for languages.

originaire *MASC & FEM ADJECTIVE*
  native
  Elle est originaire d'Afrique. She's from
  Africa.
  Gabriel est originaire de La Baule. Gabriel
  comes from La Baule.

original *MASC ADJECTIVE*, **originale** *FEM*,
originaux *MASC PL*, **originales** *FEM PL*
  original
  Le film est en version originale. The film is
  in its foreign language version.

l'**origine** *FEM NOUN*
1 origin
  Elle est d'origine écossaise. She's Scottish.
2 à l'origine originally

un **orphelin** *MASC NOUN*, une **orpheline** *FEM*
  orphan

un **orphelinat** *MASC NOUN*
  orphanage

un **orteil** *MASC NOUN*
  toe
  le gros orteil the big toe

l'**orthographe** *FEM NOUN*
  spelling

un **os** *MASC NOUN*
  bone

oser *VERB* [1]
  to dare
  Je n'ose pas y aller. I daren't go there.

un **otage** *MASC NOUN*
  hostage
  être pris en otage to be taken hostage
  Les journalistes ont été pris en otage. The
  journalists were taken hostage.

ôter *VERB* [1]
  to take off
  Je vais ôter ma veste. I'll take off my jacket.
  Ôte tes pieds du canapé! Take your feet off
  the sofa!

une **otite** *FEM NOUN*
  earache

ℓ **ou** *CONJUNCTION*
1 or
  Veux-tu une glace ou un fruit? Would you
  like an ice cream or fruit?
  Tu viens ou pas? Are you coming or not?
2 ou … ou … either … or …
  Il est ou dans ma chambre ou dans le
  salon. It's either in my bedroom or in the
  sitting-room.
3 ou bien or else
  On peut se retrouver au cinéma ou bien
  chez moi. We can meet at the cinema or
  else at my place.

ℓ **où** *ADVERB, PRONOUN*
1 where
  Où es-tu? Where are you?
  Où vont-ils? Where are they going?
  Ton frère habite où? Where does your
  brother live?
  le quartier où elle habite the area where
  she lives
  la ville d'où il vient the town he comes from
  d'où ma surprise which is why I was
  surprised
  Par où tu passes pour aller au lycée? Which
  way do you go to school?
2 when, that
  le jour où je suis arrivé the day I arrived
  Il est à l'âge où il peut sortir avec ses
  copains. He's at the age when he can go out
  with his friends.

l'**ouate** FEM NOUN
cotton wool

ℓ **oublier** VERB [1]
1 to forget
Elle oublie souvent d'éteindre la lumière. She often forgets to turn off the light.
2 to leave
Il a oublié ses clefs chez Jérôme. He's left his keys at Jérôme's.

ℓ **ouest** INVARIABLE ADJECTIVE ▸ SEE **ouest** NOUN
1 west
la côte ouest the west coast
2 western
la frontière ouest the western border

WORD TIP ouest never changes.

ℓ l'**ouest** MASC NOUN ▸ SEE **ouest** INVARIABLE ADJECTIVE
west
un vent d'ouest a westerly wind
Versailles est à l'ouest de Paris. Versailles is west of Paris.
La Bretagne se situe dans l'ouest de la France. Brittany is in the west of France.
l'Ouest the West
J'habite dans l'Ouest. I live in the West.
l'Europe de l'Ouest Western Europe

ouf EXCLAMATION
phew!

ℓ **oui** ADVERB
yes
Il a dit oui. He said yes.
'Est-ce qu'elle vient?' – 'Je crois que oui.' 'Is she coming?' – 'I think so.'

un **ouragan** MASC NOUN
hurricane

un **ours** MASC NOUN
bear

OURS

Il y a des ours bruns dans les Pyrénées mais ils sont rares.

un **outil** MASC NOUN
tool

outré MASC ADJECTIVE, **outrée** FEM
outraged

outre-Manche ADVERB
on the other side of the Channel, in Britain

outre-mer ADVERB
overseas

ℓ **ouvert** MASC ADJECTIVE, **ouverte** FEM
1 open
Laisse la fenêtre ouverte. Leave the window open.

'Ouvert le dimanche' 'Open on Sundays'
2 on
Elle a laissé le robinet ouvert. She left the tap on.

ℓ une **ouverture** FEM NOUN
opening
les heures d'ouverture opening hours
l'ouverture d'un nouveau supermarché the opening of a new supermarket

un **ouvre-boîtes** INVARIABLE MASC NOUN
tin-opener

un **ouvre-bouteilles** INVARIABLE MASC NOUN
bottle-opener

un **ouvrier** MASC NOUN, une **ouvrière** FEM
worker

ℓ **ouvrir** VERB [30]
1 to open
Elle a ouvert la porte. She opened the door.
Ouvre vite la lettre! Open your letter quick!
2 to turn on
Jessica ouvre le robinet. Jessica is turning the tap on.
s'**ouvrir** REFLEXIVE VERB ◎
Ça s'ouvre comment? How do you open it?
Sa valise s'est ouverte dans l'aéroport. His case came open in the airport.

ovale ADJECTIVE
oval

une **overdose** FEM NOUN
overdose
une overdose d'héroïne an overdose of heroine

un **ovni** NOUN MASC
(= objet volant non identifié) UFO, unidentified flying object

l'**oxygène** MASC NOUN
oxygen

l'**ozone** FEM NOUN
ozone

Pp

le **Pacifique** MASC NOUN
le Pacifique the Pacific

ℓ la **page** FEM NOUN
page
à la première page on the first page
• la page d'accueil
home page
• la page Internet
web page

- la page Web
  web page

la **paie** *FEM NOUN*
  pay, wages

le **paiement** *MASC NOUN*
  payment

la **paille** *FEM NOUN*
  straw

ℱ le **pain** *MASC NOUN*
1 bread
   du pain frais newly baked bread
   une tranche de pain a slice of bread
2 un pain a loaf of bread
   un petit pain a roll
- le pain au chocolat
  pastry with chocolate chips
- le pain complet
  wholemeal bread
- le pain grillé
  toast
- le pain de mie
  sandwich loaf
- le pain de seigle
  rye bread

pair *MASC ADJECTIVE*, **paire** *FEM* ▶ SEE **pair** *NOUN*
  even *(number)*

le **pair** *MASC NOUN* ▶ SEE **pair** *ADJECTIVE*
  au pair au pair
  une jeune fille au pair an au pair girl

la **paire** *FEM NOUN*
  pair
  une paire de chaussures a pair of shoes

la **paix** *FEM NOUN*
  peace
  faire la paix avec quelqu'un to make peace
  with somebody
  Elle veut faire la paix avec son voisin. She
  wants to make peace with her neighbour.

la **Pakistan** *FEM NOUN*
  Pakistan

pakistanais *MASC ADJECTIVE*, **pakistanaise** *FEM*
  ▶ SEE **Pakistanais**
  Pakistani

un **Pakistanais** *MASC NOUN*, une **Pakistanaise**
  FEM NOUN ▶ SEE **pakistanais**
  Pakistani

le **palais** *MASC NOUN*
  palace
- le palais de justice
  law courts
- le palais des sports
  stadium

ℱ **pâle** *MASC & FEM ADJECTIVE*
  pale

le bleu pâle pale blue

la **Palestine** *FEM NOUN*
  Palestine

le **palier** *MASC NOUN*
  landing *(on a staircase)*

pâlir *VERB* [2]
1 to turn pale
2 to fade

la **palme** *FEM NOUN*
  flipper *(for swimming)*

le **palmier** *MASC NOUN*
  palm tree

palpitant *MASC ADJECTIVE*, **palpitante** *FEM*
  thrilling
  une aventure palpitante a thrilling
  adventure

le **pamplemousse** *MASC NOUN*
  grapefruit

le **panaché** *MASC NOUN*
  shandy

la **pancarte** *FEM NOUN*
1 notice, sign
2 placard

pané *MASC ADJECTIVE*, **panée** *FEM*
  coated in breadcrumbs
  une escalope panée an escalope coated in
  breadcrumbs

ℱ le **panier** *MASC NOUN*
1 basket
2 basket *(in basketball)*
   Éva a marqué un panier. Éva scored a
   basket.
- le panier à linge
  linen basket

la **panique** *FEM NOUN*
  panic
  Pas de panique! Don't panic!

paniquer *VERB* [1]
  to panic

ℱ la **panne** *FEM NOUN*
  breakdown *(of cars, machines)*
  être en panne d'essence to run out of petrol
  La voiture est en panne. The car's broken
  down.
  Je suis tombé en panne dans
  l'embouteillage. I broke down in the traffic
  jam.
- la panne de courant
  power cut

le **panneau** *MASC NOUN*, les **panneaux** *PLURAL*
  sign
- le panneau d'affichage
  notice board

- le **panneau publicitaire**
  billboard
- le **panneau solaire**
  solar panel

le **panorama** *MASC NOUN*
  view, panorama

le **pansement** *MASC NOUN*
1 **plaster** *(for a cut)*
2 **dressing** *(for a wound)*

♀ le **pantalon** *MASC NOUN*
  trousers
  un pantalon neuf a new pair of trousers
  Où est mon pantalon? Where are my
  trousers?
  deux pantalons two pairs of trousers
  un pantalon en velours côtelé a pair of
  cords

la **panthère** *FEM NOUN*
  panther

la **pantoufle** *FEM NOUN*
  slipper

le **paon** *MASC NOUN*
  peacock

♀ le **papa** *MASC NOUN*
  Dad, Daddy

la **papaye** *FEM NOUN*
  pawpaw

le **pape** *MASC NOUN*
  pope

la **papeterie** *FEM NOUN*
  stationer's shop

le **papi** *MASC NOUN*
  grandpa, granddad

♀ le **papier** *MASC NOUN*
1 **paper**
  une feuille de papier a sheet of paper
2 **les papiers** identity papers
  Vos papiers, s'il vous plaît! Your identity
  papers, please!
- le **papier à lettres**
  writing paper
- le **papier cadeau**
  wrapping paper
- le **papier hygiénique**
  toilet paper
- le **papier peint**
  wallpaper
- les **papiers d'identité**
  identity papers

le **papillon** *MASC NOUN*
  butterfly

le **papy** *MASC NOUN*
  grandpa, granddad

le **paquebot** *MASC NOUN*
  liner

Pâques *MASC NOUN*
  Easter
  à Pâques at Easter
  un œuf de Pâques an Easter egg
  le lundi de Pâques Easter Monday

♀ le **paquet** *MASC NOUN*
1 **packet**
  un paquet de sucre a packet of sugar
2 **parcel**
3 **bundle** *(of clothes, papers)*

le **paquet-cadeau** *MASC NOUN*, les **paquets-cadeaux** *PLURAL*
  gift-wrapped present

♀ **par** *PREPOSITION*
1 *(saying how)* **by**
  passer par Rennes to go by Rennes
  payer par chèque to pay by cheque
  envoyer quelque chose par la poste to send
  something by post
  Entre par le garage! Come in through the
  garage!
2 *(giving reasons for)* par ennui out of
  boredom
  par vengeance out of revenge
3 *(saying where)* par endroits in places
  Il a jeté quelque chose par la fenêtre. He
  threw something out of the window.
4 *(saying how many)* 50 euros par personne
  50 euros per person
  deux fois par semaine twice a week
  deux par deux two by two
5 *(in expressions)* par accident by accident
  par hasard by chance
6 par contre on the other hand

le **parachute** *MASC NOUN*
  parachute

le & la **parachutiste** *MASC & FEM NOUN*
  parachutist

le **paradis** *MASC NOUN*
  heaven

le **paragraphe** *MASC NOUN*
  paragraph

paraître *VERB* [57]
1 **to seem**
  Il paraît qu'il est parti. It seems that he's
  gone.
2 **to appear**
  paraître en public to appear in public
3 **to come out** *(to be published)*
  Le roman va paraître en juin. The novel is
  coming out in June.
4 paraît-il apparently
  Elle est à Nice, paraît-il. She's in Nice,
  apparently.

⊙ means the verb takes être to form the perfect

parallèle *MASC & FEM ADJECTIVE*
  parallel
  La rue Balzac est parallèle à la rue Renoir.
  Rue Balzac is parallel to rue Renoir.

paralysé *MASC ADJECTIVE*, **paralysée** *FEM*
  paralyzed
  Il est paralysé des jambes. He's paralyzed
  in both legs.

le **parapente** *MASC NOUN*
1 **paraglider**
2 **paragliding**
  faire du parapente to go paragliding

ℒ le **parapluie** *MASC NOUN*
  umbrella

le **parasol** *MASC NOUN*
  parasol

le **parc** *MASC NOUN*
1 **park**
  Je vais au parc. I'm going to the park.
2 **grounds** *(of a large house, a château)*
• le parc d'attractions
  amusement park

ℒ **parce que** *CONJUNCTION*
  because
  Elle ne vient pas parce qu'elle est malade.
  She isn't coming because she's ill.

par-ci *ADVERB*
  par-ci par-là here and there

le **parcmètre** *MASC NOUN*
  parking meter

parcourir *VERB* [29]
  to travel around
  J'ai parcouru l'Europe. I travelled around
  Europe.

le **parcours** *MASC NOUN*
1 **route** *(of a bus, a traveller)*
2 **course** *(of a race)*

par-dessous *ADVERB*
  underneath
  La barrière est trop haute, je passe par-
  dessous. The fence is too high, I'm going
  underneath.

ℒ le **pardessus** *MASC NOUN* ▸ SEE **par-dessus** *ADV,*
PREP
  overcoat

par-dessus *ADVERB, PREPOSITION* ▸ SEE **pardessus**
1 **on top**
  une couverture et un édredon par-dessus a
  blanket and an eiderdown on top
2 **over**
  Il a sauté par-dessus. He jumped over it.
  Elle a sauté par-dessus le ruisseau. She
  jumped over the stream.

ℒ le **pardon** *MASC NOUN*
1 **sorry** *(apologizing)*
  Pardon! Sorry!
2 **sorry**, **excuse me** *(asking for something)*
  Pardon monsieur, pouvez-vous me dire où
  se trouve le cinéma? Excuse me, could you
  tell me where the cinema is?

pardonner *VERB* [1]
1 *(interrupting politely)* Pardonnez-moi, mais
  … Excuse me, but …
2 **to forgive**
  Je ne lui pardonnerai jamais son erreur. I'll
  never forgive him for his mistake.

pare-balles *MASC & FEM ADJECTIVE*
  bullet-proof
  un gilet pare-balles a bullet-proof vest

le **pare-brise** *INVARIABLE MASC NOUN*
  windscreen

le **pare-chocs** *INVARIABLE MASC NOUN*
  bumper *(on a car)*

pareil *MASC ADJECTIVE*, **pareille** *FEM*
1 **the same**
  C'est toujours pareil. It's always the same.
  Nos chaussures sont presque pareilles. Our
  shoes are almost the same.
2 **such**
  Je n'ai jamais dit une chose pareille. I never
  said any such thing.

ℒ le **parent** *MASC NOUN*
1 **parent**
  mes parents my parents
2 **relation**
  mes parents et amis my friends and
  relations

la **parenthèse** *FEM NOUN*
  bracket
  entre parenthèses in brackets

la **paresse** *FEM NOUN*
  laziness

ℒ **paresseux** *MASC ADJECTIVE*, **paresseuse** *FEM*
  lazy

parfait *MASC ADJECTIVE*, **parfaite** *FEM*
  perfect

parfaitement *ADVERB*
  perfectly
  Tu le sais parfaitement! You know that
  perfectly well!

ℒ **parfois** *ADVERB*
  sometimes

ℒ le **parfum** *MASC NOUN*
1 **perfume**, **scent**
  Elle porte du parfum. She's wearing
  perfume.
2 **flavour**

Pour la glace, quel parfum veux-tu? What flavour ice cream would you like?

parfumé MASC ADJECTIVE, **parfumée** FEM
1 flavoured
parfumé au citron a lemon-flavoured
2 fragrant
3 scented

la **parfumerie** FEM NOUN
perfume shop

le **pari** MASC NOUN
bet
faire un pari to make a bet

parier VERB [1]
to bet
Je te parie 5 euros que les bleus gagneront. I bet you 5 euros the French team will win.
Je te parie qu'il ne viendra pas. I bet you he won't come.

parisien MASC ADJECTIVE, **parisienne** FEM ▶ SEE
Parisien
Parisian, Paris
la vie parisienne Parisian life
un restaurant parisien a Paris restaurant

le **Parisien** MASC NOUN, la **Parisienne** FEM ▶ SEE
parisien
Parisian

ℒ le **parking** MASC NOUN
car park

le **Parlement** MASC NOUN
Parliament
le Parlement européen the European Parliament

ℒ **parler** VERB [1]
1 to speak
parler (le) français to speak French
Jules parle avec Juliette. Jules is speaking to Juliette.
parler à quelqu'un to speak to somebody, to talk to somebody
Elle parle à mon prof de maths. She's talking to my maths teacher.
parler de quelque chose, quelqu'un to talk about something, somebody
Parle-moi de tes vacances! Tell me about your holidays!
Grégoire parle beaucoup de toi. Grégoire talks a lot about you.
Je dois te parler de ton frère. I must talk to you about your brother.
2 to speak, to talk
parler en italien to speak in Italian
Il parle très vite. He talks very fast.
3 parler de quelque chose to be about something (books, films, articles)

se **parler** REFLEXIVE VERB ◐
to talk to each other

Ils se parlent. They are talking to each other.
Ils ne se parlent plus. They aren't on speaking terms any more.

ℒ **parmi** PREPOSITION
among
parmi les élèves among the pupils
Je dois choisir parmi tous ces livres. I must choose from all those books.

la **parole** FEM NOUN
1 word
Il n'a pas dit une parole. He didn't say a word.
2 promise
Elle viendra, elle m'a donné sa parole. She'll come, she promised.
Elle a tenu sa parole, elle est venue. She kept her word, she's come.
3 les paroles the lyrics (of a song)
4 (the opportunity to speak) prendre la parole to speak
C'est à toi de prendre la parole. It's your turn to speak.

le **parquet** MASC NOUN
wooden floor

le **parrain** MASC NOUN
1 godfather
2 sponsor (of a project, a candidate, a child)

parrainer VERB [1]
to sponsor
Nous parrainons un enfant d'un orphelinat étranger. We sponsor a child in a foreign orphanage.

parsemer VERB [50]
to sprinkle

la **part** FEM NOUN
1 share
Il a payé sa part. He paid his share.
Elle a fait sa part du travail. She did her share of the work.
faire part de quelque chose à quelqu'un to tell somebody about something
Elle m'a fait part de ses projets. She told me about her plans.
2 portion (of pie, pizza)
3 side
de toutes parts from all sides
4 à part separate separately
une chambre à part a separate bedroom
j'ai mis l'argent à part I put the money aside
à part ça, qu'est-ce qu'il t'a dit? apart from that, what did he tell you?
5 de la part de quelqu'un for somebody, on somebody's behalf
Dis-lui bonjour de ma part! Say hello to him for me!
C'est de la part de qui? Who's calling?

◐ means the verb takes être to form the perfect

partager *VERB* [52]
1 **to share** *(belongings, food, ideas)*
Elle partage ses magazines avec Camille.
She shares her magazines with Camille.
2 **to divide**
Je partage mon temps entre l'école et le sport. I divide my time between school and football.

le & la **partenaire** *MASC & FEM NOUN*
partner

le **parterre** *MASC NOUN*
flower bed

le **parti** *MASC NOUN*
party *(in politics)*
le parti communiste the communist party

la **participation** *FEM NOUN*
participation

le **participe** *MASC NOUN*
(Grammar) **participle**
le participe passé the past participle
le participe présent the present participle

participer *VERB* [1]
1 **to participate, to take part**
Nous participons à la manifestation. We're taking part in the demonstration.
2 **participer à quelque chose to contribute to something**

particulier *MASC ADJECTIVE*, **particulière** *FEM*
1 **private**
une voiture particulière a private car
en particulier in private
2 **special**
un signe particulier a special feature
en particulier especially
Il aime tous les sports, en particulier le foot. He likes all sports, especially football.
3 **particular, specific**

particulièrement *ADVERB*
especially

la **partie** *FEM NOUN*
1 **part**
la première partie the first part
les parties du corps the parts of the body
2 **en partie partly**
C'est en partie de ta faute. It's partly your fault.
3 **faire partie de quelque chose to be part of something**
Anne-Laure fait partie de la famille. Anne-Laure's one of the family.
4 **game**
Tu as gagné la partie. You've won the game.

♭ **partir** *VERB* ○ [58]
1 **to leave, to go**

Manon part. Manon is leaving.
Elle est partie en Italie. She's gone to Italy.
Nous partons en vacances. We're going away on holiday.
2 **to start**
Le chemin part de l'église. The path starts at the church.
Je suis parti à huit heures. I started out at eight o'clock.
3 **to come out, to come off**
La tache ne part pas. The stain's not coming out.
L'étiquette est partie. The label's come off.
4 **à partir de from**
à partir de lundi from Monday onwards
à partir d'ici from here onwards

la **partition** *FEM NOUN*
score *(in music)*

♭ **partout** *ADVERB*
1 **everywhere**
J'ai cherché partout. I've looked everywhere.
Ça se trouve un peu partout. You can find it almost anywhere.
2 *(Sport)* trois buts partout three goals all

parvenir *VERB* ○ [81]
1 **parvenir à to reach**
Ma lettre lui est parvenue. My letter's reached him.
2 **parvenir à faire quelque chose to manage to do something**
Il est parvenu à ouvrir la porte. He managed to open the door.

♭ **pas** *ADVERB* ▶ SEE **pas** *NOUN*
1 *(with ne to make verbs negative)* **not**
Je ne suis pas grande. I am not tall.
Je n'ai pas de stylo. I don't have a pen.
Il n'y a pas de café. There isn't any coffee.
Ils n'ont pas le téléphone. They're not on the phone.
2 *(without ne)* **not**
C'est lui qui paie, pas moi. He's paying, not me.
Tu viens ou pas? Are you coming or not?
une radio pas chère a cheap radio
3 *(in expressions)* pas du tout not at all
pas mal not bad
Pas de chance! Bad luck!

le **pas** *MASC NOUN* ▶ SEE **pas** *ADVERB*
1 **step** *(in walking)*
2 **footprint**
3 **footstep**

passable *MASC & FEM ADJECTIVE*
1 **quite good**
'Comment était le film?' – 'Passable.' 'How was the film?' – 'Quite good.'
2 **fair** *(as a mark at school)*

le **passage** MASC NOUN
1 **traffic**
2 **crossing**
   le passage en ferry the ferry crossing
   'Passage interdit' 'No through traffic'
3 **way**
   Je peux te prendre au passage. I can pick
   you up on my way.
   Dégagez le passage! Clear the way!
4 **passage** (in a book)
• le passage à niveau
   level crossing
• le passage piéton
   pedestrian crossing
• le passage protégé
   pedestrian crossing
• le passage souterrain
   subway (under a road)

passager MASC ADJECTIVE, **passagère** FEM ▶ SEE
   passager NOUN
   temporary

le **passager** MASC NOUN, la **passagère** FEM ▶ SEE
   passager ADJECTIVE
   passenger

le **passant** MASC NOUN, la **passante** FEM
   passer-by

la **passe** FEM NOUN
   pass (in sport)

passé MASC ADJECTIVE, **passée** FEM ▶ SEE **passé**
   NOUN
   past
   l'an passé last year
   Il est dix heures passées. It's past ten
   o'clock.

le **passé** MASC NOUN ▶ SEE **passé** ADJECTIVE
1 **past**
2 (Grammar) **past tense**
   Mets cette phrase au passé. Put this
   sentence into the past tense.
• le passé composé
   present perfect
• le passé simple
   past historic

le **passe-partout** INVARIABLE MASC NOUN
   master key

ℙ le **passeport** MASC NOUN
   passport
   Je dois renouveler mon passeport. I must
   renew my passport.

ℙ **passer** VERB [1]
1 ◯ **to pass, to get through**
   On ne peut pas passer. We can't get past.
   laisser passer quelqu'un, quelque chose to
   let somebody, something through
   Laisse-le passer! Let him through!
2 ◯ **to go past**

   Elle regarde passer les trains. She's
   watching the trains go by.
3 ◯ **to drop in, to call by**
   Pierre est passé ce matin. Pierre dropped in
   this morning.
   passer prendre quelqu'un, quelque chose
   to pick somebody, something up
   Je passerai te prendre à huit heures. I'll pick
   you up at eight.
4 ◯ **passer à to go to**
   Le client passe à la caisse. The customer is
   going to the checkout.
5 ◯ **passer par to go through**
   Je passe par le parc. I go through the park.
   Par où tu passes? Which way do you go?
6 ◯ **to pass**
   Le temps passe vite. Time passes quickly.
7 ◯ (in school) **passer en to move up to**
   Ludovic passe en quatrième. Ludovic is
   moving up to year 9.
8 ◯ **to be on, to be showing**
   Qu'est-ce qu'on passe comme film au
   cinéma? What's on at the cinema?
9 **to spend** (time)
   J'ai passé deux jours à Paris. I spent two
   days in Paris.
   passer son temps à faire quelque chose to
   spend your time doing something
   Le weekend, il passe son temps à faire du
   cheval. At weekends, he spends his time
   horse-riding.
10 **to lend** (a book, a video, etc)
   Aurélie m'a passé son vélo. Aurélie lent me
   her bike.
11 **to pass on** (a cold, flu, information)
   Tu m'as passé ton rhume. You've given me
   your cold.
   passer quelque chose à quelqu'un to pass
   somebody something (sauce, glasses)
   Passe-moi le sel, s'il te plaît. Pass me the
   salt, please.
12 **to cross** (a bridge)
   Le camion a passé le pont. The lorry has
   crossed the bridge.
13 **to take** (a test, an exam)
   Demain, je passe le permis de conduire.
   Tomorrow I'm taking my driving test.
14 **to put (somebody) through** (on the
   telephone)
   Je vous passe le responsable. I'll put you
   through to the manager.
   Pouvez-vous me passer Djamila, s'il vous
   plaît? Could you put me through to Djamila
   please?
15 (in expressions) passer l'aspirateur to
   vacuum

◯ means the verb takes être to form the perfect

passer le chiffon to dust

WORD TIP Use passer with être in the perfect tense with verbs of movement, showing films, etc; in other words, when the verb has no object. Use passer with avoir in the perfect tense of verbs to do with spending (time), lending, giving or crossing (a bridge), etc, when the verb has an object.

se **passer** REFLEXIVE VERB ◯
1 **to happen**
Qu'est-ce qui se passe? What's happening?
Ça s'est passé à Londres. It happened in London.
2 **to take place**
Le film se passe au début du siècle. The film takes place at the beginning of the century.
3 **to go**
Mon entretien s'est bien passé. My interview went well.
Comment se sont passées tes vacances? How did your holidays go?
4 se passer de quelque chose to do without something
Il peut se passer de son vélo. He can do without his bike.

la **passerelle** FEM NOUN
footbridge

𝒫 le **passe-temps** INVARIABLE MASC NOUN
hobby, pastime
Qu'est-ce que tu as comme passe-temps? What hobbies do you have?
Quel est ton passe-temps préféré? What's your favourite pastime?
Comme passe-temps, je fais de la danse. My hobby is ballet.

WORD TIP passe-temps does not change.

passif MASC ADJECTIVE, **passive** FEM ▸ SEE passif NOUN
passive
le **passif** MASC NOUN ▸ SEE passif ADJECTIVE
(Grammar) **passive**
la **passion** FEM NOUN
passion
𝒫 **passionnant** MASC ADJECTIVE, **passionnante** FEM
exciting
une idée passionnante an exciting idea
passionné MASC ADJECTIVE, **passionnée** FEM
▸ SEE passionné NOUN
keen
C'est une musicienne passionnée. She's a keen musician.
Marion est passionnée de chevaux. Marion is very keen on horses.

le **passionné** MASC NOUN, la **passionnée** FEM
▸ SEE passionné ADJECTIVE
enthusiast
un passionné de théâtre a theatre enthusiast

la **passoire** FEM NOUN
1 **sieve** (for flour)
2 **colander** (for vegetables, pasta)
3 **strainer** (for tea leaves)

la **pastille** FEM NOUN
pastille
des pastilles pour la gorge throat sweets

la **patate** FEM NOUN
(informal) **potato, spud**
• la patate douce
sweet potato

la **pâte** FEM NOUN
1 **pastry**
la pâte feuilletée puff pastry
2 **batter**
la pâte à crêpes pancake batter
3 **dough**
la pâte à pain bread dough
4 les pâtes pasta
• le pâte à modeler
Plasticine®

le **pâté** MASC NOUN
1 **pâté**
un sandwich au pâté de foie a liver pâté sandwich
2 un pâté de maisons a block of houses

la **patience** FEM NOUN
patience
Il faut prendre patience, ça ne sera pas long. Be patient, it won't be long.

le **patient** MASC NOUN, la **patiente** FEM
patient

patienter VERB [1]
to wait
Patientez, s'il vous plaît! Please hold the line! (telephoning)

le **patin** MASC NOUN
skate

le **patinage** MASC NOUN
skating
• le patinage artistique
figure skating
• le patinage à glace
ice skating

le **patin à glace** MASC NOUN
1 **ice skate**
2 **ice skating**
faire du patin à glace to go ice skating

le **patin à roulettes** *MASC NOUN*
1 roller skate
2 roller skating
  faire du patin à roulettes to go roller
  skating

patiner *VERB* [1]
  to skate

le **patineur** *MASC NOUN*, la **patineuse** *FEM*
  skater

♪ la **patinoire** *FEM NOUN*
  ice rink

♪ la **pâtisserie** *FEM NOUN*
1 cake shop, pâtisserie
2 pastry-making, baking
3 cake

la **patrie** *FEM NOUN*
  homeland

le **patron** *MASC NOUN*, la **patronne** *FEM*
1 boss
2 owner
  Elle est la patronne du restaurant. She's the
  owner of the restaurant.

patronner *VERB* [1]
  to sponsor

la **patrouille** *FEM NOUN*
  patrol

la **patte** *FEM NOUN*
1 leg (of an animal)
2 paw

la **paume** *FEM NOUN*
  palm (of the hand)

paumer *VERB* [1]
  (informal) to lose

la **paupière** *FEM NOUN*
  eyelid

la **pause** *FEM NOUN*
  break
  la pause café the coffee break
  la pause déjeuner the lunch break
  Faisons une pause! Let's take a break!

♪ **pauvre** *MASC & FEM ADJECTIVE* ▸ SEE **pauvre** *NOUN*
  poor
  a poor family une famille pauvre
  un vocabulaire pauvre a poor vocabulary

♪ le & la **pauvre** *MASC & FEM NOUN* ▸ SEE **pauvre**
  ADJECTIVE
  poor man, poor woman
  les pauvres the poor

♪ la **pauvreté** *FEM NOUN*
  poverty

le **pavé** *MASC NOUN*
  cobblestone

le **pavillon** *MASC NOUN*
  detached house
  un pavillon de banlieue a house in the
  suburbs

payant *MASC ADJECTIVE*, **payante** *FEM*
  not free (of a show, an event)
  un parking payant a car park where you pay

la **paye** *FEM NOUN*
  wages, pay

♪ **payer** *VERB* [59]
1 to pay (a bill, a person)
  C'est moi qui paie. I'm paying.
  J'ai payé le gaz. I paid the gas bill.
  payer quelqu'un to pay somebody
  La femme de ménage est payée à l'heure.
  The cleaning lady is paid by the hour.
2 payer quelque chose to pay for something
  Il a payé le repas. He paid for the meal.
3 (informal) payer quelque chose à quelqu'un
  to buy somebody something
  Je te paie un verre. I'll buy you a drink.

♪ le **pays** *MASC NOUN*
1 country
2 region
  des fruits du pays locally produced fruit
• le pays d'accueil
  host country
• le pays en voie de développement
  developing country

le **paysage** *MASC NOUN*
  landscape

♪ le **paysan** *MASC NOUN*, la **paysanne** *FEM*
  farmer

les **Pays-Bas** *PLURAL MASC NOUN*
  the Netherlands

♪ le **Pays de Galles** *MASC NOUN*
  Wales

  WORD TIP Countries and regions in French take
  le, la or les.

le **PC** *MASC NOUN*
  PC, personal computer

♪ le **péage** *MASC NOUN*
1 toll
  une autoroute à péage toll motorway
2 tollbooth
  On arrive au péage. Here we are at the
  tollbooths.

♪ la **peau** *FEM NOUN*, les **peaux** *PLURAL*
1 skin
  Tu as une peau de pêche. You have very
  soft skin.
2 peel (of an orange, a lemon)

♪ la **pêche** *FEM NOUN*
1 peach

⬤ means the verb takes être to form the perfect

2 fishing
la pêche au saumon salmon fishing
la pêche à la ligne angling
On va à la pêche. We're going fishing.

le **péché** *MASC NOUN*
sin

pêcher *VERB* [1]
▶SEE **pêcher** *NOUN*
1 to fish for *(trout, salmon, other fish)*
2 to catch
Denise a pêché une truite. Denise caught
a trout.

le **pêcher** *MASC NOUN* ▶SEE **pêcher** *VERB*
peach tree

le **pêcheur** *MASC NOUN*
fisherman

pédagogique *MASC & FEM ADJECTIVE*
educational

la **pédale** *FEM NOUN*
pedal

pédaler *VERB* [1]
to pedal

le **pédalo**® *MASC NOUN*
pedalo, pedal boat

℘ le **peigne** *MASC NOUN*
comb

peigner *VERB* [1]
to comb *(somebody's hair)*

se **peigner** *REFLEXIVE VERB* ◉
to comb your hair

le **peignoir** *MASC NOUN*
bathrobe

peindre *VERB* [60]
to paint
Ils peignent les bancs en vert. They're
painting the benches green.

la **peine** *FEM NOUN*
1 trouble, effort
Elle a eu beaucoup de peine à trouver un
logement. She had a lot of trouble finding
somewhere to live.
Ce n'est pas la peine. It's not worth the
trouble.
se donner de la peine pour faire quelque
chose to go to the trouble of doing
something
Elle s'est donné de la peine pour organiser
cette sortie. She went to a lot of trouble to
organize this outing.
prendre la peine de faire quelque chose to
take the trouble to do something
Il n'a même pas pris la peine d'appeler. He
didn't even take the trouble to ring.
2 sorrow, grief

Il a de la peine. He's feeling sad.
3 à peine hardly, scarcely
Je le connais à peine. I hardly know him.
Il était à peine cinq heures. It was barely
five o'clock.
4 penalty
une peine de prison a prison sentence
• la peine de mort
death penalty

le **peintre** *MASC NOUN*
painter
• le peintre en bâtiment
painter and decorator

le **peintre-décorateur** *MASC NOUN*, les
peintres-décorateurs *PLURAL*
interior decorator

la **peinture** *FEM NOUN*
1 paint
de la peinture blanche white paint
'Peinture fraîche' 'Wet paint'
2 painting
faire de la peinture to paint
3 paintwork
4 une peinture a painting
une peinture de Bacon a painting by Bacon

le **pèlerin** *MASC NOUN*
pilgrim

le **pèlerinage** *MASC NOUN*
pilgrimage

la **pelle** *FEM NOUN*
1 shovel
2 spade *(toy)*
3 dustpan
le balai et la pelle dustpan and brush
• la pelle mécanique
mechanical digger

℘ la **pellicule** *FEM NOUN*
1 film *(for a camera)*
une pellicule couleur a colour film
2 les pellicules dandruff

la **pelouse** *FEM NOUN*
lawn
'Pelouse interdite' 'Keep off the grass'

la **peluche** *FEM NOUN*
soft toy
les jouets en peluche soft toys

pencher *VERB* [1]
to tilt
Le tableau penche du côté gauche The
picture's tilting to the left.

se **pencher** *REFLEXIVE VERB* ◉
to lean out
se pencher par la fenêtre to lean out of the
window
Penche-toi et ramasse mes clés! Bend down

℘ indicates key words

and pick up my keys!

𝒫 **pendant** PREPOSITION
1 **for**
pendant longtemps for a long time
J'ai attendu pendant deux heures. I waited
for two hours.
Pendant combien de temps as-tu habité
au Pays de Galles? How long have you lived
in Wales?
Il a plu pendant toutes les vacances. It
rained throughout the holiday.
2 **during**
pendant l'hiver during the winter
3 **pendant que while**
Ils s'amusent pendant que je travaille. They
play while I work.

le **pendentif** MASC NOUN
pendant

la **penderie** FEM NOUN
wardrobe

pendre VERB [3]
pendre quelque chose to hang something
up
Elle a pendu la clé au clou. She hung the
key on the nail.

la **pendule** FEM NOUN
clock

pénétrer VERB [24]
1 **pénétrer dans to enter, to get into**
Un voleur a pénétré dans le bureau. A thief
got into the office.
2 **to seep into** (water, wax)
3 **to get to the bottom of** (a mystery)

pénible MASC & FEM ADJECTIVE
1 **difficult**
une situation pénible a difficult situation
un travail pénible hard work
2 **tiresome** (person)
Il est pénible avec ses jeux vidéo. He's so
tiresome with his video games.

la **péniche** FEM NOUN
barge

le **pénis** MASC NOUN
penis

la **pensée** FEM NOUN
1 **thought**
2 **pansy** (flower)

𝒫 **penser** VERB [1]
1 **to think**
Je pense que tu as raison. I think you're
right.
Oui, je pense. Yes, I think so.
Je ne pense pas. I don't think so.
2 **penser faire quelque chose to intend to do**
something

Nous pensons partir le soir. We're
intending to leave this evening.
3 **penser à quelque chose to remember**
something
J'ai pensé à prendre mes affaires de gym. I
remembered to take my PE kit.
4 **penser à quelque chose to think about**
something
À quoi penses-tu? What are you thinking
about?
Je pense aux enfants d'Afrique. I'm thinking
about the children in Africa.
5 **faire penser quelqu'un à quelque chose,**
à quelqu'un to remind somebody of
something, somebody
Cette chanson me fait penser à ta mère.
This song reminds me of your mother.
faire penser quelqu'un à faire quelque
chose to remind somebody to do
something
Fais-moi penser à acheter du pain. Remind
me to buy some bread.

la **pension** FEM NOUN
1 (in hotels) la pension complète full board
la demi-pension half board
2 **boarding house**
3 **pension** (in retirement)
4 **boarding school**
• la pension de famille
family hotel

le & la **pensionnaire** MASC & FEM NOUN
boarder

le **pensionnat** MASC NOUN
boarding school

la **pente** FEM NOUN
slope
Le jardin est en pente. The garden is on a
slope.

la **Pentecôte** FEM NOUN
Whitsun

le **pépé** MASC NOUN
grandpa, granddad

le **pépin** MASC NOUN
1 **pip** (in fruit)
2 (informal) **little problem**
J'ai eu un pépin avec ma mobylette. I had a
little problem with my moped.

perçant MASC ADJECTIVE, **perçante** FEM
1 **penetrating**
un regard perçant a penetrating look
le froid perçant the biting cold
2 **shrill**
un cri perçant a shrill scream

percer VERB [61]
percer un trou dans le mur to make a hole
in the wall

Karine s'est fait percer les oreilles. Karine had her ears pierced.

la **perceuse** FEM NOUN
drill

le **perdant** MASC NOUN, la **perdante** FEM
loser

ᵱ **perdre** VERB [3]
1 to lose
L'équipe de Pierre a perdu. Pierre's team lost.
2 perdre quelque chose to lose something
Sophie a perdu son appareil-photo. Sophie lost her camera.
3 perdre du temps to waste time
Nous avons perdu beaucoup de temps dans la queue. We wasted a lot of time in the queue.
se **perdre** REFLEXIVE VERB ◌
to get lost
Arthur s'est perdu dans l'hypermarché. Arthur got lost in the hypermarket.

la **perdrix** INVARIABLE FEM NOUN
partridge

perdu MASC ADJECTIVE, **perdue** FEM
lost
un enfant perdu a lost child
Je suis perdu. I'm lost.
C'est du temps perdu. It's a waste of time.
un chien perdu a stray dog

ᵱ le **père** MASC NOUN
father
un père célibataire a single father
le père Noël Father Christmas, Santa Claus

perfectionner VERB [1]
to improve
Elodie est partie à Londres pour perfectionner son anglais. Elodie went to London to improve her English.

périmé MASC ADJECTIVE, **périmée** FEM
1 out-of-date
une carte périmée an out-of-date card
2 Ce paquet de biscuit est périmé. This packet of biscuits has passed its sell-by date.

la **période** FEM NOUN
period

le **périphérique** MASC NOUN
ring road

la **perle** FEM NOUN
1 pearl
2 bead

la **permanence** FEM NOUN
1 en permanence permanently, all the time
2 service
'Permanence de 8 h à 19 h' 'Open from 8

a.m. to 7 p.m.'
3 study period
J'ai permanence le lundi de 10 h à 11 h. I have a study period on Mondays from 10 to 11 a.m.

permanent MASC ADJECTIVE, **permanente** FEM
1 permanent (job, exhibition)
2 continuous
cinéma permanent de 13 h à 23 h continuous film performances from 1 to 11 p.m.

permettre VERB [11]
Permettez-moi de vous aider! Let me help you!
Il n'est pas permis d'utiliser son portable au lycée. You aren't allowed to use your mobile at school.
permettre à quelqu'un de faire quelque chose to let somebody to do something
Ses parents lui permettent de sortir en boîte. Her parents let her to go clubbing.
Il a permis à son frère de l'accompagner. He let his brother come with him.
se **permettre** REFLEXIVE VERB ◌
to afford
Il peut se permettre d'aller au cinéma toutes les semaines. He can afford to go to the cinema every week.

le **permis** MASC NOUN
permit
Il vous faut un permis. You need a permit.
• le permis de conduire driving licence
• le permis de pêche fishing permit
• le permis de séjour residence permit

la **permission** FEM NOUN
1 permission
J'ai la permission de venir après l'école. I have permission to come after school.
2 leave (from the army)

le **perroquet** MASC NOUN
parrot

la **perruche** FEM NOUN
budgie

la **persécution** FEM NOUN
persecution

persévérer VERB [24]
to persevere

le **persil** MASC NOUN
parsley

le **personnage** MASC NOUN
1 character (in a book, a film, etc)
les personnages principaux du film the

ᵱ indicates key words

main characters in the film

2 person
un personnage célèbre a famous person

la **personnalité** *FEM NOUN*
1 personality
une forte personnalité a strong personality
2 important person
Il y avait des personnalités dans l'avion.
There were important people in the plane.

♀ la **personne** *FEM NOUN* ▸ SEE **personne** *PRONOUN*
person
les grandes personnes the adults
les personnes âgées the elderly
en personne in person
Une seule personne est venue. Only one person came.

personne *PRONOUN* ▸ SEE **personne** *NOUN*
1 nobody
Personne ne veut jouer au foot. Nobody wants to play football.
2 anybody
Je n'ai vu personne. I didn't see anybody.
Je ne l'ai dit à personne. I didn't tell anybody

WORD TIP Remember to use ne before personne in a sentence that contains a verb: Je n'ai vu personne. ▸ SEE **ne**

personnel *MASC ADJECTIVE*, **personnelle** *FEM*
▸ SEE **personnel** *NOUN*
personal

le **personnel** *MASC NOUN* ▸ SEE **personnel**
ADJECTIVE
staff

personnellement *ADVERB*
personally

la **perspective** *FEM NOUN*
1 perspective
un dessin en perspective a perspective drawing
2 view
Du sommet, la perspective est magnifique. From the top the view is magnificent.
3 prospect
Elle a la perspective d'une bonne situation. She has the prospect of a good job.

persuader *VERB* [1]
1 to persuade
persuader quelqu'un de faire quelque chose to persuade somebody to do something
Je l'ai persuadé de revenir. I persuaded him to come back.
2 être persuadé que ... to be sure that ...
Il est persuadé qu'elle le déteste. He's sure that she hates him.

la **perte** *FEM NOUN*
1 loss
la perte de son portefeuille the loss of his wallet
2 waste
une perte de temps a waste of time

perturber *VERB* [1]
to disrupt

le **pèse-personne** *FEM NOUN*
bathroom scales

peser *VERB* [50]
to weigh
Je pèse 60 kilos. I weigh 60 kilos.

pessimiste *MASC & FEM ADJECTIVE*
pessimistic

le **pétale** *MASC NOUN*
petal

la **pétanque** *FEM NOUN*
bowls

le **pétard** *MASC NOUN*
firework

pétillant *MASC ADJECTIVE*, **pétillante** *FEM*
sparkling *(wine, mineral water)*

le **petit** *MASC NOUN*, la **petite** *FEM* ▸ SEE **petit** *ADJ*
1 little boy, little girl, child
2 les petits the children

♀ **petit** *ADJECTIVE MASC*, **petite** *FEM* ▸ SEE **petit** *NOUN*
1 little, small
un petit garçon a little boy
une petite fille a little girl
une petite maison a small house
une toute petite maison a tiny house
Thibault est petit pour son âge. Thibault is small for his age.
2 short
une petite promenade a short walk
3 petit à petit little by little
• le petit ami
  boyfriend
• la petite amie
  girlfriend
• la petite annonce
  small ad
• le petit cuiller
  teaspoon
• le petit déjeuner
  breakfast
• la petite-fille
  granddaughter
• le petit- fils
  grandson
• les petits-enfants
  grandchildren
• les petits pois
  garden pea

⊙ means the verb takes être to form the perfect

le **pétrole** MASC NOUN
oil
le pétrole brut crude oil

> **WORD TIP** pétrole does not mean petrol in English; for the meaning of **petrol** ▸ SEE **essence**.

le **pétrolier** MASC NOUN
oil tanker

⌁ **peu** ADVERB
1 **not much, not many**
Camille mange peu. Camille doesn't eat much.
Il gagne très peu. He earns very little.
2 **not very**
peu intéressant not very interesting
peu réaliste unrealistic
3 **peu de** not much, not many
Il reste peu de temps. There's not much time left.
Peu d'élèves le savent. Few pupils know that.
4 **un peu** a little, a bit
Mange un peu! Eat a little!
Parle un peu plus fort! Speak a little louder!
5 **un peu de** quelque chose a little of something
Il reste un peu de café. There's a little coffee left.
Tu vas un peu plus vite. You're going a bit faster.
6 **à peu près** about
à peu près mille personnes about a thousand people
7 **peu à peu** little by little

le **peuple** MASC NOUN
people

⌁ la **peur** FEM NOUN
fear
avoir peur de quelque chose to be afraid of something
Nadine a peur des souris. Nadine's afraid of mice.
faire peur à quelqu'un to frighten somebody
Tu m'as fait peur! You gave me a fright!

peut VERB ▸ SEE **pouvoir**

⌁ **peut-être** ADVERB
perhaps, maybe
Elle a peut-être oublié. Perhaps she's forgotten.
'Tu viens ce soir?' – 'Peut-être.' 'Are you coming tonight?' – 'Maybe.'

peuvent, peux VERB ▸ SEE **pouvoir**

le **phare** MASC NOUN
1 **lighthouse**
2 **headlight** (of a car)

⌁ la **pharmacie** FEM NOUN
1 **chemist's, pharmacy**
2 **medicine cabinet**
3 **pharmacy** (at university)

le **pharmacien** MASC NOUN, la **pharmacienne** FEM
chemist, pharmacist

le **phénomène** MASC NOUN
phenomenon, happening

la **philosophie** FEM NOUN
philosophy

le **phoque** MASC NOUN
seal

la **photo** FEM NOUN
1 **photo, photograph**
une photo d'identité a passport photo
prendre quelqu'un, quelque chose en photo to take a photograph of somebody, something
2 **photography**

la **photocopie** FEM NOUN
photocopy

photocopier VERB [1]
to photocopy

la **photocopieuse** FEM NOUN
photocopier

le & la **photographe** MASC & FEM NOUN
photographer

la **photographie** FEM NOUN
1 **photography** (as a hobby, a subject)
2 **photograph**
la photographie de la classe the class photograph

photographier VERB [1]
to photograph

le **photomaton**® MASC NOUN
photo booth

⌁ la **phrase** FEM NOUN
sentence

physique MASC & FEM ADJECTIVE ▸ SEE **physique** NOUN
physical

⌁ la **physique** FEM NOUN ▸ SEE **physique** ADJECTIVE
physics (as subject)
J'étudie la physique. I study physics.

le & la **pianiste** MASC & FEM NOUN
pianist

le **piano** MASC NOUN
piano
Je joue du piano. I play the piano.

la **Picardie** FEM NOUN
Picardy

⌁ indicates key words

en Picardie in Picardy

WORD TIP Countries and regions in French take le, la or les.

le **pichet** MASC NOUN
jug

♀ la **pièce** FEM NOUN
1 **room**
un appartement de quatre pièces a four-roomed flat *(excluding kitchen and bathroom)*
2 **coin**
une pièce de deux euros a two-euro coin
3 **play**
une pièce de Feydeau a Feydeau play
4 **bit**, **piece**
les pièces d'un puzzle the pieces of a jigsaw
5 **item**
dix euros (la) pièce ten euros each
• la pièce d'identité
identification *(e.g. a passport, identity card)*
• la pièce de rechange
spare part
• la pièce de remplacement
replacement part
• la pièce de théâtre
play
• la pièce jointe
attachment, enclosure

♀ le **pied** MASC NOUN
1 **foot**
J'y vais à pied. I'm going on foot.
2 **foot**, **bottom**
au pied du lit at the foot of the bed
3 le pied de la table the table leg
4 *(when swimming)* J'ai pied. I can touch the bottom.
Je n'ai pas pied. I'm out of my depth.

le **piège** MASC NOUN
trap
être pris au piège to be trapped

piéger VERB [15]
1 **to trap**
2 **to booby-trap**

la **pierre** FEM NOUN
stone
une maison de pierre a stone house

♀ le **piéton** MASC NOUN, la **piétonne** FEM
pedestrian

piétonnier MASC ADJECTIVE, **piétonnière** FEM
pedestrian
une rue piétonnière a pedestrianized street

la **pieuvre** FEM NOUN
octopus

le **pigeon** MASC NOUN
pigeon

la **pile** FEM NOUN ▶ SEE **pile** ADVERB
1 **battery**
2 **pile** *(of clothes, magazines)*
3 **tails** *(when tossing a coin)*
Pile ou face? Heads or tails?

pile ADVERB ▶ SEE **pile** NOUN
(informal) à dix heures pile at ten o'clock on the dot
On a commencé pile à l'heure. We started dead on time.

le **pilote** MASC NOUN
pilot
• le pilote de course
racing driver

piloter VERB [1]
to fly *(a plane)*

♀ la **pilule** FEM NOUN
pill
la pilule (contraceptive) the (contraceptive) pill
la pilule du lendemain the morning-after pill

le **piment** MASC NOUN
chilli

le **pin** MASC NOUN
pine tree

la **pince** FEM NOUN
1 une pince a pair of pliers
2 pincer *(of a crab)*
• la pince à épiler
tweezers
• la pince à linge
clothes peg

le **pinceau** MASC NOUN, les **pinceaux** PLURAL
paintbrush

la **pincée** FEM NOUN
pinch *(of salt, spice)*

pincer VERB [61]
to pinch *(a person)*

le **pingouin** MASC NOUN
penguin

le **ping-pong** MASC NOUN
ping-pong

la **pintade** FEM NOUN
guinea fowl

le **pion** MASC NOUN ▶ SEE **pion** MASC & FEM NOUN
1 **counter** *(in board games)*
2 **pawn** *(in chess)*
3 **piece** *(in draughts)*

⊙ means the verb takes être to form the perfect

pion *MASC NOUN*, la **pionne** *FEM NOUN* ▸ SEE **pion**
NOUN
(informal) supervisor (in schools)

la **pipe** *FEM NOUN*
pipe

piquant *MASC ADJECTIVE*, **piquante** *FEM*
spicy (food, sauce)

le **pique** *MASC NOUN*
spades (in cards)
le trois de pique the three of spades

le **pique-nique** *MASC NOUN*
picnic

pique-niquer *VERB* [1]
to have a picnic

piquer *VERB* [1]
1 to sting
J'ai été piqué par une guêpe. I've been
stung by a wasp.
2 to bite
Il a été piqué par des moustiques. He's
been bitten by mosquitoes.
3 (informal) to pinch
On m'a piqué mon stylo. Somebody's
pinched my pen.
se **piquer** *REFLEXIVE VERB* ◌
to prick yourself
Je me suis piqué le doigt. I've pricked my
finger.

la **piqûre** *FEM NOUN*
1 injection
faire une piqûre à quelqu'un to give
somebody an injection
2 bite (of a mosquito)
3 sting (of a wasp, nettles)
4 prick (of a thorn, a pin)

le **pirate** *MASC NOUN*
pirate
• le pirate de l'air
hijacker (of a plane)
• le pirate informatique
computer hacker

pire *MASC & FEM ADJECTIVE* ▸ SEE **pire** *NOUN*
1 worse
C'est bien pire. It's much worse.
pire que worse than
C'est pire que ça! It's worse than that!
2 worst
le pire mensonge the worst lie
le **pire** *MASC NOUN* ▸ SEE **pire** *ADJECTIVE*
le pire the worst
Nous craignons le pire. We fear the worst.

℘ la **piscine** *FEM NOUN*
swimming pool
la piscine couverte the indoor swimming
pool

la **pistache** *FEM NOUN*
pistachio

la **piste** *FEM NOUN*
1 trail (escapee's, animal's)
2 track (for racing, sport)
3 piste, trail (in skiing)
4 runway (for planes)
• la piste cyclable
cycle lane

le **pistolet** *MASC NOUN*
pistol

la **pitié** *FEM NOUN*
pity
J'ai eu pitié du mendiant. I felt sorry for the
beggar.

pittoresque *MASC & FEM ADJECTIVE*
picturesque

la **pizza** *FEM NOUN*
pizza

la **pizzeria** *FEM NOUN*
pizzeria

℘ le **placard** *MASC NOUN*
cupboard

> **WORD TIP** placard does not mean **placard**
> in English; for the meaning of **placard** ▸ SEE
> **pancarte.**

℘ la **place** *FEM NOUN*
1 place
remettre les livres à leur place to put the
books back in their place
2 à la place de quelqu'un instead of
somebody
Il y est allé à ma place. He went instead of
me.
3 square
la place du village the village square
la place Rouge Red Square
4 space, room
Il y a assez de place pour deux. There's
enough room for two.
5 seat (in a theatre, a cinema, a train, a bus)
6 space (to park)
une place de parking a parking space
7 place (in ranking, grading)
en troisième place in third place
8 job
Faustine a une bonne place dans cette
société. Faustine has a good job with this
firm.

placer *VERB* [61]
1 to place
2 to seat (a person)
On m'a placé à côté de Louis. I was put next
to Louis.

♟ le **plafond** MASC NOUN
ceiling

> **WORD TIP** plafond does not mean platform in
> English; for the meaning of platform ▸ SEE quai.

♟ la **plage** FEM NOUN
beach
une plage de sable a sandy beach
des vacances à la plage holidays by the sea
On va à la plage. We're going to the beach.

la **plaie** FEM NOUN
wound

plaindre VERB [31]
to feel sorry for
Je te plains. I'm sorry for you.

se **plaindre** REFLEXIVE VERB ◎
to complain
Je ne me plains pas. I'm not complaining.
se plaindre de quelque chose à quelqu'un
to complain about something to somebody
Elle s'est plainte de la cantine au
responsable. She complained to the
manager about the canteen.

la **plaine** FEM NOUN
plain

la **plainte** FEM NOUN
complaint
porter plainte contre quelqu'un to make a
complaint about somebody
Il a porté plainte contre le directeur. He's
made a complaint about the headmaster.

plaire VERB [62]
1 La couleur me plaît. I like the colour.
La chambre vous plaît? Do you like your
room?
Le film a beaucoup plu à Jean. Jean liked the
film a lot.
2 s'il te plaît please (informal)
s'il vous plaît please (formal)
Deux billets, s'il vous plaît. Two tickets,
please.

plaisanter VERB [1]
to joke
Je l'ai dit en plaisantant. I said it as a joke.

la **plaisanterie** FEM NOUN
joke

le **plaisir** MASC NOUN
pleasure
le plaisir de chanter the pleasure of singing
'Vous venez avec nous?' – 'Oui, avec
plaisir.' 'Are you coming with us?' – 'Yes, I'd
love to.'
faire plaisir à quelqu'un to please
somebody

♟ le **plan** MASC NOUN
1 map (of a town, an underground system)
le plan du Métro the map of the Metro
le plan de ville the street map
2 plan
un plan d'action an action plan
le plan du bâtiment the plan of the building
3 au premier plan in the foreground
• le plan d'eau
artificial lake (for water sports, etc)

♟ la **planche** FEM NOUN
plank
• la planche à repasser
ironing board
• la planche à roulettes
skateboard

♟ la **planche à voile** FEM NOUN
1 windsurfing board
2 windsurfing
faire de la planche à voile to go windsurfing

♟ le **plancher** MASC NOUN
floor

planer VERB [1]
to glide

la **planète** FEM NOUN
planet

♟ la **plante** FEM NOUN
plant

planter VERB [1]
1 to plant (a tree, a shrub, a plant)
2 to hammer in (a nail)
3 to pitch (a tent)

se **planter** REFLEXIVE VERB ◎
(informal) to get it wrong
Je me suis planté dans ma division. I got my
division wrong.

le **plaquage** MASC NOUN
1 tackle
2 tackling (in football)

la **plaque** FEM NOUN
1 patch (of damp, ice)
2 sheet (of metal, glass)
• la plaque d'immatriculation
car number plate

plaqué MASC ADJECTIVE, **plaquée** FEM
plaqué or gold-plated
plaqué argent silver-plated

la **plaquette** FEM NOUN
1 bar (of chocolate)
2 pack (of butter)

le **plastique** MASC NOUN
plastic
un sac en plastique a plastic bag

◎ means the verb takes être to form the perfect

ℓ **plat** *MASC ADJECTIVE*, **plate** *FEM* ▸SEE **plat** *NOUN*
1 flat
  un pays plat a flat country
  des chaussures plates flat shoes
2 l'eau plate still water

ℓ le **plat** *MASC NOUN* ▸SEE **plat** *ADJECTIVE*
1 dish *(large plate)*
2 dish *(food)*
  un plat froid a cold dish
  Le steak-frites est mon plat préféré. Steak and chips is my favourite dish.
3 course *(of a meal)*
  le plat principal the main course
• le plat cuisiné
  cooked dish
• le plat du jour
  dish of the day

le **plateau** *MASC NOUN*, les **plateaux** *PLURAL*
1 tray
2 plateau

la **plate-bande** *FEM NOUN*, les **plates-bandes** *PL*
  flower bed

le **plâtre** *MASC NOUN*
  plaster
  avoir une jambe dans le plâtre to have a leg in plaster.

ℓ **plein** *MASC ADJECTIVE*, **pleine** *FEM* ▸SEE **plein** *NOUN*
1 full
  Le sac est plein. The bag is full.
  Élia est pleine de vie. Élia's full of life.
  un T-shirt plein de taches a T-shirt covered with stains
  un emploi à plein temps a full-time job
2 en pleine nuit in the middle of the night
  en plein centre-ville right in the middle of town
  en plein air outdoors

le **plein** *MASC NOUN* ▸SEE **plein** *ADJECTIVE*
  faire le plein to fill up *(the fuel tank)*
  Le plein, s'il vous plaît. Fill her up, please.

ℓ **pleurer** *VERB* [1]
  to cry
  Il fait toujours pleurer sa petit sœur. He always makes his little sister cry.

pleut *VERB* ▸SEE **pleuvoir**

ℓ **pleuvoir** *VERB* [63]
  to rain
  Il pleut. It's raining.
  Il a plu cette nuit. It rained last night.

le **pli** *MASC NOUN*
1 fold
2 pleat
3 crease *(in trousers)*

plier *VERB* [1]
1 to fold
2 to bend *(your arm, your leg)*

le **plomb** *MASC NOUN*
1 lead
  de l'essence sans plomb unleaded petrol
2 fuse
  Les plombs ont sauté. The fuses have blown.

le **plombage** *MASC NOUN*
  filling *(in a tooth)*

le **plombier** *MASC NOUN*
  plumber

la **plongée** *FEM NOUN*
  diving
  faire de la plongée to go diving

le **plongeoir** *MASC NOUN*
  diving board

plonger *VERB* [52]
  to dive

le **plongeur** *MASC NOUN*, la **plongeuse** *FEM*
1 diver
2 washer-up

plu *VERB* ▸SEE **plaire**, **pleuvoir**

ℓ la **pluie** *FEM NOUN*
  rain
  un jour de pluie a rainy day
  des pluies violentes heavy showers

la **plume** *FEM NOUN*
1 feather
2 nib *(of a pen)*

la **plupart** *INVARIABLE FEM NOUN*
  la plupart de most
  la plupart des gens most people
  la plupart d'entre eux most of them
  la plupart du temps most of the time

le **pluriel** *MASC NOUN*
  plural
  au pluriel in the plural

ℓ **plus** *ADVERB*
1 plus de more
  Voulez-vous un peu plus de fromage? Would you like a little more cheese?
2 plus de more than
  Il y avait plus de cent personnes. '
3 There were more than a hundred people.
4 *(in comparisons)* plus que more than
  Sa chambre est plus grande que la mienne. Her bedroom is bigger than mine.
  Le film est plus intéressant que le livre. The film's more interesting than the book.

5 *(to form a superlative)* le plus rapide the fastest
le plus joli the prettiest
le plus mal the worst

6 plus ... plus ... the more ... the more ...
Plus je gagne, plus je dépense. The more I earn the more I spend.

7 en plus more
Il nous faut trois côtelettes en plus. We need three more chops.

8 de plus more
trois chaises de plus three more chairs
une fois de plus once more

9 de plus en plus more and more
Elle travaille de plus en plus. She works more and more.
Il fait de plus en plus chaud. It's getting hotter and hotter.

10 plus ou moins more or less
La classe est plus ou moins propre. The classroom's more or less clean.

11 le plus the most
C'est lui qui gagne le plus. He earns the most.

12 *(to form a negative)* ne ... plus not any more
Elle n'habite plus ici. She doesn't live here any more.
Il n'y a plus de lait. There's no milk left.

13 *(in sums)* plus, add
Deux plus trois égalent cinq. Two plus three is five.

♪ **plusieurs** INVARIABLE PLURAL ADJECTIVE
several
Plusieurs personnes sont intéressées. Several people are interested.
Il y en a plusieurs. There are several of them.

WORD TIP plusieurs does not change.

---

plutôt ADVERB

1 *(giving preferences)* rather, instead
Je préfère envoyer un SMS plutôt que téléphoner. I'd rather text than phone.
Viens plutôt demain! Come tomorrow instead!

2 *(somewhat)* rather, quite
Elle est plutôt maigre. She's rather thin.
Le repas était plutôt bon. The meal was quite good.
C'est plutôt bien. It's pretty good.

♪ **pluvieux** MASC ADJECTIVE, **pluvieuse** FEM
rainy

♪ le **pneu** MASC NOUN
tyre
le pneu avant the front tyre

♪ la **poche** FEM NOUN
pocket
l'argent de poche pocket money

un livre de poche a paperback
Tu es parti avec seulement 50 euros en poche? You went away with only 50 euros on you?

le **poêle** MASC NOUN ▸ SEE **poêle** NOUN
stove *(for heating)*

la **poêle** FEM NOUN ▸ SEE **poêle** NOUN
frying pan

le **poème** MASC NOUN
poem

la **poésie** FEM NOUN
poetry

le **poète** MASC NOUN
poet

♪ le **poids** MASC NOUN
weight
prendre du poids to put on weight
La prof a pris un peu de poids. The teacher has put on some weight.
perdre du poids to lose weight
Gilles a perdu du poids. Gilles lost weight.

• le poids lourd
lorry, truck

la **poignée** FEM NOUN

1 handful
une poignée de cailloux a handful of pebbles

2 handle
la poignée du sac the handle of the door

• la poignée de main
handshake

le **poignet** MASC NOUN
wrist

le **poil** MASC NOUN
hair
un poil a hair
Le chat perd ses poils. The cat's moulting.

poilu MASC ADJECTIVE, **poilue** FEM
hairy

♪ le **poing** MASC NOUN
fist
un coup de poing a punch
Elle a tapé du poing sur la table. She banged her fist on the table.

le **point** MASC NOUN ▸ SEE **pointe**

1 point *(in general)*
un point de rencontre a meeting point

2 être sur le point de faire quelque chose to be just about to do something
J'étais sur le point de t'appeler. I was on the point of phoning you.

3 dot
le point sur le 'i' the dot on the 'i'

4 full stop

5 point *(in scores)*

⊙ means the verb takes être to form the perfect

six points contre sept six points to seven

6 **mark** *(in a test)*

7 **stitch** *(in sewing, knitting)*

8 **à point** just in time
Tu es arrivé à point. You arrived just in time.

9 *(for food)* un steak cuit à point a medium rare steak
un brie à point a ready-to-eat brie

- le **point cardinal**
compass point

- le **point chaud**
trouble spot

- le **point de départ**
starting point

- le **point d'exclamation**
exclamation mark

- le **point d'interrogation**
question mark

- le **point noir**
blackhead

- le **point de vue**
point of view

- le **point-virgule**
semi-colon

la **pointe** *FEM NOUN* ▸ SEE **point**

1 **point**
la pointe d'un couteau the point of a knife
sur la pointe des pieds on tip-toe

2 **tip**
la pointe de l'aiguille the tip of the needle

3 *(showing extremes)* une vitesse de pointe de 250 km/h a top speed of 250 kph
les heures de pointe the rush hour, peak time
les technologies de pointe advanced technologies
un système audio à la pointe du progrès a state-of-the-art sound system

4 **touch** *(a small quantity)*
une pointe d'ail a touch of garlic

le **pointillé** *MASC NOUN*
dotted line

pointu *MASC ADJECTIVE*, **pointue** *FEM*
pointed

ℓla **pointure** *FEM NOUN*
size *(of shoes)*
Quelle pointure fais-tu?, Quelle est ta pointure? What size do you take?

ℓla **poire** *FEM NOUN*
pear

le **poireau** *MASC NOUN*, les **poireaux** *PLURAL*
leek

le **poirier** *MASC NOUN*
pear tree

le **pois** *MASC NOUN*

1 **pea**

2 **à pois** spotted
un tissu à pois a spotted fabric

- le **pois chiche**
chick pea

le **poison** *MASC NOUN*
poison

ℓle **poisson** *MASC NOUN*
fish
J'aime le poisson. I like fish.

le **poisson d'avril** *MASC NOUN*
April fool
Il m'a fait un poisson d'avril. He played an April fool trick on me.

la **poissonnerie** *FEM NOUN*
fishmonger's

le **poissonnier** *MASC NOUN*, la **poissonnière** *FEM*
fishmonger

le **poisson rouge** *MASC NOUN*
goldfish

les **Poissons** *PLURAL MASC NOUN*
Pisces *(sign of the Zodiac)*
Odile est Poissons. Odile is Pisces.

> **WORD TIP** Signs of the zodiac do not take an article: un or une.

ℓla **poitrine** *FEM NOUN*

1 **chest**

2 **bust**
Quel est votre tour de poitrine? What is your bust size?

ℓle **poivre** *MASC NOUN*
pepper

le **poivrier** *MASC NOUN*
pepper pot

le **poivron** *MASC NOUN*
pepper *(to eat as a vegetable)*

le **poker** *MASC NOUN*
poker

le **polar** *MASC NOUN*

1 **crime novel**

2 **detective film**

le **pôle** *MASC NOUN*
pole
le pôle Nord the North Pole
le pôle Sud the South Pole

ℓ**poli** *MASC ADJECTIVE*, **polie** *FEM*
polite
Tu dois être poli avec ta grand-mère. You must be polite to your grandmother.

la **police** *FEM NOUN*

1 **police**
Ma tante est dans la police. My aunt is in

the police.
Pour appeler la police, faire le 17. To call
the police, dial 17.
2 policy
une police d'assurance an insurance policy

policier *MASC ADJECTIVE,* **policière** *FEM* ▸ SEE
policier *NOUN*
un chien policier a police dog
une enquête policière a police investigation

le policier *MASC NOUN* ▸ SEE **policier** *ADJECTIVE*
police officer
une femme policier a woman police officer

la politesse *FEM NOUN*
politeness

le politicien *MASC NOUN,* **la politicienne** *FEM*
politician

politique *MASC & FEM ADJECTIVE* ▸ SEE **politique**
NOUN
1 political
2 un homme politique a politician

la politique *FEM NOUN* ▸ SEE **politique** *ADJECTIVE*
1 politics
2 policy
la politique étrangère foreign policy

pollué *MASC ADJECTIVE,* **polluée** *FEM*
polluted

🔎 **polluer** *VERB* [1]
to pollute

la pollution *FEM NOUN*
pollution

le polo *MASC NOUN*
polo shirt

la Pologne *FEM NOUN*
Poland

polonais *MASC ADJECTIVE,* **polonaise** *FEM* ▸ SEE
Polonais
Polish

un Polonais *MASC NOUN,* **une Polonaise** *FEM*
▸ SEE **polonais**
1 Pole
2 le polonais Polish (the language)

la pommade *FEM NOUN*
ointment

🔎 **la pomme** *FEM NOUN*
apple
• la pomme de pin
pine cone
• la pomme de terre
potato
• les pommes frites
chips

le pommier *MASC NOUN*
apple tree

la pompe *FEM NOUN*
pump
• la pompe à essence
petrol pump

🔎 **les pompes funèbres** *PLURAL FEM NOUN*
undertaker's

🔎 **le pompier** *MASC NOUN*
fire fighter

le & la pompiste *MASC & FEM NOUN*
petrol pump attendant

la ponctuation *FEM NOUN*
punctuation

ponctuel *MASC ADJECTIVE,* **ponctuelle** *FEM*
punctual

le poney *MASC NOUN*
pony

🔎 **le pont** *MASC NOUN*
1 bridge
2 deck (of a ship)
3 long weekend holiday (to extend a public
holiday)
faire le pont to have a long weekend
Comme le 14 juillet est tombé un mardi,
nous avons fait le pont. As July 14th fell on
a Tuesday, we had a long weekend.

populaire *MASC & FEM ADJECTIVE*
1 working-class (housing, area, etc)
2 popular (art, writing)
3 folk

la population *FEM NOUN*
population

🔎 **le porc** *MASC NOUN*
1 pig
2 pork
un rôti de porc a pork roast

la porcelaine *FEM NOUN*
china, porcelain

la porcherie *FEM NOUN*
pigsty

🔎 **le port** *MASC NOUN*
1 port
2 harbour
• le port de plaisance
marina

portable *MASC & FEM ADJECTIVE* ▸ SEE **portable**
NOUN
portable
un ordinateur portable a laptop computer

le portable *MASC NOUN* ▸ SEE **portable** *ADJECTIVE*
1 mobile (phone)
2 laptop (computer)

⚫ means the verb takes être to form the perfect

ᴾ le **portail** *MASC NOUN*
  gate

portatif *MASC ADJECTIVE*, **portative** *FEM*
  portable *(computer)*

ᴾ la **porte** *FEM NOUN*
  1 **door** *(of a house, etc)*
    la porte d'entrée the front door
  2 **gate** *(in an airport)*
    la porte numéro douze gate number twelve
  3 mettre quelqu'un à la porte to sack
    somebody

le **porte-bagages** *MASC NOUN*
  luggage rack

le **porte-clés** *MASC NOUN*
  key-ring

ᴾ le **portefeuille** *MASC NOUN*
  wallet

le **portemanteau** *MASC NOUN*, les
  portemanteaux *PLURAL*
  1 **coat rack**
  2 **coat hanger**

le **portemine** *MASC NOUN*
  propelling pencil

ᴾ le **porte-monnaie** *MASC NOUN*
  purse

le **porte-parole** *MASC NOUN*
  spokesperson

ᴾ **porter** *VERB* [1]
  1 **to carry**
    porter un sac to carry a bag
  2 **to take**
    porter quelque chose quelque part to take
    something somewhere
    Je porte un paquet à la poste. I'm taking a
    parcel to the post office.
  3 **to wear**
    Elle portait un jean délavé. She was
    wearing faded jeans.
  se **porter** *REFLEXIVE VERB* ○
    Je me porte bien. I'm well.
    Elle se porte mal. She's unwell

le **porteur** *MASC NOUN*, la **porteuse** *FEM*
  porter

la **portière** *FEM NOUN*
  door *(of a car)*

la **portion** *FEM NOUN*
  1 **portion**
  2 **helping** *(of food)*

portoricain *MASC ADJECTIVE*, **portoricaine** *FEM*
  ▸ SEE **Portoricain**
  Puerto Rican

un **Portoricain** *MASC NOUN*, une **Portoricaine**
  FEM ▸ SEE **portoricain**
  Puerto Rican *(person)*

Porto Rico *FEM NOUN*
  Puerto Rico

  WORD TIP Unlike the names of most other
  islands, Porto Rico does not take le or la.

le **portrait** *MASC NOUN*
  portrait

portugais *MASC ADJECTIVE*, **portugaise** *FEM* ▸ SEE
  Portugais
  Portuguese

un **Portugais** *MASC NOUN*, une **Portugaise** *FEM*
  ▸ SEE **portugais**
  1 **Portuguese** *(person)*
  2 le portugais Portuguese *(the language)*

le **Portugal** *MASC NOUN*
  Portugal

ᴾ **poser** *VERB* [1]
  1 **to put down**
    Il a posé sa tasse sur la table. He put his cup
    down on the table.
  2 **to plant** *(a bomb)*
  3 **to put up** *(posters)*
  4 poser un problème à quelqu'un to pose a
    problem for somebody
    Ça ne pose pas de problème. That's no
    problem.
  5 poser une question à quelqu'un to ask
    somebody a question
    J'ai une question à te poser. I have a
    question to ask you.

positif *MASC ADJECTIVE*, **positive** *FEM*
  positive

la **position** *FEM NOUN*
  position

posséder *VERB* [24]
  to own

la **possibilité** *FEM NOUN*
  1 **possibility**
  2 **opportunity**

ᴾ **possible** *MASC & FEM ADJECTIVE*
  1 **possible**
    aussi grand que possible as big as possible
    le moins possible as little as possible
    dès que possible as soon as possible
    Ce n'est pas possible! That's not possible!
  2 **potential**
    Ils sont de possibles candidats. They are
    potential candidates.

ᴾ la **poste** *FEM NOUN* ▸ SEE **poste** *NOUN*
  post office
  mettre quelque chose à la poste to post
  something

J'ai mis ta lettre à la poste. I posted your letter.

POSTE

Les boîtes aux lettres de la Poste sont rectangulaires et jaunes.

♀ le **poste** MASC NOUN ▸ SEE **poste** NOUN
1 **job, post**
un poste de secrétaire a job as a secretary
Le poste d'assistante est vacant. The post of assistant is vacant.
2 **set** *(TV, radio)*
3 **extension** *(on a telephone system)*
Mon numéro de poste est le 3641. My extension number is 3641.
Le poste 578, s'il vous plaît. Extension 578, please.
• le poste à essence
petrol station
• le poste de police
police station

le **poster** MASC NOUN
poster

le **pot** MASC NOUN
1 **jar**
un pot de confiture a jar of jam
2 **carton**
un pot de crème a carton of cream
3 **tin**
un pot de peinture a tin of paint
4 prendre un pot to have a drink
Tu viens prendre un pot avec nous? Are you coming for a drink with us?

WORD TIP pot does not mean pot (for cooking) in English; for the meaning of pot ▸ SEE **casserole**.

potable MASC & FEM ADJECTIVE
eau potable drinking water
non potable unsuitable for drinking

♀ le **potage** MASC NOUN
soup
potage aux légumes vegetable soup

le **potager** MASC NOUN
vegetable garden

le **pot-au-feu** MASC NOUN
boiled beef with vegetables

le **poteau** MASC NOUN, les **poteaux** PLURAL
1 **post** *(a stake)*
le poteau d'arrivée the finishing post
2 **goalpost**
• le poteau indicateur
signpost

la **poterie** FEM NOUN
1 **pottery**
Aesha fait de la poterie. Aesha does pottery.

2 **piece of pottery**
Ils vendent des poteries. They sell pottery.

le **pou** MASC NOUN, les **poux** PL
louse

♀ la **poubelle** FEM NOUN
bin, dustbin
mettre quelque chose à la poubelle to throw something in the bin
Je l'ai mis à la poubelle. I threw it in the bin.

le **pouce** MASC NOUN
1 **thumb**
2 **inch**

la **poudre** FEM NOUN
powder
du lait en poudre powdered milk

le **poulain** MASC NOUN
foal

♀ la **poule** FEM NOUN
hen

♀ le **poulet** MASC NOUN
chicken
du poulet rôti roast chicken
• le poulet d'élevage
battery chicken
• le poulet fermier
free-range chicken

le **pouls** MASC NOUN
pulse
prendre le pouls de quelqu'un to take somebody's pulse
Le médecin a pris mon pouls. The doctor took my pulse.

le **poumon** MASC NOUN
lung

♀ la **poupée** FEM NOUN
doll
• la poupée mannequin
Barbie® doll

♀ **pour** PREPOSITION
1 **for**
un cadeau pour Laure a present for Laure
un billet pour Calais a ticket for Calais
le train pour Londres the train for London
Ce sera prêt pour samedi? Will it be ready for Saturday?
être pour quelque chose to be in favour of something
Je suis pour l'équipe bleue. I support the blue team.
2 **to, in order to**
pour faire quelque chose in order to do something

3 Je suis là pour t'aider. I'm here to help you.
Pour aller à la poste, prenez le bus.
To get to the post office, take the bus.

4 pour ne pas faire quelque chose so as not to do something
Je me lève tôt pour ne pas rater mon bus.
I get up early so as not to miss my bus.

5 pour que ... so that ...
Je te le dis pour que tu comprennes.
I'm telling you so that you understand.

℘ le **pourboire** MASC NOUN
tip
J'ai donné un pourboire à la serveuse. I tipped the waitress.

le **pour cent** MASC NOUN
per cent
vingt pour cent twenty per cent

le **pourcentage** MASC NOUN
percentage

℘ **pourquoi** ADVERB
why
Pourquoi est-ce que tu ris? Why are you laughing?
Pourquoi ont-ils refusé? Why did they refuse?
Je veux savoir pourquoi. I want to know why.
Pourquoi pas? Why not?

pourri MASC ADJECTIVE, **pourrie** FEM
rotten
des légumes pourris rotten vegetables

pourrir VERB [2]
to go bad (food)

poursuivre VERB [75]
1 **to chase** (a person, an animal)
2 **to continue** (a task, efforts, studies)
poursuivre son chemin to continue on your way
J'aimerais poursuivre mes études en France. I would like to continue my studies in France.

pourtant ADVERB
1 **though**
Et pourtant c'est vrai. It's true though.
Il faut pourtant leur dire. We have to tell them though.

2 **yet**
Et pourtant ça aurait pu être bien. And yet it could have been good.

pourvu que CONJUNCTION
1 **providing (that), as long as**
pourvu que tu reviennes samedi providing that you come back on Saturday
2 **let's hope (that)**
Pourvu qu'il ne pleuve pas! Let's hope that it doesn't rain!

WORD TIP Pourvu que is followed by a verb in the subjunctive.

℘ **pousser** VERB [1]
1 **to push**
Elle a poussé la porte. She pushed the door.
'Poussez' 'Push'
2 pousser quelqu'un à faire quelque chose to encourage somebody to do something
Ils m'ont poussé à participer au concours. They encouraged me to enter the competition.
3 pousser un cri to cry out
J'ai entendu quelqu'un pousser des cris. I heard somebody cry out.
4 **to grow** (child, hair, plant)
Les fraises poussent bien. The strawberries are growing well.

se **pousser** REFLEXIVE VERB ⊘
to move over
Pousse-toi! Move over!

la **poussette** FEM NOUN
pushchair

la **poussière** FEM NOUN
dust
être couvert de poussière to be covered in dust
Le bâtiment tombe en poussière. The building is crumbling away.

la **poutre** FEM NOUN
beam (in a ceiling)

pouvez VERB ▸ SEE **pouvoir**

le **pouvoir** MASC NOUN ▸ SEE **pouvoir** VERB
1 **power**
après dix ans au pouvoir after ten years in power
des pouvoirs surnaturels supernatural powers
avoir le pouvoir de faire quelque chose to have the power to do something
Ils ont le pouvoir de tout changer. They have the power to change everything.
2 les pouvoirs publics the authorities

℘ indicates key words

ℓ **pouvoir** *VERB* [12]
> ▶ SEE **pouvoir** *NOUN*

can

Je peux le faire. I can do it.

Je ne peux pas l'ouvrir. I can't open it.

Est-ce que tu peux m'aider? Can you help me?

Vous pourriez m'indiquer la gare, s'il vous plaît? Could you tell me where the station is, please?

Ils ne pouvaient pas téléphoner avant. They couldn't phone before.

Je n'ai pas pu réserver. I wasn't able to book.

Elle aurait pu nous le dire. She could have told us.

Puis-je parler à Julien, s'il vous plaît? May I speak to Julien, please?

Tu peux toujours essayer. There's no harm in trying.

WORD TIP Use puis-je and vous pourriez to ask polite questions.

pouvons *VERB* ▶ SEE **pouvoir**

la **prairie** *FEM NOUN*
1 **meadow**
2 **la prairie the prairies** *(in the US)*

pratique *MASC & FEM ADJECTIVE* ▶ SEE **pratique** *NOUN*

practical, useful

C'est un petit sac pratique. It's a handy little bag.

des renseignements pratiques useful information

la **pratique** *FEM NOUN* ▶ SEE **pratique** *ADJECTIVE*
1 **practice**
2 **practical experience**
Il manque de pratique. He lacks practical experience.

pratiquement *ADVERB*
practically
C'est pratiquement fini. It's practically finished.

pratiquer *VERB* [1]
1 **to play, to do** *(a sport, a hobby)*
Elle pratique plusieurs sports. She plays several sports.
Je pratique le yoga. I do yoga.
2 **to practise** *(a language)*
J'aurai la possibilité de pratiquer mon français. I'll be able to practise my French.

le **pré** *MASC NOUN*
meadow

préalable *MASC & FEM ADJECTIVE*
prior *(permission, notice)*

la **précaution** *FEM NOUN*
precaution
par précaution as a precaution
prendre ses précautions to take precautions

précédent *MASC ADJECTIVE*, **précédente** *FEM*
previous

précieux *MASC ADJECTIVE*, **précieuse** *FEM*
precious, valuable
une pierre précieuse a precious stone
des renseignements précieux very valuable information

le **précipice** *MASC NOUN*
precipice

la **précipitation** *FEM NOUN*
1 **haste**
avec précipitation in a hurry
2 **les précipitations rainfall**
de fortes précipitations heavy rainfall

se **précipiter** *REFLEXIVE VERB* ☺ [1]
to rush
Ils se sont précipités vers la porte. They rushed for the door.
se précipiter pour faire quelque chose to rush to do something
Je me suis précipité pour les aider. I rushed to help them.

précis *MASC ADJECTIVE*, **précise** *FEM*
1 **precise** *(time, person, etc)*
à deux heures précises at two o'clock exactly
2 **accurate** *(watch, instrument)*

précisément *ADVERB*
precisely

préciser *VERB* [1]
1 **to specify** *(a place, a date, a figure)*
On n'a pas précisé la date. They haven't specified the date.
2 **to explain**
Pouvez-vous préciser comment? Could you explain exactly how?

la **précision** *FEM NOUN*
1 **precision**
faire quelque chose avec précision to do something accurately
2 **detail**
Voici quelques précisions sur le voyage. Here are some details about the journey.

la **préfecture** *FEM NOUN*
prefecture *(France is divided into 96 départements, which are roughly equivalent to British counties. The local prefecture is responsible for the day-to-day administration of each of these départements.)*

☺ means the verb takes être to form the perfect

- la **préfecture de police**
  (local) police headquarters

préférable *MASC & FEM ADJECTIVE*
  preferable

ℓ **préféré** *MASC ADJECTIVE*, **préférée** *FEM*
  favourite
  Ma matière préférée, c'est le français. My
  favourite subject is French.

ℓ la **préférence** *FEM NOUN*
1 preference
  Les pâtes ou les nouilles, je n'ai pas de
  préférence. Pasta or noodles, I don't have a
  preference.
2 **de préférence** preferably
  Je prends le train de préférence. I prefer to
  take the train.

ℓ **préférer** *VERB* [24]
  to prefer
  **préférer quelque chose à quelque chose
  d'autre** to prefer something to something
  else
  Elle préfère le poisson à la viande. She
  prefers fish to meat.
  C'est comme tu préfères. Whatever you
  prefer.
  préférer faire quelque chose to prefer to do
  something
  Je préfère aller à l'école à pied. I prefer to
  walk to school.
  Aller au cinéma? Non, je préfère rester ici.
  Go to the cinema? No, I'd rather stay here.
  Marie préfère danser plutôt que de nager.
  Marie prefers dancing to swimming.

le **préfet** *MASC NOUN*
  prefect (*an official in charge of the
  administration of a French département*)
  ▶ SEE **préfecture**
- le **préfet de police**
  chief of police

le **préjugé** *MASC NOUN*
  prejudice
  les préjugés raciaux racial prejudice
  être plein de préjugés to be very prejudiced

ℓ **premier** *MASC ADJECTIVE*, **première** *FEM*
  ▶ SEE **premier** *MASC NOUN* ▶ SEE **première** *FEM
  NOUN*
1 **first**
  le premier immeuble à droite the first
  apartment block on the right
  au premier étage on the first floor
  la première fois the first time
  le premier juin the first of June
2 **top** (*in ranking*)
  de première qualité top quality
  être premier en biologie to be top in
  biology

ℓ le **premier** *MASC NOUN*, la **première** *FEM*
  ▶ SEE **premier** *MASC ADJECTIVE* ▶ SEE **première**
  FEM NOUN
1 **first**
  Elle est toujours la première à parler. She's
  always the first to speak.
  Nous étions les premiers à partir. We were
  the first to leave.
  être le premier de la classe to be top of
  the class
2 **en premier** first
  C'est Pierre qui est arrivé en premier.
  Pierre arrived first.

la **première** *FEM NOUN* ▶ SEE **première** *ADJ, FEM
  NOUN*
1 **première** (*of a film, a play*)
  une première mondiale a world first
  (*inventions, achievements, etc*)
2 voyager en première to travel first-class
3 (*Education*) **Year 12** (*French equivalent*)
  J'entre en première cette année. I'm going
  into Year 12 this year.

premièrement *ADVERB*
  firstly

ℓ le **premier ministre** *MASC NOUN*
  prime minister

ℓ **prendre** *VERB* [64]
1 **to take**
  Je vais prendre un taxi. I'm going to take
  a taxi.
  J'ai pris ce DVD à la bibliothèque. I got this
  DVD out of the library.
  Je dois prendre de l'argent au distributeur.
  I need to get money from the cash
  dispenser.
2 **prendre quelque chose à quelqu'un** to take
  something from somebody
  Elle a pris de l'argent à ses parents. She
  took money from her parents.
  Qui m'a pris mon vélo? Who's taken my
  bike?
3 **to have** (*something to eat, drink*)
  Je prends une bière. I'll have a beer.
  Qu'est-ce que tu prends? What would you
  like?
4 **to bring**
  Je vais prendre mon parapluie. I'm going to
  bring my umbrella.
5 **passer prendre quelqu'un** to pick
  somebody up
  Je passerai te prendre à dix heures. I'll pick
  you up at ten.

ℓ le **prénom** *MASC NOUN*
  first name

les **préparatifs** *PLURAL MASC NOUN*
  preparations
  les préparatifs du voyage the preparations

ℓ indicates key words

for the journey

la **préparation** FEM NOUN
preparation

ℰ **préparer** VERB [1]
to prepare (a room, a meal, a lesson)
Je vais préparer les légumes. I'll go and
prepare the vegetables.
Guillaume prépare le dîner. Guillaume's
getting dinner ready.
Je prépare mes examens. I'm working for
my exams.
Est-ce que tu as préparé tes affaires pour le
matin? Have you got your things ready for
the morning?
• les plats préparés
ready-to-eat meals

se **préparer** REFLEXIVE VERB ◉
to get ready
Je vais me préparer pour partir. I'll get
ready to leave.
Prépare-toi! Get ready!
se préparer à quelque chose to prepare for
something
Je me prépare aux examens. I'm preparing
for the exams.

la **préposition** FEM NOUN
(Grammar) preposition

ℰ **près** ADVERB
1 **nearby**
La poste est tout près. The post office is
quite close.
2 **près de** near
près de la gare near the station
près d'ici near here
3 **près de** nearly, almost
près de mille euros nearly a thousand euros
4 **de près** closely
Elle regarde l'écran de près. She's looking
closely at the screen.
5 **à peu près** about
à peu près deux heures about two hours
Ça coûte à peu près dix euros. It costs
about ten euros.

la **présence** FEM NOUN
presence
en présence d'une grande foule in front of
a large crowd

présent MASC ADJECTIVE, **présente** FEM ▶ SEE
présent NOUN
present
Présent! Present! (at roll-call)
Toute la famille était présente. The whole
family was there.

ℰ le **présent** MASC NOUN ▶ SEE **présent** ADJECTIVE
1 (Grammar) **present** (tense)
au présent in the present

2 **à présent** now

le **présentateur** MASC NOUN, la **présentatrice**
FEM
1 **presenter** (of a programme)
2 **newsreader**

la **présentation** FEM NOUN
presentation (of work, ideas, food)
une présentation de mode a fashion show
faire les présentations to do the
introductions

présenter VERB [1]
1 **to introduce** (people)
Je vous présente mon père. This is my
father.
Alain, je te présente Raphaël. Alain, this is
Raphaël.
2 **to show** (a ticket, a pass, a document)
Il faut présenter votre passeport. You must
show your passport.
3 **to present** (a programme, a show)

se **présenter** REFLEXIVE VERB ◉
1 **to make yourself known**
En arrivant, présentez-vous à la réception.
When you arrive, make yourself known in
reception.
2 se présenter à quelqu'un to introduce
yourself to somebody
Il s'est présenté à la classe. He introduced
himself to the class.

le **préservatif** MASC NOUN
condom

la **préservation** FEM NOUN
1 **preservation** (of heritage)
2 **conservation** (of buildings, sites)

ℰ le **président** MASC NOUN ▶ SEE **présidente**
1 **president**
2 **chairman**
• le président de la République
president of France

la **présidente** FEM NOUN ▶ SEE **président**
1 **president**
2 **chairwoman**

les **présidentielles** PLURAL FEM NOUN
presidential elections

ℰ **presque** ADVERB
1 **nearly**
Ils sont presque toujours là. They're nearly
always there.
J'ai presque fini. I've nearly finished.
2 **presque pas de** hardly any
Il ne reste presque pas de lait. There's
hardly any milk left.
3 **presque rien** hardly anything
Il n'a presque rien fait. He's done next to
nothing.

◉ means the verb takes être to form the perfect

la **presse** FEM NOUN
la presse the press, the newspapers
Que dit la presse? What do the papers say?

ℓ **pressé** MASC ADJECTIVE, **pressée** FEM
1 être pressé to be in a hurry
Elle avait l'air pressée. She looked as if she
was in a hurry.
2 urgent
Ce n'est pas pressé. It's not urgent.

presser VERB [1]
1 to squeeze (an orange, a lemon)
2 to be urgent
Ça ne presse pas. It's not urgent.

se **presser** REFLEXIVE VERB ⊘
to hurry

le **pressing** MASC NOUN
dry cleaner's

la **pression** FEM NOUN
1 pressure
sous pression pressurized
faire pression sur quelqu'un to put pressure
on somebody
2 (informal) draught beer
un demi pression a half of draught beer

le **prestidigitateur** MASC NOUN, la
prestidigitatrice FEM
conjurer

ℓ **prêt** MASC ADJECTIVE, **prête** FEM ▸ SEE **prêt** NOUN
ready
Le dîner est prêt! Dinner's ready!
Tout était prêt pour la fête. Everything was
ready for the party.
Vous êtes prêts à partir? Are you ready to
leave?

le **prêt** MASC NOUN ▸ SEE **prêt** ADJECTIVE
loan

le **prêt-à-porter** MASC NOUN
ready-to-wear clothes

prétendre VERB [3]
to claim
Elle prétend que ce n'est pas de sa faute.
She claims it's not her fault.

> **WORD TIP** prétendre does not mean pretend
> in English: for the meaning of pretend ▸ SEE faire
> semblant at semblant.

prétentieux MASC ADJECTIVE, **prétentieuse** FEM
pretentious

prêter VERB [1]
1 to lend
prêter quelque chose à quelqu'un to lend
somebody something
Je te prêterai mon vélo. I'll lend you my
bike.
Elle ne veut pas me prêter de l'argent. She

doesn't want to lend me any money.
2 prêter attention à quelqu'un to pay
attention to somebody

le **prétexte** MASC NOUN
excuse

le **prêtre** MASC NOUN
priest

la **preuve** FEM NOUN
1 proof
fournir des preuves to provide proof
Il est jaloux, la preuve c'est qu'il refuse
de me parler. He won't speak to me. That
proves that he's jealous.
2 faire preuve de quelque chose to show
something
Ils ont fait preuve de beaucoup de courage.
They showed a lot of courage.

prévenir VERB [81]
1 to tell, to warn
Ils arrivent toujours sans nous prévenir.
They always turn up without warning us.
Elle ne m'a pas prévenu qu'elle partait. She
never told me she was leaving.
2 to call (the police, a doctor, etc)
Quelqu'un a dû prévenir la police.
Somebody must have called the police.

la **prévention** FEM NOUN
prevention
• la prévention routière
road safety

la **prévision** FEM NOUN
forecast, forecasting
faire des prévisions to make forecasts
• les prévisions météo
weather forecast

prévoir VERB [65]
1 to predict
Qui aurait pu prévoir ce désastre? Who
could have predicted that disaster?
2 to plan (a journey, an arrangement)
Ça s'est passé, comme prévu. It took place,
as planned.
3 Tout a été prévu. Everything's been taken
care of.
4 Le départ est prévu pour huit heures.
Departure is scheduled for eight o'clock.
5 to allow for (in your calculations)
Prévoyez 10 euros pour le taxi. Allow 10
euros for the taxi.

prier VERB [1]
1 to pray
2 prier quelqu'un de faire quelque chose to
ask somebody to do something
Les clients sont priés de ne pas fumer.
Customers are kindly requested not to
smoke.

3 Je vous en prie. You're welcome, Don't mention it.
'Merci beaucoup.' – 'Je vous en prie.'
'Thank you very much.' – 'You're welcome.'

la **prière** *FEM NOUN*
1 prayer
2 *(on signs)* 'Prière de fermer la porte' 'Please close the door'

ℰ **primaire** *MASC & FEM ADJECTIVE*
primary

la **prime** *FEM NOUN*
1 bonus
2 free gift

le **prince** *MASC NOUN*
prince
le prince Harry Prince Harry

la **princesse** *FEM NOUN*
princess
la princesse Stéphanie Princess Stephanie

ℰ **principal** *MASC ADJECTIVE*, **principale** *FEM*, **principaux** *MASC PL*, **principales** *FEM PL*
principal
un des principaux pays industrialisés one of the main industrialized countries

le **principe** *MASC NOUN*
1 principle
2 en principe as a rule
En principe je rentre à six heures. As a rule I get back at six.
3 en principe in theory
En principe tout le monde a été informé. In theory, everybody's been informed.

ℰ le **printemps** *MASC NOUN*
spring
au printemps in (the) spring

la **priorité** *FEM NOUN*
1 priority
Les enfants ont la priorité. Children take priority.
2 right of way
'Vous n'avez pas la priorité' 'You do not have right of way' *(road sign)*

pris *MASC ADJECTIVE*, **prise** *FEM* ▸ SEE **pris** *VERB*
1 busy
Je suis très prise ce matin. I'm very busy this morning.
2 taken
Toutes les places sont prises. All the seats are taken.
3 être pris de quelque chose to be overcome with something
La foule était prise de panique. The crowd was overcome with panic.

pris *VERB* ▸ SEE **pris** *ADJECTIVE* ▸ SEE **prendre**

la **prise** *FEM NOUN*
1 (wall) socket *(for electrical appliances)*
2 plug *(for electricity)*
3 capture *(in war, etc)*
• la prise de courant
power point
• la prise de sang
blood test
• la prise multiple
adaptor plug

la **prison** *FEM NOUN*
prison

le **prisonnier** *MASC NOUN*, la **prisonnière** *FEM*
prisoner

ℰ **privé** *MASC ADJECTIVE*, **privée** *FEM* ▸ SEE **privé** *NOUN*
1 private
'Propriété privée' 'Private property'
2 être privé de quelque chose to be without something
Nous sommes privés d'électricité. We're without any electricity.

ℰ le **privé** *MASC NOUN* ▸ SEE **privé** *ADJECTIVE*
1 private sector *(of the economy, etc)*
2 en privé in private

priver *VERB* [1]
1 priver quelqu'un de quelque chose to deprive somebody of something
Le conflit les prive d'aide. They conflict deprives them of aid.
2 être privé de sortie to be grounded
On m'a privé de sortie pendant une semaine. I've been grounded for a week.

se **priver** *REFLEXIVE VERB* ☉
se priver de quelque chose to do without something
Il va falloir se priver de vacances. We'll have to do without our holidays.

privilégier *VERB* [1]
1 to favour *(a person)*
2 to give priority to *(a task, a problem)*

ℰ le **prix** *MASC NOUN*
1 price
Quel est le prix des places? What price are the seats?
Le prix a augmenté. The price has gone up.
Vous me faites un prix? Can you give me a discount?
C'est hors de prix. It's extremely expensive.
2 à tout prix at all costs
3 prize
le prix pour la meilleure traduction the prize for the best translation

☉ means the verb takes être to form the perfect

probable *MASC & FEM ADJECTIVE*
  likely
  C'est peu probable. It's unlikely.

probablement *ADVERB*
  probably

♪ le **problème** *MASC NOUN*
  problem
  Sans problème! No problem!

le **procédé** *MASC NOUN*
  process

le **procès** *MASC NOUN*
1 trial
2 lawsuit
> **WORD TIP** procès does not mean process in English; for the meaning of **process** ▶ SEE **procédé**.

la **procession** *FEM NOUN*
  procession

♪ **prochain** *MASC ADJECTIVE*, **prochaine** *FEM*
  next
  la prochaine fois the next time
  le mois prochain next month
  jeudi prochain next Thursday
  À la prochaine! See you soon!

prochainement *ADVERB*
  soon

♪ **proche** *MASC & FEM ADJECTIVE*
1 near
  La ville la plus proche est Valence. The nearest town is Valence.
  Leur maison est proche de Nice. Their house is near Nice.
2 close
  C'est un de mes amis les plus proches. He's one of my closest friends.

le **Proche-Orient** *MASC NOUN*
  le Proche-Orient the Middle East

les **proches** *PLURAL MASC NOUN*
  close family and friends

se **procurer** *REFLEXIVE VERB* ⊚ [1]
  se procurer quelque chose to get something
  se procurer le dernier exemplaire to get hold of the last copy

le **producteur** *MASC NOUN*, la **productrice** *FEM*
  producer
  les pays producteurs de pétrole the oil-producing countries

la **production** *FEM NOUN*
  production

produire *VERB* [26]
  to produce

se **produire** *REFLEXIVE VERB* ⊚
  to happen

Je me demande ce qui va se produire. I wonder what's going to happen.
Ça s'est produit au mois de mai. It happened in May.

♪ le **produit** *MASC NOUN*
  product
- les produits biologiques organic produce
- les produits congelés frozen foods
- les produits de beauté beauty products
- les produits d'entretien household products
- les produits laitiers dairy products

le **prof** *MASC NOUN*
  (informal) teacher
  notre prof de français our French teacher

♪ le **professeur** *MASC NOUN*
1 teacher
  Elle est professeur de physique. She's a physics teacher.
2 university professor

la **profession** *FEM NOUN*
  profession, occupation

professionnel *MASC ADJECTIVE*, **professionnelle** *FEM*
  professional

le **profil** *MASC NOUN*
  profile

le **profit** *MASC NOUN*
1 profit
  les profits de la société the company's profits
  vendre quelque chose à profit to sell something at a profit
2 au profit de quelque chose in aid of something
  au profit des sans-abri in aid of the homeless
3 tirer profit de quelque chose to profit from something

profiter *VERB* [1]
  profiter de quelque chose to take advantage of something
  J'ai profité des soldes pour m'acheter un PC. I took advantage of the sales to buy myself a PC.
  Profite bien de tes vacances! Make the most of your holiday!

profond *MASC ADJECTIVE*, **profonde** *FEM*
1 deep
  un trou profond de 3 mètres a hole three metres deep
2 la France profonde provincial France

♪ indicates key words

la **profondeur** FEM NOUN
depth
La piscine a une profondeur de 3 mètres.
The swimming pool is 3 metres deep.
Ils ont étudié la question en profondeur.
They've studied the issue in depth.

le **programmateur** MASC NOUN
1 **timer**
2 **programme selector** (on an appliance)

℘ le **programme** MASC NOUN
1 **programme** (for a concert, a match)
Ce n'est pas au programme. It's not on the programme.
2 **program** (for a computer)
3 **syllabus**
le programme de maths the maths syllabus

programmer VERB [1]
1 **to schedule** (TV, radio programmes)
2 (Computers) **to program**

le **programmeur** MASC NOUN, la **programmeuse** FEM
(Computers) **programmer**

le **progrès** MASC NOUN
progress
les progrès de l'informatique the advances in computer science
faire des progrès to make progress
J'ai fait des progrès en maths. I've made progress in maths.

progresser VERB [1]
1 **to progress**
2 **to make progress**

le **projecteur** MASC NOUN
1 **floodlight**
2 **spotlight**
3 **projector**

le **projet** MASC NOUN
1 **plan**
mes projets pour l'été my plans for the summer
Quels sont tes projets pour l'avenir? What plans do you have for the future?
Il a encore deux films en projet. He's planning two more films.
2 **project**
participer à un projet to take part in a project
un projet pour construire un barrage a project to build a dam
• le projet de loi
government bill (not yet law)

projeter VERB [48]
1 **to throw**
Le choc l'a projeté de sa voiture. The impact hurled him out of his car.
2 **to show** (a film, slides)

3 **to cast** (a shadow)
4 **projeter de faire quelque chose to plan to do something**
Je projette de faire le tour du monde. I'm planning to go round the world.

la **prolongation** FEM NOUN
1 **continuation** (of a conflict)
2 **extension** (of a show, a performance)
3 (Sport) **extra time**
jouer les prolongations to go into extra time

prolongé MASC ADJECTIVE, **prolongée** FEM
lengthy

prolonger VERB [52]
1 **to prolong** (a trip, a holiday)
Elle a prolongé ses vacances. She's prolonged her holidays.
2 **to continue** (a course of treatment)
se **prolonger** REFLEXIVE VERB ⊙
to go on (situation, meeting, show)
Le spectacle s'est prolongé jusqu'à 23 h. The show went on till 11 p.m.

℘ la **promenade** FEM NOUN
1 **walk**
une promenade en voiture a drive
une promenade à vélo a bike ride
une promenade en bateau a boat trip
faire une promenade to go for a walk
2 **promenade** (on the seafront)

℘ **promener** VERB [50]
to take for a walk (a child, a dog)
Je dois promener le chien. I must take the dog for a walk.
se **promener** REFLEXIVE VERB ⊙
to go for a walk
Ils sont sortis se promener. They've gone out for a walk.
se promener en voiture to go for a drive
se promener à vélo to go for a bike ride

la **promesse** FEM NOUN
promise
tenir sa promesse to keep your promise
Il m'a fait une promesse. He made me a promise.

promettre VERB [11]
to promise
promettre de faire quelque chose to promise to do something
Il a promis de téléphoner ce soir. He promised to ring this evening.
promettre à quelqu'un de faire quelque chose to promise somebody you'll do something
J'ai promis à ma mère de lui écrire souvent. I promised my mother I would write to her often.

⊙ means the verb takes être to form the perfect

ℓ la **promotion** FEM NOUN
1 **special offer**
   être en promotion to be on special offer
   Les fraises sont en promotion. Strawberries
   are on special offer.
2 **promotion** (at work)
   avoir une promotion to be promoted

le **pronom** MASC NOUN
   (Grammar) **pronoun**

ℓ **prononcer** VERB [61]
1 **to pronounce** (a word, a name)
   facile à prononcer easy to pronounce
2 **to make** (a speech)
se **prononcer** REFLEXIVE VERB ◐
   to be pronounced
   Ça se prononce comment? How do you
   pronounce it?
   Le 't' de 'mont' ne se prononce pas. You
   don't pronounce the 't' in 'mont'.

la **prononciation** FEM NOUN
   pronunciation

la **propagande** FEM NOUN
   propaganda

la **proportion** FEM NOUN
   proportion

le **propos** MASC NOUN
1 **intention**
2 **à propos** by the way
   À propos, est-ce que tu l'as appelé? By the
   way, did you ring him?
3 **à propos de** about
   Il n'a rien dit à propos de son père. He
   didn't say anything about his father.

proposer VERB [1]
1 **proposer quelque chose à quelqu'un** to
   suggest something to somebody
   Je leur ai proposé une petite promenade. I
   suggested we went for a little walk.
2 **proposer quelque chose à quelqu'un** to
   offer somebody something
   On lui a proposé un poste de technicien.
   She has been offered a job as a technician.

la **proposition** FEM NOUN
   offer

ℓ **propre** MASC & FEM ADJECTIVE
1 **clean** (after the noun)
   une chemise propre a clean shirt
   des vêtements propres clean clothes
2 **own** (before the noun)
   ma propre voiture my own car
   ses propres paroles her own words
   leurs propres enfants their own children

WORD TIP propre does not mean **proper** in
English; for the meaning of **proper** ▸SEE **correct**.

proprement ADVERB
1 **properly**
   Mange proprement! Eat properly!
2 **à proprement parler** strictly speaking

la **propreté** FEM NOUN
   cleanliness

le & la **propriétaire** MASC & FEM NOUN
1 **owner** (of a building, a business)
2 **landlord**, **landlady** (of a rented house)

la **propriété** FEM NOUN
   property
   'Propriété privée' 'Private property'

le **prospectus** MASC NOUN
   leaflet

prospère MASC & FEM ADJECTIVE
   prosperous

le **prostitué** MASC NOUN, la **prostituée** FEM
1 **male prostitute**
2 **prostitute**

protecteur MASC ADJECTIVE, **protectrice** FEM
   protective
   une crème protectrice protective cream

la **protection** FEM NOUN
   protection
   des lunettes de protection protective
   goggles

protéger VERB [15]
   to protect
   pour protéger l'environnement to protect
   the environment
   Ils se sentent protégés. They feel protected.
se **protéger** REFLEXIVE VERB ◐
   se protéger de quelque chose to protect
   yourself from something
   Je me protège du soleil. I'm protecting
   myself from the sun.

le **protestant** MASC NOUN, la **protestante** FEM
   (Religion) **Protestant**

la **protestation** FEM NOUN
   protest
   un mouvement de protestation a protest
   movement

protester VERB [1]
   to protest
   protester contre quelque chose to protest
   against something
   Ils protestent contre le racisme. They're
   protesting against racism.

prouver VERB [1]
   to prove
   Ça ne prouve rien. That doesn't prove
   anything.

265

la **provenance** *FEM NOUN*
origin
du fromage en provenance de France
cheese from France
le train en provenance de Lyon the train
arriving from Lyon

provençal *MASC ADJECTIVE,* **provençale** *FEM,*
provençaux *MASC PL,* **provençales** *FEM PL*
from Provence, Provençal

> **WORD TIP** Adjectives never have capitals in
> French, even for nationality or regional origin.

provenir *VERB* [81]
provenir de to come from
Ce fromage provient de Normandie. This
cheese is from Normandy.

le **proverbe** *MASC NOUN*
proverb

la **province** *FEM NOUN*
province
une ville de province a provincial town
Ils habitent en province. They live in the
provinces.

le & la **proviseur** *MASC & FEM NOUN*
head *(of a secondary school)*

la **provision** *FEM NOUN*
1 **supply**
faire provision de quelque chose to stock
up on something
Nous avons fait provision de charbon.
We've stocked up on coal.
2 **des provisions** food
Maman est partie prendre des provisions.
Mum's gone off shopping for food.

provisoire *MASC & FEM ADJECTIVE*
temporary

provoquer *VERB* [1]
1 **to cause**
provoquer un accident to cause an accident
provoquer une discussion to spark off a
discussion
2 **provoquer quelqu'un** to provoke somebody
Il aime bien provoquer. He likes to be
provoking.

la **proximité** *FEM NOUN*
nearness
avec des magasins à proximité with shops
close by
à proximité de quelque chose near
something
un hôtel à proximité de l'autoroute a hotel
near the motorway

prudemment *ADVERB*
carefully

la **prudence** *FEM NOUN*
caution
Conduisez avec prudence! Drive carefully!

prudent *MASC ADJECTIVE,* **prudente** *FEM*
1 **careful**
Soyez prudents par mauvais temps! Be
careful in bad weather!
2 **sensible**
Il est plus prudent de réserver. It's more
sensible to book.
Ce n'est pas prudent d'y aller seul. It's not
sensible to go there alone.

♫ la **prune** *FEM NOUN*
plum

> **WORD TIP** prune does not mean prune in
> English; for the meaning of prune ▸ SEE pruneau.

le **pruneau** *MASC NOUN,* les **pruneaux** *PLURAL*
prune

le **prunier** *MASC NOUN*
plum tree

le & la **psychanalyste** *MASC & FEM NOUN*
psychoanalyst

le & la **psychiatre** *MASC & FEM NOUN*
psychiatrist

la **psychologie** *FEM NOUN*
psychology

le & la **psychologue** *MASC & FEM NOUN*
psychologist

pu *VERB* ▸ SEE **pouvoir**

la **pub** *FEM NOUN*
1 *(informal)* **advertising**
2 **ad, advertisement**

> **WORD TIP** pub does not mean pub in English; for
> the meaning of pub ▸ SEE bar.

♫ **public** *MASC ADJECTIVE,* **publique** *FEM* ▸ SEE
public *NOUN*
public
dans un lieu public in a public place
une école publique a state school

♫ le **public** *MASC NOUN* ▸ SEE **public** *ADJECTIVE*
1 **public**
en public in public
des produits grand public consumer
products
ouvert au public open to the public
'Interdit au public' 'No entry'
2 **audience, spectators**
3 **fans** *(of a singer, etc)*

publicitaire *MASC & FEM ADJECTIVE*
une annonce publicitaire a commercial
(on TV)
une campagne publicitaire an advertising

⚫ means the verb takes être to form the perfect

campaign

_ℓ_ la **publicité** _FEM NOUN_
1 **advertising**
travailler dans la publicité to work in advertising
faire de la publicité to advertise
un coup de publicité a publicity stunt
2 **advertisement** _(in the press, on TV, etc)_
une bonne publicité a good advert

publier _VERB_ [1]
to publish

la **puce** _FEM NOUN_
1 une carte à puce a smart card
2 **flea**
un marché aux puces a fleamarket
• la puce électronique
microchip

puer _VERB_ [1]
to stink

_ℓ_ **puis** _ADVERB_
then
Nous allons à Cannes, puis à Nice. We're going to Cannes, then Nice.

puisque _CONJUNCTION_
since
Puisqu'il pleut, je vais prendre le bus. Since it's raining I'll take the bus.

la **puissance** _FEM NOUN_
power _(force, country)_

puissant _MASC ADJECTIVE_, **puissante** _FEM_
powerful

le **puits** _MASC NOUN_
well

_ℓ_ le **pull** le **pull-over** _MASC NOUN_
jumper

le **pulvérisateur** _MASC NOUN_
spray _(for perfume, etc)_

la **punaise** _FEM NOUN_
1 **drawing-pin**
2 **bug** _(insect)_

punir _VERB_ [2]
to punish
Toute la classe est punie. The whole class is being punished.

la **punition** _FEM NOUN_
punishment

pur _MASC ADJECTIVE_, **pure** _FEM_
1 **pure** _(uncontaminated)_
un shampooing très doux, très pur an ultra-mild, ultra-pure shampoo
un croissant pur beurre an all-butter croissant
2 **sheer, utter**

C'est de la folie pure. It's sheer madness.

la **purée** _FEM NOUN_
purée
purée de tomates tomato purée

le **puzzle** _MASC NOUN_
jigsaw puzzle

le **PV** _MASC NOUN_
parking ticket

_ℓ_ le **pyjama** _MASC NOUN_
(pair of) pyjamas

la **pyramide** _FEM NOUN_
pyramid

les **Pyrénées** _PLURAL FEM NOUN_
les Pyrénées the Pyrenees

Qq

_ℓ_ le **quai** _MASC NOUN_
1 **platform**
Le train à destination de Paris va arriver au quai numéro trois. The train for Paris is about to arrive at platform three.
2 **quay** _(for boats)_
3 **bank** _(of a river)_

qualifié _MASC ADJECTIVE_, **qualifiée** _FEM_
1 **qualified**
2 **skilled**

qualifier _VERB_ [1]
to qualify

se **qualifier** _REFLEXIVE VERB_ ◎
to qualify
L'équipe s'est qualifiée pour la finale. The team has qualified for the final.

la **qualité** _FEM NOUN_
quality
de première qualité top quality fruit
Jean a des qualités de leader. Jean has leadership qualities.

_ℓ_ **quand** _ADVERB, CONJUNCTION_
when
quand j'étais en France when I was in France
Quand est-ce que ton frère arrive? When does your brother arrive?
Quand tu auras dix-sept ans, tu pourras apprendre à conduire. When you're seventeen you'll be able to learn to drive.

WORD TIP When quand refers to the future, use the future tense and not the present as in English. ▸ SEE **depuis** ADVERB

quand même _ADVERB_
all the same

Il pleut mais je vais sortir quand même. It's raining but I'm going to go out all the same.

quant à PREPOSITION
as for
Quant à moi, je reste. As for me, I'm staying here.

la **quantité** FEM NOUN
amount
une petite quantité d'alcool a small amount of alcohol

la **quarantaine** FEM NOUN
about forty
une quarantaine de personnes about forty people
Il approche la quarantaine. He'll soon be forty.

ℓ **quarante** NUMBER
forty

ℓ le **quart** MASC NOUN
1 quarter (in time)
un quart d'heure a quarter of an hour
midi moins le quart a quarter to twelve
sept heures et quart a quarter past seven
Ça a duré une heure et quart. It lasted an hour and a quarter.
2 quarter (fraction)
le quart du gâteau a quarter of the cake
un quart d'eau minérale a quarter-litre bottle of mineral water
les trois quarts du paquet three quarters of the packet
• le quart de finale
quarter-final

ℓ le **quartier** MASC NOUN
area (of a town)
un quartier résidentiel a residential area
les gens du quartier the local people

WORD TIP quartier does not mean quarter in English; for the meaning of quarter ▶SEE quart.

quasi ADVERB
almost
quasi parfait almost perfect

quasiment ADVERB
practically
C'est quasiment neuf. It's practically new.

ℓ **quatorze** NUMBER
fourteen
Céline a quatorze ans. Céline's fourteen.

ℓ **quatre** NUMBER
four
le quatre mars the fourth of March

ℓ **quatre-vingt-dix** NUMBER
ninety
quatre-vingt-dix-neuf ninety-nine

ℓ **quatre-vingts** NUMBER
eighty
quatre-vingt-trois eighty-three
quatre-vingt-seize ninety-six

WORD TIP The -s of vingts is omitted when another number follows.

ℓ **quatrième** MASC & FEM ADJECTIVE ▶SEE
quatrième NOUN, NOUN
fourth
au quatrième étage on the fourth floor

le **quatrième** MASC NOUN ▶SEE quatrième
ADJECTIVE, NOUN
fourth floor

la **quatrième** FEM NOUN ▶SEE quatrième
ADJECTIVE, NOUN
Year 9 (in French schools)

ℓ **que, qu'** ADVERB, CONJUNCTION, PRONOUN
1 that (often omitted in English)
Elle dit que c'est vrai. She says (that) it's true.
Je sais qu'il y habite. I know (that) he lives there.
2 (in comparisons) than, as
plus ... que more ... than
Anaïs est plus grande que Marie. Anaïs is taller than Marie.
aussi ... que as ... as
Elle est aussi grande que moi. She's as tall as me.
moins ... que not as ... as
Elle est moins grande que toi. She's not as tall as you.
3 ne ... que only
Je n'ai que dix euros. I've only got ten euros.
▶SEE ne
4 (connecting two phrases) that, which, whom (often omitted in English)
le livre que je lis en ce moment the book (that) I'm reading at the moment
la chemise qu'il a achetée the shirt (which) he bought
5 (in questions) what
Que veut-il? What does he want?
Je ne sais pas ce qu'il veut. I don't know what he wants.
6 (in exclamations) how
Que tu as grandi! How you've grown!
7 qu'est-ce que...? what...?
qu'est-ce que tu as trouvé? what have you found?
qu'est-ce que c'est? what's that?

WORD TIP que becomes qu' before a, e, i, o, u, y or silent h.

☻ means the verb takes être to form the perfect

le **Québec** *MASC NOUN*
le Québec Quebec

> **WORD TIP** Countries and regions in French take le, la or les.

québécois *MASC ADJECTIVE*, **québécoise** *FEM*
▶ SEE **Québécois**
from Quebec, Quebecker

> **WORD TIP** Adjectives never have capitals in French, even for nationality or regional origin.

un **Québécois** *MASC NOUN*, une **Québécoise** *FEM* ▶ SEE **québécois**
1 **French Canadian**, **Quebecker**
les Québécois the French Canadians
2 le québecois Canadian French *(the language)*

> **WORD TIP** Languages never have capitals in French.

ℓ **quel** *MASC ADJECTIVE*, **quelle** *FEM*
1 *(in questions)* **which**, **what**
Quel livre lis-tu? Which book are you reading?
Quelle voiture avez-vous? Which car do you have?
Quels DVD as-tu achetés? What DVDs did you buy?
Quelles langues est-ce que tu étudies? What languages are you studying?
2 *(in exclamations)* **what**
Quel beau temps! What lovely weather!
Quelle coïncidence! What a coincidence!

quelle *FEM ADJECTIVE* ▶ SEE **quel**

ℓ **quelque** *ADJECTIVE*
some
J'ai passé quelque temps en France. I have spent some time in France.
Nous habitons ici depuis quelque temps. We've been living here for some time.

ℓ **quelque chose** *PRONOUN*
1 **something**
Il faut manger quelque chose. You must eat something.
J'ai quelque chose à te dire. I have something to tell you.
2 quelque chose de *(+ adjective)* **something + adjective**
quelque chose de nouveau something new
3 **anything**
Est-ce que tu as vu quelque chose? Did you see anything?

ℓ **quelquefois** *ADVERB*
sometimes

quelque part *ADVERB*
1 **somewhere**
J'ai laissé la clé quelque part dans le bureau. I left the key somewhere in the office.
2 **anywhere**
Est-ce que tu as vu mes lunettes quelque part? Have you seen my glasses anywhere?

quelques *PLURAL ADJECTIVE*
1 **some**
Je vais te donner quelques cerises. I'll give you some cherries.
2 **a few**
Il reste quelques fraises. There are a few strawberries left.

quelques-uns *PLURAL MASC PRONOUN*, **quelques-unes** *PL FEM*
some
quelques-uns des enfants some of the children
Les cerises sont bonnes. Prends-en quelques-unes! The cherries are good. Have some!

> **WORD TIP** Use quelques-unes for a fem plural noun.

quelqu'un *PRONOUN*
1 **somebody**
Quelqu'un a appelé pour toi. Somebody rang for you.
2 **anybody**
Il y a quelqu'un? Is there anybody there?
Est-ce que quelqu'un t'a aidé? Did anybody help you?

quels *PLURAL MASC ADJECTIVE*, **quelles** *PL FEM* ▶ SEE **quel**

la **querelle** *FEM NOUN*
quarrel

ℓ **qu'est-ce que** *PHRASE*
Qu'est-ce que ...? What ...?
Qu'est-ce que c'est? What's that?
Qu'est-ce que tu as trouvé? What have you found?
Qu'est-ce qu'il y a? What's the matter?

> **WORD TIP** qu'est-ce que becomes qu'est-ce qu' before a, e, i, o, u and silent h.

ℓ **qu'est-ce qui** *PHRASE*
Qu'est-ce qui ...? What ...?
Qu'est-ce qui fait ce bruit? What's making that noise?

> **WORD TIP** The spelling of qui never changes, even before a vowel.

ℓ la **question** *FEM NOUN*
1 **question**
Elle n'a pas répondu à mes questions. She didn't answer my questions.
Il me pose toujours des questions difficiles. He always asks me difficult questions.

ℓ **indicates key words**

2 matter, question
C'est une question de goût. It's a matter of taste.
C'est hors de question. It's out of the question.
Pas question! No way!

le **questionnaire** MASC NOUN
questionnaire

questionner VERB [1]
to question (in an interview)
On l'a questionné à propos des émeutes. He was questioned about the riots.

la **queue** FEM NOUN
1 tail
la queue du chat the cat's tail
2 queue
faire la queue to queue
3 la queue du train the rear of the train
• la queue de cheval
ponytail

ℰ **qui** PRONOUN
1 (in questions) who
Qui vient ce soir? Who's coming this evening?
Qui voulez-vous voir? Who do you want to see?
De qui parles-tu? Who are you talking about?
C'est pour qui? Who's it for?
2 (connecting two phrases) who, that
la personne qui m'a téléphoné the person who phoned me
Voilà le chien qui a mordu Victor. That's the dog that bit Victor.
3 à qui ... ? whose ... ?
À qui est ce pull? Whose is this jumper?
Je ne sais pas à qui c'est. I don't know whose it is.

WORD TIP The spelling of qui never changes.

la **quiche** FEM NOUN
quiche

la **quincaillerie** FEM NOUN
hardware shop

ℰ la **quinzaine** FEM NOUN
1 about fifteen
une quinzaine d'enfants about fifteen children
2 fortnight
une quinzaine de jours a fortnight

ℰ **quinze** NUMBER
1 fifteen
le quinze juillet the fifteenth of July
Romaine a quinze ans. Romaine is fifteen.
2 quinze jours two weeks
tous les quinze jours every two weeks

ℰ **quitter** VERB [1]
1 to leave (a place, a person, etc)
Elle quitte le bureau à cinq heures. She leaves the office at five.
Elle l'a quitté il y a deux ans. She left him two years ago.
2 (on the telephone) Ne quittez pas. Hold the line.
3 (Computers) to quit

quoi PRONOUN
1 what (in questions)
Quoi encore? What now?
Quoi de neuf? What's new?
Pour quoi faire? What for?
À quoi penses-tu? What are you thinking about?
2 (in expressions) Il n'y a pas de quoi se fâcher. There's no reason to get angry.
'Merci.' – 'Il n'y a pas de quoi.' 'Thank you.' – 'Don't mention it.'

quoique CONJUNCTION
although, though
Quoique petit, il est assez fort. Although he's small, he's quite strong.

quotidien MASC ADJECTIVE, **quotidienne** FEM
▶ SEE **quotidien** NOUN
daily
la vie quotidienne daily life

le **quotidien** MASC NOUN ▶ SEE **quotidien** ADJECTIVE
daily newspaper

Rr

le **rabais** MASC NOUN
discount
Je l'ai acheté au rabais. I bought it at a discount.

raccompagner VERB [1]
raccompagner quelqu'un chez soi to see somebody home
Je te raccompagne chez toi. I'll see you home.

le **raccourci** MASC NOUN
shortcut

ℰ **raccrocher** VERB [1]
to hang up (on the phone)

la **race** FEM NOUN
1 race
la race humaine the human race
2 breed
différentes races de chien different breeds of dogs

⬛ means the verb takes être to form the perfect

racheter VERB [16]
1 **to buy more** (bread, paper)
2 racheter quelque chose à quelqu'un **to buy something from somebody**
Il m'a racheté mon vélo. **He bought my bike from me.**

la **racine** FEM NOUN
root

raciste MASC & FEM ADJECTIVE ▸ SEE **raciste** NOUN
racist (remark)
raciste MASC & FEM NOUN ▸ SEE **raciste** ADJECTIVE
racist

raconter VERB [1]
to tell (a story)

le **radar** MASC NOUN
radar

le **radeau** MASC NOUN, les **radeaux** PLURAL
raft

le **radiateur** MASC NOUN
radiator

♪ la **radio** FEM NOUN
1 **radio**
Il a entendu la nouvelle à la radio. **He heard the news on the radio.**
2 **radio station**
3 **X-ray**
passer une radio **to have an X-ray**
• le **radio-réveil**
clock radio

le **radis** MASC NOUN
radish

raffoler VERB [1]
(informal)
raffoler de quelque chose **to be mad about something**
Je ne raffole pas des huîtres. **I'm not mad about oysters.**

rafraîchir VERB [2]
to cool (down)
La pluie a rafraîchi l'atmosphère. **The rain cooled the atmosphere.**
se **rafraîchir** REFLEXIVE VERB ◌
to get cooler (weather)

le **rafraîchissement** MASC NOUN
1 **refreshment**
2 **drop in temperature**

le **rafting** MASC NOUN
(white water) rafting

la **rage** FEM NOUN
1 **rabies**
2 être fou de rage **to be hopping mad**
• la **rage de dents**
raging toothache

le **ragoût** MASC NOUN
stew

raide MASC & FEM ADJECTIVE
1 **stiff** (body)
2 **straight** (hair)
3 **steep** (slope)

la **raie** FEM NOUN
1 **parting** (in your hair)
2 **skate** (the fish)

le **rail** MASC NOUN
rail (for trains)

♪ le **raisin** MASC NOUN
grapes
une grappe de raisin **a bunch of grapes**
un grain de raisin **a grape**

WORD TIP raisin does not mean **raisin** in English; for the meaning of **raisin** ▸ SEE **raisin sec**.

• le **raisin de Corinthe**
currant
• le **raisin sec**
raisin

♪ la **raison** FEM NOUN
1 **reason**
pour cette raison **for this reason**
pour raisons de santé **for health reasons**
2 avoir raison **to be right**
Cette fois, tu as raison. **This time, you're right.**

raisonnable MASC & FEM ADJECTIVE
sensible

le **raisonnement** MASC NOUN
reasoning

rajouter VERB [1]
to add (ingredients)

ralentir VERB [2]
to slow down

le **ralentisseur** MASC NOUN
speed hump

râler VERB [1]
(informal) **to moan**

le **râleur** MASC NOUN, la **râleuse** FEM
moaner

la **rallonge** FEM NOUN
extension lead

rallumer VERB [1]
to put back on again (light, heating)

le **ramassage** MASC NOUN
collection

ramasser VERB [1]
1 **to pick up** (papers, books)
2 **to pick** (fruit)
3 **to collect** (chestnuts, shells)

♪ **indicates key words**

4 to collect in (books, homework)

la **rame** FEM NOUN
1 oar
2 train
une rame de métro an underground train

le **rameau** MASC NOUN, les **rameaux** PLURAL
branch
les Rameaux, le dimanche des Rameaux
Palm Sunday

ramener VERB [50]
1 ramener quelqu'un (en voiture) to give
somebody a lift home
Tu veux que je te ramène? Do you want me
to give you a lift home?
2 to take back
ramener des livres à la bibliothèque to take
books back to the library

ramer VERB [1]
to row

la **rampe** FEM NOUN
1 bannister
2 ramp

la **rançon** FEM NOUN
ransom

la **rancune** FEM NOUN
resentment

la **randonnée** FEM NOUN
hike
Elle aime faire de la randonnée. She likes
to go hiking.
faire une randonnée pédestre to go on a
hike (on public footpaths)
faire une randonnée à cheval to go pony-
trekking
une randonnée à vélo a long-distance bike
ride

le **randonneur** MASC NOUN, la **randonneuse**
FEM
1 hiker
2 touring cyclist

le **rang** MASC NOUN
row

la **rangée** FEM NOUN
row (of chairs, houses)

ρ **ranger** VERB [52]
1 to put away
ranger la vaisselle to put away the dishes
2 to tidy
Je vais ranger ma chambre. I'm going to
tidy my room.
3 to arrange
rangé par ordre alphabétique arranged
alphabetically

râper VERB [1]
to grate (cheese)

ρ **rapide** MASC & FEM ADJECTIVE ▸ SEE **rapide** NOUN
1 fast
Le guépard est l'animal le plus rapide. The
cheetah is the fastest animal.
2 quick
une réaction rapide a quick reaction

ρ le **rapide** MASC NOUN ▸ SEE **rapide** ADJECTIVE
1 express train
2 rapids

rapidement ADVERB
quickly

le **rappel** MASC NOUN
1 reminder (for a bill)
2 booster (vaccination)

rappeler VERB [18]
1 to remind
Rappelle-moi de passer à la bibliothèque!
Remind me to go to the library!
Ça me rappelle mes vacances. It reminds
me of my holidays.
2 to ring back (on the phone)
Je rappellerai plus tard. I'll ring back later.

se **rappeler** REFLEXIVE VERB ◉
to remember
Je me rappelle qu'elle avait les cheveux
longs. I remember she had long hair.
Je ne me rappelle plus. I can't remember.

le **rapport** MASC NOUN
1 connection
2 relations
des rapports amicaux friendly relations
avoir des rapports sexuels to have sex
3 report
un rapport officiel an official report
4 par rapport à quelque chose compared
with something
Il fait très beau par rapport à hier. The
weather is very good compared with
yesterday.

rapporter VERB [1]
1 to bring back
2 to bring in money

rapprocher VERB [1]
1 to move something closer
Je rapproche mon bureau de la fenêtre. I'm
moving my desk closer to the window.
2 to bring together (different people, different
countries)

se **rapprocher** REFLEXIVE VERB ◉
to get closer
Elle s'est rapprochée de la table. She
moved closer to the table.

◉ means the verb takes être to form the perfect

la **raquette** FEM NOUN
1 **racket** (for tennis)
2 **bat** (for ping-pong)

ℓ **rare** MASC & FEM ADJECTIVE
rare
une fleur rare a rare flower

rarement ADVERB
rarely

ras MASC ADJECTIVE, **rase** FEM ▶ SEE **ras** ADVERB
1 **short** (hair, fur)
un chien à poil ras a short-haired dog
2 **à ras bord** to the brim
3 (informal)
**en avoir ras le bol de quelque chose,
quelqu'un** to be fed up with something,
somebody
J'en ai ras le bol! I'm fed up with it!

ras ADVERB ▶ SEE **ras** ADJECTIVE
short
des cheveux coupés ras close-cropped hair

raser VERB [1]
to shave
Il a rasé sa barbe. He's shaved off his beard.

se **raser** REFLEXIVE VERB ◎
to shave
se raser les jambes to shave your legs

le **rasoir** MASC NOUN
razor

le **rassemblement** MASC NOUN
rally (for peace, support, etc.)

rassembler VERB [1]
to gather (together)

se **rassembler** REFLEXIVE VERB ◎
to gather
Ils se sont rassemblés pour l'écouter. They
all gathered to listen to him.

rassis MASC ADJECTIVE, **rassise** FEM
stale (bread)

rassurer VERB [1]
to reassure
Ça me rassure! That puts my mind at rest!

se **rassurer** REFLEXIVE VERB ◎
to reassure yourself
Rassure-toi, tout se passera bien! Don't
worry, it'll be fine!

le **rat** MASC NOUN
rat

le **râteau** MASC NOUN, les **râteaux** PLURAL
rake

rater VERB [1]
1 **to fail** (an exam, a driving test)
2 **to miss** (a bus, a train, a plane)

la **RATP** FEM NOUN
(= Régie autonome des transports parisiens)
(transport network serving the Île-de-France
region around Paris)

rattacher VERB [1]
to fasten again (a seatbelt, a belt)

rattraper VERB [1]
1 **to catch up with** (a person)
Ils nous rattraperont. They'll catch up with
us.
2 **to make up for** (lost time)
rattraper son retard en to catch up in (a
school subject)
J'ai rattrapé mon retard en français. I've
caught up in French.
3 **to catch** (a ball)

se **rattraper** REFLEXIVE VERB ◎
to make up for it
J'ai très peu joué cet été mais je vais me
rattraper. I've played very little this summer
but I'll make up for it.

la **rature** FEM NOUN
crossing-out

ℓ **ravi** MASC ADJECTIVE, **ravie** FEM
delighted
Je suis ravi de vous voir. I'm delighted to
see you (boy speaking).
Je suis ravie de vous avoir rencontré. I'm
delighted to have met you (girl speaking).

le **ravisseur** MASC NOUN, la **ravisseuse** FEM
kidnapper

rayé MASC ADJECTIVE, **rayée** FEM
striped (fabric)

rayer VERB [59]
1 **to cross out** (a mistake)
2 **to scratch** (a surface)

ℓ le **rayon** MASC NOUN
1 **department** (in a department store)
le rayon jouets the toy department
2 **section** (in a supermarket)
3 **ray**
les rayons X X-rays
4 **radius**
dans un rayon de deux kilomètres within a
two-kilometre radius
5 **shelf**

la **rayure** FEM NOUN
1 **stripe**
2 **scratch**

le **réacteur** MASC NOUN
1 **jet engine**
2 un réacteur nucléaire a nuclear reactor

la **réaction** FEM NOUN
reaction

ℓ **indicates key words**

réagir VERB [2]
  to react

le **réalisateur** MASC NOUN, la **réalisatrice** FEM
  director (of a film, a TV programme)

la **réalisation** FEM NOUN
1 **carrying out** (of a plan, a project)
2 **production** (of a film, a radio or TV programme)

réaliser VERB [1]
1 **to carry out** (a project)
2 **to fulfil** (a dream)
3 **to make** (a film)

réaliste MASC & FEM ADJECTIVE
  realistic

la **réalité** FEM NOUN
  reality

la **réanimation** FEM NOUN
  resuscitation
  le service de réanimation the intensive care unit

le & la **rebelle** MASC & FEM NOUN
  rebel

rebondir VERB [2]
  to bounce

le **rebord** MASC NOUN
  edge (of a bathtub)
• le rebord de fenêtre
  windowsill

récemment ADVERB
  recently

ℓ **récent** MASC ADJECTIVE, **récente** FEM
  recent

ℓ la **réception** FEM NOUN
1 **welcome**
  une réception enthousiaste an enthusiastic welcome
2 **reception desk**
  Demandez la clé à la réception. Ask for the key at the reception desk.
3 **reception** (party)

le & la **réceptionniste** MASC & FEM NOUN
  receptionist

ℓ la **recette** FEM NOUN
  recipe
  la recette du gâteau au chocolat the recipe for chocolate cake

ℓ **recevoir** VERB [66]
1 **to receive, to get**
  J'ai reçu ta lettre. I received your letter.
  Il a reçu ton message. He got your message.
2 **to welcome** (a visitor, a guest)
3 **to entertain** (to invite people round)

4 **to see** (a patient, a client)
5 être reçu à un examen to pass an exam
  Il va être reçu au bac. He'll pass the baccalaureat.
  Elle a été reçue première à l'examen. She came top in the exam.

le **rechange** MASC NOUN
  de rechange spare
  des vêtements de rechange spare clothes

la **recharge** FEM NOUN
  refill

le **réchaud** MASC NOUN
  stove

le **réchauffement planétaire** MASC NOUN
  global warming

réchauffer VERB [1]
1 **to heat up** (food)
2 **to warm up** (hands, feet)

se **réchauffer** REFLEXIVE VERB ◗
1 **to warm up**
2 **to get warmer** (weather)

la **recherche** FEM NOUN
1 **research**
2 être à la recherche de quelque chose to be looking for something

rechercher VERB [1]
  to look for (a person, a job)

le **récipient** MASC NOUN
  container

réciproque MASC & FEM ADJECTIVE
  mutual

le **récit** MASC NOUN
  story

la **récitation** FEM NOUN
  text (often a poem that schoolchildren learn off by heart)
  J'ai appris ma récitation. I've learnt my text off by heart.

réciter VERB [1]
  to recite

la **réclamation** FEM NOUN
  complaint
  une lettre de réclamation a letter of complaint

ℓ la **réclame** FEM NOUN
1 **advertisement**
  une réclame pour du parfum an advertisement for perfume
2 en réclame on (special) offer (at supermarket)

réclamer VERB [1]
  to demand
  Ils réclament trois jours de plus de

◗ means the verb takes être to form the perfect

vacances. They're demanding three more days' holiday.

la **récolte** *FEM NOUN*
1 **harvest**
2 **crop**

récolter *VERB* [1]
1 **to harvest** *(wheat, corn)*
2 **to collect** *(money)*
3 *(informal)* **to get** *(a fine)*

la **recommandation** *FEM NOUN*
recommendation

recommandé *MASC ADJECTIVE,* **recommandée**
FEM
registered *(letter)*
envoyer une lettre sous pli recommandé to send a letter by registered post

℘ **recommander** *VERB* [1]
1 **to advise**
Je te recommande de ne rien dire. I advise you to say nothing.
2 **to recommend**
Pourrais-tu recommander un bon restaurant? Could you recommend a good restaurant?

recommencer *VERB* [61]
1 **to do again**
Ne recommence pas! Don't do it again!
Je recommence ma lettre, j'ai fait trop de fautes. I'm writing my letter again, I've made too many mistakes.
2 **recommencer quelque chose à zéro** to start something again from scratch
3 **to start again**
Les cours recommencent en octobre. The classes start again in October.
Ça recommence! Here we go again!

℘ la **récompense** *FEM NOUN*
reward
En récompense, j'ai eu un billet gratuit. As a reward, I got a free ticket.

récompenser *VERB* [1]
to reward

se **réconcilier** *REFLEXIVE VERB* ◉ [1]
to make up *(after a row)*
se réconcilier avec quelqu'un to make it up with somebody
Zoé s'est réconciliée avec Marine. Zoé made it up with Marine.

réconfortant *MASC ADJECTIVE,* **réconfortante**
FEM
comforting

reconnaissable *MASC & FEM ADJECTIVE*
recognizable

la **reconnaissance** *FEM NOUN*
gratitude

reconnaissant *MASC ADJECTIVE,*
reconnaissante *FEM*
grateful

reconnaître *VERB* [27]
1 **to recognize**
Je ne l'ai pas reconnue. I didn't recognize her.
2 **to admit**
Il faut reconnaître que c'est difficile. You have to admit that it's difficult.

reconstruire *VERB* [26]
to rebuild

recopier *VERB* [1]
to copy out

le **record** *MASC NOUN*
record
un record mondial a world record
Il a battu le record du 75 mètres à l'école. He broke the school record for the 75 metres.

recouvrir *VERB* [30]
to cover

la **récré** *FEM NOUN*
(informal) **break**

℘ la **récréation** *FEM NOUN*
break
à la récréation at break

le **rectangle** *MASC NOUN*
rectangle

rectangulaire *MASC & FEM ADJECTIVE*
rectangular

rectifier *VERB* [1]
to correct

℘ le **reçu** *MASC NOUN* ▶ SEE **reçu** *VERB*
receipt
Vous avez encore le reçu? Do you still have the receipt?

℘ **reçu** *VERB* ▶ SEE **reçu** *NOUN* ▶ SEE **recevoir**

le **recueil** *MASC NOUN*
collection *(of poems, essays)*

reculer *VERB* [1]
1 **to move back**
2 **to reverse** *(in a car)*

reculons *ADVERBIAL PHRASE*
à reculons backwards

récupérer *VERB* [24]
1 **to get back** *(something borrowed)*
2 **to fetch**
3 **to recover** *(from an illness)*

℘ indicates key words

le **recyclage** MASC NOUN
recycling
faire du recyclage to recycle

recycler VERB [1]
to recycle
Nous recyclons aussi les bouteilles en plastique. We recycle plastic bottles too.

la **rédaction** FEM NOUN
essay
J'ai eu une bonne note à ma rédaction. I got a good mark for my essay.

redemander VERB [1]
1 **to ask again**
Tu devrais redemander. You should ask again.
2 **to ask for more**
Il faut qu'on redemande des cahiers. We'll have to ask for more exercise books.

redescendre VERB ◒ [3]
1 **to go back down**
Elle est redescendue à la cave. She went back down to the cellar.
2 **to come back down** (from somewhere further north)
3 **to bring back down** (from upstairs)

rédiger VERB [52]
to write (an article)

redonner VERB [1]
to give again
Je leur ai redonné mon adresse. I gave them my address again

redoubler VERB [1]
to repeat a year (at school)

redresser VERB [1]
1 **to straighten** (picture, teeth)
2 **to rectify** (an error)

se **redresser** REFLEXIVE VERB ◒
to straighten up

♀ la **réduction** FEM NOUN
1 **reduction**
une réduction du nombre d'étudiants a reduction in the number of students
2 **discount**
une réduction de 20% a 20% discount
faire une réduction à quelqu'un to give somebody a discount
Ils font une réduction de 30% aux étudiants. They give students a 30% discount.
3 **concession**
une réduction pour les moins de 15 ans a concession for the under-15s

réduire VERB [68]
to cut (prices, taxes)
à prix réduit cut-price

la **rééducation** FEM NOUN
physiotherapy

réel MASC ADJECTIVE, **réelle** FEM
real

réellement ADVERB
really

refaire VERB [10]
1 **to redo**
Je dois refaire mon devoir de maths. I have to redo my maths homework.
2 **to make more**
Je refais du café. I'm making some more coffee.

la **référence** FEM NOUN
reference
la date de référence the date of reference
faire référence à quelque chose to refer to something
Il fait référence à l'article du journal. He's referring to the newspaper article.

réfléchi MASC ADJECTIVE, **réfléchie** FEM
reflexive (verb)

réfléchir VERB [2]
1 **to think**
Réfléchis bien avant d'accepter. Think carefully before accepting.
Ça fait réfléchir. It makes you think.
2 **réfléchir à quelque chose to think about something**
J'ai réfléchi à ta question. I've thought about your question.

le **reflet** MASC NOUN
1 **reflection**
regarder son reflet dans l'eau to look at your reflection in the water
2 des cheveux aux reflets blonds hair with blond highlights

refléter VERB [24]
to reflect

le **réflexe** MASC NOUN
1 **reflex**
J'ai de bons réflexes. I've got good reflexes.
2 **reaction**
Mon premier réflexe a été de crier. My first reaction was to shout.

la **réflexion** FEM NOUN
1 **thought**
Réflexion faite, je n'irai pas. On second thoughts, I won't go.
2 **comment, remark**
faire des réflexions to make remarks

le **refrain** MASC NOUN
chorus

◒ **means the verb takes être to form the perfect**

le **réfrigérateur** MASC NOUN
refrigerator

refroidir VERB [2]
1 to cool down
2 to get cold
La soupe va refroidir! The soup will get cold!

le **refuge** MASC NOUN
1 refuge
2 mountain hut (for climbers)
3 animal sanctuary
4 traffic island

le **réfugié** MASC NOUN, la **réfugiée** FEM
refugee

se **réfugier** REFLEXIVE VERB ◎ [1]
to take refuge

le **refus** MASC NOUN
refusal

refuser VERB [1]
1 to refuse
refuser de faire quelque chose to refuse to do something
Elle a refusé de répondre. She refused to answer.
2 to turn down (an application for a job)

regagner VERB [1]
to get back to
Il a regagné la plage. He got back to the beach.

le **régal** MASC NOUN
feast (delicious meal)

se **régaler** REFLEXIVE VERB ◎ [1]
Je me régale. It's delicious.
se régaler avec quelque chose to enjoy something thoroughly
On s'est régalé avec les festivals de musique. We thoroughly enjoyed the music festivals.

le **regard** MASC NOUN
look
Il jette un regard rapide à sa montre. He takes a quick look at his watch.

℘ **regarder** VERB [1]
1 to look at
Je regarde la carte. I'm looking at the map.
2 to look in (the phone book, the dictionary)
On a regardé dans le dictionnaire. We looked in the dictionary.
3 to watch (the TV)
Tu veux regarder le film? Do you want to watch the film?
4 to look
Regarde! Look!
regarder par la fenêtre to look out of the window

5 to concern
Cela ne nous regarde pas. That doesn't concern us.
Ça ne te regarde pas. That's none of your business.

se **regarder** REFLEXIVE VERB ◎
1 to look at yourself
Il se regarde dans la glace. He's looking at himself in the mirror.
2 to look at each other
3 to face each other (buildings)

la **régate** FEM NOUN
regatta

le **régime** MASC NOUN
1 diet
un régime sans sel a salt-free diet
Je fais un régime. I'm on a diet.
2 bunch (of bananas)
3 regime

℘ la **région** FEM NOUN
region, area
la région parisienne the Paris region
les vins de la région the local wines
visiter la région to visit the area
la Région Aquitaine the Aquitaine Region
(Une région is a large French administrative region made up of smaller areas called départements.)

régional MASC ADJECTIVE, **régionale** FEM, **régionaux** MASC PL, **régionales** FEM PL
regional

le **registre** MASC NOUN
register

réglable MASC & FEM ADJECTIVE
adjustable

la **règle** FEM NOUN
1 ruler
2 rule
les règles du jeu the rules of the game
En règle générale... As a general rule...
3 en règle in order (valid)
Mes papiers sont tous en règle. My papers are all in order.
4 les règles period (menstruation)
• les règles de sécurité safety regulations

℘ le **règlement** MASC NOUN
1 rules
C'est contraire au règlement de l'école. It's against the school rules.
2 payment
un mode de règlement a method of payment
3 settlement (after a dispute)

régler VERB [24]
1 to pay (a bill, a debt)

℘ indicates key words

Vous réglez comment, monsieur? How would you like to pay, sir?
2 to sort out *(details, a problem)*
3 to adjust *(the height, the width)*

la **réglisse** FEM NOUN
liquorice

le **règne** MASC NOUN
reign

régner VERB [24]
to reign

le **regret** MASC NOUN
regret
sans regret with no regrets
Mille regrets. I'm terribly sorry.

regretter VERB [1]
1 to be sorry
Je regrette, elle est partie. I'm sorry, she's left.
regretter de faire quelque chose to be sorry to do something
Je regrette de ne pas pouvoir t'aider. I'm sorry I can't help you.
2 to regret *(a decision)*
Je ne regrette rien. I have no regrets.
3 to miss
Elle regrette la vie à Paris. She misses life in Paris.

regrouper VERB [1]
to group together

se **regrouper** REFLEXIVE VERB ⬤
to gather

la **régularité** FEM NOUN
regularity

régulier MASC ADJECTIVE, **régulière** FEM
regular
un vol régulier a scheduled flight

régulièrement ADVERB
regularly

le **rein** MASC NOUN
1 kidney
2 avoir mal aux reins to have backache

♪ la **reine** FEM NOUN
queen
la reine Élisabeth Queen Elizabeth

rejeter VERB [48]
to reject

rejoindre VERB [49]
1 to meet up with
Je vous rejoins dans la cour. I'll meet you in the playground.
2 to catch up with
3 to join *(other people, a group, a movement)*

se **rejoindre** REFLEXIVE VERB ⬤
1 to meet up *(people)*

2 to merge *(motorways, lanes)*

rejouer VERB [1]
to replay

relâcher VERB [1]
1 to loosen *(a grip, a hold)*
2 to set free *(a hostage, an animal)*

le **relais** MASC NOUN
1 prendre le relais to take over
Il a pris le relais au volant. He took over the driving.
2 relay race

relatif MASC ADJECTIVE, **relative** FEM
relative

la **relation** FEM NOUN
1 connection
en relation avec in connection with
2 acquaintance
une relation de mon frère an acquaintance of my brother's
3 relationship
Il n'a pas de bonnes relations avec son père. He hasn't got a good relationship with his father.
4 les relations publiques public relations, PR

WORD TIP Relation does not mean relation in English; for the meaning of relation ▸ SEE famille.

relativement ADVERB
relatively

relax INVARIABLE MASC & FEM ADJECTIVE
1 *(informal)* laid back *(person)*
2 casual *(party, event)*

relaxer VERB [1]
to relax

le **relevé** MASC NOUN
faire le relevé de quelque chose to make a list of something
On a fait le relevé des dépenses. We made a list of the expenses.
• le relevé de compte
bank statement
• le relevé de notes
school report

relever VERB [50]
1 to raise
2 relever la tête to look up
3 to notice *(details, mistakes)*
4 to read *(the meter)*

se **relever** REFLEXIVE VERB ⬤
to pick yourself up *(after a fall)*

relier VERB [1]
1 to link
Un canal relie Brest à Nantes. A canal links Brest to Nantes.
2 to join up

⬤ means the verb takes être to form the perfect

Relie les points! Join up the dots!

religieux *MASC ADJECTIVE*, **religieuse** *FEM* ▸SEE **religieux** *NOUN*
religious

le **religieux** *MASC NOUN*, la **religieuse** *FEM* ▸SEE **religieux** *ADJECTIVE*
1 monk
2 nun

la **religion** *FEM NOUN*
religion

relire *VERB* [51]
to reread

remarié *MASC ADJECTIVE*, **remariée** *FEM*
remarried

remarquable *MASC & FEM ADJECTIVE*
remarkable
des progrès remarquables remarkable progress

la **remarque** *FEM NOUN*
1 remark
une remarque déplaisante an nasty remark
2 comment
Il y a des remarques dans la marge. There are some comments in the margin.

ℓ **remarquer** *VERB* [1]
1 to notice
Il n'a rien remarqué. He didn't notice anything.
J'ai remarqué qu'elle est arrivée en retard. I noticed she arrived late.
2 se faire remarquer to draw attention to yourself
Il n'aime pas se faire remarquer. He doesn't like to draw attention to himself.
3 faire remarquer quelque chose à quelqu'un to point something out to somebody
Elle nous a fait remarquer que c'était trop tard. She pointed out to us that it was too late.
4 Remarque, moi ça m'est égal! Mind you, it's all the same to me!

rembobiner *VERB* [1]
to rewind *(a tape)*

le **remboursement** *MASC NOUN*
refund

rembourser *VERB* [1]
1 to pay back
Je te rembourserai demain. I'll pay you back tomorrow.
2 to refund the price of *(a ticket, a purchase)*
3 to give a refund
Ce magasin ne rembourse pas. This shop doesn't give refunds.
se faire rembourser to get a refund

le **remède** *MASC NOUN*
remedy

le **remerciement** *MASC NOUN*
thanks
tous mes remerciements many thanks
une lettre de remerciement a thank-you letter

remercier *VERB* [1]
1 to thank
Je voudrais remercier tous mes amis. I would like to thank all my friends.
Je vous remercie. Thank you.
2 remercier quelqu'un d'avoir fait quelque chose to thank somebody for doing something
Il nous a remerciés de l'avoir aidé. He thanked us for helping him.

remettre *VERB* [11]
1 to put back
Il a remis la photo sur la table. He put the photo back on the table.
2 to put back on *(a sweater, a jacket)*
3 to wear again *(an item of clothing)*
4 remettre quelque chose à quelqu'un to hand something over to somebody
Pouvez-vous me remettre les clés demain? Can you hand over the keys to me tomorrow?
5 to put off *(a meeting, a trip)*
Ils ont remis la réunion à jeudi. They've put the meeting off until Thursday.

se **remettre** *REFLEXIVE VERB* ⊙
1 to start again
Charlène s'est remise au piano. Charlène's started playing the piano again.
Il se remet à pleuvoir. It's starting to rain again.
2 se remettre de quelque chose to recover from something
Elle ne s'est pas remise de sa chute. She hasn't recovered from her fall.

la **remise** *FEM NOUN*
1 handing out *(of awards)*
la remise des prix prizegiving
2 discount
une remise de 20% sur les CD a 20% discount on CDs
3 garden shed

le **remonte-pente** *MASC NOUN*, les **remonte-pentes** *PLURAL*
ski lift

remonter *VERB* [1]
1 ⊙ to go back up
Natalie est remontée dans sa chambre. Natalie's gone back up to her room.
2 ⊙ to come back up *(from somewhere further south)*

3 to get back in
Ils sont remontés dans le car. They got back into the coach.
4 to take back up *(upstairs)*
5 to put up *(in an overhead section)*
Il a remonté sa valise au filet. He put his case up in the luggage rack.
6 remonter la pente to go back up the hill
7 remonter le moral à quelqu'un to cheer somebody up
Ses blagues m'ont remonté le moral. His jokes cheered me up.

WORD TIP When you say what you **take back up**, put back up etc, use avoir in the perfect tense.

le **remords** *MASC NOUN*
remorse

la **remorque** *FEM NOUN*
trailer *(for a car)*

le **remplaçant** *MASC NOUN*, la **remplaçante** *FEM*
1 replacement *(for another person)*
2 supply teacher

remplacer *VERB* [61]
1 to stand in for *(a person)*
2 to replace
Il faut remplacer les piles. You need to replace the batteries.

ℓ **remplir** *VERB* [2]
1 to fill
remplir quelque chose de quelque chose to fill something with something
Il a rempli ses poches de bonbons. He filled his pockets with sweets.
La salle était remplie de jeunes. The hall was full of young people.
2 to fill in *(a form, a questionnaire)*
Je dois remplir un formulaire d'inscription. I have to fill in a registration form.
3 to carry out *(a duty, a role)*
Elle remplit bien son rôle de déléguée de classe. She carries out her role as class rep well.

remporter *VERB* [1]
to win *(a competition)*

le **remue-ménage** *INVARIABLE MASC NOUN*
commotion

le **remue-méninges** *INVARIABLE MASC NOUN*
brainstorming

remuer *VERB* [1]
1 to move *(your head, your hand)*
Le chien remuait la queue. The dog was wagging its tail.
2 to shake *(a branch, a tree)*
3 to stir *(a sauce, a coffee)*
4 to toss *(a salad)*

5 to upset *(a person)*

rémunérer *VERB* [24]
1 to pay *(a person)*
2 to pay for *(work)*

le **renard** *MASC NOUN*
fox

la **rencontre** *FEM NOUN*
1 meeting
Elle est venue à ma rencontre. She came to meet me.
2 *(Sport)* match
la rencontre entre la France et l'Allemagne the match between France and Germany

ℓ **rencontrer** *VERB* [1]
1 to meet *(a person)*
Je l'ai rencontré en 1999. I met him in 1999.
2 to play *(an opponent, a team)*
3 rencontrer des amis to make new friends

WORD TIP If you mean to **meet up with** existing friends use retrouver.

se **rencontrer** *REFLEXIVE VERB* ◎
to meet
Nous nous sommes rencontrés à Londres. We met in London.

ℓ le **rendez-vous** *INVARIABLE MASC NOUN*
1 appointment
prendre rendez-vous to make an appointment
J'ai pris rendez-vous avec ton professeur. I made an appointment with your teacher.
Claire a rendez-vous chez le dentiste. Claire's got a dentist's appointment.
2 donner rendez-vous à quelqu'un to arrange to meet somebody
Il m'a donné rendez-vous au café. He arranged to meet me at the cafe.
3 date
Oscar a rendez-vous avec sa copine. Oscar's got a date with his girlfriend.

se **rendormir** *REFLEXIVE VERB* ◎ [37]
to go back to sleep

rendre *VERB* [3]
1 to give back
Je te rendrai ton pull demain. I'll give you back your sweater tomorrow.
2 to make
rendre quelqu'un heureux to make somebody happy
3 to hand in *(homework)*
Elle rend ses devoirs en retard. She hands her homework in late.
4 rendre visite à quelqu'un to pay somebody a visit
André a rendu visite à son oncle. André paid his uncle a visit.
5 to be sick

◎ means the verb takes être to form the perfect

Il rend toujours sur le bateau. He always
gets sick on the boat.
J'ai envie de rendre. I feel sick.

se **rendre** *REFLEXIVE VERB* ⊙

1 **to go**
Je me rends au Québec. I'm going to
Quebec.

2 **to give yourself up**
Ils se sont rendus à la police. They gave
themselves up to the police.

3 se rendre compte de quelque chose to
realize something
Je me suis rendu compte que j'avais oublié
mon sac. I realized I had forgotten my bag.

renifler *VERB* [1]
to sniff

le **renne** *MASC NOUN*
reindeer

renommé *MASC ADJECTIVE*, **renommée** *FEM*
famous

renoncer *VERB* [61]

1 **to give up**
C'est trop difficile, je renonce! It's too
difficult, I give up!

2 renoncer à quelque chose to give
something up
Nous avons reconcé à notre projet de
visiter le Japon. We gave up our plans to
visit Japan.

renouveler *VERB* [18]
to renew *(a passport, a subscription)*

rénover *VERB* [1]

1 **to renovate** *(a house)*

2 **to restore** *(furniture)*

ℓ le **renseignement** *MASC NOUN*

1 un renseignement a piece of information
un renseignement utile a useful piece of
information

2 des renseignements information
Je cherche des renseignements. I'm looking
for information.
On va demander des renseignements
au bureau de tourisme. We'll ask for
information at the tourist office.
Adressez-vous aux renseignements! Ask at
the information desk!

3 *(for phone numbers)* les renseignements
directory enquiries

renseigner *VERB* [1]
renseigner quelqu'un to give somebody
information
La brochure vous renseigne sur les
horaires. The brochure gives you timetable
information.
être bien renseigné sur quelque chose
to be well-informed about something

se **renseigner** *REFLEXIVE VERB* ⊙
to find out
Je vais me renseigner au bureau de
tourisme. I'm going to find out at the
tourist office.

rentable *MASC & FEM ADJECTIVE*
profitable

ℓ la **rentrée** *FEM NOUN*
la rentrée (des classes) the start of the new
school year

ℓ **rentrer** *VERB* ⊙ [1]

1 ⊙ **to get home**
Il est tard, je rentre. It's late, I'm going
home.
Maman rentre à dix-huit heures. Mum will
be home at six.

2 ⊙ **to get back**
Ils rentrent de Paris jeudi. They'll be back
from Paris on Thursday.
On rentre le 6 septembre. We're going
back to school on 6 September.

3 ⊙ **to come in**
Rentrez! Do go in!

4 ⊙ rentrer dans quelque chose to go into
something
Rentre dans mon bureau! Go into my office!
Elles sont rentrées dans un magasin.
They've gone into a shop.

5 ⊙ rentrer dans quelque chose to crash into
something
La voiture est rentrée dans un mur. The car
crashed into a wall.

6 ⊙ **to get into**
Il ne rentre plus dans son pantalon. He
can't get into his trousers any more.

7 rentrer quelque chose to bring something
in *(from outside)*
Rentre les chaises, il pleut! Bring the chairs
in, it's raining!
Papa a rentré la voiture au garage. Dad put
the car in the garage.

WORD TIP When you say what you bring in etc,
use avoir in the perfect tense.

renverser *VERB* [1]

1 **to knock over** *(a glass, a vase)*

2 être renversé par une voiture to be
knocked down by a car
Antoine a été renversé par une voiture.
Antoine was knocked down by a car.

3 **to spill** *(your drink)*

renvoyer *VERB* [40]

1 **to send back**
Je renvoie le colis. I'm sending the parcel
back.
On m'a renvoyé à l'hôpital. They sent me
back to hospital.

ℓ **indicates key words**

2 to throw back (a ball)
3 to dismiss (an employee)

la **réouverture** FEM NOUN
reopening

répandu MASC ADJECTIVE, **répandue** FEM
widespread

la **réparation** FEM NOUN
repair

réparer VERB [1]
to repair
Je fais réparer ma moto. I'm having my
motorbike repaired.

repartir VERB [58]
1 to go off again
Les enfants sont déjà repartis. The children
have already gone off again.
2 to go again
Je suis reparti chez moi. I went home again.
3 repartir à zéro to start from scratch
Ils ont déménagé en Corse et sont repartis
à zéro. They moved to Corsica and started
from scratch.

répartir VERB ⊙ [2]
to share out (tasks, roles)

♫ le **repas** MASC NOUN
meal
à l'heure des repas at mealtimes
le repas de midi lunch
le repas du soir the evening meal
le repas de Noël the Christmas dinner
le repas de noces the wedding banquet

le **repassage** MASC NOUN
ironing

repasser VERB [1]
1 to drop in again
Il va repasser demain. He'll drop in again
tomorrow.
2 to iron
une planche à repasser an ironing board
3 to resit (an exam)
4 to replay (a video)

repeindre VERB [60]
to repaint

le **repère** MASC NOUN
landmark

repérer VERB [24]
1 (informal) **to spot** (a mistake)
2 to locate (a place)

le **répertoire** MASC NOUN
notebook (with a thumb index)
un répertoire d'adresses an address book

♫ **répéter** VERB [24]
1 to repeat

Pourriez-vous répéter, s'il vous plaît? Could
you repeat please?
2 to rehearse (a play)
On répète le vendredi soir. We rehearse on
Friday evenings.
3 to practise (a piece of music)

se **répéter** REFLEXIVE VERB ⊙
1 to repeat yourself
2 to happen again
Espérons que cela ne se répétera pas. Let's
hope it doesn't happen again.

la **répétition** FEM NOUN
1 rehearsal
2 repetition
• la répétition générale
dress rehearsal

replier VERB [1]
to fold up (a map, a brochure)

le **répondeur** MASC NOUN
answering machine

♫ **répondre** VERB [3]
1 to answer
Léa n'a pas répondu. Léa didn't answer.
2 répondre à quelqu'un to answer somebody
Il m'a parlé mais je ne lui ai pas répondu.
He spoke to me but I didn't answer him.
3 répondre à quelque chose to answer
something
Elle a répondu à ma question. She
answered my question.
Je vais répondre à sa lettre. I'm going to
reply to her letter.
4 to answer back

♫ la **réponse** FEM NOUN
answer
la bonne réponse the right answer
en réponse à ta question in answer to your
question

le **reportage** MASC NOUN
1 report
un reportage sur la drogue a report on
drugs
2 (news) **story**

le **reporter** MASC NOUN ▸SEE **reporter** VERB
reporter
une femme reporter a woman reporter

reporter VERB [1]
▸SEE **reporter** NOUN
to postpone
On a reporté le match à jeudi. The match
has been postponed until Thursday.

WORD TIP reporter does not mean to report
in English; for the meaning of to report ▸SEE
signaler.

⊙ means the verb takes être to form the perfect

FRENCH—ENGLISH

le **repos** *MASC NOUN*
rest
dix jours de repos ten days' rest

ℓ **reposer** *VERB* [1]
reposer quelque chose to put something
back down
Elle a reposé l'assiette sur la table. She put
the plate back down on the table.

se **reposer** *REFLEXIVE VERB* ◔
to have a rest
J'ai besoin de me reposer. I need a rest.
Repose-toi bien! Have a good rest!

repousser *VERB* [1]
1 to grow back
2 to push back *(a heavy object, a crowd)*
3 to postpone *(a match)*

reprendre *VERB* [64]
1 to have some more *(food, drink)*
2 to take back
Je reprends mes CD. I'm taking back my
CDs.
3 to start again
L'école reprend en septembre. School
starts again in September.
4 reprendre le travail to go back to work
Ils reprennent le travail lundi. They go back
to work on Monday.
5 reprendre la route to set off again

le **représentant** *MASC NOUN*, la
représentante *FEM*
sales rep

la **représentation** *FEM NOUN*
performance *(of a play)*
'Prochaine représentation à 20 heures'
'Next performance 8 p.m.'

représenter *VERB* [1]
1 to depict *(a scene, a landscape)*
2 to represent *(a team, a company)*

réprimer *VERB* [1]
to suppress

la **reprise** *FEM NOUN*
1 resumption *(of work, discussions)*
2 rerun *(of a play, a film)*
3 repeat *(of a broadcast)*
4 à plusieurs reprises on several occasions

le **reproche** *MASC NOUN*
criticism
Il m'a fait des reproches. He criticized me.

reprocher *VERB* [1]
1 to criticize *(people)*
Elle lui a reproché sa paresse. She criticized
him for his laziness.
reprocher à quelqu'un de faire quelque
chose to criticize somebody for doing
something

Il a reproché à son fils de ne pas travailler.
He criticized his son for not working.
2 to criticize *(things)*
Que reproches-tu à ma lettre? What's
wrong with my letter?

se **reprocher** *REFLEXIVE VERB* ◔
to blame yourself

la **reproduction** *FEM NOUN*
reproduction

reproduire *VERB* [26]
1 to reproduce
2 to breed *(animals)*

se **reproduire** *REFLEXIVE VERB* ◔
1 to happen again
2 to breed

républicain *MASC ADJECTIVE*, **républicaine** *FEM*
republican

la **république** *FEM NOUN*
republic
la République française the French Republic

🔵 **RÉPUBLIQUE**

La France est une république et a un président,
pas de roi ou reine.

répugnant *MASC ADJECTIVE*, **répugnante** *FEM*
revolting

la **réputation** *FEM NOUN*
reputation

le **requin** *MASC NOUN*
shark

le **RER** *MASC NOUN*
(= Réseau express régional) (the suburban
rail and metro network serving Paris)

le **réseau** *MASC NOUN*, les **réseaux** *PLURAL*
network
• le réseau social
social network

ℓ la **réservation** *FEM NOUN*
reservation

la **réserve** *FEM NOUN*
1 stock
J'ai deux bouteilles de Coca en réserve. I've
put aside two bottles of Coke.
2 reserve *(for birds, animals)*
une réserve ornithologique a bird
sanctuary

réservé *MASC ADJECTIVE*, **réservée** *FEM*
reserved

ℓ **réserver** *VERB* [1]
1 to reserve, to book
J'ai réservé deux places pour ce soir. I've
booked two seats for this evening.
2 to put aside *(some food for somebody)*
3 to keep *(for a special occasion)*

A B C D E F G H I J K L M N O P Q R S T U V W X Y Z

283

Elle réserve le grand vin pour Noël. She's keeping the really good wine for Christmas.
4 **to have in store**
Je lui réserve une surprise. I've got a surprise in store for her.

le **réservoir** MASC NOUN
1 **tank**
2 **reservoir**
• le réservoir à essence
petrol tank

la **résidence** FEM NOUN
1 **residence**
une résidence secondaire a holiday home
2 **apartment block**
• la résidence universitaire
hall of residence

le **résident** MASC NOUN, la **résidente** FEM
resident

résidentiel MASC ADJECTIVE, **résidentielle** FEM
residential

résistant MASC ADJECTIVE, **résistante** FEM ▶SEE
résistant NOUN
tough

le **résistant** MASC NOUN, la **résistante** FEM ▶SEE
résistant ADJECTIVE
Resistance fighter (in France during World War II)

résister VERB [1]
to resist
Je n'ai pas pu résister alors je l'ai acheté. I couldn't resist so I bought it.
Il faut résister aux tyrans. You've got to stand up to bullies.
résister à quelque chose to withstand something (a force, an explosion, a storm)
Les arbres n'ont pas résisté à la tempête. The trees couldn't withstand the storm.

résolu MASC ADJECTIVE, **résolue** FEM
1 **determined**
2 **resolved** (sorted out)

résoudre VERB [67]
to solve (a problem)

se **résoudre** REFLEXIVE VERB ◯
se résoudre à faire quelque chose to make up your mind to do something

le **respect** MASC NOUN
respect

respecter VERB [1]
to respect

respectueux MASC ADJECTIVE, **respectueuse** FEM
respectful

la **respiration** FEM NOUN
breathing

retenir sa respiration to hold your breath

respirer VERB [1]
to breathe
Respirez! Breathe in!
Respirez bien fort! Take a deep breath!

la **responsabilité** FEM NOUN
responsibility

responsable MASC & FEM ADJECTIVE ▶SEE
responsable NOUN
responsible
être responsable de quelque chose to be responsible for something
Il est responsable de l'incendie. He's responsible for the fire.

le & la **responsable** MASC & FEM NOUN ▶SEE
responsable ADJECTIVE
1 **person in charge**
Je voudrais parler au responsable. I'd like to speak to the person in charge.
2 **person responsible**
les responsables de la catastrophe those responsible for the disaster
• le responsable de classe
class rep

la **ressemblance** FEM NOUN
1 **likeness**
un portrait d'une grande ressemblance a very good likeness
2 **similarity**

ressembler VERB [1]
ressembler à quelqu'un to look like somebody
Elle ressemble beaucoup à sa mère. She looks very like her mother.
Cela ressemble à du bois. It looks like wood.

se **ressembler** REFLEXIVE VERB ◯
to be alike

le **ressentiment** MASC NOUN
resentment

resserrer VERB [1]
to tighten (a knot, a screw)

se **resserrer** REFLEXIVE VERB ◯
to move closer together
Resserrez-vous un peu! Squeeze up a bit!

resservir VERB [58]
1 **to give another helping**
2 **to be used again**
Ça peut toujours resservir! It can always be used again!

se **resservir** REFLEXIVE VERB ◯
to help yourself to more

le **ressort** MASC NOUN
spring (in a bed, a chair)

◯ means the verb takes être to form the perfect

ressortir *VERB* ⊘ [58]
  to go out again

la **ressource** *FEM NOUN*
1 **resource**
  des ressources énergétiques **energy resources**
2 **les ressources resources** *(income)*

le **restaurant** *MASC NOUN*
  restaurant
  manger au restaurant **to go out for a meal**
• le restaurant rapide
  fast-food restaurant

la **restauration** *FEM NOUN*
1 **catering**
2 **restoration**
• la restauration rapide
  fast-food industry

restaurer *VERB* [1]
  to restore

le **reste** *MASC NOUN*
1 **le reste the rest**
  le reste du temps **the rest of the time**
2 **les restes the leftovers**
  les restes du poulet **the leftover chicken**

ℓ **rester** *VERB* ⊘ [1]
1 **to stay**
  Reste ici, je reviens! **Stay here, I'll be back!**
  Camille est restée à la maison. **Camille stayed at home.**
2 **to remain**
3 **rester debout to remain standing**
  Je préfère rester debout. **I prefer to stand.**
4 **rester assis to remain seated**
  Elle est restée assise toute la journée. **She's been sitting down all day.**
  Reste tranquille! **Keep still!**
  Hier, je suis resté sans manger. **I didn't have anything to eat yesterday.**
5 **to be left**
  Il reste du fromage. **There's some cheese left.**
  Il nous reste combien d'argent? **How much money have we got left?**
  Il ne reste pas beaucoup à faire. **There's not much left to do.**

la **restriction** *FEM NOUN*
  restriction

ℓ le **résultat** *MASC NOUN*
  result
  les résultats des examens **the exam results**
  Il a de bons résultats à l'école. **He gets good marks at school.**

le **résumé** *MASC NOUN*
  summary
  en résumé **to sum up**

résumer *VERB* [1]
  to sum up

rétablir *VERB* [2]
  to restore
se **rétablir** *REFLEXIVE VERB* ⊘
  to recover *(after an illness)*

retaper *VERB* [1]
  to do up *(a house)*

ℓ le **retard** *MASC NOUN*
1 **delay**
  un retard d'une heure sur notre vol **an hour's delay on our flight**
  sans retard **without delay**
2 **avoir du retard to be late**
  Excusez mon retard! **I'm sorry I'm late!**
  Ils sont arrivés avec trois heures de retard. **They arrived three hours late.**
3 **être en retard to be late**
  Il est en retard pour rendre ses devoirs. **He's late handing in his homework.**

retarder *VERB* [1]
1 **to hold up**
  Le mauvais temps nous a retardés. **The bad weather held us up.**
  être retardé **to be delayed**
  Le train était retardé. **The train was delayed.**
2 **to put off**
  Il a retardé son départ. **He put off his departure.**
3 **to be slow**
  Je retarde de cinq minutes. **My watch is five minutes slow.**

retenir *VERB* [77]
1 **to keep**
  Je ne vous retiendrai pas longtemps. **I won't keep you long.**
2 **to hold up** *(to delay)*
  Elle a été retenue au bureau. **She was held up at the office.**
3 **retenir son souffle to hold your breath**
4 **to book** *(seats)*
5 **to remember**
  Je ne retiens jamais leur adresse. **I can never remember their address.**
se **retenir** *REFLEXIVE VERB* ⊘
  to stop yourself
  Je n'ai pas pu me retenir de pleurer. **I couldn't stop myself from crying.**

la **retenue** *FEM NOUN*
  detention
  être en retenue **to be in detention**

la **réticence** *FEM NOUN*
  reluctance

retirer *VERB* [1]
1 **to take off**

D'abord, je retire ma veste. I'm taking my jacket off first.

2 to take out
Attends, je vais retirer les arêtes! Wait, I'll take out the bones!
retirer de l'argent to take money out (of a bank account)
J'ai retiré 300 euros. I took out 300 euros.

3 to take away
Ils lui ont retiré son permis. They took his licence away from him.

le **retour** MASC NOUN
1 return
un billet aller-retour a return ticket
dès mon retour as soon as I get back

2 être de retour to be back
Elle sera de retour vers onze heures. She'll be back about eleven.

ℓ **retourner** VERB [1]
1 ◯ to go back
Elle est retournée à l'école. She went back to school.

2 to turn over (a steak, a pancake)

> **WORD TIP** When you say what you **turn over** etc, use avoir in the perfect tense.

la **retraite** FEM NOUN
retirement
Mon oncle est à la retraite. My uncle is retired.
prendre sa retraite to retire
une maison de retraite an old people's home

le **retraité** MASC NOUN, la **retraitée** FEM
pensioner

rétrécir VERB [2]
to shrink

retrousser VERB [1]
1 to roll up (your sleeves)
2 to hitch up (your skirt)

retrouver VERB [1]
1 to find
As-tu retrouvé ton sac? Did you find your bag?

2 to meet (friends)
Je te retrouve à la sortie. I'll meet you at the exit.

se **retrouver** REFLEXIVE VERB ◯
1 to meet
On se retrouve devant la patinoire? Shall we meet outside the ice rink?
Nous nous retrouverons à Noël. We'll see each other again at Christmas.

2 to end up
On s'est retrouvé chez Karim. We ended up at Karim's place.

3 to find your way around

Je n'arrive jamais à me retrouver dans Londres. I can never find my way around London.

le **rétroviseur** MASC NOUN
rearview mirror

ℓ la **réunion** FEM NOUN
1 meeting
Elle est en réunion. She's in a meeting.
La réunion aura lieu à 20 h 30. The meeting will take place at 8.30 p.m.

2 gathering
On fait une réunion de famille. We're having a family gathering.

3 reunion

se **réunir** REFLEXIVE VERB ◯ [2]
to meet
Nous nous réunissons entre amis. We're having a get-together with friends.

réussi MASC ADJECTIVE, **réussie** FEM
successful
une expérience réussie a successful experiment
Ta soirée était très réussie. Your party was a success.

réussir VERB [2]
1 to succeed
J'espère qu'elle va réussir. I hope she'll succeed.

2 to pass
réussir un examen to pass an exam

3 to be successful

4 réussir à faire quelque chose to manage to do something
J'ai réussi à les persuader. I managed to persuade them.

5 réussir à quelqu'un to do somebody good (food, holiday, rest)

la **réussite** FEM NOUN
success

réutilisable MASC & FEM ADJECTIVE
reusable

la **revanche** FEM NOUN
1 return match
2 revenge
prendra sa revanche sur quelqu'un to get your revenge on somebody
3 en revanche on the other hand
Je déteste les légumes, en revanche j'adore les fruits. I hate vegetables, but I love fruit.

le **rêve** MASC NOUN
dream
J'ai fait un rêve. I had a dream.
la moto de mes rêves my dream motorbike
Mon rêve, c'est d'avoir un poney. My dream is to have a pony.

◯ means the verb takes être to form the perfect

le **réveil** *MASC NOUN*
  alarm clock

ℙ **réveiller** *VERB* [1]
  réveiller quelqu'un to wake somebody up
  Elle m'a réveillé à sept heures. She woke
  me at seven.
  Nicolas est réveillé. Nicolas is awake.

se **réveiller** *REFLEXIVE VERB* ⊘
  to wake up
  D'habitude, je me réveille à sept heures. I
  usually wake up at seven.

le **réveillon** *MASC NOUN*
  le réveillon du Nouvel An the New Year's
  Eve celebrations

⊙ **RÉVEILLON**

Un réveillon, c'est un repas de fête, tard le
soir. Les Français font deux réveillons : le 24
décembre pour Noël et le 31 décembre pour le
Nouvel An.

réveillonner *VERB* [1]
1 **to celebrate Christmas Eve**
2 **to see the New Year in**

le **revenant** *MASC NOUN*, la **revenante** *FEM*
  ghost

revendre *VERB* [3]
  to sell

revenir *VERB* ⊘ [81]
1 **to come back**
   Elles sont revenues très tard. They came
   back very late.
   Je reviens de Montréal le 5 mai. I'm back
   from Montréal on 5 May.
   Je reviens tout de suite. I'll be right back.
2 **to come to**
   Ça revient à quinze euros. That comes to
   fifteen euros.
3 revenir de quelque chose to get over
   something
   Elle est revenue de ses frayeurs. She got
   over her fright.
   Je n'en reviens pas! I can't get over it!
4 faire revenir to brown (onions, meat)

le **revenu** *MASC NOUN*
  income

rêver *VERB* [1]
1 **to dream**
   Elle rêve de devenir pilote. She dreams of
   becoming a pilot.
2 **to daydream**

le **réverbère** *MASC NOUN*
  street lamp

le **revers** *MASC NOUN*
1 **back**
   d'un revers de la main with the back of

  your hand
  le revers de la médaille the other side of
  the coin
2 **lapel** (on a jacket)
3 **turn-up** (on trousers)
4 **cuff** (on a sleeve)
5 **backhand** (in tennis)

réviser *VERB* [1]
1 **to revise** (for an exam)
2 **to service** (a car, a machine)

la **révision** *FEM NOUN*
1 **revision** (for exams)
2 **service** (for a car)

revoir *VERB* [13]
1 **to see again**
   Et nous ne l'avons jamais revue. And we
   never saw her again.
2 **to revise** (for an exam)
3 **to go over** (a lesson)
   Cette leçon est à revoir. You need to go
   over this lesson again.
4 au revoir goodbye

la **révolte** *FEM NOUN*
1 **revolt**
2 **rebellion**

révolter *VERB* [1]
  to appal

se **révolter** *REFLEXIVE VERB* ⊘
  to rebel

la **révolution** *FEM NOUN*
  revolution

révolutionner *VERB* [1]
  to revolutionize

le **revolver** *MASC NOUN*
  revolver

revouloir *VERB* [14]
  (informal) **to have a second helping of**

la **revue** *FEM NOUN*
  magazine
  une revue scientifique a scientific journal

ℙ le **rez-de-chaussée** *INVARIABLE MASC NOUN*
  ground floor
  La réception est au rez-de-chaussée.
  Reception is on the ground floor.

RF *FEM NOUN*
  (= République française) **French Republic**

se **rhabiller** *VERB REFLEXIVE* ⊘ [1]
  to put your clothes on again

le **Rhin** *MASC NOUN*
  le Rhin the Rhine (the river)

le **rhinocéros** *MASC NOUN*
  rhinoceros

la **rhubarbe** *FEM NOUN*
rhubarb

le **rhum** *MASC NOUN*
rum

♪ le **rhume** *MASC NOUN*
cold
J'ai attrapé un rhume. I've caught a cold.
• le rhume de cerveau
head cold
• le rhume des foins
hay fever

ri *VERB* ▸ SEE **rire**

ricaner *VERB* [1]
to snigger

♪ **riche** *MASC & FEM ADJECTIVE*
1 well-off, rich
Sa famille est très riche. Her family is very rich.
Nous ne sommes pas très riches. We're not very well-off.
2 rich (food)
C'est riche en vitamines. It's rich in vitamins.

la **richesse** *FEM NOUN*
1 wealth
2 les richesses naturelles natural resources

la **ride** *FEM NOUN*
wrinkle (on your skin)

♪ le **rideau** *MASC NOUN*, les **rideaux** *PLURAL*
curtain

ridicule *MASC & FEM ADJECTIVE*
ridiculous
C'est totalement ridicule! That's completely ridiculous!
Tu as l'air ridicule. You look silly.

♪ un **rien** *MASC NOUN* ▸ SEE **rien** *PRONOUN*
little thing
Elle se met à hurler pour un rien. She starts shouting at the slightest thing.
en un rien de temps in next to no time

♪ **rien** *PRONOUN* ▸ SEE **rien** *NOUN*
1 nothing
Ce n'est rien. It's nothing.
Il ne reste plus rien. There's nothing left.
Rien n'a changé. Nothing's changed.
Je n'ai rien vu. I didn't see anything.
'Qu'est-ce qu'elle a dit?' – 'Rien.' 'What did she say?' – 'Nothing.'
Il n'y a rien d'autre à manger. There's nothing else to eat.
2 rien que just
'Que reste-t-il à faire?' – 'Rien que la vaisselle.' 'What's left to do?' – 'Just the washing-up.'
3 (in expressions) rien du tout nothing at all

rien de bon nothing good
'Merci.' – 'De rien.' 'Thank you.' – 'You're welcome.'
Ça ne fait rien. It doesn't matter.
4 Je n'y arrive pas, il n'y a rien à faire! I can't do it, it's no good!

WORD TIP Remember to use ne before rien in a sentence that contains a verb: Ce n'est rien.
▸ SEE **ne**

rigoler *VERB* [1] (informal)
1 to laugh
Elle rigole tout le temps. She's always laughing.
2 to have a good time
Nous avons bien rigolé. We had a great time.
3 to be joking

rigolo *MASC ADJECTIVE*, **rigolote** *FEM* (informal) funny

rigoureux *MASC ADJECTIVE*, **rigoureuse** *FEM*
1 rigorous (checks)
2 strict (discipline)
3 harsh (winter, climate)

les **rillettes** *PLURAL FEM NOUN*
les rillettes de porc potted pork

la **rime** *FEM NOUN*
rhyme

rimer *VERB* [1]
to rhyme

rincer *VERB* [61]
to rinse

se **rincer** *REFLEXIVE VERB* ◯
to rinse
se rincer les cheveux to rinse your hair

♪ le **rire** *MASC NOUN* ▸ SEE **rire** *VERB*
laughter
un rire a laugh
J'ai entendu des rires. I heard laughter.

♪ **rire** *VERB* [68]
▸ SEE **rire** *NOUN*
1 to laugh
J'ai bien ri. I laughed a lot.
Louis nous fait rire. Louis makes us laugh.
Il n'y a pas de quoi rire. It's not funny.
2 to have fun
On va bien rire. We're going to have a lot of fun.
3 to joke
C'était pour rire. It was meant as a joke.

le **risque** *MASC NOUN*
risk
J'ai pris un risque. I took a risk.
un risque d'incendie a fire hazard

◯ means the verb takes être to form the perfect

risqué *MASC ADJECTIVE*, **risquée** *FEM*
  risky

risquer *VERB* [1]
1 **to risk** *(your life)*
  Vas-y, tu ne risques rien! Go ahead, it's
  quite safe!
2 Tu risques de te brûler. You might burn
  yourself.

le **rivage** *MASC NOUN*
  shore

le **rival** *MASC NOUN*, la **rivale** *FEM* les **rivaux**
MASC PL les **rivales** *FEM PL*
  rival

la **rive** *FEM NOUN*
1 **bank** *(of a river)*
  la Rive gauche the Left Bank *(With the Seine
  in Paris and other rivers, the left bank is the
  side of the river as you face downstream.)*
2 **shore** *(by the sea)*

ℓ la **rivière** *FEM NOUN*
  river
  Elle se baigne dans la rivière. She swims in
  the river.

ℓ le **riz** *MASC NOUN*
  rice
  du gâteau de riz rice pudding
  • le riz cantonais
    egg fried rice
  • le riz au lait
    rice pudding

la **RN** *FEM NOUN*
  (= route nationale) **A road**

ℓ la **robe** *FEM NOUN*
  dress
  une robe d'été a summer dress
  • la robe de chambre
    dressing gown
  • la robe de mariée
    wedding dress
  • la robe du soir
    evening dress

ℓ le **robinet** *MASC NOUN*
  tap
  l'eau du robinet tap water
  ouvrir le robinet to turn the tap on
  fermer le robinet to turn the tap off

le **robot** *MASC NOUN*
  robot
  • le robot ménager
    food processor

la **roche** *FEM NOUN*
  rock

le **rocher** *MASC NOUN*
  rock *(large boulder)*

le **rock** *MASC NOUN*
  rock *(music)*

rôder *VERB* [1]
  to prowl

les **rognons** *PLURAL MASC NOUN*
  kidneys *(for cooking)*

le **roi** *MASC NOUN*
  king
  le roi Charles King Charles
  la fête des Rois Twelfth Night
  les Rois mages the Three Wise Men

le **rôle** *MASC NOUN*
  role

le **roller** *MASC NOUN*
1 **roller-skate**
2 **roller-skating**
  faire du roller to go roller-skating

les **ROM**
  *(= régions d'outre-mer) (French overseas
  regions)*

romain *MASC ADJECTIVE*, **romaine** *FEM*
  Roman

ℓ le **roman** *MASC NOUN*
  novel
  • le roman policier
    detective story
  • le roman d'amour
    love story

le **romancier** *MASC NOUN*, la **romancière** *FEM*
  novelist

romantique *MASC & FEM ADJECTIVE*
  romantic

le **romarin** *MASC NOUN*
  rosemary

rompre *VERB* [69]
  to split up *(couples, bands)*
  rompre avec quelqu'un to break up with
  somebody
  Anne a rompu avec son copain. Anne's
  broken up with her boyfriend.

la **ronce** *FEM NOUN*
  bramble

rond *MASC ADJECTIVE*, **ronde** *FEM* ▸ SEE **rond** *NOUN*
1 **round** *(shape, table)*
2 **plump** *(person)*

ℓ le **rond** *MASC NOUN* ▸ SEE **rond** *ADJECTIVE*
  circle
  s'asseoir en rond to sit in a circle

la **rondelle** *FEM NOUN*
1 **slice** *(of salami, cucumber, lemon)*
2 **washer** *(for a tap, a screw)*

ℓ indicates key words

♪ le **rond-point** MASC NOUN, les **ronds-points**
PLURAL
roundabout
Au rond-point, prenez à gauche! Turn left
at the roundabout!

ronfler VERB [1]
to snore

ronger VERB [52]
to gnaw

se **ronger** REFLEXIVE VERB ●
se ronger les ongles to bite your nails

ronronner VERB [1]
to purr

le **rosbif** MASC NOUN
roast beef

♪ **rose** MASC & FEM ADJECTIVE ▸ SEE **rose** NOUN
pink
une chemise rose pâle a pale pink shirt

♪ la **rose** FEM NOUN ▸ SEE **rose** ADJECTIVE
rose

le **rosé** MASC NOUN
rosé (wine)

la **rosée** FEM NOUN
dew

le **rosier** MASC NOUN
rosebush

le **rossignol** MASC NOUN
nightingale

♪ le **rôti** MASC NOUN
1 roast
du rôti de bœuf roast beef
2 joint (of pork, beef)

rôtir VERB [2]
to roast
le poulet rôti roast chicken

roucouler VERB [1]
to coo

la **roue** FEM NOUN
1 wheel
la roue de secours the spare wheel
2 cartwheel (in gymnastics)

♪ **rouge** MASC & FEM ADJECTIVE ▸ SEE **rouge** NOUN
red
tes chaussettes rouges your red socks
le feu rouge the red light

♪ le **rouge** MASC NOUN ▸ SEE **rouge** ADJECTIVE
1 red
Le rouge ne me va pas. Red doesn't suit me.
2 red traffic light
Il est passé au rouge. He jumped the lights.
Le feu est passé au rouge. The light
changed to red.

3 red wine
• le rouge-gorge
robin
• le rouge à lèvres
lipstick

la **rougeur** FEM NOUN
redness

rougir VERB [2]
to blush

la **rouille** FEM NOUN
rust

rouillé MASC ADJECTIVE, **rouillée** FEM
rusty

rouiller VERB [1]
to go rusty

la **roulade** FEM NOUN
roll (in sports)

roulant MASC ADJECTIVE, **roulante** FEM
un fauteuil roulant a wheelchair

le **rouleau** MASC NOUN, les **rouleaux** PLURAL
roll
un rouleau d'essuie-tout a roll of kitchen
towel
• le rouleau à pâtisserie
rolling pin

♪ **rouler** VERB [1]
1 to go
Le train roule très vite. The train's going
very fast.
2 to drive
Nous avons roulé toute la nuit. We drove
all night.
En France on roule à droite. In France
people drive on the right.
3 to roll
Le ballon a roulé dans le caniveau. The ball
rolled into the gutter.
4 to roll up (a carpet, a sleeping bag, a
newspaper)
5 (informal) to cheat

la **Roumanie** FEM NOUN
Romania
vivre en Roumanie to live in Romania
aller en Roumanie to go to Romania

rousse FEM ADJECTIVE ▸ SEE **roux**

♪ la **route** FEM NOUN
1 road
une grande route a main road
la route de Caen the road to Caen
un accident de la route a road accident
C'est à trois heures de route d'ici. It's three
hours' drive from here.
2 route
changer de route to change your route

● means the verb takes être to form the perfect

3 way
être sur la bonne route to be heading the right way
prendre une autre route to go a different way
La route est longue. It's a long way.
en route, en cours de route on the way *(during a journey)*
Nous sommes en route pour Nice. We're on our way to Nice.
se mettre en route to set off
Il est l'heure de se mettre en route. It's time to set off.
Bonne route! Safe journey!
- la route à quatre voies
  dual carriageway
- la route départementale
  secondary road, B road
- la route nationale
  A road

routier MASC ADJECTIVE, **routière** FEM ▸SEE **routier** NOUN
road
le transport routier road transport

le **routier** MASC NOUN ▸SEE **routier** ADJECTIVE
lorry driver

la **routine** FEM NOUN
routine

ℰ **roux** MASC ADJECTIVE, **rousse** FEM
ginger
un chat roux a ginger cat
un petit garçon roux a little red-haired boy

royal MASC ADJECTIVE, **royale** FEM, **royaux** MASC PL, **royales** FEM PL
royal

le **royaume** MASC NOUN
kingdom

le **Royaume-Uni** MASC NOUN
United Kingdom

WORD TIP Countries and regions in French take le, la or les.

le **ruban** MASC NOUN
ribbon
- le ruban adhésif
  sticky tape

la **rubéole** FEM NOUN
German measles

la **ruche** FEM NOUN
beehive

rudement ADVERB
(informal) **really**
rudement bon really tasty

ℰ la **rue** FEM NOUN
street

une rue piétonne a pedestrian street

le **rugby** MASC NOUN
rugby
jouer au rugby to play rugby

le **rugbyman** MASC, les **rugbymen** PL
rugby player

la **ruine** FEM NOUN
ruin
un château en ruine a ruined castle

ruiner VERB [1]
to ruin

le **ruisseau** MASC NOUN, les **ruisseaux** PL
stream

la **rumeur** FEM NOUN
rumour

le **rumsteck** MASC NOUN
rump steak

la **rupture** FEM NOUN
break-up *(of a relationship)*

rural MASC ADJECTIVE, **rurale** FEM, **ruraux** MASC PL, **rurales** FEM PL
country
la vie rurale country life

la **ruse** FEM NOUN
trick
les ruses du métier the tricks of the trade

rusé MASC ADJECTIVE, **rusée** FEM
crafty

russe MASC & FEM ADJECTIVE ▸SEE **Russe**
Russian
un avion russe a Russian plane

un **Russe** MASC NOUN, une **Russe** FEM ▸SEE **russe**
1 Russian *(person)*
les Russes the Russians
2 Russian *(the language)*
Je parle russe. I speak Russian.

la **Russie** FEM NOUN
Russia
Moscou est en Russie. Moscow is in Russia.
Cet été, je pars en Russie. This summer I'm going to Russia.

le **rythme** MASC NOUN
1 rhythm
un rythme lent a slow rhythm
2 pace
travailler à son propre rythme to work at your own pace

ℰ indicates key words

Ss

s' *ABBREVIATION:* **se** or **si**
▸ SEE **se, si**

WORD TIP se becomes s' before a word beginning with a, e, i, o, u or silent h.

sa *FEM DETERMINER* ▸ SEE **son**

le **sable** *MASC NOUN*
sand

sablé *MASC ADJECTIVE*, **sablée** *FEM* ▸ SEE **sablé** *NOUN*
la pâte sablée shortcrust pastry

le **sablé** *MASC NOUN* ▸ SEE **sablé** *ADJECTIVE*
shortbread biscuit

☞ le **sac** *MASC NOUN*
1 bag
un sac de sucre a bag of sugar
2 sack
un sac de charbon a sack of coal
• le sac à dos
rucksack
• le sac à main
handbag
• le sac de couchage
sleeping bag

le **sachet** *MASC NOUN*
sachet
un sachet de thé a teabag

la **sacoche** *FEM NOUN*
1 bag
2 pannier *(for a bike)*

sacré *MASC ADJECTIVE*, **sacrée** *FEM*
1 *(informal)* un sacré problème a hell of a problem
Il a un sacré culot! He's got a hell of a nerve!
2 sacred

le **sacrifice** *MASC NOUN*
sacrifice

sacrifier *VERB* [1]
to sacrifice

☞ **sage** *MASC & FEM ADJECTIVE*
1 good, well-behaved
Alors les filles, soyez sages! Right, girls! Be good!
2 sensible, wise
Ce n'est pas sage de sortir en ton état. It's not wise to go out in your state.
• la sage-femme
midwife

la **sagesse** *FEM NOUN*
wisdom
une dent de sagesse a wisdom tooth

le **Sagittaire** *MASC NOUN*
Sagittarius
Jean-Marc est Sagittaire. Jean-Marc is a Sagittarius.

WORD TIP Signs of the zodiac do not take an article: un or une.

☞ **saignant** *MASC ADJECTIVE*, **saignante** *FEM*
rare *(beef)*

saigner *VERB* [1]
to bleed
Je saigne du nez. I've got a nosebleed.

sain *MASC ADJECTIVE*, **saine** *FEM*
healthy
une alimentation saine a healthy diet

saint *MASC ADJECTIVE*, **sainte** *FEM* ▸ SEE **saint** *NOUN*
holy
le Saint-Esprit the Holy Spirit
le vendredi saint Good Friday

le **saint** *MASC NOUN*, la **sainte** *FEM* ▸ SEE **saint** *ADJECTIVE*
saint

la **Saint-Jean** *FEM NOUN*
Midsummer's Day *(June 24th)*

la **Saint-Sylvestre** *FEM NOUN*
New Year's Eve

la **Saint-Valentin** *FEM NOUN*
St Valentine's Day

sais *VERB* ▸ SEE **savoir**

saisir *VERB* [2]
1 to grab
2 saisir l'occasion to seize the opportunity
3 to understand
Je n'ai pas tout à fait saisi ... I didn't completely understand ...
4 to catch, to hear
Je n'ai pas saisi votre nom. I didn't catch your name.

☞ la **saison** *FEM NOUN*
season
la haute saison the high season

sait *VERB* ▸ SEE **savoir**

la **salade** *FEM NOUN*
1 lettuce
2 salad
une salade de fruits a fruit salad

le **salaire** *MASC NOUN*
salary, wages

le **salami** *MASC NOUN*
salami

le **salarié** *MASC NOUN*, la **salariée** *FEM*
salaried employee

☞ means the verb takes être to form the perfect

ℐ **sale** *MASC & FEM ADJECTIVE*
1 **dirty** *(when after a noun)*
avoir les mains sales to have dirty hands
2 *(informal)* **horrible** *(when before a noun)*
Quel sale temps! What horrible weather!

ℐ **salé** *MASC ADJECTIVE*, **salée** *FEM*
1 **salty**
2 **savoury**
des petits gâteaux salés savoury biscuits

la **saleté** *FEM NOUN*
dirt

salir *VERB* [2]
salir quelque chose to get something dirty
Tu vas salir ta robe. You'll get your dress
dirty.

se **salir** *REFLEXIVE VERB* ◐
to get dirty
Les enfants se sont salis. The children got
dirty.

la **salive** *FEM NOUN*
saliva

ℐ la **salle** *FEM NOUN*
1 **dining-room** *(in a restaurant)*
2 **hall**
3 **auditorium** *(in a theatre, a cinema)*
• la salle à manger
dining room
• la salle d'attente
waiting room
• la salle d'eau
shower room
• la salle de bain(s)
bathroom
• la salle de classe
classroom
• la salle de jeux
games room
• la salle d'embarquement
departure lounge
• la salle des profs
staffroom
• la salle des sports
sports hall

ℐ le **salon** *MASC NOUN*
1 **sitting room**
dans le salon in the sitting room
2 **living-room suite**
3 **trade fair**
4 **salon**
un salon de coiffure a hair salon

la **salopette** *FEM NOUN*
1 **dungarees**
2 **overalls**

saluer *VERB* [1]
1 **to say hello to**
Je l'ai salué. I said hello to him.

saluer quelqu'un de la main to wave at
somebody
Elle l'a salué de la main. She waved at him.
2 **to say goodbye to**

ℐ **salut** *GREETING*
Hi!

ℐ le **samedi** *MASC NOUN*
1 **Saturday**
samedi dernier last Saturday
samedi prochain next Saturday
Nous sommes samedi aujourd'hui. It's
Saturday today.
2 **on Saturday**
Viens me voir samedi. Come and see me on
Saturday.
À samedi! See you on Saturday!
3 **le samedi on Saturdays**
'Fermé le samedi' 'Closed on Saturdays'
4 **tous les samedis every Saturday**
Tous les samedis, je vais à la patinoire.
Every Saturday I go to the skating rink.

WORD TIP Months of the year and days of the
week start with small letters in French.

le **SAMU** *MASC NOUN*
(= Service d'assistance médicale d'urgence)
ambulance service

la **sandale** *FEM NOUN*
sandal

ℐ le **sandwich** *MASC NOUN*
sandwich
un sandwich au jambon a ham sandwich

la **sandwicherie** *FEM NOUN*
snack bar

ℐ le **sang** *MASC NOUN*
blood
être en sang to be covered in blood
• le sang-froid
calm, composure

le **sanglier** *MASC NOUN*
wild boar

le **sanglot** *MASC NOUN*
sob
éclater en sanglots to burst into tears

la **sanisette**® *FEM NOUN*
automatic public toilet

sanitaire *MASC & FEM ADJECTIVE* ▸ SEE **sanitaire**
NOUN
health
les conditions sanitaires sanitary conditions

le **sanitaire** *MASC NOUN* ▸ SEE **sanitaire** *ADJECTIVE*
les sanitaires the toilet block *(in a campsite)*

ℐ **sans** *PREPOSITION*
without

ℐ indicates key words

un café sans sucre a coffee with no sugar
Ils sont partis sans nous. They left without us.
Avec ou sans glaçons? With or without ice?
sans faire quelque chose without doing something
Il prend mes affaires sans me demander. He takes my things without asking me.
Ne sors pas sans le dire à Papa. Don't go out without telling Dad.

le & la **sans-abri** *MASC & FEM NOUN*
homeless person
les sans-abri the homeless

le & la **sans-emploi** *MASC & FEM NOUN*
unemployed person

ℓ la **santé** *FEM NOUN*
1 **health**
être en bonne santé to be in good health
2 À votre santé! Cheers!

le **sapeur-pompier** *MASC NOUN*
firefighter
les sapeurs-pompiers the fire brigade

le **sapin** *MASC NOUN*
fir tree
un sapin de Noël a Christmas tree

le **sarcasme** *MASC NOUN*
sarcasm

la **sardine** *FEM NOUN*
sardine

ℓ le **satellite** *MASC NOUN*
satellite

le **satin** *MASC NOUN*
satin

la **satisfaction** *FEM NOUN*
satisfaction

satisfaire *VERB* [10]
to satisfy

satisfaisant *MASC ADJECTIVE*, **satisfaisante** *FEM*
1 **satisfactory**
une réponse satisfaisante a satisfactory answer
2 **satisfying**
une expérience très satisfaisante a very satisfying experience

ℓ **satisfait** *MASC ADJECTIVE*, **satisfaite** *FEM*
1 **satisfied**
être satisfait de quelque chose to be satisfied with something
Êtes-vous satisfait de votre repas? Are you satisfied with your meal?
2 avoir l'air satisfait to look pleased

la **sauce** *FEM NOUN*
1 **sauce**

2 **gravy**

ℓ la **saucisse** *FEM NOUN*
sausage

ℓ le **saucisson** *MASC NOUN*
sausage

ℓ **sauf** *PREPOSITION*
1 **except**
tous les jours sauf le lundi every day except Monday
sauf quand il pleut except when it rains
2 **sauf si unless**
C'est tout, sauf s'il y a des questions? That's all, unless there are any questions?
3 **sauf que except that**
Tout va bien, sauf que ta cousine n'est pas encore arrivée. Everything's fine, except that your cousin hasn't arrived yet.

le **saule** *MASC NOUN*
willow

le **saumon** *MASC NOUN*
salmon
du saumon fumé some smoked salmon

saupoudrer *VERB* [1]
to sprinkle

le **saut** *MASC NOUN*
jump
• le saut à la perche
pole vault
• le saut à l'élastique
bungee jumping
• le saut en hauteur
high jump
• le saut en longueur
long jump

ℓ **sauter** *VERB* [1]
1 **to jump**
Elle a sauté dans un taxi. She jumped into a taxi.
sauter quelque chose to jump over something
Pierre a sauté la barrière. Pierre jumped over the gate.
sauter de quelque chose to jump out of something
J'ai sauté du lit. I jumped out of bed.
2 sauter à la corde to skip *(with a rope)*
3 **to skip** *(a class, a page)*
Nous avons sauté trois pages. We've skipped three pages.
4 faire sauter quelque chose to blow something up
Les terroristes ont fait sauter l'avion. The terrorists blew up the plane.

la **sauterelle** *FEM NOUN*
grasshopper

🔵 means the verb takes être to form the perfect

sauvage *MASC & FEM ADJECTIVE*
1 **wild**
   les animaux sauvages wild animals
2 **savage**
3 **unsociable**

sauvegarder *VERB* [1]
1 **to save** *(on a computer)*
   J'ai sauvegardé tous mes fichiers. I've saved all my files.
2 **to back up** *(a file)*

sauver *VERB* [1]
   to save
   sauver la vie à quelqu'un to save somebody's life
   Vous m'avez sauvé la vie. You saved my life.

se **sauver** *REFLEXIVE VERB* ⊘
1 **to run away**
2 Je me sauve! *(informal)* I'm off!

le **sauvetage** *MASC NOUN*
1 **rescue**
   le sauvetage en montagne mountain rescue
2 **life-saving**

savent, savez *VERB* ▸ SEE **savoir**

le **savoir** *MASC NOUN* ▸ SEE **savoir** *VERB*
   knowledge
• le savoir-faire
   know-how

ℓ **savoir** *VERB* [70]
   ▸ SEE **savoir** *NOUN*
1 **to know**
   savoir que ... to know (that) ...
   Je sais que Paul habite à Londres. I know that Paul lives in London.
   Je ne sais pas. I don't know.
   Je ne savais pas qu'elle était médecin. I didn't know she was a doctor.
   Le sais-tu? Did you know?
   Je n'en sais rien. I know nothing about it.
2 **savoir faire quelque chose** to know how to do something
   Je sais faire du ski. I know how to ski.
   Il est important de savoir lire et écrire. It's important to be able to read and write.
   Tu sais jouer du piano? Can you play the piano?
   Il ne savait pas nager. He couldn't swim.

   WORD TIP savoir is used for knowing facts or how to do things. For knowing people or places, use connaître.

ℓ le **savon** *MASC NOUN*
   soap

la **savonnette** *FEM NOUN*
   bar of soap

savons *VERB* ▸ SEE **savoir**

savoureux *MASC ADJECTIVE*, **savoureuse** *FEM*
   tasty

le **scandale** *MASC NOUN*
   scandal
   C'est un scandale! It's outrageous!

scandinave *MASC & FEM ADJECTIVE* ▸ SEE **Scandinave**
   Scandinavian

le & la **Scandinave** *MASC & FEM NOUN* ▸ SEE **scandinave**
   Scandinavian

la **Scandinavie** *FEM NOUN*
   Scandinavia

scanner *VERB* [1]
   to scan *(a document)*

le **scanneur** *MASC NOUN*
1 **scanner** *(for scanning documents)*
2 **scan** *(in medical check)*
   passer un scanneur to have a scan

le **scarabée** *MASC NOUN*
   beetle

le & la **scénariste** *MASC & FEM NOUN*
   scriptwriter

la **scène** *FEM NOUN*
1 **stage** *(in a theatre)*
   sur scène on stage
   mettre une pièce en scène to stage a play
   mise en scène de Spielberg directed by Spielberg
2 **scene**
   des scènes de panique scenes of panic
   faire une scène to throw a fit

sceptique *MASC & FEM ADJECTIVE*
   sceptical

le **schéma** *MASC NOUN*
   diagram

la **scie** *FEM NOUN*
   saw

ℓ la **science** *FEM NOUN*
   science
   Ma matière préférée, c'est la science. Science is my favourite subject.
• les sciences naturelles
   biology
• les sciences physiques
   physics

scientifique *MASC & FEM ADJECTIVE* ▸ SEE **scientifique** *NOUN*
   scientific

le & la **scientifique** *MASC & FEM NOUN* ▸ SEE **scientifique** *ADJECTIVE*
   scientist

Elle est scientifique. She's a scientist.

ᵖ **scolaire** MASC & FEM ADJECTIVE
school
les vacances scolaires the school holidays
le livret scolaire school report

la **scolarité** FEM NOUN
schooling, education

le **Scorpion** MASC NOUN
Scorpio
Delphine est Scorpion. Delphine is a
Scorpio.

WORD TIP Signs of the zodiac do not take an
article: un or une.

le **Scotch®** MASC NOUN
Sellotape®

le **scout** MASC NOUN
boy scout

la **scoute** FEM NOUN
girl guide

le **scrutin** MASC NOUN
1 **ballot** (process of voting)
2 **polls** (in an election)

le **sculpteur** MASC NOUN, la **sculpteuse** FEM
sculptor

la **sculpture** FEM NOUN
sculpture

le & la **SDF** MASC & FEM NOUN
(= sans domicile fixe) **with no fixed address**
les SDF the homeless

se, s' REFLEXIVE PRONOUN
1 **yourself** (oneself)
se faire mal to hurt yourself
2 **himself**
Il se regarde. He's looking at himself.
3 **herself**
Elle s'est fait une salade. She made herself
a salad.
4 **itself**
Le chien s'est fait mal. The dog has hurt
itself.
5 **themselves**
Ils s'amusent beaucoup. They're really
enjoying themselves.
6 **each other**
Ils s'envoient des textos. They send each
other text messages.
7 se brosser les dents to brush your teeth
Il faut se dépêcher. We have to hurry up.

WORD TIP se becomes s' before a, e i, o, u or
silent h.

ᵖ la **séance** FEM NOUN
1 **session** (for discussions, treatment)
une séance d'aromathérapie an

aromatherapy session
2 **showing** (of a film)
la séance de vingt heures the eight o'clock
showing

le **seau** MASC NOUN, les **seaux** PLURAL
bucket

ᵖ **sec** MASC ADJECTIVE, **sèche** FEM
1 **dry**
pour les peaux sèches for dry skin
2 **dried**
des abricots secs dried apricots

le **sèche-cheveux** INVARIABLE MASC NOUN
hair dryer

le **sèche-linge** MASC NOUN
tumble dryer

le **sèche-mains** MASC NOUN
hand dryer

sécher VERB [1]
1 **to dry**
2 (informal) **to skip** (a class, school)

ᵖ la **sécheresse** FEM NOUN
drought

second MASC ADJECTIVE, **seconde** FEM ▸ SEE
second NOUN
second
la seconde fois the second time

le **second** MASC NOUN ▸ SEE **second** ADJECTIVE
second floor
J'habite au second. I live on the second
floor.
Il est arrivé en second. He arrived second.

ᵖ **secondaire** MASC & FEM ADJECTIVE
secondary

la **seconde** FEM NOUN
1 **second** (in time)
2 **second class**
voyager en seconde to travel second class
3 (the French equivalent of) **Year 11**
J'entre en seconde cette année. I'm going
into Year 11 this year.

secouer VERB [1]
to shake
secouer la tête to shake your head

secourir VERB [29]
1 **to rescue** (a person in difficulty)
2 **to give first aid to** (an accident victim)

le **secourisme** MASC NOUN
first aid

secouriste MASC & FEM NOUN
first aider

ᵖ le **secours** MASC NOUN
1 **help**
Au secours! Help!

ⓔ means the verb takes être to form the perfect

2 les premiers secours first aid
3 une sortie de secours an emergency exit

secret *MASC ADJECTIVE*, **secrète** *FEM* ▶ SEE **secret**
  NOUN
  secret

le **secret** *MASC NOUN* ▶ SEE **secret** *ADJECTIVE*
  secret
  en secret in secret

ℓ le & la **secrétaire** *MASC & FEM NOUN*
1 secretary
  Elle est secrétaire. She's a secretary.
2 un secrétaire a writing desk

le **secrétariat** *MASC NOUN*
  secretary's office

le **secteur** *MASC NOUN*
  sector
  dans le secteur privé in the private sector
  dans le secteur public in the public sector

la **sécu** *FEM NOUN*
  (informal) (= Sécurité sociale) Social
  Security

la **sécurité** *FEM NOUN*
1 safety
  la sécurité routière road safety
2 être en sécurité to be safe
  se sentir en sécurité to feel safe
3 security
  la sécurité de l'emploi job security
  un problème avec le système de sécurité a
  problem with the security system

la **Sécurité sociale** *FEM NOUN*
  Social Security (the welfare system in
  France)

séduisant *MASC ADJECTIVE*, **séduisante** *FEM*
  attractive (person, idea)

le **seigle** *MASC NOUN*
  rye
  le pain de seigle rye bread

le **seigneur** *MASC NOUN*
  lord
  le Seigneur the Lord

le **sein** *MASC NOUN*
  breast
  avoir un cancer du sein to have breast
  cancer

ℓ **seize** *NUMBER*
  sixteen
  Corinne a seize ans. Corinne's sixteen.
  le seize juillet the sixteenth of July

ℓ **seizième** *NUMBER*
  sixteenth

ℓ le **séjour** *MASC NOUN*
  stay

pendant votre séjour en France during your
stay in France
Bon séjour! Enjoy your stay!

séjourner *VERB* [1]
  to stay

ℓ le **sel** *MASC NOUN*
  salt
  une pincée de sel a pinch of salt

la **sélection** *FEM NOUN*
1 selection
2 choice (of products)
3 team

sélectionner *VERB* [1]
  to select

le **self** *MASC NOUN*
  (informal) self-service restaurant
• le **self-service**
  (informal) self-service restaurant

la **selle** *FEM NOUN*
  saddle

selon *PREPOSITION*
  according to
  Selon la météo, il va pleuvoir. According to
  the forecast, it's going to rain.

ℓ la **semaine** *FEM NOUN*
  week
  cette semaine this week
  la semaine dernière last week
  la semaine prochaine next week
  une fois par semaine once a week
  une semaine de vacances a week's holiday
  une semaine sur deux every other week
  10€ d'argent de poche par semaine €10
  pocket money a week
  Elle est payée à la semaine. She's paid by
  the week.

semblable *MASC & FEM ADJECTIVE*
  similar

semblant *MASC NOUN*
  faire semblant de faire quelque chose to
  pretend to do something
  Elle fait semblant de ne pas entendre. She's
  pretending not to hear.

ℓ **sembler** *VERB* [1]
  to seem
  La maison semble vide. The house seems
  empty.

la **semelle** *FEM NOUN*
  sole (of a shoe)

semer *VERB* [1]
  to sow (seeds)

le **semestre** *MASC NOUN*
  semester

ℓ indicates key words

le **semi-remorque** *MASC NOUN*
  articulated truck

le **Sénégal** *MASC NOUN*
  Senegal
  habiter au Sénégal to live in Senegal
  Lucie va au Sénégal. Lucie's going to
  Senegal.

ℰ le **sens** *MASC NOUN*
1 direction
  dans les deux sens in both directions
  dans le sens Calais-Paris in the Calais-Paris
  direction
  sens dessus dessous upside down
2 meaning
  le sens d'un mot the meaning of a word

la **sensation** *FEM NOUN*
1 feeling
  une sensation agréable a nice feeling
2 sensation
  Le film a fait sensation à Cannes. The film
  was a sensation at Cannes.

sensationnel *MASC ADJECTIVE*, **sensationnelle**
  FEM
  sensational

le **sens commun** *MASC NOUN*
  common sense

le **sens de l'humour** *MASC NOUN*
  sense of humour

sensé *MASC ADJECTIVE*, **sensée** *FEM*
  sensible

sensibiliser *VERB* [1]
  sensibiliser quelqu'un à quelque chose
  to increase somebody's awareness of
  something (a problem)
  une campagne pour sensibiliser les gens
  au racisme a campaign to increase people's
  awareness of racism

la **sensibilité** *FEM NOUN*
  sensitivity

sensible *MASC & FEM ADJECTIVE*
1 sensitive *MASC & FEM*
  C'est une fille très sensible. She's a very
  sensitive girl.
2 noticeable
  une différence sensible a noticeable
  difference

WORD TIP Sensible does not mean sensible in
English: for the meaning of sensible ▶ SEE sage.

sensiblement *ADVERB*
  noticeably

ℰ le **sens interdit** *MASC NOUN*
1 no entry sign
2 one-way street

ℰ le **sens unique** *MASC NOUN*
  one-way street

le **sentier** *MASC NOUN*
  path
• le sentier de randonnée
  long-distance footpath (a marked route for
  ramblers)

le **sentiment** *MASC NOUN*
1 feeling
  J'ai le sentiment que... I have a feeling
  that...
2 (endings for a formal letter) Veuillez
  accepter l'expression de mes sentiments
  respectueux. Yours sincerely, Yours
  faithfully

sentimental *MASC ADJECTIVE*, **sentimentale**
  FEM, **sentimentaux** *MASC PL*,
  sentimentales *FEM PL*
  sentimental

ℰ **sentir** *VERB* [58]
1 to smell
  Ça sent bon! That smells good!
  Ce fromage sent fort. There's a strong smell
  from that cheese.
2 to smell of
  Ça sent les roses. It smells of roses.
3 to feel
  Je ne sens rien. I can't feel anything.
  Je sens qu'elle est sincère. I feel that she's
  sincere.
se **sentir** *REFLEXIVE VERB* ☉
  to feel
  Tu te sens mieux? Are you feeling better?
  Je ne me sens pas bien. I don't feel well.

séparé *MASC ADJECTIVE*, **séparée** *FEM*
1 separated
  Mes parents sont séparés. My parents are
  separated.
2 separate
  dans une chambre séparée in a separate
  bedroom

séparément *ADVERB*
  separately

séparer *VERB* [1]
  to separate
se **séparer** *REFLEXIVE VERB* ☉
  to separate
  Mes parents se sont séparés. My parents
  have separated.

ℰ **sept** *NUMBER*
  seven
  Yasmine a sept ans. Yasmine's seven.
  Il est sept heures. It's seven o'clock.
  le sept mars the seventh of March

☉ means the verb takes être to form the perfect

ℓ **septante** NUMBER
   seventy (Used in Belgium and Switzerland,
   for soixante-dix.)
   septante-sept seventy-seven

ℓ le **septembre** MASC NOUN
   September
   en septembre, au mois de septembre in
   September
   fin septembre at the end of September

   WORD TIP Months of the year and days of the
   week start with small letters in French.

ℓ **septième** MASC & FEM ADJECTIVE ▸SEE **septième**
   NOUN
   seventh

ℓ le **septième** MASC NOUN ▸SEE **septième** ADJECTIVE
   seventh floor
   J'habite au septième. I live on the seventh
   floor.

sera, serai, seras, serez VERB ▸SEE **être**

serais, serait, seraient VERB ▸SEE **être**

la **série** FEM NOUN
   series
   une série australienne an Australian series

sérieusement ADVERB
   seriously

ℓ **sérieux** MASC ADJECTIVE, **sérieuse** FEM ▸SEE
   sérieux NOUN
   1 **serious**
      Vraiment? Tu es sérieux? Really? Are you
      serious?
   2 **responsible**
      Aurélie est une jeune fille sérieuse. Aurélie
      is a responsible young woman.
   3 **reliable**
      Il est tout à fait sérieux. He's completely
      reliable.
   4 **conscientious**
      des élèves sérieux conscientious students

   WORD TIP sérieux does not mean serious in
   English: for the meaning of serious ▸SEE **grave**.

le **sérieux** MASC NOUN ▸SEE **sérieux** ADJECTIVE
   prendre quelque chose au sérieux to take
   something seriously
   Il prend tout au sérieux. He takes
   everything seriously.

le **serin** MASC NOUN
   canary

serions, seriez VERB ▸SEE **être**

séronégatif MASC ADJECTIVE, **séronégative** FEM
   HIV-negative

serons, seront VERB ▸SEE **être**

séropositif MASC ADJECTIVE, **séropositive** FEM
   HIV-positive

le **serpent** MASC NOUN
   snake

la **serpillière** FEM NOUN
   floorcloth

la **serre** FEM NOUN
   greenhouse
   l'effet de serre the greenhouse effect

serré MASC ADJECTIVE, **serrée** FEM
   1 **tight** (clothes, budget)
   2 **close** (match, competition)

serrer VERB [1]
   1 **to grip**
   2 serrer la main à quelqu'un to shake
      somebody's hand
      Nous nous sommes serré la main. We
      shook hands.
   3 serrer quelqu'un dans ses bras to hug
      somebody
      Il a serré sa fille dans ses bras. He hugged
      his daughter.
   4 serrer les poings to clench your fists
   5 **to tighten** (a screw, a belt)
   6 **to be too tight**
      Mes chaussures me serrent. My shoes are
      too tight.
   7 **to push closer together**
      Serrez les tables. Move the tables closer
      together.

se **serrer** REFLEXIVE VERB ⊙
   to squeeze up
   Serrez-vous un peu! Squeeze up a bit!

la **serrure** FEM NOUN
   lock

ℓ le **serveur** MASC NOUN
   waiter

ℓ la **serveuse** FEM NOUN
   waitress

ℓ le **service** MASC NOUN
   1 **favour**
      Je peux te demander un service? Can I ask
      a favour?
   2 **service** (on bus or train routes)
      service de dimanche Sunday service
   3 être en service to be working
      Est-ce que l'ascenseur est en service? Is the
      lift working?
      être hors service to be out of order
   4 **duty**
      Je suis de service ce soir. I am on duty this
      evening.
   5 **service** (charge)
      service non compris service not included

6 department *(in a town hall, a hospital)*
le service des urgences the casualty
department
- le service après-vente
after-sales service
- le service clientèle
customer services
- le service militaire
national service

♪ la **serviette** *FEM NOUN*
1 towel
2 table napkin
3 briefcase
- la serviette hygiénique
sanitary towel

servir *VERB* [71]
1 **to serve** *(in a shop)*
Merci, on me sert. Thank you, I'm being
served.
2 **to serve** *(with food, drink)*
Est-ce que je peux vous servir du poulet?
Can I give you some chicken?
'Servir frais' 'Serve chilled'
3 **to serve** *(in tennis)*
À toi de servir! Your service!
4 servir à quelque chose to be used for
something
À quoi ça sert? What's it for?

se **servir** *REFLEXIVE VERB* ▲
1 **to help yourself** *(at a meal)*
Sers-toi de riz. Help yourself to rice.
2 **to be served** *(food, drink)*
Ce vin se sert frais. This wine should be
served chilled.
3 se servir de quelque chose to use
something
Je sais me servir d'un scanneur. I know how
to use a scanner.

ses *DETERMINER* ▶ SEE **son** *DETERMINER*

le **set de table** *MASC NOUN*
place mat

♪ **seul** *MASC ADJECTIVE*, **seule** *FEM*
1 **only**
la seule personne the only person
être le seul à faire quelque chose to be the
only one to do something
J'étais le seul à aimer le film. I was the only
one who liked the film.
2 **alone**
Il ne faut pas y aller seul. You mustn't go
there alone.
3 se sentir seul to feel lonely
Au début, Julie s'est sentie très seule. In the
beginning, Julie felt very lonely.
4 tout seul all by yourself
Sophie sait s'habiller toute seule. Sophie
can get dressed all by herself.

♪ **seulement** *ADVERB*
1 **only**
trois fois seulement only three times
seulement une vingtaine d'élèves only
about twenty students
2 Si seulement je l'avais su. If only I'd known.

sévère *MASC & FEM ADJECTIVE*
strict

le **sexe** *MASC NOUN*
1 **sex**
2 **genitals**

sexiste *MASC & FEM ADJECTIVE*
sexist

sexuel *MASC ADJECTIVE*, **sexuelle** *FEM*
sexual

♪ le **shampooing** *MASC NOUN*
shampoo

♪ le **short** *MASC NOUN*
(pair of) shorts

♪ **si** *ADVERB* ▶ SEE **si** *CONJUNCTION*
1 **so**
Tu chantes si bien! You sing so well!
2 **yes** *(when you are contradicting somebody)*
'Tu ne viens pas avec nous?' – 'Si!' 'You're
not coming with us?' – 'Yes I am!'

♪ **si, s'** *CONJUNCTION* ▶ SEE **si** *ADVERB*
1 **if**
si tu veux if you like
Demande-lui si elle vient avec nous. Ask
her if she's coming with us.
2 s'il te plaît, s'il vous plaît please

WORD TIP si becomes s' before il or ils.

la **Sicile** *FEM NOUN*
Sicily

♪ le **sida** *MASC NOUN*
(= syndrome immuno-déficitaire acquis)
AIDS

♪ le **siècle** *MASC NOUN*
century

♪ le **siège** *MASC NOUN*
1 **seat**
2 **head office** *(of a company)*
3 **siege** *(of a castle, a town)*
- le siège social
head office

le **sien** *MASC PRONOUN*, la **sienne** *FEM* les **siens**
MASC PL les **siennes** *FEM PL*
1 **his**
J'ai prêté mon vélo à Mahmoud. Le sien est
chez lui. I've lent Mahmoud my bike. His is
at home.
'Est-ce que ces chaussures sont à Antoine?'
– 'Oui, ce sont les siennes.' 'Are these shoes

▲ means the verb takes être to form the perfect

Antoine's?' – 'Yes, they're his.'

2 hers

J'ai prêté mon vélo à Anaïs. Le sien est chez elle. I've lent Anaïs my bike. Hers is at home.
'Est-ce que ces chaussures sont à Natalie?' – 'Oui, ce sont les siennes.' 'Are these shoes Natalie's?' – 'Yes, they're hers.'

WORD TIP The article and pronoun change in French when they refer to fem and plural nouns.

la **sieste** FEM NOUN
nap
faire la sieste to have a nap

siffler VERB [1]
to whistle

le **sifflet** MASC NOUN
whistle

le **signal** MASC NOUN, les **signaux** PLURAL
signal

signaler VERB [1]
1 signaler à quelqu'un que ... to point out (to somebody) that ...
Je te signale que tu me dois de l'argent.
I'd like to point out that you owe me some money.
2 to report (a theft, an incident)
3 to indicate (roadworks, danger)

la **signalisation** FEM NOUN
signalling, signals
• la signalisation routière
road signs and markings

la **signature** FEM NOUN
signature

le **signe** MASC NOUN
sign
C'est bon signe. It's a good sign.
faire signe à quelqu'un to wave to someone
Je te faisais signe du bus. I was waving to you from the bus.
faire signe à quelqu'un de faire quelque chose to beckon somebody to do something
Il m'a fait signe de m'asseoir. He beckoned me to sit down.
Tu es de quel signe? What star sign are you?
• le signe astrologique
star sign

signer VERB [1]
to sign
N'oublie pas de signer le chèque. Don't forget to sign the cheque.
se **signer** REFLEXIVE VERB ◯
to cross oneself

la **signification** FEM NOUN
meaning

signifier VERB [1]
to mean
Qu'est-ce que ça signifie? What does that mean?

ℓ le **silence** MASC NOUN
silence
en silence in silence

silencieux MASC ADJECTIVE, **silencieuse** FEM
silent

la **silhouette** FEM NOUN
1 silhouette
2 figure

similaire MASC & FEM ADJECTIVE
similar

la **similarité** FEM NOUN
similarity

ℓ **simple** MASC & FEM ADJECTIVE ▶ SEE **simple** NOUN
simple

ℓ le **simple** MASC NOUN ▶ SEE **simple** ADJECTIVE
singles (in tennis)

simplement ADVERB
simply

la **simplicité** FEM NOUN
simplicity

simplifier VERB [1]
to simplify

simuler VERB [1]
to simulate (a situation)

simultané MASC ADJECTIVE, **simultanée** FEM
simultaneous
en simultané simultaneously

sincère MASC & FEM ADJECTIVE
sincere

la **sincérité** FEM NOUN
sincerity

le **singe** MASC NOUN
monkey
un grand singe an ape

le **singulier** MASC NOUN
singular
au singulier in the singular

sinistre MASC & FEM ADJECTIVE ▶ SEE **sinistre** NOUN
1 sinister
2 gloomy
le **sinistre** MASC NOUN ▶ SEE **sinistre** ADJECTIVE
accident, disaster (a fire, a flood)

sinistré MASC ADJECTIVE, **sinistrée** FEM ▶ SEE
sinistré NOUN
stricken
les familles sinistrées the families stricken by the disaster

A
B
C
D
E
F
G
H
I
J
K
L
M
N
O
P
Q
R
S
T
U
V
W
X
Y
Z

301

le **sinistré** MASC NOUN, la **sinistrée** FEM ▸ SEE
sinistré ADJECTIVE
disaster victim

sinon CONJUNCTION
otherwise

la **sirène** FEM NOUN
1 **siren**
une sirène d'alarme a fire alarm
2 **mermaid**

ℓ le **sirop** MASC NOUN
1 **syrup**
sirop pectoral cough mixture
2 **cordial** (drink)
sirop de menthe mint cordial

ℓ le **site** MASC NOUN
site, area
• le site classé
conservation area
• le site Internet
web site
• le site pittoresque
beauty spot
• le site touristique
place of interest (for visitors)
• le site web
web site

sitôt ADVERB
as soon as
sitôt dit, sitôt fait no sooner said than done

la **situation** FEM NOUN
1 **situation**
2 **job**

ℓ **situer** VERB [1]
être situé to be situated
L'hôtel est situé au bord de la mer. The
hotel is situated by the sea.
se **situer** REFLEXIVE VERB ⊘
1 **to be situated in**
L'appartement se situe en plein centre-
ville. The flat is right in the town centre.
2 **to be set**
Le film se situe au Japon. The film is set in
Japan.

ℓ **six** NUMBER
six
Théo a six ans. Théo's six.
Il est six heures. It's six o'clock.
le six juillet the sixth of July

ℓ **sixième** ADJECTIVE ▸ SEE **sixième** NOUN, NOUN
sixth

ℓ le **sixième** MASC NOUN ▸ SEE **sixième** ADJECTIVE,
NOUN
sixth floor
C'est au sixième. It's on the sixth floor.

ℓ la **sixième** FEM NOUN ▸ SEE **sixième** ADJECTIVE,
NOUN
(the French equivalent of) **Year 7**

le **skate** MASC NOUN
1 **skateboarding**
faire du skate to go skateboarding
2 **skateboard**

ℓ le **ski** MASC NOUN
1 **ski**
2 **skiing**
• le ski de fond
cross-country skiing
• le ski de piste
downhill skiing

skier VERB [1]
to ski
skier hors piste to ski off-piste

le **skieur** MASC NOUN, la **skieuse** FEM
skier

ℓ le **slip** MASC NOUN
1 **underpants**
2 **knickers**
• le slip de bain
trunks

la **Slovaquie** FEM NOUN
Slovakia

la **Slovénie** FEM NOUN
Slovenia

le **SMIC** MASC NOUN
(= salaire minimum interprofessionnel de
croissance) **guaranteed minimum wage**

le **SMS** MASC NOUN
text message
J'ai envoyé un SMS à David. I texted David.

le **snack** MASC NOUN
snack bar

ℓ la **SNCF** FEM NOUN
(= Société nationale des chemins de fer
français) **French national railways**

snob FEM & MASC ADJECTIVE ▸ SEE **snob** NOUN
1 **snobbish** (person)
2 **posh** (restaurant)

le & la **snob** MASC & FEM NOUN ▸ SEE **snob** ADJECTIVE
snob

sobre MASC & FEM ADJECTIVE
sober

sociable MASC & FEM ADJECTIVE
sociable

social MASC ADJECTIVE, **sociale** FEM, **sociaux**
MASC PL, **sociales** FEM PL
social

⊘ means the verb takes être to form the perfect

socialiste *MASC & FEM ADJECTIVE*
  socialist

la **société** *FEM NOUN*
1 society
  dans notre société in our society
2 company
  Il travaille pour une grande société. He
  works for a big company.
• la société de consommation
  consumer society

la **sociologie** *FEM NOUN*
  sociology

la **socquette** *FEM NOUN*
  ankle sock

le **soda**
  soda

ℓ la **sœur** *FEM NOUN*
1 sister
  ma grande sœur my big sister, my older
  sister
  J'ai deux sœurs et un frère. I have two
  sisters and a brother.
2 sister
  Sœur Emmanuelle Sister Emmanuelle
  une sœur a nun

soi *PRONOUN*
1 one, oneself
  la confiance en soi self-confidence
  la maîtrise de soi self-control
2 itself
  Le sujet n'est pas très intéressant en soi.
  The subject is not very interesting in itself.

soi-disant *MASC ADJECTIVE*, **soi-disante** *FEM*
1 so-called
  Tom est le soi-disant champion. Tom's the
  so-called champion.
2 supposedly
  Elle est soi-disant malade. She's supposedly
  ill.

la **soie** *FEM NOUN*
  silk
  un foulard en soie a silk scarf
  le papier de soie tissue paper

soient *VERB* ▶ SEE **être**

ℓ la **soif** *FEM NOUN*
  thirst
  avoir soif to be thirsty
  J'ai soif. I'm thirsty

soigné *MASC ADJECTIVE*, **soignée** *FEM*
  neat *(piece of work, writing)*
  Sophie a une écriture soignée. Sophie has
  neat writing.

soigner *VERB* [1]
1 to treat *(a wound, a patient)*

2 to look after *(a person, an animal)*
3 to take care over *(appearance, writing)*

soigneusement *ADVERB*
  carefully

soi-même *PRONOUN*
  yourself, oneself
  Il faut le faire soi-même. You have to do it
  yourself.

le **soin** *MASC NOUN*
1 care
  avec soin carefully
2 prendre soin de quelque chose to take care
  of something
3 les soins treatment
  les premiers soins first aid

ℓ le **soir** *MASC NOUN*
  evening, night
  ce soir tonight
  hier soir last night
  demain soir tomorrow night
  le soir du 15 mai on the evening of 15 May
  à six heures du soir at six in the evening
  Je sors tous les samedis soirs. I go out every
  Saturday night.
  À ce soir! See you tonight!

ℓ la **soirée** *FEM NOUN*
1 evening
  pendant la soirée during the evening
  Ils ont passé la soirée à bavarder. They
  spent the evening chatting.
2 party
  Elle donne une petite soirée. She's having
  a little party.
3 Bonne soirée! Have a nice evening!
• la soirée dansante
  dance

sois *VERB*
  ▶ SEE **être**
  Sois gentil! Be good!

soit *VERB* ▶ SEE **être** *CONJUNCTION*

soit *CONJUNCTION* ▶ SEE **soit** *VERB*
  soit... soit ... either ... or ...
  soit demain, soit jeudi either tomorrow or
  Thursday

la **soixantaine** *FEM NOUN*
1 about sixty
  une soixantaine de personnes about sixty
  people
2 avoir la soixantaine to be in your sixties
  Il a bien la soixantaine. He's in his sixties
  at least.

ℓ **soixante** *NUMBER*
  sixty

ℓ **soixante-dix** *NUMBER*
  seventy

ℓ indicates key words

soixante-dix-huit seventy-eight

le **soja** *MASC NOUN*
soya bean
la sauce de soja soy sauce

le **sol** *MASC NOUN*
1 floor
2 ground
3 soil
4 *(Music)* **G** *(the note)*

solaire *MASC & FEM ADJECTIVE*
1 solar
2 sun

le **soldat** *MASC NOUN*
soldier

℘ le **solde** *MASC NOUN*
1 balance *(of a bank account)*
2 les soldes the sales

soldé *MASC ADJECTIVE*, **soldée** *FEM*
reduced

la **sole** *FEM NOUN*
sole *(the fish)*

℘ le **soleil** *MASC NOUN*
sun
au soleil in the sun
Il fait du soleil. It's sunny.
Sophie a attrapé un coup de soleil. Sophie's
got sunburnt.

solide *MASC & FEM ADJECTIVE*
1 solid
2 strong

le & la **soliste** *MASC & FEM NOUN*
soloist

solitaire *MASC & FEM ADJECTIVE*
solitary

la **solitude** *FEM NOUN*
1 solitude
2 loneliness

la **solution** *FEM NOUN*
solution

sombre *MASC & FEM ADJECTIVE*
dark

le **somme** *MASC NOUN* ▸ SEE **somme** *NOUN*
nap
la **somme** *FEM NOUN* ▸ SEE **somme** *NOUN*
sum *(of money)*

le **sommeil** *MASC NOUN*
sleep
avoir sommeil to feel sleepy
J'ai sommeil. I feel sleepy.

sommes *VERB* ▸ SEE **être**

le **sommet** *MASC NOUN*
summit

le & la **somnambule** *MASC & FEM NOUN*
sleepwalker

son *MASC DETERMINER*, **sa** *FEM*, **ses** *PL* ▸ SEE **son** *NOUN*
1 his
son fils his son
sa fille his daughter
ses enfants his children
2 her
son fils her son
sa fille her daughter
ses enfants her children
3 its
sa patte its paw
son collier its collar
4 one's, your
Chacun son tour! Wait your turn!

le **son** *MASC NOUN* ▸ SEE **son** *DETERMINER*
1 sound
2 volume *(for radios, a hi-fi)*
3 bran

℘ le **sondage** *MASC NOUN*
survey
• le sondage d'opinion
opinion poll

sonner *VERB* [1]
1 to ring
Le téléphone sonne. The phone's ringing.
2 strike
L'horloge sonne les heures. The clock
strikes on the hour.

la **sonnerie** *FEM NOUN*
1 bell
la sonnerie d'alarme the alarm bell
2 ringtone

la **sonnette** *FEM NOUN*
1 bell
la sonnette d'alarme the alarm bell
2 doorbell

la **sono** *FEM NOUN*
(informal) **sound system**

sophistiqué *MASC ADJECTIVE*, **sophistiquée** *FEM*
sophisticated

le **sorbet** *MASC NOUN*
sorbet
un sorbet au cassis a blackcurrant sorbet

le **sorcier** *MASC NOUN*
wizard

la **sorcière** *FEM NOUN*
witch

le **sort** *MASC NOUN*
fate

WORD TIP sort does not mean **sort** in English;
for the meaning of **sort** ▸ SEE **sorte**.

◔ means the verb takes être to form the perfect

la **sorte** *FEM NOUN*
1 sort
toutes sortes d'activités all sorts of activities
C'est une sorte de poudre. It's a sort of powder.
2 en quelque sorte in a way

ℓ la **sortie** *FEM NOUN*
1 exit
Où se trouve la sortie? Where's the exit?
2 outing
Demain nous allons en sortie avec l'école. Tomorrow we're going on a school outing.
3 launch *(of a new product)*
4 release *(of a film)*
5 publication *(of a book)*
• la sortie de secours emergency exit

ℓ **sortir** *VERB* [72]
1 ◐ to go out
Elle est sortie en courant. She ran out.
2 ◐ to come out
Son nouveau film sortira en mai. Her new film is coming out in May.
3 ◐ to go out *(for pleasure)*
Mes parents sortent peu. My parents don't go out much.
Tu sors ce soir? Are you going out tonight?
4 sortir avec quelqu'un ◐ to be going out with someone
Thibault sort avec ma sœur. Thibault's going out with my sister.
5 to take out
J'ai oublié de sortir le chien. I forgot to take the dog out.

WORD TIP When you say what you **take out** etc, use avoir in the perfect tense.

se **sortir** *REFLEXIVE VERB* ◐
s'en sortir to manage
Je m'en sortirai d'une manière ou d'une autre. I'll manage one way or another.

la **sottise** *FEM NOUN*
1 silliness
2 a silly remark
Il dit des sottises. He talks nonsense.
3 faire une sottise to do something silly
Arthur a fait une sottise. Arthur's done something silly.

le **sou** *MASC NOUN*
penny
Il n'a pas un sou. He's broke.
une machine à sous a fruit machine

le **souci** *MASC NOUN*
1 worry
se faire du souci to worry
Je me fais du souci pour Chantal. I'm worried about Chantal.

2 problem
J'ai d'autres soucis à présent. I've got other problems just now.
3 marigold
un parterre de soucis a bed of marigolds

soucieux *MASC ADJECTIVE*, **soucieuse** *FEM*
worried

ℓ la **soucoupe** *FEM NOUN*
saucer

ℓ **soudain** *MASC ADJECTIVE*, **soudaine** *FEM* ▶ SEE
soudain *ADVERB*
sudden
une réaction soudaine a sudden reaction

ℓ **soudain** *ADVERB* ▶ SEE **soudain** *ADJECTIVE*
suddenly

le **souffle** *MASC NOUN*
breath
Laisse-moi reprendre mon souffle! Let me catch my breath!
être à bout de souffle to be out of breath
Après la course, il était à bout de souffle. After the race he was out of breath.
couper le souffle à quelqu'un to take someone's breath away
Ce spectacle fantastique vous coupe le souffle. This fantastic show takes your breath away.

le **soufflé** *MASC NOUN*
soufflé
un soufflé au fromage a cheese soufflé

souffler *VERB* [1]
1 to blow
2 to blow out *(a candle)*
3 to whisper
4 to tell

la **souffrance** *FEM NOUN*
1 suffering
2 misery

souffrir *VERB* [73]
to suffer
Elle a beaucoup souffert. She has suffered a lot.
souffrir de quelque chose to suffer from something
Il souffre du dos. He suffers from back problems.
Elle souffre d'asthme. She suffers from asthma.
Est-ce qu'il souffre? Is he in pain?

le **souhait** *MASC NOUN*
wish
À tes souhaits! Bless you! *(when somebody sneezes)*

souhaiter *VERB* [1]
to wish

ℓ indicates key words

souhaiter quelque chose à quelqu'un to wish somebody something
Je te souhaite bonne chance. I wish you luck.
Il souhaite se marier. He'd like to get married.

soûl MASC ADJECTIVE, **soûle** FEM
drunk

le **soulagement** MASC NOUN
relief
à mon grand soulagement to my great relief

soulever VERB [50]
1 to lift
Je n'arrive pas à soulever ta valise. I can't lift your case.
2 to raise (problems, objections)
Personne n'a soulevé la question. Nobody raised the question.

le **soulier** MASC NOUN
shoe

souligner VERB [1]
1 to underline
2 to emphasize

le **soupçon** MASC NOUN
1 suspicion
2 spot, drop (of food, drink)
juste un soupçon de lait just a drop of milk

soupçonner VERB [1]
to suspect
soupçonner quelqu'un de faire quelque chose to suspect somebody of doing something
Elle le soupçonne de voler. She suspects him of stealing.

la **soupe** FEM NOUN
soup
la soupe aux oignons onion soup

♀ **souper** VERB [1]
to have supper

le **soupir** MASC NOUN
sigh
pousser un soupir de soulagement to let out a sigh of relief

soupirer VERB [1]
to sigh

souple MASC & FEM ADJECTIVE
1 supple (person)
2 flexible (system)
3 soft (hair)

la **source** FEM NOUN
1 spring
l'eau de source spring water
2 source

Quelle est la source de tes ennuis? What's the source of your problems?

le **sourcil** MASC NOUN
eyebrow

♀ **sourd** MASC ADJECTIVE, **sourde** FEM
1 deaf
Ne crie pas, je ne suis pas sourd! Don't shout, I'm not deaf!
2 dull, muffled (noise)

souriant MASC ADJECTIVE, **souriante** FEM
cheerful

le **sourire** MASC NOUN ▸ SEE **sourire** VERB
smile
faire un sourire à quelqu'un to give somebody a smile
Le bébé m'a fait un joli sourire. The baby gave me a lovely smile.

sourire VERB [68]
▸ SEE **sourire** NOUN
to smile
Il ne sourit jamais. He never smiles.
sourire à quelqu'un to smile at somebody
Elle lui a souri. She smiled at him.

♀ la **souris** FEM NOUN
mouse (the animal, for a computer)

♀ **sous** PREPOSITION
1 under, underneath
Il est caché sous la table. He's hiding under the table.
sous terre underground
2 during
sous l'Occupation during the Occupation
3 Anne est sous antibiotiques. Anne is on antibiotics.

sous-entendu MASC ADJECTIVE, **sous-entendue** FEM ▸ SEE **sous-entendu** NOUN
implied

le **sous-entendu** MASC NOUN ▸ SEE **sous-entendu** ADJECTIVE
innuendo

sous-estimer VERB [1]
to underestimate

sous-marin MASC ADJECTIVE, **sous-marine** FEM
▸ SEE **sous-marin** NOUN
underwater
la plongée sous-marine deep-sea diving

le **sous-marin** MASC NOUN ▸ SEE **sous-marin** ADJECTIVE
submarine

♀ le **sous-sol** MASC NOUN
basement
au sous-sol in the basement

la **sous-tasse** FEM NOUN
saucer

◔ means the verb takes être to form the perfect

ℱ le **sous-titre** *MASC NOUN*
subtitle
un film avec des sous-titres en français a
film with French subtitles

la **soustraction** *FEM NOUN*
subtraction

le **sous-vêtement** *MASC NOUN*
underwear

soutenir *VERB* [77]
1 to support
Je soutiens la pétition. I support the
petition.
Il a besoin qu'on lui soutienne le moral. He
needs cheering up.
2 to withstand *(a shock, an attack)*

souterrain *MASC ADJECTIVE*, **souterraine** *FEM*
underground
un passage souterrain an underground
passage, a subway *(under a street)*

le **soutien** *MASC NOUN*
support
J'ai besoin de ton soutien moral. I need
your moral support.
• le **soutien scolaire**
learning support

le **soutien-gorge** *MASC NOUN*, les **soutiens-
gorge** *PLURAL*
bra

le **soutif** *MASC NOUN*
(informal) **bra**

ℱ le **souvenir** *MASC NOUN* ▸SEE **se souvenir** *VERB*
1 memory
mes souvenirs de Londres my memories
of London
Je n'ai aucun souvenir de l'avoir
rencontrée. I have no memory of meeting
her.
2 souvenir
C'est un souvenir de mon voyage en Chine.
It's something I brought back from my trip
to China.
se **souvenir** *REFLEXIVE VERB* [81]
▸SEE **souvenir** *NOUN*
se souvenir de quelqu'un, quelque chose to
remember somebody or something
Je me souviens d'elle. I remember her.
Il se souvient très bien de sa première
école. He remembers his first school very
well.

ℱ **souvent** *ADVERB*
often
Je ne la vois pas très souvent. I don't see
her very often.
Il faut manger des légumes le plus souvent
possible. You must eat vegetables as often

as possible.

soyons, soyez *VERB* ▸SEE **être**

spacieux *MASC ADJECTIVE*, **spacieuse** *FEM*
spacious

les **spaghettis** *PLURAL MASC NOUN*
spaghetti
des spaghettis à la bolognaise spaghetti
bolognese

ℱ le **sparadrap** *MASC NOUN*
sticking plaster

le **speaker** *MASC NOUN*, la **speakerine** *FEM*
announcer

ℱ **spécial** *MASC ADJECTIVE*, **spéciale** *FEM*, **spéciaux**
MASC PL, **spéciales** *FEM PL*
1 special
les effets spéciaux special effects
'Que fais-tu ce week-end?' – 'Rien
de spécial.' 'What are you doing this
weekend?' – 'Nothing special.'
2 odd
Stan est vraiment très spécial. Stan's really
very odd.

spécialement *ADVERB*
specially
Elle est venue spécialement pour te voir.
She came especially to see you.

se **spécialiser** *REFLEXIVE VERB* [1]
to specialize
Elle se spécialise dans la génétique. She's
specializing in genetics.

le & la **spécialiste** *MASC & FEM NOUN*
specialist

ℱ la **spécialité** *FEM NOUN*
speciality

ℱ le **spectacle** *MASC NOUN*
1 show
Nous allons au spectacle. We're going to
see a show.
un spectacle son et lumière a son et
lumière
2 sight
un spectacle familier a familiar sight

spectaculaire *MASC & FEM ADJECTIVE*
spectacular

ℱ le **spectateur** *MASC NOUN*, la **spectatrice** *FEM*
1 member of the audience
Les spectateurs ont applaudi
frénétiquement. The audience applauded
wildly.
2 spectator
Il y avait 30 000 spectateurs au match de
football. There were 30,000 spectators at
the football match.

ℱ **indicates key words**

la **spéléologie** *FEM NOUN*
  potholing

spirituel *MASC ADJECTIVE*, **spirituelle** *FEM*
1 witty
2 spiritual

la **splendeur** *FEM NOUN*
  splendour

splendide *MASC & FEM ADJECTIVE*
  splendid

sponsoriser *VERB* [1]
  to sponsor

spontané *MASC ADJECTIVE*, **spontanée** *FEM*
  spontaneous

ℰ le **sport** *MASC NOUN*
  sport, sports
  J'aime le sport. I like sport.
  Il fait beaucoup de sport. He does a lot of sport.
  Que fais-tu comme sport? What sport do you do?
  Camille est bonne en sport. Camille is good at sports.
  les sports extrêmes extreme sports
  les sports d'hiver winter sports
  Le foot est un sport d'équipe. Football is a team sport.

ℰ **sportif** *MASC ADJECTIVE*, **sportive** *FEM* ▸SEE
  sportif *NOUN*
1 sports
  un club sportif a sports club
  un journaliste sportif a sports correspondent
2 sporty
  Émeline n'est pas sportive. Émeline is not sporty.

ℰ le **sportif** *MASC NOUN*, la **sportive** *FEM* ▸SEE
  sportif *ADJECTIVE*
  sportsman, sportswoman
  une sportive de haut niveau a top sportswoman

le **spot** *MASC NOUN*
  spotlight
• le spot publicitaire
  commercial

le **square** *MASC NOUN*
  park *(public garden)*
  La nounou emmène les enfants au square.
  The nanny is taking the children to the park.

le **squelette** *MASC NOUN*
  skeleton

stable *MASC & FEM ADJECTIVE*
  stable
  L'échelle n'est pas stable. The ladder isn't stable.

Il a trouvé un emploi stable. He's found a steady job.

ℰ le **stade** *MASC NOUN*
  stadium
  Le nouveau stade accueille 80 000 personnes. The new stadium can seat 80,000 people.

ℰ le **stage** *MASC NOUN*
1 course
  suivre un stage faire un stage aller en stage to go on a course
  un stage de formation a training course
  J'ai suivi un stage intensif de français de trois mois. I went on a 3-month intensive French course.
2 un stage professionnel, un stage pratique work experience
  Elle fait un stage dans un supermarché. She's doing work experience in a supermarket.

ℰ le & la **stagiaire** *MASC & FEM NOUN*
  trainee

le **stand** *MASC NOUN*
1 stand *(in a market, an exhibition)*
2 stall *(in a fairground)*

le **standard** *MASC NOUN*
  switchboard
  Il faut passer par le standard. You have to go through the switchboard.

le & la **standardiste** *MASC & FEM NOUN*
  switchboard operator

le **standing** *MASC NOUN*
  un appartement de standing a luxury flat

la **star** *FEM NOUN*
  star *(in a film, show)*

le **starter** *MASC NOUN*
  choke *(in a car)*

ℰ la **station** *FEM NOUN*
1 station
  une station de métro an underground station
  Nous descendons à la station Péreire. We get off at Péreire.
2 une station de taxis a taxi rank
3 resort
  une station de ski a ski resort
  une station balnéaire a seaside resort
  une station thermale a spa
4 une station de radio a radio station
• la station de travail
  (computer) work station

stationnaire *MASC & FEM ADJECTIVE*
1 stationary
2 stable

ℐ le **stationnement** *MASC NOUN*
parking
'Stationnement interdit' 'No parking'

ℐ **stationner** *VERB* [1]
to park
'Défense de stationner' 'No parking'

la **station-service** *FEM NOUN*, les **stations-service** *PLURAL*
service station, filling station

la **statistique** *FEM NOUN*
statistics

la **statue** *FEM NOUN*
statue

le **statut** *MASC NOUN*
1 statute
2 status

le **steak** *MASC NOUN*
steak
un steak-frites steak and chips
un steak haché a hamburger
du steak haché minced beef

stéréo *INVARIABLE MASC & FEM ADJECTIVE* ▶ SEE
stéreo *NOUN*
stereo

la **stéréo** *FEM NOUN* ▶ SEE **stéreo** *ADJ*
stereo
en stéréo in stereo

stérile *MASC & FEM ADJECTIVE*
sterile

stériliser *VERB* [1]
to sterilize

le **steward** *MASC NOUN*
flight attendant *(male)*

stimulant *MASC ADJECTIVE*, **stimulante** *FEM*
stimulating

le **stock** *MASC NOUN*
stock
en stock in stock

le **stop** *MASC NOUN*
1 stop sign
2 hitchhiking
faire du stop to hitchhike
Nous allons faire l'Espagne en stop. We're going to hitchhike round Spain.

stopper *VERB* [1]
to stop

le **store** *MASC NOUN*
1 blind
2 awning

le **strapontin** *MASC NOUN*
fold-down seat

la **stratégie** *FEM NOUN*
strategy

stratégique *MASC & FEM ADJECTIVE*
strategic

le **stress** *MASC NOUN*
stress

stressant *MASC ADJECTIVE*, **stressante** *FEM*
stressful
un travail stressant a stressful job

stressé *MASC ADJECTIVE*, **stressée** *FEM*
stressed
Je suis très stressé en ce moment. I'm stressed out at the moment.

strict *MASC ADJECTIVE*, **stricte** *FEM*
1 strict
Le prof est très strict. The teacher is very strict.
2 severe
une coiffure stricte a severe hairstyle

studieux *MASC ADJECTIVE*, **studieuse** *FEM*
studious

le **studio** *MASC NOUN*
1 studio flat
Il habite dans un studio. He lives in a studio flat.
2 studio
les studios de cinéma film studios

stupéfait *MASC ADJECTIVE*, **stupéfaite** *FEM*
astounded

les **stupéfiants** *PLURAL MASC NOUN*
narcotics

la **stupeur** *FEM NOUN*
astonishment

stupide *MASC & FEM ADJECTIVE*
stupid

la **stupidité** *FEM NOUN*
stupidity

le **style** *MASC NOUN*
style
un style de vie a lifestyle
C'est bien son style! That's just like him!

le & la **styliste** *MASC & FEM NOUN*
designer

ℐ le **stylo** *MASC NOUN*
pen
• le stylo bille
ball-point pen
• le stylo à encre
fountain pen
• le stylo feutre
felt-tip pen
• le stylo plume
fountain pen

ℐ indicates key words

su VERB ▶ SEE **savoir**

subir VERB [2]
1 **to be subjected to** (violence, pressure)
2 **to suffer** (a defeat, discrimination)
3 **to undergo** (an operation)

subitement ADVERB
suddenly

le **subjonctif** MASC NOUN
subjunctive
au subjonctif in the subjunctive

substituer VERB [1]
to substitute

subtil MASC ADJECTIVE, **subtile** FEM
subtle

la **subvention** FEM NOUN
subsidy

le **succès** MASC NOUN
success
C'est un grand succès! It's a great success!
avoir du succès auprès de quelqu'un to be
a favourite with somebody
La nouvelle BD a du succès auprès des
jeunes. The new comic book is a favourite
with young people.

la **succursale** FEM NOUN
branch (of a company)

sucer VERB [61]
to suck

la **sucette** FEM NOUN
lollipop

♂ le **sucre** MASC NOUN
1 **sugar**
un chewing-gum sans sucre sugar-free
chewing-gum
2 un sucre a lump of sugar
Tu veux combien de sucres dans ton café?
How many sugars do you take in your
coffee?
• le sucre cristallisé
granulated sugar
• le sucre glace
icing sugar
• le sucre en morceaux
sugar lumps
• le sucre en poudre
caster sugar
• le sucre roux
brown sugar

♂ **sucré** MASC ADJECTIVE, **sucrée** FEM
sweet
C'est trop sucré pour moi. It's too sweet
for me.
sucré au miel sweetened with honey
non sucré unsweetened

les **sucreries** PLURAL FEM NOUN
sweet things

♂ **sud** INVARIABLE MASC & FEM ADJECTIVE ▶ SEE **sud** NOUN
1 **south**
la côte sud the south coast
2 **southern**
la région sud the southern area

WORD TIP sud never changes.

♂ le **sud** MASC NOUN ▶ SEE **sud** INVARIABLE MASC & FEM
ADJECTIVE
south
le sud de la France southern France
un vent du sud a south wind
Je suis du sud d'Angleterre. I'm from the
south of England.
J'habite dans le sud (de l'Écosse). I live in
the south (of Scotland).
C'est au sud de Paris. It's south of Paris.

sud-africain MASC ADJECTIVE, **sud-africaine** FEM
▶ SEE **Sud-africain** NOUN
South African

le **Sud-Africain** MASC NOUN, la **Sud-Africaine**
FEM ▶ SEE **sud-africain**
South African

sud-américain MASC ADJECTIVE, **sud-
américaine** FEM ▶ SEE **Sud-américain** NOUN
South American

le **Sud-Américain** MASC NOUN, la **Sud-
Américaine** FEM ▶ SEE **sud-américain**
South American

sud-est INVARIABLE MASC & FEM ADJECTIVE ▶ SEE
sud-est NOUN
south-east

le **sud-est** MASC NOUN ▶ SEE **sud-est** INVARIABLE
MASC & FEM ADJECTIVE
south-east
le sud-est de l'Angleterre south-east
England

sud-ouest INVARIABLE MASC & FEM ADJECTIVE ▶ SEE
sud-ouest NOUN
south-west

le **sud-ouest** MASC NOUN ▶ SEE **sud-ouest**
INVARIABLE MASC & FEM ADJECTIVE
south-west
le sud-ouest de l'Irlande south-west Ireland

la **Suède** FEM NOUN
Sweden

suédois MASC ADJECTIVE, **suédoise** FEM ▶ SEE
Suédois
Swedish

un **Suédois** MASC NOUN, une **Suédoise** FEM ▶ SEE
suédois
1 **Swede** (person from Sweden)
les Suédois the Swedes

⊙ means the verb takes être to form the perfect

2 le suédois Swedish *(the language)*

suer *VERB* [1]
   to sweat

la **sueur** *FEM NOUN*
   sweat
   Je suis en sueur. I'm sweating.

suffire *VERB* [74]
1 to be enough
   Un kilo d'abricots suffit pour faire une
   tarte. One kilo of apricots is enough to
   make a tarte.
   Ça suffit! That's enough!
2 il suffit de faire ... all you have to do is ...
   Il suffit de nous téléphoner. All you have to
   do is give us a call.

suffisamment *ADVERB*
   enough
   Nous ne sommes pas suffisamment
   informés. We don't have enough
   information.
   Il n'y a pas suffisamment de verres. There
   aren't enough glasses.

suffisant *MASC ADJECTIVE*, **suffisante** *FEM*
   sufficient
   100 euros, c'est bien suffisant! 100 euros,
   that's quite enough!

suffoquer *VERB* [1]
   to suffocate

suggérer *VERB* [24]
   to suggest

la **suggestion** *FEM NOUN*
   suggestion

se **suicider** *REFLEXIVE VERB* ⬮ [1]
   to commit suicide

suis *VERB* ▶ SEE **être, suivre**

suisse *MASC & FEM ADJECTIVE* ▶ SEE **Suisse** *NOUN*
   Swiss
   un mot suisse a Swiss word
   la cuisine suisse Swiss cooking

   WORD TIP Adjectives never have capitals in
   French, even for nationality or regional origin.

un & une **Suisse** *MASC & FEM NOUN* ▶ SEE **suisse**
1 Swiss *(person)*
   les Suisses romands the French-speaking
   Swiss
   les Suisses allemands the German-speaking
   Swiss
2 la Suisse Switzerland
   Verbier est en Suisse. Verbier is in
   Switzerland.
   la Suisse romande French-speaking
   Switzerland
   la Suisse allemande German-speaking

Switzerland

   WORD TIP Countries and regions in French take
   le, la, or les.

la **suite** *FEM NOUN*
1 rest
   Je te raconterai la suite plus tard. I'll tell
   you the rest later.
   Et on connaît la suite. And we all know
   what happened next.
2 continuation
   'Suite page 67.' 'Continued on page 67.'
   Regardez la suite jeudi. Watch the next
   instalment on Thursday.
3 suite *(in a hotel)*
4 in succession
   trois fois de suite three times in succession
5 tout de suite straightaway
   J'arrive tout de suite. I'll be right there.
6 par la suite later
   On s'est rendu compte par la suite que
   c'était une erreur. We realized later that it
   was a mistake.

suivant *MASC ADJECTIVE*, **suivante** *FEM* ▶ SEE
   suivant *NOUN*
1 following
   le jour suivant the following day
2 next
   le chapitre suivant the next chapter

le **suivant** *MASC NOUN*, la **suivante** *FEM* ▶ SEE
   suivant *ADJECTIVE*
   next one
   pas ce lundi mais le suivant not this
   Monday but the next
   Au suivant! Next please!

suivre *VERB* [75]
1 to follow
   Suivez-moi! Follow me!
   Tu devrais suivre ses conseils. You should
   follow his advice.
   Elle ne suit jamais la recette. She nevers
   follows the recipe.
   Il a décidé de suivre un régime. He decided
   to go on a diet.
2 'À suivre' 'To be continued'
3 to keep up
   Luc n'arrive pas à suivre en maths. Luc
   can't keep up in maths.
   Je suis l'actualité. I keep up with the news.
4 suivre un cours to do a course
   Éric suit un cours d'informatique. Éric is
   doing a computing course.
5 to pay attention *(at school)*
   Alexis ne suit pas en classe, il bavarde trop.
   Alexis is not paying attention in class, he
   chatters too much.
6 to follow *(to understand)*
   Je ne te suis pas, c'est trop compliqué! I
   don't follow you, it's too complicated!

7 faire suivre to forward
J'ai fait suivre ton email. I forwarded your email.
Il fait suivre son courrier à sa nouvelle adresse. He has his mail forwarded to his new address.

le **sujet** MASC NOUN
1 subject
un sujet de conversation a topic of conversation
au sujet de quelque chose about something
C'est au sujet de votre sœur. It's about your sister.
C'est à quel sujet? What's it about?
2 question
un sujet d'examen an exam question
un sujet d'histoire a history question
une dissertation sur sujet libre an essay on a subject of your choice

ℙ **super** INVARIABLE MASC & FEM ADJECTIVE ▸ SEE **super** ADVERB
(informal) great
Mais c'est super! But that's great!
Ses parents sont super! Her parents are great!

ℙ **super** ADVERB ▸ SEE **super** INVARIABLE MASC & FEM ADJECTIVE
really
C'est super bon! It's really good!

superbe MASC & FEM ADJECTIVE
superb, magnificent

la **superficie** FEM NOUN
area

superficiel MASC ADJECTIVE, **superficielle** FEM
superficial

supérieur MASC ADJECTIVE, **supérieure** FEM ▸ SEE **supérieur** NOUN
1 upper
l'étage supérieur the upper floor
2 greater
à une vitesse supérieure at a faster speed
à une température supérieure at a higher temperature
3 superior, better (work, quality)
Cet album est de loin supérieur à l'autre. This album's much better than the other one.

le **supérieur** MASC NOUN, la **supérieure** FEM ▸ SEE **supérieur** ADJECTIVE
superior

le **superlatif** MASC NOUN
superlative

ℙ le **supermarché** MASC NOUN
supermarket
Nous faisons nos courses au supermarché. We do our shopping in the supermarket.

superposer VERB [1]
1 to stack up (chairs, boxes)
des lits superposés bunk beds
2 to superimpose (an image)

superstitieux MASC ADJECTIVE, **superstitieuse** FEM
superstitious

la **superstition** FEM NOUN
superstition

ℙ le **supplément** MASC NOUN
1 extra charge
Le vin est en supplément. Wine is extra.
Il y a un supplément de 5 euros pour le plateau de fruits de mer. The seafood platter is 5 euros extra.
2 supplement (in a newspaper)

supplémentaire MASC & FEM ADJECTIVE
1 additional
des dépenses supplémentaires extra expenses
2 les heures supplémentaires overtime

le **supplice** MASC NOUN
torture

supplier VERB [1]
to beg

le **support** MASC NOUN
support
un support audiovisuel an audiovisual aid

supportable MASC & FEM ADJECTIVE
bearable

supporter VERB [1]
1 to stand
Je ne supporte pas cette musique. I can't stand this music.
Elle ne supporte pas d'attendre. She can't stand waiting.
2 to withstand
Les plantes ont bien supporté le gel. The plants withstood the frost.
Il supporte mal les longs voyages en voiture. Long car journeys are too much for him.
3 to support (a weight)
se **supporter** REFLEXIVE VERB ◎
to stand each other
Ils ne peuvent plus se supporter. They can't stand each other any longer.

supposer VERB [1]
to suppose
Je suppose que tu n'as toujours pas fini. I suppose you still haven't finished.

supprimer VERB [1]
1 to delete
J'ai supprimé un paragraphe de ma dissertation. I deleted a paragraph in my

◎ means the verb takes être to form the perfect

essay.
2 **to cut**
Ils ont supprimé la dernière scène du film.
They cut the last scene of the film.
La direction a supprimé dix emplois.
Management cut ten jobs.
3 **to cancel**
Ils ont supprimé le train de 14 heures. They
cancelled the 2 o'clock train.

ᵖ **sur** *PREPOSITION*
1 **on**
Le chat est sur ton lit. The cat's on your bed.
Il l'a écrit sur un morceau de papier. He
wrote it on a piece of paper.
un débat sur le racisme a discussion on
racism
Le cinéma est sur la droite. The cinema's on
the right.
2 **over**
un pont sur la Tamise a bridge over the
Thames
sur une période de trois ans over a three-
year period
3 **by** *(in measurements)*
La pièce mesure deux mètres sur trois. The
room is two metres by three.
4 **out of**
trois élèves sur cinq three pupils out of five
J'ai eu douze sur vingt en géographie. I got
twelve out of twenty in geography.

ᵖ **sûr** *MASC ADJECTIVE*, **sûre** *FEM*
1 **sure**
Tu es sûr? Are you sure?
Oui, bien sûr! Yes, of course!
Elle est sûre qu'il viendra. She's sure that
he'll come.
2 **sûr de soi, de lui, d'elle ...** self-confident
Elle est très sûre d'elle. She's very self-
confident.
3 **safe**
en lieu sûr in a safe place

surcharger *VERB* [52]
to overload

la **surdité** *FEM NOUN*
deafness

la **surdose** *FEM NOUN*
overdose *(of medicine)*

sûrement *ADVERB*
1 **certainly**
Sûrement pas! Certainly not!
2 **most probably**
Tu as sûrement entendu la nouvelle. You've
most probably heard the news.

la **sûreté** *FEM NOUN*
safety

le **surf** *MASC NOUN*
1 **surfing**
faire du surf to go surfing
2 **netsurf** *(on Internet)*

la **surface** *FEM NOUN*
1 **surface**
2 **area**
Je calcule la surface du triangle. I'm
working out the area of the triangle.
3 une grande surface a hypermarket
• la surface de réparation
penalty area

le **surf des neiges** *MASC NOUN*
snowboarding
Vanessa va faire du surf des neiges.
Vanessa's going snowboarding.

ᵖ **surfer** *VERB* [1]
1 **to go surfing**
2 **to surf**
surfer sur Internet to surf the Net

le **surfeur** *MASC NOUN*, la **surfeuse** *FEM*
1 **surfer** *(on the sea)*
2 **netsurfer** *(on Internet)*

surgelé *MASC ADJECTIVE*, **surgelée** *FEM* ▶SEE
surgelé *NOUN*
frozen
les légumes surgelés frozen vegetables
le **surgelé** *MASC NOUN* ▶SEE **surgelé** *ADJECTIVE*
les surgelés frozen food

sur-le-champ *ADVERB*
right away

le **surlendemain** *MASC NOUN*
two days later
Elle est arrivée le surlendemain. She
arrived two days later.

surmonter *VERB* [1]
to overcome

surnaturel *MASC ADJECTIVE*, **surnaturelle** *FEM*
supernatural

le **surnom** *MASC NOUN*
nickname

surnommer *VERB* [1]
to nickname

surpeuplé *MASC ADJECTIVE*, **surpeuplée** *FEM*
overpopulated

surprenant *MASC ADJECTIVE*, **surprenante** *FEM*
surprising

surprendre *VERB* [64]
1 **to surprise**
J'ai été agréablement surprise. I was
pleasantly surprised.
Ça m'a beaucoup surpris. I found that really
surprising.

ᵖ **indicates key words**

2 surprendre quelqu'un en train de faire quelque chose to catch somebody doing something
Je l'ai surprise en train de lire mon courrier. I caught her reading my mail.

3 se laisser surprendre par quelque chose to get caught by something
Il s'est laissé surprendre par la marée montante. He got caught by the rising tide.

surpris MASC ADJECTIVE, **surprise** FEM
surprised
Je suis surpris de te voir. I'm surprised to see you.

la **surprise** FEM NOUN
surprise
Quelle surprise! What a surprise!
Ne dis rien, c'est une surprise! Don't say a word, it's a surprise!
À ma grande surprise, elle a accepté. To my great surprise she agreed.
Il y avait un invité surprise. There was a surprise guest.
faire une surprise à quelqu'un to give somebody a surprise
Nous allons faire une surprise à nos parents. We're going to give our parents a surprise.

• la surprise-partie
surprise party

surréaliste MASC & FEM ADJECTIVE ▸ SEE **surréaliste** NOUN
surreal

le & la **surréaliste** MASC & FEM NOUN ▸ SEE **surréaliste** ADJECTIVE
surrealist

⚬ **surtout** ADVERB
1 especially
Il y a beaucoup de touristes, surtout en été. There is a lot of tourists, especially in the summer.
2 above all
Il faut surtout rester calme. Above all, we must stay calm.

le **surveillant** MASC NOUN, la **surveillante** FEM
supervisor (In a school, responsible for maintaining school discipline outside the classroom.)

surveiller VERB [1]
1 to watch, to keep an eye on
Est-ce que tu peux surveiller mon sac? Can you keep an eye on my bag?
2 surveiller une maison to keep a house under surveillance
3 to supervise (work, progress)
surveiller le travail des élèves to supervise the students' work
4 surveiller un examen to invigilate an exam

5 watch
Je surveille ma ligne. I'm watching my figure.
Surveille ton langage! Watch your language!

le **survêtement** MASC NOUN
tracksuit

la **survie** FEM NOUN
survival

le **survivant** MASC NOUN, la **survivante** FEM
survivor

survivre VERB [82]
to survive
survivre à quelque chose to survive something
Elle a survécu au tsunami. She survived the tsunami.

survoler VERB [1]
to fly over

suspect MASC ADJECTIVE, **suspecte** FEM ▸ SEE **suspect** NOUN
suspicious

le **suspect** MASC NOUN, la **suspecte** FEM ▸ SEE **suspect** ADJECTIVE
suspect

le **suspense** MASC NOUN
suspense (as in a thriller)

la **suture** FEM NOUN
un point de suture a stitch (in a wound)

svelte MASC & FEM ADJECTIVE
slender

⚬ la **SVP** ABBREVIATION
(= s'il vous plaît) please

le **sweat** MASC NOUN ▸ SEE **sweatshirt**

le **sweatshirt** MASC NOUN
sweatshirt

la **syllabe** FEM NOUN
syllable

le **symbole** MASC NOUN
symbol

symbolique MASC & FEM ADJECTIVE
symbolic
un geste symbolique a token gesture

⚬ **sympa** INVARIABLE MASC & FEM ADJECTIVE
(informal) nice
Je le trouve très sympa, ton copain. He's really nice, your boyfriend.

la **sympathie** FEM NOUN
J'ai beaucoup de sympathie pour elle. I like her a lot.

sympathique MASC & FEM
nice

⚬ means the verb takes être to form the perfect

C'est un type sympathique. He's a nice guy.

sympathiser *VERB* [1]
sympathiser avec quelqu'un to get on well with someone
Il sympathise avec le nouvel élève. He gets on well with the new student.

le **symptôme** *MASC NOUN*
symptom

la **synagogue** *FEM NOUN*
synagogue

le **syndicat** *MASC NOUN*
trade union
- le syndicat d'initiative
tourist information office

synthétique *MASC & FEM*
synthetic

le **synthétiseur** *MASC NOUN*
synthesizer

le **système** *MASC NOUN*
system

Tt

t' *ABBREVIATION:* **te**

> **WORD TIP** te becomes t' before a word beginning with a, e, i, o, u or silent h.

ta *FEM ADJECTIVE* ▸ SEE **ton**

♃ le **tabac** *MASC NOUN*
1 tobacco
2 un bureau de tabac a tobacconist's

le **tabagisme** *MASC NOUN*
smoking, nicotine addiction
le tabagisme passif passive smoking

♃ la **table** *FEM NOUN*
table
Léa met la table. Léa's laying the table.
À table! Dinner's ready!
- la table de chevet
bedside table
- la table de nuit
bedside table

♃ le **tableau** *MASC NOUN*
1 painting
un tableau de Renoir a painting by Renoir
2 table, chart
un tableau horaire a timetable
- le tableau d'affichage
notice board
- le tableau noir
blackboard

la **tablette** *FEM NOUN*
1 bar
une tablette de chocolat a bar of chocolate
2 tablet *(computer)*
un ordinateur tablette a tablet computer

le **tableur** *MASC NOUN*
spreadsheet

le **tablier** *MASC NOUN*
apron

le **tabouret** *MASC NOUN*
stool

la **tache** *FEM NOUN*
1 stain
2 spot
- les taches de rousseur *FEM PL*
freckles

la **tâche** *FEM NOUN*
task
- les tâches ménagères *FEM PL*
household chores

tacher *VERB* [1]
to stain

le **tacle** *MASC NOUN*
tackle *(in soccer)*

le **tact** *MASC NOUN*
tact

la **tactique** *FEM NOUN*
tactics

la **taie d'oreiller** *FEM NOUN*
pillowcase

♃ la **taille** *FEM NOUN*
1 size
la taille au-dessus the next size up
la taille au-dessous the next size down
Quelle taille faites-vous? What size are you?
'Taille unique' 'One size'
2 height
une personne de taille moyenne a person of average height
3 waist

le **taille-crayon** *MASC NOUN*, les **taille-crayons** *PLURAL*
pencil sharpener

tailler *VERB* [1]
1 to cut
2 to carve *(wood)*
3 to prune *(a tree)*
4 to sharpen *(a pencil)*

le **tailleur** *MASC NOUN*
1 suit *(for a woman)*
2 tailor
être assis en tailleur to be sitting cross-legged

♃ indicates key words

se **taire** *REFLEXIVE VERB* ⬆ [76]
 to stop talking
 Taisez-vous! Be quiet!

le **talent** *MASC NOUN*
 talent
 Il a du talent. He's talented

ℰ le **talon** *MASC NOUN*
 1 **heel** *(of your foot, a shoe)*
 chaussures à talons hauts high-heeled
 shoes
 2 **stub** *(of a ticket)*

le **tambour** *MASC NOUN*
 drum

le **tambourin** *MASC NOUN*
 tambourine

la **Tamise** *FEM NOUN*
 la Tamise the Thames

le **tampon** *MASC NOUN*
 stamp
 • le tampon à récurer
 scouring pad
 • le tampon hygiénique
 tampon

tamponneuse *FEM ADJECTIVE*
 les autos tamponneuses the dodgems

tandis que *CONJUNCTION*
 while

tant *ADVERB*
 1 **so much**
 J'ai tant mangé! I've eaten so much!
 ce qu'elle avait tant voulu what she had
 wanted so much
 2 **tant de** so much, so many
 tant d'argent so much money
 tant d'amis so many friends
 3 Tant pis. Never mind.
 4 Tant mieux. It's just as well.
 5 tant que while
 Allons se promener tant qu'il fait beau!
 Let's go for a walk while it's nice!
 6 tant que as long as
 Je reste dehors tant qu'il y aura du soleil.
 I'm staying outside as long as there's some
 sunshine.

ℰ la **tante** *FEM NOUN*
 aunt

tantôt *ADVERB*
 sometimes

taper *VERB* [1]
 1 taper quelqu'un to hit somebody
 Lydia m'a tapé. Lydia hit me.
 2 taper à la machine to type
 3 taper des mains to clap your hands
 4 taper à quelque chose to knock on

something
 Il y a quelqu'un qui tape à la porte. There's
 someone knocking at the door.

se **taper** *REFLEXIVE VERB* ⬆
 se taper dessus to knock each other about

le **tapis** *INVARIABLE MASC NOUN*
 carpet
 • le tapis de souris
 mousemat

le **tapis roulant** *MASC NOUN*
 1 moving walkway
 2 carousel *(for airport luggage)*
 3 conveyor belt

tapisser *VERB* [1]
 to wallpaper

la **tapisserie** *FEM NOUN*
 1 tapestry
 2 wallpaper

taquiner *VERB* [1]
 to tease

ℰ **tard** *ADVERB*
 late
 Il est tard. It's late.
 trop tard too late
 plus tard later

tardif *MASC ADJECTIVE*, **tardive** *FEM*
 late

ℰ le **tarif** *MASC NOUN*
 1 **rate**
 le tarif horaire the hourly rate
 2 **fare**
 le plein tarif full fare
 le tarif réduit reduced fare
 à tarif réduit at a reduced price
 3 **price list**
 tarif des consommations price list *(in a
 French cafe)*

ℰ la **tarte** *FEM NOUN*
 tart
 une tarte aux abricots an apricot tart

ℰ la **tartine** *FEM NOUN*
 slice of bread and butter
 une tartine de confiture a slice of bread
 and jam

tartiner *VERB* [1]
 to spread *(on bread)*

le **tas** *INVARIABLE MASC NOUN*
 1 **pile**
 un tas de bois a pile of wood
 2 *(informal)* un tas de quelque chose stacks
 of something
 J'ai un tas de choses à faire ce soir. I've got
 stacks of things to do tonight.

⬆ means the verb takes être to form the perfect

ℐ la **tasse** *FEM NOUN*
  cup
  une tasse de thé a cup of tea

le **tatouage**
  tattoo

la **taupe** *FEM NOUN*
  mole *(the animal)*

la **taupinière** *FEM NOUN*
  molehill

le **taureau** *MASC NOUN*, les **taureaux** *PLURAL*
  ▸ SEE **Taureau**
  bull

le **Taureau** *MASC NOUN* ▸ SEE **taureau**
  Taurus
  Camille est Taureau. Camille is a Taurus.

WORD TIP Signs of the zodiac do not take an article: un or une.

le **taux** *INVARIABLE MASC NOUN*
  rate
  le taux de natalité the birth rate
• le taux de change
  exchange rate

la **taxe** *FEM NOUN*
  tax
  la boutique hors taxes the duty-free shop

le **taxi** *MASC NOUN*
  taxi
  appeler un taxi to call a taxi
  On a pris un taxi. We took a taxi.

tchatter *VERB* [1]
  to chat online

tchèque *MASC & FEM ADJECTIVE*
  Czech
  la République tchèque the Czech Republic

te *PRONOUN*
1 *(as a direct object)* **you**
  Elle te taquine. She's teasing you.
  Il ne t'aime pas. He doesn't like you.
2 *(as an indirect object)* **(to) you**
  Écoute, elle te parle! Listen, she's talking to you!
  Il t'a expliqué le problème? Did he explain the problem to you?
3 *(with reflexive verbs)* **yourself**
  Tu te lèves à quelle heure? What time do you get up? *(se lever is a reflexive verb)*
4 **(for) yourself**
  Tu t'es acheté un jean? Did you buy yourself a pair of jeans?

WORD TIP te becomes t' before a, e, i, o, u or silent h.

le **technicien** *MASC NOUN*, la **technicienne** *FEM*
  technician

technique *MASC & FEM ADJECTIVE* ▸ SEE **technique**
  NOUN
  technical

la **technique** *FEM NOUN* ▸ SEE **technique**
  ADJECTIVE
  technique

la **technologie** *FEM NOUN*
  technology

le **tee-shirt** *MASC NOUN*
  T-shirt

le **teint** *MASC NOUN*
  complexion
  avoir le teint clair to have a fair complexion
  avoir le teint mat to have olive skin

le **teinturier** *MASC NOUN*, la **teinturière** *FEM*
  dry-cleaner's

tel *MASC ADJECTIVE*, **telle** *FEM*
1 **such**
  un tel talent such talent
  une telle aventure such an adventure
  de tels mensonges such lies
  Je n'ai jamais rien vu de tel. I've never seen anything like it.
2 tel que **such as**
  les animaux tels que le lion et le tigre animals such as the lion and the tiger
  les grandes villes telles que Paris et Lyon big cities such as Paris and Lyons
3 rien de tel que ... **nothing like ...**
  Il n'y a rien de tel qu'un bon repas. There's nothing like a good meal.
4 tel quel **as it is**
  Servir le saumon tel quel. Serve the salmon just as it is.
  J'ai acheté la veste telle quelle. I bought the jacket just as it was.

ℐ la **télé** *FEM NOUN*
  (informal) **telly**
  à la télé on telly
• la télécabine
  cable car
• la télécarte®
  phonecard
• la télécommande
  remote control
• la télécopie
  fax
• le télécopieur
  fax machine
• le télégramme
  telegram
• le téléphérique
  cable car

télécharger [52] *VERB*
  to download

A B C D E F G H I J K L M N O P Q R S **T** U V W X Y Z

♀ le **téléphone** MASC NOUN
telephone
au téléphone on the phone
un numéro de téléphone a phone number
• le téléphone portable
mobile phone

♀ **téléphoner** VERB [1]
to phone
téléphoner à quelqu'un to phone
somebody
Je vais téléphoner à Nicolas. I'm going to
phone Nicolas.

téléphonique MASC & FEM ADJECTIVE
une cabine téléphonique a phone box

la **télé-réalité** FEM NOUN
reality TV

le **télésiège** MASC NOUN
chairlift

♀ le **téléspectateur** MASC NOUN, la
téléspectatrice FEM
viewer (of TV programme)

♀ le **téléviseur** MASC NOUN
television (set)

♀ la **télévision** FEM NOUN
television
Nous regardons la télévision. We're
watching television.
• la télévision par câble
cable television
• la télévision par satellite
satellite television

telle FEM ADJECTIVE ▶ SEE **tel**

tellement ADVERB
1 so
C'est tellement compliqué. It's so
complicated.
2 so much
Il a tellement plu. It rained so much.
'Tu aimes lire?' – 'Pas tellement.' 'Do you
like reading?' – 'Not much.'
3 tellement de so much, so many
J'ai tellement de travail. I've got so much
work.
Il y avait tellement de monde. There were
so many people there.

tels PLURAL MASC ADJECTIVE, **telles** FEM PL ▶ SEE **tel**

le **témoignage** MASC NOUN
1 story (of a person's life)
le témoignage d'une adolescente africaine
an African teenager's story
2 account
selon les témoignages de quelques
passants according to accounts given by
some passers-by
3 evidence (used in court)

témoigner VERB [1]
to give evidence

le **témoin** MASC NOUN
witness

♀ la **température** FEM NOUN
temperature
La température est de 20°C. The
temperature is 20°C.
Martine est malade, elle a de la
température. Martine is ill, she has a
temperature.
prendre la température de quelqu'un to
take somebody's temperature
L'infirmière m'a pris la température. The
nurse took my temperature.

la **tempête** FEM NOUN
storm

le **temple** MASC NOUN
1 temple
2 (Protestant) church

temporaire MASC & FEM ADJECTIVE
temporary

♀ le **temps** INVARIABLE MASC NOUN
1 weather
le mauvais temps the bad weather
par temps de pluie in rainy weather
Quel temps fait-il? What's the weather like?
2 time
Je n'ai pas le temps. I haven't got time.
Il nous reste combien de temps? How
much time have we got left?
Il est temps de partir. It's time to go.
mettre du temps à faire quelque chose
to take time to do something
Ça a mis beaucoup de temps. It took a long
time.
Il met beaucoup de temps à s'habiller. He
takes his time to get dressed.
passer son temps à faire quelque chose to
spend your time doing something
Elle passe son temps à écouter de la
musique. She spends her time listening to
music.
perdre son temps to waste your time
Tu perds ton temps. You're wasting your
time.
Il était temps! About time too!
à temps in time, on time
de temps en temps from time to time
en même temps at the same time
un travail à plein temps a full-time job
un travail à temps partiel a part-time job
3 tense (of a verb)

la **tendance** FEM NOUN
1 tendency
Elle a une tendance à l'étourderie. She can

318

be a bit absent-minded.
avoir tendance à faire quelque chose to
tend to do something
Il a tendance à croire tout ce qu'on dit. He
tends to believe everything you say.

2 trend

tendre *MASC & FEM ADJECTIVE* ▸ SEE **tendre** *VERB*

1 tender
de la viande tendre tender meat

2 soft
C'est un dur au cœur tendre. He's got a soft
heart beneath that tough exterior.

tendre *VERB* [3]
▸ SEE **tendre** *ADJECTIVE*

1 to stretch *(something elastic)*

2 to hold out
tendre quelque chose à quelqu'un to hold
something out to somebody
Elle m'a tendu un crayon. She held out a
pencil to me.

3 tendre le bras to reach out

la **tendresse** *FEM NOUN*
tenderness

tendu *MASC ADJECTIVE*, **tendue** *FEM*
tense

ℱ **tenir** *VERB* [77]

1 to hold
Peux-tu tenir la corde? Can you hold the
rope?
Elle tenait l'enfant par la main. She was
holding the child by the hand.

2 to run *(a business)*
Mon oncle tient un restaurant. My uncle
runs a restaurant.

3 to keep
'Tenir hors de la portée des enfants' 'Keep
away from children'

4 to take up
tenir de la place to take up space

5 to fit
Nous ne tiendrons pas tous à table. We
won't all fit around the table.

6 tenir à faire quelque chose to be
determined to do something
Je tiens à le finir aujourd'hui. I'm
determined to finish it today.

7 Tiens! Oh!

se **tenir** *REFLEXIVE VERB* ◉

1 to hold
Tiens-toi à la rampe! Hold the banister!

2 to stand
Elle se tenait devant l'entrée. She was
standing by the entrance.
Tiens-toi droit! Stand up straight!

3 *(meeting)* **to be held**
La réunion se tiendra à 19 heures. The
meeting will be held at 7 p.m.

le **tennis** *INVARIABLE MASC NOUN*
tennis
Victor joue au tennis. Victor plays tennis.
un terrain de tennis, un court de tennis a
tennis court

• le tennis de table
table tennis

la **tension** *FEM NOUN*

1 tension *(of a rope)*

2 blood pressure

tentant *MASC ADJECTIVE*, **tentante** *FEM*
tempting

la **tentation** *FEM NOUN*
temptation

la **tentative** *FEM NOUN*
attempt

ℱ la **tente** *FEM NOUN*
tent
une tente pour 6 personnes a six-man tent
monter la tente to pitch the tent

tenter *VERB* [1]

1 to attempt
tenter de faire quelque chose to try to do
something
Il a tenté de s'échapper. He tried to escape.

2 to tempt

la **tenue** *FEM NOUN*

1 clothes
changer de tenue to change clothes
en tenue décontractée wearing casual
clothes
la tenue de sport sports kit
'Tenue correcte exigée' 'Appropriate
clothing must be worn' *(in a church, a
museum)*

2 behaviour
Sa tenue en classe est irréprochable. Her
behaviour in class is impeccable.

le **terme** *MASC NOUN*

1 word
un terme technique a technical term

2 end
à court terme short-term
à long terme long-term

3 les termes the terms

WORD TIP terme does not mean school term in
English; for the meaning of term ▸ SEE **trimestre**.

la **terminale** *FEM NOUN*
(the French equivalent of) Year 13

terminer *VERB* [1]
to finish
'Avez-vous terminé?' – 'Oui, merci.' 'Have
you finished?' – 'Yes, thanks.'

ℱ indicates key words

se **terminer** REFLEXIVE VERB ⬅
to end
La réunion s'est terminée à 18 heures. The meeting ended at 6 p.m.

le **terminus** INVARIABLE MASC NOUN
terminus

♀ le **terrain** MASC NOUN
1 land, ground
du terrain marécageux some marshy land
2 plot of land
un terrain à bâtir a site (for building on)
3 ground, pitch (for sports)
un nouveau terrain de sport a new sports ground
• le terrain de camping
campsite
• le terrain de football
football pitch
• le terrain de golf
golf course
• le terrain de jeu(x)
playground

la **terrasse** FEM NOUN
terrace
Je me suis assis à la terrasse d'un café. I sat at a table outside a cafe.

la **terre** FEM NOUN
1 ground
Il était à terre. He was lying on the ground.
2 soil
La terre ici est fertile. The soil here is rich.
3 land (not sea)
4 par terre on the floor, on the ground
Le verre est tombé par terre. The glass fell on the floor.
5 earth
vivre sur terre to live on earth
6 la Terre the Earth
• la terre cuite
terracotta

♀ **terrible** MASC & FEM ADJECTIVE
1 terrible
des événements terribles terrible events
2 (informal) terrific
Le concert était terrible! The concert was terrific!

terrifiant MASC ADJECTIVE, **terrifiante** FEM
terrifying

terrifier VERB [1]
terrify

la **terrine** FEM
1 (round) bowl (for cooking)
2 terrine de canard terrine of duck

le **territoire** MASC NOUN
1 territory

2 country

le **terrorisme** MASC NOUN
terrorism

le & la **terroriste** MASC & FEM NOUN
terrorist

tes PLURAL ADJECTIVE
▶ SEE **ton** your

le **test** MASC NOUN
test

WORD TIP test does not mean a school test in English; for the meaning of **test** ▶ SEE **contrôle**.

le **testament** MASC NOUN
will

tester VERB [1]
to test

le **tétanos** INVARIABLE MASC NOUN
tetanus

le **têtard** MASC NOUN
tadpole

♀ la **tête** FEM NOUN
1 head
Tu t'es cogné la tête. You banged your head.
Elle a mal à la tête. She has a headache.
se laver la tête to wash your hair
2 face
Pourquoi fait-il cette tête? Why is he pulling such a face?
3 mind
J'ai quelque chose en tête. I've got something in mind.
4 faire la tête to sulk
Il fait la tête car il n'est pas invité. He's sulking because he isn't invited.
5 en tête à tête in private
un dîner en tête à tête an intimate dinner for two
6 top
Tu es en tête de la liste. You're first on the list.
7 front (of a train)
les deux wagons de tête the two front coaches

têtu MASC ADJECTIVE, **têtue** FEM
stubborn

le **texte** MASC NOUN
text

le **texto**® MASC NOUN
text message
envoyer un texto à quelqu'un to text somebody
Jeanne m'a envoyé un texto pour dire qu'elle arrive. Jeanne texted me to say she's on her way.

⬅ means the verb takes être to form the perfect

𝒫 le **TGV®** *MASC NOUN*
(= *train à grande vitesse*) **high-speed train**

la **thalassothérapie** *FEM NOUN*
sea-water treatment (*at a health spa*)

𝒫 le **thé** *MASC NOUN*
tea
un thé au lait tea with milk
un thé au citron a lemon tea
une tasse de thé a cup of tea
Je vais faire du thé. I'll make some tea.
Deux thés, s'il vous plaît! Two teas please!
un salon de thé a tea room
• le thé à la bergamote
Earl Grey tea
• le thé vert
green tea

𝒫 le **théâtre** *MASC NOUN*
1 **theatre**
Demain, nous allons au théâtre. Tomorrow
we're going to the theatre.
une pièce de théâtre a play
un coup de théâtre a dramatic turn of
events
2 **plays**
le théâtre de Molière Molière's plays
3 **drama**
une école de théâtre a drama school
Lou fait du théâtre. Lou's in a drama group.

la **théière** *FEM NOUN*
teapot

le **thème** *MASC NOUN*
subject

la **théorie** *FEM NOUN*
theory

la **thérapie** *FEM NOUN*
1 **(medical) treatment**
2 **therapy**

thermal *MASC ADJECTIVE*, **thermale** *FEM*,
thermaux *MASC PL*, **thermales** *FEM PL*
thermal
une station thermale a spa

le **thermomètre** *MASC NOUN*
thermometer

le or la **thermos®** *INVARIABLE MASC & FEM NOUN*
vacuum flask

le **thon** *MASC NOUN*
tuna

le **tibia** *MASC NOUN*
Il a reçu un coup de pied dans les tibias. He
got a kick in the shins.

le **tic** *MASC NOUN*
nervous twitch

𝒫 le **ticket** *MASC NOUN*
ticket
• le ticket de caisse
till receipt
• le ticket de métro
underground ticket
• le ticket de quai
platform ticket

tiède *MASC & FEM ADJECTIVE*
1 **warm**
2 **lukewarm**

le **tien** *MASC PRONOUN*, la **tienne** *FEM* les **tiens**
MASC PL les **tiennes** *FEM PL*
yours
Est-ce que ce stylo est le tien? Is this pen
yours?
J'ai laissé ma moto chez moi. On va
prendre la tienne. I left my motorbike at
home. We'll take yours.
Je n'aime pas ces baskets. Je préfère les
tiens. I don't like those trainers. I prefer
yours.
Ces chaussures, ce sont les tiennes, n'est-ce
pas? Those shoes – they're yours, aren't
they?

WORD TIP The article and pronoun change in
French when they refer to fem and plural nouns.

tiens *VERB* ▸ SEE **tenir**

tiers *MASC ADJECTIVE*, **tierce** *FEM* ▸ SEE **tiers** *NOUN*
third

𝒫 le **tiers** *MASC NOUN* ▸ SEE **tiers** *ADJECTIVE*
third
les deux tiers de la population two-thirds
of the population

𝒫 le **tiers-monde** *MASC NOUN*
Third World

le **tigre** *MASC NOUN*
tiger

le **tilleul** *MASC NOUN*
1 **lime tree**
2 **herbal tea** (*made from lime flowers*)

𝒫 le **timbre** *MASC NOUN*
stamp
un timbre tarif rapide a first-class stamp
un timbre tarif lent a second-class stamp
un timbre à 55 centimes a 55-cent stamp
Je voudrais un timbre pour la Grande-
Bretagne. I'd like a stamp for Great Britain.

𝒫 **timide** *MASC & FEM ADJECTIVE*
shy

la **timidité** *FEM NOUN*
shyness

le **tir** *MASC NOUN*
1 **shooting**

A B C D E F G H I J K L M N O P Q R S **T** U V W X Y Z

2 shot *(in football)*
- le tir à l'arc
  archery

le **tirage** *MASC NOUN*
  draw
  le tirage de la loterie the lottery draw
  le tirage au sort the draw

le **tire-bouchon** *MASC NOUN*
  corkscrew

la **tirelire** *FEM NOUN*
  money box

tirer *VERB* [1]
1 to pull
  Le bébé tire les cheveux. The baby pulls
  my hair.
  Il m'a tiré par le bras. He pulled my arm.
  'Tirez' 'Pull' *(on doors)*
2 to draw
  tirer les rideaux to draw the curtains
  tirer au sort to draw lots
  tirer des conclusions to draw conclusions
3 to fire *(a gun)*
4 to shoot *(in ball games)*

le **tiret** *MASC NOUN*
  dash

le **tiroir** *MASC NOUN*
  drawer

la **tisane** *FEM NOUN*
  herbal tea

le **tissu** *MASC NOUN*
  material, fabric

> **WORD TIP** tissu does not mean a tissue in
> English; for the meaning of tissue ▸ SEE kleenex®.

le **titre** *MASC NOUN*
1 title
  le titre du livre the book title
2 headline
  les gros titres the headlines
  les titres de l'actualité the news headlines
- le titre de transport
  travel ticket

tituber *VERB* [1]
  to stagger

le **toast** *MASC NOUN*
1 piece of toast
2 toast *(in champagne)*

le **toboggan** *MASC NOUN*
  slide

> **WORD TIP** toboggan does not mean toboggan
> in English; for the meaning of toboggan ▸ SEE
> luge.

♀**toi** *PRONOUN*
1 you *(as opposed to anybody else)*

C'était toi! It was you!
chez toi at your house
Elle pense à toi. She's thinking of you.
2 *(after prepositions like avec or sans and in
comparisons)* **you**
  Je peux venir avec toi? Can I come with
  you?
  C'est pour toi. It's for you.
  Louis est plus grand que toi. Louis is taller
  than you.
3 à toi yours *(belonging to you)*
  J'ai vu des amis à toi. I saw some friends of
  yours.
  Ce n'est pas a toi. That's not yours.
4 *(for emphasis)* **you**
  Toi, tu restes là. You stay there.
  C'est toi qui as oublié. You're the one who
  forgot.
  C'est à toi de jouer. It's your turn to play.

la **toile** *FEM NOUN*
1 cloth
2 canvas
3 painting
  une toile de Picasso a painting by Picasso
4 la toile the web *(Internet)*
- la toile d'araignée
  cobweb

la **toilette** *FEM NOUN*
1 wash
  faire sa toilette to have a wash
  les produits de toilette toiletries
2 outfit
  Je me suis acheté une nouvelle toilette. I've
  bought a new outfit.

> **WORD TIP** toilette does not mean toilet in
> English; for the meaning of toilet ▸ SEE toilettes.

♀les **toilettes** *PLURAL FEM NOUN*
  toilet
  Où sont les toilettes, s'il vous plaît? Where
  are the toilets please?
  les toilettes pour dames the ladies
  les toilettes pour hommes the gents

toi-même *PRONOUN*
  yourself
  Est-ce que tu l'as fait toi-même? Did you
  make it yourself?

le **toit** *MASC NOUN*
  roof

tolérant *MASC ADJECTIVE*, **tolérante** *FEM*
  tolerant

tolérer *VERB* [24]
  to tolerate

♀la **tomate** *FEM NOUN*
  tomato
  des tomates en salade, une salade de

⬤ means the verb takes être to form the perfect

tomates a tomato salad
la sauce tomate tomato sauce

la **tombe** *FEM NOUN*
grave

le **tombeau** *MASC NOUN*, les **tombeaux** *PLURAL*
tomb

♪ **tomber** *VERB* ☁ [1]
1 to fall
Attention, tu vas tomber! Careful, you'll fall!
La chaise est tombée. The chair fell over.
Lucy est tombée à l'eau. Lucy fell into the water.
La nuit tombe. It's getting dark.
2 tomber malade to fall ill
Je suis tombé malade pendant les vacances. I fell ill during the holidays.
tomber amoureux de quelqu'un to fall in love with somebody
Nadjette est tombée amoureuse de Kevin.
Nadjette fell in love with Kevin.
3 to come
C'est tombé au bon moment. It came at the right time.
4 faire tomber quelqu'un, quelque chose to knock somebody, something over
J'ai fait tomber le vase. I knocked the vase over.
5 laisser tomber to drop
J'ai laissé tomber mon porte-monnaie. I've dropped my purse.
6 laisser tomber to give up (an activity)
Elle a laissé tomber l'espagnol. She's given up Spanish.
Laisse tomber! Forget it!
laisser tomber quelqu'un to drop somebody
Il a laissé tomber sa petite amie. He dumped his girlfriend.

WORD TIP When you use faire or laisser before tomber to talk about the past, use avoir in the perfect tense.

ton *MASC ADJECTIVE*, **ta** *FEM*, **tes** *PLURAL* ▶SEE **ton** *NOUN*
your
ton frère your brother
ta sœur your sister
tes amis your friends
tes yeux your eyes

le **ton** *MASC NOUN* ▶SEE **ton** *ADJECTIVE*
1 tone of voice
Ne me parle pas sur ce ton! Don't speak to me in that tone of voice!
2 shade
des tons de bleu shades of blue

la **tonalité** *FEM NOUN*
1 tone (of voice)

2 (Telephones) dialling tone

la **tondeuse** *FEM NOUN*
lawnmower

tondre *VERB* [3]
1 to mow (a lawn)
2 to clip (a dog, a horse)

les **tongs** *PLURAL FEM NOUN*
flip-flops

tonique *MASC & FEM ADJECTIVE*
1 tonic (drink)
2 lively (child)

la **tonne** *FEM NOUN*
1 tonne (1,000 kg)
2 ton
J'ai des tonnes de choses à faire. I've got tons of things to do.

le **tonneau** *MASC NOUN*, les **tonneaux** *PLURAL*
barrel

le **tonnerre** *MASC NOUN*
thunder
un coup de tonnerre a clap of thunder
il fait du tonnerre, il y a du tonnerre there is thunder

le **tonton** *MASC NOUN*
(informal) uncle

le **tonus** *INVARIABLE MASC NOUN*
1 energy (for a person)
avoir du tonus to be dynamic
2 tone (for your muscles)

la **toque** *FEM NOUN*
1 chef's hat
2 cap (for a jockey)

le **torchon** *MASC NOUN*
1 tea towel
2 (informal) rag (newspaper)
3 (informal) messy piece of work
La prof a dit que je lui ai rendu un torchon. The teacher said that the piece of work I handed in was a real mess.

tordre *VERB* [3]
1 to twist (your arm, your wrist)
tordre le bras à quelqu'un to twist somebody's arm
Il m'a tordu le bras. He twisted my arm.
2 to wring out (the washing, a towel)
3 to bend (metal, a bumper)

se **tordre** *REFLEXIVE VERB* ☁
to twist
se tordre le bras to twist your arm
Je me suis tordu la cheville. I twisted my ankle.

tordu *MASC ADJECTIVE*, **tordue** *FEM*
bent

la **tornade** FEM NOUN
tornado

le **torrent** MASC NOUN
mountain stream

le **torse** MASC NOUN
chest

♂ le **tort** MASC NOUN
avoir tort to be wrong
Je crois que tu as tort. I think you're wrong.
avoir tort de faire quelque chose to be
wrong to do something
Il a tort de dire ça. He's wrong to say that.

le **torticolis** INVARIABLE MASC NOUN
stiff neck
avoir un torticolis to have a stiff neck

se **tortiller** REFLEXIVE VERB ◯ [1]
to wriggle

la **tortue** FEM NOUN
tortoise

la **torture** FEM NOUN
torture

torturer VERB [1]
to torture

♂ **tôt** ADVERB
1 early
On va partir tôt. We're leaving early.
2 soon
Je viendrai le plus tôt possible. I'll come as
soon as possible.
tôt ou tard sooner or later
au plus tôt at the earliest
(informal) 'J'ai fini.' – 'Eh bien, ce n'est pas
trop tôt!' – 'I've finished.' – 'About time too!'

total MASC ADJECTIVE, **totale** FEM, **totaux** MASC
PL, **totales** FEM PL ▶ SEE **total** NOUN
total

le **total** MASC NOUN, les **totaux** PLURAL ▶ SEE **total**
ADJECTIVE
total
au total in total

totalement ADVERB
totally

la **totalité** FEM NOUN
la totalité du groupe the whole group

touchant MASC ADJECTIVE, **touchante** FEM
touching

la **touche** FEM NOUN
1 key (on a keyboard)
2 button (on a machine)
Appuyez sur la touche. Press the button.
3 la (ligne de) touche the touchline
Le ballon est sorti en touche. The ball went
into touch.

♂ **toucher** VERB [1]
1 to touch
Ne touche pas à ma peinture. Don't touch
my painting.
2 to touch (emotionally)
Cette histoire m'a beaucoup touché. That
story really touched me.
3 to affect, to concern
Ce problème nous touche tous. This
problem affects us all.
4 to get (money, wages)
Il touche 350 euros par semaine. He's
getting 350 euros a week.

touffu MASC ADJECTIVE, **touffue** FEM
bushy

♂ **toujours** ADVERB
1 always
comme toujours as always
pour toujours forever
Il est toujours en retard. He's always late.
2 still
Nous habitons toujours au même endroit.
We're still living in the same place.
Ton paquet n'est toujours pas arrivé. Your
parcel still hasn't arrived.

le **tour** MASC NOUN ▶ SEE **tour** NOUN
1 faire le tour de quelque chose to go round
something
faire le tour des magasins to go round all
the shops
faire le tour du monde to go round the
world
2 walk
On va faire un petit tour. We'll go for a little
walk.
3 ride
Allons faire un tour à vélo! Let's go for a
bike ride!
4 drive
Nous avons fait un tour en voiture dans
la campagne. We went for a drive in
countryside.
5 turn
C'est ton tour de jouer. It's your turn to
play.
À qui le tour? Whose turn is it?
6 trick
un tour de cartes a card trick

WORD TIP un tour does not mean a **tour** in
English; for the meaning of **tour** ▶ SEE **visite**,
voyage organisé.

la **tour** FEM NOUN ▶ SEE **tour** NOUN
1 tower
la tour Eiffel the Eiffel Tower
2 tower block

◯ means the verb takes être to form the perfect

3 **castle**, **rook** *(in chess)*

⊙ **TOUR**

On a construit la Tour Eiffel en 1889 pour les 100 ans de la Révolution française.

le **tourbillon** *MASC NOUN*
1 **whirlwind**
2 **whirlpool**

le **tourisme** *MASC NOUN*
  tourism
• le tourisme solidaire
  responsible tourism

le & la **touriste** *MASC & FEM NOUN*
  tourist

touristique *MASC & FEM ADJECTIVE*
  un guide touristique a tourist guide(book)
  une ville touristique a town which attracts tourists

le **tournant** *MASC NOUN*
1 **bend** *(in a road)*
2 **turning-point**

la **tournée** *FEM NOUN*
1 **round** *(by a postman, a baker)*
2 **round** *(of drinks)*
  C'est ma tournée. It's my round.
3 **tour** *(by a performer)*
  être en tournée to be on tour
  Le groupe est en tournée au Japon. The band is on tour in Japan.

ℓ **tourner** *VERB* [1]
1 **to turn**
  Tournez à gauche à l'église. Turn left at the church.
  J'ai tourné la tête et je l'ai vu. I looked around and I saw him.
2 **to go round and round**
  Leur discussion tourne en rond. Their discussion is going round in circles.
3 **to shoot** *(a film)*
  Ils tournent un film dans notre école. There're shooting a film in our school.
4 **mal tourner to go badly**
  La soirée a mal tourné. The evening went badly.
  Son frère a mal tourné. His brother turned out badly.

se **tourner** *REFLEXIVE VERB* ⊙
1 **to turn**
  Elle s'est tournée vers moi. She turned to face me.
2 **to turn round**
  Tourne-toi, je me change! Turn around, I'm getting changed!

le **tournevis** *INVARIABLE MASC NOUN*
  screwdriver

le **tournoi** *MASC NOUN*
  tournament
  le Tournoi des Six Nations the Six Nations Championship *(in rugby)*

tous *ADJECTIVE, PRONOUN* ▸SEE **tout** *ADJECTIVE*

la **Toussaint** *FEM NOUN*
  All Saints' Day *(1 November)*

tousser *VERB* [1]
  to cough

ℓ **tout** *MASC ADJECTIVE,* **toute** *FEM,* **tous** *MASC PL,* **toutes** *FEM PL* ▸SEE **tout** *ADVERB, PRON*
1 **all**
  Il a mangé tout le pain. He ate all the bread.
  Tous les garçons jouent au tennis. All the boys play tennis.
  Toutes les filles jouent au foot. All the girls play football.
  Toute la classe est punie. The whole class is punished.
  tout le monde everybody
  Ils sont invités tous les deux. They are both invited.
  Elles sont invitées toutes les deux. They are both invited.
  Elle a voyagé en Europe pendant toute une année. She travelled through Europe for a whole year.
2 **any**
  'Service à toute heure' 'Service at any time'
3 **every**
  Je me lève à 6 heures tous les jours. I get up at 6 a.m. every day.
  Nicole voit son père tous les lundis. Nicole sees her dad every Monday.
  Prenez un comprimé toutes les quatre heures. Take one pill every four hours.
  Ils se voient tous les mois. They see each other every month.
  toutes directions all directions

WORD TIP tout changes when it refers to fem and plural nouns.

ℓ **tout** *ADVERB* ▸SEE **tout** *ADJECTIVE, PRON*
1 **very**
  tout droit straight ahead
  tout petit very small
2 **all**
  Je suis tout mouillé. I'm all wet.
  Elle est toute seule. She's all alone.

ℓ **tout** *MASC PRONOUN,* **toute** *FEM,* **tous** *MASC PL,* **toutes** *FEM PL* ▸SEE **tout** *ADJECTIVE, ADVERB*
1 **everything**
  Ils ont tout pris. They took everything.
  Tout va bien. Everything's fine.
2 **all**
  C'est tout? Is that all?
  J'en compte 14 en tout. I count 14 in all.

3 all
Allons-y tous ensemble! Let's all go together!
Écoutez-moi tous! Listen to me, all of you!
Elles étaient toutes là. They were all there.

4 pas du tout not at all

WORD TIP Tous becomes toutes when it refers to fem people or things.

♂ **tout à coup** ADVERB
suddenly

tout à fait ADVERB
1 absolutely
Elle avait tout à fait raison. She was absolutely right.
'Tu es d'accord?' – 'Tout à fait.' 'Do you agree?' – 'Absolutely.'
2 quite
Je n'ai pas tout à fait fini. I haven't quite finished.
Ce n'est pas tout à fait pareil. It's not quite the same thing.

♂ **tout à l'heure** ADVERB
a little while
Je l'ai vu tout à l'heure. I saw him a little while ago.
À tout à l'heure! See you later!

tout de même ADVERB
1 all the same
C'est tout de même bizarre. All the same, it's odd.
2 honestly
Tout de même, tu exagères! Honestly! You're going a bit far.

♂ **tout de suite** ADVERB
at once, straight away
Fais-le tout de suite! Do it at once!

toute ADJECTIVE, PRONOUN ▶ SEE **tout** ADJECTIVE

toutefois ADVERB
however

toutes ADJECTIVE, PRONOUN ▶ SEE **tout** ADJECTIVE

la **toux** INVARIABLE FEM NOUN
cough

le & la **toxicomane** MASC & FEM NOUN
drug addict

toxique MASC & FEM ADJECTIVE
toxic

le **trac** MASC NOUN (informal)
1 stage fright
2 nerves

la **trace** FEM NOUN
1 les traces tracks
des traces de pas footprints
2 mark

des traces de doigts fingermarks

tracer VERB [61]
to draw

WORD TIP tracer does not mean to trace (somebody) in English; for the meaning of to trace ▶ SEE retrouver, localiser.

le **tracteur** MASC NOUN
tractor

la **tradition** FEM NOUN
tradition

traditionnel MASC ADJECTIVE, **traditionnelle** FEM
traditional

le **traducteur** MASC NOUN, la **traductrice** FEM
translator

la **traduction** FEM NOUN
translation

traduire VERB [26]
to translate
Je traduis un article en français. I'm translating an article into French.

le **trafic** MASC NOUN
1 dealing (usually illegal)
le trafic de drogue drug dealing
2 traffic (by air, sea, rail)

le **trafiquant** MASC NOUN, la **trafiquante** FEM
dealer (in drugs, arms)

tragique MASC & FEM ADJECTIVE
tragic

trahir VERB [2]
to betray

la **trahison** FEM NOUN
1 betrayal
2 treason

♂ le **train** MASC NOUN
1 train
en train by train
le train de dix heures the ten o'clock train
Le train pour Nice partira du quai 1. The train for Nice will be leaving from platform 1.
Le train est à l'heure. The train is on time.
Le train a une heure de retard. The train is an hour late.
2 être en train de faire quelque chose to be doing something
Je suis en train de faire mes devoirs. I'm

⬤ means the verb takes être to form the perfect

doing my homework.

TRAIN

Le TGV (« train à grande vitesse ») roule depuis 1981. Il va très vite ! Son record : plus de 500 km/h (300 mph). Il fait Paris-Marseille en 3 heures.

traîner *VERB* [1]
1 **to drag** *(your feet, a bag)*
2 **to hang around**
3 **to lie around**
4 **to dawdle**
5 **to drag on** *(time, classes)*

WORD TIP traîner does not mean **to train (in sport)** in English; for the meaning of **train** ▶ SEE **s'entraîner**.

traire *VERB* [78]
to milk

le **trait** *MASC NOUN*
1 **line**
Tirez un trait en bas de page. Draw a line at the end of the page.
2 **trait**
C'est un trait de caractère bien français. It's a typically French trait.
3 les **traits features** *(of your face)*
Il avait les traits tirés. He looked tired and drawn.
4 **d'un seul trait in one go**
Il a bu son verre d'un seul trait. He drank his glass down in one go.
• le **trait d'union**
hyphen

le **traité** *MASC NOUN*
treaty

le **traitement** *MASC NOUN*
1 **treatment**
Henri est sous traitement. Henri's undergoing treatment.
2 **processing**
le traitement de texte word processing
3 **salary**

traiter *VERB* [1]
1 **to treat**
Il la traite très mal. He treats her very badly.
le médecin qui me traite the doctor who's treating me
2 **to deal with** *(a question, a problem)*
3 **traiter quelqu'un de quelque chose to call someone something**
Il m'a traité de menteur. He called me a liar.
Il l'a traitée de tricheuse. He called her a cheat.

le **traiteur** *MASC NOUN*
caterer

ℓ le **trajet** *MASC NOUN*
1 **journey**
un trajet de deux heures a two-hour journey
2 **route**

le **trampoline** *MASC NOUN*
trampoline
faire du trampoline to do trampolining

le **tramway** *MASC NOUN*
1 **tram**
2 **tramway**

tranchant *MASC ADJECTIVE*, **tranchante** *FEM*
sharp

ℓ la **tranche** *FEM NOUN*
1 **slice**
deux tranches de jambon two slices of ham
Il faut couper le saucisson en tranches. You have to slice up the sausage.
2 **phase** *(of work)*
3 **period** *(of time)*

trancher *VERB* [1]
1 **to slice**
2 **to come to a decision**

ℓ **tranquille** *MASC & FEM ADJECTIVE*
1 **quiet**
une rue tranquille a quiet street
Tiens-toi tranquille! Keep still!
2 **Laisse-moi tranquille! Leave me alone!**
3 **ne pas être tranquille to worry**
Maman n'est pas tranquille si je n'appelle pas. Mum worries if I don't ring.
Sois tranquille, je ne dirai rien! Don't worry, I won't say anything!

la **tranquillité** *FEM NOUN*
peace

le **transat** *MASC NOUN*
(informal) **deck chair**

transférer *VERB* [24]
to transfer *(an employee, a player)*

le **transfert** *MASC NOUN*
transfer *(of an employee, a footballer)*

transformer *VERB* [1]
to change
Ils ont tout transformé dans leur salon. They've changed everything in their sitting room.
transformer quelque chose en quelque chose to turn something into something
Nous avons transformé le garage en salle de jeux. We've turned the garage into a playroom.

se **transformer** *REFLEXIVE VERB* ◎
to change

la **transfusion** *FEM NOUN*
  transfusion
  une transfusion sanguine a blood
  transfusion

le **transistor** *MASC NOUN*
  transistor

transmettre *VERB* [11]
1 transmettre quelque chose à quelqu'un to
  pass something on to somebody
  Je leur ai transmis tes instructions. I passed
  your instructions on to them.
  Il m'a transmis un virus par email. He
  passed a virus on to me through my email.
2 to transmit
  transmettre des chaînes de télévision par
  satellite to transmit TV channels by satellite

la **transpiration** *FEM NOUN*
  sweat

transpirer *VERB* [1]
  to sweat

la **transplantation** *FEM NOUN*
1 transplant *(medical)*
2 transplantation *(of plants)*

♂ le **transport** *MASC NOUN*
  transport
  un mode de transport a means of transport
  le transport aérien air transport
  le transport par route road transport
  le transport des déchets nucléaires the
  transport of nuclear waste
• les transports en commun
  public transport

transporter *VERB* [1]
1 to transport
2 to carry

la **trappe** *FEM NOUN*
  trap door

  WORD TIP trappe does not mean trap in English;
  for the meaning of trap ▸ SEE **piège**.

♂ le **travail** *MASC NOUN*, les **travaux** *PL*
1 work
  J'ai beaucoup de travail à faire. I've got a lot
  of work to do.
2 job
  un travail à mi-temps a part-time job
  Sylvie cherche un travail. Sylvie's looking
  for a job.
  Ma mère a cessé le travail. My mother
  stopped work.
3 les travaux work
  des travaux de construction building work
4 des travaux roadworks
  On ne peut pas passer à cause des travaux.
  We can't drive through because of the
  roadworks.

• les travaux dirigés
  classwork
• les travaux manuels
  arts and crafts
• les travaux ménagers
  housework

♂ **travailler** *VERB* [1]
1 to work
  Nous travaillons dur. We're working hard.
  Jacques travaille dans l'édition. Jacques
  works in publishing.
  Dominique travaille comme secrétaire.
  Dominique works as a secretary.
  travailler quelque chose to work on
  something
  Il faut que je travaille mon français. I must
  work on my French.
  Va travailler ton piano! Go and practise
  your piano!
2 travailler quelqu'un to bother somebody
  Qu'est-ce qui te travaille? What's bothering
  you?
  C'est ça qui me travaille. That's what's
  bothering me.

travailleur *MASC ADJECTIVE*, **travailleuse** *FEM*
  ▸ SEE **travailleur** *NOUN*
  hard-working

le **travailleur** *MASC NOUN*, la **travailleuse** *FEM*
  ▸ SEE **travailleur** *ADJECTIVE*
  worker

travailliste *MASC & FEM ADJECTIVE*
  Labour *(in British politics)*
  le parti travailliste the Labour party

les **travaux** *PLURAL MASC NOUN* ▸ SEE **travail**

le **travers** *INVARIABLE MASC NOUN*
1 à travers quelque chose through something
  passer à travers les mailles du filet to slip
  through the net
  Quelqu'un regardait à travers les rideaux.
  Somebody was looking through the
  curtains.
2 à travers quelque chose across something
  Elles ont marché à travers la campagne.
  They walked across country.
  Il voyage à travers le monde. He travels all
  over the world.
3 de travers crooked
  Le tableau est de travers. The picture's
  crooked.
4 de travers wrongly
  Tout va de travers aujourd'hui. Everything
  is going wrong today.

la **traversée** *FEM NOUN*
  crossing
  une traversée de l'Atlantique an Atlantic
  crossing
  Nous avons fait une bonne traversée. We

had a good crossing.

_ρ_ **traverser** _VERB_ [1]
1 to cross
Regardez avant de traverser la rue. Look before you cross the road.
Allez, on traverse! Let's cross over!
2 to go through
Ils ont traversé la France pour aller en Italie. They went through France on the way to Italy.
La pluie a traversé ma veste. The rain's gone right through my jacket.
Ils ont traversé une crise. They went through a crisis.

trébucher _VERB_ [1]
to stumble

le **trèfle** _MASC NOUN_
1 clover
un trèfle à quatre feuilles a four-leaved clover
2 clubs _(in cards)_
la dame de trèfle the queen of clubs

_ρ_ **treize** _INVARIABLE NUMBER_
thirteen
à treize heures at one p.m.
le treize juillet the thirteenth of July
Aurélie a treize ans. Aurélie's thirteen.

_ρ_ **treizième** _NUMBER_
thirteenth

le **tremblement de terre** _MASC NOUN_
earthquake

trembler _VERB_ [1]
to shake
Elle tremble de tout son corps. She's shaking all over.
La terre a encore tremblé en Inde. There's been another earthquake in India.

trempé _MASC ADJECTIVE_, **trempée** _FEM_
soaked

tremper _VERB_ [1]
to soak

le **tremplin** _MASC NOUN_
springboard

la **trentaine** _FEM NOUN_
about thirty
une trentaine de personnes about thirty people
Elle a la trentaine. She's in her thirties.

_ρ_ **trente** _INVARIABLE NUMBER_
thirty
le trente juillet the thirtieth of July
Elle a trente ans. She's thirty.

_ρ_ **très** _ADVERB_
very

Ils sont très heureux. They are very happy.
Il est très amoureux. He's very much in love.
Nous sommes très en avance. We're very early.
Je vais très bien. I'm very well.
J'ai très faim. I'm very hungry.

le **trésor** _MASC NOUN_
treasure

la **tresse** _FEM NOUN_
plait

triangulaire _MASC & FEM ADJECTIVE_
triangular

la **tribu** _FEM NOUN_
tribe

le **tribunal** _MASC NOUN_, les **tribunaux** _PLURAL_
court
paraître devant le tribunal to appear in court _(on a charge)_

tricher _VERB_ [1]
to cheat
Il m'a accusé d'avoir triché. He accused me of cheating.

tricolore _MASC & FEM ADJECTIVE_
three-coloured
le drapeau tricolore the French flag _(in three vertical bands of blue, white, and red)_

le **tricot** _MASC NOUN_
knitting
faire du tricot to knit

tricoter _VERB_ [1]
to knit

trier _VERB_ [1]
to sort (out)
Hier soir, nous avons trié toutes les photos. Last night we sorted out all the photographs.

_ρ_ le **trimestre** _MASC NOUN_
term
au premier trimestre in the first term

trinidadien _MASC ADJECTIVE_, **trinidadienne**
FEM ▸SEE **Trinidadien**
Trinidadian

le **Trinidadien** _MASC NOUN_, la **Trinidadienne**
FEM ▸SEE **trinidadien**
Trinidadian _(person)_

la **Trinité** _FEM NOUN_
l'île de la Trinité Trinidad

le **triomphe** _MASC NOUN_
triumph

triompher _VERB_ [1]
to triumph

A
B
C
D
E
F
G
H
I
J
K
L
M
N
O
P
Q
R
S
T
U
V
W
X
Y
Z

_ρ_ indicates key words

les tripes *PLURAL FEM NOUN*
  tripe *(for eating)*

le triple *MASC NOUN*
  three times as much
  Ça m'a coûté le triple. It cost me three times as much.

tripler *VERB* [1]
  to treble

les triplés *PLURAL MASC NOUN*
  triplets

♀ **triste** *MASC & FEM ADJECTIVE*
  1 **sad**
    Tu as l'air triste. You look sad.
    Ne sois pas triste! Don't be sad!
  2 **sorry** *(state, sight)*
    Ton anorak est dans un triste état. Your anorak's in a sorry state.

la tristesse *FEM NOUN*
  sadness

le trognon *MASC NOUN*
  1 **core** *(of an apple, a pear)*
  2 **stalk** *(of a lettuce)*

♀ **trois** *INVARIABLE NUMBER*
  three
    à trois heures at three o'clock
    le trois mars the third of March
    Tom a trois ans. Tom's three.

♀ **troisième** *MASC & FEM ADJECTIVE* ▶ SEE **troisième** *NOUN*
  third
  • le troisième âge
    the elderly

♀ **la troisième** *FEM NOUN* ▶ SEE **troisième** *ADJECTIVE*
  Year 10 *(in the French system)*

le trombone *MASC NOUN*
  1 **trombone**
  2 **paperclip**

la trompe *FEM NOUN*
  trunk *(of an elephant)*

tromper *VERB* [1]
  to deceive
se tromper *REFLEXIVE VERB* ◯
  to make a mistake
    Il se trompe souvent. He often makes mistakes.
    se tromper de quelque chose to get something wrong
    Vous vous êtes trompé de numéro. You've got the wrong number.

la trompette *FEM NOUN*
  trumpet
    Charlotte joue de la trompette. Charlotte plays the trumpet.

le tronc *MASC NOUN*
  trunk *(of a tree)*

la tronçonneuse *FEM NOUN*
  chainsaw

♀ **trop** *ADVERB*
  1 **too**
    C'est trop loin. It's too far.
    C'est beaucoup trop cher. It's far too expensive.
  2 **too much**
    J'ai trop mangé. I've eaten too much.
    Tu m'en as donné trop. You've given me too much.
  3 **trop de too much, too many**
    J'ai acheté trop de pain. I bought too much bread.
    Tu as mangé trop de bonbons. You've eaten too many sweets.
    Il y a trop de monde. There are too many people.
  4 **de trop too many, too much**
    Il y a une chaise de trop. There's one chair too many.
    Il y a dix euros de trop. That's ten euros too much.

♀ **le trottoir** *MASC NOUN*
  pavement
    Reste sur le trottoir. Stay on the pavement.
    le bord du trottoir the kerb

le trou *MASC NOUN*
  hole
    le trou dans la couche d'ozone the hole in the ozone layer
  • le trou de la serrure
    keyhole

troublant *MASC ADJECTIVE*, **troublante** *FEM*
  disturbing

trouer *VERB* [1]
  to make a hole in
    des chaussettes trouées socks with holes in them
    J'ai troué mon jean neuf. I put a hole in my new jeans.

la trouille *FEM NOUN*
  (informal) **fear**
    avoir la trouille to be scared
    Elle a la trouille du prof. She's scared of the teacher.

la troupe *FEM NOUN*
  1 **troop** *(of soldiers)*
  2 **troop** *(of tourists, children)*
  3 **flock** *(of birds)*
  • la troupe de théâtre
    theatre company

le troupeau *MASC NOUN*, **les troupeaux** *PLURAL*
  1 **herd** *(of cattle)*

◯ **means the verb takes être to form the perfect**

2 **flock** (of sheep)

ρ la **trousse** FEM NOUN
pencil case
- la trousse de maquillage
  make-up bag
- la trousse de secours
  first-aid kit

le **trousseau** MASC NOUN, les **trousseaux**
    PLURAL
bunch
un trousseau de clés a bunch of keys

ρ **trouver** VERB [1]
1 **to find**
J'ai trouvé un portefeuille dans le bus. I
found a wallet on the bus.
As-tu trouvé ton passeport? Did you find
your passport?
Il a trouvé son chemin. He found his way.
Savez-vous où je peux trouver des ciseaux?
Do you know where I can find a pair of
scissors?
2 trouver que ... to think that ...
Moi, je trouve que c'est intéressant. I think
it's interesting.
Ah bon, tu trouves? Really, do you think so?
J'ai trouvé le film passionnant. I thought
the film was wonderful.

se **trouver** REFLEXIVE VERB ⌃
1 **to be** (in a place)
Cette semaine elle se trouve à Montpellier.
She's in Montpellier this week.
Le musée se trouve près de la mairie. The
museum is next to the town hall.
2 **to find yourself**
Trouve-toi quelque chose à faire! Find
yourself something to do!

ρ le **truc** MASC NOUN
1 (informal) **thing**
un petit truc en bois a little thing made of
wood
Qu'est-ce que c'est que ce truc? What on
earth is that thing?
Il y a un truc qui ne va pas. Something's
wrong.
Le jazz, ce n'est pas mon truc. Jazz just isn't
my thing.
2 **trick**
Il doit y avoir un truc. There must be a trick
to it.

ρ la **truite** FEM NOUN
trout

TSVP ABBREVIATION
(= tournez s'il vous plaît) **PTO, please turn
over**

TTC ABBREVIATION
(= toutes taxes comprises) **inclusive of tax**

tu PRONOUN
you (singular)
Toi, tu restes ici. You stay here.
Tu as fait tes devoirs? Have you done your
homework?

WORD TIP tu is used to speak to a family
member, a person you know well or a person of
your own age; otherwise vous is used.

le **tube** MASC NOUN
1 **tube**
2 (informal) **hit** (in pop music)
un des tubes de l'été dernier one of last
summer's hits

tuer VERB [1]
to kill
se **tuer** REFLEXIVE VERB ⌃
1 **to be killed**
Elle s'est tuée dans un accident de voiture.
She was killed in a car accident.
2 **to kill yourself**

tue-tête IN PHRASE
crier à tue-tête to shout at the top of your
voice

la **tuile** FEM NOUN
1 **tile** (on a roof)
2 **thin almond biscuit**

la **Tunisie** FEM NOUN
Tunisia

tunisien MASC ADJECTIVE, **tunisienne** FEM ▸ SEE
Tunisien
Tunisian

le **Tunisien** MASC NOUN, la **Tunisienne** FEM ▸ SEE
tunisien
Tunisian

ρ le **tunnel** MASC NOUN
tunnel
le tunnel sous la Manche the Channel
Tunnel

turc MASC ADJECTIVE, **turque** FEM ▸ SEE **Turc**
Turkish

le **Turc** MASC NOUN, la **Turque** FEM ▸ SEE **turc**
1 **Turk**
les Turcs the Turks
2 le turc **Turkish** (the language)

la **Turquie** FEM NOUN
Turkey

le **tuteur** MASC NOUN, la **tutrice** FEM
1 **guardian**
2 **tutor**

tutoyer VERB [39]
tutoyer quelqu'un to use 'tu' with someone
Il ne faut pas tutoyer ton professeur. You
shouldn't use 'tu' with your teacher.

ρ **indicates key words**

Tu peux me tutoyer. You can use 'tu' with me.
▶ SEE **tu**

se **tutoyer** REFLEXIVE VERB ⊘
to use 'tu' with each other
On peut se tutoyer? Can we use 'tu' with each other?

le **tuyau** MASC NOUN, les **tuyaux** PLURAL
1 pipe (for water, drainage, etc)
2 (informal) tip (a helpful hint)
Tu as des tuyaux pour les examens? Do you have any exam tips?
• le tuyau d'arrosage
hosepipe

la **TVA** FEM NOUN
(= taxe à la valeur ajoutée) VAT, value added tax

le **type** MASC NOUN
1 kind
Quel type de papier? What type of paper?
2 (informal) guy
un drôle de type a strange guy
Je le connais, c'est le type qui m'a vendu la moto. I know him, he's the guy who sold me the motorbike.

typique MASC & FEM ADJECTIVE
typical

tyranniser VERB [1]
to tyrannize

tzigane MASC & FEM ADJECTIVE ▶ SEE **tzigane** NOUN
gypsy

le & la **tzigane** MASC & FEM NOUN ▶ SEE **tzigane** ADJECTIVE
gypsy

Uu

l'**UE** FEM NOUN
EU

un **ulcère** MASC NOUN
ulcer

un MASC DETERMINER, **une** FEM, **des** PL ▶ SEE **un** NUMBER, PRON
1 (with masc singular nouns) a, an
un film a film
un animal an animal
2 (with fem singular nouns) a, an
une moto a motorbike
une orange an orange
▶ SEE **de, des**

un MASC PRONOUN, **une** FEM, **uns** MASC PL, **unes** FEM PL ▶ SEE **un** DETERMINER, NUMBER
one

l'un d'entre nous one of us
l'une d'entre les filles one of the girls
Les uns pensent que ... Some think that ...
l'un(e) et l'autre the one and the other
L'un est français et l'autre est allemand. One's French and the other's German.
l'un(e) ou l'autre either of them
Prends l'une ou l'autre, ça n'a pas d'importance. Take either of them, it doesn't matter.

WORD TIP l'un changes to l'une when used for a fem noun, to les uns when used for masc plural nouns, and to les unes when used for fem plural nouns.

un MASC NUMBER, **une** FEM ▶ SEE **un** DETERMINER, PRONOUN
one
Il y a un paquet pour moi et deux pour toi. There's one parcel for me and two for you.
un par un one by one
trente et une personnes thirty-one people
un jour sur deux every other day

uni MASC ADJECTIVE, **unie** FEM
1 close-knit (family, group)
2 plain (not patterned)
un tissu uni a plain fabric

ℓ un **uniforme** MASC NOUN
uniform
Dans mon école, on ne porte pas d'uniforme. In my school we don't wear a uniform.

une **union** FEM NOUN
union
l'ex-Union soviétique the former Soviet Union
• l'Union européenne
European Union

ℓ **unique** MASC & FEM ADJECTIVE
1 only
Elle est fille unique. She's an only child.
Il est fils unique. He's an only child.
C'est l'unique solution à tous tes problèmes. That's the only solution to all your problems.
2 single
'Prix unique' 'All one price'
3 unique
C'est une occasion unique de le rencontrer. This is a unique opportunity to meet him.
Ce musée est unique au monde. This museum is unique in the world.

uniquement ADVERB
only

une **unité** FEM NOUN
1 unity
2 unit (of currency, measurement)

⊘ means the verb takes être to form the perfect

un **univers** *INVARIABLE MASC NOUN*
1 universe
2 world
   l'univers de Dali Dali's world

universitaire *MASC & FEM ADJECTIVE*
1 university *(degree, town)*
2 academic *(work)*

une **université** *FEM NOUN*
   university
   Audrey est à l'université. Audrey is at university.
   Je voudrais aller à l'université. I would like to go to university.

un **urbanisme** *MASC NOUN*
   town planning

une **urgence** *FEM NOUN*
1 urgency
   Il y a urgence! It's urgent!
2 d'urgence immediately, at once
   Il faut téléphoner d'urgence. You must phone at once.
3 emergency
   Je te donne mon numéro de portable en cas d'urgence. I'll give you my mobile number in case of emergency.
4 les urgences, le service des urgences accident and emergency *(in a hospital)*
   On l'a emmené aux urgences. He was taken to casualty.

ℱ **urgent** *MASC ADJECTIVE*, **urgente** *FEM*
   urgent
   Je dois lui parler, c'est urgent! I must speak to him, it's urgent!

les **USA** *PLURAL MASC NOUN*
   USA
   Patsy habite aux USA. Patsy lives in the USA.
   Mon père va en voyage d'affaires aux USA. My father is going on a business trip to the USA.

> **WORD TIP** Countries and regions in French take le, la or les.

un **usage** *MASC NOUN*
   use
   hors d'usage out of order
   L'usage d'une calculatrice est interdit à l'examen. The use of a calculator is forbidden in the exam.
   'À usage externe' 'For external use only'

usagé *MASC ADJECTIVE*, **usagée** *FEM*
1 worn
2 used

un **usager** *MASC NOUN*
   user
   un usager de la route a road user

les usagers des transports en commun the users of public transport

usé *MASC ADJECTIVE*, **usée** *FEM*
   worn *(shoes, clothing, tyre)*

user *VERB* [1]
   to wear out *(shoes, clothing)*

ℱ une **usine** *FEM NOUN*
   factory
   Mon frère travaille dans une usine. My brother works in a factory.

un **ustensile** *MASC NOUN*
   utensil

ℱ **utile** *MASC & FEM ADJECTIVE*
   useful
   un renseignement utile a useful piece of information
   se rendre utile to make oneself useful
   Si tu veux te rendre utile, mets-moi la table! If you'd like to make yourself useful, lay the table for me!

utilisable *MASC & FEM ADJECTIVE*
   usable

un **utilisateur** *MASC NOUN*, une **utilisatrice** *FEM*
   user

ℱ **utiliser** *VERB* [1]
   to use
   J'utilise un dictionnaire pour vérifier l'orthographe d'un mot nouveau. I use a dictionary to check the spelling of a new word.

l'**utilité** *FEM NOUN*
   use
   'Tu n'as pas de portable?' – 'Non, je n'en ai pas l'utilité.' 'You don't have a mobile phone?' – 'No, I have no use for one.'

Vv

va *VERB* ▶ SEE **aller** *VERB*

ℱ les **vacances** *PLURAL FEM NOUN*
   holidays
   les vacances d'hiver the winter holidays
   les vacances scolaires the school holidays
   les grandes vacances the summer holidays
   être en vacances to be on holiday
   Nous sommes en vacances pendant deux semaines. We're on holiday for two weeks.
   aller en vacances to go on holiday
   Nous allons en vacances en Irlande. We're going on holiday to Ireland.
   Bonnes vacances! Have a good holiday!
• les vacances à la neige
   skiing holiday

le **vacancier** MASC NOUN, la **vacancière** FEM
holidaymaker

le **vacarme** MASC NOUN
din

la **vaccination** FEM NOUN
vaccination

vacciner VERB [1]
to vaccinate
se faire vacciner to be vaccinated
Je me suis fait vacciner contre le tétanos.
I've been vaccinated against tetanus.

♪ **vache** MASC & FEM ADJECTIVE ▶ SEE **vache** NOUN
(informal) **mean**
être vache avec quelqu'un to be mean to
somebody
Il a été vache avec elle. He was mean to her.

♪ la **vache** FEM NOUN ▶ SEE **vache** ADJECTIVE
1 **cow**
2 (informal)
Oh, la vache! Wow!

vachement ADVERB
(informal) **really**
C'était vachement bien! It was really good!

le **vagabond** MASC NOUN, la **vagabonde** FEM
tramp

le **vagin** MASC NOUN
vagina

vague MASC & FEM ADJECTIVE ▶ SEE **vague** NOUN
vague

la **vague** FEM NOUN ▶ SEE **vague** ADJECTIVE
wave (in the sea)
• la vague de chaleur
heatwave

vain MASC ADJECTIVE, **vaine** FEM
1 **useless**
2 en vain in vain

> **WORD TIP** vain does not mean vain in English:
> for the meaning of vain ▶ SEE **vaniteux**.

vaincre VERB [79]
1 to defeat (an enemy)
2 to overcome (an illness)

le **vainqueur** MASC NOUN
winner

vais VERB ▶ SEE **aller** VERB

le **vaisseau** MASC NOUN, les **vaisseaux** PLURAL
vessel
• le vaisseau spatial
spaceship

♪ la **vaisselle** FEM NOUN
dishes
faire la vaisselle to wash up
C'est ton tour de faire la vaisselle. It's your

turn to wash up.

valable MASC & FEM ADJECTIVE
valid

le **valet** MASC NOUN
jack
le valet de pique the jack of spades

la **valeur** FEM NOUN
value
des objets de valeur valuables
d'une grande valeur valuable

valider VERB [1]
to stamp (a ticket)

♪ la **valise** FEM NOUN
suitcase
faire ses valises to pack
Je n'ai pas encore fait mes valises! I haven't
packed yet!

la **vallée** FEM NOUN
valley

valoir VERB [80]
1 to be, to cost
Ça vaut combien? How much is that?
Combien valent ces bottes? How much are
those boots?
2 ça vaut la peine de faire quelque chose it's
worth doing something
Ça vaut la peine d'essayer. It's worth trying.
Ça ne vaut pas la peine d'y aller. It's not
worth going.
3 il vaut mieux faire quelque chose it's better
to do something
Il vaut mieux demander la permission. It's
better to ask permission.

la **valse** FEM NOUN
waltz

le **vandalisme** MASC NOUN
vandalism

♪ la **vanille** FEM NOUN
vanilla
une glace à la vanille a vanilla ice cream

vaniteux MASC ADJECTIVE, **vaniteuse** FEM,
vaniteux MASC PL, **vaniteuses** FEM PL
vain

se **vanter** REFLEXIVE VERB ✪ [1]
to boast

♪ la **vapeur** FEM NOUN
steam
faire cuire quelque chose à la vapeur to
steam something
Je fais cuire les légumes à la vapeur. I steam
the vegetables.

variable ADJ
variable

la **varicelle** FEM NOUN
  chickenpox

ℱ **varié** MASC ADJECTIVE, **variée** FEM
1 varied
  un menu varié a varied menu
2 various
  sous des formes variées in various forms

varier VERB [1]
  to vary

la **variété** FEM NOUN
1 variety
2 popular music
  un spectacle de variétés a variety show

vas VERB ▸ SEE **aller** VERB

le **vase** MASC NOUN
  vase

vaste MASC & FEM ADJECTIVE
  huge
  un vaste choix a huge selection

vaudrait VERB ▸ SEE **valoir**

vaut VERB ▸ SEE **valoir**

va-vite ADVERB
  à la va-vite in a rush

ℱ le **veau** MASC NOUN, les **veaux** PLURAL
1 calf
2 veal

vécu VERB ▸ SEE **vivre**

ℱ la **vedette** FEM NOUN
  star
  un enfant vedette a child star

végétal MASC ADJECTIVE, **végétale** FEM,
  végétaux MASC PL, **végétales** FEM PL
  vegetable
  l'huile végétale vegetable oil

végétalien MASC ADJECTIVE, **végétalienne** FEM
  vegan

ℱ **végétarien** MASC ADJECTIVE, **végétarienne** FEM
  ▸ SEE **végétarien** NOUN
  vegetarian
  Elle est végétarienne. She's a vegetarian.

ℱ le **végétarien** MASC NOUN, la **végétarienne**
  FEM ▸ SEE **végétarien** ADJECTIVE
  vegetarian

ℱ le **véhicule** MASC NOUN
  vehicle

ℱ la **veille** FEM NOUN
  la veille the day before
  la veille de Noël Christmas Eve

le **veinard** MASC NOUN, la **veinarde** FEM
  (informal)
  Petit veinard! You lucky little devil!

la **veine** FEM NOUN
1 vein
2 (informal) luck
  Il a de la veine. He's lucky.

ℱ le **vélo** MASC NOUN
  bike
  Je suis venu à vélo. I came by bike.
  faire du vélo to go cycling
  Le dimanche matin, je fais du vélo. On
  Sunday mornings I go cycling.
• le vélo tout terrain
  mountain bike

le **vélomoteur** MASC NOUN
  moped

le **velours** INVARIABLE MASC NOUN
  velvet
  une écharpe en velours a velvet scarf
• le velours côtelé
  corduroy

le **velouté** MASC NOUN
  cream soup
  un velouté de champignons cream of
  mushroom soup

les **vendanges** PLURAL FEM NOUN
  grape harvest

🔵 **VENDANGES**

Des étudiants du monde entier viennent faire
les vendanges en France début septembre.

ℱ le **vendeur** MASC NOUN, la **vendeuse** FEM
1 shop assistant
2 salesperson
3 seller

ℱ **vendre** VERB [3]
  to sell
  vendre quelque chose à quelqu'un to sell
  something to somebody
  J'ai vendu mon ordinateur à Céline. I've
  sold my computer to Céline.
  'À vendre' 'For sale'

ℱ le **vendredi** MASC NOUN
1 Friday
  vendredi dernier last Friday
  vendredi prochain next Friday
  Nous sommes vendredi aujourd'hui. It's
  Friday today.
2 on Friday
  À vendredi! See you on Friday!
3 on Fridays
  'Fermé le vendredi' 'Closed on Fridays'
4 tous les vendredis every Friday
  Tous les vendredis, je fais de l'athlétisme.
  Every Friday I do athletics.

WORD TIP Months of the year and days of the
week start with small letters in French.

- le **vendredi saint**
  Good Friday

vénéneux MASC ADJECTIVE, **vénéneuse** FEM
  poisonous (plant)

la **vengeance** FEM NOUN
  revenge

se **venger** REFLEXIVE VERB ☺ [52]
  to have your revenge

venimeux MASC ADJECTIVE, **venimeuse** FEM
  poisonous (snake, spider)

♀ **venir** VERB ☺ [81]
  1 to come
    Il vient de Provence. He comes from
    Provence.
    Elles sont venues mardi. They came on
    Tuesday.
    Viens voir! Come and see!
    Venez nous aider! Come and help us!
  2 **faire venir quelqu'un** to send for somebody
    Il faut faire venir le médecin. We must send
    for the doctor.
  3 **venir de faire quelque chose** to have just
    done something
    Ils viennent d'arriver. They've just arrived.
    Elle venait de partir. She had just left.

♀ le **vent** MASC NOUN
  wind
    Il y a du vent. It's windy.

♀ la **vente** FEM NOUN
  sale
    être en vente to be for sale
    Leur maison est en vente. Their house is
    for sale.
    Il travaille au service des ventes. He works
    in the sales department.
  - la **vente aux enchères**
    auction sale

le **ventilateur** MASC NOUN
  (electric) fan

♀ le **ventre** MASC NOUN
  stomach
    avoir mal au ventre to have stomach ache
    Lili a mal au ventre. Lili's got stomach ache.

venu VERB ▸ SEE **venir**

le **ver** MASC NOUN
  worm

le **verbe** MASC NOUN
  verb

le **verger** MASC NOUN
  orchard

le **verglas** INVARIABLE MASC NOUN
  black ice

♀ **vérifier** VERB [1]
  to check
    vérifier que ... to check that ...
    Il vérifie que ses réponses sont correctes.
    He's checking that his answers are correct.

véritable MASC & FEM ADJECTIVE
  real

la **vérité** FEM NOUN
  truth
    Dis-moi la vérité. Tell me the truth.
    À la vérité ... To tell the truth ...

vernir VERB [2]
  to varnish

le **vernis** MASC NOUN
  varnish
  - le **vernis à ongles**
    nail varnish

♀ le **verre** MASC NOUN
  1 glass
    une table en verre a glass table
  2 glass (to drink from)
    un verre de vin a glass of wine
  3 drink
    Tu veux prendre un verre? Do you want to
    go for a drink?
  4 lens (for glasses)

le **verrou** MASC NOUN
  bolt (on a door)

verrouiller VERB [1]
  to bolt (a door)

la **verrue** FEM NOUN
  wart

♀ le **vers** INVARIABLE MASC NOUN ▸ SEE **vers**
    PREPOSITION
  line (of poetry)

♀ **vers** PREPOSITION ▸ SEE **vers** INVARIABLE MASC NOUN
  1 towards
    Tu vas vers la mairie ... You go towards the
    town hall ...
  2 near
    Ils habitent vers Tours. They live near Tours.
  3 about (in time)
    Il arrivera vers midi. He'll arrive about
    twelve.

le **Verseau** MASC NOUN
  Aquarius
    Catherine est Verseau. Catherine is an
    Aquarius.

    WORD TIP Signs of the zodiac do not take an
    article: un or une.

le **versement** MASC NOUN
  payment

☺ means the verb takes être to form the perfect

verser *VERB* [1]
1 **to pour** *(a drink)*
2 **to pay in** *(at a bank, etc)*
3 **to shed** *(tears, blood)*

ℐ la **version** *FEM NOUN*
1 **version**
2 **translation** *(into your own language)*
• la version originale
original version *(of a film)*

le **verso** *MASC NOUN*
back *(of a piece of paper)*
voir au verso see overleaf

ℐ **vert** *MASC ADJECTIVE*, **verte** *FEM*
green
le feu vert the green light

vertical *MASC ADJECTIVE*, **verticale** *FEM*,
verticaux *MASC PL*, **verticales** *FEM PL*
vertical

le **vertige** *MASC NOUN*
vertigo *(dizziness)*
avoir le vertige to be scared of heights

la **verveine** *FEM NOUN*
herbal tea *(with verbena)*

ℐ la **veste** *FEM NOUN*
jacket

WORD TIP veste does not mean vest in English;
for the meaning of vest ▸ SEE **maillot de corps**.

le **vestiaire** *MASC NOUN*
1 **cloakroom** *(in a theatre)*
2 **changing room** *(in a gym)*

ℐ le **vestibule** *MASC NOUN*
hall

ℐ le **vêtement** *MASC NOUN*
garment
les vêtements clothes

le & la **vétérinaire** *MASC & FEM NOUN*
vet

ℐ **veuf** *MASC ADJECTIVE*, **veuve** *FEM* ▸ SEE **veuf** *NOUN*
▸ SEE **veuve**
Le directeur est veuf. The headmaster is a
widower.
Ma voisine est veuve. My neighbour is a
widow.

ℐ le **veuf** *MASC NOUN* ▸ SEE **veuf** *ADJECTIVE*
a widower

ℐ la **veuve** *FEM NOUN* ▸ SEE **veuf** *NOUN*
widow

vexer *VERB* [1]
to upset

ℐ la **viande** *FEM NOUN*
meat
la viande hachée mince

la viande rouge red meat

vibrer *VERB* [1]
to vibrate

la **victime** *FEM NOUN*
victim

la **victoire** *FEM NOUN*
victory

ℐ **vide** *MASC & FEM ADJECTIVE* ▸ SEE **vide** *NOUN*
empty

ℐ le **vide** *MASC NOUN* ▸ SEE **vide** *ADJECTIVE*
1 **space**
dans le vide in space, into space
2 **vacuum**
du café emballé sous vide vacuum-packed
coffee

le **vide-greniers** *INVARIABLE MASC NOUN*
car boot sale

ℐ **vidéo** *INVARIABLE MASC & FEM ADJECTIVE* ▸ SEE **vidéo**
NOUN
video
une caméra vidéo a video camera
un jeu vidéo a video game

ℐ la **vidéo** *FEM NOUN* ▸ SEE **vidéo** *INVARIABLE MASC &*
FEM ADJECTIVE
video

le **vidéoclip** *MASC NOUN*
music video

vider *VERB* [1]
to empty

ℐ la **vie** *FEM NOUN*
life
la vie urbaine city life
leur mode de vie their lifestyle
C'est la vie! That's life!
être en vie to be alive
Il est encore en vie. He's still alive.

vieil *ADJECTIVE* ▸ SEE **vieux**

le **vieillard** *MASC NOUN*, la **vieillarde** *FEM*
1 un vieillard an old man
les vieillards old people
2 une vieillarde an old woman
▸ SEE **vieux**

vieille *FEM ADJECTIVE* ▸ SEE **vieux**

la **vieillesse** *FEM NOUN*
old age

vieillir *VERB* [2]
to age

vierge *MASC & FEM ADJECTIVE* ▸ SEE **vierge** *NOUN*
1 **virgin**
2 **blank**
une cassette vierge a blank cassette

la **vierge** FEM NOUN ▶SEE **vierge** ADJECTIVE
virgin
la Sainte Vierge the Virgin Mary

la **Vierge** FEM NOUN, NOUN
Virgo
Nicolas est du signe de la Vierge. Nicolas is a Virgo.

WORD TIP Signs of the zodiac do not take an article: un or une.

♟ **vieux, vieil** MASC ADJECTIVE, **vieille** FEM ▶SEE **vieux** NOUN
old
un vieux tableau an old picture
un vieil arbre an old tree
une vieille dame an old lady
Cléo est plus vieille que Bess. Cléo is older than Bess.
Oscar est moins vieux qu'Hugo. Oscar is younger than Hugo.

WORD TIP vieux becomes vieil before a, e, i, o, u or silent h.

♟ le **vieux** MASC NOUN, la **vieille** FEM ▶SEE **vieux** ADJ
un vieux an old man
une vieille an old woman
les vieux old people

WORD TIP It's more polite to use un vieil homme, une vieille femme or les personnes âgées to refer to elderly people in French.

vif MASC ADJECTIVE, **vive** FEM
1 alive
2 lively (colours, discussion)
3 brisk (gesture, action)

la **vigne** FEM NOUN
1 vine
2 vineyard

le **vigneron** MASC NOUN, la **vigneronne** FEM
winegrower

la **vignette** FEM NOUN
1 tax disc (for cars)
2 label (on prescribed medicines)

le **vignoble** MASC NOUN
vineyard

♟ **vilain** MASC ADJECTIVE, **vilaine** FEM
1 ugly
une vilaine robe an ugly dress
2 naughty
Liliane est vilaine. Liliane is naughty.
3 nasty
Il a attrapé un vilain rhume. He's caught a nasty cold.

la **villa** FEM NOUN
villa

♟ le **village** MASC NOUN
village
dans un village in a village

♟ la **ville** FEM NOUN
town, city
une grande ville a city
Ce matin, je vais en ville. This morning I'm going into town.

♟ le **vin** MASC NOUN
wine
du vin blanc white wine
du vin rouge red wine
du vin rosé rosé wine
du vin pétillant sparkling wine
• le vin chaud
mulled wine

♟ le **vinaigre** MASC NOUN
vinegar

la **vinaigrette** FEM NOUN
French dressing

♟ **vingt** NUMBER
twenty
le vingt juillet the twentieth of July
à vingt heures at 8 p.m.
vingt-trois twenty-three
Marion a vingt ans. Marion's twenty.

la **vingtaine** FEM NOUN
about twenty
Elle a la vingtaine. She's about twenty.
une vingtaine de personnes about twenty people

♟ **vingtième** MASC & FEM ADJECTIVE
twentieth

le **viol** MASC NOUN
rape

violemment ADVERB
violently

la **violence** FEM NOUN
violence

violent MASC ADJECTIVE, **violente** FEM
violent

violer VERB [1]
to rape

violet MASC ADJECTIVE, **violette** FEM
purple

la **violette** FEM NOUN
violet (the flower)

le **violon** MASC NOUN
violin
jouer du violon to play the violin

⬥ means the verb takes être to form the perfect

le **violoncelle** *MASC NOUN*
cello
jouer du violoncelle to play the cello

le **virage** *MASC NOUN*
bend *(in the road)*

la **virgule** *FEM NOUN*
1 comma
2 *(Maths)* decimal point
sept virgule trois seven point three

le **virus** *INVARIABLE MASC NOUN*
virus
le virus du sida the Aids virus

la **vis** *INVARIABLE FEM NOUN* ▸ SEE **vis** *VERB*
screw

vis *VERB* ▸ SEE **vis** *INVARIABLE FEM NOUN* ▸ SEE **vivre**

le **visa** *MASC NOUN*
visa

ℙ le **visage** *MASC NOUN*
face

viser *VERB* [1]
1 to aim *(with a weapon)*
2 to aim for *(a target, a result)*
une campagne qui vise les jeunes a
campaign aimed at young people
viser à faire quelque chose to aim to do
something
Cette loi vise à protéger les minorités. This
law aims to protect minorities.

la **visibilité** *FEM NOUN*
visibility

visible *MASC & FEM ADJECTIVE*
1 visible
2 obvious

la **visite** *FEM NOUN*
visit
rendre visite à quelqu'un to visit somebody
Demain, nous allons rendre visite à ma
grand-mère. Tomorrow we're going to visit
my grandmother.
• la visite guidée
guided tour

ℙ **visiter** *VERB* [1]
to visit *(a place)*
Je voudrais visiter le Louvre. I'd like to visit
the Louvre.

le **visiteur** *MASC NOUN*, la **visiteuse** *FEM*
visitor

vit *VERB* ▸ SEE **vivre**

la **vitamine** *FEM NOUN*
vitamin

ℙ **vite** *ADVERB*
1 fast
Tu conduis trop vite. You drive too fast.

2 quick
Vite! Le bus arrive! Quick! Here's the bus!
3 soon
Elle a vite compris. She soon understood.

la **vitesse** *FEM NOUN*
1 speed
en vitesse quickly
Elle est partie à toute vitesse. She rushed
off.
2 gear *(in a car)*
en deuxième vitesse in second gear

le **vitrail** *MASC NOUN*, les **vitraux** *PLURAL*
stained-glass window

la **vitre** *FEM NOUN*
1 window pane
2 window *(of a car, a train)*

ℙ la **vitrine** *FEM NOUN*
shop window
faire les vitrines to go window-shopping

vivant *MASC ADJECTIVE*, **vivante** *FEM*
1 living
Il est vivant. He's alive.
2 lively
C'est un enfant très vivant. He's a very
lively child.

vive *FEM ADJECTIVE* ▸ SEE **vive** *EXCLAMATION* ▸ SEE **vif**

vive *EXCLAMATION* ▸ SEE **vive** *ADJECTIVE*
Vive le roi! Long live the king!

vivement *ADVERB*
1 strongly
2 Vivement samedi! I can't wait for Saturday!

ℙ **vivre** *VERB* [82]
1 to live
Ils vivent ensemble. They live together.
2 to live through
Elle a vécu une période difficile. She's been
through a difficult period.
Ils vivent une vie tranquille. They lead a
quiet life.

le **vocabulaire** *MASC NOUN*
vocabulary

le **vœu** *MASC NOUN*, les **vœux** *PLURAL*
1 wish
faire un vœu to make a wish
Meilleurs vœux! Best wishes! *(especially at
New Year)*
2 vow
faire un vœu to make a vow

la **vogue** *FEM NOUN*
fashion
en vogue in fashion

ℙ **voici** *ADVERB*
1 here is, here are
Voici l'addition. Here's the bill.

Voici les clés. Here are the keys.

2 this is, these are

Voici ma sœur. This is my sister.

Voici mes copines. These are my friends.

WORD TIP voici never changes.

la **voie** FEM NOUN

1 way

2 track (for trains)

la voie ferrée the railway track

3 lane (on a main road)

une autoroute à trois voies a three-lane motorway

ℓ **voilà** ADVERB

1 there is, there are

Voilà ta trousse, là-bas sur la table. There's your pencil case, over there on the table.

La voilà! There she is!

2 here is, here are

Voilà ton jus d'orange. Here's your orange juice.

Voilà tes frites. Here are your chips.

Voilà Anna qui arrive. Here comes Anna now.

3 Voilà pourquoi elle est triste. That's why she's sad.

Voilà comment ça se fait. That's how it's done.

Voilà, c'est tout. Right, that's all.

WORD TIP voilà never changes.

le **voile** MASC NOUN ▶SEE **voile** NOUN

veil, headscarf

la **voile** FEM NOUN ▶SEE **voile** NOUN

1 sail (of a boat)

2 sailing

faire de la voile to go sailing

le **voilier** MASC NOUN

sailing boat

ℓ **voir** VERB [13]

1 to see

Je te vois. I can see you.

Je vois mon médecin à 11 heures. I'm seeing the doctor at 11 am.

Il va voir son copain. He's going to see his friend.

Je viendrai te voir un de ces jours. I'll come and see you one of these days.

Oui, je vois... Yes, I see...

Peut-être, on verra. Maybe, we'll see.

Voir page 50. See page 50.

2 faire voir quelque chose à quelqu'un to show somebody something

Je te ferai voir mes photos. I'll show you my photos.

se **voir** REFLEXIVE VERB ◯

1 to show

La tache ne se verra pas. The stain won't show.

2 to see each other

Ils se voient à Noël. They see each other at Christmas.

ℓ le **voisin** MASC NOUN, la **voisine** FEM

neighbour

chez les voisins at the neighbours'

le **voisinage** MASC NOUN

neighbourhood

ℓ la **voiture** FEM NOUN

1 car

en voiture by car

2 carriage (on a train)

la voiture de première classe the first-class carriage

ℓ la **voix** INVARIABLE FEM NOUN

1 voice

lire à haute voix to read out loud

2 vote

Samuel a eu 10 voix et Manon 17. Samuel got 10 votes and Manon got 17.

ℓ le **vol** MASC NOUN

1 flight

le vol pour Edimbourg the flight to Edinburgh

Il y a deux heures de vol. It's a two-hour flight.

2 theft

un vol à main armée an armed robbery

la **volaille** FEM NOUN

poultry

volant MASC ADJECTIVE, **volante** FEM ▶SEE **volant** NOUN

flying

le **volant** MASC NOUN ▶SEE **volant** ADJECTIVE

1 steering wheel

être au volant to be driving

2 shuttlecock

le **volcan** MASC NOUN

volcano

la **volée** FEM NOUN

1 (Sport) **volley**

2 flock (of birds)

ℓ **voler** VERB [1]

1 to steal

voler quelque chose à quelqu'un to steal something from someone

Quelqu'un m'a volé mon passeport. Somebody's stolen my passport.

se faire voler quelque chose to have

◯ means the verb takes être to form the perfect

something stolen
Il s'est fait voler son vélo. He's had his bicycle stolen.

2 voler quelqu'un to rob somebody
Ils volent leurs clients. They're robbing their customers.

3 **to fly**
L'avion volait juste au-dessus de leurs têtes. The plane was flying just above their heads.

le **volet** MASC NOUN
shutter

ℰ le **voleur** MASC NOUN, la **voleuse** FEM
thief

le **volley** MASC NOUN
volleyball
jouer au volley to play volleyball

WORD TIP volley does not mean **volley** (in tennis) in English; for the meaning of **volley** ▸ SEE **volée**.

le & la **volontaire** MASC & FEM NOUN
volunteer

volontaire MASC & FEM ADJECTIVE
voluntary
le travail volontaire voluntary work

la **volonté** FEM NOUN
1 **will**
2 **willpower**
3 à volonté unlimited
'Pizza à volonté' 'As much pizza as you want'

volontiers ADVERB
gladly
'Volontiers!' 'I'd love to!'

ℰ **vomir** VERB [2]
to be sick
Elle a envie de vomir. She's feeling sick.

ℰ **vos** PLURAL MASC & FEM ADJECTIVE
your
vos cahiers your notebooks
vos amies françaises your French friends

WORD TIP Use vos for **your** with plural French nouns. ▸ SEE **votre**

voter VERB [1]
to vote

ℰ **votre** MASC & FEM ADJECTIVE, **vos** PLURAL
your
votre professeur your teacher
votre voiture your car

WORD TIP Use votre for **your** with singular French nouns. ▸ SEE **vos**.

le **vôtre** MASC PRONOUN, la **vôtre** FEM les **vôtres** PL
1 **yours**
un pays comme le vôtre a country like yours
une maison comme la vôtre a house like yours
mes parents et les vôtres my parents and yours
'Ces photos sont à vous?' – 'Non, ce sont les vôtres.' 'Are these photos yours?' – 'No, they're yours.'
2 (as a toast) À la vôtre! Cheers!

WORD TIP The article and pronoun change in French when they refer to fem and plural nouns.

ℰ **vouloir** VERB [14]
1 **to want**
Je veux du chocolat. I want some chocolate.
vouloir faire quelque chose to want to do something
Veux-tu venir avec nous? Do you want to come with us?
Il n'a pas voulu venir. He didn't want to come.
2 **to like**
si tu veux if you like
Je voudrais un verre d'eau. I'd like a glass of water.
Elle voudrait visiter Versailles. She'd like to go to Versailles.
3 Voulez-vous m'excuser? Would you excuse me?
Veux-tu fermer la porte? Would you shut the door?
Veuillez accepter mes excuses. Please accept my apologies.
4 bien vouloir quelque chose not to mind something
Je voudrais bien de la confiture. I wouldn't mind some jam.
5 bien vouloir faire quelque chose to be happy to do something
Je veux bien le faire. I'm happy to do it.
6 vouloir dire to mean
Qu'est-ce que tu veux dire? What do you mean?
7 en vouloir à quelqu'un to bear a grudge against somebody
Elle en veut à ses parents. She's never forgiven her parents.

voulu VERB ▸ SEE **vouloir**

ℰ **vous** PRONOUN
1 (PLURAL speaking to more than one person)
you
Vous avez fait vos devoirs? Have you done

341

your homework?
Elle va vous aider. She's going to help
you.

2 *(polite form of* **vous** *for one or more persons)*
you
Vous voulez du vin, monsieur? Would you
like some wine, sir?
Je vais vous montrer le chemin. I'll show
you the way.

3 *(after prepositions like* **avec** *or* **contre** *and in
comparisons)* **you**
Je viens avec vous. I'm coming with you.
Ils sont plus âgés que vous. They're older
than you.

4 *(as a direct object)* **you**
Elle vous aide. She helps you.
Elle vous a aidés. She helped you. *(to several
people)*
Elle vous a aidé. She helped you. *(politely to
one person)*

5 *(as an indirect object)* **(to) you**
Je vous écrirai. I'll write to you.
Je vous ai donné mon adresse. I've given
you my address.

6 **à vous** yours
Ceci est à vous. This is yours.
Ce sont des amis à vous? Are they friends
of yours?

7 *(with reflexive verbs)* **Vous vous levez à sept
heures.** You get up at seven o'clock.

8 *(polite form with reflexive verbs)* **yourself,
yourselves**
Ne vous coupez pas! Don't cut yourself!

9 **chez vous** at your house

vous-même *PRONOUN*
yourself
Vous me l'avez dit vous-même. You told
me yourself.

> **WORD TIP** This is the polite form to one person.

vous-mêmes *PLURAL PRONOUN*
yourselves
Est-ce que vous l'avez fait vous-mêmes?
Did you make it yourselves?

> **WORD TIP** This is the plural form used to speak
> to several people.

vouvoyer *VERB* [39]
vouvoyer quelqu'un to use 'vous' with
someone
Il faut vouvoyer le professeur. You should
use 'vous' with the teacher.
▶ SEE **tutoyer**

se vouvoyer *REFLEXIVE VERB* ⊛
to use 'vous' with each other
**Après tant d'années, ils continuent à se
vouvoyer.** After all these years, they still use
'vous' with each other.
Use vous to people you don't know well,

*especially adults. You may be asked to use
tu when you get to know someone well.*

ℓ **le voyage** *MASC NOUN*
1 **trip**
On fait un voyage en Chine. We're going on
a trip to China.
Bon voyage! Have a good trip!
2 **journey**
un voyage de 10 000 kilomètres a
10,000-kilometre journey
• **le voyage organisé**
package holiday

ℓ **voyager** *VERB* [52]
to travel
Il a beaucoup voyagé. He's travelled a lot.

le voyageur *MASC NOUN,* **la voyageuse** *FEM*
passenger

la voyelle *FEM NOUN*
vowel

le voyou *MASC NOUN*
hooligan

vrac *ADVERB*
acheter des olives en vrac to buy olives
loose *(not packaged)*

ℓ **vrai** *MASC ADJECTIVE,* **vraie** *FEM*
real, genuine
un vrai diamant a real diamond
C'est vrai? Really?

vraiment *ADVERB*
really

vraisemblable *ADJECTIVE*
likely

le VTT *MASC NOUN*
(= vélo tout-terrain) mountain bike

vu *MASC ADJECTIVE,* **vue** *FEM* ▶ SEE **vu** *VERB*
1 **être mal vu** to be disapproved of
Il est plutôt mal vu. People don't think
much of him.
C'est mal vu de faire beaucoup de bruit.
They don't like people making a lot of noise.
2 **être bien vu** to be well thought of
Elle est très bien vue à l'école. People at the
school think highly of her.
3 **Bien vu!** Good point!

vu *VERB* ▶ SEE **vu** *ADJECTIVE* ▶ SEE **voir**

ℓ **la vue** *FEM NOUN*
1 **eyesight**
Tu as une bonne vue. You've got good
eyesight.
2 **sight**
à première vue at first sight
connaître quelqu'un de vue to know
somebody by sight
Je le connais de vue. I know him by sight.

⊛ **means the verb takes être to form the perfect**

perdre quelqu'un de vue to lose touch with somebody
Nous l'avons perdue de vue. We've lost touch with her.

3 view
une vue de mer a sea view
une chambre avec vue sur le lac a room with a view of the lake

vulgaire *MASC & FEM ADJECTIVE*
1 vulgar
Ne sois pas si vulgaire! Don't be so vulgar!
2 common

Ww

ℓ le **wagon** *MASC NOUN*
1 railway carriage
Nos places sont dans le wagon numéro 2. Our seats are in carriage number 2.
2 waggon
- le **wagon-lit**
sleeper *(on a train)*
- le **wagon-restaurant**
dining car

le **walkman** *MASC NOUN*
walkman

wallon *MASC ADJECTIVE,* **wallonne** *FEM* ▶ SEE
Wallon
Walloon *(from French-speaking Belgium)*

> **WORD TIP** Adjectives never have capitals in French, even for nationality or regional origin.

le **Wallon** *MASC NOUN,* la **Wallonne** *FEM* ▶ SEE
wallon
1 Walloon *(French-speaking Belgian)*
les Wallons the Walloons
2 le wallon Walloon *(the language of Wallonia, Belgium)*
Je parle wallon. I speak Walloon.

> **WORD TIP** Languages never have capitals in French.

ℓ les **WC** *PLURAL MASC NOUN*
toilet
Où sont les WC? Where's the toilet?
J'ai besoin d'aller aux WC. I need to go to the toilet.
Il est aux WC. He's in the loo.

le **web** *MASC NOUN*
the web
un site web a website

le **week-end** *MASC NOUN*
weekend

le **western** *MASC NOUN*
western
Il n'aime que les vieux westerns. He only likes old westerns.

Xx

la **xénophobie** *FEM NOUN*
xenophobia
continuer la lutte contre la xénophobie to continue the fight against xenophobia

le **xylophone** *MASC NOUN*
xylophone
Simon joue du xylophone. Simon plays the xylophone.

Yy

ℓ **y** *PRONOUN*
1 there *(not always translated)*
J'y vais demain. I'm going there tomorrow.
Ils vont faire une fête. Tu y vas? They're going to have a party. Are you going?
N'y va pas! Don't go!
2 il y a there is, there are
Il y a un café à côté. There's a cafe next door.
Il y a des poissons dans l'étang. There are some fish in the pond.
Il y a de la limonade dans le frigo. There's some lemonade in the fridge.
Des cerises? Il n'y en a pas. Cherries? There aren't any.
Il n'y en a plus. There are none left.
3 *(y is used for the preposition à with verbs like penser à, croire à, réfléchir à and is translated in different ways)*
J'y pense. I'm thinking about it.
Tu n'y peux rien. You can't do anything about it.
Laisse-moi y réfléchir. Let me have a think about it.
Il n'y comprend rien. He doesn't understand a thing.
Attends, j'y viens. Just wait, I'm coming to that point.
Le Père Noël? Tu y crois? Father Christmas? Do you believe in him?

ℓ le **yaourt** *MASC NOUN*
yoghurt
- le yaourt aux fruits
fruit yoghurt
- le yaourt nature
natural yogurt

A B C D E F G H I J K L M N O P Q R S T U V W X Y Z

ℐ les **yeux** *PLURAL MASC NOUN*
  eyes
  ▶SEE **œil**

le **yoga** *MASC NOUN*
  yoga

Zz

zapper *VERB* [1]
  to channel-hop *(with a TV)*

le **zèbre** *MASC NOUN*
  zebra

le **zéro** *MASC NOUN*
1 zero *(when counting)*
  Elle a le moral à zéro. She's really
  depressed.
2 nil
  Ils ont gagné deux à zéro. They won two
  nil.
3 love *(in tennis)*
  15 zéro 15 love

le **zeste** *MASC NOUN*
  peel *(of oranges, lemons)*

zézayer *VERB* [59]
  to lisp

le **zigzag** *MASC NOUN*
  zigzag
  une route en zigzag a winding road
  faire des zigzags to zigzag

zinzin *INVARIABLE ADJECTIVE*
  crazy

le **zodiaque** *MASC NOUN*
  zodiac
  Quel est ton signe du zodiaque? What sign
  of the zodiac are you?

la **zone** *FEM NOUN*
1 zone, area
2 la zone the slums
  un enfant de la zone a child who grew up
  in the slums
• la zone euro
  eurozone
• la zone industrielle
  industrial estate
• la zone piétonne
  pedestrian area

le **zoo** *MASC NOUN*
  zoo

zoologique *MASC & FEM ADJECTIVE*
  zoological

zut *EXCLAMATION*
  (informal) damn!

Using your French

Important words and phrases

When does it happen?

d'habitude usually

normalement normally

généralement generally

la plupart du temps most of the time

tous les jours every day

souvent often

quelquefois sometimes

de temps en temps from time to time

toujours always

une fois par semaine once a week

deux fois par an twice a year

rarement rarely

jamais never

Formal or informal?

Speaking to a friend

Tu peux m'aider, s'il te plaît?
Can you help me, please?

Tu veux aller au cinéma? Do you want
to go to the cinema?

Je peux sortir ce soir? Can I go out tonight?

Je t'en prie. don't mention it.

Excuse-moi de te déranger. Sorry for
disturbing you.

Je voudrais te voir. I'd like to see you.

Speaking to an adult

Vous pouvez m'aider, s'il vous plaît?
Can you help me, please?

Vous voulez me voir? Do you want to
see me?

Je vous en prie. Don't mention it.

Excusez-moi de vous déranger Sorry for
disturbing you.

Je voudrais vous aider. I'd like to help you.

Pourriez-vous me dire … ? Could you
tell me …?

Agreeing and disagreeing

Je suis tout à fait d'accord.
I completely agree.

Exactement! exactly!

Je suis pour … I'm in favour of …

Tu as raison. you are right.

Je suis du même avis. I'm of the same
opinion.

C'est sans doute vrai that's probably.
true.

Je ne suis pas du tout d'accord.
I don't agree at all.

Absolument pas! certainly not!

je suis contre … I'm against …

Tu as tort. You're wrong.

Je ne partage pas ton opinion.
I don't share your opinion.

Ce n'est pas du tout vrai. that's not
true at all.

Opinions

à mon avis in my opinion

je crois/pense que I believe that

je suis convaincu(e) que I'm convinced
that

je m'intéresse à I'm interested in

je me passionne pour I really love

j'ai horreur de I hate

je ne peux pas supporter I can't stand

ça ne m'intéresse pas that doesn't
interest me

parce que c'est … because it is

amusant fun, amusing

passionnant exciting

intéressant interesting

agréable pleasant

ennuyeux boring

affreux awful

une perte de temps a waste of time

Asking questions

Où est-ce que tu vas ce soir?
Where are you going tonight?
Avec qui? Who with?
À quelle heure commencent les
cours? What time do lessons start?
Quelle sorte de sports préfères-tu
What kind of sports do you prefer?
Quand pars-tu en vacances? When are
you going on holiday?

Experiences

j'ai commencé à I began to
j'ai décidé de I decided to
j'ai réussi à I managed to
j'ai refusé de I refused to
j'ai essayé de I tried to
je suis allé(e) I went
je me suis amusé(e) I had a good time

je vais/je ne vais pas I'm going/
not going to
je voudrais/j'aimerais I'd like to
je ne veux pas I don't want to
j'ai l'intention de I intend to
j'espère I hope to
je rêve de I dream of

Connectives

parce que because
comme as/since/like
car since, for
puisque since
tandis que whereas
donc so, therefore
en plus what's more
quand when
où where
pendant que while
également also
dès que as soon as

Role play phrases

J'ai oublié ... I've forgotten ...
J'ai perdu ... I've lost...
Je cherche ... I'm looking for ...
Qu'est-ce que tu as/vous avez?
What's the matter?
Pouvez-vous/peux-tu me donner ...
Can you give me ... ?
J'ai besoin de ... I need ...
Pour aller au centre-ville? How do I
get to the town centre?
Ça s'écrit comment? How do you
spell that?
Qu'est-ce qui s'est passé? What's
happened?

Prepositions

avec/sans
with/without
malgré in spite of
sauf except
à cause de
because of
à côté de next to
en face de opposite

devant
in front of
derrière behind
à gauche de
to the left of
à droite de
to the right of
au milieu (de)
in the middle (of)
au fond
at the back
au premier plan
at the front
entre between

Letters, emails and social media

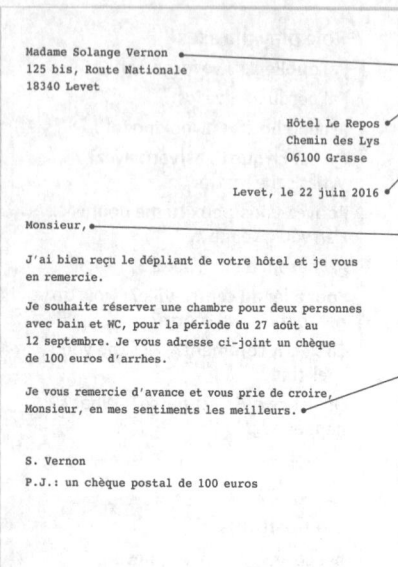

Formal letters

Madame Solange Vernon
125 bis, Route Nationale
18340 Levet
— the sender's name and address

Hôtel Le Repos
Chemin des Lys
06100 Grasse
— the name and the address the letter is being sent to

Levet, le 22 juin 2016
— the name of the town and the date the letter is being written

Monsieur,
Monsieur *(to a man)*
Madame *(to a woman)*

J'ai bien reçu le dépliant de votre hôtel et je vous en remercie.

Je souhaite réserver une chambre pour deux personnes avec bain et WC, pour la période du 27 août au 12 septembre. Je vous adresse ci-joint un chèque de 100 euros d'arrhes.

Salutations distinguées.
Kind regards

Je vous remercie d'avance et vous prie de croire, Monsieur, en mes sentiments les meilleurs.
Je vous prie d'agréer, Madame/Monsieur, l'expression des mes salutations distinguées./de mes sentiments distingués.
Yours faithfully/Yours sincerely

S. Vernon
P.J.: un chèque postal de 100 euros

To a whole family or group:

Bonjour à tous Hello everyone
Cher/Chère Dear
Chers amis Dear Friends

À (très) bientôt See you (very) soon
Grosses bises Love and kisses
Je t'embrasse/Je vous embrasse. I send you a big kiss.
Amicalement/Très amicalement Best wishes/Very best wishes
Amitiés With best wishes

Emails

un mail, un email, un courriel an email
une adresse électronique an email address
une boîte de réception an inbox
envoyer un mail to send an email
recevoir un mail to receive an email
une pièce jointe an attachment
un arobase an @ sign
un site Web a website
cliquer (sur) to click (on)
une page d'accueil a homepage
une rubrique a heading
faire suivre to forward
envoyer en copie to CC
effacer to delete

Pierre,

Salut! J'ai trouvé un site génial: www.schooldictionaries.co.uk.
Tu devrais l'ajouter à ta liste de sites favoris. La page d'accueil te donne les noms de tous les dictionnaires qui conviennent aux étudiants, et des jeux de mots amusants. Tu peux cliquer sur les rubriques pour trouver un dictionnaire qui te convienne parfaitement! Envoie-moi un mail quand tu y auras jeté un coup d'œil.

@+
Tim

P.J. Est-ce que tu peux faire suivre ce message à Marc? Je voulais le lui envoyer en copie, mais je ne trouve plus son adresse, j'ai effacé son dernier message de ma boîte de réception. Je suis sûr que ça l'intéressera aussi.

La télévision et les films
Television and films

Il y a … There's …

- une émission sportive. a sports programme.
- un documentaire. a documentary.
- un feuilleton. a soap.
- un jeu. a game show.
- les infos. the news.

Ma série préférée, c'est …
My favourite series is …

Allons au cinéma. Let's go to the cinema.

On passe … They're showing …

- un film policier. a detective film.
- un dessin animé. a cartoon.
- une comédie. a drama/a comedy.
- un film d'horreur/d'épouvante.
  a horror film.

Au téléphone
On the telephone

Allô! Hello!

Est-ce que je peux parler à … ?
Can I speak to … ?

Qui est à l'appareil? Who's calling?

Ne quittez pas. Hold on.

Je peux laisser un message?
Can I leave a message?

Je rappellerai plus tard.
I'll call back later.

Je vous mets en communication.
I'll put you through.

Qu'est-ce que tu en penses?
What do you think?

Les portables sont pratiques pour la sécurité. Mobiles are practical for safety.

La facture de mon portable est très chère. My mobile bill is very dear.

Les sonneries m'énervent.
Ring tones annoy me.

La fraude sur Internet est un gros problème. Internet fraud is a big problem.

La cyberintimidation m'inquiète.
Cyberbullying concerns me.

Il y a trop de pression dans les réseaux sociaux. There is too much pressure in social media.

Sur mon ordinateur,
On my computer,

- Je surfe sur le Web/la Toile. I surf the web.
- Je télécharge de la musique, des vidéoclips et des jeux. I download music, videos and games.
- Je fais mes devoirs. I do homework.
- Internet est indispensable pour trouver des renseignements. The Internet is indispensible for finding information.

- un portable a laptop
- un forum a chatroom
- un réseau social a social network
- un blog a blog
- une webcam a webcam

Careers and future plans

Lucy Belmont

Adresse

34, Darlington Street
London NW4 5RT
tél: 0208 203 5687

Née le 30 juillet 1995, à Londres
Nationalité britannique

Formation

Préparation des A levels (équivalent du baccalauréat)
options: anglais, français, allemand, musique
depuis 2011   Owen's Sixth Form Centre (lycée)

2011   GCSEs (équivalent du Brevet des Collèges)

                options: mathématiques, sciences, anglais,
                français, allemand, géographie, histoire,
                musique

2006—2011   Ashworth Secondary School (collège)

Expérience professionnelle

2011   Emploi d'été:
                stage dans un journal local
2010   Emploi d'été:
                vendeuse en magasin
2010   baby-sitting

Divers

Langues étrangères:
français (bonnes connaissances orales et écrites),
allemand (bonnes connaissances), espagnol (notions)

Informatique:
bonne connaissance de Microsoft Word

Qualités personnelles:
calme, responsable, sociable, énergique

Centres d'intérêt:
les voyages, les langues, la lecture, la musique,
le cinéma

Membre de l'orchestre et du groupe de théâtre du lycée

Writing a CV

In France, it is quite usual to include a passport-sized photo with your CV (le CV).

Always handwrite a covering letter (la lettre de motivation) – it's quite common for French companies to use a graphologist (handwriting expert).

Qu'est-ce que tu en penses? What do you think?

La formation professionnelle est utile pour trouver un travail. Vocational training is useful for finding a job.

Je veux trouver un travail bien payé. I want to find a well-paid job.

J'ai envie de voyager beaucoup. I want to travel a lot.

Je ne veux pas travailler dans un bureau. I don't want to work in an office.

Je trouve le travail trop monotone. I find the work too monotonous.

J'aime mieux travailler en plein air. I prefer to work in the open air/outdoors.

Je veux collecter de l'argent pour des associations caritatives. I want to collect money for charities.

Je veux devenir professeur parce que j'aime les enfants. I want to become a teacher because I like children.

Le contact avec le public est important pour moi. Contact with the public is important for me.

Tu as déjà fait un stage en entreprise? Have you done any work experience?

J'ai déjà travaillé dans … I've already worked in …

- un bureau an office
- une usine a factory
- une station-service a filling-station
- un supermarché a supermarket

- pendant une semaine/un mois/un an. for a week/month/a year.

L'année dernière j'ai travaillé dans une école primaire près de chez moi. J'ai aidé les enfants avec leur travail ce qui m'a beaucoup plu mais j'ai trouvé le travail très fatigant. Last year I worked in a primary school near where I live. I helped the children with their work which I enjoyed a lot but I found the work very tiring.

Après le collège/le lycée je veux … After school I want …

- faire un apprentissage. to do an apprenticeship.
- trouver un emploi. to find a job.
- faire une année sabbatique. to have a gap year.
- un job d'été. a summer job.
- un emploi à temps partiel. a part-time job.

Mon ambition, c'est …
My ambition is …

• d'être comptable.
to be an accountant.

• d'être coiffeur/coiffeuse.
to be a hairdresser.

• d'aller à l'étranger.
to go abroad.

• travailler dans un magasin.
work in a shop.

• aider les sans-abris.
to help the homeless.

Je veux devenir mécanicien parce que je m'intéresse aux voitures.
I want to become a mechanic because I am interested in cars.

Je rêve de travailler comme médecin car je veux aider les autres. I dream of working as a doctor because I want to help others.

Je fais du travail bénévole pour aider les personne âgées. I do voluntary work to help the elderly.

Je veux faire du bénévolat mais je n'ai pas le temps. I want to do voluntary work but I don't have the time.

Il faut promouvoir l'égalité des chances. We must promote equal opportunities.

Il faut combattre la pauvreté. We must fight poverty.

Les droits des animaux sont importants, à mon avis. Animal rights are important, in my opinion.

➤ **Qu'est-ce qu'il y a sur la photo?**
What's in the photo?

Il y a une jeune fille qui travaille dans un garage. Elle est en train de réparer une voiture. Je pense qu'elle est mécanicienne. Elle porte une salopette de travail et elle se sert d'un ordinateur portable. There is a girl who is working in a garage. She is repairing a car. I think she is a mechanic. She's wearing overalls and is using a laptop.

➤ **Quelle sorte de travail t'intéresse et pourquoi?**
What sort of job interests you and why ?

Je ne sais pas encore. D'abord j'ai l'intention d'aller à l'université et puis de faire une année sabbatique parce que je veux voyager un peu. Ensuite je chercherai un travail bien payé. I don't know yet. First of all I intend to go to university and then to have a gap year because I want to travel a little. Afterwards I will look for a well-paid job.

Family

Dans ma famille ...
In my family ...

il y a ... there are ...

- mes parents. my parents.
- mon père/ma mère. my father/ my mother.
- mon beau-père/ma belle-mère. my stepfather/my stepmother.

Il a/Elle a ... He/She has ...

- des enfants. children.
- un fils/une fille. a son/a daughter.

J'ai ... I have ...

- un frère/une sœur. a brother/ a sister.
- un demi-frère/une demi-sœur. a half-brother *or* stepbrother/ a half-sister *or* stepsister.
- un jumeau/une jumelle. a twin brother/a twin sister.

Je suis fils/fille unique. I'm an only child *(boy/girl speaking)*.

Je m'entends bien/Je ne m'entends pas avec ... I get on well/I don't get on well with ...

- mon cousin *(boy)*/ma cousine *(girl)*. my cousin.

Il est/Elle est ...
He is/She is ...

- célibataire. single.
- fiancé(e). engaged.
- marié(e). married.
- séparé(e). separated.
- divorcé(e). divorced.
- mort(e). dead.

- grand(e). tall.
- petit(e). short.
- blond(e). blond.
- brun(e). dark-haired.
- sympa. really nice.
- pénible. a pain.

Qu'est-ce que tu en penses?
What do you think?

Je m'entends bien avec mes parents parce qu'ils m'écoutent et et qu'ils me font confiance. I get on well with my parents because they listen to me and trust me.

Je ne m'entends pas avec mes parents parce qu'ils sont stricts et me traitent comme un enfant. I don't get on with my parents because they are strict and treat me like a child.

Mon frère m'énerve, on se dispute tout le temps. My brother annoys me, we argue all the time.

Mes amis sont importants pour moi, je peux toujours compter sur eux. My friends are important for me, I can always count on them.

Shopping and eating out

At the restaurant/cafe

Je voudrais réserver une table pour quatre personnes. I'd like to reserve a table for four people.

Vous désirez? What would you like?

Je voudrais ... I'd like ...

- un café. a coffee.
- un thé. a cup of tea.
- un jus d'orange. an orange juice.

L'addition, s'il vous plaît?
The bill, please?

Je fais des courses ...
I go shopping *(for food)* ...

- au supermarché.
  at the supermarket.
- à la charcuterie.
  at the delicatessen.
- à l'épicerie.
  at the grocer's.
- sur Internet.
  on the Internet.
- à la boulangerie.
  at the baker's.
- à la boucherie.
  at the butcher's.
- au marché.
  at the market.
- à la pâtisserie.
  at the cake shop.

➤ **Qu'est-ce qu'il y a sur la photo?**
What's in the photo?

C'est une famille qui est en train de manger. La mère est à gauche et le père à droite. Entre les parents il y a les deux enfants. Ils mangent à l'extérieur et ils s'amusent beaucoup. It's a family who are eating. The mother is on the left and the father on the right. Between the parents there are two children. They are eating outside and they are having a very good time.

➤ **Qu'est-ce que tu as fait avec ta famille le weekend dernier? What did you do with your family last weekend?**

On est allés à un restaurant italien pour fêter l'anniversaire de ma sœur. On a très bien mangé et le service était excellent. On a bien rigolé. We went to an Italian restaurant to celebrate my sister's birthday. We ate very well and the service was excellent. We had a good laugh.

353

Healthy living

Je mange des fruits deux fois par jour.
I eat fruit twice a day.

J'ai faim. I'm hungry.

J'ai soif. I'm thirsty.

J'ai envie de dormir. I'm sleepy.

J'ai mal à la tête. I have a headache.

J'ai une allergie/Je suis allergique
au/à la/aux ... I have an allergy/
I'm allergic to ...

Qu'est-ce que tu en penses?
What do you think?

Le tabagisme passif est très
dangereux. Passive smoking is very
dangerous.

L'alcool est mauvais pour le foie et
provoque la violence. Alcohol is bad
for the liver and causes violence.

Les jeunes se droguent à cause de
la pression des pairs. Young people
takes drugs because of peer pressure.

J'aime bien/Je n'aime pas faire
du sport. I like/I don't like
playing sport.

Mon sport préféré, c'est ...
My favourite sport is ...

- le foot. football.
- le tennis. tennis.
- le volley. volleyball.
- l'athlétisme. athletics.
- le vélo tout terrain. mountain biking.
- l'alpinisme. mountaineering.
- la plongée sous marine. scuba diving.
- la planche à voile. windsurfing.
- le skateboard. skateboarding.
- le patin/le pain à glace. skating/
  ice skating.

Pour rester en bonne santé, il faut ...
To stay healthy, you have to ...

- manger des fruits et des légumes.
  eat fruit and vegetables.
- se lever tôt. get up early.
- ne pas se coucher tard. not go to
  bed late.
- faire du sport. get exercise.
- aller à pied. walk.

C'est bon pour la santé.
It's healthy.

Il faut être actif pour garder la forme.
You need to be active to keep fit.

Il faut éviter de boire des boissons
gazeuses/de l'alcool/du café. You must
avoid drinking fizzy drinks/alcohol/
coffee.

Il ne faut pas fumer.
You mustn't smoke.

Je suis/Il est/Elle est ...
I am/He is/She is ...

- sportif/sportive. sporty. (boy/girl
  speaking)
- blessé/blessée. injured. (boy/girl
  speaking)
- en bonne santé. in good health.

J'aime me maintenir en forme.
I like to keep fit.

> **Qu'est-ce qu'il y a sur la photo?**
What's in the photo?

C'est un groupe de jeunes qui regardent un film au cinéma. Ils boivent des boissons gazeuses et mangent du popcorn. C'est un film d'horreur parce qu'ils ont l'air effrayé et qu'ils laissent tomber le popcorn. It's a group of young people who are watching a film at the cinema. They are drinking fizzy drinks and eating popcorn. It's a horror film because they look scared and are dropping the popcorn.

> **Quel genre de films préfères-tu?** What kind of films do you prefer?

Je préfère les films comiques parce que j'aime rire avec mes copains. J'aime aussi les films d'aventures qui sont passionnants. Cependant, je ne peux pas supporter les films de science-fiction que je trouve ennuyeux. I prefer comedy films because I like a good laugh with my friends. I also like adventure films which are exciting. However, I can't stand science fiction films which I find boring.

> **Parle-moi de ta dernière visite au cinéma.** Tell me about your last visit to the cinema.

Il y a deux semaines, je suis allée au cinéma avec ma meilleure amie pour voir un film d'amour. On a acheté de quoi manger mais c'était cher. Le film n'était pas très bien car l'intrigue n'était pas intéressante et les acteurs étaient médiocres. Two weeks ago, I went to the cinema with my best friend to see a romantic film. We bought something to eat but it was expensive. The film wasn't too good because the plot wasn't interesting and the actors were average.

Si on allait au parc? Shall we go to the park?

On se retrouve à la salle de gym! Let's meet up at the gym!

J'aimerais mieux aller au stade de football. I'd rather go to the football stadium.

Rendez-vous ...
See you ...

• au cinéma!
  at the cinema!
• à la discothèque!
  at the disco!
• au match!
  at the match!
• au centre de loisirs!
  at the leisure centre!
• à la fête! at the party!

Mon passe-temps préféré, c'est ...
My favourite pastime is ...

• sortir avec des copains. going out with friends.
• aller en ville. going into town.
• faire les magasins. going shopping.
• aller à des concerts. going to concerts.
• lire. reading.
• écouter de la musique. listening to music.
• regarder la télévision. watching TV.
• jouer sur une console. playing on a games console.
• aller à des fêtes/ aller en discothèque. going to parties/discos.
• faire du vélo. going cycling.

Environment

Qu'est-ce que tu en penses?
What do you think?

Il faut créer plus de zones piétonnes et de pistes cyclables. We must create more pedestrian zones and cycle lanes.

Il faut planter plus d'arbres pour rendre l'air plus propre. We must plant more trees to make the air cleaner.

Les supermarchés utilisent trop d'emballages. Supermarkets use too much packaging.

le tourisme vert ecotourism
l'environnement the environment
écologique environmentally friendly
la préservation conservation
sauver la planète saving the planet
passer au vert: Mon école passe au vert. 'going green': My school is going green.
le dioxyde de carbone carbon dioxide
le réchauffement de la planète global warming
la pollution pollution

➤ **Qu'est-ce qu'il y a sur la photo?**
What's in the photo?

Il y a six éoliennes qui produisent de l'énergie à partir du vent ce qui est bon pour l'environnement. La photo a été prise soit au lever ou coucher du soleil. There are six wind turbines which produce energy from the wind. This is good for the environment. The photo was taken either at sunrise or sunset.

➤ **Qu'est-ce que tu as fait récemment pour protéger la planète?** **What have you done recently to protect the planet?**

J'ai recyclé le verre et le papier et j'ai pris une douche plutôt qu'un bain pour économiser de l'eau. La semaine dernière je suis allée au collège à pied. I have recycled glass and paper and I had a shower rather than a bath to save water. Last week I went to school on foot.

➤ **Quels sont les problèmes environnementaux dans ta région?** **What are the envoirnmental problems in your area?**

Malheureusement, des gens laissent tomber des papiers et il y a trop de circulation donc l'air est pollué. Unfortunately, people drop litter and there is too much traffic so the air is polluted.

➤ **Que vas-tu faire à l'avenir pour protéger l'environnement?** **What are you going to do in the future to protect the environment?**

Je n'utiliserai plus de sacs en plastique parce qu'ils causent des dégâts environnementaux et qu'ils peuvent tuer des animaux. Je vais utiliser les déchets du jardin pour faire du compost. I won't use plastic bags because they cause environmental damage and can kill animals. I'm going to use garden waste to make compost.

Travel

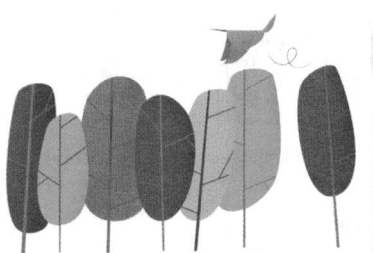

Je voudrais ...
I'd like ...

- un aller simple/un aller-retour pour Paris, s'il vous plaît. a single/a return to Paris, please.
- acheter un billet. to buy a ticket.
- réserver une place. to reserve a seat.
- consulter l'horaire. to check the timetable.

Je voyage ...
I'm going ...

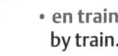

- à moto. on a motorbike

- en voiture. by car.

- en car. by coach.

- en taxi. by taxi.

- en avion. by plane.

- en train. by train.

- à vélo. by bike.

- en bus. by bus.

- en bateau. by ship.

On se retrouve ... ?
Shall we meet ... ?

- à l'aéroport. at the airport.
- au port. at the port.
- à la gare. at the station.
- à la gare routière. at the coach station.

Il faut encourager les gens à à ne pas prendre leur voiture pour les petits trajets.
We must encourage people not to take their cars for short journeys.

Il y a trop d'embouteillages aux heures d'affluence. There are too many traffic jams at rush hour.

Le train part de quel quai?
What platform does the train leave from?

Où est l'arrêt de bus? Where is the bus stop?

La station de métro est tout près.
The underground station is close by.

Le vol dure combien de temps?
How long is the flight?

On a voyagé en car. We travelled by coach.

Je ne suis jamais allé(e) à l'étranger.
I have never been abroad.

Le tourisme est mauvais pour l'environnement et peut menacer la culture régionale d'un pays. Tourism is bad for the environment and can threaten the local culture of a country.

School and home

Ma matière préférée, c'est …
My favourite subject is …

• le dessin.
art.

• les sciences.
science.

• le français.
French.

• la géographie.
geography.

• la musique.
music.

• l'EPS.
PE.

• l'histoire.
history.

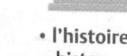

• l'anglais.
English.

• l'informatique.
computing.

• les mathématiques.
mathematics.

Je vais à l'école à pied.
I walk to school.

Il y a 25 élèves dans ma classe. There are 25 pupils in my class.

Les cours commencent à neuf heures. Lessons start at nine o'clock.

Un cours dure 45 minutes. A lesson lasts 45 minutes.

À midi, je mange à la cantine. At lunchtime, I eat in the canteen.

On a beaucoup de devoirs. We have a lot of homework.

➤ **Qu'est-ce qu'il y a sur la photo?**
What's in the photo?

Il fait beau. La scène se passe sur un terrain de football. Un garçon, qui porte des gants, joue au football et il a attrapé le ballon. It's fine weather. The scene takes place on a football pitch. A boy, who is wearing gloves, is playing football and he has caught the ball.

➤ **Quelle est ta matière préférée et pourquoi? What is your favourite subject and why?**

J'aime beaucoup l'anglais parce que je m'intéresse aux langues et que le professeur est très amusant et sympa. Je suis assez fort(e) en anglais. I like English a lot because I'm interested in languages and the teacher is very funny and pleasant. I'm quite good at English.

➤ **Parle-moi d'une visite scolaire à laquelle tu as participé. Talk about a school trip you've taken part in.**

L'année dernière, je suis allé(e) en France avec mes camarades de classe. On y a voyagé en car et en bateau ce que j'ai trouvé fatigant et ennuyeux. On a passé quatre jours à Paris. Pendant le séjour, on a visité tous les monuments célèbres et on s'est très bien amusés. Je voudrais y retourner un jour. Last year, I went to France with my classmates. We went there by coach and boat which I found tiring and boring. We spent four days in Paris. During our stay we visited all the famous monuments and we had a good time. I'd like to go back one day.

Tu habites ...
Do you live ...

- dans le centre-ville? in the city centre?
- dans la banlieue? in the suburbs?
- à la campagne? in the country?
- au bord de la mer? at the seaside?
- à la montagne? in the mountains?

J'habite dans le nord/le sud/l'est/l'ouest/le centre de ... I live in the north/south/east/west/centre of ...

C'est une ville industrielle/moderne/animée. It's an industrial/a modern/a lively town.

C'est un village agricole/calme/touristique. It's a farming/quiet/touristy village.

Qu'est-ce que tu en penses?
What do you think?

J'aime ma maison parce qu'elle se trouve près des magasins ce qui est pratique. I like my house because it is situated neat the shops which is practical.

J'habite ma maison depuis cinq ans mais en ce moment je partage ma chambre avec mon frère. Je voudrais avoir ma propre chambre. I've lived in my house for five years but at the moment I share my room with my brother. I would like to have my own bedroom.

Dans ma ville, il y a toujours quelque chose à faire. In my town, there is always something to do.

Dans mon village, il n'y a rien à faire pour les jeunes mais c'est tranquille et l'air n'est pas pollué. In my village, there's nothing for young people to do but it's quiet and the air is not polluted.

J'habite dans ...
I live in ...

- une maison. a house.
- un appartement au deuxième étage/aau rez-de-chaussée/au premier étage. a flat on the second floor/on the ground floor/on the first floor.

Chez moi, c'est petit/grand/moderne/ancien. My home is small/big/modern/old.

- un garage. a garage.

Il y a ...
There is ...

- un jardin. a garden.

- une cuisine. a kitchen.

- un salon/un séjour. a lounge/a living room.

- une chambre. a bedroom.

- des WC/des toilettes. a toilet.

- une salle à manger. a dining room.

- une salle de bains. a bathroom.

- un bureau. an office/a study.

Holidays and Festivals

➤ **Qu'est-ce qu'il y a sur la photo?**
What's in the photo?

J'aime bien/
Je n'aime pas …
I like/I don't like …

- le temps.
  the weather.
- la cuisine.
  the food.
- la musique.
  the music.
- la culture.
  the culture.

La scène se passe à un festival de musique dans un champ. À gauche et à droite, on voit des tentes et des drapeaux de différentes couleurs. Malheureusement, le ciel est gris et il va peut-être pleuvoir. The scene takes place at a music festival in a field. To the left and right, you can see tents and flags in different colours. Unfortunately, the sky is grey and it's going to rain.

➤ **Tu as déjà participé à un festival de musique?** **Have you ever been to a music festival ?**

Non, je ne suis jamais allé(e) à un festival mais l'année prochaine j'espère y aller.

Je dois économiser de l'argent parce que le prix des billets est très cher. On fera du camping et on s'amusera beaucoup même s'il pleut. No, I've never been to a festival but next year I hope to go. I must save money because the price of tickets is very expensive. We will go camping and have a good time even if it rains.

Qu'est-ce que tu en penses?
What do you think?

Quelle sorte de logement est-ce que tu préfères et pourquoi ? What sort of accommodation do you prefer and why?

Le camping, ce n'est pas agréable quand il fait froid. J'aime mieux loger dans un appartement ou une villa parce que c'est moins cher qu'un hôtel et on a plus de liberté. Camping is not pleasant when it's cold. I prefer to stay in a flat or a villa because it's cheaper than a hotel and you have more freedom.

En vacances on peut se faire de nouveaux amis et voir des endroits différents. On holiday, you can make new friends and see new places.

Je voudrais partir en vacances avec mes copains parce que ce serait plus amusant. Mes parents sont un peu trop stricts. I'd like to go on holiday with my friends because it would be more fun. My parents are a bit too strict.

Pendant les vacances …
During the holidays …

- je vais à l'hôtel I go to a hotel
- je vais dans une auberge de jeunesse I go to a youth hostel
- je vais dans un gîte I go to a holiday home

- au bord de la mer. by the sea.
- à la montagne. in the mountains.
- à la campagne. in the country.

Tous les étés, je vais au Maroc.
Every summer, I go to Morocco.

L'été prochain, je vais aller à Paris.
Next summer, I'll be going to Paris.

One is **une** in French when it agrees with a feminine noun,
so **un crayon** but **une table, une des tables, vingt-et-une tables,** etc.

0	zéro			
1	un (sometimes une)	1st	1er	premier (fem première)
2	deux	2nd	2e	second (fem seconde) *or* deuxième
3	trois	3rd	3e	troisième
4	quatre	4th	4e	quatrième
5	cinq	5th	5e	cinquième
6	six	6th	6e	sixième
7	sept	7th	7e	septième
8	huit	8th	8e	huitième
9	neuf	9th	9e	neuvième
10	dix	10th	10e	dixième
11	onze	11th	11e	onzième
12	douze	12th	12e	douzième
13	treize	13th	13e	treizième
14	quatorze	14th	14e	quatorzième
15	quinze	15th	15e	quinzième
16	seize	16th	16e	seizième
17	dix-sept	17th	17e	dix-septième
18	dix-huit	18th	18e	dix-huitième
19	dix-neuf	19th	19e	dix-neuvième
20	vingt	20th	20e	vingtième
21	vingt -et-un	21st	21e	vingt et unième
22	vingt-deux	22nd	22e	vingt-deuxième
30	trente	30th	30e	trentième
40	quarante	40th	40e	quarantième
50	cinquante	50th	50e	cinquantième
60	soixante	60th	60e	soixantième

70 is **soixante-dix** and 80 is **quatre-vingts.**
Quatre-vingts loses the **-s** when another number joins it.

70	soixante-dix	70th	70e	soixante-dixième
71	soixante-et-onze	71st	71e	soixante-et-onzième
80	quatre-vingts	80th	80e	quatre-vingtième
81	quatre-vingt-un	81st	81e	quatre-vingt-unième
82	quatre-vingt-deux	82nd	82e	quatre-vingt-deuxième
90	quatre-vingt-dix	90th	90e	quatre-vingt-dixième
91	quatre-vingt-onze	91st	91e	quatre-vingt-onzième
92	quatre-vingt-douze	92nd	92e	quatre-vingt-douzième
99	quatre-vingt-dix-neuf	99th	99e	quatre-vingt-dix-neuvième
100	cent	100th	100e	centième
101	cent un	101st	101e	cent-et-unième
102	cent deux	102nd	102e	cent-deuxième
200	deux cents	200th	200e	deux centième
201	deux cent un	201st	201e	deux cent et unième
202	deux cent deux	202nd	202e	deux cent deuxième

When writing longer numbers French uses a space
or a full stop instead of a comma – for example,
1 000 or **1.000** rather than **1,000.**

1 000	mille	1000th	1 000e	millième
1 001	mille un	1001st	1 001e	mille et unième
1 002	mille deux	1002nd	1 002e	mille deuxième
2 000	deux mille	2000th	2 000e	deux millième
1 000 000	un million	1000000th	1 000 000e	millionième

Time

Months

janvier January
février February
mars March
avril April
mai May
juin June
juillet July
août August
septembre September
octobre October
novembre November
décembre December
NB: *in + month* = en

Mon anniversaire est en février.
My birthday is in February.
Elle est partie en mars.
She left in March.
On arrive le 11 novembre.
We're arriving on 11th November.
Richard est né le 2 août.
Richard was born on 2nd August.
en 2007 in 2007
en 1999 in 1999

Days of the week

lundi Monday
mardi Tuesday
mercredi Wednesday
jeudi Thursday
vendredi Friday
samedi Saturday
dimanche Sunday

Seasons

le printemps spring
l'été summer
l'automne autumn
l'hiver winter

Time

Il est quelle heure?
What time is it?
Il est une heure.
It's one o'clock.
Il est quatre heures et demie.
It's half past four.
Il est six heures et quart.
It's quarter past six.
Il est six heures moins le quart.
It's quarter to six.
Il est neuf heures dix.
It's ten past nine.
Il est neuf heures moins dix.
It's ten to nine.
Il est midi.
It's midday.
Il est minuit.
It's midnight.
Il est dix-neuf heures.
It's 7pm (19.00).
Il est treize heures quinze.
It's 1.15pm (13.15).

 une heure
one o'clock

 quatre heures
et demie
half past four

 six heures
et quart
quarter past six

 six heures
moins le quart
quarter to six

 neuf heures dix
ten past nine

 neuf heures
moins dix
ten to nine

 dix-neuf heures
7pm (19.00)

 treize heures
quinze
1.15pm (13.15)

 midi
midday

 minuit
midnight

Verb tables

This section contains full conjugations for regular -er, -ir and -re verbs plus the most common irregular verbs. On both sides of the dictionary, each French verb is followed by a number. Use this number to locate the verb in these tables.

Model French regular verbs (pages 364–367)

There are three regular verb families in French: -er, -ir and -re verbs.
Models of the way these verbs are formed are given on pages 364-367.
When you look up an entry in this dictionary, you will see a number in square brackets ([1], [2], etc.). This number tells you which verb model you need to follow for that verb.

[1]	-er	e.g. parler	to speak
[2]	-ir	e.g. finir	to finish
[3]	-re	e.g. attendre	to wait
[4]	reflexive (-er)	e.g. se laver	to wash (oneself)

Main French irregular verbs (pages 368–377)

The following verbs are unlike the regular verbs. They are irregular and don't follow a particular pattern so their forms are given for you on pages 368-377. Again, when you look up an entry, use the number in square brackets to bring you to these tables to see how to form the parts of the verb you need.

[5]	avoir	to have
[6]	être	to be
[7]	aller	to go
[8]	devoir	to have to
[9]	dire	to say
[10]	faire	to do or to make
[11]	mettre	to put
[12]	pouvoir	to be able
[13]	voir	to see
[14]	vouloir	to want

Other irregular verb forms (see pages 378–384)

Verbs that take être ○

The ○ in the dictionary reminds you which verbs are conjugated with être in the perfect tense. They are:
– all reflexive verbs e.g. se laver
– the following verbs:
aller arriver décéder descendre* devenir* entrer monter* mourir naître partir rentrer* rester retourner* revenir sortir* tomber* venir
*These verbs occasionally take avoir in the perfect tense – see the Word Tips at the individual entries in the dictionary for details.

[1] parler
to speak

Present

je	parle	I speak or I am speaking
tu	parles	
il/elle/on	parle	
nous	parlons	
vous	parlez	
ils/elles	parlent	

Imperative

parle   speak
Parle à ton prof.   Speak to your teacher.
parlons   let's speak
Parlons français maintenant.
Let's speak French now.
parlez   speak
Ne parlez pas aussi vite!   Don't speak so fast!

Perfect*

j'	ai parlé	I have spoken or I spoke
tu	as parlé	
il/elle/on	a parlé	
nous	avons parlé	
vous	avez parlé	
ils/elles	ont parlé	

*uses avoir plus the past participle to describe completed events in the past

Imperfect*

je	parlais	I spoke or I used to speak or I was speaking
tu	parlais	
il/elle/on	parlait	
nous	parlions	
vous	parliez	
ils/elles	parlaient	

*used to describe what something was like, what used to happen or what was happening

past participle

parlé   spoken
J'ai parlé au prof.
I've spoken to the teacher.

Future

je	parlerai	I will speak
tu	parleras	
il/elle/on	parlera	
nous	parlerons	
vous	parlerez	
ils/elles	parleront	

Conditional

je	parlerais	I would speak
tu	parlerais	
il/elle/on	parlerait	
nous	parlerions	
vous	parleriez	
ils/elles	parleraient	

Present subjunctive*

(que) je	parle	I speak or I am speaking
(que) tu	parles	
(qu') il/elle/on	parle	
(que) nous	parlions	
(que) vous	parliez	
(qu') ils/elles	parlent	

*usually used after que: J'ai peur qu'il parle à mes parents. I'm scared he'll talk to my parents.

[Use the tu (informal singular) form when speaking to one person who you know well, such as a friend; use the vous (formal singular, or plural) form when speaking to someone you don't know well, or when speaking to more than one person.]

[2] finir
to finish

Present

je	finis	I finish or I am finishing
tu	finis	
il/elle/on	finit	
nous	finissons	
vous	finissez	
ils/elles	finissent	

Perfect*

j'	ai fini	I have finished or I finished
tu	as fini	
il/elle/on	a fini	
nous	avons fini	
vous	avez fini	
ils/elles	ont fini	

*uses avoir plus the past participle to describe completed events in the past

past participle

fini   finished
Il a fini de regarder le match de foot.
He's finished watching the football match.

Future

je	finirai	I will finish
tu	finiras	
il/elle/on	finira	
nous	finirons	
vous	finirez	
ils/elles	finiront	

Present subjunctive*

(que) je	finisse	I finish or I am finishing
(que) tu	finisses	
(qu') il/elle/on	finisse	
(que) nous	finissions	
(que) vous	finissiez	
(qu') ils/elles	finissent	

*usually used after que: Le prof veut que je finisse ça pour demain. The teacher wants me to finish this for tomorrow.

Imperative

finis   finish
Finis tes devoirs!   Finish your homework!
finissons   let's finish
Finissons cette question.
Let's finish this question.
finissez   finish
Finissez votre phrase et posez votre stylo.
Finish your sentence and put your pen down.

Imperfect*

je	finissais	I finished or I used to finish or I was finishing
tu	finissais	
il/elle/on	finissait	
nous	finissions	
vous	finissiez	
ils/elles	finissaient	

*used to describe what something was like, what used to happen or what was happening

Conditional

je	finirais	I would finish
tu	finirais	
il/elle/on	finirait	
nous	finirions	
vous	finiriez	
ils/elles	finiraient	

[Use the **tu** (informal singular) form when speaking to one person who you know well, such as a friend; use the **vous** (formal singular, or plural) form when speaking to someone you don't know well, or when speaking to more than one person.]

[3] attendre
to wait

Present

j'	attend**s**	I wait or I am waiting
tu	attend**s**	
il/elle/on	attend	
nous	attend**ons**	
vous	attend**ez**	
ils/elles	attend**ent**	

Imperative

attend**s** wait
Attend**s**-moi, s'il te plaît!
Wait for me, please!
attend**ons** let's wait
Attend**ons** le début du jeu.
Let's wait for the game to start.
attend**ez** wait
Attend**ez**, il n'y a pas assez d'essence dans la
voiture! Wait, there's not enough petrol in
the tank!

Perfect*

j'	ai attend**u**	I have waited
		or I waited
tu	as attend**u**	
il/elle/on	a attend**u**	
nous	avons attend**u**	
vous	avez attend**u**	
ils/elles	ont attend**u**	

*uses avoir plus the past participle to describe
completed events in the past

Imperfect*

j'	attend**ais**	I waited or I used to
		wait or I was waiting
tu	attend**ais**	
il/elle/on	attend**ait**	
nous	attend**ions**	
vous	attend**iez**	
ils/elles	attend**aient**	

*used to describe what something was like, what used
to happen or what was happening

past participle

attend**u** waited
Ils ont attend**u** leurs amis au cinéma.
They waited for their friends at the cinema.

Future

j'	attend**rai**	I will wait
tu	attend**ras**	
il/elle/on	attend**ra**	
nous	attend**rons**	
vous	attend**rez**	
ils/elles	attend**ront**	

Conditional

j'	attend**rais**	I would wait
tu	attend**rais**	
il/elle/on	attend**rait**	
nous	attend**rions**	
vous	attend**riez**	
ils/elles	attend**raient**	

Present subjunctive*

(que) j'	attend**e**	I wait or I am waiting
(que) tu	attend**es**	
(qu') il/elle/on	attend**e**	
(que) nous	attend**ions**	
(que) vous	attend**iez**	
(qu') ils/elles	attend**ent**	

*usually used after que: Il faut que tu attend**es** les
autres. You must wait for the others.

[Use the **tu** (informal singular) form when speaking to one person who you know well, such as a
friend; use the **vous** (formal singular, or plural) form when speaking to someone you don't know
well, or when speaking to more than one person.]

[4] se laver
to wash (oneself)

Present

je	me lave	I wash (myself) or I am washing (myself)
tu	te laves	
il/elle/on	se lave	
nous	nous lavons	
vous	vous lavez	
ils/elles	se lavent	

Perfect*

je	me suis lavé(e)	I have washed (myself) or I washed (myself)
tu	t'es lavé(e)	
il	s'est lavé	
elle	s'est lavée	
on	s'est lavé(e)(s)	
nous	nous sommes lavé(e)s	
vous	vous êtes lavé(e)(s)	
ils	se sont lavés	
elles	se sont lavées	

*uses être plus the past participle to describe completed events in the past

past participle

lavé   washed
Elle s'est lavée à toute vitesse ce matin.
She had a quick wash this morning.

Future

je	me laverai	I will wash (myself)
tu	te laveras	
il/elle/on	se lavera	
nous	nous laverons	
vous	vous laverez	
ils/elles	se laveront	

Present subjunctive*

(que) je	me lave	I wash (myself) or I am washing (myself)
(que) tu	te laves	
(qu') il/elle/on	se lave	
(que) nous	nous lavions	
(que) vous	vous laviez	
(qu') ils/elles	se lavent	

*usually used after que: Il est important que vous vous laviez les mains. It's important that you wash your hands.

Imperative

lave-toi   wash yourself or have a wash
Lave-toi après ton entraînement!
Have a wash after your training!
lavons-nous   let's wash ourselves or let's have a wash
Lavons-nous aux douches du camping.
Let's have a wash at the campsite showers.
lavez-vous   wash yourselves or wash yourself or have a wash
Lavez-vous tous les matins avec cette lotion traitante.
Use this treatment when you wash yourself every morning.

Imperfect*

je	me lavais	I washed (myself) or I used to wash (myself) or I was washing (myself)
tu	te lavais	
il/elle/on	se lavait	
nous	nous lavions	
vous	vous laviez	
ils/elles	se lavaient	

*used to describe what something was like, what used to happen or what was happening

Conditional

je	me laverais	I would wash (myself)
tu	te laverais	
il/elle/on	se laverait	
nous	nous laverions	
vous	vous laveriez	
ils/elles	se laveraient	

[Use the tu (informal singular) form when speaking to one person who you know well, such as a friend; use the vous (formal singular, or plural) form when speaking to someone you don't know well, or when speaking to more than one person.]

[5] avoir
to have

Present

j'	ai	I have or I am having
tu	as	
il/elle/on	a	
nous	av**ons**	
vous	av**ez**	
ils/elles	ont	

Imperative

aie   have
Aie un peu de patience!   Be patient!
ayons   let's have
Ayons courage!   Let's be brave!
ayez   have
Ayons du courage!   Don't be afraid!

Perfect*

j'	ai eu	I have had or I had
tu	as eu	
il/elle/on	a eu	
nous	avons eu	
vous	avez eu	
ils/elles	ont eu	

*uses avoir plus the past participle to describe completed events in the past

Imperfect*

j'	av**ais**	I had or I used to have or I was having
tu	av**ais**	
il/elle/on	av**ait**	
nous	av**ions**	
vous	av**iez**	
ils/elles	av**aient**	

*used to describe what something was like, what used to happen or what was happening

past participle

eu   had
J'ai eu un portable pour mon anniversaire.
I had a mobile for my birthday.

Future

j'	aurai	I will have
tu	auras	
il/elle/on	aura	
nous	aurons	
vous	aurez	
ils/elles	auront	

Conditional

j'	aurais	I would have
tu	aurais	
il/elle/on	aurait	
nous	aurions	
vous	auriez	
ils/elles	auraient	

Present subjunctive*

(que) j'	aie	I have or I am having
(que) tu	aies	
(qu') il/elle/on	ait	
(que) nous	ayons	
(que) vous	ayez	
(qu') ils/elles	aient	

*usually used after que: Il faut que j'aie ce jeu.
I must have that game.

[Use the **tu** (informal singular) form when speaking to one person who you know well, such as a friend; use the **vous** (formal singular, or plural) form when speaking to someone you don't know well, or when speaking to more than one person.]

[6] être
to be

Present

je	suis	I am
tu	es	
il/elle/on	est	
nous	sommes	
vous	êtes	
ils/elles	sont	

Imperative

sois be
Sois gentil et occupe-toi de ton frère.
Be a good boy and look after your brother.
soyons let's be.
Ne soyons pas déçus.
Let's not be disappointed.
soyez be
Soyez patient avec les enfants.
Be patient with the children.

Perfect*

j'	ai été	I have been or I was
tu	as été	
il/elle/on	a été	
nous	avons été	
vous	avez été	
ils/elles	ont été	

*uses avoir plus the past participle to describe completed events in the past

Imperfect*

j'	étais	I was or I used to be or I was being
tu	étais	
il/elle/on	était	
nous	étions	
vous	étiez	
ils/elles	étaient	

*used to describe what something was like, what used to happen or what was happening

past participle

été been
J'ai été ravi de ma visite.   I was delighted with my visit.

Future

je	serai	I will be
tu	seras	
il/elle/on	sera	
nous	serons	
vous	serez	
ils/elles	seront	

Conditional

je	serais	I would be
tu	serais	
il/elle/on	serait	
nous	serions	
vous	seriez	
ils/elles	seraient	

Present subjunctive*

(que) je	sois	I am
(que) tu	sois	
(qu') il/elle/on	soit	
(que) nous	soyons	
(que) vous	soyez	
(qu') ils/elles	soient	

*usually used after que: J'ai peur qu'elle soit là.
I'm afraid she may be here.

[Use the **tu** (informal singular) form when speaking to one person who you know well, such as a friend; use the **vous** (formal singular, or plural) form when speaking to someone you don't know well, or when speaking to more than one person.]

[7] aller
to go

Present

je	vais	I go or I am going
tu	vas	
il/elle/on	va	
nous	allons	
vous	allez	
ils/elles	vont	

Imperative

va   go
Va voir ce que fait ta petite sœur!
Go and check on your little sister!
allons   let's go
Allons au cinéma ce soir.
Let's go to the cinema tonight.
allez   go
Allez vous laver les mains avant de manger!
Go and wash your hands before lunch!

Perfect*

je	suis allé(e)	I have gone or I went
tu	es allé(e)	
il	est allé	
elle	est allée	
on	est allé(e)(s)	
nous	sommes allé(e)s	
vous	êtes allé(e)(s)	
ils	sont allés	
elles	sont allées	

*uses être plus the past participle to describe completed events in the past

Imperfect*

j'	allais	I went to or I used to go or I was going
tu	allais	
il/elle/on	allait	
nous	allions	
vous	alliez	
ils/elles	allaient	

*used to describe what something was like, what used to happen or what was happening

past participle

allé   gone
Elle est allée se baigner à la rivière.
She went for a swim in the river.

Future

j'	irai	I will go
tu	iras	
il/elle/on	ira	
nous	irons	
vous	irez	
ils/elles	iront	

Conditional

j'	irais	I would go
tu	irais	
il/elle/on	irait	
nous	irions	
vous	iriez	
ils/elles	iraient	

Present subjunctive*

(que) j'	aille	I go or I am going
(que) tu	ailles	
(qu') il/elle/on	aille	
(que) nous	allions	
(que) vous	alliez	
(qu') ils/elles	aillent	

*usually used after que: Mamie veut que tu ailles faire les courses avec elle. Gran wants you to go shopping with her.

[Use the **tu** (informal singular) form when speaking to one person who you know well, such as a friend; use the **vous** (formal singular, or plural) form when speaking to someone you don't know well, or when speaking to more than one person.]

[8] devoir
to have to

Present
je	dois	I have to or I must
tu	dois	
il/elle/on	doit	
nous	dev**ons**	
vous	dev**ez**	
ils/elles	doivent	

Perfect*
j'	ai dû	I have had to or I had to
tu	as dû	
il/elle/on	a dû	
nous	avons dû	
vous	avez dû	
ils/elles	ont dû	

*uses avoir plus the past participle to describe completed events in the past

past participle
dû   had

J'ai dû ranger ma chambre avant de sortir.
I've had to tidy up my room before going out.

Future
je	dev**rai**	I will have to
tu	dev**ras**	
il/elle/on	dev**ra**	
nous	dev**rons**	
vous	dev**rez**	
ils/elles	dev**ront**	

Present subjunctive*
(que) je	doive	I have to or I must
(que) tu	doives	
(qu') il/elle/on	doive	
(que) nous	dev**ions**	
(que) vous	dev**iez**	
(qu') ils/elles	doivent	

*usually used after que: J'ai bien peur que nous devions aller le voir. I'm afraid we may have to visit him.

Imperative
The imperative of devoir is not used.

Imperfect*
je	dev**ais**	I had to or I used to have to
tu	dev**ais**	
il/elle/on	dev**ait**	
nous	dev**ions**	
vous	dev**iez**	
ils/elles	dev**aient**	

*used to describe what something was like, what used to happen or what was happening

Conditional
je	dev**rais**	I ought to
tu	dev**rais**	
il/elle/on	dev**rait**	
nous	dev**rions**	
vous	dev**riez**	
ils/elles	dev**raient**	

[Use the **tu** (informal singular) form when speaking to one person who you know well, such as a friend; use the **vous** (formal singular, or plural) form when speaking to someone you don't know well, or when speaking to more than one person.]

[9] dire
to say

Present

je	dis	I say or I am saying
tu	dis	
il/elle/on	dit	
nous	disons	
vous	dites	
ils/elles	disent	

Imperative

dis   say
Dis ce que tu as à dire!
Say what you've got to say!
disons   let's say
Disons que ça fait à peu près huit euros.
Let's say it's about eight euros.
dites   say
Dites-le avec des fleurs!   Say it with flowers!

Perfect*

j'	ai dit	I have said or I said
tu	as dit	
il/elle/on	a dit	
nous	avons dit	
vous	avez dit	
ils/elles	ont dit	

*uses avoir plus the past participle to describe completed events in the past

Imperfect*

je	disais	I said or I used to say or I was saying
tu	disais	
il/elle/on	disait	
nous	disions	
vous	disiez	
ils/elles	disaient	

*used to describe what something was like, what used to happen or what was happening

past participle

dit   said
Vous avez dit dix-neuf heures ce soir, c'est bien ça?
You did say seven tonight, didn't you?

Future

je	dirai	I will say
tu	diras	
il/elle/on	dira	
nous	dirons	
vous	direz	
ils/elles	diront	

Conditional

je	dirais	I would say
tu	dirais	
il/elle/on	dirait	
nous	dirions	
vous	diriez	
ils/elles	diraient	

Present subjunctive*

(que) je	dise	I say or I am saying
(que) tu	dises	
(qu') il/elle/on	dise	
(que) nous	disions	
(que) vous	disiez	
(qu') ils/elles	disent	

*usually used after que: Il faut que tu le lui dises. You must tell her.

[Use the **tu** (informal singular) form when speaking to one person who you know well, such as a friend; use the **vous** (formal singular, or plural) form when speaking to someone you don't know well, or when speaking to more than one person.]

[10] faire
to do or to make

Present

je	fais	I do or I make or I am doing or I am making
tu	fais	
il/elle/on	fait	
nous	faisons	
vous	faites	
ils/elles	font	

Imperative

fais   do or make
Fais comme chez toi!
Make yourself at home!
faisons   let's do or let's make
Faisons un gâteau pour son anniversaire!
Let's make a cake for her birthday!
faites   do or make
Faites attention aux voitures!
Watch out for the cars!

Perfect*

j'	ai fait	I have done or I have made or I did or I made
tu	as fait	
il/elle/on	a fait	
nous	avons fait	
vous	avez fait	
ils/elles	ont fait	

*uses avoir plus the past participle to describe completed events in the past

Imperfect*

je	faisais	I did or I made or I used to do or I used to make or I was doing or I was making
tu	faisais	
il/elle/on	faisait	
nous	faisions	
vous	faisiez	
ils/elles	faisaient	

*used to describe what something was like, what used to happen or what was happening

past participle

fait   done or made
Qu'est-ce que tu as fait?   What have you done? or What have you made?

Future

je	ferai	I will do or I will make
tu	feras	
il/elle/on	fera	
nous	ferons	
vous	ferez	
ils/elles	feront	

Conditional

je	ferais	I would do or I would make
tu	ferais	
il/elle/on	ferait	
nous	ferions	
vous	feriez	
ils/elles	feraient	

Present subjunctive*

(que) je	fasse	I do or I make or I am doing or I am making
(que) tu	fasses	
(qu') il/elle/on	fasse	
(que) nous	fassions	
(que) vous	fassiez	
(qu') ils/elles	fassent	

*usually used after que: La prof veut que nous fassions tous nos devoirs. The teacher wants us to do all our homework.

[Use the **tu** (informal singular) form when speaking to one person who you know well, such as a friend; use the **vous** (formal singular, or plural) form when speaking to someone you don't know well, or when speaking to more than one person.]

[11] mettre
to put

Present

je	mets	I put or I am putting
tu	mets	
il/elle/on	met	
nous	mettons	
vous	mettez	
ils/elles	mettent	

Imperative

mets   put

Mets ton manteau pour avoir chaud.
Put on your coat to keep warm.

mettons   let's put

Mettons le couvert!   Let's lay the table!

mettez   put

Mettez de l'argent de côté pour acheter une console de jeux.
Save up for a games console.

Perfect*

j'	ai mis	I have put or I put
tu	as mis	
il/elle/on	a mis	
nous	avons mis	
vous	avez mis	
ils/elles	ont mis	

*uses avoir plus the past participle to describe completed events in the past

Imperfect*

je	mettais	I put or I used to put or I was putting
tu	mettais	
il/elle/on	mettait	
nous	mettions	
vous	mettiez	
ils/elles	mettaient	

*used to describe what something was like, what used to happen or what was happening

past participle

mis   put

Elles ont mis la clé sous le paillasson.
They put the key under the doormat.

Future

je	mettrai	I will put
tu	mettras	
il/elle/on	mettra	
nous	mettrons	
vous	mettrez	
ils/elles	mettront	

Conditional

je	mettrais	I would put
tu	mettrais	
il/elle/on	mettrait	
nous	mettrions	
vous	mettriez	
ils/elles	mettraient	

Present subjunctive*

(que) je	mette	I put or I am putting
(que) tu	mettes	
(qu') il/elle/on	mette	
(que) nous	mettions	
(que) vous	mettiez	
(qu') ils/elles	mettent	

*usually used after que: Il faut qu'elle mette aussi un casque. She must also wear a helmet.

[Use the tu (informal singular) form when speaking to one person who you know well, such as a friend; use the vous (formal singular, or plural) form when speaking to someone you don't know well, or when speaking to more than one person.]

[12] pouvoir
to be able

Present

je	peux	I am able *or* I can
tu	peux	
il/elle/on	peut	
nous	pouvons	
vous	pouvez	
ils/elles	peuvent	

Imperative
The imperative of pouvoir is not used.

Perfect*

j'	ai pu	I have been able to *or* I was able to *or* I could
tu	as pu	
il/elle/on	a pu	
nous	avons pu	
vous	avez pu	
ils/elles	ont pu	

*uses avoir plus the past participle to describe completed events in the past

Imperfect*

je	pouvais	I was able to *or* I could *or* I used to be able to
tu	pouvais	
il/elle/on	pouvait	
nous	pouvions	
vous	pouviez	
ils/elles	pouvaient	

*used to describe what something was like, what used to happen or what was happening

past participle
pu   been able to
Ils ont pu acheter des billets pour le concert.
They were able to buy tickets for the concert.

Future

je	pourrai	I will be able to
tu	pourras	
il/elle/on	pourra	
nous	pourrons	
vous	pourrez	
ils/elles	pourront	

Conditional

je	pourrais	I would be able to *or* I could
tu	pourrais	
il/elle/on	pourrait	
nous	pourrions	
vous	pourriez	
ils/elles	pourraient	

Present subjunctive*

(que) je	puisse	I am able *or* I can
(que) tu	puisses	
(qu') il/elle/on	puisse	
(que) nous	puissions	
(que) vous	puissiez	
(qu') ils/elles	puissent	

*usually used after que: Ça m'étonnerait qu'elle puisse le faire. I'd be surprised if she could do it.

[Use the **tu** (informal singular) form when speaking to one person who you know well, such as a friend; use the **vous** (formal singular, or plural) form when speaking to someone you don't know well, or when speaking to more than one person.]

[13] voir
to see

Present

je	vois	I see *or* I am seeing
tu	vois
il/elle/on	voit
nous	voyons
vous	voyez
ils/elles	voient

Imperative

vois   see
Vois comme le coucher de soleil est beau!
See how beautiful the sunset is!
voyons   let's see.
Voyons, où en étions-nous?
Let's see, where were we?
voyez   have
Voyez comme ce n'est pas difficile!
See how easy it is!

Perfect*

j'	ai vu	I have seen *or* I saw
tu	as vu
il/elle/on	a vu
nous	avons vu
vous	avez vu
ils/elles	ont vu

*uses avoir plus the past participle to describe completed events in the past

Imperfect*

je	voyais	I saw *or* I used to see *or* I was seeing
tu	voyais
il/elle/on	voyait
nous	voyions
vous	voyiez
ils/elles	voyaient

*used to describe what something was like, what used to happen or what was happening

past participle

vu   seen
J'ai vu un joli sac à main dans la vitrine.
I've seen a nice handbag in the shop window.

Future

je	verrai	I will see
tu	verras
il/elle/on	verra
nous	verrons
vous	verrez
ils/elles	verront

Conditional

je	verrais	I would see
tu	verrais
il/elle/on	verrait
nous	verrions
vous	verriez
ils/elles	verraient

Present subjunctive*

(que) je	voie	I see *or* I am seeing
(que) tu	voies
(qu') il/elle/on	voie
(que) nous	voyions
(que) vous	voyiez
(qu') ils/elles	voient

*usually used after que: Il faut que vous voyiez mon nouveau VTT. You must see my new mountain bike.

[Use the tu (informal singular) form when speaking to one person who you know well, such as a friend; use the vous (formal singular, or plural) form when speaking to someone you don't know well, or when speaking to more than one person.]

[14] vouloir
to want

Present

je	veux	I want or I am wanting
tu	veux	
il/elle/on	veut	
nous	voulons	
vous	voulez	
ils/elles	veulent	

Imperative

The veuille and veuillons forms of the imperative are not used.

veuillez ... please ...

Veuillez noter que notre magasin sera fermé pendant le mois d'août.

Please note that our shop will be closed in August.

Perfect*

j'	ai voulu	I have wanted or I wanted
tu	as voulu	
il/elle/on	a voulu	
nous	avons voulu	
vous	avez voulu	
ils/elles	ont voulu	

*uses avoir plus the past participle to describe completed events in the past

Imperfect*

je	voulais	I wanted or I used to want or I was wanting
tu	voulais	
il/elle/on	voulait	
nous	voulions	
vous	vouliez	
ils/elles	voulaient	

*used to describe what something was like, what used to happen or what was happening

past participle

voulu   wanted

J'ai voulu tourner à gauche, mais la rue était bloquée.

I wanted to turn left, but the street was blocked.

Conditional

je	voudrais	I would like
tu	voudrais	
il/elle/on	voudrait	
nous	voudrions	
vous	voudriez	
ils/elles	voudraient	

Future

je	voudrai	I will want
tu	voudras	
il/elle/on	voudra	
nous	voudrons	
vous	voudrez	
ils/elles	voudront	

Present subjunctive*

(que) je	veuille	I want or I am wanting
(que) tu	veuilles	
(qu') il/elle/on	veuille	
(que) nous	voulions	
(que) vous	vouliez	
(qu') ils/elles	veuillent	

*usually used after que: Ça m'étonnerait qu'il veuille venir avec nous. I'd be surprised if he came with us.

[Use the tu (informal singular) form when speaking to one person who you know well, such as a friend; use the vous (formal singular, or plural) form when speaking to someone you don't know well, or when speaking to more than one person.]

Other *irregular* verbs (pages 378–384)

The following verbs are only irregular in certain forms. Again, when you look up an entry, use the number in square brackets to find the verb model below.

[15]	abréger	to shorten
[16]	acheter	to buy
[17]	acquérir	to acquire
[18]	appeler	to call; to phone
[19]	apprendre	to learn; to hear; to teach
[20]	s'asseoir	to sit down
[21]	battre	to beat; to clap; to bang
[22]	boire	to drink
[23]	bouillir	to boil
[24]	céder	to give in; to give up
[25]	conclure	to conclude
[26]	conduire	to drive; to take (somebody) to
[27]	connaître	to know; to meet
[28]	coudre	to sew
[29]	courir	to run
[30]	couvrir	to cover
[31]	craindre	to be afraid of
[32]	créer	to create
[33]	croire	to think; to believe
[34]	croître	to grow
[35]	cueillir	to pick
[36]	cuire	to cook; to bake; to roast
[37]	dormir	to sleep
[38]	écrire	to write
[39]	employer	to employ; to use
[40]	envoyer	to send
[41]	essuyer	to wipe
[42]	faillir	use faillir faire to say something nearly happened
[43]	falloir	use falloir to say something must be done
[44]	fuir	to run away, to flee; to leak
[45]	geler	to freeze
[46]	haïr	to hate
[47]	interdire	to forbid
[48]	jeter	to throw; to throw away
[49]	joindre	to get hold of; to enclose; to put together
[50]	lever	to raise
[51]	lire	to read
[52]	manger	to eat
[53]	mentir	to lie
[54]	mourir	to die

[55] naître	to be born
[56] offrir	to offer; to give; to buy
[57] paraître	to seem; to appear; to come out *(to be published)*
[58] partir	to leave, to go; to start; to come out, to come off
[59] payer	to pay
[60] peindre	to paint
[61] placer	to place; to seat
[62] plaire	use plaire to talk about likes and dislikes
[63] pleuvoir	to rain
[64] prendre	to take; to have *(something to eat, drink)*; to bring; to pick up *(someone)*
[65] prévoir	to predict; to plan; to allow for
[66] recevoir	to receive, to get; to welcome; to entertain; to see
[67] résoudre	to solve
[68] rire	to laugh; to have fun; to joke
[69] rompre	to split up
[70] savoir	to know
[71] servir	to serve; to be used for something
[72] sortir	to go out; to come out; to be going out with someone; to take out
[73] souffrir	to suffer
[74] suffire	to be enough
[75] suivre	to follow
[76] se taire	to stop talking
[77] tenir	to hold; to run; to keep; to take up; to fit; to be determined to do something
[78] traire	to milk
[79] vaincre	to defeat; to overcome
[80] valoir	to be, to cost
[81] venir	to come
[82] vivre	to live; to live through

Irregular verb forms

This list shows the main forms of other irregular verbs. The number before the infinitive is the number given after verbs in the dictionary which follow this pattern.

1 = Present   **2** = Past participle   **3** = Imperfect   **4** = Future

[15] abréger
1 j'abrège, nous abrégeons, ils abrègent
2 abrégé
3 j'abrégeais
4 j'abrégerai

[16] acheter
1 j'achète, nous achetons, ils achètent
2 acheté
3 j'achetais
4 j'achèterai

[17] acquérir
1 j'acquiers, il acquiert, nous acquérons, vous acquérez, ils acquièrent
2 acquis
3 j'acquérais
4 j'acquerrai

[18] appeler
1 j'appelle, nous appelons
2 appelé
3 j'appelais
4 j'appellerai

[19] apprendre
1 j'apprends, nous apprenons, vous apprenez, ils apprennent
2 appris
3 j'apprenais
4 j'apprendrai

[20] s'asseoir
1 je m'assieds, nous nous asseyons, vous vous asseyez, ils s'asseyent
2 assis
3 je m'asseyais
4 je m'assiérai

[21] battre
1 je bats, il bat, nous battons
2 battu
3 je battais
4 je battrai

[22] boire
1 je bois, nous buvons, ils boivent
2 bu
3 je buvais
4 je boirai

[23] bouillir
1 je bous, nous bouillons
2 bouilli
3 je bouillais
4 je bouillirai

[24] céder
1 je cède, nous cédons, ils cèdent
2 cédé
3 je cédais
4 je céderai

[25] conclure
1 je conclus, nous concluons
2 conclu
3 je concluais
4 je conclurai

[26] conduire
1 je conduis, nous conduisons
2 conduit
3 je conduisais
4 je conduirai

[27] connaître
1 je connais, nous connaissons
2 connu
3 je connaissais
4 je connaîtrai

[28] coudre
1 je couds, nous cousons,
   vous cousez, ils cousent
2 cousu
3 je cousais
4 je coudrai

[29] courir
1 je cours, nous courons
2 couru
3 je courais
4 je courrai

[30] couvrir
1 je couvre, nous couvrons
2 couvert
3 je couvrais
4 je couvrirai

[31] craindre
1 je crains, nous craignons
2 craint
3 je craignais
4 je craindrai

[32] créer
1 je crée, nous créons
2 créé
3 je créais
4 je créerai

[33] croire
1 je crois, nous croyons,
   ils croient
2 cru
3 je croyais
4 je croirai

[34] croître
1 je croîs, nous croissons
2 crû
3 je croissais
4 je croîtrai

[35] cueillir
1 je cueille, nous cueillons
2 cueilli
3 je cueillais
4 je cueillerai

[36] cuire
1 je cuis, nous cuisons, ils cuisent
2 cuit
3 je cuisais
4 je cuirai

[37] dormir
1 je dors, nous dormons
2 dormi
3 je dormais
4 je dormirai

[38] écrire
1 j'écris, nous écrivons
2 écrit
3 j'écrivais
4 j'écrirai

[39] employer
1 j'emploie, nous employons,
   vous employez, ils emploient
2 employé
3 j'employais
4 j'emploierai

[40] envoyer
1 j'envoie, nous envoyons,
   vous envoyez, ils envoient
2 envoyé
3 j'envoyais
4 j'enverrai

[41] essuyer
1 j'essuie, nous essuyons,
   vous essuyez, ils essuient
2 essuyé
3 j'essuyais
4 j'essuierai

[42] faillir
2 failli

[43] falloir
1 il faut
2 fallu
3 il fallait
4 il faudra

[44] fuir
1 je fuis, nous fuyons, ils fuient
2 fui
3 je fuyais
4 je fuirai

[45] geler
1 je gèle, nous gelons,
vous gelez, ils gèlent
2 gelé
3 je gelais
4 je gèlerai

[46] haïr
1 je hais, nous haïssons,
ils haïssent
2 haï
3 je haïssais
4 je haïrai

[47] interdire
1 j'interdis, nous interdisons,
vous interdisez
2 interdit
3 j'interdisais
4 j'interdirai

[48] jeter
1 je jette, nous jetons, ils jettent
2 jeté
3 je jetais
4 je jetterai

[49] joindre
1 je joins, nous joignons
2 joint
3 je joignais
4 je joindrai

[50] lever
1 je lève, nous levons, ils lèvent
2 levé
3 je levais
4 je lèverai

[51] lire
1 je lis, nous lisons
2 lu
3 je lisais
4 je lirai

[52] manger
1 je mange, nous mangeons
2 mangé
3 je mangeais
4 je mangerai

[53] mentir
1 je mens, nous mentons
2 menti
3 je mentais
4 je mentirai

[54] mourir
1 je meurs, nous mourons,
ils meurent
2 mort
3 je mourais
4 je mourrai

[55] naître
1 je nais, il naît, nous naissons
2 né
3 je naissais
4 je naîtrai

[56] offrir
1 j'offre, nous offrons
2 offert
3 j'offrais
4 j'offrirai

[57] paraître
1 je parais, il paraît, nous paraissons
2 paru
3 je paraissais
4 je paraîtrai

[58] partir
1 je pars, nous partons
2 parti
3 je partais
4 je partirai

[59] payer
1 je paie/je paye, nous payons, vous payez, ils paient/ils payent
2 payé
3 je payais
4 je paierai/je payerai

[60] peindre
1 je peins, nous peignons
2 peint
3 je peignais
4 je peindrai

[61] placer
1 je place, nous plaçons
2 placé
3 je plaçais
4 je placerai

[62] plaire
1 je plais, il plaît, nous plaisons
2 plu
3 je plaisais
4 je plairai

[63] pleuvoir
1 il pleut
2 plu
3 il pleuvait
4 il pleuvra

[64] prendre
1 je prends, nous prenons, ils prennent
2 pris
3 je prenais
4 je prendrai

[65] prévoir
1 je prévois, nous prévoyons, vous prévoyez, ils prévoient
2 prévu
3 je prévoyais
4 je prévoirai

[66] recevoir
1 je reçois, il reçoit, ils reçoivent
2 reçu
3 je recevais
4 je recevrai

[67] résoudre
1 je résous, nous résolvons, vous résolvez, ils résolvent
2 résolu
3 je résolvais
4 je résoudrai

[68] rire
1 je ris, nous rions
2 ri
3 je riais
4 je rirai

[69] rompre
1 je romps, il rompt, nous rompons
2 rompu
3 je rompais
4 je romprai

[70] savoir
1 je sais, nous savons, ils savent
2 su
3 je savais
4 je saurai

[71] servir
1 je sers, nous servons
2 servi
3 je servais
4 je servirai

[72] sortir
1 je sors, nous sortons
2 sorti
3 je sortais
4 je sortirai

[73] souffrir
1 je souffre, nous souffrons
2 souffert
3 je souffrais
4 je souffrirai

[74] suffire
1 je suffis, nous suffisons
2 suffi
3 je suffisais
4 je suffirai

[75] suivre
1 je suis, nous suivons
2 suivi
3 je suivais
4 je suivrai

[76] taire
1 je me tais, nous nous taisons
2 tu
3 je me taisais
4 je me tairai

[77] tenir
1 je tiens, nous tenons, ils tiennent
2 tenu
3 je tenais
4 je tiendrai

[78] traire
1 je trais, nous trayons, ils traient
2 trait
3 je trayais
4 je trairai

[79] vaincre
1 je vaincs, il vainc, nous vainquons
2 vaincu
3 je vainquais
4 je vaincrai

[80] valoir
1 je vaux, il vaut, nous valons
2 valu
3 je valais
4 je vaincrai

[81] venir
1 je viens, nous venons, ils viennent
2 venu
3 je venais
4 je viendrai

[82] vivre
1 je vis, nous vivons
2 vécu
3 je vivais
4 je vivrai

Aa

ℓ **a, an** DETERMINER
1 *(before a masc singular noun)* **un**
   a shop un magasin
   a tree un arbre
   a man un homme
2 *(before a fem singular noun)* **une**
   a house une maison
   a school une école
   a woman une femme
3 *(showing how much, how many, how often)*
   five euros a kilo cinq euros le kilo
   fifty kilometres an hour cinquante
   kilomètres à l'heure
   three times a day trois fois par jour
   I do athletics twice a week. Je fais de
   l'athlétisme deux fois par semaine.
4 *(when saying what you do)* **She's a dentist.**
   Elle est dentiste.
   I'm a student. Je suis étudiant *(boy
   speaking),* Je suis étudiante *(girl speaking).*

   WORD TIP a before an occupation is not
   translated into French.

to **abandon** VERB
   abandonner [1]

abbey NOUN
   une **abbaye** FEM
   Westminster Abbey l'Abbaye de
   Westminster

abbreviation NOUN
   une **abréviation** FEM

ability NOUN
   la **capacité** FEM
   the ability to do something la capacité de
   faire quelque chose

ℓ **able** ADJECTIVE
   to be able to do something pouvoir [12]
   faire quelque chose
   I wasn't able to sleep. Je n'ai pas pu dormir.

to **abolish** VERB
   abolir [2]

abortion NOUN
   un **avortement** MASC
   She had an abortion. Elle s'est fait avorter.

ℓ **about** PREPOSITION ▶ SEE **about** ADVERB
1 *(telling the story of)* **sur**
   a book about a rock band un livre sur un
   groupe de rock
   What's the film about? De quoi le film
   parle-t-il?
2 *(concerning)* **au sujet de**
   He wants to talk to you about your exam.

Il veut te parler au sujet de ton examen.
   (emails, letters, messages) **What's it about?**
   De quoi s'agit-il?
   It's about the school trip. Il s'agit du
   voyage scolaire.
3 **to talk about something** parler de quelque
   chose
   What's she talking about? De quoi parle-
   t-elle?

ℓ **about** ADVERB ▶ SEE **about** PREPOSITION
1 *(nearly)* **environ**
   There are about twenty people here. Il y a
   environ vingt personnes ici.
2 *(talking about the time)* **vers**
   at about three o'clock vers trois heures
3 **to be about to do something** être [6] sur le
   point de faire quelque chose
   She's just about to leave. Elle est sur le
   point de partir.

ℓ **above** PREPOSITION
1 **au-dessus de**
   the shelf above the TV l'étagère au-dessus
   de la télévision
2 **above all** surtout
   Above all, wait for me. Surtout, attendez-
   moi!

ℓ **abroad** ADVERB
   à l'étranger
   They live abroad. Ils vivent à l'étranger.
   to go abroad aller ◎ [7] à l'étranger
   I'd like to go abroad next summer.
   J'aimerais aller à l'étranger l'été prochain.

abseiling NOUN
   la **descente en rappel** FEM

absent ADJECTIVE
   absent MASC, **absente** FEM
   He was absent yesterday. Il était absent
   hier.

absolute ADJECTIVE
   complet MASC, **complète** FEM
   The party was an absolute disaster. La fête
   a été un désastre complet.

ℓ **absolutely** ADVERB
   absolument
   You're absolutely right. Tu as tout à fait
   raison.
   Absolutely not! Pas du tout!

abuse NOUN ▶ SEE **abuse** VERB
1 *(of drugs, alcohol)* l'**abus** MASC
2 *(violence)* le **mauvais traitement** MASC
3 *(insulting words)* les **injures** FEM PL

to **abuse** VERB ▶ SEE **abuse** NOUN
   to abuse somebody maltraiter [1]
   quelqu'un

ℓ indicates key words

to **accelerate** *VERB*
accélérer [24]

accelerator *NOUN*
un accélérateur *MASC*

accent *NOUN*
un accent *MASC*
She has a French accent. Elle a l'accent français.

to **accept** *VERB*
accepter [1]

acceptable *ADJECTIVE*
acceptable *MASC & FEM*

access *NOUN* ▸ SEE **access** *VERB*
un accès *MASC*

to **access** *VERB* ▸ SEE **access** *NOUN*
to access the file accéder [24] au fichier

accessory *NOUN*
un accessoire *MASC*

ℓ **accident** *NOUN*
1 *(something bad)* un **accident** *MASC*
a car accident un accident de voiture
a road accident un accident de la route
to have an accident avoir [5] un accident
2 *(chance)* un **hasard** *MASC*
by accident par hasard
I found it by accident. Je l'ai trouvé par hasard.

accident & emergency *NOUN*
(Medicine) les urgences *FEM PL*

ℓ **accidentally** *ADVERB*
1 *(without meaning to)* accidentellement
I accidentally sent this email. J'ai envoyé cet email accidentellement.
2 *(by chance)* par hasard
Amy accidentally discovered that ... Amy a découvert par hasard que ...

to **accommodate** *VERB*
recevoir [66]
The centre accommodates sixty people. Le centre reçoit soixante personnes.

ℓ **accommodation** *NOUN*
le **logement** *MASC*
We are looking for accommodation. Nous cherchons un logement.

to **accompany** *VERB*
to accompany somebody accompagner [1] quelqu'un

ℓ **according to** *PHRASE*
selon
According to Laura they've split up. Selon Laura ils ne sont plus ensemble.

accordion *NOUN*
un accordéon *MASC*

ℓ **account** *NOUN*
1 *(in a bank, shop, post office)* le **compte** *MASC*
to open an account ouvrir un compte
I have twenty pounds in my account. J'ai vingt livres sur mon compte.
2 *(of an event)* le **compte rendu** *MASC*
3 **on account of something** à cause de quelque chose
There are no buses on account of the strike. Il n'y a pas de bus à cause de la grève.
4 **to take something into account** tenir compte de quelque chose
You have to take travel expenses into account. Il faut tenir compte des frais de voyage.

accountant *NOUN*
le & la **comptable** *MASC & FEM*
She's an accountant. Elle est comptable.

accuracy *NOUN*
la précision *FEM*

accurate *ADJECTIVE*
précis *MASC*, précise *FEM*

ℓ to **accuse** *VERB*
to accuse somebody of doing something accuser [1] quelqu'un d'avoir fait quelque chose
She accused me of stealing her pen. Elle m'a accusé d'avoir volé son stylo.
He is accused of killing many people. On l'accuse d'avoir tué beaucoup de gens.

accustomed *ADJECTIVE*
to be accustomed to something être [6] habitué à quelque chose
She is accustomed to life in the city. Elle est habituée à la vie en ville.

ace *ADJECTIVE* ▸ SEE **ace** *NOUN*
(informal) super *MASC & FEM INVARIABLE*
He's an ace drummer. C'est un super batteur.

ace *NOUN* ▸ SEE **ace** *ADJECTIVE*
un **as** *MASC*
the ace of hearts l'as de cœur

to **ache** *VERB*
My head aches. J'ai mal à la tête.
My feet are aching. J'ai mal aux pieds.

to **achieve** *VERB*
accomplir [2]
She's achieved great things. Elle a accompli de grandes choses.

achievement *NOUN*
la réussite *FEM*

🔵 means the verb takes être to form the perfect

It's a great achievement. C'est une grande réussite.

acid NOUN
un **acide** MASC
- **acid rain**
les pluies acides

acne NOUN
l'**acné** FEM

acorn NOUN
le **gland** MASC

acrobat NOUN
un & une **acrobate** MASC & FEM

ℐ **across** PREPOSITION
1 (to the other side of)
to walk across something traverser [1] quelque chose
We walked across the park. On a traversé le parc.
2 (on the other side of) **de l'autre côté de**
the house across the canal la maison de l'autre côté du canal
3 (opposite) **across from** en face de
She was sitting across from me. Elle était assise en face de moi.

act NOUN ▶ SEE **act** VERB
un **acte** MASC

ℐ to **act** VERB ▶ SEE **act** NOUN
1 (in plays, films) **jouer** [1]
He acts in the Bond films. Il joue dans les films de James Bond.
2 (to take action) **agir** [2]
They acted quickly. Ils ont agi rapidement.

acting NOUN
le **jeu** MASC
She wants to go into acting. Elle veut devenir actrice.
The acting was terrible. Les acteurs jouaient très mal.

action NOUN
une **action** FEM
- **action replay**
le replay

active ADJECTIVE
actif MASC, **active** FEM

ℐ **activity** NOUN
une **activité** FEM
They have lots of sports activities. Ils ont beaucoup d'activités sportives.
- **activity holiday**
les vacances sportives

actor NOUN
un **acteur** MASC
your favourite actor ton acteur préféré

actress NOUN
une **actrice** FEM
my favourite actress mon actrice préférée

actual ADJECTIVE
1 (exact) **exact** MASC, **exacte** FEM
I don't remember the actual words. Je ne me rappelle pas les mots exacts.
2 (real) **the actual house where he was born** la maison même où il est né

ℐ **actually** ADVERB
1 (in fact) **en fait**
Actually, I've changed my mind. En fait, j'ai changé d'avis.
2 (really and truly) **vraiment**
Did she actually say that? Est-ce qu'elle a vraiment dit ça?

acute ADJECTIVE
1 (intense) **vif** MASC, **vive** FEM
The pain was acute. La douleur était vive.
2 (Grammar) **an acute accent** un accent aigu (as in café)

ℐ **ad** NOUN
1 (on television) la **pub** FEM (informal)
That ad annoys me. Cette pub m'agace.
2 (in a newspaper) une **annonce** FEM
to put an ad in the paper mettre une annonce dans le journal
the small ads les petites annonces

AD ABBREVIATION
après Jésus-Christ, apr. J-C
in AD 400 en quatre cents après Jésus-Christ

to **adapt** VERB
1 **to adapt something for something** adapter [1] quelque chose pour quelque chose
The book has been adapted for television. Le livre a été adapté pour la télévision.
2 **to adapt to something** s'adapter [1] ◔ à quelque chose
She has adapted well to the new school. Elle s'est bien adaptée à la nouvelle école.

adaptor NOUN
un **adaptateur** MASC

ℐ to **add** VERB
ajouter [1]
Add three eggs. Ajoutez trois œufs.
- **to add something up**
additionner [1] quelque chose
Add up the scores. Additionnez les points.

addict NOUN
1 (drug addict) le **drogué** MASC, la **droguée** FEM
2 (fan) un & une **accro** MASC & FEM
She's a telly addict. C'est une accro de la télé.

ℐ indicates key words

addicted *ADJECTIVE*
1 to be addicted to drugs avoir une
dépendance à la drogue
She's addicted to heroin. Elle a une
dépendance à l'héroïne.
2 *(to sweets, junk food)* to be addicted to
something être [6] accro de quelque chose
(informal)
I'm addicted to chocolate. Je suis accro de
chocolat.

addition *NOUN*
(adding up) l'**addition** *FEM*
in addition to something en plus de
quelque chose

additional *ADJECTIVE*
supplémentaire *MASC & FEM*

additive *NOUN*
un **additif** *MASC*

ℰ**address** *NOUN*
une **adresse** *FEM*
an email address une adresse électronique,
une adresse email
What's your address? Quelle est ton
adresse?
to change your address changer [52]
d'adresse
• address book
le carnet d'adresses

adhesive *ADJECTIVE* ▸ SEE **adhesive** *NOUN*
collant *MASC*, collante *FEM*
some adhesive tape du ruban adhésif

adhesive *NOUN* ▸ SEE **adhesive** *ADJECTIVE*
la **colle** *FEM*

adjective *NOUN*
un **adjectif** *MASC*

to **adjust** *VERB*
1 to adjust something régler [24] quelque
chose
to adjust the screen régler l'écran.
2 to adjust to something s'adapter [1] ◎ à
quelque chose
He didn't adjust to the changes. Il ne s'est
pas adapté aux changements.

adjustable *ADJECTIVE*
réglable *MASC & FEM*

administration *NOUN*
une **administration** *FEM*

admiral *NOUN*
un **amiral** *MASC*

admiration *NOUN*
l'**admiration** *FEM*

ℰto **admire** *VERB*
admirer [1]

I admire her a lot. Je l'admire beaucoup.

admission *NOUN*
une **entrée** *FEM*
'No admission' 'Entrée interdite'
'Admission free' 'Entrée gratuite'

ℰto **admit** *VERB*
1 *(to confess)* reconnaître [27]
She admits that she lied. Elle reconnaît
qu'elle a menti.
I admit I was wrong. Je reconnais que j'ai
eu tort.
2 to be admitted to hospital être [6]
hospitalisé
She was admitted to hospital. Elle a été
hospitalisée.

adolescence *NOUN*
l'**adolescence** *FEM*

adolescent *NOUN*
un **adolescent** *MASC*, une **adolescente** *FEM*

to **adopt** *VERB*
adopter [1]

adopted *ADJECTIVE*
adoptif *MASC*, adoptive *FEM*

adoption *NOUN*
une **adoption** *FEM*

to **adore** *VERB*
adorer [1]

Adriatic Sea *NOUN*
the Adriatic Sea la mer Adriatique

adult *ADJECTIVE* ▸ SEE **adult** *NOUN*
adulte *MASC & FEM*
the adult population la population adulte

adult *NOUN* ▸ SEE **adult** *ADJECTIVE*
un & une **adulte** *MASC & FEM*

advance *NOUN* ▸ SEE **advance** *VERB*
le **progrès** *MASC*
advances in technology les progrès de la
technologie

to **advance** *VERB* ▸ SEE **advance** *NOUN*
progresser [1]
**Technology has advanced a lot in ten
years.** La technologie a beaucoup progressé
en dix ans.

advanced *ADJECTIVE*
avancé *MASC*, avancée *FEM*

ℰ**advantage** *NOUN*
un **avantage** *MASC*
There are several advantages. Il y a
plusieurs avantages.
to take advantage of something profiter
[1] de quelque chose
**We took advantage of the good weather
and got a tan.** Nous avons profité du beau

◎ means the verb takes être to form the perfect

temps et nous avons bronzé.

Advent NOUN
l'Avent MASC

adventure NOUN
une aventure FEM

adventurous ADJECTIVE
aventureux MASC, aventureuse FEM

adverb NOUN
un adverbe MASC

advert NOUN ▸ SEE **advertisement** NOUN

ℰ to **advertise** VERB
1 to advertise something in the newspaper mettre [11] une annonce pour quelque chose dans le journal
I saw a bike advertised in the paper. J'ai vu une annonce pour un vélo dans le journal.
2 to advertise a product faire [10] de la publicité pour un produit

advertisement NOUN
1 (on TV) la publicité FEM
2 (in a newspaper) une annonce FEM
3 (small ad) une petite annonce FEM

advertising NOUN
la publicité FEM
I'd like to work in advertising. J'aimerais travailler dans la publicité.

ℰ **advice** NOUN
les conseils MASC PL
a piece of advice un conseil
She gave us some good advice. Elle nous a donné de bons conseils.
to ask for advice about something demander [1] des conseils à propos de quelque chose
Ask for advice about the exam. Demande des conseils à propos de l'examen.

ℰ to **advise** VERB
to advise somebody to do something conseiller [1] à quelqu'un de faire quelque chose
I advised my brother to leave. J'ai conseillé à mon frère de partir.
I advised her not to wait. Je lui ai conseillé de ne pas attendre.

adviser NOUN
le conseiller MASC, la conseillère FEM

aerial NOUN
une antenne FEM

aerobics NOUN
l'aérobic MASC
to do aerobics faire [10] de l'aérobic

aeroplane NOUN
un avion MASC
We went by aeroplane. Nous avons voyagé en avion.

aerosol NOUN
an aerosol can une bombe aérosol

affair NOUN
1 (event) une affaire FEM
international affairs les affaires internationales
2 (romance) une liaison FEM

ℰ to **affect** VERB
toucher [1]
the people most affected by the floods les gens les plus touchés par les inondations
The changes don't affect us yet. Les changements ne nous concernent pas encore.

affectionate ADJECTIVE
affectueux MASC, affectueuse FEM

ℰ to **afford** VERB
to afford something avoir [5] les moyens d'acheter quelque chose
They can afford it. Ils ont les moyens de l'acheter.
They can't afford it. Ils n'ont pas les moyens de l'acheter.
to be able to afford to do something avoir les moyens de faire quelque chose
They can afford to go out a lot. Ils ont les moyens de sortir beaucoup.

ℰ **afraid** ADJECTIVE
1 to be afraid of something avoir [5] peur de quelque chose
She's afraid of dogs. Elle a peur des chiens.
2 (when giving bad news) I'm afraid ... Je suis désolé mais ...
I'm afraid there are no seats left. Je suis désolée mais il ne reste plus de places.

Africa NOUN
l'Afrique FEM

African ADJECTIVE ▸ SEE **African** NOUN
africain MASC, africaine FEM

African NOUN ▸ SEE **African** ADJECTIVE
un Africain MASC, une Africaine FEM

ℰ **after** ADVERB, PREPOSITION, CONJUNCTION
après
after 10 o'clock après dix heures
after lunch après le déjeuner
after school après l'école
the day after tomorrow après-demain
the day after le lendemain
soon after peu après
After I had tidied my room, I watched TV. Après avoir rangé ma chambre, j'ai regardé

la télévision.
After I've done my homework, I'll call you. Quand j'aurai fait mes devoirs, je t'appellerai.
The dog ran after us. Le chien nous a couru après.

after all ADVERB
après tout
After all, she's only six. Elle n'a que six ans après tout.

ℓ **afternoon** NOUN
un & une **après-midi** INVARIABLE MASC & FEM
this afternoon cet après-midi
every afternoon tous les après-midi
at four o'clock in the afternoon à quatre heures de l'après-midi
on Saturday afternoon samedi après-midi
on Saturday afternoons le samedi après-midi

afters NOUN
le **dessert** MASC

after-shave NOUN
un **après-rasage** MASC

afterwards ADVERB
après
shortly afterwards peu de temps après

ℓ **again** ADVERB
1 *(one more time)* encore une fois
Try again. Essaie encore une fois.
I've forgotten it again. Je l'ai encore oublié.
Oh no, not again! Ah non, pas encore!
2 *(once more)* de nouveau
She's ill again. Elle est de nouveau malade.
3 *(with verbs)* to start again recommencer
I'm going to do it again. Je vais le refaire.
I phoned her again yesterday. Je lui ai retéléphoné hier.
I've told him again and again. Je lui ai dit et redit.

ℓ **against** PREPOSITION
contre
the fight against racism la lutte contre le racisme
I'm against the idea. Je suis contre l'idée.
They're playing against Scotland. Ils jouent contre l'Écosse.

ℓ **age** NOUN
1 un **âge** MASC
at the age of fifteen à l'âge de quinze ans
She's the same age as me. Elle a le même âge que moi.
to be under age être [6] mineur
Those boys are under age. Ces garçons sont mineurs.
2 **... for ages** Ça fait une éternité que ...

I haven't seen Johnny for ages. Ça fait une éternité que je n'ai pas vu Johnny.
We've lived here for ages. Ça fait une éternité que nous habitons ici.

aged ADJECTIVE
âgé de MASC, **âgée de** FEM
a girl aged eleven une fille âgée de onze ans

aggressive ADJECTIVE
agressif MASC, **agressive** FEM

ℓ **ago** ADVERB
an hour ago il y a une heure
three days ago il y a trois jours
five years ago il y a cinq ans
a long time ago il y a longtemps
How long ago was it? C'était il y a combien de temps?

ℓ to **agree** VERB
1 to agree with somebody être [6] d'accord avec quelqu'un
I agree with Sophie. Je suis d'accord avec Sophie.
I really don't agree. Je ne suis pas du tout d'accord.
2 to agree to do something accepter [1] de faire quelque chose
Steve has agreed to help us. Steve a accepté de nous aider.

agreement NOUN
un **accord** MASC
an agreement between France and Britain un accord entre la France et la Grande-Bretagne

agricultural ADJECTIVE
agricole MASC & FEM

agriculture NOUN
l'**agriculture** FEM

ℓ **ahead** ADVERB
1 **straight ahead** tout droit
2 **Go straight ahead until you get to the crossroads.** Allez tout droit jusqu'au carrefour.
3 **Go ahead!** *(polite form)* Allez-y!, *(familiar form)* Vas-y!
Go ahead, try it. It's good. Vas-y, goûte! C'est bon.

aid NOUN
une **aide** FEM
to give aid to developing countries donner de l'aide aux pays en voie de développement
a concert in aid of the homeless un concert au profit des sans-abri

🔵 **means the verb takes être to form the perfect**

AIDS *NOUN*
le **sida** *MASC*
(short for) **syndrome immunodéficitaire acquis**
to have AIDS avoir [5] le sida

aim *NOUN* ▶ SEE **aim** *VERB*
un **objectif** *MASC*
to achieve our aims atteindre [60] nos objectifs
Their aim is to control pollution. Leur objectif est de contrôler la pollution.

to **aim** *VERB* ▶ SEE **aim** *NOUN*
1 **to aim to do something** avoir [5] l'intention de faire quelque chose
We're aiming to finish it today. Nous avons l'intention de le finir aujourd'hui.
2 **to aim a gun at somebody** braquer [1] un revolver sur quelqu'un
She aimed the pistol at him. Elle a braqué le revolver sur lui.
an advertising campaign aimed at young people une campagne publicitaire qui vise les jeunes

ℰ **air** *NOUN*
1 l'**air** *MASC*
in the open air en plein air
We're going to get some fresh air. Nous sortons prendre l'air.
2 **by air** en avion
We came by air. Nous sommes venus en avion.
• **airbag**
un airbag
• **air-conditioned**
climatisé *MASC*, climatisée *FEM*
• **air-conditioning**
la climatisation

air force *NOUN*
l'**armée de l'air** *FEM*
My brother's in the air force. Mon frère est dans l'armée de l'air.

air hostess *NOUN*
une **hôtesse de l'air**
She's an air hostess. Elle est hôtesse de l'air.

airline *NOUN*
la **compagnie aérienne** *FEM*

airmail *NOUN*
by airmail par avion

ℰ **airport** *NOUN*
un **aéroport** *MASC*
to pick somebody up at the airport aller ◎ [7] chercher quelqu'un à l'aéroport

air transport *NOUN*
le **transport aérien** *MASC*

alarm *NOUN*
une **alarme** *FEM*
to set off the alarm déclencher [1] l'alarme
▶ SEE **burglar alarm, fire alarm**
• **alarm clock**
le **réveil**

album *NOUN*
un **album** *MASC*
a photo album un album photos

alcohol *NOUN*
l'**alcool** *MASC*
There's no alcohol in it. Il n'y a pas d'alcool dedans.
• **alcohol abuse**
l'abus d'alcool

alcoholic *ADJECTIVE* ▶ SEE **alcoholic** *NOUN*
alcoolisé *MASC*, alcoolisée *FEM*

alcoholic *NOUN* ▶ SEE **alcoholic** *ADJECTIVE*
un & une **alcoolique** *MASC & FEM*
She's an alcoholic. C'est une alcoolique.
• **alcoholic drink**
la boisson alcoolisée

alert *ADJECTIVE*
vif *MASC*, vive *FEM*

A levels *PLURAL NOUN*
le **baccalauréat** *MASC*, le **bac** *MASC* *(informal)*
Students take 'le bac' at the same age as A levels are taken in Britain. You can explain A levels briefly as follows: Les A levels sont répartis en deux niveaux, AS et A2. On passe les examens AS au bout d'une année de préparation, généralement dans quatre ou cinq matières. On passe les examens A2 l'année suivante, dans un plus petit nombre de matières, en choisissant parmi celles qui ont déjà fait l'objet d'un examen AS. La meilleure note que l'on peut obtenir est A et la note la plus basse est N. Les A levels permettent de s'inscrire à l'université.
▶ SEE **baccalauréat**

Algeria *NOUN*
l'**Algérie** *FEM*

alien *NOUN*
un & une **extra-terrestre** *MASC & FEM*
Bart is kidnapped by aliens. Bart est enlevé par des extra-terrestres.

alike *ADJECTIVE*
(in behaviour, attitudes) pareil *MASC*, pareille *FEM*
to look alike se ressembler ◎ [1]
The brothers look very alike. Les frères se ressemblent beaucoup.

ℰ **alive** *ADJECTIVE*
vivant *MASC*, vivante *FEM*

She was still alive. Elle était encore vivante.

♪ **all** ADJECTIVE, ADVERB, PRONOUN
1 *(with masc singular nouns)* **tout**
   all my money tout mon argent
   He complains all the time. Il se plaint tout le temps.
   We're doing all the work! C'est nous qui faisons tout le travail!
2 *(with fem singular nouns)* **toute**
   all day toute la journée
   I was at home all week. J'ai passé toute la semaine à la maison.
3 *(with masc plural nouns)* **tous**
   all the boys tous les garçons
   They all got your text. Ils ont tous reçu ton texto.
   All of us decided to leave. Nous avons tous décidé de partir.
4 *(with fem plural nouns)* **toutes**
   all the girls toutes les filles
   all my holidays toutes mes vacances
5 *(everything)* **tout**
   Is that all? C'est tout?
   I spent it all. J'ai tout dépensé.
6 *(completely)* **tout** MASC, **toute** FEM
   to be all wet être [6] tout mouillé
7 *(in scores)* **partout**
   They're two all. Il y a deux partout.
• **all along**
   depuis le début
• **all over**
   (everywhere) partout

allergic ADJECTIVE
   allergique MASC & FEM
   to be allergic to something être [6] allergique à quelque chose

allergy NOUN
   une **allergie** FEM
   to have an allergy to something être [6] allergique à quelque chose
   I have an allergy to cats. Je suis allergique aux chats.

alligator NOUN
   un **alligator** MASC

♪ to **allow** VERB
1 **to allow somebody to do something**
   permettre [11] à quelqu'un de faire quelque chose
   The teacher allows them to go out. Le professeur leur permet de sortir.
2 **to be allowed to do something** avoir [5] le droit de faire quelque chose
   I'm allowed to go out during the week. J'ai le droit de sortir en semaine.
   It's not allowed. C'est interdit.

all right ADVERB
1 *(yes)* **d'accord**
   'Come round to my house at six.' — 'All right.' 'Passe chez moi à six heures.' — 'D'accord.'
2 *(fine, well)* **bien**
   Is everything all right? Est-ce que tout va bien?
   She's all right now. Elle va bien maintenant.
   Are you all right? Ça va?
3 *(not bad)* **pas mal**
   The meal was all right. Le repas n'était pas mal.
4 *(allowable)* **Is it all right to ...** Est-ce qu'on peut ...?
   Is it all right to leave the door open? Est-ce qu'on peut laisser la porte ouverte?

almond NOUN
   une **amande** FEM

almost ADVERB
   presque
   almost every day presque tous les jours
   almost everybody presque tout le monde
   She's almost five. Elle a presque cinq ans.

♪ **alone** ADJECTIVE, ADVERB
1 *(on your own)* **seul** MASC, **seule** FEM
   I'm all alone. Je suis tout seul *(boy speaking)*, Je suis toute seule *(girl speaking)*.
   She hates travelling alone. Elle déteste voyager seule.
2 *(in peace)* **to leave somebody alone** laisser [1] quelqu'un tranquille
   She wants to be left alone. Elle veut qu'on la laisse tranquille.
3 *(undisturbed)* **to leave something alone** ne pas toucher [1] à quelque chose
   Leave those sweets alone! Ne touche pas à ces bonbons!

along PREPOSITION
1 *(showing where)* **le long de**
   There are trees along the road. Il y a des arbres tout le long de la route.
2 *(with to come, to go)* **avec quelqu'un**
   Would you like to come along? Est-ce que tu veux venir avec nous?

aloud ADVERB
   à haute voix
   He read the poem aloud. Il a lu le poème à haute voix.

alphabet NOUN
   l'**alphabet** MASC

alphabetical ADJECTIVE
   alphabétique MASC & FEM
   in alphabetical order par ordre alphabétique

◉ **means the verb takes être to form the perfect**

Alps PLURAL NOUN
the Alps les Alpes FEM PL

ℰ**already** ADVERB
déjà
They've already left. Ils sont déjà partis.
It's six o'clock already! Il est déjà six heures!

alright ADVERB ▸ SEE **all right**

Alsatian NOUN
le berger allemand (dog)

ℰ**also** ADVERB
1 (as well) aussi
I've also invited Karen. J'ai aussi invité Karen.
She also plays the piano. Elle joue aussi du piano.
2 (in addition) en plus
It's too cold. Also, I've got homework to do. Il fait trop froid. En plus, j'ai des devoirs à faire.

to **alter** VERB
changer [52]

alternative ADJECTIVE ▸ SEE **alternative** NOUN
autre
an alternative solution une autre solution

alternative NOUN ▸ SEE **alternative** ADJECTIVE
la possibilité FEM
There are several alternatives. Il y a plusieurs possibilités.

alternative medicine NOUN
la médecine douce FEM

although CONJUNCTION
bien que
Although she's ill, she wants to go to school. Bien qu'elle soit malade, elle veut aller en cours.

altitude NOUN
l'altitude FEM

altogether ADVERB
en tout
I've spent thirty pounds altogether. J'ai dépensé trente livres en tout.
Altogether, there were five of us. Nous étions cinq en tout.

aluminium NOUN
l'aluminium MASC

ℰ**always** ADVERB
toujours
I always phone her on Saturdays. Je lui téléphone toujours le samedi.

am VERB ▸ SEE **be**

ℰ**a.m.** ADVERB
du matin
at eight a.m. à huit heures du matin ▸ SEE **p.m.**

amateur NOUN
un amateur MASC

to **amaze** VERB
surprendre [64]
What amazes me is how easy it is. Ce qui me surprend, c'est que c'est si facile.

amazed ADJECTIVE
stupéfait MASC, stupéfaite FEM
He was amazed to see her. Il était stupéfait de la voir.
I'm amazed that … Ça m'étonne que …
I'm amazed that you still speak to him. Ça m'étonne que tu lui parles encore.

amazement NOUN
la stupéfaction FEM
He looked at us in amazement. Il nous a regardés avec stupéfaction.

amazing ADJECTIVE
1 (surprising) extraordinaire
She has an amazing number of friends. Elle a un nombre extraordinaire d'amis.
He told me an amazing story. Il m'a raconté une histoire extraordinaire.
2 (very good) fantastique
Your dress is amazing! Ta robe est fantastique!
She's got an amazing tan. Elle a un bronzage fantastique.

ambassador NOUN
un ambassadeur MASC, une ambassadrice FEM

ambition NOUN
une ambition FEM

ambitious ADJECTIVE
ambitieux MASC, ambitieuse FEM

ambulance NOUN
une ambulance FEM
• **ambulance driver**
un ambulancier, une ambulancière

amenities PLURAL NOUN
les équipements MASC PL

America NOUN
l'Amérique FEM
in America en Amérique
to America en Amérique

WORD TIP Countries and regions in French take le, la or les.

ℰ indicates key words

A
B
C
D
E
F
G
H
I
J
K
L
M
N
O
P
Q
R
S
T
U
V
W
X
Y
Z

American *ADJECTIVE* ▶ SEE **American** *NOUN*
américain *MASC*, américaine *FEM*

> **WORD TIP** Adjectives never have capitals in French, even for nationality or regional origin.

American *NOUN* ▶ SEE **American** *ADJECTIVE*
un **Américain** *MASC*, une **Américaine** *FEM*
the Americans les **Américains**

ammunition *NOUN*
la **munition** *FEM*

among, **amongst** *PREPOSITION*
1 *(with)* parmi
I found it amongst my books. Je l'ai trouvé parmi mes livres.
2 *(between)* entre
You can decide amongst yourselves. Vous pouvez décider entre vous.

amount *NOUN*
1 *(of food, effort, time)* la **quantité** *FEM*
an enormous amount of time énormément de temps
an enormous amount of bread une énorme quantité de pain
2 *(of money)* la **somme** *FEM*
a large amount of money une grosse somme d'argent

amp *NOUN*
1 *(in electricity)* une **ampère** *MASC*
2 *(amplifier)* un **ampli** *MASC* *(informal)*

amplifier *NOUN*
un **amplificateur** *MASC*

to **amuse** *VERB*
amuser [1]
The teacher is not amused. La prof ne trouve pas ça drôle.

amusement arcade *NOUN*
la **salle de jeux électroniques** *FEM*

amusing *ADJECTIVE*
amusant *MASC*, amusante *FEM*

an *DETERMINER*
un *(masculine)*, une *(feminine)* ▶ SEE **a**

to **analyse** *VERB*
analyser [1]

analysis *NOUN*
une **analyse** *FEM*

ancestor *NOUN*
un & une **ancêtre** *MASC & FEM*

anchor *NOUN*
une **ancre** *FEM*

ancient *ADJECTIVE*
1 *(historic)* ancien *MASC*, ancienne *FEM*
an ancient abbey une abbaye ancienne
2 *(very old)* très vieux *MASC*, très vieille *FEM*

an ancient pair of jeans un très vieux jean
3 *(Greece, Rome)* antique
ancient Greece la Grèce antique

♪ **and** *CONJUNCTION*
1 et
Ben and Amy Ben et Amy
Rosie and me Rosie et moi
your shoes and socks tes chaussures et tes chaussettes
2 louder and louder de plus en plus fort
faster and faster de plus en plus rapide

angel *NOUN*
un **ange** *MASC*

anger *NOUN*
la **colère** *FEM*

angle *NOUN*
un **angle** *MASC*

♪ **angry** *ADJECTIVE*
to be angry être [6] en colère
The teacher was angry. La prof était en colère.
to be angry with somebody être [6] en colère contre quelqu'un
I'm not angry with you. Je ne suis pas en colère contre toi.
to get angry se fâcher ◎ [1]
He gets angry easily. Il se fâche facilement.

animal *NOUN*
un **animal** *MASC* *(PL* les **animaux***)*

ankle *NOUN*
la **cheville** *FEM*
to break your ankle se casser ◎ [1] la cheville

anniversary *NOUN*
un **anniversaire** *MASC*
a wedding anniversary un anniversaire de mariage

to **announce** *VERB*
annoncer [61]
to announce the winner annoncer le gagnant

announcement *NOUN*
une **annonce** *FEM*
to make an announcement faire [10] une annonce

to **annoy** *VERB*
agacer [61]
She really annoys me! Vraiment elle m'agace!

annoyed *ADJECTIVE*
fâché *MASC*, fâchée *FEM*
to get annoyed se fâcher ◎ [1]
I got annoyed. Je me suis fâché.

◎ means the verb takes être to form the perfect

He's very annoyed with us! Il est très fâché contre nous!

annoying *ADJECTIVE*
agaçant *MASC*, agaçante *FEM*
I find that very annoying. Je trouve ça très agaçant.

annual *ADJECTIVE*
annuel *MASC*, annuelle *FEM*

anorak *NOUN*
un anorak *MASC*

anorexia *NOUN*
l'anorexie *FEM*

ℰ **another** *ADJECTIVE*
1 *(different)* un autre *MASC*, une autre *FEM*
Would you like another ice cream? Voulez-vous une autre glace?
2 *(more of the same)* encore
another two years encore deux ans
She had another coffee. Elle a pris un autre café.
We need another three chairs. Il nous faut encore trois chaises.

ℰ **answer** *NOUN* ▸ SEE **answer** *VERB*
1 *(to a question)* la réponse *FEM*
the right answer la bonne réponse
the wrong answer la mauvaise réponse
2 *(to a problem)* la solution *FEM*
That's not the answer! Ce n'est pas une solution!

ℰ to **answer** *VERB* ▸ SEE **answer** *NOUN*
répondre [3]
He's afraid to answer. Il a peur de répondre.
Answer the question. Réponds à la question.
You didn't answer my email. Tu n'as pas répondu à mon mail.
to answer somebody répondre à quelqu'un
She answered me immediately. Elle m'a tout de suite répondu.

answering machine *NOUN*
le répondeur *MASC*
to leave a message on the answering machine laisser [1] un message sur le répondeur

ant *NOUN*
la fourmi *FEM*

Antarctic *NOUN*
l'Antarctique *MASC*
in the Antarctic dans l'Antarctique

antibiotic *NOUN*
un antibiotique *MASC*
to be on antibiotics être [6] sous antibiotiques

antique *ADJECTIVE* ▸ SEE **antique** *NOUN*
ancien *MASC*, ancienne *FEM*
an antique table une table ancienne

antique *NOUN* ▸ SEE **antique** *ADJECTIVE*
1 *(piece of furniture)* le meuble ancien
2 antiques *(for collectors)* les antiquités *FEM PL*

antiseptic *NOUN*
un antiseptique *MASC*

anxious *ADJECTIVE*
inquiet *MASC*, inquiète *FEM*
to get anxious s'inquiéter [24]

ℰ **any** *DETERMINER, ADVERB, PRONOUN*
1 *(before a masc singular noun)* du
Is there any butter? Y a-t-il du beurre?
Is there any cake left? Est-ce qu'il reste du gâteau?
2 *(before a fem singular noun)* de la
Is there any flour? Y a-t-il de la farine?
3 *(before singular nouns beginning with a, e, i, o, u or silent h)* de l'
Do you have any money? Avez-vous de l'argent?
Is there any oil? Y a-t-il de l'huile?
4 *(before plural nouns)* des
Are there any eggs? Y a-t-il des œufs?
Do you have any stamps? Est-ce que tu as des timbres?
5 *(saying no, not)* de
There isn't any flour. Il n'y a pas de farine.
There aren't any eggs. Il n'y a pas d'œufs.
6 *(when any is by itself without a noun)* en
I don't want any. Je n'en veux pas.
Don't you have any? Tu n'en as pas?
7 not ... any more ne ... plus
There isn't any more butter. Il n'y a plus de beurre.
She doesn't eat meat any more. Elle ne mange plus de viande.

ℰ **anybody**, **anyone** *PRONOUN*
1 *(in questions and after if)* quelqu'un
Is anybody in? Est-ce qu'il y a quelqu'un?
If anybody wants water, it's ... Si quelqu'un veut de l'eau, elle ...
Does anybody want some tea? Qui veut du thé?
2 not ... anybody ne ... personne
He doesn't talk to anybody. Il ne parle à personne.
There isn't anybody in the office. Il n'y a personne dans le bureau.
3 *(anybody at all)* n'importe qui
I'm not giving it to anybody. Je ne vais pas le donner à n'importe qui.

ℰ indicates key words

anyhow ADVERB ▸ SEE **anyway**

anyone PRONOUN ▸ SEE **anybody**

ℓ **anything** PRONOUN
1 (in questions and after if) **quelque chose**
   Is there anything I can do to help? Est-ce que je peux faire quelque chose pour t'aider?
   If you find out anything, tell me. Si tu découvres quelque chose, dis-le-moi.
2 **not ... anything** ne ... rien
   There isn't anything on the table. Il n'y a rien sur la table.
   I can't understand anything! Je ne comprends rien!
   She hasn't said anything to me. Elle ne m'a rien dit.
3 (anything at all) **n'importe quoi**
   Anything could happen. Il pourrait arriver n'importe quoi.

anyway, **anyhow** ADVERB
   de toute façon
   Anyway, I'll ring you. De toute façon, je t'appellerai.

ℓ **anywhere** ADVERB
1 (in questions) **quelque part**
   Have you seen my keys anywhere? Est-ce que tu as vu mes clés quelque part?
   Are you going anywhere tomorrow? Est-ce que tu vas quelque part demain?
2 **not ... anywhere** ne ... nulle part
   I can't find my keys anywhere. Je ne trouve mes clés nulle part .
   You're not going anywhere tonight! Tu ne sors pas ce soir!
3 (anywhere at all) **n'importe où**
   Put your cases down anywhere. Pose tes valises n'importe où.

apart ADJECTIVE, ADVERB
1 (separate) **séparé** MASC, **séparée** FEM
   We don't like being apart. Nous n'aimons pas être séparés.
2 (indicating distance) **to be two metres apart** être [6] à deux mètres l'un de l'autre
3 **apart from** à part, sauf
   Apart from Jack, everybody was there. À part Jack, tout le monde était là.
   I eat everything apart from shellfish. Je mange de tout sauf des fruits de mer.

ℓ **apartment** NOUN
   un **appartement** MASC
   an apartment on the fourth floor un appartement au quatrième étage
• **apartment block**
   un **immeuble**

ape NOUN
   le **(grand) singe** MASC

to **apologize** VERB
   s'excuser ☺ [1]
   I apologize. Je m'excuse.
   to apologize for something s'excuser de quelque chose
   He apologizes for his behaviour. Il s'excuse de son comportement.
   to apologize to someone s'excuser auprès de quelqu'un
   She apologized to Peter. Elle s'est excusée auprès de Peter.

apology NOUN
   an apology des excuses FEM PL
   I owe you an apology. Je te dois des excuses.

apostrophe NOUN
   une **apostrophe** FEM

apparently ADVERB
   apparemment
   Apparently they know each other. Apparemment, ils se connaissent.

appeal NOUN ▸ SEE **appeal** VERB
   un **appel** MASC
   an appeal for help un appel à l'aide

to **appeal** VERB ▸ SEE **appeal** NOUN
1 **to appeal for something** lancer [61] un appel pour quelque chose
   They appealed for a million euros. Ils ont lancé un appel pour un million d'euros.
2 (to interest) **to appeal to somebody** tenter [1] quelqu'un
   Horror films don't appeal to me. Les films d'épouvante ne me tentent pas.

to **appear** VERB
1 (to turn up) **apparaître** ☺ [57]
   Sophie appeared at the door. Sophie est apparue à la porte.
2 **to appear on TV** passer ☺ [1] à la télévision
   the day I appeared on TV le jour où je suis passé à la télévision
3 (to seem) **paraître** [57]
   It appears that somebody has stolen the key. Il paraît que quelqu'un a volé la clé.

appendicitis NOUN
   l'**appendicite** FEM

appendix NOUN
   un **appendice** MASC
   I've had my appendix out. Je me suis fait opérer de l'appendicite.

appetite NOUN
   l'**appétit** MASC

to **applaud** VERB
   applaudir [2]

☺ **means the verb takes être to form the perfect**

applause *NOUN*
les **applaudissements** *MASC PL*

ℰ **apple** *NOUN*
la **pomme** *FEM*
- **apple juice**
le jus de pomme
- **apple tart**
la tarte aux pommes
- **apple tree**
le pommier

applicant *NOUN*
le **candidat** *MASC*, la **candidate** *FEM*

application *NOUN*
(for a job) la **candidature** *FEM*
- **application form**
le dossier de candidature

to **apply** *VERB*
1 **to apply for something** poser [1] sa candidature à quelque chose
He has applied for the job. Il a posé sa candidature au poste.
I'm applying for that sailing course. Je fais une demande d'inscription à ce cours de voile.
2 **to apply to somebody** s'appliquer ◉ [1] à quelqu'un
The rule doesn't apply to students. La règle ne s'applique pas aux élèves.

appointment *NOUN*
le **rendez-vous** *MASC*
to make an appointment at the dentist's prendre rendez-vous chez le dentiste

apprentice *NOUN*
un **apprenti** *MASC*, une **apprentie** *FEM*

apprenticeship *NOUN*
un **apprentissage** *MASC*

to **approach** *VERB*
1 **to approach something** s'approcher [1] ◉ de quelque chose
We are approaching the stadium. Nous nous approchons du stade.
2 **to approach somebody** s'approcher [1] ◉ de quelqu'un
Do not approach him. Ne t'approche pas de lui.

approval *NOUN*
l'**approbation** *FEM*

to **approve** *VERB*
to approve of somebody apprécier [1] quelqu'un
They don't approve of her boyfriend. Ils n'apprécient pas son copain.

apricot *NOUN*
un **abricot** *MASC*

- **apricot jam**
la confiture d'abricots

ℰ **April** *NOUN*
avril *MASC*
in April en avril
- **April Fool**
le poisson d'avril
- **April Fool's Day**
le premier avril

> **WORD TIP** Months of the year and days of the week start with small letters in French.

apron *NOUN*
le **tablier** *MASC*

aquarium *NOUN*
un **aquarium** *MASC*

Aquarius *NOUN*
Verseau *MASC*
Lucy's Aquarius. Lucy est Verseau.

> **WORD TIP** Signs of the zodiac do not take an article: un or une.

Arab *ADJECTIVE* ► SEE **Arab** *NOUN*
arabe *MASC & FEM*
the Arab countries les pays arabes

Arab *NOUN* ► SEE **Arab** *ADJECTIVE*
un & une **Arabe** *MASC & FEM*

Arabic *NOUN*
(the language) l'**arabe** *MASC*

arch *NOUN*
une **arche** *FEM*

archaeologist *NOUN*
un & une **archéologue** *MASC & FEM*

archaeology *NOUN*
l'**archéologie** *FEM*

archbishop *NOUN*
un **archevêque** *MASC*

architect *NOUN*
un & une **architecte** *MASC & FEM*

architecture *NOUN*
l'**architecture** *FEM*

Arctic *NOUN*
l'**Arctique** *MASC*
in the Arctic dans l'Arctique

are *VERB* ► SEE **be**

area *NOUN*
1 *(part of a town)* le **quartier** *MASC*
a nice area un beau quartier
a rough area un quartier mal fréquenté
2 *(region)* la **région** *FEM*
in the Leeds area dans la région de Leeds

ℰ indicates key words

to argue VERB
1 **se disputer** ⊙ [1]
We never argue. Nous ne nous disputons jamais.
2 **to argue about something** discuter [1] de quelque chose
They're arguing about the result. Ils sont en train de discuter du résultat.

argument NOUN
la **dispute** FEM
to have an argument se disputer ⊙ [1]
Julie and Emma had an argument. Julie et Emma se sont disputées.

Aries NOUN
Bélier MASC
Rachel's Aries. Rachel est Bélier.

WORD TIP Signs of the zodiac do not take an article: un or une.

arithmetic NOUN
l'**arithmétique** FEM

♪ **arm** NOUN
le **bras** MASC
to fold your arms croiser [1] les bras
They went off arm in arm. Ils sont partis bras dessus bras dessous.
to break your arm se casser ⊙ [1] le bras
She's broken her arm. Elle s'est cassé le bras.

armchair NOUN
le **fauteuil** MASC

armed ADJECTIVE
armé MASC, **armée** FEM

armpit NOUN
une **aisselle** FEM

army NOUN
une **armée** FEM
to join the army s'engager ⊙ [1] dans l'armée
He joined the army. Il s'est engagé dans l'armée.

♪ **around** ADVERB, PREPOSITION
1 (with time) **vers**
at around midnight vers minuit
We'll arrive around ten. On va arriver vers dix heures.
2 (with ages, amounts) **environ**
She's around fifteen. Elle a environ quinze ans.
We need around six kilos. Il nous faut environ six kilos.
It costs around ten euros. Ça coûte environ dix euros.
3 (surrounding) **autour de**
the countryside around Edinburgh la campagne autour d'Édimbourg
4 (near) **Is Phil around?** Est-ce que Phil est là?
Is there a post office around here? Est-ce qu'il y a un bureau de poste près d'ici?
There was nobody around. Il n'y avait personne.
5 (wrapped around) **autour de**
She had a scarf around her neck. Elle avait une écharpe autour du cou.

to arrange VERB
to arrange to do something prévoir [65] de faire quelque chose
We've arranged to see a film on Saturday. Nous avons prévu de voir un film samedi.
I haven't arranged anything yet. Je n'ai encore rien prévu.

arrangement NOUN
arrangements les **préparatifs** MASC PL
the arrangements for the trip les préparatifs pour le voyage
to make arrangements to do something s'arranger ⊙ [52] pour faire quelque chose

arrest NOUN ▸ SEE **arrest** VERB
to be under arrest être [6] en état d'arrestation
to arrest VERB ▸ SEE **arrest** NOUN
arrêter [1]
They're going to arrest her. Ils vont l'arrêter.

arrival NOUN
l'**arrivée** FEM

♪ **to arrive** VERB
arriver ⊙ [1]
They arrive in Poitiers at 3 p.m. Ils arrivent à Poitiers à quinze heures.

arrow NOUN
la **flèche** FEM

art NOUN
1 l'**art** MASC
modern art l'art moderne
2 (school subject) le **dessin** MASC

artery NOUN
une **artère** FEM

art gallery NOUN
1 (museum) le **musée des beaux arts** MASC
2 (private) la **galerie d'art** FEM

artichoke NOUN
un **artichaut** MASC

♪ **article** NOUN
1 (in a newspaper, magazine) un **article** MASC
a magazine article un article de magazine
2 (Grammar) un **article** MASC
the definite article l'article défini (in French these are le, la, les)

⊙ **means the verb takes être to form the perfect**

the indefinite article l'article indéfini *(in French these are un, une, des)*

artificial *ADJECTIVE*
artificiel *MASC*, artificielle *FEM*

artist *NOUN*
un & une **artiste** *MASC & FEM*
She's an artist. C'est une artiste.

artistic *ADJECTIVE*
artistique *MASC & FEM*

art school *NOUN*
une **école de beaux arts**

ℱ **as** *ADVERB, CONJUNCTION, PREPOSITION*
1 *(like)* **comme**
as you know comme vous le savez
as I told you comme je t'avais dit
as usual comme d'habitude
2 *(because)* **puisque**
As there were no trains, we took the bus. Puisqu'il n'y avait pas de trains, nous avons pris le bus.
3 **as ... as** aussi ... que
He's as tall as his brother. Il est aussi grand que son frère.
4 **as much ... as** autant de ... que
You have as much time as I do. Tu as autant de temps que moi.
5 **as many ... as** autant de ... que
We have as many problems as he does. Nous avons autant de problèmes que lui.
6 **as long as** pourvu que
We'll go tomorrow, as long as it's a nice day. On va y aller demain, pourvu qu'il fasse beau.
7 **as soon as possible** dès que possible
8 **to work as something** travailler [1] comme quelque chose
He works as a taxi driver. Il travaille comme chauffeur de taxi.

ashamed *ADJECTIVE*
to be ashamed avoir [5] honte
I was so ashamed! J'avais tellement honte!

ashes *PLURAL NOUN*
les **cendres** *FEM PL*

ashtray *NOUN*
le **cendrier** *MASC*

Asia *NOUN*
l'**Asie** *FEM*

Asian *ADJECTIVE* ▸ SEE **Asian** *NOUN*
1 *(from Asia generally)* asiatique *MASC & FEM*
2 *(from India)* indien *MASC*, indienne *FEM*
3 *(from Pakistan)* pakistanais *MASC*, pakistanaise *FEM*

Asian *NOUN* ▸ SEE **Asian** *ADJECTIVE*
1 *(from the Far East)* un & une **Asiatique** *MASC*

& *FEM*
2 *(from India)* un **Indien** *MASC*, une **Indienne** *FEM*
3 *(from Pakistan)* un **Pakistanais** *MASC*, une **Pakistanaise** *FEM*

ℱ **to ask** *VERB*
1 **demander** [1]
You can ask at reception. Tu peux demander à l'accueil.
to ask somebody something demander quelque chose à quelqu'un
I'll ask him where he lives. Je lui demanderai où il habite.
to ask for something demander quelque chose
I asked for three coffees. J'ai demandé trois cafés.
to ask somebody for something demander quelque chose à quelqu'un
Did you ask her for the DVD? Est-ce que tu lui as demandé le DVD?
to ask somebody to do something demander à quelqu'un de faire quelque chose
Ask Jake to give you a hand. Demande à Jake de te donner un coup de main.
2 **to ask somebody a question** poser [1] une question à quelqu'un
I asked you a question! Je t'ai posé une question!
3 *(to invite)* **inviter** [1]
They've asked us to a party at their house. Ils nous ont invités à une fête chez eux.
Adam's asked Julie out on Friday. Adam a invité Julie à sortir avec lui vendredi.

ℱ **asleep** *ADJECTIVE*
to be asleep dormir [37]
The baby's asleep. Le bébé dort.
to fall asleep s'endormir ◊ [37]
She's fallen asleep! Elle s'est endormie!

asparagus *NOUN*
une **asperge** *FEM*

aspirin *NOUN*
l'**aspirine** *FEM*

assembly *NOUN*
(at school) le **rassemblement** *MASC*

assignment *NOUN*
(at school) le **devoir** *MASC*
I finished my assignment on Paris. J'ai fini mon devoir sur Paris.

assistance *NOUN*
l'**aide** *FEM*

assistant *NOUN*
1 un **assistant** *MASC*, une **assistante** *FEM*
2 **a shop assistant** un vendeur, une vendeuse

ℱ **indicates key words**

association NOUN
une association FEM

assorted ADJECTIVE
variés MASC PL, variées FEM PL
assorted colours des couleurs variées

assortment NOUN
le mélange MASC

to **assume** VERB
supposer [1]
I assume she's coming too. Je suppose
qu'elle vient aussi.

to **assure** VERB
assurer [1]

asterisk NOUN
un astérisque MASC

asthma NOUN
l'asthme MASC
She has asthma. Elle a de l'asthme.

astonishing ADJECTIVE
étonnant MASC, étonnante FEM

astrologer NOUN
un & une astrologue MASC & FEM

astrology NOUN
l'astrologie FEM

astronaut NOUN
un & une astronaute MASC & FEM

astronomer NOUN
un & une astronome MASC & FEM

astronomy NOUN
l'astronomie FEM

♂ **at** PREPOSITION
1 (saying where) à
at home à la maison
at school à l'école
at my office à mon bureau
at the market au marché
at meetings aux réunions

WORD TIP à + le becomes au; à + les becomes
aux.

2 (at person's house, office) chez
at Emma's house chez Emma
at her brother's chez son frère
at the hairdresser's chez le coiffeur
3 (talking about time) à
at eight o'clock à huit heures
4 at night la nuit
at the weekend le week-end
She's never there at weekends. Elle n'est
jamais là le week-end.
5 at last enfin
He's found a job at last. Il a enfin trouvé un
emploi.

6 (@ in emailing) une arobase FEM
jane-dot-smith@easyconnect-dot-com
jane-point-smith-arobase-easyconnect-
point-com

athlete NOUN
un & une athlète MASC & FEM

athletic ADJECTIVE
athlétique MASC & FEM

athletics NOUN
l'athlétisme MASC

Atlantic NOUN
l'Atlantique MASC
to sail across the Atlantic traverser [1]
l'Atlantique à la voile.

atlas NOUN
un atlas MASC

atmosphere NOUN
l'atmosphère FEM

atom NOUN
un atome MASC

atomic ADJECTIVE
atomique

to **attach** VERB
attacher [1]

attached ADJECTIVE
to be attached to something être [6]
attaché à quelque chose
The chain is attached to the wall. La chaîne
est attachée au mur.
Please find my invoice attached attached.
Veuillez trouver ma facture ci-jointe.

attachment NOUN
la pièce jointe FEM
to open the attachment ouvrir [30] la pièce
jointe

attack NOUN ▶ SEE **attack** VERB
une attaque FEM
to **attack** VERB ▶ SEE **attack** NOUN
1 (armies, in sport) attaquer [1]
2 (muggers) agresser [1]
He was attacked in the street. Il s'est fait
agresser dans la rue.

attacker NOUN
un agresseur MASC

attempt NOUN ▶ SEE **attempt** VERB
la tentative FEM
at the first attempt à la première tentative
to **attempt** VERB ▶ SEE **attempt** NOUN
to attempt to do something essayer [59]
de faire quelque chose
She's attempting to break the record. Elle
essaie de battre le record.

⬤ means the verb takes être to form the perfect

attendance NOUN
(at meetings) la **présence** FEM
school attendance la fréquentation scolaire

attention NOUN
l'**attention** FEM
to pay attention faire attention
I wasn't paying attention. Je ne faisais pas attention.
for the attention of à l'attention de

attic NOUN
le **grenier** MASC
in the attic au grenier

attitude NOUN
une **attitude** FEM
He's got an attitude problem. Son attitude lui vaut des problèmes

to **attract** VERB
attirer [1]
to attract attention attirer l'attention

attraction NOUN
une **attraction** FEM

attractive ADJECTIVE
séduisant MASC, **séduisante** FEM

aubergine NOUN
une **aubergine** FEM

auction NOUN
la **vente aux enchères**

audience NOUN
le **public** MASC
a lively audience un public animé

⚘ **August** NOUN
août MASC
in August en août

> **WORD TIP** Months of the year and days of the week start with small letters in French.

aunt, **auntie** NOUN
la **tante** FEM
my aunt Ruth ma tante Ruth

au pair NOUN
une **jeune fille au pair** FEM, un **jeune homme au pair** MASC
I'm looking for a job as an au pair. Je cherche un emploi de jeune fille au pair.

Australia NOUN
l'**Australie** FEM
in Australia en Australie
to Australia en Australie

> **WORD TIP** Countries and regions in French take le, la or les.

Australian ADJECTIVE ▶ SEE **Australian** NOUN
australien MASC, **australienne** FEM

> **WORD TIP** Adjectives never have capitals in French, even for nationality or regional origin.

Australian NOUN ▶ SEE **Australian** ADJECTIVE
un **Australien** MASC, une **Australienne** FEM
the Australians les Australiens

Austria NOUN
l'**Autriche** FEM

Austrian ADJECTIVE ▶ SEE **Austrian** NOUN
autrichien MASC, **autrichienne** FEM

Austrian NOUN ▶ SEE **Austrian** ADJECTIVE
un **Autrichien** MASC, une **Autrichienne** FEM

author NOUN
un **auteur** MASC

autobiography NOUN
une **autobiographie** FEM

automatic ADJECTIVE
automatique MASC & FEM

automatically ADVERB
automatiquement

⚘ **autumn** NOUN
l'**automne** MASC
in autumn en automne
next autumn l'automne prochain
last autumn l'automne dernier

availability NOUN
la **disponibilité** FEM

available ADJECTIVE
disponible MASC & FEM
The film is not available yet. Le film n'est pas encore disponible.

avalanche NOUN
une **avalanche** FEM

avenue NOUN
une **avenue** FEM

average ADJECTIVE ▶ SEE **average** NOUN
moyen MASC, **moyenne** FEM
the average age l'âge moyen
the average height la hauteur moyenne

average NOUN ▶ SEE **average** ADJECTIVE
la **moyenne** FEM
on average en moyenne
above average au-dessus de la moyenne
below average au-dessous de la moyenne

avocado NOUN
un **avocat** MASC

to **avoid** VERB
éviter [1]
She's avoiding us. Elle nous évite.
to avoid doing something éviter de faire

⚘ indicates key words

quelque chose
I avoid speaking to him. J'évite de lui parler.

awake ADJECTIVE
to be awake être [6] réveillé
Is Chloë awake? Est-ce que Chloë est réveillée?
I was awake all night. Je n'ai pas dormi de la nuit.

award NOUN
le **prix** MASC
to win an award remporter [1] un prix

aware ADJECTIVE
to be aware of something être [6] au courant de quelque chose
I wasn't aware of the problem. Je n'étais pas au courant du problème.

♪ away ADVERB
1 (describing distances) **It's two kilometres away.** C'est à deux kilomètres d'ici.
How far away is it? C'est à quelle distance d'ici?
It's not far away. Ce n'est pas loin d'ici.
2 (absent) **to be away** être [6] absent
while he was away pendant qu'il était absent
She'll be away next week. Elle sera absente la semaine prochaine.
3 (with verbs) **to give something away** donner quelque chose
to go away partir ◉ [58]
Go away! Va-t'en!
to put something away ranger [52] quelque chose
to run away partir ◉ [58] en courant
• **away match**
le match à l'extérieur

awful ADJECTIVE
1 (no good) **affreux** MASC, **affreuse** FEM
The weather was awful! Le temps était affreux!
It tastes awful. C'est dégoûtant.
2 (ill) **I feel awful.** Je ne me sens pas bien du tout.
You look awful. Tu as très mauvaise mine.
3 (embarrassed, unhappy) **I feel awful about it.** Ça m'ennuie vraiment.
4 (to say how much, many, etc) **an awful lot of something** énormément de quelque chose
It costs an awful lot of money. Ça coûte énormément d'argent.
He knows an awful lot of people. Il connaît énormément de gens.

awkward ADJECTIVE
1 (problem, situation) **difficile** MASC & FEM
It's an awkward situation. C'est une situation difficile.
2 (person) **difficile** MASC & FEM
She's really awkward. Elle est vraiment difficile.

axe NOUN
la **hache** FEM

Bb

♪ baby NOUN
le **bébé** MASC

to babysit VERB
faire [10] du baby-sitting

babysitter NOUN
le & la **baby-sitter** MASC & FEM

babysitting NOUN
le **baby-sitting** MASC

♪ bachelor NOUN
le **célibataire** MASC

♪ back ADJECTIVE ▶ SEE **back** ADVERB, VERB, NOUN
1 (wheel, seat) **arrière**
the back seat of the car le siège arrière de la voiture
2 (door, gate, etc) **de derrière**
the back gate la porte de derrière
the back garden le jardin de derrière

♪ back ADVERB ▶ SEE **back** ADJECTIVE, VERB, NOUN
1 (showing movement to and from places) **rentrer** ◉ [1]
to go back rentrer
Lucy's gone back home. Lucy est rentrée chez elle.
to go back to school rentrer à l'école
When do we go back to school? Quand est-ce qu'on rentre à l'école?
to come back from a place rentrer
They've come back from Normandy. Ils sont rentrés de Normandie.
We went by bus and walked back. Nous avons pris le bus pour y aller et nous sommes rentrés à pied.
2 (showing where someone is now) **to be back** être [6] rentré
Emma's not back yet. Emma n'est pas encore rentrée.
I'll be right back. Je reviens tout de suite.
Hannah's back at work. Hannah a repris le travail.
3 **to give something back to somebody** rendre [3] quelque chose à quelqu'un
I gave him back his books. Je lui ai rendu ses livres.
Give it back! Rends-le-moi!

◉ **means the verb takes être to form the perfect**

ᵖ to **back** VERB ▸ SEE **back** ADJECTIVE, ADVERB, NOUN
1 *(a candidate)* soutenir [77]
2 *(a horse)* parier [1] sur
• **to back up**
1 *(Computing)* **to back up a file** sauvegarder [1] un fichier
You must back up your work. Il faut sauvegarder votre travail.
2 *(in an argument, discussion)* **to back somebody up** soutenir [77] quelqu'un
Josh backed me up. Josh m'a soutenu.

ᵖ **back** NOUN ▸ SEE **back** ADJECTIVE, ADVERB, VERB
1 *(of a person, animal, hand)* le **dos** MASC
Write your name on the back of the sheet. Écrivez votre nom au dos du papier.
2 *(of a car, a plane, a building)* l'**arrière** MASC
There are seats at the back. Il y a des places à l'arrière.
There's a garden at the back of our house. Il y a un jardin à l'arrière de notre maison.
3 *(of a room)* le **fond** MASC
Tom was at the back of the room. Tom était au fond de la salle.
4 *(of a chair, sofa)* le **dossier** MASC
5 *(in football, etc)* un **arrière** MASC
the left back l'arrière gauche
• **backache**
le mal de dos
• **backbone**
la colonne vertébrale

back door NOUN
1 *(of a building)* la **porte de derrière**
2 *(of a car)* la **portière arrière**

background NOUN
1 *(of a person)* le **milieu** MASC
2 *(of events, a situation)* le **contexte** MASC
3 *(of a picture, view)* un **arrière-plan** MASC
in the background les arbres à l'arrière-plan
• **background music**
la musique d'ambiance

backhand NOUN
le **revers** MASC

backing NOUN
1 *(on sticky-backed plastic)* le **revêtement intérieur**
2 *(moral support)* le **soutien** MASC

backpack NOUN
le **sac à dos** MASC

backpacking NOUN
to go backpacking partir ⊘ [58] en randonnée
I'm going backpacking in August. En août je pars en randonnée.

backside NOUN
le **derrière** MASC

backstage ADVERB
to go backstage aller ⊘ [7] dans les coulisses

backstroke NOUN
le **dos crawlé** MASC

back to front ADVERB
à l'envers

backup NOUN
1 *(support)* le **soutien** MASC
2 *(in computing)* la **sauvegarde** FEM
a backup disk un disque de sauvegarde

backwards ADVERB
(to lean, fall) en arrière

bacon NOUN
1 *(streaky)* le **lard** MASC
2 *(smoked)* le **bacon** MASC
bacon and eggs les œufs au bacon

ᵖ **bad** ADJECTIVE
1 *(not good)* **mauvais** MASC, **mauvaise** FEM
a bad meal un mauvais repas
a bad experience une mauvaise expérience
His new film's not bad. Son nouveau film n'est pas mauvais.
to be bad at something être [6] mauvais en quelque chose
I'm bad at physics. Je suis mauvais en physique *(boy speaking)*, Je suis mauvaise en physique *(girl speaking)*.
Smoking is bad for your health. Fumer est mauvais pour la santé.
2 *(serious)* **grave** MASC & FEM
a bad accident un accident grave
a bad cold un gros rhume
3 *(rotten)* **pourri** MASC, **pourrie** FEM
a bad apple une pomme pourrie
to go bad se gâter ⊘ [1]
This meat has gone bad. La viande s'est gâtée.
4 *(naughty)* **vilain** MASC, **vilaine** FEM
Bad dog! Vilain!
5 *(rude)* **grossier** MASC, **grossière** FEM
bad language un langage grossier

badge NOUN
le **badge** MASC

ᵖ **badly** ADVERB
1 *(not well)* **mal**
I slept badly. J'ai mal dormi.
He writes very badly. Il écrit très mal.
to go badly se passer ⊘ [1] mal
The exam went badly. L'examen s'est mal passé.
2 *(damaged)* **sérieusement**
My bike was badly damaged. Mon vélo a

été sérieusement endommagé.
3 *(injured)* **to be badly hurt**
être [6] grièvement blessé
Her sister was badly hurt. Sa sœur a été
grièvement blessée.

bad-mannered *ADJECTIVE*
mal élevé *MASC*, mal élevée *FEM*

badminton *NOUN*
le badminton *MASC*
to play badminton jouer [1] au badminton

♪ **bag** *NOUN*
le sac *MASC*

baggage *NOUN*
les bagages *MASC PL*
• **baggage allowance**
la franchise de bagages
• **baggage reclaim**
la réception des bagages

bagpipes *PLURAL NOUN*
la cornemuse *FEM*
to play the bagpipes jouer [1] de la
cornemuse

bags *PLURAL NOUN*
les bagages *MASC PL*
to pack your bags faire [10] ses bagages

Bahamas *PLURAL NOUN*
the Bahamas les Bahamas *FEM PL*
We had a holiday in the Bahamas. Nous
avons passé les vacances aux Bahamas.

to **bake** *VERB*
1 *(a dish, vegetables)* faire [10] cuire
2 *(a cake, bread)* faire [10]
I like baking cakes. J'aime faire des
gâteaux.

baked *ADJECTIVE*
(fish, fruit, vegetables) au four
a baked potato une pomme de terre au
four
• **baked beans**
les haricots blancs à la sauce tomate

♪ **baker** *NOUN*
le boulanger *MASC*, la boulangère *FEM*
I bought croissants at the baker's. J'ai
acheté des croissants à la boulangerie.
to go to the baker's aller ◎ [7] à la
boulangerie

bakery *NOUN*
la boulangerie *FEM*

balance *NOUN*
1 *(of a person)* l'équilibre *MASC*
to lose your balance perdre [3] l'équilibre
2 *(of a bank account)* le solde *MASC*

♪ **balcony** *NOUN*
le balcon *MASC*

bald *ADJECTIVE*
chauve *MASC & FEM*

♪ **ball** *NOUN*
1 *(for tennis, golf)* la balle *FEM*
2 *(for football, volleyball)* le ballon *MASC*
3 *(of string, wool)* la pelote *FEM*

ballet *NOUN*
le ballet *MASC*
• **ballet dancer**
le danseur de ballet, la danseuse de ballet

♪ **balloon** *NOUN*
1 *(for a party)* le ballon *MASC*
2 *(hot air)* la montgolfière *FEM*

ballot *NOUN*
le scrutin *MASC*

ballpoint pen *NOUN*
le stylo à bille

ban *NOUN* ▸ SEE **ban** *VERB*
une interdiction *FEM*
a ban on smoking une interdiction de
fumer
to **ban** *VERB* ▸ SEE **ban** *NOUN*
interdire [47]

♪ **banana** *NOUN*
la banane *FEM*

band *NOUN*
1 *(musical)* le groupe *MASC*
a rock band un groupe de rock
a jazz band un orchestre de jazz
2 *(for your head)* le bandeau *MASC*

bandage *NOUN* ▸ SEE **bandage** *VERB*
le bandage *MASC*
to **bandage** *VERB* ▸ SEE **bandage** *NOUN*
faire [10] un bandage à
She will bandage your arm. Elle te fera un
bandage au bras.

bang *NOUN* ▸ SEE **bang** *VERB, EXCLAMATION*
1 *(noise)* le boum *MASC*
2 *(of a door, shutter, window)* le claquement
MASC
to **bang** *VERB* ▸ SEE **bang** *NOUN, EXCLAMATION*
1 *(to hit)* taper [1] sur *(a drum)*
He banged his fist on the table. Il a tapé du
poing sur la table.
2 *(to knock)* cogner [1]
to bang your head se cogner ◎ la tête
to bang into heurter [1]
I banged into the table. J'ai heurté la table.
3 *(to slam)* claquer [1]
to bang the door claquer la porte

◎ means the verb takes être to form the perfect

bang EXCLAMATION ▶ SEE **bang** NOUN, VERB
(like a gun) **pan!**

Bangladesh NOUN
le **Bangladesh** MASC
in Bangladesh au Bangladesh

Bangladeshi ADJECTIVE ▶ SEE **Bangladeshi** NOUN
du Bangladesh

Bangladeshi NOUN ▶ SEE **Bangladeshi** ADJECTIVE
Bangladais MASC, **Bangladaise** FEM

bangle NOUN
le **bracelet** MASC

banisters PLURAL NOUN
la **rampe** (d'escalier)

ℰ **bank** NOUN
1 (for money) la **banque** FEM
I'm going to the bank. Je vais à la banque.
2 (of a river, lake) le **bord** MASC
• **bank account**
le compte bancaire
• **bank balance**
le solde bancaire
• **bank card**
la carte bancaire
• **bank holiday**
le jour férié
• **banknote**
le billet de banque
• **bank statement**
le relevé de compte

to **baptize** VERB
baptiser [1]

ℰ **bar** NOUN ▶ SEE **bar** VERB
1 (selling drinks) le **bar** MASC
Her brother works in a bar. Son frère
travaille dans un bar.
2 (the counter) le **comptoir** MASC
3 (a block of something) la **barre** FEM
a metal bar une barre en métal
a bar of chocolate une tablette de chocolat
a bar of soap une savonnette
4 (in music) la **mesure** FEM

ℰ to **bar** VERB ▶ SEE **bar** NOUN
(to block) **barrer** [1]
to bar someone's way barrer le passage à
quelqu'un
A tall man barred my way. Un homme
grand m'a barré le passage.

Barbadian ADJECTIVE ▶ SEE **Barbadian** NOUN
de la Barbade

Barbadian NOUN ▶ SEE **Barbadian** ADJECTIVE
Barbadien MASC, **Barbadienne** FEM

Barbados NOUN
la **Barbade** FEM
to be in Barbados être [6] à la Barbade

to go to Barbados aller à la Barbade

barbecue NOUN ▶ SEE **barbecue** VERB
le **barbecue** MASC

to **barbecue** VERB ▶ SEE **barbecue** NOUN
faire [10] **griller au barbecue**
to barbecue a chicken faire griller un
poulet au barbecue

bare ADJECTIVE
nu MASC, **nue** FEM

barefoot ADJECTIVE
to be barefoot être [6] nu-pieds
to walk barefoot marcher pieds nus

bargain NOUN
une **affaire** FEM
It's a bargain! C'est une bonne affaire!

barge NOUN
la **péniche** FEM

bark NOUN ▶ SEE **bark** VERB
1 (of a dog) l'**aboiement** MASC
2 (of a tree) une **écorce** FEM

to **bark** VERB ▶ SEE **bark** NOUN
aboyer [39]

barley NOUN
l'**orge** MASC

barmaid NOUN
la **barmaid** FEM

barman NOUN
le **barman** MASC

barn NOUN
la **grange** FEM

barometer NOUN
le **baromètre** MASC

barrel NOUN
le **tonneau** MASC (PL les **tonneaux**)

barrier NOUN
la **barrière** FEM

base NOUN
la **base** FEM

baseball NOUN
le **base-ball** MASC

based ADJECTIVE
to be based on something être [6] fondé
sur quelque chose
The film is based on a true story. Le film est
tiré d'une histoire vraie.

ℰ **basement** NOUN
le **sous-sol** MASC
in the basement au sous-sol

bash NOUN ▶ SEE **bash** VERB
1 (a knock) la **bosse** FEM

ℰ indicates key words

It's got a bash on the wing. L'aile est cabossée.

2 *(a try)* **to have a bash** essayer [59] un coup
I'll have a bash. Je vais essayer un coup.

to **bash** VERB ▶ SEE **bash** NOUN
cogner [1]
I bashed my head. Je me suis cogné la tête.

basic ADJECTIVE
1 *(at the bottom level)* de base
basic knowledge des connaissances de base
her basic salary son salaire de base
2 *(essential)* essentiel MASC, essentielle FEM
the basic facts les faits essentiels
3 *(not luxurious)* rudimentaire MASC & FEM

basically ADVERB
1 *(essentially)* au fond
It's basically all right. Au fond, ça va.
2 *(to be honest)* à vrai dire
Basically, I don't want to go. À vrai dire, je ne veux pas y aller.

basics NOUN
les rudiments MASC PL

basin NOUN
(washbasin) le lavabo MASC

basis NOUN
la base FEM

ℓ**basket** NOUN
1 *(for shopping)* le panier MASC
2 *(other)* la corbeille FEM

basketball NOUN
le basketball MASC
to play basketball jouer [1] au basketball

bass NOUN
la basse FEM
to play bass jouer [1] de la basse
• **bass drum**
la grosse caisse
• **bass guitar**
la guitare basse

bassoon NOUN
le basson MASC
to play the bassoon jouer [1] du basson

bat NOUN
1 *(for cricket, baseball)* la batte FEM
2 *(for table tennis)* la raquette FEM
3 *(the animal)* la chauve-souris FEM

batch NOUN
1 *(of books, orders)* le lot MASC
2 *(of cakes)* la fournée FEM

ℓ**bath** NOUN
1 *(act of washing)* le bain MASC
I was in the bath. J'étais dans mon bain.

I'm going to have a bath. Je vais prendre un bain.
2 *(bathtub)* la baignoire FEM
The bath's pink. La baignoire est rose.

to **bathe** VERB
(a wound) laver [1]

ℓ**bathroom** NOUN
la salle de bains *(PL* les salles de bains*)*

baths PLURAL NOUN
la piscine FEM

bath towel NOUN
la serviette de bain

batter NOUN
(for frying) la pâte à frire
pancake batter la pâte à crêpes

battery NOUN
1 *(for a torch, radio)* la pile FEM
2 *(for a car)* la batterie FEM

battle NOUN
la bataille FEM

bay NOUN
1 *(on the coast)* la baie FEM
2 *(for coaches)* la travée FEM

BC ABBREVIATION
(short for before Christ) avant Jésus-Christ, av. J-C

ℓto **be** VERB
1 *(showing where or how something is)* être [6]
Gita is in the kitchen. Gita est dans la cuisine.
Where is the butter? Où est le beurre?
I'm tired. Je suis fatigué *(boy speaking)*, Je suis fatiguée *(girl speaking)*.
I saw the film when we were in France. J'ai vu le film quand nous étions en France.
2 *(with jobs and professions)* être [6]
Mum's a teacher. Ma mère est professeur.
He's a taxi driver. Il est chauffeur de taxi.

WORD TIP a before the name of the job is not translated into French.

3 *(telling the time)* être [6]
It's three o'clock. Il est trois heures.
It's half past five. Il est cinq heures et demie.
4 *(days of the week and dates)* **What day is it today?** Nous sommes quel jour aujourd'hui?
It's Tuesday today. On est mardi aujourd'hui.
It's the tenth of May. On est le dix mai.
5 *(talking about age)* avoir [5]
How old are you? Quel âge as-tu?
I'm fifteen. J'ai quinze ans.

☁ means the verb takes être to form the perfect

Harry's twenty. Harry a vingt ans.
6 *(cold, hot, hungry)* avoir [5]
to be hot avoir chaud
I'm hot. J'ai chaud.
to be cold avoir froid
I'm cold. J'ai froid.
to be hungry avoir faim
I'm hungry. J'ai faim.
7 *(with weather expressions)* faire [10]
It's cold today. Il fait froid aujourd'hui.
It's a nice day. Il fait beau.
8 to have been to a place être [6] allé à un endroit
I've never been to Paris. Je ne suis jamais allé à Paris *(boy speaking)*, Je ne suis jamais allée à Paris *(girl speaking)*.
Have you ever been to Greece? Est-ce que tu as jamais été en Grèce?
9 *(with -ed forms of verbs)* to be loved être [6] aimé
Jackson is adored by his fans. Jackson est adoré par ses fans.
The president has been assassinated. Le président a été assassiné.

ᴘ **beach** NOUN
la **plage** FEM
on the beach sur la plage
The children are playing on the beach. Les enfants jouent sur la plage.
to go to the beach aller ◎ [7] à la plage
Let's go to the beach! Allons à la plage!

bead NOUN
la **perle** FEM

beak NOUN
le **bec** MASC

beam NOUN
1 *(of light)* le **rayon** MASC
2 *(for a roof)* la **poutre** FEM

bean NOUN
un **haricot** MASC
green beans les haricots verts

bear NOUN ▶ SEE **bear** VERB
un **ours** MASC

to **bear** VERB ▶ SEE **bear** NOUN
(something bad) supporter [1]
I can't bear him. Je ne peux pas le supporter.
• to bear up
tenir [77] le coup
'How's your mum?' — 'She's bearing up.'
'Comment va ta mère?' — 'Elle tient le coup.'

beard NOUN
la **barbe** FEM

bearded ADJECTIVE
barbu MASC, **barbue** FEM

beast NOUN
1 *(an animal)* la **bête** FEM
2 *(a person)* le **chameau** MASC

beat NOUN ▶ SEE **beat** VERB
le **rythme** MASC

to **beat** VERB ▶ SEE **beat** NOUN
1 *(an army, other players)* battre [21]
We beat them! On les a battus!
2 *(eggs, mixture)* battre [21]
Beat the eggs. Battez les œufs.
• to beat somebody up
tabasser [1] quelqu'un

beautician NOUN
un **esthéticien** MASC, une **esthéticienne** FEM

ᴘ **beautiful** ADJECTIVE
beau MASC, **bel** MASC, **belle** FEM, **beaux** MASC PL, **belles** FEM PL
a beautiful day un beau jour
a beautiful girl une belle fille
beautiful pictures de beaux tableaux
a beautiful place un bel endroit

WORD TIP beau, belle etc go before the noun. bel is for singular masc nouns starting with a, e, i, o, u or silent h.

beautifully ADVERB
1 *(to behave, write, play)* admirablement
2 *(decorated, set)* magnifiquement
She dresses beautifully. Elle s'habille toujours avec beaucoup de goût.

beauty NOUN
la **beauté** FEM
• beauty spot
le site pittoresque

ᴘ **because** CONJUNCTION
parce que
I'm late because I missed the bus. Je suis en retard parce que j'ai raté le bus.
because of à cause de
because of the accident à cause de l'accident
I got into trouble because of you. C'est à cause de toi que j'ai des ennuis.

to **become** VERB
devenir ◎ [81]

ᴘ **bed** NOUN
1 *(for sleeping)* le **lit** MASC
to make the bed faire le lit
a double bed un grand lit
in bed au lit
Are the children in bed? Les enfants sont-ils au lit?
to go to bed aller ◎ [7] se coucher

ᴘ indicates key words

I usually go to bed at 11 o'clock.
D'habitude, je me couche à onze heures.
2 *(for flowers)* le **parterre** *MASC*
• **bedclothes**
les **couvertures**
• **a bed and breakfast**
une chambre d'hôte

bedding *NOUN*
la **literie** *FEM*

♪ **bedroom** *NOUN* ▸ SEE **bedroom** *ADJECTIVE*
la **chambre** *FEM*

bedside *NOUN*
le **chevet** *MASC*
a bedside table une table de chevet

bedsit *NOUN*
la **chambre meublée**

bedspread *NOUN*
le **dessus-de-lit** *MASC*

bedtime *NOUN*
It's bedtime. C'est l'heure d'aller se
coucher.

bee *NOUN*
une **abeille** *FEM*

beech *NOUN*
un **hêtre** *MASC*

♪ **beef** *NOUN*
le **bœuf** *MASC*
We had beef for dinner. On a mangé du
bœuf au dîner.
• **beefburger** un **hamburger** *MASC*

♪ **beer** *NOUN*
la **bière** *FEM*
Two beers, please. Deux bières, s'il vous
plaît.
a beer can une canette de bière

beetle *NOUN*
le **scarabée** *MASC*

beetroot *NOUN*
la **betterave** *FEM*

♪ **before** *ADVERB* ▸ SEE **before** *CONJUNCTION,*
PREPOSITION
1 *(already)* **déjà**
I've seen him before. Je l'ai déjà vu.
I had seen the film before. J'avais déjà vu
le film.
2 *(earlier)* **the day before** la veille
the day before the wedding la veille du
mariage
the day before yesterday avant-hier
the week before la semaine d'avant

♪ **before** *PREPOSITION* ▸ SEE **before** *ADVERB, CONJUNCTION*
avant

before Monday avant lundi
He left before me. Il est parti avant moi.
There's a to be done before the exams. On
a beaucoup à faire avant les examens.

♪ **before** *CONJUNCTION* ▸ SEE **before** *ADV, PREP*
1 **before doing something** avant de faire
quelque chose
I closed the windows before I left. J'ai
fermé les fenêtres avant de partir.
2 **avant que**
Phone me before they leave. Appelle-moi
avant qu'ils s'en aillent.
Oh, before I forget … Avant que j'oublie …

WORD TIP avant que is followed by a verb in the
subjunctive.

beforehand *ADVERB*
à l'avance
Phone beforehand. Appelle à l'avance.

to beg *VERB*
1 *(for money)* **mendier** [1]
2 *(somebody)* **supplier** [1]
to beg somebody to do something
supplier quelqu'un de faire quelque chose
She begged me not to leave. Elle m'a
supplié de ne pas partir.

♪ **to begin** *VERB*
commencer [61]
Lessons begin at nine. Les cours
commencent à neuf heures.
words beginning with P les mots qui
commencent par un P
to begin to do something commencer à
faire quelque chose
I'm beginning to understand. Je
commence à comprendre.
It began to rain. Il a commencé à pleuvoir.

beginner *NOUN*
le **débutant** *MASC*, la **débutante** *FEM*

beginning *NOUN*
le **début** *MASC*
at the beginning au début
**We went away at the beginning of the
holidays.** Nous sommes partis au début des
vacances.

♪ **behalf** *NOUN*
on behalf of pour
**The headmaster spoke on behalf of the
school.** Le directeur a parlé pour l'école.

♪ **to behave** *VERB*
se comporter ⊘ [1]
He behaved badly. Il s'est mal comporté.
She behaved even worse. Elle s'est
comportée encore plus mal.
to behave yourself être [6] sage
Behave yourselves! Soyez sages!

⊘ **means the verb takes être to form the perfect**

℘**behaviour** NOUN
le **comportement** MASC

℘**behind** ADVERB ▸ SEE **behind** NOUN, PREPOSITION
(to forget) **to leave something behind**
oublier [1] quelque chose
I left my phone behind on the train. J'ai
oublié mon portable dans le train.

℘**behind** PREPOSITION ▸ SEE **behind** ADVERB, NOUN
1 (in a place) **derrière**
behind them derrière eux
He hid behind the sofa. Il s'est caché
derrière le canapé.
2 (in class, at school)
to be behind avoir [5] du retard
Joe's behind in Maths. Joe a du retard en
math.

℘**behind** NOUN ▸ SEE **behind** ADVERB, PREPOSITION
le **derrière** MASC

beige ADJECTIVE
beige MASC & FEM

Belgian ADJECTIVE ▸ SEE **Belgian** NOUN
belge MASC & FEM
Belgian chocolates des chocolats belges

WORD TIP Adjectives never have capitals in
French, even for nationality.

℘**Belgian** NOUN ▸ SEE **Belgian** ADJECTIVE
un **Belge** MASC, une **Belge** FEM

℘**Belgium** NOUN
la **Belgique**
to be in Belgium être [6] en Belgique
to go to Belgium aller ◎ [7] en Belgique

belief NOUN
la **conviction** FEM
his political beliefs ses convictions
politiques

℘to **believe** VERB
croire [33]
I believe you. Je te crois.
They believed what I said. Ils ont cru ce
que j'ai dit.
I don't believe you! Ce n'est pas vrai!
to believe in something croire à quelque
chose
Do you believe in ghosts? Tu crois aux
fantômes?
to believe in God croire en Dieu
I believe in God. Je crois en Dieu.

bell NOUN
1 (in a church) la **cloche** FEM
2 (on a door) la **sonnette** FEM
Ring the bell! Appuyez sur la sonnette!

℘to **belong** VERB
1 (to be somebody's) **to belong to somebody**
appartenir [81] à quelqu'un
That watch belongs to Nick. Cette montre-
là appartient à Nick.
2 (to be part of something) **to belong to a
club** faire [10] partie d'un club
Paul belongs to a tennis club. Paul fait
partie d'un club de tennis.
3 (to be kept somewhere) aller ◎ [7]
That chair belongs in the study. Cette
chaise va dans le bureau.
Where does this vase belong? Ce vase va
où?

belongings PLURAL NOUN
les **affaires** FEM PL
All my belongings are at my dad's. Toutes
mes affaires sont chez mon père.

℘**below** ADVERB, PREPOSITION
1 (under something else) **au-dessous de**
(quelque chose)
below the window au-dessous de la
fenêtre
She lives in the flat below yours. Elle
habite l'appartement au-dessous du tien.
2 (underneath) **de dessous**
She lives in the flat below. Elle habite
l'appartement de dessous.

℘**belt** NOUN
la **ceinture** FEM

bench NOUN
le **banc** MASC

bend NOUN ▸ SEE **bend** VERB
1 (in a road) le **virage** MASC
2 (in a river) la **courbe** FEM

to **bend** VERB ▸ SEE **bend** NOUN
1 (your arm, your leg, a wire) **plier** [1]
to bend down se pencher ◎ [1]
2 (roads, paths) **tourner** [1]
The road bends to the right. La route
tourne à droite.

beneath PREPOSITION
sous
beneath the window sous la fenêtre
She lives in the flat beneath yours. Elle
habite l'appartement sous le tien.

benefit NOUN
un **avantage** MASC

bent ADJECTIVE
tordu MASC, **tordue** FEM

beret NOUN
le **béret** MASC

berry NOUN
la **baie** FEM

℘**berth** NOUN
la **couchette** FEM

℘ **indicates key words**

beside PREPOSITION
à côté de
She was sitting beside me. Elle était assise à côté de moi.

besides ADVERB
(anyway) d'ailleurs
Besides, it's too late. D'ailleurs, il est trop tard.

best ADJECTIVE, ADVERB ▸ SEE **best** NOUN
1 *(with nouns)* **meilleur** MASC, **meilleure** FEM
That's the best car. Cette voiture-là est la meilleure.
She's my best friend. C'est ma meilleure amie.
He's my best friend. C'est mon meilleur ami.
The best thing to do is to phone them. La meilleure chose à faire, c'est de leur téléphoner.
2 *(with verbs)* **le mieux**
Harry plays best. Harry joue le mieux.
I like Paris best. C'est Paris que je préfère.
best of all mieux que tout
I like Science best of all. J'aime les sciences plus que tout.

best NOUN ▸ SEE **best** ADJ, ADV
le **meilleur** MASC, la **meilleure** FEM
It's the best. C'est le meilleur.
It's the best I can do. Je ne peux pas faire mieux.
All the best! *(good luck)* Bonne chance!, *(cheers)* À ta santé!
He's the best at tennis. C'est lui le meilleur au tennis.
to do your best to do something faire [10] de son mieux pour faire quelque chose
I did my best to help her. J'ai fait de mon mieux pour l'aider.
• **best man**
le garçon d'honneur

bet NOUN ▸ SEE **bet** VERB
le **pari** MASC

to **bet** VERB ▸ SEE **bet** NOUN
parier [1]
He bet on the winning horse. Il a parié sur le cheval gagnant.
I bet you he'll forget! Je te parie qu'il va oublier!

better ADJECTIVE, ADVERB ▸ SEE **better** NOUN
1 *(showing improvement)* **mieux**
This pen writes better. Ce stylo écrit mieux.
even better encore mieux
to get better s'améliorer ◎ [1]
My French is getting better. Mon français s'améliore.

2 *(in comparisons)* **It works better than the other one.** Il fonctionne mieux que l'autre.
He's better at English than French. Il est meilleur en anglais qu'en français.
It's even better than before. C'est encore mieux qu'avant.
3 *(less ill)* **to be better** aller ◎ [7] mieux
He's a bit better today. Il va un peu mieux aujourd'hui.
to feel better se sentir ◎ [58] mieux
I feel better. Je me sens mieux.
4 *(to say you must do something)* **You had better do something.** Tu ferais mieux de faire quelque chose.
I'd better go now. Je dois partir maintenant.
He'd better not go. Il ferait mieux de ne pas y aller.
You had better phone at once. Tu ferais mieux d'appeler tout de suite.

better NOUN ▸ SEE **better** ADJECTIVE, ADVERB
the sooner the better le plus vite possible
I need to see you, and the sooner the better. Je dois te voir, et le plus vite possible.
so much the better tant mieux
If Will can come, so much the better. Si Will peut venir, tant mieux.

better off ADJECTIVE
1 *(richer)* **plus riche** MASC & FEM
They're better off than us. Ils sont plus riches que nous.
2 *(more comfortable)* **mieux** MASC & FEM
You'd be better off in bed. Tu serais mieux au lit.

between PREPOSITION
entre
between London and Dover entre Londres et Douvres
between the two entre les deux
I'll get there between 5 and 6 o'clock. J'arriverai entre cinq et six heures.

to **beware** VERB
Beware of the dog! Chien méchant!

beyond PREPOSITION
(in time and space) au-delà de
They went beyond the village. Ils sont allés au-delà du village.

Bible NOUN
the Bible la Bible

bicycle NOUN
le **vélo** MASC
by bicycle à vélo
I come to school by bicycle. Je viens à l'école à vélo.

◎ **means the verb takes être to form the perfect**

- **bicycle lane**
  la piste cyclable
- **bicycle rack**
  le parc à bicyclettes

ℓ **bidet** NOUN
  le bidet MASC

ℓ **big** ADJECTIVE
  1 (place, person, clothing) **grand** MASC,
    grande FEM
    a big garden un grand jardin
    a big city une grande ville
    my big sister ma grande sœur
    It's too big for me. C'est trop grand pour
    moi.
  2 (animal, car, box) **gros** MASC, **grosse** FEM
    a big dog un gros chien
    a big car une grosse voiture
    a big mistake une grosse erreur

  WORD TIP grand and gros go before the noun.

bigheaded ADJECTIVE
  to be bigheaded avoir [5] la grosse tête

big toe NOUN
  le gros orteil

ℓ **bike** NOUN
  1 (with pedals) le **vélo** MASC
    by bike à vélo
    to go for a bike ride se promener ◎ [1] à
    vélo
    He came by bike. Il est venu à vélo.
  2 (with motor) la **moto** FEM

bikini NOUN
  le bikini MASC

bilingual ADJECTIVE
  bilingue MASC & FEM

ℓ **bill** NOUN
  1 (in a restaurant) une **addition** FEM
    Can we have the bill, please? L'addition, s'il
    vous plaît.
  2 (for gas, electricity, etc) la **facture** FEM

billiards NOUN
  le billard MASC
  to play billiards jouer [1] au billard

billion NOUN
  le milliard MASC

bin NOUN
  la poubelle FEM

ℓ **binoculars** NOUN
  les jumelles FEM PL

biochemistry NOUN
  la biochimie FEM

biography NOUN
  la biographie FEM

biologist NOUN
  le & la **biologiste** MASC & FEM

ℓ **biology** NOUN
  la biologie FEM

ℓ **bird**
  un **oiseau** MASC (PL les **oiseaux**)
- **bird flu**
  la grippe aviaire
- **bird sanctuary**
  la réserve ornithologique

birdwatching NOUN
  to go birdwatching observer [1] les oiseaux

Biro® NOUN
  le bic® MASC

ℓ **birth** NOUN
  la naissance FEM
- **birth certificate**
  un acte de naissance
- **birth control**
  la contraception

ℓ **birthday** NOUN
  un **anniversaire** MASC
  a birthday present un cadeau
  d'anniversaire
  Happy birthday! Joyeux anniversaire!

ℓ **birthday party** NOUN
  1 (children's) le **goûter d'anniversaire**
  2 (adult's) la **soirée d'anniversaire**

ℓ **biscuit** NOUN
  le biscuit MASC

bishop NOUN
  un évêque MASC

ℓ **bit** NOUN
  1 (of bread, cheese, wood) le **morceau** MASC
    a bit of coal un morceau de charbon
  2 (of string, paper, garden) le **bout** MASC
    a bit of string un bout de ficelle
    with a little bit of garden avec un petit
    bout de jardin
  3 (a small amount)
    a bit un peu
    a bit hot un peu chaud
    a bit early un peu trop tôt
    Wait a bit! Attends un peu!
    a bit of un peu de
    a bit of sugar un peu de sucre
    a bit of news une nouvelle
    bit by bit petit à petit
    With a bit of luck we will win. Avec un peu
    de chance, nous gagnerons.
  4 (of a book, film, etc) le **passage** MASC
    This bit is brilliant! Ce passage est génial!
  5 (piece) **to fall to bits** tomber ◎ [1] en
    morceaux

ℓ indicates key words

My old diary fell to bits. Mon vieux journal est tombé en morceaux.

♂ **bite** NOUN ▶ SEE **bite** VERB
1 *(snack)* le **morceau** MASC
   I'll just have a bite before I go. Je vais juste manger un morceau avant de partir.
2 *(insect's)* la **piqûre** FEM
   a mosquito bite une piqûre de moustique
3 *(dog's)* la **morsure** FEM

♂ to **bite** VERB ▶ SEE **bite** NOUN
1 *(person, dog)* **mordre** [3]
2 *(insect)* **piquer** [1]
3 **to bite your nails** se **ronger** ◎ [52] les ongles

bitter ADJECTIVE
   (taste) **amer** MASC, **amère** FEM

black NOUN ▶ SEE **black** ADJECTIVE
   le **noir** MASC

♂ **black** ADJECTIVE ▶ SEE **black** NOUN
1 *(colour)* **noir** MASC, **noire** FEM
   a black cat un chat noir
   my black jacket ma veste noire
   a black coffee un café noir
   to turn black **noircir** [2]
   The plant turned black. La plante a noirci.
2 *(skin)* **a Black man** un **Noir**
   a Black woman une **Noire**
• **blackberry**
   la **mûre**
• **blackbird**
   le **merle**
• **blackboard**
   le **tableau noir**
• **blackcurrant**
   le **cassis**
• **black eye**
   un **œil au beurre noir**
• **black pudding**
   le **boudin noir**

blade NOUN
   la **lame** FEM

blame NOUN ▶ SEE **blame** VERB
   la **responsabilité** FEM
   to take the blame for something **prendre** [64] la responsabilité de quelque chose

to **blame** VERB ▶ SEE **blame** NOUN
   to blame someone for something **tenir** [77] quelqu'un responsable de quelque chose
   They blamed him for the accident. Ils l'ont tenu responsable de l'accident.
   She is to blame for it. Elle en est responsable.

blank ADJECTIVE ▶ SEE **blank** NOUN
1 *(page, piece of paper, cheque)* **blanc** MASC,

blanche FEM
2 *(tape, disk)* **vierge** MASC & FEM
3 *(screen)* **vide** MASC & FEM

blank NOUN ▶ SEE **blank** ADJECTIVE
   le **blanc** MASC

♂ **blanket** NOUN
   la **couverture** FEM

blast NOUN
1 *(an explosion)* une **explosion** FEM
2 *(of air)* le **souffle** MASC
3 *(of sounds)* **at full blast** à plein volume
   She plays her music at full blast. Elle met sa musique à plein volume.

blaze NOUN ▶ SEE **blaze** VERB
   un **incendie** MASC

to **blaze** VERB ▶ SEE **blaze** NOUN
   brûler [1]

bleach NOUN
   l'**eau de javel** FEM

to **bleed** VERB
   saigner [1]

blend NOUN
   le **mélange** MASC

blender NOUN
   le **mixer** MASC

to **bless** VERB
   bénir [2]
   Bless you! À tes souhaits! *(after a sneeze)*

blind ADJECTIVE ▶ SEE **blind** NOUN
   aveugle MASC & FEM
   to go blind **perdre la vue**

blind NOUN ▶ SEE **blind** ADJECTIVE
   (in a window) le **store** MASC

blindness NOUN
   la **cécité** FEM

to **blink** VERB
   cligner [1] des yeux

blister NOUN
   une **ampoule** FEM

blizzard NOUN
   la **tempête de neige**

blob NOUN
   la **goutte** FEM

♂ **block** NOUN ▶ SEE **block** VERB
1 *(building)*
   a block of flats un **immeuble**
   an office block un immeuble de bureaux
2 *(square group of buildings)* le **pâté de maisons**
   We drove round the block. Nous avons fait le tour du pâté de maisons.

◎ **means the verb takes être to form the perfect**

ρ to **block** *VERB* ▸SEE **block** *NOUN*
1 *(an exit, road)* **bloquer** [1]
2 *(a drain, hole)* **boucher** [1]
   The sink's blocked. L'évier est bouché.

blog *NOUN*
   le **blog** *MASC*

blogger *NOUN*
   le **blogueur** *MASC*, la **blogueuse** *FEM*

ρ **blonde** *ADJECTIVE*
   blond *MASC*, **blonde** *FEM*

ρ **blood** *NOUN*
   le **sang** *MASC*
   • **blood test**
     la prise de sang

blossom *NOUN*
   les **fleurs** *FEM PL*
   to be in blossom être [6] en fleurs

blot *NOUN*
   la **tache** *FEM*

blotchy *ADJECTIVE*
   (skin) **marbré** *MASC*, **marbrée** *FEM*

ρ **blouse** *NOUN*
   le **chemisier** *MASC*

ρ **blow** *NOUN* ▸SEE **blow** *VERB*
   le **coup** *MASC*

ρ to **blow** *VERB* ▸SEE **blow** *NOUN*
1 *(wind, person)* **souffler** [1]
   to blow your nose se moucher ⊘ [1]
2 *(explosion)* **to blow a hole in something**
   faire un trou dans quelque chose
   The bomb blew a hole in the wall. La
   bombe a fait un trou dans le mur.
   • **to blow something out** *(a candle)*
     souffler [1], *(flames)* éteindre [60]
   • **to blow up** *(to explode)*
     exploser [1]
     The plane blew up. L'avion a explosé.
   • **to blow something up** *(a balloon, tyre)*
     gonfler [1], *(a building)* faire [10] sauter

blow-dry *NOUN*
   le **brushing** *MASC*

ρ **blue** *ADJECTIVE* ▸SEE **blue** *NOUN*
   bleu *MASC*, **bleue** *FEM*
   blue eyes les yeux bleus

   blue *NOUN* ▸SEE **blue** *ADJECTIVE*
1 le **bleu** *MASC*
2 *(Music)*
   the blues le blues
   • **bluebell**
     la jacinthe des bois

blunder *NOUN*
   la **gaffe** *FEM*

blunt *ADJECTIVE*
1 *(knife, scissors)* **émoussé** *MASC*, **émoussée** *FEM*
2 *(pencil)* **mal taillé** *MASC*, **mal taillée** *FEM*
3 *(person)* **brusque** *MASC & FEM*

blurred *ADJECTIVE*
1 *(view, colours)* **indistinct** *MASC*, **indistincte** *FEM*
2 *(photo)* **flou** *MASC*, **floue** *FEM*

to **blush** *VERB*
   rougir [2]

board *NOUN*
1 *(plank)* la **planche** *FEM*
2 *(blackboard)* le **tableau noir**
3 *(whiteboard)* le **tableau blanc**
4 *(notice board)* le **panneau d'affichage**
5 *(for a board game)* le **jeu** *MASC*
   a chess board un échiquier
6 *(accommodation in a hotel)*
   full board la pension complète
   half board la demi-pension
7 *(on a boat)* **on board** à bord
   We were on board the ferry. Nous étions à
   bord du ferry.

boarder *NOUN*
   (in a school) l'**interne** *MASC & FEM*

board game *NOUN*
   le **jeu de société** *(PL* les **jeux de société***)*

boarding *NOUN*
   l'**embarquement** *MASC*
   • **boarding card**
     la carte d'embarquement
   • **boarding school**
     un internat

to **boast** *VERB*
   se **vanter** ⊘ [1]

ρ **boat** *NOUN*
1 *(in general)* le **bateau** *MASC*
2 *(sailing boat)* le **voilier** *MASC*
3 *(rowing boat)* la **barque** *FEM*

ρ **body** *NOUN*
1 *(of a person, animal)* le **corps** *MASC*
2 *(dead body)* le **cadavre** *MASC*
   • **bodybuilding**
     le culturisme
   • **bodyguard**
     le garde du corps

bodyboard *NOUN*
   le **bodyboard** *MASC*

ρ **boil** *NOUN* ▸SEE **boil** *VERB*
1 *(swelling)* le **furoncle** *MASC*
2 *(in cooking)* **Bring the water to the boil.**
   Portez l'eau à ébullition.

ρ **indicates key words**

ℰ to **boil** VERB ► SEE **boil** NOUN
bouillir [23]
The water's boiling. L'eau bout.
to boil something faire [10] bouillir quelque chose
I'm going to boil some water. Je vais faire bouillir de l'eau.
to boil an egg faire cuire un œuf
• boil over
déborder [1]

boiled egg NOUN
un œuf à la coque

boiler NOUN
la **chaudière** FEM

boiling ADJECTIVE
1 (water) bouillant MASC, bouillante FEM
2 (weather)
It's boiling hot today! Il fait une chaleur infernale aujourd'hui!

bolt NOUN ► SEE **bolt** VERB
le **verrou** MASC

to **bolt** VERB ► SEE **bolt** NOUN
verrouiller [1]

bomb NOUN ► SEE **bomb** VERB
la **bombe** FEM

to **bomb** VERB ► SEE **bomb** NOUN
bombarder [1]

bombing NOUN
1 (in a war) le bombardement MASC
2 (terrorist attack) un attentat à la bombe

bone NOUN
1 (of a person, animal) un os MASC
2 (of a fish) une arête FEM

bonfire NOUN
1 (for rubbish) le feu de jardin
2 (for a celebration) le feu de joie

bonnet NOUN
(of a car) le capot MASC

bony ADJECTIVE
1 (fish) plein d'arêtes MASC, pleine d'arêtes FEM
2 (body) anguleux MASC, anguleuse FEM
3 (knee) osseux MASC, osseuse FEM

to **boo** VERB
huer [1]

ℰ **book** NOUN ► SEE **book** VERB
1 (that you read) le **livre** MASC
a book about dinosaurs un livre sur les dinosaures
a biology book un livre de biologie
2 (that you write in) le **cahier** MASC
3 (of cheques, stamps, etc) le **carnet** MASC

• bookcase
la bibliothèque

ℰ to **book** VERB ► SEE **book** NOUN
réserver [1]
I booked a table for 8 o'clock. J'ai réservé une table pour vingt heures.

ℰ **booking** NOUN
(for holidays, etc) la **réservation** FEM
• booking office
le bureau de location

ℰ **booklet** NOUN
la **brochure** FEM

bookshelf NOUN
une **étagère** FEM

ℰ **bookshop** NOUN
la **librairie** FEM

boom NOUN
1 (of thunder) le grondement MASC
2 (time of prosperity) le boom MASC

ℰ **boot** NOUN
1 (for football, climbing, skiing) la **chaussure** FEM
walking boots des chaussures de randonnée
2 (short fashion boot) le bottine FEM
3 (knee-high boots, wellingtons) la botte FEM
4 (of a car) le coffre MASC

border NOUN
(between countries) la **frontière** FEM

bore NOUN
1 (person) raseur MASC, raseuse FEM (informal)
2 (nuisance)
What a bore! Quelle barbe!

bored ADJECTIVE
to be bored s'ennuyer ◎ [41]
I'm bored. Je m'ennuie.
to get bored s'ennuyer

ℰ **boring** ADJECTIVE
ennuyeux MASC, ennuyeuse FEM
It's boring at school. On s'ennuie en cours.

ℰ **born** ADJECTIVE
né MASC, née FEM
to be born naître ◎ [55]
I was born on 12 June in Chester. Je suis né le douze juin à Chester (boy speaking), Je suis née le douze juin à Chester (girl speaking).

to **borrow** VERB
emprunter [1]
Can I borrow your bike? Je peux emprunter ton vélo?
to borrow something from someone emprunter quelque chose à quelqu'un

◎ means the verb takes être to form the perfect

I'll borrow some money from Dad. Je vais emprunter de l'argent à papa.

ᵖ **boss** NOUN
le **patron** MASC, la **patronne** FEM

bossy ADJECTIVE
autoritaire MASC & FEM

both PRONOUN
1 *(when you talk about people)* **tous les deux** MASC, **toutes les deux** FEM
They both came. Ils sont venus tous les deux *(two boys or a boy and a girl).*
Both my sisters were there. Mes sœurs y étaient toutes les deux.
2 *(when you talk about things)* **les deux**
both my feet mes deux pieds
They have both been sold. Les deux sont vendus.
3 both ... and ...
I like to go to the seaside both in winter and in summer. J'aime aller à la mer en hiver comme en été.

ᵖ **bother** NOUN ▸ SEE **bother** VERB
l'**ennui** MASC
I've had a lot of bother with the car. J'ai eu beaucoup d'ennuis avec la voiture.
It's too much bother. C'est trop de tracas.
I answered the question without any bother. J'ai répondu à la question sans aucune difficulté.

ᵖ to **bother** VERB ▸ SEE **bother** NOUN
1 *(to disturb)* **déranger** [52]
I'm sorry to bother you. Je suis désolé de vous déranger *(boy speaking)*, Je suis désolée de vous déranger *(girl speaking).*
2 *(to worry)* **inquiéter** [24]
That doesn't bother me at all. Ça ne m'inquiète pas du tout.
Don't bother about the change. Ne t'inquiète pas pour la monnaie.
3 *(to take the trouble)* **prendre la peine**
She didn't even bother to come. Elle n'a même pas pris la peine de venir.
Don't bother! Ce n'est pas la peine!

ᵖ **bottle** NOUN
la **bouteille** FEM
• bottle bank
le conteneur à verre
• bottle opener
un ouvre-bouteille *(PL les ouvre-bouteilles)*

ᵖ **bottom** ADJECTIVE ▸ SEE **bottom** NOUN
1 *(lowest)* **inférieur** MASC, **inférieure** FEM
the bottom shelf le rayon inférieur
2 *(division, team, place)* **dernier** MASC, **dernière** FEM
His team is in bottom place in the league. Son équipe se trouve à la dernière place du

championnat.
3 *(sheet, blanket)* **de dessous**
Change the bottom sheet. Changez le drap de dessous.
4 *(flat)* **du rez-de-chaussée**
I live in the bottom flat. J'habite l'appartement du rez-de-chaussée.

ᵖ **bottom** NOUN ▸ SEE **bottom** ADJECTIVE
1 *(of a hill, wall, steps)* le **pied** MASC
She was waiting at the bottom of the hill. Elle attendait au pied de la colline.
2 *(of a bag, bottle, hole, pond, garden)* le **fond** MASC
The car was at the bottom of the lake. La voiture se trouvait au fond du lac.
3 *(of a page)* le **bas** MASC
at the bottom of the page en bas de la page
4 *(buttocks)* le **derrière** MASC

to **bounce** VERB
rebondir [2]

bouncer NOUN
(in a club) le **videur** MASC

bound ADJECTIVE
He's bound to be late. Il va sûrement être en retard.
That was bound to happen. Cela devait arriver.

boundary NOUN
la **limite** FEM

bow NOUN
1 *(in a shoelace, ribbon)* le **nœud** MASC
2 *(for a violin)* un **archet** MASC
3 *(for archery)* un **arc** MASC
a bow and arrow un arc et une flèche

ᵖ **bowl** NOUN ▸ SEE **bowl** VERB
1 *(to eat from)* le **bol** MASC
2 *(larger, for salad, mixing)* le **saladier** MASC
3 *(for washing up)* la **cuvette** FEM

ᵖ to **bowl** VERB ▸ SEE **bowl** NOUN
(a ball) **lancer** [61]

bowler NOUN
(in cricket) le **lanceur** MASC, la **lanceuse** FEM

bowling NOUN
(tenpin) le **bowling** MASC
to go bowling jouer [1] au bowling

ᵖ **box** NOUN
1 *(container)* la **boîte** FEM
a box of chocolates une boîte de chocolats
2 a cardboard box un carton
3 *(in printed form)* la **case** FEM

boxer NOUN
1 *(fighter)* le **boxeur** MASC

2 (dog) le **boxer** MASC
- **boxer shorts**
le caleçon

boxing NOUN
la **boxe** FEM
a boxing match un match de boxe

Boxing Day NOUN
le lendemain de Noël

box office NOUN
le **guichet** MASC

♀ **boy** NOUN
le **garçon** MASC
a little boy un petit garçon

♀ **boyfriend** NOUN
le **copain** MASC

bra NOUN
le **soutien-gorge** MASC

brace NOUN
(for teeth) un **appareil** MASC

bracelet NOUN
le **bracelet** MASC

bracket NOUN
la **parenthèse** FEM
in brackets entre parenthèses

brain NOUN
le **cerveau** MASC (PL les **cerveaux**)
- **brainwave**
une idée géniale

♀ **brake** NOUN ▶ SEE **brake** VERB
le **frein** MASC

♀ to **brake** VERB ▶ SEE **brake** NOUN
freiner [1]

bramble NOUN
la **ronce** FEM

branch NOUN
1 (of a tree) la **branche** FEM
2 (of a shop) la **succursale** FEM
3 (of a bank) une **agence** FEM

♀ **brand** NOUN
la **marque** FEM

brand new ADJECTIVE
tout neuf MASC, toute neuve FEM

brandy NOUN
le **cognac** MASC

brass NOUN
le **laiton** MASC, le **cuivre jaune**
a brass candlestick un chandelier en cuivre jaune
- **brass band**
la fanfare

brave ADJECTIVE
courageux MASC, courageuse FEM

bravery NOUN
le **courage** MASC

Brazil NOUN
le **Brésil** MASC

Brazilian ADJECTIVE ▶ SEE **Brazilian** NOUN
brésilien MASC, brésilienne FEM

Brazilian NOUN ▶ SEE **Brazilian** ADJECTIVE
le **Brésilien** MASC, la **Brésilienne** FEM

♀ **bread** NOUN
le **pain** MASC
a loaf of bread un pain
a slice of bread une tranche de pain

♀ **break** NOUN ▶ SEE **break** VERB
1 (short rest) la **pause** FEM
fifteen minutes' break une pause de quinze minutes
to take a break faire [10] une pause
Let's take a break for five minutes. Faisons une pause de cinq minutes.
2 (in school) la **récréation** FEM
3 (holiday) les **vacances** FEM PL
the Christmas break les vacances de Noël

♀ to **break** VERB ▶ SEE **break** NOUN
1 (a plate, vase) casser [1]
He broke a glass. Il a cassé un verre.
2 (by itself – window, cup, eggs) se casser ⊚ [1]
The eggs broke. Les œufs se sont cassés.
3 (an arm, leg, tooth) se casser ⊚ [1]
to break your arm se casser le bras
I broke my arm. Je me suis cassé le bras.
4 (a record) battre [21]
The French swimmer broke the record. Le nageur français a battu le record.
5 **to break a promise** ne pas tenir [77] sa promesse
You broke your promise. Tu n'as pas tenu ta promesse.
to break the rules ne pas respecter [1] le règlement
You mustn't break the rules. Il faut respecter le règlement.
- **to break down**
tomber ⊚ [1] en panne
The car broke down. La voiture est tombée en panne.
- **to break in** (thief)
entrer ⊚ [1] par effraction
Someone broke in and stole our TV. Quelqu'un est entré et nous a volé la télé.
- **to break out**
1 (fire) se déclarer ⊚ [1]
2 (fight, storm) éclater [1]
3 (prisoner) s'évader ⊚ [1]

⊚ means the verb takes être to form the perfect

- **to break up**
1 *(family, couple)* se séparer ◎ [1]
2 *(crowd, clouds)* se disperser ◎ [1]
3 *(from school)* **We break up on Thursday.**
Les cours finissent jeudi.

ℱ **breakdown** *NOUN*
1 *(of a vehicle)* la **panne** *FEM*
We had a breakdown on the motorway.
Nous sommes tombés en panne sur
l'autoroute.
2 *(in talks, negotiations)* la **rupture** *FEM*
3 *(mental)* la **dépression** *FEM*
to have a breakdown faire [10] une
dépression
She had a breakdown after the accident.
Après l'accident, elle a fait une dépression.
- **breakdown truck**
le camion de dépannage

ℱ **breakfast** *NOUN*
le **petit déjeuner** *MASC*

break-in *NOUN*
le **cambriolage** *MASC*

breast *NOUN*
1 *(of a woman)* le **sein** *MASC*
2 *(of a chicken)* le **blanc** *MASC*
- **breaststroke**
la brasse

breath *NOUN*
1 *(when you breathe in)* le **souffle** *MASC*
out of breath à bout de souffle
to get your breath reprendre [64] son
souffle
2 *(when you breathe out)* l'**haleine** *FEM*
to have bad breath avoir [5] mauvaise
haleine

to **breathe** *VERB*
respirer [1]

breathing *NOUN*
la **respiration** *FEM*

breed *NOUN* ▸ SEE **breed** *VERB*
(of dog, cat, etc) la **race** *FEM*

to **breed** *VERB* ▸ SEE **breed** *NOUN*
1 *(animals)* élever [50]
2 *(to have young)* se reproduire ◎ [26]

breeze *NOUN*
la **brise** *FEM*

to **brew** *VERB*
1 *(tea)* préparer [1]
2 *(beer)* brasser [1]

brewery *NOUN*
la **brasserie** *FEM*

brick *NOUN*
la **brique** *FEM*

ℱ **bride** *NOUN*
la **mariée** *FEM*
the bride and groom les mariés *MASC PL*

ℱ **bridegroom** *NOUN*
le **marié** *MASC*

bridesmaid *NOUN*
la **demoiselle d'honneur**

ℱ **bridge** *NOUN*
1 *(on a river)* le **pont** *MASC*
a bridge over the Seine un pont sur la Seine
2 *(card game)* le **bridge** *MASC*
to play bridge jouer [1] au bridge

bridle *NOUN*
la **bride** *FEM*

brief *ADJECTIVE*
bref *MASC*, brève *FEM*

briefcase *NOUN*
la **serviette** *FEM*

briefly *ADVERB*
brièvement

briefs *PLURAL NOUN*
le **slip** *MASC*

bright *ADJECTIVE*
1 *(colour, light)* vif *MASC*, vive *FEM*
bright green le vert vif
Try to look on the bright side. Essayez de
voir le bon côté des choses.
2 *(sunshine)* éclatant *MASC*, éclatante *FEM*
3 *(clever)* intelligent *MASC*, intelligente *FEM*
She's very bright. Elle est très intelligente.

to **brighten up** *VERB*
(weather, day) s'éclaircir ◎ [3]
The weather's brightening up. Le temps
s'éclaircit.

brilliant *ADJECTIVE*
1 *(very clever)* brillant *MASC*, brillante *FEM*
a brilliant surgeon un chirurgien brillant
He's brilliant at maths. Il est très doué en
maths.
2 *(wonderful)* génial *MASC*, géniale *FEM*,
géniaux *MASC PL*, géniales *FEM PL*
The party was brilliant! La fête était
géniale!

ℱ to **bring** *VERB*
1 *(something you carry)* apporter [1]
They brought a present. Ils ont apporté un
cadeau.
Bring your camera! Apporte ton appareil
photo!
Bring the garden chairs in. Rentrez les
chaises de jardin.
2 *(a person, animal)* amener [50]
She's bringing all the children. Elle va

amener tous les enfants.
- **to bring something back**
rapporter [1] quelque chose
She brought me back a present. Elle m'a
rapporté un cadeau.
- **to bring somebody up** *(children)*
élever [50] quelqu'un
He was brought up by his aunt. Il a été
élevé par sa tante.

Britain, Great Britain NOUN
la **Grande-Bretagne** FEM
Britain's amabassadeur l'ambassadeur de
la Grande-Bretagne
to go to Britain aller ◎ [7] en Grande-
Bretagne
to be in Britain être [6] en Grande-Bretagne
They came to Britain in 1995. Ils sont
arrivés en Grande-Bretagne en 1995.
We have lived in Britain for three years.
Nous vivons en Grande-Bretagne depuis
trois ans.

British ADJECTIVE ▶ SEE **British** PL NOUN
britannique MASC & FEM
the British Isles les îles Britanniques

WORD TIP Adjectives never have capitals in
French, even for nationality.

British PLURAL NOUN ▶ SEE **British** ADJECTIVE
the British les Britanniques MASC & FEM PLURAL

Brittany NOUN
la **Bretagne** FEM
a region of north-west France
to be in Brittany être [6] en Bretagne
to go to Brittany aller ◎ [7] en Bretagne

broad ADJECTIVE
large MASC & FEM
- **broad bean**
la fève

broadcast NOUN ▶ SEE **broadcast** VERB
une **émission** FEM

to broadcast VERB ▶ SEE **broadcast** NOUN
(a programme) **diffuser** [1]

broccoli NOUN
le **brocoli** MASC

brochure NOUN
la **brochure** FEM

broke ADJECTIVE
to be broke être [6] fauché

broken ADJECTIVE
cassé MASC, **cassée** FEM
The phone's broken. Le téléphone est
cassé.
My car has broken down. Ma voiture est
en panne.

bronchitis NOUN
la **bronchite** FEM
to have bronchitis avoir [5] une bronchite

brooch NOUN
la **broche** FEM

broom NOUN
1 *(for sweeping)* le **balai** MASC
2 *(plant)* le **genêt** MASC

brother NOUN
le **frère** MASC
my little brother mon petit frère
- **brother-in-law**
le **beau-frère** *(PL les **beaux-frères**)*

brown ADJECTIVE
1 *(colour)* **marron** INVARIABLE ADJECTIVE
my brown jacket ma veste marron
your brown shoes tes chaussures marron
light brown marron clair
dark brown marron foncé
2 *(tanned in the sun)* **bronzé** MASC, **bronzée**
FEM
to go brown bronzer [1]
I go brown easily. Je bronze facilement.
3 *(hair)* **châtain** INVARIABLE ADJECTIVE

WORD TIP châtain and marron do not change in
the feminine or plural.

- **brown bread**
le pain complet
- **brown sugar**
le sucre roux

bruise NOUN
1 *(on a person)* le **bleu** MASC
2 *(on fruit)* la **tache** FEM

brush NOUN ▶ SEE **brush** VERB
1 *(for hair, clothes, shoes)* la **brosse** FEM
my hair brush ma brosse à cheveux
2 *(for sweeping)* le **balai** MASC
3 *(for painting)* le **pinceau** MASC

to brush VERB ▶ SEE **brush** NOUN
1 *(the floor, clothes)* **brosser** [1]
2 *(your hair, teeth)* se **brosser** ◎ [1]
to brush your hair se brosser les cheveux
to brush your teeth se brosser les dents
She brushed her hair. Elle s'est brossé les
cheveux.

Brussels NOUN
Bruxelles
- **Brussels sprout**
le chou de Bruxelles

bubble NOUN
la **bulle** FEM
- **bubble bath**
le bain moussant

◎ means the verb takes être to form the perfect

bucket NOUN
le **seau** MASC (PL les **seaux**)

buckle NOUN
la **boucle** FEM

Buddhism NOUN
le **bouddhisme** MASC

Buddhist NOUN
le & la **bouddhiste** MASC & FEM

> **WORD TIP** Adjectives and nouns of religion start with a small letter in French

budget NOUN
le **budget** MASC

budgie NOUN
la **perruche** FEM

ℓ **buffet** NOUN
le **buffet** MASC
• **buffet car**
la **voiture-buffet**

bug NOUN
1 (insect) la **bestiole** FEM (informal)
2 (germ) le **microbe** MASC
   a stomach bug une gastroentérite
3 (in a computer) le **virus** MASC

to **build** VERB
construire [26]

builder NOUN
le **maçon** MASC

ℓ **building** NOUN
1 (house, church, etc) le **bâtiment** MASC
2 (with offices, flats) un **immeuble** MASC
• **building site**
le **chantier**
• **building society**
la **société d'investissement et de crédit immobilier**

built-up ADJECTIVE
urbanisé MASC, **urbanisée** FEM
a built-up area une agglomération

bulb NOUN
1 (for a light) une **ampoule** FEM
2 (that you plant) un **oignon** MASC

bull NOUN
le **taureau** MASC (PL les **taureaux**)

bulldozer NOUN
le **bulldozer** MASC

ℓ **bullet** NOUN
la **balle** FEM

bulletin NOUN
le **bulletin** MASC

bully NOUN ▸ SEE **bully** VERB
la **brute** FEM
He's a bully. C'est une brute.

to **bully** VERB ▸ SEE **bully** NOUN
1 **tyranniser** [1]
2 (at school) **harceler** [45]

bullying NOUN
1 la **brutalité** FEM
2 (at school) le **harcèlement** MASC

bum NOUN
le **derrière** MASC

bump NOUN ▸ SEE **bump** VERB
1 (that sticks up) la **bosse** FEM
   a bump on the head une bosse à la tête
   a bump in the road une bosse sur la route
2 (jolt) la **secousse** FEM
3 (noise) le **bruit sourd**

to **bump** VERB ▸ SEE **bump** NOUN
1 (to bang) **cogner** [1]
   I bumped my head. Je me suis cogné la tête.
   She bumped into the wall. Elle est rentrée dans le mur.
2 **to bump into somebody croiser** [1] quelqu'un
   I bumped into Sue in the supermarket. J'ai croisé Sue au supermarché.

bumper NOUN
le **pare-chocs** MASC

bumpy ADJECTIVE
1 (road) **accidenté** MASC, **accidentée** FEM
2 (plane landing) **agité** MASC, **agitée** FEM

bun NOUN
1 (for a burger) le **petit pain** MASC
2 (sugary) le **petit cake** MASC

bunch NOUN
1 (of flowers) le **bouquet** MASC
2 (of carrots, radishes) la **botte** FEM
3 (of keys) le **trousseau** MASC
4 (of grapes) la **grappe** FEM

bundle NOUN
le **tas** MASC

bungalow NOUN
le **pavillon** MASC

bunk NOUN
(on a train, boat) la **couchette** FEM
• **bunk beds**
les **lits superposés** MASC PL

bureau NOUN
une **agence** FEM

burger NOUN
le **hamburger** MASC

burglar NOUN
le **cambrioleur** MASC, la **cambrioleuse** FEM
- **burglar alarm**
la sonnerie d'alarme

🔑 **burglary** NOUN
le **cambriolage** MASC

burn NOUN ▸ SEE **burn** VERB
la **brûlure** FEM

to **burn** VERB ▸ SEE **burn** NOUN
1 (paper, wood, etc) **brûler** [1]
2 (to burn yourself) se **brûler** ⬤ [1]
She burnt herself on the grill. Elle s'est brûlée au gril.
3 (by accident) **laisser** [1] **brûler**
Mum's burnt her cake. Maman a laissé brûler son gâteau.
4 (in the sun) **I burn easily.** J'attrape facilement des coups de soleil.

burnt ADJECTIVE
brûlé MASC, **brûlée** FEM

🔑 **burst** ADJECTIVE ▸ SEE **burst** VERB
crevé MASC, **crevée** FEM
a burst tyre un pneu crevé

🔑 to **burst** VERB ▸ SEE **burst** ADJECTIVE
1 (balloon, tyre) **crever** [50]
2 (to do something suddenly) **to burst out laughing** éclater [1] de rire
Jo burst out laughing. Jo a éclaté de rire.
to burst into tears fondre [3] en larmes
The baby burst into tears. Le bébé a fondu en larmes.
to burst into flames prendre [64] feu
The bus burst into flames. Le bus a pris feu.

to **bury** VERB
enterrer [1]

🔑 **bus** NOUN
1 (public transport) un **autobus** MASC, le **bus** MASC
a bus ticket un ticket de bus
I get the bus to school. Je prends le bus pour aller à l'école.
2 (coach) le **car** MASC
I usually go to London by bus. D'habitude je vais à Londres en car.
- **bus driver**
le conducteur de bus, la conductrice de bus

bush NOUN
le **buisson** MASC

🔑 **business** NOUN
1 (commercial dealings) les **affaires** FEM PL
a business letter une lettre d'affaires
to be in business être [6] dans les affaires
Her father's in business. Son père est dans les affaires.
He's in Leeds on business. Il est à Leeds en voyage d'affaires.
She's in the insurance business. Elle travaille dans les assurances.
2 (company) une **entreprise** FEM
small businesses les petites entreprises
- **business class**
la classe affaires
- **businessman**
un homme d'affaires
- **business trip**
le voyage d'affaires
- **businesswoman**
une femme d'affaires

bus lane NOUN
le couloir d'autobus

bus pass NOUN
la carte de bus

bus route NOUN
la ligne d'autobus

bus shelter NOUN
un Abribus® MASC

bus station NOUN
la gare routière

🔑 **bus stop** NOUN
l'arrêt de bus

🔑 **bust** NOUN
la **poitrine** FEM
bust size le tour de poitrine

🔑 **busy** ADJECTIVE
1 (person) **occupé** MASC, **occupée** FEM
He's busy. Il est occupé.
to be busy doing something être [6] en train de faire quelque chose
Dad's busy washing the car. Papa est en train de laver la voiture.
2 (day, week) **chargé** MASC, **chargée** FEM
a busy day une journée chargée
3 (street, shop) très **fréquenté** MASC, très **fréquentée** FEM
The shops were busy. Il y avait beaucoup de monde dans les magasins.
4 (phone) **occupé** MASC, **occupée** FEM
The line's busy. La ligne est occupée.

🔑 **but** CONJUNCTION
mais
not Thursday but Friday pas jeudi mais vendredi
Max is small but strong. Max est petit mais fort.
I'll try, but it's difficult. J'essaierai, mais c'est difficile.

🔑 **butcher** NOUN
le **boucher** MASC, la **bouchère** FEM
He's a butcher. Il est boucher.

⬤ means the verb takes être to form the perfect

I'm going to the butcher's. Je vais chez le boucher.
Where is the nearest butcher's? Où est la boucherie la plus proche?

ℱ **butter** NOUN ▸ SEE **butter** VERB
le **beurre** MASC
- **buttercup**
  le **bouton-d'or**
- **butterfly**
  le **papillon**

to **butter** VERB ▸ SEE **butter** NOUN
beurrer [1]

ℱ **button** NOUN
le **bouton** MASC
Press the record button. Appuyez sur la touche d'enregistrement.
- **buttonhole**
  la **boutonnière**

ℱ **buy** NOUN ▸ SEE **buy** VERB
a good buy une bonne affaire
a bad buy une mauvaise affaire

ℱ to **buy** VERB ▸ SEE **buy** NOUN
acheter [16]
I bought the tickets. J'ai acheté les billets.
to buy something for somebody acheter quelque chose pour quelqu'un
Sarah bought him a sweater. Sarah lui a acheté un pull.
to buy something from someone acheter quelque chose à quelqu'un
I bought my bike from Tom. J'ai acheté mon vélo à Tom.

buyer NOUN
un **acheteur** MASC, une **acheteuse** FEM

to **buzz** VERB
(flies, bees) **bourdonner** [1]

buzzer NOUN
la **sonnerie** FEM

ℱ **by** PREPOSITION
1 (using, because of) **par**
by telephone par téléphone
by mistake par erreur
The hamster was eaten by the dog. Le hamster a été mangé par le chien.
to take somebody by the hand prendre quelqu'un par la main
Lucy took me by the hand. Lucy m'a pris par la main.
2 (when saying how you travel) **en**
Ravi came by bus. Ravi est venu en bus.
They're leaving by train. Ils partent en train.
I come to school by car. Je viens à l'école en voiture.
3 (near a place) **à côté de**

She was sitting by the fire. Elle était assise à côté du feu.
I'd love to live by the sea. J'aimerais bien habiter au bord de la mer.
His family lives close by. Sa famille habite tout près.
4 (before a time) **avant**
Kevin was back by four. Kevin est rentré avant quatre heures.
5 (with myself, yourself, etc) **tout seul** MASC, **toute seule** FEM
by yourself tout seul (boy, man), toute seule (girl, woman)
I was by myself. J'étais tout seul (boy speaking), J'étais toute seule (girl speaking).
She did it by herself. Elle l'a fait toute seule.
6 **to go by** passer ◎ [1]
A car went by. Une voiture est passée.

bye EXCLAMATION
au revoir
Bye for now! À bientôt!

bypass NOUN
la **rocade** FEM

Cc

cab NOUN
le **taxi** MASC

ℱ **cabbage** NOUN
le **chou** MASC (PL les **choux**)

cabin NOUN
la **cabine** FEM

ℱ **cable** NOUN
1 (electrical) le **câble** MASC
2 (TV) la **télévision par câble**
They've got cable. Ils ont le câble.
- **cable car**
  le **téléphérique** MASC
- **cable TV**
  la **télévision par câble**

cactus NOUN
le **cactus** MASC

ℱ **cafe** NOUN
le **café** MASC

cage NOUN
la **cage** FEM

ℱ **cake** NOUN
le **gâteau** MASC (PL les **gâteaux**)
a piece of cake un morceau de gâteau
a birthday cake un gâteau d'anniversaire

to **calculate** VERB
calculer [1]

ℱ **indicates key words**

calculation NOUN
le calcul MASC
to do some calculations faire [10] des calculs

calculator NOUN
la calculatrice FEM

calendar NOUN
le calendrier MASC

ℰ **calf** NOUN
1 (animal) le veau MASC (PL les veaux)
2 (of your leg) le mollet MASC

ℰ **call** NOUN ▶ SEE **call** VERB
un appel MASC
Thanks for your call. Merci de votre appel.
I've had several calls. J'ai eu plusieurs appels.
There was a call for you. Quelqu'un t'a téléphoné.
I got a phone call from her. J'ai eu un coup de téléphone d'elle.

ℰ to **call** VERB ▶ SEE **call** NOUN
1 (to phone) appeler [18]
to call a taxi appeler un taxi
Let's call a taxi! Appelons un taxi!
to call the doctor appeler le médecin
Call this number. Appelez ce numéro.
2 (to name) appeler [18]
They've called the baby Rachel. Ils ont appelé le bébé Rachel.
3 **to be called** ... s'appeler ◯ [18] ...
She's called Salma. Elle s'appelle Salma.
I've got a brother called Josh. J'ai un frère qui s'appelle Josh.
What's he called? Comment s'appelle-t-il?
It's called 'babyfoot'. Ça s'appelle un 'babyfoot'.
What's it called in French? Ça s'appelle comment en français?
4 (to insult) **to call somebody something** traiter [1] quelqu'un de quelque chose
She called him an idiot. Elle l'a traité d'imbécile.
5 (to wake up) réveiller [1]
Call me at eight o'clock. Réveille-moi à huit heures.
• **to call back**
rappeler [18]
I'll call back later. Je rappellerai plus tard.
He won't call her back. Il ne va pas la rappeler.
• **to call in**
passer ◯ [1]
She called in briefly yesterday. Elle est passée rapidement hier.

call box NOUN
la cabine téléphonique

ℰ **calm** ADJECTIVE ▶ SEE **calm** VERB
calme MASC & FEM
The sea is calm. La mer est calme.
We remained calm. Nous sommes restés calmes.

ℰ to **calm** VERB ▶ SEE **calm** NOUN
calmer [1]
• **to calm down**
1 se calmer ◯ [1]
He's calmed down. Il s'est calmé.
2 **to calm somebody down** calmer quelqu'un
I tried to calm her down. J'ai essayé de la calmer.

calmly ADVERB
calmement

calorie NOUN
la calorie FEM

camcorder NOUN
le caméscope MASC

camel NOUN
le chameau MASC (PL les chameaux)

camera NOUN
1 (for photos) un appareil photo (PL les appareils photo)
2 (for film, TV) la caméra FEM
• **cameraman**
le caméraman MASC

ℰ **camp** NOUN ▶ SEE **camp** VERB
le camp MASC

ℰ to **camp** VERB ▶ SEE **camp** NOUN
camper [1]
We camped in the forest. Nous avons campé dans la forêt.

campaign NOUN
la campagne FEM
an advertising campaign une campagne publicitaire

ℰ **camper van** NOUN
le camping-car MASC

ℰ **camping** NOUN
le camping MASC
to go camping faire [10] du camping
We're going camping in Italy. Nous allons faire du camping en Italie.

ℰ **campsite** NOUN
le terrain de camping

can NOUN ▶ SEE **can** VERB
1 (for food, drinks) la boîte FEM
a can of tuna une boîte de thon
2 (for beer) la canette FEM
3 (for petrol, oil) le bidon MASC

◯ means the verb takes être to form the perfect

𝒫 **can** VERB ▸ SEE **can** NOUN
1 (to be able to do something) **pouvoir** [12]
   You can leave your bag here. Tu peux laisser ton sac ici.
   They cannot believe it. Ils ne peuvent pas le croire.
   They couldn't come. Ils n'ont pas pu venir.
2 (to know how to do something) **savoir** [70]
   She can drive. Elle sait conduire.
   I can't swim. Je ne sais pas nager.
   Can you play the guitar? Tu sais jouer de la guitare?
3 (when **can** is not translated in French)
   Can you hear me? Est-ce que tu m'entends?
   I can't see him. Je ne le vois pas.
   Can you understand? Tu comprends?
   I can't remember. Je ne me souviens pas.
4 (to ask for, to offer help) **pouvoir** [12]
   Can you open the door, please? Est-ce que tu peux ouvrir la porte, s'il te plaît?
   Can I help you? Est-ce que je peux t'aider?
   ▸ SEE **could**

Canada NOUN
   le **Canada** MASC
   to be in Canada être [6] au Canada
   to go to Canada aller ⊙ [7] au Canada

   WORD TIP Countries and regions in French take le, la or les.

🔵 **CANADA**
   The second largest French-speaking city in the world is Montreal, in Canada.

𝒫 **Canadian** ADJECTIVE ▸ SEE **Canadian** NOUN
   canadien MASC, **canadienne** FEM

   WORD TIP Adjectives never have capitals in French, even for nationality or regional origin.

𝒫 **Canadian** NOUN ▸ SEE **Canadian** ADJECTIVE
   le **Canadien** MASC, la **Canadienne** FEM

canal NOUN
   le **canal** MASC (PL les **canaux**)

canary NOUN
   le **canari** MASC

to **cancel** VERB
   annuler [1]
   to cancel a concert annuler un concert

cancer NOUN
   le **cancer** MASC
   lung cancer le cancer du poumon
   to have cancer avoir [5] le cancer

Cancer NOUN
   Cancer MASC
   I'm Cancer. Je suis Cancer.

   WORD TIP Signs of the zodiac do not take an article: un or une.

candidate NOUN
   le **candidat** MASC, la **candidate** FEM

candle NOUN
   la **bougie** FEM

candyfloss NOUN
   la **barbe à papa**

canned ADJECTIVE
   en conserve
   canned tuna le thon en conserve

cannon NOUN
   le **canon** MASC

cannot VERB ▸ SEE **can**

canoe NOUN
   le **canoë** MASC

canoeing NOUN
   to go canoeing faire [10] du canoë

can-opener NOUN
   un **ouvre-boîtes** MASC (PL les **ouvre-boîtes**)

𝒫 **canteen** NOUN
   la **cantine** FEM
   to eat in the canteen manger [52] à la cantine.

canvas NOUN
   la **toile** FEM

cap NOUN
1 (hat) la **casquette** FEM
   a baseball cap une casquette de baseball
2 (on a bottle, tube) le **bouchon** MASC

capable ADJECTIVE
   capable MASC & FEM
   a capable girl une fille capable
   We're quite capable of doing it. Nous sommes bien capables de le faire.

capital NOUN
1 (city) la **capitale** FEM
   Paris is the capital of France. Paris est la capitale de la France.
2 (letter) la **majuscule** FEM
   in capitals en majuscules

capitalism NOUN
   le **capitalisme** MASC

Capricorn NOUN
   Capricorne MASC
   Linda's Capricorn. Linda est Capricorne.

   WORD TIP Signs of the zodiac do not take an article: un or une.

to **capsize** VERB
   chavirer [1]
   to capsize a boat faire [10] chavirer un bateau

𝒫 indicates key words

captain NOUN
le **capitaine** MASC

captivity NOUN
in captivity en captivité
They're kept in captivity. Ils sont gardés en captivité.

to **capture** VERB
1 (an animal, a person) **capturer** [1]
2 (a town, a castle) **prendre** [64]

ℓ **car** NOUN
la **voiture** FEM
in the car dans la voiture
The car was parked here. La voiture était garée ici.
We're going by car. Nous y allons en voiture.

caramel NOUN
le **caramel** MASC

ℓ **caravan** NOUN
la **caravane** FEM
a caravan holiday des vacances en caravane

carbon dioxide NOUN
le **gaz carbonique** MASC

car crash NOUN
un **accident de voiture**

ℓ **card** NOUN
1 (for playing games) la **carte** FEM
a pack of cards un jeu de cartes
a game of cards une partie de cartes
to play cards jouer [1] aux cartes
2 (for birthdays, etc) la **carte** FEM
I sent her a card from Nice. Je lui ai envoyé une carte de Nice. ▸ SEE **birthday card, postcard**

cardboard NOUN
le **carton** MASC
• **cardboard box**
le **carton**

cardigan NOUN
le **cardigan** MASC

cardphone NOUN
le **téléphone à carte**

ℓ **care** NOUN ▸ SEE **care** VERB
1 (doing your best) le **soin** MASC
with great care avec beaucoup de soin
to take care to do something prendre [64] soin de faire quelque chose
I take care to eat well. Je prends soin de bien manger. ▸ SEE **medical care**
2 **to take care of somebody** (to look after) s'occuper ◯ [1] de quelqu'un
She takes care of us. Elle s'occupe de nous.

3 **to take care of something** (to sort out) s'occuper ◯ [1] de quelque chose
I'll take care of the present. Je vais m'occuper du cadeau.
4 **to take care (when) doing something** (to watch out) faire [10] attention en faisant quelque chose
Take care typing the password. Fais attention en tapant le mot de passe.
5 **Bye, take care!** Salut! À bientôt!

ℓ to **care** VERB ▸ SEE **care** NOUN
1 **to care about something** se soucier ◯ [1] de quelque chose
They don't care about recycling. Ils ne se soucient pas du recyclage.
2 **She doesn't care.** Ça lui est égal.
I couldn't care less! Ça m'est complètement égal!
Who cares! On s'en fiche! (informal)
3 **to care about somebody** aimer [1] quelqu'un
They don't care about me. Ils ne m'aiment pas.

career NOUN
la **carrière** FEM
• **careers adviser**
le **conseiller d'orientation**, la **conseillère d'orientation**

ℓ **careful** ADJECTIVE
prudent MASC, **prudente** FEM
to be careful faire [10] attention
Be careful! Fais attention!
to be careful not to do something faire [10] attention de ne pas faire quelque chose
Be careful not to bang your head. Fais attention de ne pas te cogner la tête.

carefully ADVERB
1 (paying attention) **attentivement**
Read the questions carefully. Lisez attentivement les questions.
2 (with great care) **avec précaution**
3 (to avoid mistakes) **soigneusement**

careless ADJECTIVE
1 (person) **to be careless** ne pas faire [10] attention à ce qu'on fait
She's very careless. Elle ne fait pas attention à ce qu'elle fait.
2 (piece of work) **peu soigné** MASC, **peu soignée** FEM
This is careless work. C'est du travail peu soigné.
careless mistakes des fautes d'inattention

ℓ **caretaker** NOUN
le **gardien** MASC, la **gardienne** FEM

car ferry NOUN
le **ferry** MASC

◯ **means the verb takes être to form the perfect**

car hire NOUN
la location de voitures

Caribbean NOUN
the Caribbean les Caraïbes FEM PL
the Caribbean Sea la mer des Caraïbes
to be in the Caribbean être [6] aux Caraïbes
to go to the Caribbean aller ⊘ [7] aux Caraïbes

carnation NOUN
un œillet MASC

carnival NOUN
le carnaval MASC (PL les carnavals)

ℐ **car park** NOUN
le parking MASC

carpenter NOUN
le menuisier MASC
He's a carpenter. Il est menuisier.

carpentry NOUN
la menuiserie FEM

carpet NOUN
1 (fitted) la moquette FEM
2 (large rug) le tapis MASC

car phone NOUN
le téléphone de voiture

car radio NOUN
un autoradio MASC

carriage NOUN
(of a train) la voiture FEM

carrier bag NOUN
le sac en plastique

ℐ **carrot** NOUN
la carotte FEM

ℐ to **carry** VERB
1 (people) porter [1]
She was carrying a parcel. Elle portait un paquet.
I carried the suitcase into the hall. J'ai porté la valise dans le vestibule.
2 (vehicles, planes) transporter [1]
The coach was carrying schoolchildren. Le car transportait des élèves.
• to carry on
continuer [1]
to carry on doing something continuer à faire quelque chose
They carried on talking. Ils ont continué à parler.

carrycot NOUN
le porte-bébé INVARIABLE MASC

carsick ADJECTIVE
to be carsick être [6] malade en voiture

cart NOUN
la charrette FEM

carton NOUN
1 (of cream, yoghurt) le pot MASC
2 (of milk, orange) la brique FEM

ℐ **cartoon** NOUN
1 (film) le dessin animé
2 (comic strip) la bande dessinée, la BD
3 (amusing drawing) le dessin humoristique

cartridge NOUN
(for a pen, a video) la cartouche FEM

to **carve** VERB
(meat) découper [1]

case NOUN
1 (suitcase) la valise FEM
to pack a case faire une valise
2 (large wooden crate) la caisse FEM
3 (for your glasses, etc) un étui MASC
4 (situation) le cas MASC
In that case, I'm not going. En ce cas, je n'y vais pas.
.In any case, it's too late. De toute façon, c'est trop tard.

cash NOUN
1 (money in general) l'argent MASC
I haven't got any cash on me. Je n'ai pas d'argent.
2 (notes and coins) les espèces FEM PL
I paid £50 in cash. J'ai payé cinquante livres en espèces.
• cash desk
la caisse
• cash dispenser
le guichet automatique

cashier NOUN
le caissier MASC, la caissière FEM

cash point NOUN
le distributeur d'argent MASC

cassette NOUN
la cassette FEM

cast NOUN
the cast les acteurs MASC PL

ℐ **castle** NOUN
le château MASC (PL les châteaux)
a medieval castle un château du Moyen Âge

casual ADJECTIVE
décontracté MASC, décontractée FEM
• casual clothes
les vêtements décontractés MASC PL

casualty NOUN
1 (in an accident, explosion) la victime FEM
many casualties plusieurs victimes

ℐ indicates key words

2 *(in a crash)* le **blessé** MASC, la **blessée** FEM
3 **to be in casualty** être [6] aux urgences

ℰ **cat** NOUN
1 le **chat** MASC
  a big black cat un gros chat noir
2 *(female)* la **chatte** FEM

catalogue NOUN
le **catalogue** MASC

catastrophe NOUN
la **catastrophe** FEM

catch NOUN ▸ SEE **catch** VERB
(on a window, door) la **fermeture** FEM

ℰ to **catch** VERB ▸ SEE **catch** NOUN
1 *(a ball, a person, an animal)* **attraper** [1]
  Jack caught a mouse. Jack a attrapé une souris.
  You can't catch me! Tu ne m'attraperas pas!
  I caught hold of a branch. J'ai attrapé une branche.
2 **to catch somebody doing something** attraper quelqu'un en train de faire quelque chose
  They caught her stealing. On l'a attrapée en train de voler.
  to get caught doing something se faire ⬡ [10] attraper en train de faire quelque chose
  He got caught copying. Il s'est fait attraper en train de copier.
3 *(a bus, plane, train)* **prendre** [64]
4 *(an illness)* **attraper** [1]
  I've caught a cold. J'ai attrapé un rhume.
5 **to catch your finger in something** se **prendre** ⬡ [64] les doigts dans quelque chose
  I caught my finger in the door. Je me suis pris le doigt dans la porte.
6 ▸ SEE **fire** VERB
• **to catch up with somebody** rattraper [1] quelqu'un

category NOUN
la **catégorie** FEM

catering NOUN
la **restauration** FEM

caterpillar NOUN
la **chenille** FEM

ℰ **cathedral** NOUN
la **cathédrale** FEM
  Wells cathedral la cathédrale de Wells

Catholic NOUN, ADJECTIVE
un & une **catholique** MASC & FEM

WORD TIP Adjectives and nouns of religion start with a small letter in French

cattle PLURAL NOUN
le **bétail** MASC SINGULAR

caught ▸ SEE **catch**

ℰ **cauliflower** NOUN
le **chou-fleur** MASC (PL les **choux-fleurs**)

cause NOUN ▸ SEE **cause** VERB
1 *(of fire, accident, problem)* la **cause** FEM
  the main causes of pollution les causes principales de la pollution
2 *(charity, political goal)* la **cause** FEM
  a good cause une bonne cause

ℰ to **cause** VERB ▸ SEE **cause** NOUN
1 *(problems, damage)* **causer** [1]
  to cause trouble créer [32] des problèmes
  Stop causing trouble! Arrête de créer des problèmes!
2 *(chaos, disease)* **provoquer** [1]
  It caused delays. Ça a provoqué des retards.

caution NOUN
la **prudence** FEM

cautious ADJECTIVE
prudent MASC, **prudente** FEM

cave NOUN
la **grotte** FEM

caving NOUN
la **spéléologie** FEM
  to go caving faire [10] de la spéléologie

ℰ **CD** NOUN
le **CD** MASC
  to put a CD on mettre [11] un CD

WORD TIP CD never changes.

• **CD player**
la **platine laser**

ℰ **CD-ROM** NOUN
le **CD-ROM** MASC
  I've got it on CD-ROM. Je l'ai sur CD-ROM.

WORD TIP CD-ROM never changes.

ℰ **ceiling** NOUN
le **plafond** MASC

to **celebrate** VERB
fêter [1]
  I'm celebrating my birthday. Je fête mon anniversaire.

celebrity NOUN
la **célébrité** FEM
  to become a celebrity devenir ⬡ [81] une célébrité

426

⬡ means the verb takes être to form the perfect

celery NOUN
le **céleri** MASC

cell NOUN
la **cellule** FEM

ℱ**cellar** NOUN
la **cave** FEM

cello NOUN
le **violoncelle** MASC
to play the cello jouer [1] du violoncelle

cement NOUN
le **ciment** MASC

cemetery NOUN
le **cimetière** MASC

ℱ**cent** NOUN
1 *(in euro system)* le **centime** MASC *(usual term)* le **cent** *(official term)*
2 *(in dollar system)* le **cent** MASC

centenary NOUN
le **centenaire** MASC

centigrade ADJECTIVE
centigrade
ten degrees centigrade dix degrés centigrade

ℱ**centimetre** NOUN
le **centimètre** MASC

ℱ**central** ADJECTIVE
central MASC, centrale FEM, centraux MASC PL, centrales FEM PL
in central London dans le centre de Londres
• **central heating**
le chauffage central

ℱ**centre** NOUN
1 *(middle)* le **centre** MASC
in the centre of the forest au centre de la forêt
2 *(of a town, city)* le **centre-ville** MASC
right in the centre en plein centre-ville
3 ►SEE **shopping centre, leisure centre, sports centre**

ℱ**century** NOUN
le **siècle** MASC
in the twenty-first century au vingt-et-unième siècle

cereal NOUN
(breakfast) cereal les **céréales** FEM PL pour le petit déjeuner
I have cereal for breakfast. Je prends des céréales au petit déjeuner.

ceremony NOUN
la **cérémonie** FEM

ℱ**certain** ADJECTIVE
certain MASC, certaine FEM

a certain number of people un certain nombre de personnes
to be certain that … être [6] sûr que …
Lucy's certain that you're wrong. Lucy est sûre que tu as tort.
Nobody knows for certain. Personne ne sait au juste.
I can't say for certain. Je ne sais pas au juste.

certainly ADVERB
certainement
certainly not certainement pas

ℱ**certificate** NOUN
1 *(document, qualification)* le **certificat** MASC
2 *(award for a skill)* le **brevet** MASC
3 **an 18-certificate film** un film interdit aux moins de 18 ans

ℱ**chain** NOUN
la **chaîne** FEM
a gold chain une chaîne en or

ℱ**chair** NOUN
1 *(in class, at dining table)* la **chaise** FEM
2 *(armchair)* le **fauteuil** MASC
• **chair lift**
le télésiège

chalet NOUN
1 *(in the mountains)* le **chalet** MASC
2 *(in a holiday camp)* le **bungalow** MASC

chalk NOUN
la **craie** FEM

challenge NOUN
1 *(that excites you)* le **défi** MASC
We rose to the challenge and beat them. Nous avons relevé le défi et nous les avons battus.
2 *(test)* une **épreuve** FEM
The exam was a challenge for him. L'examen l'a mis à l'épreuve.

ℱ**champion** NOUN
le **champion** MASC, la **championne** FEM
She was world champion at 17. Elle a été championne du monde à 17 ans.

ℱ**chance** NOUN
1 *(opportunity)* une **occasion** FEM
to have the chance to do something avoir [5] l'occasion de faire quelque chose
If you have the chance to go there … Si tu as l'occasion d'y aller …
I didn't get the chance to go. Je n'ai pas eu l'occasion d'y aller.
2 *(hope)*
not to stand a chance of doing something n'avoir [5] aucune chance de faire quelque chose
We don't stand a chance of beating them.

ℱ **indicates key words**

Nous n'avons aucune chance de les battre.
3 *(luck)*
by chance par hasard
You haven't seen him, by any chance? Tu ne l'as pas vu, par hasard?
4 *(risk)*
to take a chance prendre [64] un risque
I'm not taking any chances. Je ne prends pas de risques.

ℰ **change** NOUN ▸ SEE **change** VERB
1 *(something new, different)* le **changement** MASC
a change of plan un changement de programme
I've made some changes to my room. J'ai fait des changements dans ma chambre.
Take a change of clothes. Prends des vêtements de rechange.
to do something for a change faire [10] quelque chose pour changer
Let's go to the ice rink for a change! Allons à la patinoire pour changer!
It makes a change from burgers. Ça change un peu des hamburgers.
2 *(cash)* la **monnaie** FEM
I don't have any change. Je n'ai pas de monnaie.
The machine doesn't give change. La machine ne rend pas la monnaie.

ℰ **to change** VERB ▸ SEE **change** NOUN
1 *(to transform completely)* **changer** [52]
It changed my life. Cela m'a changé la vie.
Amy will never change. Amy ne changera jamais.
Josh has changed a lot. Josh a beaucoup changé.
2 *(to switch from one thing to another)* **changer** [52] de
I must change my jeans. Je dois changer de jean.
They changed places. Ils ont changé de place.
We changed trains in Paris. Nous avons changé de train à Paris.
to change your mind changer [52] d'avis
Well, I've changed my mind. Eh bien, j'ai changé d'avis.
3 *(to exchange in a shop)* **échanger** [52]
to change something for something échanger quelque chose contre quelque chose
Can I change it for the larger size? Puis-je l'échanger contre la taille au-dessus?
4 *(to change your clothes)* **se changer** ⊙ [52]
John's gone up to change. John est monté se changer.
Go and get changed. Va te changer.
5 *(money)* **changer** [52]

to change some money changer de l'argent

changing room NOUN
1 *(in pool, club)* le **vestiaire** MASC
2 *(in a shop)* le **salon d'essayage**

ℰ **channel** NOUN
1 *(on TV)* la **chaîne** FEM
to change channels changer [52] de chaîne
2 **the Channel** la Manche
• **Channel Islands** les îles Anglo-Normandes
• **Channel Tunnel** le tunnel sous la Manche

chaos NOUN
la **pagaille** FEM *(informal)*
It was chaos! C'était la pagaille!

chapel NOUN
la **chapelle** FEM

chapter NOUN
le **chapitre** MASC
in chapter two au chapitre deux

character NOUN
1 *(personality)* le **caractère** MASC
She's got character. Elle a du caractère.
2 *(somebody in a book, play, film)* le **personnage** MASC

characteristic ADJECTIVE
caractéristique MASC & FEM

charcoal NOUN
(for burning) le **charbon de bois**

ℰ **charge** NOUN ▸ SEE **charge** VERB
1 *(payment)* les **frais** MASC PL
to pay a booking charge payer [59] des frais de réservation
free of charge gratuit
There's no charge. C'est gratuit.
2 **to be in charge** être [6] responsable
Who's in charge? Qui est responsable?
I'm in charge of the money. Je suis responsable de l'argent.

ℰ **to charge** VERB ▸ SEE **charge** NOUN
1 *(to ask a specific sum)* **prendre** [64]
They charge twenty euros an hour. Ils prennent vingt euros de l'heure.
How much do you charge? Vous prenez combien?
2 *(to ask people to pay)* **faire** [10] **payer**
They don't charge, it's free. Ils ne font pas payer, c'est gratuit.
They charged me for the phone call. Il m'ont fait payer l'appel téléphonique.
3 **to charge somebody with something** inculper [1] quelqu'un de quelque chose
to be charged with murder être [6] inculpé de meurtre

⊙ means the verb takes être to form the perfect

charity *NOUN*
une **organisation caritative**

charm *NOUN*
le **charme** *MASC*

ℰ **charming** *ADJECTIVE*
charmant *MASC*, **charmante** *FEM*

chart *NOUN*
1 *(table)* le **tableau** *MASC*
Our names are on the chart. Nos noms sont dans le tableau.
2 *(for weather)* **the weather chart** la carte du temps
3 **the charts** le hit-parade *MASC*
number one in the charts numéro un au hit-parade

chase *NOUN* ▸ SEE **chase** *VERB*
a car chase une poursuite en voiture

to **chase** *VERB* ▸ SEE **chase** *NOUN*
(a person, an animal) pourchasser [1]
They chased us for a long time. Ils nous ont longtemps pourchassés.
• **to chase somebody away**
chasser [1] quelqu'un

ℰ **chat** *NOUN* ▸ SEE **chat** *VERB*
la **conversation** *FEM*
to have a chat with somebody bavarder [1] avec quelqu'un
I was having a chat with my friends. Je bavardais avec mes copains.
• **chatroom**
le chatroom
• **chat show**
le talk-show

to **chat** *VERB* ▸ SEE **chat** *NOUN*
1 **causer** [1]
2 *(online)* tchater [1]
• **to chat somebody up**
draguer [1] quelqu'un *(informal)*
He's trying to chat her up. Il essaie de la draguer.

to **chatter** *VERB*
1 *(to gossip)* bavarder [1]
2 *(with cold)* **My teeth are chattering.** Je claque des dents.

chatty *ADJECTIVE*
bavard *MASC*, **bavarde** *FEM*

ℰ **cheap** *ADJECTIVE*
1 *(low in price)* **pas cher** *MASC*, **pas chère** *FEM*
a cheap holiday des vacances pas chères
Wow! That's really cheap! Ça alors! Ce n'est vraiment pas cher!
2 *(shoddy)* de mauvaise qualité
It won't last. It's cheap. Ça ne va pas durer. C'est de la mauvaise qualité.

ℰ **cheaper** *ADJECTIVE*
moins cher *MASC*, **moins chère** *FEM*
This ring is cheaper than the others. Cette bague est moins chère que les autres.
It's cheaper to go by bus. Ça revient moins cher d'y aller en bus.

cheapest *ADJECTIVE*
le **moins cher** *MASC*, la **moins chère** *FEM*
the cheapest shoes les chaussures les moins chères

cheaply *ADVERB*
pas cher
You can eat cheaply there. On y mange pour pas cher.

cheap rate *ADJECTIVE*
(phone call) à tarif réduit

cheat *NOUN* ▸ SEE **cheat** *VERB*
le **tricheur** *MASC*, la **tricheuse** *FEM*

to **cheat** *VERB* ▸ SEE **cheat** *NOUN*
tricher [1]
to cheat in an exam tricher à un examen

ℰ **check** *NOUN* ▸ SEE **check** *VERB*
le **contrôle** *MASC*
a passport check un contrôle des passeports

ℰ to **check** *VERB* ▸ SEE **check** *NOUN*
(to make sure) **vérifier** [1]
He checked the time. Il a vérifié l'heure.
Check the spelling. Vérifie l'orthographe.
Check that they're all back. Vérifiez qu'ils sont tous rentrés.
to check with somebody demander [1] à quelqu'un
Check with your father. Demande à ton père.
• **to check in**
1 *(at the airport)* enregistrer [1]
2 *(at a hotel)* arriver ◐ [1] à l'hôtel
• **to check out**
(of a hotel) quitter [1] l'hôtel

ℰ **check-in** *NOUN*
l'**enregistrement** *MASC*

ℰ **checkout** *NOUN*
la **caisse** *FEM*

check-up *NOUN*
un **examen médical**

cheek *NOUN*
1 *(part of face)* la **joue** *FEM*
2 *(nerve)*
What a cheek! Quel culot! *(informal)*

cheeky *ADJECTIVE*
1 *(playful)* **coquin** *MASC*, **coquine** *FEM*
2 *(rude)* **impoli** *MASC*, **impolie** *FEM*

to cheer VERB
(to shout hurray) applaudir [2]
• to **cheer somebody on**
encourager [52] quelqu'un
• to **cheer up**
reprendre [64] courage
Cheer up! Courage!
That's to cheer you up. Ça c'est pour te remonter le moral.

cheerful ADJECTIVE
gai MASC, gaie FEM

cheers NOUN
1 *(when you have a drink)*
Cheers! À la vôtre!
2 *(when you say thanks)*
Cheers! Merci!

cheese NOUN
le fromage MASC
blue cheese le fromage bleu
a cheese sandwich un sandwich au fromage

chef NOUN
le chef cuisinier
She's a chef. Elle est chef cuisinier.

chemical NOUN ▶ SEE **chemical** ADJECTIVE
le produit chimique

chemical ADJECTIVE ▶ SEE **chemical** NOUN
chimique MASC & FEM

chemist NOUN
1 *(selling medicines)* le pharmacien MASC, la pharmacienne FEM
2 **a chemist's** une pharmacie
at the chemist's à la pharmacie
3 *(scientist)* le & la chimiste MASC & FEM

chemistry NOUN
la chimie FEM

cheque NOUN
le chèque MASC
to pay by cheque payer par chèque
to write a cheque faire un chèque
traveller's cheque le chèque de voyage
• **chequebook**
le carnet de chèques

cherry NOUN
la cerise FEM
• **cherry tree**
le cerisier

chess NOUN
les échecs MASC PL
to play chess jouer [1] aux échecs
• **chessboard**
un échiquier
• **chess set**
le jeu d'échecs

chest NOUN
1 *(part of the body)* la poitrine FEM
2 *(box)* le coffre MASC
• **chest of drawers**
la commode

chestnut NOUN
le marron MASC

to chew VERB
(food, gum) mâcher [1]

chewing gum NOUN
le chewing-gum MASC

chick NOUN
(of a hen) le poussin MASC

chicken NOUN
le poulet MASC
roast chicken du poulet rôti
a chicken sandwich un sandwich au poulet

chickenpox NOUN
la varicelle FEM

chief NOUN
le chef MASC
the chief of police le préfet de police

child NOUN
un & une enfant MASC & FEM
a two-year old child un enfant de deux ans
I'm an only child. Je suis enfant unique.

childish ADJECTIVE
puéril MASC, puérile FEM

childminder NOUN
la nourrice FEM

chill NOUN
1 *(in weather)* la fraîcheur FEM
2 *(illness)* le coup de froid

chilli NOUN
le piment MASC

to chill out VERB
décompresser [1] *(informal)*

chilly ADJECTIVE
froid MASC, froide FEM
to be chilly faire [10] froid

chimney NOUN
la cheminée FEM

chimpanzee NOUN
le chimpanzé MASC

chin NOUN
le menton MASC

china NOUN
la porcelaine FEM

China NOUN
la Chine FEM

means the verb takes être to form the perfect

to be in China être [6] en Chine
to go to China aller ◎ [7] en Chine

Chinese ADJECTIVE ▸SEE **Chinese** NOUN
chinois MASC, chinoise FEM

Chinese NOUN ▸SEE **Chinese** ADJECTIVE
1 (person) le Chinois MASC, la Chinoise FEM
the Chinese les Chinois
2 (language) le chinois MASC

ℓ**chip** NOUN
1 (fried potato) la frite FEM
steak and chips le steak frites
2 (microchip) la puce FEM

ℓ**chocolate** NOUN
le chocolat MASC
a bar of chocolate une tablette de chocolat
a box of chocolates une boîte de chocolats
a chocolate ice cream une glace au chocolat ▸SEE **hot chocolate**

ℓ**choice** NOUN
le choix MASC
a difficult choice un choix difficile
to have a choice avoir [5] le choix
You have a choice of two colours. Vous avez le choix entre deux couleurs.

choir NOUN
(in a school) la chorale FEM
to sing in a choir faire [10] partie d'une chorale

to **choke** VERB
1 (on food, drink) s'étouffer ◎ [1]
to choke on a bone s'étouffer avec une arête
2 (on smoke, fumes) étouffer [1]

ℓto **choose** VERB
choisir [2]
Alice chose the present. Alice a choisi le cadeau.
I can't choose between the red and the blue. Je n'arrive pas à choisir entre le rouge et le bleu.
It's hard to choose from all these colours. Il est difficile de choisir parmi toutes ces couleurs.
There isn't much to choose from. Il y a très peu de choix.

chop NOUN ▸SEE **chop** VERB
la côtelette FEM
a lamb chop une côtelette d'agneau

to **chop** VERB ▸SEE **chop** NOUN
(food) hacher [1]

chopstick NOUN
la baguette FEM

chord NOUN
un accord MASC

chorus NOUN
le refrain MASC

Christ NOUN
le Christ MASC

christening NOUN
le baptême MASC

Christian NOUN ▸SEE **Christian** ADJECTIVE
le chrétien MASC, la chrétienne FEM

WORD TIP Adjectives and nouns of religion start with a small letter in French.

Christian ADJECTIVE ▸SEE **Christian** NOUN
chrétien MASC, chrétienne FEM
• **Christian name**
le prénom ▸SEE **first name**

ℓ**Christmas** NOUN
Noël MASC
at Christmas à Noël
Happy Christmas! Joyeux Noël!
What did you get for Christmas? Qu'est-ce que tu as eu à Noël?
We go to their house for Christmas. Nous allons chez eux pour Noël.
• **Christmas card**
la carte de Noël
• **Christmas carol**
le chant de Noël
• **Christmas cracker**
le diablotin
• **Christmas Day**
le jour de Noël
• **Christmas dinner**
le repas de Noël
• **Christmas Eve**
la veille de Noël
• **Christmas present**
le cadeau de Noël
• **Christmas tree**
le sapin de Noël

chunk NOUN
(of wood, bread) le morceau MASC

ℓ**church** NOUN
une église FEM
to go to church aller ◎ [7] à l'église
• **churchyard**
le cimetière

chute NOUN
(in a pool, playground) le toboggan MASC

ℓ**cider** NOUN
le cidre MASC

cigar NOUN
le cigare MASC

ℓ**cigarette** NOUN
la cigarette FEM

ℓ indicates key words

- **cigarette stub**
  le mégot

ρ **cinema** *NOUN*
le cinéma *MASC*
Let's go to the cinema. Allons au cinéma.
What's on at the cinema? Qu'est-ce qu'on
joue au cinéma?

ρ **circle** *NOUN*
le cercle *MASC*
I drew a circle. J'ai dessiné un cercle.
to sit in a circle s'asseoir ⊙ [20] en cercle
to go round in circles tourner [1] en rond

circuit *NOUN*
1 *(for athletes)* la **piste** *FEM*
2 *(for cars)* le **circuit** *MASC*

circumference *NOUN*
(Grammar) la **circonférence** *FEM*

circumflex *NOUN*
un **accent circonflexe**

circumstances *PLURAL NOUN*
les **circonstances** *FEM PL*

ρ **circus** *NOUN*
le cirque *MASC*
to go to the circus aller ⊙ [7] au cirque
- **circus act**
  le numéro de cirque

city *NOUN*
la **(grande) ville** *FEM*
the city of Paris la ville de Paris
- **city centre**
  le centre-ville *MASC*

civilian *NOUN*
le **civil** *MASC*, la **civile** *FEM*

civilization *NOUN*
la **civilisation** *FEM*

civil servant *NOUN*
le & la **fonctionnaire** *MASC & FEM*
She's a civil servant. Elle est fonctionnaire.

civil service *NOUN*
la **fonction publique**

civil war *NOUN*
la **guerre civile**

to **claim** *VERB*
to claim that ... prétendre [3] que ...
She claims that I'm telling lies. Elle prétend
que je dis des mensonges.

to **clap** *VERB*
1 *(at a performance)* applaudir [2]
Everyone clapped. Tout le monde a
applaudi.
2 **to clap your hands** battre [21] des mains

clapping *NOUN*
les **applaudissements** *MASC PL*

clarinet *NOUN*
la **clarinette** *FEM*
to play the clarinet jouer [1] de la clarinette

to **clash** *VERB*
1 *(rivals)* s'affronter ⊙ [1]
Fans clashed outside the stadium. Les
supporters se sont affrontés devant le
stade.
to clash with somebody se heurter ⊙ [1] à
quelqu'un
They clashed with the police. Ils se sont
heurtés à la police.
2 *(colours)* jurer [1]
The skirt and shirt clash. La jupe jure avec
la chemise.

ρ **class** *NOUN*
1 *(of students, pupils)* la **classe** *FEM*
She's in the same class as me. Elle est dans
la même classe que moi.
There are fifteen boys in my class. Il y a
quinze garçons dans ma classe.
2 *(lesson)* le **cours** *MASC*
an art class un cours de dessin
I was chatting in class. Je bavardais en
cours.

classic *ADJECTIVE*
classique *MASC & FEM*

classical *ADJECTIVE*
classique *MASC & FEM*
- **classical music**
  la musique classique

classmate *NOUN*
le & la **camarade de classe** *MASC & FEM*

ρ **classroom** *NOUN*
la **salle de classe** *FEM*

claw *NOUN*
1 *(of a cat, dog)* la **griffe** *FEM*
2 *(of a crab)* la **pince** *FEM*

clay *NOUN*
(for modelling) l'**argile** *FEM*

ρ **clean** *ADJECTIVE* ▶ SEE **clean** *VERB*
1 *(not dirty)* **propre** *MASC & FEM*
My hands are clean. J'ai les mains propres.
Your room isn't clean. Ta chambre n'est
pas propre.
to keep something clean ne pas salir [2]
quelque chose
Keep your trainers clean. Ne salis pas tes
baskets.
2 *(not polluted)* **pur** *MASC*, **pure** *FEM*

ρ to **clean** *VERB* ▶ SEE **clean** *ADJECTIVE*
nettoyer [39]

⊙ means the verb takes être to form the perfect

She's cleaning her room. Elle est en train de nettoyer sa chambre.
I cleaned the car. J'ai nettoyé la voiture.
to clean your teeth se laver ⊘ [1] les dents

cleaner NOUN
1 *(cleaning lady)* la **femme de ménage**
2 *(of public places)* l'**agent de nettoyage** MASC
3 ▸ SEE **dry cleaner**

ℰ **cleaning** NOUN
to do the cleaning faire [10] le ménage

cleanser NOUN
(for the face) le **démaquillant** MASC

ℰ **clear** ADJECTIVE ▸ SEE **clear** VERB
1 *(that you can see through)* **transparent** MASC, **transparente** FEM
2 *(cloudless)* **clair** MASC, **claire** FEM
The sky was clear. Le ciel était clair.
3 *(easy to understand)* **clair** MASC, **claire** FEM
a clear example un exemple clair
Is that clear? Est-ce que c'est clair?
It wasn't very clear. Ce n'était pas très clair.
It's clear he's lying. Il est clair qu'il ment.

ℰ to **clear** VERB ▸ SEE **clear** ADJECTIVE
1 *(papers, rubbish, clothes)* **to clear something out of something** enlever [50] quelque chose
I cleared my stuff out of the room. J'ai enlevé mes affaires de la chambre.
2 *(a table, a room)* **débarrasser** [1]
Can I clear the table? Puis-je débarrasser la table?
3 *(a road, path)* **dégager** [52]
4 *(fog, snow)* se **dissiper** ⊘ [1]
(your throat) **to clear your throat** se racler ⊘ [1] la gorge
• **to clear something out**
(a cupboard, a room) **vider** [1] quelque chose

clearly ADVERB
(to think, speak, hear) **clairement**

clementine NOUN
la **clémentine** FEM

ℰ **clever** ADJECTIVE
1 **intelligent** MASC, **intelligente** FEM
clever children des enfants intelligents
2 *(ingenious)* **astucieux** MASC, **astucieuse** FEM
a clever idea une idée astucieuse

click NOUN ▸ SEE **click** VERB
1 *(noise)* le **petit bruit sec**
I heard a click. J'ai entendu un petit bruit sec.
2 *(with mouse)* le **clic** MASC
a double-click un double-clic

to **click** VERB ▸ SEE **click** NOUN
1 *(using a mouse)* **cliquer** [1]

Click on the icon. Cliquer sur l'icône.
2 *(with a person)* **sympathiser** [1] *(informal)*

cliff NOUN
la **falaise** FEM

ℰ **climate** NOUN
le **climat** MASC
a mild climate un climat doux
• **climate change**
le changement climatique

to **climb** VERB
1 *(a hill, stairs)* **monter** [1]
I climbed the stairs in the dark. J'ai monté l'escalier dans le noir.
2 *(a mountain)* **faire l'escalade de**
They climbed Mont Blanc. Ils ont fait l'escalade du Mont Blanc.

climber NOUN
un & une **alpiniste** MASC & FEM

ℰ **climbing** NOUN
l'**escalade** FEM
to go climbing faire [10] de l'escalade

clinic NOUN
le **centre médical** *(PL les **centres médicaux**)*

clip NOUN ▸ SEE **clip** VERB
1 *(from a film)* un **extrait** MASC
a clip from the film un extrait du film
2 *(for your hair)* la **barrette** FEM

to **clip** VERB ▸ SEE **clip** NOUN
(a hedge) **couper** [1]

cloakroom NOUN
le **vestiaire** MASC

ℰ **clock** NOUN
1 *(large)* une **horloge** FEM
the town hall clock l'horloge de la mairie
2 *(smaller)* la **pendule** FEM
to put the clocks back reculer [1] les pendules
to put the clocks forward an hour avancer [61] les pendules d'une heure
3 ▸ SEE **alarm clock, o'clock**
• **clock radio**
le **radio-réveil**
• **clockwise**
(to turn) dans le sens des aiguilles d'une montre

ℰ **close** ADVERB, ADJECTIVE ▸ SEE **close** NOUN, VERB
1 *(near)* **près**
not very close pas tout près
The school's very close. L'école est tout près.
She lives close by. Elle habite tout près.
to be close to something être [6] près de quelque chose

ENGLISH—FRENCH

The shop's close to the cinema. Le magasin est près du cinéma.
2 *(friend, relation)* **proche** MASC & FEM
They're very close. Ils sont très proches l'un de l'autre.
I'm close to my Dad. Je suis proche de mon père.
3 *(result, match)* **serré** MASC, **serrée** FEM
It was a close match. C'était un match serré.

P to **close** VERB ▸ SEE **close** ADJECTIVE, ADVERB
(by itself) **se fermer** ⊙ [1]
The door closed. La porte s'est fermée.
• to close down
fermer [1]
The school's closing down. L'école ferme.
They closed the club down. Ils ont fermé le club.

P **closed** ADJECTIVE
fermé MASC, **fermée** FEM
Too late, it's closed! Trop tard, c'est fermé!

closely ADVERB
(to examine, look at) **de près**

closing date NOUN
la **date limite**

closing-down sale NOUN
la **liquidation** FEM

P **closing time** NOUN
l'**heure de fermeture**

cloth NOUN
1 *(for the floor)* la **serpillière** FEM
2 *(for polishing)* le **chiffon** MASC
3 *(for sewing, dressmaking)* le **tissu** MASC

P **clothes** PLURAL NOUN
les **vêtements** MASC PL
some great clothes des vêtements super
to put your clothes on **s'habiller** ⊙ [1]
I put my clothes on. Je me suis habillé *(boy speaking)*, Je me suis habillée *(girl speaking)*.
to take your clothes off **se déshabiller** ⊙ [1]
to change your clothes **se changer** ⊙ [52]
I had to change my clothes. J'ai dû me changer.
• clothes line
la corde à linge
• clothes peg
la pince à linge

clothing NOUN
les **vêtements** MASC PL

cloud NOUN
le **nuage** MASC

P **cloudy** ADJECTIVE
nuageux MASC, **nuageuse** FEM
to become cloudy **se couvrir** ⊙ [30]

The weather was cloudy. Le temps était couvert.

clove NOUN
1 *(spice)* le **clou de girofle**
2 a clove of garlic une **gousse d'ail**

clown NOUN
le **clown** MASC

P **club** NOUN
1 *(association)* le **club** MASC
to be in a club **faire** [10] partie d'un club
2 *(in cards)* le **trèfle** MASC
the four of clubs le quatre de trèfle
3 *(in golf)* le **club** MASC

clue NOUN
1 *(in problems)* un **indice** MASC
Look for clues. Cherchez des indices.
Give me a clue. Aide-moi.
(understanding) I haven't a clue. Je n'en ai pas la moindre idée.
2 *(in a crossword)* la **définition** FEM
to work out a clue **comprendre** [64] une définition

clumsy ADJECTIVE
maladroit MASC, **maladroite** FEM

to **clutch** VERB
tenir [77] fermement

P **coach** NOUN
1 *(bus)* le **car** MASC
on the coach dans le car
We travelled to Metz by coach. Nous sommes allés à Metz en car.
to go on a coach trip **faire** [10] une excursion en car
Our class is going on a coach trip. Notre classe va faire une excursion en car.
2 *(in sports)* un **entraîneur** MASC, une **entraîneuse** FEM
3 *(railway carriage)* le **wagon** MASC
• coach station
la gare routière

coal NOUN
le **charbon** MASC
• coal mine
la mine de charbon
• coal miner
le mineur

coast NOUN
la **côte** FEM
We went to the coast. Nous sommes allés sur la côte.

P **coat** NOUN
1 *(clothing)* le **manteau** MASC (PL les **manteaux**)
2 *(layer)* la **couche** FEM

⊙ means the verb takes être to form the perfect

a coat of red paint une couche de peinture rouge
- **coat hanger**
le cintre

cobweb NOUN
la **toile d'araignée**

cock, **cockerel** NOUN
le **coq** MASC

cocoa NOUN
1 *(drink)* le **chocolat (chaud)**
2 *(powder)* le **cacao** MASC

coconut NOUN
la **noix de coco**

cod NOUN
le **cabillaud** MASC

code NOUN
1 *(set of rules)* le **code** MASC
the highway code le code de la route
2 *(in phone number)* un **indicatif** MASC
the code for Bristol l'indicatif pour Bristol

ℓ **coffee** NOUN
le **café** MASC
a cup of coffee un café
a black coffee un café
a white coffee un café au lait
- **coffee break**
la **pause-café**
- **coffee machine**
la **cafetière électrique**

coffin NOUN
le **cercueil** MASC

ℓ **coin** NOUN
la **pièce de monnaie**
a pound coin une pièce d'une livre
a two-euro coin une pièce de deux euros

coincidence NOUN
la **coïncidence** FEM

Coke® NOUN
le **coca** MASC
Two Cokes®, please. Deux cocas, s'il vous plaît.

ℓ **cold** ADJECTIVE ▶ SEE **cold** NOUN
1 *(weather, places)*
to be cold faire [10] froid
It's cold today. Il fait froid aujourd'hui.
It was very cold outside. Il faisait très froid dehors.
2 *(the feeling)*
to be cold avoir [5] froid
I'm cold. J'ai froid.
I'm very cold. J'ai très froid.
I was too cold. J'avais trop froid.
Your hands are cold. Tu as les mains

froides.

ℓ **cold** NOUN ▶ SEE **cold** ADJECTIVE
1 *(cold weather)* le **froid** MASC
out in the cold dehors dans le froid
2 *(illness)* le **rhume** MASC
to have a cold être [6] enrhumé
to get a cold s'enrhumer [1]
I got a cold. Je me suis enrhumé *(boy speaking)*, Je me suis enrhumée *(girl speaking)*.
- **cold sore**
le **bouton de fièvre**

to collapse VERB
1 *(walls, rooves)* s'**écrouler** ◎ [1]
2 *(buildings)* s'**effondrer** ◎ [1]

collar NOUN
1 *(on a shirt)* le **col** MASC
2 *(for a dog)* le **collier** MASC
- **collarbone**
la **clavicule** FEM

colleague NOUN
le & la **collègue** MASC & FEM

ℓ **to collect** VERB
1 *(as a hobby)* **collectionner** [1]
She collects phone cards. Elle collectionne les télécartes.
2 *(a person)* **aller** ◎ [7] **chercher**
He collects the children from school. Il va chercher les enfants à l'école.
I'll come and collect you. Je vais venir te chercher.
3 *(a thing)* **passer** ◎ [1] **prendre**
I'll collect my jacket later. Je passerai prendre ma veste plus tard.
4 *(fares, money)* **encaisser** [1]
5 *(to gather up)* **ramasser** [1]
Who collected the exercise books? Qui a ramassé les cahiers?

collection NOUN
1 *(of stamps, jewellery, posters)* la **collection** FEM
2 *(of money)* la **collecte** FEM
We'll organize a collection. Nous ferons une collecte.

college NOUN
1 *(school)* le **collège** MASC
2 *(for higher education)* un **établissement d'études supérieures**
to go to college faire [10] des études supérieures

collision NOUN
la **collision** FEM

to colour VERB ▶ SEE **colour** NOUN
1 *(with paints, crayons)* **colorier** [1]
I've coloured the sky pink. J'ai colorié le

ℓ **indicates key words**

ciel en rose.
2 **to get your hair coloured** se faire ⊙ [10]
faire une couleur

ℐ **colour** NOUN ▸ SEE **colour** VERB
la **couleur** FEM
What colour is it? C'est de quelle couleur?
What colour is your bag? De quelle couleur
est ton sac?
What colour are her eyes? Elle a les yeux
de quelle couleur?
Do you have it in a different colour? Est-ce
que vous l'avez dans une autre couleur?

• **colour blind** ADJECTIVE
daltonien MASC, daltonienne FEM
• **colour film**
la pellicule couleur (PL les pellicules
couleur)

colourful ADJECTIVE
(picture, display) aux couleurs vives

colouring book NOUN
un album à colorier

column NOUN
la colonne FEM

ℐ **comb** NOUN ▸ SEE **comb** VERB
le peigne MASC

ℐ to **comb** VERB ▸ SEE **comb** NOUN
to comb your hair se peigner ⊙ [1]

combination NOUN
la combinaison FEM

to **combine** VERB
1 (two or more things) combiner [1]
2 (colours, tastes) se combiner ⊙ [1]

ℐ to **come** VERB
1 (to a place) venir ⊙ [81]
Come quick! Viens vite!
Come and see! Venez voir!
Did Jess come to school? Est-ce que Jess est
venue à l'école?
Do you want to come to my house? Tu
veux venir chez moi?
She came on holiday with us. Elle est
venue en vacances avec nous.
Peter comes from Scotland. Peter vient
d'Écosse.
2 (to arrive) arriver ⊙ [1]
Coming! J'arrive!
The bus is coming. Le bus arrive.
as soon as the train comes dès que le train
arrive
3 (to collect) **to come for somebody** passer ⊙
[1] prendre quelqu'un
My father's coming for me. Mon père
passe me prendre.
4 **Come on!** Allez!
Come on, hurry up! Allez, dépêche-toi!

• **to come apart**
1 (drawers, boxes, machines) se casser ⊙ [1]
2 (books, seams) se déchirer ⊙ [1]
• **to come back**
revenir ⊙ [81]
Come back! Reviens!
to come back home rentrer ⊙ [1]
• **to come down**
descendre ⊙ [3]
Come down right now! Descends tout de
suite!
• **to come down something**
(a street, a hill, the stairs) descendre ⊙ [3]
quelque chose
Max is coming down the stairs. Max
descend l'escalier.
• **to come in**
1 entrer ⊙ [1]
Come in! Entrez!
He came in through the window. Il est
entré par la fenêtre.
2 **The tide is coming in.** La marée monte.
• **to come off**
1 (buttons, handle) se détacher ⊙ [1]
2 (stains, dirt) partir ⊙ [58]
• **to come out**
1 sortir ⊙ [72]
Are you coming out with us? Est-ce que tu
sors avec nous?
2 (book, film, game) sortir ⊙ [72]
3 (sun, moon) se montrer ⊙ [1]
• **to come round**
passer ⊙ [1]
I'll come round later. Je passerai plus tard.
• **to come up**
monter ⊙ [1]
Can you come up a moment? Peux-tu
monter un instant?
• **to come up something**
(a street, a hill, the stairs) monter [1]
quelque chose
They came up the stairs. Ils ont monté
l'escalier.

comedian NOUN
le comique MASC, l'actrice comique FEM

comedy NOUN
la comédie FEM

ℐ **comfortable** ADJECTIVE
1 (chair, bed) confortable MASC & FEM
This bed's comfortable. Ce lit est
confortable.
I'm quite comfortable here. Je suis bien là.
2 (at ease) à l'aise
I'm not too comfortable. Je ne suis pas très
à l'aise.

comfortably ADVERB
confortablement

⊙ means the verb takes être to form the perfect

ꝑ**comic** NOUN
 (*magazine*) une **bande dessinée** FEM
• **comic strip**
 la bande dessinée

command NOUN
 un **ordre** MASC

comment NOUN
 (*in a conversation*) la **remarque** FEM
 He made a rude comment about you. Il a
 fait une remarque impolie sur toi.

commentary NOUN
 le **reportage en direct**
 the match commentary le reportage du
 match

commentator NOUN
 le **commentateur** MASC, la **commentatrice**
 FEM
 a sports commentator un commentateur
 sportif

commercial ADJECTIVE ▶ SEE **commercial** NOUN
 commercial MASC, **commerciale** FEM,
 commerciaux MASC PL, **commerciales** FEM PL

commercial NOUN ▶ SEE **commercial** ADJECTIVE
 le **spot publicitaire**

to **commit** VERB
 to commit a crime commettre [11] un
 crime

committee NOUN
 le **comité** MASC

common ADJECTIVE
1 (*happening a lot*) **courant** MASC, **courante**
 FEM
 a common problem un problème courant
 It's not very common. Ce n'est pas très
 courant.
2 (*interests, activities*) **in common** en
 commun
 We don't have a lot in common. On n'a pas
 grand-chose en commun.
• **common sense**
 le bon sens

to **communicate** VERB
 communiquer [1]

communication NOUN
1 (*being in contact*) la **communication** FEM
2 (*telephone, fax etc*)
 communications les communications FEM PL

communion NOUN
 la **communion** FEM

communism NOUN
 le **communisme** MASC

community NOUN
 la **communauté** FEM

 to be part of the community faire [10]
 partie de la communauté

to **commute** VERB
 to commute between Oxford and London
 faire [10] le trajet entre Oxford et Londres
 tous les jours

commuter NOUN
 le **banlieusard** MASC, la **banlieusarde** FEM

compact disc NOUN
 le **disque compact**
• **compact disc player**
 la platine laser

company NOUN
1 (*business*) la **société** FEM
 an insurance company une société
 d'assurances
2 (*group*) la **compagnie** FEM
 a theatre company une compagnie
 théâtrale
3 **to keep somebody company** tenir [77]
 compagnie à quelqu'un
 I'll keep you company. Je vais te tenir
 compagnie.

ꝑto **compare** VERB
 comparer [1]
 to compare the French with the English
 comparer les Français aux Anglais
 I compared my photo with hers. J'ai
 comparé ma photo à la sienne.
 compared with something par rapport à
 quelque chose
 Our house is small compared with yours.
 Notre maison est petite par rapport à la
 tienne.

comparison NOUN
 la **comparaison** FEM
 in comparison with England par rapport à
 l'Angleterre

ꝑ**compartment** NOUN
 le **compartiment** MASC

compass NOUN
 la **boussole** FEM

compatible ADJECTIVE
 (*printer, scanner, webcam*) compatible MASC
 & FEM

to **compete** VERB
 to compete in something participer [1] à
 quelque chose
 I competed in the relay race. J'ai participé à
 la course de relais.
 to compete for first prize se disputer ◎ [1]
 le premier prix

competition NOUN
1 (*event*) le **concours** MASC

ꝑ indicates key words

to take part in a competition participer [1] à un concours

2 *(the drive to win)* la **concurrence** FEM
• **There's a lot of competition.** Il y a beaucoup de concurrence.

competitor NOUN
le **concurrent** MASC, la **concurrente** FEM

to **complain** VERB
se **plaindre** ⊘ [31]
• **He's always complaining!** Il se plaint sans arrêt!
• **to complain about something** se plaindre de quelque chose

complaint NOUN
la **plainte** FEM
• **to make a complaint** se plaindre ⊘ [31]

ℓ **complete** ADJECTIVE ▸ SEE **complete** VERB
1 *(entire, full)* **complet** MASC, **complète** FEM
• **the complete collection** la collection complète
2 *(total, utter)* **total** MASC, **totale** FEM
• **a complete disaster** un désastre total
• **a complete nightmare** un vrai cauchemar

ℓ to **complete** VERB ▸ SEE **complete** ADJECTIVE
(to finish) **compléter** [24]
• **Complete the sentence.** Complétez la phrase.

ℓ **completely** ADVERB
complètement

complexion NOUN
le **teint** MASC
• **to have a pale complexion** avoir [5] le teint pâle

complicated ADJECTIVE
compliqué MASC, **compliquée** FEM
• **to get complicated** se compliquer ⊘ [1]

compliment NOUN
le **compliment** MASC
• **to pay somebody a compliment** faire [10] un compliment à quelqu'un

to **compose** VERB
(music, score) **composer** [1]

composer NOUN
le **compositeur** MASC, la **compositrice** FEM

comprehension NOUN
la **compréhension** FEM
• **a comprehension test** un test de compréhension

compromise NOUN
le **compromis** MASC

ℓ **compulsory** ADJECTIVE
obligatoire MASC & FEM

ℓ **computer** NOUN
un **ordinateur** MASC
• **to work on computer** travailler sur ordinateur
• **He's got his homework on computer.** Il a des devoirs sur ordinateur.
• **The computers are down.** Les ordinateurs sont en panne.
• **computer engineer**
le **technicien en informatique**, la **technicienne en informatique**
• **computer game**
le **jeu électronique** *(PL les **jeux électroniques**)*
• **computer programmer**
le **programmeur**, la **programmeuse**
• **computer science**
l'**informatique** FEM

computing NOUN
l'**informatique** FEM

conceited ADJECTIVE
vaniteux MASC, **vaniteuse** FEM

to **concentrate** VERB
se **concentrer** ⊘ [1]
• **I can't concentrate.** Je n'arrive pas à me concentrer.
• **I was concentrating on the film.** Je me concentrais sur le film.

concentration NOUN
la **concentration** FEM

concern NOUN ▸ SEE **concern** VERB
(worry) une **inquiétude** FEM
• **It's causing concern.** C'est inquiétant.

to **concern** VERB ▸ SEE **concern** NOUN
1 *(to affect)* **concerner** [1]
• **The environment concerns us all.** L'environnement nous concerne tous.
2 *(showing your opinion)*
• **as far as I'm concerned, ...** en ce qui me concerne, ...

concerned ADJECTIVE
inquiet MASC, **inquiète** FEM
• **We're very concerned.** Nous sommes très inquiets.

ℓ **concert** NOUN
le **concert** MASC
• **to go to a concert** aller ⊘ [7] à un concert
• **I got tickets for the concert.** J'ai acheté des billets pour le concert.
• **concert hall**
la **salle de concert**

conclusion NOUN
la **conclusion** FEM

concrete NOUN
le **béton** MASC

⊘ **means the verb takes être to form the perfect**

a concrete floor un sol en béton

to **condemn** VERB
condamner [1]

ℱ **condition** NOUN
1 (state) la **condition** FEM
in good condition en bonne condition
The bike was in good condition. Le vélo était en bonne condition.
in bad condition en mauvaise condition
The tyres are in bad condition. Les pneus sont en mauvaise condition.
2 (state of the weather) **weather conditions** les conditions météorologiques
3 (when you make a deal) la **condition** FEM
Ok, but on one condition - you tidy up. D'accord, mais à une condition: c'est toi qui ranges.
on condition that ... à condition que ...
I'll go on condition that you come too. J'irai à condition que tu viennes aussi.

conditional NOUN
le conditionnel MASC

conditioner NOUN
un après-shampooing MASC

condom NOUN
le préservatif MASC

conduct NOUN ▶ SEE **conduct** VERB
la conduite FEM
good conduct la bonne conduite

to **conduct** VERB ▶ SEE **conduct** NOUN
(an orchestra, a choir) diriger [52]

conductor NOUN
(of an orchestra) le chef d'orchestre

cone NOUN
1 (for ice cream) le cornet MASC
2 (for traffic) la balise FEM

confectionery NOUN
la confiserie FEM

conference NOUN
la conférence FEM

to **confess** VERB
avouer [1]

confession NOUN
la confession FEM

confidence NOUN
1 (faith in somebody else) la confiance FEM
I don't have confidence in them. Je n'ai pas confiance en eux.
2 (self-confidence) l'assurance FEM
to be lacking in confidence manquer [1] d'assurance
to have lots of confidence être [6] très assuré

Emma has lots of confidence. Emma est très assurée.

ℱ **confident** ADJECTIVE
1 (sure of yourself) assuré MASC, assurée FEM
2 (optimistic) sûr MASC, sûre FEM
They're confident that we'll win. Ils sont sûrs que nous allons gagner.

to **confirm** VERB
(a date, a time) confirmer [1]

ℱ to **confuse** VERB
1 (to mix up) confondre [69]
It's easy to confuse the two words. Il est facile de confondre les deux mots.
I always confuse him with his brother. Je le confonds toujours avec son frère.
2 (to bother, upset) troubler [1]
The whole thing confuses me. Tout ça me trouble.

ℱ **confused** ADJECTIVE
confus MASC, confuse FEM
a confused story une histoire confuse
I'm completely confused! Là je n'y comprends plus rien!

confusing ADJECTIVE
pas clair MASC, pas claire FEM
The message is confusing. Le message n'est pas clair.

confusion NOUN
la confusion FEM

to **congratulate** VERB
féliciter [1]
I congratulated her on winning. Je l'ai félicitée d'avoir gagné.

ℱ **congratulations** PLURAL NOUN
les félicitations FEM PL
Congratulations! Félicitations!

conjurer NOUN
le prestidigitateur MASC, la prestidigitatrice FEM

to **connect** VERB
1 (a computer, printer, TV) brancher [1]
2 (Internet) connecter [1]
We're not connected yet. Nous ne sommes pas encore connectés.
3 (the parts, wires, etc) raccorder [1]

connection NOUN
1 (between two ideas, events) le rapport MASC
I don't see the connection. Je ne vois pas le rapport.
2 (between trains or planes) la correspondance FEM
We'll miss our connection. Nous allons rater notre correspondance.
3 (electrical) le contact MASC

439

a faulty connection un mauvais contact

conscience NOUN
la **conscience** FEM
to have a guilty conscience avoir [5] mauvaise conscience

conscious ADJECTIVE
conscient MASC, **consciente** FEM

consequence NOUN
la **conséquence** FEM
as a consequence par conséquent

conservation NOUN
(of nature, environment) la **protection** FEM

conservative ADJECTIVE
conservateur MASC, **conservatrice** FEM

Conservative NOUN
le **conservateur** MASC
the Conservative Party le parti conservateur

conservatory NOUN
la **véranda** FEM

to **consider** VERB
to consider doing something envisager [52] de faire quelque chose
I'm considering changing schools. J'envisage de changer d'école.

considerable ADJECTIVE
considérable MASC & FEM

considerate ADJECTIVE
gentil MASC, **gentille** FEM

consideration NOUN
la **considération** FEM
You must take holidays into consideration. Il faut prendre les vacances en considération.

considering PREPOSITION
étant donné
Considering that Tom did it all himself, it's great. Étant donné que Tom a tout fait lui-même, c'est génial.

to **consist** VERB
to consist of être [6] composé de
This dish consists of vegetables and rice. Ce plat est composé de légumes et de riz.

consonant NOUN
la **consonne** FEM

constant ADJECTIVE
permanent MASC, **permanente** FEM

constipated ADJECTIVE
constipé MASC, **constipée** FEM

to **construct** VERB
construire [26]

consulate NOUN
le **consulat** MASC

to **consult** VERB
consulter [1]
The students were consulted. On a consulté les étudiants.

consumer NOUN
le **consommateur** MASC, la **consommatrice** FEM

consumption NOUN
la **consommation** FEM

contact NOUN ▸SEE **contact** VERB
1 (communication) le **contact** MASC
We've lost contact. Nous avons perdu contact.
to be in contact with somebody être [6] en contact avec quelqu'un
Are you still in contact with Marie? Est-ce que tu es toujours en contact avec Marie?
2 (person you know) la **connaissance** FEM

to **contact** VERB ▸SEE **contact** NOUN
contacter [1]
I'll contact you tomorrow. Je te contacterai demain.

contact lens NOUN
la **lentille de contact** (PL les **lentilles de contact**)
to wear contact lenses porter [1] des lentilles de contact

to **contain** VERB
contenir [77]
It contains salt. Ça contient du sel.

container NOUN
(for food, for small objects) le **récipient** MASC

to **contaminate** VERB
contaminer [1]
The water has been contaminated. L'eau a été contaminée.

contents PLURAL NOUN
(of a suitcase, bag, box) le **contenu** MASC

contest NOUN
le **concours** MASC

contestant NOUN
le **concurrent** MASC, la **concurrente** FEM

continent NOUN
le **continent** MASC
on the Continent en Europe continentale

continental ADJECTIVE
a continental holiday des vacances en Europe continentale

⏳to **continue** VERB
continuer [1]
We continued our journey. Nous avons

⏳ means the verb takes être to form the perfect

continué notre voyage.
to continue doing something continuer de
faire quelque chose
Mark continued chatting. Mark a continué
de bavarder.

continuous ADJECTIVE
continu MASC, **continue** FEM
• **continuous assessment**
le contrôle continu

contraception NOUN
la contraception FEM

contraceptive NOUN
le contraceptif MASC

contract NOUN
le contrat MASC

to **contradict** VERB
contredire [47]

contradiction NOUN
la contradiction FEM

contrary NOUN
on the contrary au contraire
On the contrary, she's funny. Au contraire,
elle est marrante.

contrast NOUN
le contraste MASC

to **contribute** VERB
1 (money) donner [1]
2 (in class, in discussion) participer [1]

contribution NOUN
(to charity, for a good cause) le don MASC
to make a contribution faire [10] un don

control NOUN ▶ SEE **control** VERB
(of a crowd) le contrôle MASC
Max lost control of his motorbike. Max a
perdu le contrôle de sa moto.
Everything's under control. Tout va bien.
The fire was out of control. On ne
maîtrisait plus l'incendie.

to **control** VERB ▶ SEE **control** NOUN
1 (a crowd, animals, a fire) maîtriser [1]
They can't control the fans. Ils ne
maîtrisent plus les supporters.
2 (yourself) **to control yourself** se contrôler
⊜ [1]
I couldn't control myself. Je n'arrivais plus à
me contrôler.

controversial ADJECTIVE
(decision, choice) discutable MASC & FEM

ℓ **convenient** ADJECTIVE
1 (appliance) pratique MASC & FEM
The microwave is very convenient. Le
micro-ondes est très pratique.
2 (plan) **to be convenient for somebody**

convenir [81] à quelqu'un
It's not convenient for me. Ça ne me
convient pas.
If it's more convenient for you, ... Si ça
vous convient mieux, ...
3 (place) bien situé MASC, bien située FEM
It's convenient for the shops. C'est bien
situé par rapport aux magasins.

convent NOUN
le couvent MASC

conventional ADJECTIVE
(person) conformiste MASC & FEM

conversation NOUN
la conversation FEM
a conversation in French une conversation
en français

to **convert** VERB
transformer [1]
to convert a garage into a games room
transformer un garage en salle de jeux

to **convince** VERB
convaincre [79]
I couldn't convince them. Je n'ai pas pu les
convaincre.
I'm convinced that Jack's wrong. Je suis
convaincu que Jack a tort.

convincing ADJECTIVE
convaincant MASC, **convaincante** FEM

ℓ **cook** NOUN ▶ SEE **cook** VERB
le cuisinier MASC, la cuisinière FEM
She's a cook. Elle est cuisinière.

ℓ to **cook** VERB ▶ SEE **cook** NOUN
1 (to prepare food) faire [10] la cuisine
I like cooking. J'aime faire la cuisine.
Dad never cooks. Papa ne fait jamais la
cuisine.
2 (vegetables, pasta) faire [10] cuire
Cook the carrots for five minutes. Faire
cuire les carottes pendant cinq minutes.
3 (a meal) préparer [1]
Zoë's cooking supper. Zoë est en train de
préparer le dîner.
4 (food) cuire [36]
It's cooked. C'est cuit.
The stew's cooking. Le ragoût est en train
de cuire.

ℓ **cooker** NOUN
la cuisinière FEM

cookery NOUN
la cuisine FEM
• **cookery book**
le livre de cuisine

ℓ **cooking** NOUN
la cuisine FEM

ℓ indicates key words

French cooking la cuisine française
to do the cooking faire [10] la cuisine

ρ **cool** ADJECTIVE ▸ SEE **cool** NOUN, VERB
1 *(food, drink)* frais MASC, fraîche FEM
  a cool drink une boisson fraîche
  to keep something cool tenir [77] quelque
  chose au frais
2 *(the weather, a place)* **to be cool** faire [10]
  frais
  It's cool at night. Il fait frais la nuit.
3 *(laid-back)* décontracté MASC,
  décontractée FEM
4 *(sophisticated)* branché MASC, branchée FEM
  It looks cool. Ça fait branché.
  She's so cool! Elle est vraiment branchée!
5 *(great)* super MASC & FEM
  a cool bike un vélo super
  Cool! Super!
  That's cool! C'est cool!
  Your parents are cool. Tes parents sont
  cool.

to **cool** VERB ▸ SEE **cool** ADJ, NOUN
  (a liquid) refroidir [2]
• **to cool down**
  (food, hot drinks) se refroidir ◉ [2]
  It's cooling down. Ça se refroidit.

ρ **cool** NOUN ▸ SEE **cool** ADJ, VERB
1 *(coldness)* la fraîcheur FEM
  Stay in the cool. Reste au frais.
2 *(calm)* le sang-froid MASC
  I lost my cool. J'ai perdu mon sang-froid.
  She always keeps her cool. Elle garde
  toujours son sang-froid.

to **cooperate** VERB
  coopérer [24]
  He won't cooperate with anyone. Il ne
  veut coopérer avec personne.

ρ **cop** NOUN
  le flic MASC *(informal)*

to **cope** VERB
1 *(with a new situation)* se débrouiller ◉ [1]
  She's coping well. Elle se débrouille bien.
2 *(with a difficult situation)* faire [10] face à
  He can't cope with school any more. Il
  n'arrive plus à faire face à l'école.

copper NOUN
  le cuivre MASC

copy NOUN ▸ SEE **copy** VERB
1 *(photocopy)* la copie FEM
  ten copies of the worksheet dix copies de
  la feuille d'exercices
2 *(of a book)* un exemplaire MASC
  the very last copy le tout dernier
  exemplaire

to **copy** VERB ▸ SEE **copy** NOUN
1 *(a document, file)* copier [1]
  Copy the file onto a disk. Copiez le fichier
  sur disquette.
  He copied Amy's project. Il a copié le
  dossier d'Amy.
2 *(a person)* copier sur
  She copies you. Elle copie sur toi.

cord NOUN
  (on a blind) le cordon MASC

cordless phone NOUN
  le téléphone sans fil

core NOUN
  (of an apple, pear) le trognon MASC

cork NOUN
  (in a bottle) le bouchon MASC
• **corkscrew**
  le tire-bouchon

corn NOUN
1 *(wheat)* le blé MASC
2 *(sweetcorn)* le maïs MASC

ρ **corner** NOUN
  le coin MASC
  at the corner of the street au coin de la rue
  out of the corner of your eye du coin de
  l'œil
  just round the corner tout près

cornflakes NOUN
  les corn-flakes MASC PL

Cornwall NOUN
  la Cornouailles FEM
  in Cornwall en Cornouailles

corpse NOUN
  le cadavre MASC

ρ **correct** ADJECTIVE ▸ SEE **correct** VERB
1 *(true)* exact MASC, exacte FEM
  Yes, that's correct. Oui, c'est exact.
2 *(right)* bon MASC, bonne FEM
  the correct result le bon résultat
  the correct answers les bonnes réponses

to **correct** VERB ▸ SEE **correct** ADJECTIVE
  (a mistake, a typo) corriger [52]

correction NOUN
  la correction FEM

correctly ADVERB
  (to fill in, write, pronounce) correctement

corridor NOUN
  le couloir MASC

Corsica NOUN
  la Corse FEM
  to be in Corsica être [6] en Corse
  to go to Corsica aller ◉ [7] en Corse

◉ **means the verb takes** être **to form the perfect**

cosmetics PLURAL NOUN
les **produits de beauté**

ρ **cost** NOUN ▸SEE **cost** VERB
le **prix** MASC
the cost of a new computer le prix d'un nouvel ordinateur

ρ to **cost** VERB ▸SEE **cost** NOUN
coûter [1]
How much does it cost? Ça coûte combien?
The tickets cost £10. Les billets coûtent dix livres.
It doesn't cost much to hire bikes. Ça ne coûte pas cher de louer des vélos.

ρ **costume** NOUN
le **costume** MASC

cosy ADJECTIVE
(room) **douillet** MASC, **douillette** FEM
It's cosy by the fire. On est bien à côté du feu.

cot NOUN
le **lit d'enfant**

cottage NOUN
la **petite maison**

ρ **cotton** NOUN
1 (fabric) le **coton** MASC
a cotton shirt une chemise en coton
2 (thread) le **fil de coton**
• **cotton wool**
la **ouate**

couch NOUN
le **canapé** MASC

cough NOUN ▸SEE **cough** VERB
la **toux** FEM
to have a cough tousser [1]

to **cough** VERB ▸SEE **cough** NOUN
tousser [1]

ρ **could** VERB
1 (able to do something) **They couldn't believe it.** Ils ne pouvaient pas le croire.
They asked if he could pay. Ils ont demandé s'il pouvait payer.
I did everything I could. J'ai fait tout ce que j'ai pu.
2 (knowing how to do something) **She could drive at fifteen.** Elle savait conduire à quinze ans.
I couldn't even swim. Je ne savais même pas nager.
3 (when 'could' is not translated in French) **I could hear the police car.** J'entendais la voiture de police.
They could smell gas. Ça sentait le gaz.
She couldn't see anything. Elle ne voyait rien.

I could understand some French. Je comprenais un peu de français.
4 (to ask for, to offer help) **Could I speak to David?** Pourrais-je parler à David?
You could phone him. Tu pourrais lui téléphoner.

council NOUN
le **conseil** MASC
the town council le conseil municipal

ρ to **count** VERB
1 (to add up) **compter** [1]
I counted my money. J'ai compté mon argent.
That makes eight, not counting Mel. Ça fait huit, sans compter Mel.
2 (to be treated as) **être** [6] **considéré comme**
Teenagers count as adults. Les adolescents sont considérés comme des adultes.
3 (to be allowed) **compter** [1]
That doesn't count. Ça ne compte pas.

counter NOUN
1 (in a shop, cafe) le **comptoir** MASC
2 (in a post office, bank) le **guichet** MASC
3 (in a big store) le **rayon** MASC
the cheese counter le rayon fromagerie
4 (for board games) le **jeton** MASC

ρ **country** NOUN
1 (France, England, etc) le **pays** MASC
foreign countries les pays étrangers
from another country d'un autre pays
2 (countryside) la **campagne** FEM
a country road une route de campagne
a holiday in the country des vacances à la campagne
• **countryside**
la **campagne**

county NOUN
le **comté** MASC

ρ **couple** NOUN
1 (pair) le **couple** MASC
a young couple from London un jeune couple de Londres
2 (one or two)
a couple of students deux ou trois étudiants
a couple of times deux ou trois fois
I've got a couple of things to do. J'ai deux ou trois choses à faire.

courage NOUN
le **courage** MASC

courgette NOUN
la **courgette** FEM

courier NOUN
1 (travel courier) un **accompagnateur** MASC,

une **accompagnatrice** FEM
2 *(delivery service)* le **coursier** MASC
by courier par coursier

♀ **course** NOUN
1 *(set of lessons)* le **cours** MASC
a computer course un cours d'informatique
I'm going on a course. Je vais suivre un cours.
2 *(part of a meal)* le **plat** MASC
For the main course, there's chicken.
Comme plat principal, il y a du poulet.
3 *(certainly)* **of course** bien sûr
Of course not! Bien sûr que non!
He's forgotten, of course. Il a oublié, bien sûr.
4 ▸ SEE **golf course**

court NOUN
1 *(for tennis, squash)* le **court** MASC
2 *(for basketball)* le **terrain** MASC
• **courtyard**
la **cour**

♀ **cousin** NOUN
le **cousin** MASC, la **cousine** FEM
my cousin Janet ma cousine Janet ▸ SEE **first cousin**

♀ **cover** NOUN ▸ SEE **cover** VERB
1 *(for a book, magazine)* la **couverture** FEM
2 *(for a duvet, cushion)* la **housse** FEM
3 *(cover version)* la **version** FEM
a cover of a French hit une version d'un tube français

♀ to **cover** VERB ▸ SEE **cover** NOUN
1 *(to protect)* **couvrir** [30]
Cover the wound. Couvrez la blessure.
to be covered in something être [6] couvert de quelque chose
She was covered in spots. Elle était couverte de boutons.
2 *(with leaves, snow, fabric)* **recouvrir** [30]
covered with snow recouvert de neige

♀ **cow** NOUN
la **vache** FEM

coward NOUN
le & la **lâche** MASC & FEM

cowboy NOUN
le **cowboy** MASC

crab NOUN
le **crabe** MASC

crack NOUN ▸ SEE **crack** VERB
1 *(in a wall, cup)* la **fêlure** FEM
2 *(cracking noise)* le **craquement** MASC
I heard a crack. J'ai entendu un craquement.

to **crack** VERB ▸ SEE **crack** NOUN
1 *(a plate, the ice)* **fêler** [1]
2 *(to break)* **casser** [1]
You cracked the eggs! Tu as cassé les œufs!
3 *(to split by itself)* se **fêler** ○ [1]
The ice is starting to crack. La glace commence à se fêler.

cracker NOUN
1 *(biscuit)* le **cracker** MASC
2 *(Christmas cracker)* le **diablotin** MASC

to **crackle** VERB
(fire) **crépiter** [1]

crafts NOUN
(at school) les **travaux manuels**

crafty ADJECTIVE
ingénieux MASC, **ingénieuse** FEM

cramp NOUN
la **crampe** FEM
a cramp in your leg une crampe à la jambe

crane NOUN
la **grue** FEM

to **crash** VERB ▸ SEE **crash** NOUN
1 *(cars, planes)* s'**écraser** ○ [1]
The plane crashed. L'avion s'est écrasé.
2 **to crash into** **rentrer** ○ [1] **dans**
They crashed into a tree. Ils sont rentrés dans un arbre.

crash NOUN ▸ SEE **crash** VERB
1 *(accident)* un **accident** MASC
a car crash un accident de voiture
2 *(of broken glass)* le **fracas** MASC
• **crash course**
le **cours intensif**
• **crash helmet**
le **casque** MASC

♀ **crate** NOUN
1 *(for bottles, china)* la **caisse** FEM
2 *(for fruit)* le **cageot** MASC

crawl NOUN ▸ SEE **crawl** VERB
(in swimming) le **crawl** MASC

to **crawl** VERB ▸ SEE **crawl** NOUN
1 *(person, baby)* **marcher** [1] **à quatre pattes**
2 *(cars in a traffic jam)* **rouler** [1] **au pas**

crayon NOUN
1 *(wax)* le **crayon gras**
2 *(coloured pencil)* le **crayon de couleur**

craze NOUN
la **vogue** FEM
the craze for rollerblades la vogue des rollers

♀ **crazy** ADJECTIVE
fou MASC, **folle** FEM
She's crazy! Elle est folle!

○ means the verb takes être to form the perfect

to go crazy devenir ◎ [81] fou

to **creak** *VERB*
1 *(door)* grincer [61]
2 *(floorboard)* craquer [1]

ℱ **cream** *NOUN*
la **crème** *FEM*
strawberries and cream des fraises à la crème
• **cream cheese**
le fromage à tartiner

creased *ADJECTIVE*
froissé *MASC*, froissée *FEM*

to **create** *VERB*
(problems) créer [32]

creative *ADJECTIVE*
créatif *MASC*, créative *FEM*

creature *NOUN*
la **créature** *FEM*

crèche *NOUN*
la **crèche** *FEM*

credit *NOUN*
le **crédit** *MASC*
We bought it on credit. On l'a acheté à crédit.
• **credit card**
la carte de crédit

creepy *ADJECTIVE*
a creepy film un film qui donne la chair de poule

crew *NOUN*
1 *(on a ship, plane)* un **équipage** *MASC*
2 *(rowing, filming)* une **équipe** *FEM*
• **crew cut**
les cheveux en brosse

cricket *NOUN*
1 *(game)* le **cricket** *MASC*
to play cricket jouer [1] au cricket
2 *(insect)* le **grillon** *MASC*
• **cricket bat**
la batte de cricket

crime *NOUN*
1 *(illegal act)* le **crime** *MASC*
2 *(trend within society)* la **criminalité** *FEM*

criminal *NOUN*
le **criminel** *MASC*, la **criminelle** *FEM*

crimson *ADJECTIVE*
pourpre *MASC & FEM*

crisis *NOUN*
la **crise** *FEM*

ℱ **crisp** *ADJECTIVE* ▶ SEE **crisp** *NOUN*
croustillant *MASC*, croustillante *FEM*

ℱ **crisp** *NOUN* ▶ SEE **crisp** *ADJECTIVE*
la **chip** *FEM*
a packet of crisps un paquet de chips

critical *ADJECTIVE*
critique *MASC & FEM*
She's too critical. Elle est trop critique.

criticism *NOUN*
la **critique** *FEM*

to **criticize** *VERB*
critiquer [1]

crockery *NOUN*
la **vaisselle** *FEM*

crocodile *NOUN*
le **crocodile** *MASC*

crook *NOUN*
(criminal) un **escroc** *MASC*

crooked *ADJECTIVE*
(picture, hat) **to be crooked** être [6] de travers

crop *NOUN*
la **récolte** *FEM*

cross *NOUN* ▶ SEE **cross** *ADJ, VERB*
la **croix** *FEM*
a silver cross une croix en argent

ℱ **cross** *ADJECTIVE* ▶ SEE **cross** *NOUN, VERB*
fâché *MASC*, fâchée *FEM*
She's very cross. Elle est très fâchée.
I'm cross with you. Je suis fâché contre toi.
to get cross se fâcher ◎ [1]
My mum got cross. Ma mère s'est fâchée.

ℱ to **cross** *VERB* ▶ SEE **cross** *NOUN, ADJ*
1 *(a road, a river)* traverser [1]
Watch out crossing the road. Faites attention en traversant la rue.
2 *(your fingers, legs)* croiser [1]
I'll keep my fingers crossed. Je croise les doigts.
3 *(a border)* passer ◎ [1]
to cross into Italy passer en Italie
4 *(to meet each other)* se croiser ◎ [1]
• **to cross out something**
(a mistake, your name) rayer [59] quelque chose

cross-Channel *ADJECTIVE*
(ferry) transmanche *INVARIABLE ADJECTIVE*

cross-country *NOUN*
le **cross** *MASC*
• **cross-country skiing**
le ski de fond

ℱ **crossing** *NOUN*
la **traversée** *FEM*
a Channel crossing une traversée

transmanche ►SEE **level crossing,
pedestrian crossing**

cross-legged ADJECTIVE
to sit cross-legged être [6] assis en tailleur

ℓ **crossroads** NOUN
le **carrefour** MASC
at the crossroads au carrefour

crossword NOUN
les **mots croisés**
to do the crossword faire [10] les mots
croisés

to **crouch** VERB
s'accroupir [2]

crow NOUN ►SEE **crow** VERB
le **corbeau** MASC

to **crow** VERB ►SEE **check** NOUN
(cockerels) chanter [1]

ℓ **crowd** NOUN ►SEE **crowd** VERB
la **foule** FEM
in the crowd dans la foule
a crowd of 5,000 une foule de cinq mille
personnes
to avoid the crowds éviter [1] la foule

crowded ADJECTIVE
bondé MASC, bondée FEM
The hall was crowded. La salle était
bondée.

crown NOUN
la **couronne** FEM

cruel ADJECTIVE
cruel MASC, cruelle FEM

cruelty NOUN
la **cruauté** FEM

cruise NOUN
la **croisière** FEM
They're on a cruise. Ils font une croisière.

crumb NOUN
la **miette** FEM

to **crumple** VERB
froisser [1]

to **crunch** VERB
(an apple) croquer [1]

crunchy ADJECTIVE
croquant MASC, croquante FEM

to **crush** VERB
écraser [1]

crust NOUN
la **croûte** FEM

crusty ADJECTIVE
(bread) croustillant MASC, croustillante FEM

crutch NOUN
la **béquille** FEM
He's on crutches. Il marche avec des
béquilles.

ℓ **cry** NOUN ►SEE **cry** VERB
le **cri** MASC

ℓ to **cry** VERB ►SEE **cry** NOUN
1 (to weep) pleurer [1]
Don't cry. Ne pleure pas.
to make somebody cry faire [10] pleurer
quelqu'un
They made me cry. Ils m'ont fait pleurer.
2 (to call out) crier [1]
to cry out loudly crier fort
to cry for help appeler [18] au secours

crystal NOUN
le **cristal** MASC

cub NOUN
1 (young animal) le **petit** MASC
2 (scout) le **louveteau** MASC

Cuba NOUN
la **Cuba** FEM
to be in Cuba être [6] à Cuba
to go to Cuba aller ⊚ [7] à Cuba

Cuban NOUN
un **Cubain** MASC, une **Cubaine** FEM

Cuban ADJECTIVE
cubain MASC, cubaine FEM

cube NOUN
le **cube** MASC
an ice cube un glaçon

cubicle NOUN
1 (in a changing room) la **cabine** FEM
2 (in a public toilet) le **cabinet** MASC

cuckoo NOUN
le **coucou** MASC

cucumber NOUN
le **concombre** MASC

cuddle NOUN
to give somebody a cuddle faire [10] un
câlin à quelqu'un
She gave him a cuddle. Elle lui a fait un
câlin.

cue NOUN
(in billiards, etc) la **queue de billard**

cuff NOUN
(on a shirt) la **manchette** FEM

cul-de-sac NOUN
une **impasse** FEM

culture NOUN
la **culture** FEM

⊚ means the verb takes être to form the perfect

cunning ADJECTIVE
rusé MASC, rusée FEM

ℓ **cup** NOUN
1 (for drinking) la **tasse** FEM
a cup of tea une tasse de thé
2 (trophy) la **coupe** FEM
the World Cup la Coupe du Monde
• cup final
la finale de la coupe
• cup tie
le match de coupe

cupboard NOUN
le **placard** MASC

cure NOUN ▶ SEE **cure** VERB
le **remède** MASC
a cure for warts un remède contre les verrues

to **cure** VERB ▶ SEE **cure** NOUN
(a sick person) **guérir** [2]

curiosity NOUN
la **curiosité** FEM
I asked out of curiosity. J'ai demandé par curiosité.

curious ADJECTIVE
curieux MASC, curieuse FEM

curl NOUN ▶ SEE **curl** VERB
la **boucle** FEM

to **curl** VERB ▶ SEE **curl** NOUN
(your hair) **friser** [1]

curly ADJECTIVE
bouclé MASC, bouclée FEM
curly hair les cheveux bouclés

currant NOUN
le **raisin de Corinthe** MASC

ℓ **currency** NOUN
(money) les **devises** FEM PL

current NOUN ▶ SEE **adjective** ADJ
(of electricity, in sea) le **courant** MASC

current ADJECTIVE ▶ SEE **current** NOUN
(present-day) actuel MASC, actuelle FEM
• current affairs
l'actualité FEM

curriculum NOUN
le **programme** MASC

curry NOUN
le **curry** MASC
chicken curry le curry de poulet

ℓ **cursor** NOUN
le **curseur** MASC

ℓ **curtain** NOUN
le **rideau** MASC (PL les **rideaux**)

cushion NOUN
le **coussin** MASC

custard NOUN
1 (runny) la **crème anglaise**
2 (baked) le **flan** MASC

custom NOUN
la **coutume** FEM

ℓ **customer** NOUN
le **client** MASC, la **cliente** FEM
full of customers plein de clients

ℓ **customs** PLURAL NOUN
la **douane** FEM SINGULAR
We went through customs. Nous sommes passés à la douane.
• customs hall
la douane FEM
• customs officer
le douanier MASC

ℓ **cut** NOUN ▶ SEE **cut** VERB
1 (injury) la **coupure** FEM
2 (haircut) la **coupe** FEM

ℓ to **cut** VERB ▶ SEE **cut** NOUN
1 (with scissors, a knife) **couper** [1]
I've cut the bread. J'ai coupé le pain.
Cut the pizza in half. Coupe la pizza en deux.
to cut yourself se couper ◎ [1]
Ruth's cut her finger. Ruth s'est coupé le doigt.
2 (with lawnmower) **tondre** [3]
I cut the grass. J'ai tondu le gazon.
3 to get your hair cut se faire ◎ [10] couper les cheveux
Sophie's had her hair cut. Sophie s'est fait couper les cheveux.
4 (on computer) **couper** [1]
I cut the image and pasted it into the file. J'ai coupé l'image et je l'ai collée dans le fichier.
5 (prices) **baisser** [1]
• to cut something down
(a tree) abattre [21] quelque chose
• to cut something out
1 (a photo, an article) découper [1] quelque chose
2 (sugar, salt) supprimer [1] quelque chose
• to cut something up
1 (carrots) couper [1] quelque chose
2 (a chicken) découper [1] quelque chose

cutlery NOUN
les **couverts** MASC PL

CV NOUN
le **CV** MASC

cyberbullying NOUN
le **cyberharcèlement** MASC

to **cycle** VERB
faire [10] **du vélo**
I enjoy cycling. J'aime faire du vélo.
I cycle to school every day. Tous les jours,
je vais à l'école à vélo.

cycle lane NOUN
la **piste cyclable**

cycle race NOUN
la **course cycliste**

⚲ **cycling** NOUN
le **cyclisme** MASC
to go on a cycling holiday faire [10] du
cyclotourisme

🔵 **CYCLING**

The Tour de France cycle race takes place in
France every summer. The 4,000 kilometre
route changes every year but always finishes in
Paris. The previous day's winner wears a special
yellow jersey.

⚲ **cyclist** NOUN
le & la **cycliste** MASC & FEM

cylinder NOUN
le **cylindre** MASC

Dd

⚲ **dad** NOUN
1 (in general) le **père** MASC
Anna's dad le père d'Anna
Dad works in a bank. Mon père travaille
dans une banque.
2 (within the family) **papa** MASC
Dad's not home yet. Papa n'est pas encore
rentré.

daffodil NOUN
la **jonquille** FEM

daily ADJECTIVE ▸ SEE **daily** ADVERB
quotidien MASC, **quotidienne** FEM
a daily newspaper un journal quotidien

daily ADVERB ▸ SEE **daily** ADJECTIVE
quotidiennement
She visits him daily. Elle lui rend visite tous
les jours.

dairy products PLURAL NOUN
les **produits laitiers** MASC PL
Connor is allergic to dairy products.
Connor est allergique aux produits laitiers.

dam NOUN
le **barrage** MASC

⚲ to **damage** VERB ▸ SEE **damage** NOUN
1 (a car, building) **endommager** [52]

2 (your health) **s'abîmer** [1]
You're going to damage your eyesight. Tu
vas t'abîmer la vue.

damage NOUN ▸ SEE **damage** VERB
les **dégâts** MASC PL

damn NOUN ▸ SEE **damn** EXCLAMATION
(informal) **not to give a damn** s'en ficher
He doesn't give a damn. Il s'en fiche
complètement.

damn EXCLAMATION ▸ SEE **damn** NOUN
(informal) zut!

damp ADJECTIVE ▸ SEE **damp** NOUN
humide MASC & FEM

damp NOUN ▸ SEE **damp** ADJECTIVE
l'**humidité** FEM

⚲ **dance** NOUN ▸ SEE **dance** VERB
1 (like salsa, waltz) la **danse** FEM
a folk dance une danse traditionnelle
2 (party) la **soirée dansante**

⚲ to **dance** VERB ▸ SEE **dance** NOUN
danser [1]

dancer NOUN
le **danseur** MASC, la **danseuse** FEM

dancing NOUN
la **danse** FEM
I like dancing. J'aime danser.
• **dancing class**
le cours de danse

dandruff NOUN
les **pellicules** FEM PL

danger NOUN
le **danger** MASC
to be in danger être [6] en danger
The world is in danger. Le monde est en
danger.

⚲ **dangerous** ADJECTIVE
dangereux MASC, **dangereuse** FEM
to be dangerous to do something être [6]
dangereux de faire quelque chose
It's dangerous to drive fast. Il est
dangereux de conduire vite.

Danish ADJECTIVE ▸ SEE **Danish** NOUN
danois MASC, **danoise** FEM

Danish NOUN ▸ SEE **Danish** ADJECTIVE
(language) le **danois** MASC

to **dare** VERB
1 **to dare to do something** oser [1] faire
quelque chose
I didn't dare to suggest it. Je n'ai pas osé le
suggérer.
2 (in orders) **Don't you dare tell her I'm here!**
Je t'interdis de lui dire que je suis là!
3 **I dare you!** Chiche! (informal)

⚲ means the verb takes être to form the perfect

I **dare you to drink it all!** Chiche que tu bois tout!

daring ADJECTIVE
osé MASC, **osée** FEM
a daring choice un choix osé

dark ADJECTIVE ▸ SEE **dark** NOUN
1 (colour) **foncé** MASC, **foncée** FEM
a dark blue skirt une jupe bleu foncé
2 (night) **It's dark already.** Il fait nuit déjà.
It gets dark around five. La nuit commence à tomber vers cinq heures.
3 (hair, skin) **brun** MASC, **brune** FEM
She has dark brown hair. Elle est brune.
4 (room) **sombre** MASC & FEM
It's dark in here. Il fait sombre ici.

dark NOUN ▸ SEE **dark** ADJECTIVE
in the dark dans l'obscurité
after dark après la tombée de la nuit
My little brother's afraid of the dark. Mon petit frère a peur du noir.

darkness NOUN
l'obscurité FEM
in darkness dans l'obscurité

darling NOUN
chéri MASC, **chérie** FEM
See you later, darling! À tout à l'heure, chéri!

dart NOUN
la fléchette FEM
to play darts jouer [1] aux fléchettes

data PLURAL NOUN
les données FEM PL

database NOUN
la base de données

℘ **date** NOUN
1 (in time) **la date** FEM
What's the date today? On est le combien aujourd'hui?
to fix a date for something fixer [1] une date pour quelque chose
They've fixed a date for their wedding. Ils ont fixé la date de leur mariage.
2 (to go out with somebody) **to have a date with somebody** sortir ◐ [72] avec quelqu'un
Laura's got a date with Mick tonight. Laura sort avec Mick ce soir.
3 (fruit) **la datte** FEM
• **date of birth**
la date de naissance

℘ **daughter** NOUN
la fille FEM
Tina's daughter la fille de Tina

daughter-in-law NOUN
la belle-fille FEM (PL **les belles-filles**)

dawn NOUN
l'aube FEM

℘ **day** NOUN
1 **le jour** MASC
three days later trois jours plus tard
the day I met my girlfriend le jour où j'ai rencontré ma copine
2 (as a period of time) **la journée** FEM
It rained all day. Il a plu toute la journée.
3 (when you refer to the weather) **It's a nice day.** Il fait beau.
4 (in expressions) **the day after** le lendemain
the day after tomorrow après-demain
5 **the day before** la veille
the day before yesterday avant-hier
• **day off**
le jour de congé
When's your day off? Quel est ton jour de congé?

℘ **dead** ADJECTIVE ▸ SEE **dead** ADVERB
mort MASC, **morte** FEM
Her mother's dead. Sa mère est morte.
The cat's dead. Le chat est mort.

dead ADVERB ▸ SEE **dead** ADJECTIVE
1 (very, really) **vachement**
It's dead easy. C'est vachement facile.
2 (completely) **absolument**
You're dead right. Tu as absolument raison.
dead on time à l'heure pile
• **dead end**
une impasse
• **deadline**
la date limite

℘ **deaf** ADJECTIVE
sourd MASC, **sourde** FEM

deafening ADJECTIVE
assourdissant MASC, **assourdissante** FEM

deal NOUN ▸ SEE **deal** VERB
1 (buying and selling) **une affaire** FEM
It's a good deal. C'est une bonne affaire.
2 (agreement) **le marché** MASC
It's a deal! Marché conclu!
I'll make a deal with you. Je ferai un marché avec toi.
3 **a great deal of something** beaucoup de quelque chose
a great deal of money beaucoup d'argent
I don't have a great deal of time. Je n'ai pas beaucoup de temps.

to **deal** VERB ▸ SEE **deal** NOUN
(in cards) **donner** [1]
• **to deal with something**
s'occuper [1] de quelque chose
I'll deal with it. Je m'en occuperai.

℘ **indicates key words**

I dealt with the repairs. Je me suis occupé des réparations.

ℓ **dear** ADJECTIVE
1 (in letters) **cher** MASC, **chère** FEM
Dear Sylvie Chère Sylvie
2 (expensive) **cher** MASC, **chère** FEM
That's dear. Ça coûte cher.

death NOUN
la **mort** FEM
after his father's death après la mort de son père
I was bored to death. Je m'ennuyais à mourir.
I'm sick to death of it! J'en ai vraiment marre! (informal)
• **death penalty**
la peine de mort

debate NOUN ▸ SEE **debate** VERB
le **débat** MASC

to **debate** VERB ▸ SEE **debate** NOUN
débattre [21]

debt NOUN
la **dette** FEM
to get into debt s'endetter ☺ [1]
Students are getting into too much debt.
Les étudiants s'endettent trop.

decade NOUN
la **décennie** FEM

decaffeinated ADJECTIVE
décaféiné MASC, décaféinée FEM

to **deceive** VERB
tromper [1]

December NOUN
décembre MASC
in December en décembre

WORD TIP Months of the year and days of the week start with small letters in French.

decent ADJECTIVE
(adequate) **convenable** MASC & FEM
a decent salary un salaire convenable
a decent meal un bon repas

ℓ to **decide** VERB
décider [1]
I haven't decided yet. Je n'ai pas encore décidé.
to decide to do something décider de faire quelque chose
She's decided to buy a car. Elle a décidé d'acheter une voiture.
She's decided not to look for a job. Elle a décidé de ne pas chercher de petit boulot.

decimal ADJECTIVE
décimal MASC, décimale FEM, décimaux

MASC PL, décimales FEM PL
• **decimal point**
la virgule

WORD TIP In French a comma is used for a dot in decimals.

decision NOUN
la **décision** FEM
the right decision la bonne décision
the wrong decision la mauvaise décision
to take a decision prendre [64] une décision

deck NOUN
1 (on a ship) le **pont** MASC
2 (on a bus, plane) un **étage** MASC
• **deckchair**
le transat

to **declare** VERB
déclarer [1]

to **decorate** VERB
1 décorer [1]
I love decorating the Christmas tree.
J'aime décorer le sapin de Noël.
2 (paint) peindre [60]
Dad is going to decorate the kitchen. Papa va peindre la cuisine.

decoration NOUN
la **décoration** FEM

decorator NOUN
le **peintre-décorateur** MASC, la **peintre-décoratrice** FEM

decrease NOUN
la **diminution** FEM
a decrease in the number of marriages une diminution du nombre de mariages

to **decrease** VERB
diminuer [1]

to **deduct** VERB
déduire [26]

deep ADJECTIVE
profond MASC, **profonde** FEM
a deep hole un trou profond
a hole two metres deep un trou de deux mètres de profondeur
The river is very deep. La rivière est très profonde.
How deep is the swimming pool? Quelle est la profondeur de la piscine?
• **deep end**
(of a swimming pool) le grand bassin
• **deep freeze**
le congélateur

deeply ADVERB
profondément

☺ means the verb takes être to form the perfect

deer NOUN
(*male*) le **cerf** MASC (*female*) la **biche** FEM

defeat NOUN ▸ SEE **defeat** VERB
la **défaite** FEM

to **defeat** VERB ▸ SEE **defeat** NOUN
battre [21]

defect NOUN
le **défaut** MASC

defence NOUN
la **défense** FEM

to **defend** VERB
défendre [3]

defender NOUN
le **défenseur** MASC

to **define** VERB
définir [2]

definite ADJECTIVE
1 (*clear*) **net** MASC, **nette** FEM
a definite change un net changement
a definite improvement une nette
amélioration
2 (*certain*) **sûr** MASC, **sûre** FEM
It's not definite yet. Ce n'est pas encore sûr.
3 (*exact*) **précis** MASC, **précise** FEM
a definite answer une réponse précise
I don't have a definite idea of what I want.
Je n'ai pas une idée précise de ce que je
veux.
• definite article
l'article défini MASC

definitely ADVERB
1 (*when giving your opinion*) **sans aucun
doute**
The blue one is definitely the biggest. Le
bleu est sans aucun doute le plus grand.
Your French is definitely better than mine.
Ton français est sans aucun doute meilleur
que le mien.
'Do you like this one better?' —
'Definitely!' 'Tu préfères celui-ci?' — 'Sans
aucun doute!'
2 (*certainly*) She's definitely going to be
there. Elle va y être, c'est sûr.
I'm definitely not going. C'est décidé, je
n'y vais pas.

definition NOUN
la **définition** FEM

deforestation NOUN
le **déboisement** MASC

ℒ **degree** NOUN
1 (*in temperatures, angles*) le **degré** MASC
thirty degrees trente degrés
2 (*qualification*) a university degree un
diplôme universitaire

ℒ **delay** NOUN ▸ SEE **delay** VERB
le **retard** MASC
a two-hour delay un retard de deux heures

ℒ to **delay** VERB ▸ SEE **delay** NOUN
1 (*to make late*) retarder [1]
The flight was delayed by bad weather. Le
vol a été retardé par le mauvais temps.
2 (*to postpone*) différer [24]
The decision has been delayed until
Thursday. La décision a été différée jusqu'à
jeudi.

to **delete** VERB
effacer [61]

deliberate ADJECTIVE
délibéré MASC, **délibérée** FEM

deliberately ADVERB
exprès
He left it there deliberately. Il a fait exprès
de le laisser là.

delicate ADJECTIVE
délicat MASC, **délicate** FEM

delicatessen NOUN
une **épicerie fine**

● DELICATESSEN

Charcuteries were originally pork butchers.
Modern charcuteries are delicatessens selling
a range of cooked meats, pâtés, quiches or
pizzas and salads. Many have a range of ready-
cooked, takeaway meals— from choucroute
to couscous.

ℒ **delicious** ADJECTIVE
délicieux MASC, **délicieuse** FEM

ℒ **delighted** ADJECTIVE
ravi MASC, **ravie** FEM
I'm delighted to hear you can come. Je suis
ravi d'apprendre que tu peux venir (*boy
speaking*), Je suis ravie d'apprendre que tu
peux venir (*girl speaking*).
They're delighted with their new car. Ils
sont ravis de leur nouvelle voiture.

to **deliver** VERB
1 (*goods*) livrer [1]
They're delivering the computer
tomorrow. Ils vont livrer l'ordinateur
demain.
2 (*mail*) distribuer [1]

delivery NOUN
la **livraison** FEM

demand NOUN ▸ SEE **demand** VERB
la **demande** FEM

to **demand** VERB ▸ SEE **demand**
exiger [52]

ℒ **indicates key words**

democracy NOUN
la démocratie FEM

democratic ADJECTIVE
démocratique MASC & FEM

to **demolish** VERB
démolir [2]

to **demonstrate** VERB
1 (a product, a machine, etc) faire [10] la démonstration de
2 (to protest) manifester [1]
to demonstrate against something manifester contre quelque chose
Millions of people demonstrated against the war. Des millions de gens ont manifesté contre la guerre.

demonstration NOUN
1 (of a product, a machine, etc) la démonstration FEM
2 (protest) la manifestation FEM

demonstrator NOUN
le manifestant MASC, la manifestante FEM

denim NOUN
le jean MASC
a denim jacket un blouson en jean

Denmark NOUN
Danemark MASC
in Denmark au Danemark
to Denmark au Danemark

dense ADJECTIVE
dense MASC & FEM

dent NOUN ▶ SEE dent VERB
la bosse FEM

to **dent** VERB ▶ SEE dent
cabosser [1]

dental ADJECTIVE
dentaire MASC & FEM
dental floss du fil dentaire
a dental appointment un rendez-vous chez le dentiste
• **dental hygiene**
l'hygiène dentaire FEM
• **dental surgeon**
le chirurgien-dentiste, la chirurgienne-dentiste

ᵖ **dentist** NOUN
le & la dentiste MASC & FEM
My mum's a dentist. Ma mère est dentiste.

to **deny** VERB
nier [1]

deodorant NOUN
le déodorant MASC

to **depart** VERB
partir ⊙ [58]

ᵖ **department** NOUN
1 (in a shop) le rayon MASC
the men's department le rayon hommes
2 (in schools) le département MASC
the language department le département de langues étrangères
• **department store**
le grand magasin

ᵖ **departure** NOUN
le départ MASC
• **departure lounge**
la salle d'embarquement

to **depend** VERB
It depends. Ça dépend.
to depend on something dépendre [3] de quelque chose
It depends on the price. Ça dépend du prix.
It depends on what you want. Ça dépend de ce que tu veux.

ᵖ **deposit** NOUN
1 (with a booking) les arrhes FEM PL
to pay a deposit verser des arrhes
We paid a deposit of 50 euros. Nous avons versé des arrhes de 50 euros.
2 (for hiring something) la caution FEM
3 (on a bottle) la consigne FEM

depressed ADJECTIVE
déprimé MASC, déprimée FEM

depressing ADJECTIVE
déprimant MASC, déprimante FEM

depth NOUN
la profondeur FEM

deputy NOUN
adjoint MASC, adjointe FEM
• **deputy head**
le directeur adjoint, la directrice adjointe

to **descend** VERB
descendre ⊙ [3]

ᵖ to **describe** VERB
décrire [38]

ᵖ **description** NOUN
la description FEM

desert NOUN
le désert MASC
in the desert dans le désert
• **desert island**
une île déserte

to **deserve** VERB
mériter [1]

⊙ means the verb takes être to form the perfect

design NOUN ▸ SEE **design** VERB
1 (artistic) le **design** MASC
  fashion design le stylisme
2 (pattern) le **motif** MASC
  a floral design un motif floral
3 (technological) la **conception** FEM
  the design of the plane la conception de
  l'avion

to **design** VERB ▸ SEE **design** NOUN
1 (costumes, clothes, scenery) **créer** [32]
2 (a machine, a plane, a system) **concevoir**
  [66]

designer NOUN
1 (in fashion) le & la **styliste** MASC & FEM
2 (in graphics) le & la **graphiste** MASC & FEM

desire NOUN ▸ SEE **desire** VERB
  le **désir** MASC

to **desire** VERB ▸ SEE **desire**
  désirer [1]

ℓ **desk** NOUN
1 (in an office, at home) le **bureau** MASC
  the information desk le bureau des
  renseignements
  the reception desk la réception
2 (at school) la **table** FEM

despair NOUN ▸ SEE **despair** VERB
  le **désespoir** MASC

to **despair** VERB ▸ SEE **despair**
  to despair of doing something désespérer
  [24] de faire quelque chose
  **We despaired of ever finishing this
  project.** Nous nous désespérions de ne
  jamais finir ce projet.

desperate ADJECTIVE
1 **désespéré** MASC, **désespérée** FEM
  a desperate attempt une tentative
  désespérée
2 **to be desperate to do something** avoir [5]
  très envie de faire quelque chose
  I'm desperate to see you. J'ai très envie de
  te voir.

to **despise** VERB
  mépriser [1]

ℓ **dessert** NOUN
  le **dessert** MASC
  What's for dessert? Qu'est-ce qu'il y a
  comme dessert?
  For dessert, we have ... Comme dessert,
  nous avons ...

ℓ **destination** NOUN
  la **destination** FEM

to **destroy** VERB
  détruire [26]

destruction NOUN
  la **destruction** FEM

detached house NOUN
  le **maison individuelle**

detail NOUN
  le **détail** MASC

detailed ADJECTIVE
  détaillé MASC, **détaillée** FEM

detective NOUN
  un **inspecteur de police**, une **inspectrice
  de police**
  a private detective le détective, la
  détective
• **detective story**
  le roman policier

detention NOUN
  la **retenue** FEM

detergent NOUN
  le **détergent** MASC

determined ADJECTIVE
  résolu MASC, **résolue** FEM
  He's determined to leave. Il est résolu de
  partir.

determiner NOUN
  (Grammar) le **déterminant** MASC

  WORD TIP In English these are a, an and the. In
  French they are un, une, des and le, la, les.

detour NOUN
  le **détour** MASC

to **develop** VERB
1 (a film) **faire** [10] **développer**
  I got the film developed. J'ai fait
  développer la pellicule.
2 (people, children) se **développer** ◌ [1]
  how children develop comment les enfants
  se développent

developing country NOUN
  le **pays en voie de développement**

development NOUN
  le **développement** MASC

devil NOUN
  le **diable** MASC

devoted ADJECTIVE
  dévoué MASC, **dévouée** FEM

dew NOUN
  la **rosée** FEM

diabetes NOUN
  le **diabète** MASC

diabetic ADJECTIVE, NOUN
  diabétique MASC & FEM

A
B
C
D
E
F
G
H
I
J
K
L
M
N
O
P
Q
R
S
T
U
V
W
X
Y
Z

453

to be diabetic être [6] diabétique
Diane is diabetic. Diane est diabétique.
Jack is a diabetic. Jack est diabétique.

diagnosis NOUN
le diagnostic MASC

diagonal ADJECTIVE
diagonal MASC, diagonale FEM, diagonaux
MASC PL, diagonales FEM PL

diagram NOUN
le schéma MASC

to **dial** VERB
composer [1] le numéro
Dial 999. Composez le 999.
Dial 00 33 for France. Faîtes le 00 33 pour
la France.

dialling tone NOUN
la tonalité FEM

dialogue NOUN
le dialogue MASC

diameter NOUN
le diamètre MASC

diamond NOUN
1 (jewel) le diamant MASC
2 (shape) le losange MASC
3 (in cards) le carreau MASC
the jack of diamonds le valet de carreau

diarrhoea NOUN
la diarrhée FEM
to have diarrhoea avoir [5] la diarrhée
The baby had diarrhoea. Le bébé avait la
diarrhée.

diary NOUN
1 (for appointments) un agenda MASC
I've noted it in my diary. Je l'ai marqué
dans mon agenda.
2 (of what you do) le journal intime
to keep a diary tenir [77] un journal
Do you keep a diary? Est-ce que tu tiens un
journal?

dice NOUN
le dé MASC
Throw the dice! Jette le dé!

dictation NOUN
la dictée FEM

dictionary NOUN
le dictionnaire MASC
to look up a word in the dictionary
chercher [1] un mot dans le dictionnaire
You can look it up in your dictionary. Tu
peux le chercher dans ton dictionnaire.

did VERB ▸ SEE **do**

to **die** VERB
1 mourir ⊜ [54]
My grandmother died in January. Ma
grand-mère est morte en janvier.
2 **to be dying to do something** mourir
d'envie de faire quelque chose
I'm dying to see them! Je meurs d'envie de
les voir!
• **to die out**
disparaître [27]

diesel NOUN
le gazole MASC
a diesel car une voiture diesel
a diesel engine un moteur diesel

ℓ **diet** NOUN
1 (what you eat) une alimentation FEM
I try to have a healthy diet. J'essaye d'avoir
une alimentation saine.
2 (for slimming) le régime MASC
a salt-free diet un régime sans sel
to be on a diet être [6] au régime
She's on a diet. Elle est au régime.

ℓ **difference** NOUN
1 la différence FEM
the difference between the two la
différence entre les deux
**What's the difference between adopt
and adapt?** Quelle est la différence entre
adopter et adapter?
2 **to make a difference** changer [52] quelque
chose
It makes a difference. Ça change quelque
chose.
It makes no difference. Ça ne change rien.

ℓ **different** ADJECTIVE
différent MASC, différente FEM
The sisters are very different. Les sœurs
sont très différentes.
to be different from somebody être [6]
différent de quelqu'un
She's very different from her sister. Elle est
très différente de sa sœur.

ℓ **difficult** ADJECTIVE
difficile MASC & FEM
It's very difficult. C'est très difficile.
to be difficult to do something être [6]
difficile de faire quelque chose
It's difficult to decide. Il est difficile de
décider.

difficulty NOUN
1 la difficulté FEM
2 **to have difficulty doing something** avoir
[5] du mal à faire quelque chose
I had difficulty answering the questions.
J'ai eu du mal à répondre aux questions.

⊜ means the verb takes être to form the perfect

to **dig** *VERB*
   (a hole) creuser [1]
   The dog had dug a deep hole. Le chien
   avait creusé un trou profond.

digestion *NOUN*
   la digestion *FEM*

digital *ADJECTIVE*
   numérique *MASC & FEM*
   a digital recording un enregistrement
   numérique
   a digital watch une montre à affichage
   numérique

dim *ADJECTIVE*
1 *(weak)* **a dim light** une lumière faible
2 *(not clever)* **She's a bit dim.** Elle est un peu
   bouchée.

dimension *NOUN*
   la dimension *FEM*

din *NOUN*
   le vacarme *MASC*
   What a din! Quel vacarme!

dinghy *NOUN*
   a sailing dinghy un dériveur *MASC*
   a rubber dinghy un canot pneumatique

ℓ **dining room** *NOUN*
   la salle à manger *FEM*

ℓ **dinner** *NOUN*
1 *(in the evening)* le dîner *MASC*
   Mum invited him to dinner. Maman l'a
   invité à dîner.
2 *(at midday)* le déjeuner *MASC*
   to have school dinners déjeuner [1] à la
   cantine
• **dinner time** *NOUN*
1 *(at midday)* l'heure du déjeuner
2 *(in the evening)* l'heure du dîner

dinosaur *NOUN*
   le dinosaure *MASC*

ℓ **diploma** *NOUN*
   le diplôme *MASC*

ℓ **direct** *ADJECTIVE* ▸ SEE **direct** *ADVERB, VERB*
   direct *MASC*, directe *FEM*
   a direct flight un vol direct

ℓ **direct** *ADVERB* ▸ SEE **direct** *ADJECTIVE, VERB*
   directement
   The bus goes direct to the airport. Le bus
   va directement à l'aéroport.

ℓ to **direct** *VERB* ▸ SEE **direct** *ADJECTIVE, ADVERB*
1 *(a film, a programme)* réaliser [1]
2 *(a play)* mettre [11] en scène
3 *(the traffic)* régler [24]

ℓ **direction** *NOUN*
1 *(the way you go)* la direction *FEM*
   in the other direction dans l'autre direction
2 *(instructions)* **to ask somebody for**
   directions demander [1] son chemin à
   quelqu'un
   We asked a woman for directions. Nous
   avons demandé notre chemin à une dame.
   Directions for use Mode d'emploi

directly *ADVERB*
   directement

ℓ **director** *NOUN*
1 *(of a company)* le directeur *MASC*, la
   directrice *FEM*
2 *(of a film, programme)* le réalisateur *MASC*,
   la réalisatrice *FEM*
3 *(of a play)* le metteur en scène

ℓ **directory** *NOUN*
   l'annuaire *MASC*
   to be ex-directory être [6] sur la liste rouge
   We are ex-directory. Nous sommes sur la
   liste rouge.

dirt *NOUN*
   la saleté *FEM*

ℓ **dirty** *ADJECTIVE*
   sale *MASC & FEM*
   a dirty sweater un pull sale
   My hands are dirty. J'ai les mains sales.
   Your trainers are dirty. Tes baskets sont
   sales.
   to get something dirty salir [2] quelque
   chose
   I got my jeans dirty. J'ai sali mon jean.
   to get dirty se salir ☉ [2]
   Trainers get dirty quickly. Les baskets se
   salissent vite.

disability *NOUN*
   l'infirmité *FEM*
   Does he have a disability? Est-il infirme?

disabled *ADJECTIVE*
   handicapé *MASC*, handicapée *FEM*
   to work with disabled people travailler [1]
   avec les handicapés

disadvantage *NOUN*
1 le désavantage *MASC*
2 **to be at a disadvantage** être [6]
   désavantagé
   Without experience you're at a
   disadvantage. Sans expérience, on est
   désavantagé.

to **disagree** *VERB*
   ne pas être [6] d'accord
   I disagree. Je ne suis pas d'accord.
   I disagree with you. Je ne suis pas d'accord
   avec toi.

A
B
C
D
E
F
G
H
I
J
K
L
M
N
O
P
Q
R
S
T
U
V
W
X
Y
Z

ℓ **indicates key words**

to **disappear** VERB
disparaître [27]

disappearance NOUN
la disparition FEM

♪ **disappointed** ADJECTIVE
déçu MASC, déçue FEM
I was disappointed with my results. J'ai été déçu par mes résultats.

disappointment NOUN
la déception FEM

disaster NOUN
le désastre MASC
It was a complete disaster. Ça a été un désastre complet.

disastrous ADJECTIVE
désastreux MASC, désastreuse FEM

disc NOUN
1 (in general) le disque MASC
a compact disc un disque compact
2 a slipped disc une hernie discale
3 (for a vehicle) a tax disc la vignette FEM

discipline NOUN
la discipline FEM

disc-jockey NOUN
le disc-jockey MASC

♪ **disco** NOUN
1 (party) la soirée disco
They're having a disco. Ils font une soirée disco.
2 (club) la discothèque FEM

to **disconnect** VERB
1 (the telephone, electricity) couper [1]
2 (a cooker, a fridge) débrancher [1]

discount NOUN
la réduction FEM

to **discourage** VERB
décourager [52]

to **discover** VERB
découvrir [30]

discovery NOUN
la découverte FEM

discreet ADJECTIVE
discret MASC, discrète FEM

discrimination NOUN
la discrimination FEM
racial discrimination la discrimination raciale

♪ to **discuss** VERB
to discuss something discuter [1] de quelque chose
to discuss the problem discuter du problème
I'm going to discuss it with Phil. Je vais en discuter avec Phil.

discussion NOUN
la discussion FEM

disease NOUN
la maladie FEM

disgraceful ADJECTIVE
scandaleux MASC, scandaleuse FEM

disguise NOUN ▶ SEE disguise VERB
le déguisement MASC
to be in disguise être [6] déguisé
Nobody recognised him because he was in disguise. Personne ne l'a reconnu parce qu'il était déguisé.

to **disguise** VERB ▶ SEE disguise NOUN
déguiser [1]
He was disguised as a woman. Il était déguisé en femme.

disgust NOUN
le dégoût MASC

disgusted ADJECTIVE
dégoûté MASC, dégoûtée FEM

♪ **disgusting** ADJECTIVE
dégoûtant MASC, dégoûtante FEM

♪ **dish** NOUN
1 (plate, food) le plat MASC
a large white dish un grand plat blanc
my favourite dish. mon plat favori.
2 to do the dishes faire [10] la vaisselle
It's my turn to do the dishes. C'est à moi de faire la vaisselle.
3 (TV) une antenne parabolique
• dishcloth
le torchon

dishonest ADJECTIVE
malhonnête MASC & FEM

dishonesty NOUN
la malhonnêteté FEM

♪ **dishwasher** NOUN
la lave-vaisselle INVARIABLE MASC

disinfectant NOUN
le désinfectant MASC

♪ **disk** NOUN
le disque MASC
the hard disk le disque dur
• disk drive
une unité de disque

♪ **diskette** NOUN
la disquette FEM

to **dislike** VERB
ne pas aimer [1]

⬤ means the verb takes être to form the perfect

I dislike sport. Je n'aime pas le sport.
She dislikes Becky. Elle n'aime pas Becky.

to **dismiss** VERB
(employees) licencier [1]

disobedient ADJECTIVE
désobéissant MASC, désobéissante FEM

to **disobey** VERB
1 (a person) désobéir à [2]
2 (the rules) enfreindre [60]

display NOUN ▸ SEE **display** VERB
1 une exposition FEM
a handicrafts display une exposition d'artisanat
to be on display être [6] exposé
2 (in a shop) **a window display** une vitrine
3 (of fireworks) un feu d'artifice
There will be a firework display in the square. Il y aura un feu d'artifice dans la place.

to **display** VERB ▸ SEE **display** NOUN
exposer [1]

disposable ADJECTIVE
jetable MASC & FEM

dispute NOUN
la dispute FEM

to **disqualify** VERB
disqualifier [1]

to **disrupt** VERB
perturber [1]

to **dissolve** VERB
dissoudre [67]

ℓ **distance** NOUN
la distance FEM
It's within walking distance. On peut y aller à pied.
from a distance de loin
I didn't recognise Adam from a distance. Je n'ai pas reconnu Adam de loin.
in the distance au loin
We saw the fire in the distance. Nous avons vu l'incendie au loin.

distant ADJECTIVE
lointain MASC, lointaine FEM

distinct ADJECTIVE
net MASC, nette FEM

distinctly ADVERB
distinctement
It's distinctly odd. C'est vraiment bizarre.

to **distract** VERB
distraire [78]

to **distribute** VERB
distribuer [1]

district NOUN
1 (in a town) le quartier MASC
a poor district of Paris un quartier pauvre de Paris
2 (in the country) la région FEM

to **disturb** VERB
déranger [52]
Do not disturb. Ne pas déranger.
Sorry to disturb you. Je suis désolé de vous déranger.

ditch NOUN ▸ SEE **ditch** VERB
le fossé MASC

to **ditch** VERB ▸ SEE **ditch**
(informal) **to ditch somebody** plaquer [1] quelqu'un
I ditched him. Je l'ai plaqué.

dive NOUN ▸ SEE **dive** VERB
le plongeon MASC

to **dive** VERB ▸ SEE **dive** NOUN
plonger [52]

diver NOUN
le plongeur MASC, la plongeuse FEM

ℓ **diversion** NOUN
(on the roads) la déviation FEM

to **divide** VERB
diviser [1]

diving NOUN
la plongée FEM
to go diving faire [10] de la plongée
Let's go diving! Faisons de la plongée!
• **diving board**
le plongeoir

division NOUN
la division FEM

divorce NOUN ▸ SEE **divorce** VERB
le divorce MASC

to **divorce** VERB ▸ SEE **divorce**
divorcer [61]
They divorced last year. Ils ont divorcé l'année dernière.

divorced ADJECTIVE
divorcé MASC, divorcée FEM
My parents are divorced. Mes parents sont divorcés.

DIY NOUN
le bricolage MASC
to do DIY faire [10] du bricolage
Dad doesn't like doing DIY. Mon père n'aime pas le bricolage.
a DIY shop un magasin de bricolage

dizzy ADJECTIVE
I feel dizzy. J'ai la tête qui tourne.

DJ *NOUN*
le **disc-jockey** *MASC*

♀to **do** *VERB*
1 (*to carry out*) faire [10]
What are you doing? Qu'est-ce que tu fais?
I'm doing my homework. Je fais mes devoirs.
What have you done with the hammer? Qu'est-ce que tu as fait du marteau?
2 (*to make sentences with **no, not***) ne … pas
I do not like mushrooms, I don't like mushrooms. Je n'aime pas les champignons.
She does not like spinach, She doesn't like spinach. Elle n'aime pas les épinards.
You did not shut the door, You didn't shut the door. Tu n'as pas fermé la porte.
It doesn't matter. Ça ne fait rien.
3 (*when **do** refers to another verb, it is not translated*) **'Do you live here?' — 'Yes, I do.'** 'Est-ce que tu habites ici?' — 'Oui.'
She has more money than I do. Elle a plus d'argent que moi.
'I live in Chester.' — 'So do I.' 'J'habite à Chester.' — 'Moi aussi.'
'I didn't phone Gemma.' — 'Neither did I.' 'Je n'ai pas appelé Gemma.' — 'Moi non plus.'
4 (*used to form questions*) **Do you want some strawberries?** Est-ce que tu veux des fraises?, Veux-tu des fraises?
When does it start? Quand est-ce que ça commence?
How did you open it? Comment l'as-tu ouvert?
5 (*in question tags*) **don't you?, doesn't he? etc** n'est-ce pas?
You know Bill, don't you? Tu connais Bill, n'est-ce pas?
She left on Thursday, didn't she? Elle est partie jeudi, n'est-ce pas?
6 (*to say enough*) **That'll do.** Ça ira.
Fifteen will do. Avec quinze ça suffit.
7 (*to concern*) **It has to do with money.** Il s'agit d'argent.
It has nothing to do with her. Ça ne la regarde pas.
• **could do with something** avoir [5] besoin de
I could do with a rest. J'ai bien besoin de me reposer.
• **to do something up**
1 (*your shoes*) lacer [61]
2 (*a jacket, cardigan*) boutonner [1]
3 (*a house*) retaper [1]
• **to do without something** se passer ◉ [1] de quelque chose
We did without butter. Nous nous sommes

passés de beurre.

♀**doctor** *NOUN*
le **médecin** *MASC*
Her mother's a doctor. Sa mère est médecin.

document *NOUN*
le **document** *MASC*

documentary *NOUN*
le **documentaire** *MASC*

dodgems *PLURAL NOUN*
the dodgems les autos tamponneuses *FEM PL*

♀**dog** *NOUN*
le **chien** *MASC* (*female*) la **chienne** *FEM*

♀**do-it-yourself** *NOUN*
le **bricolage** *MASC*

dole *NOUN*
les **allocations chômage**
to be on the dole être [6] au chômage
Ken is on the dole. Ken est au chômage.

♀**doll** *NOUN*
la **poupée** *FEM*

dollar *NOUN*
le **dollar** *MASC*

dolphin *NOUN*
le **dauphin** *MASC*

Dominican *ADJECTIVE* ▸ SEE **Dominican** *NOUN*
dominicain *MASC*, **dominicaine** *FEM*

Dominican *NOUN* ▸ SEE **Dominican** *ADJECTIVE*
le **Dominicain** *MASC*, la **Dominicaine** *FEM*

Dominican Republic *NOUN*
la **République dominicaine**

domino *NOUN*
le **domino** *MASC*
to play dominoes jouer [1] aux dominos
Do you want to play dominoes? Tu veux jouer aux dominos?

donation *NOUN*
le **don** *MASC*

donkey *NOUN*
un **âne** *MASC*

don't ▸ SEE **do**

♀**door** *NOUN*
1 (*of a house*) la **porte** *FEM*
Could you open the door? Tu peux ouvrir la porte?
Please shut the door! Ferme la porte, s'il te plaît!
2 (*of a car*) la **portière** *FEM*

◉ **means the verb takes être to form the perfect**

doorbell NOUN
  la **sonnerie** FEM
  to ring the doorbell sonner [1] à la porte
  There's the doorbell! On sonne!

dormitory NOUN
  le **dortoir** MASC

dot NOUN
1 (written) le **point** MASC
2 (on fabric) le **pois** MASC
3 **on the dot** pile
  The train arrived at ten on the dot. Le train est arrivé à dix heures pile.

double ADJECTIVE ▶ SEE **double** ADVERB
1 (twice as much) **double**
  a double whisky un double whisky
  a double helping of chips une double portion de frites
2 (for two people) **a double room** une chambre pour deux personnes
  a double bed un grand lit

double ADVERB ▶ SEE **double** ADJECTIVE
  le **double**
  double the time le double du temps
  I paid double the price. J'ai payé le double du prix.
• **double bass**
  la contrebasse
• **double-decker bus**
  un autobus à impériale
• **double-glazing**
  le double vitrage

doubles NOUN
  (in tennis, squash) le **double** MASC
  to play a game of doubles faire [10] un double
  We played a game of doubles. Nous avons fait un double.

doubt NOUN ▶ SEE **doubt** VERB
  le **doute** MASC
  There's no doubt about it. Il n'y a aucun doute là-dessus.
  I have my doubts. J'ai des doutes.

to **doubt** VERB ▶ SEE **doubt** NOUN
  to doubt something douter [1] de quelque chose
  I doubt it. J'en doute.
  I doubt that ... douter que ... (+ subjunctive)
  I doubt that they'll do it. Je doute qu'ils le fassent.

doubtful ADJECTIVE
1 pas sûr MASC, pas sûre FEM
  It's doubtful. Ce n'est pas sûr.
2 **to be doubtful about doing something** hésiter [1] à faire quelque chose
  I'm doubtful about inviting them together. J'hésite à les inviter ensemble.

dough NOUN
  la **pâte** FEM

doughnut NOUN
  le **beignet** MASC

Dover NOUN
  Douvres
  the ferry from Dover to Calais le ferry qui relie Douvres à Calais

down ADVERB, PREPOSITION
1 (below) **en bas**
  He's down in the cellar. Il est en bas dans la cave.
2 (showing movement) **She came down** . Elle est descendue.
  She was walking down the street. Elle descendait la rue.
  She sat down on the sofa. Elle s'est assise sur le canapé.
  Jenny ran down the stairs. Jenny a descendu l'escalier en courant.
  Paul went down to the kitchen. Paul est descendu dans la cuisine.
3 (nearby) **à côté**
  There's a chemist's just down the road. Il y a une pharmacie juste à côté.

download VERB
  télécharger [52]

ℓ **downstairs** ADJECTIVE, ADVERB
1 (showing where) **en bas**
  She's downstairs in the sitting-room. Elle est en bas dans le salon.
  The dog sleeps downstairs. Le chien dort en bas.
2 (showing belonging) **du dessous**
  Who lives in the downstairs flat ? Qui habite l'appartement du dessous?
  Have you met the people downstairs? As-tu rencontré les voisins du dessous?

to **doze** VERB
  sommeiller [1]

dozen NOUN
  la **douzaine** FEM
  a dozen eggs une douzaine d'œufs

drag NOUN ▶ SEE **drag** VERB
  (informal) **What a drag!** Quelle barbe!
  She's a bit of a drag. Elle n'est pas marrante.

to **drag** VERB ▶ SEE **drag** NOUN
  (informal) **traîner** [1]

dragon NOUN
  le **dragon** MASC

drain NOUN ▶ SEE **drain** VERB
  un **égout** MASC

ℓ indicates key words

to **drain** VERB ▸ SEE **drain** NOUN
(vegetables, pasta) **égoutter** [1]

drama NOUN
1 (in theatre) l'**art dramatique** MASC
2 (fuss)
(informal) **He made a big drama out of it.** Il en a fait tout un cinéma.

dramatic ADJECTIVE
spectaculaire MASC & FEM

draught NOUN
le **courant d'air** MASC

draughts NOUN
les **dames** FEM PL
to play draughts jouer [1] aux dames
Grandad taught me to play draughts. Mon grand-père m'a appris à jouer aux dames.

♀ **draw** VERB ▸ SEE **draw** NOUN
1 (a picture, an object) **dessiner** [1]
She can draw really well. Elle dessine vraiment bien.
I can't draw horses. Je ne sais pas dessiner les chevaux.
2 **to draw a picture** faire [10] un dessin
3 (the curtains) **tirer** [1] les rideaux
Shall I draw the curtains? Tu veux que je tire les rideaux?
4 (a crowd) **attirer** [1] une foule de spectateurs
The concert drew a big crowd. Le concert a attiré une foule de spectateurs.
5 (Sports) **faire** [10] match nul
We drew three all. Nous avons fait match nul trois à trois.
6 **to draw lots** tirer [1] au sort
They drew lots for the winner. Ils ont tiré le gagnant au sort.

♀ **draw** NOUN ▸ SEE **draw** VERB
1 (Sports) le **match nul**
It was a draw. Ils ont fait match nul.
2 (in a lottery) le **tirage au sort**
• **drawback**
un **inconvénient** MASC

drawer NOUN
le **tiroir** MASC

♀ **drawing** NOUN
le **dessin** MASC
• **drawing pin**
la **punaise** FEM

dreadful ADJECTIVE
affreux MASC, **affreuse** FEM

dreadfully ADVERB
terriblement
I was dreadfully late. J'étais terriblement en retard.

I'm dreadfully sorry. Je suis vraiment navré.

dream NOUN ▸ SEE **dream** VERB
le **rêve** MASC
my dream holiday mes vacances de rêve
to have a dream faire [10] un rêve
I had a horrible dream. J'ai fait un rêve horrible.

to **dream** VERB ▸ SEE **dream** NOUN
rêver [1]
to dream about something rêver de quelque chose
I was dreaming about the sea. Je rêvais de la mer.

drenched ADJECTIVE
trempé MASC, **trempée** FEM
to get drenched se faire ◉ [10] tremper
We got drenched. On s'est fait tremper.

♀ **dress** NOUN ▸ SEE **dress** VERB
la **robe** FEM

♀ to **dress** VERB ▸ SEE **dress** NOUN
to dress a child habiller [1] un enfant
I dressed Billy while mum ... J'ai habillé Billy pendant que maman ...
• **to dress up**
se **déguiser** ◉ [1]
Nick dressed up as a vampire. Nick s'est déguisé en vampire.

♀ **dressed** ADJECTIVE
1 **habillé** MASC, **habillée** FEM
Is he dressed yet? Est-ce qu'il est habillé?
to be dressed in something être [6] habillé de quelque chose
She was dressed in black trousers and a yellow shirt. Elle était habillée d'un pantalon noir et d'une chemise jaune.
2 **to get dressed** s'habiller ◉ [1]
I got dressed quickly. Je me suis vite habillé (boy speaking), Je me suis vite habillée (girl speaking).

dressing gown NOUN
la **robe de chambre**

dressing table NOUN
la **coiffeuse** FEM

drier NOUN
1 (for hair) le **sèche-cheveux**
2 (for clothes) le **sèche-linge**

drill NOUN
la **perceuse** FEM

♀ **drink** NOUN ▸ SEE **drink** VERB
1 la **boisson** FEM
a hot drink une boisson chaude
a cold drink une boisson fraîche
2 **Would you like a drink?** Tu veux boire quelque chose?

◉ **means the verb takes être to form the perfect**

to go out for a drink aller ◉ [7] prendre un pot
Let's go out for a drink! Allons prendre un pot!

𝒫 to **drink** VERB ▸ SEE **drink** NOUN
boire [22]
What would you like to drink? Qu'est-ce que tu veux boire?
He drank a glass of water. Il a bu un verre d'eau.

𝒫 **drive** NOUN ▸ SEE **drive** VERB
1 (to a house) une **allée** FEM
2 (in a car) **to go for a drive** faire [10] un tour en voiture
We went for a drive. Nous avons fait un tour en voiture.

𝒫 to **drive** VERB ▸ SEE **drive** NOUN
1 (a car, a bus) **conduire** [26]
to drive a car conduire une voiture
Can you drive? Tu sais conduire?
Yes, I can drive. Oui, je sais conduire.
Suzie drives very fast. Suzie conduit très vite.
I'd like to learn to drive. J'aimerais apprendre à conduire.
2 (to go by car) **aller** ◉ [7] **en voiture**
We drove to Toulouse. Nous sommes allés à Toulouse en voiture.
3 **to drive somebody to a place** emmener [50] quelqu'un à un endroit en voiture
She drove me to the station. Elle m'a emmené en voiture à la gare.
to drive somebody home raccompagner [1] quelqu'un
Peter drove me home. Peter m'a raccompagnée.
4 **to drive somebody mad** rendre [3] quelqu'un fou MASC, rendre quelqu'un folle FEM
She drives me mad! Elle me rend fou! (boy speaking), Elle me rend folle! (girl speaking).

𝒫 **driver** NOUN
1 (of a car) le **conducteur** MASC, la **conductrice** FEM
2 (of a taxi, a bus) le **chauffeur** MASC

driving instructor NOUN
le **moniteur d'auto-école**, la **monitrice d'auto-école**

driving lesson NOUN
la **leçon de conduite**

𝒫 **driving licence** NOUN
le **permis de conduire**

driving school NOUN
l'**école de conduite** FEM

driving test NOUN
l'**examen du permis de conduire** MASC
to take your driving test passer [1] son permis
I'm going to take my driving test soon. Je vais bientôt passer mon permis.
to pass your driving test avoir [5] son permis
Misha's passed her driving test. Misha a eu son permis.

drop NOUN ▸ SEE **drop** VERB
la **goutte** FEM

𝒫 to **drop** VERB ▸ SEE **drop** NOUN
1 **to drop something** laisser [1] tomber quelque chose
I dropped my glasses. J'ai laissé tomber mes lunettes.
I'm dropping history next year. Je vais laisser tomber l'histoire l'année prochaine.
Drop it! Laisse tomber!
2 (a person) **déposer** [1]
Could you drop me at the station? Est-ce que tu peux me déposer à la gare?

𝒫 **drought** NOUN
la **sécheresse** FEM

𝒫 to **drown** VERB
se **noyer** ◉ [39]
She drowned in the lake. Elle s'est noyée dans le lac.
He nearly drowned. Il a failli se noyer.

𝒫 **drug** NOUN
1 (medicine) le **médicament** MASC
2 (illegal) **drugs** la **drogue** FEM
soft drugs les drogues douces
hard drugs les drogues dures
to take drugs se droguer ◉ [1]
He used to take drugs. Il se droguait.
• **drug abuse**
l'usage des stupéfiants MASC
• **drug addict**
le & la toxicomane
• **drug addiction**
la toxicomanie

drum NOUN
1 le **tambour** MASC
2 **the drums** la batterie
Baz plays the drums. Baz joue de la batterie.
• **drum kit**
la batterie

drummer NOUN
le **batteur** MASC, la **batteuse** FEM

drunk ADJECTIVE ▸ SEE **drunk** NOUN
ivre MASC & FEM

𝒫 **indicates key words**

drunk NOUN ▸ SEE **drunk** ADJECTIVE
un & une **ivrogne** MASC & FEM

ℓ **dry** ADJECTIVE ▸ SEE **dry** VERB
1 (clothes, paint, etc) **sec** MASC, **sèche** FEM
   My hair's dry. J'ai les cheveux secs.
2 (weather) **a dry day** un jour de soleil
   in wet weather quand il fait beau
   It's going to be wet tomorrow. Il va faire
   beau demain.

ℓ to **dry** VERB ▸ SEE **dry** ADJECTIVE
1 **sécher** [24]
   She let the towels dry in the sun. Elle a
   laissé sécher les serviettes au soleil.
   to dry the washing faire [10] sécher le linge
   I dried the washing. J'ai fait sécher le linge.
2 **to dry your hair** se sécher ◉ [1] les cheveux
3 (to wipe dry) **essuyer** [41]
   Can you dry the dishes, please? Peux-tu
   essuyer la vaisselle, s'il te plaît?
   to dry your hands s'essuyer ◉ [41] les
   mains
   Dry your hands carefully! Essuie-toi bien
   les mains!
• **dry cleaner's**
   la **teinturerie**

dryer NOUN ▸ SEE **drier**

dual carriageway NOUN
la **route à quatre voies**

dubbed ADJECTIVE
   a dubbed film un film doublé

ℓ **duck** NOUN
le **canard** MASC

due ADJECTIVE, ADVERB
1 **due to** en raison de
   **The match has been cancelled due to bad
   weather.** Le match a été annulé en raison
   du mauvais temps.
2 **to be due to do something** devoir [8] faire
   quelque chose
   We're due to leave on Thursday. Nous
   devons partir jeudi.
   Pria's due back soon. Pria doit bientôt
   revenir.

duke NOUN
le **duc** MASC

dull ADJECTIVE
1 (day, weather) **maussade** MASC & FEM
   dull weather un temps maussade
   It's dull today. Il fait un temps maussade
   aujourd'hui.
2 (boring) **ennuyeux** MASC, **ennuyeuse** FEM

dumb ADJECTIVE
   bête MASC & FEM
   He asked some dumb questions. Il a posé

des questions bêtes.

to **dump** VERB
1 (rubbish) **jeter** [48]
2 (a boyfriend, a girlfriend) **plaquer** [1]
   She's dumped her boyfriend. Elle a plaqué
   son copain.

dune NOUN
la **dune** FEM

dungarees PLURAL NOUN
la **salopette** FEM

dungeon NOUN
le **cachot** MASC

Dunkirk NOUN
Dunkerque

ℓ **during** PREPOSITION
   pendant
   during the night pendant la nuit
   I saw her during the holidays. Je l'ai vue
   pendant les vacances.

dusk NOUN
   at dusk à la nuit tombante

dust NOUN ▸ SEE **dust** VERB
la **poussière** FEM

to **dust** VERB ▸ SEE **dust** NOUN
   épousseter [48]

ℓ **dustbin** NOUN
la **poubelle** FEM
   Put the bag in the dustbin. Jette le sac à la
   poubelle.

dustman NOUN
un **éboueur** MASC

dusty ADJECTIVE
   poussiéreux MASC, **poussiéreuse** FEM

Dutch ADJECTIVE ▸ SEE **Dutch** NOUN
   hollandais MASC, **hollandaise** FEM

Dutch NOUN ▸ SEE **Dutch** ADJECTIVE
1 (the people) **the Dutch** les Hollandais MASC
   PL, les Hollandaises FEM PL
2 (the language) le **hollandais** MASC

duty NOUN
1 le **devoir** MASC
   to have a duty to do something avoir [5] le
   devoir de faire quelque chose
   You have a duty to inform us. Vous avez le
   devoir de nous informer.
2 **to be on duty** être [6] de service
   Dad is on duty at the weekend. Papa est de
   service pendant le week-end.
   to be on night duty être [6] de service de
   nuit
   She's on night duty next week. Elle est de
   service de nuit la semaine prochaine.
   to be off duty ne pas être de service

◉ means the verb takes être to form the perfect

I'm off duty tonight. Je ne suis pas de service ce soir.

duty-free *ADJECTIVE*
hors taxes *MASC & FEM*
the duty-free shops les boutiques hors taxes
duty-free purchases les achats hors taxes

duvet *NOUN*
la **couette** *FEM*
• **duvet cover**
la housse de couette

DVD *NOUN*
le **DVD** *INVARIABLE MASC*
• **DVD player**
le lecteur DVD

dwarf *NOUN*
le **nain** *MASC*, la **naine** *FEM*

dye *NOUN* ▸SEE **dye** *VERB*
la **teinture** *FEM*

to **dye** *VERB* ▸SEE **dye** *NOUN*
teindre [60]
to dye your hair se teindre ⊙ [60] les cheveux
I'm going to dye my hair pink. Je vais me teindre les cheveux en rose.

dynamic *ADJECTIVE*
dynamique *MASC & FEM*

dyslexia *NOUN*
la **dyslexie** *FEM*

dyslexic *ADJECTIVE*
dyslexique *MASC & FEM*

Ee

ℓ **each** *DETERMINER* ▸SEE **each** *PRONOUN*
chaque *MASC & FEM*
each time chaque fois
5 euros for each child cinq euros pour chaque enfant

ℓ **each** *PRONOUN* ▸SEE **each** *DETERMINER*
chacun *MASC*, **chacune** *FEM*
My sisters each have a computer. Mes sœurs ont chacune un ordinateur.
She gave us a pound each. Elle nous a donné une livre chacun.
The posters cost ten pounds each. Les affiches coûtent dix livres chacune.
I have a present for each of you. J'ai un cadeau pour chacun de vous.
We each got a present. Chacun de nous a reçu un cadeau.

each other *PRONOUN*
They love each other. Ils s'aiment.
We write to each other every day. Nous nous écrivons chaque jour.
Do you see each other often? Est-ce que vous vous voyez souvent?

WORD TIP each other is usually translated with a reflexive verb in French.

eagle *NOUN*
un **aigle** *MASC*

ℓ **ear** *NOUN*
une **oreille** *FEM*

earache *NOUN*
une **otite** *FEM*
to have earache avoir [5] une otite

earlier *ADVERB*
1 *(a while ago)* **tout à l'heure**
He phoned earlier. Il a appelé tout à l'heure.
2 *(not as late)* **plus tôt**
I started earlier this time. J'ai commencé plus tôt cette fois.
We had seen him earlier in the day. Nous l'avions vu plus tôt dans la journée.

ℓ **early** *ADVERB* ▸SEE **early** *ADJECTIVE*
1 *(in the day)* **tôt**
early in the morning tôt le matin
It's too early. Il est trop tôt.
John gets up early. John se lève tôt.
2 *(for an appointment)* **en avance**
to be early être [6] en avance
Alice likes to be early. Alice aime être en avance.

ℓ **early** *ADJECTIVE* ▸SEE **early** *ADVERB*
1 *(one of the first)* **premier** *MASC*, **première** *FEM*
in the early months pendant les premiers mois
I'm getting the early train. Je prends le premier train.
2 *(before the usual time)* **tôt**
I had an early lunch. J'ai déjeuné tôt.
Jane's having an early night. Jane va se coucher tôt.
We're making an early start. Nous partons tôt.
3 *(in expressions)* **in the early afternoon** en début d'après-midi
in the early hours au petit matin

to **earn** *VERB*
(money) **gagner** [1]
He earns seven pounds an hour. Il gagne sept livres de l'heure.

earnings PLURAL NOUN
le **salaire** MASC

earphones NOUN
les **écouteurs** MASC PL

earring NOUN
la **boucle d'oreille**

earth NOUN
la **terre** FEM
life on earth la vie sur terre
What on earth are you doing? Mais qu'est-ce que tu fais là?
• **earthquake**
le tremblement de terre

easily ADVERB
1 (without difficulty) **facilement**
2 (by far) **de loin**
Pete's easily the best. Pete est de loin le meilleur.

♂ **east** ADJECTIVE, ADVERB ► SEE **east** NOUN
est
the east side of the city le côté est de la ville
an east wind un vent d'est
a town east of Bordeaux une ville à l'est de Bordeaux
We're going east. Nous allons vers l'est.

WORD TIP **est** never changes.

♂ **east** NOUN ► SEE **east** ADJECTIVE, ADVERB
l'**est** MASC
in the east à l'est
in the east of Scotland dans l'est de l'Écosse

Easter NOUN
Pâques
They're coming at Easter. Ils viennent à Pâques.
Happy Easter! Joyeuses Pâques!
• **Easter Day**
le dimanche de Pâques
• **Easter egg**
un œuf de Pâques

Eastern Europe NOUN
l'**Europe de l'Est** FEM

♂ **easy** ADJECTIVE
facile MASC & FEM
an easy exam un examen facile
It's easy! C'est facile!
It was easy to make. C'était facile à faire.

♂ to **eat** VERB
1 **manger** [52]
He was eating a croissant. Il mangeait un croissant.
We're going to have something to eat. On va manger quelque chose.

2 (a meal) **prendre** [64]
We were eating breakfast. Nous prenions le petit déjeuner.
3 **to eat out** manger au restaurant
Let's eat out tonight. Mangeons au restaurant ce soir.

echo NOUN ► SEE **echo** VERB
un **écho** MASC

to **echo** VERB ► SEE **echo** NOUN
retentir [2]

eclipse NOUN
(of the sun, moon) une **éclipse** FEM

ecological ADJECTIVE
écologique MASC & FEM

ecologist NOUN
un & une **écologiste** MASC & FEM

ecology NOUN
l'**écologie** FEM

economic ADJECTIVE
1 (relating to economics) **économique** MASC & FEM
2 (profitable) **rentable** MASC & FEM

economical ADJECTIVE
1 (person) **économe** MASC & FEM
2 (method) **économique** MASC & FEM

economics NOUN
l'**économie** FEM
to study economics étudier l'économie

economy NOUN
une **économie** FEM

eczema NOUN
l'**eczéma** MASC

♂ **edge** NOUN
1 le **bord** MASC
the edge of the table le bord de la table
at the edge of the lake au bord du lac
2 **to be on edge** être [6] **énervé**
She was all on edge. Elle était vraiment énervée.

edible ADJECTIVE
comestible MASC & FEM

Edinburgh NOUN
Édimbourg

to **edit** VERB
éditer [1]

editor NOUN
1 (of a newspaper) le **rédacteur en chef**, la **rédactrice en chef**
2 (of texts) le **correcteur** MASC, la **correctrice** FEM
3 (Computers) un **éditeur** MASC

⬛ means the verb takes **être** to form the perfect

to educate VERB
(a student) instruire [26]

education NOUN
une **éducation** FEM

educational ADJECTIVE
éducatif MASC, **éducative** FEM
educational toys des jouets éducatifs

effect NOUN
un **effet** MASC
the effect of the accident l'effet de
l'accident
brilliant special effects des effets spéciaux
sensationnels
to have an effect on somebody avoir [5] un
effet sur quelqu'un
It had a good effect on the whole family.
Cela a eu un bon effet sur toute la famille.

effective ADJECTIVE
efficace MASC & FEM

efficient ADJECTIVE
efficace MASC & FEM

effort NOUN
un **effort** MASC
to make an effort faire [10] un effort
David made an effort to help us. David a
fait un effort pour nous aider.
He didn't even make the effort to go. Il n'a
même pas fait l'effort d'y aller.

e.g. ABBREVIATION
(for: for example) par ex, par exemple

ℒ **egg** NOUN
un **œuf** MASC
a dozen eggs une douzaine d'œufs
a fried egg un œuf au plat
two boiled eggs deux œufs à la coque
a hard-boiled egg un œuf dur
scrambled eggs les œufs brouillés
• **egg-cup**
le coquetier
• **eggshell**
la coquille d'œuf
• **egg-white**
le blanc d'œuf
• **egg-yolk**
le jaune d'œuf

eight NUMBER
huit
Maya's eight. Maya a huit ans.

eighteen NUMBER
dix-huit
Jason's eighteen. Jason a dix-huit ans.

eighth ADJECTIVE
1 **huitième** MASC & FEM
on the eighth floor au huitième étage

2 (in dates) **the eighth of July** le huit juillet

eighty NUMBER
quatre-vingts
eighty-five quatre-vingt-cinq

> **WORD TIP** The s of -vingts is omitted when
> another number follows.

Éire NOUN
la **République d'Irlande** FEM

ℒ **either** PRONOUN ▸ SEE **either** CONJUNCTION
1 (one or the other) **l'un ou l'autre** MASC, **l'une
ou l'autre** FEM
Choose either. Choisis l'un ou l'autre.
I don't like either of them. Je n'aime ni l'un
ni l'autre.
2 (both) **les deux** MASC & FEM
Either is possible. Tous les deux sont
possibles.

ℒ **either** CONJUNCTION ▸ SEE **either** PRONOUN
1 (when you give alternatives)
either ... or ou ... ou
either Thursday or Friday ou jeudi ou
vendredi
I'll take either Susie or Judy.
J'accompagnerai ou Susie ou Judy.
2 (in negative statements) **non plus**
He doesn't want to either. Il ne veut pas
non plus.
I don't know them either. Je ne les connais
pas non plus.

elastic ADJECTIVE ▸ SEE **elastic** NOUN
élastique MASC & FEM

elastic NOUN ▸ SEE **elastic** ADJECTIVE
l'élastique MASC
• **elastic band**
un élastique MASC

ℒ **elbow** NOUN
le **coude** MASC

ℒ **elder** ADJECTIVE
aîné MASC, **aînée** FEM
her elder brother son frère aîné
his elder sister sa sœur aînée

elderly ADJECTIVE
âgé MASC, **âgée** FEM
the elderly les personnes âgées

ℒ **eldest** ADJECTIVE
aîné MASC, **aînée** FEM
her eldest brother son frère aîné
his eldest sister sa sœur aînée

to elect VERB
(a leader, a politician) élire [51]

ℒ **election** NOUN
une **élection** FEM
in the elections aux élections

to win an election gagner aux élections
They lost the election. Ils ont perdu aux
élections.

electric ADJECTIVE
électrique MASC & FEM

electrical ADJECTIVE
électrique MASC & FEM

electrician NOUN
un **électricien** MASC, une **électricienne** FEM

℘ **electricity** NOUN
l'**électricité** FEM
the electricity bill la facture d'électricité
to turn off the electricity couper [1] le
courant.

electronic ADJECTIVE
électronique MASC & FEM
• **electronic mail**
le courrier électronique

electronics NOUN
l'**électronique** FEM

℘ **elegant** ADJECTIVE
élégant MASC, élégante FEM

element NOUN
un **élément** MASC

elephant NOUN
un **éléphant** MASC

℘ **eleven** NUMBER
1 onze
Josh is eleven. Josh a onze ans.
2 (a team) **a football eleven** une équipe de
football

eleventh ADJECTIVE
1 onzième MASC & FEM
on the eleventh floor au onzième étage
2 (in dates) **the eleventh of May** le onze mai

to **eliminate** VERB
éliminer [1]

else ADVERB
1 d'autre
somebody else, anybody else quelqu'un
d'autre
Pick somebody else. Choisis quelqu'un
d'autre.
Did you see anybody else? As-tu vu
quelqu'un d'autre?
nothing else, anything else rien d'autre
I don't want anything else. Je ne veux rien
d'autre.
2 **something else, anything else** autre chose
Would you like something else? Désirez-
vous autre chose?
3 **somewhere else, anywhere else** ailleurs
Do you want to go anywhere else? Est-ce

que tu veux aller ailleurs?
4 **or else** sinon
Hurry, or else we'll be late. Dépêche-toi,
sinon nous serons en retard.

℘ to **email** VERB ▶ SEE email NOUN
envoyer [40] un mail
Email me! Envoie-moi un mail!

℘ **email** NOUN ▶ SEE email VERB
1 (a message) le **mail**, un **email**
Did you get my email? As-tu reçu mon
mail?
2 (system) le **courrier électronique**
• **email address**
une adresse email

embarrassed ADJECTIVE
gêné MASC, gênée FEM

embarrassing ADJECTIVE
gênant MASC, gênante FEM

embarrassment NOUN
l'**embarras** MASC

embassy NOUN
une **ambassade** FEM
the French Embassy l'ambassade de France

embroidery NOUN
la **broderie** FEM

℘ **emergency** NOUN
le **cas d'urgence**
It's an emergency! C'est urgent!
In an emergency, break the glass. En cas
d'urgence, casser la vitre.
• **emergency exit**
la sortie de secours
• **emergency landing**
un atterrissage forcé

emotion NOUN
une **émotion** FEM

emotional ADJECTIVE
1 (person) ému MASC, émue FEM
2 (speech, occasion) chargé d'émotion MASC,
chargée d'émotion FEM

emperor NOUN
un **empereur** MASC

emphasis NOUN
un **accent** MASC
to put the emphasis on mettre [11] l'accent
sur

to **emphasize** VERB
1 (to highlight) mettre [11] l'accent sur
2 (to stress a point) insister [1] sur le fait que

empire NOUN
un **empire** MASC
the Roman Empire l'Empire Romain

⬤ means the verb takes être to form the perfect

to **employ** VERB
employer [39]

ℰ **employee** NOUN
le **salarié** MASC, la **salariée** FEM

employer NOUN
un **employeur** MASC, une **employeuse** FEM

employment NOUN
le **travail** MASC

empress NOUN
une **impératrice** FEM

ℰ **empty** ADJECTIVE ▸ SEE **empty** VERB
vide MASC & FEM
an empty bottle une bouteille vide
The room was empty. La pièce était vide.

ℰ to **empty** VERB ▸ SEE **empty** ADJECTIVE
vider [1]
I emptied the teapot into the sink. J'ai vidé
la théière dans l'évier.

to **enclose** VERB
(in a letter) joindre [49]
Please find enclosed a cheque. Veuillez
trouver ci-joint un chèque.

encore NOUN
le **bis** MASC
to give an encore jouer [1] un bis

to **encourage** VERB
encourager [52]
to encourage somebody to do something
encourager quelqu'un à faire quelque chose
She encouraged me to try again. Elle m'a
encouragé à recommencer.

encouragement NOUN
un **encouragement** MASC

encouraging ADJECTIVE
encourageant MASC, **encourageante** FEM

encyclopedia NOUN
une **encyclopédie** FEM

ℰ **end** NOUN ▸ SEE **end** VERB
1 (last part) la **fin** FEM
at the end of the film à la fin du film
I was exhausted by the end of the day.
J'étais épuisé à la fin de la journée.
In the end I went home. Finalement je suis
rentré chez moi.
Sally's coming at the end of June. Sally
viendra fin juin.
2 (in a book, a film) 'The End' 'Fin'
3 (of a table, garden, stick, road) le **bout** MASC
Hold the other end. Tiens l'autre bout.
She lives at the end of the street. Elle
habite au bout de la rue.
4 (in tennis, football) le **côté** MASC
We change ends at half-time. Nous

changeons de côté à la mi-temps.

ℰ to **end** VERB ▸ SEE **end** NOUN
1 (to put an end to) mettre [11] fin à
They've ended the strike. Ils ont mis fin à
la grève.
2 (to come to an end) se terminer [1]
The day ended with a dance. La journée
s'est terminée par un bal.
• to end up
to end up doing something finir [2] par
faire quelque chose
We ended up taking a taxi. Nous avons fini
par prendre un taxi.
end to end up somewhere se retrouver [1]
quelque part
Mark ended up in San Francisco. Mark s'est
retrouvé à San Francisco.

endangered ADJECTIVE
menacé MASC, **menacée** FEM
an endangered species une espèce en voie
d'extinction

ending NOUN
la **fin** FEM

endless ADJECTIVE
interminable MASC & FEM

enemy NOUN
un **ennemi** MASC, une **ennemie** FEM
to make enemies se faire ◎ [10] des
ennemis

energetic ADJECTIVE
énergique MASC & FEM

energy NOUN
l'**énergie** FEM

ℰ **engaged** ADJECTIVE
1 (to be married) **fiancé** MASC, **fiancée** FEM
Kate's engaged. Kate est fiancée.
They're engaged. Ils sont fiancés.
They're going to get engaged. Ils vont se
fiancer.
2 (phones, toilets) **occupé** MASC, **occupée** FEM
It's engaged, I'll ring later. C'est occupé,
j'appellerai plus tard.

engagement NOUN
(to marry) les **fiançailles** FEM PL
• engagement ring
la bague de fiançailles

ℰ **engine** NOUN
1 (in a car) le **moteur** MASC
2 (pulling a train) la **locomotive** FEM

ℰ **engineer** NOUN
1 (repair person) le **technicien** MASC
2 (graduate) un **ingénieur** MASC

ℰ indicates key words

engineering NOUN
l'**ingénierie** FEM
to study engineering faire [10] des études d'ingénieur

♀ **England** NOUN
l'**Angleterre** FEM
in England en Angleterre
Richard lives in England. Richard vit en Angleterre.
to England en Angleterre
He came to England in 1999. Il est venu en Angleterre en 1999.
I'm from England. Je suis anglais *(boy speaking)*, Je suis anglaise *(girl speaking)*.

WORD TIP Countries and regions in French take le, la or les.

♀ **English** ADJECTIVE ▸ SEE **English** NOUN
1 *(of or from England)* **anglais** MASC, **anglaise** FEM
  the English team l'équipe anglaise
2 *(of the English language)* **d'anglais**
  an English lesson un cours d'anglais
  our English teacher notre professeur d'anglais

WORD TIP Adjectives never have capitals in French, even for nationality or regional origin.

♀ **English** NOUN ▸ SEE **English** ADJECTIVE
1 *(the people)* **the English** les Anglais MASC PL
2 *(the language)* **Do you speak English?** Parlez-vous anglais?
  He answered in English. Il a répondu en anglais.

WORD TIP Languages never have capitals in French.

• **English Channel**
  la Manche
• **Englishman**
  un Anglais
• **Englishwoman**
  une Anglaise

♀ to **enjoy** VERB
1 **aimer** [1]
  Did you enjoy the party? As-tu aimé la soirée?
  We really enjoyed the concert. Nous avons beaucoup aimé le concert.
2 **to enjoy doing something** aimer [1] faire quelque chose
  I enjoy swimming. J'aime nager.
3 **to enjoy yourself** s'amuser [1]
  We really enjoyed ourselves. Nous nous sommes bien amusés.
  Did you enjoy yourself? Tu t'es bien amusé?
  Enjoy your meal! Bon appétit!

enjoyable ADJECTIVE
agréable MASC & FEM

to **enlarge** VERB
(a photo) **agrandir** [2]

enlargement NOUN
(of a photo) un **agrandissement** MASC

enormous ADJECTIVE
énorme MASC & FEM

♀ **enough** ADVERB, PRONOUN
1 **assez**
  There's enough for everyone. Il y en a assez pour tout le monde.
  That's enough. Ça suffit.
2 *(followed by a noun)* **assez de**
  enough water assez d'eau
  Is there enough bread? Est-ce qu'il y a assez de pain?
3 *(following an adjective or adverb)* **assez**
  This jacket's big enough for you. Cette veste est assez grande pour toi.
  Am I walking slowly enough? Est-ce que je marche assez lentement?

to **enquire** VERB
se renseigner [1]
to enquire about the trains se renseigner sur les trains

enquiry NOUN
la **demande de renseignements**
to make enquiries about something demander [1] des renseignements sur quelque chose

to **enrol** VERB
s'inscrire [38]
to enrol on a course s'inscrire à un cours

♀ to **enter** VERB
1 *(to go inside)* **entrer** ⊙ [1] **dans**
  We all entered the church. Nous sommes tous entrés dans l'église.
2 **to enter for something** s'inscrire [38] à quelque chose
  I'm going to enter for seven GCSEs. Je vais m'inscrire à sept épreuves de GCSE.

to **entertain** VERB
divertir [2]
Find something to entertain the children. Trouve quelque chose pour divertir les enfants.

entertaining ADJECTIVE
amusant MASC, **amusante** FEM

entertainment NOUN
les **distractions** FEM PL
There wasn't much entertainment at night. Il n'y avait pas beaucoup de distractions le soir.

⊙ means the verb takes être to form the perfect

enthusiasm NOUN
l'**enthousiasme** MASC

enthusiast NOUN
passionné MASC, **passionnée** FEM
He's a rugby enthusiast. C'est un passionné de rugby.

enthusiastic ADJECTIVE
enthousiaste MASC & FEM

entire ADJECTIVE
entier MASC, **entière** FEM
The entire class went to the theatre. La classe entière est allée au théâtre.

entirely ADVERB
complètement

entrance NOUN
une **entrée** FEM

entry NOUN
(the way in) une **entrée** FEM
'No entry' 'Défense d'entrer'
• **entry phone**
un **interphone** MASC

envelope NOUN
une **enveloppe** FEM

envious ADJECTIVE
envieux MASC, **envieuse** FEM
to be envious of être [6] jaloux de
She's envious of my results. Elle est jalouse de mes résultats.

environment NOUN
l'**environnement** MASC

environmental ADJECTIVE
écologique MASC & FEM

environment-friendly ADJECTIVE
écologique MASC & FEM

envy NOUN
l'**envie** FEM

epidemic NOUN
une **épidémie** FEM

epileptic NOUN
un & une **épileptique** MASC & FEM

episode NOUN
un **épisode** MASC

equal ADJECTIVE ▸ SEE **equal** VERB
égal MASC, **égale** FEM, **égaux** MASC PL, **égales** FEM PL
in equal quantities en quantités égales
to **equal** VERB ▸ SEE **equal** ADJECTIVE
égaler [1]

equality NOUN
l'**égalité** FEM

to **equalize** VERB
(in a contest, match) **égaliser** [1]

equally ADVERB
(to share, divide up) **en parts égales**

equator NOUN
l'**équateur** MASC

to **equip** VERB
équiper [1]
Joe's well equipped for the hike. Joe est bien équipé pour la randonnée.
I was rather ill equipped. J'étais plutôt mal équipé.
to be equipped with something être [6] équipé de quelque chose

equipment NOUN
1 *(for sport)* l'**équipement** MASC
2 *(in an office, a lab)* le **matériel** MASC
laboratory equipment le matériel de laboratoire

equivalent ADJECTIVE
to be equivalent to something être [6] équivalent à quelque chose
Grade A is equivalent to 16 out of 20. Un A est équivalent à 16 sur 20.

error NOUN
1 *(in spelling, typing)* la **faute** FEM
a spelling error une faute d'orthographe
2 *(in maths, on a PC)* une **erreur** FEM
• **error message**
le message d'erreur

escalator NOUN
un **escalier mécanique**

escape NOUN ▸ SEE **escape** VERB
(from prison) une **évasion** FEM

escape VERB ▸ SEE **escape** NOUN
1 *(person)* **s'évader** [1]
an escaped prisoner un évadé
2 *(animal)* **s'échapper** [1]

escort NOUN
l'**escorte** FEM
a police escort une escorte de police

♪ **especially** ADJECTIVE
1 *(above all)* **surtout**
There are lots of tourists, especially in August. Il y a beaucoup de touristes, surtout en août.
2 *(unusually)* **particulièrement**
'Was it funny?' — 'Not especially'. 'C'était drôle?' — 'Pas particulièrement'.

essay NOUN
la **rédaction** FEM
an essay on pollution une rédaction sur la pollution

essential ADJECTIVE
essentiel MASC, essentielle FEM
It's essential to reply quickly. Il est
essentiel de répondre vite.

establishment NOUN
un établissement MASC

estate NOUN
1 (housing estate) la cité FEM
2 (car) le break MASC
3 (big house and grounds) le domaine MASC
• estate agent
un agent immobilier
• estate agency
une agence immobilière

estimate NOUN ▶ SEE **estimate** VERB
1 (quote for work) le devis MASC
2 (rough guess) une estimation FEM
to **estimate** VERB ▶ SEE **estimate** NOUN
évaluer [1]

etc ABBREVIATION
etc

ethnic ADJECTIVE
ethnique MASC & FEM
an ethnic minority une minorité ethnique

EU NOUN
(short for European Union) la UE FEM, l'Union
européenne FEM

euro NOUN
un euro MASC
The euro is divided into cents. L'euro est
divisé en centimes.

Europe NOUN
l'Europe FEM
to travel outside Europe voyager en dehors
de l'Europe

European ADJECTIVE ▶ SEE **European** NOUN
européen MASC, européenne FEM

European NOUN ▶ SEE **European** ADJECTIVE
un Européen MASC, une Européenne FEM
• European Union
l'Union européenne FEM

eurozone NOUN
la zone euro

to **evacuate** VERB
faire [10] évacuer
The police evacuated the building. La
police a fait évacuer l'immeuble.

to **evaporate** VERB
s'évaporer [1]

ℓ **eve** NOUN
la veille FEM
Christmas Eve la veille de Noël
New Year's Eve la Saint-Sylvestre

ℓ **even** ADVERB ▶ SEE **even** ADJECTIVE
1 (when you talk about something surprising)
même
Even Lisa didn't like it. Même Lisa ne l'a
pas aimé.
He did it without even asking. Il l'a fait
sans même demander.
even if même si
Even if they arrive now, we'll be late.
Même s'ils arrivent maintenant, nous
serons en retard.
I don't like animals, not even dogs. Je
n'aime pas les animaux, même pas les
chiens.
even so quand même
Even so, we had a good time. Nous nous
sommes bien amusés quand même.
2 (in comparisons) encore plus
Her suitcase was even bigger. Sa valise
était encore plus grande.
Omar drove even faster. Omar est allé
encore plus vite.
I like this song even more than the last.
J'aime cette chanson encore plus que la
dernière.

ℓ **even** ADJECTIVE ▶ SEE **even** ADVERB
1 (surface, layer) régulier MASC, régulière FEM
2 (number) pair MASC, paire FEM
Six is an even number. Six est un numéro
pair.
3 (with the same score) à égalité
Lee and Barry are even. Lee et Barry sont
à égalité.

ℓ **evening** NOUN ▶ SEE **evening** ADJECTIVE
1 le soir MASC
at six o'clock in the evening à six heures
du soir
See you this evening! À ce soir!
Let's eat out tomorrow evening! Allons
manger au restaurant demain soir!
I saw the film on Thursday evening. J'ai vu
le film jeudi soir.
I'd spoken to him the evening before. Je lui
avais parlé la veille au soir.
Bill watches TV every evening. Bill regarde
la télé tous les soirs.
I work in the evenings. Je travaille le soir.
2 (from beginning to end) la soirée FEM
an evening with Madonna une soirée avec
Madonna
Did you go out during the evening? Est-ce
que tu es sorti pendant la soirée?

evening ADJECTIVE ▶ SEE **evening** NOUN
du soir
the evening meal le repas du soir
• evening class
le cours du soir

ℰ **event** NOUN
1 *(happening)* un **événement** *MASC*
   an important event un événement important
2 *(in athletics)* une **épreuve** *FEM*
   track events les épreuves de vitesse

eventful ADJECTIVE
   mouvementé *MASC*, **mouvementée** *FEM*

eventually ADVERB
   finalement

ℰ **ever** ADVERB
1 *(at any time)* **jamais**
   Have you ever been to France? As-tu jamais été en France?
   Haven't you ever noticed that? Tu n'as jamais remarqué ça?
   Nobody ever came. Personne n'est jamais venu.
   I hardly ever see her. Je ne la vois presque jamais.
   It was hotter than ever. Il faisait plus chaud que jamais.
2 *(always)* **toujours**
   Harry was as cheerful as ever. Harry était toujours aussi gai.
   Dad's the same as ever. Papa est toujours le même.
3 **ever since** depuis
   And it's been raining ever since. Et depuis il pleut tout le temps.

ℰ **every** ADJECTIVE
1 *(all)* **tous** *MASC PL*, **toutes** *FEM PL*
   Every house has a garden. Toutes les maisons ont un jardin.
   He sees her every day. Il la voit tous les jours.
   I've seen every one of his films. J'ai vu tous ses films.
2 *(showing repetition)* **every other week** une semaine sur deux
   every now and then de temps en temps
   to stop every ten kilometres s'arrêter tous les dix kilomètres
   It rains every time we go there. Il pleut chaque fois qu'on y va.

ℰ **everybody**, **everyone** PRONOUN
1 **tout le monde**
   Everybody knows she likes Sam. Tout le monde sait qu'elle aime bien Sam.
2 **everybody else** tous les autres
   We stayed but everyone else left. Nous sommes restés mais tous les autres sont partis.

ℰ **everything** PRONOUN
   tout
   Everything is ready. Tout est prêt.

Everything's fine. Tout va bien.
Everything you said was true. Tout ce que tu as dit était vrai.
everything else tout le reste

ℰ **everywhere** ADVERB
   partout
   There were tourists everywhere. Il y avait des touristes partout.
   Everywhere she went, people recognised her. Partout où elle allait, les gens la reconnaissaient.
   I've looked everywhere else. J'ai cherché partout ailleurs.

evidently ADVERB
   manifestement

evil ADJECTIVE ▶ SEE **evil** NOUN
   mauvais *MASC*, **mauvaise** *FEM*

evil NOUN ▶ SEE **evil** ADJECTIVE
   le **mal** *MASC*

exact ADJECTIVE
   exact *MASC*, **exacte** *FEM*
   the exact amount la somme exacte
   It's the exact opposite. C'est exactement le contraire.

exactly ADVERB
   exactement
   Yes, exactly. Oui, exactement.
   They're exactly the same age. Ils ont exactement le même âge.

to **exaggerate** VERB
   exagérer [24]

exaggeration NOUN
   une **exagération** *FEM*

ℰ **exam** NOUN
   un **examen** *MASC*
   a history exam un examen d'histoire
   to take an exam passer [1] un examen
   to pass an exam réussir [2] un examen
   I passed all my exams. J'ai réussi tous mes examens.
   to fail an exam échouer [1] à un examen
   Adam failed the Latin exam. Adam a échoué à l'examen de latin.

examination NOUN
   un **examen** *MASC*

to **examine** VERB
   examiner [1]

examiner NOUN
   un **examinateur** *MASC*, une **examinatrice** *FEM*

ℰ **example** NOUN
   un **exemple** *MASC*
   for example par exemple

ℰ indicates key words

Camping, for example, is fun.
Le camping, par exemple, est un plaisir.
to set a good example donner l'exemple

_ℐ_ **excellent** ADJECTIVE
excellent MASC, **excellente** FEM

_ℐ_ **except** PREPOSITION
1 **sauf**
except in March sauf au mois de mars
except when it rains sauf quand il pleut
I train every day except Tuesday. Je
m'entraîne tous les jours sauf le mardi.
2 **except for** sauf
We all went except for Liz. Nous y sommes
tous allés sauf Liz.

exception NOUN
une **exception** FEM
without exception sans exception
with the exception of à l'exception de

_ℐ_ **exchange** NOUN ▸ SEE **exchange** VERB
1 un **échange** MASC
in exchange for the shoes en échange des
chaussures
2 (an exchange visit) un **échange**
I went on an exchange to France. J'ai fait
un échange en France.

_ℐ_ **exchange** VERB ▸ SEE **exchange** NOUN
échanger [52]
**Can I exchange this sweatshirt for a
smaller one?** Puis-je échanger ce sweatshirt
contre le même la taille au-dessous?

exchange rate NOUN
le **taux de change**

to excite VERB
exciter [1]

excited ADJECTIVE
excité MASC, **excitée** FEM
The children are excited. Les enfants sont
excités.
to get excited s'exciter [1]
They get excited when they hear the car.
Ils s'excitent quand ils entendent la voiture.

excitement NOUN
l'**excitation** FEM

_ℐ_ **exciting** ADJECTIVE
passionnant MASC, **passionnante** FEM
a really exciting film un film vraiment
passionnant

exclamation mark NOUN
le **point d'exclamation**

excursion NOUN
une **excursion** FEM

excuse NOUN ▸ SEE **excuse** VERB
une **excuse** FEM

I've got a good excuse. J'ai une bonne
excuse.

_ℐ_ **to excuse** VERB ▸ SEE **excuse** NOUN
excuser [1]
Excuse me! Excuse-moi!, Excusez-moi!
(formal)

to execute VERB
exécuter [1]

_ℐ_ **exercise** NOUN
un **exercice** MASC
a maths exercise un exercice de maths
physical exercise l'exercice physique
• **exercise bike**
le vélo d'appartement
• **exercise book**
le cahier

exhaust (pipe) NOUN
le **pot d'échappement**

_ℐ_ **exhausted** ADJECTIVE
épuisé MASC, **épuisée** FEM

exhaust fumes PLURAL NOUN
le **gaz d'échappement**

exhibition NOUN
une **exposition** FEM

to exist VERB
exister [1]

_ℐ_ **exit** NOUN
la **sortie** FEM

to expand VERB
s'agrandir [2]
The town is expanding. La ville se
développe.

to expect VERB
1 (guests, a baby) **attendre** [3]
We're expecting thirty people. Nous
attendons trente personnes.
2 (something to happen) **s'attendre** [3] à
I didn't expect that. Je ne m'attendais pas
à ça.
I didn't expect it at all. Je ne m'y attendais
pas du tout.
3 (to suppose) **imaginer** [1]
I expect she'll bring her boyfriend.
J'imagine qu'elle amènera son copain.
Yes, I expect so. Oui, j'imagine.

expedition NOUN
une **expédition** FEM

to expel VERB
to be expelled se faire ◉ [10] renvoyer
Lee has been expelled. Lee s'est fait
renvoyer.

◉ means the verb takes **être** to form the perfect

expenses *PLURAL NOUN*
les **frais** *MASC PL*

*ᵖ***expensive** *ADJECTIVE*
cher *MASC*, **chère** *FEM*
expensive trainers des baskets chers
an expensive meal un repas cher
the most expensive computers les
ordinateurs les plus chers
Those shoes are too expensive for me. Ces
chaussures sont trop chères pour moi.

experience *NOUN*
une **expérience** *FEM*

experienced *ADJECTIVE*
expérimenté *MASC*, **expérimentée** *FEM*

experiment *NOUN* ▸ SEE **experiment** *VERB*
une **expérience** *FEM*
Let's do an experiment! Faisons une
expérience!

to **experiment** *VERB* ▸ SEE **experiment** *NOUN*
expérimenter [1]

expert *NOUN*
le & la **spécialiste** *MASC & FEM*
He's a computer expert. C'est un
spécialiste en informatique.

expiry date *NOUN*
la **date d'expiration** *FEM*

*ᵖ*to **explain** *VERB*
expliquer [1]
Can you explain it to me? Tu peux me
l'expliquer?

*ᵖ***explanation** *NOUN*
une **explication** *FEM*

to **explode** *VERB*
exploser [1]

to **explore** *VERB*
explorer [1]

explosion *NOUN*
une **explosion** *FEM*

export *NOUN* ▸ SEE **export** *VERB*
une **exportation** *FEM*
the chief export le premier produit
d'exportation

to **export** *VERB* ▸ SEE **export** *NOUN*
exporter [1]
France exports a lot of cars. La France
exporte beaucoup de voitures.

exposure *NOUN*
(of a film) la **pose** *FEM*
a 24-exposure film une pellicule de vingt-
quatre poses

express *ADJECTIVE* ▸ SEE **express** *NOUN, VERB*
1 *(train)* **rapide** *MASC & FEM*

2 *(letter)* **exprès** *MASC*, **expresse** *FEM*

express *NOUN* ▸ SEE **express** *ADJ, VERB*
le **rapide** *MASC*
to take the express prendre [64] le rapide

to **express** *VERB* ▸ SEE **express** *ADJ, NOUN*
1 **exprimer** [1]
2 **to express yourself** s'exprimer
She expresses herself well. Elle s'exprime
bien.

expression *NOUN*
une **expression** *FEM*

to **extend** *VERB*
(a house, room, etc) **agrandir** [2]

extension *NOUN*
1 *(to a house)* un **agrandissement** *MASC*
2 *(telephone)* le **poste** *MASC*
Can I have extension 4055, please?
Est-ce que je peux avoir le poste quarante-
cinquante-cinq, s'il vous plaît? *(The French
say telephone numbers in pairs.)*
3 *(extension lead)* la **rallonge** *FEM*
• **extension number**
le **numéro de poste**

exterior *ADJECTIVE*
extérieur *MASC*, **extérieure** *FEM*

extinct *ADJECTIVE*
1 *(species)* **disparu** *MASC*, **disparue** *FEM*
2 *(volcano)* **éteint** *MASC*, **éteinte** *FEM*

to **extinguish** *VERB*
éteindre [60]

extinguisher *NOUN*
(for fires) un **extincteur** *MASC*

extra *ADJECTIVE* ▸ SEE **extra** *ADVERB*
supplémentaire *MASC & FEM*
extra homework des devoirs
supplémentaires
at no extra charge sans supplément
I paid extra. J'ai payé un supplément.

extra *ADVERB* ▸ SEE **extra** *ADJECTIVE*
extra hot très chaud
extra large très grand

*ᵖ***extraordinary** *ADJECTIVE*
extraordinaire *MASC & FEM*

extra-special *ADJECTIVE*
exceptionnel *MASC*, **exceptionnelle** *FEM*

extra time *NOUN*
(in football) la **prolongation** *FEM*
to go into extra time jouer [1] les
prolongations

extreme *ADJECTIVE* ▸ SEE **extreme** *NOUN*
extrême *MASC & FEM*

extreme *NOUN* ▸ SEE **extreme** *ADJECTIVE*
un **extrême** *MASC*

ᵖ **indicates key words**

to go to extremes pousser [1] les choses à l'extrême

♀ **extremely** ADVERB
extrêmement

extreme sports PLURAL NOUN
les **sports extrêmes** MASC PL

♀ **eye** NOUN
un **œil** MASC (PL les **yeux**)
my left eye mon œil gauche
a girl with blue eyes une fille aux yeux bleus
Shut your eyes! Ferme les yeux!
to keep an eye on something surveiller [1] quelque chose
Could you keep an eye on my bag? Tu peux surveiller mon sac?
to make eyes at somebody faire [10] les yeux doux à quelqu'un
She's making eyes at my boyfriend. Elle fait les yeux doux à mon copain.

• **eyebrow**
le sourcil

• **eyelash**
le cil

• **eyelid**
la paupière

• **eyeliner**
un eye-liner

• **eye make-up**
le maquillage pour les yeux

• **eye shadow**
le fard à paupières

• **eyesight**
la vue

Ff

fabric NOUN
(cloth) le **tissu** MASC

fabulous ADJECTIVE
sensationnel MASC, sensationnelle FEM

♀ **face** NOUN ▸ SEE **face** VERB
1 (of a person) le **visage** MASC
You've got chocolate on your face. Tu as du chocolat sur le visage.
2 **to pull a face** faire [10] une grimace
Lucy tasted it and pulled a face. Lucy l'a goûté et a fait une grimace.
3 (of a clock, watch) le **cadran** MASC

♀ **to face** VERB ▸ SEE **face** NOUN
1 (a person) faire [10] face à
She faced her attacker. Elle a fait face à son agresseur.
2 (to look onto) **The house faces the park.** La

maison donne sur le jardin public.
3 (to stand the idea of) avoir [5] le courage de
I can't face going back. Je n'ai pas le courage de rentrer.

• **face up to something**
faire [10] face à quelque chose
You have to face up to the fact that you're going to fail. Tu dois faire face au fait que tu vas échouer.

• **face cloth**
le gant de toilette

facilities PLURAL NOUN
1 **The school has good sports facilities.**
L'école dispose de bonnes installations sportives.
2 **The flat has cooking facilities.**
L'appartement a une cuisine équipée.

fact NOUN
le **fait** MASC
The fact is that we lost the match. Le fait est que nous avons perdu le match.
in fact en fait
In fact, he's right. En fait, il a raison.
Is that a fact? Vraiment?

♀ **factory** NOUN
une **usine** FEM

to fade VERB
1 (fabrics) se décolorer [1]
faded jeans un jean délavé
2 (colours) passer [1]
The colours have faded. Les couleurs ont passé.

♀ **to fail** VERB
1 (an exam) rater [1]
I failed my driving test. J'ai raté mon permis.
2 (students) échouer [1]
Three students failed. Trois étudiants ont échoué.
3 (to be unable to do) **to fail to do something** ne pas réussir [2] à faire quelque chose
He failed to finish the exam. Il n'a pas réussi à terminer l'épreuve.
4 **without fail** sans faute
Ring me without fail! Appelle-moi sans faute!

failure NOUN
1 (in general) un **échec** MASC
It was a terrible failure. C'était un échec terrible.
2 (breakdown) la **panne** FEM
There was a power failure. Il y avait une panne de courant.

♀ **faint** ADJECTIVE ▸ SEE **faint** VERB
1 **to feel faint** se sentir [58] mal

I feel faint. Je me sens mal.
2 *(smell, taste)* **léger** *MASC*, **légère** *FEM*
a faint smell of gas une légère odeur de gaz
I haven't the faintest idea. Je n'en ai pas la moindre idée.
3 *(voice, sound)* **faible** *MASC & FEM*

faint *VERB* ▸ SEE **faint** *ADJECTIVE*
s'évanouir [2]
Lisa fainted. Lisa s'est évanouie.

℘**fair** *ADJECTIVE* ▸ SEE **fair** *NOUN*
1 *(even-handed)* **juste** *MASC & FEM*
It's not fair! Ce n'est pas juste!
2 *(hair)* **blond** *MASC*, **blonde** *FEM*
He's fair-haired. Il a les cheveux blonds.
3 *(skin)* **clair** *MASC*, **claire** *FEM*
people with fair skin les gens qui ont la peau claire
4 *(quite good)* **assez bon** *MASC*, **assez bonne** *FEM*
Her history is fair. Elle est assez bonne en histoire.
5 *(weather)* **If it's fair we'll go out.** S'il ne pleut pas, nous irons nous promener.

fair *NOUN* ▸ SEE **fair** *ADJECTIVE*
la **foire** *FEM*
• **fairground**
le champ de foire

℘**fairly** *ADVERB*
(quite) **assez**
She's fairly happy. Elle est assez contente.

fair trade *NOUN*
le **commerce équitable** *MASC*

fairy *NOUN*
la **fée** *FEM*
• **fairy tale**
le conte de fées

faith *NOUN*
1 *(trust)* la **confiance** *FEM*
I have faith in him. J'ai confiance en lui.
2 *(in God)* la **foi** *FEM*

faithful *ADJECTIVE*
fidèle *MASC & FEM*

faithfully *ADVERB*
(in a letter ending to someone you don't know) **Yours faithfully,** Veuillez agréer l'expression de mes sentiments distingués.

fake *ADJECTIVE* ▸ SEE **fake** *NOUN*
faux *MASC*, **fausse** *FEM*
a fake passport un faux passeport

fake *NOUN* ▸ SEE **fake** *ADJECTIVE*
le **faux** *MASC* (PL les **faux**)
The diamonds are fakes. Les diamants sont des faux.

fall *NOUN* ▸ SEE **fall** *VERB*
la **chute** *FEM*
to have a fall tomber ◎ [1]
Granny had a fall. Mamie est tombée.

℘**fall** *VERB* ▸ SEE **fall** *NOUN*
1 *(people, things)* **tomber** ◎ [1]
Mind, you'll fall! Attention, tu vas tomber!
Tony fell off his bike. Tony est tombé de son vélo.
Katie fell downstairs. Katie est tombée dans l'escalier.
My jacket fell on the floor. Ma veste est tombée par terre.
2 *(temperature)* **descendre** ◎ [3]
The temperature fell to minus eleven last night. La température est descendue à moins onze cette nuit.
3 *(prices)* **baisser** [1]

℘**false** *ADJECTIVE*
faux *MASC*, **fausse** *FEM*
a false alarm une fausse alerte
• **false teeth**
le dentier

fame *NOUN*
la **renommée** *FEM*

familiar *ADJECTIVE*
familier *MASC*, **familière** *FEM*
Your face is familiar. Votre visage m'est familier.

℘**family** *NOUN*
la **famille** *FEM*
a family of six une famille de six personnes
the Barnes family la famille Barnes
Ben's one of the family. Ben fait partie de la famille.
• **family name**
le nom de famille
• **family room**
la chambre de famille

famine *NOUN*
la **famine** *FEM*

℘**famous** *ADJECTIVE*
célèbre *MASC & FEM*

fan *NOUN*
1 *(of a team)* le **supporter** *MASC*
Matt's a Chelsea fan. Matt est un supporter de Chelsea.
2 *(of a star, a band)* le & la **fan** *MASC & FEM*
Sophie's an Oasis fan. Sophie est une fan de Oasis.
3 *(electric)* le **ventilateur** *MASC*
4 *(hand-held)* l'**éventail** *MASC*

fanatic *NOUN*
le & la **fanatique** *MASC & FEM*

fancy ADJECTIVE ▸ SEE **fancy** NOUN, VERB
1 (equipment) **sophistiqué** MASC, **sophistiquée** FEM
2 (clothes) **chic** MASC & FEM
3 (price) **cher** MASC, **chère** FEM

fancy NOUN ▸ SEE **fancy** ADJECTIVE, VERB
to take someone's fancy faire [10] envie à quelqu'un
The cake took his fancy. Le gâteau lui a fait envie.

to **fancy** VERB ▸ SEE **fancy** ADJECTIVE, NOUN
1 (to want) **Do you fancy a coffee?** Tu veux un café?
Do you fancy going to see the film? Ça te dirait d'aller voir le film?
2 (a person) **I really fancy him.** Il me plaît beaucoup.
3 (expressing surprise) **Fancy that!** Pas possible!
Fancy you being here! Tiens donc, toi ici!

fancy dress NOUN
in fancy dress déguisé MASC, déguisée FEM
a fancy-dress party une soirée déguisée

ℱ **fantastic** ADJECTIVE
génial MASC, **géniale** FEM, **géniaux** MASC PL, **géniales** FEM PL
a fantastic holiday des vacances géniales
Really? That's fantastic! Vraiment? C'est génial!

ℱ **far** ADJECTIVE, ADVERB
1 **loin**
It's not far. Ce n'est pas loin.
Is it far to Cambridge? Est-ce que Cambridge est loin d'ici?
How far is it to Bristol? Bristol est à quelle distance d'ici?
as far as jusqu'à
He took us as far as Newport. Il nous a emmenés jusqu'à Newport.
2 **by far** de loin
the prettiest by far de loin le plus joli
3 (much) **beaucoup**
You're working is far better. Tu travailles beaucoup mieux.
This bike goes far faster. Ce vélo va beaucoup plus vite.
There were far too many people in the lift. Il y avait beaucoup trop de monde dans l'ascenseur.
4 **so far** jusqu'ici
So far everything's going well. Jusqu'ici tout va bien.
5 **as far as I know** pour autant que je sache

ℱ **fare** NOUN
1 (on a bus, in the metro) le **prix du ticket** MASC
2 (on a train, plane) le **prix du billet** MASC

half fare le demi-tarif
full fare le plein tarif
What's the return fare to Cardiff? Quel est le prix d'un aller-retour à Cardiff?

Far East NOUN
l'Extrême-Orient MASC

ℱ **farm** NOUN
la **ferme** FEM

ℱ **farmer** NOUN
un **agriculteur** MASC, une **agricultrice** FEM

farmhouse NOUN
la **ferme** FEM

farming NOUN
l'agriculture FEM

farthest ADJECTIVE ▸ SEE **farthest** ADVERB
le plus éloigné MASC, **la plus éloignée** FEM

farthest ADVERB ▸ SEE **farthest**
le plus loin

fascinating ADJECTIVE
fascinant MASC, **fascinante** FEM

fashion NOUN
1 la **mode** FEM
in fashion à la mode
Short skirts are in fashion. Les jupes courtes sont à la mode.
2 **out of fashion** démodé MASC, démodée FEM
Cowboy boots are out of fashion. Les bottes de cow-boy sont démodées.

fashionable ADJECTIVE
à la mode

fashion designer NOUN
un **dessinateur de mode** MASC, une **dessinatrice de mode** FEM

fashion model NOUN
le **mannequin** MASC

fashion show NOUN
la **présentation de collection** FEM

ℱ **fast** ADJECTIVE ▸ SEE **fast** ADVERB
1 **rapide** MASC & FEM
a fast car une voiture rapide
2 (clocks, watches) **My watch is fast.** Ma montre avance.
You're ten minutes fast. Ta montre avance de dix minutes.

ℱ **fast** ADVERB ▸ SEE **fast** ADJECTIVE
1 **vite**
He swims fast. Il nage vite.
2 **to be fast asleep** être [6] profondément endormi
The baby was fast asleep. Le bébé était profondément endormi.

⬤ means the verb takes être to form the perfect

- **fast food**
  le fast-food
- **fast forward**
  l'avance rapide

ℱ **fat** ADJECTIVE ▶ SEE **fat** NOUN
  gros MASC, **grosse** FEM
  a fat man un gros monsieur
  a fat woman une grosse femme
  to get fat grossir
  I'm getting a bit fat. Je grossis.

fat NOUN ▶ SEE **fat** ADJECTIVE
1 (on your body) la **graisse** FEM
2 (on meat) le **gras** MASC
3 (in food) les **matières grasses** FEM PL

fatal ADJECTIVE
  (accident) **mortel** MASC, **mortelle** FEM

ℱ **father** NOUN
  le **père** MASC
  my father's office le bureau de mon père
- **Father Christmas**
  le père Noël
- **father-in-law**
  le beau-père

Father's Day NOUN
  la **fête des Pères**

ℱ **fault** NOUN
1 (responsibility) la **faute** FEM
  It's Stephen's fault. C'est la faute de
  Stephen.
  It's not my fault. Ce n'est pas ma faute.
2 (defect) le **défaut** MASC
  There's a fault in this sweater. Il y a un
  défaut dans ce pull.
3 (in tennis) la **faute** FEM

ℱ **favour** NOUN
1 (kindness) le **service** MASC
  to do somebody a favour rendre service à
  quelqu'un
  Can you do me a favour? Peux-tu me
  rendre service?
  to ask somebody a favour demander un
  service à quelqu'un
  Can I ask you a favour? Puis-je te demander
  un service?
2 **to be in favour of something** être [6] pour
  quelque chose
  **I'm in favour of introducing identity
  cards.** Je suis pour l'introduction des cartes
  d'identité.

ℱ **favourite** ADJECTIVE
  préféré MASC, **préférée** FEM
  my favourite band mon groupe préféré

ℱ **fear** NOUN ▶ SEE **fear** VERB
  la **peur** FEM

ℱ to **fear** VERB ▶ SEE **fear** NOUN
  craindre [31]
  He fears the worst. Il craint le pire.

feather NOUN
  la **plume** FEM

feature NOUN
1 (of a car, a mobile phone) la **caractéristique**
  FEM
2 (of your face) le **trait** MASC

February NOUN
  février MASC
  in February en février

  WORD TIP Months of the year and days of the
  week start with small letters in French.

ℱ **fed up** ADJECTIVE
  I'm fed up. J'en ai marre. (informal)
  I'm fed up with working every day. J'en ai
  marre de travailler tous les jours.

to **feed** VERB
  donner [1] à manger à
  Have you fed the dog? Est-ce que tu as
  donné à manger au chien?

to **feel** VERB
1 (tired, well) se **sentir** [58]
  I feel tired. Je me sens fatigué.
  I don't feel well. Je ne me sens pas bien.
2 (a pain) **sentir** [58]
  I didn't feel a thing. Je n'ai rien senti.
3 (afraid, cold) **to feel afraid** avoir [5] peur
  She felt afraid to move. Elle avait peur de
  bouger.
  to feel cold avoir [5] froid
  Do you feel cold? As-tu froid?
4 **to feel like doing something** avoir [5] envie
  de faire quelque chose
  I feel like going to the cinema. Je ai envie
  d'aller au cinéma.
5 (to touch) **toucher** [1]
  Feel this! It's really soft. Touche! C'est
  vraiment doux.

feeling NOUN
1 (mental) le **sentiment** MASC
  a feeling of embarrassment un sentiment
  de gêne
  to show your feelings montrer [1] ses
  sentiments
  Oliver never shows his feelings. Oliver ne
  montre jamais ses sentiments.

A B C D E **F** G H I J K L M N O P Q R S T U V W X Y Z

ℱ **indicates key words**

to hurt somebody's feelings **blesser [1]**
quelqu'un
You hurt her feelings. Tu l'as blessée.
2 *(physical)* la **sensation** *FEM*
a dizzy feeling une sensation de vertige
3 *(idea)* une **impression** *FEM*
I have the feeling James doesn't like me.
J'ai l'impression que James ne m'aime pas.

felt-tip (pen) *NOUN*
le **feutre** *MASC*

female *ADJECTIVE* ▸ SEE **female** *NOUN*
1 *(person, population)* **féminin** *MASC*,
féminine *FEM*
2 *(animal, insect)* **femelle** *MASC & FEM*

female *NOUN* ▸ SEE **female** *ADJECTIVE*
(of a species) la **femelle** *FEM*

feminine *ADJECTIVE* ▸ SEE **feminine** *NOUN*
féminin *MASC*, **féminine** *FEM*
a feminine noun un nom féminin

feminine *NOUN* ▸ SEE **feminine** *ADJECTIVE*
(Grammar) le **féminin** *MASC*
in the feminine au féminin

feminist *NOUN*
le & la **féministe** *MASC & FEM*

fence *NOUN*
la **clôture** *FEM*

fern *NOUN*
la **fougère** *FEM*

ferry *NOUN*
le **ferry** *MASC*

fertilizer *NOUN*
l'**engrais** *MASC*

festival *NOUN*
le **festival** *MASC*

to **fetch** *VERB*
aller ⓔ [7] **chercher**
Tom's fetching the children. Tom est allé
chercher les enfants.
Fetch me the other knife! Va me chercher
l'autre couteau!

fever *NOUN*
la **fièvre** *FEM*

ᵖ **few** *ADJECTIVE, PRONOUN*
1 *(followed by a noun)* **peu de**
few people think that ... peu de gens
pensent que...
Very few houses have a swimming-pool.
Très peu de maisons ont une piscine.
2 a few **quelques**
a few weeks earlier quelques semaines
plus tôt
I'll be ready in a few minutes. Je serai prêt
dans quelques minutes.

3 *(by itself)* a few **quelques-uns** *MASC*,
quelques-unes *FEM*
Have you any tomatoes? We want a few
for the salad. Avez-vous des tomates? Nous
en voulons quelques-unes pour la salade.
4 quite a few **pas mal de**
There are quite a few tourists. Il y avait
pas mal de touristes.

ᵖ **fewer** *ADJECTIVE*
moins de
There are fewer tourists this year. Il y a
moins de touristes cette année.

ᵖ **fiancé** *NOUN*
le **fiancé** *MASC*

ᵖ **fiancée** *NOUN*
la **fiancée** *FEM*

fiction *NOUN*
les **romans** *MASC PL*
I read a lot of fiction. Je lis beaucoup de
romans.

ᵖ **field** *NOUN*
1 *(on a farm)* le **champ** *MASC*
a field of wheat un champ de blé
2 *(for sport)* le **terrain** *MASC*
3 *(of work, study)* le **domaine** *MASC*

fierce *ADJECTIVE*
1 *(animal, person)* **féroce** *MASC & FEM*
2 *(storm, battle)* **violent** *MASC*, **violente** *FEM*

ᵖ **fifteen** *NUMBER*
quinze
Laura's fifteen. Laura a quinze ans.

fifth *ADJECTIVE*
1 **cinquième** *MASC & FEM*
on the fifth floor au cinquième étage
2 *(in dates)* the fifth of January le cinq janvier

fifty *NUMBER*
cinquante
My uncle's fifty. Mon oncle a cinquante ans.

fig *NOUN*
la **figue** *FEM*

fight *NOUN* ▸ SEE **fight** *VERB*
1 *(in the street)* la **bagarre** *FEM*
2 *(in boxing)* le **combat** *MASC*
3 *(against illness)* la **lutte** *FEM*

fight *VERB* ▸ SEE **fight** *NOUN*
1 *(to have a fight)* se **battre** [21]
They were fighting. Ils se battaient.
2 *(to quarrel)* se **disputer** [1]
They're always fighting. Ils sont toujours
en train de se disputer.
3 *(against cancer)* **lutter** [1] contre

fighting *NOUN*
1 *(in the street)* la **bagarre** *FEM*

ⓔ means the verb takes être to form the perfect

2 *(in a war)* le **combat** *MASC*

ℓ **figure** *NOUN*
1 *(number)* le **chiffre** *MASC*
   a four-figure number un nombre de quatre
   chiffres
2 *(body shape)* la **ligne** *FEM*
   Swimming is good for your figure. La
   natation, c'est bon pour la ligne.
3 *(person)* le **personnage** *MASC*
   a familiar figure un personnage familier
4 *(diagram)* la **figure** *FEM*

file *NOUN* ► SEE **file** *VERB*
1 *(for records)* le **dossier** *MASC*
2 *(ring binder)* le **classeur** *MASC*
3 *(cardboard folder)* la **chemise** *FEM*
4 *(on a computer)* le **fichier** *MASC*
5 **a nail file** une **lime**

to **file** *VERB* ► SEE **file** *VERB*
1 *(a document)* **classer** [1]
2 **to file your nails** se **limer** [1] les ongles

ℓ to **fill** *VERB*
   (a bottle, jar) **remplir** [2]
   She filled my glass. Elle a rempli mon verre.
   a smoke-filled room une pièce remplie de
   fumée
• **to fill in**
   (a form) **remplir** [2] quelque chose
• **to fill in for someone**
   remplacer [61] quelqu'un

filling *NOUN*
1 *(for a sandwich)* la **garniture** *FEM*
2 *(of meat, vegetables)* la **farce** *FEM*
3 *(in a chocolate, pastry)* **with an apricot
   filling** fourré à l'abricot
4 *(in a tooth)* le **plombage** *MASC*

ℓ **film** *NOUN*
1 *(in a cinema)* le **film** *MASC*
   the new film about Picasso le nouveau film
   au sujet de Picasso
   Shall we go and see a film? Si on allait voir
   un film?
2 *(for a camera)* la **pellicule** *FEM*

film star *NOUN*
   la **vedette de cinéma** *FEM*

filter *NOUN*
   le **filtre** *MASC*

ℓ **filthy** *ADJECTIVE*
   dégoûtant *MASC*, **dégoûtante** *FEM*

fin *NOUN*
   la **nageoire** *FEM*

final *ADJECTIVE* ► SEE **final** *NOUN*
   dernier *MASC*, **dernière** *FEM*
   the final instalment le dernier épisode
   the final result le résultat final

final *NOUN* ► SEE **final** *ADJECTIVE*
   (Sports) la **finale** *FEM*

ℓ **finally** *ADVERB*
   finalement

ℓ to **find** *VERB*
   trouver [1]
   Did you find your passport? As-tu trouvé
   ton passeport?
   I can't find my keys. Je ne trouve pas mes
   clefs.
• **to find out**
   (to enquire) se **renseigner** ◎ [1]
   I don't know, I'll find out. Je ne sais pas, je
   me renseignerai.
   find to find something out **découvrir** [30]
   quelque chose
   Luke found out the truth. Luke a découvert
   la vérité.

fine *ADJECTIVE* ► SEE **fine** *NOUN*
1 *(in good health)* **bien** *INVARIABLE MASC & FEM*
   'How are you?' — 'Fine, thanks'.
   'Comment ça va?' — 'Très bien merci.'
2 *(very good)* **excellent** *MASC*, **excellente** *FEM*
   She's a fine athlete. C'est une excellente
   athlète.
3 *(convenient)* **très bien** *INVARIABLE MASC & FEM*
   Ten o'clock? Yes, that's fine. Dix heures?
   Oui, très bien.
   Friday will be fine. Vendredi sera très bien.
4 *(weather, day)* **beau** *MASC*, **belle** *FEM*
   a fine day une belle journée
5 *(cloth, silk)* **fin** *MASC*, **fine** *FEM*
   in fine wool en laine fine

fine *NOUN* ► SEE **fine** *ADJECTIVE*
1 *(in general)* l'**amende** *FEM*
2 *(for parking, speeding)* la **contravention** *FEM*

ℓ **finger** *NOUN*
   le **doigt** *MASC*
   I'll keep my fingers crossed for you. Je
   croise les doigts pour toi.
• **fingernail**
   l'**ongle** *MASC*

finish *NOUN* ► SEE **finish** *VERB*
1 *(end)* la **fin** *FEM*
2 *(in a race)* l'**arrivée** *FEM*

ℓ to **finish** *VERB* ► SEE **finish** *NOUN*
1 *(to stop)* **finir** [2]
   I've finished. J'ai fini.
   When does school finish? À quelle heure
   finit l'école?
2 *(to come to the end of)* **terminer** [1]
   Have you finished the book? Est-ce que tu
   as terminé le livre?
3 **to finish doing something** **finir** [2] de faire
   quelque chose
   Have you finished telephoning? As-tu fini

de téléphoner?
- **to finish with something**
finir avec quelque chose
Have you finished with the computer? As-tu fini avec l'ordinateur?

finishing line NOUN
la **ligne d'arrivée** FEM

Finland NOUN
la **Finlande** FEM

Finnish ADJECTIVE ▶ SEE **Finnish** NOUN
finlandais MASC, **finlandaise** FEM

Finnish NOUN ▶ SEE **Finnish** ADJECTIVE
(the language) le **finnois** MASC

ℓ **fire** NOUN ▶ SEE **fire** VERB
1 (for heating) le **feu** MASC
to light a fire allumer un feu
Dad lit a fire. Papa a allumé un feu.
She was sitting by the fire. Elle était assise près du feu.
2 **to catch fire** prendre [64] feu
The newspaper caught fire. Le journal a pris feu.
3 (accidental) un **incendie** MASC
a fire in a factory un incendie dans une usine

ℓ **fire** VERB ▶ SEE **fire** NOUN
1 (to shoot) **tirer** [1]
The soldiers were firing. Les soldats tiraient.
to fire at somebody tirer sur quelqu'un
Someone had fired at them. Quelqu'un avait tiré sur eux.
2 (a gun) **décharger**
- **fire alarm**
une alarme incendie
- **fire brigade**
les pompiers MASC PL
- **fire engine**
la voiture des pompiers
- **fire escape**
un escalier de secours
- **fire extinguisher**
un extincteur
- **fire fighter**
le pompier
- **fireplace**
la cheminée
- **fire station**
la caserne de pompiers
- **firework**
le feu d'artifice (PL les feux d'artifice)
There will be a firework display. Il y aura un feu d'artifice.

firm ADJECTIVE ▶ SEE **firm** NOUN
ferme MASC & FEM

firm NOUN ▶ SEE **firm** ADJECTIVE
(business) une **entreprise** FEM

ℓ **first** ADJECTIVE, ADVERB
1 (in order) **premier** MASC, **première** FEM
the first of May le premier mai
I met him for the first time yesterday. Je l'ai rencontré hier pour la première fois.
Susan's the first. Susan est la première.
I came first in the 200 metres. Je suis arrivé premier aux 200 mètres (boy speaking), Je suis arrivée première aux 200 mètres (girl speaking).
2 (to begin with) **d'abord**
First, I'm going to have a shower. D'abord je vais prendre une douche.
3 **at first** au début
At first he was shy. Au début il était timide.

first aid NOUN
les **premiers secours** MASC PL
- **first-aid kit**
la trousse de secours

first class ADJECTIVE
1 (ticket, carriage, hotel) de **première classe**
a first-class compartment un compartiment de première classe
He always travels first class. Il voyage toujours en première.
2 (stamp, letter) **au tarif rapide**
six first-class stamps six timbres au tarif rapide

first floor NOUN
le **premier étage** MASC
on the first floor au premier étage

firstly ADVERB
premièrement

ℓ **first name** NOUN
le **prénom** MASC

fir tree NOUN
le **sapin** MASC

ℓ **fish** NOUN ▶ SEE **fish** VERB
le **poisson** MASC
Do you like fish? Aimez-vous le poisson?

to **fish** VERB ▶ SEE **fish** NOUN
pêcher [1]
Dad was fishing for trout. Papa pêchait la truite.
- **fish and chips**
le poisson frit avec des frites

fisherman NOUN
le **pêcheur** MASC

ℓ **fishing** NOUN
la **pêche** FEM
I love fishing. J'adore la pêche.
to go fishing aller ⊚ [7] à la pêche

⊚ means the verb takes être to form the perfect

Tom's gone fishing. Tom est allé à la pêche.
- **fishing rod**
  la canne à pêche
- **fishing tackle**
  le matériel de pêche

fist NOUN
le **poing** MASC

ℓ **fit** ADJECTIVE ▸ SEE **fit** NOUN, VERB
(healthy) **en forme**
I feel really fit. Je me sens vraiment en forme.
to keep fit se maintenir [81] en forme
I'm trying to keep fit. J'essaie de me maintenir en forme.

fit NOUN ▸ SEE **fit** ADJECTIVE, VERB
1 (of rage) **to have a fit** piquer [1] une crise
Your dad'll have a fit when he sees your tattoo! Ton père va piquer une crise quand il va voir ton tatouage!
2 (illness) **an epileptic fit** une crise d'épilepsie

ℓ to **fit** VERB ▸ SEE **fit** ADJECTIVE, NOUN
1 (clothes) **être** [6] à la taille
This skirt doesn't fit me. Cette jupe n'est pas à ma taille.
2 (shoes) **être** [6] à la pointure de
3 (to go into) **aller** ◐ [7] **dans**
Will my cases fit in the car? Est-ce que mes valises iront dans la voiture?
The key doesn't fit in the lock. La clé ne va pas dans la serrure.
4 (to install) **installer** [1]
They've fitted an alarm. Ils ont installé une alarme.

fitness NOUN
la **forme** FEM
fitness training les exercices de mise en forme

fitted carpet NOUN
la **moquette** FEM

fitted kitchen NOUN
la **cuisine intégrée**

fitting room NOUN
la **cabine d'essayage**

five NUMBER
cinq
Beth's five. Beth a cinq ans.
It's five o'clock. Il est cinq heures.

to **fix** VERB
1 (a machine) **réparer** [1]
Rob's fixed the computer. Rob a réparé l'ordinateur.
2 (a date, a price) **fixer** [1]
to fix a date fixer une date
They've fixed a date for the wedding. Ils ont fixé une date pour le mariage.

at a fixed price à prix fixe
3 (a meal) **préparer** [1]
I'll fix supper. Je vais préparer le dîner.

fizzy ADJECTIVE
gazeux MASC, **gazeuse** FEM
fizzy water l'eau gazeuse

flag NOUN
le **drapeau** MASC (PL les **drapeaux**)

> ⓘ **FLAG**
>
> The French flag (le Tricolore) has three vertical stripes: blue, white and red. It dates from the French Revolution (1794), combining the colours of Paris (blue/red) with that of the king (white).

flame NOUN
la **flamme** FEM

flamingo NOUN
le **flamant rose** MASC

flan NOUN
la **tarte** FEM
an onion flan une tarte à l'oignon

to **flap** VERB
battre [21]
The bird flapped its wings. L'oiseau battait des ailes.

flash NOUN ▸ SEE **flash** VERB
1 (bright light) **a flash of lightning** un éclair
2 (short time) **in a flash** en un clin d'œil
He was ready in a flash. Il était prêt en un clin d'œil.
3 (for a camera) le **flash** MASC

to **flash** VERB ▸ SEE **flash** NOUN
1 (lights) **clignoter** [1]
2 **to flash by** passer [1] comme un éclair
The ambulance flashed by. L'ambulance est passée comme un éclair.
3 **to flash your headlights** faire [10] des appels de phares
- **flashback**
  le **flash-back** MASC

flask NOUN
1 (insulated bottle) le or la **thermos**® MASC OR FEM
2 (of spirits) le **flacon** MASC

ℓ **flat** ADJECTIVE ▸ SEE **flat** NOUN
plat MASC, **plate** FEM
flat shoes des chaussures plates
a flat landscape un paysage plat
a flat tyre un pneu crevé

ℓ **flat** NOUN ▸ SEE **flat** ADJECTIVE
un **appartement** MASC
a third-floor flat un appartement au troisième étage

ℓ **indicates key words**

- **flatmate**
le & la colocataire MASC & FEM

to **flatter** VERB
flatter [1]

flattering ADJECTIVE
flatteur MASC, flatteuse FEM

♂ **flavour** NOUN ▸ SEE **flavour** VERB
1 (taste) le goût MASC
The sauce had no flavour. La sauce n'avait aucun goût.
2 (of a drink, an ice cream) le parfum MASC
What flavour of ice cream would you like? Tu veux quel parfum de glace?

to **flavour** VERB ▸ SEE **flavour** NOUN
parfumer [1]
vanilla-flavoured parfumé à la vanille

flea NOUN
la puce FEM
- **flea market**
le marché aux puces

fleet NOUN
1 (of ships) la flotte FEM
2 (of vehicles) le parc MASC

flesh NOUN
la chair FEM

flex NOUN
le fil MASC

flexible ADJECTIVE
flexible MASC & FEM

♂ **flight** NOUN
1 le vol MASC
a charter flight un vol charter
The flight from Moscow is delayed. Le vol de Moscou est retardé.
2 **a flight of stairs** un escalier
four flights of stairs quatre étages
- **flight attendant**
1 (male) le steward
2 (female) une hôtesse de l'air

to **fling** VERB
lancer [61]

flipper NOUN
(for a swimmer) la palme FEM

to **flirt** VERB
flirter [1]

to **float** VERB
flotter [1]

flood NOUN ▸ SEE **flood** VERB
1 (of water) une inondation FEM
the floods in the south les inondations au sud
to be in floods of tears verser [1] des

torrents de larmes
Rosie was in floods of tears. Rosie versait des torrents de larmes.
2 (of letters, complaints) le déluge MASC

to **flood** VERB ▸ SEE **flood** NOUN
inonder [1]
- **floodlight**
le projecteur

♂ **floor** NOUN
1 (wooden) le plancher MASC
to sweep the floor balayer
I've swept the kitchen floor. J'ai balayé la cuisine.
Your glasses are on the floor. Tes lunettes sont par terre.
2 (concrete) le sol MASC
3 (storey) un étage MASC
on the second floor au deuxième étage

florist NOUN
le & la fleuriste MASC & FEM

flour NOUN
la farine FEM

to **flow** VERB
couler [1]

♂ **flower** NOUN ▸ SEE **flower** VERB
la fleur FEM
a bunch of flowers un bouquet

to **flower** VERB ▸ SEE **flower** NOUN
fleurir [2]

♂ **flu** NOUN
la grippe FEM
to have flu avoir [5] la grippe
Sally has flu. Sally a la grippe.

fluent ADJECTIVE
She speaks fluent Italian. Elle parle couramment l'italien.

fluently ADVERB
couramment

fluid NOUN
le liquide MASC

to **flush** VERB
to flush the toilet tirer [1] la chasse

flute NOUN
la flûte FEM
to play the flute jouer [1] de la flûte
Jo plays the flute. Jo joue de la flûte.

fly NOUN ▸ SEE **fly** VERB
la mouche FEM
- **fly spray**
la bombe insecticide

◆ means the verb takes être to form the perfect

_ℓ_ to **fly** _VERB_ ▸ SEE **fly** _NOUN_
1 _(birds, bees, planes)_ **voler** [1]
2 _(in a plane)_ **prendre** [64] **l'avion**
   We flew to Edinburgh. Nous sommes allés à Édimbourg en avion.
   We flew from Gatwick. Nous sommes partis de Gatwick.
3 _(a kite)_ **faire** [10] **voler**
4 _(time)_ **passer** ○ [1] **très vite**

foam _NOUN_
1 _(foam rubber)_ la **mousse** _FEM_
   a foam mattress un matelas mousse
2 _(on a drink)_ la **mousse** _FEM_

focus _NOUN_ ▸ SEE **focus** _VERB_
   to be in focus être [6] au point
   to be out of focus être flou
   All the photos were out of focus. Toutes les photos étaient floues.

to **focus** _VERB_ ▸ SEE **focus** _NOUN_
   (a camera) **mettre** [11] **au point**

_ℓ_ **fog** _NOUN_
   le **brouillard** _MASC_

foggy _ADJECTIVE_
   (weather) **brumeux** _MASC_, **brumeuse** _FEM_
   It was foggy. Il y avait du brouillard.

fold _NOUN_ ▸ SEE **fold** _VERB_
   le **pli** _MASC_

to **fold** _VERB_ ▸ SEE **fold** _NOUN_
1 **plier** [1]
   to fold something up plier quelque chose
   I folded up the towels. J'ai plié les serviettes.
2 **to fold your arms** croiser [1] les bras

folder _NOUN_
   la **chemise** _FEM_

folding _ADJECTIVE_
   pliant _MASC_, **pliante** _FEM_
   a folding table une table pliante

to **follow** _VERB_
   (a person, advice, a path) **suivre** [75]
   Follow me! Suivez-moi!
   You must follow the instructions. Il faut suivre les instructions.
   Do you follow me? Vous me suivez?

following _ADJECTIVE_
   suivant _MASC_, **suivante** _FEM_
   the following year l'année suivante

fond _ADJECTIVE_
   to be fond of somebody aimer beaucoup quelqu'un
   I'm very fond of him. Je l'aime beaucoup.

_ℓ_ **food** _NOUN_
1 _(to keep you alive)_ la **nourriture** _FEM_

   to buy food acheter à manger
   I like French food. J'aime la cuisine française.
2 _(stocks)_ les **provisions** _FEM PL_
   We bought food for the holiday. Nous avons acheté des provisions pour les vacances.
• **food poisoning**
   une intoxication alimentaire

fool _NOUN_
   un **idiot** _MASC_, une **idiote** _FEM_

_ℓ_ **foot** _NOUN_
1 le **pied** _MASC_
   on foot à pied
   Hannah came on foot. Hannah est venue à pied.
2 _(the bottom)_ **at the foot of the stairs** en bas de l'escalier

_ℓ_ **football** _NOUN_
1 _(game)_ le **football** _MASC_
   to play football jouer [1] au football
   George loves playing football. George aime beaucoup jouer au football.
2 _(ball)_ le **ballon de football**

footballer _NOUN_
   le **joueur de football** _MASC_, la **joueuse de football** _FEM_

footpath _NOUN_
   le **sentier** _MASC_

footprint _NOUN_
   une **empreinte** _FEM_

footstep _NOUN_
   le **pas** _MASC_

_ℓ_ **for** _PREPOSITION_
1 _(in general)_ **pour**
   a present for my mother un cadeau pour ma mère
   petrol for the car de l'essence pour la voiture
   sausages for lunch des saucisses pour le déjeuner
   It's for cleaning. C'est pour nettoyer.
   What's it for? C'est pour quoi faire?
   What's the French for 'bee'? Comment dit-on 'bee' en français?
2 _(in time expressions in the past or future)_ **pendant**
   I studied French for six years. J'ai étudié le français pendant six ans _(but I no longer do)_.
   I'll be away for four days. Je serai absent pendant quatre jours.
3 _(in time expressions continuing into the present)_ **depuis**
   I've been waiting here for an hour. J'attends ici depuis une heure _(and am still_

waiting).
My brother's been living in Paris for three years. Mon frère habite à Paris depuis trois ans *(and is still living there).*

4 *(with prices)* **I sold my bike for fifty pounds.** J'ai vendu mon vélo cinquante livres.

to **forbid** VERB
défendre [3]
to forbid somebody to do something défendre [3] à quelqu'un de faire quelque chose
I forbid you to go out. Je te défends de sortir.

ℱ **forbidden** ADJECTIVE
défendu MASC, défendue FEM

force NOUN ▸ SEE **force** VERB
la force FEM

to **force** VERB ▸ SEE **force** NOUN
forcer [61]
to force somebody to do something forcer quelqu'un à faire quelque chose
No-one forced you to go. Personne ne t'a forcé à y aller.

forefinger NOUN
un index MASC

foreground NOUN
le premier plan MASC
in the foreground au premier plan

forehead NOUN
le front MASC

foreign ADJECTIVE
étranger MASC, étrangère FEM
in a foreign country dans un pays étranger

ℱ **foreigner** NOUN
un étranger MASC, une étrangère FEM

to **foresee** VERB
prévoir [65]

ℱ **forest** NOUN
la forêt FEM

forever ADVERB
1 pour toujours
I'd like to stay here forever. J'aimerais rester là pour toujours.
2 *(non-stop)* sans arrêt
He's forever asking questions. Il pose des questions sans arrêt.

forgery NOUN
1 *(painting)* un faux MASC
2 *(signature, banknote)* une contrefaçon FEM

ℱ to **forget** VERB
oublier [1]
I forget his name. J'oublie son nom.
We've forgotten the bread! Nous avons oublié le pain!
to forget to do something oublier de faire quelque chose
I forgot to phone. J'ai oublié d'appeler.
to forget about something oublier quelque chose
I forgot all about it. Je l'ai complètement oublié.

to **forgive** VERB
pardonner [1] à
to forgive somebody pardonner à quelqu'un
I forgave him. Je lui ai pardonné.
to forgive somebody for doing something pardonner à quelqu'un d'avoir fait quelque chose
I forgave her for losing my ring. Je lui ai pardonné d'avoir perdu ma bague.

ℱ **fork** NOUN
la fourchette FEM

ℱ **form** NOUN ▸ SEE **form** VERB
1 *(for applications)* le formulaire MASC
to fill in a form remplir un formulaire
I've filled in the forms. J'ai rempli les formulaires.
2 *(shape, type)* la forme FEM
in the form of a letter sous forme de lettre
3 **to be on form** être [6] en forme
Mandy was on good form. Mandy était en pleine forme.
4 *(school class)* la classe FEM

to **form** VERB ▸ SEE **form** NOUN
former [1]

formal ADJECTIVE
(invitation, event, complaint) officiel MASC, officielle FEM

format NOUN
le format MASC

ℱ **former** ADJECTIVE
ancien MASC, ancienne FEM
a former pupil un ancien élève

formula NOUN
la formule FEM

fortnight NOUN
quinze jours MASC PL
We're going to Spain for a fortnight. Nous allons passer quinze jours en Espagne.

⊙ means the verb takes être to form the perfect

fortress *NOUN*
la **forteresse** *FEM*

fortunate *ADJECTIVE*
to be fortunate avoir [5] de la chance
You were very fortunate. Tu avais bien de la chance.

fortunately *ADVERB*
heureusement

fortune *NOUN*
la **fortune** *FEM*
to make a fortune gagner [1] beaucoup d'argent
Will makes a fortune at the bank. Will gagne beaucoup d'argent à la banque.

forty *NUMBER*
quarante
My aunt's forty. Ma tante a quarante ans.

forum *NOUN*
le **forum** *MASC*

forward *ADVERB* ▶ SEE **forward** *NOUN*
to move forward avancer
Move forward a little! Avancez un peu!

forward *NOUN* ▶ SEE **forward** *ADVERB*
(in sport) un **avant** *MASC*

foster child *NOUN*
un **enfant adoptif**, une **enfant adoptive**

foul *ADJECTIVE* ▶ SEE **foul** *NOUN*
infect *MASC*, infecte *FEM*
The weather's foul. Il fait un temps infect.

foul *NOUN* ▶ SEE **foul** *ADJECTIVE*
(Sports) la **faute** *FEM*

fountain *NOUN*
la **fontaine** *FEM*
• fountain pen
un **stylo à encre**

four *NUMBER*
quatre
Simon's four. Simon a quatre ans.
It's four o'clock. Il est quatre heures.
Sam was on all fours looking for his contact lens. Sam était à quatre pattes pour chercher sa lentille de contact.

fourteen *NUMBER*
quatorze
Susie's fourteen. Susie a quatorze ans.

fourth *ADJECTIVE*
1 **quatrième** *MASC & FEM*
on the fourth floor au quatrième étage
2 (in dates) the fourth of July le quatre juillet

fox *NOUN*
le **renard** *MASC*

fracture *NOUN*
la **fracture** *FEM*

ℓ **fragile** *ADJECTIVE*
fragile *MASC & FEM*

frame *NOUN*
1 (of a picture) le **cadre** *MASC*
2 (of a door) un **encadrement** *MASC*

ℓ **franc** *NOUN*
le **franc** *MASC*
Switzerland's money; name of the money used in France, Belgium and Luxembourg before the euro; 100 French francs = 15.24 euros

ℓ **France** *NOUN*
la **France** *FEM*
I like France. J'aime la France.
in France en France
They live in France. Ils vivent en France.
to France en France
She's going to France. Elle part en France.
Nadine's from France. Nadine est française.

> **WORD TIP** Countries and regions in French take le, la or les.

frantic *ADJECTIVE*
1 (very upset) fou *MASC*, folle *FEM*
Mum was frantic with worry. Maman était folle d'inquiétude.
2 (efforts, search) désespéré *MASC*, désespérée *FEM*

freckle *NOUN*
la **tache de rousseur** *FEM*

ℓ **free** *ADJECTIVE* ▶ SEE **free** *VERB*
1 (when you don't pay) gratuit *MASC*, gratuite *FEM*
The bus is free. Le bus est gratuit.
a free ticket un billet gratuit
2 (not occupied) libre *MASC & FEM*
Are you free on Thursday? Es-tu libre jeudi?
3 sugar-free sans sucre
lead-free sans plomb

ℓ indicates key words

A B C D E F G H I J K L M N O P Q R S T U V W X Y Z

to **free** VERB ▸ SEE **free** ADJECTIVE
libérer [24]

freedom NOUN
la liberté FEM

free gift NOUN
le cadeau MASC (PL les cadeaux)

free kick NOUN
le coup franc MASC

♁to **freeze** VERB
1 (in a freezer) congeler [45]
frozen peas des petits pois congelés
2 (in cold weather) geler [45]
It's freezing outside. Il gèle dehors.

♁**freezer** NOUN
le congélateur MASC

freezing ADJECTIVE ▸ SEE **freezing** NOUN
I'm freezing. Je suis gelé.
It's freezing outside. Il fait très froid
dehors.

freezing NOUN ▸ SEE **freezing** ADJECTIVE
zéro MASC
Three degrees below freezing. Trois degrés
en-dessous de zéro.

♁**French** ADJECTIVE ▸ SEE **French** NOUN
1 français MASC, française FEM
Jean-Marc is French. Jean-Marc est français.
Élodie is French. Élodie est française.
2 (teacher, lesson) de français
the French class le cours de français

WORD TIP Adjectives never have capitals in
French, even for nationality or regional origin.

♁**French** NOUN ▸ SEE **French** ADJECTIVE
1 (the language) le français MASC
to speak French parler français
Say it in French. Dis-le en français.
to learn French apprendre [64] le français
Adam's learning French. Adam apprend le
français.
2 (the people) the French les Français MASC PL
most of the French la plupart des
Français
• French bean
le haricot vert
• French dressing
la vinaigrette
• French fries
les frites FEM PL
• Frenchman
un Français
• French stick
la baguette

• **Frenchwoman**
une Française

Ⓕ **FRENCH**

There are around 80 million native speakers
of French around the world and a further 150
million non-native speakers.

frequent ADJECTIVE
fréquent MASC, fréquente FEM

frequently ADVERB
souvent

♁**fresh** ADJECTIVE
frais MASC, fraîche FEM
fresh eggs des œufs frais
I'm going out for some fresh air. Je vais
prendre l'air.
• fresh water
l'eau douce FEM

♁**Friday** NOUN
le vendredi MASC
next Friday vendredi prochain
last Friday vendredi dernier
on Friday vendredi
I'll phone you on Friday evening. Je
t'appellerai vendredi soir.
on Fridays le vendredi
closed on Fridays fermé le vendredi
I see her every Friday. Je la vois tous les
vendredis.
Good Friday le Vendredi saint

WORD TIP Months of the year and days of the
week start with small letters in French. Note,
however, that Vendredi saint always starts with
a capital V.

fridge NOUN
le frigo MASC
Put it in the fridge. Mets-le au frigo.

♁**friend** NOUN
un ami MASC, une amie FEM
a friend of mine un ami à moi (a boy), une
amie à moi (a girl)
to make friends se faire ◎ [10] des amis
You'll soon make new friends. Tu te feras
vite de nouveaux amis.
He made friends with Danny. Il est devenu
ami avec Danny.

friendly ADJECTIVE
sympathique MASC & FEM

friendship NOUN
l'amitié FEM

fries PLURAL NOUN
les frites FEM PL

fright NOUN
la peur FEM

◎ means the verb takes être to form the perfect

to get a fright avoir [5] peur
I got such a fright. J'ai eu tellement peur.
You gave me a fright! Tu m'as fait peur!

to **frighten** VERB
effrayer [59]

ℱ **frightened** ADJECTIVE
to be frightened avoir [5] peur
Martin's frightened of snakes. Martin a
peur des serpents.

frightening ADJECTIVE
effrayant MASC, effrayante FEM

fringe NOUN
la frange FEM

frog NOUN
la grenouille FEM
a frog's leg une cuisse de grenouille

ℱ **from** PREPOSITION
de
a letter from Tina une lettre de Tina
100 metres from the cinema à cent mètres
du cinéma
from Monday to Friday du lundi jusqu'au
vendredi
He comes from Dublin. Il vient de Dublin.
two years from now d'ici deux ans
from seven o'clock onwards à partir de
sept heures

WORD TIP de + le gives du. de + les gives des. de
+ a, e, i, o, u gives d'.

ℱ **front** ADJECTIVE ▸ SEE **front** NOUN
1 de devant
his front paw sa patte de devant
in the front row au premier rang
2 avant
the front seat
of a car le siège avant
the front wheel la roue avant

ℱ **front** NOUN ▸ SEE **front** ADJECTIVE
1 (of a building, garment) le **devant** MASC
2 (of a car) l'**avant** MASC
He was sitting in the front. Il était assis à
l'avant.
3 (of a train, queue) la **tête** FEM
There are seats at the front of the train. Il y
a des places en tête du train.
4 (of a card, envelope) le **recto** MASC
The address is on the front. L'adresse est
au recto.
5 (in a theatre, cinema, class) le **premier rang**
MASC
seats at the front des places au premier
rang
6 in front of devant
in front of the TV devant la télé
Jack sat in front of me. Jack s'est assis

devant moi.
• front door
la porte d'entrée

frontier NOUN
la frontière FEM

frost NOUN
le gel MASC

frosty ADJECTIVE
1 (weather)
It's frosty this morning. Il gèle ce matin.
2 (windscreen, grass) couvert de givre MASC,
couverte de givre FEM

to **frown** VERB
froncer [61] les sourcils
He frowned at us. Il nous a regardés en
fronçant les sourcils.

frozen ADJECTIVE
1 (fingers, ground, lake) gelé MASC, gelée FEM
2 (food) surgelé MASC, surgelée FEM

ℱ **fruit** NOUN
les fruits MASC PL
I like fruit. J'aime les fruits.
a piece of fruit un fruit
fruit juice le jus de fruits
We bought cheese and fruit. Nous avons
acheté du fromage et des fruits.
• fruit machine
la machine à sous
• fruit salad
la salade de fruits

frustrated ADJECTIVE
frustré MASC, frustrée FEM

frustrating ADJECTIVE
frustrant MASC, frustrante FEM

to **fry** VERB
faire [10] frire
a fried egg un œuf au plat
We fried the fish. Nous avons fait frire les
poissons.

frying pan NOUN
la poêle FEM

fuel NOUN
(for vehicles, planes) le carburant MASC

ℱ **full** ADJECTIVE
1 (in general) plein MASC, pleine FEM
This glass is full. Ce verre est plein.
The train was full of tourists. Le train était
plein de touristes.
I'm full. J'ai assez mangé.
2 (hotels, flights) complet MASC, complète FEM
3 (in expressions) at full speed à toute vitesse
at full volume à plein volume
Write your name out in full. Écris ton nom

A
B
C
D
E
F
G
H
I
J
K
L
M
N
O
P
Q
R
S
T
U
V
W
X
Y
Z

ℱ indicates key words

en toutes lettres.
- **full stop**
le point

full-time ADJECTIVE ▶ SEE **full time** NOUN
à plein temps
a full-time job un travail à plein temps

full time NOUN ▶ SEE **full-time**
(in sport) la fin du match

fully ADVERB
entièrement

fun NOUN
le **plaisir** MASC
Skiing is fun. C'est amusant de faire du ski.
I do it for fun. Je le fais pour m'amuser.
to have fun s'amuser [4]
Have fun! Amusez-vous bien!
We had lots of fun. Nous nous sommes
beaucoup amusés.
to make fun of somebody se moquer ◎ [1]
de quelqu'un
They all made fun of her. Ils se sont tous
moqués d'elle.

funds PLURAL NOUN
les **fonds** MASC PL

funeral NOUN
l'**enterrement** MASC

funfair NOUN
la **fête foraine** FEM

ℐ**funny** ADJECTIVE
1 *(when you laugh)* **drôle** MASC & FEM
How funny you are! Que tu es drôle!
2 *(strange)* **bizarre** MASC & FEM
a funny noise un bruit bizarre
That's funny, I'm sure I paid. C'est bizarre,
je suis certain d'avoir payé.

fur NOUN
1 *(animal's)* les **poils** MASC PL
2 *(for coats)* la **fourrure** FEM
a fur coat un manteau de fourrure

furious ADJECTIVE
furieux MASC, **furieuse** FEM
She's furious with Steve. Elle est furieuse
contre Steve.

ℐ**furniture** NOUN
les **meubles** MASC PL
a piece of furniture un meuble
I want to buy some furniture. Je veux
acheter des meubles.

further ADVERB
plus loin
further than the station plus loin que la
gare
ten kilometres further on dix kilomètres
plus loin

further forward plus en avant
further back plus en arrière

fuse NOUN
le **fusible** MASC

fuss NOUN
to make a fuss faire [10] toute une histoire
He made a fuss about the bill. Il a fait toute
une histoire à propos de l'addition.

fussy ADJECTIVE
difficile MASC & FEM
to be fussy about something être [6]
difficile sur quelque chose
He's fussy about what he eats. Il est
difficile sur ce qu'il mange.

future NOUN
1 l'**avenir** MASC
in future à l'avenir
Be more careful in future! Faites plus
attention à l'avenir!
in the future dans l'avenir
In the future we'll all have electric cars.
Dans l'avenir on aura tous les voitures
électriques.
2 *(Grammar)* le **futur** MASC
a verb in the future un verbe au futur

Gg

gadget NOUN
le **gadget** MASC

to **gain** VERB
1 **gagner** [1]
We have nothing to gain. Nous n'avons
rien à gagner.
in order to gain time pour gagner du
temps
2 **to gain speed** prendre [64] de la vitesse
The car behind is gaining speed. La voiture
de derrière prend de la vitesse.
to gain weight prendre [64] du poids
Hayley's gained five kilos. Hayley a pris
cinq kilos.

galaxy NOUN
la **galaxie** FEM
a galaxy of film stars une constellation de
vedettes

gale NOUN
le **vent violent**

gallery NOUN
an art gallery *(public)* un musée, *(private)*
une galerie

◎ means the verb takes être to form the perfect

to **gamble** VERB
jouer [1]

gambling NOUN
le **jeu** MASC

game NOUN
1 (in general) le **jeu** MASC
children's games les jeux d'enfant
a game of chance un jeu de hasard
a board game un jeu de société
2 (of cards) la **partie de cartes**
Let's have a game of cards. Faisons une partie de cartes.
3 le **match** MASC
a game of football un match de foot
4 **games** le **sport** MASC
Jack's very good at games. Jack est très bon en sport.

game show NOUN
le **jeu télévisé** MASC

gang NOUN
1 (of friends) la **bande** FEM
All the gang were there. Toute la bande y était.
2 (of criminals) le **gang** MASC

gangster NOUN
le **gangster** MASC

gap NOUN
1 (hole) le **trou** MASC
2 (in time) un **intervalle** MASC
a two-year gap un intervalle de deux ans
3 (difference) la **différence** FEM
an age gap une différence d'âge
• **gap year**
une année sabbatique avant d'entrer à l'université

ℰ **garage** NOUN
le **garage** MASC

ℰ **garden** NOUN
le **jardin** MASC

gardener NOUN
le **jardinier** MASC
Paul wants to be a gardener. Paul veut être jardinier.

gardening NOUN
le **jardinage** MASC

garlic NOUN
l'**ail** MASC
• **garlic mayonnaise**
l'**aïoli** MASC

garment NOUN
le **vêtement** MASC

ℰ **gas** NOUN
le **gaz** MASC

• **gas cooker**
la cuisinière à gaz
• **gas fire**
un appareil de chauffage au gaz
• **gas meter**
le compteur à gaz

gate NOUN
1 (in a garden) le **portail** MASC
2 (in a field) la **barrière** FEM
3 (at the airport) la **porte** FEM

to **gather** VERB
1 (people) se **rassembler** ◔ [1]
A crowd gathered. Une foule s'est rassemblée.
2 (fruit, vegetables, flowers) cueillir [35]
3 (to understand) **As far as I can gather ...**
Autant que je sache ...

gay ADJECTIVE
homosexuel MASC, **homosexuelle** FEM

to **gaze** VERB
to gaze at something regarder [1] quelque chose
Joe was gazing longingly at the cake. Joe regardait le gâteau avec convoitise.

GCSEs PLURAL NOUN
You can explain GCSEs briefly as follows:
Ce sont des examens que l'on passe à environ 16 ans dans un certain nombre de matières (12 au maximum). La meilleure note que l'on peut obtenir est A-star et la note la plus basse est N. Une fois qu'ils ont obtenu leurs GCSEs, de nombreux étudiants se préparent pour les A levels.
▸ SEE **A levels**

gear NOUN
1 (in a car) la **vitesse** FEM
to change gear changer de vitesse
2 (equipment) le **matériel** MASC
camping gear du matériel de camping
3 (things) les **affaires** FEM PL
I've left all my gear at Gary's. J'ai laissé toutes mes affaires chez Gary.
• **gear lever**
le levier de vitesses

gel NOUN
hair gel le gel pour les cheveux

Gemini NOUN
les **Gémeaux** MASC PL
Stuart's Gemini. Stuart est Gémeaux.

WORD TIP Signs of the zodiac do not take an article: un or une.

gender NOUN
(of a word) le **genre** MASC
What is the gender of 'maison'? Quel est le

genre de 'maison'?

ℓ **general** *ADJECTIVE* ▸ SEE **general** *NOUN*
général *MASC*, **générale** *FEM*, **généraux** *MASC PL*, **générales** *FEM PL*
in general en général
I like fantasy books in general. J'aime les romans fantastiques en général.
- **general election**
les élections législatives
- **general knowledge**
les connaissances générales

general *NOUN* ▸ SEE **general** *ADJECTIVE*
le **général** *MASC* (PL les **généraux**)
General Jackson le général Jackson

ℓ **generally** *ADVERB*
généralement

generation *NOUN*
la **génération** *FEM*

generator *NOUN*
le **générateur** *MASC*

generous *ADJECTIVE*
généreux *MASC*, **généreuse** *FEM*

genetics *NOUN*
la **génétique** *FEM*

Geneva *NOUN*
Genève
to Geneva à Genève
We went to Geneva in 1999. Nous sommes allés à Genève en 1999.
in Geneva à Genève
Sally works in Geneva. Sally travaille à Genève.
Lake Geneva le lac Léman

genius *NOUN*
le **génie** *MASC*
Lisa, you're a genius! Lisa, tu es un génie!

ℓ **gentle** *ADJECTIVE*
doux *MASC*, **douce** *FEM*

ℓ **gentleman** *NOUN*
le **monsieur** *MASC* (PL les **messieurs**)
ladies and gentlemen mesdames et messieurs

ℓ **gently** *ADVERB*
doucement

gents *NOUN*
1 les **toilettes** *FEM PL* **(pour hommes)**
Where's the gents? Où sont les toilettes?
2 *(men's toilets)* 'Messieurs'

genuine *ADJECTIVE*
1 *(real)* **véritable** *MASC & FEM*
a genuine diamond un véritable diamant
2 *(authentic)* **authentique** *MASC & FEM*
a genuine signature une signature authentique
3 *(person)* **sincère** *MASC & FEM*
She's very genuine. Elle est très sincère.

ℓ **geography** *NOUN*
la **géographie** *FEM*

geology *NOUN*
la **géologie** *FEM*

geometry *NOUN*
la **géométrie** *FEM*

germ *NOUN*
le **microbe** *MASC*

German *ADJECTIVE* ▸ SEE **German** *NOUN*
allemand *MASC*, **allemande** *FEM*
a German car une voiture allemande

WORD TIP Adjectives never have capitals in French, even for nationality or regional origin.

German *NOUN* ▸ SEE **German** *ADJECTIVE*
1 un **Allemand** *MASC*, une **Allemande** *FEM*
the Germans les Allemands
2 *(the language)* l'**allemand** *MASC*
I speak German. Je parle allemand.

Germany *NOUN*
l'**Allemagne** *FEM*
to Germany en Allemagne
in Germany en Allemagne

ℓ **to get** *VERB*
1 *(to receive)* **avoir** [5]
I got a bike for my birthday. J'ai eu un vélo pour mon anniversaire.
I got your letter yesterday. J'ai eu ta lettre hier.
I got fifteen for my French homework. J'ai eu quinze pour mon devoir de français.
2 *(to have)* **have got** avoir [5]
He's got lots of money. Il a beaucoup d'argent.
She's got long hair. Elle a les cheveux longs.
3 *(to fetch)* **chercher** [1]
I'll go and get some bread. J'irai chercher du pain.
I'll get your bag for you. Je te chercherai ton sac.
4 *(to obtain)* **trouver** [1]
Maya's got a job. Maya a trouvé un emploi.
Where did you get that jacket? Où est-ce que tu as trouvé cette veste?
5 **to have got to do something** devoir [8] faire quelque chose
I've got to phone before midday. Je dois appeler avant midi.
6 **to get to somewhere** arriver ◎ [1] quelque part
I rang when we got to London. J'ai téléphoné quand nous sommes arrivés à Londres.

◎ means the verb takes **être** to form the perfect

to get here, to get there arriver ◎ [1]
We got here this morning. Nous sommes arrivés ce matin.
What time did they get there? Ils sont arrivés à quelle heure?

7 *(to become)* commencer [61] à être
I'm getting tired. Je commence à être fatigué *(boy speaking)*, Je commence à être fatiguée *(girl speaking)*.
It's getting late. Il se fait tard.
It's getting dark. Il commence à faire nuit.
I'm getting hungry. Je commence à avoir faim.

8 *(to become)* **to get something done** faire [10] faire quelque chose
I'm getting my hair cut this afternoon. Je vais me faire couper les cheveux cet après-midi.

• **to get back**
rentrer ◎ [1]
Mum gets back at six. Maman rentre à six heures.

• **to get something back**
récupérer [24] quelque chose
Did you get your books back? Est-ce que tu as récupéré tes livres?

• **to get into something**
(a car, lorry, taxi) monter ◎ [1] dans quelque chose
He got into the car. Il est monté dans la voiture.

• **to get off something**
descendre ◎ [3] de quelque chose
We got off the train at Bristol. Nous sommes descendus du train à Bristol.

• **to get on**
aller ◎ [7]
How's Amanda getting on? Comment va Amanda?

• **to get on something**
(a bus, train, plane) monter ◎ [1] dans quelque chose
She got on the train at Reading. Elle est montée dans le train à Reading.

• **to get on with somebody**
s'entendre [3] avec quelqu'un
Sita doesn't get on with her brother. Sita ne s'entend pas avec son frère.

• **to get out of something**
(a car, lorry, taxi) descendre ◎ [3] de quelque chose
Laura got out of the car. Laura est descendue de la voiture.

• **to get something out**
sortir [72] quelque chose
Robert got his guitar out. Robert a sorti sa guitare.

• **to get together**
se voir ◎ [13]

We must get together soon. Il faut qu'on se voie bientôt.

• **to get up**
se lever ◎ [50]
I get up at seven. Je me lève à sept heures.

ghost *NOUN*
le **fantôme** *MASC*

giant *ADJECTIVE* ▶ SEE **giant** *NOUN*
énorme *MASC & FEM*
a giant lorry un énorme camion

giant *NOUN* ▶ SEE **giant** *ADJECTIVE*
le **géant** *MASC*, la **géante** *FEM*

giddy *ADJECTIVE*
to feel giddy avoir [5] la tête qui tourne
I'm feeling giddy. J'ai la tête qui tourne.

♪ **gift** *NOUN*
1 le **cadeau** *MASC* (*PL* les **cadeaux**)
a Christmas gift un cadeau de Noël
2 *(talent)* **to have a gift for something** avoir [5] un don pour quelque chose
Jenny has a real gift for languages. Jenny a vraiment un don pour les langues.

gifted *ADJECTIVE*
doué *MASC*, **douée** *FEM*

gig *NOUN*
le **concert de rock**

gigabyte *NOUN*
le **gigaoctet** *MASC*
a twenty gigabyte hard disk un disque dur de 20 gigaoctets

gigantic *ADJECTIVE*
gigantesque *MASC & FEM*

gin *NOUN*
le **gin** *MASC*

ginger *NOUN*
le **gingembre** *MASC*

gipsy *NOUN*
1 *(in general)* le **bohémien** *MASC*, la **bohémienne** *FEM*
2 *(from Spain)* le **gitan** *MASC*, la **gitane** *FEM*
3 *(from Eastern Europe)* le & la **tzigane** *MASC & FEM*

giraffe *NOUN*
la **girafe** *FEM*

♪ **girl** *NOUN*
1 *(in general)* la **fille** *FEM*
three boys and four girls trois garçons et quatre filles
a little girl une petite fille
when I was a little girl quand j'étais petite
2 *(teenager, young woman)* une **jeune fille** *FEM*
an eighteen-year-old girl une jeune fille de dix-huit ans

♪ **indicates key words**

P **girlfriend** *NOUN*
la **copine** *FEM*
Darren's gone out with his girlfriend.
Darren est sorti avec sa copine.
Lizzie and her girlfriends have gone to the cinema. Lizzie et ses copines sont allées au cinéma.

P to **give** *VERB*
donner [1]
to give something to somebody to give somebody something donner quelque chose à quelqu'un
She gave her address to me. Elle m'a donné son adresse.
Give me the key. Donne-moi la clé.
Yasmin's dad gave her the money. Le père de Yasmin lui a donné l'argent.
• **to give something away**
donner quelque chose
She's given away all her books. Elle a donné tous ses livres.
• **to give something back to somebody**
rendre [3] quelque chose à quelqu'un
I gave her back the keys. Je lui ai rendu les clés.
• **to give in**
céder [24]
My mum said no but she gave in in the end. Maman a dit non, mais elle a fini par céder.
• **to give up**
abandonner [1]
I give up! J'abandonne!
• **to give up doing something**
arrêter [1] de faire quelque chose
She's given up smoking. Elle a arrêté de fumer.

glacier *NOUN*
le **glacier** *MASC*

P **glad** *ADJECTIVE*
content *MASC*, contente *FEM*
I'm glad to hear he's better. Je suis content d'apprendre qu'il va mieux *(boy speaking)*
I'm glad to be back. Je suis contente d'être de retour *(girl speaking)*.

glamorous *ADJECTIVE*
1 *(life)* luxueux *MASC*, luxueuse *FEM*
2 *(job)* prestigieux *MASC*, prestigieuse *FEM*
3 *(woman)* élégant *MASC*, élégante *FEM*

glance *NOUN* ▸ SEE **glance** *VERB*
un **coup d'œil** *MASC*

glance *VERB* ▸ SEE **glance** *NOUN*
to glance at something jeter [48] un coup d'œil à quelque chose
Sara glanced at the envelope. Sara a jeté un coup d'œil à l'enveloppe.

glass *ADJECTIVE* ▸ SEE **glass** *NOUN*
en verre
a glass table une table en verre

P **glass** *NOUN* ▸ SEE **glass** *ADJECTIVE*
le **verre** *MASC*
a glass of water un verre d'eau

P **glasses** *PLURAL NOUN*
les **lunettes** *FEM PL*
to wear glasses porter des lunettes
Does Katie wear glasses? Est-ce que Katie porte des lunettes?

glider *NOUN*
le **planeur** *MASC*

global *ADJECTIVE*
mondial *MASC*, mondiale *FEM*, mondiaux *MASC PL*, mondiales *FEM PL*

global warming *NOUN*
le **réchauffement de la planète**

globe *NOUN*
le **globe** *MASC*

gloomy *ADJECTIVE*
1 *(expression)* lugubre *MASC & FEM*
2 *(weather)* déprimant *MASC*, déprimante *FEM*

glory *NOUN*
la **gloire** *FEM*

glove *NOUN*
le **gant** *MASC*
a pair of gloves une paire de gants
• **glove compartment**
la boîte à gants

glue *NOUN*
la **colle** *FEM*

P **go** *NOUN* ▸ SEE **go** *VERB*
1 *(turn)* **Whose go is it?** C'est à qui de jouer?
It's my go. C'est à moi de jouer.
2 *(a try)* **to have a go at doing something**
essayer [59] de faire quelque chose
I'll have a go at mending it for you. Je vais essayer de te le réparer.

P to **go** *VERB* ▸ SEE **go** *NOUN*
1 *(in general)* aller ⊙ [7]
We're going to London tomorrow. Nous allons à Londres demain.
Mark's gone to the dentist's. Mark est allé chez le dentiste.
Beth's gone home. Beth est rentrée chez elle.
to go for a walk aller ⊙ [7] se promener
We went for a walk on the beach. Nous sommes allés nous promener sur la plage.
2 **to be going to do something** aller ⊙ [7]
faire quelque chose
I'm going to make some coffee. Je vais

⊙ **means the verb takes être to form the perfect**

faire du café.
He was going to phone me. Il allait m'appeler.

3 *(to leave)* **partir** ☺ **[58]**
Pam's already gone. Pam est déjà partie.
We're going on holiday tomorrow. Nous partons en vacances demain.

4 *(parties, meetings, events)* **se passer [1]**
Did the party go well? Est-ce que la soirée s'est bien passée?

- **to go away**
s'en aller ☺ **[7]**
He's going away. Il s'en va.
She's gone away. Elle est partie.
Go away! Va-t'en!

- **to go back**
1 **retourner** ☺ **[1]**
I'm going back to France in March. En mars je retourne en France.
I'm not going back there again! Je n'y retourne plus!

2 *(to home, school, office)* **rentrer** ☺ **[1]**
She went back home. Elle est rentrée chez moi.

- **to go down**
1 **descendre** ☺ **[3]**
She's gone down to the kitchen. Elle est descendue dans la cuisine.
to go down the stairs descendre l'escalier
You go down the stairs, then turn left. Vous descendez l'escalier puis vous tournez à gauche.

2 *(prices, temperature)* **baisser [1]**
Prices have gone down. Les prix ont baissé.

3 *(tyres, balloons, etc)* **se dégonfler** ☺ **[1]**

- **to go in**
entrer ☺ **[1]**
He went in and shut the door. Il est entré et il a fermé la porte.

- **to go into something**
1 *(person)* **entrer** ☺ **[1]** dans quelque chose
Fran went into the kitchen. Fran est entrée dans la cuisine.

2 *(thing)* **rentrer** ☺ **[1]** dans quelque chose
This file won't go into my bag. Ce classeur ne rentre pas dans mon sac.

- **to go off**
1 **exploser [1]**
A bomb went off in the city centre. Une bombe a explosé dans le centre-ville.

2 *(alarm clocks)* **sonner [1]**
My alarm clock went off at six. Mon réveil a sonné à six heures.

3 *(fire alarms, burglar alarms)* **se déclencher** ☺ **[1]**
The fire alarm went off. L'alarme d'incendie s'est déclenchée.

- **to go on**
1 *(to happen)* **se passer** ☺ **[1]**

What's going on? Qu'est-ce qui se passe?

2 *(to continue)* **to go on doing something** continuer **[1]** à faire quelque chose
She went on talking. Elle a continué à parler.

3 **to go on about something** ne pas arrêter **[1]** de parler de quelque chose
Rob's always going on about his dog. Rob n'arrête pas de parler de son chien.

- **to go out**
1 **sortir** ☺ **[72]**
I'm going out tonight. Je sors ce soir.
She went out of the kitchen. Elle est sortie de la cuisine.

2 *(light, fire)* **s'éteindre** ☺ **[60]**
The light went out. La lumière s'est éteinte.

- **to go out with somebody**
sortir ☺ **[72]** avec quelqu'un
Anna's going out with my brother. Anna sort avec mon frère.

- **to go past something**
passer ☺ **[1]** devant quelque chose
We went past your house. Nous sommes passés devant chez toi.

- **to go round**
to go round to somebody's house aller ☺ **[7]** chez quelqu'un
I went round to Imran's last night. Je suis allé chez Imran hier soir.

- **to go round something**
1 *(a building, garden, park)* **faire [10]** le tour de quelque chose

2 *(a museum, monument)* **visiter [1]** quelque chose

- **to go through something**
passer ☺ **[1]** par quelque chose
This train goes through Dijon. Ce train passe par Dijon.
You can go through my office. Tu peux passer par mon bureau.

- **to go up**
1 *(people)* **monter** ☺ **[1]**
She's gone up to her room. Elle est montée dans sa chambre.
to go up the stairs monter l'escalier
I saw someone going up the stairs. J'ai vu quelqu'un qui montait l'escalier.

2 *(prices)* **augmenter [1]**
The price of petrol has gone up. Le prix de l'essence a augmenté.

goal NOUN
le **but** MASC
to score a goal marquer un but
Adam scored two goals! Adam a marqué deux buts!
We won by three goals to two. On a gagné trois buts à deux.

- **goalkeeper**
  le gardien de but

goat NOUN
  la **chèvre** FEM
  goat's cheese le fromage de chèvre

god NOUN ▸SEE **God**
  le **dieu** MASC (PL les **dieux**)

God NOUN ▸SEE **god**
  le **Dieu** MASC
  to believe in God croire en Dieu
  Do you believe in God? Est-ce que tu crois
  en Dieu?

- **goddaughter**
  la **filleule** FEM

goddess NOUN
  la **déesse** FEM

godfather NOUN
  le **parrain** MASC

godmother NOUN
  la **marraine** FEM

godson NOUN
  le **filleul** MASC

goggles PLURAL NOUN
  les **lunettes** FEM PL
  swimming goggles les lunettes de plongée
  skiing goggles les lunettes de ski

go-karting NOUN
  le **karting** MASC
  to go go-karting faire [10] du karting
  I love to go go-karting with my friends.
  J'aime bien faire du karting avec mes amis.

gold ADJECTIVE ▸SEE **gold** NOUN
  en or
  a gold bracelet un bracelet en or

gold NOUN ▸SEE **gold** ADJECTIVE
  l'**or** MASC

- **goldfish**
  le **poisson rouge**

golf NOUN
  le **golf** MASC
  to play golf jouer [1] au golf
  More young people are playing golf. De
  plus en plus de jeunes jouent au golf.

golf club NOUN
  (place, stick) le **club de golf**

golf course NOUN
  le **terrain de golf**

golfer NOUN
  le **golfeur** MASC, la **golfeuse** FEM

♪ **good** ADJECTIVE
  1 (in general) **bon** MASC, **bonne** FEM
  He's a good teacher. C'est un bon

professeur.
  The cherries are very good. Les cerises
  sont très bonnes.
  2 to be good for you être [6] bon pour la
  santé
  Tomatoes are good for you. Les tomates
  sont bonnes pour la santé.
  3 to be good at something être [6] bon
  MASC en quelque chose, être bonne FEM en
  quelque chose
  She's good at art. Elle est bonne en dessin.
  4 (well-behaved) **sage** MASC & FEM
  Be good! Sois sage!
  5 (kind) **gentil** MASC, **gentille** FEM
  She's been very good to me. Elle a été très
  gentille avec moi.
  6 for good pour de bon
  I've stopped smoking for good. J'ai arrêté
  de fumer pour de bon.

- **good afternoon**
  bonjour
- **goodbye**
  au revoir
- **good evening**
  bonsoir
- **Good Friday**
  le Vendredi saint

good-looking ADJECTIVE
  beau MASC, **belle** FEM, **beaux** MASC PL, **belles**
  FEM PL
  Maria's boyfriend is really good-looking.
  Le copain de Maria est très beau.

good morning EXCLAMATION
  bonjour

goodness EXCLAMATION
  mon Dieu!
  For goodness sake! Au nom du ciel!

good night EXCLAMATION
  bonne nuit

goods PLURAL NOUN
  les **marchandises** FEM PL
- **goods train**
  le **train de marchandises**

goose NOUN
  une **oie** FEM
- **goose pimples**
  la **chair de poule**

gorgeous ADJECTIVE
  superbe MASC & FEM
  a gorgeous dress une robe superbe
  It's a gorgeous day. Il fait un temps
  superbe.

gorilla NOUN
  le **gorille** MASC

● means the verb takes être to form the perfect

gorse NOUN
les **ajoncs** MASC PL

gosh EXCLAMATION
ça alors!

gossip NOUN ▸ SEE **gossip** VERB
1 (person) le **bavard** MASC, la **bavarde** FEM
2 (news) les **nouvelles** FEM PL
   What's the latest gossip? Quoi de neuf?

gossip VERB ▸ SEE **gossip** NOUN
bavarder [1]

government NOUN
le **gouvernement** MASC

to **grab** VERB
1 saisir [2]
   She grabbed my arm. Elle m'a saisi par le bras.
2 (to take away) **to grab something from somebody** arracher [1] quelque chose à quelqu'un
   He grabbed the book from me. Il m'a arraché le livre.

graceful ADJECTIVE
élégant MASC, élégante FEM

grade NOUN
(mark) la **note** FEM
to get good grades avoir [5] de bonnes notes
Kat always gets good grades. Kat a toujours de bonnes notes.

gradual ADJECTIVE
progressif MASC, progressive FEM

gradually ADVERB
petit à petit
The weather got gradually better. Le temps s'est amélioré petit à petit.

graffiti PLURAL NOUN
les **graffiti** MASC PL

grain NOUN
le **grain** MASC

grammar NOUN
la **grammaire** FEM

grammar school NOUN
1 (from age 11 to 15) le **collège** MASC
2 (from age 15 to 18) le **lycée** MASC

grammatical ADJECTIVE
a grammatical error une faute de grammaire

ℰ **gramme** NOUN
le **gramme** MASC

gran NOUN
la **mamie** FEM

ℰ **grandchildren** PLURAL NOUN
les **petits-enfants** MASC PL

granddad NOUN
le **papy** MASC

ℰ **granddaughter** NOUN
la **petite-fille** FEM

ℰ **grandfather** NOUN
le **grand-père** MASC

grandma NOUN
la **mamie** FEM

ℰ **grandmother** NOUN
la **grand-mère** FEM

grandpa NOUN
le **papi** MASC

ℰ **grandparents** PLURAL NOUN
les **grands-parents** MASC PL

ℰ **grandson** NOUN
le **petit-fils** MASC

granny NOUN
la **mamie** FEM

ℰ **grape** NOUN
a grape un grain de raisin
to buy some grapes acheter du raisin
Do you like grapes? Est-ce que tu aimes le raisin?
a bunch of grapes une grappe de raisin

grapefruit NOUN
le **pamplemousse** MASC

graph NOUN
le **graphique** MASC

graphic designer NOUN
le & la **graphiste** MASC & FEM

graphics NOUN
la **visualisation graphique**

to **grasp** VERB
saisir [2]

ℰ **grass** NOUN
1 l'**herbe** FEM
   Ben was sitting on the grass. Ben était assis dans l'herbe.
2 (lawn) la **pelouse** FEM
   to cut the grass tondre la pelouse
   Could you cut the grass this afternoon? Pourrais-tu tondre la pelouse cet après-midi?
• **grasshopper**
   la **sauterelle**

to **grate** VERB
râper [1]
grated cheese du fromage râpé

A B C D E F G H I J K L M N O P Q R S T U V W X Y Z

grateful ADJECTIVE
reconnaissant MASC, reconnaissante FEM

grater NOUN
la râpe FEM

grave NOUN
1 (burial site) la tombe FEM
2 (Grammar) un accent grave (as in grève)

gravel NOUN
les gravillons MASC PL

graveyard NOUN
le cimetière MASC

gravity NOUN
la pesanteur FEM

gravy NOUN
la sauce (au jus de rôti)

grease NOUN
la graisse FEM

ℰ **greasy** ADJECTIVE
gras MASC, grasse FEM
to have greasy skin avoir [5] la peau grasse
I hate greasy food. Je déteste la nourriture grasse.

ℰ **great** ADJECTIVE
1 grand MASC, grande FEM
a great poet un grand poète
2 (terrific) génial MASC, géniale FEM, géniaux MASC PL, géniales FEM PL
It was a great party! Ça a été une soirée géniale!
Great! Génial!
3 a great deal of something beaucoup de quelque chose
a great deal of money beaucoup d'argent
a great many beaucoup de
There are a great many things still to be done. Il reste encore beaucoup de choses à faire.

Great Britain NOUN
la Grande-Bretagne FEM
to Great Britain en Grande-Bretagne
Many tourists come to Great Britain.
Beaucoup de touristes viennent en Grande-Bretagne.
in Great Britain en Grande-Bretagne
There are beautiful places to visit in Great Britain. Il y a des beaux endroits à visiter en Grande-Bretagne.
to be from Great Britain être [6] britannique
Todd's grandparents were from Great Britain. Les grands-parents de Todd étaient britanniques.

WORD TIP Countries and regions in French take le, la or les.

Greece NOUN
la Grèce FEM
to go to Greece aller ◎ [7] en Grèce
to be in Greece être [6] en Grèce

greedy ADJECTIVE
(with food) gourmand MASC, gourmande FEM

Greek NOUN ▶ SEE **Greek** ADJECTIVE
1 (person) un Grec MASC, une Grecque FEM
2 (the language) le grec MASC
Greek ADJECTIVE ▶ SEE **Greek** NOUN
grec MASC, grecque FEM

ℰ **green** ADJECTIVE ▶ SEE **green** NOUN
1 vert MASC, verte FEM
a green door une porte verte
2 écologiste MASC & FEM
the Green Party le parti écologiste

ℰ **green** NOUN ▶ SEE **green** ADJECTIVE
1 (colour) le vert MASC
a pale green un vert pâle
2 (vegetables) greens les légumes verts
3 (Politics) the Greens les Verts MASC PL

greengrocer NOUN
le marchand de fruits et légumes

greenhouse NOUN
la serre FEM
• greenhouse effect
l'effet de serre MASC

greetings PLURAL NOUN
Season's Greetings! Meilleurs vœux! MASC PL
• greetings card
la carte de vœux

ℰ **grey** ADJECTIVE
gris MASC, grise FEM
a grey skirt une jupe grise
to have grey hair avoir [5] les cheveux gris

greyhound NOUN
le lévrier MASC

grid NOUN
1 (grating) la grille FEM
2 (network) le réseau MASC (PL les réseaux)

grief NOUN
le chagrin MASC

grill NOUN ▶ SEE **grill** VERB
(of a cooker) le gril MASC
to **grill** VERB ▶ SEE **grill** NOUN
to grill something faire [10] griller quelque chose
I grilled the sausages. J'ai fait griller les saucisses.

grim ADJECTIVE
sinistre MASC & FEM

◎ means the verb takes être to form the perfect

grin *NOUN* ▸ SEE **grin** *VERB*
le **sourire** *MASC*

to **grin** *VERB* ▸ SEE **grin** *NOUN*
sourire [68]

grip *NOUN* ▸ SEE **grip** *VERB*
la **prise** *FEM*

to **grip** *VERB* ▸ SEE **grip** *NOUN*
serrer [1]

grit *NOUN*
(for roads) les **gravillons** *MASC PL*

groan *NOUN* ▸ SEE **groan** *VERB*
1 *(of pain)* le **gémissement** *MASC*
2 *(of disgust, boredom)* le **grognement** *MASC*

to **groan** *VERB* ▸ SEE **groan** *NOUN*
1 *(in pain)* gémir [2]
2 *(in disgust, boredom)* grogner [1]

⨍ **grocer** *NOUN*
un **épicier** *MASC*, une **épicière** *FEM*
My dad's a grocer. Mon père est épicier.

⨍ **groceries** *PLURAL NOUN*
les **provisions** *FEM PL*
to buy some groceries faire [10] ses
provisions

grocer's *NOUN*
une **épicerie** *FEM*
I met Jake in the grocer's. J'ai rencontré
Jake à l'épicerie.

groom *NOUN*
(bridegroom) le **marié** *MASC*
the bride and groom les jeunes mariés

gross *ADJECTIVE*
1 a gross injustice une injustice flagrante
2 a gross error une erreur grossière
3 *(disgusting)* dégoûtant *MASC*, dégoûtante
FEM
The food was gross! La nourriture était
dégoûtante!

ground *ADJECTIVE* ▸ SEE **ground** *NOUN, VERB*
moulu *MASC*, moulue *FEM*
ground coffee du café moulu

⨍ **ground** *NOUN* ▸ SEE **ground** *ADJECTIVE, VERB*
1 la **terre** *FEM*
to sit on the ground s'asseoir par terre
The children were sitting on the ground.
Les enfants étaient assis par terre.
to throw something on the ground jeter
quelque chose par terre
Jim threw the book on the ground. Jim a
jeté le livre par terre.
2 *(for sport)* le **terrain** *MASC*
a football ground un terrain de foot

to **ground** *VERB* ▸ SEE **ground** *ADJECTIVE, NOUN*
priver [1] quelqu'un de sorties
You're grounded for a week! Tu es privé de

sorties pendant une semaine!

ground floor *NOUN*
le **rez-de-chaussée** *MASC*
They live on the ground floor. Ils habitent
au rez-de-chaussée.

⨍ **group** *NOUN*
le **groupe** *MASC*

⨍ to **grow** *VERB*
1 *(plant, hair)* pousser [1]
Your hair's grown! Tes cheveux ont poussé!
2 *(person)* grandir [2]
My little sister's grown a lot this year. Ma
petite sœur a beaucoup grandi cette année.
3 *(numbers)* augmenter [1]
The number of students has grown. Le
nombre d'étudiants a augmenté.
4 *(a plant, fruit, vegetables)* faire [10] pousser
Our neighbours grow strawberries. Nos
voisins font pousser des fraises.
5 to grow a beard se laisser ⊘ [1] pousser la
barbe
6 to grow old vieillir [2]
Granddad's growing old. Papy vieillit.
• to grow up
grandir [2]
The children are growing up. Les enfants
grandissent.
She grew up in Scotland. Elle a grandi en
Écosse.

to **growl** *VERB*
grogner [1]

grown-up *NOUN*
l'**adulte** *MASC & FEM*

growth *NOUN*
la **croissance** *FEM*

grudge *NOUN*
to bear a grudge against somebody en
vouloir à quelqu'un
She bears me a grudge. Elle m'en veut.

gruesome *ADJECTIVE*
horrible *MASC & FEM*

to **grumble** *VERB*
se plaindre ⊘ [31]
She's always grumbling. Elle est toujours
en train de se plaindre.
to grumble about something se plaindre
de quelque chose
Stop grumbling about the weather. Arrête
de te plaindre du temps.

guarantee *NOUN* ▸ SEE **guarantee** *VERB*
la **garantie** *FEM*
a year's guarantee une garantie d'un an

guarantee *VERB* ▸ SEE **guarantee** *NOUN*
garantir [2]

⨍ **indicates key words**

guard NOUN ▸ SEE **guard** VERB
1 a prison guard un **gardien** de prison
2 (on a train) le **chef** de train
3 a security guard un **vigile**
to **guard** VERB ▸ SEE **guard** NOUN
   surveiller [1]
• guard dog
   le **chien** de garde

guardian NOUN
   (of child) le **tuteur** MASC, la **tutrice** FEM

guess NOUN ▸ SEE **guess** VERB
   Have a guess! **Devine**!
   It's a good guess. Tu as **deviné**.
to **guess** VERB ▸ SEE **guess** NOUN
   deviner [1]
   Guess who I saw last night! **Devine** qui j'ai
   vu hier soir!
   You'll never guess! Tu ne **devineras** jamais!

guest NOUN
1 un **invité** MASC, une **invitée** FEM
   We've got guests coming tonight. **Nous
   avons** des invités ce soir.
2 (in a hotel) le **client** MASC, la **cliente** FEM
3 (in somebody's home) a paying guest un
   hôte payant

guesthouse NOUN
   la **pension** de famille

⸓ **guide** NOUN
1 (person, book) le **guide** MASC
2 (girl guide) la **guide** FEM
• guidebook
   le **guide**
• guide dog
   le **chien** d'aveugle
• guideline
   une **indication**

guided tour NOUN
   la **visite** guidée FEM

guilty ADJECTIVE
   coupable MASC & FEM
   to feel guilty se **sentir** [58] coupable
   It wasn't my fault but I feel guilty. Ce
   n'était pas ma faute mais je me **sens**
   coupable.

guinea pig NOUN
1 (pet) le **cochon** d'Inde
2 (in an experiment) le **cobaye** MASC
   They want me to be a guinea pig. Ils
   veulent que je serve de cobaye.

guitar NOUN
   la **guitare** FEM
   to play the guitar **jouer** [1] de la guitare
   I can play the guitar. Je sais **jouer** de la
   guitare.

on the guitar à la guitare

guitarist NOUN
   le & la **guitariste** MASC & FEM

gum NOUN
1 (in your mouth) la **gencive** FEM
2 (chewing gum) le **chewing-gum** MASC

gun NOUN
1 le **revolver** MASC
2 (rifle) le **fusil** MASC

gust NOUN
   a gust of wind une **rafale** de vent

gutter NOUN
   (in the street) le **caniveau** MASC (PL les
   caniveaux)

guy NOUN
   le **type** MASC (informal)
   a guy from Newcastle un **type** qui vient de
   Newcastle
   He's a nice guy. C'est un **type** sympa.
• guy rope
   la **corde** d'attache

⸓ **gym** NOUN
   la **gym** FEM
   to go to the gym **aller** [7] à la gym
   Alex goes to the gym three times a week.
   Alex **va** à la gym trois fois par semaine.

gymnasium NOUN
   le **gymnase** MASC

gymnast NOUN
   le & la **gymnaste** MASC & FEM

gymnastics NOUN
   la **gymnastique** FEM

gym shoe NOUN
   la **chaussure** de gym

Hh

⸓ **habit** NOUN
   une **habitude** FEM
   It's a bad habit. C'est une mauvaise
   habitude.
   to be in the habit of doing something **avoir**
   [5] l'habitude de faire quelque chose

haddock NOUN
   un **églefin** MASC
   smoked haddock le **haddock**

hail NOUN ▸ SEE **hail** VERB
   la **grêle** FEM
to **hail** VERB ▸ SEE **hail** NOUN
   grêler [1]

It's hailing. Il grêle.

hailstone NOUN
le **grêlon** MASC

hailstorm NOUN
une **averse de grêle**

ℓ **hair** NOUN
1 (one hair on your head) un **cheveu**
2 (one hair on your body) un **poil**
3 (those on your head) les **cheveux** MASC PL
to have short hair avoir [5] les cheveux courts
Lucy has long hair. Lucy a les cheveux longs.
She's brushing her hair. Elle se brosse les cheveux.
Gita washes her hair every day. Gita se lave les cheveux tous les jours.
She's had her hair cut. Elle s'est fait couper les cheveux.
I'm getting my hair done. Je me fais coiffer.
• **hairbrush**
la brosse à cheveux
• **haircut**
la coupe

hairdresser NOUN
le **coiffeur** MASC, la **coiffeuse** FEM
She's a hairdresser. Elle est coiffeuse.
Mum's at the hairdresser's. Maman est chez le coiffeur.

hair dryer NOUN
le **sèche-cheveux** MASC

hairgel NOUN
le **gel pour les cheveux**

hairgrip NOUN
la **pince à cheveux**

hair remover NOUN
la **crème dépilatoire**

hairslide NOUN
la **barrette** FEM

hairspray NOUN
la **laque** FEM

hairstyle NOUN
la **coiffure** FEM

hairy ADJECTIVE
poilu MASC, **poilue** FEM

Haiti NOUN
Haïti MASC

WORD TIP Unlike other names of countries, Haïti does not take le or la.

Haitian ADJECTIVE ▸ SEE **Haitian** NOUN
haïtien MASC, **haïtienne** FEM

Haitian NOUN ▸ SEE **Haitian** ADJECTIVE
un **Haïtien** MASC, une **Haïtienne** FEM

ℓ **half** NOUN
1 (of something) la **moitié** FEM
half an apple la moitié d'une pomme
half of the money la moitié de l'argent
You've only eaten half of it. Tu n'en as mangé que la moitié.
half the people la moitié des gens
2 (as a fraction) **demi**
three and a half trois et demi
She's five and a half. Elle a cinq ans et demi.
to cut something in half couper [1] quelque chose en deux
3 (when telling the time) **demi** MASC, **demie** FEM
half an hour une demi-heure
an hour and a half une heure et demie
It's half past three. Il est trois heures et demie.
4 (in weights and measures) **demi** MASC, **demie** FEM
half a litre un demi-litre
half a cup une demi-tasse
a litre and a half un litre et demi

half hour NOUN
la **demi-heure** FEM
every half hour toutes les demi-heures

half-price ADJECTIVE, ADVERB
à **moitié prix**
half-price books des livres à moitié prix
I bought it half price. Je l'ai acheté à moitié prix.

half time NOUN
la **mi-temps** FEM
at half time à la mi-temps

halfway ADVERB
1 (in distance) à **mi-chemin**
halfway between Paris and Dijon à mi-chemin entre Paris et Dijon
2 (in time) to be halfway through something avoir [5] à moitié fini quelque chose
I'm halfway through my homework. J'ai à moitié fini mes devoirs.

ℓ **hall** NOUN
1 (in a house) une **entrée** FEM
2 (for meetings, events) la **salle** FEM
the village hall la salle des fêtes

Hallowe'en NOUN
la **veille de la Toussaint** (Hallowe'en is not celebrated in France.)

ℓ **ham** NOUN
le **jambon** MASC
a slice of ham une tranche de jambon
a ham sandwich un sandwich au jambon

hamburger NOUN
un **hamburger** MASC

hammer NOUN
le **marteau** MASC (PL les **marteaux**)

hammock NOUN
un **hamac** MASC

hamster NOUN
un **hamster** MASC

ℰ **hand** NOUN ► SEE **hand** VERB
1 (part of the body) la **main** FEM
to have something in your hand avoir [5] quelque chose à la main
to hold somebody's hand tenir [77] quelqu'un par la main
They were holding hands. Ils se tenaient par la main.
2 (help) a hand un **coup de main**
Can you give me a hand? Est-ce que tu peux me donner un coup de main?
Do you need a hand? Est-ce que tu as besoin d'un coup de main?
3 (of a watch, clock) l' **aiguille** FEM
the hour hand l'aiguille des heures

ℰ to **hand** VERB ► SEE **hand** NOUN
passer [1]
I handed him the keys. Je lui ai passé les clés.
• **to hand something in**
rendre [3] quelque chose
I've handed in my homework. J'ai rendu mon devoir.
• **to hand something out**
distribuer [1] quelque chose
Claire handed out the exercise books. Claire a distribué les cahiers.
• **handbag**
le **sac à main** (PL les **sacs à main**)
• **handcuffs**
les **menottes** FEM PL

handful NOUN
poignée FEM
a handful of something une poignée de quelque chose

ℰ **handkerchief** NOUN
le **mouchoir** MASC

handle NOUN ► SEE **handle** VERB
1 (of a door, drawer) la **poignée** FEM
2 (of a knife, tool) le **manche** MASC
3 (of a frying pan, saucepan) la **queue** FEM
4 (of a cup, basket) une **anse** FEM

to **handle** VERB ► SEE **handle** NOUN
s'occuper [1] de
Gina handles the accounts. Gina s'occupe de la comptabilité.
Leave it to me, I can handle it. Laisse-moi

faire, je peux m'en occuper.
She's good at handling people. Elle a un bon contact avec les gens.

handlebars PLURAL NOUN
le **guidon** MASC

hand luggage NOUN
les **bagages à main** MASC PL

handmade ADJECTIVE
fait à la main MASC, **faite à la main** FEM

ℰ **handsome** ADJECTIVE
beau MASC, **belle** FEM, **beaux** MASC PL, **belles** FEM PL
He's a handsome guy. C'est un beau type.

handwriting NOUN
l' **écriture** FEM

ℰ **handy** ADJECTIVE
1 (useful) **pratique** MASC & FEM
This bag's very handy. Ce sac est très pratique.
2 (nearby) **sous la main**
I keep a notebook handy. Je garde un calepin sous la main.

ℰ to **hang** VERB
1 (to be hanging) être [6] accroché
A painting was hanging on the wall. Une peinture était accrochée au mur.
A light hung from the ceiling. Une lumière pendait du plafond.
2 (a picture, a painting) accrocher [1]
We hung the mirror on the wall. Nous avons accroché le miroir au mur.
• **to hang around**
traîner [1]
We were hanging around in the street. On traînait dans la rue.
• **to hang on**
attendre [3]
Hang on a second! Attends une seconde!
• **to hang up**
(on the phone) raccrocher [1]
She hung up on me. Elle m'a raccroché au nez.
Do not hang up. Ne quittez pas.
• **to hang something up**
accrocher [1] quelque chose
Hang your coat up. Accroche ton manteau.

hang-gliding NOUN
le **deltaplane** MASC
to go hang-gliding faire [10] du deltaplane

hangover NOUN
la **gueule de bois**
to have a hangover avoir [5] la gueule de bois

⬤ means the verb takes être to form the perfect

to **happen** *VERB*
se passer ◐ [1]
What's happening? Qu'est-ce qui se passe?
It happened in June. Ça s'est passé en juin.
What happened at school? Qu'est-ce qui
s'est passé à l'école?

happily *ADVERB*
1 *(cheerfully)* joyeusement
2 *(willingly)* volontiers
I'll happily do it for you. Je le ferai pour toi
volontiers.

happiness *NOUN*
le **bonheur** *MASC*

ℱ **happy** *ADJECTIVE*
heureux *MASC*, heureuse *FEM*
a happy child un enfant heureux
a happy family une famille heureuse
Happy Birthday! Bon anniversaire!

ℱ **harbour** *NOUN*
le **port** *MASC*

ℱ **hard** *ADJECTIVE* ▸ SEE **hard** *ADVERB*
1 *(not soft)* dur *MASC*, dure *FEM*
to go hard durcir
The cheese has gone hard. Le fromage a
durci.
2 *(difficult)* difficile *MASC & FEM*
a hard question une question difficile
It's hard to know ... Il est difficile de savoir
...

ℱ **hard** *ADVERB* ▸ SEE **hard** *ADJECTIVE*
1 **to work hard** travailler dur
He works hard. Il travaille dur.
2 **to try hard** faire [10] beaucoup d'efforts
• **hard-boiled egg**
un œuf dur
• **hard disk**
le disque dur

hardly *ADVERB*
1 à peine
I can hardly hear him. Je l'entends à peine.
2 *(in expressions)* **hardly any** presque pas de
There's hardly any milk. Il n' y a presque
pas de lait.
hardly ever presque jamais
I hardly ever see them. Je ne les vois
presque jamais.
hardly anyone presque personne
There was hardly anyone there. Il n'y avait
presque personne.

hare *NOUN*
le **lièvre** *MASC*

harm *NOUN* ▸ SEE **harm** *VERB*
mal
It won't do you any harm. Ça ne te fera pas
de mal.

to **harm** *VERB* ▸ SEE **harm** *NOUN*
to harm somebody faire [10] du mal à
quelqu'un
They did not harm him. Ils ne lui ont pas
fait de mal.

harmful *ADJECTIVE*
nuisible *MASC & FEM*

harmless *ADJECTIVE*
inoffensif *MASC*, inoffensive *FEM*

harvest *NOUN*
la **récolte** *FEM*

ℱ **hat** *NOUN*
le **chapeau** *MASC (PL* les **chapeaux)**

ℱ to **hate** *VERB*
détester [1]
I hate spiders. Je déteste les araignées.

hatred *NOUN*
la **haine** *FEM*

ℱ to **have** *VERB*
1 *(to possess)* avoir [5]
Anna has three brothers. Anna a trois
frères.
How many sisters do you have? Tu as
combien de sœurs?
We've got a dog. Nous avons un chien.
What have you got in your hand? Qu'est-ce
que tu as dans la main?
2 *(in English past tenses with have, had + -ed
words – some French verbs take avoir)* **I've
finished.** J'ai fini.
Have you seen the film? Est-ce que tu as
vu le film?
We had already eaten. Nous avions déjà
mangé.
3 *(some French verbs take être)* **Rosie hasn't
arrived yet.** Rosie n'est pas encore arrivée.
He had left. Il était parti.
They have sat down. Ils se sont assis.
4 **to have to do something** devoir [8] faire
quelque chose
I have to phone Nathalie. Je dois appeler
Nathalie.
5 *(food, a drink, a shower)* prendre [64]
We had a coffee. Nous avons pris un café.
I'll have an omelette. Je prends une
omelette.
I'm going to have a shower. Je vais prendre
une douche.
6 *(with meals)* **to have breakfast** prendre [64]
le petit déjeuner
to have lunch déjeuner [1]
to have dinner dîner [1] *(in the evening)*
7 **to have something done** se faire ◐ [10]
faire quelque chose
I'm going to have my hair cut. Je vais me

faire couper les cheveux.

> **WORD TIP** Verbs taking être for the -ed tenses in English do not have direct objects: Je suis arrivé. = I have arrived. Il est entré. = He has come in. Reflexive verbs (with se) also take être in the tenses where English uses **have, had**: Elle s'est lavée. = She has washed herself.

hawk NOUN
le **faucon** MASC

hay NOUN
le **foin** MASC

• hay fever
le **rhume des foins**

hazelnut NOUN
la **noisette** FEM

♪ **he** PRONOUN
il
He's a student. Il est étudiant.
He lives in Manchester. Il habite à Manchester.
He's a musician. C'est un musicien.
Who is he? C'est qui?
Here he is! Le voici!
There he is! Le voilà!

♪ **head** NOUN ▸ SEE **head** VERB
1 (part of your body) la **tête** FEM
He has a cap on his head. Il a une casquette sur la tête.
at the head of the queue en tête de queue
2 (of a school) le **directeur** MASC, la **directrice** FEM (of a lycée) le **proviseur** MASC
3 (when tossing a coin) **'Heads or tails?'** — **'Heads.'** 'Pile ou face?' — 'Face.'

to **head** VERB ▸ SEE **head** NOUN
• to head for something
se **diriger** ⊙ [52] vers quelque chose
Liz headed for the door. Liz s'est dirigée vers la porte.

headache NOUN
I've got a headache. J'ai mal à la tête.

headlight NOUN
le **phare** MASC

headline NOUN
le **gros titre** MASC

headmaster NOUN
le **directeur** MASC

headmistress NOUN
la **directrice** FEM

headphones PLURAL NOUN
le **casque** MASC SINGULAR

headquarters NOUN
1 (of an organization) le **siège social**
2 (military) le **quartier général**

headteacher NOUN
le **directeur** MASC, la **directrice** FEM

♪ **health** NOUN
la **santé** FEM

• health centre
le **centre médico-social**

healthy ADJECTIVE
1 (person) en **bonne santé**
to be healthy être [6] en bonne santé
2 (diet) **sain** MASC, **saine** FEM

heap NOUN
le **tas** MASC

♪ to **hear** VERB
1 (a sound, a noise) **entendre** [3]
I can hear you. Je t'entends.
I can't hear anything. Je n'entends rien.
2 (some news) **apprendre** [64]
I hear you've bought a dog. J'apprends que tu as acheté un chien.
• to hear about something
entendre [3] parler de quelque chose
Have you heard about the concert? As-tu entendu parler du concert?
• to hear of something
entendre parler de quelque chose
She's never heard of crêpes. Elle ne sait pas ce que c'est qu'une crêpe.

hearing aid NOUN
le **Sonotone®** MASC

heart NOUN
1 (part of the body) le **cœur** MASC
to learn something by heart apprendre [64] quelque chose par cœur
2 (in cards) le **cœur** MASC
the jack of hearts le valet de cœur
• heart attack
la **crise cardiaque**

♪ **heat** NOUN ▸ SEE **heat** VERB
la **chaleur** FEM

♪ to **heat** VERB ▸ SEE **heat** NOUN
chauffer [1]
to heat the house with gas chauffer la maison au gaz
The soup's heating. La soupe est en train de chauffer.
• to heat something up
faire [10] chauffer quelque chose
I'll heat up the soup. Je vais faire chauffer la soupe.

heater NOUN
le **radiateur** MASC

heather NOUN
la **bruyère** FEM

ℱ **heating** NOUN
le **chauffage** MASC

heatwave NOUN
la **vague de chaleur**

heaven NOUN
le **paradis** MASC

ℱ **heavy** ADJECTIVE
(weight, weather, defeat) **lourd** MASC, **lourde** FEM
My rucksack's heavy. Mon sac à dos est lourd.
heavy rain de fortes pluies
heavy traffic une circulation dense
• **heavy metal**
le **hard rock**

hedge NOUN
la **haie** FEM

hedgehog NOUN
un **hérisson** MASC

ℱ **heel** NOUN
le **talon** MASC

ℱ **height** NOUN
1 (of a person) la **taille** FEM
a man of average height un homme de taille moyenne
2 (of a building) la **hauteur** FEM
3 (of a mountain) l'**altitude** FEM

helicopter NOUN
un **hélicoptère** MASC

hell NOUN
l'**enfer** MASC
It's hell here! C'est infernal ici!

ℱ **hello** EXCLAMATION
1 (polite) **bonjour!**
2 (informal) **salut!**
3 (on the telephone) **allô!**

helmet NOUN
le **casque** MASC

ℱ **help** NOUN ▸ SEE **help** VERB
l'**aide** FEM
Do you need any help? Est-ce que tu as besoin d'aide?

ℱ to **help** VERB ▸ SEE **help** NOUN
1 **aider** [1]
to help somebody to do something aider [1] quelqu'un à faire quelque chose
Can you help me move the table? Peux-tu m'aider à déplacer la table?
2 **Help yourself!** Sers-toi!
Help yourselves to vegetables. Prenez des légumes.
3 **Help!** Au secours!

helper NOUN
un & une **aide** MASC & FEM

helpful ADJECTIVE
(person) **serviable** MASC & FEM

helping NOUN
la **portion** FEM
Would you like a second helping of chips? Est-ce que tu veux encore des frites?

hem NOUN
un **ourlet** MASC

ℱ **hen** NOUN
la **poule** FEM

ℱ **her** PRONOUN ▸ SEE **her** DETERMINER
1 (as a direct object) **la**
I know her. Je la connais.
I don't know her. Je ne la connais pas.
I saw her last week. Je l'ai vue la semaine dernière.
Watch her! Regarde-la!
Don't forget her. Ne l'oublie pas.

> **WORD TIP** la as a direct object becomes l' before a, e, i, o, u or silent h.

2 (as the indirect object) **lui**
Give the book to her. Donne-lui le livre.
Can you write to her? Est-ce que tu peux lui écrire?
I gave her my address. Je lui ai donné mon adresse.
Don't give her my number. Ne lui donne pas mon numéro.

> **WORD TIP** lui as an indirect object never changes.

3 (after prepositions) **elle**
I'll go with her. J'irai avec elle.
We left without her. Nous sommes partis sans elle.
It's a present for her. C'est un cadeau pour elle.

> **WORD TIP** elle is used after prepositions like avec or sans.

4 (in comparisons) **elle**
I'm older than her. Je suis plus âgé qu'elle.

ℱ **her** DETERMINER ▸ SEE **her** PRONOUN
1 (with masc singular nouns) **son**
her brother son frère
her computer son ordinateur
2 (with fem singular nouns) **sa**
her sister sa sœur
her house sa maison
What's her address? Quelle est son adresse?
3 (with plural nouns) **ses**
her friends ses amis
4 (with parts of the body) **le, la, les**

ℱ **indicates key words**

She's washing her hands. Elle se lave les mains.
She had a glass in her hand. Elle avait un verre à la main.

WORD TIP Use son with feminine nouns beginning with a, e, i, o, u or silent h.

herb NOUN
l'herbe FEM

herd NOUN
le troupeau MASC (PL les troupeaux)

here ADVERB
1 (close to the speaker) ici
Leave it here. Laisse-le ici.
Come here. Viens ici.
We're in here in the kitchen. Nous sommes ici dans la cuisine.
2 (in this general area) ici
the shops around here les magasins par ici
It's sunnier over here. Il fait plus de soleil ici.
The cashpoint's not far from here. Le guichet automatique n'est pas loin d'ici.
Is Tom here? Est-ce que Tom est là?
He isn't here at the moment. Il n'est pas là en ce moment.
3 (when you point things out) here is voici, voilà
Here's my address. Voici mon adresse.
Look, here comes Ben now. Tiens, voilà Ben qui arrive.
here are voici, voilà
Here are the photos. Voici les photos.
And here they are! Et les voilà!

hero NOUN
un héros MASC

heroin NOUN
l'héroïne FEM

heroine NOUN
une héroïne FEM

herring NOUN
un hareng MASC

hers PRONOUN
1 (for masc singular nouns) le sien
I took my hat and she took hers. J'ai pris mon chapeau et elle a pris le sien.
2 (for fem singular nouns) la sienne
I gave her my address and she gave me hers. Je lui ai donné mon adresse et elle m'a donné la sienne.
3 (for masc plural nouns) les siens
I invited my parents and Karen invited hers. J'ai invité mes parents et Karen a invité les siens.
4 (for fem plural nouns) les siennes
I showed her my photos and she showed

me hers. Je lui ai montré mes photos et elle m'a montré les siennes.
5 (belonging to her) à elle
It's hers. C'est à elle.
Is that hers? C'est à elle, ça?
The green one's hers. Le vert est à elle.

herself PRONOUN
1 se
She's going to hurt herself. Elle va se blesser.
She enjoyed herself. Elle s'est amusée.

WORD TIP se becomes s' before a, e, i, o, u or silent h. amusée agrees with se, which refers to elle.

2 (for emphasis) elle-même
She said it herself. Elle l'a dit elle-même.
3 (on her own) by herself toute seule
She did it by herself. Elle l'a fait toute seule.

to **hesitate** VERB
hésiter [1]

heterosexual ADJECTIVE
hétérosexuel MASC, hétérosexuelle FEM

hi EXCLAMATION
(informal) salut!

hiccups PLURAL NOUN
to have the hiccups avoir [5] le hoquet

hidden ADJECTIVE
caché MASC, cachée FEM

to **hide** VERB
1 (to hide yourself) se cacher ⊙ [1]
She hid behind the door. Elle s'est cachée derrière la porte.
2 (something) cacher [1]
Who's hidden the chocolate? Qui a caché le chocolat?

hide-and-seek NOUN
to play hide-and-seek jouer [1] à cache-cache

hi-fi NOUN
la chaîne hi-fi

high ADJECTIVE
1 (in general) haut MASC, haute FEM
a high shelf une étagère haute
The wall is very high. Le mur est très haut.
The wall is two metres high. Le mur fait deux mètres de hauteur.
How high is the Eiffel Tower? Quelle est la hauteur de la tour Eiffel?
2 (numbers, prices, temperatures) élevé MASC, élevée FEM
The prices are very high. Les prix sont très élevés.
3 (speed) grand MASC, grande FEM
at high speed à grande vitesse

⊙ means the verb takes être to form the perfect

high winds des vents forts
4 *(voice, note)* aigu *MASC*, aiguë *FEM*
    a high voice une voix aiguë

higher education *NOUN*
    l'enseignement supérieur *MASC*

Highers, Advanced Highers *PLURAL NOUN*
    le baccalauréat *MASC*, le **bac** *MASC (informal)*
    the exam taken at the end of secondary school

high-heeled *ADJECTIVE*
    à hauts talons
    high-heeled shoes des chaussures à hauts talons

high jump *NOUN*
    le **saut en hauteur**

highly *ADVERB*
    extrêmement

to **hijack** *VERB*
    to hijack a plane détourner [1] un avion

hijacker *NOUN*
    le **pirate de l'air**

hijacking *NOUN*
    le **détournement** *MASC*

hike *NOUN*
    la **randonnée** *FEM*
    to go on a hike faire [10] une randonnée

hiker *NOUN*
    le **randonneur** *MASC* la **randonneuse** *FEM*

hiking *NOUN*
    la **randonnée** *FEM*
    We like hiking. Nous aimons faire de la randonnée.

hilarious *ADJECTIVE*
    hilarant *MASC*, hilarante *FEM*

ℰ **hill** *NOUN*
1 *(in the landscape)* la **colline** *FEM*
    You can see the hills. On voit les collines.
2 *(steep slope)* le **coteau** *MASC (PL* les **coteaux***)*
    the houses on the hill les maisons sur le coteau
3 *(sloping street, road)* **to go up the hill** monter
    You go up the hill as far as the church ... Vous montez jusqu'à l'église ...

ℰ **him** *PRONOUN*
1 *(as a direct object)* le
    I know him. Je le connais.
    I don't know him. Je ne le connais pas.
    I saw him last week. Je l'ai vu la semaine dernière.
    Watch him! Regarde-le!

Don't forget him. Ne l'oublie pas.

WORD TIP le as a direct object becomes l'before a, e, i, o, u or silent h.

2 *(as an indirect object)* lui
    Give the book to him. Donne-lui le livre.
    Can you write to him? Est-ce que tu peux lui écrire?
    I gave him my address. Je lui ai donné mon adresse.
    Don't give him my number. Ne lui donne pas mon numéro.

WORD TIP lui as an indirect object never changes.

3 *(after prepositions)* lui
    I'll go with him. J'irai avec lui.
    We left without him. Nous sommes partis sans lui.
    It's a present for him. C'est un cadeau pour lui.

WORD TIP lui is used after prepositions like avec or sans.

4 *(in comparisons)* lui
    She's older than him. Elle est plus âgée que lui.

himself *PRONOUN*
1 se
    He's going to hurt himself. Il va se blesser.
    He enjoyed himself. Il s'est beaucoup amusé.

WORD TIP se becomes s' before a, e, i, o, u or silent h. amusé above, agrees with se, which refers to il.

2 *(for emphasis)* lui-même
    He said it himself. Il l'a dit lui-même.
3 *(on his own)* **by himself** tout seul
    He did it by himself. Il l'a fait tout seul.

Hindu *ADJECTIVE*
    hindou *MASC*, hindoue *FEM*

WORD TIP Adjectives and nouns of religion start with a small letter in French.

hip *NOUN*
    la **hanche** *FEM*

hippie *NOUN*
    le & la **hippy** *MASC & FEM*

hippopotamus *NOUN*
    un **hippopotame** *MASC*

ℰ **hire** *NOUN* ▶ SEE **hire** *VERB*
    la **location** *FEM*
    car hire la location de voitures
    for hire à louer

ℰ to **hire** *VERB* ▶ SEE **hire** *NOUN*
    louer [1]

ℰ **indicates key words**

We always hire a car. Nous louons toujours une voiture.

his DETERMINER ▶ SEE **his** PRONOUN
1 *(with masc singular nouns)* **son**
   his brother son frère
   his computer son ordinateur
2 *(with fem singular nouns)* **sa**
   his sister sa sœur
   his house sa maison
   What's his address? Quelle est son adresse?
3 *(with plural nouns)* **ses**
   his friends ses amis
4 *(with parts of the body)* **le, la, les**
   He's washing his hands. Il se lave les mains.
   He had a glass in his hand. Il avait un verre à la main.

WORD TIP Use son with fem nouns beginning with a, e, i, o, u or silent h.

his PRONOUN ▶ SEE **his** DETERMINER
1 *(for masc singular nouns)* **le sien**
   I took my hat and he took his. J'ai pris mon chapeau et il a pris le sien.
2 *(for fem singular nouns)* **la sienne**
   I gave him my address and he gave me his. Je lui ai donné mon adresse et il m'a donné la sienne.
3 *(for masc plural nouns)* **les siens**
   I've invited my parents and Steve's invited his. J'ai invité mes parents et Steve a invité les siens.
4 *(for fem plural nouns)* **les siennes**
   I showed him my photos and he showed me his. Je lui ai montré mes photos et il m'a montré les siennes.
5 *(belonging to him)* **à lui**
   It's his. C'est à lui.
   Is that his? C'est à lui, ça?
   The green car's his. La voiture verte est à lui.

historic ADJECTIVE
   historique MASC & FEM

ℰ **history** NOUN
   une **histoire** FEM

hit NOUN ▶ SEE **hit** VERB
1 *(song)* le **tube** MASC
   their latest hit leur dernier tube
2 *(success)* le **succès** MASC
   The film was a huge hit. Le film a eu un succès fou.

ℰ to **hit** VERB ▶ SEE **hit** NOUN
1 **frapper** [1]
   to hit the ball frapper la balle
2 **to hit your head on something** se cogner ⬥ [1] la tête contre quelque chose
3 *(to go into)* **heurter** [1]

The car hit a tree. La voiture a heurté un arbre.
4 **to be hit by a car** être [6] renversé par une voiture
   She was hit by a car. Elle a été renversée par une voiture.

hitch NOUN ▶ SEE **hitch** VERB
   le **problème** MASC

to **hitch** VERB ▶ SEE **hitch** NOUN
   to hitch a lift faire [10] du stop
   Harry hitched a lift home. Harry est rentré en stop.

ℰ to **hitchhike** VERB
   faire [10] du stop
   We hitchhiked for a week. Nous avons fait du stop pendant une semaine.
   We hitchhiked to Dijon. Nous sommes allés à Dijon en stop.

hitchhiker NOUN
   un **auto-stoppeur** MASC, une **auto-stoppeuse** FEM

ℰ **hitchhiking** NOUN
   l'**auto-stop** MASC

HIV-negative ADJECTIVE
   séronégatif MASC, **séronégative** FEM

HIV-positive ADJECTIVE
   séropositif MASC, **séropositive** FEM

ℰ **hobby** NOUN
   le **passe-temps** MASC
   My favourite hobby is skiing. Mon passe-temps préféré, c'est le ski.

hockey NOUN
   le **hockey** MASC
   to play hockey jouer [1] au hockey
• **hockey stick**
   la crosse de hockey

to **hold** VERB
1 *(in your hands)* **tenir** [77]
   Can you hold the torch? Est-ce que tu peux tenir la lampe?
2 *(to contain)* **contenir** [77]
   a jug which holds a litre un pichet qui contient un litre
3 *(a meeting, an event)* **tenir** [77]
   A meeting was held in the village hall. On a tenu une réunion dans la salle des fêtes.
4 *(when telephoning)* **Hold the line.** Ne quittez pas.
• **to hold on**
   (to wait) **attendre** [3]
   Hold on! Attends!, *(on the telephone)* Ne quittez pas!
• **to hold somebody up**
   retenir [77] quelqu'un
   I was held up at the dentist's. J'ai été

⬥ means the verb takes être to form the perfect

retenu chez le dentiste.
- **to hold something up**
  lever [50] quelque chose
  He held up his glass. Il a levé son verre.

hold-up NOUN
1 (delay) le **retard** MASC
2 (traffic jam) le **bouchon** MASC
3 (robbery) le **hold-up** MASC

hole NOUN
le **trou** MASC

ℰ **holiday** NOUN
1 (non-working day) **a public holiday** un jour férié
  Monday's a holiday. Lundi est férié.
2 (time for relaxation) les **vacances** FEM PL
  the school holidays les vacances scolaires
  Where are you going for your holiday? Où est-ce que vous partez en vacances?
  Leyla is away on holiday. Leyla est en vacances.
  to go on holiday partir ◎ [58] en vacances
  When are you going on holiday? Quand est-ce que tu pars en vacances?
  Have a good holiday! Bonnes vacances!
3 (from work) le **congé** MASC
  I'm taking two days' holiday. Je prends deux jours de congé.
- **holiday home**
  la résidence secondaire

Holland NOUN
la **Hollande** FEM
They went to Holland at Easter. Ils sont allés en Hollande à Pâques.
Laura works in Holland. Laura travaille en Hollande.

WORD TIP Countries and regions in French take **le**, **la** or **les**.

hollow ADJECTIVE
creux MASC, **creuse** FEM

holly NOUN
le **houx** MASC

holy ADJECTIVE
saint MASC, **sainte** FEM

ℰ **home** NOUN ▸ SEE **home** ADVERB
la **maison** FEM
I was at home. J'étais à la maison.
We stayed at home. Nous sommes restés à la maison.
Make yourself at home! Fais comme chez toi!

ℰ **home** ADVERB ▸ SEE **home** NOUN
1 **chez ...**
  I'll call on my way home. Je passerai te voir en rentrant chez moi.

Susie came home with us. Susie est venue chez nous.

WORD TIP You show whose home with **chez** **moi** my house, **chez toi** your house, **chez Emma** Emma's house, etc.

2 **to get home** rentrer ◎ [1]
  We got home at midnight. Nous sommes rentrés à minuit.

home economics NOUN
les **arts ménagers** MASC PL

ℰ **homeless** NOUN
the homeless les **sans-abri** MASC PL

homemade ADJECTIVE
fait maison MASC, **faite maison** FEM
homemade cakes des gâteaux faits maison

home match NOUN
le **match à domicile**

homeopathic ADJECTIVE
homéopathique MASC & FEM

homesick ADJECTIVE
to be homesick avoir [5] le mal du pays
I'm homesick. J'ai le mal du pays.

ℰ **homework** NOUN
les **devoirs** MASC PL
I did my homework. J'ai fait mes devoirs.
my French homework mes devoirs de français

homosexual ADJECTIVE
homosexuel MASC, **homosexuelle** FEM

ℰ **honest** ADJECTIVE
honnête MASC & FEM

honestly ADVERB
franchement

honesty NOUN
l'**honnêteté** FEM

honey NOUN
le **miel** MASC

honeymoon NOUN
le **voyage de noces**
They're going to Paris on their honeymoon. Ils partent à Paris en voyage de noces.

honeysuckle NOUN
le **chèvrefeuille** MASC

honour NOUN
un **honneur** MASC

hood NOUN
la **capuche** FEM

hoodie NOUN
le **pull à capuche** MASC

ℰ indicates key words

hook NOUN
1 le **crochet** MASC
2 **to take the phone off the hook** décrocher le téléphone

hooligan NOUN
le **voyou** MASC

hooray EXCLAMATION
hourra!

to **hoover** VERB
passer [1] l'aspirateur
I hoovered my bedroom. J'ai passé l'aspirateur dans ma chambre.

Hoover® NOUN
un **aspirateur** MASC

hope NOUN ▸ SEE **hope** VERB
un **espoir** MASC
to give up hope perdre l'espoir
They gave up hope of finding her. Ils ont perdu l'espoir de lui trouver.

♪ to **hope** VERB ▸ SEE **hope** NOUN
espérer [24]
We hope you'll be able to come. Nous espérons que vous pourrez venir.
Hoping to see you on Friday. En espérant te voir vendredi.
I hope so. Je l'espère.
I hope not. J'espère que non.

hopefully ADVERB
avec un peu de chance
Hopefully, the film won't have started. Avec un peu de chance, le film n'aura pas commencé.

hopeless ADJECTIVE
nul MASC, nulle FEM
I'm hopeless at maths. Je suis nul en maths.

horizon NOUN
l'**horizon** MASC

horizontal ADJECTIVE
horizontal MASC, horizontale FEM, horizontaux MASC PL, horizontales FEM PL

horn NOUN
1 (of an animal) la **corne** FEM
2 (of a car) le **klaxon** MASC
to sound your horn klaxonner
3 (musical instrument) le **cor** MASC
to play the horn jouer [1] du cor

horoscope NOUN
un **horoscope** MASC

♪ **horrible** ADJECTIVE
1 (weather, experience) **affreux** MASC, **affreuse** FEM
The weather was horrible. Il a fait un temps affreux.

2 (person) **désagréable** MASC & FEM
She's really horrible! Elle est vraiment désagréable!
He was horrible to me. Il a été désagréable avec moi.

horrific ADJECTIVE
terrible MASC & FEM

horror NOUN
l'**horreur** FEM
• **horror film**
le film d'épouvante

♪ **horse** NOUN
le **cheval** MASC (PL les **chevaux**)

horse chestnut NOUN
1 (tree) le **marronnier** MASC
2 (nut) le **marron** MASC

horse racing NOUN
les **courses hippiques** FEM PL

horseshoe NOUN
le **fer à cheval**

hose NOUN
le **tuyau** MASC (PL les **tuyaux**)

hosepipe NOUN
le **tuyau d'arrosage**

♪ **hospital** NOUN
un **hôpital** MASC (PL les **hôpitaux**)
to be in hospital être [6] à l'hôpital
Nina was in hospital for three weeks. Nina était à l'hôpital pendant trois semaines.
to be taken into hospital être hospitalisé MASC, être hospitalisée FEM

hospitality NOUN
l'**hospitalité** FEM

host NOUN
1 un **hôte** MASC, une **hôtesse** FEM
2 (in exchanges) **host family** la famille d'accueil
My host family is very nice. Ma famille d'accueil est très sympathique.

hostage NOUN
un **otage** MASC

hostel NOUN
le **foyer** MASC

hostess NOUN
une **hôtesse** FEM
an air hostess une hôtesse de l'air

♪ **hot** ADJECTIVE
1 (food, drink) **chaud** MASC, **chaude** FEM
a hot drink une boisson chaude
hot meals des repas chauds
Be careful, the plates are hot! Fais attention, les assiettes sont très chaudes!

🌀 **means the verb takes être to form the perfect**

2 *(weather, places)* **to be hot** faire [10] chaud
It's hot today. Il fait chaud aujourd'hui.
It won't be too hot. Il ne fera pas trop chaud.
It was very hot in the kitchen. Il faisait très chaud dans la cuisine.

3 *(the feeling)* **to be hot** avoir [5] chaud
I'm hot. J'ai chaud.
I'm very hot. J'ai très chaud.
I'm too hot. J'ai trop chaud.
Your hands are hot. Tu as les mains chaudes.

4 *(spicy)* **épicé** MASC, **épicée** FEM
• **hot dog**
un hot-dog

℘ **hotel** NOUN
un **hôtel** MASC

℘ **hour** NOUN
une **heure** FEM
an hour ago il y a une heure
two hours later deux heures plus tard
We waited for three hours. Nous avons attendu trois heures.
There's a train every hour. Il y a un train toutes les heures.
an hour and a half une heure et demie
to be paid by the hour être [6] payé à l'heure

hourly ADJECTIVE, ADVERB
1 *(every hour)* **toutes les heures**
There is an hourly bus. Il y a un bus toutes les heures.
2 *(by the hour)* **à l'heure**
We're paid on an hourly basis. On nous paye à l'heure.

℘ **house** NOUN
1 la **maison** FEM
to buy a house acheter une maison
2 **at somebody's house** chez quelqu'un
I'm at Jake's house. Je suis chez Jake.
I'm going to Hannah's house. Je vais chez Hannah.
• **housewife**
la femme au foyer

housework NOUN
le **ménage** MASC
to do the housework faire [10] le ménage

℘ **how** ADVERB
1 *(asking in what way)* **comment**
How are you? Comment allez-vous?
How did you do it? Comment l'as-tu fait?
2 *(asking about quantity)* **how much, how many** combien
How much is it? Ça coûte combien?
How much money do you have? Tu as combien d'argent?

How many brothers do you have? Tu as combien de frères?
3 *(asking general questions)* **How old are you?** Quel âge as-tu?
How far is it? C'est à quelle distance d'ici?
How long will it take? Ça va prendre combien de temps?
How long have you known her? Tu la connais depuis combien de temps?

however ADVERB
cependant

hug NOUN
to give somebody a hug serrer [1] quelqu'un dans ses bras
She gave me a hug. Elle m'a serré dans ses bras.
They gave each other a hug. Ils se sont serrés dans ses bras.

huge ADJECTIVE
immense MASC & FEM

to **hum** VERB
fredonner [1]

human ADJECTIVE
humain MASC, **humaine** FEM
• **human being**
un être humain

humour NOUN
l'**humour** MASC
to have a sense of humour avoir [5] le sens de l'humour

℘ **hundred** NUMBER
1 *(exactly 100)* **cent**
a hundred people cent personnes
two hundred deux cents
two hundred and ten deux cent dix

WORD TIP cent does not take an -s when another number follows it.
---

2 *(around 100)* **about a hundred** une centaine
about a hundred people une centaine de personnes
hundreds of people des centaines de personnes

Hungary NOUN
la **Hongrie** FEM

WORD TIP Countries and regions in French take le, la or les.
---

hunger NOUN
la **faim** FEM

℘ **hungry** ADJECTIVE
to be hungry avoir [5] faim
I'm hungry. J'ai faim.

to **hunt** VERB
1 *(an animal)* chasser [1]
2 *(a person)* rechercher [1]

hunting NOUN
la **chasse** FEM
fox-hunting la chasse au renard

hurricane NOUN
un **ouragan** MASC

♪ **hurry** NOUN ▸ SEE **hurry** VERB
to be in a hurry être [6] pressé MASC, être
pressée FEM
He's always in a hurry. Il est toujours
pressé.
Dina was in a hurry. Dina était pressée.

♪ to **hurry** VERB ▸ SEE **hurry** NOUN
se dépêcher ⊙ [50]
I must hurry. Je dois me dépêcher.
He hurried home. Il s'est dépêché de
rentrer chez lui.
She hurried to catch the bus. Elle s'est
dépêchée d'attraper le bus.
Hurry up! Dépêche-toi!, Dépêchez-vous!
(formal or plural form)

♪ **hurt** ADJECTIVE ▸ SEE **hurt** VERB
blessé MASC, blessée FEM
Three people were hurt. Trois personnes
ont été blessées.

♪ to **hurt** VERB ▸ SEE **hurt** ADJECTIVE
1 *(to injure)* **to hurt somebody** faire [10]
mal à quelqu'un
You're hurting me! Tu me fais mal!
That hurts! Ça fait mal!
2 *(to give pain)* **My back hurts.** J'ai mal au dos.
3 **to hurt yourself** se faire ⊙ [10] mal
Did you hurt yourself? Est-ce que tu t'es
fait mal?

♪ **husband** NOUN
le **mari** MASC

hygienic ADJECTIVE
hygiénique MASC & FEM

hymn NOUN
le **cantique** MASC

♪ **hypermarket** NOUN
un **hypermarché** MASC

hyphen NOUN
le **trait d'union** MASC

to **hypnotize** VERB
hypnotiser [1]

Ii

♪ **I** PRONOUN
1 *(before the verb)* je, j'
I'm Scottish. Je suis écossais *(boy speaking)*,
Je suis écossaise *(girl speaking)*.
I have two sisters. J'ai deux sœurs.
I live in London. J'habite à Londres.
I'm learning French. J'apprends le français.
2 *(in other positions)* moi
my brother and I mon frère et moi
I'm the person who ... C'est moi qui ...
Tom and I left before you. Tom et moi
sommes partis avant vous.
Here I am at last! Me voici enfin!

WORD TIP je becomes j' before a, e, i, o, u or a
silent h.

♪ **ice** NOUN
1 *(frozen water)* la **glace** FEM
2 *(on the roads)* le **verglas** MASC
3 *(in a drink)* les **glaçons** MASC PL

iceberg NOUN
un **iceberg** MASC

ice cream NOUN
la **glace** FEM
a chocolate ice cream une glace au
chocolat

ice-cube NOUN
le **glaçon** MASC

ice hockey NOUN
le **hockey sur glace** MASC

ice rink NOUN
la **patinoire** FEM

ice-skating NOUN
to go ice-skating faire [10] du patin à glace
We went ice-skating on Saturday. Nous
avons fait du patin à glace samedi.

icing NOUN
le **glaçage** MASC

icon NOUN
une **icône** FEM

icy ADJECTIVE
1 *(road)* verglacé MASC, verglacée FEM
2 *(very cold)* glacial MASC, glaciale FEM
an icy wind un vent glacial

♪ **idea** NOUN
une **idée** FEM
What a good idea! Quelle bonne idée!
I have an idea. J'ai une idée.
I have no idea. Je n'en ai aucune idée.

⊙ means the verb takes être to form the perfect

ideal *ADJECTIVE*
idéal *MASC*, idéale *FEM*, idéaux *MASC PL*,
idéales *FEM PL*

identical *ADJECTIVE*
identique *MASC & FEM*
identical twins des vrais jumeaux

ᵖ **identification** *NOUN*
une **identification** *FEM*

to **identify** *VERB*
identifier [1]

ᵖ **identity card** *NOUN*
la **carte d'identité**

> **IDENTITY CARD**
>
> By law, all French people must carry an identity
> card, called une carte d'identité.

ᵖ **idiot** *NOUN*
un **idiot** *MASC*, une **idiote** *FEM*

idiotic *ADJECTIVE*
bête *MASC & FEM*

i.e. *ABBREVIATION*
c-à-d *(short for* c'est-à-dire*)*

ᵖ **if** *CONJUNCTION*
1 si, s'
If Sophie's there, he'll be happy. Si Sophie
est là, il sera content.
If it rains, we won't go. S'il pleut, nous
n'irons pas.
If I won the lottery, I would buy a flat.
Si je gagnais la loterie, j'achèterais un
appartement.
if not sinon
2 if only … si seulement …
**If only you'd told me, I would have helped
you.** Si seulement tu me l'avais dit, je
t'aurais aidé.
3 even if même si
We're going out, even if it snows. On sort,
même s'il neige.
4 if I were you … à ta place …
If I were you, I'd forget about it. À ta place
je n'y penserais plus.

WORD TIP si becomes s' before il and ils.
---

to **ignore** *VERB*
1 *(a person)* ignorer [1]
2 *(what somebody says)* ne pas écouter [1]
3 **Ignore it.** Ne fais pas attention.

ᵖ **ill** *ADJECTIVE*
malade *MASC & FEM*
I feel ill. Je ne me sens pas bien.
to be taken ill tomber ⊘ [1] malade
Her grandmother has been taken ill. Sa
grand-mère est tombée malade.

illegal *ADJECTIVE*
illégal *MASC*, illégale *FEM*, illégaux *MASC PL*,
illégales *FEM PL*

illness *NOUN*
la **maladie** *FEM*

illusion *NOUN*
une **illusion** *FEM*

illustrated *ADJECTIVE*
illustré *MASC*, illustrée *FEM*

illustration *NOUN*
une **illustration** *FEM*

ᵖ **image** *NOUN*
une **image** *FEM*

imagination *NOUN*
l'**imagination** *FEM*
to show imagination faire [10] preuve
d'imagination
Joe shows real imagination. Joe fait preuve
de beaucoup d'imagination.

to **imagine** *VERB*
imaginer [1]
Imagine that you're very rich. Imagine que
tu es très riche.
You can't imagine how hard it was! Tu
ne peux pas t'imaginer combien c'était
difficile!

to **imitate** *VERB*
imiter [1]

imitation *NOUN*
une **imitation** *FEM*

immediate *ADJECTIVE*
immédiat *MASC*, immédiate *FEM*

ᵖ **immediately** *ADVERB*
immédiatement
I rang them immediately. Je les ai appelés
immédiatement.
immediately before the party juste avant
la soirée

immigrant *NOUN*
un **immigré** *MASC*, une **immigrée** *FEM*

immigration *NOUN*
l'**immigration** *FEM*

impact *NOUN*
un **impact** *MASC*

impatience *NOUN*
l'**impatience** *FEM*

impatient *ADJECTIVE*
1 impatient *MASC*, impatiente *FEM*
2 **to get impatient with somebody**
s'impatienter [1] contre quelqu'un

impatiently ADVERB
avec impatience

imperfect NOUN
(Grammar) l'**imparfait** MASC
in the imperfect à l'imparfait

import NOUN ▸ SEE **import** VERB
le **produit importé**

to **import** VERB ▸ SEE **import** NOUN
importer [1]
wine imported from France du vin importé de France

importance NOUN
l'**importance** FEM

ℰ **important** ADJECTIVE
important MASC, importante FEM
It's not important. Ça n'a pas d'importance.

ℰ **impossible** ADJECTIVE
impossible MASC & FEM
It's impossible to find a telephone. Il est impossible de trouver un téléphone.

impressed ADJECTIVE
impressionné MASC, impressionnée FEM

impression NOUN
une **impression** FEM
to make a good impression on somebody faire [10] bonne impression sur quelqu'un
He made a good impression on me. Il a fait bonne impression sur moi.
I got the impression that ... J'avais l'impression que ...

impressive ADJECTIVE
impressionnant MASC, impressionnante FEM
an impressive performance une interprétation impressionante

to **improve** VERB
1 (a design, grades etc) améliorer [1]
I'm trying to improve my grades. J'essaye d'améliorer mes notes.
2 (to get better) s'améliorer [1]
The weather is improving. Le temps s'améliore.

improvement NOUN
1 (change for the better) une **amélioration** FEM
2 (gradual progress) les **progrès** MASC PL

ℰ **in** ADVERB, PREPOSITION
1 (in general) dans
in the kitchen dans la cuisine
in the newspaper dans le journal
in my class dans ma classe
I was in the bath. J'étais dans mon bain.
2 (in named towns, places) à

in Dover à Douvres
in town en ville
a house in the country une maison à la campagne
in the sun au soleil
3 (dressed in) à
the girl in the pink blouse la fille à la chemise rose
dressed in white habillé en blanc (boy), habillée en blanc (girl)
4 (in langues, countries) en
in French en français
in France en France
in Portugal au Portugal

> **WORD TIP** en is used for feminine countries, au for most masculine countries.

5 (in time expressions)
in May en mai
in 2006 en deux mil six
in winter en hiver
in summer en été
in autumn en automne
in spring au printemps
in the morning le matin
at eight in the morning à huit heures du matin
in the night pendant la nuit
I'll phone you in ten minutes. Je t'appellerai dans dix minutes.
She did it in five minutes. Elle l'a fait en cinq minutes.
6 (with biggest, greatest, etc) de
the tallest boy in the class le garçon le plus grand de la classe
the biggest city in the world la ville la plus grande du monde
7 (at home) **to be in** être [6] là
Mick's not in at the moment. Mick n'est pas là en ce moment.
8 (in expressions) **in the photo** sur la photo
in the rain sous la pluie
9 (with verbs) **to come in** entrer ⬭ [1]
to run in entrer ⬭ en courant
to go in entrer

incident NOUN
un **incident** MASC

ℰ to **include** VERB
comprendre [64]
service included service compris
Dinner is included in the price. Le dîner est compris dans le prix.

ℰ **including** PREPOSITION
(y) compris
including Sundays y compris les dimanches
£50 including VAT cinquante livres TVA comprise
not including Sundays sans compter les

⬭ means the verb takes être to form the perfect

dimanches
everyone, including children tout le
monde, y compris les enfants

income NOUN
le **revenu** MASC
- **income tax**
l'impôt sur le revenu MASC

inconvenient ADJECTIVE
1 *(place, arrangement)* **incommode** MASC & FEM
2 *(time)* **inopportun** MASC, **inopportune** FEM

increase NOUN ▸ SEE **increase** VERB
une **augmentation** FEM

ℐ to **increase** VERB ▸ SEE **increase** NOUN
augmenter [1]
The price has increased by £10. Le prix a
augmenté de dix livres.

incredible ADJECTIVE
incroyable MASC & FEM

incredibly ADVERB
extrêmement
The film's incredibly boring. Le film est
extrêmement ennuyeux.

indeed ADVERB
1 *(for emphasis)* **vraiment**
I'm very hungry indeed. J'ai vraiment très
faim.
Thank you very much indeed. Merci
beaucoup.
2 *(certainly)* **bien sûr**
'Can you hear his radio?' — 'Indeed I can!'
'Tu entends sa radio?' — 'Bien sûr que oui!'

indefinite article NOUN
(Grammar) l'**article indéfini** MASC

independence NOUN
l'**indépendance** FEM

independent ADJECTIVE
indépendant MASC, **indépendante** FEM

index NOUN
un **index** MASC
- **index finger**
l'**index** MASC

India NOUN
l'**Inde** FEM
in India en Inde

Indian ADJECTIVE ▸ SEE **Indian** NOUN
indien MASC, **indienne** FEM
Indian NOUN ▸ SEE **Indian** ADJECTIVE
un **Indien** MASC, une **Indienne** FEM

to **indicate** VERB
indiquer [1]

indigestion NOUN
une **indigestion** FEM

to have indigestion avoir [5] une
indigestion

indirect ADJECTIVE
indirect MASC, **indirecte** FEM

individual ADJECTIVE ▸ SEE **individual** NOUN
1 *(portion, contribution)* **individuel** MASC,
individuelle FEM
2 **individual tuition** des cours particuliers
individual NOUN ▸ SEE **individual** ADJECTIVE
un **individu** MASC

indoor ADJECTIVE
couvert MASC, **couverte** FEM
an indoor swimming pool une piscine
couverte

indoors ADVERB
à l'intérieur
It's cooler indoors. Il fait plus frais à
l'intérieur.
to go indoors rentrer ◉ [1]
Shall we go indoors? On rentre?

industrial ADJECTIVE
industriel MASC, **industrielle** FEM
- **industrial estate**
la zone industrielle

ℐ**industry** NOUN
une **industrie** FEM
the advertising industry l'industrie de la
publicité

inefficient ADJECTIVE
inefficace MASC & FEM

inevitable ADJECTIVE
inévitable MASC & FEM

inexperienced ADJECTIVE
inexpérimenté MASC, **inexpérimentée** FEM

infant school NOUN
une **école maternelle**

infected ADJECTIVE
1 *(wound)* **infecté** MASC, **infectée** FEM
2 *(person, blood)* **contaminé** MASC,
contaminée FEM

infection NOUN
une **infection** FEM
an eye infection une infection de l'œil
a throat infection une angine

infectious ADJECTIVE
contagieux MASC, **contagieuse** FEM

infinitive NOUN
(Grammar) l'**infinitif** MASC
in the infinitive à l'infinitif

inflammable ADJECTIVE
inflammable MASC & FEM

inflatable ADJECTIVE
pneumatique MASC & FEM

to **inflate** VERB
(a mattress, a boat) gonfler [1]

inflation NOUN
l'inflation FEM

influence NOUN ▸ SEE **influence** VERB
une influence FEM
to be a good influence on somebody avoir
[5] une bonne influence sur quelqu'un
My brother was a good influence on me.
Mon frère a eu une bonne influence sur
moi.

to **influence** VERB ▸ SEE **influence** NOUN
influencer [61]

to **inform** VERB
informer [1]
to inform somebody that ... informer
quelqu'un du fait que ...
They informed us that there was a
problem. Ils nous ont informés du fait qu'il
y avait un problème.
to inform somebody of something
informer quelqu'un de quelque chose
Please inform us of any change of
address. Prière de nous informer de tout
changement de domicile.

informal ADJECTIVE
1 (meal, event) simple MASC & FEM
2 (phrase, expression) familier MASC, familière
FEM

ℙ **information** NOUN
les renseignements MASC PL
a piece of information un renseignement
I need information on flights to Paris. J'ai
besoin de renseignements sur les vols vers
Paris.
• information desk
le bureau des renseignements
• information technology
l'informatique FEM

ingredient NOUN
un ingrédient MASC

inhabitant NOUN
un habitant MASC, une habitante FEM

inhaler NOUN
un inhalateur MASC

initials PLURAL NOUN
les initiales FEM PL
Write your initials here. Mettez vos
initiales ici.

initiative NOUN
une initiative FEM

injection NOUN
la piqûre FEM
The doctor gave me an injection. Le
médecin m'a fait une piqûre.

ℙ to **injure** VERB
blesser [1]
No one was injured. Il n'y avait pas de
blessés.

injured ADJECTIVE
blessé MASC, blessée FEM

injury NOUN
la blessure FEM

ink NOUN
l'encre FEM

in-laws NOUN
les beaux-parents MASC PL

inner ADJECTIVE
intérieur MASC, intérieure FEM

innocent ADJECTIVE
innocent MASC, innocente FEM

inscription NOUN
une inscription FEM

ℙ **insect** NOUN
un insecte MASC
an insect bite une piqûre d'insecte
• insect repellent
un insectifuge

to **insert** VERB
insérer [24]

ℙ **inside** ADVERB ▸ SEE **inside** NOUN, PREPOSITION
à l'intérieur
She's inside, I think. Elle est à l'intérieur,
je crois.
to go inside entrer ◎ [1]
He went inside. Il est entré.

ℙ **inside** PREPOSITION ▸ SEE **inside** ADVERB, NOUN
à l'intérieur de
inside the cinema à l'intérieur du cinéma
inside the house à l'intérieur de la maison

inside NOUN ▸ SEE **inside** ADVERB, PREPOSITION
l'intérieur MASC
the inside of the box l'intérieur de la boîte

inside out ADVERB
à l'envers
Your sweater's inside out. Tu as mis ton
pull à l'envers.

insincere ADJECTIVE
peu sincère MASC & FEM

to **insist** VERB
1 (to demand) insister [1]
if you insist puisque tu insistes
to insist on doing something insister pour

faire quelque chose
He insisted on paying. Il a insisté pour payer.
2 to insist that affirmer [1] que
Rob insisted I was wrong. Rob a affirmé que j'avais tort.

inspector *NOUN*
un **inspecteur** *MASC*, une **inspectrice** *FEM*

to **install** *VERB*
installer [1]

instalment *NOUN*
1 *(of a story, serial)* un **épisode** *MASC*
2 *(payment)* le **versement** *MASC*

instance *NOUN*
for instance par exemple

instant *ADJECTIVE* ▸ SEE **instant** *NOUN*
1 *(coffee, soup)* instantané *MASC*, instantanée *FEM*
2 *(milk)* en poudre
3 *(effect, success)* immédiat *MASC*, immédiate *FEM*

instant *NOUN* ▸ SEE **instant** *ADJECTIVE*
un **instant** *MASC*
in an instant dans un instant
Come here this instant! Viens ici tout de suite!

instantly *ADVERB*
immédiatement

ℰ **instead** *ADVERB*
1 **I couldn't go, so Lisa went instead.** Je ne pouvais pas y aller, donc Lisa est allée à ma place.
2 **instead of** au lieu de
Instead of pudding I had cheese. J'ai pris le fromage au lieu du dessert.
Instead of playing tennis we went swimming. Au lieu de jouer au tennis nous sommes allés à la piscine.

instinct *NOUN*
l'**instinct** *MASC*

institute *NOUN*
un **institut** *MASC*

institution *NOUN*
une **institution** *FEM*

to **instruct** *VERB*
to instruct somebody to do something donner [1] l'ordre à quelqu'un de faire quelque chose
The teacher instructed us to stay together. Le professeur nous a donné l'ordre de rester en groupe.

ℰ **instructions** *PLURAL NOUN*
les **instructions** *FEM PL*

'**Instructions for use.**' 'Mode d'emploi.'
Follow the instructions on the packet. Suivez les instructions sur l'emballage.

instructor *NOUN*
le **moniteur** *MASC*, la **monitrice** *FEM*
my skiing instructor mon moniteur de ski

ℰ **instrument** *NOUN*
un **instrument** *MASC*
to play an instrument jouer [1] d'un instrument

insult *NOUN* ▸ SEE **insult** *VERB*
une **insulte** *FEM*

to **insult** *VERB* ▸ SEE **insult** *NOUN*
insulter [1]

insurance *NOUN*
l'**assurance** *FEM*
travel insurance l'assurance voyage
Do you have medical insurance? Est-ce que vous avez une assurance maladie?

intelligence *NOUN*
l'**intelligence** *FEM*

ℰ **intelligent** *ADJECTIVE*
intelligent *MASC*, intelligente *FEM*

to **intend** *VERB*
1 vouloir [14]
as I intended comme je le voulais
2 **to intend to do something** avoir [5] l'intention de faire quelque chose
We intend to spend the night in Rome. Nous avons l'intention de passer la nuit à Rome.

intensive *ADJECTIVE*
intensif *MASC*, intensive *FEM*

intensive care *NOUN*
in intensive care en réanimation

intention *NOUN*
une **intention** *FEM*
I have no intention of paying. Je n'ai aucune intention de payer.

interest *NOUN* ▸ SEE **interest** *VERB*
1 *(hobby)* le **centre d'intérêt**
What are your interests? Quels sont vos centres d'intérêt?
2 *(enthusiasm)* un **intérêt** *MASC*
to take an interest in something s'intéresser [1] à quelque chose
He has an interest in jazz. Il s'intéresse au jazz.
Katie has no interest in politics. Katie ne s'intéresse pas à la politique.
3 *(on a loan)* les **intérêts** *MASC PL*

ℰ to **interest** *VERB* ▸ SEE **interest** *NOUN*
intéresser [1]

ℰ indicates key words

That doesn't interest me. Ça ne
m'intéresse pas.

interested ADJECTIVE
   to be interested in something s'intéresser
   ⊚ [1] à quelque chose
   Sean's very interested in cars. Sean
   s'intéresse beaucoup aux voitures.

ℐ **interesting** ADJECTIVE
   intéressant MASC, intéressante FEM

to **interfere** VERB
   to interfere with something toucher [1]
   quelque chose
   to interfere in something se mêler ⊚ [1] de
   quelque chose
   He always interferes in everything. Il se
   mêle de tout.

ℐ **interior** ADJECTIVE
   intérieur MASC, intérieure FEM
   • **interior designer**
     un & une architecte d'intérieur

ℐ **international** ADJECTIVE
   international MASC, internationale FEM,
   internationaux MASC PL, internationales
   FEM PL

Internet NOUN
   l'Internet MASC
   to find something on the Internet trouver
   [1] quelque chose sur Internet
   Jack's on the Internet all the time. Jack est
   tout le temps sur Internet
   • **Internet café**
     le cybercafé
   • **Internet service provider**
     le fournisseur d'accès Internet

to **interpret** VERB
   1 (act as an interpreter) faire [10] l'interprète
   2 (a remark, an action) interpréter [1]

interpreter NOUN
   un & une interprète MASC & FEM

to **interrupt** VERB
   interrompre [69]

interruption NOUN
   une interruption FEM

interval NOUN
   (in a play, concert) un entracte MASC

ℐ **interview** NOUN ▸ SEE **interview** VERB
   1 (for a job) un entretien MASC
     a job interview un entretien
   2 (in a newspaper, on TV, radio) une interview
     FEM

ℐ to **interview** VERB ▸ SEE **interview** NOUN
   (on TV, radio, etc) interviewer [1]

interviewer NOUN
   (on TV, radio, etc) un intervieweur MASC,
   une intervieweuse FEM

ℐ **into** PREPOSITION
   1 (showing movement) dans
     He's gone into the bank. Il est entré dans
     la banque.
     Mum's gone into town. Maman est allée
     en ville.
     We got into the car. Nous sommes montés
     dans la voiture.
     Get into bed ! Va au lit!
   2 (showing change) en
     to translate into French traduire [26] en
     français
     to change pounds into euros changer [52]
     des livres sterling en euros
   3 **to be into something** être [6] fana de
     quelque chose
     Pete's really into Afro music. Pete est
     vraiment fana de musique africaine.

to **introduce** VERB
   présenter [1]
   She introduced me to her brother. Elle m'a
   présenté à son frère.
   Can I introduce you to my mother? Je te
   présente ma mère.

introduction NOUN
   1 (in a book) une introduction FEM
   2 (of a person) la présentation FEM

intuition NOUN
   l'intuition FEM

to **invade** VERB
   envahir [2]

invalid NOUN
   le & la malade MASC & FEM

invasion NOUN
   une invasion FEM

to **invent** VERB
   inventer [1]

invention NOUN
   une invention FEM

inventor NOUN
   un inventeur MASC, une inventrice FEM

inverted commas PLURAL NOUN
   (Grammar) les guillemets MASC PL
   in inverted commas entre guillemets

investigation NOUN
   une enquête FEM
   an investigation into the fire une enquête
   sur l'incendie

invisible ADJECTIVE
   invisible MASC & FEM

⊚ means the verb takes être to form the perfect

invitation *NOUN*
une **invitation** *FEM*
an invitation to dinner une invitation à
dîner

♪ to **invite** *VERB*
inviter [1]
Kirsty invited me to lunch. Kirsty m'a invité
à déjeuner *(boy speaking)*
He's invited me out on Tuesday. Il m'a
invitée à sortir avec lui mardi *(girl speaking)*.

invoice *NOUN*
la **facture** *FEM*

to **involve** *VERB*
1 *(to require)* nécessiter [1]
It involves a lot of work. Cela nécessite
beaucoup de travail.
2 *(to affect)* concerner [1]
Two cars were involved. Deux voitures
étaient concernées.
3 **to be involved in something** participer [1] à
quelque chose
I am involved in the new project. Je
participe au nouveau projet.

Iran *NOUN*
l'**Iran** *MASC*

Iraq *NOUN*
l'**Iraq** *MASC*

♪ **Ireland** *NOUN*
l'**Irlande** *FEM*
in Ireland en Irlande
We went to Ireland at Christmas. Nous
sommes allés en Irlande à Noël.
the Republic of Ireland la République
d'Irlande

WORD TIP Countries and regions in French take
le, la or les.

♪ **Irish** *NOUN* ▸ SEE **Irish** *ADJECTIVE*
1 *(the people)* **the Irish** les Irlandais *MASC PL*
2 *(the language)* l'**irlandais** *MASC*

WORD TIP Languages never have capitals in
French.

♪ **Irish** *ADJECTIVE* ▸ SEE **Irish** *NOUN*
irlandais *MASC*, irlandaise *FEM*

WORD TIP Adjectives never have capitals in
French, even for nationality or regional origin.

• **Irishman**
un Irlandais
• **Irish Sea**
la mer d'Irlande
• **Irishwoman**
une Irlandaise

iron *NOUN* ▸ SEE **iron** *VERB*
1 *(the metal)* le **fer** *MASC*

2 *(for clothes)* le **fer à repasser**
to **iron** *VERB* ▸ SEE **iron** *NOUN*
repasser [1]

ironing *NOUN*
le **repassage** *MASC*
to do the ironing faire [10] le repassage
• **ironing board**
la planche à repasser

ironmonger's *NOUN*
la **quincaillerie** *FEM*

irregular *ADJECTIVE*
irrégulier *MASC*, irrégulière *FEM*

irresponsible *ADJECTIVE*
irresponsable *MASC & FEM*

irritable *ADJECTIVE*
irritable *MASC & FEM*

to **irritate** *VERB*
irriter [1]

irritating *ADJECTIVE*
irritant *MASC*, irritante *FEM*

Islam *NOUN*
(Religion) l'**islam** *MASC*

WORD TIP Adjectives and nouns of religion start
with a small letter in French.

Islamic *ADJECTIVE*
islamique *MASC & FEM*

island *NOUN*
une **île** *FEM*

isolated *ADJECTIVE*
isolé *MASC*, isolée *FEM*

Israel *NOUN*
Israël *MASC*

WORD TIP Unlike other names of countries
Israël does not take l', la or les.

Israeli *ADJECTIVE* ▸ SEE **Israeli** *NOUN*
israélien *MASC*, israélienne *FEM*
Israeli *NOUN* ▸ SEE **Israeli** *ADJECTIVE*
un Israélien *MASC*, une Israélienne *FEM*

issue *NOUN* ▸ SEE **issue** *VERB*
1 *(discussion point)* la **question** *FEM*
a political issue une question politique
2 *(of a magazine)* le **numéro** *MASC*

♪ **it** *PRONOUN*
1 *(referring to masc singular nouns, as subject)*
il
'Where's my bag?' — **'It's in the kitchen.'**
'Où est mon sac?' — 'Il est dans la cuisine.'
2 *(referring to fem singular nouns, as subject)*
elle
'How old is your TV?' — **'It's five years**

♪ indicates key words

old.' 'Quel âge a ta télévision?' — 'Elle a cinq ans.'

3 *(referring to masc singular nouns, as object)* **le**

His new book? I know it. Son nouveau livre? Je le connais.

I like your coat. Can I borrow it? J'aime bien ton manteau. Je peux l'emprunter?

4 *(referring to fem singular nouns, as object)* **la**

His address? I know it. Son addresse? Je la connais.

Where's my key? I've lost it. Où est ma clé? Je l'ai perdue.

5 *(when the gender is not given)* Yes, it's true. Oui, c'est vrai.

It's a bit strange. C'est un peu bizarre.

It doesn't matter. Ça ne fait rien.

6 Who is it? Qui c'est?

It's me. C'est moi.

What is it? Qu'est-ce que c'est?

It's a ring. C'est une bague.

7 *(when talking about the weather and clock time)* **il**

It's raining. Il pleut.

It's a nice day. Il fait beau.

It's two o'clock. Il est deux heures.

8 *(after prepositions like* **to** *or* **of***)* Jake's having a party. I'm going to it. Jake fait une fête. J'y vais.

I'm going to think about it. Je vais y réfléchir.

I've had enough of it. J'en ai assez.

WORD TIP le and la become l' before a, e, i, o, u or silent h, when used as objects.

IT NOUN

(Computers) l'**informatique** FEM

Italian ADJECTIVE ▸ SEE **Italian** NOUN

1 **italien** MASC, **italienne** FEM

Italian food la cuisine italienne

2 *(teacher, lesson)* **d'italien** MASC & FEM

my Italian class mon cours d'italien

Italian NOUN ▸ SEE **Italian** ADJECTIVE

1 *(person)* un **Italien** MASC, une **Italienne** FEM

2 *(the language)* l'**italien** MASC

italics NOUN

l'**italique** MASC

in italics en italique

Italy NOUN

l'**Italie** FEM

in Italy en Italie

to Italy en Italie

to **itch** VERB

1 *(hands, arm, etc)* My back is itching. J'ai le dos qui me démange.

2 *(clothes, material)* This sweater itches. Ce pull me gratte.

item NOUN

un **article** MASC

its ADJECTIVE

1 *(for masc and fem nouns beginning with a, e, i, o, u or silent h)* **son**

The dog has lost its collar. Le chien a perdu son collier.

its ear son oreille *(oreille is feminine)*

2 *(for fem nouns)* **sa**

The dog's in its kennel. Le chien est dans sa niche.

3 *(for plural nouns)* **ses**

its toys ses jouets

Its eyes were shining. Ses yeux brillaient.

itself PRONOUN

1 **se, s'**

The cat is washing itself. Le chat se lave.

The animal injured itself. L'animal s'est blessé.

2 all by itself **tout seul**

He left the dog all by itself. Il a laissé le chien tout seul.

WORD TIP se becomes before a, e, i, o, u or silent h.

ivy NOUN

le **lierre** MASC

Jj

jack NOUN

1 *(in cards)* le **valet** MASC

2 *(for a car)* le **cric** MASC

jacket NOUN

la **veste** FEM

• jacket potato

la pomme de terre en robe des champs

jackpot NOUN

le **gros lot**

to win the jackpot gagner [1] le gros lot

jagged ADJECTIVE

dentelé MASC, **dentelée** FEM

jail NOUN ▸ SEE **jail** VERB

la **prison** FEM

to **jail** VERB ▸ SEE **jail** NOUN

emprisonner [1]

jam NOUN

1 *(for eating)* la **confiture** FEM

raspberry jam la confiture de framboises

2 *(in traffic)* un **embouteillage** MASC

Jamaica NOUN

la **Jamaïque** FEM

⬤ means the verb takes être to form the perfect

Jamaican *ADJECTIVE* ▸ SEE **Jamaican** *NOUN*
  jamaïquain *MASC*, jamaïquaine *FEM*

Jamaican *NOUN* ▸ SEE **Jamaican** *ADJECTIVE*
  un Jamaïquain *MASC*, une Jamaïquaine *FEM*

jammed *ADJECTIVE*
  coincé *MASC*, coincée *FEM*

ℐ **January** *NOUN*
  janvier *MASC*
  in January en janvier

> **WORD TIP** Months of the year and days of the
> week start with small letters in French.

Japan *NOUN*
  le Japon *MASC*
  in Japan au Japon

Japanese *ADJECTIVE* ▸ SEE **Japanese** *NOUN*
  japonais *MASC*, japonaise *FEM*
  a Japanese car une voiture japonaise

Japanese *NOUN* ▸ SEE **Japanese** *ADJECTIVE*
1 *(person)* un Japonais *MASC*, une Japonaise *FEM*
  the Japanese les Japonais
2 *(the language)* le japonais *MASC*
  I speak Japanese. Je parle japonais.

jar *NOUN*
1 *(small)* le **pot** *MASC*
  a jar of jam un pot de confiture
2 *(large)* le **bocal** *MASC* (*PL* les **bocaux**)

javelin *NOUN*
  le javelot *MASC*

jaw *NOUN*
  la mâchoire *FEM*

jazz *NOUN*
  le jazz *MASC*
• **jazz band**
  un orchestre de jazz

jealous *ADJECTIVE*
  jaloux *MASC*, jalouse *FEM*

jealousy *NOUN*
  la jalousie *FEM*

jeans *NOUN*
  le jean *MASC*
  a pair of jeans un jean

> **🔵 JEANS**
>
> Jeans (a singular word in French: **le jean**, or
> **le blue-jean**) are made of the strong cotton
> material that originally came from the French
> town of Nîmes — **de Nîmes** was shortened to
> 'denim'.

jelly *NOUN*
  la gelée *FEM*

jellyfish *NOUN*
  la méduse *FEM*

jersey *NOUN*
1 *(jumper)* le pull *MASC*
2 *(for sport)* le maillot *MASC*

Jersey *NOUN*
  Jersey *FEM*
  in the Channel Islands

> **WORD TIP** Unlike the names of most other
> islands, Jersey does not take le or la.

Jesus *NOUN*
  Jésus *MASC*
  Jesus Christ Jésus-Christ

jet *NOUN*
  le jet *MASC*
• **jet lag**
  le décalage horaire
• **jet-ski**
  le jet-ski

jetty *NOUN*
  la jetée *FEM*

Jew *NOUN*
  un juif *MASC*, une juive *FEM*

> **WORD TIP** Adjectives and nouns of religion start
> with a small letter in French.

jewel *NOUN*
  le bijou *MASC* (*PL* les **bijoux**)

jeweller *NOUN*
  le bijoutier *MASC*, la bijoutière *FEM*
• **jeweller's shop**
  la bijouterie

jewellery *NOUN*
  les bijoux *MASC PL*

Jewish *ADJECTIVE*
  juif *MASC*, juive *FEM*

> **WORD TIP** Adjectives and nouns of religion start
> with a small letter in French.

jigsaw *NOUN*
  le puzzle *MASC*

ℐ **job** *NOUN*
1 *(paid work)* un **emploi** *MASC*
  a job as a secretary un emploi comme
  secrétaire
  He's got a job at the supermarket. Il a un
  emploi au supermarché.
  What's your job? Qu'est-ce que vous faites
  comme travail?
  to be out of a job être [6] sans emploi
  I'm out of a job right now. En ce moment je
  suis sans emploi.
  a job application une demande d'emploi
  a job offer une offre d'emploi
2 *(a task)* le **travail** *MASC*
  It's not an easy job. Ce n'est pas un travail

A
B
C
D
E
F
G
H
I
J
K
L
M
N
O
P
Q
R
S
T
U
V
W
X
Y
Z

A
B
C
D
E
F
G
H
I
J
K
L
M
N
O
P
Q
R
S
T
U
V
W
X
Y
Z

facile.
She made a good job of it. Elle a fait un bon travail.

jobless ADJECTIVE
sans emploi

jockey NOUN
le **jockey** MASC

to **jog** VERB
to go jogging faire [10] du jogging
She goes jogging every day. Elle fait du jogging tous les jours.

to **join** VERB
1 (parts, ends) joindre [49]
2 (to become a member of) s'inscrire [38] à
I've joined the judo club. Je me suis inscrit au club de judo.
3 (to meet up with) rejoindre [49]
I'll join you later. Je te rejoins tout à l'heure.
• **to join in**
participer [1]
Ruth never joins in. Ruth ne participe jamais.
• **to join in something**
participer [1] à quelque chose
Won't you join in the game? Veux-tu participer au jeu?

joiner NOUN
le **menuisier** MASC, la **menuisière** FEM

joint ADJECTIVE ▶ SEE **joint** NOUN
the joint winners les lauréats ex aequo

joint NOUN ▶ SEE **joint** ADJECTIVE
1 (of meat) le **rôti** MASC
2 (in your body) une **articulation** FEM

joke NOUN ▶ SEE **joke** VERB
(a funny story) la **plaisanterie** FEM
to tell a joke raconter une plaisanterie

to **joke** VERB ▶ SEE **joke** NOUN
plaisanter [1]
You're joking! Tu plaisantes!

joker NOUN
1 (in cards) le **joker** MASC
2 (in class) le **farceur** MASC, la **farceuse** FEM

Jordan NOUN
la **Jordanie** FEM

journalism NOUN
le **journalisme** MASC

ℓ**journalist** NOUN
le & la **journaliste** MASC & FEM
Sean's dad is a journalist. Le père de Sean est journaliste.

ℓ**journey** NOUN
1 (long distance) le **voyage** MASC
our journey to Morocco notre voyage au

Maroc
2 (to work, school) le **trajet** MASC
a bus journey un trajet en bus
My journey to school takes half an hour. Le trajet à l'école dure trente minutes.

joy NOUN
la **joie** FEM

joy-riding NOUN
le **rodéo à la voiture volée**

joystick NOUN
(for computer games) la **manette de jeu**

Judaism NOUN
le **judaïsme** MASC

> **WORD TIP** Adjectives and nouns of religion start with a small letter in French.

judge NOUN ▶ SEE **judge** VERB
le **juge** MASC

to **judge** VERB ▶ SEE **judge**
1 (a time, a distance) estimer [1]
2 (a person) juger [52]

judgement NOUN
le **jugement** MASC

judo NOUN
le **judo** MASC
She does judo. Elle fait du judo.

jug NOUN
le **pot** MASC

to **juggle** VERB
jongler [1]

juggler NOUN
le **jongleur** MASC, la **jongleuse** FEM

ℓ**juice** NOUN
le **jus** MASC
Two orange juices, please. Deux jus d'orange, s'il vous plaît.

juicy ADJECTIVE
juteux MASC, **juteuse** FEM

jukebox NOUN
le **jukebox** MASC

ℓ**July** NOUN
juillet MASC
in July en juillet

> **WORD TIP** Months of the year and days of the week start with small letters in French.

jumble sale NOUN
la **vente de charité**

jumbo jet NOUN
le **gros-porteur** MASC

jump NOUN ▶ SEE **jump** VERB
le **saut** MASC

⊘ means the verb takes être to form the perfect

a parachute jump un saut en parachute

ℱ to **jump** VERB ▸ SEE **jump** NOUN
sauter [1]

ℱ **jumper** NOUN
le **pull** MASC

junction NOUN
1 *(of roads)* le **carrefour** MASC
2 *(of motorways)* un **échangeur** MASC
3 *(on a railway)* le **nœud ferroviaire**

ℱ **June** NOUN
juin MASC
in June en juin

> **WORD TIP** Months of the year and days of the week start with small letters in French.

jungle NOUN
la **jungle** FEM

ℱ **junior** ADJECTIVE ▸ SEE **junior** NOUN
primaire MASC & FEM
a junior school une école primaire

ℱ **junior** NOUN ▸ SEE **junior** ADJECTIVE
un & une **élève du primaire**
the juniors les élèves du primaire

junk NOUN
(useless things) le **bric-à-brac** MASC
• **junk food**
la nourriture industrielle
• **junk shop**
la brocante

jury NOUN
le **jury** MASC

just ADVERB
1 *(immediately, simply)* **juste**
just before midday juste avant midi
just after the church juste après l'église
just for fun juste pour rire
2 **to have just done something** venir ◎ [81]
juste de faire quelque chose
Tom has just arrived. Tom vient juste
d'arriver.
Helen had just called. Helen venait juste
d'appeler.
3 *(right now)* **I'm just finishing my
homework.** Je suis en train de finir mes
devoirs.
I'm just coming! J'arrive!
4 *(only)* ne ... que
It's just for you. Ce n'est que pour toi.
There's just me and Justine. Il n'y a que
Justine et moi.
Just a moment, please. Un moment, s'il
vous plait.
5 *(exactly)* **exactement**
It's just what I need. C'est exactement ce
que je veux.

justice NOUN
la **justice** FEM

to **justify** VERB
justifier [1]

Kk

kangaroo NOUN
le **kangourou** MASC

karaoke NOUN
le **karaoké** MASC

karate NOUN
le **karaté** MASC
• **karate chop** NOUN
le coup de karaté

kebab NOUN
la **brochette** FEM

keen ADJECTIVE
1 **passionnée** FEM, **passionné** MASC
She's a keen photographer. C'est une
photographe passionnée.
I'm keen to see it. J'ai envie de le voir.
You don't look very keen. Tu n'as pas l'air
très enthousiaste.
2 **to be keen on something** aimer bien
quelque chose
I'm keen on tennis. J'aime bien le tennis.
3 **to be keen on doing something** avoir [5]
très envie de faire quelque chose
I'm not keen on camping. Je n'ai pas très
envie de faire du camping.
4 **to be keen on someone** être [6] très attiré
par quelqu'une *(boy by a girl)*, être très
attirée par quelqu'un *(girl by a boy)*
He is keen on her. Il est très attiré par elle.
She is keen on him. Elle est très attirée
par lui.

ℱ to **keep** VERB
1 *(a letter, a seat)* garder [1]
I kept the letter. J'ai gardé la lettre.
Will you keep my seat? Tu peux garder ma
place?
They kept her in hospital. Ils l'ont gardée
à l'hôpital.
2 *(a promise, a secret)* **to keep a promise** tenir
[77] sa promesse
He kept his promise. Il a tenu sa promesse.
to keep a secret garder un secret
He kept it to himself. Il l'a gardé pour soi.
3 *(to stay)* rester ◎ [1]
Keep calm! Restez calme!
4 *(to store)* ranger
I keep my bike in the garage. Je range mon
vélo dans le garage.

- **to keep on**
  continuer [1]
  Keep straight on. Continuez tout droit.
  She kept on talking. Elle a continué à
  parler.
  He keeps on ringing me up. Il n'arrête pas
  de m'appeler.
- **to keep out**
  Keep out! Ne pas entrer!
- **to keep up**
1 *(to be as good as the rest)* suivre [75]
  He can't keep up in chemistry. Il ne suit pas
  bien en chimie.
2 *(to continue)* continuer [1]
  Keep up the good work! Continuez comme
  ça!

keep fit NOUN
  la **gymnastique d'entretien** FEM

kennel NOUN
1 *(for one dog)* la **niche** FEM
2 **kennels** *(for boarding)* le **chenil** MASC

kerb NOUN
  le **bord du trottoir** MASC

ketchup NOUN
  le **ketchup** MASC

kettle NOUN
  la **bouilloire** FEM
  to put the kettle on mettre [11] l'eau à
  chauffer
  The kettle's boiling. L'eau bout.

key NOUN
1 *(for a lock)* la **clé** FEM
  a bunch of keys un trousseau de clés
2 *(on a piano, a computer)* la **touche** FEM
3 *(in music)* le **ton** MASC
  What key is it in? Dans quel ton est-il?
  It is in the key of C minor. Il est en Do
  mineur.

keyboard NOUN
  (of a piano, a computer) le **clavier** MASC
  the numeric keyboard le clavier numérique
  ... and on the keyboards, Jean-Baptiste ...
  et au clavier, Jean-Baptiste

keyhole NOUN
  le **trou de serrure** MASC

keyring NOUN
  le **porte-clés** MASC

ℱ **kick** NOUN ▸ SEE **kick** VERB
1 *(from a person, a horse)* le **coup de pied**
  MASC
  to give somebody a kick donner [1] un
  coup de pied à quelqu'un
  He gave him a good kick. Il lui a donné un
  bon coup de pied.

2 *(in football)* le **tir** MASC
  a free kick un coup franc
  Mata took a kick at goal. Mata a tiré vers
  le but.
3 **to get a kick out of something** prendre [64]
  plaisir à faire quelque chose
  She gets a kick out of it. Elle prend plaisir
  à faire ça.

to kick VERB ▸ SEE **kick** NOUN
  donner [1] un coup de pied
  She kicked him. Elle lui a donné un coup de
  pied.
  to kick the ball donner un coup de pied
  dans le ballon
  Jean-Luc kicked the ball over the goalpost.
  Jean-Luc a envoyé le ballon par-dessus le
  poteau de but d'un coup de pied.

kick-off NOUN
  le **coup d'envoi** MASC
  What time's the kick-off? À quelle heure
  on décolle?

kid NOUN ▸ SEE **kid** VERB
1 *(child)* le & la **gosse** MASC & FEM *(informal)*
  Dad's looking after the kids. Papa s'occupe
  des gosses.
2 *(young goat)* le **chevreau** MASC, la **chevrette**
  FEM

kid VERB ▸ SEE **kid** VERB
  rigoler [1]
  I'm only kidding! Je rigole!
  You've got to be kidding! Tu veux rire!

to kidnap VERB
  enlever [50]
  He was kidnapped. Il a été enlevé.

kidnapper NOUN
  le **kidnappeur** MASC, la **kidnappeuse** FEM

kidney NOUN
1 *(part of the body)* le **rein** MASC
2 *(food)* le **rognon** MASC

to kill VERB
1 *(to cause death to)* tuer [1]
  He killed the wasp. Il a tué la guêpe.
  She was killed in an accident. Elle a été
  tuée dans un accident.
  My feet are killing me. J'ai mal aux pieds.
2 **to kill oneself** se suicider ◉ [1]
  He killed himself. Il s'est suicidé.

killer NOUN
  (murderer) le **meurtrier** MASC, la **meurtrière**
  FEM

ℱ **kilo** NOUN ▸ SEE **kilogramme**
  le **kilo** MASC
  a kilo of sugar un kilo de sucre
  five euros a kilo cinq euros le kilo

◉ means the verb takes être to form the perfect

_ƥ_ **kilogramme** NOUN ▸SEE **kilo**
    le **kilogramme** MASC

_ƥ_ **kilometre** NOUN
    le **kilomètre** MASC
    All road distances in France and Belgium are
    measured in kilometres.

_ƥ_ **kind** ADJECTIVE ▸SEE **kind** NOUN
    gentil MASC, **gentille** FEM
    Marion was very kind to me. Marion a été
    très gentille avec moi.
    That's very kind of you. C'est très gentil de
    votre part.

kind NOUN ▸SEE **kind** ADJECTIVE
    la **sorte** FEM
    all kinds of people toutes sortes de gens
    He's kind of cute. Il est plutôt mignon.

kindness NOUN
    la **gentillesse** FEM

king NOUN
    le **roi** MASC
    King George le roi Georges
    the king of hearts le roi de cœur

> **WORD TIP** le is used with names of kings and a
> small letter is used for roi in French.

kingdom NOUN
    le **royaume** MASC
    the United Kingdom le Royaume-Uni
    the animal kingdom le règne animal

kiosk NOUN
1 _(for newspapers, snacks)_ le **kiosque** MASC
2 _(phonebox)_ la **cabine** FEM

kipper NOUN
    un **hareng fumé** MASC

kiss NOUN ▸SEE **kiss** VERB
    le **baiser** MASC
    to give somebody a kiss embrasser
    quelqu'un
• **the kiss of life**
    le bouche-à-bouche

to **kiss** VERB ▸SEE **kiss** NOUN
    embrasser [1]
    Kiss me! Embrasse-moi!
    We kissed each other. Nous nous sommes
    embrassés.

kit NOUN
1 _(set of tools)_ la **trousse** FEM
    a tool kit une trousse à outils
2 _(clothes)_ les **affaires** FEM PL
    Where's my football kit? Où sont mes
    affaires de foot?
3 _(for making models, furniture)_ le **kit** MASC
    a hands-free kit un kit mains libres
    conducteur

_ƥ_ **kitchen** NOUN
    la **cuisine** FEM
    the kitchen table la table de la cuisine
• **kitchen foil**
    le papier d'aluminium
• **kitchen roll**
    l'essuie-tout MASC

kite NOUN
    (toy) le **cerf-volant** MASC
    to fly a kite faire [10] voler un cerf-volant

kitten NOUN
    le **chaton** MASC
    to have kittens avoir [5] des chatons

kiwi fruit NOUN
    le **kiwi** MASC

knack NOUN
    le **don** MASC
    I think I've got the knack of it. Je crois que
    j'en ai attrapé le tour de main.

knee NOUN
    le **genou** MASC _(PL_ les **genoux**_)_
    on hands and knees à quatre pattes

to **kneel** VERB
    se **mettre** ◉ [11] à genoux

knickers PLURAL NOUN
    la **petite culotte** FEM

knife NOUN
    le **couteau** MASC _(PL_ les **couteaux**_)_
    a bread knife un couteau à pain
    a sharp knife un couteau tranchant

knight NOUN
1 _(in chess)_ le **cavalier** MASC
2 _(in history)_ le **chevalier** MASC

to **knit** VERB
    tricoter [1]

knitting NOUN
    le **tricot** MASC

knob NOUN
    le **bouton** MASC

knock NOUN ▸SEE **knock** VERB
    le **coup** MASC
    a knock on the head un coup à la tête
    a knock at the door un coup à la porte
to **knock** VERB ▸SEE **knock** NOUN
1 _(to bang)_ cogner [1]
    I knocked my arm on the table. Je me suis
    cogné le bras contre la table.
2 _(on the door)_ frapper [1]
    I'll knock on the door around 7.30. Je
    frapperai à ta porte vers 7 h 30.
• **to knock down**
1 _(a pedestrian, child)_ renverser [1]
    She was knocked down by a car. Elle a été

renversée par une voiture.
2 *(an old building)* démolir [2]
• to knock out
1 *(in boxing)* assommer [1]
2 *(in competitions)* éliminer [1]
They were knocked out in the first round.
Ils ont été éliminé au premier tour.

knocker *NOUN*
un **heurtoir** *MASC*

knot *NOUN*
le **nœud** *MASC*
to tie a knot in something nouer [1]
quelque chose

♪ to **know** *VERB*
1 *(a fact, something)* savoir [70]
Do you know where Tim is? Tu sais où est
Tim?
I don't know. Je ne sais pas.
I know they've moved house. Je sais qu'ils
ont déménagé.
Yes, I know. Oui, je sais.
You never know! On ne sait jamais!
Who knows? Va savoir!
to know how to do something savoir [70]
faire quelque chose
Steve knows how to make couscous. Steve
sait faire du couscous.
Liz knows how to mend it. Liz sait le
réparer.
2 *(a person, a place, a book, some music)*
connaître [27]
Do you know the Jacksons? Est-ce que tu
connais les Jackson?
all the people I know tous les gens que je
connais
Yes, I know Paris. Oui, je connais Paris.
I know him. Je le connais.
I don't know his mother. Je ne connais pas
sa mère.
• to know about
1 *(a situation, a person)* être [6] au courant de
quelque chose
She knows about the situation. Elle est au
courant de la situation.
Do you know about Mark? Est-que vous
êtes au courant pour Mark?
2 *(how things work)* s'y connaître ◎ [27] en
quelque chose
She knows about computers Elle s'y
connaît en informatique.

knowledge *NOUN*
la **connaissance** *FEM*
It's common knowledge. C'est de notoriété
publique.

knuckle *NOUN*
l'**articulation des doigts** *FEM*

Koran *NOUN*
(Religion) le **Coran** *MASC*
a verse of the Koran un verset du Coran
to follow the teachings of the Koran suivre
le Coran

kosher *ADJECTIVE*
casher *MASC & FEM*
a kosher restaurant un restaurant casher

Ll

lab *NOUN*
le **labo** *MASC (informal)*

label *NOUN*
une **étiquette** *FEM*

laboratory *NOUN*
le **laboratoire** *MASC*

Labour *NOUN*
les **travaillistes** *MASC PL*
the Labour Party le parti travailliste

lace *NOUN*
1 *(for a shoe)* le **lacet** *MASC*
2 *(material)* la **dentelle** *FEM*

lad *NOUN*
le **gars** *INVARIABLE MASC*

ladder *NOUN*
une **échelle** *FEM*

ladies *NOUN*
1 *(lavatory)* les **toilettes** *FEM PL*
2 *(on a sign)* '**Ladies**' 'Dames'

♪ **lady** *NOUN*
la **dame** *FEM*
ladies and gentlemen mesdames et
messieurs

lager *NOUN*
la **bière blonde**

laid-back *ADJECTIVE*
décontracté *MASC*, **décontractée** *FEM*

♪ **lake** *NOUN*
le **lac** *MASC*
Lake Geneva le lac Léman

♪ **lamb** *NOUN*
un **agneau** *MASC (PL les agneaux)*

♪ **lamp** *NOUN*
la **lampe** *FEM*
• lamp-post
le **réverbère**

♪ **land** *NOUN* ▶ SEE **land** *VERB*
1 *(from the sea)* la **terre** *FEM*
2 *(property)* le **terrain** *MASC*

◎ means the verb takes être to form the perfect

a piece of land un terrain
They've bought some land there. Ils ont acheté du terrain là-bas.

to **land** VERB ▸ SEE **land** NOUN
1 *(planes, passengers)* **atterrir** [2]
2 *(from a ship)* **débarquer** [1]

landing NOUN
1 *(on the stairs)* le **palier** MASC
2 *(of a plane)* un **atterrissage** MASC
3 *(from a boat)* le **débarquement** MASC

landlady NOUN
la **propriétaire** FEM

landlord NOUN
le **propriétaire** MASC

landmark NOUN
le **point de repère**

landscape NOUN
le **paysage** MASC

lane NOUN
1 *(country road)* le **chemin** MASC
2 *(of a motorway)* la **voie** FEM

ℓ **language** NOUN
1 *(French, Italian, etc)* la **langue** FEM
a foreign language une langue étrangère
She speaks three languages. Elle parle trois langues.
2 *(way of speaking)* le **langage** MASC
bad language le langage grossier
• **language lab**
le laboratoire de langues
• **language school**
une école de langue

lap NOUN
1 *(your knees)* les **genoux** MASC PL
The cat was on my lap. Le chat était sur mes genoux.
2 *(in races)* le **tour de piste**
They're on the last lap. Ils font le dernier tour.
• **laptop**
le portable

ℓ **large** ADJECTIVE
1 *(in general)* **grand** MASC, **grande** FEM
a large number un grand nombre
a large crowd une grande foule
Do you have a larger size? Vous avez la taille au-dessus?
2 *(piece, part, animal)* **gros** MASC, **grosse** FEM
a large piece of cake un gros morceau de gâteau
a large amount of money une grosse somme d'argent
a large family une famille nombreuse

laser NOUN
le **laser** MASC
• **laser beam**
le rayon laser
• **laser printer**
une imprimante à laser
• **laser surgery**
la chirurgie au laser

ℓ **last** ADJECTIVE ▸ SEE **last** ADVERB, VERB
1 *(after the noun)* **dernier** MASC, **dernière** FEM
last week la semaine dernière
last month le mois dernier
2 *(before the noun)* **dernier** MASC, **dernière** FEM
the last time I played tennis la dernière fois que j'ai joué au tennis

ℓ **last** ADVERB ▸ SEE **last** ADJECTIVE, VERB
1 *(in final position)* **en dernier**
Mark arrived last. Mark est arrivé en dernier.
At last! Enfin!
2 *(most recently)* **I last saw her in May.** La dernière fois que je l'ai vue c'était en mai.

ℓ to **last** VERB ▸ SEE **last** ADJECTIVE, ADVERB
durer [1]
How long does it last? Ça dure combien de temps?
It lasts two hours. Ça dure deux heures.

ℓ **late** ADJECTIVE, ADVERB
1 **en retard**
I was late. J'étais en retard.
They arrived late. Ils sont arrivés en retard.
We were late for the film. Nous étions en retard pour le film.
2 *(buses, trains)* **to be late** avoir [5] du retard
The train was an hour late. Le train a eu une heure de retard.
3 *(in the day)* **tard**
late last night tard hier soir
I got up late. Je me suis levé tard.
It's getting late. Il se fait tard.

lately ADVERB
ces derniers temps

ℓ **later** ADVERB
plus tard
I'll explain later. J'expliquerai plus tard.
See you later! À tout à l'heure!

latest ADJECTIVE ▸ SEE **latest** NOUN
dernier MASC, **dernière** FEM
the latest news les dernières nouvelles
her latest album son dernier album

latest NOUN ▸ SEE **latest** ADJECTIVE
at the latest au plus tard
the latest in audio equipment le dernier cri en matière d'équipement hi-fi

A B C D E F G H I J K L M N O P Q R S T U V W X Y Z

Latin NOUN
  (language) le latin MASC

laugh NOUN ▸ SEE **laugh** VERB
1 le **rire** MASC
2 **I did it for a laugh.** Je l'ai fait pour rigoler.

♂ to **laugh** VERB ▸ SEE **laugh** NOUN
1 **rire [68]**
    Everybody laughed. Tout le monde a ri.
2 **to laugh at somebody** se moquer ● [1] de
    quelqu'un
    They laughed at me. Ils se sont moqués
    de moi.
    Don't laugh! Ne te moque pas!

launch NOUN ▸ SEE **launch** VERB
1 (of a product, a rocket) le **lancement** MASC
2 (boat) la **vedette** FEM

to **launch** VERB ▸ SEE **launch** NOUN
1 (a product, a spacecraft) **lancer [61]**
2 (a ship) **mettre [11] à l'eau**

launderette NOUN
  la **laverie automatique**

laundry NOUN
1 (in a hotel) la **laverie** FEM
2 (shop) la **blanchisserie** FEM

lavatory NOUN
  les **toilettes** FEM PL

law NOUN
1 (rules) la **loi** FEM
    It's against the law. C'est interdit.
2 (subject of study) le **droit** MASC

♂ **lawn** NOUN
  la **pelouse** FEM
  to mow the lawn tondre [3] la pelouse
• **lawnmower**
  la **tondeuse**

lawyer NOUN
  un **avocat** MASC, une **avocate** FEM

♂ to **lay** VERB
1 **to lay the table** mettre [11] la table
    I usually lay the table. D'habitude c'est moi
    qui mets la table.
2 (rugs, newspaper) **étaler [1]**
    We laid newspaper on the floor. Nous
    avons étalé du papier journal par terre.
3 (your hand, bricks) **poser [1]**
• **lay-by**
  une **aire de stationnement**

layer NOUN
  la **couche** FEM

laziness NOUN
  la **paresse** FEM

♂ **lazy** ADJECTIVE
  paresseux MASC, **paresseuse** FEM

Don't be so lazy! Ne sois pas si paresseux!

lead NOUN ▸ SEE **lead** VERB
1 **to be in the lead** être [6] en tête
    Harry's in the lead. Harry est en tête.
2 (cable) le **fil** MASC
3 (for a dog) la **laisse** FEM
4 (metal) le **plomb** MASC

to **lead** VERB ▸ SEE **lead** NOUN
1 **to lead to a place** mener [50] à quelque
    chose
    The path leads to the sea. Le chemin mène
    à la mer.
2 **to lead to something** entraîner [1] quelque
    chose
    It could lead to difficulties. Ça pourrait
    entraîner des difficultés.
3 **to be leading** être [6] en tête
    Who's leading? Qui est en tête?

♂ **leader** NOUN
1 (of a political party, a gang) le **chef** MASC
2 (in a competition) le **premier** MASC, la
    première FEM

lead-free petrol NOUN
  l'**essence sans plomb** FEM

lead singer NOUN
  le **chanteur principal**, la **chanteuse
  principale**

leaf NOUN
  la **feuille** FEM

♂ **leaflet** NOUN
  le **dépliant** MASC

league NOUN
  le **championnat** MASC

leak NOUN ▸ SEE **leak** VERB
  la **fuite** FEM
  a gas leak une fuite de gaz

to **leak** VERB ▸ SEE **leak** NOUN
  (bottles, roof) **fuir [44]**
  The roof is leaking! Le toit fuit!

to **lean** VERB
1 **to lean on something** s'appuyer ● [41] sur
    quelque chose
    She was leaning on my arm. Elle s'appuyait
    sur mon bras.
2 **to lean something against something**
    appuyer [41] quelque chose contre quelque
    chose
    to lean the ladder against the tree
    Appuyer l'échelle contre l'arbre
3 (person) se **pencher** ● [1]
    to lean out of the window se pencher par
    la fenêtre

to **leap** VERB
  sauter [1]

● means the verb takes être to form the perfect

to leap over something franchir [2] quelque chose d'un bond

• leap year
une année bissextile

P to **learn** *VERB*
apprendre [64]
Sally's learning Russian. Sally apprend le russe.
We learned a lot. On a appris beaucoup de choses.
to learn how to do something apprendre [64] à faire quelque chose
I want to learn to drive. Je veux apprendre à conduire.

learner *NOUN*
un **apprenant** *MASC*, une **apprenante** *FEM*
Alex is a fast learner. Alex apprend vite.

• learner driver
un & une élève d'auto-école

P **least** *ADVERB, ADJECTIVE, PRONOUN*
1 *(followed by an adjective)* **the least** le moins, la moins, les moins
the least expensive hotel l'hôtel le moins cher
the least expensive car la voiture la moins chère
2 *(followed by a noun)* **the least** le moins de
I've got the least food. C'est moi qui ai le moins de nourriture.
3 *(after verb)* **(the) least** le moins
I like the blue shirt least. C'est la chemise bleue que j'aime le moins.
4 *(with numbers)* **at least** au moins
at least twenty people au moins vingt personnes
5 *(at any rate)* **at least** du moins
At least, I think she's a teacher. Du moins, je crois qu'elle est professeur.

P **leather** *NOUN*
le **cuir** *MASC*
a leather jacket un blouson en cuir

P to **leave** *VERB*
1 *(to go away)* **partir** ◎ [58]
They leave tomorrow. Ils vont partir demain.
He has already left. Il est déjà parti.
We left at six. Nous sommes partis à six heures.
2 *(a place)* **quitter** [1]
I left the office at five. J'ai quitté le bureau à cinq heures.
John left school at sixteen. John a quitté l'école à seize ans.
3 *(to go out of)* **sortir** ◎ [72] de
She left the cinema at ten. Elle est sortie du cinéma à dix heures.
4 *(to put, to put off)* **laisser** [1]

You can leave your coats in the hall. Vous pouvez laisser vos manteaux dans l'entrée.
I left it till the last minute. Je l'ai laissé jusqu'à la dernière minute.
5 *(to forget)* **oublier** [1]
He left his bag on the train. Il a oublié son sac dans le train.
to leave something behind laisser quelque chose
Don't leave your mobile behind. Ne laisse pas ton portable.
6 **to be left** rester ◎ [1]
There are two pancakes left. Il reste deux crêpes.
We have ten minutes left. Il nous reste dix minutes.

• to leave something out
omettre [11] quelque chose
You left out that information. Tu as omis cette information.

lecture *NOUN*
1 *(for the public)* la **conférence** *FEM*
2 *(at university)* le **cours magistral** *(PL* les **cours magistraux)**

lecturer *NOUN*
le **professeur d'université**, la **professeure d'université**

leek *NOUN*
le **poireau** *MASC (PL* les **poireaux)**

P **left** *ADJECTIVE* ▶ SEE **left** *NOUN*
gauche *MASC & FEM*
his left foot son pied gauche

P **left** *NOUN* ▶ SEE **left** *ADJECTIVE*
la **gauche** *FEM*
on my left à ma gauche
to drive on the left conduire [26] à gauche
Turn left at the church. Tournez à gauche à l'église.

to **left-click** *VERB*
to left-click on the icon cliquer [1] sur l'icône en appuyant sur le bouton gauche de la souris

left-hand *ADJECTIVE*
the left-hand side la gauche

left-handed *ADJECTIVE*
gaucher *MASC*, **gauchère** *FEM*

left luggage office *NOUN*
la **consigne** *FEM*

leftovers *PLURAL NOUN*
les **restes** *MASC PL*

P **leg** *NOUN*
1 *(of a person, horse)* la **jambe** *FEM*
my left leg ma jambe gauche
My leg hurts. J'ai mal à la jambe.

to break your leg se casser ⊝ [1] la jambe
2 *(of other animals)* la **patte** *FEM*
3 *(of a table, chair)* le **pied** *MASC*
4 *(in cooking)* **a leg of chicken** une cuisse de poulet
a leg of lamb un gigot

legal *ADJECTIVE*
légal *MASC*, **légale** *FEM*, **légaux** *MASC PL*, **légales** *FEM PL*

legend *NOUN*
la **légende** *FEM*

leggings *PLURAL NOUN*
le **caleçon** *MASC*

legible *ADJECTIVE*
lisible *MASC & FEM*

♪**leisure** *NOUN*
les **loisirs** *MASC PL*
in my leisure time pendant mes loisirs

♪**leisure activities** *PLURAL NOUN*
les **loisirs** *MASC PL*
What sort of leisure activities are there? Qu'est-ce qu'il y a comme loisirs?

leisure centre *NOUN*
le **centre de loisirs**

♪**lemon** *NOUN*
le **citron** *MASC*
a lemon yoghurt un yaourt au citron

♪**lemonade** *NOUN*
la **limonade** *FEM*
a can of lemonade une boîte de limonade

lemon juice *NOUN*
le **jus de citron**

♪**to lend** *VERB*
to lend something to somebody prêter [1] quelque chose à quelqu'un
I lent my bike to Janet. J'ai prêté mon vélo à Janet.
I'm lending Dan some money. Je prête de l'argent à Dan.
Will you lend it to me? Veux-tu me le prêter?

length *NOUN*
la **longueur** *FEM*
What length is the garden? Quelle est la longueur du jardin?
It's 20 metres in length. Il est long de 20 mètres.

♪**lens** *NOUN*
1 *(in a camera)* un **objectif** *MASC*
2 *(in spectacles)* le **verre** *MASC*
3 *(contact lenses)* **to wear lenses** porter des lentilles de contact

Lent *NOUN*
le **Carême** *MASC*

lentil *NOUN*
la **lentille** *FEM*

Leo *NOUN*
le **Lion** *MASC*
I'm a Leo. Je suis Lion.

WORD TIP Signs of the zodiac do not take an article: un or une.

leotard *NOUN*
le **justaucorps** *INVARIABLE MASC*

lesbian *NOUN*
la **lesbienne** *FEM*

♪**less** *ADJECTIVE, ADVERB, PRONOUN*
1 *(before a noun)* **moins de**
less traffic moins de circulation
less energy moins d'énergie
I have less time now. J'ai moins de temps maintenant.
2 *(before adjectives, adverbs)* **moins**
less interesting moins intéressant
less quickly than us moins vite que nous
3 *(after a verb)* **moins**
Richard eats less. Richard mange moins.
She travels less. Elle voyage moins.
4 *(in amounts)* **less than** moins de
less than three hours moins de trois heures
less than a kilo moins d'un kilo
5 *(in comparisons)* **less than** moins que
You spend less than me. Tu dépenses moins que moi.

♪**lesson** *NOUN*
1 *(class)* le **cours** *MASC*
the history lesson le cours d'histoire
2 *(in a series)* la **leçon** *FEM*
a driving lesson une leçon de conduite
3 **That taught them a lesson!** Ça leur a servi de leçon!

♪**to let** *VERB*
1 **to let somebody do something** laisser [1] quelqu'un faire quelque chose
She lets me borrow her bike. Elle me laisse lui emprunter son vélo.
Will you let me go alone? Tu me laisses y aller toute seule?
Let me help you. Laisse-moi t'aider.
Let me see it. Fais voir.
2 *(as a suggestion)* **Let's go!** Allons-y!
Let's not talk about it. N'en parlons pas.
Let's eat out. Si on allait manger au restaurant?
3 **to let go of somebody** lâcher [1] quelqu'un
Let go of me! Lâche-moi!
4 *(a house, a flat)* louer [1]
'Flat to let.' 'Appartement à louer.'

⊝ **means the verb takes être to form the perfect**

- **to let somebody in**
  faire [10] entrer quelqu'un
- **to let something off**
1 *(fireworks)* tirer [1] quelque chose
2 *(a bomb)* faire [10] exploser quelque chose
- **to let somebody off something**
  dispenser [1] quelqu'un de quelque chose
  He let me off my homework. Il m'a
  dispensé de mes devoirs.
- **to let somebody out**
  laisser [1] sortir quelqu'un
  She won't let us out. Elle ne va pas nous
  laisser sortir.

lethal ADJECTIVE
  mortel MASC, **mortelle** FEM

⅃ **letter** NOUN
1 *(sent by post)* la **lettre** FEM
  I wrote her a letter. Je lui ai écrit une lettre.
2 *(in the alphabet)* la **lettre** FEM
  a word with five letters un mot de cinq
  lettres
- **letterbox**
  la boîte à lettres

lettuce NOUN
  la **salade** FEM
  two lettuces deux salades

leukaemia NOUN
  la **leucémie** FEM

level ADJECTIVE ▶ SEE **level** NOUN
1 *(shelf, floor)* **droit** MASC, **droite** FEM
2 *(ground)* **plat** MASC, **plate** FEM
level NOUN ▶ SEE **level** ADJECTIVE
  le **niveau** MASC *(PL les niveaux)*
  at street level au niveau de la rue
- **level crossing**
  le passage à niveau

lever NOUN
  le **levier** MASC

liar NOUN
  le **menteur** MASC, la **menteuse** FEM

liberal ADJECTIVE
  libéral MASC, **libérale** FEM, **libéraux** MASC PL,
  libérales FEM PL

Liberal Democrats PLURAL NOUN
  le **parti libéral-démocrate**

liberty NOUN
  la **liberté** FEM

Libra NOUN
  la **Balance** FEM
  Sean's a Libra. Sean est Balance.

  WORD TIP Signs of the zodiac do not take an
  article: un or une.

librarian NOUN
  le & la **bibliothécaire** MASC & FEM

⅃ **library** NOUN
  la **bibliothèque** FEM

⅃ **licence** NOUN
1 *(for driving, fishing)* le **permis** MASC
2 *(for a TV)* la **redevance** FEM

to **lick** VERB
  lécher [24]
  to lick your fingers se lécher ◐ [24] les
  doigts

lid NOUN
  le **couvercle** MASC
  to take off the lid enlever [50] le couvercle

lie NOUN ▶ SEE **lie** VERB
  le **mensonge** MASC
  to tell lies mentir [53]

⅃ to **lie** VERB ▶ SEE **lie** NOUN
1 **to lie on something** être [6] allongé sur
  quelque chose
  Alice was lying on the sofa. Alice était
  allongée sur le canapé.
  My coat lay on the bed. Mon manteau était
  sur le lit.
2 *(not to tell the truth)* mentir [53]
  I know when she's lying. Je sais quand elle
  ment.
  He lied to them. Il leur a menti.
- **to lie down**
1 *(to sleep)* se coucher ◐ [1]
2 *(to relax)* s'allonger ◐ [52]

lie-in NOUN
  to have a lie-in faire la grasse matinée

lieutenant NOUN
  le **lieutenant** MASC

⅃ **life** NOUN
  la **vie** FEM
  all her life toute sa vie
  That's life! C'est la vie!
  to save somebody's life sauver [1] la vie à
  quelqu'un
  You saved my life. Tu m'as sauvé la vie.
- **lifebelt**
  la bouée de sauvetage
- **lifeboat**
  le canot de sauvetage

lifeguard NOUN
  le **maître nageur**

life jacket NOUN
  le **gilet de sauvetage**

lifestyle NOUN
  le **style de vie**

⅃ indicates key words

P **lift** NOUN ▸ SEE **lift** VERB
1 (between floors) un **ascenseur** MASC
Let's take the lift. Prenons l'ascenseur.
2 (a ride) **to give somebody a lift home** déposer [1] quelqu'un chez soi
Tom gave me a lift home. Tom m'a déposé chez moi.
Could you give us a lift to the station? Tu pourrais nous déposer à la gare?

P to **lift** VERB ▸ SEE **lift** NOUN
soulever [50]
He lifted the box. Il a soulevé le carton.

P **light** ADJECTIVE ▸ SEE **light** NOUN, VERB
1 (not heavy) **léger** MASC, **légère** FEM
a light sweater un pull léger
a light meal un repas léger
a light breeze une brise légère
2 **to get light** faire [10] jour
It gets light at six. Il fait jour à six heures.
3 (in colour) **clair** MASC & FEM

P **light** NOUN ▸ SEE **light** ADJECTIVE, VERB
1 (electric) la **lumière** FEM
to turn on the light allumer [1] la lumière
to turn off the light éteindre [3] la lumière
2 (streetlight) le **réverbère** MASC
3 (headlight) le **phare** MASC
His lights aren't on. Il n'a pas allumé ses phares.
4 (indicator on a machine) le **voyant** MASC
5 (at cross-roads) les **feux** MASC PL
The lights were green. Le feu était au vert.
She didn't stop at the lights. Elle ne s'est pas arrêtée au feu.
6 (match) **Have you got a light?** Tu as du feu?
to **light** VERB ▸ SEE **light** ADJECTIVE, NOUN
1 (an oven, a cigarette) allumer [1]
to light a fire faire [10] un feu
2 (a match) craquer [1]
• **light bulb** une ampoule

lighter NOUN
le **briquet** MASC

lighthouse NOUN
le **phare** MASC

P **lightning** NOUN
les **éclairs** MASC PL
a flash of lightning un éclair
The tree was struck by lightning. L'arbre a été frappé par la foudre.

light switch NOUN
un **interrupteur** MASC

P **like** CONJUNCTION, PREPOSITION ▸ SEE **like** VERB
1 (in descriptions) **comme**
like me comme moi
like this comme ça

like a dog comme un chien
like I said comme j'ai dit
something like that quelque chose comme ça
You're just like my sister! Tu es exactement comme ma sœur!
2 **to look like somebody** ressembler [1] à quelqu'un
Katie looks like her father. Katie ressemble à son père.
3 (in questions) **What's it like?** C'est comment?
What's she like? Elle est comment?
What was the weather like? Quel temps faisait-il?

P to **like** VERB ▸ SEE **like** CONJUNCTION, PREPOSITION
1 (saying what you enjoy) **aimer** [1] **(bien)**
I like fish. J'aime bien le poisson.
I don't like snakes. Je n'aime pas les serpents.
Do you like the campsite? Il te plaît le camping?
I really like it. Ça me plaît beaucoup.
to like somebody aimer [1] bien quelqu'un
I like Peter . J'aime bien Peter.
2 **to like doing something,** aimer [1] (bien) faire quelque chose
Mum likes travelling. Maman aime bien voyager.
I like to write stories. J'aime bien écrire des histoires.
3 **to like something best** préférer [24] quelque chose
I like Spielberg films best. Je préfère les films de Spielberg.
4 (talking about what you want) **What would you like to eat?** Qu'est-ce que tu veux manger?
I'd like some soup. Je voudrais de la soupe.
Would you like a coffee? Est-ce que tu voudrais un café?
I'd like a hot chocolate. Je voudrais un chocolat chaud.

likely ADJECTIVE
probable MASC & FEM
It's not very likely. Ce n'est pas très probable.

lilac NOUN
le **lilas** MASC

lily NOUN
le **lys** MASC

lime NOUN
le **citron vert**

limit NOUN
la **limitation** FEM
the speed limit la limitation de vitesse

◯ means the verb takes être to form the perfect

ℓ**line** NOUN
1 *(on paper)* la **ligne** FEM
  a straight line une ligne droite
  to draw a line tirer [1] un trait
2 *(for telephones)* la **ligne** FEM
  Hold the line, please! Ne quittez pas!
3 *(electric cable)* la **ligne** FEM
  All the lines are down. Toutes les lignes ont été abattues.

ℓ**linen** NOUN
  le **lin** MASC

lining NOUN
  la **doublure** FEM

link NOUN ▶ SEE **link** VERB
1 *(connection)* le **rapport** MASC
  Is there a link between the two? Quel est le rapport entre les deux?
2 *(on a web page)* le **lien** MASC
  Click on the link. Cliquez sur le lien.

to **link** VERB ▶ SEE **link** NOUN
  (two places) **relier** [1]
  the motorway which links Cardiff to London l'autoroute qui relie Cardiff à Londres

lion NOUN
  le **lion** MASC

lip NOUN
  la **lèvre** FEM
• **lipstick**
  le **rouge à lèvres**

liquid ADJECTIVE, NOUN
  le **liquide** MASC

liquidizer NOUN
  le **mixer** MASC

list NOUN
  la **liste** FEM
  the shopping list la liste des courses
  to make a list faire [10] une liste

ℓ to **listen** VERB
  écouter [1]
  I wasn't listening. Je n'écoutais pas.
  to listen to something écouter [1] quelque chose
  Listen to me. Écoute-moi.
  Listen to the music. Écoutez la musique.
  You're not listening to me. Tu ne m'écoutes pas.

listener NOUN
  (Radio) un **auditeur** MASC, une **auditrice** FEM

literally ADVERB
  littéralement

literature NOUN
  la **littérature** FEM

ℓ**litre** NOUN
  le **litre** MASC
  a litre of milk un litre de lait

litter NOUN
  les **détritus** MASC PL
• **litter bin**
  la **poubelle** FEM

ℓ**little** ADJECTIVE, PRONOUN
1 *(small)* **petit** MASC, **petite** FEM
  a little boy un petit garçon
  a little break une petite pause
  my little brother mon petit frère
  little by little petit à petit
2 *(not much)* **peu de**
  They have little money. Ils ont peu d'argent.
  We have very little time. Nous avons très peu de temps.
3 **a little** un peu (de)
  It's a little late. C'est un peu tard.
  We have a little money. Nous avons un peu d'argent.
  a little more un peu plus de
  Could I have a little more cake? Je peux prendre encore un peu de gâteau?
• **little finger**
  le **petit doigt**

ℓ**live** ADJECTIVE ▶ SEE **live** VERB
1 *(broadcast)* **en direct**
  a live concert un concert en direct
2 *(animals)* **vivant** MASC, **vivante** FEM
  live animals. des animaux vivants

ℓ to **live** VERB ▶ SEE **live** ADJECTIVE
1 *(in a house, town, country)* **habiter** [1]
  We live at number 57. Nous habitons au numéro cinquante-sept.
  Shazia lives in Newcastle. Shazia habite Newcastle, Shazia habite à Newcastle.
  They live in a flat. Ils habitent dans un appartement.
  They live in France. Ils habitent en France.
  We're living in the country now. Nous habitons à la campagne maintenant.
  He's not living at home any more. Il n'habite plus chez ses parents.
2 *(to be alive, stay alive, spend your life)* **vivre** [82]
  They live together. Ils vivent ensemble.
  I like living here. J'aime bien vivre ici.
  to live on something vivre de quelque chose
  They live on fruit. Ils vivent de fruits.

lively ADJECTIVE
  (party, restaurant) **animé** MASC, **animée** FEM
  a very lively street une rue très animée

ℓ **indicates key words**

liver NOUN
le **foie** MASC

living NOUN
la **vie** FEM
What do they do for a living? Qu'est-ce qu'ils font dans la vie?
to earn a living gagner [1] sa vie
• **living room**
la salle de séjour

lizard NOUN
le **lézard** MASC

ℓ**load** NOUN ▸ SEE **load** VERB
1 (on a lorry) le **chargement** MASC
2 **a bus-load of tourists** un autobus plein de touristes
3 **loads of** des tas de
We bought loads of things. Nous avons acheté des tas de choses.
They've got loads of money. Ils sont bourrés de fric.

ℓto **load** VERB ▸ SEE **load** NOUN
charger [52]
a lorry loaded with wood un camion chargé de bois
to load a program charger un programme

loaf NOUN
le **pain** MASC
a loaf of bread un pain

loan NOUN ▸ SEE **loan** VERB
le **prêt** MASC
to **loan** VERB ▸ SEE **loan** NOUN
prêter [1]

lobster NOUN
le **homard** MASC

local ADJECTIVE ▸ SEE **local** NOUN
(shops, school, pool) du coin
the local library la bibliothèque du coin
the local newspaper le journal local
local NOUN ▸ SEE **local** ADJECTIVE
1 (pub, bar) le **pub du coin**
2 **the locals** les gens du coin

locality NOUN
la **région** FEM

lock NOUN ▸ SEE **lock** VERB
1 (for a door, cupboard) la **serrure** FEM
2 (for a bike, steering wheel) un **antivol** MASC
3 (on a canal) une **écluse** FEM
to **lock** VERB ▸ SEE **lock** NOUN
to lock the door fermer [1] la porte à clé
All the doors are locked. Toutes les portes sont fermées à clé.

locker NOUN
le **casier** MASC

• **locker room**
le vestiaire

lodger NOUN
le & la **locataire** MASC & FEM

loft NOUN
le **grenier** MASC

log NOUN
la **bûche** FEM

logical ADJECTIVE
logique MASC & FEM

lollipop NOUN
la **sucette** FEM

London NOUN
Londres
to London à Londres
a day in London une journée à Londres

Londoner NOUN
le **Londonien** MASC, la **Londonienne** FEM

loneliness NOUN
la **solitude** FEM

ℓ**lonely** ADJECTIVE
1 **seul** MASC, **seule** FEM
to feel lonely se sentir ◌ [53] seul
I felt lonely at first. Au début je me sentais seul (boy speaking), Au début je me sentais seule (girl speaking).
2 (place) **isolé** MASC, **isolée** FEM
a lonely farmhouse une ferme isolée

ℓ**long** ADJECTIVE, ADVERB ▸ SEE **long** VERB
1 (in general) **long** MASC, **longue** FEM
a long film un film long
a long dress une robe longue
The pool's 50 metres long. La piscine fait 50 mètres de long.
2 **a long way** loin MASC & FEM
It's quite a long way. C'est assez loin.
It's a long way to the pool. La piscine est loin d'ici.
3 (in time expressions) **all day long** toute la journée
all night long toute la nuit
It's an hour long. Ça dure une heure.
a long time longtemps
He stayed for a long time. Il est resté longtemps.
I've been here for a long time. Je suis là depuis longtemps.
4 (with ago) **long ago, a long time ago** il y a longtemps
They lived here long ago. Ils habitaient ici il y a longtemps.
It happened a long time ago. Cela s'est passé il y a longtemps.
5 **How long?** Combien de temps?

◌ **means the verb takes être to form the perfect**

How long did it last? Ça a duré combien de temps?
How long have you been here? Tu es là depuis combien de temps?

to **long** VERB ▸ SEE **long** ADJECTIVE, ADVERB
1 to long to do something avoir [5] très envie de faire quelque chose
I'm longing to see you. J'ai très envie de te voir.
2 to long for something attendre [3] quelque chose avec impatience
I'm longing for the holidays. J'attends les vacances avec impatience.

long-distance call NOUN
un **appel interurbain**

long-distance runner NOUN
le **coureur de fond**, la **coureuse de fond**

longer ADVERB
no longer ne … plus
I no longer know. Je ne sais plus.
They no longer live here. Ils n'habitent plus ici.

long jump NOUN
le **saut en longueur**

loo NOUN
les **toilettes** FEM PL
Where's the loo? Où sont les toilettes?

ℓ **look** NOUN ▸ SEE **look** VERB
1 (glance) le **coup d'œil**
to have a look at something jeter [1] un coup d'œil à quelque chose
Could you have a look at my homework? Tu peux jeter un coup d'œil à mes devoirs?
2 to have a look round faire [10] un tour
We had a look round the town. On a fait un tour en ville.
Let's have a look round the shops. Si on faisait les magasins?

ℓ to **look** VERB ▸ SEE **look** NOUN
1 regarder [1]
to look out of the window regarder par la fenêtre
I wasn't looking. Je ne regardais pas.
2 to look at something regarder [1] quelque chose
Martin was looking at the photos. Martin regardait les photos.
3 (to seem) avoir [5] l'air + adjective
Melanie looks pleased. Melanie a l'air contente.
The salad looks delicious. La salade a l'air délicieuse.
4 (to look like) What does the house look like? Comment est la maison?
It looks like a palace. On dirait un palais.
They look like each other. Ils se

ressemblent.
It looks like rain. On dirait qu'il va pleuvoir.
to look like somebody ressembler [1] à quelqu'un
Alicia looks like her sister. Alicia ressemble à sa sœur.
• to look after
1 to look after somebody s'occuper [1] de quelqu'un
Dad's looking after the baby. Papa s'occupe du bébé.
2 to look after something surveiller [1] quelque chose
Can you look after my suitcase? Tu peux surveiller ma valise?
• to look for something chercher [1] quelque chose
I'm looking for the keys. Je cherche les clés.
• to look forward to something (a party, a holiday) attendre [3] quelque chose avec impatience
I'm looking forward to your visit. J'attends ta visite avec impatience.
• to look onto something donner [1] sur quelque chose
My room looks onto the garden. Ma chambre donne sur le jardin.
• to look round se retourner ○ [1]
I looked round to see. Je me suis retourné pour voir.
• to look up lever [1] les yeux
When I looked up, she was gone. Quand j'ai levé les yeux, elle n'était plus là.
• to look up something chercher [1] quelque chose
Look it up in the dictionary. Cherche-le dans le dictionnaire.

loony ADJECTIVE (informal)
dingue MASC & FEM (informal)
a loony idea une idée dingue

loose ADJECTIVE
1 (screw, knot) **desserré** MASC, **desserrée** FEM
2 (trousers, jacket, dress) **ample** MASC & FEM

ℓ **lorry** NOUN
le **camion** MASC
• lorry driver
le **routier**

ℓ to **lose** VERB
1 (a game, glasses) perdre [3]
We lost. Nous avons perdu.
We lost the match. Nous avons perdu le match.
Sam's lost his watch. Sam a perdu sa montre.
2 to lose your way se perdre ○ [3]

We lost our way in the suburbs. Nous nous sommes perdus dans la banlieue.

loss NOUN
la **perte** FEM

lost ADJECTIVE
perdu MASC, **perdue** FEM
Are you lost? Vous êtes perdus?
I'm lost. Je suis perdu.
to get lost se perdre ⬤ [3]
I got lost on the way. Je me suis perdu en route.

♟ **lost property** NOUN
les **objets trouvés**
• **lost property office**
le bureau des objets trouvés

♟ **lot** NOUN
1 a lot beaucoup
Josh eats a lot. Josh mange beaucoup.
He's a lot better. Il va beaucoup mieux.
She's a lot nicer. Elle est beaucoup plus sympa.
Thanks a lot! Merci beaucoup!
2 **a lot of, lots of** beaucoup de
a lot of coffee beaucoup de café
lots of people beaucoup de gens
lots of friends beaucoup d'amis
a lot of money beaucoup d'argent

WORD TIP beaucoup de becomes beaucoup d' before a, e, i, o, u or silent h.

lottery NOUN
la **loterie** FEM
to win the lottery gagner [1] à la loterie
• **lottery ticket**
le ticket de loto

♟ **loud** ADJECTIVE
1 **fort** MASC, **forte** FEM
in a loud voice d'une voix forte
a little louder un peu plus fort
2 **out loud** à haute voix
Ellie read the letter out loud. Ellie a lu la lettre à haute voix.

loudly ADVERB
fort

loudspeaker NOUN
le **haut-parleur** MASC (PL les **haut-parleurs**)

♟ **to love** VERB ▸ SEE **love** NOUN
1 (a person) **aimer** [1]
I love you. Je t'aime.
They love each other. Ils s'aiment.
2 (a place, a suggestion) **aimer** [1] beaucoup
She loves London. Elle aime beaucoup Londres.
I'd love to come. J'aimerais beaucoup venir.
3 (an activity, a thing) **adorer** [1]

Sophie loves seafood. Sophie adore les fruits de mer.
to love doing something adorer faire quelque chose
I love dancing. J'adore danser.

♟ **love** NOUN ▸ SEE **love** VERB
1 l'**amour** MASC
Gina sends her love. Gina t'embrasse.
to be in love with somebody être [6] amoureux MASC, amoureuse FEM de quelqu'un
She's in love with Jake. Elle est amoureuse de Jake.
He's in love with Liz. Il est amoureux de Liz.
to fall in love with somebody tomber ⬤ [1] amoureux MASC, amoureuse FEM de quelqu'un
Pete fell in love with her. Pete est tombé amoureux d'elle.
(in letters) **With love from Charlie** Amitiés, Charlie
Lots of love, ... Grosses bises, ...
2 (in tennis) le **zéro** MASC
15 love 15 à zéro
• **love affair**
la **liaison** FEM
• **love story**
une histoire d'amour

♟ **lovely** ADJECTIVE
1 (to look at) **joli** MASC, **jolie** FEM
a lovely dress une jolie robe
It's a lovely village. C'est un joli village.
2 (weather) **It's a lovely day.** Il fait très beau.
We had lovely weather. Il a fait très beau.
3 (food, meals) **délicieux** MASC, **délicieuse** FEM
That was really lovely! C'était vraiment délicieux!
4 **a lovely surprise** une belle surprise
5 (person) très aimable MASC & FEM

lover NOUN
1 (in general) le & la **partenaire** MASC & FEM
2 (married man's) la **maîtresse** FEM
3 (married woman's) un **amant** MASC

♟ **low** ADJECTIVE
bas MASC, **basse** FEM
a low table une table basse
at a low price à prix bas
in a low voice à voix basse

lower ADJECTIVE ▸ SEE **lower** VERB
inférieur MASC, **inférieure** FEM

to lower VERB ▸ SEE **lower** ADJECTIVE
(lights, prices, sound) **baisser** [1]

low-fat milk NOUN
le lait écrémé

♟ **luck** NOUN
la **chance** FEM

⬤ means the verb takes être to form the perfect

Good luck! Bonne chance!
Bad luck! Pas de chance!
with a bit of luck avec un peu de chance

luckily *ADVERB*
heureusement
luckily for them heureusement pour eux

ℰ **lucky** *ADJECTIVE*
to be lucky avoir [5] de la chance
We were lucky. Nous avons eu de la chance.
That's my lucky number. C'est mon numéro porte-bonheur.

ℰ **luggage** *NOUN*
les **bagages** *MASC PL*
My luggage is in the boot. Mes bagages sont dans le coffre.

lump *NOUN*
1 *(of earth)* la **motte** *FEM*
2 *(swelling)* la **grosseur** *FEM*
3 *(in sauce, gravy)* le **grumeau** *MASC (PL* les **grumeaux)**

ℰ **lunch** *NOUN*
le **déjeuner** *MASC*
to have lunch déjeuner [1]
We had lunch in Boulogne. Nous avons déjeuné à Boulogne.
• **lunch break**
la **pause-déjeuner**
• **lunch hour**
l'**heure du déjeuner** *FEM*

lung *NOUN*
le **poumon** *MASC*

Luxembourg *NOUN*
1 *(country)* le **Luxembourg** *MASC*
to go to Luxembourg aller ◎ [7] au Luxembourg
2 *(city)* **Luxembourg**
in Luxembourg à Luxembourg

luxurious *ADJECTIVE*
luxueux *MASC*, **luxueuse** *FEM*

luxury *NOUN*
le **luxe** *MASC*
a luxury hotel un hôtel de luxe

lyrics *PLURAL NOUN*
les **paroles** *FEM PL*

Mm

mac *NOUN*
un **imper** *MASC (informal)*

macaroni *NOUN*
les **macaronis** *MASC PL*

machine *NOUN*
la **machine** *FEM*

machinery *NOUN*
les **machines** *FEM PL*

mackerel *NOUN*
le **maquereau** *MASC (PL* les **maquereaux)**

ℰ **mad** *ADJECTIVE*
1 *(crazy)* **fou** *MASC* **folle** *FEM*
She's completely mad! Elle est complètement folle!
2 *(angry)* **furieux** *MASC*, **furieuse** *FEM*
My mum will be mad! Ma mère sera furieuse!
3 **to be mad about something** adorer [1] quelque chose
Fiona's mad about horses. Fiona adore les chevaux.

madam *NOUN*
madame *FEM*

madman *NOUN*
le **fou** *MASC*

madness *NOUN*
la **folie** *FEM*

ℰ **magazine** *NOUN*
le **magazine** *MASC*

maggot *NOUN*
un **asticot** *MASC*

magic *ADJECTIVE* ▶ SEE **magic** *NOUN*
1 *(supernatural)* **magique** *MASC & FEM*
2 *(great)* **super** *INVARIABLE ADJECTIVE*

magic *NOUN* ▶ SEE **magic** *ADJECTIVE*
la **magie** *FEM*

magician *NOUN*
1 *(wizard)* le **magicien** *MASC*
2 *(conjurer)* le **prestidigitateur** *MASC*

magnet *NOUN*
un **aimant** *MASC*

magnificent *ADJECTIVE*
magnifique *MASC & FEM*

magnifying glass *NOUN*
la **loupe** *FEM*

mahogany *NOUN*
l'**acajou** *MASC*

maiden name *NOUN*
le **nom de jeune fille**

ℰ **mail** *NOUN*
1 *(post)* le **courrier** *MASC*
2 *(email)* l'**email** *MASC*, le **courrier électronique**

mail order NOUN
to buy something by mail order acheter [1]
quelque chose par correspondance

ℬ **main** ADJECTIVE
principal MASC, principale FEM, principaux
MASC PL, principales FEM PL
the main entrance l'entrée principale
The main thing is to eat well. Le principal,
c'est de bien manger.
• main course
le plat principal

mainly ADVERB
principalement

main road NOUN
la route principale

maize NOUN
le maïs MASC

major ADJECTIVE ▸ SEE **major** NOUN
majeur MASC, majeure FEM

major NOUN ▸ SEE **major** ADJECTIVE
le commandant MASC

Majorca NOUN
Majorque FEM

> **WORD TIP** Unlike the names of most other
> islands, Majorque does not take le or la.

majority NOUN
la majorité FEM

ℬ to **make** VERB ▸ SEE **make** NOUN
1 (in general) faire [10]
She made her bed. Elle a fait son lit.
I'm making an omelette. Je fais une
omelette.
Two and three make five. Deux et trois
font cinq.
to make friends se faire ◎ [10] des amis
I've made some friends. Je me suis fait des
amis.
to make a meal préparer [1] un repas
to make a phone call passer [1] un coup
de fil
2 to make somebody do something faire [10]
faire quelque chose à quelqu'un
He made me wait. Il m'a fait attendre.
She makes me laugh. Elle me fait rire.
3 (to produce) fabriquer [1]
They make computers. Ils fabriquent des
ordinateurs.
'Made in France' 'Fabriqué en France'
4 to make somebody happy, sad rendre [3]
quelqu'un heureux, triste
Her comments made us proud. Ses
remarques nous ont rendus fiers.
It makes me nervous. Ça m'angoisse.
5 (to earn) gagner [1]

He makes forty pounds a day. Il gagne
quarante livres par jour.
to make a living gagner [1] sa vie
6 to make somebody do something obliger
[52] quelqu'un à faire quelque chose
She made him return the money. Elle l'a
obligé à rendre l'argent.
7 I can't make it tonight. Je ne peux pas venir
ce soir.
• to make something up
1 (an excuse, a story) inventer [1] quelque
chose
2 to make it up se réconcilier ◎ [1]
They've made it up. Ils se sont réconciliés.

make NOUN ▸ SEE **make** VERB
la marque FEM
What make is your bike? De quelle marque
est ton vélo?

ℬ **make-up** NOUN
le maquillage MASC
to wear make-up se maquiller ◎ [1]
I don't wear make-up. Je ne me maquille
pas.
to put on (your) make-up se maquiller

male ADJECTIVE
1 (animal) mâle MASC
2 (sex, gender) masculin MASC, masculine FEM
• male chauvinist
le macho

malicious ADJECTIVE
malveillant MASC, malveillante FEM

mall NOUN
le centre commercial

Malta NOUN
Malte FEM

> **WORD TIP** Unlike the names of most other
> islands, Malte does not take le or la.

mammal NOUN
le mammifère MASC

ℬ **man** NOUN
un homme MASC
modern man l'homme moderne

to **manage** VERB
1 (a business) diriger [52]
2 (to cope) se débrouiller ◎ [1]
I can manage. Je me débrouille.
3 to manage to do something réussir [2] à
faire quelque chose
He managed to open the door. Il a réussi à
ouvrir la porte.

management NOUN
1 (of a business) la gestion FEM
2 (the people in charge) la direction FEM

◎ means the verb takes être to form the perfect

ℱ **manager** NOUN
1 *(of a company, bank)* le **directeur** MASC, la **directrice** FEM
2 *(of a shop, restaurant)* le **gérant** MASC, la **gérante** FEM
3 *(in sport, entertainment)* le **manager** MASC

manageress NOUN
la **gérante** FEM

managing director NOUN
le **directeur général**, la **directrice générale**

mandarin orange NOUN
la **mandarine** FEM

mango NOUN
la **mangue** FEM

maniac NOUN
le **fou** MASC, la **folle** FEM

mankind NOUN
l'**humanité** FEM

man-made ADJECTIVE
(fibre) **synthétique** MASC & FEM

manners PLURAL NOUN
to have good manners être [6] poli
It's bad manners to talk like that. Ce n'est pas poli de parler comme ça.

mansion NOUN
le **manoir** FEM

mantelpiece NOUN
la **cheminée** FEM

manual NOUN
le **manuel** MASC

to **manufacture** VERB
fabriquer [1]

manufacturer NOUN
le **fabricant** MASC

manure NOUN
le **fumier** MASC

many DETERMINER, PRONOUN
1 **beaucoup de**
Many people came. Beaucoup de gens sont venus.
many of them beaucoup d'entre eux
Are there many left? Est-ce qu'il en reste beaucoup?
not many pas beaucoup de
There weren't many young people. Il n'y avait pas beaucoup de jeunes.
Onions? There aren't many left. Des oignons? Il n'en reste pas beaucoup.
2 **very many** beaucoup de
There aren't very many seats. Il n'y a pas beaucoup de places.

3 **so many** *(such a lot of)* tant de
so many places to visit tant d'endroits à visiter
I have so many things to do! J'ai tant de choses à faire!
4 **so many** *(as many)* autant de
I've never eaten so many sweets! Je n'ai jamais mangé autant de bonbons!
as many as autant que
Take as many as you like. Prends autant que tu veux.
I've got as many friends as he has. J'ai autant d'amis que lui.
5 **too many** trop (de)
too many people trop de monde
I have too many things to do. J'ai trop de choses à faire.
That's far too many! C'est beaucoup trop!
6 **how many?** combien?
How many are there? Il y en a combien?
How many are there left? Il en reste combien?
How many sisters do you have? Tu as combien de sœurs?

ℱ **map** NOUN
1 *(of a country, region)* la **carte** FEM
a road map une carte routière
2 *(of a city)* le **plan** MASC
Can you point it out on the map? Pouvez-vous l'indiquer sur le plan?

marathon NOUN
le **marathon** MASC

marble NOUN
1 *(the stone)* le **marbre** MASC
2 *(in a game)* la **bille** FEM
to play marbles jouer [1] aux billes

to **march** VERB ▸ SEE **march** NOUN
1 *(demonstrators)* **défiler** [1]
2 *(soldiers)* **marcher** [1]
march NOUN ▸ SEE **march** VERB
la **manifestation** FEM
a peace march une manifestation pour la paix

March NOUN
mars MASC
in March en mars

WORD TIP Months of the year and days of the week start with small letters in French.

mare NOUN
la **jument** FEM

margarine NOUN
la **margarine** FEM

margin NOUN
la **marge** FEM

ℱ indicates key words

ℓ to **mark** VERB ▸ SEE **mark** NOUN
1 *(to correct)* corriger [52]
   The teacher marks our homework. Le professeur corrige nos devoirs.
2 *(to stain)* marquer [1]
3 *(in sport)* marquer [1]

ℓ **mark** NOUN ▸ SEE **mark** VERB
1 *(for school work)* la **note** FEM
   I got a good mark. J'ai eu une bonne note.
   What mark did you get for French? Tu as eu combien en français?
2 *(stain)* la **tache** FEM
   to leave a mark faire une tache

ℓ **market** NOUN
   le **marché** MASC
   to go to the market aller ◎ [7] au marché

marketing NOUN
   le **marketing** MASC

marmalade NOUN
   la **confiture d'oranges amères**

maroon ADJECTIVE
   bordeaux INVARIABLE ADJECTIVE

ℓ **marriage** NOUN
   le **mariage** MASC

ℓ **married** ADJECTIVE
   marié MASC, **mariée** FEM
   a married couple un couple marié

ℓ to **marry** VERB
1 **to marry somebody** épouser [1] quelqu'un
   She married a Frenchman. Elle a épousé un Français.
2 **to get married** se marier ◎ [1]
   They got married in July. Ils se sont mariés en juillet.

martial arts PLURAL NOUN
   les **arts martiaux** MASC PL

ℓ **marvellous** ADJECTIVE
   merveilleux MASC, **merveilleuse** FEM
   The weather's marvellous. Il fait un temps merveilleux.

marzipan NOUN
   la **pâte d'amandes**

mascara NOUN
   le **mascara** MASC

ℓ **masculine** ADJECTIVE ▸ SEE **masculine** NOUN
   masculin MASC, **masculine** FEM
   a masculine noun un nom masculin

masculine NOUN ▸ SEE **masculine** ADJECTIVE
   (Grammar) le **masculin** MASC
   in the masculine au masculin

to **mash** VERB
   (vegetables) écraser [1]

mashed potatoes PLURAL NOUN
   la **purée de pommes de terre**

mask NOUN
   le **masque** MASC

mass NOUN
1 *(amount)* la **masse** FEM
2 *(lots)* **masses of** beaucoup de
   masses of money beaucoup d'argent
   There's masses left over. Il en reste beaucoup.
3 *(Church)* la **messe** FEM
   to go to mass aller ◎ [7] à la messe

massacre NOUN
   le **massacre** MASC

massage NOUN
   le **massage** MASC

massive ADJECTIVE
   énorme MASC & FEM

to **master** VERB
   (a skill, a technique) maîtriser [1]
• **master bedroom**
   la **chambre principale**
• **masterpiece**
   le **chef-d'œuvre** *(PL les chefs-d'œuvre)*

mat NOUN
1 *(doormat)* le **paillasson** MASC
2 **a table mat** un set de table

to **match** VERB ▸ SEE **match** NOUN
   to match something être [6] assorti à quelque chose
   The jacket matches the skirt. La veste est assortie à la jupe.

ℓ **match** NOUN ▸ SEE **match** VERB
1 *(for lighting a fire)* une **allumette** FEM
2 *(in sport)* le **match** MASC *(PL les **matchs**)*
   a football match un match de foot
   United won the match. United a gagné le match.
   We lost the match 3-0. Nous avons perdu le match trois à zéro.

matching ADJECTIVE
   (curtains, clothes) **assorti** MASC, **assortie** FEM

ℓ **mate** NOUN
   copain MASC, **copine** FEM *(informal)*
   She's my best mate. C'est ma meilleure copine.
   to go out with your mates sortir ◎ [2] avec les copains

material NOUN
1 *(fabric)* le **tissu** MASC
2 *(information)* la **documentation** FEM
   some material for my project de la documentation pour mon dossier

◎ means the verb takes être to form the perfect

ℊ **mathematics** *NOUN*
les **mathématiques** *FEM PL*

ℊ **maths** *NOUN*
les **maths** *FEM PL*
Anna's good at maths. Anna est forte en maths.

ℊ to **matter** *VERB* ▸ SEE **matter** *NOUN*
être [6] important
to matter to somebody être [6] important pour quelqu'un
It matters a lot to me. C'est très important pour moi.
It doesn't matter. Ça n'a pas d'importance.
Don't worry, it doesn't matter. Ne t'inquiète pas, ça ne fait rien.
It doesn't matter if it rains. Ça ne fait rien s'il pleut.

matter *NOUN* ▸ SEE **matter** *VERB*
What's the matter? Qu'est-ce qu'il y a?
What's the matter with you? Qu'est-ce que tu as?
What's the matter with Emily? Qu'est-ce qu'elle a, Emily?

mattress *NOUN*
le **matelas** *MASC*
a foam mattress un matelas de mousse

mature *ADJECTIVE*
mûr *MASC*, mûre *FEM*
to be mature for your age être [6] mûr pour son âge

maximum *ADJECTIVE* ▸ SEE **maximum** *NOUN*
maximum *INVARIABLE ADJECTIVE*
the maximum temperature la température maximum
a maximum speed of 70 mph une vitesse maximum de 110km/h

maximum *NOUN* ▸ SEE **maximum** *ADJECTIVE*
le **maximum** *MASC*
a maximum of four hours a day un maximum de quatre heures par jour
a maximum of 30 students 30 élèves au maximum

may *VERB*
1 *(when you suggest a possibility)* **She may be ill.** Elle est peut-être malade.
We may go to Spain. Nous irons peut-être en Espagne.
They may have left. Ils sont peut-être partis.
2 *(when you ask politely)* **May I close the door?** Est-ce que je peux fermer la porte?

May *NOUN*
mai *MASC*

in May en mai

WORD TIP Months of the year and days of the week start with small letters in French.

ℊ **maybe** *ADVERB*
peut-être
maybe not peut-être pas
Maybe I'm wrong. J'ai peut-être tort.
Maybe he's forgotten. Il a peut-être oublié.
Maybe they've got lost. Ils se sont peut-être perdus.

May Day *NOUN*
le Premier Mai

mayonnaise *NOUN*
la **mayonnaise** *FEM*

mayor *NOUN*
le **maire** *MASC*

mayoress *NOUN*
la **mairesse** *FEM*

ℊ **me** *PRONOUN*
1 *(as object)* me, m' *(before a, e, i, o, u or silent h)*
She knows me. Elle me connaît.
Can you help me, please? Est-ce que tu peux m'aider, s'il te plaît?
Can you give me your address? Peux-tu me donner ton adresse?
Can you give it to me? Peux-tu me la donner?
2 *(after prepositions like avec, sans)* moi
I took her with me. Je l'ai emmenée avec moi.
They left without me. Ils sont partis sans moi.
That parcel's for me. Ce paquet est pour moi.
3 *(in commands)* moi
Listen to me! Écoute-moi!
Excuse me! Excusez-moi!
Give me the key. Donne-moi la clé.
4 *(in comparisons)* moi
She's older than me. Elle est plus âgée que moi.
He's not as smart as me. Il n'est pas aussi intelligent que moi.
5 **Me too!** Moi aussi!

meadow *NOUN*
le **pré** *MASC*

ℊ **meal** *NOUN*
le **repas** *MASC*
a family meal un repas de famille
to go out for a meal aller ◎ [7] manger au restaurant

ℊ to **mean** *VERB* ▸ SEE **mean** *ADJECTIVE*
1 vouloir [14] dire

What do you mean? Qu'est-ce que tu veux dire?
What does that mean? Qu'est-ce que ça veut dire?
It means that we don't pay. Ça veut dire que nous ne payons pas.
That's not what I meant. Ce n'est pas ce que je voulais dire.

2 **to mean to do something** avoir [5] l'intention de faire quelque chose
I meant to phone you. J'avais l'intention de t'appeler.
I didn't mean to annoy her. Je n'ai pas voulu la contrarier.
I didn't mean it. Je ne l'ai pas fait exprès.

3 **to be meant to do something** devoir [8] faire quelque chose
You were meant to be here at six. Tu devais être là à six heures.

ℰ **mean** ADJECTIVE ▸ SEE **mean** VERB

1 *(with money)* radin MASC, radine FEM *(informal)*

2 *(unkind)* méchant MASC, méchante FEM
to be mean to somebody être [6] méchant avec quelqu'un
She was mean to you. Elle a été méchante avec toi.

meaning NOUN
le sens MASC

ℰ **means** NOUN

1 le moyen MASC
a means of transport un moyen de transport
a means of doing something un moyen de faire quelque chose
I have no means of checking. Je n'ai aucun moyen de vérifier.

2 **by all means** certainement
'Can I come in?' — 'By all means, do.' 'Je peux entrer?' — 'Certainement.'

meantime NOUN
for the meantime pour le moment
in the meantime pendant ce temps
In the meantime, I looked it up on the Internet. Pendant ce temps, je l'ai cherché sur Internet.

meanwhile ADVERB
pendant ce temps
Meanwhile, she was waiting at the station. Pendant ce temps, elle attendait à la gare.

measles NOUN
la rougeole FEM

to **measure** VERB
mesurer [1]

measurements PLURAL NOUN

1 *(of a room, an object)* les **dimensions** FEM PL

2 *(for clothes)* les **mensurations** FEM PL
my chest measurement mon tour de poitrine
my waist measurement mon tour de taille

ℰ **meat** NOUN
la viande FEM
Georgia doesn't eat meat. Georgia ne mange pas de viande.

Mecca NOUN
la Mecque FEM

ℰ **mechanic** NOUN
le mécanicien MASC, la mécanicienne FEM
He's a mechanic. Il est mécanicien.

mechanical ADJECTIVE
mécanique MASC & FEM

medal NOUN
la médaille FEM
the gold medal la médaille d'or

to **meddle** VERB
to meddle in something se mêler ◎ [1] à quelque chose
He meddles in people's business. Il se mêle aux affaires des autres.

media NOUN
the media les médias MASC PL

medical ADJECTIVE ▸ SEE **medical** NOUN
médical MASC, médicale FEM, médicaux MASC PL, médicales FEM PL
a medical student un étudiant en médecine

medical NOUN ▸ SEE **medical** ADJECTIVE
la **visite médicale**
to have a medical passer [1] une visite médicale

ℰ **medicine** NOUN

1 *(remedy)* le médicament MASC
some cough medicine un médicament pour la toux

2 *(medical studies)* la médecine FEM
to study medicine faire [10] des études de médecine

medieval ADJECTIVE
médiéval MASC, médiévale FEM, médiévaux MASC PL, médiévales FEM PL
medieval castles des châteaux médiévaux
medieval knights des chevaliers du Moyen Âge

Mediterranean NOUN
the Mediterranean la Méditerranée

ℰ **medium** ADJECTIVE
moyen MASC, moyenne FEM
He's about medium height. Il est de taille

◎ **means the verb takes être to form the perfect**

moyenne.
- **medium-sized**
  (school, building) de taille moyenne

ℳ to **meet** *VERB*
1 *(by chance)* **rencontrer** [1]
  I met them outside the pool. Je les ai rencontrés devant la piscine.
2 *(by arrangement)* **retrouver** [1]
  I'll meet you there at six. Je t'y retrouverai à six heures.
3 *(to get to know)* **faire** [10] la **connaissance de**
  I met some French people. J'ai fait la connaissance de quelques Français.
  Tom, have you met Oliver? Tom, est-ce que tu connais Oliver?
4 *(at a station, airport)* **venir** ◎ [81] **chercher**
  He's meeting me at the station. Il vient me chercher à la gare.

ℳ **meeting** *NOUN*
  la **réunion** *FEM*
  She's in a meeting. Elle est en réunion.

megabyte *NOUN*
  le **mégaoctet** *MASC*

melody *NOUN*
  la **mélodie** *FEM*

ℳ **melon** *NOUN*
  le **melon** *MASC*

to **melt** *VERB*
1 **fondre** [3]
  It melts in your mouth. Ça fond dans la bouche.
2 **to melt something faire** [10] **fondre quelque chose**
  Melt the butter. Faites fondre le beurre.

member *NOUN*
  le **membre** *MASC*
  to be a member of something être [6] membre de quelque chose

Member of Parliament *NOUN*
  le **député** *MASC*, la **députée** *FEM*

membership *NOUN*
  l'**adhésion** *FEM*
- **membership card**
  la carte de membre
- **membership fee**
  la cotisation

memorial *NOUN*
  a war memorial un monument aux morts

to **memorize** *VERB*
  to memorize something apprendre [64] quelque chose par cœur
  to memorize your verb endings apprendre ses conjugaisons

memory *NOUN*
1 *(person's, computer's)* la **mémoire** *FEM*
  You have a good memory! Tu as bonne mémoire!
  I have a bad memory. Je n'ai pas de mémoire.
2 *(of the past)* le **souvenir** *MASC*
  I've good memories of my stay. J'ai de bons souvenirs de mon séjour.
- **memory card**
  la carte mémoire

to **mend** *VERB*
  réparer [1]

meningitis *NOUN*
  la **méningite** *FEM*

mental *ADJECTIVE*
  mental *MASC*, **mentale** *FEM*, **mentaux** *MASC PL*, **mentales** *FEM PL*
  a mental illness une maladie mentale
  a mental hospital un hôpital psychiatrique

to **mention** *VERB*
  mentionner [1]
  She mentioned your name. Elle a mentionné ton nom.
  Mention three French regions. Mentionne trois régions françaises.

ℳ **menu** *NOUN*
  le **menu** *MASC*
  a set menu un menu
  a children's menu un menu pour enfants
  on the menu au menu
  I'm having the €15 menu. Je prends le menu à 15€.

mercy *NOUN*
  la **pitié** *FEM*

to **merge** *VERB*
1 *(roads)* **se rejoindre** ◎ [49]
2 *(the data)* **fusionner** [1]

meringue *NOUN*
  la **meringue** *FEM*

merit *NOUN*
  le **mérite** *MASC*

mermaid *NOUN*
  la **sirène** *FEM*

merry *ADJECTIVE*
  (happy) **joyeux** *MASC*, **joyeuse** *FEM*
  Merry Christmas! Joyeux Noël!
- **merry-go-round**
  le **manège**

mess *NOUN*
  le **désordre** *MASC*
  My things are in a mess. Mes affaires sont dans le désordre.

to make a mess mettre [11] du désordre
What a mess! Quelle pagaille! *(informal)*
- to mess about
faire [10] l'imbécile
- to mess about with something
(with matches, alcohol) jouer [1] avec
quelque chose
- to mess something up
(files, belongings) mettre [11] la pagaille
dans quelque chose

message *NOUN*
le **message** *MASC*
a phone message un message
téléphonique
to leave a message laisser [1] un message
He didn't leave a message. Il n'a pas laissé
de message.

messenger *NOUN*
le **messager** *MASC*

messy *ADJECTIVE*
1 **a messy job** un travail salissant
2 **messy handwriting** une écriture peu
soignée

metal *NOUN*
le **métal** *MASC* (PL les **métaux**)

meter *NOUN*
1 *(for electricity, gas, in a taxi)* le **compteur**
MASC
2 *(parking meter)* le **parcmètre** *MASC*

method *NOUN*
la **méthode** *FEM*
- method of transport
le moyen de transport

Methodist *NOUN*
le & la **méthodiste** *MASC & FEM*

> **WORD TIP** Adjectives never have capitals in
> French, even for religions.

ℐ **metre** *NOUN*
le **mètre** *MASC*
a 50-metre pool une piscine de 50 mètres
The hedge is two metres high. La haie fait
deux mètres de haut.

metric *ADJECTIVE*
métrique *MASC & FEM*

Mexican *ADJECTIVE* ▸ SEE **Mexican** *NOUN*
mexicain *MASC*, **mexicaine** *FEM*

Mexican *NOUN* ▸ SEE **Mexican** *ADJECTIVE*
un **Mexicain** *MASC*, une **Mexicaine** *FEM*

Mexico *NOUN*
le **Mexique** *MASC*
in Mexico au Mexique
to Mexico au Mexique

microphone *NOUN*
le **microphone** *MASC*

microscope *NOUN*
le **microscope** *MASC*

microwave (oven) *NOUN*
le (four à) micro-ondes
Heat it up in the microwave. Fais-le
chauffer au micro-ondes.

ℐ **midday** *NOUN*
midi *MASC*
at midday à midi
The shops close at midday. Les magasins
ferment à midi.

ℐ **middle** *NOUN*
1 le **milieu** *MASC*
in the middle of the night au milieu de la
nuit
in the middle of the room au milieu de la
pièce
2 **to be in the middle of doing something**
être [6] en train de faire quelque chose
I was in the middle of washing my hair.
J'étais en train de me laver les cheveux.
- middle-aged
d'un certain âge
- middle-class
de la classe moyenne
- Middle East
le Moyen-Orient
- middle finger
le majeur

midge *NOUN*
le **moucheron** *MASC*

mid-length *ADJECTIVE*
mi-long *MASC*, **mi-longue** *FEM*

ℐ **midnight** *NOUN*
minuit *MASC*
at midnight à minuit
It was almost midnight. Il était presque
minuit.

Midsummer's Day *NOUN*
la **Saint Jean**

midwife *NOUN*
la **sage-femme** *FEM* (PL les **sages-femmes**)

ℐ **might** *VERB*
'Will you phone him?' — 'I might.' Est-ce
que tu vas l'appeler? — 'Peut-être.'
I might invite Jess. J'inviterai peut-être Jess.
He might have forgotten. Il a peut-être
oublié.

migraine *NOUN*
la **migraine** *FEM*

⬤ means the verb takes être to form the perfect

mike NOUN
le **micro** MASC (informal)

mild ADJECTIVE
doux MASC, **douce** FEM
It's mild today. Il fait doux aujourd'hui.

mile NOUN
le MASC (to convert miles to kilometres, multiply by 8 and divide by 5)
The village is ten miles from Newhaven. Le village est à seize kilomètres de Newhaven.
We walked for miles. On a marché pendant des kilomètres.

mileage NOUN
le **kilométrage** MASC
What's the mileage on the car? Elle a combien de kilomètres, la voiture?

military ADJECTIVE
militaire MASC & FEM

to **milk** VERB ▶ SEE **milk** NOUN
(a cow) **traire** [78]

ℓ **milk** NOUN ▶ SEE **milk** VERB
le **lait** MASC
full-cream milk le lait entier
skimmed milk le lait écrémé
semi-skimmed milk le lait demi-écrémé
• **milk chocolate**
le chocolat au lait
• **milkman**
le laitier
• **milk round**
la tournée de laitier
• **milk shake**
le milk-shake

millennium NOUN
le **millénaire** MASC

millimetre NOUN
le **millimètre** MASC

million NOUN
le **million** MASC
a million people un million de personnes
two million people deux millions de personnes

WORD TIP Use de after million in French.

millionaire NOUN
le & la **millionnaire** MASC & FEM

millionth ADJECTIVE
millionième MASC & FEM

to **mimic** VERB
imiter [1]

mince NOUN
la **viande hachée** FEM

ℓ to **mind** VERB ▶ SEE **mind** NOUN
1 (to keep an eye on) **surveiller** [1]
Can you mind my bag for me? Est-ce que tu peux surveiller mon sac?
2 (to be bothered by) **I don't mind the heat.** La chaleur ne me dérange pas.
Do you mind if ...? Est-ce que cela vous dérange si ...?
Do you mind if I close the door? Est-ce que cela vous dérange si je ferme la porte?
3 (to be careful) **Mind the step!** Attention à la marche!
Mind your fingers! Attention à tes doigts!
4 (to care) **Never mind!** Peu importe!
'What shall we do?' — 'I don't mind.' 'Qu'est-ce qu'on va faire?' — 'Ça m'est égal.'

ℓ **mind** NOUN ▶ SEE **mind** VERB
1 un **esprit** MASC
to have a logical mind avoir [5] l'esprit logique.
It never even crossed my mind! Ça ne m'est même pas venu à l'esprit!
It's on my mind. Ça me préoccupe.
to have a lot on your mind être [6] très préoccupé
2 **to change your mind** changer [52] d'avis
I've changed my mind. J'ai changé d'avis.
3 **to make up your mind** se décider ◎ [1]
I can't make up my mind. Je n'arrive pas à me décider.

mine NOUN ▶ SEE **mine** PRONOUN
la **mine** FEM
a coal mine une mine de charbon

ℓ **mine** PRONOUN ▶ SEE **mine** NOUN
1 (for masc singular nouns) **le mien**
She took her bag and I took mine. Elle a pris son sac et j'ai pris le mien.
2 (for fem singular nouns) **la mienne**
She gave me her address and I gave her mine. Elle m'a donné son adresse et je lui ai donné la mienne.
3 (for masc plural nouns) **les miens**
Karen's invited her parents and I've invited mine. Karen a invité ses parents et j'ai invité les miens.
4 (for fem plural nouns) **les miennes**
She showed me her photos and I showed her mine. Elle m'a montré ses photos et je lui ai montré les miennes.
5 (belonging to me) **à moi**
It's mine. C'est à moi.
The green one's mine. Le vert est à moi.

miner NOUN
le **mineur** MASC

ℓ **mineral water** NOUN
l'**eau minérale** FEM
two bottles of mineral water deux

bouteilles d'eau minérale

miniature ADJECTIVE ▶ SEE **miniature** NOUN
miniature MASC & FEM

miniature NOUN ▶ SEE **miniature** ADJECTIVE
la miniature FEM

minibus NOUN
le minibus MASC

minimum ADJECTIVE ▶ SEE **minimum** NOUN
minimum INVARIABLE ADJECTIVE
the minimum age l'âge minimum
minimum safety measures des mesures de
sécurité minimum
the minimum amount le minimum

minimum NOUN ▶ SEE **minimum** ADJECTIVE
le minimum MASC
a minimum of 10 minutes a day un
minimum de 10 minutes par jour
a minimum of eight people un minimum
de huit personnes
I did the minimum. J'ai fait le minimum.

miniskirt NOUN
la minijupe FEM

minister NOUN
1 (in a government) le ministre MASC
the minister of health le ministre de la
santé
2 (in a church) le pasteur MASC

ministry NOUN
le ministère MASC

minor ADJECTIVE
mineur MASC, mineure FEM

minority NOUN
la minorité FEM

mint NOUN
1 (herb) la menthe FEM
2 (sweet) le bonbon à la menthe

minus PREPOSITION
moins
Seven minus three is four. Sept moins trois
égale quatre.
It was minus five last night. Il a fait moins
cinq la nuit dernière.

minute ADJECTIVE ▶ SEE **minute** NOUN
minuscule MASC & FEM

♀ **minute** NOUN ▶ SEE **minute** ADJECTIVE
la minute FEM
at the last minute à la dernière minute
Just a minute! Une minute!
It's five minutes' walk from here. C'est à
cinq minutes à pied d'ici.
We'll be ready in two minutes. Nous
serons prêts dans deux minutes.

miracle NOUN
le miracle MASC

♀ **mirror** NOUN
1 la glace FEM
He looked at himself in the mirror. Il s'est
regardé dans la glace.
2 (in a car) le rétroviseur MASC

to **misbehave** VERB
se conduire ◎ [26] mal

mischief NOUN
to get up to mischief faire [10] des bêtises
He's always getting up to mischief. Il fait
toujours des bêtises.

mischievous ADJECTIVE
coquin MASC, coquine FEM

miser NOUN
un & une avare MASC & FEM

miserable ADJECTIVE
1 (unhappy) malheureux MASC, malheureuse
FEM
He's miserable without her. Il est
malheureux sans elle.
I feel really miserable. Je n'ai vraiment pas
le moral.
It's miserable weather. Il fait un sale
temps.
2 (pay, salary) de misère
They're paid a miserable wage. Ils gagnent
un salaire de misère.

misery NOUN
la souffrance FEM

misfortune NOUN
1 (unfortunate event) le malheur MASC
2 (bad luck) la malchance
She had the misfortune of losing her
passport. Elle a eu la malchance de perdre
son passeport.

to **misjudge** VERB
1 (an amount, a distance) mal évaluer [1]
I misjudged the distance. J'ai mal évalué la
distance.
2 (a person) mal juger [52]
Everybody had misjudged her. Tout le
monde l'avait mal jugée.

to **mislay** VERB
(the keys, money, passport) égarer [1]

misleading ADJECTIVE
trompeur MASC, trompeuse FEM
a misleading advertisement une publicité
trompeuse

♀ to **miss** VERB
1 (a bus, a target, an event) rater [1]
She missed her train. Elle a raté son train.

◎ means the verb takes être to form the perfect

The ball missed the goal. Le ballon a raté le but.
Missed! Raté!
2 *(a class)* **manquer [1]**
  He's missed several classes. Il a manqué plusieurs cours.
3 **to miss an opportunity** manquer une occasion
  It's an opportunity not to be missed! C'est une occasion à ne pas manquer!
4 **to be missed by somebody** manquer [1] à quelqu'un
  He'll be missed. Il va nous manquer.
  I miss you. Tu me manques.
  She's missing her sister. Sa sœur lui manque.
  I miss France. La France me manque.

> **WORD TIP** The subject of the verb manquer is the thing or person that you miss.

ℙ**Miss** *NOUN*
  Mademoiselle *FEM*
  Miss Jones Mademoiselle Jones, Mlle Jones *(usual written form)*

missile *NOUN*
  le **missile** *MASC*

missing *ADJECTIVE*
1 **manquant** *MASC*, **manquante** *FEM*
  the missing pieces les pièces manquantes
2 **to be missing** manquer [1]
  What's missing? Qu'est-ce qui manque?
  There's a plate missing. Il manque une assiette.
  There are three forks missing. Il manque trois fourchettes.
3 **to go missing** disparaître [27]
  Several computers have gone missing. Plusieurs ordinateurs ont disparu.
  Three people are missing. Trois personnes ont disparu.

missionary *NOUN*
  le & la **missionnaire** *MASC & FEM*

mist *NOUN*
  la **brume** *FEM*

to **mistake** *VERB* ▸ SEE **mistake** *NOUN*
  to mistake somebody for somebody else prendre [64] quelqu'un pour quelqu'un d'autre
  I mistook you for your brother. Je vous ai pris pour votre frère.

ℙ**mistake** *NOUN* ▸ SEE **mistake** *VERB*
1 *(in a calculation, judgement)* une **erreur** *FEM*
  by mistake par erreur
  It was my mistake. C'était une erreur de ma part.
2 *(in spelling, typing)* la **faute** *FEM*

a spelling mistake une faute d'orthographe
  You've made lots of mistakes. Tu as fait beaucoup de fautes.
3 *(to be wrong)* **to make a mistake** se tromper ◌ [1]
  I've made a mistake. Je me suis trompé *(boy speaking)*, Je me suis trompée *(girl speaking)*.

mistaken *ADJECTIVE*
  to be mistaken se tromper ◌ [1]

mistletoe *NOUN*
  le **gui** *MASC*

misty *ADJECTIVE*
  brumeux *MASC*, **brumeuse** *FEM*
  a misty morning un matin brumeux
  It's misty this morning. Il y a de la brume ce matin.

to **misunderstand** *VERB*
  mal comprendre [64]
  I misunderstood. J'ai mal compris.

misunderstanding *NOUN*
  le **malentendu** *MASC*
  There's been a misunderstanding. Il y a eu un malentendu.

ℙto **mix** *VERB* ▸ SEE **mix** *NOUN*
1 **mélanger [52]**
  Mix the ingredients together. Mélangez les ingrédients.
  Oil and water don't mix. L'eau et l'huile ne se mélangent pas.
2 **to mix with people** fréquenter [1] des gens
  I don't like the kind of people she mixes with. Je n'aime pas trop les gens qu'elle fréquente.
  They're mixing with the local people. Ils se mêlent aux gens du coin.
• to **mix up**
1 **to mix something up** mélanger [52] quelque chose
  You've mixed up my files! Tu as mélangé mes fichiers!
  to get something mixed up mélanger [52] quelque chose
  You've got it all mixed up! Tu mélanges tout!
2 **to get mixed up in something** se trouver ◌ [1] mêlé à quelque chose
  He got mixed up in a fight. Il s'est trouvé mêlé à une bagarre.
3 **to mix somebody up with somebody else** confondre [69] quelqu'un avec quelqu'un d'autre
  I get her mixed up with her sister. Je la confonds avec sa sœur.

mix *NOUN* ▸ SEE **mix** *VERB*
  le **mélange** *MASC*

a good mix of people un bon mélange de gens

ₚ **mixed** ADJECTIVE
varié MASC, variée FEM
a mixed programme un programme varié
- **mixed salad**
la salade composée
- **mixed school**
une école mixte

mixer NOUN
le batteur électrique

mixture NOUN
le mélange MASC
It's a mixture of jazz and rock. C'est un mélange de jazz et de rock.

mix-up NOUN
la confusion FEM
a mix-up with the names une confusion sur les noms

to **moan** VERB
1 (to complain) râler [1] (informal)
Stop moaning! Arrête de râler!
She was moaning about you. Elle râlait contre toi.
2 (to make a low noise) gémir [2]

mobile home NOUN
le mobile home

mobile phone NOUN
le téléphone portable
to call somebody on their mobile appeler quelqu'un au portable

to **mock** VERB
to mock somebody se moquer ◎ [1] de quelqu'un
They're mocking us. Ils se moquent de nous.
Don't mock! Ne te moque pas de moi!

mock exam NOUN
un examen blanc

model NOUN
1 (in a series) le modèle MASC
the latest model le dernier modèle
2 (fashion worker) le mannequin (man or woman)
She's a top model. Elle est top-modèle.
3 (of a plane, car) le modèle réduit
He makes models. Il fait des modèles réduits.
4 (scale model) la maquette FEM
a model of the prototype une maquette du prototype
- **model aeroplane**
le modèle réduit d'avion

- **model railway**
le chemin de fer miniature
- **model village**
le village miniature

modem NOUN
le modem MASC

moderate ADJECTIVE
modéré MASC, modérée FEM

ₚ **modern** ADJECTIVE
moderne MASC & FEM
I like modern buildings. J'aime les bâtiments modernes.
life in the modern world la vie dans le monde contemporain

to **modernize** VERB
moderniser [1]
It needs to be modernized. Il a besoin d'être modernisé.

modern languages PLURAL NOUN
les langues vivantes FEM PL

modest ADJECTIVE
modeste MASC & FEM

to **modify** VERB
modifier [1]

moisture NOUN
l'humidité FEM

moisturizer NOUN
1 (lotion) le lait hydratant
2 (cream) la crème hydratante

mole NOUN
1 (animal) la taupe FEM
2 (on skin) le grain de beauté

ₚ **moment** NOUN
1 un instant MASC
He'll be here in a moment. Il sera là dans un instant.
It could happen at any moment. Ça pourrait se produire à tout instant.
2 at the moment en ce moment
She's studying at the moment. Elle étudie en ce moment.
You rang at just the right moment. Tu as téléphoné au bon moment.

Monaco NOUN
Monaco MASC
to go to Monaco aller ◎ [7] à Monaco

WORD TIP Monaco does not take le or la.

ₚ **monarchy** NOUN
la monarchie FEM

monastery NOUN
le monastère MASC

◎ means the verb takes être to form the perfect

ℐ **Monday** NOUN
le **lundi** MASC
on Monday lundi
last Monday lundi dernier
next Monday lundi prochain
every Monday tous les lundis
on Mondays le lundi
I'm going out on Monday. Je sors lundi.
See you on Monday! À lundi!

WORD TIP Months of the year and days of the week start with small letters in French.

ℐ **money** NOUN
l'**argent** MASC
to make money gagner [1] de l'argent
I've got enough money. J'ai assez d'argent.
I've got no money left. Je n'ai plus d'argent.
to get money back *(in a shop)* être [6] remboursé
They gave me my money back. Ils m'ont remboursé.
• **money box**
la tirelire

mongrel NOUN
le **chien bâtard**

monitor NOUN
(Computers) le **moniteur** MASC

monk NOUN
le **moine** MASC

monkey NOUN
le **singe** MASC

monotonous ADJECTIVE
(voice, music) **monotone** MASC & FEM

monster NOUN
le **monstre** MASC

ℐ **month** NOUN
le **mois** MASC
last month le mois dernier
next month le mois prochain
this month ce mois-ci
every month tous les mois
in the month of May au mois de mai
in two months' time dans deux mois
at the end of the month à la fin du mois

monthly ADJECTIVE
mensuel MASC, **mensuelle** FEM

ℐ **monument** NOUN
le **monument** MASC

ℐ **mood** NOUN
l'**humeur** FEM
to be in a good mood être [6] de bonne humeur
Paul's in a good mood. Paul est de bonne humeur.

to be in a bad mood être de mauvaise humeur
Sally's in a bad mood. Sally est de mauvaise humeur.

moody ADJECTIVE
lunatique MASC & FEM

ℐ **moon** NOUN
1 la **lune** FEM
to put a man on the moon envoyer [40] un homme sur la lune
2 **to be over the moon** être [6] aux anges
She's over the moon about winning. Elle est aux anges depuis qu'elle a gagné.
• **moonlight**
le clair de lune

moor NOUN
la **lande** FEM
the Yorkshire moors les landes du Yorkshire

moped NOUN
la **mobylette** FEM

moral ADJECTIVE ▶ SEE **moral** NOUN
moral MASC, **morale** FEM, **moraux** MASC PL, **morales** FEM PL

moral NOUN ▶ SEE **moral** ADJECTIVE
la **morale** FEM
the moral of the story la morale de l'histoire

morale NOUN
le **moral** MASC
Our morale is high. Notre moral est bon.
It will raise the team's morale. Ça va remonter le moral à l'équipe.

morals NOUN
la **moralité** FEM

ℐ **more** DETERMINER, ADVERB, PRONOUN
1 *(with verbs)* **plus**
She's studying more. Elle étudie plus.
I train more in the summer. Je m'entraîne plus en été.
2 *(before a noun)* **plus de**
more time plus de temps
more money plus d'argent
We need more light. Il nous faut plus de lumière.
Would you like some more milk? Voulez-vous encore du lait?
Is there any more pasta? Il reste encore des pâtes?
3 *(for a noun)* **plus**
I'll have some more. J'en prendrai un peu plus.
Do you want some more? Tu en veux encore?
I don't want any more. Je n'en veux plus.

ℐ **indicates key words**

We need more. Il nous en faut plus.
4 *(before an adjective or adverb)* **plus**
more entertaining plus amusant
more difficult plus difficile
more slowly plus lentement
more easily plus facilement
5 **more than** *(in amounts)* **plus de**
more than a hundred people plus de cent personnes
more than a thousand pounds plus de mille livres
6 **more than** *(in comparisons)* **plus que**
She eats more than me. Elle mange plus que moi.
The game's more interesting than the film. Le jeu est plus intéressant que le film.
7 **more and more** de plus en plus
It's getting more and more expensive. Ça coûte de plus en plus cher.
It takes more and more time. Ça prend de plus en plus de temps.
8 **more or less** plus ou moins
It's more or less finished. C'est plus ou moins fini.

♯ **morning** NOUN
1 *(early in the day)* **le matin** MASC
this morning ce matin
tomorrow morning demain matin
yesterday morning hier matin
in the morning le matin
on Friday mornings le vendredi matin
She works in the mornings. Elle travaille le matin.
at six o'clock in the morning à six heures du matin
2 *(as period of time)* **la matinée** FEM
sometime during the morning au cours de la matinée
I spent the morning reading. J'ai passé la matinée à lire.

Morocco NOUN
le Maroc MASC
in Morocco au Maroc

mortgage NOUN
le crédit (immobilier)

Moscow NOUN
Moscou

Moslem NOUN
le musulman MASC, **la musulmane** FEM

WORD TIP Adjectives never have capitals in French, even for religions.
---

mosque NOUN
la mosquée FEM

mosquito NOUN
le moustique MASC

a mosquito bite une piqûre de moustique
I got bitten by mosquitoes. Je me suis fait piquer par des moustiques.

♯ **most** DETERMINER, ADVERB, PRONOUN
1 *(followed by a plural noun)* **la plupart de**
Most of my friends live in London. La plupart de mes amis habitent à Londres.
Most children like chocolate. La plupart des enfants aiment le chocolat.
Most people go home at 6 p.m. La plupart des gens rentrent chez eux à 18 heures.
2 *(followed by a singular noun)* **presque tout, presque toute**
They've eaten most of the chocolate. Ils ont mangé presque tout le chocolat.
I spent most of the day in bed. J'ai passé presque toute la journée au lit.
3 **most of the time** la plupart du temps
They quarrel most of the time. Ils se disputent la plupart du temps.
4 *(followed by an adjective)* **the most** le plus, la plus, les plus
the most interesting film le film le plus intéressant
the most exciting story l'histoire la plus passionnante
the most boring books les livres les plus ennuyeux
5 *(followed by a noun)* **the most** le plus de
I've got the most time. C'est moi qui ai le plus de temps.
6 *(after a verb)* **(the) most** le plus
I like Paris the most. C'est Paris que j'aime le plus.
What I hate most is the noise. Ce que je déteste le plus, c'est le bruit.

moth NOUN
1 *(large insect)* **le papillon de nuit**
2 *(clothes moth)* **la mite**

♯ **mother** NOUN
la mère FEM
my mother ma mère
Kate's mother la mère de Kate

♯ **mother-in-law** NOUN
la belle-mère FEM (PL les **belles-mères**)

Mother's Day NOUN
la fête des Mères *(the last Sunday in May)*

motivated ADJECTIVE
motivé MASC, **motivée** FEM

motivation NOUN
la motivation FEM

♯ **motor** NOUN
le moteur MASC
• **motorbike**
la moto

⚪ means the verb takes être to form the perfect

- **motorboat**
le bateau à moteur
- **motorcyclist**
le & la motocycliste

motorist NOUN
un & une **automobiliste** MASC & FEM

motor racing NOUN
la **course automobile**

motorway NOUN
une **autoroute** FEM
to take the motorway prendre [64]
l'autoroute

> **MOTORWAY**
> France has 9,000 kilometres of motorways,
> numbered A1, A2, etc (A = autoroute). Some
> also have names, like the motorway to the
> south: l'Autoroute du soleil. You have to pay a
> toll to use many French motorways.

mouldy ADJECTIVE
moisi MASC, **moisie** FEM

ᵖ **mountain** NOUN
la **montagne** FEM
in the mountains à la montagne
We spent a week in the mountains. Nous
avons passé une semaine à la montagne.
- **mountain bike**
le VTT (= vélo tout-terrain)

> **MOUNTAIN**
> The highest mountain in Europe is Mont Blanc
> (4,897m) in the French Alps.

mountaineer NOUN
un & une **alpiniste** MASC & FEM

mountaineering NOUN
l'**alpinisme** MASC
to go mountaineering faire [10] de
l'alpinisme

mountainous ADJECTIVE
montagneux MASC, **montagneuse** FEM

mouse NOUN
(the animal, for computers) la **souris** FEM
- **mouse mat**
(Computers) le tapis de souris
- **mousetrap**
la souricière

mousse NOUN
la **mousse** FEM
chocolate mousse la mousse au chocolat

moustache NOUN
la **moustache** FEM
a man with a moustache un moustachu

ᵖ **mouth** NOUN
la **bouche** FEM

- **mouthful**
la bouchée
- **mouth organ**
un harmonica

ᵖ to **move** VERB ▶ SEE **move** NOUN
1 (people, things) **bouger** [52]
Don't move! Ne bouge pas!
The dog wasn't moving. Le chien ne
bougeait pas.
2 (a piece of furniture, a car) **déplacer** [61]
I can't move the wardrobe. Je n'arrive pas à
déplacer l'armoire.
3 (your personal items, a bag, a phone)
enlever [50] quelque chose
Can you move your bag, please? Est-ce que
tu peux enlever ton sac, s'il te plaît?
Someone's moved my things. Quelqu'un a
enlevé mes affaires.
Move the chairs out of the way. Enlève les
chaises de là.
4 (traffic) **avancer** [61]
The traffic was moving slowly. La
circulation avançait lentement.
5 (vehicles) **rouler** [1]
The cars were moving at high speed. Les
voitures roulaient à grande vitesse.
6 (to go to a new address) **déménager** [52]
We're moving house on Tuesday. Nous
déménageons mardi.
They've moved to France. Ils se sont
installés en France.
7 (to make space, get out of the way) **Move up
a bit.** Pousse-toi un peu.
Move your head, I can't see! Pousse ta tête,
je ne vois rien!
- **to move forward**
s'avancer [61]
He moved forward a step. Il s'est avancé
d'un pas.
- **to move in**
emménager [52]
They've just moved in. Ils viennent
d'emménager.
- **to move out**
déménager [52]
We're moving out soon. Nous
déménageons bientôt.

move NOUN ▶ SEE **move** VERB
1 (to a different address) le **déménagement**
MASC
2 (in games) **Your move!** À toi de jouer!

movement NOUN
1 (of waves, of trees, of your body) le
mouvement MASC
2 (group, organization) le **mouvement** MASC
the peace movement le mouvement pour
la paix

ᵖ indicates key words

movie NOUN
1 (film) le **film** MASC
2 the movies le cinéma
  I love going to the movies. J'aime beaucoup aller au cinéma.

moving ADJECTIVE
1 (vehicle) en marche
  a moving vehicle un véhicule en marche
2 (experience, story) **émouvant** MASC, **émouvante** FEM

to **mow** VERB
  tondre [3]
  to mow the lawn tondre la pelouse

mower NOUN
  la **tondeuse à gazon**

MP NOUN
  le **député** MASC, la **députée** FEM
  She's an MP. Elle est députée.

mp3 player NOUN
  le **lecteur mp3** MASC

♂ **Mr** NOUN
  Monsieur (abbreviated to M.)
  Mr Angus Brown M. Angus Brown

♂ **Mrs** NOUN
  Madame (abbreviated to Mme)
  Mrs Mary Hendry Mme Mary Hendry

Ms NOUN
  Madame (abbreviated to Mme)
  Ms has no equivalent in French. Madame is used for all women.

♂ **much** DETERMINER, ADVERB, PRONOUN
1 **beaucoup**
  She doesn't eat much. Elle ne mange pas beaucoup.
  We don't go out much. Nous ne sortons pas beaucoup.
  much more beaucoup plus
  much shorter beaucoup plus court
  much easier beaucoup plus facile
  It's much more fun. C'est beaucoup plus marrant.
2 **beaucoup de**
  We don't have much time. Nous n'avons pas beaucoup de temps.
  Is there much left? Est-ce qu'il en reste beaucoup?
3 **not much** pas beaucoup
  'Do you have any homework?' — 'Yes, but not much.' 'Est-ce que tu as des devoirs?' — 'Oui, mais pas beaucoup.'
4 **very much** (a lot) beaucoup
  Thanks very much. Merci beaucoup.
  I don't train very much. Je ne m'entraîne pas beaucoup.
5 **very much** (a lot of) beaucoup de

There isn't very much milk. Il n'y a pas beaucoup de lait.
6 (such a lot) **so much** tellement
  I have so much to do! J'ai tellement de choses à faire!
7 (all of that) **so much** autant
  You shouldn't have given me so much. Tu n'aurais pas dû m'en donner autant.
8 **as much as** autant que
  You can take as much as you like. Tu peux en prendre autant que tu veux.
  I spent as much money as you did. J'ai dépensé autant d'argent que toi.
9 **too much** trop (de)
  too much money trop d'argent
  That's far too much! C'est beaucoup trop!
10 **how much?** combien?
  How much is it? Ça coûte combien?
  How much money do you have? Tu as combien d'argent?
  How much time do you have left? Il te reste combien de temps?

mud NOUN
  la **boue** FEM

muddle NOUN
1 le **désordre** MASC
  to be in a muddle être [6] en désordre
  to leave something in a muddle laisser [1] quelque chose en désordre
2 **to get into a muddle** s'embrouiller [1]
  We got into a muddle. Nous nous sommes embrouillés.

muddy ADJECTIVE
1 (path, road) **boueux** MASC, **boueuse** FEM
2 (shoes, clothes) **couvert de boue** MASC, **couverte de boue** FEM
  My boots are all muddy. Mes bottes sont couvertes de boue.

to **mug** VERB ▸ SEE **mug** NOUN
  agresser [1]
  The old lady was mugged. La vieille dame a été agressée.
  to get mugged se faire ☺ [10] agresser
  My brother got mugged in the park. Mon frère s'est fait agresser au parc.

mug NOUN ▸ SEE **mug** VERB
  la **grande tasse** FEM
  a mug of coffee une grande tasse de café

mugging NOUN
  une **agression** FEM

multicultural ADJECTIVE
  multiculturel MASC, **multiculturelle** FEM

multiplication NOUN
  la **multiplication** FEM

☺ means the verb takes être to form the perfect

to **multiply** VERB
multiplier [1]

ℬ **mum**, **mummy** NOUN
1 (mother) la **mère** FEM
Jim's mum la mère de Jim
I'll ask my mum. Je vais demander à ma mère.
2 (within the family, as a name) la **maman** FEM
Mum's not back yet. Maman n'est pas encore rentrée.

mumps NOUN
les **oreillons** MASC PL

to **murder** VERB ▶ SEE **murder** NOUN
assassiner [1]

murder NOUN ▶ SEE **murder** VERB
le **meurtre** MASC
to be accused of murder être [6] accusé de meurtre

murderer NOUN
un **assassin** MASC

muscle NOUN
le **muscle** MASC

muscular ADJECTIVE
musclé MASC, musclée FEM

ℬ **museum** NOUN
le **musée** MASC
to go to the museum aller ◎ [7] au musée
I can't stand museums! J'ai horreur des musées!

ℬ **mushroom** NOUN
le **champignon** MASC
a mushroom pizza une pizza aux champignons

ℬ **music** NOUN
la **musique** FEM
classical music la musique classique
reggae music le reggae
I prefer pop music. J'aime mieux la musique pop.

musical NOUN ▶ SEE **musical** ADJECTIVE
la **comédie musicale**

musical ADJECTIVE ▶ SEE **musical** NOUN
to be musical être [6] musicien
Lauren's musical. Lauren est musicienne.
They're a very musical family. Ils sont très musiciens dans la famille.

musical instrument NOUN
un **instrument de musique**
to play a musical instrument jouer [1] d'un instrument de musique

musician NOUN
le **musicien** MASC, la **musicienne** FEM
He wants to be a musician. Il veut être musicien.

Muslim NOUN
le **Musulman** MASC, la **Musulmane** FEM

ℬ **mussel** NOUN
la **moule** FEM

ℬ **must** VERB
1 (to have to) falloir [43] (only used with the il faut form)
We must leave now. Il faut partir maintenant.
We mustn't forget Jake. Il ne faut pas oublier Jake.
I must tell you something. Il faut que je te dise quelque chose.
2 (if you assume something to be true) devoir [8]
You must be tired. Tu dois être fatigué.
It must be five o'clock. Il doit être cinq heures.
They must have forgotten. Ils ont dû oublier.

ℬ **mustard** NOUN
la **moutarde** FEM

to **mutter** VERB
marmonner [1]

my ADJECTIVE
1 (with masc singular nouns) **mon**
my brother mon frère
my book mon livre
my computer mon ordinateur
2 (with fem singular nouns) **ma**
my sister ma sœur
my house ma maison
Here's my address. Voici mon adresse.

WORD TIP Use mon with feminine nouns beginning with a, e, i, o, u or silent h.

3 (with plural nouns) **mes**
my children mes enfants
my friends mes amis
my sisters mes sœurs
4 (with parts of the body) **le, la, les**
I'm washing my hands. Je me lave les mains.
I had a glass in my hand. J'avais un verre à la main.
My eyes are sore. J'ai mal aux yeux.

myself PRONOUN
1 **me, m'** (before a, e, i, o, u or silent h)
I've hurt myself. Je me suis blessé.
I'm really enjoying myself. Je m'amuse beaucoup.
2 (for emphasis) **moi-même**
I said it myself. Je l'ai dit moi-même.
3 (on my own) by myself **tout seul** (boy speaking), **toute seule** (girl speaking)

I did it by myself. Je l'ai fait tout seul.

ℰ **mysterious** ADJECTIVE
mystérieux MASC, mystérieuse FEM
mysterious noises des bruits mystérieux

mystery NOUN
1 (puzzle) le **mystère** MASC
It's a mystery to me how they won. Je ne comprends vraiment pas comment ils ont gagné.
2 (book) le **roman policier**

myth NOUN
le **mythe** MASC

mythology NOUN
la **mythologie** FEM

Nn

to **nail** VERB ▶ SEE **nail** NOUN
clouer [1]
a sign nailed to the gate un panneau cloué à la barrière

nail NOUN ▶ SEE **nail** VERB
1 (on fingers, toes) un **ongle** MASC
2 (for wood) le **clou** MASC
• nailbrush
la brosse à ongles
• nailfile
la lime à ongles
• nail scissors
les ciseaux à ongles

naked ADJECTIVE
nu MASC, nue FEM

ℰ **name** NOUN
1 (person's) le **nom** MASC
What's your name? Comment vous appelez-vous?
My name is Debbie. Je m'appelle Debbie.
2 (of a book, film) le **titre** MASC

ⓘ NAMES

The most common surname in France is Martin.

nap NOUN
le **petit somme** MASC
to have a nap faire [10] un petit somme

napkin NOUN
la **serviette** FEM

ℰ **narrow** ADJECTIVE
étroit MASC, étroite FEM
the narrow streets les rues étroites
The trousers are too narrow. Le pantalon est trop étroit.

ℰ **nasty** ADJECTIVE
1 (mean) méchant MASC, méchante FEM
That was a nasty thing to do. Ça, c'était méchant.
to be nasty to somebody être [6] méchant avec quelqu'un
The girls are nasty to her. Les filles sont méchantes avec elle.
2 (unpleasant) désagréable MASC & FEM
a nasty job une tâche désagréable
a nasty cold un gros rhume
3 (food, smell) mauvais MASC, mauvaise FEM
The soup tastes nasty. La soupe a mauvais goût.

nation NOUN
la **nation** FEM

national ADJECTIVE
national MASC, nationale FEM, nationaux MASC PL, nationales FEM PL
• national anthem
un hymne national

National 5s PLURAL NOUN
You can explain National 5s as follows: Ce sont des examens que les lycéens écossais passent à l'âge d'environ 16 ans dans six ou sept matières. La meilleure note que l'on peut obtenir est A et la note la plus basse est 'no award'. Une fois qu'ils ont obtenu leurs National 5s, de nombreux étudiants se préparent pour les Highers.
▶ SEE **Highers**

nationality NOUN
la **nationalité** FEM
What nationality are you? Vous êtes de quelle nationalité?

national park NOUN
le **parc national** (PL les **parcs nationaux**)

Nativity NOUN
la **nativité** FEM

ℰ **natural** ADJECTIVE
1 (from nature) naturel MASC, naturelle FEM
the planet's natural resources les ressources naturelles de la planète
2 (understandable) normal MASC, normale FEM
It's natural to be curious. Il est normal d'être curieux.

naturally ADVERB
naturellement
Naturally, he said no. Naturellement, il a refusé.

ℰ **nature** NOUN
la **nature** FEM
• nature reserve
la réserve naturelle

naughty ADJECTIVE
vilain MASC, vilaine FEM
a naughty little girl une vilaine petite fille

nausea NOUN
la nausée FEM

navel NOUN
le nombril MASC

to **navigate** VERB
naviguer [1]

navy NOUN
1 la marine FEM
to join the navy s'engager [52] dans la marine
My uncle's in the navy. Mon oncle est dans la marine.
2 (colour) le bleu marine MASC

navy-blue ADJECTIVE
bleu marine INVARIABLE ADJECTIVE
navy-blue gloves des gants bleu marine

ℓ **near** ADJECTIVE ▸ SEE **near** ADVERB, PREPOSITION
proche MASC & FEM
the nearest phone booth la cabine téléphonique la plus proche
The supermarket is quite near. Le supermarché est assez proche.

ℓ **near** ADVERB, PREPOSITION ▸ SEE **near** ADJECTIVE
1 près
I live quite near. J'habite tout près.
to come nearer s'approcher [1]
As the bull came nearer, ... Comme le taureau s'approchait de plus en plus, ...
2 near (to) something près de quelque chose
It's near the station. C'est près de la gare.
Is there a cafe near here? Est-ce qu'il y a un café près d'ici?
We live near Edinburgh. Nous habitons près d'Édimbourg.

nearby ADVERB
tout près

ℓ **nearly** ADVERB
presque
nearly empty presque vide
I've nearly finished. J'ai presque fini.
I nearly forgot. J'ai failli oublier.

ℓ **neat** ADJECTIVE
1 (room, house) bien rangé MASC, bien rangée FEM
2 (appearance, writing) soigné MASC, soignée FEM
She always looks neat. Elle est toujours soignée.

neatly ADVERB
avec soin

ℓ **necessary** ADJECTIVE
nécessaire MASC & FEM
That's not necessary. Cela n'est pas nécessaire.
If necessary, they'll collect us. Si besoin est, ils viendront nous chercher.

ℓ **neck** NOUN
1 (of a person) le cou MASC
2 (of a top, a shirt) une encolure FEM

necklace NOUN
le collier MASC

nectarine NOUN
la nectarine FEM

ℓ to **need** VERB ▸ SEE **need** NOUN
1 to need something, somebody avoir [5] besoin de quelqu'un, quelque chose
We need bread. Nous avons besoin de pain.
Is that everything you need? C'est tout ce qu'il vous faut?
That's all I need. C'est tout ce qu'il me faut.
2 to need to do something devoir [8] faire quelque chose
We need to call Paul. Nous devons appeler Paul.
3 I don't need to go now. Je ne suis pas obligé d'y aller maintenant.
We needn't wait. Nous ne sommes pas obligés d'attendre.

ℓ **need** NOUN ▸ SEE **need** VERB
There's no need, I've done it. Inutile, c'est fait.
There's no need to wait. Inutile d'attendre.

needle NOUN
une aiguille FEM

negative ADJECTIVE ▸ SEE **negative** NOUN
négatif MASC, négative FEM

negative NOUN ▸ SEE **negative** ADJECTIVE
1 (of photos) le négatif MASC
2 (Grammar) la forme négative

neglected ADJECTIVE
mal entretenu MASC, mal entretenue FEM

ℓ **neighbour** NOUN
le voisin MASC, la voisine FEM
I'm going round to the neighbours'. Je vais chez les voisins.

ℓ **neighbourhood** NOUN
le quartier MASC
to live in a good neighbourhood habiter [1] un quartier agréable
It's a tough neighbourhood. C'est un quartier dur.

ℓ **neither** CONJUNCTION
1 neither ... nor ne ... ni ... ni
I have neither the time nor the money. Je

n'ai ni le temps ni l'argent.
2 *(when there is no verb)* **ni l'un ni l'autre** *(ni l'une ... with feminine nouns)*
'Which do you like?' — 'Neither.' 'Lequel aimes-tu?' — 'Ni l'un ni l'autre.'
3 *(in replies)* **Neither do I.** Moi non plus.
'I don't like fish.' — 'Neither do I.' 'Je n'aime pas le poisson.' — 'Moi non plus.'
'I didn't like the film.' — 'Neither did we.' 'Je n'ai pas aimé le film.' — 'Nous non plus.'

WORD TIP non plus can be used for 'nor do they', etc eux non plus, etc.

ℓ **nephew** NOUN
le **neveu** MASC (PL les **neveux**)

ℓ **nerve** NOUN
1 *(in the body)* le **nerf** MASC
He gets on my nerves. Il me tape sur les nerfs.
2 *(daring)* le **courage** MASC
You've got a nerve! Tu as un sacré culot!

nervous ADJECTIVE
nerveux MASC, **nerveuse** FEM
nervous students des élèves nerveux
• **nervous breakdown**
la dépression nerveuse

nest NOUN
le **nid** MASC
a bird's nest un nid d'oiseau

ℓ **net** NOUN
1 *(for fishing, in tennis)* le **filet** MASC
2 *(in football)* les **filets** MASC PL
3 **the Net** l'Internet MASC
to look something up on the Net chercher [1] quelque chose sur Internet
We can look it up on the Net. On peut le chercher sur Internet.
• **netball**
le netball

Netherlands NOUN
the Netherlands les Pays-Bas MASC PL

nettle NOUN
une **ortie** FEM

network NOUN
le **réseau** MASC (PL les **réseaux**)
a television network un réseau de télévision

neutral ADJECTIVE
neutre MASC & FEM
neutral colours des couleurs neutres

ℓ **never** ADJECTIVE
1 *(when used with a verb)* **ne ... jamais**
Ben never smokes. Ben ne fume jamais.
I've never seen the film. Je n'ai jamais vu le film.

2 *(when used alone)* **jamais**
'Have you ever been to Spain?' — 'Never.'
'Est-ce que tu es déjà allé en Espagne?' — 'Jamais.'
3 *(in expressions)* **Never again.** Plus jamais.
Never mind! Peu importe!

WORD TIP ne comes before the verb or verb group, including pronouns, with jamais coming after. ▸ SEE **nobody** ▸ SEE **not** ▸ SEE **nothing**.

ℓ **new** ADJECTIVE
1 *(different, unknown to you)* **nouveau** MASC, **nouvel** MASC, **nouvelle** FEM, **nouveaux** MASC PL, **nouvelles** FEM PL
my new coat mon nouveau manteau
a new album un nouvel album
Liam's new girlfriend la nouvelle copine de Liam
our new neighbours les nouveaux voisins

WORD TIP nouveau, etc come before the noun; nouvel is used before a, e, i, o, u or silent h.

2 *(brand new)* **neuf** MASC, **neuve** FEM
a new house une maison neuve
It's a new bike. C'est un vélo neuf.

newcomer NOUN
le **nouveau venu** MASC (PL les **nouveaux venus**), la **nouvelle venue** FEM (PL les **nouvelles venues**)

ℓ **news** PLURAL NOUN
1 *(in conversation)* la **nouvelle** FEM, les **nouvelles** FEM PL
a piece of news une nouvelle
She got some bad news. Elle a eu une mauvaise nouvelle.
I've got good news. J'ai de bonnes nouvelles.
2 *(on the radio, TV)* le **journal** MASC, les **informations** FEM PL
the midday news le journal de midi
They're watching the news. Ils regardent le journal.

ℓ **newsagent** NOUN
le **marchand de journaux**
at the newsagent's chez le marchand de journaux

ℓ **newspaper** NOUN
le **journal** MASC (PL les **journaux**)
I read it in the newspaper. Je l'ai lu dans le journal.

newsreader NOUN
le **présentateur** MASC, la **présentatrice** FEM

ℓ **New Year** NOUN
le **Nouvel An**
Happy New Year! Bonne Année!
• **New Year's Day**
le jour de l'An

- **New Year's Eve**
  la Saint-Sylvestre

New Zealand *NOUN*
la **Nouvelle-Zélande** *FEM*
in New Zealand en Nouvelle-Zélande
to go to New Zealand aller ⊘ [7] en
Nouvelle-Zélande

> **WORD TIP** Countries and regions in French take
> le, la or les.

New Zealander *NOUN*
un **Néo-Zélandais** *MASC*, une **Néo-
Zélandaise** *FEM*
the New Zealanders les Néo-Zélandais

> **WORD TIP** Adjectives never have capitals in
> French, even for nationality or regional origin.

ℰ **next** *ADJECTIVE* ▸ SEE **next** *ADVERB*
1 *(in the future)* **prochain** *MASC*, **prochaine**
  FEM
  next week la semaine prochaine
  next Thursday jeudi prochain
  next year l'année prochaine
  The next train is at ten. Le prochain train
  est à dix heures.
2 *(in a series)* **suivant** *MASC*, **suivante** *FEM*
  the next page la page suivante
  the next day le lendemain
3 *(office, room)* **voisin** *MASC*, **voisine** *FEM*

ℰ **next** *ADVERB* ▸ SEE **next** *ADJECTIVE*
1 *(afterwards)* **ensuite**
  What did he say next? Qu'est-ce qu'il a dit
  ensuite?
2 *(now)* **maintenant**
  What shall we do next? Qu'est-ce qu'on
  fait maintenant?
3 **next to** à côté de
  the girl next to Emma la fille à côté
  d'Emma

next door *ADVERB*
à côté
Who lives next door? Qui habite à côté?

ℰ **nice** *ADJECTIVE*
1 *(place, time)* **agréable** *MASC & FEM*
  I had a nice evening. J'ai passé une soirée
  agréable.
  Have a nice time! Amusez-vous bien!
2 *(clothes)* **joli** *MASC*, **jolie** *FEM*
  I bought a nice ring. J'ai acheté une jolie
  bague.
3 *(people)* **sympathique** *MASC & FEM*
  Amy's really nice. Amy est vraiment
  sympathique.
4 **to be nice to somebody** être [6] gentil avec
  quelqu'un
  She's been very nice to us. Elle a été très
  gentille avec nous.

5 *(taste, drink)* **bon** *MASC*, **bonne** *FEM*
  a nice meal un bon repas
  a nice cup of tea une bonne tasse de thé
6 *(weather)* **to be nice** faire [10] beau
  It's a nice day. Il fait beau.
  The weather was nice. Il a fait beau.

> **WORD TIP** joli and bon come before the noun.

nickname *NOUN*
le **surnom** *MASC*
My nickname is Mizz. On m'a surnommé
Mizz.

ℰ **niece** *NOUN*
la **nièce** *FEM*

ℰ **night** *NOUN*
1 *(before bedtime)* le **soir** *MASC*
  tomorrow night demain soir
  on Saturday night samedi soir
  I saw Jason last night. J'ai vu Jason hier soir.
2 *(after bedtime)* la **nuit** *FEM*
  in the middle of the night au milieu de la
  nuit
  It's cold at night. Il fait froid la nuit.
  We stayed the night at Rachel's. Nous
  avons couché chez Rachel.
- **night club**
  la boîte de nuit

nightie *NOUN*
la chemise de nuit

nightmare *NOUN*
le **cauchemar** *MASC*
to have a nightmare faire [10] un
cauchemar

nil *NOUN*
le **zéro** *MASC*
They won four-nil. Ils ont gagné quatre à
zéro.

nine *NUMBER*
neuf
Jake's nine. Jake a neuf ans.

nineteen *NUMBER*
dix-neuf
Kate's nineteen. Kate a dix-neuf ans.

nineteenth *ADJECTIVE*
1 **dix-neuvième** *MASC & FEM*
2 *(in dates)* **the nineteenth of September** le
  dix-neuf septembre

ninetieth *ADJECTIVE*
quatre-vingt-dixième *MASC & FEM*
It's his ninetieth birthday. Il fête ses
quatre-vingt-dix ans.

ninety *NUMBER*
quatre-vingt-dix
My great-uncle is ninety. Mon grand-oncle

a quatre-vingt-dix ans.

ninth ADJECTIVE
1 **neuvième** MASC & FEM
on the ninth floor au neuvième étage
2 *(in dates)* **the ninth of June** le neuf juin

♪ **no** ADVERB ▶ SEE **no** ADJECTIVE
non
'Are you hungry?' — 'No.' 'Tu as faim?' —
'Non.'
No, thank you. Non merci.

♪ **no** ADJECTIVE ▶ SEE **no** ADVERB
1 *(in general)* **pas de**
No problem! Pas de problème!
No way! Pas question!
2 *(on notices)* **'No smoking'** 'Défense de
fumer'
'No parking' 'Stationnement interdit'
3 *(with a verb)* **ne ... pas de**
We've got no bread. Nous n'avons pas de
pain.
He has no friends. Il n'a pas d'amis.

WORD TIP ne comes before the verb, or verb
group, and pas de comes after it. Ne becomes n'
before a, e, i, o, u or silent h.

♪ **nobody** PRONOUN
1 *(without a verb)* **personne**
'Who's there?' — 'Nobody.' 'Qui est là?' —
'Personne.'
2 *(with a verb)* **ne ... personne**
There's nobody in the classroom. Il n'y a
personne dans la salle de classe.
Nobody knows me. Personne ne me
connaît.
Nobody answered. Personne n'a répondu.

WORD TIP ne comes before the verb or verb
group, including pronouns, with personne
coming after. ▶ SEE **never** ▶ SEE **not** ▶ SEE **nothing**.

to **nod** VERB
hocher [1] **la tête**

♪ **noise** NOUN
le bruit MASC
too much noise trop de bruit
to make a noise faire [10] du bruit
I heard strange noises. J'ai entendu des
bruits bizarres.

♪ **noisy** ADJECTIVE
bruyant MASC, **bruyante** FEM
It's too noisy here. Ici c'est trop bruyant.

♪ **none** PRONOUN
1 *(not one)* **aucun** MASC, **aucune** FEM
'How many students failed the exam?'
— 'None.' 'Combien d'étudiants ont raté
l'examen?' — 'Aucun.'
2 *(with a verb)* **ne ... aucun** *(aucune with*

feminine nouns)
None of the girls knows him. Aucune des
filles ne le connaît.
None of these biros works. Aucun de ces
bics ne marche.
3 *(no more)* **ne ... plus**
There's none left. Il n'y en a plus.
There are none left. Il n'y en a plus.

WORD TIP ne comes before the verb or verb
group, including pronouns, no matter where
aucun or aucune appears in the sentence. ... plus
follows the verb or verb group. ne becomes n'
before a, e, i, o, u or silent h. ▶ SEE **nothing** ▶ SEE
nobody ▶ SEE **not**.

nonsense NOUN
les bêtises FEM PL
to talk nonsense dire [47] des bêtises

♪ **non-smoker** NOUN
le non-fumeur, la non-fumeuse

non-stop ADJECTIVE ▶ SEE **non-stop**
(train, bus service) **direct**

non-stop ADVERB ▶ SEE **non-stop**
sans arrêt
She talks non-stop. Elle parle sans arrêt.

noodles PLURAL NOUN
les nouilles FEM PL

♪ **noon** NOUN
midi MASC
at (twelve) noon à midi

♪ **no one, no-one** PRONOUN ▶ SEE **nobody**

♪ **nor** CONJUNCTION
1 **neither ... nor** ne ... ni ... ni
I have neither the time nor the money. Je
n'ai ni le temps ni l'argent.
2 *(in replies)* **Nor do I.** Moi non plus.
'I don't like fish.' — 'Nor do I.' 'Je n'aime
pas le poisson.' — 'Moi non plus.'
'I wasn't invited.' — 'Nor were we.' 'Je n'ai
pas été invité.' — 'Nous non plus.'

WORD TIP ne becomes n' before a, e, i, o, u or
silent h. non plus can be used for 'nor do they',
etc.: eux non plus, etc.

♪ **normal** ADJECTIVE
1 *(natural)* **normal** MASC, **normale** FEM,
normaux MASC PL, **normales** FEM PL
a normal reaction une réaction normale
That's normal. C'est normal.
2 *(usual)* **habituel** MASC, **habituelle** FEM
my normal work mon travail habituel
We'll come at the normal time. On viendra
à l'heure habituelle.

normally ADVERB
normalement

⬤ means the verb takes être to form the perfect

Normandy *NOUN*
la **Normandie** *FEM*
in Normandy en Normandie

ℰ **north** *ADJECTIVE, ADVERB* ▸ SEE **north** *NOUN*
nord *INVARIABLE ADJECTIVE*
the north side le côté nord
a north wind un vent du nord
north of Paris au nord de Paris
We're going north. Nous allons vers le nord.

WORD TIP **nord** never changes.

ℰ **north** *NOUN* ▸ SEE **north** *ADJECTIVE, ADVERB*
le **nord** *MASC*
in the north au nord
in the north of France dans le nord de la France

North America *NOUN*
l'**Amérique du Nord** *FEM*
in North America en Amérique du Nord

North American *ADJECTIVE* ▸ SEE **North American** *NOUN*
nord-américain *MASC*, **nord-américaine** *FEM*

North American *NOUN* ▸ SEE **North American** *ADJECTIVE*
un **Nord-Américain** *MASC*, une **Nord-Américaine** *FEM*

northeast *ADJECTIVE* ▸ SEE **northeast** *NOUN*
in northeast England au nord-est de l'Angleterre

northeast *NOUN* ▸ SEE **northeast** *ADJECTIVE*
le **nord-est** *MASC*

Northern Ireland *NOUN*
l'**Irlande du Nord** *FEM*
in Northern Ireland en Irlande du Nord

WORD TIP Countries and regions in French take **le**, **la**, or **les**.

Northern Irish *ADJECTIVE*
d'**Irlande du Nord**
I'm Northern Irish. Je suis d'Irlande du Nord.

North Pole *NOUN*
the North Pole le pôle Nord

North Sea *NOUN*
the North Sea la mer du Nord

northwest *ADJECTIVE* ▸ SEE **northwest** *NOUN*
in northwest Scotland au nord-ouest de l'Écosse

northwest *NOUN* ▸ SEE **northwest** *ADJECTIVE*
le **nord-ouest** *MASC*

Norway *NOUN*
la **Norvège** *FEM*

Norwegian *ADJECTIVE* ▸ SEE **Norwegian** *NOUN*
norvégien *MASC*, **norvégienne** *FEM*

Norwegian *NOUN* ▸ SEE **Norwegian** *ADJECTIVE*
1 *(person)* un **Norvégien** *MASC*, une **Norvégienne** *FEM*
2 *(the language)* le **norvégien** *MASC*

ℰ **nose** *NOUN*
le **nez** *MASC*
to blow your nose se moucher ◎ [1]

nostril *NOUN*
la **narine** *FEM*

ℰ **not** *ADVERB*
1 *(without a verb)* **pas**
not bad pas mal
not yet pas encore
not on Saturdays pas le samedi
Not me! Pas moi!
Not again! Pas encore!
2 *(when used with a verb)* **ne ... pas**
I don't know. Je ne sais pas.
It's not my watch. Ce n'est pas ma montre.
It doesn't matter. Ça ne fait rien.
I haven't replied. Je n'ai pas répondu.
Will didn't phone. Will n'a pas appelé.
They won't come. Ils ne viendront pas.
We decided not to wait. Nous avons décidé de ne pas attendre. *(ne pas comes before an infinitive)*

WORD TIP **ne** comes before the verb or verb group, including pronouns, with **pas** coming after. **ne** becomes **n'** before a, e, i, o, u or silent h. ▸ SEE **never** ▸ SEE **nobody** ▸ SEE **nothing**.

ℰ **note** *NOUN*
1 *(message)* le **mot** *MASC*
She left me a note. Elle m'a laissé un mot.
2 *(in order to remember)* la **note** *FEM*
to take notes prendre [64] des notes
to make a note of something noter [1] quelque chose
I made a note of the date. J'ai noté la date.
3 *(banknote)* le **billet** *MASC*
a ten-pound note un billet de dix livres
4 *(in music)* la **note** *FEM*
• **notebook**
le **carnet**
• **notepad**
le **bloc-notes** *(PL les **blocs-notes**)*

ℰ **nothing** *PRONOUN*
1 *(without a verb)* **rien**
'What did you buy?' — 'Nothing.' 'Qu'est-ce que tu as acheté?' — 'Rien.'
'What's going on?' — 'Nothing.' 'Qu'est-ce qui se passe?' — 'Rien.'
2 **nothing + adjective** rien de *(+ adjective)*
nothing new rien de nouveau
There's nothing interesting on TV. Il n'y a

rien d'intéressant à la télé.
3 *(with a verb as object)* ne ... rien
She knows nothing. Elle ne sait rien.
I heard nothing. Je n'ai rien entendu.
There's nothing left. Il ne reste rien.
We've got nothing to do. On n'a rien à
faire.
I've decided to do nothing. J'ai décidé de
ne rien faire.
4 *(with a verb as subject)* Nothing has
changed. Rien n'a changé.
Nothing's happening. Il ne se passe rien.

WORD TIP ne comes before the verb or verb
group, including pronouns, no matter where
rien appears in the sentence. ne becomes n'
before a, e, i, o, u or silent h. ▶ SEE **never** ▶ SEE
nobody ▶ SEE **not**

ℓ to **notice** VERB ▶ SEE **notice** NOUN
remarquer [1]
I noticed the box. J'ai remarqué la boîte.
to notice that ... remarquer que ...
Did you notice that she was talking? Est-ce
que tu as remarqué qu'elle parlait?

ℓ **notice** NOUN ▶ SEE **notice** VERB
1 *(sign)* le **panneau** MASC *(PL les **panneaux**)*
It's written on the notice. C'est marqué sur
le panneau.
2 *(advertisement)* une **annonce** FEM
3 to take no notice ne pas faire [10] attention
You never take any notice. Tu ne fais jamais
attention.
Don't take any notice of her! Ne fais pas
attention à elle!

noticeable ADJECTIVE
visible MASC & FEM

noticeboard NOUN
le panneau d'affichage

nought NOUN
le zéro MASC

noun NOUN
le nom MASC

ℓ **novel** NOUN
le roman MASC

novelist NOUN
le romancier MASC, la romancière FEM

November NOUN
novembre MASC
in November en novembre

WORD TIP Months of the year and days of the
week take a small letter in French.

ℓ **now** ADVERB
1 *(in general)* maintenant
Where is he now? Où est-il maintenant?
I have two cats now. J'ai deux chats

maintenant.
Bye for now. À bientôt.
2 *(this minute)* just now en ce moment
I'm busy just now. Je suis occupé en ce
moment.
3 *(a minute ago)* just now
I saw Jack just now. Je viens de voir Jack.
4 right now tout de suite
5 to be doing something right now être [6]
en train de faire quelque chose
I'm reading your text right now. Je suis en
train de lire ton texto.
6 now and then de temps en temps

WORD TIP venir de + infinitive verb is for very
recent actions. être en train de + infinitive verb
is for actions as they happen.

nowadays ADVERB
de nos jours
Nowadays people use computers. De nos
jours, on se sert des ordinateurs.

ℓ **nowhere** ADVERB
nulle part
nowhere in France nulle part en France
There's nowhere to play ball. Il n'y a aucun
endroit pour jouer au ballon.

nuclear ADJECTIVE
nucléaire MASC & FEM
a nuclear power station une centrale
nucléaire

nude ADJECTIVE
nu MASC, nue FEM
in the nude nu

nuisance NOUN
That's a nuisance. Ça, c'est embêtant.
She's a nuisance. Elle est pénible.

numb ADJECTIVE
1 *(with cold)* engourdi MASC, engourdie FEM
My foot's numb. J'ai le pied engourdi.
2 *(without feeling)* insensible MASC & FEM

ℓ **number** NOUN
1 *(of a house, a phone, an account, in a list)* le
numéro MASC
my mobile number mon numéro de
portable
What's your number? Ton numéro de
téléphone, c'est quoi?
2 *(written figure)* le chiffre MASC
the third number is a 7 le troisième chiffre
est un 7
3 *(amount)* le nombre MASC
a large number of visitors un grand
nombre de visiteurs
• number plate
la plaque d'immatriculation

⬤ means the verb takes être to form the perfect

nun *NOUN*
la **religieuse** *FEM*

ℰ **nurse** *NOUN*
un **infirmier** *MASC*, une **infirmière** *FEM*
Janet's a nurse Janet est infirmière.

nursery *NOUN*
1 *(for children)* la **crèche** *FEM*
2 *(for plants)* la **pépinière** *FEM*
• **nursery school**
une école maternelle

nursing *NOUN*
la **profession d'infirmière** *(for a female nurse)*, d'**infirmier** *(for a male nurse)*
to go into nursing devenir ◐ [81] infirmière *(female nurse)*, infirmier *(male nurse)*

nut *NOUN*
1 *(walnut)* la **noix** *FEM*
2 *(almond)* une **amande** *FEM*
3 *(peanut)* la **cacahuète** *FEM*
4 *(for a bolt)* un **écrou** *MASC*

nylon *NOUN*
le **nylon** *MASC*
made of nylon en nylon

Oo

oak *NOUN*
le **chêne** *MASC*

oar *NOUN*
la **rame** *FEM*

oasis *NOUN*
une **oasis** *FEM*

oats *NOUN*
l'**avoine** *FEM*

obedient *ADJECTIVE*
obéissant *MASC*, **obéissante** *FEM*

obese *ADJECTIVE*
obèse *MASC & FEM*

obesity *NOUN*
l'**obésité** *FEM*

to **obey** *VERB*
1 *(a person)* **obéir** [2] **à**
You must obey your team leader.
Il faut que tu obéisses à ton chef d'équipe.
2 **to obey the rules** **respecter** [1] **le règlement**
You must obey the rules. Il faut que tu respectes le règlement.

to **object** *VERB* ▸ SEE **object** *NOUN*
soulever [50] **des objections**

object *NOUN* ▸ SEE **object** *VERB*
un **objet** *MASC*

objection *NOUN*
une **objection** *FEM*

oblong *ADJECTIVE*
rectangulaire *MASC & FEM*

oboe *NOUN*
le **hautbois** *MASC*
to play the oboe jouer [1] du hautbois

obscene *ADJECTIVE*
obscène *MASC & FEM*

obsessed *ADJECTIVE*
obsédé *MASC*, **obsédée** *FEM*
Kat's obsessed with her diet. Kat est obsédée par son régime.

obsession *NOUN*
une **obsession**
She has an obsession with cleanliness. Elle est obsédée par la propreté.

obstacle *NOUN*
un **obstacle** *MASC*

obstinate *ADJECTIVE*
têtu *MASC*, **têtue** *FEM*

to **obstruct** *VERB*
(the traffic, a person) **gêner** [1]

to **obtain** *VERB*
obtenir [77]

obvious *ADJECTIVE*
évident *MASC*, **évidente** *FEM*

obviously *ADVERB*
1 *(of course)* **bien sûr**
'Do you want to come too?' — 'Obviously.'
'Veux-tu venir avec nous?' — 'Bien sûr.'
2 *(visibly)* **manifestement**
The house is obviously empty. La maison est manifestement vide.

occasion *NOUN*
une **occasion** *FEM*
a special occasion une grande occasion

occasionally *ADVERB*
de temps en temps
I see her occasionally. Je la vois de temps en temps.

occupation *NOUN*
1 *(job)* la **profession** *FEM*
2 *(of a country)* l'**occupation** *FEM*

occupied *ADJECTIVE*
occupé *MASC*, **occupée** *FEM*

to **occur** *VERB*
1 *(to happen)* **avoir** [5] **lieu**
The accident occurred on Monday.

L'accident a eu lieu lundi.
2 *(to come to mind)* **It occurs to me that ...** Il me vient à l'esprit que ...
It never occurred to me. Cela ne m'est pas venu à l'idée.

ocean NOUN
un **océan** MASC

o'clock ADVERB
It's one o'clock. Il est une heure.
Jane's arriving at ten o'clock. Jane arrive à dix heures.

October NOUN
octobre MASC
Alex's birthday is in October. L'anniversaire d'Alex est en octobre.

WORD TIP Months of the year and days of the week start with small letters in French.

octopus NOUN
la **pieuvre** FEM

ℰ **odd** ADJECTIVE
1 *(strange)* **bizarre** MASC & FEM
an odd flavour un goût bizarre
That's odd. C'est bizarre.
2 *(in numbers)* **impair** MASC, **impaire** FEM
Three is an odd number. Trois est un chiffre impair.

ℰ **of** PREPOSITION
1 *(in general)* **de**
a kilo of tomatoes un kilo de tomates
the end of my work la fin de mon travail
two of us deux d'entre nous
2 *(in dates)* **the sixth of June** le six juin
3 **made of** en
a bracelet made of silver un bracelet en argent
4 *(followed by the)* **the name of the flower** le nom de la fleur
the beginning of the concert le début du concert
the parents of the children les parents des enfants
5 **of it, of them** en
We ate a lot of it. Nous en avons mangé beaucoup.
He's selling three of them. Il en vend trois.

WORD TIP en goes before the verb.

off ADJECTIVE, ADVERB, PREPOSITION
1 *(electrical things)* **éteint** MASC, **éteinte** FEM
Is the telly off? Est-ce que la télé est éteinte?
Could you turn off the light? Est-ce que tu peux éteindre la lumière?
2 *(tap, water, gas)* **fermé** MASC, **fermée** FEM
The tap's off. Le robinet est fermé.

3 *(when supply is cut)* **coupé** MASC, **coupée** FEM
The gas and electricity were off. Le gaz et l'électricité étaient coupés.
4 **to be off** s'en aller ☉ [7]
I'm off. Je m'en vais.
5 **a day off** un jour de congé
to be off sick être [6] malade
Maya's off school today. Maya n'est pas à l'école aujourd'hui.
6 *(cancelled)* **annulé** MASC, **annulée** FEM
The match is off. Le match est annulé.
7 *(in prices)* **'20% off shoes'** '20% de remise sur les chaussures'

offence NOUN
1 *(crime)* le **délit** MASC
2 **to take offence** s'offenser [1]

to **offer** VERB ▶ SEE **offer** NOUN
1 *(a present, reward, job)* **offrir** [56]
He offered her a chair. Il lui a offert une chaise.
2 **to offer to do something** proposer [1] de faire quelque chose
Ben offered to drive me to the station. Ben m'a proposé de me conduire à la gare.

offer NOUN ▶ SEE **offer** VERB
1 une **offre** FEM
a job offer une offre d'emploi
2 **'On special offer'** 'En promotion'

ℰ **office** NOUN
le **bureau** MASC *(PL* les **bureaux***)*
He's at the office. Il est au bureau.

officer NOUN
un **officier** NOUN

official ADJECTIVE
officiel MASC, **officielle** FEM

off-licence NOUN
le **magasin de vins et de spiritueux**

offside ADJECTIVE
(player) **hors jeu**

ℰ **often** ADVERB
souvent
He's often late. Il est souvent en retard.
Do you see Rosie often? Est-ce que tu vois Rosie souvent?

ℰ **oil** NOUN
1 *(in general)* l'**huile** FEM
2 *(crude oil)* le **pétrole** MASC
• **oil painting**
la peinture à l'huile
• **oil rig**
la plateforme pétrolière
• **oil slick**
la marée noire
• **oil tanker**
le pétrolier

☉ means the verb takes être to form the perfect

ointment NOUN
   la **pommade** FEM

ℓ **okay** ADJECTIVE
1 **d'accord**
    Okay, tomorrow at ten. D'accord, demain
    à dix heures.
2 (all right) **pas mal**
    The film was okay. Le film n'était pas mal.
3 (not ill) **Are you okay?** Ça va?
    I'm okay now. Ça va mieux maintenant.
4 (person) **sympa** INVARIABLE ADJECTIVE
    Daisy's okay. Daisy est sympa.

   WORD TIP sympa never changes.

ℓ **old** ADJECTIVE
1 (in general) **vieux** MASC, **vieil** MASC, **vieille**
    FEM, **vieux** MASC PL, **vieilles** FEM PL
    an old man un vieux monsieur
    an old lady une vieille dame
    an old tree un vieil arbre
2 (when talking about age) **a two-year-old**
    child un enfant de deux ans
    old people les personnes âgées
    How old are you? Tu as quel âge?
    James is ten years old. James a dix ans.
3 (when comparing ages) **my older sister** ma
    sœur aînée
    She's older than me. Elle est plus âgée que
    moi.
    He's a year older than me. Il a un an de plus
    que moi.
4 (previous) **ancien** MASC, **ancienne** FEM
    It's their old address. C'est leur ancienne
    adresse.

   WORD TIP ancien and ancienne come before
   the noun.

• **old age**
  la vieillesse
• **old age pensioner**
  le retraité (man), la retraitée (woman)

old-fashioned ADJECTIVE
1 (clothes, music, style) **démodé** MASC,
    démodée FEM
2 (person) **vieux jeu**
    My parents are so old-fashioned. Mes
    parents sont si vieux jeu.

olive NOUN
   une **olive** FEM
• **olive oil**
  l'**huile** d'olive FEM

Olympic Games, **Olympics** PLURAL NOUN
   les **Jeux Olympiques** MASC PL

🔵 **OLYMPIC GAMES**

A Frenchman, Baron Pierre de Coubertin,
organised the first modern Olympic Games in
1896.

omelette NOUN
   une **omelette** FEM
   a cheese omelette une omelette au
   fromage

ℓ **on** ADJECTIVE ► SEE **on** PREPOSITION
1 (TV, light, oven) **to be on** être [6] allumé
    MASC, **allumée** FEM
    All the lights were on. Toutes les lumières
    étaient allumées.
2 (machine) être [6] **en marche**
    The dishwasher is on. Le lave-vaisselle est
    en marche.
3 (showing) **What's on on TV?** Qu'est-ce qu'il
    y a à la télé?
    What's on at the cinema? Qu'est-ce qui
    passe au cinéma?

ℓ **on** PREPOSITION ► SEE **on** ADJECTIVE
1 (saying where) **sur**
    on the desk sur le bureau
    on the beach sur la plage
2 (saying when) **on 21st March** le 21 mars
    He's arriving on Tuesday. Il arrive mardi.
    It's shut on Saturdays. C'est fermé le
    samedi.
    On rainy days I take the train. Quand il
    pleut je prends le train.
3 (on buses, trains) **She arrived on the bus.**
    Elle est arrivée en bus.
    I met Jackie on the bus. J'ai vu Jackie dans
    le bus.
    I slept on the plane. J'ai dormi dans l'avion.
    Let's go on our bikes! Allons-y à vélo!
4 (with activities) **on holiday** en vacances
    to be on strike être en grève
5 (with media) **on TV** à la télé
    on the radio à la radio
    on video en vidéo

ℓ **once** ADVERB
1 **une fois**
    once a day une fois par jour
    more than once plus d'une fois
    I've tried once already. J'ai déjà essayé une
    fois.
    Try once more. Essaie encore une fois.
2 (without delay) **at once** tout de suite
    The doctor came at once. Le médecin est
    venu tout de suite.
3 (at the same time) **at once** à la fois
    I can't do two things at once. Je ne peux
    pas faire deux choses à la fois.

ℓ indicates key words

one NUMBER ▶ SEE **one** PRONOUN
  un MASC, une FEM
  one son un fils
  one apple une pomme
  at one o'clock à une heure

one PRONOUN ▶ SEE **one** NUMBER
  1 on
    One never knows. On ne sait jamais.
  2 this one celui-ci MASC, celle-ci FEM
    I like that bike, but this one's cheaper.
    J'aime bien ce vélo-là, mais celui-ci est
    moins cher.
    Do you want the red dress or this one?
    Veux-tu la robe rouge ou celle-ci?
    these ones ceux-ci MASC, celles-ci FEM
    I'd like these trainers but my brother
    wants these ones. Je voudrais ces baskets
    mais mon frère veut ceux-ci.
    'Which shoes do you like best?' — 'I like
    these ones.' 'Quelles chaussures préfères-
    tu?' — 'J'aime celles-ci.'
  3 that one celui-là MASC, celle-là FEM
    'Which video?' — 'That one.' 'Quelle
    vidéo?' — 'Celle-là.'
    those ones ceux-là MASC PL, celles-là FEM PL
    And as for the earrings, I prefer those
    ones. Et quant aux boucles d'oreille, je
    préfère celles-là.
  4 which one? lequel? MASC, laquelle? FEM
    'She borrowed a skirt from me.' — 'Which
    one?' 'Elle m'a emprunté une jupe.' —
    'Laquelle?'
    'My foot's hurting.' — 'Which one?' 'J'ai
    mal au pied.' — 'Auquel?'

    WORD TIP à+ lequel become auquel.

one's ADJECTIVE
  (before a masc noun) son, (before a fem
  noun) sa, (before a plural noun) ses
  One does one's best. On fait de son mieux.
  to wash one's hands se laver ⬤ [1] les mains

oneself PRONOUN
  1 to wash oneself se laver ⬤ [1]
    to hurt oneself se blesser ⬤ [1]
  2 (for emphasis) soi-même
    One has to do everything oneself. Il faut
    tout faire soi-même.
  3 by oneself tout seul MASC, toute seule FEM

ℓ **one-way street** NOUN
  le sens unique

ℓ **onion** NOUN
  un oignon MASC

ℓ **only** ADJECTIVE ▶ SEE **only** ADVERB
  1 (one) seul MASC, seule FEM
    the only free seat la seule place libre
    It was the only thing to do. C'était la seule
    chose à faire.

  2 (children) an only child un enfant unique
    I'm an only child. Je suis enfant unique.

ℓ **only** ADVERB, CONJUNCTION ▶ SEE **only** ADJECTIVE
  1 (with a verb) ne ... que
    They've only got two bedrooms. Ils n'ont
    que deux chambres.
    Anne's only free on Fridays. Anne n'est
    libre que le vendredi.
    There are only three left. Il n'en reste que
    trois.
  2 (just) seulement
    'How long did they stay?' — 'Only two
    days.' 'Ils sont restés combien de temps?'
    — 'Deux jours seulement.'

onto PREPOSITION
  sur

ℓ to **open** VERB ▶ SEE **open** ADJECTIVE, NOUN
  1 (a door, a box) ouvrir [30]
    Can you open the door? Est-ce que tu peux
    ouvrir la porte?
    The bank opens at nine. La banque ouvre à
    neuf heures.
    What time do you open? Vous ouvrez à
    quelle heure?
  2 (by itself) s'ouvrir [30]
    The door opened slowly. La porte s'est
    ouverte lentement.

ℓ **open** ADJECTIVE ▶ SEE **open** VERB, NOUN
  ouvert MASC, ouverte FEM
  The door's open. La porte est ouverte.
  Are the shops still open? Est-ce que les
  magasins sont toujours ouverts?

open NOUN ▶ SEE **open** VERB, ADJECTIVE
  in the open en plein air
  I love eating in the open. J'adore manger
  en plein air.

open-air ADJECTIVE
  en plein air
  an open-air swimming pool une piscine en
  plein air

opening NOUN
  1 (space) une ouverture FEM
  2 (opportunity) une occasion FEM
  3 (for a job) un débouché MASC

opera NOUN
  un opéra MASC

to **operate** VERB
  (medically) opérer [24]

operation NOUN
  une opération FEM
  to have an operation se faire ⬤ [10] opérer
  She's had an operation. Elle s'est fait
  opérer.

⬤ means the verb takes être to form the perfect

℘ **opinion** NOUN
un **avis** MASC
in my opinion à mon avis
• **opinion poll** le sondage

opponent NOUN
un & une **adversaire** MASC & FEM

opportunity NOUN
une **occasion** FEM
to have the opportunity of doing something avoir [5] l'occasion de faire quelque chose

opposed ADJECTIVE
to be opposed to something être [6] opposé à quelque chose

℘ **opposite** ADJECTIVE ▸ SEE **opposite** ADVERB, NOUN, PREPOSITION
1 *(direction, side, view)* **opposé** MASC, **opposée** FEM
She went off in the opposite direction. Elle est partie dans la direction opposée.
2 *(facing)* **d'en face**
Joe lives in the house opposite. Joe habite dans la maison d'en face.

℘ **opposite** ADVERB, PREPOSITION ▸ SEE **opposite** ADJECTIVE, NOUN
1 **en face**
They live opposite. Ils habitent en face.
2 **en face de**
The school's opposite the station. L'école est en face de la gare.

opposite NOUN ▸ SEE **opposite** ADJECTIVE, ADVERB, PREPOSITION
le **contraire** MASC

opposition NOUN
l'**opposition** FEM

℘ **optician** NOUN
un **opticien** MASC, une **opticienne** FEM

optimistic ADJECTIVE
optimiste MASC & FEM

option NOUN
le **choix** MASC
We have no option. Nous n'avons pas le choix.

optional ADJECTIVE
facultatif MASC, **facultative** FEM
an optional course un cours facultatif

℘ **or** CONJUNCTION
1 *(in general)* **ou**
today or Tuesday? aujourd'hui ou mardi?
Is he English or French? Il est anglais ou français?
2 *(after not)* **ni**
not in June or July ni en juin ni en juillet
I don't have a cat or a dog. Je n'ai ni chat

ni chien.
3 *(or else)* **sinon**
Phone Mum, or she'll worry. Appelle maman, sinon elle va s'inquiéter.

oral NOUN
(an exam) un **oral** MASC *(PL* les **oraux)**
the French oral l'oral de français

℘ **orange** ADJECTIVE ▸ SEE **orange** NOUN
orange INVARIABLE ADJ
my orange socks mes chaussettes orange

WORD TIP orange never changes.

orange NOUN ▸ SEE **orange** ADJECTIVE
(the fruit) une **orange** FEM
an orange juice un jus d'orange

orchestra NOUN
un **orchestre** MASC

℘ **to order** VERB ▸ SEE **order** NOUN
1 *(in a restaurant, shop)* **commander** [1]
2 *(a taxi)* **réserver** [1]

℘ **order** NOUN ▸ SEE **order** VERB
1 *(arrangement)* l'**ordre** MASC
in the right order dans le bon ordre
in the wrong order dans le mauvais ordre
in alphabetical order dans l'ordre alphabétique
2 *(for buying)* la **commande** FEM
Can I take your orders? Puis-je prendre vos commandes?
3 **out of order** en panne
The lift is out of order again. L'ascenseur est de nouveau en panne.
4 **in order to do something** pour faire quelque chose
We hurried in order to be on time. Nous nous sommes dépêchés pour arriver à l'heure.

℘ **ordinary** ADJECTIVE
ordinaire MASC & FEM

organ NOUN
1 *(musical instrument)* un **orgue** MASC
to play the organ jouer de l'orgue
2 *(of the body)* un **organe** MASC

organic ADJECTIVE
(food) **biologique** MASC & FEM

organization NOUN
une **organisation** FEM

to organize VERB
organiser [1]

orienteering NOUN
la **course d'orientation**

original ADJECTIVE
original MASC, **originale** FEM, **originaux**

MASC PL, **originales** FEM PL
the original version la version originale

originally ADVERB
à l'origine
Originally we wanted to take the car. À l'origine, nous voulions prendre la voiture.

Orkneys PLURAL NOUN
the Orkneys les Orcades FEM PL

ornament NOUN
le bibelot MASC

orphan NOUN
un orphelin MASC, une orpheline FEM

ostrich NOUN
une autruche FEM

♂ **other** DETERMINER, PRONOUN
1 autre MASC & FEM
the other day l'autre jour
the other two cars les deux autres voitures
Where are the others? Où sont les autres?
Give me the other one. Donne-moi l'autre.
2 (in expressions) every other week une semaine sur deux
somebody or other quelqu'un
something or other quelque chose
somewhere or other quelque part

otherwise ADVERB, CONJUNCTION
1 (or else) sinon
I'll phone home, otherwise they'll worry. Je vais appeler chez moi, sinon ils vont s'inquiéter.
2 (in other ways) à part ça
The flat's a bit small but otherwise it's lovely. L'appartement n'est pas très grand mais à part ça il est très bien.

♂ **ought** VERB [8]
I ought to go now. Je devrais partir maintenant.
They ought to know the address. Ils devraient connaître l'adresse.
You oughtn't to have any problems. Vous ne devriez pas avoir de problèmes.

WORD TIP ought is translated by the conditional tense of devoir: je devrais, tu devrais etc.

our ADJECTIVE
1 (with singular nouns) notre
our house notre maison
our family notre famille
Do you like our garden? Est-ce que tu aimes notre jardin?
2 (with plural nouns) nos
our parents nos parents
3 (with parts of the body) le, la, les
We're washing our hands. Nous nous lavons les mains.

ours PRONOUN
1 (for masc singular nouns) le nôtre
Their garden's bigger than ours. Leur jardin est plus grand que le nôtre.
2 (for fem singular nouns) la nôtre
Their house is smaller than ours. Leur maison est plus petite que la nôtre.
3 (for plural nouns) les nôtres
They've invited their friends and we've invited ours. Ils ont invité leurs amis et nous avons invité les nôtres.
4 (belonging to us) à nous
It's ours. C'est à nous.
The green one's ours. Le vert est à nous.
Will is a friend of ours. Will est un ami à nous.

ourselves PRONOUN
1 nous (second nous in these examples)
We introduced ourselves. Nous nous sommes présentés.
We really enjoyed ourselves. Nous nous sommes bien amusés.
2 (for emphasis) nous-mêmes
In the end we did it ourselves. Finalement nous l'avons fait nous-mêmes.

out ADJECTIVE ▶ SEE **out** ADVERB
éteint MASC, éteinte FEM
Are all the lights out? Est-ce que toutes les lumières sont éteintes?

♂ **out** ADVERB ▶ SEE **out** ADJECTIVE
1 (outside) It's cold out there. Il fait froid dehors.
out in the rain sous la pluie
They're out in the garden. Ils sont dans le jardin.
2 (showing movement) to go out sortir ⬤ [72]
She went out an hour ago. Elle est sortie il y a une heure.
to go out of the room sortir de la pièce
Are you going out this evening? Est-ce que tu sors ce soir?
3 (out of something) to drink out of a glass boire [22] dans un verre
He threw it out of the window. Il l'a jeté par la fenêtre.
She took the photo out of her bag. Elle a pris la photo dans son sac.
4 (not at home) to be out être [6] sorti MASC, sortie FEM
Mrs Barnes is out. Madame Barnes est sortie.

outdoor ADJECTIVE
1 (activity, sport) de plein air
2 (cinema, theatre, restaurant) en plein air

outdoors ADVERB
en plein air

⬤ means the verb takes être to form the perfect

outing NOUN
la **sortie** FEM

out-of-date ADJECTIVE
1 (not valid) **périmé** MASC, **périmée** FEM
My passport's out-of-date. Mon passeport est périmé.
2 (old-fashioned) **démodé** MASC, **démodée** FEM
This music is so out-of-date! Cette musique est tellement démodée!

ℓ **outside** ADJECTIVE, ADVERB, NOUN, PREPOSITION
1 (wall) **extérieur** MASC, **extérieure** FEM
2 (outside surface) l'**extérieur** MASC
It's blue on the outside. C'est bleu à l'extérieur.
3 (in the open) **dehors**
It's cold outside. Il fait froid dehors.
4 (a cafe, theatre) **devant**
I'll meet you outside the cinema. On se retrouve devant le cinéma.

outskirts NOUN
la **périphérie** FEM
on the outskirts of Glasgow à la périphérie de Glasgow

outstanding ADJECTIVE
exceptionnel MASC, **exceptionnelle** FEM

oven NOUN
le **four** MASC
I've put it in the oven. Je l'ai mis au four.

over ADJECTIVE ▸ SEE **over** ADVERB, PREPOSITION
terminé MASC, **terminée** FEM
when the meeting's over quand la réunion sera terminée
It's all over now. C'est terminé maintenant.

ℓ **over** ADVERB, PREPOSITION ▸ SEE **over** ADJECTIVE
1 (above) **au-dessus de**
There's a mirror over the sideboard. Il y a un miroir au-dessus du buffet.
2 (showing movement) **par-dessus**
She jumped over the fence. Elle a sauté par-dessus la clôture.
3 **over here** par ici
The drinks are over here. Les boissons sont par ici.
4 **over there** là-bas
She's over there. Elle est là-bas.
5 (with numbers) **plus de**
It will cost over a hundred pounds. Ça coûtera plus de cent livres.
He's over sixty. Il a plus de soixante ans.
6 (during) **pendant**
over the weekend pendant le week-end
over Christmas à Noël
7 (in expressions) over the phone par téléphone
all over the place partout

overcast ADJECTIVE
couvert MASC, **couverte** FEM
The sky was overcast. Le ciel était couvert.

overcrowded ADJECTIVE
bondé MASC, **bondée** FEM
an overcrowded room une pièce bondée

overdose NOUN
1 (of drugs) une **overdose** FEM
2 (of medicine) la **surdose** FEM

to **overflow** VERB
déborder [1]

overseas ADVERB
à l'**étranger**
Dave works overseas. Dave travaille à l'étranger.

to **oversleep** VERB
se **réveiller** ◎ [1] trop tard
Matt overslept this morning. Matt s'est réveillé trop tard ce matin.

ℓ to **overtake** VERB
(cars) **doubler** [1]

ℓ **overtime** NOUN
to work overtime **faire** [10] des heures supplémentaires
Dad works a lot of overtime. Papa fait beaucoup d'heures supplémentaires.

overweight ADJECTIVE
trop gros MASC, **trop grosse** FEM

ℓ to **owe** VERB
devoir [8]
to owe somebody something devoir quelque chose à quelqu'un
I owe Rick ten pounds. Je dois dix livres à Rick.

owing ADJECTIVE
owing to en **raison de**
The school is closed owing to the snow. L'école est fermée en raison des chutes de neige.

ℓ **owl** NOUN
le **hibou** MASC (PL les **hiboux**)

ℓ to **own** VERB ▸ SEE **own** ADJECTIVE
posséder [24]

ℓ **own** ADJECTIVE ▸ SEE **own** VERB
1 **propre** MASC & FEM
my own computer mon propre ordinateur
I've got my own room. J'ai une chambre à moi.

> **WORD TIP** propre comes before the noun when it means own.

2 **on your own** tout seul MASC, **toute seule** FEM

ℓ indicates key words

Amy did it on her own. Amy l'a fait toute
seule.

owner NOUN
le & la **propriétaire** MASC & FEM

oxygen NOUN
l'**oxygène** MASC

oyster NOUN
une **huître** FEM

ozone layer NOUN
la **couche d'ozone**
a hole in the the ozone layer un trou dans
la couche d'ozone

Pp

pace NOUN
1 (step) le **pas** MASC
2 (the speed you walk at) une **allure** FEM
They were walking at a brisk pace. Ils
marchaient à vive allure.

Pacific NOUN
the Pacific Ocean l'océan Pacifique MASC

ℓ to **pack** VERB ▸ SEE **pack** NOUN
1 faire [10] ses bagages
I've packed. J'ai fait mes bagages.
2 to pack your case faire sa valise
I'll pack my case. Je ferai ma valise.
Have you packed your trainers? Est-ce que
tu as mis tes baskets dans la valise?

pack NOUN ▸ SEE **pack** VERB
1 le **paquet** MASC
2 a pack of cards un jeu de cartes

ℓ **package** NOUN
le **paquet** MASC
A package came in the post. Un paquet est
arrivé par la poste.

package holiday, **package tour** NOUN
le **voyage organisé**
to go on a package holiday to Greece aller
◎[7] en Grèce en voyage organisé

packed ADJECTIVE
bondé MASC, bondée FEM
The hall was packed. La salle était bondée.
The beach is packed with tourists in
summer. La plage est pleine de touristes
en été.
• packed lunch
le panier-repas

ℓ **packet** NOUN
1 le **paquet** MASC
a packet of biscuits un paquet de biscuits
2 (bag) le **sachet** MASC

packing NOUN
to do your packing faire [10] ses bagages

pad NOUN
(of paper) le **bloc-notes** MASC

paddle NOUN
(for a canoe) la **pagaie** FEM

padlock NOUN
le **cadenas** MASC

ℓ **page** NOUN
la **page** FEM
on page seven à la page sept

ℓ **pain** NOUN
1 la **douleur** FEM
to have a pain in ... avoir [5] mal à ...
I've got a pain in my leg. J'ai mal à la
jambe.
The pain's gone. Je n'ai plus mal.
2 to be a pain in the neck être [6] pénible
She's a real pain in the neck! Elle est
vraiment pénible!

painful ADJECTIVE
douloureux MASC, douloureuse FEM

painkiller NOUN
un **analgésique** MASC

to **paint** VERB ▸ SEE **paint** NOUN
peindre [60]
to paint the walls blue peindre les murs
en bleu
The door is painted red. La porte est peinte
en rouge.

paint NOUN ▸ SEE **paint** VERB
la **peinture** FEM
two pots of paint deux pots de peinture
'Wet paint' 'Peinture fraîche'
• paintbrush
le pinceau (PL les pinceaux)

painter NOUN
le **peintre** MASC

ℓ **painting** NOUN
1 (picture) le **tableau** MASC (PL les **tableaux**)
a painting by Bacon un tableau de Bacon
2 (the activity) la **peinture**
I love painting. J'adore la peinture.

ℓ **pair** NOUN
1 (in general) la **paire** FEM
a pair of socks une paire de chaussettes
a pair of scissors une paire de ciseaux
a pair of jeans un jean
2 to work in pairs travailler [1] en groupes
de deux
We're working in pairs. Nous travaillons en
groupes de deux.

◎ means the verb takes être to form the perfect

Pakistan NOUN
le Pakistan MASC

Pakistani ADJECTIVE ▸ SEE **Pakistani** NOUN
pakistanais MASC, pakistanaise FEM

Pakistani NOUN ▸ SEE **Pakistani** ADJECTIVE
un Pakistanais MASC, une Pakistanaise FEM

palace NOUN
le palais MASC
the Palace of Versailles le palais de
Versailles

℘ **pale** ADJECTIVE
pâle MASC & FEM
pale green vert pâle
She looks very pale. Elle est très pâle.
to go pale pâlir [2]

palm NOUN
1 (of your hand) la paume FEM
2 (tree) le palmier MASC

pan NOUN
1 (saucepan) la casserole FEM
a pan of water une casserole d'eau
2 (frying-pan) la poêle FEM
Heat some oil in a pan. Faire chauffer de
l'huile dans une poêle.

℘ **pancake** NOUN
la crêpe FEM
pancakes with jam des crêpes à la confiture

panda NOUN
le panda MASC

panel NOUN
1 (in a TV show) les invités MASC PL
Let me introduce our panel. Je vous
présente nos invités.
2 (for walls) le panneau MASC (PL les
panneaux)
a wooden panel un panneau en bois

to **panic** VERB ▸ SEE **panic** NOUN
s'affoler [1]
I panicked. Je me suis affolé.
Don't panic! Pas de panique!

panic NOUN ▸ SEE **panic** VERB
la panique FEM
She's in a complete panic. Elle est
complètement affolée.
to cause panic provoquer [1] la panique

pannier NOUN
la sacoche FEM

panther NOUN
la panthère FEM

panties NOUN
la petite culotte

pantomime NOUN
le spectacle pour enfants

pants PLURAL NOUN
le slip MASC
a pair of pants un slip

℘ **paper** NOUN
1 le papier MASC
a sheet of paper une feuille de papier
2 (made of paper) a paper cup un gobelet en
carton
3 (newspaper) le journal MASC (PL les
journaux)
the Sunday papers les journaux de
dimanche
• paperback
le livre de poche
• paper towel
un essuie-tout (PL les essuie-tout)

parachute NOUN
le parachute MASC

parachuting NOUN
le parachutisme MASC
to go parachuting faire [10] du
parachutisme

parade NOUN
le défilé MASC
There are street parades. Il y a des défilés
dans la rue.

paradise NOUN
le paradis MASC

paraffin NOUN
le pétrole MASC

paragraph NOUN
le paragraphe MASC
I wrote a paragraph in French. J'ai écrit un
paragraphe en français.

parallel ADJECTIVE
parallèle MASC & FEM
parallel lines des lignes parallèles

paralysed ADJECTIVE
paralysé MASC, paralysée FEM

℘ **parcel** NOUN
le paquet MASC

pardon EXCLAMATION
Pardon? Pardon?

℘ **parent** NOUN
le parent MASC
a parents' evening une réunion pour les
parents d'élèves
My parents are Scottish. Mes parents sont
écossais.

Paris NOUN
Paris
to live in Paris habiter à Paris
to go to Paris aller ◎ [7] à Paris

A B C D E F G H I J K L M N O P Q R S T U V W X Y Z

℘ indicates key words

Parisian *ADJECTIVE* ▶ SEE **Parisian** *NOUN*
parisien *MASC*, parisienne *FEM*

> **WORD TIP** Adjectives never have capitals in French, even for nationality or regional origin.

Parisian *NOUN* ▶ SEE **Parisian** *ADJECTIVE*
un Parisien *MASC*, une Parisienne *FEM*

to **park** *VERB* ▶ SEE **park** *NOUN*
1 se garer ⊚ [1]
Can we park here? Est-ce qu'on peut se garer ici?
2 *(a car)* garer [1]
Where did you park the car? Où avez-vous garé la voiture?

🎵 **park** *NOUN* ▶ SEE **park** *VERB*
1 le parc *MASC*
We're going for a walk in the park. On va se promener dans le parc.
2 **a car park** un parking

> ⊙ **PARK**
> There are two great theme parks (parcs d'attractions or parcs de loisirs) in the Paris region: Disneyland Paris at Marne-la-Vallée and Parc Astérix, based on the cartoon character, at Plailly.

parking *NOUN*
le stationnement *MASC*
'No parking' 'Stationnement interdit'
• **parking meter**
le parcmètre
• **parking ticket**
la contravention

parliament *NOUN*
le parlement *MASC*

parrot *NOUN*
le perroquet *MASC*

parsley *NOUN*
le persil *MASC*

🎵 **part** *NOUN*
1 la partie *FEM*
part of the garden une partie du jardin
the funniest part of the film le passage le plus drôle du film
2 **to be part of something** faire [10] partie de quelque chose
It's part of my homework. Ça fait partie de mes devoirs.
3 **to take part in something** participer [1] à quelque chose
I didn't take part in the competition. Je n'ai pas participé au concours.
4 *(in a play)* le rôle *MASC*
I play the part of Juliet. Je joue le rôle de Juliet.

particular *ADJECTIVE*
particulier *MASC*, particulière *FEM*
nothing in particular rien de particulier
I don't like that particular song. Je n'aime pas cette chanson-là.

particularly *ADVERB*
1 *(very much)* particulièrement
It's not particularly interesting. Ce n'est pas particulièrement intéressant.
2 *(in particular)* surtout
Particularly as it was our last day. Surtout que c'était notre dernier jour.

parting *NOUN*
(in your hair) la raie *FEM*

partly *ADVERB*
en partie
That's partly why we missed the train. C'est en partie pourquoi nous avons raté notre train.

partner *NOUN*
1 *(in games, in life)* le partenaire *MASC*
Who's your partner? Ton partenaire, c'est qui?
2 *(in business)* un associé *MASC*, une associée *FEM*

partridge *NOUN*
la perdrix *FEM*

part-time *ADJECTIVE, ADVERB*
à temps partiel
part-time work le travail à temps partiel
to work part-time travailler [1] à temps partiel
She works part-time. Elle travaille à temps partiel.

🎵 **party** *NOUN*
1 *(in general)* la fête *FEM*
a Christmas party une fête de Noël
We've been invited to a party. Nous sommes invités à une fête.
There's a party at Josh's. Il y a une fête chez Josh.
2 *(formal evening event)* la soirée *FEM*
3 *(group)* le groupe *MASC*
a party of schoolchildren un groupe d'élèves
a rescue party une équipe de secours
4 *(in politics)* le parti *MASC*
a political party un parti politique
• **party game**
le jeu de société (PL les jeux de société)

🎵 to **pass** *VERB* ▶ SEE **pass** *NOUN*
1 *(a place, building)* passer [1] ⊚ devant
We passed your house. Nous sommes passés devant chez toi.
2 *(a car)* doubler [1]

⊚ means the verb takes être to form the perfect

A truck tried to pass us. Un camion a
essayé de nous doubler.
3 **to pass something to somebody** passer
quelque chose à quelqu'un
Could you pass me the paper? Peux-tu me
passer le journal?
She passed me a plate. Elle m'a passé une
assiette.
Pass the ball! Passe-moi le ballon!
4 *(time)* passer [1]
The time passed slowly. Le temps passait
lentement.
5 *(in an exam)* être [6] reçu
to pass an exam être reçu à un examen
Did you pass? Est-ce que tu as été reçu?

pass NOUN ▶ SEE **pass** VERB
1 *(to let you in)* le **laissez-passer** MASC *(PL les
laissez-passer)*
2 *(for transport)* la **carte** FEM
a bus pass une carte de bus
3 *(in sport)* la **passe** FEM
4 *(in the mountains)* le **col** MASC

passage NOUN
1 *(corridor)* le **couloir** MASC
2 *(text)* le **passage** MASC
Read the passage aloud. Lis le passage à
haute voix.

ℓ**passenger** NOUN
1 *(in a car, plane, ship)* le **passager** MASC, la
passagère FEM
2 *(in trains, buses)* le **voyageur** MASC, la
voyageuse FEM

passerby NOUN
le **passant** MASC, la **passante** FEM

passion NOUN
la **passion** FEM

passionate ADJECTIVE
passionné MASC, **passionnée** FEM

passive NOUN
(Grammar) le **passif** MASC

Passover NOUN
la **Pâque juive**

ℓ**passport** NOUN
le **passeport** MASC
an EU passport un passeport de l'UE
They check passports at the border. Ils
contrôlent les passeports à la frontière.

password NOUN
le **mot de passe**
What's your password? Quel est ton mot
de passe?
to change your password changer [52] ton
mot de passe.

past ADJECTIVE ▶ SEE ADVERB, NOUN, PREPOSITION
1 *(recent)* **dernier** MASC, **dernière** FEM
in the past few weeks pendant les
dernières semaines
2 *(over)* **fini** MASC, **finie** FEM
Winter is past. L'hiver est fini.

past NOUN ▶ SEE **past** ADJECTIVE, ADVERB, PREPOSITION
1 *(the old days)* le **passé** MASC
in the past dans le passé
2 *(Grammar)* **the past (tense)** le **passé**
a verb in the past un verbe au passé

ℓ**past** ADVERB, PREPOSITION ▶ SEE **past** ADJ, NOUN
1 **to go past something** passer ◎ [1] devant
quelque chose
We went past the school. Nous sommes
passés devant l'école.
Peter went past on his bike. Peter est passé
sur son vélo.
2 *(the other side of)* **après**
It's just past the post office. C'est juste
après la poste.
3 *(in time expressions)* **ten past six** six heures
dix
half past four quatre heures et demie
a quarter past two deux heures et quart

pasta NOUN
les **pâtes** FEM PL

to **paste** VERB
coller [1]
to paste cards into a notebook coller des
cartes dans un carnet
to cut and paste a table couper-coller un
tableau

pasteurized ADJECTIVE
pasteurisé MASC, **pasteurisée** FEM

pastry NOUN
1 *(dough)* la **pâte** FEM
to make pastry faire [10] une pâte
2 *(small cake)* la **pâtisserie** FEM

patch NOUN
1 *(for mending)* la **pièce** FEM
2 *(of snow, ice)* la **plaque** FEM
patches of black ice des plaques de verglas
3 *(of fog)* la **nappe** FEM
fog patches des nappes de brouillard
4 *(of blue sky)* le **coin** MASC

ℓ**path** NOUN
1 *(track)* le **chemin** MASC
a path through the wood un chemin à
travers le bois
2 *(very narrow)* le **sentier** MASC
a mountain path un sentier de montagne

pathetic ADJECTIVE
lamentable MASC & FEM
That's so pathetic! C'est vraiment

lamentable!

patience NOUN
1 la **patience** FEM
2 *(card game)* la **réussite** FEM

patient ADJECTIVE ▸ SEE **patient** NOUN
patient MASC, **patiente** FEM
She's very patient. Elle est très patiente.
Be patient! Patience!

patient NOUN ▸ SEE **patient** ADJECTIVE
le **patient** MASC, la **patiente** FEM

patiently ADVERB
avec **patience**

patio NOUN
la **terrasse** FEM
on the patio sur la terrasse

patrol NOUN
la **patrouille** FEM
to be out on patrol être [6] de patrouille
• **patrol car**
la voiture de police

pattern NOUN
1 *(on wallpaper, fabric)* le **motif** MASC
a pattern with stripes un motif à rayures
2 *(for dressmaking)* le **patron** MASC

pause NOUN
1 *(in a conversation)* le **silence** MASC
2 *(in an activity)* la **pause** FEM

ℓ **pavement** NOUN
le **trottoir** MASC
on the pavement sur le trottoir

paw NOUN
la **patte** FEM

pawn NOUN
le **pion** MASC

ℓ **to pay** VERB ▸ SEE **pay** NOUN
1 **payer** [59]
I'm paying. C'est moi qui paie.
Are they paying for you? Est-ce qu'ils
paient pour toi?
You have to pay cash. Il faut payer
comptant.
2 to pay for something **payer** [59] quelque
chose
Sophie paid for the pizzas. Sophie a payé
les pizzas.
It's all paid for. C'est tout payé.
3 to pay by credit card **régler** [24] par carte
de crédit
to pay by cheque régler par chèque
4 to pay somebody back **rembourser** [1]
quelqu'un
I haven't paid them back yet. Je ne les ai
pas encore remboursés.
5 to pay attention faire [10] attention

We weren't paying attention. On ne faisait
pas attention.
6 to pay a visit to somebody **rendre** [3] visite
à quelqu'un
I'm paying a visit to my cousins. Je rends
visite à mes cousins.
• **paydesk**
la **caisse**

pay NOUN ▸ SEE **pay** VERB
le **salaire** MASC

payment NOUN
1 le **paiement** MASC
to make a payment of £50 faire un
paiement de 50 livres sterling
2 *(of a bill)* le **règlement** MASC

pay phone NOUN
le **téléphone public**
I'm looking for a pay phone. Je cherche un
téléphone public.

PC NOUN
le **PC** MASC

ℓ **pea** NOUN
le **petit pois** MASC
I don't eat peas. Je ne mange pas de petits
pois.

ℓ **peace** NOUN
1 la **paix** FEM
They're trying to make peace. Ils essaient
de faire la paix.
2 *(of a place)* peace and quiet la **tranquillité**

peaceful ADJECTIVE
1 *(tranquil)* **paisible** MASC & FEM
It's a peaceful place. C'est un endroit
paisible.
2 *(without conflict)* **pacifique** MASC & FEM
to find a peaceful solution trouver une
solution pacifique

ℓ **peach** NOUN
la **pêche** FEM
a kilo of peaches un kilo de pêches

peacock NOUN
le **paon** MASC

peak NOUN
(of a mountain) le **pic** MASC
• **peak period**
la **période de pointe**
• **peak rate**
(Telephones) le **tarif rouge**

peak time NOUN
(for traffic) les **heures de pointe** FEM PL
at peak time aux heures de pointe

peanut NOUN
la **cacahuète** FEM

means the verb takes être to form the perfect

- **peanut butter**
  le beurre de cacahuètes

ℰ **pear** NOUN
  la **poire** FEM
  The pears are ripe. Les poires sont mûres.

pearl NOUN
  la **perle** FEM

ℰ **peasant** NOUN
  le **paysan** MASC, la **paysanne** FEM
  The word paysan is less old-fashioned than peasant.

pebble NOUN
1 *(on the road)* le **caillou** MASC *(PL les* **cailloux***)*
2 *(on a beach)* le **galet** MASC
  a pebble beach une plage de galets

peculiar ADJECTIVE
  bizarre MASC & FEM
  a peculiar noise un bruit bizarre

to **pedal** VERB ▶ SEE **pedal** NOUN
  pédaler [1]

pedal NOUN ▶ SEE **pedal** VERB
  la **pédale** FEM

pedal boat NOUN
  le **pédalo®** MASC

ℰ **pedestrian** NOUN
  le **piéton** MASC, la **piétonne** FEM
  It's dangerous for pedestrians. C'est dangereux pour les piétons.
- **pedestrian crossing**
  le passage piéton
- **pedestrian precinct**
  la zone piétonne

pee NOUN
  le **pipi** MASC *(informal)*
  to have a pee faire [10] pipi

to **peel** VERB ▶ SEE **peel** NOUN
  éplucher [1]
  Peel the potatoes. Épluchez les pommes de terre.

peel NOUN ▶ SEE **peel** VERB
1 *(of an apple)* la **peau** FEM
2 *(of an orange)* une **écorce** FEM

to **peer** VERB
  to peer at something regarder [1] quelque chose attentivement
  He was peering at the screen. Il regardait l'écran attentivement.

peg NOUN
1 *(hook)* la **patère** FEM
2 **a clothes peg** une pince à linge
3 **a tent peg** un piquet de tente

ℰ **pen** NOUN
  le **stylo** MASC

a felt pen un stylo-feutre
  I lent her my red pen. Je lui ai prêté mon stylo rouge.

to **penalize** VERB
  désavantager [52]
  This law penalizes the elderly. Cette loi désavantage les personnes âgées.

penalty NOUN
1 *(a fine)* une **amende** FEM
2 *(in football)* le **penalty** MASC
  to take a penalty tirer [1] un penalty
  to give a penalty siffler [1] un penalty
3 *(in rugby)* la **pénalité** FEM
- **penalty area**
  la surface de réparation

pence PLURAL NOUN
  les **pence** MASC PL

ℰ **pencil** NOUN
  le **crayon** MASC
  coloured pencils les crayons de couleur
  I wrote it in pencil first. Je l'ai écrit au crayon d'abord.
- **pencil case**
  la trousse
- **pencil sharpener**
  le taille-crayon

pendant NOUN
  le **pendentif** MASC

ℰ **penfriend** NOUN
  le **correspondant** MASC, la **correspondante** FEM
  I'd like to have a French penfriend. J'aimerais avoir un correspondant français.
  My penfriend's name is Maryse. Ma correspondante s'appelle Maryse.

penguin NOUN
  le **pingouin** MASC

penis NOUN
  le **pénis** MASC

penknife NOUN
  le **canif** MASC

penny NOUN
  le **penny** MASC

pension NOUN
  la **pension** FEM

pensioner NOUN
  le **retraité** MASC, la **retraitée** FEM

ℰ **people** PLURAL NOUN
1 les **gens** MASC PL
  people round here les gens d'ici
  most people la plupart des gens
  They're nice people. Ce sont des gens sympathiques.

I enjoy working with people. J'aime travailler avec les gens.

2 *(when you count them)* les **personnes** FEM PL
ten people dix personnes
several people plusieurs personnes
How many people have you invited? Tu as invité combien de personnes?

3 **people say that ...** on dit que ...
People say he's very rich. On dit qu'il est très riche.

pepper NOUN
1 *(spice)* le **poivre** MASC
2 *(vegetable)* le **poivron** MASC
a green pepper un poivron vert
• **peppermill**
le moulin à poivre

peppermint NOUN
1 *(herb)* la **menthe** FEM
2 *(sweet)* le **bonbon à la menthe**
• **peppermint tea**
le thé à la menthe

per PREPOSITION
par
It costs ten pounds per person. Ça coûte dix livres par personne.

per cent ADVERB
pour cent
sixty per cent of students soixante pour cent des étudiants

percentage NOUN
le **pourcentage** MASC

percussion NOUN
la **percussion** FEM
to play percussion jouer des percussions

♂ **perfect** ADJECTIVE ▸ SEE **perfect** NOUN
1 *(flawless)* **parfait** MASC, **parfaite** FEM
She speaks perfect French. Elle parle un français parfait.
The weather's perfect. Il fait un temps parfait.
2 *(ideal)* **idéal** MASC, **idéale** FEM, **idéaux** MASC PL, **idéales** FEM PL
It's the perfect place for a picnic. C'est l'endroit idéal pour un pique-nique.
We've found the perfect solution. Nous avons trouvé la solution idéale.

perfect NOUN ▸ SEE **perfect** ADJECTIVE
(Grammar) le **parfait** MASC
in the perfect au parfait

perfectly ADVERB
parfaitement

to **perform** VERB
1 *(a piece of music, play)* **jouer** [1]
2 *(a song)* **chanter** [1]

♂ **performance** NOUN
1 *(show)* le **spectacle** MASC
The performance starts at eight. Le spectacle commence à huit heures.
2 *(acting, playing a role)* une **interprétation** FEM
a wonderful performance of Macbeth une superbe interprétation de Macbeth

performer NOUN
un **artiste** MASC, une **artiste** FEM

♂ **perfume** NOUN
le **parfum** MASC
I bought her some perfume. Je lui ai acheté du parfum.

♂ **perhaps** ADVERB
peut-être
Perhaps it's in the drawer? Il est peut-être dans le tiroir?
Perhaps he's missed the train. Il a peut-être raté le train.

♂ **period** NOUN
1 *(length of time)* la **période** FEM
a two-year period une période de deux ans
the holiday period la période des vacances
over a period of three weeks pendant trois semaines
2 *(a lesson)* le **cours** MASC
a forty-five-minute period un cours de quarante-cinq minutes
I have a double period of French. J'ai deux cours de français à la suite.
3 *(menstruation)* les **règles** FEM PL
during your period pendant vos règles

perm NOUN
la **permanente** FEM
to have a perm se faire ◎ [10] faire une permanente

permanent ADJECTIVE
permanent MASC, **permanente** FEM

permanently ADVERB
en permanence
They're going to stay there permanently. Ils vont rester là définitivement.

permission NOUN
la **permission** FEM
to ask permission demander [1] la permission
Let's ask permission first. Demandons la permission d'abord.
to get permission to do something obtenir [77] la permission de faire quelque chose
We didn't get permission to go out. Nous n'avons pas obtenu la permission de sortir.

♂ to **permit** VERB ▸ SEE **permit** NOUN
permettre [11]

◎ means the verb takes être to form the perfect

Her parents will not permit it. Ses parents ne le permettrons pas.
to permit somebody to do something permettre à quelqu'un de faire quelque chose
They are not permitted to go out at night. On ne les permet pas de sortir le soir.
Smoking is not permitted. Il est interdit de fumer.
Weather permitting, we'll go camping. Si le temps le permet, on va faire du camping.

permit NOUN ▸ SEE **permit** VERB
(for fishing) le **permis** MASC

ℓ **person** NOUN
    la **personne** FEM
There's room for one more person. Il y a de la place pour une autre personne.
He's the sort of person who always complains. C'est le genre de personne qui se plaint toujours.
to do something in person faire quelque chose en personne
He wrote to me in person. Il m'a écrit en personne.

personal ADJECTIVE
    personnel MASC, **personnelle** FEM
personal belongings les affaires personnelles
my personal appearance mon apparence
She's got personal problems. Elle a des problèmes personnels.

personality NOUN
    1 *(a person's character)* la **personnalité** FEM
to have a strong personality avoir [5] une forte personnalité
    2 *(a celebrity)* la **vedette** FEM
a TV personality une vedette de la télévision

personally ADVERB
    personnellement
Personally, I'm against it. Personnellement, je suis contre.

personal stereo NOUN
    le **baladeur** MASC

perspiration NOUN
    la **transpiration** FEM

to **perspire** VERB
    transpirer [1]

ℓ to **persuade** VERB
    persuader [1]
to persuade somebody to do something persuader quelqu'un de faire quelque chose
Can you persuade them to come too? Est-ce que tu peux les persuader de venir aussi?
We persuaded Tim to sing. Nous avons

persuadé Tim de chanter.

pessimistic ADJECTIVE
    pessimiste MASC & FEM

pest NOUN
    (annoying person) le **casse-pieds** MASC, la **casse-pieds** FEM
She can be a pest. Elle peut être casse-pieds.

to **pester** VERB
    harceler [45]
to pester somebody for something harceler quelqu'un pour obtenir quelque chose
They pester people for money. Ils harcèlent les gens pour obtenir de l'argent.

ℓ **pet** NOUN
    1 un **animal de compagnie** *(PL* les **animaux de compagnie)**
Do you have a pet? Avez-vous un animal de compagnie?
I've got a pet dog. J'ai un chien.
They're not allowed pets. Ils n'ont pas le droit d'avoir des animaux.
    2 *(favourite person)* le **chouchou** MASC, la **chouchoute** FEM
Julie's the teacher's pet. Julie est la chouchoute du prof.

petal NOUN
    le **pétale** MASC

pet name NOUN
    le **petit nom** MASC

ℓ **petrol** NOUN
    l'**essence** FEM
unleaded petrol l'essence sans plomb
to fill up with petrol faire [10] le plein d'essence
to run out of petrol tomber ⊙ [1] en panne d'essence
We ran out of petrol. Nous sommes tombés en panne d'essence.
• **petrol station**
    la **station-service**

petticoat NOUN
    le **jupon** MASC

pharmacist NOUN
    le **pharmacien** MASC, la **pharmacienne** FEM

pharmacy NOUN
    la **pharmacie** FEM

pheasant NOUN
    le **faisan** MASC

philosophy NOUN
    la **philosophie** FEM

A
B
C
D
E
F
G
H
I
J
K
L
M
N
O
P
Q
R
S
T
U
V
W
X
Y
Z

P to **phone** VERB ▸ SEE **phone** NOUN
1 téléphoner [1]
while I was phoning pendant que je téléphonais
It's quicker to phone. Ça va plus vite de téléphoner.
Phone up and ask for information. Téléphone et demande-leur des renseignements.
2 **to phone somebody** appeler [18] quelqu'un
I'll phone you later. Je t'appellerai plus tard.
It's too late to phone her. Il est trop tard pour l'appeler.

P **phone** NOUN ▸ SEE **phone** VERB
le téléphone MASC
She's on the phone. Elle est au téléphone.
to be on the phone to somebody être [6] au téléphone avec quelqu'un
I was on the phone to Claire. J'étais au téléphone avec Claire.
Can you book by phone? Est-ce qu'on peut réserver par téléphone?
Nobody answered the phone. Personne n'a répondu au téléphone.

P **phone book** NOUN
un annuaire MASC
Look it up in the phone book. Cherche dans l'annuaire.

P **phone box** NOUN
la cabine téléphonique
the nearest phone box la cabine téléphonique la plus proche

P **phone call** NOUN
un appel MASC
Phone calls are free. Les appels sont gratuits.
May I make a phone call? Puis-je téléphoner?

P **phone card** NOUN
la télécarte FEM
Do you sell phone cards? Est-ce que vous vendez les télécartes?

phone number NOUN
le numéro de téléphone
to get somebody's phone number prendre [64] le numéro de téléphone de quelqu'un

P **photo** NOUN
la photo FEM
to take a photo prendre [64] une photo
to take a photo of somebody prendre quelqu'un en photo
Could you take a photo of us? Pourriez-vous nous prendre en photo?
I took a photo of their house J'ai pris leur maison en photo.

I'd like to get some photos developed. Je voudrais faire développer des photos.

photocopier NOUN
la photocopieuse FEM

to **photocopy** VERB ▸ SEE **photocopy** NOUN
photocopier [1]

photocopy NOUN ▸ SEE **photocopy** VERB
la photocopie FEM
I made a few photocopies. J'ai fait quelques photocopies.

to **photograph** VERB ▸ SEE **photograph** NOUN
photographier [1]

photograph NOUN ▸ SEE **photograph** VERB
la photo FEM
to take a photograph prendre [64] une photo
to take a photograph of somebody prendre quelqu'un en photo
He took a photograph of the family. Il a pris la famille en photo.

photographer NOUN
le & la photographe MASC & FEM

photography NOUN
la photographie FEM
I'm interested in photography. Je m'intéresse à la photographie.

P **phrase** NOUN
une expression FEM
a French expression une expression française
• **phrasebook**
le guide de conversation

physical ADJECTIVE
physique MASC & FEM

physicist NOUN
le physicien MASC, la physicienne FEM

P **physics** NOUN
la physique FEM
She's good at physics. Elle est bonne en physique.

physiotherapist NOUN
le & la kinésithérapeute MASC & FEM

physiotherapy NOUN
la kinésithérapie FEM

pianist NOUN
le & la pianiste MASC & FEM

P **piano** NOUN
le piano MASC
a piano lesson une leçon de piano
to play the piano jouer du piano
I know how to play it on the piano. Je sais le jouer au piano.

◉ means the verb takes être to form the perfect

ρ to **pick** VERB ▶ SEE **pick** NOUN

1 *(to choose)* **choisir** [2]
Pick a card. Choisis une carte.
We picked a good present. Nous avons choisi un bon cadeau.

2 *(for a team)* **sélectionner** [1]
I've been picked for Saturday. J'ai été sélectionné pour samedi.

3 *(fruit, flowers)* **cueillir** [35]
I like picking strawberries. J'aime cueillir les fraises.

- **to pick something up**

1 *(lift)* **prendre** [64] quelque chose
She picked up her bag and went out. Elle a pris son sac et elle est sortie.

2 *(collect together)* **ramasser** [1] quelque chose
Could you pick up the toys? Est-ce que tu peux ramasser les jouets?

3 *(to collect)* **venir** ◐ [81] **chercher** quelque chose
I'll pick up the keys tomorrow. Je viendrai chercher les clés demain.

4 *(learn)* **apprendre** [64] quelque chose
I picked up a few words of French. J'ai appris quelques mots de français.
You'll soon pick it up. Tu vas vite l'apprendre.

- **to pick somebody up**
venir ◐ [81] **chercher** quelqu'un
My mum's picking me up at six. Ma mère vient me chercher à six heures.

pick NOUN ▶ SEE **pick** VERB
Take your pick! Choisis!

pickpocket NOUN
le **pickpocket** MASC

picnic NOUN
le **pique-nique** MASC
to have a picnic pique-niquer [1]
We went for a picnic by the lake. Nous sommes allés pique-niquer au bord du lac.

ρ **picture** NOUN

1 *(a painting)* le **tableau** MASC *(PL les tableaux)*
a picture by Matisse un tableau de Matisse
It's a lovely picture. C'est un beau tableau.
to paint a picture of something peindre quelque chose
He painted a picture of a horse. Il a peint un cheval.

2 *(a drawing)* le **dessin** MASC
She draws brilliant pictures. Elle fait des dessins superbes.
to draw a picture of something dessiner quelque chose
Can you draw a picture of the house? Est-ce que tu peux dessiner la maison?

3 *(in a book)* une **illustration** FEM
a book with lots of pictures un livre avec beaucoup d'illustrations

4 *(the cinema)* **the pictures** le **cinéma**
I love going to the pictures. J'adore aller au cinéma.

pie NOUN

1 *(sweet)* la **tarte** FEM
an apple pie une tarte aux pommes

2 *(savoury)* la **tourte** FEM
a meat pie une tourte à la viande

ρ **piece** NOUN

1 *(a bit)* le **morceau** MASC *(PL les morceaux)*
a big piece of cheese un gros morceau de fromage

2 *(that you fit together)* la **pièce** FEM
the pieces of a jigsaw les pièces d'un puzzle
There was a piece missing. Il manquait une pièce.
to take something to pieces démonter [1] quelque chose
He took the radio to pieces. Il a démonté la radio.
The vase was smashed to pieces. Le vase était cassé en mille morceaux.

3 **a piece of furniture** un meuble
a piece of fruit un fruit
a piece of good news une bonne nouvelle
a useful piece of information un renseignement utile
We have four pieces of luggage. Nous avons quatre valises.
That's a piece of luck! C'est un coup de chance!

4 *(coin)* la **pièce** FEM
a ten-pence piece une pièce de dix pence

pier NOUN
la **jetée** FEM

pierced ADJECTIVE
percé MASC, **percée** FEM
to have pierced ears avoir [5] les oreilles percées
I'm having my ears pierced. Je me fais percer les oreilles.

ρ **pig** NOUN
le **cochon** MASC

pigeon NOUN
le **pigeon** MASC

piggy bank NOUN
la **tirelire** FEM

pigsty NOUN
la **porcherie** FEM
Your room is a pigsty. Ta chambre est une vraie porcherie.

ρ indicates key words

pigtail NOUN
la natte FEM

to **pile** VERB ▶ SEE **pile** NOUN
to be piled with something être [6] recouvert de quelque chose
The table was piled with plates. La table était recouverte d'assiettes.
• **to pile up**
1 (leaves, rubbish) s'entasser [1]
The rubbish is starting to pile up. Les ordures commencent à s'entasser.
2 (work, problems) s'accumuler [1]
• **to pile something up**
1 (neatly) empiler [1] quelque chose
I piled the books up on the shelf. J'ai empilé les livres sur l'étagère.
2 (in a heap) entasser [1] quelque chose

𝒫 **pile** NOUN ▶ SEE **pile** VERB
1 (a neat stack) la **pile** FEM
a pile of plates une pile d'assiettes
2 (a heap) le **tas** MASC
a pile of dirty shirts un tas de chemises sales

pilgrimage NOUN
le pèlerinage MASC
to go on a pilgrimage faire [10] un pèlerinage

𝒫 **pill** NOUN
1 (tablet) le **comprimé** MASC
2 **the pill** la pilule
to be on the pill prendre [64] la pilule

pillar NOUN
le pilier MASC
• **pillar box**
la boîte aux lettres

pillow NOUN
un oreiller MASC
• **pillowcase**
la taie d'oreiller

pilot NOUN
le pilote MASC
an airline pilot un pilote de ligne
a fighter pilot un pilote de chasse

pimple NOUN
le bouton MASC
He's got pimples. Il a des boutons.

to **pin** VERB ▶ SEE **pin** NOUN
to pin something to something accrocher [1] quelque chose à quelque chose
I pinned the balloons to the door. J'ai accroché les ballons à la porte.
• **to pin something up**
1 (a notice) accrocher [1]
Can you pin up the ad? Est-ce que tu peux accrocher l'annonce?

2 (a hem) épingler [1]

pin NOUN ▶ SEE **pin** VERB
1 (for sewing) une épingle FEM
2 **a three-pin plug** une prise à trois fiches

PIN NOUN
(personal identification number) le **code confidentiel**
I've forgotten my PIN. J'ai oublié le code confidentiel.

pinball NOUN
le flipper MASC
to play pinball jouer au flipper
a pinball machine un flipper

to **pinch** VERB ▶ SEE **pinch** NOUN
1 (nip) pincer [61]
to pinch somebody pincer quelqu'un
Stop pinching me! Arrête de me pincer!
She pinched my arm. Elle m'a pincé le bras.
2 (steal) piquer [1] (informal)
Somebody's pinched my bike. On m'a piqué mon vélo.

pinch NOUN ▶ SEE **pinch** VERB
la pincée FEM
a pinch of salt une pincée de sel

pine NOUN
le pin MASC
• **pineapple**
un ananas
• **pine cone**
la pomme de pin
• **pine needles**
les aiguilles de pin
• **pine nuts**
les pignons de pin
• **pine tree**
le pin

ping-pong NOUN
le ping-pong MASC
to play ping-pong jouer au ping-pong

𝒫 **pink** ADJECTIVE
rose MASC & FEM
a pink skirt une jupe rose

pip NOUN
(in a fruit) le pépin MASC

pipe NOUN
1 (for gas, water) le **tuyau** MASC (PL les tuyaux)
The pipes have burst. Les tuyaux ont éclaté.
2 (for smoking) la **pipe** FEM
He smokes a pipe. Il fume la pipe.

pirate NOUN
le pirate MASC

● means the verb takes être to form the perfect

pirated *ADJECTIVE*
piraté *MASC*, piratée *FEM*
a pirated video une vidéo piratée

Pisces *NOUN*
les Poissons *MASC PL*
Valerie is Pisces. Valerie est Poissons.

WORD TIP Signs of the zodiac do not take an article: un or une.

pistachio *NOUN*
la pistache *FEM*

pit *NOUN*
la fosse *FEM*

to **pitch** *VERB* ▸ SEE **pitch** *NOUN*
to pitch a tent dresser [1] une tente

ℙ **pitch** *NOUN* ▸ SEE **pitch** *VERB*
le terrain *MASC*
a football pitch un terrain de foot
The pitch was flooded. Le terrain a été inondé.

pitch dark *ADJECTIVE*
tout noir *MASC*, toute noire *FEM*
It was pitch dark outside. Dehors, il faisait tout noir.

to **pity** *VERB* ▸ SEE **pity** *NOUN*
to pity somebody plaindre [31] quelqu'un
I pity them. Je les plains.

ℙ **pity** *NOUN* ▸ SEE **pity** *VERB*
1 (a shame) le dommage *MASC*
That's a pity! C'est dommage!
It would be a pity to miss the film. Ce serait dommage de rater le film.
It's a pity she's not coming. C'est dommage qu'elle ne vienne pas.
2 (feeling of sympathy) la pitié *FEM*
to take pity on avoir [5] pitié de
They took pity on me. Ils ont eu pitié de moi.

pizza *NOUN*
la pizza *FEM*
a mushroom pizza une pizza aux champignons

to **place** *VERB* ▸ SEE **place** *NOUN*
mettre [11]
He placed his cup on the table. Il a mis sa tasse sur la table.

ℙ **place** *NOUN* ▸ SEE **place** *VERB*
1 (location) un endroit *MASC*
in a warm place dans un endroit chaud
a wonderful place un endroit merveilleux
a good place to have a picnic un bon endroit pour pique-niquer
It's my favourite place. C'est mon endroit préféré.

Bath is a nice place to live. Bath est agréable à vivre.
all over the place partout
We looked all over the place for the keys. On a cherché les clés partout.
There was water all over the place. Il y avait de l'eau partout.
2 (a space) la place *FEM*
a place for the car une place pour la voiture
Is there a place for me? Y a-t-il une place pour moi?
Will you keep my place? Veux-tu me garder ma place?
to change places changer de place
I changed places with Jessica. J'ai changé de place avec Jessica.
3 (in a race) la place *FEM*
in first place à la première place
4 (house) chez quelqu'un
at your place chez toi
Come to my place. Viens chez moi.
We'll go round to Hassan's place. On ira chez Hassan.
5 to take place avoir [5] lieu
The competition will take place at four. Le concours aura lieu à seize heures.

plain *NOUN* ▸ SEE **plain** *ADJECTIVE*
la plaine *FEM*

ℙ **plain** *ADJECTIVE* ▸ SEE **plain** *NOUN*
1 (not fussy) simple *MASC & FEM*
plain cooking une cuisine simple
2 (not patterned) uni *MASC*, unie *FEM*
plain curtains des rideaux unis
3 (unflavoured) nature *INVARIABLE ADJECTIVE*
some plain yoghurt du yaourt nature

WORD TIP As an adjective, nature never changes.

plait *NOUN*
la natte *FEM*

ℙ to **plan** *VERB* ▸ SEE **plan** *NOUN*
1 to plan to do something avoir [5] l'intention de faire quelque chose
We're planning to leave early. Nous avons l'intention de partir tôt.
Jack was planning to look for a job. Jack avait l'intention de chercher un travail.
2 (make plans for) préparer [1]
Mr Smith's planning a trip to Italy. M. Smith prépare un voyage en Italie.
I'm planning a surprise for my parents. Je prépare une surprise à mes parents.
3 (organize) organiser [1]
I need to plan my day. J'ai besoin d'organiser ma journée.
She loves planning the holiday. Elle aime organiser les vacances.

4 *(a house, garden)* concevoir [66]
  a well-planned kitchen une cuisine bien
  conçue

𝓟 **plan** NOUN ▸ SEE **plan** VERB
  1 *(idea, scheme)* le projet MASC
  my plans for the future mes projets
  d'avenir
  What are your plans for this summer?
  Quels sont vos projets pour cet été?
  I don't have any plans yet. Je n'ai pas
  encore de projets.
  She's got plans tonight. Elle a prévu
  quelque chose pour ce soir.
  to go according to plan se passer ⬆ [1]
  comme prévu
  Everything went according to plan. Tout
  s'est passé comme prévu.
  2 *(a map)* le plan MASC
  a plan of the city un plan de la ville

𝓟 **plane** NOUN
  un avion MASC
  to catch a plane to Paris prendre [64] un
  avion pour Paris
  We went by plane. Nous avons pris l'avion.
  I nearly missed my plane. J'ai failli rater
  mon avion.

planet NOUN
  la planète FEM

plank NOUN
  la planche FEM

to **plant** VERB ▸ SEE **plant** NOUN
  planter [1]
  We planted some tomatoes. Nous avons
  planté des tomates.

𝓟 **plant** NOUN ▸ SEE **plant** VERB
  la plante FEM
  a house plant une plante d'intérieur
  to water the plants arroser [1] les plantes

plaster NOUN
  1 *(sticking plaster)* le pansement adhésif
  She put a plaster on my hand. Elle m'a mis
  un pansement à la main.
  2 *(to heal a fracture)* le plâtre MASC
  to have your leg in plaster avoir [5] la
  jambe dans le plâtre
  My arm was in plaster for a month. J'avais
  le bras dans le plâtre pendant un mois.
  3 *(for walls)* le plâtre MASC

plastic NOUN
  le plastique MASC
  a plastic bag un sac en plastique
  The table is made of plastic. La table est en
  plastique.

𝓟 **plate** NOUN
  une assiette FEM

  paper plates des assiettes en carton

𝓟 **platform** NOUN
  1 *(in a station)* le quai MASC
  at platform three au quai numéro trois
  the train arriving at platform six le train
  qui entre en gare quai numéro six
  2 *(for lecturing or performing on)* une estrade
  FEM

𝓟 to **play** VERB ▸ SEE **play** NOUN
  1 jouer [1]
  I play with my little sister. Je joue avec ma
  petite sœur.
  The children were playing with matches.
  Les enfants jouaient avec des allumettes.
  2 *(in sport)* jouer [1] à
  to play tennis jouer au tennis
  Who wants to play football? Qui veut jouer
  au football?
  I was playing cards. Je jouais aux cartes.
  3 *(in music)* jouer [1] de
  to play the violin jouer du violon
  She plays the drums. Elle joue de la
  batterie.
  Can you play the flute? Tu sais jouer de la
  flûte?
  They play all kinds of music. Ils jouent
  toutes sortes de musique.
  I don't play pop music. Je ne joue pas de
  musique pop.
  4 *(a CD, DVD, video)* mettre [11]
  Play me your CD. Mets-moi ton CD.
  5 *(a trick)* jouer [1]
  to play a trick on somebody jouer un tour
  à quelqu'un
  They played a trick on me. Ils m'ont joué
  un tour.
  6 *(a part, role)* jouer [1]
  Who's playing Hamlet? Qui joue Hamlet?
  She plays the doctor in the film. Elle joue le
  rôle du médecin dans le film.

𝓟 **play** NOUN ▸ SEE **play** VERB
  la pièce FEM
  a play by Molière une pièce de Molière
  to put on a play monter [1] une pièce
  Our school is putting on a play. Notre école
  monte une pièce.
  I'm acting in the play. Je joue dans la pièce.

𝓟 **player** NOUN
  1 *(in sport)* le joueur MASC, la joueuse FEM
  a football player un joueur de foot
  a tennis player un joueur de tennis
  She's my favourite player. C'est ma joueuse
  préférée.
  2 *(musician)* le musicien MASC, la musicienne
  FEM

playground NOUN
  la cour de récréation FEM

⬆ means the verb takes être to form the perfect

playgroup NOUN
la **halte-garderie** FEM

playing card NOUN
la **carte à jouer**

playing field NOUN
le **terrain de sport**

playroom NOUN
la **salle de jeux**

plaza NOUN
a shopping plaza un **centre commercial**

ℙ **pleasant** ADJECTIVE
agréable MASC & FEM
I spent a pleasant day there. J'y ai passé
une journée agréable.

ℙ **please** ADVERB
1 **s'il vous plaît**
Two coffees, please. Deux cafés, s'il vous
plaît.
Follow me, please. Voulez-vous me suivre?
2 (less formal) **s'il te plaît**
Could you turn the TV off, please? Est-ce
que tu peux éteindre la télé, s'il te plaît?

ℙ **pleased** ADJECTIVE
content MASC, **contente** FEM
I was really pleased! J'étais vraiment
content! (boy speaking), J'étais vraiment
contente! (girl speaking).
to be pleased with something **être** [6]
content de quelque chose
She's very pleased with her present. Elle
est très contente de son cadeau.
He was quite pleased with himself! Il était
assez content de soi!
Pleased to meet you! Enchanté! (boy
speaking), Enchantée! (girl speaking).

pleasure NOUN
le **plaisir** MASC

ℙ **plenty** PRONOUN
1 (lots) **beaucoup**
plenty of something **beaucoup de quelque
chose**
There's plenty of bread. Il y a beaucoup
de pain.
He's got plenty of money. Il a beaucoup
d'argent.
We have plenty of friends here. Nous
avons beaucoup d'amis ici.
2 (quite enough) We've got plenty of time
to chat. Nous avons largement le temps de
bavarder.
Thanks, that's plenty! Merci, ça suffit!

pliers NOUN
la **pince** FEM
a pair of pliers une pince

plot NOUN
(of a film, novel) une **intrigue** FEM
I couldn't follow the plot. Je n'ai pas réussi
à suivre l'intrigue.

to **plough** VERB
labourer [1]

plug NOUN
1 (electrical) la **prise** FEM
2 (in a bath, sink) la **bonde** FEM
to pull out the plug retirer la bonde

plum NOUN
la **prune** FEM
a plum tart une tarte aux prunes

plumber NOUN
le **plombier** MASC
He's a plumber. Il est plombier.

plump ADJECTIVE
potelé MASC, **potelée** FEM

to **plunge** VERB
plonger [52]
He plunged into the river. Il a plongé dans
la rivière.

plural NOUN
(Grammar) le **pluriel** MASC
a noun in the plural un nom au pluriel

plus PREPOSITION
plus
three children plus the dog trois enfants
plus le chien

ℙ **p.m.** ADVERB
1 French people usually use the 24-hour clock
to refer to times after midday
at two p.m. à quatorze heures
at nine p.m. à vingt-et-une heures
2 You can also use 'de l'après-midi' for times
up to 6 p.m. and 'du soir' for times
after that
at two p.m. à deux heures de l'après-midi
at nine p.m. à neuf heures du soir

poached egg NOUN
un **œuf poché**

ℙ **pocket** NOUN
la **poche** FEM
to have your hands in your pockets avoir
[5] les mains dans les poches
to put your hand in your pocket mettre
[11] sa main dans sa poche
• pocket money
l'argent de poche

poem NOUN
le **poème** MASC
I've written a poem. J'ai écrit un poème.

A B C D E F G H I J K L M N O P Q R S T U V W X Y Z

ℙ indicates key words

poet NOUN
le poète MASC

poetry NOUN
la poésie FEM
to write poetry écrire [38] de la poésie

ℰ to **point** VERB ▸ SEE point NOUN
1 (to give directions) indiquer [1]
to point to something indiquer quelque chose
a sign pointing to the station un flèche qui indiquait la gare
2 (with your finger) montrer [1] du doigt
to point at somebody montrer quelqu'un du doigt
Don't point at her. Ne la montre pas du doigt.
He pointed at one of the children. Il a montré l'un des enfants du doigt.
• to point out something
1 (a building, a sight, an object) montrer [1]
James pointed out the cathedral to us. James nous a montré la cathédrale.
2 (to make it clear) to point out that ... signaler [1] que ...
I'd like to point out that I'm paying. Je vous signale que c'est moi qui paie.
He pointed out that it was a mistake. Il a fait remarquer que c'était une erreur.

ℰ **point** NOUN ▸ SEE point VERB
1 (tip) la pointe FEM
the point of a nail la pointe d'un clou
I removed it with the point of the knife. Je l'ai enlevé avec la pointe du couteau.
2 (in time) le moment MASC
at that point à ce moment-là
At that point, the police arrived. À ce moment-là, la police est arrivée.
3 (in a discussion, argument)
to get the point comprendre [64]
I don't get the point. Je ne comprends pas.
That's not the point. Il ne s'agit pas de ça.
Let's stick to the point. Restons dans le sujet.
That's a good point! C'est vrai!
I see your point but ... Je vois ce que tu veux dire mais ...
what's the point of doing...? ça sert à quoi de faire...?
What's the point of waiting? Ça sert à quoi d'attendre?
there's no point in doing... ça ne sert à rien de faire...
There's no point in phoning, he's out. Ça ne sert à rien d'appeler, il est sorti.
4 (in somebody's personality) le point MASC
her strong point son point fort
It's one of her weak points. C'est un de ses

points faibles.
It's not my strong point! Ce n'est pas mon point fort!
5 (in scoring) le point MASC
fifteen points to eleven quinze points à onze
6 (in decimals) virgule
6 point 4 six virgule quatre (this is how you say it aloud)

WORD TIP When writing in French, a comma is used for the decimal point: 6,75.

pointless ADJECTIVE
inutile MASC & FEM
The whole thing is pointless! Tout ça, c'est inutile!
it's pointless to do (something) il est inutile de faire (quelque chose)
It's pointless to keep on walking. Il est inutile de continuer à marcher.

ℰ **point of view** NOUN
le point de vue
from my point of view de mon point de vue
Everyone has a point of view. Chacun a son point de vue.

to **poison** VERB ▸ SEE poison NOUN
empoisonner [1]
to poison the water empoisonner l'eau
poison NOUN ▸ SEE poison VERB
le poison MASC
That's poison. C'est du poison.

poisonous ADJECTIVE
1 (chemical, gas) toxique MASC & FEM
poisonous gases des gaz toxiques
2 (toadstool, berry) vénéneux MASC, vénéneuse FEM
poisonous mushrooms des champignons vénéneux
3 (snake, insect) venimeux MASC, venimeuse FEM

poker NOUN
1 (for fire) le tisonnier MASC
2 (card game) le poker MASC
to play poker jouer [1] au poker

Poland NOUN
la Pologne FEM

polar bear NOUN
un ours polaire

pole NOUN ▸ SEE Pole
1 (for a tent) le mât MASC
One of the poles snapped. Un des mâts s'est cassé.
2 (for skiing) le bâton MASC
3 the North Pole le pôle Nord

⬤ means the verb takes être to form the perfect

the South Pole le pôle Sud

Pole NOUN ▸ SEE **pole**
un **Polonais** MASC, une **Polonaise** FEM
the Poles les Polonais

ℓ **police** NOUN
the police la police
to join the police entrer ◎ [1] dans la police
Somebody called the police. Quelqu'un a appelé la police.
The police are coming. La police arrive.
- police car
la voiture de police
- police dog
le chien policier
- policeman
un agent de police
- police record
le casier judiciaire
- police station
le commissariat de police
- police van
le fourgon cellulaire
- policewoman
la femme policier

policy NOUN
1 (plan of action) la **politique** FEM
2 (document) la **police** FEM

to **polish** VERB ▸ SEE **polish** NOUN
(shoes, furniture) **cirer** [1]

polish NOUN ▸ SEE **polish** VERB
1 (for furniture) la **cire** FEM
2 (for shoes) le **cirage** MASC

Polish ADJECTIVE ▸ SEE **Polish** NOUN
polonais MASC, polonaise FEM

Polish NOUN ▸ SEE **Polish** ADJECTIVE
(the language) le polonais ▸ SEE **Pole**

ℓ **polite** ADJECTIVE
poli MASC, polie FEM
a polite girl une jeune fille polie
to be polite to somebody être poli avec quelqu'un
They weren't very polite to us. Ils n'étaient pas très polis avec nous.

political ADJECTIVE
politique MASC & FEM
the political situation la situation politique

politician NOUN
un homme politique MASC, une femme politique FEM

politics NOUN
la politique FEM
I'm very interested in politics. La politique m'intéresse beaucoup.

ℓ to **pollute** VERB
polluer [1]
It pollutes the atmosphere. Ça pollue l'atmosphère.

ℓ **polluted** ADJECTIVE
pollué MASC, polluée FEM
to become polluted devenir ◎ [81] pollué

pollution NOUN
la pollution FEM
The fish die because of pollution. Les poissons meurent à cause de la pollution.

polo-necked ADJECTIVE
à col roulé
a polo-necked jumper un pull à col roulé

polythene bag NOUN
le sac en plastique

pond NOUN
1 (large) un **étang** MASC
2 (smaller) la **mare** FEM
3 (in a garden) le **bassin** MASC

pony NOUN
le **poney** MASC
- ponytail
la queue de cheval

poodle NOUN
le **caniche** MASC

pool NOUN
1 (swimming pool) la **piscine** FEM
The pool's closed. La piscine est fermée.
2 (in the country) un **étang** MASC
3 (puddle) la **flaque** FEM
There were pools of water everywhere. Il y avait des flaques d'eau partout.
4 (game) le **billard américain**
Who wants a game of pool? Qui veut jouer au billard américain?
5 the football pools le loto sportif
to do the pools jouer au loto sportif

ℓ **poor** ADJECTIVE
1 pauvre MASC & FEM
a poor area un quartier pauvre
a poor family une famille pauvre
poor people les pauvres
Poor Jane's failed her exam. La pauvre Jane a raté son examen.
You poor thing! Mon pauvre! (to a boy), Ma pauvre! (to a girl)
2 (bad) mauvais MASC, mauvaise FEM
a poor mark une mauvaise note
This is poor work. C'est du mauvais travail.
The weather was pretty poor. Le temps était plutôt mauvais.

to **pop** VERB ▸ SEE **pop** NOUN
to pop into a shop faire [10] un saut dans

un magasin
I'll just pop into the post office. Je vais
juste faire un saut au bureau de poste.
I popped home to eat. J'ai mangé en
vitesse à la maison.
She'll pop by tomorrow. Elle va passer en
vitesse demain.

pop NOUN ▶ SEE **pop** VERB
(music) le **pop** MASC
She can't stand pop. Elle ne supporte pas
le pop.

pop concert NOUN
le concert de pop

popcorn NOUN
le pop-corn MASC

pope NOUN
le pape MASC

poppy NOUN
le coquelicot MASC

pop song NOUN
la chanson pop

pop star NOUN
la pop star

ℓ **popular** ADJECTIVE
populaire MASC & FEM
a popular actor un acteur populaire
a popular hobby among young people un
passe-temps répandu chez les jeunes
to be popular avoir [5] beaucoup d'amis
She's very popular. Elle a beaucoup d'amis.
He's very popular with the girls. Il a
beaucoup de succès auprès des filles.

population NOUN
la population FEM
most of the population la majorité de la
population

porch NOUN
le porche MASC

ℓ **pork** NOUN
le porc MASC
a pork chop une côtelette de porc
I don't eat pork. Je ne mange pas de porc.

porridge NOUN
le porridge MASC

ℓ **port** NOUN
le port MASC
a fishing port un port de pêche
The ferry was in port. Le ferry était au port.

portable computer NOUN
(Computers) un ordinateur portable

portable DVD player NOUN
le lecteur DVD portable

porter NOUN
1 (at a station, airport) le porteur MASC
2 (in a hotel) le portier MASC

portion NOUN
la portion FEM
half a portion une demi-portion
a portion of chips une portion de frites

portrait NOUN
le portrait MASC

Portugal NOUN
le Portugal MASC

Portuguese ADJECTIVE ▶ SEE **Portuguese** NOUN
portugais MASC, portugaise FEM

Portuguese NOUN ▶ SEE **Portuguese** ADJECTIVE
1 un Portugais MASC, une Portugaise FEM
the Portuguese les Portugais
2 (the language) le portugais MASC

posh ADJECTIVE
chic INVARIABLE ADJECTIVE
a posh house une maison chic
a posh area un quartier chic

WORD TIP chic never changes.

position NOUN
1 (where something is) la position FEM
to get into position se mettre ◉ [11] en
place
2 (in a competition) la position FEM
in third position en troisième position

ℓ **positive** ADJECTIVE
1 (very sure) sûr MASC, sûre FEM
I'm positive he's left. Je suis sûr qu'il est
parti.
2 (enthusiastic) positif MASC, positive FEM
a positive reaction une réaction positive
to stay positive rester ◉ [1] positif
Try to be more positive. Essaie d'être plus
positif.

to possess VERB
posséder [24]

possessions PLURAL NOUN
les affaires FEM PL
They lost all their possessions. Ils ont
perdu toutes leurs affaires.

possibility NOUN
la possibilité FEM
That's another possibility. C'est une autre
possibilité.
There are a number of possibilities. Il y a
plusieurs possibilités.

ℓ **possible** ADJECTIVE
possible MASC & FEM
if possible si possible
as quickly as possible le plus vite possible

◉ means the verb takes être to form the perfect

I'll do it as quickly as possible. Je le ferai le plus vite possible.
It's quite possible. C'est tout à fait possible.
Is it possible to book online? Est-ce qu'il est possible de réserver en ligne?
It's not yet possible. Ce n'est pas encore possible.

possibly ADVERB
1 *(maybe)* **peut-être**
   'Are they back already?' — 'Possibly.' 'Est-ce qu'ils sont déjà rentrés?' — 'Peut-être.'
2 *(to express a strong feeling)* **I can't possibly arrive before Thursday.** Je ne peux vraiment pas arriver avant jeudi.
   You can't possibly say that! Mais tu ne peux vraiment pas dire ça!

℔ to **post** VERB ▸ SEE **post** NOUN
   to post a letter mettre [11] une lettre à la poste
   Post that as soon as possible. Mets ça à la poste le plus vite possible.

℔ **post** NOUN ▸ SEE **post** VERB
1 la **poste** FEM
   to send something by post envoyer quelque chose par la poste
   I sent her the book by post. Je lui ai envoyé le livre par la poste.
2 *(letters)* le **courrier** MASC
   Is there any post for me? Y a-t-il du courrier pour moi?
   You haven't got any post. Tu n'as pas de courrier.
3 *(job)* le **poste** MASC
   He was offered a post abroad. On lui a proposé un poste à l'étranger.
4 *(pole)* le **poteau** MASC

postbox NOUN
   la **boîte aux lettres**
   The postboxes are yellow. Les boîtes aux lettres sont jaunes.

℔ **postcard** NOUN
   la **carte postale**
   to send postcards envoyer des cartes postales

postcode NOUN
   le **code postal**

℔ **poster** NOUN
1 *(for decoration)* le **poster** MASC
   I've got posters all over my room. J'ai des posters partout dans ma chambre.
2 *(advertising)* une **affiche** FEM
   I saw a poster for the concert. J'ai vu une affiche pour le concert.
   We're putting up posters at school. On met des affiches à l'école.

℔ **postman** NOUN
   le **facteur** MASC
   Has the postman been? Est-ce que le facteur est passé?

℔ **post office** NOUN
   la **poste** FEM
   I'm looking for the post office. Je cherche la poste.
   The post office is on the right. La poste est à droite.

to **postpone** VERB
   to postpone something remettre [11] quelque chose à plus tard
   The trip was postponed until August. On a remis l'excursion au mois d'août.

postwoman NOUN
   la **factrice** FEM

pot NOUN
1 *(jar)* le **pot** MASC
   a pot of honey un pot de miel
   three pots of paint trois pots de peinture
2 *(teapot)* la **théière** FEM
   I'll make a pot of tea. Je vais faire du thé.
3 *(pan)* la **casserole** FEM
   to put away the pots and pans ranger [52] les casseroles

℔ **potato** NOUN
   la **pomme de terre**
   fried potatoes les pommes de terre sautées
   some mashed potatoes de la purée
• **potato crisps**
   les **chips** MASC PL

pottery NOUN
   la **poterie** FEM
   a piece of pottery une poterie
   to make pottery fabriquer [1] des poteries

℔ **pound** NOUN
1 *(money)* la **livre** FEM
   fourteen pounds quatorze livres
   How much is that in pounds? C'est combien en livres sterling?
2 *(in weight)* la **livre** FEM
   a pound of apples une livre de pommes

℔ to **pour** VERB
1 *(a liquid)* **verser** [1]
   I poured the milk into the pan. J'ai versé le lait dans la casserole.
2 *(a drink)* **servir** [71]
   to pour the tea servir le thé
   to pour somebody a drink servir à boire à quelqu'un
   I poured him a drink. Je lui ai servi à boire.
3 **to be pouring with rain** pleuvoir [63] à verse
   It's pouring. Il pleut à verse.

℔ **indicates key words**

ℐ poverty NOUN
la **pauvreté** FEM
to fight against poverty lutter [1] contre la pauvreté

powder NOUN
la **poudre** FEM

ℐ power NOUN
1 (electricity) le **courant** MASC
They've turned on the power. Ils ont mis le courant.
2 (energy) l'**énergie** FEM
nuclear power l'énergie nucléaire
3 (over other people) le **pouvoir** MASC
to have a lot of power avoir [5] beaucoup de pouvoir
to be in power être [6] au pouvoir
He wants to stay in power. Il veut rester au pouvoir.

power cut NOUN
la **coupure de courant**

powerful ADJECTIVE
puissant MASC, **puissante** FEM
a powerful computer un ordinateur puissant

power point NOUN
la **prise de courant**

power station NOUN
la **centrale électrique**

practical ADJECTIVE
pratique MASC & FEM
to be a practical person avoir [5] l'esprit pratique
• **practical joke**
la **farce**

practically ADVERB
pratiquement
They've practically all gone. Ils sont pratiquement tous partis.

ℐ practice NOUN
1 (for sport) l'**entraînement** MASC
hockey practice l'entraînement de hockey
2 (for an instrument) **to do your piano practice** travailler [1] son piano
I've got to do some flute practice. Je dois travailler ma flûte.
3 **to be out of practice** être [6] rouillé
She's a bit out of practice. Elle est un peu rouillée.

ℐ to practise VERB
1 (music, a language) travailler [1]
an opportunity to practise my French une occasion pour travailler mon français
She's practising the violin. Elle est en train de travailler son violon.

2 (in a sport) **s'entraîner** [1]
The team practises on Wednesdays. L'équipe s'entraîne le mercredi.
I've got to practise for the match. Je dois m'entraîner pour le match.

to praise VERB
to praise somebody for something féliciter [1] quelqu'un de quelque chose
They praised her for her achievement. Ils l'ont félicitée de son succès.

pram NOUN
le **landau** MASC

prawn NOUN
la **crevette** FEM

to pray VERB
prier [1]

prayer NOUN
la **prière** FEM

precaution NOUN
la **précaution** FEM
to take precautions prendre ses précautions

precinct NOUN
a shopping precinct un quartier commerçant
a pedestrian precinct une zone piétonne

precious ADJECTIVE
précieux MASC, **précieuse** FEM
precious stones les pierres précieuses

precise ADJECTIVE
précis MASC, **précise** FEM
at 2 a.m. to be precise à deux heures du matin, pour être précis

precisely ADVERB
précisément
at eleven o'clock precisely à onze heures précises
That's precisely why they don't get on. C'est précisément pour ça qu'ils ne s'entendent pas bien.

preface NOUN
la **préface** FEM

ℐ to prefer VERB
préférer [24]
Which dress do you prefer? Tu préfères quelle robe?
I prefer the red one. Je préfère la rouge.
to prefer something to something préférer quelque chose à quelque chose
I prefer coffee to tea. Je préfère le café au thé.
to prefer to do something préférer faire quelque chose

means the verb takes être to form the perfect

I'd prefer to go to the gym. Je préfère aller au gymnase.
She prefers swimming. Elle préfère la natation.

pregnancy NOUN
la **grossesse** FEM

pregnant ADJECTIVE
enceinte FEM

prejudice NOUN
le **préjugé** MASC
a prejudice un préjugé
to fight against racial prejudice lutter contre les préjugés raciaux

prejudiced ADJECTIVE
to be prejudiced avoir [5] des préjugés

preliminary ADJECTIVE
préliminaire MASC & FEM

première NOUN
(of a play, film) la **première** FEM

prep NOUN
les **devoirs** MASC PL
my English prep mes devoirs d'anglais

preparation NOUN
1 la **préparation** FEM
2 (for a trip, event) **preparations** les préparatifs MASC PL
the preparations for something les préparatifs pour quelque chose
our preparations for Christmas nos préparatifs pour Noël

ℱ to **prepare** VERB
préparer [1]
to prepare for something se préparer ◎ à quelque chose
We're preparing for the exam. Nous nous préparons à l'examen.
Prepare yourselves! Préparez-vous!
to prepare somebody for something préparer quelqu'un à quelque chose
I wasn't prepared for the shock. On ne m'a pas préparé au choc.

prepared ADJECTIVE
prêt MASC, **prête** FEM
to be prepared to do something être [6] prêt à faire quelque chose
I'm prepared to pay half. Je suis prêt à en payer la moitié.
We weren't prepared to wait. Nous n'étions pas prêts à attendre.
to be prepared for something s'attendre [3] à quelque chose
I was prepared for the worst. Je m'attendais au pire.

preposition NOUN
(Grammar) la **préposition** FEM

prep school NOUN
une **école primaire privée**

to **prescribe** VERB
prescrire [38]
He prescribed antibiotics for me. Il m'a prescrit des antibiotiques.

prescription NOUN
une **ordonnance** FEM
on prescription sur ordonnance
I got it on prescription. Je l'ai eu sur ordonnance.

presence NOUN
la **présence** FEM
in my presence en ma présence

presence of mind NOUN
la **présence d'esprit**

to **present** VERB ▶ SEE **present** ADJECTIVE, NOUN
1 (a prize) **remettre** [11]
Who's going to present the prizes? Qui va remettre les prix?
to present somebody with something remettre quelque chose à quelqu'un
He presented me with the cup. Il m'a remis la coupe.
2 (on TV, radio) **présenter** [1]
She presents the programme every year. Elle présente l'émission chaque année.

ℱ **present** ADJECTIVE ▶ SEE **present** VERB, NOUN
1 (attending a class, ceremony) **présent** MASC, **présente** FEM
Is Jenny present? Est-ce que Jenny est présente?
• **to be present at something** assister [1] à quelque chose
Fifty people were present at the funeral. Cinquante personnes ont assisté à l'enterrement.
2 (existing now) **actuel** MASC, **actuelle** FEM
the present situation la situation actuelle
3 **at the present time** actuellement

ℱ **present** NOUN ▶ SEE **present** VERB, ADJECTIVE
1 (gift) le **cadeau** MASC (PL les **cadeaux**)
to give somebody a present offrir [56] un cadeau à quelqu'un
We gave Rashid a present. Nous avons offert un cadeau à Rashid.
to give something to somebody as a present offrir [56] quelque chose à quelqu'un
I'll give him the tickets as a present. Je vais lui offrir les billets.
2 (at the moment) **for the present** pour le moment

ℱ indicates key words

That's all for the present. C'est tout pour le moment

3 *(Grammar)* le présent *MASC*
in the present (tense) au présent

presenter *NOUN*
(on TV) le **présentateur** *MASC*, la **présentatrice** *FEM*

presently *ADVERB*
(soon) bientôt

ℓ **president** *NOUN*
le **président** *MASC*, la **présidente** *FEM*
the first woman president la première présidente
to run for president être [6] candidat à la présidence
She wants to run for president. Elle veut être candidate à la présidence.

ℓ to **press** *VERB* ▶ SEE **press** *NOUN*
1 *(to push)* appuyer [41]
You have to press here to open it. Il faut appuyer ici pour l'ouvrir.
Press hard. Appuyez fort.
2 *(a button, switch, pedal)* appuyer [41] sur
I pressed the bell. J'ai appuyé sur la sonnette.
Don't press that button. N'appuie pas sur ce bouton.

press *NOUN* ▶ SEE **press** *VERB*
the press la presse
the tabloid press la presse populaire

press conference *NOUN*
la **conférence de presse**

pressure *NOUN*
la **pression** *FEM*
She did it under pressure from the others. Elle l'a fait sous la pression des autres.
to put pressure on somebody faire [10] pression sur quelqu'un
They put pressure on him. Ils ont fait pression sur lui.
- **pressure gauge**
un indicateur de pression
- **pressure group**
le groupe de pression

ℓ to **pretend** *VERB*
to pretend to do something faire [10] semblant de faire quelque chose
I pretended to be asleep. J'ai fait semblant de dormir.
He's pretending not to hear. Il fait semblant de ne pas entendre.
Let's pretend that we missed class. Faisons semblant d'avoir manqué le cours.

pretentious *ADJECTIVE*
prétentieux *MASC*, prétentieuse *FEM*

pretty *ADVERB* ▶ SEE **pretty** *ADJECTIVE*
plutôt
It was pretty stupid. C'était plutôt bête.
The exam's pretty easy. L'examen est plutôt facile.

ℓ **pretty** *ADJECTIVE* ▶ SEE **pretty** *ADVERB*
joli *MASC*, jolie *FEM*
a pretty village un joli village
They've got pretty things in that shop. Ils ont de jolies choses dans ce magasin.

WORD TIP joli goes before the noun.

ℓ to **prevent** *VERB*
to prevent somebody from doing something empêcher [1] quelqu'un de faire quelque chose
It's preventing me from having fun. Ça m'empêche de m'amuser.
There's nothing to prevent you from leaving. Rien ne vous empêche de partir.

previous *ADJECTIVE*
précédent *MASC*, précédente *FEM*
during the previous week pendant la semaine précédente

previously *ADVERB*
auparavant

ℓ **price** *NOUN*
le **prix** *MASC*
the price per kilo le prix du kilo
Prices are high. Les prix sont élevés.
to go up in price augmenter [1]
Cars have gone up in price. Les voitures ont augmenté.
- **price list**
la liste des prix
- **price ticket**
une étiquette

to **prick** *VERB*
piquer [1]
to be pricked by thorns se faire ⊙ [10] piquer par des épines
to prick your finger se piquer ⊙ le doigt
I pricked my finger with the needle. Je me suis piqué le doigt avec l'aiguille.

pride *NOUN*
la **fierté** *FEM*

priest *NOUN*
le **prêtre** *MASC*

ℓ **primary (school) teacher** *NOUN*
un **instituteur** *MASC*, une **institutrice** *FEM*
My mother's a primary teacher. Ma mère est institutrice.

ℓ **primary school** *NOUN*
une **école primaire**

⊙ means the verb takes être to form the perfect

the local **primary school** l'école primaire
du quartier

ℱ**prime minister** NOUN
le **Premier ministre** MASC
the **Prime Minister of France** le Premier
ministre de la France

prince NOUN
le **prince** MASC
Prince William le prince William

princess NOUN
la **princesse** FEM
Princess Anne la princesse Anne

ℱ**principal** NOUN ▸ SEE **principal** ADJECTIVE
(of a college) le **directeur** MASC, la **directrice**
FEM
at the **principal's office** au bureau du
directeur

principal ADJECTIVE ▸ SEE **principal** NOUN
(main) **principal** MASC, **principale** FEM,
principaux MASC PL, **principales** FEM PL
one of the **principal reasons** une des
raisons principales

principle NOUN
le **principe** MASC
on **principle** par principe
That's true in principle. Cela est vrai en
principe.
It's against my principles. C'est contraire à
mes principes.

print NOUN
1 (printed letters) les **caractères** MASC PL
in **small print** en petits caractères
2 (a photo) le **tirage** MASC
a **colour print** un tirage en couleur

ℱ**printer** NOUN
une **imprimante** FEM
a **laser printer** une imprimante à laser

print-out NOUN
la **copie papier**

prison NOUN
la **prison** FEM
in **prison** en prison

prisoner NOUN
le **prisonnier** MASC, la **prisonnière** FEM
to **take somebody prisoner** faire quelqu'un
prisonnier
She was taken prisoner. On l'a fait
prisonnière.
• **prisoner of war**
le prisonnier de guerre, la prisonnière de
guerre

ℱ**private** ADJECTIVE
1 **privé** MASC, **privée** FEM
a **private school** une école privée

'**Private property**' 'Propriété privée'
in **private** en privé
Can we talk to you in private? Est-ce qu'on
peut vous parler en privé?
It's my private business. Ce sont mes
affaires personnelles.
2 (one-to-one) **particulier** MASC, **particulière**
FEM
to **have private lessons** prendre [64] des
cours particuliers
She has private lessons in music. Elle prend
des cours particuliers de musique.

privately ADVERB
en privé

ℱ**prize** NOUN
le **prix** MASC
to **win a prize** gagner un prix
I won first prize. J'ai gagné le premier prix.
• **prize-giving**
la **distribution des prix**
• **prizewinner**
le **gagnant**, la **gagnante**

probable ADJECTIVE
probable MASC & FEM
one of the **probable effects** un des effets
probables

probably ADVERB
probablement
I'll probably be late. Je serai probablement
en retard.

ℱ**problem** NOUN
le **problème** MASC
a **serious problem** un grave problème
What's the problem? Quel est le problème?
No problem! Pas de problème!
I had a bit of a problem. J'ai eu un petit
problème.

process NOUN
1 le **processus** MASC
2 to **be in the process of doing something**
être en train de faire quelque chose
We're in the process of making dinner.
Nous sommes en train de préparer le repas.

procession NOUN
1 (in parade) le **défilé** MASC
2 (at religious festival) la **procession** FEM

to **produce** VERB ▸ SEE **produce** NOUN
produire [26]
I produced my passport. J'ai produit mon
passeport.
It produces a lot of heat. Ça produit
beaucoup de chaleur.
He has produced some fine work. Il a
produit un beau travail.

ℱ indicates key words

produce NOUN ▸ SEE **produce** VERB
les **produits** MASC PL
organic produce les produits biologiques

producer NOUN
(of a film, programme) le **producteur** MASC,
la **productrice** FEM
a famous film producer un célèbre
producteur de cinéma

ℓ **product** NOUN
le **produit** MASC
a range of products une gamme de
produits
to import cheap products importer des
produits bon marché

production NOUN
1 (of a film, opera) la **production** FEM
She's in charge of the production. Elle est
responsable de la production.
2 (of a play) la **mise en scène** FEM
a new production of Hamlet une nouvelle
mise en scène de Hamlet
3 (by a factory) la **production** FEM
**That motorbike has gone out of
production.** On ne fabrique plus cette
moto.
• **production line**
la chaîne de fabrication

profession NOUN
la **profession** FEM

professional NOUN ▸ SEE **professional** ADJECTIVE
le **professionnel** MASC, la **professionnelle**
FEM
They're professionals. Ce sont des
professionnels.

professional ADJECTIVE ▸ SEE **professional** NOUN
professionnel MASC, **professionnelle** FEM
professional players les joueurs
professionnels
She's a professional singer. C'est une
chanteuse professionnelle.

professor NOUN
le **professeur** MASC, la **professeure** FEM

profile NOUN
le **profil** MASC

profit NOUN
le **bénéfice** MASC
to make a profit faire [10] un bénéfice
We sold the cakes at a profit. Nous avons
fait un bénéfice sur la vente des gâteaux.

profitable ADJECTIVE
rentable MASC & FEM

program NOUN ▸ SEE **programme**
a computer program un programme
informatique

ℓ **programme** NOUN ▸ SEE **program**
1 (on TV, radio) une **émission** FEM
a popular TV programme une émission
télévisée grand public
2 (for a play, event) le **programme** MASC
Could I see the programme? Est-ce que je
peux voir le programme?

programmer NOUN
le **programmateur** MASC, la
programmatrice FEM

ℓ **progress** NOUN
1 le **progrès** MASC
That's progress! C'est ça le progrès!
to make progress faire [10] des progrès
I'm making progress in French. Je fais des
progrès en français.
2 **to be in progress** être en cours
Talks are in progress. Les négociations sont
en cours.

ℓ **project** NOUN
1 (at school) le **dossier** MASC
a project on something un dossier sur
quelque chose
my project on the rain forest mon dossier
sur la forêt tropicale
2 (a plan) le **projet** MASC
Our school is taking part in the project.
Notre école participe au projet.
a project to do something un projet pour
faire quelque chose
a project to build a bridge un projet pour
construire un pont
• **project manager**
le directeur de projet, la directrice de projet

projector NOUN
le **projecteur** MASC

ℓ **to promise** VERB ▸ SEE **promise** NOUN
to promise to do something promettre [11]
de faire quelque chose
I've promised to be home by ten. J'ai
promis de rentrer avant dix heures.
I promise I'll phone when I get there. Je
t'appelle quand j'y arriverai, je le promets.

ℓ **promise** NOUN ▸ SEE **promise** VERB
la **promesse** FEM
to make a promise faire [10] une promesse
She's always making promises. Elle fait
toujours des promesses.
to break a promise manquer [1] à sa
promesse
I never break a promise. Je ne manque
jamais à ma promesse.
It's a promise! C'est promis!

to promote VERB
to be promoted être [6] promu
She's been promoted. Elle a été promue.

◔ means the verb takes être to form the perfect

promotion NOUN
la **promotion** FEM
to get a promotion être [6] promu

prompt ADJECTIVE
rapide MASC & FEM
a prompt reply une réponse rapide

promptly ADJECTIVE
1 (at once) **immédiatement**
He promptly fell off again. Il est retombé
immédiatement.
2 (quickly) **rapidement**
Please reply promptly. Répondez
rapidement s'il vous plaît.
3 **Lessons begin promptly at nine o'clock.**
Les cours commencent à neuf heures
précises.

pronoun NOUN
(Grammar) le **pronom** MASC

ℱto **pronounce** VERB
prononcer [61]
It's hard to pronounce. C'est difficile à
prononcer.
I can't pronounce the word. Je ne peux pas
prononcer le mot.
How do you pronounce it? Ça se prononce
comment?

pronunciation NOUN
la **prononciation** FEM
Your pronunciation is good. Tu as une
bonne prononciation.

ℱ**proof** NOUN
la **preuve** FEM
They still have no proof. Ils n'ont toujours
aucune preuve.
I've got proof. J'ai des preuves.
There's no proof that ... Rien ne prouve
que ...
There's no proof that it's dangerous. Rien
ne prouve que c'est dangereux.

propaganda NOUN
la **propagande** FEM

propeller NOUN
une **hélice** FEM

ℱ**proper** ADJECTIVE
1 (real, genuine) **vrai** MASC, **vraie** FEM
a proper doctor un vrai médecin
I need a proper meal. J'ai besoin d'un vrai
repas.
We haven't had a proper holiday. Nous
n'avons pas eu de vraies vacances.
2 (correct) **bon** MASC, **bonne** FEM
the proper tools les bons outils
That's not the proper answer. Ce n'est pas
la bonne réponse.
The TV wasn't in its proper place. La télé

n'était pas à sa place.

WORD TIP The adjectives vrai and bon come
before the noun.

ℱ**properly** ADVERB
comme il faut
Hold it properly. Tiens-le comme il faut.
Is it properly wrapped? Est-ce que c'est
emballé comme il faut?

property NOUN
1 la **propriété** FEM
'Private property' 'Propriété privée'
2 (belongings) les **affaires** FEM PL
my personal property mes affaires
personnelles
to be somebody's property appartenir [81]
à quelqu'un
It's not your property. Cela ne t'appartient
pas.

proposal NOUN
la **proposition** FEM

to **propose** VERB
1 (suggest) **proposer** [1]
2 **to propose (marriage) to somebody**
demander quelqu'un en mariage
He proposed to her. Il l'a demandée en
mariage.

prostitute NOUN
la **prostituée** FEM
a male prostitute un prostitué

ℱto **protect** VERB
protéger [15]
to protect the environment protéger
l'environnement
to protect somebody from something
protéger quelqu'un contre quelque chose
to protect children from drugs protéger
les enfants contre la drogue

protection NOUN
la **protection** FEM

protein NOUN
la **protéine** FEM

ℱto **protest** VERB ▸ SEE **protest** NOUN
1 (to grumble) **protester** [1]
We protested, but it was pointless. Nous
avons protesté, mais c'était inutile.
2 (demonstrate) **manifester** [1]
They're protesting against poverty. Ils
manifestent contre la pauvreté.

protest NOUN ▸ SEE **protest** VERB
1 (opposition) la **protestation** FEM
in spite of their protests malgré leurs
protestations
**to do something in protest against
something** faire quelque chose en signe de

ℱ **indicates key words**

protestation contre quelque chose
2 *(a demonstration)* la **manifestation** FEM
   a street protest une manifestation
   to organize a protest organiser [1] une
   manifestation

Protestant ADJECTIVE ▶ SEE **Protestant** NOUN
protestant MASC, protestante FEM

Protestant NOUN ▶ SEE **Protestant** ADJECTIVE
le protestant MASC, la protestante FEM

> **WORD TIP** Adjectives never have capitals in
> French, even for religions.

protester NOUN
le **manifestant** MASC, la **manifestante** FEM

protest march NOUN
la **manifestation** FEM

♪ **proud** ADJECTIVE
fier MASC, fière FEM
   to be proud of something être [6] fier de
   quelque chose
   She's proud of her garden. Elle est fière de
   son jardin.
   to be proud of yourself être [6] fier de soi
   I was very proud of myself. J'étais très fier
   de moi.

♪ to **prove** VERB
prouver [1]
   What does it prove? Qu'est-ce que ça
   prouve?
   That doesn't prove anything. Ça ne prouve
   rien.
   to prove that ... prouver que ...
   It proves that we're right. Ça prouve que
   nous avons raison.

proverb NOUN
le **proverbe** MASC

to **provide** VERB
fournir [2]
   Are meals provided? Est-ce que les repas
   sont fournis?
   to provide somebody with something
   fournir quelque chose à quelqu'un
   It provides people with work. Ça fournit
   du travail aux gens.
   to provide training assurer [1] la formation

♪ **provided** CONJUNCTION
à condition que
   provided you do it now à condition que tu
   le fasses maintenant

province NOUN
la **province** FEM

prune NOUN
le **pruneau** MASC (PL les **pruneaux**)

ps ABBREVIATION
(in a letter) P.S.

psychiatrist NOUN
le & la **psychiatre** MASC & FEM
   He's a psychiatrist. Il est psychiatre.

psychological ADJECTIVE
psychologique MASC & FEM

psychologist NOUN
le & la **psychologue** MASC & FEM
   She's a psychologist Elle est psychologue.

psychology NOUN
la **psychologie** FEM

PTO ABBREVIATION
TSVP (= *tournez s'il vous plaît*)

pub NOUN
le **pub** MASC
   They went to the pub. Ils sont allés au pub.

♪ **public** ADJECTIVE ▶ SEE **public** NOUN
1 public MASC, publique FEM
   public opinion l'opinion publique
2 **the public library** la bibliothèque
   municipale
• **public address system**
   la sonorisation

♪ **public** NOUN ▶ SEE **public** ADJECTIVE
the public le public
   open to the public ouvert au public
   in public en public

♪ **public holiday** NOUN
le **jour férié**
   January 1 is a public holiday. Le premier
   janvier est férié.

publicity NOUN
la **publicité** FEM

public school NOUN
une **école privée**

public transport NOUN
les **transports en commun** MASC PL

to **publish** VERB
publier [1]

publisher NOUN
un **éditeur** MASC

♪ **pudding** NOUN
le **dessert** MASC
   What's for pudding? Qu'est-ce qu'il y a
   comme dessert?
   For pudding we've got strawberries.
   Comme dessert nous avons des fraises.

puddle NOUN
la **flaque** FEM

⊙ means the verb takes être to form the perfect

Puerto Rico NOUN
Porto Rico FEM

> **WORD TIP** Unlike the names of most other islands, Porto Rico does not take le or la.

puff NOUN
(of smoke) la **bouffée** FEM
- **puff pastry**
la pâte feuilletée

ℙ to **pull** VERB
1 tirer [1]
Pull hard! Tire fort!
to pull a rope tirer sur une corde
to pull the chain tirer sur la chasse d'eau
She was pulling me by the arm. Elle me tirait par le bras.
to pull something out of something tirer quelque chose de quelque chose
He pulled a mobile out of his pocket. Il a tiré un portable de sa poche.
to pull somebody out of something sortir [72] quelqu'un de quelque chose
They pulled me out of the water. Ils m'ont sorti de l'eau.
We pulled the sledge up the hill. Nous avons monté la côte en tirant la luge.
2 **to pull faces** faire [10] des grimaces
- **to pull away**
(car, bus) démarrer [1]
As the bus was pulling away, ... Comme le bus démarrait, ...
- **to pull something down**
(a blind) baisser [1]
Pull down the blind. Baissez le store.
- **to pull in**
(at the roadside) s'arrêter [1]
We pulled in to have a rest. Nous nous sommes arrêtés pour nous reposer.
- **to pull through**
(after an accident, illness) s'en sortir ◎ [2]
Luckily, she pulled through. Heureusement, elle s'en est sortie.

pullover NOUN
le **pull-over** MASC, le **pull** MASC

pulse NOUN
le **pouls** MASC
The doctor took my pulse. Le médecin a pris mon pouls.

to **pump** VERB ▸ SEE **pump** NOUN
pomper [1]
They were pumping the water out of the cellar. Ils pompaient l'eau de la cave.
- **to pump something up**
(a tyre) gonfler [1]
The tyres need to be pumped up. Il faut gonfler les pneus.

pump NOUN ▸ SEE **pump** VERB
1 (for tyres) la **pompe** FEM
a bicycle pump une pompe à vélo
2 (shoe) la **ballerine** FEM
ballet pumps des ballerines

pumpkin NOUN
la **citrouille** FEM

to **punch** VERB ▸ SEE **punch** NOUN
1 **to punch somebody** donner [1] un coup de poing à quelqu'un
He punched me. Il m'a donné un coup de poing.
2 (a ticket) composter [1]
Don't forget to punch your tickets. N'oubliez pas de composter vos billets.

punch NOUN ▸ SEE **punch** VERB
1 (a blow) le **coup de poing**
a punch on the nose un coup de poing dans le nez
to give somebody a punch donner un coup de poing à quelqu'un
2 (drink) le **punch** MASC
We had some punch. Nous avons bu du punch.

punctual ADJECTIVE
ponctuel MASC, ponctuelle FEM

punctuation NOUN
la **ponctuation** FEM
punctuation errors des erreurs de ponctuation
- **punctuation mark**
le signe de ponctuation

puncture NOUN
la **crevaison** FEM
to get a puncture crever [1]
I got a puncture on the way. J'ai crevé en route.

to **punish** VERB
punir [2]
to punish somebody for doing something punir quelqu'un pour avoir fait quelque chose
We'll be punished for missing class. On va nous punir pour avoir séché le cours.

punishment NOUN
la **punition** FEM

ℙ **pupil** NOUN
un **élève** MASC, une **élève** FEM
They're good pupils. Ce sont de bons élèves.

puppet NOUN
la **marionnette** FEM

puppy NOUN
le **chiot** MASC

A B C D E F G H I J K L M N O P Q R S T U V W X Y Z

a labrador puppy un chiot labrador

pure ADJECTIVE
pur MASC, pure FEM

ℓ **purple** ADJECTIVE
violet MASC, violette FEM
She's got purple hair. Elle a les cheveux violets.

ℓ **purpose** NOUN
1 on purpose exprès
to do something on purpose faire exprès de faire quelque chose
He closed the door on purpose. Il a fait exprès de fermer la porte.
Did she do it on purpose? Est-ce qu'elle l'a fait exprès?
I didn't do it on purpose. Je ne l'ai pas fait exprès.
2 (aim) le but MASC
to have a purpose in life avoir [5] un but dans la vie
What's the purpose of this meeting? Quel est le but de cette réunion?

to **purr** VERB
ronronner [1]

ℓ **purse** NOUN
le porte-monnaie MASC (PL les porte-monnaie)
My purse was stolen. On m'a volé mon porte-monnaie.

ℓ to **push** VERB ▶ SEE **push** NOUN
1 pousser [1]
He pushed me. Il m'a poussé.
Can you help me to push the table? Tu peux m'aider à pousser la table?
2 (a bell, button) appuyer [41] sur
Push the red button. Appuyez sur le bouton rouge.
3 to push somebody to do something pousser [1] quelqu'un à faire quelque chose
His teacher's pushing him to learn German. Son prof le pousse à apprendre l'allemand.
• to push somebody around
bousculer [1] quelqu'un
Stop pushing me around. Arrête de me bousculer.
• to push something away
repousser [1] quelque chose
I pushed my plate away. J'ai repoussé mon assiette.
• to push on
(with a journey, task) continuer [1]
We pushed on for another hour. Nous avons continué pendant une heure encore.

push NOUN ▶ SEE **push** VERB
to give something a push pousser [1]

quelque chose
We had to give the car a push. Nous avons dû pousser la voiture.

pushchair NOUN
la poussette FEM

ℓ to **put** VERB
1 (to place) mettre [11]
Put your suitcases here. Mettez vos valises ici.
I didn't put the cream in the fridge. Je n'ai pas mis la crème au frigo.
Where did you put my skirt? Où est-ce que tu as mis ma jupe?
2 (to write) écrire [38]
Put your address here. Écris ton adresse ici.
• to put something away
ranger [52] quelque chose
I put the shopping away. J'ai rangé les courses.
• to put something back
1 remettre [11] quelque chose
Put it back in the drawer. Remets-le dans le tiroir.
2 (to postpone) remettre [11]
The trip has been put back until Thursday. La sortie a été remise à jeudi.
• to put something down
poser [1] quelque chose
She put the plant down on the floor. Elle a posé la plante par terre.
• to put somebody off
1 décourager [52] quelqu'un
The experience hasn't put me off. L'expérience ne m'a pas découragé.
to be put off se décourager ◔ [52]
She's easily put off. Elle se décourage facilement.
Don't be put off! Ne te décourage pas!
2 to put somebody off something dégoûter [1] quelqu'un de quelque chose
It really put me off meat! Ça m'a vraiment dégoûté de la viande!
• to put something off
1 (a class, match) remettre [11]
He's put off my lesson till Thursday. Il a remis ma leçon à jeudi.
2 (a light, TV) éteindre [60]
Don't forget to put off the TV. N'oublie pas d'éteindre la télé.
• to put something on
1 (clothing, make-up, music) mettre [11]
I'll just put my shoes on. Je vais juste mettre mes chaussures.
He's put on his favourite music. Il a mis sa musique préférée.
2 (a light, the heating) allumer [1]
Who put the lamp on? Qui a allumé la lampe?

◔ means the verb takes être to form the perfect

3 *(a play)* monter [1]
We're putting on a French play. Nous sommes en train de monter une pièce française.

• **to put something out**
1 *(a bin, the rubbish)* sortir [72]
Have you put the rubbish out? Est-ce que tu as sorti les ordures?
2 *(a fire, light, cigarette)* éteindre [60]
I've put the lights out. J'ai éteint la lumière.
3 **to put out your hand** tendre [3] la main

• **to put somebody through to**
passer [52] quelqu'un à
Could you put me through to the secretary? Pourriez-vous me passer la secrétaire?

• **to put something up**
1 *(your hand)* lever [50]
I put up my hand. J'ai levé la main.
2 *(a picture, poster)* mettre [11]
I've put up some photos in my room. J'ai mis des photos dans ma chambre.
3 *(a notice)* afficher [1]
4 *(the price)* augmenter [1]
They've put up the price of the tickets. Ils ont augmenté le prix des billets.

• **to put somebody up**
(for the night) héberger [52] quelqu'un
Can you put me up on Friday? Est-ce que tu peux m'héberger vendredi?

• **to put up with something**
supporter [1] quelque chose
We can't put up with this situation any more. Nous ne pouvons plus supporter cette situation.
I don't know how she puts up with it. Je ne sais pas comment elle le supporte.

puzzle NOUN
(jigsaw) le **puzzle** MASC
• **puzzle book**
le livre de jeux

puzzled ADJECTIVE
perplexe MASC & FEM
He looked puzzled. Il avait l'air perplexe.

ℙ **pyjamas** PLURAL NOUN
le **pyjama** MASC SINGULAR
a pair of pyjamas un pyjama
Where are my pyjamas? Où est mon pyjama?

pylon NOUN
le **pylône** MASC

Pyrenees NOUN
the Pyrenees les **Pyrénées** FEM PL

Qq

qualification NOUN
1 *(exam pass, degree)* le **diplôme** MASC
2 *(in general)* **qualifications** qualifications FEM PL
vocational qualifications les qualifications professionnelles

qualified ADJECTIVE
1 *(experienced, trained)* **qualifié** MASC, **qualifiée** FEM
2 *(having a degree, diploma)* **diplômé** MASC, **diplômée** FEM

to **qualify** VERB
1 *(in sport)* se **qualifier** ◎ [1]
Our team qualified for the semifinal. Notre équipe s'est qualifiée pour la demi-finale.
2 **to qualify for something** avoir [5] droit à
I qualify for a reduction. J'ai droit à une réduction.
3 *(to get a qualification)* obtenir [77] son diplôme
She qualified as a nurse. Elle a obtenu son diplôme d'infirmière.
• **qualifying match**
le match de qualification

quality NOUN
la **qualité** FEM
good quality clothes des vêtements de bonne qualité
It's poor quality. C'est de la mauvaise qualité.

quantity NOUN
la **quantité** FEM
They grow large quantities of vegetables. Ils cultivent de grandes quantités de légumes.

WORD TIP quantité is followed by de before a noun.

to **quarrel** VERB ▸SEE **quarrel** NOUN
se **disputer** ◎ [1]
quarrel NOUN ▸SEE **quarrel** VERB
la **dispute** FEM
to have a quarrel se disputer ◎ [1]

quarry NOUN
la **carrière** FEM

ℙ **quarter** NOUN
1 le **quart** MASC
A quarter of the class is ill. Le quart de la classe est malade.
Three quarters of the class are absent. Les trois quarts de la classe sont absents.
2 *(talking about time)* le **quart**

a quarter to ten dix heures moins le quart
a quarter past ten dix heures et quart
a quarter of an hour un quart d'heure
three quarters of an hour trois quarts
d'heure
• **quarter-final**
le quart de finale

quartet NOUN
le **quatuor** MASC

quay NOUN
le **quai** MASC

Quebec NOUN
le **Québec**

> **WORD TIP** Countries and regions in French take
> le, la or les.

Quebecker NOUN
le **Québecois** MASC, la **Québecoise** FEM

℗ **queen** NOUN
la **reine** FEM
Queen Elizabeth la reine Elizabeth
the Queen of Spain la reine d'Espagne

> **WORD TIP** la is used with names of queens and a
> small letter is used for reine in French.

query NOUN
la **question** FEM

to **question** VERB ▸ SEE **question** NOUN
interroger [52]

℗ **question** NOUN ▸ SEE **question** VERB
1 (query) la **question** FEM
You haven't answered my question. Tu
n'as pas répondu à ma question.
to ask somebody a question poser [1] une
question à quelqu'un
I asked her a question. Je lui ai posé une
question.
2 (matter) la **question**
It's a question of time. C'est une question
de temps.
It's out of the question! C'est hors de
question!
• **question mark**
le point d'interrogation

questionnaire NOUN
le **questionnaire** MASC

to **queue** VERB ▸ SEE **queue** NOUN
faire [10] **la queue**
We queued for hours. Nous avons fait la
queue pendant des heures.

queue NOUN ▸ SEE **queue** VERB
1 (of people) la **queue** FEM
2 (of cars) la **file** FEM

℗ **quick** ADJECTIVE
1 **rapide** MASC & FEM
We had a quick lunch Nous avons déjeuné
rapidement
It's quicker on the motorway. C'est plus
rapide par l'autoroute.
2 (as an order) **Quick! There's the bus!** Vite!
Voilà le bus!
Be quick! Dépêche-toi!, Dépêchez-vous!

℗ **quickly** ADVERB
vite
I ate too quickly. J'ai mangé trop vite.
Come quickly! Viens vite!, Venez vite!

℗ **quiet** ADJECTIVE
1 (person, class) **silencieux** MASC, **silencieuse**
FEM
The children are very quiet. Les enfants
sont très silencieux.
Keep quiet. Tais-toi (to one person).
Taisez-vous (to two or more people).
2 (in character) **réservé** MASC, **réservée** FEM
Zoë's a quiet girl. Zoë est une fille réservée.
3 (voice, music) **doux** MASC, **douce** FEM
She was speaking in a quiet voice. Elle
parlait à voix basse.
4 (street, evening, life) **tranquille** MASC & FEM
a quiet area un quartier tranquille

℗ **quietly** ADVERB
1 (to move) **sans bruit**
to get up quietly se lever ◯ [50] sans bruit
2 (to speak, sing) **doucement**
to talk quietly parler doucement
3 (to read, play) **en silence**
to work quietly travailler en silence

quilt NOUN
la **couette** FEM

to **quit** VERB
1 (school) **quitter** [1]
to quit doing something arrêter [1] de faire
quelque chose
2 (from a computer game) **sortir** ◯ [72]

℗ **quite** ADVERB
1 (in general) **assez, plutôt**
I draw quite well. Je dessine assez bien.
It's quite cold outside. Il fait assez froid
dehors.
It's quite expensive. C'est plutôt cher.
That's quite a good idea. C'est une assez
bonne idée.
quite often assez souvent
You're quite right! Tu as tout à fait raison!
2 **not quite** pas tout à fait
That's not quite true. Ce n'est pas tout à
fait vrai.
3 **quite a lot of** pas mal de
quite a lot of homework pas mal de devoirs

◯ means the verb takes être to form the perfect

We have quite a lot of friends. Nous avons pas mal d'amis.

quiz NOUN
le **quiz** MASC
a TV quiz **show** un jeu télévisé

quotation NOUN
la **citation** FEM
• quotation **marks**
les **guillemets** MASC PL
in quotation marks entre guillemets

to **quote** VERB ▸ SEE **quote** NOUN
citer [1]

quote NOUN ▸ SEE **quote** VERB
1 *(from a book)* la **citation** FEM
2 in quotes entre guillemets

Rr

rabbi NOUN
le **rabbin** MASC

ℛ **rabbit** NOUN
le **lapin** MASC
• rabbit **hutch**
le **clapier**

rabies NOUN
la **rage** FEM

to **race** VERB ▸ SEE **race** NOUN
to race against somebody faire [10] la course avec quelqu'un

ℛ **race** NOUN ▸ SEE **race** VERB
1 *(sports event)* la **course** FEM
a cycle race une course cycliste
She came third in the race. Elle est arrivée troisième dans la course.
to have a race faire [10] la course
Two children were having a race. Deux enfants faisaient la course.
2 *(ethnic group)* la **race** FEM
the human race la race humaine
• race **relations**
les relations inter-raciales FEM PL
• race **riots**
les émeutes raciales FEM PL

racehorse NOUN
le **cheval de course**

racer NOUN
(bike) le **vélo de course**

racetrack NOUN
1 *(for horses)* le **champ de course**
2 *(for cars)* le **circuit** MASC
3 *(for cycles)* la **piste** FEM

racial ADJECTIVE
racial MASC, **raciale** FEM, **raciaux** MASC PL, **raciales** FEM PL
racial discrimination la discrimination raciale

racing NOUN
les **courses** FEM PL
He's watching the racing. Il regarde les courses.
• racing **car**
la **voiture de course**
• racing **driver**
le **pilote de course**

racism NOUN
le **racisme** MASC

racist ADJECTIVE ▸ SEE **racist** NOUN
raciste MASC & FEM
a racist comment une réflexion raciste

racist NOUN ▸ SEE **racist** ADJECTIVE
le & la **raciste** MASC & FEM

rack NOUN
1 *(for luggage)* le **porte-bagages** MASC *(PL les porte-bagages)*
2 *(for bicycles)* le **parc à bicyclettes**

racket NOUN
1 *(for tennis, badminton)* la **raquette** FEM
Here's your tennis racket. Voici ta raquette de tennis.
2 *(noise)* le **vacarme** MASC
The boys were making a racket. Les garçons faisaient du vacarme.
3 *(swindle)* l'**escroquerie** FEM

radar NOUN
le **radar** MASC
by radar au radar

radiation NOUN
la **radiation** FEM
• radiation **sickness**
le **mal des rayons**
• radiation **therapy**
la **radiothérapie**

radiator NOUN
le **radiateur** MASC

ℛ **radio** NOUN
la **radio** FEM
to listen to the radio écouter [1] la radio
I was listening to the radio when he arrived. J'écoutais la radio quand il est arrivé.
to hear something on the radio entendre [3] quelque chose à la radio
I heard it on the radio. Je l'ai entendu à la radio.
to be on the radio passer ⊘ [1] à la radio
She was on the radio. Elle est passée à la radio.

radioactive ADJECTIVE
radioactif MASC, radioactive FEM

radio-controlled ADJECTIVE
(toy) téléguidé MASC, téléguidée FEM

radio station NOUN
la station de radio

radish NOUN
le radis MASC

radius NOUN
le rayon MASC
all houses within a 10-kilometre radius
toutes les maisons dans un rayon de 10
kilomètres

raffle NOUN
la tombola FEM

raft NOUN
le radeau MASC

rag NOUN
le chiffon MASC

rage NOUN
1 la colère FEM
to be in a rage être [6] furieux
She's in a rage. Elle est furieuse.
He flew into a rage. Il s'est mis dans une
colère noire.
2 **to be all the rage** faire [10] fureur
It's all the rage now. Ça fait fureur à
présent.

raging ADJECTIVE
to be raging être [6] fou de rage (boy), être
[6] folle de rage (girl)

to **raid** VERB ▶ SEE **raid** NOUN
1 (robbers) attaquer [1]
2 (police) faire [10] une rafle dans

raid NOUN ▶ SEE **raid** VERB
1 (on a bank) le hold-up MASC
2 (by the police) la rafle FEM

rail NOUN
1 **to go by rail** prendre [64] le train
2 (on a balcony, bridge) la balustrade FEM
3 (on stairs) la rampe FEM
4 (for a train) le rail MASC
The train went off the rails. Le train a
déraillé.

railing NOUN
la grille FEM

rail strike NOUN
la grève des cheminots

ℓ **railway** NOUN
1 (the system) le chemin de fer
the railways les chemins de fer

2 (from one place to another) **a railway line**
une ligne de chemin de fer
**the railway line between London and
Oxford** la ligne entre Londres et Oxford
3 **an accident on the railway line** un accident
sur la voie ferrée
• **railway carriage**
le wagon
• **railway track**
la voie ferrée

ℓ **railway station** NOUN
la gare FEM

ℓ **rain** NOUN ▶ SEE **rain** VERB
la pluie FEM
in the rain sous la pluie
I like walking in the rain. J'aime bien me
promener sous la pluie.
when the rain stopped quand il s'est arrêté
de pleuvoir
• **rainbow**
un arc-en-ciel (PL les **arcs-en-ciel**)
• **raincoat**
un imperméable
• **raindrop**
la goutte de pluie
• **rainfall**
le niveau de précipitations
• **rain forest**
la forêt tropicale

ℓ to **rain** VERB ▶ SEE **rain** NOUN
pleuvoir [63]
It's raining. Il pleut.
It's going to rain. Il va pleuvoir.
It rained all night. Il a plu toute la nuit.

ℓ **rainy** ADJECTIVE
pluvieux MASC, pluvieuse FEM
a rainy day un jour pluvieux

to **raise** VERB
1 (to lift up) lever [50]
She raised her head. Elle a levé la tête.
Raise your hands, please! Levez la main, s'il
vous plaît!
2 (so as to be heard) **to raise your voice** parler
[1] plus fort
3 (a price, a salary) augmenter [1]
4 **The school is raising money for
computers.** L'école collecte des fonds pour
acheter des ordinateurs.
5 (a child, a family) élever
I was raised in Scotland. J'ai été élevé en
Écosse (boy speaking), J'ai été élevée en
Écosse (girl speaking).
Helen was raised by her grandmother.
Helen a été élevée par sa grand-mère.
6 **to raise the alarm** donner [1] l'alarme

⊙ **means the verb takes être to form the perfect**

raisin NOUN
le **raisin** sec

rake NOUN
le **râteau** MASC (PL les **râteaux**)

rally NOUN
1 (public gathering) le **rassemblement** MASC
2 (for sport) le **rallye** MASC
3 (in tennis) un **échange** MASC

rambler NOUN
le **randonneur** MASC, la **randonneuse** FEM

rambling NOUN
la **randonnée** FEM
to go rambling faire [10] une randonnée

ramp NOUN
la **rampe** FEM

ranch NOUN
le **ranch** MASC

range NOUN
1 (of activities, prices) la **gamme** FEM
We offer a range of sports activities. Nous vous proposons une gamme d'activités sportives.
The computer is top of the range. C'est un ordinateur haut de gamme.
2 (of colours, products) le **choix** MASC
They have a very large range of bikes. Ils ont un très grand choix de vélos.
3 (of mountains) la **chaîne** FEM

to **ransack** VERB
fouiller [1] dans

to **rap** VERB ▶ SEE **rap** NOUN
to rap at the door **frapper** [1] à la porte

rap NOUN ▶ SEE **rap** VERB
le **rap** MASC
• **rap music**
la musique rap
• **rap singer**
le chanteur rap, la chanteuse rap

to **rape** VERB ▶ SEE **rape** NOUN
violer [1]

rape NOUN ▶ SEE **rape** VERB
le **viol** MASC

ℓ **rare** ADJECTIVE
1 **rare** MASC & FEM
a rare bird un oiseau rare
2 (meat) **saignant** MASC, **saignante** FEM
I like my steak rare. J'aime le steak saignant.
a bit too rare un peu trop saignant
a medium-rare steak un steak à point

rarely ADVERB
rarement

rash ADJECTIVE ▶ SEE **rash** NOUN
irréfléchi MASC, **irréfléchie** FEM
a rash decision une décision irréfléchie

rash NOUN ▶ SEE **rash** ADJECTIVE
les **rougeurs** FEM PL
I've got a rash on my arms. J'ai des rougeurs sur les bras.
to come out in a rash se couvrir ◎ [30] de rougeurs
I came out in a rash. Je me suis couvert de rougeurs.

ℓ **raspberry** NOUN
la **framboise** FEM
raspberry jam la confiture de framboises
a raspberry tart une tarte aux framboises
raspberry-flavoured yoghurt le yaourt à la framboise

rat NOUN
le **rat** MASC

ℓ **rate** NOUN
1 (charge) le **tarif** MASC
a special rate un tarif spécial
an hourly rate un tarif horaire
Children travel at a reduced rate. Les enfants bénéficient d'un tarif réduit.
2 (level) le **taux** MASC
the birth rate le taux de natalité
the high crime rate le taux élevé de criminalité
3 at any rate en tout cas
I hope I've passed, at any rate. En tout cas, j'espère avoir réussi.

rather ADVERB
1 **plutôt**
It's rather expensive. C'est plutôt cher.
2 rather a lot of **pas mal de**
I've got rather a lot of homework to do. J'ai pas mal de devoirs à faire.
3 rather than **plutôt que**
Go there in summer rather than winter. Allez-y en été plutôt qu'en hiver.
4 (showing preference) I'd rather go to the cinema. Je préférerais aller au cinéma.
Would you rather stay here? Est-ce que tu préférerais rester ici?
I'd rather walk than wait for the bus. Je préférerais aller à pied plutôt que d'attendre le bus.

rave NOUN
(party) le **rave** MASC

raw ADJECTIVE
cru MASC, **crue** FEM
raw fish le poisson cru
• **raw materials**
les matières premières FEM

ℓ **indicates key words**

ray NOUN
1 le **rayon** MASC
   rays of sunshine des rayons de soleil
2 (fish) la **raie** FEM

razor NOUN
   le **rasoir** MASC
• **razor blade**
   la lame de rasoir

RE NOUN
   l'**éducation religieuse** FEM

ℰ to **reach** VERB ▸ SEE **reach** NOUN
1 **arriver** ◉ [1] à quelque chose
   When you reach the church, turn left.
   Quand vous arrivez à l'église, tournez à
   gauche.
2 **to reach a decision** arriver ◉ [1] à une
   décision
   **The committee still hasn't reached a
   decision.** Le comité n'est pas encore arrivé
   à une décision.
   to reach the final parvenir ◉ [81] en finale
   **The defending champions didn't reach
   the final.** Les tenants du titre ne sont pas
   parvenus en finale.
3 (a particular age, level) **atteindre** [60]
   when you reach the age of 18 quand on
   atteint la majorité

reach NOUN ▸ SEE **reach** VERB
   la **portée** FEM
   out of reach hors de portée
   within reach (of your hand) à portée de
   main
   **We've rented a villa within easy reach
   of the sea.** Nous avons loué une villa à
   proximité de la mer.

to **react** VERB
   réagir [2]
   How did you react? Comment est-ce que
   tu as réagi?

reaction NOUN
   la **réaction** FEM

ℰ to **read** VERB
   lire [51]
   What are you reading at the moment?
   Qu'est-ce que tu lis en ce moment?
   I didn't read the instructions. Je n'ai pas lu
   les instructions.
   I'd like to read that book again. J'aimerais
   relire ce livre.
• **to read something out**
   lire [51] quelque chose à haute voix
   He read out the list. Il a lu la liste à haute
   voix.
• **to read up on something**
   étudier [1] quelque chose
   I have to read up on the subject. Je dois

   étudier le sujet.

ℰ **reading** NOUN
   la **lecture** FEM
   I don't much like reading. Je n'aime pas
   beaucoup la lecture.

ℰ **ready** ADJECTIVE
1 **prêt** MASC, **prête** FEM
   Jane's not ready yet. Jane n'est pas encore
   prête.
   Dinner's ready! À table!
   to be ready to do something être [6] prêt à
   faire quelque chose
   Are you ready to leave? Est-ce que tu es
   prêt à partir?
2 **to get ready** se préparer ◉ [1]
   I need to get ready. Je dois me préparer.
   to get ready to do something se préparer à
   faire quelque chose
   I'm getting ready to go out. Je me prépare
   à sortir.
3 **to get something ready** préparer [1]
   quelque chose
   I'll get your room ready. Je vais préparer ta
   chambre.
• **ready-made meal**
   le plat préparé

ℰ **real** ADJECTIVE
   vrai MASC, **vraie** FEM
   They're real diamonds. Ce sont de vrais
   diamants.
   That's the real reason. Ça, c'est la vraie
   raison.
   He's a real bore. C'est un vrai casse-pieds.
   Is that his real name? Est-ce que c'est son
   vrai nom?
   His real name is Jack. Son vrai nom, c'est
   Jack.
   Her real father is dead. Son vrai père est
   mort.
   She's a real friend. C'est une véritable amie.

   WORD TIP vrai comes before the noun.

realistic ADJECTIVE
   réaliste MASC & FEM

reality NOUN
   la **réalité** FEM
• **reality TV**
   la télé réalité

ℰ to **realize** VERB
1 **to realize something** se rendre ◉ [3]
   compte de quelque chose
   when I realized my mistake quand je me
   suis rendu compte de mon erreur
   They don't realize how hard it is. Ils ne se
   rendent pas compte de la difficulté.
   Do you realize what time it is? Tu te rends

◉ means the verb takes être to form the perfect

compte de l'heure qu'il est?
I hadn't realized. Je ne m'en étais pas rendu compte.
to realize (that) ... se rendre compte que ...
I didn't realize he was French. Je ne m'étais pas rendu compte qu'il était français.
2 *(an ambition, a dream)* réaliser [1]

ℱ **really** ADVERB
vraiment
The film was really good. Le film était vraiment très bon.
Is it really midnight? Est-ce qu'il est vraiment minuit?
not really pas vraiment
'Are you pleased?' — 'Not really.' 'Tu es content?' — 'Pas vraiment.'
I really don't know. Je ne sais vraiment pas.
Really? C'est vrai?

rear ADJECTIVE ▸ SEE **rear** NOUN
arrière MASC & FEM
(of a car) **the rear door** la portière arrière

rear NOUN ▸ SEE **rear** ADJECTIVE
(of a building) l'arrière MASC
to get on at the rear of the train monter [1] en queue de train

to **rearrange** VERB
1 *(a room, a house)* réaménager [52]
2 *(your plans)* modifier [1]

ℱ **reason** NOUN
la raison FEM
the reason why ... la raison pour laquelle ...
I nearly forgot the reason why I phoned. J'ai presque oublié la raison pour laquelle j'appelais.
That's the reason why I'm not going. C'est pourquoi je n'y vais pas.
What's the reason for the delay? Quelle est la raison du retard?

reasonable ADJECTIVE
raisonnable MASC & FEM
Be reasonable! Sois raisonnable!

to **reassure** VERB
rassurer [1]

reassuring ADJECTIVE
rassurant MASC, rassurante FEM

rebel NOUN
le & la rebelle MASC & FEM

rebellion NOUN
la rébellion FEM, la révolte FEM

to **rebuild** VERB
reconstruire [26]

ℱ **receipt** NOUN
le reçu MASC
I've kept the receipt. J'ai gardé le reçu.

ℱ to **receive** VERB
recevoir [66]

ℱ **receiver** NOUN
le combiné MASC
to pick up the receiver décrocher [1]

ℱ **recent** ADJECTIVE
récent MASC, récente FEM
It's quite a recent discovery. C'est une découverte assez récente.

recently ADVERB
récemment

ℱ **reception** NOUN
1 la réception FEM
a big wedding reception une grande réception de mariage
at (the) reception à la réception
He's waiting at reception. Il attend à la réception.
2 *(for a mobile phone)* la réception FEM
The reception is good. La réception est bonne.
• **reception desk**
le bureau d'accueil

receptionist NOUN
le & la réceptionniste MASC & FEM
She's a receptionist. Elle est réceptionniste.

ℱ **recipe** NOUN
la recette FEM
the recipe for risotto la recette du risotto
Can I have the recipe for this cake? Est-ce que je peux avoir la recette de ce gâteau?

to **reckon** VERB
penser [1]
I reckon it's a good idea. Je pense que c'est une bonne idée.
What do you reckon? Qu'est-ce que tu en penses?

ℱ to **recognize** VERB
reconnaître [27]
She recognized my voice. Elle a reconnu ma voix.
I didn't recognize him. Je ne l'ai pas reconnu.
to recognize each other se reconnaître ⊙ [27]
We recognized each other immediately. Nous nous sommes reconnus tout de suite.

ℱ to **recommend** VERB
to recommend something to somebody recommander [1] quelque chose à quelqu'un
I recommend the fish soup. Je vous recommande la soupe de poisson.
Can you recommend a dentist? Est-ce que vous pouvez me recommander un dentiste?

ℱ **indicates key words**

They recommended the hotel to us. Ils
nous ont recommandé l'hôtel.

recommendation NOUN
la recommandation FEM

ℰ to **record** VERB ▶ SEE **record** NOUN
enregistrer [1]
They're recording a new album. Ils sont en
train d'enregistrer un nouvel album.

ℰ **record** NOUN ▶ SEE **record** VERB
1 le record MASC
She broke the record. Elle a battu le record.
It's a world record. C'est le record mondial.
the hottest summer on record l'été le plus
chaud qu'on ait jamais enregistré
We finished it in record time. Nous l'avons
terminé en un temps record.
2 to keep a record of something noter [1]
quelque chose
Could you please keep a record of the
results? Est-ce que tu peux noter les
résultats?
3 le disque MASC
a huge record collection une énorme
collection de disques
4 (office files) le dossier MASC
I'll just check your records. Je vais juste
vérifier votre dossier.

recorder NOUN
1 la flûte à bec
to play the recorder jouer [1] de la flûte
à bec
2 a DVD recorder un enregistreur DVD
a video recorder un magnétoscope

record-holder NOUN
le recordman MASC, la recordwoman FEM

ℰ **recording** NOUN
un enregistrement MASC

record player NOUN
le tourne-disque MASC

to **recover** VERB
se remettre ◎ [11]
to recover from something se remettre de
quelque chose
I'm still recovering from flu. Je me remets
encore de la grippe.

recovery NOUN
(from an illness) le rétablissement MASC
He's made a full recovery. Il s'est
complètement rétabli.
• recovery vehicle
le camion de dépannage

rectangle NOUN
le rectangle MASC

rectangular ADJECTIVE
rectangulaire MASC & FEM

to **recycle** VERB
recycler [1]

recycling NOUN
le recyclage MASC
• recycling centre
le centre de recyclage

ℰ **red** ADJECTIVE
1 rouge MASC & FEM
a red shirt une chemise rouge
a bright red car une voiture rouge vif
to go red rougir [2]
He went red when he saw her. Il a rougi
quand il l'a vue.
2 (hair) roux MASC, rousse FEM
to have red hair avoir [5] les cheveux roux
Rachel has red hair. Rachel a les cheveux
roux.
• red card
le carton rouge

Red Cross NOUN
the Red Cross la Croix-Rouge

redcurrant NOUN
la groseille FEM
redcurrant jelly la gelée de groseilles

to **redecorate** VERB
refaire [10]
They've had the kitchen redecorated. Ils
ont fait refaire la cuisine.

to **redo** VERB
refaire [10]

to **reduce** VERB
réduire [68]
They've reduced all the bags by 20%. Ils
ont réduit tous les sacs de 20%.
to reduce your speed ralentir [2]

ℰ **reduction** NOUN
la réduction FEM

redundancy NOUN
1 (a lost job) le licenciement MASC
2 (unemployment) le chômage MASC

redundant ADJECTIVE
to be made redundant être [6] licencié

reel NOUN
(of cotton) la bobine FEM

to **refer** VERB
to refer to someone, something parler [1]
de quelqu'un, quelque chose
She's referring to you. Elle parle de toi.
Did he refer to the trip? Est-ce qu'il a parlé
de l'excursion?

◎ means the verb takes être to form the perfect

referee NOUN
un **arbitre** MASC

reference NOUN
(for a job, course) les **références** FEM PL
to give somebody a reference fournir [2]
des références à quelqu'un
• **reference book**
un ouvrage de référence

refill NOUN
(for a pen, a lighter) la **recharge** FEM

to **reflect** VERB
refléter [24]

reflection NOUN
1 (in a mirror) une **image** FEM
2 (thought) la **réflexion** FEM
on reflection à la réflexion

reflex NOUN
le **réflexe** MASC

reflexive ADJECTIVE
(Grammar) **réfléchi** MASC, **réfléchie** FEM
a reflexive verb un verbe pronominal

refreshing ADJECTIVE
rafraîchissant MASC, **rafraîchissante** FEM

refreshment NOUN
le **rafraîchissement** MASC

refrigerator NOUN
le **réfrigérateur** MASC

refuge NOUN
le **refuge** MASC
to take refuge in something se réfugier ©
[1] dans quelque chose

refugee NOUN
le **réfugié** MASC, la **réfugiée** FEM

to **refund** VERB ▸SEE **refund** NOUN
rembourser [1]

refund NOUN ▸SEE **refund** VERB
le **remboursement** MASC
to get a refund se faire © [10] rembourser

refusal NOUN
le **refus** MASC

to **refuse** VERB ▸SEE **refuse** NOUN
refuser [1]
I refused. J'ai refusé.
to refuse to do something refuser de faire
quelque chose

refuse NOUN ▸SEE **refuse** VERB
(rubbish) les **ordures** FEM PL

regards PLURAL NOUN
les **amitiés** FEM PL
'Regards to your parents.' 'Mes amitiés à
vos parents.'

reggae NOUN
le **reggae** MASC

℘ **region** NOUN
la **région** FEM

regional ADJECTIVE
régional MASC, **régionale** FEM, **régionaux**
MASC PL, **régionales** FEM PL

℘ to **register** VERB ▸SEE **register** NOUN
s'inscrire [38]
I've registered for the class. Je me suis
inscrit au cours.

register NOUN ▸SEE **register** VERB
(in school) le **cahier des absences**
to take the register faire [10] l'appel

registered letter NOUN
la **lettre recommandée**

registration number NOUN
le **numéro d'immatriculation**

to **regret** VERB
regretter [1]
to regret doing something regretter
d'avoir fait quelque chose

regular ADJECTIVE
régulier MASC, **régulière** FEM

regularly ADVERB
régulièrement

℘ **regulation** NOUN
le **règlement** MASC
It's against regulations. C'est contraire au
règlement.

rehearsal NOUN
la **répétition** FEM

to **rehearse** VERB
répéter [24]

to **reheat** VERB
réchauffer [1]

reign NOUN
le **règne** MASC

rein NOUN
la **rêne** FEM

reindeer NOUN
le **renne** MASC

to **reject** VERB
rejeter [48]

related ADJECTIVE
1 (person, language) **apparenté** MASC,
apparentée FEM
2 (connected) **lié** MASC, **liée** FEM
a work-related accident un accident lié au
travail

ℓ **relation** NOUN
le **parent** MASC, la **parente** FEM
a close relation un parent proche
my relations ma famille
I met all her relations. J'ai rencontré toute sa famille.
There were just relations and close friends. Il n'y avait que la famille et des amis proches.
Rashid's got relations in France. Rashid a de la famille en France.

relationship NOUN
les **relations** FEM PL
to have a good relationship with somebody s'entendre [3] très bien

relative NOUN
le **membre de la famille**
We've invited a few relatives. Nous avons invité quelques membres de la famille.
All my relatives were there. Il y avait toute ma famille.

relatively ADVERB
relativement

ℓ to **relax** VERB
se **détendre** ⊙ [3]
to relax by doing something se détendre en faisant quelque chose
I relax by playing squash. Je me détends en jouant au squash.
I'm going to relax and watch telly tonight. Je vais me détendre en regardant la télé ce soir.

relaxation NOUN
la **détente** FEM
a form of relaxation une détente

relaxed ADJECTIVE
détendu MASC, **détendue** FEM

relaxing ADJECTIVE
reposant MASC, **reposante** FEM

relay race NOUN
la **course de relais**

to **release** VERB ▸ SEE **release** NOUN
1 (film, album) **sortir** [72]
2 (a prisoner) **libérer** [24]

release NOUN ▸ SEE **release** VERB
1 (film, album) la **nouveauté** FEM
2 (of a prisoner, a hostage) la **libération** FEM

relevant ADJECTIVE
pertinent MASC, **pertinente** FEM

ℓ **reliable** ADJECTIVE
(person, car) **fiable** MASC & FEM
She's extremely reliable. Elle est très fiable.

relief NOUN
1 le **soulagement** MASC
2 (aid) l'**aide** FEM
famine relief l'aide aux victimes de la famine

to **relieve** VERB
soulager [52]

relieved ADJECTIVE
soulagé MASC, **soulagée** FEM
I was relieved to hear you'd arrived. J'ai été soulagé d'apprendre que tu étais arrivé.

religion NOUN
la **religion** FEM

religious ADJECTIVE
1 (person) **croyant** MASC, **croyante** FEM
2 (art, music) **religieux** MASC, **religieuse** FEM

reluctant ADJECTIVE
réticent MASC, **réticente** FEM
to be reluctant to do something être peu disposé à faire quelque chose

ℓ to **rely** VERB
to rely on somebody compter [1] sur quelqu'un
I'm relying on you for Saturday. Je compte sur toi pour samedi.
You can't rely on them. On ne peut pas compter sur eux.

ℓ to **remain** VERB
rester ⊙ [1]
She remained calm. Elle est restée calme.
That remains to be seen. Ça reste à voir.

remains PLURAL NOUN
les **restes** MASC PL

remark NOUN
la **remarque** FEM
an odd remark une remarque bizarre
to make remarks about somebody faire des réflexions sur quelqu'un

remarkable ADJECTIVE
remarquable MASC & FEM

remarkably ADVERB
remarquablement

ℓ to **remember** VERB
1 se **souvenir** ⊙ [81]
I don't remember. Je ne me souviens pas.
2 **to remember something** se souvenir ⊙ [81] de quelque chose
Do you remember his name? Est-ce que tu te souviens de son nom?
I can't remember the number. Je ne me souviens pas du numéro.
3 **to remember somebody** se souvenir ⊙ [81] de quelqu'un

⊙ **means the verb takes être to form the perfect**

I remember Lucy well. Je me souviens très bien de Lucy.
4 *(to recall)* to remember doing something se souvenir ◉ [81] d'avoir fait quelque chose
I remember switching off the TV. Je me souviens d'avoir éteint la télévision.
5 *(not to forget)* to remember to do something ne pas oublier [1] de faire quelque chose
Remember to shut the door. N'oublie pas de fermer la porte.

ℓ to **remind** *VERB*
1 rappeler [18]
to remind somebody to do something rappeler à quelqu'un de faire quelque chose
Remind your father to pick me up. Rappelle à ton père de venir me chercher.
Remind me to buy some milk. Rappelle-moi d'acheter du lait.
2 to remind somebody of something faire [10] penser quelqu'un à quelque chose
It reminds me of Paris. Ça me fait penser à Paris.
He reminds me of Frank. Il me fait penser à Frank.
Oh, that reminds me ... Tiens, à ce propos...

remote *ADJECTIVE*
isolé *MASC*, isolée *FEM*
• remote control
la télécommande

to **remove** *VERB*
enlever [50]
He removed the packaging. Il a enlevé l'emballage.
It's for removing stains. C'est pour enlever les taches.

to **renew** *VERB*
renouveler [18]

renewable *ADJECTIVE*
(form of energy) renouvelable *MASC & FEM*

ℓ to **rent** *VERB* ▸ SEE **rent** *NOUN*
louer [1]
Simon's rented a flat. Simon a loué un appartement.
We rented a house in Brittany. Nous avons loué une maison en Bretagne.

ℓ **rent** *NOUN* ▸ SEE **rent** *VERB*
le loyer *MASC*

ℓ **rental** *NOUN*
la location *FEM*

to **reorganize** *VERB*
réorganiser [1]

ℓ to **repair** *VERB* ▸ SEE **repair** *NOUN*
réparer [1]
to get something repaired faire [10] réparer quelque chose
We got the television repaired. Nous avons fait réparer la télévision.

repair *NOUN* ▸ SEE **repair** *VERB*
la réparation *FEM*

to **repay** *VERB*
rembourser [1]
to repay somebody something rembourser quelque chose à quelqu'un

ℓ to **repeat** *VERB* ▸ SEE **repeat** *NOUN*
1 répéter [24]
Repeat after me. Répétez après moi.
2 *(at school)* redoubler [1]
She has to repeat a year. Elle doit redoubler.

repeat *NOUN* ▸ SEE **repeat** *VERB*
(of a TV programme) la reprise *FEM*

repeatedly *ADVERB*
à plusieurs reprises

repertoire *NOUN*
le répertoire *MASC*

repetitive *ADJECTIVE*
répétitif *MASC*, répétitive *FEM*

ℓ to **replace** *VERB*
remplacer [61]
I replaced the broken plate. J'ai remplacé l'assiette cassée.
to be replaced by something être [6] remplacé par quelque chose
Records had been replaced by CDs. Les disques avaient été remplacés par les CD.
Replace each noun with the correct pronoun. Remplace chaque nom par le pronom qui convient.

replacement *NOUN*
1 *(person)* le remplaçant *MASC*, la remplaçante *FEM*
2 to find a replacement for something remplacer [6] quelque chose
The chain broke and I couldn't find a replacement for it. La chaîne s'est cassée et je n'ai pas pu la remplacer.
• replacement part
la pièce de remplacement

to **replay** *VERB*
1 *(a game)* rejouer [1]
2 *(a DVD, a video)* repasser [1]

ℓ to **reply** *VERB* ▸ SEE **reply** *NOUN*
répondre [3]
to reply to something répondre à quelque chose

ℓ indicates key words

I still haven't replied to the letter. Je n'ai toujours pas répondu à la lettre.

ℰ **reply** NOUN ▸ SEE **reply** VERB
la **réponse** FEM
We're still waiting for a reply. Nous attendons toujours une réponse.
I didn't get a reply to my letter. Je n'ai pas reçu de réponse à ma lettre.
(on the telephone) There's no reply. Ça ne répond pas.

ℰ to **report** VERB ▸ SEE **report** NOUN
1 (a problem, an accident) **signaler** [1]
We've reported the theft. Nous avons signalé le vol.
There's nothing to report. Il n'y a rien à signaler.
Two people were reported dead. On a signalé deux morts.
2 to report somebody to somebody **dénoncer** [1] quelqu'un à quelqu'un
They reported him to the teacher. Ils l'ont dénoncé au professeur.
3 (to present yourself) **se présenter** ◐ [1]
I had to report to reception. Je devais me présenter à la réception.
4 to report on something **faire** [10] un reportage sur quelque chose
the journalists reporting on the conflict les journalistes qui font des reportages sur le conflit

ℰ **report** NOUN ▸ SEE **report** VERB
1 (description, account) le **compte rendu** MASC, le **rapport** MASC
to write a report **faire** [10] un compte rendu
Write a report on today's events. Fais un compte rendu des événements d'aujourd'hui.
2 (school report) le **bulletin scolaire**
3 (on the news) le **reportage**

reporter NOUN
le & la **journaliste** MASC & FEM
She's a reporter. Elle est journaliste.

to **represent** VERB
représenter [1]

representative NOUN
le **représentant** MASC, la **représentante** FEM

to **reproach** VERB ▸ SEE **reproach** NOUN
to reproach somebody **faire** [10] des reproches à quelqu'un

reproach NOUN ▸ SEE **reproach** VERB
le **reproche** MASC

reproduction NOUN
la **reproduction** FEM

reptile NOUN
le **reptile** MASC

republic NOUN
la **république** FEM

reputation NOUN
la **réputation** FEM
The town has a bad reputation. La ville a mauvaise réputation.
Claire has a reputation for honesty. Claire a la réputation d'être honnête.

to **request** VERB ▸ SEE **request** NOUN
demander [1]

request NOUN ▸ SEE **request** VERB
la **demande** FEM
I've got a special request. J'ai quelque chose à te demander.
on request sur demande
prices on request tarifs sur demande

to **rescue** VERB ▸ SEE **rescue** NOUN
sauver [1]
They rescued the dog. Ils ont sauvé le chien.

ℰ **rescue** NOUN ▸ SEE **rescue** VERB
le **secours** MASC
to come to somebody's rescue **venir** ◐ [81] au secours de quelqu'un
A policeman came to the woman's rescue. Un agent de police est venu au secours de la dame.
Jack to the rescue! Jack à la rescousse!
• rescue operation
une opération de sauvetage
• rescue party
une équipe de secours
• rescue worker
le & la secouriste

to **research** VERB ▸ SEE **research** NOUN
to research into something **faire** [10] des recherches sur quelque chose
to be well researched **être** [6] bien documenté

research NOUN ▸ SEE **research** VERB
la **recherche** FEM
to do research into something **faire** [10] des recherches sur quelque chose
She wants to do research into autism. Elle veut faire des recherches sur l'autisme.

resemblance NOUN
la **ressemblance** FEM
There's a strong resemblance between them. Ils se ressemblent beaucoup.
a family resemblance un air de famille

to **resemble** VERB
ressembler [1] à
She resembles her aunt. Elle ressemble à

◐ means the verb takes être to form the perfect

sa tante.

to **resent** VERB
    to resent somebody en vouloir [14] à quelqu'un
    She resents me because I won, not her. Elle m'en veut parce que c'est moi qui ai gagné et pas elle.

ℓ **reservation** NOUN
    la **réservation** FEM
    to make a reservation faire [10] une réservation
    Have you made a reservation? Avez-vous fait une réservation?
    We don't have a reservation. Nous n'avons pas fait de réservation.

ℓ to **reserve** VERB ▸ SEE **reserve** NOUN
    réserver [1]
    This table is reserved. Cette table est réservée.

reserve NOUN ▸ SEE **reserve** VERB
  1 *(supply)* la **réserve** FEM
    We have some in reserve. Nous en avons en réserve.
  2 *(for wildlife)* la **réserve** FEM
    a nature reserve une réserve naturelle
  3 *(person)* le **remplaçant** MASC, la **remplaçante** FEM
    Ella's on the reserve team. Ella fait partie de l'équipe de réserve.

reserved ADJECTIVE
    réservé MASC, réservée FEM

reservoir NOUN
    le **réservoir** MASC

resident NOUN
    le **résident** MASC, la **résidente** FEM

residential ADJECTIVE
    résidentiel MASC, résidentielle FEM

to **resign** VERB
    démissionner [1]

resignation NOUN
    la **démission** FEM

to **resist** VERB
    résister [1] à

to **resit** VERB
    repasser [1]

ℓ **resort** NOUN
  1 *(for holidays)* le **lieu de villégiature**
    a popular holiday resort un lieu de villégiature très visité
    a ski resort une station de ski
    a seaside resort une station balnéaire
  2 **as a last resort** en dernier recours
    I'll call her only as a last resort. Je ne

l'appellerai qu'en dernier recours.

to **respect** VERB ▸ SEE **respect** NOUN
    respecter [1]

respect NOUN ▸ SEE **respect** VERB
    le **respect** MASC
    out of respect for par respect pour

respectable ADJECTIVE
    respectable MASC & FEM

respectful ADJECTIVE
    respectueux MASC, respectueuse FEM

responsibility NOUN
    la **responsabilité** FEM

ℓ **responsible** ADJECTIVE
  1 *(to blame)* **responsable** MASC & FEM
    to be responsible for something être [6] responsable de quelque chose
    He's responsible for the delay. Il est responsable du retard.
  2 *(in charge)* **responsable** MASC & FEM
    Kirsty's responsible for booking the rooms. Kirsty est responsable de la réservation des chambres.
    to make somebody responsible for doing something charger [52] quelqu'un de faire quelque chose
    They made me responsible for collecting the money. On m'a chargé de collecter l'argent.
  3 *(reliable)* **sérieux** MASC, **sérieuse** FEM
    Daniel's not very responsible. Daniel n'est pas très sérieux.
  4 **to have a responsible job** avoir [5] un poste à responsabilités

ℓ to **rest** VERB ▸ SEE **rest** NOUN
    se reposer ◎ [1]
    Try to rest. Essaie de te reposer.

ℓ **rest** NOUN ▸ SEE **rest** VERB
  1 *(the remainder)* **the rest** le **reste** MASC
    the rest of the bread le reste du pain
    the rest of the day le reste de la journée
  2 *(the others)* **the rest** les **autres** MASC PL
    The rest have gone home. Les autres sont rentrés.
    What about the rest of them? Et les autres?
  3 *(from work)* le **repos** MASC
    ten days' complete rest dix jours de repos complet
    to have a rest se reposer ◎ [1]
    You need to have a rest. Tu as besoin de te reposer.
  4 *(a break)* la **pause** FEM
    to stop for a rest faire [10] une pause
    We stopped for a rest at two o'clock. Nous avons fait une pause à deux heures.

ℓ indicates key words

restaurant NOUN
le **restaurant** MASC
a Chinese restaurant un restaurant chinois
We had a meal in a restaurant. Nous avons mangé au restaurant.

restful ADJECTIVE
reposant MASC, reposante FEM

restless ADJECTIVE
nerveux MASC, nerveuse FEM

to **restore** VERB
1 (order, peace) rétablir [2]
It will restore his confidence. Ça va lui redonner confiance.
2 (a building, a work of art) restaurer [1]

to **restrain** VERB
1 (a person) retenir [77]
2 (a crowd) contenir [77]

to **restrict** VERB
limiter [1]

restriction NOUN
la **limitation** FEM

result NOUN
1 le **résultat** MASC
the exam results les résultats des examens
Laura's just got her results. Laura vient d'avoir ses résultats.
2 as a result par conséquent
As a result we missed the ferry. Par conséquent nous avons raté le ferry.

to **retire** VERB
(older person) prendre [64] sa retraite
holidays for retired people des vacances pour les retraités

retirement NOUN
la **retraite** FEM

to **return** VERB ▸ SEE **return** NOUN
1 (to come back) revenir ◎ [81]
He returned ten minutes later. Il est revenu dix minutes plus tard.
2 (to go back) retourner ◎ [1]
when they return to school quand ils retournent à l'école
He won't be returning to France. Il ne va pas retourner en France.
3 (to get home) rentrer ◎ [1]
to return from holiday rentrer de vacances
4 (to give back) rendre [3]
Gemma hasn't returned the DVD yet. Gemma n'a pas encore rendu le DVD.
5 (to a shop) rapporter [1]
I had to return the shoes. J'ai dû rapporter les chaussures.
6 (a phone call) to return somebody's call rappeler [18] quelqu'un

She never returns my calls. Elle ne me rappelle jamais.
• return fare
le prix d'un billet aller-retour
• return ticket
le billet aller-retour
• return trip
le voyage de retour

return NOUN ▸ SEE **return** VERB
1 le **retour** MASC
on my return à mon retour
the return to normal le retour à la normale
2 in return for something en échange de quelque chose
in return for his help en échange de son aide
3 Many happy returns! Bon anniversaire!

reunion NOUN
la **réunion** FEM
a class reunion une réunion d'anciens élèves

to **reunite** VERB
réunir [2]

to **reveal** VERB
révéler [24]

revenge NOUN
la **vengeance** FEM
to get your revenge se venger ◎ [52]

to **reverse** VERB ▸ SEE **reverse** NOUN
1 (car, bus) faire [10] marche arrière
The truck was reversing. Le camion faisait marche arrière.
Dad reversed the car out of the garage. Papa a sorti la voiture du garage en marche arrière.
2 to reverse the charges faire [10] un appel en PCV

reverse NOUN ▸ SEE **reverse** VERB
1 (of a coin) le **revers** MASC
2 (of a page) le **dos** MASC
3 (the opposite) le **contraire** MASC
4 (gear in car) la **marche arrière**

to **review** VERB ▸ SEE **review** NOUN
faire [10] la critique de
The film was well reviewed. Le film a eu une bonne critique.

review NOUN ▸ SEE **review** VERB
(of a play, a book, a film) la **critique** FEM

to **revise** VERB
réviser [1]

revision NOUN
la **révision** FEM
to do your revision faire [10] ses révisions
I still haven't done my revision. Je n'ai pas

◎ means the verb takes être to form the perfect

encore fait mes révisions.

to **revive** VERB
ranimer [1]

revolting ADJECTIVE
infect MASC, infecte FEM

revolution NOUN
la révolution FEM

revolving door NOUN
la porte à tambour

to **reward** VERB ▸ SEE **reward** NOUN
récompenser [1]

℘ **reward** NOUN ▸ SEE **reward** VERB
la récompense FEM
They're offering a reward of £50. On offre
50 livres de récompense.
as a reward for something en récompense
de quelque chose
as a reward for all their work en
récompense de tout leur travail

rewarding ADJECTIVE
enrichissant MASC, enrichissante FEM

to **rewind** VERB
rembobiner [1]

rhinoceros NOUN
le rhinocéros MASC

rhubarb NOUN
la rhubarbe FEM

rhyme NOUN
la rime FEM

rhythm NOUN
le rythme MASC

rib NOUN
la côte FEM

ribbon NOUN
le ruban MASC

℘ **rice** NOUN
le riz MASC
chicken and rice du poulet avec du riz
rice pudding le riz au lait

℘ **rich** ADJECTIVE
riche MASC & FEM
We're not very rich. Nous ne sommes pas
très riches.
the rich and the poor les riches et les
pauvres

℘ **rid** ADJECTIVE
to get rid of something se débarrasser ◉
[1] de quelque chose
We got rid of the car. Nous nous sommes
débarrassés de la voiture.
Can't you get rid of them? Tu ne peux pas

te débarrasser d'eux?

riddle NOUN
la devinette FEM

℘ to **ride** VERB ▸ SEE **ride** NOUN
1 **to ride a bike** faire [10] du vélo
Sam's learning to ride a bike. Sam apprend
à faire du vélo.
2 **to ride a horse** monter ◉ [1] à cheval
I've never ridden a horse. Je ne suis jamais
monté à cheval (boy speaking), Je ne suis
jamais montée à cheval (girl speaking).
to learn to ride apprendre [64] à monter
à cheval

℘ **ride** NOUN ▸ SEE **ride** VERB
1 le tour à vélo
to go for a (bike) ride faire [10] un tour à
vélo
We went for a ride in the park. Nous avons
fait un tour à vélo au parc.
2 la promenade à cheval
to go for a ride faire [10] une promenade
à cheval
You can go for rides at the weekend. On
peut faire des promenades le week-end.

rider NOUN
1 (on a horse) le cavalier MASC, la cavalière
FEM
2 (on a bike) le & la cycliste MASC & FEM
3 (on a motorbike) le & la motocycliste MASC
& FEM

ridiculous ADJECTIVE
ridicule MASC & FEM

℘ **riding** NOUN
l'équitation FEM
to go riding faire [10] de l'équitation
We went riding every day. Nous avons fait
de l'équitation tous les jours.
• **riding lesson**
la leçon d'équitation
• **riding school**
le centre équestre

rifle NOUN
le fusil MASC

℘ **right** ADJECTIVE ▸ SEE **right** ADVERB, NOUN
1 (not left) droit MASC, droite FEM
my right hand ma main droite
2 (correct) bon MASC, bonne FEM
the right answer la bonne réponse
the right amount of sugar la bonne
quantité de sucre
Is this the right address? Est-ce que c'est la
bonne adresse?
3 **to be right** avoir [5] raison
I'm right. J'ai raison.
You're absolutely right. Tu as tout à

A
B
C
D
E
F
G
H
I
J
K
L
M
N
O
P
Q
R
S
T
U
V
W
X
Y
Z

fait raison.
4 *(morally)* **to be right to do something** bien
faire [10] de faire quelque chose
You're right to stay at home. Tu fais bien
de rester chez toi.
He was right not to say anything. Il a bien
fait de ne rien dire.

ℓ **right** ADVERB ▸ SEE **right** ADJECTIVE, NOUN
1 *(direction)* **à droite**
Turn right at the junction. Tournez à droite
au carrefour.
2 *(correctly)* **comme il faut**
If you do it right, you'll learn faster. Si tu le
fais comme il faut, tu apprendras plus vite.
I'm not doing it right. Je ne le fais pas
comme il faut.
3 *(exactly)* **tout**
right at the beginning tout au début
right in the middle of the street en plein
milieu de la rue
**My keys were right at the bottom of my
bag.** Mes clés étaient tout au fond de mon
sac.
**The headmaster wants to see you right
now.** Le directeur veut te voir tout de suite.
4 *(okay)* **bon**
Right, let's go! Bon, allons-y!

ℓ **right** NOUN ▸ SEE **right** ADJECTIVE, ADVERB
1 *(not left)* **la droite** FEM
on the right à droite
to drive on the right rouler [1] à droite
The supermarket is on the right. Le
supermarché est à droite.
on my right à ma droite
Becky sat on my right. Becky était assise à
ma droite.
2 *(to do something)* **le droit** MASC
the right to strike le droit de grève
human rights les droits de l'homme
to have the right to do something avoir [5]
le droit de faire quelque chose
You have no right to say that. Tu n'as pas le
droit de dire ça.

to **right-click** VERB ▸ SEE **right-click** NOUN
to right-click on the icon cliquer [1] sur
l'icône en appuyant sur le bouton droit de
la souris

right-click NOUN ▸ SEE **right-click** VERB
le clic sur le bouton droit de la souris

right-hand ADJECTIVE
on the right-hand side à droite

right-handed ADJECTIVE
droitier MASC, **droitière** FEM

rind NOUN
1 *(on fruit)* **la peau** FEM
2 *(on cheese)* **la croûte** FEM

ℓ to **ring** VERB ▸ SEE **ring** NOUN
1 *(bell, phone)* **sonner** [1]
The phone rang. Le téléphone a sonné.
2 *(to phone)* **appeler** [18]
Ring me when you get back. Appelle-moi
quand tu rentres.
I tried to ring you. J'ai essayé de t'appeler.
to ring for something appeler quelque
chose
Could you ring for a taxi? Est-ce que tu
peux appeler un taxi?
• **to ring back**
rappeler [18]
I'll ring you back later. Je te rappellerai tout
à l'heure.
• **to ring off**
raccrocher [1]
• **ring road**
la rocade

ring NOUN ▸ SEE **ring** VERB
1 *(on the phone)* **to give somebody a ring**
appeler [18] quelqu'un
2 *(for your finger)* **la bague** FEM
3 *(circle)* **le cercle** MASC
4 **There was a ring at the door.** On a sonné
à la porte.

ringtone NOUN
la sonnerie FEM

to **rinse** VERB
rincer [61]

riot NOUN
une émeute FEM

rioting NOUN
les émeutes FEM PL

to **rip** VERB
déchirer [1]
• **to rip something apart**
déchiqueter [1] quelque chose
• **to rip somebody off**
arnaquer *(informal)* [1] quelqu'un
to get ripped off se faire ◎ [10] arnaquer
• **to rip something open**
déchirer [1] quelque chose

ripe ADJECTIVE
mûr MASC, **mûre** FEM

rip-off NOUN
une arnaque FEM *(informal)*
It's a total rip-off! C'est de l'arnaque!

ℓ to **rise** VERB ▸ SEE **rise** NOUN
1 *(sun)* **se lever** ◎ [50]
2 *(prices, temperatures)* **augmenter** [1]
Prices are rising fast. Les prix augmentent
rapidement.
Temperatures are still rising. Les
températures augmentent encore.

◎ means the verb takes être to form the perfect

3 *(water, path)* monter ◌ [1]

rise NOUN ▸ SEE **rise** VERB
1 la **hausse** FEM
2 a pay rise une augmentation

to **risk** VERB ▸ SEE **risk** NOUN
risquer [1]
She even risked her life. Elle a même risqué sa vie.
to risk doing something risquer de faire quelque chose
He risks getting suspended from school. Il risque d'être exclu du lycée.
I don't want to risk it. Je ne veux pas prendre le risque.

ℛ **risk** NOUN ▸ SEE **risk** VERB
le **risque** MASC
to take risks prendre [10] des risques
You take too many risks. Tu prends trop de risques.

rival NOUN
le **rival** MASC, la **rivale** FEM *(PL les **rivaux**)*

ℛ **river** NOUN
1 la **rivière** FEM
We picnicked on the edge of a river. Nous avons pique-niqué au bord d'une rivière.
2 le **fleuve** MASC
the rivers of Europe les fleuves d'Europe

> **WORD TIP** fleuve is only used for a river which flows directly into the sea like the Thames in Britain or the Seine in France.

• **river bank**
la berge

Riviera NOUN
the French Riviera la Côte d'Azur

ℛ **road** NOUN
1 la **route** FEM
the road to London la route de Londres
Is this the right road for Bradford? C'est bien la route pour Bradford?
2 *(in a town)* la **rue** FEM
on the other side of the road de l'autre côté de la rue
The bus stop's on the other side of the road. L'arrêt de bus est de l'autre côté de la rue.
3 across the road en face
They live just across the road from us. Ils habitent juste en face de chez nous.
4 *(to success, disaster)* la **voie** FEM
to be on the road to success être [6] sur la voie du succès
• **road accident**
un accident de la route
• **road map**
la carte routière

• **road rage**
la violence au volant

roadside NOUN
by the roadside au bord de la route

ℛ **road sign** NOUN
le **panneau de signalisation** *(PL les **panneaux de signalisation**)*

roadworks NOUN
les **travaux** MASC PL

ℛ **roast** ADJECTIVE ▸ SEE **roast** NOUN
rôti MASC, **rôtie** FEM
roast potatoes les pommes de terre rôties
roast beef le rôti de bœuf

ℛ **roast** NOUN ▸ SEE **roast** ADJECTIVE
le **rôti** MASC

to **rob** VERB
1 *(a person)* **voler** [1]
2 *(a bank)* **dévaliser** [1]

robber NOUN
le **voleur** MASC, la **voleuse** FEM

robbery NOUN
le **vol** MASC
a bank robbery un hold-up

robot NOUN
le **robot** MASC

rock NOUN
1 *(large stone)* le **rocher** MASC
2 *(material)* la **roche** FEM
3 *(music)* le **rock** MASC
a rock band un groupe de rock
a rock concert un concert rock
to dance rock and roll danser [1] le rock

rock climbing NOUN
l'**escalade** FEM
to go rock climbing faire [10] de l'escalade

rocket NOUN
1 la **fusée** FEM
2 *(in salad)* la **roquette** FEM

rocking horse NOUN
le **cheval à bascule**

rock star NOUN
la **rock-star** FEM

rocky ADJECTIVE
rocailleux MASC, **rocailleuse** FEM

rod NOUN
(for fishing) la **canne à pêche**

role NOUN
le **rôle** MASC

ℛ to **roll** VERB ▸ SEE **roll** NOUN
1 *(ball, coin, pen)* **rouler** [1]
The coins rolled everywhere. Les pièces

ont roulé partout.
The pen rolled off the table. Le stylo est
tombé de la table.
2 **to roll around on the grass** se rouler ⊜ [1]
dans l'herbe
3 **to roll your eyes** rouler [1] des yeux
Why are you rolling your eyes? Pourquoi
est-ce que tu roules des yeux?
4 **to roll something into a ball** rouler [1]
quelque chose en boule
I rolled my sweater into a ball. J'ai roulé
mon pull en boule.
• **to roll something out**
(pastry) étendre [3] quelque chose
• **to roll something up**
1 *(a carpet, a newspaper, a sleeping bag)*
rouler [1] quelque chose
2 *(your sleeves)* retrousser [1] quelque chose
Ross rolled up his sleeves. Ross a retroussé
ses manches.

roll NOUN ▶ SEE **roll** VERB
1 le **rouleau** MASC *(PL* les **rouleaux)**
a roll of fabric un rouleau de tissu
a toilet roll un rouleau de papier
hygiénique
a roll of film une pellicule
2 le **petit pain**
six bread rolls six petits pains
a ham roll un sandwich au jambon

roller NOUN
1 *(for paint)* le **rouleau** MASC *(PL* les **rouleaux)**
2 *(for hair)* le **bigoudi** MASC
3 *(for surfers)* le **rouleau** *(PL* les **rouleaux)**
• **rollerblades**
les **rollers** MASC PL
• **rollercoaster**
les **montagnes russes** FEM PL
• **roller skates**
les **patins à roulettes** MASC PL

Roman Catholic ADJECTIVE ▶ SEE **Roman**
Catholic NOUN
catholique MASC & FEM

Roman Catholic NOUN ▶ SEE **Roman Catholic**
ADJECTIVE
le & la **catholique** MASC & FEM

> **WORD TIP** Adjectives never have capitals in
> French, even for religions.

Romania NOUN
la **Roumanie**

Romanian ADJECTIVE ▶ SEE **Romanian** NOUN
roumain MASC, **roumaine** FEM
Romanian NOUN ▶ SEE **Romanian** ADJECTIVE
un **Roumain** MASC, une **Roumaine** FEM

romantic ADJECTIVE
romantique MASC & FEM

roof NOUN
le **toit** MASC
• **roof rack**
la **galerie**

rook NOUN
1 *(in chess)* la **tour** FEM
2 *(bird)* le **freux** MASC

♪ **room** NOUN
1 la **pièce** FEM
Mum's in the other room. Maman est dans
l'autre pièce.
She lives in a three-room flat. Elle habite
dans un appartement de trois pièces.
2 *(bedroom)* la **chambre** FEM
Leila's in her room. Leila est dans sa
chambre.
3 *(space)* la **place** FEM
There's very little room. Il y a très peu de
place.
Is there enough room for two? Est-ce qu'il
y a assez de place pour deux?
There's no room left. Il n'y a plus de place.
to make room for something faire [10] de
la place pour quelque chose
I have to make room for the table. Je dois
faire de la place pour la table.
• **roommate**
le & la **camarade de chambre**

root NOUN
la **racine** FEM

rope NOUN
la **corde** FEM

♪ **rose** NOUN
la **rose** FEM
• **rosebush**
le **rosier**

to rot VERB
pourrir [2]

rota NOUN
le **tableau de service**

rotten ADJECTIVE
(fruit, wood, weather) **pourri** MASC, **pourrie**
FEM

rough ADJECTIVE
1 *(scratchy, bumpy)* **rugueux** MASC, **rugueuse**
FEM
2 *(vague)* **approximatif** MASC, **approximative**
FEM
a rough idea une idée approximative
3 *(stormy)* **agité** MASC, **agitée** FEM
4 **to have a rough time** traverser [1] une
période difficile
5 **to sleep rough** dormir [2] à la dure
They're sleeping rough on the streets. Ils
dorment à la dure dans les rues.

⊜ **means the verb takes être to form the perfect**

roughly ADVERB
  à peu près
  roughly ten per cent à peu près dix pour
  cent

round ADVERB ▸ SEE **round** ADJECTIVE, NOUN,
PREPOSITION
1 **to go round to somebody's house** aller ⊘
  [7] chez quelqu'un
  We invited Josh round for lunch. Nous
  avons invité Josh à déjeuner.
2 **It's sunny all the year round.** Il y a du soleil
  toute l'année.

round PREPOSITION ▸ SEE **round** ADJECTIVE, ADVERB,
NOUN
1 autour de
  round the city autour de la ville
2 **to go round the shops** faire [10] les
  magasins
  to go round a museum visiter [1] un musée
  It's just round the corner. C'est juste au
  coin de la rue.
  There aren't many shops round here. Il n'y
  a pas beaucoup de magasins par ici.

ℱ **round** ADJECTIVE ▸ SEE **round** ADVERB, NOUN,
PREPOSITION
  rond MASC, ronde FEM
  a round table une table ronde
  a round face un visage rond

round NOUN ▸ SEE **round** ADJECTIVE, ADVERB,
PREPOSITION
1 (in a tournament) la **manche** FEM
2 (of cards) la **partie** FEM
3 **a round of drinks** une tournée

roundabout NOUN
1 (for traffic) le **rond-point** MASC (PL les **ronds-
points**)
2 (in fairground) le **manège** MASC

round trip NOUN
  un **aller-retour**

ℱ **route** NOUN
1 (that you plan) un **itinéraire** MASC
  The best route is via Calais. Le meilleur
  itinéraire passe par Calais.
  They went by another route. Ils ont pris un
  autre chemin.
2 (of a bus, race) le **parcours** MASC
  The 13 takes the same route. Le numéro 13
  suit le même parcours.

routine NOUN
  la **routine** FEM

row VERB ▸ SEE **row** NOUN
  ramer [1]
  We rowed across the lake. Nous avons
  traversé le lac à la rame.

row NOUN ▸ SEE **row** VERB
1 (quarrel) la **dispute** FEM
  to have a row se disputer ⊘ [1]
  I had a row with my parents. Je me suis
  disputé avec mes parents.
2 (noise) le **vacarme** MASC
3 (of houses) la **rangée** FEM
4 (of seats) le **rang** MASC

rowing NOUN
  l'**aviron** MASC
  to go rowing faire [10] de l'aviron
• **rowing boat**
  la barque

royal ADJECTIVE
  royal MASC, royale FEM, royaux MASC PL,
  royales FEM PL
  the royal family la famille royale

to **rub** VERB
  frotter [1]
  to rub your eyes se frotter ⊘ les yeux
• **to rub something out**
  effacer [61] quelque chose

rubber NOUN
1 (eraser) la **gomme** FEM
2 (material) le **caoutchouc** MASC
• **rubber band**
  un élastique

rubbish ADJECTIVE ▸ SEE **rubbish** NOUN
  nul MASC, nulle FEM
  The film was rubbish. Le film était nul.
  I'm rubbish at maths. Je suis nul en maths.

rubbish NOUN ▸ SEE **rubbish** ADJECTIVE
1 (for the bin) les **ordures** FEM PL
2 (nonsense) les **bêtises** FEM PL
  to talk rubbish dire [9] des bêtises
• **rubbish bin**
  la poubelle

ℱ **rucksack** NOUN
  le **sac à dos**
  I put on my rucksack. J'ai mis mon sac à
  dos.

rude ADJECTIVE
1 (impolite) impoli MASC, impolie FEM
  That's rude. C'est impoli.
2 (crude) grossier MASC, grossière FEM
  a rude joke une plaisanterie grossière
  a rude word un gros mot

rug NOUN
1 le **tapis** MASC
2 (blanket) la **couverture** FEM

rugby NOUN
  le **rugby** MASC
  a rugby match un match de rugby
  to play rugby jouer [1] au rugby

A B C D E F G H I J K L M N O P Q R S T U V W X Y Z

ℱ indicates key words

to **ruin** VERB ▸ SEE **ruin** NOUN
1 *(clothes, shoes, a carpet, a book)* abîmer [1]
  to ruin your eyesight s'abîmer [1] la vue
2 *(a day, a holiday)* gâcher [1]
  It ruined my evening. Ça m'a gâché la soirée.
3 *(to make poor)* ruiner [1]

ruin NOUN ▸ SEE **ruin** VERB
  la **ruine** FEM
  The house was in ruins. La maison était en ruines.

to **rule** VERB ▸ SEE **rule** NOUN
1 *(king, queen)* régner [24] sur
2 *(political party)* gouverner [1]

♀ **rule** NOUN ▸ SEE **rule** VERB
1 la **règle** FEM
  the rules of the game les règles du jeu
  a grammar rule une règle de grammaire
2 *(in an organization)* le **règlement**
  the school rules le règlement de l'école
  It's against the rules. C'est contraire au règlement.
3 **as a rule** en général
  As a rule, I don't eat fish. En général, je ne mange pas de poisson.

ruler NOUN
  la **règle** FEM

rum NOUN
  le **rhum** MASC

to **rummage** VERB
  fouiller [1]

rumour NOUN
  la **rumeur** FEM

♀ to **run** VERB ▸ SEE **run** NOUN
1 courir [29]
  I ran ten kilometres. J'ai couru dix kilomètres.
  He ran across the pitch. Il a traversé le terrain en courant.
  I ran down the stairs. J'ai descendu l'escalier en courant.
  Somebody was running after us. Quelqu'un nous courait après.
2 *(to organize)* organiser [1]
  Who's running this concert? Qui organise ce concert?
3 *(a business)* diriger [52]
  My parents run a small company. Mes parents dirigent une petite entreprise.
4 *(train, bus)* circuler [1]
  The buses don't run on Sundays. Les bus ne circulent pas le dimanche.
5 **to run a bath** faire [10] couler un bain
  I'll run you a bath. Je vais te faire couler un bain.

• **to run away**
1 s'enfuir [44]
  The thieves ran away. Les voleurs se sont enfuis.
2 *(child, teenager)* faire [10] une fugue
  She ran away from home. Elle a fait une fugue.
• **to run into something**
  rentrer ◎ [1] dans quelque chose
  The car ran into a lamppost. La voiture est rentrée dans un réverbère.
• **to run out of something**
  We've run out of bread. Il ne reste plus de pain.
  I'm running out of money. Je n'ai presque plus d'argent.
• **to run somebody over**
  écraser [1] quelqu'un
  to get run over se faire ◎ [10] écraser

run NOUN ▸ SEE **run** VERB
1 **to go for a run** aller ◎ [7] courir
2 *(in cricket)* le **point** MASC
3 **in the long run** à long terme

runner NOUN
  le **coureur** MASC, la **coureuse** FEM

runner-up NOUN
  le **second** MASC, la **seconde** FEM

running ADJECTIVE ▸ SEE **running** NOUN
1 **running water** l'eau courante
2 *(in a row)* de suite
  three days running trois jours de suite

running NOUN ▸ SEE **running** ADJECTIVE
  la **course à pied**
  to take up running se mettre ◎ [11] à la course à pied

runway NOUN
  la **piste** FEM

to **rush** VERB ▸ SEE **rush** NOUN
1 *(to hurry)* se dépêcher ◎ [1]
2 *(to make a person hurry)* bousculer [1]
3 *(to run)* se précipiter ◎ [1]
  She rushed into the street. Elle s'est précipitée dans la rue.
4 **to rush somebody to hospital** emmener [50] quelqu'un d'urgence à l'hôpital

rush NOUN ▸ SEE **rush** VERB
  to be in a rush être [6] pressé
  There's no rush. Ça ne presse pas.

rush hour NOUN
  les **heures de pointe** FEM PL
  in the rush hour aux heures de pointe

Russia NOUN
  la **Russie** FEM
  in Russia en Russie
  to Russia en Russie

◎ means the verb takes être to form the perfect

Russian ADJECTIVE ▶ SEE **Russian** NOUN
  russe MASC & FEM

Russian NOUN ▶ SEE **Russian** ADJECTIVE
1 un & une **Russe** MASC & FEM
  the Russians les Russes
2 (the language) le **russe** MASC

rust NOUN
  la **rouille** FEM

rusty ADJECTIVE
  rouillé MASC, **rouillée** FEM

rye NOUN
  le **seigle** MASC
  rye bread le pain de seigle

Ss

Sabbath NOUN
1 (Christian) le **dimanche** MASC
2 (Jewish) le **sabbat** MASC

> **WORD TIP** Months of the year and days of the week start with small letters in French.

sack NOUN
  le **sac** MASC
  sacks of corn des sacs de maïs

sacred ADJECTIVE
  sacré MASC, **sacrée** FEM

sacrifice NOUN
  le **sacrifice** MASC
  to make sacrifices faire [10] des sacrifices

ℰ **sad** ADJECTIVE
1 (unhappy) **triste** MASC & FEM
  She looks sad. Elle a l'air triste.
  to make somebody sad rendre [3] quelqu'un triste
  It makes me sad. Ça me rend triste.
2 (pathetic) **nul** MASC, **nulle** FEM
  You're so sad! Vous êtes vraiment nuls!

saddle NOUN
  la **selle** FEM

saddlebag NOUN
  la **sacoche** FEM

sadly ADVERB
1 **tristement**
2 (unfortunately) **malheureusement**
  Sadly, they never saw him again. Malheureusement, ils ne l'ont jamais revu.

ℰ **safe** ADJECTIVE ▶ SEE **safe** NOUN
1 (unharmed) **hors de danger**
  The children are safe. Les enfants sont hors de danger.
  to feel safe se sentir ◎ [58] en sécurité

  I don't feel safe here. Je ne me sens pas en sécurité ici.
2 (not dangerous) **pas dangereux** MASC, **pas dangereuse** FEM
  It's a safe activity. Cette activité n'est pas dangereuse.
  Is it safe to swim here? Est-ce qu'on peut se baigner ici sans danger?
  The paths are safe. Les sentiers ne sont pas dangereux.
  Your bag is safe there. Ton sac ne risque rien là.

safe NOUN ▶ SEE **safe** ADJECTIVE
  le **coffre-fort** (PL les **coffres-forts**)

safety NOUN
  la **sécurité** FEM
  safety on the roads la sécurité routière
• **safety belt**
  la ceinture de sécurité
• **safety pin**
  une épingle de nourrice

Sagittarius NOUN
  le **Sagittaire** MASC
  Debbie's Sagittarius. Debbie est Sagittaire.

> **WORD TIP** Signs of the zodiac do not take an article: un or une.

to **sail** VERB ▶ SEE **sail** NOUN
  to sail around the world faire [10] le tour du monde en bateau

sail NOUN ▶ SEE **sail** VERB
  la **voile** FEM

sailing NOUN
  la **voile** FEM
  She does a lot of sailing. Elle fait beaucoup de voile.
  We went sailing in Corsica. Nous avons fait de la voile en Corse.
• **sailing boat**
  le voilier
• **sailing club**
  le club de voile

sailor NOUN
  le **marin** MASC

saint NOUN
  le **saint** MASC, la **sainte** FEM

salad NOUN
  la **salade** FEM
  a tomato salad une salade de tomates
• **salad dressing**
  la vinaigrette

ℰ **salami** NOUN
  le **saucisson** MASC

salary NOUN
  le **salaire** MASC

ℰ indicates key words

ℱ **sale** NOUN
1 (selling) la **vente** FEM
the sale of the house la vente de la maison
on sale at the post office en vente au
bureau de poste
'For sale' 'À vendre'
2 the sales les **soldes** FEM PL
There's a sale on. Il y a des soldes.
I bought it in the sales. Je l'ai acheté en
solde.
• sales assistant
le vendeur, la vendeuse
• salesman
le représentant
• saleswoman
la représentante

saliva NOUN
la **salive** FEM

salmon NOUN
le **saumon** MASC

ℱ **salt** NOUN
le **sel** MASC
• salt water
l'eau salée FEM

ℱ **salty** ADJECTIVE
salé MASC, salée FEM

ℱ **same** ADJECTIVE
1 **même** MASC & FEM
the same thing la même chose
the same people les mêmes gens
We arrived at the same time. Nous
sommes arrivés en même temps.
2 the same **pareil** MASC, **pareille** FEM
It's not the same. Ce n'est pas pareil.
The two bikes are the same. Les deux vélos
sont pareils.
3 the same as **comme**
We did the same as everyone else. On a
fait comme tous les autres.

sample NOUN
un **échantillon** MASC

sand NOUN
le **sable** MASC

ℱ **sandal** NOUN
la **sandale** FEM
a pair of sandals une paire de sandales

sand castle NOUN
le **château de sable** (PL les **châteaux de
sable**)

sand dune NOUN
la **dune** FEM

sandpaper NOUN
le **papier de verre**

ℱ **sandwich** NOUN
le **sandwich** MASC
a ham sandwich un sandwich au jambon

sanitary towel NOUN
la **serviette hygiénique**

Santa Claus NOUN
le **père Noël**
to believe in Santa Claus croire [33] au
père Noël

sarcasm NOUN
le **sarcasme** MASC

sarcastic ADJECTIVE
sarcastique MASC & FEM
sarcastic comments des remarques
sarcastiques

sardine NOUN
la **sardine** FEM

satchel NOUN
le **cartable** MASC

ℱ **satellite** NOUN
la **satellite** MASC
to be transmitted by satellite être [6]
transmis par satellite
• satellite dish
une antenne parabolique
• satellite television
la télévision par satellite

satisfactory ADJECTIVE
satisfaisant MASC, **satisfaisante** FEM

ℱ **satisfied** ADJECTIVE
satisfait MASC, **satisfaite** FEM
satisfied customers des clients satisfaits
The teacher wasn't satisfied. La prof n'était
pas satisfaite.
to be satisfied with something être [6]
satisfait de quelque chose
He's satisfied with my progress. Il est
satisfait de mes progrès.

to **satisfy** VERB
satisfaire [10]

satisfying ADJECTIVE
1 (pleasing) **satisfaisant** MASC, **satisfaisante**
FEM
a satisfying result un résultat satisfaisant
2 (meal) **consistant** MASC, **consistante** FEM

ℱ **Saturday** NOUN
le **samedi** MASC
last Saturday samedi dernier
next Saturday samedi prochain
every Saturday tous les samedis
on Saturdays le samedi
I'm going out on Saturday. Je sors samedi.

◆ means the verb takes être to form the perfect

See you on Saturday! À samedi!

WORD TIP Months of the year and days of the week start with small letters in French.

sauce NOUN
la **sauce** FEM
in tomato sauce à la sauce tomate

♪ **saucepan** NOUN
la **casserole** FEM

♪ **saucer** NOUN
la **soucoupe** FEM

♪ **sausage** NOUN
1 la **saucisse** FEM
2 (salami) le **saucisson** MASC

♪ to **save** VERB
1 (to rescue) **sauver** [1]
to save somebody's life sauver la vie à quelqu'un
The doctors saved his life. Les médecins lui ont sauvé la vie.
2 (money, food) **mettre** [11] de côté
I've saved £60. J'ai mis soixante livres de côté.
I walk to school to save money. Je vais à l'école à pied pour économiser de l'argent.
3 **to save time** gagner [1] du temps
We took a taxi to save time. On a pris un taxi pour gagner du temps.
4 (work, a document) **sauvegarder** [1]
Always save your documents. Il faut toujours sauvegarder tes documents.
5 (a penalty, a shot) **arrêter** [1]
• **to save up**
mettre [11] de l'argent de côté
I'm saving up to go to Spain. Je mets de l'argent de côté pour aller en Espagne.

savings PLURAL NOUN
les **économies** FEM PL
• **savings account**
la compte d'épargne

♪ **savoury** ADJECTIVE
salé MASC, **salée** FEM
I prefer savoury things to sweet things. J'aime mieux les choses salées que les choses sucrées.

saw NOUN
la **scie** FEM
to cut wood with a saw scier [1] du bois

saxophone NOUN
le **saxophone** MASC
to play the saxophone jouer [1] du saxophone

♪ to **say** VERB
1 **dire** [9]
What did you say? Qu'est-ce que tu as dit?

to say that ... dire que ...
She says (that) she's tired. Elle dit qu'elle est fatiguée.
They say (that) there's no class. Ils disent qu'il n'y a pas de cours.
How do you say 'money' in French? Comment dire 'money' en français?
I didn't know what to say. Je ne savais quoi dire.
2 **to say something again** répéter [24] quelque chose
Could you say it again, please? Pouvez-vous répéter, s'il vous plaît?
3 (in expressions) **let's say** disons
Let's say, 15 cm. Disons, quinze centimètres.
as they say comme on dit
'À bientôt', as they say in French. 'À bientôt', comme on dit en français.

saying NOUN
le **dicton** MASC

scab NOUN
la **croûte** FEM

scale NOUN
1 (of a map, a model) l'**échelle** FEM
a large-scale map une carte à grande échelle
2 (extent) l'**ampleur** FEM
to estimate the scale of the disaster évaluer l'ampleur du désastre
3 (in music) la **gamme** FEM
to practise your scales faire [10] ses gammes
4 (of a fish) une **écaille** FEM

scales NOUN
1 (for food) la **balance** FEM
2 (for people) le **pèse-personne** MASC

scallop NOUN
la **coquille Saint-Jacques**

scalp NOUN
le **cuir chevelu**

to **scan** VERB
scanner [1]
to scan a photograph scanner une photo

scandal NOUN
le **scandale** MASC

Scandinavia NOUN
la **Scandinavie** FEM

Scandinavian ADJECTIVE
scandinave MASC & FEM

scanner NOUN
le **scanner** MASC

scar NOUN
la **cicatrice** FEM

ℓ **scarce** ADJECTIVE
rare MASC & FEM
to become scarce devenir ⊘ [81] rare
Water is scarce. L'eau est rare.

scarcely ADVERB
à peine
She scarcely spoke to us. Elle nous a parlé à peine.

ℓ **to scare** VERB ▸ SEE **scare** NOUN
to scare somebody faire [10] peur à quelqu'un
You scared me! Tu m'as fait peur!

scare NOUN ▸ SEE **scare** VERB
1 la **panique** FEM
It caused a scare. Cela a provoqué une panique.
We got quite a scare. Nous avons vraiment eu peur.
2 **a bomb scare** une alerte à la bombe

scarecrow NOUN
un **épouvantail** MASC

ℓ **scared** ADJECTIVE
to be scared avoir [5] peur
I'm scared! J'ai peur!
to be scared of something avoir [5] peur de quelque chose
She's scared of spiders. Elle a peur des araignées.
He's scared of his grandmother. Il a peur de sa grand-mère.
to be scared of doing something avoir [5] peur de faire quelque chose
I'm scared of failing the exam. J'ai peur d'échouer l'examen.

scarf NOUN
1 (silky) le **foulard** MASC
2 (long, warm) une **écharpe** FEM

scary ADJECTIVE
effrayant MASC, **effrayante** FEM
a scary experience une expérience effrayante
It's quite scary. Ça fait plutôt peur.

ℓ **scene** NOUN
1 (of an incident, a crime) le **lieu** MASC
the scene of the crime le lieu du crime
to be at the scene être [6] sur les lieux
The police were at the scene. La police était sur les lieux.
2 (world) le **monde** MASC
on the music scene dans le monde de la musique
3 **scenes of violence** des incidents violents

scenery NOUN
1 (landscape) le **paysage** MASC
2 (theatrical) les **décors** MASC PL

scent NOUN
le **parfum** MASC

scented ADJECTIVE
parfumé MASC, **parfumée** FEM

ℓ **schedule** NOUN
le **programme** MASC
We have a tight schedule. Nous avons un programme serré.

scheme NOUN
le **projet** MASC
It's a scheme to solve traffic problems. C'est un projet pour résoudre les problèmes de circulation.

scholarship NOUN
la **bourse** FEM
to win a scholarship gagner [1] une bourse

ℓ **school** NOUN
une **école** FEM
at school à l'école
to go to school aller ⊘ [7] à l'école
She goes to the same school as me. Elle va à la même école que moi.
I take the bus to school. Je prends le bus pour aller à l'école.
I'm going to change schools. Je vais changer d'école.
There's no school on Friday. Il n'y a pas de classe vendredi.
• **schoolbag**
le cartable
• **schoolbook**
le livre scolaire
• **schoolboy**
un écolier
• **schoolchildren**
les écoliers MASC PL
• **school day**
la journée scolaire
• **schoolfriend**
le & la camarade de classe
• **schoolgirl**
une écolière
• **school trip**
le voyage scolaire
• **school uniform**
un uniforme scolaire
• **school year**
une année scolaire

ℓ **science** NOUN
la **science** FEM
the science teacher le prof des sciences
I like science. J'aime la science.

science fiction NOUN
la **science-fiction** FEM
science fiction films les films de science-fiction

scientific ADJECTIVE
scientifique MASC & FEM
a scientific experiment une expérience scientifique

scientist NOUN
le & la **scientifique** MASC & FEM

ℓ **scissors** PLURAL NOUN
les **ciseaux** MASC PL

to **scoff** VERB
(to eat) **bouffer** [1] *(informal)*
He's scoffed everything! Il a tout bouffé!

scoop NOUN
(of ice cream) la **boule** FEM
How many scoops would you like? Vous voulez combien de boules?
Two scoops of vanilla. Deux boules de vanille.

scooter NOUN
1 *(motor scooter)* le **scooter** MASC
2 *(for a child)* la **trottinette** FEM

ℓ to **score** VERB ▸ SEE **score** NOUN
marquer [1]
She scored twice. Elle a marqué deux buts.
to score a goal marquer un but
Ollie scored a goal. Ollie a marqué un but.
I scored three points. J'ai marqué trois points.

score NOUN ▸ SEE **score** VERB
le **score** MASC
The score was five two. Le score était cinq à deux.
to keep score compter [1] les points

Scorpio NOUN
le **Scorpion** MASC
Jessica's Scorpio. Jessica est Scorpion.

WORD TIP Signs of the zodiac do not take an article: un or une.

ℓ **Scot** NOUN
un **Écossais** MASC, une **Écossaise** FEM
the Scots les Écossais MASC PL

ℓ **Scotland** NOUN
l'**Écosse** FEM
in Scotland en Écosse
to go to Scotland aller ◎ [7] en Écosse
Pauline's from Scotland. Pauline est écossaise.

WORD TIP Countries and regions in French take le, la or les.

Scots ADJECTIVE
écossais MASC, **écossaise** FEM
a Scots accent un accent écossais

WORD TIP Adjectives never have capitals in French, even for nationality or regional origin.

Scotsman NOUN
un **Écossais** MASC

Scotswoman NOUN
une **Écossaise** FEM

ℓ **Scottish** ADJECTIVE
écossais MASC, **écossaise** FEM
a Scottish dance une danse écossaise
Scottish people les Écossais

WORD TIP Adjectives never have capitals in French, even for nationality or regional origin.

scout NOUN
le **scout** MASC

scrambled eggs NOUN
les **œufs brouillés**

scrap NOUN
1 *(of cloth, food)* le **bout** MASC
a scrap of paper un bout de papier
some scraps of bread quelques bouts de pain
2 *(a fight)* la **bagarre** FEM
a scrap in the playground une bagarre dans la cour
• **scrapbook**
un album

to **scrape** VERB
1 **gratter** [1]
2 **to scrape your knees** s'écorcher [1] les genous

to **scratch** VERB ▸ SEE **scratch** NOUN
1 **to scratch (yourself)** se gratter ◎ [1]
to scratch your head se gratter ◎ [1] la tête
2 *(the paintwork)* **érafler** [1]

scratch NOUN ▸ SEE **scratch** VERB
1 *(on your skin)* une **égratignure** FEM
2 *(on a surface)* la **rayure** FEM
3 *(from the start)* **from scratch**
We had to start from scratch. Nous avons dû partir de zéro.

ℓ to **scream** VERB ▸ SEE **scream** NOUN
crier [1]
to scream with fright crier de peur

scream NOUN ▸ SEE **scream** VERB
le **cri** MASC

ℓ **screen** NOUN
un **écran** MASC
on the screen à l'écran
on the computer screen sur l'écran d'ordinateur

to **screw** VERB ▶ SEE **screw** NOUN
visser [1]
to screw the top on a bottle visser le bouchon sur une bouteille.

screw NOUN ▶ SEE **screw** VERB
la **vis** FEM

screwdriver NOUN
le **tournevis** MASC

to **scribble** VERB
griffonner [1]

to **scrub** VERB
(a saucepan) récurer [1]
to scrub your nails se brosser ◎ [1] les ongles

scuba diving NOUN
la plongée sous-marine
to go scuba diving faire [10] la plongée sous-marine

sculptor NOUN
le **sculpteur** MASC, la **sculptrice** FEM

sculpture NOUN
la **sculpture** FEM

ℙ **sea** NOUN
la **mer** FEM
a holiday by the sea des vacances au bord de la mer
a sea view une vue de mer

ℙ **seafood** NOUN
les **fruits de mer**
I love seafood. J'adore les fruits de mer.

seagull NOUN
la **mouette** FEM

to **seal** VERB ▶ SEE **seal** NOUN
(an envelope) coller [1]
It wasn't sealed properly. Ce n'était pas bien collé.

seal NOUN ▶ SEE **seal** VERB
(animal) le **phoque** MASC

seaman NOUN
le **marin** MASC

ℙ to **search** VERB ▶ SEE **search** NOUN
1 (a house, a bag) fouiller [1]
The police are searching the area. La police est en train de fouiller le quartier.
They searched us at the airport. Ils nous ont fouillé à l'aéroport.
2 (for something, someone) chercher [1]
They're still searching for the family. Ils cherchent encore la famille.
I've searched everywhere for the scissors. J'ai cherché les ciseaux partout.

search NOUN ▶ SEE **search** VERB
1 la **fouille** FEM

to carry out a search of something fouiller [1] quelque chose
2 (Computers) la **recherche**
to do a search effectuer [1] une recherche

seashell NOUN
le **coquillage** MASC

seasick ADJECTIVE
to be seasick avoir [5] le mal de mer

seaside NOUN
at the seaside au bord de la mer
We spent a week at the seaside. Nous avons passé une semaine au bord de la mer.
• **seaside resort**
la station balnéaire

ℙ **season** NOUN
la **saison** FEM
the rugby season la saison de rugby
during the holiday season pendant la période des vacances
Strawberries are in season. C'est la saison des fraises.
• **season ticket**
la carte d'abonnement

ℙ **seat** NOUN
1 (part of a chair) le **siège** MASC
the front seat le siège avant
the back seat le siège arrière
to be sitting in the front seat être [6] assis à l'avant.
Have a seat. Asseyez-vous.
2 (that you book) la **place** FEM
to book a seat réserver [1] une place
I'd like a window seat. Je voudrais une place côté fenêtre.
There are no more seats. Il n'y a plus de places.

seatbelt NOUN
la **ceinture de sécurité**
to fasten your seatbelt attacher [1] sa ceinture de sécurité

seaweed NOUN
les **algues** FEM PL

ℙ **second** ADJECTIVE ▶ SEE **second** NOUN
1 **deuxième** MASC & FEM
for the second time pour la deuxième fois
to come second arriver ◎ [1] en deuxième position
2 (in dates) **the second of July** le deux juillet
3 **the Second World War** la Seconde Guerre mondiale

ℙ **second** NOUN ▶ SEE **second** ADJECTIVE
la **seconde** FEM
Can you wait a second? Est-ce que tu peux attendre une seconde?
It takes a second. Ça prend une seconde.

◎ means the verb takes être to form the perfect

ℰ **secondary school** *NOUN*
1 le **collège** *MASC*
up to the end of the equivalent of Year 10
2 le **lycée** *MASC*
for the equivalent of Years 11 to 13

second class *ADJECTIVE, ADVERB*
1 **to travel second class** voyager [52] en deuxième classe
a seat in second class une place en deuxième classe
2 *(average)* **a second class team** une équipe de niveau très moyen

ℰ **secondhand** *ADJECTIVE, ADVERB*
d'occasion
a secondhand bike un vélo d'occasion
I bought it secondhand. Je l'ai acheté d'occasion.

secondly *ADVERB*
deuxièmement

secret *ADJECTIVE* ▶ SEE **secret** *NOUN*
secret *MASC*, secrète *FEM*

ℰ **secret** *NOUN* ▶ SEE **secret** *ADJECTIVE*
le **secret** *MASC*
to keep a secret garder [1] un secret
Can you keep a secret? Est-ce que tu peux garder un secret?
He sees her in secret. Il la voit en secret.

secretarial college *NOUN*
une école de secrétariat

ℰ **secretary** *NOUN*
le & la **secrétaire** *MASC & FEM*
She's a secretary. Elle est secrétaire.

secretly *ADVERB*
secrètement

sect *NOUN*
la **secte** *FEM*

ℰ **section** *NOUN*
1 la **partie** *FEM*
a section of the train une partie du train
2 *(in a shop, a library)* le **rayon** *MASC*
in the children's section au rayon enfants

security *NOUN*
la **sécurité** *FEM*
• **security guard**
le **vigile**

ℰ **to see** *VERB*
1 *(in general)* **voir** [13]
I saw Becky yesterday. J'ai vu Becky hier.
Have you seen the film? Est-ce que tu as vu le film?
Did you see that programme? Est-ce que tu as vu cette émission?

I'm going to see the doctor. Je vais voir le médecin.
'Can Luke come?' — 'We'll see.' 'Est-ce que Luke peut venir?' — 'On verra.'
2 **to be able to see** voir [13]
Can you see it? Est-ce que tu le vois?
I can't see anything. Je ne vois rien.
3 *(saying goodbye)* **See you!** Salut!, À plus! *(informal)*
See you on Saturday! À samedi!
See you soon! À bientôt!
• **to see to something**
s'occuper [1] de quelque chose
Could you see to the drinks, please? Tu peux t'occuper des boissons, s'il te plaît?

seed *NOUN*
la **graine** *FEM*
to plant seeds semer [50] des graines

ℰ **to seem** *VERB*
1 **paraître** [57]
it seems that ... il paraît que ...
It seems that he's left. Il paraît qu'il est parti.
It seems odd to me. Ça me paraît bizarre.
2 *(to look, to appear to be)* **avoir** [5] **l'air**
to seem shy avoir l'air timide
Amy seemed tired. Amy avait l'air fatiguée.
to seem to be ... avoir [5] l'air d'être ...
The pool seems to be closed. La piscine a l'air d'être fermée.

seesaw *NOUN*
la **balançoire** *FEM*

to select *VERB*
sélectionner [1]
to be selected for the team être [6] sélectionné pour l'équipe

selection *NOUN*
la **sélection** *FEM*

self-confidence *NOUN*
la **confiance en soi**
He has a lot of self-confidence. Il a beaucoup de confiance en lui.

self-confident *ADJECTIVE*
assuré *MASC*, assurée *FEM*
to be self-confident être [6] sûr de soi

self-conscious *ADJECTIVE*
timide *MASC & FEM*

self-employed *ADJECTIVE*
a self-employed person un travailleur indépendant
to be self-employed travailler [1] à son compte

selfish ADJECTIVE
   égoïste MASC & FEM

ℰ to **sell** VERB
   vendre [3]
   Do you sell stamps? Est-ce que vous vendez
   des timbres?
   The house has been sold. La maison a été
   vendue.
   to sell something to somebody vendre
   quelque chose à quelqu'un
   I sold him my bike. Je lui ai vendu mon vélo.
   • sell-by date
     la date limite de vente

seller NOUN
   le **vendeur** MASC, la **vendeuse** FEM

Sellotape® NOUN
   le **Scotch®** MASC
   to stick something with Sellotape scotcher
   [1] quelque chose (informal)

semicircle NOUN
   le **demi-cercle** MASC

semicolon NOUN
   le **point-virgule** MASC

semi-detached house NOUN
   la **maison jumelée**
   We live in a semi-detached house. Nous
   habitons dans une maison jumelée.

semi-final NOUN
   la **demi-finale** FEM

semi-skimmed milk NOUN
   le **lait demi-écrémé**

ℰ to **send** VERB
   envoyer [40]
   to send an email envoyer un email
   to send something to somebody envoyer
   quelque chose à quelqu'un
   I sent her a Valentine card. Je lui ai envoyé
   une carte de la Saint-Valentin.
   Send me a text. Envoie-moi un texto.
   • to send somebody back
     renvoyer [40] quelqu'un
     She sent me back home. Elle m'a renvoyé
     chez moi.
   • to send something back
     renvoyer [40] quelque chose
     I'm going to send the book back. Je vais
     renvoyer le livre.

sender NOUN
   un **expéditeur** MASC, une **expéditrice** FEM

senior citizen NOUN
   une **personne âgée**

sensation NOUN
   1 (feeling) la **sensation** FEM

   2 (impact) la **sensation** FEM
   She caused a sensation. Elle a fait
   sensation.

sensational ADJECTIVE
   sensationnel MASC, sensationnelle FEM

ℰ **sense** NOUN
   le **sens** MASC
   It doesn't make sense. Ça n'a pas de sens.
   That makes sense. Ça paraît logique.
   to have the sense to do something avoir
   [5] le bon sens de faire quelque chose
   She had the sense to tell me. Elle a eu le
   bon sens de me le dire.
   I can't make sense of it. Je ne le comprends
   pas.
   • sense of humour
     le sens de l'humour
   • sense of smell
     l'odorat MASC
   • sense of touch
     le toucher

ℰ **sensible** ADJECTIVE
   raisonnable MASC & FEM
   He's very sensible. Il est très raisonnable.
   It's a sensible decision. C'est une décision
   raisonnable.

ℰ **sensitive** ADJECTIVE
   sensible MASC & FEM
   I've got sensitive skin. J'ai la peau sensible.
   She's very sensitive. Elle est très sensible.

   to **sentence** VERB ▸ SEE **sentence** NOUN
   condamner [1]
   to be sentenced to death être [6]
   condamné à mort

ℰ **sentence** NOUN ▸ SEE **sentence** VERB
   1 (in writing) la **phrase** FEM
   Écris une phrase en français. Write a
   sentence in French.
   2 (Law) the death sentence la peine de mort

sentimental ADJECTIVE
   sentimental MASC, sentimentale FEM,
   sentimentaux MASC PL, sentimentales
   FEM PL

to **separate** VERB ▸ SEE **separate** ADJECTIVE
   1 séparer [1]
   The teacher separated them. Le prof les a
   séparés.
   2 (couple) se séparer ⊙ [1]
   Her parents have separated. Ses parents se
   sont séparés.

ℰ **separate** ADJECTIVE ▸ SEE **separate** VERB
   1 (apart) à part
   in a separate pile dans une pile à part
   on a separate sheet of paper sur une feuille
   à part

⊙ means the verb takes être to form the perfect

2 *(different)* **autre** *MASC & FEM*
in a separate box dans une autre boîte
That's a separate problem. C'est un autre problème.

3 **We have separate rooms.** Nous avons chacun notre chambre.

separately *ADVERB*
séparément

separation *NOUN*
la **séparation** *FEM*

September *NOUN*
septembre *MASC*
in September en septembre

> **WORD TIP** Months of the year and days of the week start with small letters in French.

sequel *NOUN*
la **suite** *FEM*
in the film's sequel dans la suite au film

sequence *NOUN*
1 *(of events)* la **série** *FEM*
2 *(in a film)* la **séquence** *FEM*

sergeant *NOUN*
1 *(in the police)* le **brigadier** *MASC*
2 *(in the army)* le **sergent** *MASC*

ℱ **serial** *NOUN*
le **feuilleton** *MASC*
a TV serial un feuilleton télévisé
• **serial killer**
un auteur de meurtres en série

series *NOUN*
la **série** *FEM*
a television series une série télévisée
a series of strange events une série d'événements bizarres

ℱ **serious** *ADJECTIVE*
1 *(illness, injury, mistake, problem)* **grave** *MASC & FEM*
a serious problem un grave problème.
It's not a serious mistake. Ce n'est pas une grave erreur.

2 *(earnest)* **sérieux** *MASC*, **sérieuse** *FEM*
a serious discussion une discussion sérieuse
Are you serious? Sérieusement?
to be serious about doing something avoir [5] vraiment l'intention de faire quelque chose
I'm serious about looking for a job. J'ai vraiment l'intention de chercher un travail.

ℱ **seriously** *ADVERB*
1 *(ill, injured)* **gravement**
She's seriously ill. Elle est gravement malade.

2 *(no joking)* **sérieusement**

Seriously, I have to go. Sérieusement, je dois partir.

3 **to take somebody seriously** prendre [64] quelqu'un au sérieux
She doesn't take me seriously. Elle ne me prend pas au sérieux.

servant *NOUN*
le & la **domestique** *MASC & FEM*

to **serve** *VERB* ▶ SEE **serve** *NOUN*
1 *(food, a meal)* **servir** [71]
They served the fish with a lemon sauce. Ils ont servi le poisson accompagné d'une sauce au citron.
2 *(in tennis)* **servir** [71]
3 **It serves him right!** C'est bien fait pour lui!

serve *NOUN* ▶ SEE **serve** *VERB*
(in tennis) le **service** *MASC*
Whose serve is it? C'est à qui de servir?

to **service** *VERB* ▶ SEE **service** *NOUN*
réviser [1]
to have your car serviced faire [10] réviser sa voiture

ℱ **service** *NOUN* ▶ SEE **service** *VERB*
1 *(in a restaurants, hotels)* le **service** *MASC*
room service le service de chambre
Is service included? Est-ce que le service est compris?
Service is not included. Le service n'est pas compris.
2 *(for the public)* le **service** *MASC*
a bus service un service d'autobus
Call the emergency services! Appelle police-secours!
3 *(for cars)* la **révision** *FEM*
4 *(in church)* un **office** *MASC*

service area *NOUN*
une **aire de services**

service charge *NOUN*
le **service** *MASC*
There's no service charge. Le service est compris.

ℱ **service station** *NOUN*
la **station-service** *FEM* (*PL* les **stations-service**)

serviette *NOUN*
la **serviette** *FEM*

ℱ **session** *NOUN*
la **séance** *FEM*
a training session une séance d'entraînement
a recording session une séance d'enregistrement

ℱ to **set** *VERB* ▶ SEE **set** *ADJECTIVE*, *NOUN*
1 *(a date, a time)* **fixer** [1]

They've set the date. Ils ont fixé la date.
2 *(a record)* établir [2]
She set a new world record. Elle a établi un nouveau record mondial.
3 *(the table, an alarm clock)* mettre [11]
Who's setting the table? Qui met la table?
I've set my alarm for seven. J'ai mis mon réveil à sept heures.
to set your watch régler [24] sa montre
4 *(sun)* se coucher ⊙ [1]
• to set off
partir ⊙ [58]
We're setting off at ten. Nous allons partir à dix heures.
• to set off something
1 *(a firework)* faire [10] partir
2 *(a bomb)* faire [10] exploser
3 *(an alarm)* déclencher [1]
• to set out
partir ⊙ [58]
They set out for Calais yesterday. Ils sont partis pour Calais hier.

set ADJECTIVE ▸ SEE **set** NOUN, VERB
fixe MASC & FEM
at a set time à une heure fixe
a set menu un menu à prix fixe

ℰ **set** NOUN ▸ SEE **set** ADJECTIVE, VERB
1 *(games)* le **jeu** MASC (PL les **jeux**)
a chess set un jeu d'échecs
2 **a train set** un petit train
3 *(in tennis)* le **set** MASC

ℰ **settee** NOUN
le canapé MASC

ℰ to **settle** VERB
(a bill, an argument) régler [24]
Have you settled the bill? Est-ce que tu as réglé l'addition?

seven NUMBER
sept
Lucy's seven. Lucy a sept ans.

seventeen NUMBER
dix-sept
Matt's seventeen. Matt a dix-sept ans.

seventeenth ADJECTIVE
1 dix-sept MASC & FEM
2 *(in dates)* **the seventeenth of June** le dix-sept juin

seventh ADJECTIVE
1 septième MASC & FEM
on the seventh floor au septième étage
2 *(in dates)* **the seventh of July** le sept juillet

seventies PLURAL NOUN
the seventies les années soixante-dix
in the seventies aux années soixante-dix

seventieth ADJECTIVE
soixante-dixième MASC & FEM
It's her seventieth birthday. Elle fête ses soixante-dix ans.

seventy NUMBER
soixante-dix
Grandma's seventy. Ma grand-mère a soixante-dix ans.

ℰ **several** ADJECTIVE, PRONOUN
plusieurs MASC & FEM
several people plusieurs personnes
several times plusieurs fois
I've seen several of her films. J'ai vu plusieurs de ses films.

severe ADJECTIVE
1 *(serious)* grave MASC & FEM
severe injuries des blessures graves
2 *(weather)* rigoureux MASC, rigoureuse FEM
3 *(in manner)* sévère MASC & FEM

to **sew** VERB
coudre [28]

sewer NOUN
un égout MASC

sewing NOUN
la couture FEM
• sewing machine
la machine à coudre

sex NOUN
1 *(gender)* le sexe MASC
2 *(intercourse)* les rapports sexuels MASC PL
to have sex with someone coucher [1] avec quelqu'un
• sex education
l'éducation sexuelle FEM

sexism NOUN
le sexisme MASC

sexist ADJECTIVE
sexiste MASC & FEM
sexist remarks des propos sexistes

sexual ADJECTIVE
sexuel MASC, sexuelle FEM
• sexual harassment
le harcèlement sexuel

sexuality NOUN
la sexualité FEM

sexy ADJECTIVE
sexy INVARIABLE ADJECTIVE

shade NOUN
1 *(out of the sun)* l'ombre FEM
in the shade à l'ombre
The tent is in the shade. La tente est à l'ombre.
2 *(of a colour)* le ton MASC

⊙ **means the verb takes** être **to form the perfect**

a paler shade un ton plus pâle

shadow NOUN
une **ombre** FEM

ᵖto **shake** VERB
1 (to tremble) **trembler** [1]
My hands are shaking. J'ai les mains qui tremblent.
2 **to shake something** secouer [1] quelque chose
Shake the bottle before you open it. Secoue la bouteille avant de l'ouvrir.
The event shook the world. L'événement a secoué le monde entier.
3 **to shake hands with somebody** serrer [1] la main à quelqu'un
She shook hands with me. Elle m'a serré la main.
We shook hands. Nous nous sommes serré la main.

shaken ADJECTIVE
bouleversé MASC, **bouleversée** FEM
She looked shaken. Elle avait l'air bouleversée.

ᵖ**shall** VERB
Shall I come with you? Tu veux que je t'accompagne?
Shall we stop now? Si on s'arrêtait maintenant?
What shall we do? Qu'est-ce qu'on fait?

shallow ADJECTIVE
peu profond MASC, **peu profonde** FEM
The water's very shallow here. L'eau est très peu profonde ici.
• **shallow end**
la partie la moins profonde de la piscine

shambles NOUN
la **pagaille** FEM (informal)
It was a complete shambles! Ça a été la pagaille complète!

ᵖ**shame** NOUN
1 **What a shame!** Quel dommage!
It's a real shame. C'est vraiment dommage.
It's a shame that she can't come. C'est dommage qu'elle ne puisse pas venir.
2 (guilty thought) la **honte** FEM

ᵖ**shampoo** NOUN
le **shampooing** MASC
I bought some shampoo. J'ai acheté du shampooing.

shamrock NOUN
le **trèfle** MASC

shandy NOUN
le **panaché** MASC

ᵖ**shape** NOUN
la **forme** FEM
in the shape of something en forme de quelque chose
a building in the shape of a boat un bâtiment en forme de bateau

ᵖto **share** VERB ▸ SEE **share** NOUN
1 (a room, costs with one person) **partager** [52]
I'm sharing a room with Emma. Je partage une chambre avec Emma.
2 (between several people) **se partager** ◉ [52]
It will be quicker if we share the task. Ça ira plus vite si nous nous partageons la tâche.
• (to) **share out something**
partager [52] quelque chose
We shared out the pizza. Nous avons partagé la pizza.

ᵖ**share** NOUN ▸ SEE **share** VERB
1 (proportion) la **part** FEM
the biggest share la plus grande part
your share of the bill ta part de l'addition
He paid his fair share. Il a payé sa part.
2 (in a company) une **action** FEM

shark NOUN
le **requin** MASC

ᵖ**sharp** ADJECTIVE
1 (scissors) **bien aiguisé** MASC, **bien aiguisée** FEM
2 (knife) **tranchant** MASC, **tranchante** FEM
3 (pencil) **bien taillé** MASC, **bien taillée** FEM
4 (bend) **brusque** MASC & FEM
5 (clever) **intelligent** MASC, **intelligente** FEM

to **sharpen** VERB
1 (a pencil) **tailler** [1]
2 (a knife) **aiguiser** [1]

sharpener NOUN
le **taille-crayon** MASC

to **shave** VERB
1 (to have a shave) **se raser** ◉ [1]
2 (to shave something) **to shave your beard** se raser la barbe
to shave your legs se raser ◉ [1] les jambes

shaver NOUN
le **rasoir** MASC

shaving cream NOUN
la **crème à raser**

shaving foam NOUN
la **mousse à raser**

ᵖ**she** PRONOUN
elle
She's a student. Elle est étudiante.
She lives in Glasgow. Elle habite à Glasgow.

She's a teacher. C'est un professeur.
Who is she? C'est qui?
Here she is! La voici!
There she is! La voilà!

shed NOUN
la **remise** FEM

sheep NOUN
le **mouton** MASC
- **sheepdog**
le **chien de berger** (PL les **chiens de berger**)

sheet NOUN
1 (for a bed) le **drap** MASC
2 (of paper) la **feuille** FEM
a sheet of wrapping paper une feuille de papier-cadeau

ℰ **shelf** NOUN
1 (in the home) une **étagère** FEM
I have shelves in my room. J'ai une étagère dans ma chambre.
2 (in shops, fridges) le **rayon** MASC
It's on the top shelf. C'est au rayon le plus haut.

shell NOUN
1 (of an egg, a nut) la **coquille** FEM
2 (seashell) le **coquillage** MASC
3 (explosive) un **obus** MASC
- **shellfish**
les **fruits de mer**

ℰ **shelter** NOUN
1 l'**abri** MASC
in the shelter of a tree à l'abri d'un arbre
to take shelter from something se mettre ⬆ [11] à l'abri de quelque chose
They took shelter from the rain. Ils se sont mis à l'abri de la pluie.
2 a bus shelter un **abribus**®

shepherd NOUN
le **berger** MASC

sheriff NOUN
le **shérif** MASC

Shetland Islands PLURAL NOUN
les **îles Shetland**

shield NOUN
le **bouclier** MASC

to **shift** VERB ▸ SEE **shift** NOUN
to shift something **déplacer** [61] quelque chose
Can you help me shift this table? Est-ce que tu peux m'aider à déplacer cette table?

shift NOUN ▸ SEE **shift** VERB
le **service** MASC
the night shift le service de nuit
to be on night shift être [6] de nuit

shifty ADJECTIVE
louche MASC & FEM
He looks a bit shifty. Il a l'air un peu louche.

shin NOUN
le **tibia** MASC

ℰ to **shine** VERB
briller [1]
The sun's shining again. Le soleil brille encore.
The tiles shone. Les carreaux brillaient.

shiny ADJECTIVE
brillant MASC, **brillante** FEM
shiny hair des cheveux brillants

ℰ **ship** NOUN
1 (in general) le **bateau** MASC
a passenger ship un paquebot
2 (naval ship) le **navire** MASC
- **shipbuilding**
la **construction navale**
- **shipyard**
le **chantier naval**

ℰ **shirt** NOUN
1 (man's) la **chemise** FEM
2 (woman's) le **chemisier** MASC

to **shiver** VERB
frissonner [1]
We were shivering with cold. On frissonnait de froid.

to **shock** VERB ▸ SEE **shock** NOUN
choquer [1]
He likes to shock people. Il aime choquer les gens.

ℰ **shock** NOUN ▸ SEE **shock** VERB
1 le **choc** MASC
It was a shock. Ça a été un choc.
It gave me a shock. J'ai eu un choc.
to be in shock être [6] en état de choc
2 (electric) la **décharge**
She got an electric shock. Elle a pris une décharge.

shocked ADJECTIVE
choqué MASC, **choquée** FEM
We were shocked. Nous avons été choqués.

shocking ADJECTIVE
choquant MASC, **choquante** FEM

ℰ **shoe** NOUN
la **chaussure** FEM
a pair of shoes une paire de chaussures
to take off your shoes enlever [50] ses chaussures
to put on your shoes mettre [11] ses chaussures

⬆ means the verb takes être to form the perfect

- **shoelace**
  le lacet
- **shoe polish**
  le cirage
- **shoe shop**
  le magasin de chaussures

ℯ to **shoot** *VERB*
1 *(to fire)* **tirer** [1]
   She shot him in the leg. Elle lui a tiré une
   balle dans la jambe.
   He shot himself in the head. Il s'est tiré une
   balle dans la tête.
2 *(to kill)* **abattre** [21]
   He was shot by terrorists. Il a été abattu
   par des terroristes.
3 *(a film)* **tourner** [1]
   The film was shot in Dublin. Le film a été
   tourné à Dublin.
4 *(in football, hockey)* **shooter** [1]
5 *(to execute)* **fusiller** [1]

shooting *NOUN*
1 *(as a sport)* le **tir** *MASC*
2 *(murder)* le **meurtre** *MASC*

ℯ **shop** *NOUN*
1 le **magasin** *MASC*
   a shoe shop un magasin de chaussures
   to go round the shops faire [10] les
   magasins
   We went round the shops. On a fait les
   magasins.
2 **to go to the shops** aller ◉ [7] faire les
   courses
   She's gone to the shops. Elle est allée faire
   les courses.
- **shop assistant**
  le vendeur, la vendeuse
- **shopkeeper**
  le commerçant, la commerçante
- **shoplifter**
  le voleur à l'étalage, la voleuse à l'étalage
- **shoplifting**
  le vol à l'étalage

ℯ **shopping** *NOUN*
1 les **courses** *FEM PL*
2 *(to buy food)* **to do the shopping** faire [10]
   des courses
   I've got a lot of shopping to do. J'ai
   beaucoup de courses à faire.
3 *(for clothes, presents)* **to go shopping** faire
   [10] du shopping
   Mark hates going shopping. Mark déteste
   faire du shopping.
- **shopping bag**
  le sac à provisions
- **shopping centre**
  le centre commercial

- **shopping mall**
  le centre commercial
- **shopping trolley**
  le chariot

shop window *NOUN*
   la **vitrine** *FEM*

ℯ **short** *ADJECTIVE*
1 *(in length)* **court** *MASC*, **courte** *FEM*
   a short dress une robe courte
   She has short hair. Elle a les cheveux
   courts.
   She's quite short. Ele est assez petite.
2 *(not lasting long)* **petit** *MASC*, **petite** *FEM*
   for a short while pendant un petit moment
   I went for a short walk. J'ai fait une petite
   promenade.
3 **to be short of something** ne pas avoir [5]
   beaucoup de quelque chose
   I'm short of money. Je n'ai pas d'argent.

shortage *NOUN*
   la **pénurie** *FEM*

shortbread *NOUN*
   le **sablé** *MASC*

short cut *NOUN*
   le **raccourci** *MASC*
   to take a short cut prendre [64] un
   raccourci

to **shorten** *VERB*
1 *(a skirt, a sleeve)* **raccourcir** [2]
2 *(a stay, a journey)* **écourter** [1]

shortly *ADVERB*
   bientôt

ℯ **shorts** *PLURAL NOUN*
   le **short** *MASC*
   Where are my red shorts? Où est mon
   short rouge?

short-sighted *ADJECTIVE*
   myope *MASC & FEM*

short story *NOUN*
   la **nouvelle** *FEM*

shot *NOUN*
1 *(from a gun)* le **coup de feu** *MASC* *(PL* les
   **coups de feu)*
   There were shots. Il y a eu des coups de
   feu.
2 *(photo)* la **photo** *FEM*
   I took a few shots of the castle. J'ai pris
   quelques photos du château.
- **shotgun**
  le fusil de chasse *(PL* les **fusils de chasse)*

ℯ **should** *VERB*
1 *(ought to)* **devoir** [8]
   You should ask Farida. Tu devrais

demander à Farida.
The pasta should be cooked now. Les pâtes devraient être cuites maintenant.

2 *(with conditional)* **You should have checked.** Tu aurais dû vérifier.
I shouldn't have told her. Je n'aurais pas dû le lui dire.

3 *(in suggestions)* **I should forget it if I were you.** À ta place je l'oublierais.

4 *(expressing opinion, surprise)* **I should think he's forgotten.** À mon avis, il a oublié.
'I had to apologize.' — 'I should think so too!' 'J'ai dû m'excuser.' — 'Je pense bien!'

ℰ **shoulder** NOUN
une **épaule** FEM
Straighten your shoulders. Redressez les épaules.
• **shoulder bag**
le sac à bandoulière

ℰ to **shout** VERB ▶ SEE **shout** NOUN
crier [1]
Stop shouting! Arrêtez de crier!
There's no need to shout. Ce n'est pas la peine de crier.
to shout for help crier au secours

shout NOUN ▶ SEE **shout** VERB
le **cri** MASC

shovel NOUN
la **pelle** FEM

ℰ to **show** VERB ▶ SEE **show** NOUN
montrer [1]
to show something to somebody montrer quelque chose à quelqu'un
I'll show you my photos. Je te montrerai mes photos.
Show me what you found. Montre-moi ce que tu as trouvé.
to show somebody how to do something montrer à quelqu'un comment on fait quelque chose
He showed me how to download songs. Il m'a montré comment on télécharge les chansons.
• **to show somebody around**
faire [10] visiter quelqu'un
I'll show you around. Je te ferai visiter.
She showed me around the apartment. Elle m'a fait visiter l'appartement.
• **to show off**
frimer [1] *(informal)*

ℰ **show** NOUN ▶ SEE **show** VERB
1 *(on stage)* le **spectacle** MASC
We went to see a show. Nous sommes allés voir un spectacle.
We're putting on a show. Nous montons un spectacle.

2 *(on TV)* une **émission**
He has a TV show. Il a une émission à la télé.

3 *(on exhibition)* **to be on show** être [6] exposé
The photos are on show this week. Les photos sont exposées cette semaine.

ℰ **shower** NOUN
1 *(in a bathroom)* la **douche** FEM
to have a shower prendre [64] une douche
I'll have a shower now. Je prendrai maintenant ma douche.
2 *(of rain)* une **averse** FEM
There'll be showers. Il y aura des averses.

show-jumping NOUN
le **saut d'obstacles**

show-off NOUN
le **frimeur** MASC, la **frimeuse** FEM

shrimp NOUN
la **crevette** FEM

shrine NOUN
1 *(in a church)* un **autel** MASC
2 *(for pilgrims)* le **lieu de pèlerinage**

to **shrink** VERB
rétrécir [2]
My jeans shrank. Mon jean a rétréci.

Shrove Tuesday NOUN
le **mardi gras**

to **shrug** VERB
to shrug your shoulders hausser [1] les épaules

to **shuffle** VERB
to shuffle the cards battre [21] les cartes

ℰ to **shut** VERB ▶ SEE **shut** ADJECTIVE
(windows, shops, factories) fermer [1]
When do the shops shut? Les magasins ferment à quelle heure?
The shops shut at six. Les magasins ferment à six heures.
to shut the window fermer la fenêtre
• **to shut up**
se taire ⊚ [76]
Shut up! Tais-toi!

ℰ **shut** ADJECTIVE ▶ SEE **shut** VERB
fermé MASC, fermée FEM
The shops are shut. Les magasins sont fermés.
The door's not shut properly. La porte n'est pas bien fermée.

shutter NOUN
le **volet** MASC

shuttle NOUN
la **navette** FEM

⊚ **means the verb takes être to form the perfect**

There's a shuttle service from the airport.
Il y a une navette de l'aéroport.

shuttlecock NOUN
le **volant** MASC

ᵖ **shy** ADJECTIVE
timide MASC & FEM
She's a bit shy. Elle est un peu timide.
He's too shy to say it in French. Il n'ose pas
le dire en français.

shyness NOUN
la **timidité** FEM

Sicily NOUN
la **Sicile** FEM

ᵖ **sick** ADJECTIVE
1 (ill) **malade** MASC & FEM
She's sick today. Elle est malade
aujourd'hui.
a sick joke une plaisanterie malsaine
2 to be sick **vomir** [2]
I was sick several times. J'ai vomi plusieurs
fois.
to feel sick avoir [5] mal au cœur
I felt really sick. J'ai eu vraiment mal au
cœur.
3 to be sick of something en avoir [5] assez
de quelque chose
I'm sick of staying at home every night.
J'en ai assez de rester à la maison tous les
soirs.

sickness NOUN
la **maladie** FEM

ᵖ **side** NOUN
1 le **côté** MASC
on the wrong side du mauvais côté
on each side de chaque côté
side by side côte à côte
on the other side of the street de l'autre
côté de la rue
from one side to the other d'un côté
jusqu'à l'autre
2 (of the road, pool) le **bord** MASC
at the side of the road au bord de la route
3 (team) une **équipe** FEM
She plays on our side. Elle joue dans notre
équipe.
• **side-effect**
un effet secondaire
• **sideline**
la ligne de touche
• **side street**
la petite rue

siege NOUN
le **siège** MASC

sieve NOUN
la **passoire** FEM

to **sigh** VERB ▸ SEE **sigh** NOUN
pousser [1] un soupir

sigh NOUN ▸ SEE **sigh** VERB
le **soupir** MASC

ᵖ **sight** NOUN
1 (vista) le **spectacle** MASC
What a sight! Quel spectacle!
It was a marvellous sight. C'était un
spectacle merveilleux.
2 (eyesight) la **vue** FEM
to have poor sight avoir [5] une mauvaise
vue
to know somebody by sight connaître [27]
quelqu'un de vue
3 out of sight **caché**
We stayed out of sight. Nous sommes
restés cachés.
4 (place to see) to see the sights visiter [1] les
attractions touristiques

ᵖ **sightseeing** NOUN
le **tourisme** MASC
to do some sightseeing faire [10] du
tourisme
Shall we do some sightseeing? Si on faisait
un peu de tourisme?

ᵖ to **sign** VERB ▸ SEE **sign** NOUN
(documents) **signer** [1]
to sign a cheque signer un chèque
You need to sign there. Il faut signer là.

ᵖ **sign** NOUN ▸ SEE **sign** VERB
1 (notice) le **panneau** MASC (PL les **panneaux**)
2 (trace, indication) le **signe** MASC
It's a good sign. C'est bon signe.
There's no sign of life at Paul's. Il n'y a
aucun signe de vie chez Paul.
3 (of the Zodiac) le **signe** MASC
What sign are you? Tu es de quel signe?

signal NOUN
le **signal** MASC (PL les **signaux**)
a danger signal un signal de danger

signature NOUN
la **signature** FEM

significance NOUN
l'**importance** FEM

significant ADJECTIVE
important MASC, **importante** FEM
a significant victory une victoire
importante

sign language NOUN
le **langage par signes**
to talk in sign language communiquer [1]
par signes

signpost NOUN
le **poteau indicateur** (PL les **poteaux**

indicateurs)

silence NOUN
le **silence** MASC
Silence, please! Silence, s'il vous plaît!

silent ADJECTIVE
silencieux MASC, **silencieuse** FEM
the silent streets les rues silencieuses

silicon chip NOUN
la **puce électronique**

silk ADJECTIVE ▶ SEE **silk** NOUN
en **soie**
a silk shirt une chemise en soie

silk NOUN ▶ SEE **silk** ADJECTIVE
la **soie** FEM

silky ADJECTIVE
soyeux MASC, **soyeuse** FEM

silly ADJECTIVE
idiot MASC, **idiote** FEM
It was a really silly thing to do. C'était vraiment idiot.
I said some silly things. J'ai dit des bêtises.
Don't be silly! Ne dis pas de bêtises!

silver ADJECTIVE ▶ SEE **silver** NOUN
en **argent**
a silver chain une chaîne en argent
a silver medal une médaille d'argent

silver NOUN ▶ SEE **silver** ADJECTIVE
l'**argent** MASC

SIM card NOUN
la **carte SIM**

similar ADJECTIVE
semblable MASC & FEM

similarity NOUN
la **ressemblance** FEM

simple ADJECTIVE
1 **simple** MASC & FEM
It's so simple. C'est tellement simple.
2 **facile** MASC & FEM
It's a simple question. C'est une question facile.

to simplify VERB
simplifier [1]

simply ADVERB
simplement

sin NOUN
(Religion) le **péché** MASC

since ADVERB, CONJUNCTION, PREPOSITION
1 (because) **puisque**
Since it was raining, the match was cancelled. Puisqu'il pleuvait, le match a été annulé.
2 (with a specific time) **depuis**

I have been in Paris since Saturday. Je suis à Paris depuis samedi.
I've been learning French since last year. J'apprends le français depuis l'année dernière.
I haven't seen her since Monday. Je ne l'ai pas revue depuis lundi.
Since when? Depuis quand?
3 (with a vague time) **depuis que**
Since I have known Jessica... Depuis que je connais Jessica...
Since I've been learning French... Depuis que j'apprends le français...

WORD TIP When what you are talking about is still going on, use the present tense in French followed by depuis and the length of time.

sincere ADJECTIVE
sincère MASC & FEM
She seemed sincere. Elle semblait sincère.

sincerely ADVERB
sincèrement
He spoke sincerely. Il a parlé sincèrement.
(ending a formal letter) **Yours sincerely, ...** Veuillez agréer, Monsieur, l'expression de mes sentiments les meilleurs (Madame, if to a woman)

to sing VERB
chanter [1]
Everyone was singing on the way home. Tout le monde chantait en rentrant.

singer NOUN
le **chanteur** MASC, la **chanteuse** FEM
my favourite female singer ma chanteuse préférée
He's a good singer. Il chante bien.

singing NOUN
1 le **chant** MASC
a singing lesson une leçon de chant
2 **I like singing.** J'aime chanter.

single ADJECTIVE ▶ SEE **single** NOUN
1 (not married) **célibataire** MASC & FEM
to stay single rester ◎ [1] célibataire
I'm staying single. Je reste célibataire.
a single father un père célibataire
2 (room, bed) **a single room** une chambre pour une personne
a single bed un lit pour une personne
3 **not a single ...** pas un seul ... MASC, pas une seule ... FEM
I haven't had a single reply. Je n'ai pas reçu une seule réponse.

single NOUN ▶ SEE **single** ADJECTIVE
un **aller simple**
A single to Lyons, please. Un aller simple pour Lyon, s'il vous plaît.

◎ means the verb takes être to form the perfect

single parent NOUN
   to be a single parent élever [50] ses enfants tout seul
   She's a single parent. Elle élève ses enfants toute seule.
- **single-parent family**
la famille monoparentale

singles PLURAL NOUN
   (in tennis) le **simple** MASC
   the women's singles le simple dames
   the men's singles le simple messieurs

singular NOUN
   le **singulier** MASC
   a noun in the singular un nom au singulier

to **sink** VERB ▸ SEE **sink** NOUN
   couler [1]
   The Titanic sank. Le Titanic a coulé.
   to sink a ship faire [10] couler un navire

ℱ **sink** NOUN ▸ SEE **sink** VERB
   un **évier** MASC

sir NOUN
   le **monsieur** MASC
   Yes, sir. Oui, Monsieur.

siren NOUN
   la **sirène** FEM

ℱ **sister** NOUN
   la **sœur** FEM
   my older sister ma sœur aînée
   my youngest sister ma sœur cadette
   my twin sister ma jumelle

sister-in-law NOUN
   la **belle-sœur** FEM *(PL les **belles-sœurs**)*

ℱ to **sit** VERB
  1 s'asseoir ◔ [20]
    I can sit on the floor. Je peux m'asseoir par terre.
    Sit beside me. Assieds-toi à côté de moi.
  2 to be sitting être [6] assis
    Leila was sitting on the sofa. Leila était assise sur le canapé.
  3 to sit an exam passer [1] un examen
    She's sitting the exam today. Elle passe l'examen aujourd'hui.
- **to sit down**
s'asseoir ◔ [20]
    He sat down on a chair. Il s'est assis sur une chaise.
    Do sit down. Asseyez-vous.

sitcom NOUN
   la **comédie de situation** *(PL les **comédies de situation**)*

site NOUN
   a building site un chantier
   an archaeological site un site archéologique

ℱ **sitting room** NOUN
   le **salon** MASC

ℱ **situated** ADJECTIVE
   to be situated être [6] situé
   The house is situated in a small village. La maison est située dans un petit village.

situation NOUN
   la **situation** FEM

six NUMBER
   six
   David's six. David a six ans.

sixteen NUMBER
   seize
   Shahnaz is sixteen. Shahnaz a seize ans.

sixteenth ADJECTIVE
  1 seizième MASC & FEM
  2 *(in dates)* **the sixteenth of January** le seize janvier

sixth ADJECTIVE
  1 sixième MASC & FEM
    on the sixth floor au sixième étage
  2 *(in dates)* **the sixth of July** le six juillet

sixtieth ADJECTIVE
   soixantième MASC & FEM
   It's his sixtieth birthday. Il fête ses soixante ans.

sixty NUMBER
   soixante
   She's sixty. Elle a soixante ans.

ℱ **size** NOUN
  1 *(in general)* la **grandeur** FEM
    the size of the house. la grandeur de la maison.
    It's the size of my bedroom. C'est de la grandeur de ma chambre.
  2 *(precise measurements)* les **dimensions** FEM PL
    What size is the window? Quelles sont les dimensions de la fenêtre?
  3 *(for clothes)* la **taille** FEM
    What size do you take? Quelle taille faites-vous?
    I take a size 8. Je fais du 8.
  4 *(for shoes)* la **pointure** FEM
    What size shoe do you take? Tu fais quelle pointure?
    I take a size thirty-eight. Je fais du trente-huit.

to **skate** VERB ▸ SEE **skate** NOUN
  1 *(on ice)* faire [10] du patin à glace
  2 *(on rollerskates)* faire [10] du patin à roulettes

ℱ indicates key words

skate NOUN ▸ SEE **skate** VERB
le **patin** MASC
an ice skate un patin à glace

skateboard NOUN
le **skateboard** MASC

skateboarding NOUN
le **skateboard** MASC
to do skateboarding faire [10] du
skateboard

skater NOUN
le **patineur** MASC, la **patineuse** FEM

skating NOUN
1 (on ice) le **patin à glace**
2 (on rollerskates) le **patin à roulettes**

ℰ**skating rink** NOUN
la **patinoire** FEM
Is there a skating rink here? Est-ce qu'il y a
une patinoire ici?

skeleton NOUN
le **squelette** MASC

sketch NOUN
1 (drawing) le **croquis** MASC
2 (comedy routine) le **sketch** MASC

ℰ**to ski** VERB ▸ SEE **ski** NOUN
faire [10] du ski
I can ski. Je sais faire du ski.
I'm learning to ski. J'apprends à faire du ski.

ski NOUN ▸ SEE **ski** VERB
le **ski** MASC
to put on your skis mettre [11] ses skis

ski boot NOUN
la **chaussure de ski**

to skid VERB
(cars, bikes) **déraper** [1]
The car skidded. La voiture a dérapé.

skier NOUN
le **skieur** MASC, la **skieuse** FEM

ℰ**skiing** NOUN
le **ski** MASC
to go skiing faire [10] du ski
• **skiing holiday**
les **vacances de neige**
• **skiing instructor**
le **moniteur de ski**, la **monitrice de ski**

ski lift NOUN
le **remonte-pente** MASC (PL les **remonte-
pentes**)

skill NOUN
la **compétence** FEM

skimmed milk NOUN
le **lait écrémé**

ℰ**skin** NOUN
la **peau** FEM (PL les **peaux**)
to have lovely skin avoir [5] une belle peau
She's got dark skin. Elle a la peau brune.
• **skinhead**
le & la **skinhead**

skinny ADJECTIVE
maigre MASC & FEM
a bit too skinny un peu trop maigre

to skip VERB ▸ SEE **skip** NOUN
1 (a meal, a chapter) **sauter** [1]
2 **to skip a lesson** sécher un cours (informal)
3 (with a rope) **sauter** [1] à la corde

skip NOUN ▸ SEE **skip** VERB
la **benne** FEM

ski pants PLURAL NOUN
le **fuseau** MASC SINGULAR
I bought some ski pants. J'ai acheté un
fuseau.

skipping rope NOUN
la **corde à sauter**

ℰ**skirt** NOUN
la **jupe** FEM
a long skirt une jupe longue
a mini-skirt une mini-jupe

ski suit NOUN
la **combinaison de ski**

skittles PLURAL NOUN
les **quilles** FEM PL
to play skittles jouer [1] aux quilles

skull NOUN
le **crâne** MASC

ℰ**sky** NOUN
le **ciel** MASC
a cloudy sky un ciel nuageux
The sky is clear. Le ciel est clair.
• **skyscraper**
le **gratte-ciel** (PL les **gratte-ciel**)

to slam VERB
claquer [1]
I slammed the door. J'ai claqué la porte.

slang NOUN
l'**argot** MASC

to slap VERB ▸ SEE **slap** NOUN
to slap somebody donner [1] une claque à
quelqu'un

slap NOUN ▸ SEE **slap** VERB
la **claque** FEM

slate NOUN
une **ardoise** FEM

slave NOUN
un & une **esclave** MASC & FEM

● means the verb takes être to form the perfect

sledge NOUN
la **luge** FEM

sledging NOUN
to go sledging faire [10] de la luge

ℰ to **sleep** VERB ▸ SEE **sleep** NOUN
dormir [37]
She's sleeping. Elle dort.
Sleep well! Dors bien!
• to **sleep in**
faire [10] la grasse matinée
I like to sleep in on Saturdays. J'aime faire la grasse matinée le samedi.

ℰ **sleep** NOUN ▸ SEE **sleep** VERB
le **sommeil** MASC
I had a good sleep. J'ai bien dormi.
We got no sleep. Nous n'avons pas dormi du tout.
to go to sleep s'endormir [37]
I couldn't get to sleep. Je n'arrivais pas à m'endormir.

ℰ **sleeping bag** NOUN
le **sac de couchage**

sleeping pill NOUN
le **somnifère** MASC

ℰ **sleepy** ADJECTIVE
to be sleepy avoir [5] sommeil
I feel sleepy. J'ai sommeil.
He was getting sleepy. Il commençait à avoir sommeil.

sleet NOUN
la **neige fondue**

sleeve NOUN
la **manche** FEM
a long-sleeved jumper un pull à manches longues
a short-sleeved shirt une chemise à manches courtes
to roll up your sleeves retrousser [1] ses manches

to **slice** VERB ▸ SEE **slice** NOUN
to slice something couper [1] quelque chose en tranches
I sliced the cheese. J'ai coupé le fromage en tranches.

ℰ **slice** NOUN ▸ SEE **slice** VERB
1 (of bread, meat) la **tranche** FEM
two slices of ham deux tranches de jambon
2 (of cake, pie) la **part** FEM
a slice of pizza une part de pizza

slide NOUN
1 (photo) la **diapositive** FEM
2 (for sliding down) le **toboggan** MASC

ℰ **slight** ADJECTIVE
léger MASC, **légère** FEM
a slight delay un léger retard
There is a slight problem. Il y a un léger problème.

slightly ADVERB
légèrement
He's slightly better. Il va un peu mieux.

to **slim** VERB ▸ SEE **slim** ADJECTIVE
to be slimming faire [10] un régime
I'm slimming. Je fais un régime.

slim ADJECTIVE ▸ SEE **slim** VERB
mince MASC & FEM

sling NOUN
une **écharpe** FEM

ℰ to **slip** VERB ▸ SEE **slip** NOUN
1 (to fall) glisser [1]
I slipped on the ice. J'ai glissé sur la glace.
Be careful not to slip. Attention de ne pas glisser.
2 (to forget) **It had slipped my mind.** J'avais oublié.

slip NOUN ▸ SEE **slip** VERB
1 (mistake) une **erreur** FEM
2 (from the waist) le **jupon** MASC
3 (full-length) la **combinaison** FEM

slipper NOUN
la **pantoufle** FEM

slippery ADJECTIVE
glissant MASC, **glissante** FEM

slope NOUN
la **pente** FEM

slot NOUN
la **fente** FEM

slot machine NOUN
1 (for games) la **machine à sous**
2 (dispenser) le **distributeur automatique**

ℰ **slow** ADJECTIVE
1 **lent** MASC, **lente** FEM
a slow train un train lent
2 (clock, watch) **to be slow** retarder [1]
My watch is slow. Ma montre retarde.

to **slow down** VERB
ralentir [2]
The train is slowing down. Le train ralentit.

ℰ **slowly** ADVERB
lentement
to work slowly travailler lentement
He got up slowly. Il s'est levé lentement.
Can you speak more slowly, please? Est-ce que vous pouvez parler plus lentement, s'il vous plaît?

ℰ **indicates key words**

slug NOUN
la **limace** FEM

slum NOUN
le **quartier démuni**

slush NOUN
la **neige fondue**

sly ADJECTIVE
rusé MASC, **rusée** FEM
to do something on the sly faire quelque chose en douce

to **smack** VERB ▸ SEE **smack** NOUN
to smack somebody donner [1] une claque à quelqu'un

smack NOUN ▸ SEE **smack** VERB
la **claque** FEM

♪ **small** ADJECTIVE
petit MASC, **petite** FEM
a small dog un petit chien
a small country town une petite ville de province

> **WORD TIP** petit always goes before the noun.

♪ **smart** ADJECTIVE
1 (well-dressed) **chic** (doesn't change)
a smart restaurant un restaurant chic
smart young women les jeunes femmes chic
2 (clever) **intelligent** MASC, **intelligente** FEM
She's a smart girl. Elle est très intelligente.
to try to be smart faire [10] le malin
Stop trying to be smart! Arrête de faire le malin!
• **smart card**
la **carte à puce**

to **smash** VERB ▸ SEE **smash** NOUN
1 (a plate, a mirror) **casser** [1]
They smashed a window. Ils ont cassé une vitre.
The windscreen was smashed. Le pare-brise était cassé.
2 (by itself) **se casser** ⊙ [1]
The vase fell and it smashed. Le vase est tombé et il s'est cassé.

smash NOUN ▸ SEE **smash** VERB
a car smash un accident de voiture

smashing ADJECTIVE
formidable MASC & FEM

♪ to **smell** VERB ▸ SEE **smell** NOUN
1 (in general) **sentir** [58]
I can't smell anything. Je ne sens rien.
I can smell lavender. Ça sent la lavande.
2 (to smell bad) **sentir** [58] **mauvais**
The bins smell. Les poubelles sentent mauvais.

3 (to smell good) **sentir** [58] **bon**
That smells really good! Ça sent vraiment bon!

♪ **smell** NOUN ▸ SEE **smell** VERB
une **odeur** FEM
a nasty smell une mauvaise odeur
There's a smell of burning. Ça sent le brûlé.

smelly ADJECTIVE
qui sent mauvais
her smelly dog son chien qui sent mauvais
to be smelly sentir [58] mauvais
My trainers are smelly. Mes baskets sentent mauvais.

♪ to **smile** VERB ▸ SEE **smile** NOUN
sourire [68]
to smile at somebody sourire à quelqu'un
Everyone was smiling at James. Tout le monde souriait à James.

♪ **smile** NOUN ▸ SEE **smile** VERB
le **sourire** MASC
to give somebody a smile faire un sourire à quelqu'un
He gave me a big smile. Il m'a fait un gros sourire.

♪ to **smoke** VERB ▸ SEE **smoke** NOUN
fumer [1]
She doesn't smoke. Elle ne fume pas.
He smokes a pipe. Il fume la pipe.

smoke NOUN ▸ SEE **smoke** VERB
la **fumée** FEM

smoked ADJECTIVE
fumé MASC, **fumée** FEM
smoked salmon du saumon fumé

smoker NOUN
le **fumeur** MASC, la **fumeuse** FEM

smoking NOUN
'No smoking' 'Défense de fumer'
to give up smoking arrêter [1] de fumer
Adam has given up smoking. Adam a arrêté de fumer.

♪ **smooth** ADJECTIVE
1 (surfaces) **lisse** MASC & FEM
to have smooth skin avoir [5] la peau lisse
She's got smooth hair. Elle a les cheveux lisses.
2 (person) **mielleux** MASC, **mielleuse** FEM
He's too smooth. Il est trop mielleux.

smug ADJECTIVE
suffisant MASC, **suffisante** FEM

to **smuggle** VERB
to smuggle something faire [10] passer quelque chose en contrebande

⊙ **means the verb takes être to form the perfect**

smuggler NOUN
1 *(of goods)* le **contrebandier** MASC, la **contrebandière** FEM
2 *(of drugs, arms)* le **passeur** MASC, la **passeuse** FEM

smuggling NOUN
1 *(of goods)* la **contrebande** FEM
2 *(of drugs, arms)* le **trafic** MASC

snack NOUN
le **casse-croûte** MASC *(PL les **casse-croûte**)*

snack bar NOUN
la **sandwicherie** FEM, le **snack-bar** MASC

snail NOUN
un **escargot** MASC

> **◯ SNAILS**
>
> The French eat snails, but only occasionally:
> they are expensive! There are two edible
> varieties. You can get them in cans, frozen or in
> restaurants, often served with garlic butter.

snake NOUN
le **serpent** MASC

to **snap** VERB ▶ SEE **snap** NOUN
1 *(to break)* se **casser** ◎ [1]
The fishing rod snapped in two. La canne à pêche s'est cassée en deux.
2 **to snap your fingers** faire [10] claquer ses doigts
3 **to snap at somebody** être [6] agressif avec quelqu'un
She's always snapping at me. Elle est toujours agressive avec moi.

snap NOUN ▶ SEE **snap** VERB
(cards) la **bataille** FEM

snapshot NOUN
la **photo** FEM

to **snarl** VERB
gronder [1]

to **snatch** VERB
to snatch something from somebody arracher [1] quelque chose à quelqu'un
He snatched my book from me. Il m'a arraché mon livre.
She had her bag snatched. On lui a arraché son sac.

to **sneak** VERB
to sneak in entrer ◎ [1] furtivement
to sneak out sortir ◎ [72] furtivement
to sneak up on somebody s'approcher ◎ [1] de quelqu'un sans faire de bruit
He sneaked up on me. Il s'est approché de moi sans faire de bruit.

to **sneeze** VERB
éternuer [1]
I can't stop sneezing. Je n'arrête pas d'éternuer.

to **sniff** VERB
renifler [1]

snob NOUN
le & la **snob** MASC & FEM

snobbery NOUN
le **snobisme** MASC

snooker NOUN
le **snooker** MASC

snooze NOUN
le **somme** MASC
to have a snooze faire [10] un petit somme

to **snore** VERB
ronfler [1]

ℐ to **snow** VERB ▶ SEE **snow** NOUN
neiger [52]
It's snowing. Il neige.
It's going to snow. Il va neiger.
It snowed last night. Il a neigé cette nuit.

ℐ **snow** NOUN ▶ SEE **snow** VERB
la **neige** FEM
a fall of snow une chute de neige

snowball NOUN
la **boule de neige** *(PL les **boules de neige**)*
to throw snowballs at each other se lancer ◎ [61] des boules de neige

snowdrift NOUN
la **congère** FEM

snowman NOUN
le **bonhomme de neige** *(PL les bonshommes de neige)*

snowy ADJECTIVE
enneigé MASC, **enneigée** FEM

ℐ **so** CONJUNCTION, ADVERB
1 **tellement**
He's so lazy. Il est tellement paresseux.
She's so sweet! Elle est tellement mignonne!
so ... that ... tellement ... que ...
The coffee's so hot that I can't drink it. Le café est tellement chaud que je n'arrive pas à le boire.
2 **not so** *(+ adjective)* moins *(+ adjective)*
Our house is like yours, but not so big. Notre maison est comme la vôtre, mais moins grande.
I'm not so tired today. Je suis moins fatigué aujourd'hui.
3 **so much** tellement
I hate it so much! Je le déteste tellement!
4 **so much, so many** tellement de
I have so much work to do. J'ai tellement de travail à faire.

We've got so many problems. Nous avons tellement de problèmes.

5 *(therefore)* **donc**
He got up late, so he missed his train. Il s'est levé tard, donc il a raté son train.

6 *(starting a sentence)* **alors**
So, what's your name? Alors, tu t'appelles comment?
So, what shall we do? Alors, qu'est-ce qu'on fait?
So what? Et alors?

7 *(with be, do + I, you, he, she, we, etc)* **So am I, So was I.** Moi aussi.
So do I, So did I. Moi aussi.
'I live in Leeds.' — 'So do I.' 'J'habite à Leeds.' — 'Moi aussi.'
So do we. Nous aussi.
So does Zara. Zara aussi.
So do the French. Les Français aussi.

8 *(with think, hope + so)* **I think so.** Je crois.
We hope so. Nous espérons.

to **soak** *VERB*
tremper [1]

soaked *ADJECTIVE*
trempé *MASC*, **trempée** *FEM*
We got soaked. Nous avons été trempés.
to be soaked to the skin être [6] trempé jusqu'aux os

soaking *ADJECTIVE*
trempé *MASC*, **trempée** *FEM*
It's soaking wet. C'est trempé.

℘**soap** *NOUN*
le **savon** *MASC*
a bar of soap un savon
• **soap opera**
le **feuilleton**
• **soap powder**
la **lessive**

sober *ADJECTIVE*
to be sober ne pas avoir [5] bu
He's sober. Il n'a pas bu.

℘**soccer** *NOUN*
le **football** *MASC*

sociable *ADJECTIVE*
sociable *MASC & FEM*
I'm quite sociable. Je suis assez sociable.

social *ADJECTIVE*
social *MASC*, **sociale** *FEM*, **sociaux** *MASC PL*, **sociales** *FEM PL*
a social class une classe sociale
social groups des groupes sociaux

socialism *NOUN*
le **socialisme** *MASC*

socialist *NOUN*
le & la **socialiste** *MASC & FEM*

social network *NOUN*
le **réseau social** *MASC*

social security *NOUN*
1 *(benefit)* l'**aide sociale** *FEM*
to be on social security recevoir [66] de l'aide sociale
2 *(the system)* la **sécurité sociale**

social worker *NOUN*
le **travailleur social** *(PL les **travailleurs sociaux**)*, la **travailleuse sociale**

society *NOUN*
la **société** *FEM*
a multicultural society une société multiculturelle

sociology *NOUN*
la **sociologie** *FEM*

℘**sock** *NOUN*
la **chaussette** *FEM*
a pair of socks une paire de chaussettes
my yellow socks mes chaussettes jaunes

socket *NOUN*
(power point) la **prise de courant** *(PL les prises de courant)*

℘**sofa** *NOUN*
le **canapé** *MASC*
a leather sofa un canapé en cuir
• **sofa bed**
le **canapé-lit** *MASC*

℘**soft** *ADJECTIVE*
1 *(in general)* **doux** *MASC*, **douce** *FEM*
a soft voice une voix douce
soft music une musique douce
I like soft fabrics. J'aime les tissus doux.
2 **The butter's too soft.** Le beurre est trop mou.
3 *(not strict)* **indulgent** *MASC*, **indulgente** *FEM*
• **soft drink**
la **boisson non alcoolisée**
• **soft toy**
la **peluche**
• **software**
le **logiciel**

soil *NOUN*
la **terre** *FEM*

solar energy *NOUN*
l'**énergie solaire** *FEM*

soldier *NOUN*
le **soldat** *MASC*
a woman soldier une femme soldat

solicitor *NOUN*
1 *(for legal disputes)* un **avocat** *MASC*, une

◉ means the verb takes être to form the perfect

avocate *FEM*
She's a solicitor. Elle est avocate.
2 *(for property)* le **notaire** *MASC*

solid *ADJECTIVE*
1 *(not flimsy)* **solide** *MASC & FEM*
a solid structure une structure solide
That shed looks solid. Cette remise a l'air solide.
2 *(pure)* **massif** *MASC*, **massive** *FEM*
a solid gold ring une bague en or massif

solo *ADJECTIVE, ADVERB* ▸ SEE **solo** *NOUN*
en solo
a solo album un album en solo
to play solo jouer [1] en solo
I sing solo. Je chante en solo.

solo *NOUN* ▸ SEE **solo** *ADJECTIVE, ADVERB*
le **solo** *MASC*
a guitar solo un solo de guitare

soloist *NOUN*
le & la **soliste** *MASC & FEM*

solution *NOUN*
la **solution** *FEM*

to **solve** *VERB*
résoudre [67]
I think I've solved the problem. Je pense que j'ai résolu le problème.

ℓ **some** *ADJECTIVE, ADVERB, PRONOUN*
1 *(with masc singular nouns)* **du**
some paper du papier
Would you like some orange juice? Voulez-vous du jus d'orange?
2 *(with fem singular nouns)* **de la**
some meat de la viande
May I have some salad? Puis-je avoir de la salade?
3 *(with nouns beginning with a, e, i, o, u or silent h)* **de l'**
some help de l'aide
Can you lend me some money? Est-ce que tu peux me prêter de l'argent?
4 *(with plural nouns)* **des**
some friends des amis
I've bought some apples. J'ai acheté des pommes.
5 *(referring to something that has been mentioned)* **en**
'Would you like butter?' — 'Thanks, I've got some.' 'Veux-tu du beurre?' — 'Merci, j'en ai.'
He's eaten some of it. Il en a mangé un peu.
I'm going to have some more. Je vais en reprendre.
6 **some day** un de ces jours
maybe some day un de ces jours, peut-être

ℓ **somebody**, **someone** *PRONOUN*
quelqu'un

There's somebody in the garden. Il y a quelqu'un dans le jardin.
Somebody phoned this morning. Quelqu'un a téléphoné ce matin.

ℓ **somehow** *ADVERB*
d'une manière ou d'une autre
I've got to finish it somehow. Je dois le finir d'une manière ou d'une autre.

someone *PRONOUN* ▸ SEE **somebody**

somersault *NOUN*
1 *(child's)* la **galipette** *FEM*
2 *(gymnast's)* le **roulade** *FEM*
3 *(diver's)* le **saut périlleux**

ℓ **something** *PRONOUN*
1 **quelque chose**
I've got something to tell you. J'ai quelque chose à te dire.
He had something to do. Il avait quelque chose à faire.
2 **something + adjective** quelque chose de (+ *adjective*)
something pretty quelque chose de joli
I did something interesting today. J'ai fait quelque chose d'intéressant aujourd'hui.
There's something wrong. Il y a quelque chose qui ne va pas.
3 *(in expressions)* **Their house is really something!** Leur maison c'est vraiment quelque chose!
a guy called Colin something or other un type qui s'appelle Colin quelque chose

sometime *ADVERB*
un de ces jours
Give me a ring sometime. Appelle-moi un de ces jours.
I'll ring you sometime next week. Je t'appellerai dans le courant de la semaine prochaine.

ℓ **sometimes** *ADVERB*
quelquefois
I sometimes take the train. Quelquefois, je prends le train.

ℓ **somewhere** *ADVERB*
quelque part
somewhere in Scotland quelque part en Écosse
I've left my bag somewhere. J'ai posé mon sac quelque part.
I've seen you before somewhere. Je vous ai déjà vu quelque part.

ℓ **son** *NOUN*
le **fils** *MASC*
the eldest son le fils aîné
the adopted son le fils adoptif

𝒫 **song** NOUN
la **chanson** FEM
the song that won the contest la chanson qui a gagné le concours

son-in-law NOUN
le **gendre** MASC

𝒫 **soon** ADVERB
1 **bientôt**
See you soon! À bientôt!
It will soon be the holidays. C'est bientôt les vacances.
I'll be back soon. Je reviendrai bientôt.
It's too soon. C'est trop tôt.
2 **as soon as ...** dès que ...
as soon as she arrives dès qu'elle arrivera
as soon as possible dès que possible
I'll come as soon as possible. Je viendrai dès que possible.

sooner ADVERB
1 **plus tôt**
We should have started sooner. Nous aurions dû commencer plus tôt.
2 **sooner or later** tôt ou tard
It must be done sooner or later. Il va falloir le faire tôt ou tard.

soprano NOUN
le & la **soprano** MASC & FEM

𝒫 **sore** ADJECTIVE ▸ SEE **sore** NOUN
to have a sore throat avoir [5] mal à la gorge
My arm's sore. J'ai mal au bras.

sore NOUN ▸ SEE **sore** ADJECTIVE
la **plaie** FEM

𝒫 **sorry** ADJECTIVE
1 (in apologies) **désolé** MASC, **désolée** FEM
I'm really sorry. Je suis vraiment désolé (boy speaking), Je suis vraiment désolée (girl speaking).
2 **to be sorry you've done something** être [6] désolé d'avoir fait quelque chose
I'm sorry I forgot your birthday Je suis désolé d'avoir oublié ton anniversaire.
3 **to say sorry** s'excuser [1]
I wanted to say sorry. Je voulais m'excuser.
Sorry! Excusez-moi!
4 (interrupting) **Sorry to disturb you.** Je suis désolé de vous déranger.
5 (saying what politely) **Sorry?** Comment?
Sorry? Could you repeat that, please? Comment? Pouvez-vous répéter s'il vous plaît?
6 (to pity) **to feel sorry for somebody** plaindre [31] quelqu'un
I feel sorry for them. Je les plains.

to **sort** VERB ▸ SEE **sort** NOUN
classer [1]
• **to sort something out**
1 (room, papers, belongings) **mettre** [11] de l'ordre dans
2 (a problem, arrangements) **s'occuper** [1] de
I'll sort out the tickets. Je m'en occuperai des billets.

𝒫 **sort** NOUN ▸ SEE **sort** VERB
la **sorte** FEM, le **genre** MASC
a sort of une sorte de
what sort of ...? quelle sorte de ...
What sort of music do you like? Tu aimes quelle sorte de musique?
I don't like that sort of music. Je n'aime pas ce genre de musique.
I like all sorts of music. J'aime toutes sortes de musique.
It's a sort of hostel. C'est une sorte d'auberge.
He's not that sort of person. Ce n'est pas son genre.

so-so ADJECTIVE
moyen MASC, **moyenne** FEM
'How was the film?' — 'So-so.' 'C'était comment le film?' — 'Moyen.'

soul NOUN
1 (person's) une **âme** FEM
2 (Music) le **soul** MASC

𝒫 to **sound** VERB ▸ SEE **sound** NOUN
You sound bored. Tu as l'air ennuyé.
It sounds easy. Ça a l'air facile.
She sounded tired. Elle avait l'air fatiguée.
It sounds as if she's happy. Elle a l'air d'être heureuse.

𝒫 **sound** NOUN ▸ SEE **sound** VERB
1 (noise) le **bruit** MASC
the sound of voices le bruit des voix
We left without making a sound. Nous sommes partis sans faire de bruit.
2 (volume) le **volume** MASC
to turn down the sound baisser [1] le volume
• **sound asleep**
profondément endormi
• **sound card**
la carte son
• **sound effect**
un effet sonore
• **soundtrack**
la bande sonore

𝒫 **soup** NOUN
la **soupe** FEM
mushroom soup la soupe aux champignons
• **soup plate**
une assiette creuse à soupe

⊙ means the verb takes **être** to form the perfect

- **soup spoon**
  la cuillère à soupe

sour *ADJECTIVE*
1 *(taste)* **aigre** *MASC & FEM*
2 **to go sour** tourner [1]
   The milk has gone sour. Le lait a tourné.

ℓ **south** *ADJECTIVE, ADVERB* ▸ SEE **south** *NOUN*
   sud *INVARIABLE ADJECTIVE*
   the south side le côté sud
   a south wind un vent du sud
   south of Paris au sud de Paris
   We're going south. Nous allons vers le sud.

   WORD TIP sud never changes.

ℓ **south** *NOUN* ▸ SEE **south** *ADJECTIVE, ADVERB*
   le **sud** *MASC*
   in the south au sud
   in the south of France dans le sud de la
   France

South Africa *NOUN*
   l'**Afrique** *FEM* **du Sud**
   in South Africa en Afrique du Sud

   WORD TIP Countries and regions in French take
   le, la or les.

South African *ADJECTIVE* ▸ SEE **South African**
   NOUN
   sud-africain *MASC*, **sud-africaine** *FEM*

   WORD TIP Adjectives never have capitals in
   French, even for nationality or regional origin.

South African *NOUN* ▸ SEE **South African**
   ADJECTIVE
   un **Sud-Africain** *MASC*, une **Sud-Africaine**
   FEM

South America *NOUN*
   l'**Amérique** *FEM* **du Sud**
   in South America en Amérique du Sud

southeast *ADJECTIVE* ▸ SEE **southeast** *NOUN*
   in southeast England au sud-est de
   l'Angleterre

southeast *NOUN* ▸ SEE **southeast** *ADJECTIVE*
   le **sud-est** *MASC*

South Pole *NOUN*
   le **pôle Sud**

southwest *ADJECTIVE* ▸ SEE **southwest** *NOUN*
   in southwest Scotland au sud-ouest de
   l'Écosse

southwest *NOUN* ▸ SEE **southwest** *ADJECTIVE*
   le **sud-ouest** *MASC*

souvenir *NOUN*
   le **souvenir** *MASC*

soya *NOUN*
   le **soja** *MASC*

soy sauce *NOUN*
   la **sauce de soja**

ℓ **space** *NOUN*
1 *(room)* la **place** *FEM*
   Is there enough space? Est-ce qu'il y a de
   la place?
   There's space for two. Il y a de la place pour
   deux.
2 *(gap)* un **espace** *MASC*
   Leave a space. Laissez un espace.
3 *(Astronomy)* l'**espace** *MASC*
   in space dans l'espace
   She was staring into space. Elle regardait
   dans le vide.
- **spacecraft**
  le vaisseau spatial
- **space exploration**
  l'exploration *FEM* de l'espace

spade *NOUN*
1 la **pelle** *FEM*
2 *(in cards)* le **pique** *MASC*
   the queen of spades la reine de pique

spaghetti *NOUN*
   les **spaghetti** *MASC PL*

Spain *NOUN*
   l'**Espagne** *FEM*

Spaniard *NOUN*
   un **Espagnol** *MASC*, une **Espagnole** *FEM*

spaniel *NOUN*
   un **épagneul** *MASC*

Spanish *ADJECTIVE* ▸ SEE **Spanish** *NOUN*
   espagnol *MASC*, **espagnole** *FEM*
   Pedro is Spanish. Pedro est espagnol.

Spanish *NOUN* ▸ SEE **Spanish** *ADJECTIVE*
1 *(language)* l'**espagnol** *MASC*
2 *(people)* **the Spanish** les **Espagnols** *MASC PL*

spanner *NOUN*
   la **clé anglaise**

to **spare** *VERB* ▸ SEE **spare** *ADJECTIVE*
   I can't spare the time. Je n'ai pas le temps.
   Can you spare a moment? Est-ce que tu as
   un instant?

spare *ADJECTIVE* ▸ SEE **spare** *VERB*
   de rechange
   a spare battery une pile de rechange
   I've got a spare ticket. J'ai un billet de trop.
   There's a spare seat here. Il y a une place
   disponible ici.
- **spare part**
  la pièce de rechange
- **spare room**
  la chambre d'amis
- **spare time**
  le temps libre

- **spare wheel**
  la roue de secours

sparkling ADJECTIVE
  sparkling (mineral) water l'eau (minérale)
  pétillante
  sparkling wine le vin mousseux

sparrow NOUN
  le **moineau** MASC (PL les **moineaux**)

ℰ to **speak** VERB
  1 **parler** [1]
  Do you speak French? Est-ce que vous
  parlez français?
  I can speak a little French. Je parle un peu
  français.
  2 **to speak to somebody** parler [1] à
  quelqu'un
  May I speak to Mrs Brown? Puis-je parler à
  Mrs Brown?
  She's speaking to Ahmed. Elle parle à
  Ahmed.
  to speak to somebody about something
  parler [1] de quelque chose à quelqu'un
  Did you speak to Tom about the party?
  Est-ce que tu as parlé de la fête à Tom?
  I'll speak to him about it. Je vais lui en
  parler.
  3 **to speak to each other** se parler ◎ [1]
  They speak to each other in Chinese. Ils se
  parlent en chinois.
  4 (on the phone) **Who's speaking?** C'est qui à
  l'appareil?

speaker NOUN
  1 (on a music system) une **enceinte** FEM
  2 (at a public lecture) le **conférencier** MASC, la
  conférencière FEM
  3 (of a language) **a French speaker** un & une
  francophone
  an English speaker un & une anglophone

spear NOUN
  la **lance** FEM

ℰ **special** ADJECTIVE
  spécial MASC, **spéciale** FEM, **spéciaux** MASC
  PL, **spéciales** FEM PL
  the special effects les effets spéciaux
  special training une formation spéciale
  to be on special offer être [6] en promotion
  They have it on special offer. Ils l'ont en
  promotion.
  There's no special reason. Il n'y a pas de
  raison particulière.

specialist NOUN
  le & la **spécialiste** MASC & FEM

to **specialize** VERB
  to specialize in something être [6]
  spécialisé dans quelque chose

They specialize in French cars. Ils sont
spécialisés dans les voitures françaises.

ℰ **specially** ADVERB
  1 (in general) **spécialement**
  not specially pas spécialement
  The songs were chosen specially for her.
  Les chansons ont été spécialement choisies
  pour elle.
  2 (specifically) **exprès**
  I came specially to see you. Je suis venu
  exprès pour te voir.
  I bought this cheese specially for you. J'ai
  acheté ce fromage exprès pour toi.

species NOUN
  une **espèce** FEM
  an endangered species une espèce en voie
  de disparition

specific ADJECTIVE
  précis MASC, **précise** FEM

spectacular ADJECTIVE
  spectaculaire MASC & FEM

ℰ **spectator** NOUN
  le **spectateur** MASC, la **spectatrice** FEM

speech NOUN
  le **discours** MASC
  to make a speech faire [10] un discours

speechless ADJECTIVE
  muet MASC, **muette** FEM
  to be speechless with rage rester ◎ [1]
  muet de colère

to **speed** VERB ▶ SEE **speed** NOUN
  rouler [1] trop vite
  She was speeding. Elle roulait trop vite.
- **to speed up**
  accélérer [24]

ℰ **speed** NOUN ▶ SEE **speed** VERB
  la **vitesse** FEM
  a twelve-speed bike un vélo à douze
  vitesses
  What speed was he doing? Il roulait à
  quelle vitesse?
  He was travelling at top speed. Il roulait à
  toute vitesse.

speeding NOUN
  l'**excès de vitesse** MASC
  He was fined for speeding. Il a reçu une
  contravention pour excès de vitesse.

speed limit NOUN
  la **limitation de vitesse**

ℰ to **spell** VERB ▶ SEE **spell** NOUN
  1 (in writing) **écrire** [38]
  How do you spell it? Ça s'écrit comment?
  It's spelt with an 'e'. Ça s'écrit avec un 'e'.

◎ means the verb takes être to form the perfect

How do you spell your surname? Ça s'écrit comment, ton nom de famille?
2 *(out loud)* **épeler** [18]
I'll spell it for you. Je vais l'épeler pour vous.

spell *NOUN* ▸ SEE **spell** *VERB*
(of time) la **période** *FEM*
a cold spell une période de temps froid
sunny spells des belles éclaircies

spell checker *NOUN*
le **correcteur orthographique**

spelling *NOUN*
l'**orthographe** *FEM*
a spelling mistake une faute d'orthographe

ℙ to **spend** *VERB*
1 *(money)* **dépenser** [1]
I've spent all my money. J'ai dépensé tout mon argent.
How much money did you spend? Tu as dépensé combien d'argent?
to spend money on something dépenser de l'argent en quelque chose
I spend money on clothes. Je dépense de l'argent en vêtements.
2 *(time)* **passer** [1]
We spent three days in Paris. Nous avons passé trois jours à Paris.
to spend time doing something passer du temps à faire quelque chose
I spend my time sending texts. Je passe mon temps à envoyer des textos.

spice *NOUN*
une **épice** *FEM*

spicy *ADJECTIVE*
épicé *MASC*, **épicée** *FEM*

spider *NOUN*
une **araignée** *FEM*

ℙ to **spill** *VERB*
renverser [1]
to spill coffee on the carpet renverser du café sur la moquette

spin *NOUN*
le **tour** *MASC*
to go for a spin aller ◎ [7] faire un tour
We went for a spin on our bikes. Nous sommes allés faire un tour à vélo.

spinach *NOUN*
les **épinards** *MASC PL*

spine *NOUN*
la **colonne vertébrale**

spiral *NOUN*
la **spirale** *FEM*

spire *NOUN*
la **flèche** *FEM*

spirit *NOUN*
1 *(energy)* l'**énergie** *FEM*
2 **to get into the spirit of things** se mettre ◎ [11] dans l'ambiance

spirits *NOUN*
1 *(alcohol)* les **alcools forts** *MASC PL*
2 **to be in good spirits** être [6] de bonne humeur

to **spit** *VERB*
cracher [1]

spite *NOUN*
1 **in spite of something** malgré quelque chose
We decided to go in spite of the rain. Nous avons décidé d'y aller malgré la pluie.
2 *(nastiness)* la **méchanceté** *FEM*
He said that out of spite. Il a dit ça par méchanceté.

spiteful *ADJECTIVE*
méchant *MASC*, **méchante** *FEM*

splash *NOUN*
1 *(noise)* le **plouf** *MASC*
2 **a splash of colour** une touche de couleur

splendid *ADJECTIVE*
splendide *MASC & FEM*

splinter *NOUN*
une **écharde** *FEM*

ℙ to **split** *VERB*
1 *(a log, a stone)* **fendre** [3]
to split a piece of wood fendre un morceau de bois
2 *(to come apart)* se **fendre** ◎ [3]
The lining has split. La doublure s'est fendue.
3 *(the cost, expense)* **partager** [52]
They split the money between them. Ils ont partagé l'argent entre eux.
• to **split up**
1 *(couples, groups)* se **séparer** ◎ [1]
Her parents have split up. Ses parents se sont séparés.
2 **to split up with somebody** **rompre** [69]
She's split up with her boyfriend. Elle a rompu avec son copain.

to **spoil** *VERB*
1 *(an occasion, an event)* **gâcher** [1]
2 *(a child)* **gâter** [1]

spoiled *ADJECTIVE*
gâté *MASC*, **gâtée** *FEM*

spoilsport *NOUN*
le & la **trouble-fête** *MASC & FEM*

ℙ **indicates key words**

spoke NOUN
(of a wheel) le **rayon** MASC

spokesman NOUN
le **porte-parole** MASC (PL les **porte-parole**)

spokeswoman NOUN
la **porte-parole** MASC (PL les **porte-parole**)

sponge NOUN
une **éponge** FEM
• **sponge bag**
la trousse de toilette
• **sponge cake**
la génoise

to **sponsor** VERB ▸ SEE **sponsor** NOUN
sponsoriser [1]
to be sponsored by somebody être [6]
sponsorisé par quelqu'un

sponsor NOUN ▸ SEE **sponsor** VERB
le **sponsor** MASC

spontaneous ADJECTIVE
spontané MASC, spontanée FEM

spooky ADJECTIVE
sinistre MASC & FEM
a spooky house une maison sinistre
a spooky story une histoire qui fait froid
dans le dos

ℰ **spoon** NOUN
la **cuillère** FEM

spoonful NOUN
la **cuillère** FEM
a spoonful of cinnamon une cuillère de
cannelle

ℰ **sport** NOUN
le **sport** MASC
My favourite sport is tennis. Mon sport
préféré, c'est le tennis.
to be good at sport être [6] bon en sport
to do a lot of sport faire [10] beaucoup de
sport
Chloë does a lot of sport. Chloë fait
beaucoup de sport.
• **sports bag**
le sac de sport
• **sports car**
la voiture de sport
• **sports centre**
le centre sportif
• **sports club**
le club sportif
• **sports hall**
la salle de sports
• **sportsman**
le sportif
• **sportswear**
les vêtements de sport

• **sportswoman**
la sportive

ℰ **sporty** ADJECTIVE
sportif MASC, sportive FEM
Sarah's very sporty. Sarah est très sportive.

to **spot** VERB ▸ SEE **spot** NOUN
repérer [24]
I spotted her in the crowd. Je l'ai repérée
dans la foule.

ℰ **spot** NOUN ▸ SEE **spot** VERB
1 (in a fabric design) le **pois** MASC
a white scarf with black spots une écharpe
blanche aux pois noirs
2 (pimple) le **bouton** MASC
I've got spots. J'ai des boutons.
Amy was covered in spots. Amy était
couverte de boutons.
3 (stain) la **tache** FEM
You have a spot on your blouse. Tu as une
tache sur ta chemise.
4 (in a theatre) le **projecteur** MASC
5 (at home) le **spot** MASC
6 (in expressions) **on the spot**
an on-the-spot repair une réparation sur-
le-champ.
They have advisers on the spot. Ils ont des
conseillers sur place.

spotless ADJECTIVE
impeccable MASC & FEM

spotlight NOUN
1 (in theatre) le **projecteur** MASC
2 (at home) le **spot** MASC

spouse NOUN
un **époux** MASC, une **épouse** FEM

to **sprain** VERB ▸ SEE **sprain** NOUN
to sprain your ankle se faire ◉ [10] une
entorse à la cheville

sprain NOUN ▸ SEE **sprain** VERB
une **entorse** FEM

to **spray** VERB ▸ SEE **spray** NOUN
1 (a liquid, flowers) vaporiser [1]
2 (a person) asperger [52]
3 (an oilslick) arroser [1]

spray NOUN ▸ SEE **spray** VERB
(spray can) la **bombe** FEM
a paint spray une bombe de peinture

ℰ to **spread** VERB ▸ SEE **spread** NOUN
1 (news, diseases, fire, panic) se propager
◉ [52]
The fire spread quickly. L'incendie s'est
propagée rapidement.
2 (butter, jam, glue) étaler [1]
3 (a rumour) faire [10] circuler la rumeur
He's spreading a rumour that I'm going

◉ means the verb takes être to form the perfect

away. Il fait circuler la rumeur que je pars.

spread NOUN ▶ SEE **spread** VERB
la **pâte à tartiner**
cheese spread le fromage à tartiner

spreadsheet NOUN
le **tableur** MASC

℘ **spring** NOUN
1 *(the season)* le **printemps** MASC
in the spring au printemps
next spring le printemps prochain
last spring le printemps dernier
2 *(in a mattress, a seat)* le **ressort** MASC
3 *(for water)* la **source** FEM
• **spring-cleaning**
le grand nettoyage de printemps
• **springtime**
le printemps
• **spring water**
l'eau de source FEM

to **sprint** VERB ▶ SEE **sprint** NOUN
courir [2] à toute vitesse
I sprinted after the bus. J'ai couru à toute
vitesse après le bus.

sprint NOUN ▶ SEE **sprint** VERB
le **sprint** MASC

sprinter NOUN
le **sprinteur** MASC, la **sprinteuse** FEM

sprout NOUN
(Brussels sprout) le **chou de Bruxelles** (PL les
choux de Bruxelles)

to **spy** VERB ▶ SEE **spy** NOUN
to spy on somebody espionner [1]
quelqu'un

spy NOUN ▶ SEE **spy** VERB
un **espion** MASC, une **espionne** FEM

spying NOUN
l'**espionnage** MASC

℘ **square** ADJECTIVE ▶ SEE **square** NOUN
carré MASC, **carrée** FEM
a square box une boîte carrée
three square metres trois mètres carrés
The room is four metres square. La pièce
fait quatre mètres carrés.

℘ **square** NOUN ▶ SEE **square** ADJECTIVE
1 *(shape)* le **carré**
black and white squares des carrés noirs
et blancs
2 *(in a town, a village)* la **place** FEM
the village square la place du village

to **squash** VERB ▶ SEE **squash** NOUN
écraser [1]

squash NOUN ▶ SEE **squash** VERB
1 *(drink)* le **sirop** MASC
orange squash le sirop d'orange

2 *(the sport)* le **squash** MASC
to play squash jouer au squash

to **squeak** VERB
1 *(doors, hinges)* grincer [61]
2 *(people, animals)* pousser [1] un petit cri

to **squeeze** VERB
1 *(someone's arm, hand)* serrer [1]
to squeeze somebody's arm serrer le bras
à quelqu'un
2 *(a toothpaste tube, a lemon)* presser [1]
to squeeze an orange presser une orange

squid NOUN
le **calmar** MASC

squirrel NOUN
un **écureuil** MASC

to **stab** VERB
poignarder [1]

stable ADJECTIVE ▶ SEE **stable** NOUN
stable MASC & FEM

stable NOUN ▶ SEE **stable** ADJECTIVE
une **écurie** FEM

stack NOUN
1 *(of plates, magazines)* la **pile** FEM
2 **stacks of** plein de
She's got stacks of books. Elle a plein de
livres.

℘ **stadium** NOUN
le **stade** MASC
We train at the stadium. Nous nous
entraînons au stade.

staff NOUN
1 *(of a company)* le **personnel** MASC
2 *(in a school)* les **professeurs** MASC PL

staffroom NOUN
la **salle des professeurs** FEM

℘ **stage** NOUN
1 *(for performers)* la **scène** FEM
on stage sur scène
The band came on stage. Le groupe est
entré en scène.
2 *(phase)* le **stade** MASC
at this stage of the project à ce stade du
projet

staggered ADJECTIVE
(amazed) stupéfié MASC, stupéfiée FEM

to **stain** VERB ▶ SEE **stain** NOUN
tacher [1]

stain NOUN ▶ SEE **stain** VERB
la **tache** FEM
to leave a stain faire [10] une tache
to remove a stain enlever [50] une tache

stainless steel NOUN
l'inox MASC

staircase NOUN
un **escalier** MASC

♀**stairs** NOUN
l'**escalier** MASC
to go up the stairs monter ◯ [1] l'escalier
to go down the stairs descendre ◯ [3] l'escalier
I met her on the stairs. Je l'ai croisée dans l'escalier.
She fell down the stairs. Elle est tombée dans l'escalier.

stale ADJECTIVE
(bread) rassis MASC, rassise FEM

stalemate NOUN
(in chess) le **pat** MASC

stall NOUN
1 (in markets, fairs) le **stand** MASC
2 (in theatres) the stalls l'**orchestre** MASC SINGULAR

to **stammer** VERB ▸ SEE **stammer** NOUN
bégayer [59]

stammer NOUN ▸ SEE **stammer** VERB
to have a stammer bégayer [59]

to **stamp** VERB ▸ SEE **stamp** NOUN
1 (a letter) affranchir [2]
2 to stamp your foot taper [1] du pied

♀**stamp** NOUN ▸ SEE **stamp** VERB
le **timbre** MASC
I have to buy stamps. Je dois acheter des timbres.
How much is a stamp for England? Un timbre pour l'Angleterre, c'est combien?

stamp album NOUN
un album de timbres

stamp collection NOUN
la collection de timbres

♀to **stand** VERB
1 être [6] debout
Several people were standing. Plusieurs personnes étaient debout.
2 (to put up with) supporter [1]
I can't stand her. Je ne la supporte pas.
I can't stand waiting. Je ne supporte pas d'attendre.
3 (to be) to be standing somewhere être [6] quelque part
They're still standing there. Ils sont toujours là.
• to stand back
se reculer ◯ [1]
Stand back from the road. Reculez-vous de la route.

• to stand for something
être [6] l'abréviation de quelque chose
'UN' stands for 'United Nations'. 'UN' est l'abréviation de 'United Nations'.
• to stand up
se lever ◯ [50]
Everybody stood up. Tout le monde s'est levé.

standard ADJECTIVE ▸ SEE **standard** NOUN
standard INVARIABLE ADJECTIVE
the standard price le prix standard

standard NOUN ▸ SEE **standard** ADJECTIVE
le **niveau** MASC
to be of a high standard être [6] d'un bon niveau
They must reach the required standard. Ils doivent atteindre le niveau exigé.

standard of living NOUN
le niveau de vie
a higher standard of living un niveau de vie supérieur

stands PLURAL NOUN
la tribune FEM SINGULAR
a seat in the stands une place à la tribune

to **staple** VERB ▸ SEE **staple** NOUN
agrafer [1]

staple NOUN ▸ SEE **staple** VERB
une agrafe FEM

stapler NOUN
une agrafeuse FEM

to **star** VERB ▸ SEE **star** NOUN
to star in a film être [6] la vedette d'un film

♀**star** NOUN ▸ SEE **star** VERB
1 (in the sky) une étoile FEM
2 (personality) une vedette
He's a film star. C'est une vedette de cinéma.

♀to **stare** VERB
regarder [1] fixement
He was staring at me. Il me regardait fixement.
What are you staring at? Qu'est-ce que tu regardes?

♀**star sign** NOUN
le signe astrologique
What star sign are you? De quelle signe êtes-vous?

♀to **start** VERB ▸ SEE **start** NOUN
1 commencer [61]
When does it start? Ça commence à quelle heure?
It starts at eight. Ça commence à huit heures.
I've started the book. J'ai commencé

◯ means the verb takes être to form the perfect

le livre.

2 **to start doing something** commencer [61] à faire quelque chose
I've started learning Spanish. J'ai commencé à apprendre l'espagnol.

3 **to start again** recommencer
We'll have to start all over again. Il va falloir recommencer à zéro.

4 *(cars)* démarrer [1]
The car won't start. La voiture ne veut pas démarrer.
She started the car. Elle a fait démarrer la voiture.

ℓ **start** NOUN ▸ SEE **start** VERB

1 le **début** MASC
at the start au début
at the start of the book au début du livre
from the start dès le début

2 **to make a start on something** commencer [61] à faire quelque chose
I've made a start on my homework. J'ai commencé à faire mes devoirs.

3 *(of a race)* le **départ** MASC

4 **the start of the school year** la rentrée scolaire

ℓ **starter** NOUN
une **entrée** FEM
What would you like as a starter? Qu'est-ce que vous voulez comme entrée?
I'd like the melon as a starter. Je prendrai le melon comme entrée.

to **starve** VERB
mourir ◎ [54] **de faim**
I'm starving! Je meurs de faim!

to **state** VERB ▸ SEE **state** NOUN

1 *(an opinion, an intention)* déclarer [1]

2 *(your address, occupation)* indiquer [1]

ℓ **state** NOUN ▸ SEE **state** VERB

1 *(condition)* un **état** MASC
in a very bad state en très mauvais état

2 *(in a country)* un **état** MASC

3 *(in politics)* **the state** l'État

4 *(USA)* **the States** les États-Unis MASC PL
They live in the States. Ils habitent aux États-Unis.

• **state school**
l'école publique FEM

stately home NOUN
le **château** MASC *(PL les **châteaux**)*

statement NOUN
la **déclaration** FEM

ℓ **station** NOUN
la **gare** FEM
the railway station la gare
the bus station la gare routière

She dropped me off at the station. Elle m'a déposé à la gare.

stationer's NOUN
la **papeterie** FEM

stationery NOUN
la **papeterie** FEM

statistics NOUN

1 *(subject)* la **statistique** FEM

2 *(figures)* **the statistics** les statistiques FEM PL

statue NOUN
la **statue** FEM

status NOUN
la **position** FEM
social status la position sociale

ℓ **to stay** VERB ▸ SEE **stay** NOUN

1 *(in general)* rester ◎ [1]
I'll stay here. Je reste ici.
How long are you staying? Vous restez combien de temps?
I'll be staying here for two nights. Je reste deux nuits ici.

2 *(with periods of time)* passer [1]
We stayed in Nice for a week. Nous avons passé une semaine à Nice.

3 **to stay with somebody** aller ◎ [7] chez quelqu'un
We stayed with friends. Nous sommes allés chez des amis.

4 *(to be living temporarily)* loger [52]
Where are you staying? Où est-ce que vous logez?
We're staying at the youth hostel. Nous logeons à l'auberge de jeunesse.

• **to stay in**
rester ◎ [1] à la maison
I'm staying in tonight. Je reste à la maison ce soir.

• **to stay out**
to stay out late rentrer ◎ [1] tard
Don't stay out too late. Ne rentre pas trop tard.

• **(to) stay up**
to stay up late se coucher ◎ [1] tard

ℓ **stay** NOUN ▸ SEE **stay** VERB
le **séjour** MASC
during our stay in Dijon pendant notre séjour à Dijon
Enjoy your stay! Bon séjour!

ℓ **steady** ADJECTIVE

1 *(job)* stable MASC & FEM

2 *(increase, decrease)* régulier MASC, régulière FEM

3 *(hand, voice)* ferme MASC & FEM

4 **to hold something steady** bien tenir [77] quelque chose

ℓ **indicates key words**

I held the ladder steady. J'ai bien tenu l'échelle.

steak *NOUN*
le steack *MASC*
steak and chips un steack frites

♟ to **steal** *VERB*
voler [1]
The purse was stolen. Le porte-monnaie a été volé.
to steal something from somebody voler quelque chose à quelqu'un
They stole money from us. Ils nous ont volé de l'argent.
My camera's been stolen. On m'a volé mon appareil photo.

steam *NOUN*
la vapeur *FEM*
• steam engine
la locomotive à vapeur
• steam iron
le fer à vapeur

steel *NOUN*
l'acier *MASC*
made of steel en acier

steep *ADJECTIVE*
raide *MASC & FEM*

steeple *NOUN*
1 (spire) la flèche *FEM*
2 (bell tower) le clocher *MASC*

steering wheel *NOUN*
le volant *MASC*

to **step** *VERB* ▶ SEE **step** *NOUN*
to step into something entrer ◎ [1] dans quelque chose
I stepped into the office. Je suis entré dans le bureau.
• to step back
faire [10] un pas en arrière
• to step forward
faire [10] un pas en avant

♟ **step** *NOUN* ▶ SEE **step** *VERB*
1 (in walking) le pas *MASC*
to take a step forwards faire [10] un pas en avant
to take a step backwards faire [10] un pas en arrière
I heard steps. J'ai entendu des pas.
2 (on stairs) la marche *FEM*
'Mind the step' 'Attention à la marche'

stepbrother *NOUN*
le demi-frère *MASC* (PL les demi-frères)

stepdaughter *NOUN*
la belle-fille *FEM* (PL les belles-filles)

stepfather *NOUN*
le beau-père *MASC* (PL les beaux-pères)

stepladder *NOUN*
un escabeau *MASC* (PL les escabeaux)

stepmother *NOUN*
la belle-mère *FEM* (PL les belles-mères)

stepsister *NOUN*
la demi-sœur *FEM* (PL les demi-sœurs)

stepson *NOUN*
le beau-fils *MASC* (PL les beaux-fils)

stereo *NOUN*
la chaîne stéréo (PL les chaînes stéréo)

stew *NOUN*
le ragoût *MASC*

steward *NOUN*
le steward *MASC*

stewardess *NOUN*
une hôtesse *FEM*

♟ to **stick** *VERB* ▶ SEE **stick** *NOUN*
1 (with glue) coller [1]
I stuck it on with tape. Je l'ai collé avec du Scotch®.
2 (to put) mettre [11]
Stick them on my desk. Mets-les sur mon bureau.
3 to stick out your tongue tirer [1] la langue
• to stick together
1 (to stay together) rester ◎ [1] ensemble
2 (to be loyal) être [6] solidaire

stick *NOUN* ▶ SEE **stick** *VERB*
le bâton *MASC*

sticker *NOUN*
un autocollant *MASC*

sticky *ADJECTIVE*
1 (hands, fingers) poisseux *MASC*, poisseuse *FEM*
2 (paper, tape) adhésif *MASC*, adhésive *FEM*

sticky tape *NOUN*
le Scotch® *MASC*

♟ **stiff** *ADJECTIVE*
1 to feel stiff avoir [5] des courbatures
to have stiff legs avoir [5] des courbatures dans les jambes
I was stiff all over. J'avais des courbatures partout.
2 to be bored stiff s'ennuyer [41] à mourir
3 to be scared stiff être [6] mort de peur

still *ADJECTIVE* ▶ SEE **still** *ADVERB*
1 (not moving) Sit still! Tiens-toi tranquille!
Keep still! Ne bouge pas!
2 (not fizzy) non-gazeux *MASC*, non-gazeuse *FEM*

◎ means the verb takes être to form the perfect

ℐ **still** ADVERB ▸ SEE **still** ADJECTIVE
1 toujours
  I still go there. J'y vais toujours.
  I've still not finished. Je n'ai toujours pas fini.
  He's still working. Il est toujours en train de travailler.
  Do you still live in Hull? Est-ce que tu habites toujours à Hull?
2 encore
  There's still a lot of cake left. Il reste encore beaucoup de gâteau.
  I've still got some money. Il me reste encore de l'argent.
3 **better still** encore mieux

ℐ to **sting** VERB ▸ SEE **sting** NOUN
  piquer [1]
  to be stung se faire ◎ [10] piquer
  I was stung by a bee. Je me suis fait piquer par une abeille.

sting NOUN ▸ SEE **sting** VERB
  la piqûre FEM

to **stink** VERB ▸ SEE **stink** NOUN
  puer [1]
  It stinks of cigarettes. Ça pue la cigarette ici.

stink NOUN ▸ SEE **stink** VERB
  une odeur FEM
  the stink of fish l'odeur de poisson
  What a stink! Ça pue!

ℐ to **stir** VERB
1 (a liquid, a sauce) remuer [1]
2 (to move) bouger [52]
  He was stirring in his sleep. Il bougeait en dormant.
3 **to stir up trouble** faire [10] des histoires
  Why is she stirring up trouble? Pourquoi est-ce qu'elle fait des histoires?

stitch NOUN
1 (in sewing) le point MASC
2 (in knitting) la maille FEM
3 (for a wound) le point de souture (PL les points de souture)
  I got ten stitches. On m'a fait dix points de souture.
4 **to get a stitch** attraper [1] un point de côté

to **stock** VERB ▸ SEE **stock** NOUN
  vendre [3]
  They don't stock fireworks. Ils ne vendent pas les feux d'artifice.
• **to stock up on something** s'approvisionner [1] en quelque chose
  We must stock up on fruit. Il faut s'approvisionner en fruits.

stock NOUN ▸ SEE **stock** VERB
1 (in store) le stock MASC

  in stock en stock
  Do you have any others in stock? Vous en avez d'autres en stock?
2 (supply) la réserve
  I always have a stock of pencils. J'ai toujours une réserve de crayons.
3 (for cooking) le bouillon MASC
  chicken stock le bouillon de poulet

stock cube NOUN
  le bouillon-cube MASC

stock exchange NOUN
  la Bourse (des valeurs)

stocking NOUN
  le bas MASC
  a pair of stockings une paire de bas

stomach NOUN
  l'estomac MASC

stomach ache NOUN
  to have stomach ache avoir [5] mal au ventre

ℐ **stone** NOUN
1 (in general) la pierre FEM
  a stone wall un mur en pierre
2 (small) le caillou MASC (PL les cailloux)
  to throw stones lancer [61] des cailloux
3 (in fruit) le noyau MASC (PL les noyaux)
  to remove the stone enlever [50] le noyau

stool NOUN
  le tabouret MASC

ℐ to **stop** VERB ▸ SEE **stop** NOUN
1 s'arrêter ◎ [1]
  The music stopped. La musique s'est arrêtée.
  Paul stopped in front of the shop. Paul s'est arrêté devant le magasin.
  The train only stops once. Le train s'arrête une fois seulement.
  Does the train stop in Dijon? Est-ce que le train s'arrête à Dijon?
2 (a person, a car) arrêter [1]
  She stopped me in the street. Elle m'a arrêté dans la rue.
  They're stopping the coach. Ils arrêtent le car.
3 **to stop doing something** arrêter [1] de faire quelque chose
  Everyone stopped laughing. Tout le monde a arrêté de rire.
  He's stopped smoking. Il a arrêté de fumer.
  She never stops asking questions. Elle n'arrête pas de poser des questions.
4 **to stop somebody doing something** empêcher [1] quelqu'un de faire quelque chose
  It stopped me sleeping. Ça m'a empêché

ℐ indicates key words

A
B
C
D
E
F
G
H
I
J
K
L
M
N
O
P
Q
R
S
T
U
V
W
X
Y
Z

de dormir.

ℰ **stop** NOUN ▸ SEE **stop** VERB
un **arrêt** MASC
at the bus stop à l'arrêt de bus
the next stop le prochain arrêt

stopwatch NOUN
le **chronomètre** MASC

to **store** VERB ▸ SEE **store** NOUN
1 (wine, food) **garder** [1]
2 (Computers) **mémoriser** [1]

store NOUN ▸ SEE **store** VERB
(shop) le **magasin** MASC

ℰ **storey** NOUN
un **étage** MASC
a three-storey house une maison à trois étages
I live on the second storey. J'habite au deuxième étage.

stork NOUN
la **cigogne** FEM

ℰ **storm** NOUN
1 (wind) la **tempête** FEM
a snowstorm une tempête de neige
2 (thunderstorm) un **orage** MASC
There's going to be a storm. Il va y avoir de l'orage.

stormy ADJECTIVE
orageux MASC, **orageuse** FEM
It's stormy today. Il fait de l'orage aujourd'hui.

ℰ **story** NOUN
1 (a tale) une **histoire** FEM
a true story une histoire vécue
a ghost story une histoire de fantômes
to tell a story raconter [1] une histoire
to make up a story inventer [1] une histoire
2 (in a newspaper) un **article** MASC
a front-page story un article à la une

stove NOUN
1 (cooker) la **cuisinière** FEM
2 (heater) le **poêle** MASC

ℰ **straight** ADJECTIVE ▸ SEE **straight** ADVERB
1 **droit** MASC, **droite** FEM
a straight line une ligne droite
to have straight hair avoir [5] les cheveux raides
2 (clear) **clair** MASC, **claire** FEM
a straight answer une réponse claire

ℰ **straight** ADVERB ▸ SEE **straight** ADJECTIVE
1 (in direction) **droit**
straight ahead tout droit
Go straight ahead. Continuez tout droit.
2 (in time) **directement**
He went straight to the doctor's. Il est allé directement chez le médecin.
3 **straight away** tout de suite
I called back straight away. J'ai rappelé tout de suite.

straightforward ADJECTIVE
1 (explanation, question) **simple** MASC & FEM
2 (honest) **franc** MASC, **franche** FEM

to **strain** VERB ▸ SEE **strain** NOUN
1 (your back, eyes) **se faire** ◉ [10] **mal à**
2 (a muscle) **se froisser** ◉ [1]
Dan strained a muscle during the match. Dan s'est froissé un muscle pendant le match.
3 (rice, pasta) **égoutter** [1]

strain NOUN ▸ SEE **strain** VERB
le **stress** MASC
the strain of the last few weeks le stress de ces dernières semaines
They're under a lot of strain. Ils sont stressés.

ℰ **strange** ADJECTIVE
bizarre MASC & FEM
a strange situation une situation bizarre
It seems very strange to me. Ça me paraît très bizarre.

stranger NOUN
un **inconnu** MASC, une **inconnue** FEM
They were strangers. C'étaient des inconnus.

to **strangle** VERB
étrangler [1]

strap NOUN
1 (of a case, camera) la **courroie** FEM
2 (of a shoulder bag) la **bandoulière** FEM
3 (of a dress, a bra) la **bretelle** FEM
4 (of a watch) le **bracelet** MASC
5 (of a shoe) la **lanière** FEM

strapless ADJECTIVE
(dress, bra) **sans bretelles**

straw NOUN
1 (for drinking with) la **paille** FEM
2 (material) la **paille** FEM
a straw hat un chapeau de paille

ℰ **strawberry** NOUN
la **fraise** FEM
strawberry jam la confiture de fraises

stray ADJECTIVE
a stray dog un chien perdu

stream NOUN
le **ruisseau** MASC (PL les **ruisseaux**)

ℰ **street** NOUN
la **rue** FEM
The streets are always busy. Les rues sont

toujours animées.
I met Ben in the street. J'ai croisé Ben dans
la rue.
- **streetlamp**
le réverbère
- **street map**
le plan de la ville

streetwise *ADJECTIVE*
dégourdi *MASC*, dégourdie *FEM*

ℓ **strength** *NOUN*
1 *(of a person)* la **force** *FEM*
with all your strength de toutes ses forces
He pulled with all his strength. Il a tiré de
toutes ses forces.
I hadn't got the strength to shout. Je n'ai
pas eu la force de crier.
2 *(of a country)* la **puissance**
military strength la puissance militaire

to **stress** *VERB* ▸ SEE **stress** *NOUN*
(a point) **souligner** [1]

stress *NOUN* ▸ SEE **stress** *VERB*
le **stress** *MASC*
to be under a lot of stress être [6] stressé

ℓ to **stretch** *VERB*
1 *(fabrics, woollens)* se **déformer** ◌ [1]
This jumper has stretched. Ce pull s'est
déformé.
2 *(your muscles)* **étirer** [1]
to stretch out your arms étirer les bras
to stretch your legs se dégourdir ◌ [2] les
jambes
3 *(with your whole body)* s'**étirer** ◌ [1]
4 *(shoes)* s'**élargir** ◌ [2]

stretcher *NOUN*
le **brancard** *MASC*

stretchy *ADJECTIVE*
élastique *MASC & FEM*

strict *ADJECTIVE*
strict *MASC*, **stricte** *FEM*

to **strike** *VERB* ▸ SEE **strike** *NOUN*
1 *(to hit)* **frapper** [1]
2 *(clock)* **sonner** [1]
The clock struck six. L'horloge a sonné six
heures.
3 *(workers)* **faire** [10] grève

ℓ **strike** *NOUN* ▸ SEE **strike** *VERB*
la **grève** *FEM*
to go on strike faire [10] grève
to be on strike être [6] en grève

striker *NOUN*
1 *(in football)* le **buteur** *MASC*
2 *(worker)* le & la **gréviste** *MASC & FEM*

striking *ADJECTIVE*
frappant *MASC*, **frappante** *FEM*

a striking resemblance une ressemblance
frappante

string *NOUN*
1 *(for parcels)* la **ficelle** *FEM*
2 *(for musical instruments)* la **corde** *FEM*

to **strip** *VERB* ▸ SEE **strip** *NOUN*
(to undress) se **déshabiller** ◌ [1]

strip *NOUN* ▸ SEE **strip** *VERB*
la **bande** *FEM*

strip cartoon *NOUN*
la **bande dessinée**

stripe *NOUN*
la **rayure** *FEM*

striped *ADJECTIVE*
rayé *MASC*, **rayée** *FEM*

to **stroke** *VERB* ▸ SEE **stroke** *NOUN*
caresser [1]

stroke *NOUN* ▸ SEE **stroke** *VERB*
1 *(in swimming)* la **nage** *FEM*
2 *(medical)* une **attaque** *FEM*
to have a stroke avoir [5] une attaque
3 **to have a stroke of luck** avoir [5] un coup
de chance

to **stroll** *VERB* ▸ SEE **stroll** *NOUN*
se **promener** ◌ [50]

stroll *NOUN* ▸ SEE **stroll** *VERB*
to go for a stroll faire [10] une petite
promenade

ℓ **strong** *ADJECTIVE*
1 *(in general)* **fort** *MASC*, **forte** *FEM*
She's as strong as you. Elle est aussi forte
que toi.
There are strong currents. Il y a des
courants forts.
2 *(material)* **solide** *MASC & FEM*
strong shoes des chaussures solides
Is the shelf strong enough? Est-ce que
l'étagère est assez solide?
3 *(country, state)* **puissant** *MASC*, **puissante**
FEM

strongly *ADVERB*
1 *(to believe)* **fermement**
2 *(to support)* **fortement**
3 *(to advise, oppose)* **vivement**

to **struggle** *VERB* ▸ SEE **struggle** *NOUN*
1 *(to get something)* se **battre** ◌ [21]
They have struggled to survive. Ils se sont
battus pour survivre.
2 *(physically)* se **débattre** ◌ [21]
I was struggling to stay awake. Je me
débattais pour rester éveillé.

struggle *NOUN* ▸ SEE **struggle** *VERB*
la **lutte** *FEM*
a power struggle une lutte pour le pouvoir

the struggle for independence la lutte
pour l'indépendance

to **stub** VERB
1 **to stub your toe on something** se cogner ⊜
[1] l'orteil contre quelque chose
2 **to stub a cigarette out** écraser [1] une
cigarette

stubborn ADJECTIVE
têtu MASC, têtue FEM

stuck ADJECTIVE
1 (jammed) coincé MASC, coincée FEM
The drawer's stuck. Le tiroir est coincé.
2 **to get stuck** rester ⊜ [1] coincé
We got stuck in the traffic. Nous sommes
restés coincés dans la circulation.

stud NOUN
1 (on a belt, jacket) le clou MASC
2 (on a boot) le clou MASC
3 (earring) la boucle d'oreille

student NOUN
un étudiant MASC, une étudiante FEM

studio NOUN
1 (film, TV) le studio MASC
2 (artist's) un atelier MASC
• studio flat
le studio

ℐ to **study** VERB ► SEE **study** NOUN
1 (to revise) réviser [1]
He's studying for his exams. Il est en train
de réviser pour ses examens.
2 (a subject) faire [10] des études de
She's studying medicine. Elle fait des
études de médecine.

study NOUN ► SEE **study** VERB
le bureau MASC

to **stuff** VERB ► SEE **stuff** NOUN
1 (to push) fourrer [1]
She stuffed some things into a backpack.
Elle a fourré quelques affaires dans un sac.
2 (a chicken, vegetables) farcir [2]
stuffed aubergines des aubergines farcies
3 **to be stuffed up** avoir [5] le nez bouché

stuff NOUN ► SEE **stuff** VERB
1 (personal belongings) les affaires FEM PL
all my stuff toutes mes affaires
You can leave your stuff at my house. Tu
peux laisser tes affaires chez moi.
2 (general things) les trucs MASC PL
I put all that stuff in the attic. J'ai mis tous
ces trucs au grenier.
3 (substance) le truc MASC
some antiseptic stuff un truc antiseptique

stuffing NOUN
la farce FEM

stuffy ADJECTIVE
étouffant MASC, étouffante FEM

to **stumble** VERB
trébucher [1]

stunned ADJECTIVE
stupéfait MASC, stupéfaite FEM

stunning ADJECTIVE
sensationnel MASC, sensationnelle FEM

stunt NOUN
(in a film) la cascade FEM
• stuntman
le cascadeur
• stuntwoman
la cascadeuse

ℐ **stupid** ADJECTIVE
bête MASC & FEM
That was really stupid. C'était vraiment
bête.
They're so stupid. Ils sont tellement bêtes.
to do something stupid faire [10] une
bêtise
Don't do anything stupid. Ne fais pas de
bêtises.

stutter NOUN ► SEE **stutter** VERB
to have a stutter bégayer [59]

to **stutter** VERB ► SEE **stutter** NOUN
bégayer [59]

ℐ **style** NOUN
1 (way) le style MASC
a style of living un style de vie
2 (fashion) la mode FEM
It's the latest style. C'est la dernière mode.
They have no sense of style. Ils n'ont aucun
sens de la mode.

ℐ **subject** NOUN
1 (in general) le sujet MASC
the subject of my talk le sujet de mon
exposé
Can we change the subject? Est-ce qu'on
peut parler d'autre chose?
2 (at school) la matière FEM
My favourite subject is biology. Ma
matière préférée, c'est la biologie.

submarine NOUN
le sous-marin MASC (PL les sous-marins)

subscription NOUN
un abonnement MASC
to take out a subscription to a magazine
s'abonner [1] à un magazine

subsidy NOUN
la subvention FEM

substance NOUN
la substance FEM

⊜ means the verb takes être to form the perfect

to **substitute** *VERB* ▸ SEE **substitute** *NOUN*
substituer [1]

substitute *NOUN* ▸ SEE **substitute** *VERB*
(person) le **remplaçant** *MASC*, la
remplaçante *FEM*

subtitled *ADJECTIVE*
sous-titré *MASC*, sous-titrée *FEM*

subtitles *PLURAL NOUN*
les **sous-titres** *MASC PL*

subtle *ADJECTIVE*
subtil *MASC*, subtile *FEM*

to **subtract** *VERB*
soustraire [78]

ℓ **suburb** *NOUN*
la **banlieue** *FEM*
a suburb of Edinburgh une banlieue
d'Édimbourg
in the suburbs of London dans la banlieue
de Londres

suburban *ADJECTIVE*
(house, estate) de **banlieue**
large suburban estates les cités de
banlieue

subway *NOUN*
1 (underpass) le **passage souterrain**
2 (in New York, Tokyo, etc) le **métro**

ℓ to **succeed** *VERB*
réussir [2]
Will they succeed? Est-ce qu'ils vont
réussir?
to succeed in doing something réussir à
faire quelque chose
We've succeeded in contacting her. Nous
avons réussi à la contacter.

ℓ **success** *NOUN*
le **succès** *MASC*
a great success un grand succès
to have a lot of success avoir [5] beaucoup
de succès

successful *ADJECTIVE*
réussi *MASC*, réussie *FEM*
a successful operation une opération
réussie
He's a successful writer. C'est un écrivain
à succès.

successfully *ADVERB*
avec succès

ℓ **such** *ADVERB*
1 tellement
They're such nice people! Ils sont tellement
gentils!
I've had such a busy day! J'ai eu une
journée tellement chargée!

It's such a long way. C'est tellement loin.
It's such a pity. C'est tellement dommage.
2 such a lot of tellement de
such a lot of homework tellement de
devoirs
3 **such as** comme
in big cities such as Glasgow dans les
grandes villes comme Glasgow

to **suck** *VERB*
sucer [61]

sudden *ADJECTIVE*
soudain *MASC*, soudaine *FEM*
a sudden noise un bruit soudain
all of a sudden tout d'un coup

ℓ **suddenly** *ADVERB*
1 tout d'un coup
Suddenly the light went out. Tout d'un
coup la lumière s'est éteinte.
2 **to die suddenly** mourir ◎ [54] subitement

suede *NOUN*
le **daim** *MASC*

to **suffer** *VERB*
souffrir [73]

sufficiently *ADVERB*
suffisamment

ℓ **sugar** *NOUN*
le **sucre** *MASC*
Would you like sugar? Est-ce que tu veux
du sucre?

ℓ to **suggest** *VERB*
suggérer [24]
**to suggest to somebody that they should
do something** suggérer à quelqu'un de
faire quelque chose
**He suggested I should speak to you about
it.** Il m'a suggéré de vous en parler.

suggestion *NOUN*
la **suggestion** *FEM*

suicide *NOUN*
le **suicide** *MASC*
to commit suicide se suicider ◎ [1]

ℓ to **suit** *VERB*
1 **to suit somebody** convenir [81] à quelqu'un
Eight p.m., does that suit you? Vingt
heures, ça te convient?
It doesn't suit me. Ça ne me convient pas.
2 (to look well on) **to suit somebody** aller ◎
[7] (bien) à quelqu'un
Does it suit me? Est-ce que ça me va?
Blue really suits you. Le bleu te va bien.

ℓ **suit** *NOUN* ▸ SEE **suit** *VERB*
1 (man's) le **costume** *MASC*
2 (woman's) le **tailleur** *MASC*

suitable *ADJECTIVE*
1 *(clothes, presents)* **approprié** *MASC*,
   appropriée *FEM*
   I don't have any suitable shoes. Je n'ai pas
   de chaussures appropriées.
2 **to be suitable for somebody** **convenir** [81]
   à quelqu'un
   It's more suitable for children. Ça convient
   mieux aux enfants.

℗ **suitcase** *NOUN*
   la valise *FEM*
   to pack your suitcase **faire** [10] sa valise

to **sulk** *VERB*
   bouder [1]

sum *NOUN* ▶ SEE **sum** *VERB*
1 *(quantity)* **la somme** *FEM*
   a large sum of money une grosse somme
   d'argent
2 *(calculation)* **le calcul** *MASC*

to **summarize** *VERB*
   résumer [1]

summary *NOUN*
   le résumé *MASC*

℗ **summer** *NOUN*
   l'été *MASC*
   in summer en été
   next summer l'été prochain
   summer clothes les vêtements d'été
   the summer holidays les grandes vacances
   I'm going there for the summer. J'y vais
   pour l'été.
   We went to Brittany last summer. Nous
   sommes allés en Bretagne l'été dernier.

summertime *NOUN*
   l'été *MASC*
   in summertime en été

summit *NOUN*
   le sommet *MASC*
   at the summit au sommet

℗ **sun** *NOUN*
   le soleil *MASC*
   in the sun au soleil
• **sunbathe**
   se bronzer ◎ [1]
• **sunblock**
   la crème écran total
• **sunburn**
   le coup de soleil

℗ **sunburned** *ADJECTIVE*
   to get sunburned **attraper** [1] un coup de
   soleil
   I got sunburned. J'ai attrapé un coup de
   soleil.

℗ **Sunday** *NOUN*
   le dimanche *MASC*
   on Sunday dimanche
   last Sunday dimanche dernier
   next Sunday dimanche prochain
   every Sunday tous les dimanches
   on Sundays le dimanche
   The museum is closed on Sundays. Le
   musée est fermé le dimanche.
   I'm going out on Sunday. Je sors dimanche.
   See you on Sunday! À dimanche!

WORD TIP Months of the year and days of the
week start with small letters in French.

sunflower *NOUN*
   le tournesol *MASC*
• **sunflower oil**
   l'huile *FEM* de tournesol

sunglasses *PLURAL NOUN*
   les lunettes de soleil *FEM PL*

sunlight *NOUN*
   le soleil *MASC*

℗ **sunny** *ADJECTIVE*
1 **to be sunny** **faire** [10] du soleil
   It's very sunny. Il fait du soleil.
   It's going to be sunny. Il va faire du soleil.
2 *(place)* **ensoleillé** *MASC*, **ensoleillée** *FEM*
   in a sunny corner of the garden dans un
   coin ensoleillé du jardin

sunrise *NOUN*
   le lever du soleil

sunroof *NOUN*
   le toit ouvrant

sunset *NOUN*
   le coucher du soleil

sunshine *NOUN*
   le soleil *MASC*
   in the sunshine au soleil

sunstroke *NOUN*
   une insolation *FEM*
   to get sunstroke **attraper** [1] une insolation

℗ **suntan** *NOUN*
   le bronzage *MASC*
   to get a suntan **bronzer** [1]
• **suntan lotion**
   la lotion solaire

super *ADJECTIVE*
   super *INVARIABLE ADJ*, **formidable** *MASC & FEM*
   We had a super time! C'était super!

℗ **supermarket** *NOUN*
   le supermarché *MASC*

supernatural *ADJECTIVE*
   surnaturel *MASC*, **surnaturelle** *FEM*

◎ means the verb takes être to form the perfect

superstitious *ADJECTIVE*
  superstitieux *MASC*, **superstitieuse** *FEM*

to **supervise** *VERB*
  surveiller [1]

supervisor *NOUN*
1 *(in a shop)* le & la **responsable** *MASC & FEM*
2 *(in a factory)* le **contremaître** *MASC*

ℓ **supper** *NOUN*
  le **dîner** *MASC*
  to have supper dîner [1]
  I had supper at Helen's. J'ai dîné chez Helen.

ℓ **supplement** *NOUN*
  le **supplément** *MASC*
  There's a supplement. Il y a un supplément à payer.
  There's no supplement. Il n'y a pas de supplément.

supplies *PLURAL NOUN*
  les **provisions** *FEM PL*

ℓ to **supply** *VERB* ▸ SEE **supply** *NOUN*
  fournir [2]
  The school supplies the paper. C'est l'école qui fournit le papier.
  to supply somebody with something fournir quelque chose à quelqu'un
  They supply us with the books. Ils nous fournissent les livres.

ℓ **supply** *NOUN* ▸ SEE **supply** *VERB*
1 *(stock)* les **réserves** *FEM PL*
  food supplies les réserves de nourriture
2 *(of oil, gas, electricity)* l'**alimentation** *FEM*
3 **to be in short supply** être [6] difficile à trouver
  Work is in short supply. Le travail est difficile à trouver.

supply teacher *NOUN*
  le **suppléant** *MASC*, la **suppléante** *FEM*

ℓ to **support** *VERB* ▸ SEE **support** *NOUN*
1 *(to back up)* soutenir [77]
  Her teachers have really supported her. Ses professeurs l'ont vraiment soutenue.
2 *(a team)* être [6] supporter de
  Dave supports Liverpool. Dave est supporter de Liverpool.
3 **to support a family** subvenir [81] aux besoins d'une famille

support *NOUN* ▸ SEE **support** *VERB*
  le **soutien** *MASC*
  He has a lot of support. Il a beaucoup de soutien.

supporter *NOUN*
  le & la **supporter** *MASC & FEM*
  a Rangers supporter un supporter de Rangers

to **suppose** *VERB*
  I suppose she's forgotten. Elle a sans doute oublié.
  Suppose she doesn't come? Et si elle ne vient pas?

ℓ **supposed** *ADJECTIVE*
  to be supposed to do something être [6] censé faire quelque chose
  You're supposed to wear a helmet. On est censé porter un casque.
  We're not supposed to chat. Nous ne sommes pas censés bavarder.
  He was supposed to be here at six. Il devait être là à six heures.

ℓ **sure** *ADJECTIVE*
  sûr *MASC*, **sûre** *FEM*
  Are you sure? Tu es sûr?
  Yes, I'm sure. Oui, j'en suis sûr.
  Are you sure you've had enough to eat? Tu es sûr que tu as assez mangé?
  Are you sure you saw her? Tu es sûr de l'avoir vue?
  I'm sure I recognized her. Je suis sûr de l'avoir reconnue.
  'Can you shut the door?' — 'Sure!' 'Peux-tu fermer la porte?' — 'Bien sûr!'

surely *ADVERB*
  quand même
  Surely you've checked! Tu as vérifié quand même!

ℓ to **surf** *VERB* ▸ SEE **surf** *NOUN*
  to surf the Net surfer [1] sur Internet

surf *NOUN* ▸ SEE **surf** *VERB*
  l'**écume** *FEM*

surface *NOUN*
  la **surface** *FEM*
  on the surface à la surface

surfboard *NOUN*
  la **planche de surf** *(PL les **planches de surf**)*

surfer *NOUN*
1 *(in the sea)* le **surfeur** *MASC*, la **surfeuse** *FEM*
2 *(on the Internet)* un & une **internaute** *MASC & FEM*

surfing *NOUN*
  le **surf** *MASC*
  to go surfing faire [10] du surf

surgeon *NOUN*
  le **chirurgien**, la **chirurgienne** *FEM*
  She's a surgeon. Elle est chirurgienne.

surgery *NOUN*
1 *(procedure)* la **chirurgie** *FEM*
  cosmetic surgery la chirurgie esthétique
  to have surgery se faire ◉ [10] opérer

Rangers

ℓ indicates key words

She had to have surgery. Elle a dû se faire opérer.
2 *(doctor's)* le **cabinet médical**
the dentist's surgery le cabinet dentaire

♪ **surname** NOUN
le **nom de famille** *(PL les **noms de famille**)*
What's your surname? Quel est votre nom de famille?

to **surprise** VERB ▸ SEE **surprise** NOUN
to surprise somebody faire [10] une surprise à quelqu'un
Let's surprise them. On va leur faire une surprise.

♪ **surprise** NOUN ▸ SEE **surprise** VERB
la **surprise** FEM
What a surprise! Quelle surprise!
I want it to be a surprise. Je veux que ce soit une surprise.

surprised ADJECTIVE
étonné MASC, **étonnée** FEM
I was surprised to see her. J'ai été étonné de la voir.

♪ **surprising** ADJECTIVE
étonnant MASC, **étonnante** FEM
I find that surprising. Je trouve ça étonnant.
It's not surprising. Ce n'est pas étonnant.

to **surrender** VERB ▸ SEE **surrender** NOUN
1 *(soldiers)* se **rendre** ◎ [3]
2 *(country)* **capituler** [1]
3 *(a town, a castle)* **livrer** [1]

surrender NOUN ▸ SEE **surrender** VERB
1 *(by a sportsman)* l'**abandon** MASC
2 *(by an army)* la **capitulation** FEM

♪ to **surround** VERB
1 *(police, enemy)* **encercler** [1]
Police have surrounded the building. La police a encerclé le bâtiment.
2 to be surrounded by something être [6] entouré de quelque chose
The house is surrounded by trees. La maison est entourée d'arbres.

survey NOUN
une **enquête** FEM
to carry out a survey faire [10] une enquête

to **survive** VERB
survivre [82]

survivor NOUN
le **survivant** MASC, la **survivante** FEM

to **suspect** VERB ▸ SEE **suspect** NOUN
soupçonner [1]
They're suspected of having stolen the money. Ils sont soupçonnés d'avoir volé l'argent.

suspect NOUN ▸ SEE **suspect** VERB
le **suspect** MASC, la **suspecte** FEM

to **suspend** VERB
1 *(to hang)* **suspendre** [3]
suspended in mid air suspendu dans le vide
2 to be suspended *(from school)* être [6] exclu

suspense NOUN
le **suspense** MASC

♪ **suspicious** ADJECTIVE
1 *(wary)* **méfiant** MASC, **méfiante** FEM
The locals are suspicious. Les gens du coin sont méfiants.
I'm suspicious of her. Je me méfie d'elle.
2 *(worrying)* **suspect** MASC, **suspecte** FEM
a suspicious parcel un paquet suspect
3 *(person)* **louche** MASC & FEM
He looks suspicious. Il a l'air louche.

to **swallow** VERB ▸ SEE **swallow** NOUN
avaler [1]

swallow NOUN ▸ SEE **swallow** VERB
(bird) une **hirondelle** FEM

swan NOUN
le **cygne** MASC

♪ to **swap** VERB
1 **échanger** [52]
Do you want to swap? Tu veux qu'on échange?
to swap something for something échanger quelque chose contre quelque chose
I've swapped my bike for a computer. J'ai échangé mon vélo contre un ordinateur.
2 to swap places with somebody changer [52] de place avec quelqu'un
I swapped places with Rebecca. J'ai changé de place avec Rebecca.

to **swear** VERB
utiliser [1] des gros mots
He swears a lot. Il utilise beaucoup de gros mots.

swearword NOUN
le **gros mot**

to **sweat** VERB ▸ SEE **sweat** NOUN
transpirer [1]

sweat NOUN ▸ SEE **sweat** VERB
la **transpiration** FEM

♪ **sweater** NOUN
le **pull** MASC

sweatshirt NOUN
le **sweatshirt** MASC, le **sweat** MASC

swede NOUN
(vegetable) le **rutabaga** MASC

◎ means the verb takes être to form the perfect

Swede NOUN ▸ SEE **swede** NOUN
un **Suédois** MASC, une **Suédoise** FEM

Sweden NOUN
la **Suède** FEM

Swedish ADJECTIVE ▸ SEE **Swedish** NOUN
suédois MASC, **suédoise** FEM ▸ SEE **Swede**

Swedish NOUN ▸ SEE **Swedish** ADJECTIVE
(language) le **suédois** MASC

to **sweep** VERB
balayer [59]
to sweep away the leaves balayer les
feuilles

℘ **sweet** ADJECTIVE ▸ SEE **sweet** NOUN
1 (food) **sucré** MASC, **sucrée** FEM
Avoid eating sweet things. Évitez les
choses sucrées.
2 (kind) **gentil** MASC, **gentille** FEM
It was really sweet of him. C'était vraiment
gentil de sa part.
3 (cute) **mignon** MASC, **mignonne** FEM
You look really sweet in that hat! Tu es
mignon avec ce chapeau!

sweet NOUN ▸ SEE **sweet** ADJECTIVE
1 (wrapped) le **bonbon** MASC
2 (dessert) le **dessert** MASC

sweetcorn NOUN
le **maïs** MASC

to **swell** VERB
enfler [1]

swelling NOUN
une **enflure** FEM
He has a swelling on his knee. Il a le genou
enflé.

to **swerve** VERB
faire [10] **un écart**
The car swerved to avoid the dog. La
voiture a fait un écart pour éviter le chien.

℘ to **swim** VERB ▸ SEE **swim** NOUN
nager [52]
Can he swim? Est-ce qu'il sait nager?
He can't swim very well. Il ne sait pas très
bien nager.
to swim across a lake traverser [1] un lac
à la nage

℘ **swim** NOUN ▸ SEE **swim** VERB
to go for a swim aller ◎ [7] se baigner
We went for a swim every morning. Nous
sommes allés nous baigner tous les matins.

swimmer NOUN
le **nageur** MASC, la **nageuse** FEM

℘ **swimming** NOUN
la **natation** FEM
to go swimming faire [10] de la natation

- **swimming cap**
le **bonnet de bain**
- **swimming costume**
le **maillot de bain**
- **swimming instructor**
le **maître-nageur** (PL les **maîtres-nageurs**)
- **swimming pool**
la **piscine**
- **swimming trunks**
le **maillot de bain**

℘ **swimsuit** NOUN
le **maillot de bain**

swindle NOUN
l'**escroquerie** FEM
What a swindle! Quelle escroquerie!

swing NOUN
la **balançoire** FEM

Swiss ADJECTIVE ▸ SEE **Swiss** NOUN
suisse MASC & FEM

WORD TIP Adjectives never have capitals in
French, even for nationality or regional origin.

Swiss NOUN ▸ SEE **Swiss** ADJECTIVE
(person) un & une **Suisse** MASC & FEM
the Swiss les **Suisses** MASC PL

℘ to **switch** VERB ▸ SEE **switch** NOUN
(change) **changer** [52] **de**
to switch places changer de place
to switch from French to English passer [1]
du français à l'anglais
- **to switch something off**
éteindre [60] quelque chose
I switched the light off. J'ai éteint la
lumière.
- **to switch something on**
allumer [1] quelque chose
Can you switch on the computer? Est-ce
que tu peux allumer l'ordinateur?

switch NOUN ▸ SEE **switch** VERB
1 (button type) le **bouton** MASC
2 (up-down type) un **interrupteur** MASC

Switzerland NOUN
la **Suisse** FEM
in Switzerland en Suisse
to Switzerland en Suisse

WORD TIP Countries and regions in French take
le, la or les.

---

swollen ADJECTIVE
enflé MASC, **enflée** FEM
My finger's swollen. J'ai le doigt enflé.

to **swop** VERB ▸ SEE **swap**

sword NOUN
une **épée** FEM

- **swordfish**
  un **espadon** MASC

syllabus NOUN
le **programme** MASC
to be on the syllabus être [6] au
programme

symbol NOUN
le **symbole** MASC

symbolic ADJECTIVE
symbolique MASC & FEM

sympathetic ADJECTIVE
compréhensif MASC, **compréhensive** FEM
a sympathetic attitude une attitude
compréhensive

to **sympathize** VERB
to sympathize with somebody
comprendre [64] quelqu'un
I sympathize with her. Je la comprends.

sympathy NOUN
la **compassion** FEM
out of sympathy par compassion

symphony NOUN
la **symphonie** FEM
- **symphony orchestra**
  un orchestre symphonique

symptom NOUN
le **symptôme** MASC

synagogue NOUN
la **synagogue** FEM

synthesizer NOUN
le **synthétiseur** MASC

synthetic ADJECTIVE
synthétique MASC & FEM

syringe NOUN
la **seringue** FEM

system NOUN
le **système** MASC

Tt

♟**table** NOUN
la **table** FEM
on the table sur la table
to lay the table mettre [11] la table
to clear the table débarrasser [1] la table
- **tablecloth**
  la **nappe**

tablemat NOUN
1 *(for individual plates)* le **set de table**
2 *(for a dish)* le **dessous-de-plat**

tablespoon NOUN
la **grande cuillère**

♟**tablet** NOUN
1 *(medicine)* le **comprimé** MASC
2 *(computer)* la **tablette** FEM

table tennis NOUN
le **ping-pong**® MASC
to play table tennis jouer [1] au ping-pong

tabloid NOUN
le **quotidien populaire**

to **tackle** VERB ▸ SEE **tackle** NOUN
1 *(in football, hockey)* **tacler** [1]
2 *(in rugby)* **plaquer** [1]
3 *(a job, a problem)* **s'attaquer** [1] à

tackle NOUN ▸ SEE **tackle** VERB
1 *(in football)* le **tacle** MASC
2 *(in rugby)* le **plaquage** MASC

tactful ADJECTIVE
plein de tact MASC, **pleine de tact** FEM
a tactful answer une réponse pleine de tact

tadpole NOUN
le **têtard** MASC

tail NOUN
la **queue** FEM

♟to **take** VERB
1 *(in general)* **prendre** [64]
I took the bus. J'ai pris le bus.
Who's taken my keys? Qui a pris mes clefs?
Take lots of photos. Prenez beaucoup de
photos.
Did you take notes? Est-ce que tu as pris
des notes?
2 *(to a place)* **emmener** [50]
She's taking Jack to the doctor's. Elle
emmène Jack chez le médecin.
3 *(to carry away)* **emporter** [1]
She's taken some work home. Elle a
emporté du travail chez elle.
4 **to take something upstairs monter** [1]
quelque chose
Could you take these towels up? Est-ce que
tu peux monter ces serviettes?
5 **to take something downstairs descendre**
[3] quelque chose
Molly's taken the cups down. Molly a
descendu les tasses.
6 *(a credit card)* **accepter** [1]
Do you take cheques? Est-ce que vous
acceptez les chèques?
7 *(an exam)* **passer** [1]
She's taking her driving test. Elle passe son
permis.
8 *(to need)* **falloir** [43] *(falloir is used only in
the il faut form)*
It takes a lot of courage. Il faut beaucoup

⬤ means the verb takes être to form the perfect

de courage.

9 *(with clothes, shoes)* faire **[10]**
What size shoe do you take? Quelle
pointure faites-vous?
I take a size 36. Je fais du 36.

• **to take something away**
(fast food) emporter **[1]**
They have meals to take away. Ils ont des
plats à emporter.

• **to take something apart**
démonter **[1]** quelque chose

• **to take something back**
1 *(customers)* rapporter **[1]** quelque chose
I have to take those shoes back. Je dois
rapporter ces chaussures.
2 *(shops)* reprendre **[64]**

• **to take off**
(plane) décoller **[1]**

• **to take something off**
1 *(clothes, shoes)* enlever **[50]**
2 *(to reduce)* déduire **[26]**
She took five pounds off the price. Elle a
réduit le prix de cinq livres.

• **to take something out**
sortir **[72]**
He took out his wallet. Il a sorti son portefeuille.

• **to take somebody out**
to take somebody out somewhere
emmener **[50]** quelqu'un quelque part
My mum took us out to the cinema. Ma
mère nous a emmenés au cinéma.

• **to take up something**
1 *(time, space)* prendre **[64]**
The table takes up too much space. La
table prend trop de place.
2 *(the piano, tennis)* se mettre ◎ **[11]** à
Josh has taken up the guitar. Josh s'est mis
à la guitare.

takeaway *NOUN*
1 *(meal)* le **repas à emporter**
2 *(outlet)* le **restaurant qui fait des plats à
emporter**

tale *NOUN*
une **histoire** *FEM*

talent *NOUN*
le **talent** *MASC*
to have a talent for something être **[6]**
doué pour quelque chose

talented *ADJECTIVE*
doué *MASC*, douée *FEM*

ℱto **talk** *VERB*
1 **to talk about something** parler **[1]** de
quelque chose
What's she talking about? De quoi est-ce
qu'elle parle?
She's talking about work. Elle parle du

travail.
to talk to somebody about something
parler de quelque chose avec quelqu'un
I was talking to Ibrahim about cars. Je
parlais de voitures avec Ibrahim.
2 *(to chat)* bavarder **[1]**
They're always talking. Ils sont toujours en
train de bavarder.

ℱ**talk** *NOUN* ▸ SEE **talk** *VERB*
1 *(chat)* la **conversation** *FEM*
to have a talk about something avoir **[5]**
une conversation au sujet de quelque chose
I had a talk with Matt about the concert.
J'ai eu une conversation avec Matt au sujet
du concert.
2 *(peace)* **talks** les **négociations** (sur la paix)

ℱ**tall** *ADJECTIVE*
1 **grand** *MASC*, **grande** *FEM*
She's very tall. Elle est très grande.
How tall are you? Tu mesures combien?
I'm 1.7 metres tall. Je mesure un mètre
soixante-dix.
2 *(building, wall, tree)* **haut** *MASC*, **haute** *FEM*

tame *ADJECTIVE*
apprivoisé *MASC*, **apprivoisée** *FEM*

tampon *NOUN*
le **tampon** *MASC*

tan *NOUN*
le **bronzage** *MASC*

ℱto **tan** *VERB*
bronzer **[1]**
I tan easily. Je bronze facilement.

tank *NOUN*
1 *(for petrol, water)* le **réservoir** *MASC*
2 *(for fish)* un **aquarium** *MASC*
3 *(military)* le **char** *MASC*

tanker *NOUN*
1 *(ship)* le **navire-citerne** *INVARIABLE MASC*
2 *(on road)* le **camion-citerne** *INVARIABLE MASC*

tanned *ADJECTIVE*
bronzé *MASC*, **bronzée** *FEM*

to **tap** *VERB* ▸ SEE **tap** *NOUN*
taper **[1]**
to tap on the window taper sur la fenêtre
to tap your feet taper du pied

ℱ**tap** *NOUN* ▸ SEE **tap** *VERB*
1 *(for water, gas)* le **robinet** *MASC*
the hot tap le robinet d'eau chaude
to turn on the tap ouvrir **[30]** le robinet
to turn off the tap fermer **[1]** le robinet
2 *(knock)* la **petite tape** *FEM*

tap-dancing *NOUN*
les **claquettes** *FEM PL*

to do tap-dancing faire [10] des claquettes

♫ to **tape** VERB ▶ SEE **tape** NOUN
enregistrer [1]
I want to tape the film. Je veux enregistrer
le film.

tape NOUN ▶ SEE **tape** VERB
1 (video, audio) la **cassette** FEM
2 (adhesive) le **scotch**®
• tape recorder
le magnétophone

tapestry NOUN
la **tapisserie** FEM

target NOUN
la **cible** FEM

♫ **tart** NOUN
la **tarte** FEM
a raspberry tart une tarte aux framboises

tartan ADJECTIVE
écossais MASC, écossaise FEM

task NOUN
la **tâche** FEM

to **taste** VERB ▶ SEE **taste** NOUN
goûter [1]
Do you want to taste? Tu veux goûter?
The steak tastes good. Le bifteck a bon
goût.
The soup tasted horrible. La soupe avait un
goût infect.

♫ **taste** NOUN ▶ SEE **taste** VERB
1 (of food, drink) le **goût** MASC
She hates the taste of garlic. Elle déteste
le goût d'ail.
2 (what you like) le **goût** MASC
Zoë has good taste in clothes. Zoë s'habille
avec goût.
That joke was in really bad taste. Cette
blague était vraiment de mauvais goût.

tasty ADJECTIVE
savoureux MASC, savoureuse FEM

tattoo NOUN
le **tatouage** MASC

Taurus NOUN
Taureau
Joe's Taurus. Joe est Taureau.

WORD TIP Signs of the zodiac do not take an
article: un or une.

tax NOUN
les **impôts** MASC PL

taxi NOUN
le **taxi** MASC
to take a taxi prendre [64] un taxi
Let's go by taxi. Allons-y en taxi.
• taxi driver
le chauffeur de taxi
• taxi rank
la station de taxis

♫ **tea** NOUN
1 le **thé** MASC
a cup of tea une tasse de thé
2 (evening meal) le **dîner** MASC
• tea room
le salon de thé

teabag NOUN
le **sachet de thé** MASC

♫ to **teach** VERB
1 to teach something to somebody
apprendre [64] quelque chose à quelqu'un
She's teaching me Italian. Elle m'apprend
l'italien.
to teach somebody how to do something
apprendre à quelqu'un à faire quelque
chose
Lee's teaching me to drive. Lee m'apprend
à conduire.
2 enseigner [1]
Her mum teaches maths. Sa mère enseigne
les maths.
She teaches children tennis. Elle enseigne
le tennis aux enfants.

♫ **teacher** NOUN
1 (in a secondary school) le **professeur** MASC,
la **professeure** FEM
My mother's a biology teacher. Ma mère
est professeure de biologie.
2 (in a primary school) un **instituteur** MASC,
une **institutrice** FEM
She's a primary school teacher. Elle est
institutrice.

♫ **team** NOUN
une **équipe** FEM
a football team une équipe de foot
Our team won. Notre équipe a gagné.
He wants to be in the team. Il veut faire
partie de l'équipe.
• team-mate
le coéquipier, la coéquipière
• teamwork
le travail d'équipe

teapot NOUN
la **théière** FEM

⬆ means the verb takes être to form the perfect

to **tear** VERB ▸ SEE **tear** NOUN
  déchirer [1]
  You've torn the wrapping paper! Tu as
  déchiré le papier cadeau!
  It tears easily. Ça se déchire
  facilement.
  • **to tear something off**
    (a coupon, a label) détacher [1] quelque
    chose
  • **to tear something open**
    arracher [1] quelque chose
    She tore open the envelope. Elle a arraché
    l'enveloppe.
  • **to tear something up**
    déchirer [1] quelque chose
    Tear the letter up. Déchire la lettre.

tear NOUN ▸ SEE **tear** VERB
1 *(when you cry)* la **larme** FEM
  to burst into tears fondre [3] en larmes
2 *(in clothing)* un **accroc** MASC

to **tease** VERB
  taquiner [1]

teaspoon NOUN
1 la **petite cuillère** FEM
2 *(in recipes)* la **cuillère à café**

ℱ**teatime** NOUN
  l'**heure du dîner** FEM

tea towel NOUN
  le **torchon** MASC

technical ADJECTIVE
  technique MASC & FEM

technician NOUN
  le **technicien** MASC, la **technicienne** FEM
  She's a technician. Elle est
  technicienne.

technique NOUN
  la **technique** FEM

techno NOUN
  (Music) la **techno** FEM

technological ADJECTIVE
  technologique MASC & FEM

technology NOUN
  la **technologie** FEM

ℱ**teenage** ADJECTIVE
1 adolescent MASC, adolescente FEM
  a teenage son un fils adolescent
2 *(films, magazines)* pour les jeunes
  a teenage magazine un magazine pour
  les jeunes

ℱ**teenager** NOUN
1 *(young person)* le & la **jeune** MASC & FEM
  a group of teenagers une bande de
  jeunes
2 *(more precisely)* un **adolescent** MASC, une
  adolescente FEM

teens PLURAL NOUN
  l'**adolescence** FEM
  She's in her teens. C'est une
  adolescente.

tee-shirt NOUN
  le **tee-shirt** MASC

ℱ to **telephone** VERB ▸ SEE **telephone** NOUN
  appeler [18]
  I'll telephone Susie. Je vais appeler Susie.

ℱ**telephone** NOUN ▸ SEE **telephone** VERB
  le **téléphone** MASC
  He's on the telephone. Il est au
  téléphone.
  • **telephone call**
    le coup de téléphone
  • **telephone card**
    la carte de téléphone
  • **telephone directory**
    un annuaire
  • **telephone kiosk**
    la cabine téléphonique
  • **telephone number**
    le numéro de téléphone

telescope NOUN
  le **télescope** MASC

ℱ**television** NOUN
  la **télévision** FEM
  She's watching television. Elle regarde la
  télévision.
  I saw it on television. Je l'ai vu à la
  télévision.
  • **television channel**
    la chaîne de télévision
  • **television news**
    le journal télévisé
  • **television programme**
    une émission de télévision

ℱ to **tell** VERB
1 **to tell somebody something** dire [9]
  quelque chose à quelqu'un
  I've told Sarah. Je l'ai dit à Sarah.
  Tell me the truth! Dis-moi la vérité!
  You mustn't tell anyone. Il ne faut le dire
  à personne.

A B C D E F G H I J K L M N O P Q R S T U V W X Y Z

2 to tell somebody to do something dire [9] à quelqu'un de faire quelque chose
He told me to do it myself. Il m'a dit de le faire moi-même.
She told me not to wait. Elle m'a dit de ne pas attendre.

3 to tell somebody how to do something expliquer [1] à quelqu'un comment faire quelque chose
Joe will tell you how to save the file. Joe va t'expliquer comment sauver le fichier.
Can you tell me how to do it? Est-ce que vous pouvez m'expliquer comment on le fait?

4 (a story, a joke) raconter [1]
to tell somebody about something raconter quelque chose à quelqu'un
Tell me about your holiday. Raconte-moi tes vacances.

5 (to see) voir [13]
You can tell she's cross. On voit bien qu'elle est fâchée.
to tell somebody from somebody else distinguer [1] quelqu'un de quelqu'un d'autre
I can't tell them apart. Je n'arrive pas à les distinguer.

telly NOUN
la **télé** FEM
to watch telly regarder [1] la télé
I saw her on telly. Je l'ai vue à la télé.

temper NOUN
to lose your temper se mettre ◯ [11] en colère

ℓ **temperature** NOUN
1 la **température** FEM
The temperature is 25° Celsius. La température est de 25°.
2 to have a temperature avoir [5] de la fièvre
She took my temperature. Elle m'a pris la température.

temple NOUN
le **temple** MASC

temporary ADJECTIVE
temporaire MASC & FEM

temptation NOUN
la **tentation** FEM
to resist the temptation résister [1] à la tentation

tempted ADJECTIVE
tenté MASC, **tentée** FEM
to be tempted to do something être [6] tenté de faire quelque chose

tempting ADJECTIVE
tentant MASC, **tentante** FEM

ℓ **ten** NUMBER
dix
Imran's ten. Imran a dix ans.

to **tend** VERB
to tend to do something avoir [5] tendance à faire
He tends to talk a lot. Il a tendance à beaucoup parler.

tendency NOUN
la **tendance** FEM
to have a tendency to do something avoir [5] tendance à faire quelque chose

tender ADJECTIVE
tendre MASC & FEM

tennis NOUN
le **tennis** MASC
to play tennis jouer [1] au tennis
• **tennis ball**
  la balle de tennis
• **tennis court**
  le tennis
• **tennis player**
  le joueur de tennis, la joueuse de tennis
• **tennis racket**
  la raquette de tennis

tenor NOUN
le **ténor** MASC

tense ADJECTIVE ▸ SEE **tense** NOUN
(atmosphere, person) **tendu** MASC, **tendue** FEM
to get tense se crisper ◯ [1]

tense NOUN ▸ SEE **tense** ADJECTIVE
(Grammar) the present tense le présent
the future tense le futur

ℓ **tent** NOUN
la **tente** FEM
to put up a tent dresser [1] une tente
to sleep in a tent dormir [2] sous la tente

tenth ADJECTIVE
1 dixième MASC & FEM
on the tenth floor au dixième étage
2 (in dates) the tenth of April le dix avril

ℓ **term** NOUN
le **trimestre** MASC
during term pendant le trimestre
at the end of term à la fin du trimestre

terminal NOUN
1 (at an airport) une **aérogare** FEM
at terminal two à l'aérogare numéro deux
2 (for ferries) une **gare maritime**
3 (Computers) le **terminal** MASC (PL les terminaux)

◯ means the verb takes être to form the perfect

terrace NOUN
1 (of a hotel) la **terrasse** FEM
2 (at a stadium) **the terraces** les gradins MASC PL

ℓ **terrible** ADJECTIVE
épouvantable MASC & FEM
The weather was terrible. Il a fait un temps épouvantable.
I feel terrible. Je ne me sens pas bien du tout.

terribly ADVERB
(badly) **affreusement mal**
I played terribly. J'ai joué affreusement mal.

terrific ADJECTIVE
1 (impressive) **épouvantable** MASC & FEM
at a terrific speed à une vitesse folle
2 (exclamation) **Terrific!** Formidable!

terrified ADJECTIVE
terrifié MASC, **terrifiée** FEM

to **terrify** VERB
terrifier [1]

territory NOUN
le **territoire** MASC

terrorism NOUN
le **terrorisme** MASC

terrorist NOUN
le & la **terroriste** MASC & FEM

to **test** VERB ▶ SEE **test** NOUN
(in school) **contrôler** [1]
to test somebody on something interroger [52] quelqu'un sur quelque chose
Can you test me on my verbs? Tu peux m'interroger sur les verbes?

ℓ **test** NOUN ▶ SEE **test** VERB
1 (in school) le **contrôle** MASC
We've got a maths test tomorrow. Nous avons un contrôle de maths demain.
2 (of your skills, patience) le **test** MASC
a personality test un test de personnalité
3 (medical) une **analyse** FEM
a blood test une analyse de sang
an eye test un examen des yeux

test tube NOUN
une **éprouvette** FEM

ℓ to **text** VERB
to text somebody envoyer [40] un texto à quelqu'un
I'll text you tomorrow. Je t'enverrai un texto demain.

ℓ **text** NOUN
1 (of a book) le **texte** MASC

2 (by mobile) le **texto**

🔘 **TEXTING**

Here are some common abbreviations to help you understand text messages in French: jé = j'ai, Gt = j'étais, ya = il y a and parske = parce que. Number 1 replaces the sounds un, en or in (b1 = bien), 2 replaces de (pa2koi = pas de quoi).

textbook NOUN
le **manuel** MASC

text message NOUN
le **texto** MASC

ℓ **than** CONJUNCTION, PREPOSITION
1 (in comparisons) **plus** + ADJECTIVE + **que** (except for irregular forms)
bigger than plus grand que
better than meilleur que
worse than pire que
You're taller than her. Tu es plus grand qu'elle.
It's worse than ever. C'est pire que jamais.
2 (for quantities) **plus de** + NUMBER
more than 20 pounds plus de 20 livres
more than a year plus d'un an

to **thank** VERB
remercier [1]
I forgot to thank you. J'ai oublié de vous remercier.

ℓ **thanks** EXCLAMATION
merci
Thanks a lot. Merci beaucoup.
No thanks. Non merci.
Thanks for helping us. Merci de nous avoir aidé.

ℓ **thank you** EXCLAMATION
merci
No thank you. Non merci.
Thank you for the card. Merci pour la carte.

ℓ **that** DETERMINER ▶ SEE **that** ADVERB, CONJUNCTION, PRONOUN
1 (with masc singular nouns) **ce**
that dog ce chien
2 (with masc singular nouns starting a, e, i, o, u or silent h) **cet**
that money cet argent
3 (with fem singular nouns) **cette**
that colour cette couleur
4 **that one** celui-là (for masc nouns)
'Which cake would you like?' — 'That one'. 'Tu veux quel gâteau?' — 'Celui-là'.
5 **that one** celle-là (for fem nouns)
I like all the jackets but I'm going to buy that one. J'aime toutes les vestes mais je

vais acheter celle-là.

> **WORD TIP** Add -là to a noun for emphasis: cet homme-là that **particular** man.

that *ADVERB* ▶ SEE **that** *DETERMINER, CONJUNCTION, PRONOUN*

The wall was that high. Le mur était haut comme ça.

It isn't all that good. Ce n'est pas si bon que ça.

ℙ **that** *CONJUNCTION, PRONOUN* ▶ SEE **that** *DETERMINER, ADVERB*

1 *(before e-)* **ce, c'**
That's true. C'est vrai.
Is that true? C'est vrai?
What's that? Qu'est-ce que c'est?
Who's that? C'est qui?
Where's that? C'est où?
Is that Mandy? C'est Mandy?

2 **ça**
That smells good. Ça sent bon.
Did you see that? Tu as vu ça?
What does that mean? Ça veut dire quoi?

3 *(in place of a noun: subject)* **qui**
the book that is on the table le livre qui est sur la table

4 *(in place of a noun: object)* **que, qu'** *(a, e, i, o, u or silent h)*
the film that I liked the best le film que j'ai aimé le mieux
the house that he built la maison qu'il a construite

5 *(as a conjunction)* **que, qu'** *(a, e, i, o, u or silent h)*
I thought (that) you knew. Je croyais que tu le savais.
I knew (that) he was wrong. Je savais qu'il avait tort.

> **WORD TIP** that is often left out in English, but que is always needed in French.

to **thaw** *VERB*
dégeler [45]

ℙ **the** *DETERMINER*

1 *(with masc singular nouns)* **le**
the cat le chat
the building le bâtiment

2 *(with fem singular nouns)* **la**
the table la table
the meeting la réunion

3 *(with singular nouns starting a, e, i, o, u or silent h)* **l'**
the engineer l'ingénieur *MASC*
the nurse l'infirmière *FEM*
the tree l'arbre *MASC*

4 *(with plural nouns)* **les**
the holidays les vacances
the students les élèves

from the Netherlands des Pays-Bas
to go to the United States aller ◉ [7] aux États-Unis

> **WORD TIP** ▶ SEE **from, of** de + le = du; de + la = de la; de + les = des. ▶ SEE **to** à + le = au; à + la = à la; à + les = aux.

ℙ **theatre** *NOUN*
le théâtre *MASC*

ℙ **theft** *NOUN*
le vol *MASC*

ℙ **their** *DETERMINER*

1 *(with singular nouns)* **leur**
their flat leur appartement
their mother leur mère

2 *(with plural nouns)* **leurs**
their presents leurs cadeaux
their friends leurs amis

3 *(with parts of the body)* **le, la, les**
They're washing their hands. Elles se lavent les mains.

ℙ **theirs** *PRONOUN*

1 *(for masc singular nouns)* **le leur**
Our garden's smaller than theirs. Notre jardin est plus petit que le leur.

2 *(for fem singular nouns)* **la leur**
Your house is bigger than theirs. Ta maison est plus grande que la leur.

3 *(for plural nouns)* **les leurs**
Our holidays are longer than theirs. Nos vacances sont plus longues que les leurs.

4 *(belonging to them)* **à eux** *(male or mixed group)*
He's a friend of theirs. C'est un ami à eux.

5 *(belonging to them)* **à elles** *(all-female group)*
The rackets are theirs. Les racquettes sont à elles.

ℙ **them** *PRONOUN*

1 *(for plural nouns as direct object)* **les**
I know them. Je les connais.
I saw them last week. Je les ai vus la semaine dernière.
Watch them! Regarde-les!
Give them to me. Donne-les-moi.

2 *(for plural nouns as indirect object)* **leur**
I gave them my address. Je leur ai donné mon adresse.
Give the book to them. Donne-leur le livre.
Can you write to them? Est-ce que tu peux leur écrire?

3 *(after prepositions like avec, sans)* **eux** *(male or mixed group)*, **elles** *(all-female group)*
I'll go with them. J'irai avec eux.
We left without them. On est parti sans elles.

4 *(in comparisons)* **than them** qu'eux *(male or mixed group)*, qu'elles *(all-female group)*

◉ means the verb takes être to form the perfect

He's older than them. Il est plus âgé qu'eux.
She's younger than them. Elle est plus jeune qu'elles.

theme *NOUN*
  la **thème** *FEM*
• **theme park**
  le parc de loisirs

themselves *PRONOUN*
1 se, s'
  They all helped themselves. Ils se sont tous servis.
2 *(for emphasis)* **eux-mêmes** *(male or mixed group)*, **elles-mêmes** *(all-female group)*
  The boys can do it themselves. Les garçons peuvent le faire eux-mêmes.
  The girls will tell you themselves. Les filles vous le diront elles-mêmes.

> **WORD TIP** se becomes s' before a, e, i, o, u or silent h.

ℱ **then** *ADVERB*
1 *(next)* ensuite
  I went to the post office and then the shops. Je suis allé à la poste et ensuite aux magasins.
2 *(at that time)* à l'époque
  We were living in Leeds then. Nous habitions à Leeds à l'époque.
3 *(in that case)* alors
  Then why worry? Alors pourquoi s'inquiéter?
4 **by then** déjà
5 **from then on** à partir de ce moment-là

theory *NOUN*
  la **théorie** *FEM*

ℱ **there** *ADVERB, PRONOUN*
1 *(not far from the speaker)* là
  Put it there. Mets-le là.
  They're in there. Ils sont là.
2 **over there** là-bas
3 **down there** là-bas
4 **up there** là-haut
5 **y** *(referring to a place that was mentioned before)*
  We've never been there. Nous n'y sommes jamais allés.
  Yes, I'm going there on Tuesday. Oui, j'y vais mardi.
6 *(with facts and questions: singular)* **there is** il y a
  There's a cat in the garden. Il y a un chat dans le jardin.
  There was no bread. Il n'y avait pas de pain.
  Is there any milk? Est-ce qu'il y a du lait?
  (: plural) **there are** il y a
  Are there any seats? Est-ce qu'il y a des

places?
  There are plenty of seats. Il y a beaucoup de places.
7 *(when you point things out)* **There she is!** La voilà!
  There they are! Les voilà!

ℱ **therefore** *ADVERB*
  donc

thermometer *NOUN*
  le **thermomètre** *MASC*

these *ADJECTIVE, PRONOUN*
1 *(with plural nouns)* **ces**
  these books ces livres
  these books here ces livres-ci
2 *(for plural masc nouns)* **these (ones)** ceux-ci
  If you want some knives, take these. Si tu veux des couteaux, prends ceux-ci.
3 *(for plural fem nouns)* **these (ones)** celles-ci
  If you want some plates, take these. Si tu veux des assiettes, prends celles-ci.

ℱ **they** *PRONOUN*
1 *(for plural masc nouns)* **ils**
  'Where are the knives?' — 'They're in the drawer.' 'Où sont les couteaux?' — 'Ils sont dans le tiroir.'
2 *(for plural fem nouns)* **elles**
  I bought some apples but they're not good. J'ai acheté des pommes mais elles ne sont pas bonnes.

ℱ **thick** *ADJECTIVE*
  épais *MASC*, **épaisse** *FEM*
  a thick layer of snow une couche épaisse de neige

ℱ **thief** *NOUN*
  le **voleur** *MASC*, la **voleuse** *FEM*
  Look out for thieves. Attention aux voleurs.

thigh *NOUN*
  la **cuisse** *FEM*

ℱ **thin** *ADJECTIVE*
1 *(not fat)* **mince** *MASC & FEM*
  Joe's tall and thin. Joe est grand et mince.
2 *(too thin)* **maigre** *MASC & FEM*
  to get thin maigrir [2]

ℱ **thing** *NOUN*
1 *(in general)* la **chose** *FEM*
  I've got lots of things to do. J'ai beaucoup de choses à faire.
  How are things? Comment ça va?
2 *(whatsit)* le **truc** *MASC* *(informal)*
  that thing next to the hammer ce truc à côté du marteau
3 *(belongings)* **things** les **affaires** *FEM PL*
  I can't find my things. Je ne trouve pas mes affaires.
4 **not ... a thing** ne ... rien

I can't see a thing. Je ne vois rien.

☌ to **think** VERB

1 *(to believe)* **croire** [33]
I think he's already left. Je crois qu'il est déjà parti.
Do you think they'll come? Tu crois qu'ils vont venir?
No, I don't think so. Non, je ne crois pas.

2 *(to have an opinion)* **penser** [1]
What do you think of my new jacket? Qu'est-ce que tu penses de ma nouvelle veste?
What do you think of that? Qu'en penses-tu?

3 **to think about somebody** penser [1] à quelqu'un
I'm thinking about you. Je pense à toi.

4 **to think of doing something** penser [1] faire quelque chose
I'm thinking of buying a mobile. Je pense acheter un portable.

5 *(to think carefully)* **réfléchir** [2]
Let me think. Laisse-moi réfléchir.

6 *(to imagine)* **imaginer** [1]
Just think! We'll soon be in Spain! Imagine! On va bientôt être en Espagne!

third ADJECTIVE ▸ SEE **third** NOUN

1 **troisième** MASC & FEM
on the third floor au troisième étage

2 *(in dates)* **the third of March** le trois mars

third NOUN ▸ SEE **third** ADJECTIVE
le **tiers** MASC
a third of the population un tiers de la population

☌ **Third World** NOUN
le **tiers-monde** MASC
Third-World countries les pays du tiers-monde

thirst NOUN
la **soif** FEM

☌ **thirsty** ADJECTIVE
to be thirsty avoir [5] soif
I'm very thirsty. J'ai très soif.

thirteen NUMBER
treize
My brother's thirteen. Mon frère a treize ans.

thirteenth ADJECTIVE

1 **treizième** MASC & FEM
my thirteenth birthday mon treizième anniversaire

2 *(in dates)* **the thirteenth of May** le treize mai

thirtieth ADJECTIVE

1 **trentième** MASC & FEM

2 *(in dates)* **the thirtieth of October** le trente octobre

thirty NUMBER
trente
My cousin is thirty. Mon cousin a trente ans.

☌ **this** DETERMINER ▸ SEE **this** PRONOUN

1 *(with masc singular nouns)* **ce**
this paintbrush ce pinceau

2 *(with masc singular nouns beginning with a, e, i, o, u or silent h)* **cet**
this tree cet arbre

3 *(with fem singular nouns)* **cette**
this cup cette tasse

4 *(in place of masc nouns)* **this one** celui-ci
If you need a pen you can use this one. Si tu as besoin d'un stylo tu peux utiliser celui-ci.

5 *(in place of fem nouns)* **this one** celle-ci
I like all the lamps but I'll take this one. Toutes les lampes me plaisent mais je prendrai celle-ci.

☌ **this** PRONOUN ▸ SEE **this** DETERMINER

1 *(with être)* **ce, c'** *(before e-)*
This is painful! C'est pénible!
What's this? Qu'est-ce que c'est?
Who's this? C'est qui?

2 *(introducing someone)* **This is ...** Je te présente ...
This is my sister Carla. Je te présente ma sœur Carla.

3 *(with other verbs)* **ça**
I bought this in the sales. J'ai acheté ça aux soldes.
This means we've missed the train. Ça veut dire qu'on a raté le train.

thorn NOUN
une **épine** FEM

thorough ADJECTIVE

1 *(search)* **minutieux** MASC, **minutieuse** FEM

2 *(person)* **consciencieux** MASC, **consciencieuse** FEM

those DETERMINER, PRONOUN

1 *(with plural masc nouns)* **ces**
those books ces livres
those books there ces livres-là

2 *(for plural masc nouns)* **those (ones)** ceux-là
If you want some knives, take those. Si tu veux des couteaux, prends ceux-là.

3 *(for plural fem nouns)* **those (ones)** celles-là
If you want some plates, take those. Si tu veux des assiettes, prends celles-là.

though ADVERB, CONJUNCTION

1 *(although)* **bien que**
Though it's cold, it's sunny. Bien qu'il fasse froid, il y a du soleil.

☺ means the verb takes être to form the perfect

2 *(however)* **pourtant**
It was a good idea though. Pourtant, c'était une bonne idée.

thought NOUN
1 *(thinking)* la **pensée** FEM
2 *(idea)* une **idée**
What a thought! Quelle idée!

thousand NUMBER
mille
a thousand mille
three thousand trois mille
five thousand euros cinq mille euros
thousands of rats des milliers de rats

> **WORD TIP** mille does not take an -s in the plural.

thousandth ADJECTIVE
millième MASC & FEM

thread NOUN
le **fil** MASC

threat NOUN
la **menace** FEM

to **threaten** VERB
menacer [61]
to threaten to do something menacer de faire quelque chose
She's threatening to leave school. Elle menace de quitter l'école.

three NUMBER
trois
My little sister's three. Ma petite sœur a trois ans.

three-quarters NOUN
les **trois-quarts** MASC PL
in three-quarters of an hour en trois-quarts d'heure
to be three-quarters full être [6] plein aux trois-quarts

thrilled ADJECTIVE
ravi MASC, **ravie** FEM
She's thrilled with her presents. Elle est ravie de ses cadeaux.

thriller NOUN
le **thriller** MASC

ℱ **throat** NOUN
la **gorge** FEM
Emma has a sore throat. Emma a mal à la gorge.

through ADJECTIVE ▸ SEE **through** ADVERB, PREPOSITION
(train, service) **direct** MASC, **directe** FEM

ℱ **through** ADVERB, PREPOSITION ▸ SEE **through** ADJECTIVE
1 *(across)* **à travers**

a path through the forest un chemin à travers la forêt
The police let us through. La police nous a laissés passer.
2 *(by, via)* **par**
I saw her through the window. Je l'ai vue par la fenêtre.
We went through the park. Nous avons traversé le parc.
3 *(during)* **through the night** toute la nuit

throughout PREPOSITION
1 *(during the whole of)* **pendant tout** MASC, **pendant toute** FEM
throughout the day pendant toute la journée
2 *(all over)* **dans tout** MASC, **dans toute** FEM
throughout the country dans tout le pays
known throughout the world connu partout dans le monde

ℱ to **throw** VERB
1 *(in general)* **jeter** [48]
I threw the letter into the bin. J'ai jeté la lettre dans la poubelle.
He threw it on the floor. Il l'a jeté par terre.
2 *(stones, a ball)* **lancer** [61]
to throw something to somebody lancer quelque chose à quelqu'un
Throw me the ball! Lance-moi le ballon!
• **to throw something away**
jeter [48] quelque chose
I've thrown away the old newspapers. J'ai jeté les vieux journaux.
• **to throw up**
vomir [2]

thumb NOUN
le **pouce** MASC

thunder NOUN
le **tonnerre** MASC
• **thunderstorm**
un **orage**

thundery ADJECTIVE
orageux MASC, **orageuse** FEM

ℱ **Thursday** NOUN
le **jeudi**
last Thursday jeudi dernier
next Thursday jeudi prochain
every Thursday tous les jeudis
on Thursdays le jeudi
See you on Thursday! À jeudi!

> **WORD TIP** Months of the year and days of the week start with small letters in French.

to **tick** VERB
1 *(clock)* **faire** [10] **tic-tac**
2 *(on paper)* **cocher** [1]
Tick the box. Cochez la case.

ℱ indicates key words

⚘**ticket** NOUN
1 *(for planes, trains, films)* le **billet** MASC
   I have two tickets for the concert. J'ai deux billets pour le concert.
2 *(for the metro, buses, left luggage)* le **ticket** MASC
   a bus ticket un ticket de bus
3 *(a parking fine)* le **pv**
• **ticket inspector**
   le **contrôleur**
• **ticket office**
   le **guichet**

to **tickle** VERB
   chatouiller [1]

⚘**tide** NOUN
   la **marée** FEM

⚘to **tidy** VERB ▸ SEE **tidy** ADJECTIVE
   ranger [52]
   I'll tidy up the kitchen. Je rangerai la cuisine.

tidy ADJECTIVE ▸ SEE **tidy** VERB
1 *(room)* **bien rangé** MASC, **bien rangée** FEM
2 *(piece of work, writing)* **soigné** MASC, **soignée** FEM
3 *(person)* **ordonné** MASC, **ordonnée** FEM

⚘to **tie** VERB ▸ SEE **tie** NOUN
1 **nouer** [1]
2 **to tie a knot in something** faire [10] un nœud à quelque chose
   I tied a knot in my scarf. J'ai fait un nœud à mon foulard.
• **to tie something up**
1 *(a parcel)* **ficeler** [18] quelque chose
2 *(a boat)* **amarrer** [1] quelque chose
3 *(an animal)* **attacher** [1] quelque chose

⚘**tie** NOUN ▸ SEE **tie** VERB
1 la **cravate** FEM
2 *(in games)* le **match nul** MASC

tiger NOUN
   le **tigre** MASC

tight ADJECTIVE
1 *(not comfortable)* **juste** MASC & FEM
   The skirt's a bit tight. La jupe est un peu juste.
2 *(close-fitting)* **moulant** MASC, **moulante** FEM

to **tighten** VERB
   serrer [1]

tightly ADVERB
   fermement

⚘**tights** PLURAL NOUN
   le **collant** MASC SINGULAR
   a pair of tights un collant

tile NOUN
1 *(on wall)* le **carreau** MASC (PL les **carreaux**)

2 *(on roof)* la **tuile** FEM

⚘**till** CONJUNCTION, PREPOSITION ▸ SEE **till** NOUN
1 **jusqu'à**
   till now jusqu'à présent
2 **not till** ne ... pas avant
   We won't be back till ten. Nous ne serons pas rentrés avant dix heures.

till NOUN ▸ SEE **till** CONJUNCTION, PREPOSITION
   la **caisse** FEM

⚘**time** NOUN
1 *(on the clock)* l'**heure** FEM
   What time is it? Quelle heure est-il?
   It's time for lunch. C'est l'heure du déjeuner.
   to arrive on time arriver ⊚ [1] à l'heure
2 *(an amount of time)* le **temps** MASC
   We've got lots of time. Nous avons beaucoup de temps.
   There's not much time left. Il ne reste plus beaucoup de temps.
   I waited for a long time. J'ai attendu longtemps.
   I see her from time to time. Je la vois de temps en temps.
3 *(moment)* le **moment** MASC
   Is this a good time to phone? Est-ce que c'est le bon moment pour vous appeler?
   She'll arrive any time now. Elle devrait arriver d'un moment à l'autre.
4 *(in a series)* la **fois** FEM
   six times six fois
   three times a year trois fois par an
   the first, last time I saw you la première, dernière fois que je t'ai vu
5 **to have a good time** bien s'amuser [1]
   Have a good time! Amusez-vous bien!
   We had a really good time. Nous nous sommes très bien amusés.
6 *(in a person's life)* la **période**
   the happiest time of her life la période la plus heureuse de sa vie

time off NOUN
1 *(free time)* le **temps libre**
2 *(holiday)* le **congé** MASC

timetable NOUN
1 *(in school)* un **emploi du temps**
2 *(for trains, buses)* un **horaire**

⚘**tin** NOUN
1 *(container)* la **boîte** FEM
   a tin of tomatoes une boîte de tomates
2 *(metal)* l'**étain** MASC

tinned ADJECTIVE
   en conserve

tin opener NOUN
   un **ouvre-boîtes** MASC (PL les **ouvre-boîtes**)

⊚ means the verb takes être to form the perfect

tiny ADJECTIVE
  minuscule MASC & FEM

℘ to **tip** VERB ▶ SEE **tip** NOUN
  1 to tip somebody donner [1] un pourboire
    à quelqu'un
    We tipped the waiter. Nous avons donné
    un pourboire au garçon.
  2 (liquid) verser [1]
    I tipped it down the sink. Je l'ai versé dans
    l'évier.

℘ **tip** NOUN ▶ SEE **tip** VERB
  1 (of your finger, a pen) le **bout** MASC
    on the tips of your toes sur la pointe des
    pieds
  2 (money) le **pourboire** MASC
    a 10-euro tip un pourboire de 10 euros
  3 (hint) le **tuyau** MASC (PL les **tuyaux**)
    She gave me some good tips. Elle m'a
    donné de bons tuyaux.
  4 (mess) la **pagaille**
    This place is a tip! C'est la pagaille ici!

tiptoe NOUN
  la pointe des pieds

℘ **tired** ADJECTIVE
  1 fatigué MASC, **fatiguée** FEM
    We're tired. Nous sommes fatigués.
    You look tired. Tu as l'air fatigué.
  2 to be tired of something en avoir [5] assez
    de quelque chose
    I'm tired of London. J'en ai assez de
    Londres.
    to be tired of doing something en avoir
    assez de faire quelque chose
    I'm tired of watching TV. J'en ai assez de
    regarder la télé.
  3 to get tired se fatiguer ☺ [1]
    She gets tired easily. Elle se fatigue
    facilement.
  4 to get tired of something se lasser ☺ [1] de
    quelque chose
    You get tired of it after a while. On s'en
    lasse au bout d'un moment.

tiring ADJECTIVE
  fatigant MASC, **fatigante** FEM

tissue NOUN
  le **kleenex**®
  • **tissue paper**
    le papier de soie

title NOUN
  1 (of a film, book, play) le **titre**
  2 (in sport) le **titre** MASC
    to win the world title remporter [1] le titre
    mondial

℘ **to** PREPOSITION
  1 (a town, person) à

    Leah's gone to London. Leah est allée à
    Londres.
    Give the book to Leila. Donne le livre à
    Leila.
  2 (with fem singular nouns) à
    Come to the pool. Viens à la piscine.
  3 (with masc singular nouns) **au**
    She's gone to the office. Elle est partie au
    bureau.
    John works from Monday to Friday. John
    travaille du lundi au vendredi.
  4 (with singular nouns beginning with a, e, i, o,
    u or silent h) à l'
    I'm going to school. Je vais à l'école.
  5 (with plural nouns) **aux**
    We've sent a letter to the parents. On a
    envoyé une lettre aux parents.
  6 (with fem country names) **en**
    to go to Spain aller en Espagne
  7 (with masc country names) **au**
    to go to Portugal aller au Portugal
  8 (with plural country names) **aux**
    to go to the United States aller aux États-
    Unis
  9 (to somebody's house, shop, surgery) **chez**
    to go to Paul's house aller chez Paul
    I'm going to the dentist's. Je vais chez le
    dentiste.
  10 (with verb infinitives) **à**
    We're ready to go. Nous sommes prêts à
    partir.
    I have a lot of homework to do. J'ai
    beaucoup de devoirs à faire.
  11 (talking about the time) **moins**
    It's ten to nine. Il est neuf heures moins dix.
  12 (in order to) to do something **pour** faire
    quelque chose
    We need money to pay for the tickets.
    Nous avons besoin d'argent pour payer les
    billets.
  13 (towards) **avec**
    They're mean to me. Ils sont méchants
    avec moi.
    She's kind to animals. Elle est gentille avec
    les animaux.

toad NOUN
  le **crapaud** MASC
  • **toadstool**
    le champignon vénéneux

toast NOUN
  1 le **pain grillé**
  2 (to someone's health) le **toast** MASC
    We drank a toast to the future. Nous avons
    levé un verre à l'avenir.

toaster NOUN
  le **grille-pain** INVARIABLE MASC

ᴾ **tobacco** NOUN
le **tabac** MASC

ᴾ **tobacconist's** NOUN
le **bureau de tabac**

ᴾ **today** NOUN
aujourd'hui MASC
today's teenagers les adolescents d'aujourd'hui
What's the date today? On est le combien aujourd'hui?
Today's her birthday. C'est son anniversaire aujourd'hui.

ᴾ **toe** NOUN
le **doigt de pied**
my big toe mon gros orteil

toffee NOUN
le **caramel** MASC

together ADVERB
1 (with one another) **ensemble**
Kate and David arrived together. Kate et David sont arrivés ensemble.
2 (at the same time) **en même temps**
They all left together. Ils sont tous partis en même temps.

ᴾ **toilet** NOUN
les **toilettes** FEM PL
Where's the toilet? Où sont les toilettes?
• **toilet block**
(in campsite) le **bloc sanitaire**
• **toilet paper**
le **papier hygiénique**

tolerant ADJECTIVE
tolérant MASC, **tolérante** FEM

toll NOUN
1 (on a motorway, a bridge) le **péage** MASC
2 death toll le **nombre de victimes**
• **toll booth**
le **poste de péage**
• **toll road**
la **route à péage**

ᴾ **tomato** NOUN
la **tomate** FEM
tomato soup la soupe à la tomate
tomato sauce la sauce tomate

ᴾ **tomorrow** ADVERB
demain
tomorrow afternoon demain après-midi
tomorrow morning demain matin
tomorrow night demain soir
She's coming the day after tomorrow. Elle arrive après-demain.

ton NOUN
la **tonne** FEM
She gets tons of letters. Elle reçoit des tonnes de lettres.

tone NOUN
1 (on an answerphone) la **tonalité** FEM
Speak after the tone. Parlez après la tonalité.
2 (of a voice, letter) le **ton** MASC
a tone of voice un ton

ᴾ **tongue** NOUN
la **langue** FEM
It's on the tip of my tongue. Je l'ai sur le bout de la langue.

tonic NOUN
le **Schweppes®** MASC
a gin and tonic un gin tonic

tonight ADVERB
1 (this evening) **ce soir**
What are you doing tonight? Qu'est-ce que tu fais ce soir?
See you tonight! À ce soir!
2 (after bedtime) **cette nuit**
It's going to be cold tonight. Il va faire froid cette nuit.

tonsillitis NOUN
une **angine** FEM

ᴾ **too** ADVERB
1 (excessively) **trop**
too often trop souvent
It's too expensive. C'est trop cher.
You're too tired. Tu es trop fatigué.
2 too much, too many trop (de)
It takes too much time. Ça prend trop de temps.
There are too many accidents. Il y a trop d'accidents.
He eats too much. Il mange trop.
3 (also) **aussi**
Karen's coming too. Karen vient aussi.
Me too! Moi aussi!

tool NOUN
un **outil** MASC
• **tool box**
la **boîte à outils**

ᴾ **tooth** NOUN
la **dent** FEM
to brush your teeth se brosser ❍ [1] les dents

toothache NOUN
le **mal de dents**
to have toothache avoir [5] mal aux dents
I've got toothache. J'ai mal aux dents.

toothbrush NOUN
la **brosse à dents**

toothpaste NOUN
le **dentifrice**

❍ means the verb takes être to form the perfect

top *ADJECTIVE* ▸ SEE **top** *NOUN*
1 *(step, floor)* **dernier** *MASC*, **dernière** *FEM*
It's on the top floor. C'est au dernier étage.
2 *(shelf, bunk)* **du haut**
in the top bunk dans le lit du haut
in the top left-hand corner en haut à gauche

top *NOUN* ▸ SEE **top** *ADJECTIVE*
1 *(of a page, a ladder, the stairs)* le **haut** *MASC*
at the top of the stairs en haut de l'escalier
from top to bottom du haut en bas
It's on top of the wardrobe. C'est sur l'armoire.
2 *(of a container, box)* le **dessus** *MASC*
3 *(of a mountain)* le **sommet** *MASC*
4 *(lid for a pen)* le **capuchon** *MASC*
5 *(lid for a bottle)* la **capsule** *FEM*
6 *(clothing)* un **haut** *MASC*
7 *(of a list, of the charts)* la **tête** *FEM*
8 **Salma's top of the class.** Salma est la première de la classe.
9 *(to succeed)* **to get to the top** réussir [2]

topic *NOUN*
le **sujet** *MASC*

topping *NOUN*
la **garniture** *FEM*
Which topping would you like on your pizza? Vous voulez une pizza à quoi?

torch *NOUN*
la **lampe de poche**

torn *ADJECTIVE*
déchiré *MASC*, **déchirée** *FEM*

tornado *NOUN*
la **tornade** *FEM*

tortoise *NOUN*
la **tortue** *FEM*

to torture *VERB* ▸ SEE **torture** *NOUN*
torturer [1]

torture *NOUN* ▸ SEE **torture** *VERB*
la **torture** *FEM*

Tory *NOUN*
conservateur *MASC*, **conservatrice** *FEM*

total *ADJECTIVE* ▸ SEE **total** *NOUN*
total *MASC*, **totale** *FEM*, **totaux** *MASC PL*, **totales** *FEM PL*
What's the total cost? Le prix total, c'est quoi?
The party was a total failure. La soirée était un échec total.

total *NOUN* ▸ SEE **total** *ADJECTIVE*
le **total** *MASC*
20 euros in total 20 euros au total

totally *ADVERB*
complètement
You're totally wrong. Tu as complètement tort.
I totally agree. Je suis complètement d'accord.

to touch *VERB* ▸ SEE **touch** *NOUN*
toucher [1]
Don't touch my things! Ne touche pas à mes affaires!

touch *NOUN* ▸ SEE **touch** *VERB*
1 **to get in touch with somebody** prendre [64] contact avec quelqu'un
to stay in touch with somebody rester ☉ [1] en contact avec quelqu'un
2 **to lose touch with somebody** perdre [3] quelqu'un de vue
We've lost touch. On s'est perdu de vue.
3 **a touch of something** un petit peu de quelque chose
a touch of vanilla un petit peu de vanille

touching *ADJECTIVE*
touchant *MASC*, **touchante** *FEM*

touchscreen *NOUN*
l'**écran tactile** *MASC*

tough *ADJECTIVE*
1 *(in general)* **dur** *MASC*, **dure** *FEM*
The meat's tough. La viande est dure.
Chris is a tough guy. Chris est un dur.
2 *(strong)* **robuste** *MASC & FEM*
a tough fabric un tissu robuste
3 *(strict)* **sévère** *MASC & FEM*
tough measures des mesures sévères
to be tough on somebody être [6] dur avec quelqu'un
4 *(too bad)* **tant pis**
That's just tough! Tant pis!

to tour *VERB* ▸ SEE **tour** *NOUN*
1 *(holidaymakers)* **faire** [10] **du tourisme**
We toured around a bit. Nous avons fait un peu de tourisme.
2 *(performers)* **être** [6] **en tournée**
They're touring the States. Ils sont en tournée aux États-Unis.

tour *NOUN* ▸ SEE **tour** *VERB*
1 *(around a place)* la **visite** *FEM*
a guided tour of the city une visite guidée de la ville
to do a tour of something faire [1] la visite de quelque chose
We did a tour of the castle. Nous avons fait la visite du château.
2 *(by a band, theatre group)* la **tournée** *FEM*
to go on tour partir ☉ [58] en tournée
The band is going on tour to Japan. Le groupe part en tournée au Japon.

A B C D E F G H I J K L M N O P Q R S T U V W X Y Z

- **tour guide**
le & la **guide**

tourism NOUN
le **tourisme** MASC

tourist NOUN
le & la **touriste** MASC & FEM
The town is popular with tourists. C'est une ville touristique.
- **tourist attraction**
l'**attraction touristique** FEM
- **tourist information office**
le **syndicat d'initiative**
- **tourist trap**
le **piège à touristes**

tournament NOUN
le **tournoi** MASC

to **tow** VERB
remorquer [1]
- **to tow something away**
(breakdown truck) remorquer [1] quelque chose

ℓ **towards** PREPOSITION
1 **en direction de**
She went off towards the park. Elle est partie en direction du parc.
They were coming towards us. Il s'approchaient de nous.
2 (approximately) **vers**
towards the end of the month vers la fin du mois
3 (to) **envers**
my attitude towards my parents mon attitude envers mes parents

ℓ **towel** NOUN
la **serviette** FEM

tower NOUN
la **tour** FEM
the Eiffel Tower la tour Eiffel
- **tower block**
la **tour**

ℓ **town** NOUN
la **ville** FEM
to go into town aller ⊘ [7] en ville
- **town centre**
le **centre-ville**
- **town hall**
la **mairie**

toxic ADJECTIVE
toxique MASC & FEM

ℓ **toy** NOUN
le **jouet** MASC
a toy car une petite voiture
- **toyshop**
le **magasin de jouets**

to **trace** VERB ▸ SEE **trace** NOUN
1 (a missing person) **retrouver** [1]
2 (a phone call) **localiser** [1]

trace NOUN ▸ SEE **trace** VERB
la **trace** FEM
There was no trace of it. Il n'en restait aucune trace.

ℓ **track** NOUN
1 (for athletics) la **piste** FEM
ten laps of the track dix tours de piste
2 (for cars) le **circuit**
3 (path) le **chemin** MASC
4 (song) la **chanson** FEM
This is my favourite track. C'est ma chanson préférée.
5 **to be on the right track** être [6] sur la bonne piste
I think we're on the right track. Je crois que nous sommes sur la bonne piste.
- **track and field**
l'**athlétisme** MASC
- **track suit**
le **survêtement**

tractor NOUN
le **tracteur** MASC

trade NOUN
1 (job) le **métier** MASC
He's a plumber by trade. C'est un plombier de son métier.
2 (business) le **commerce**

trademark NOUN
la **marque**
a registered trademark une marque déposée

tradition NOUN
la **tradition** FEM

traditional ADJECTIVE
traditionnel MASC, **traditionnelle** FEM

ℓ **traffic** NOUN
la **circulation** FEM
The traffic's heavy. Il y a beaucoup de circulation.
- **traffic jam**
un **embouteillage**
- **traffic lights**
les **feux** MASC PL
- **traffic warden**
le **gardien de la paix**, la **gardienne de la paix**

tragedy NOUN
la **tragédie** FEM

tragic ADJECTIVE
tragique MASC & FEM

trail NOUN
le **sentier** MASC

⊘ means the verb takes être to form the perfect

a nature trail un sentier écologique

trailer NOUN
la **remorque** FEM
- trailer tent
la tente-remorque

ℓ to **train** VERB ▸ SEE **train** NOUN
1 (for a career) **former** [1]
2 to train to be something **suivre** [75] une formation de quelque chose
He's training to be a plumber. Il suit une formation de plombier.
My mother trained as a teacher. Ma mère a reçu une formation de professeur.
3 (for sport) **s'entraîner** [1]
The team trains on Saturdays. L'équipe s'entraîne le samedi.

ℓ **train** NOUN ▸ SEE **train** VERB
le **train** MASC
the train to Rouen le train pour Rouen
He's coming by train. Il prend le train.
We went to Rennes by train. Nous sommes allés à Rennes en train.

train crash NOUN
un **accident ferroviaire**

ℓ **trainee** NOUN
le & la **stagiaire** MASC & FEM

trainer NOUN
1 (shoe) le **basket** MASC
2 (coach) un **entraîneur** MASC, une **entraîneuse** FEM

ℓ **training** NOUN
1 (for a career) la **formation** FEM
a training centre un centre de formation
2 (for sport) l'**entraînement** MASC

tram NOUN
le **tramway** MASC

tramp NOUN
le **clochard** MASC, la **clocharde** FEM

trampoline NOUN
le **trampoline** MASC

to **transfer** VERB ▸ SEE **transfer** NOUN
1 (an employee, a player, data) **transférer** [1]
2 (money) **virer** [1]

transfer NOUN ▸ SEE **transfer** VERB
1 (of money) le **virement** MASC
2 (of an employee, a footballer) le **transfert** MASC
3 (sticker) la **décalcomanie** FEM

to **transform** VERB
transformer [1]

transistor NOUN
le **transistor** MASC

to **translate** VERB
traduire [26]
Translate the sentences into French.
Traduisez les phrases en français.

translation NOUN
la **traduction** FEM

translator NOUN
le **traducteur** MASC, la **traductrice** FEM

transparent ADJECTIVE
transparent MASC, **transparente** FEM

transplant NOUN
1 (operation) la **transplantation** FEM
2 (organ) le **transplant** MASC

ℓ **transport** NOUN ▸ SEE **transport** VERB
le **transport** MASC
public transport les transports en commun

to **trap** VERB ▸ SEE **trap** NOUN
to be trapped **être** [6] coincé

trap NOUN ▸ SEE **trap** VERB
le **piège** MASC

ℓ to **travel** VERB ▸ SEE **travel** NOUN
voyager [52]
I love travelling abroad. J'aime beaucoup voyager à l'étranger.
He hates travelling by plane. Il déteste voyager par avion.

travel NOUN ▸ SEE **travel** VERB
les **voyages** MASC PL
some travel brochures des brochures de voyage
- travel agency
une agence de voyages
- travel agent
un agent de voyages

traveller NOUN
1 (in general) le **voyageur** MASC, la **voyageuse** FEM
2 (gypsy) le & la **nomade** MASC & FEM

ℓ **traveller's cheque** NOUN
le **chèque-voyage** MASC (PL les **chèques-voyage**)

travelling NOUN
les **voyages** MASC PL

travel-sick ADJECTIVE
to get travel-sick **souffrir** [73] du mal de voyage

travel-sickness NOUN
le **mal de voyage**

tray NOUN
le **plateau** MASC (PL les **plateaux**)

to **tread** VERB
to tread on something **marcher** [1] sur

quelque chose
Somebody trod on my toe. Quelqu'un m'a marché sur l'orteil.

treasure NOUN
le **trésor** MASC

to **treat** VERB ▸ SEE **treat** NOUN
1 *(in general)* traiter [1]
They treat me like an adult. Ils me traitent comme un adulte.
2 **to treat somebody to something** offrir [56] quelque chose à quelqu'un
I'll treat you to a drink. Je vous offre à boire.
to treat yourself to something s'offrir [56] quelque chose
I treated myself to some chocolates. Je me suis offert quelques chocolats.

treat NOUN ▸ SEE **treat** VERB
1 *(something enjoyable)* le **petit plaisir**
I took them to the circus as a treat. Je les ai emmenés au cirque pour leur faire plaisir.
2 *(food)* la **gâterie** FEM
It's a little treat. C'est une petite gâterie.

treatment NOUN
le **traitement** MASC

treaty NOUN
le **traité** MASC

ℰ **tree** NOUN
un **arbre** MASC

to **tremble** VERB
trembler [1]

tremendous ADJECTIVE
fantastique MASC & FEM

trend NOUN
1 *(fashion)* la **mode** FEM
2 *(tendency)* la **tendance** FEM

trendy ADJECTIVE
branché MASC, branchée FEM

trial NOUN
(legal) le **procès** MASC
to go on trial passer [1] en jugement

triangle NOUN
le **triangle** MASC

triathlon NOUN
le **triathlon** MASC

tribe NOUN
la **tribu** FEM

tribute NOUN
un **hommage** MASC
to pay tribute to somebody rendre [3] hommage à quelqu'un

ℰ to **trick** VERB ▸ SEE **trick** NOUN
rouler [1]
He tricked me! Il m'a roulé!

ℰ **trick** NOUN ▸ SEE **trick** VERB
1 *(by a conjuror, as a joke)* le **tour** MASC
to play a trick on somebody jouer un tour à quelqu'un
Rebecca played a trick on me. Rebecca m'a joué un tour.
2 **to do the trick** faire [10] l'affaire
That hat will do the trick. Ce chapeau fera l'affaire.

tricky ADJECTIVE
délicat MASC, délicate FEM
It's a tricky situation. C'est une situation délicate.

to **trim** VERB
couper [1]

Trinidad NOUN
(l'île de) la Trinité

Trinidadian ADJECTIVE ▸ SEE **Trinidadian** NOUN
trinidadien MASC, trinidadienne FEM

Trinidadian NOUN ▸ SEE **Trinidadian** ADJECTIVE
un Trinidadien MASC, une Trinidadienne FEM

to **trip** VERB ▸ SEE **trip** NOUN
trébucher [1]
to trip over something trébucher sur quelque chose

ℰ **trip** NOUN ▸ SEE **trip** VERB
le **voyage** MASC
a trip to Florida un voyage en Floride
a coach trip un voyage en car
a business trip un voyage d'affaires
a trip to Disneyworld une visite à Disneyworld
We went on a day-trip to France. Nous avons fait une excursion d'une journée en France.

to **triple** VERB
tripler [1]

triumph NOUN
le **triomphe** MASC

ℰ **trolley** NOUN
le **chariot** MASC

trombone NOUN
le **trombone** MASC
to play the trombone jouer [1] du trombone

trophy NOUN
le **trophée** MASC

tropical ADJECTIVE
tropical MASC, tropicale FEM, tropicaux MASC PL, tropicales FEM PL

◎ means the verb takes être to form the perfect

to **trot** *VERB*
  trotter [1]

ℐ **trouble** *NOUN*
1 *(problems)* les **problèmes** *MASC PL*
  We've had trouble with the car. Nous avons eu des problèmes avec la voiture.
2 *(personal problems)* les **ennuis** *MASC PL*
  to be in trouble avoir [5] des ennuis
  Steph's in trouble (with the school). Steph a des ennuis (avec l'école).
  What's the trouble? Qu'est-ce qui ne va pas?
3 **to have trouble doing something** avoir [5] du mal à faire quelque chose
  I had trouble finding a seat. J'ai eu du mal à trouver une place.
4 **to go to a lot of trouble to do something** se donner ◎ [1] beaucoup de mal pour faire quelque chose
  She went to a lot of trouble to get the tickets. Elle s'est donné beaucoup de mal pour avoir les billets.
  to be worth the trouble valoir [80] la peine
  It's not worth the trouble. Cela ne vaut pas la peine.

ℐ **trousers** *PLURAL NOUN*
  le **pantalon** *MASC SINGULAR*
  a new pair of trousers un pantalon neuf

ℐ **trout** *NOUN*
  la **truite** *FEM*

truant *NOUN*
  to play truant faire [10] l'école buissonnière

ℐ **truck** *NOUN*
  le **camion** *MASC*

ℐ **true** *ADJECTIVE*
  vrai *MASC*, vraie *FEM*
  a true story une histoire vraie
  Is that true? C'est vrai?
  That's not true. Ce n'est pas vrai.

trump *NOUN*
  un **atout** *MASC*
  Spades are trumps. Atout pique.

trumpet *NOUN*
  la **trompette** *FEM*
  to play the trumpet jouer [1] de la trompette

trunk *NOUN*
1 *(of a tree)* le **tronc** *MASC*
2 *(elephant's)* la **trompe** *FEM*
3 *(for clothes, belongings)* la **malle** *FEM*

trunks *PLURAL NOUN*
  le **maillot de bain**
  my new swimming trunks mon maillot de bain neuf

to **trust** *VERB* ► SEE **trust** *NOUN*
  to trust somebody faire [10] confiance à quelqu'un
  I trust her. Je lui fais confiance.
  They don't trust each other. Ils ne se font pas confiance.

trust *NOUN* ► SEE **trust** *VERB*
  la **confiance** *FEM*

truth *NOUN*
  la **vérité** *FEM*
  She's telling the truth. Elle dit la vérité.

ℐ to **try** *VERB* ► SEE **try** *NOUN*
  essayer [59]
  to try to do something essayer de faire quelque chose
  I'm trying to open the door. J'essaie d'ouvrir la porte.
  Did you try calling her? Est-ce que tu as essayé de l'appeler?
  I'm trying not to think about it. J'essaie de ne pas y penser.
  to try hard to do something faire [10] de gros efforts pour faire quelque chose
  She was trying hard to concentrate. Elle faisait de gros efforts pour se concentrer.
• **to try something on**
  essayer [59] quelque chose

try *NOUN* ► SEE **try** *VERB*
1 **to have a try** essayer [59]
  I'll have a try. J'essaierai.
  It's worth a try. Cela vaut la peine d'essayer.
2 *(in rugby)* un **essai** *MASC*
  to score a try marquer [1] un essai

T-shirt *NOUN*
  le **tee-shirt** *MASC*

tub *NOUN*
  le **pot** *MASC*

tube *NOUN*
1 *(in general)* le **tube** *MASC*
2 **the Tube** le métro (à Londres)

Tuesday *NOUN*
  le **mardi** *MASC*
  last Tuesday mardi dernier
  next Tuesday mardi prochain
  every Tuesday tous les mardis
  on Tuesdays le mardi
  See you on Tuesday! À mardi!

WORD TIP Months of the year and days of the week start with small letters in French.

to **tug** *VERB*
  tirer [1]
  to tug at something tirer sur quelque chose

tuition NOUN
les **cours** MASC PL
piano tuition des cours de piano
private tuition des cours particuliers

tumble-drier NOUN
le **sèche-linge** MASC (PL les **sèche-linge**)

tumbler NOUN
le **verre droit**

tummy NOUN
l'**estomac** MASC

tuna NOUN
le **thon** MASC

to **tune** VERB ▸ SEE **tune** NOUN
(musical instruments) **accorder** [1]

tune NOUN ▸ SEE **tune** VERB
1 un **air** MASC
2 **to sing in tune** chanter [1] juste

Tunisia NOUN
la **Tunisie** FEM

Tunisian ADJECTIVE ▸ SEE **Tunisian** NOUN
tunisien MASC, **tunisienne** FEM

Tunisian NOUN ▸ SEE **Tunisian** ADJECTIVE
un **Tunisien**, une **Tunisienne**

ℓ **tunnel** NOUN
le **tunnel** MASC
the Channel Tunnel le tunnel sous la
Manche

> **TUNNEL**
The Eurotunnel – linking Britain and France
since 1994 – is the longest rail tunnel in the
world.

turban NOUN
le **turban** MASC

turkey NOUN ▸ SEE **Turkey**
la **dinde** FEM

Turkey NOUN
la **Turquie** FEM

Turkish ADJECTIVE ▸ SEE **Turkish** NOUN
turc MASC, **turque** FEM

Turkish NOUN ▸ SEE **Turkish** ADJECTIVE
le **turc** MASC

ℓ to **turn** VERB ▸ SEE **turn** NOUN
1 (in general) **tourner** [1]
Turn left at the next set of lights. Tournez à
gauche aux prochains feux.
I turned to look out of the window. J'ai
tourné la tête pour regarder par la fenêtre.
2 (to become) **devenir** ⊘ [81]
She turned red. Elle est devenue rouge.
3 **to turn to somebody for something**
tourner [1] vers quelqu'un pour demander
quelque chose

They turn to us for advice. Ils tournent vers
nous pour demander des conseils.
• **to turn around**
se retourner ⊘ [1]
When I turned around, I saw her. Quand je
me suis retourné, je l'ai vue.
• **to turn something around**
tourner [1] quelque chose
Turn your chair around. Tourne ta chaise.
• **to turn back**
faire [10] demi-tour
We turned back. Nous avons fait demi-tour.
• **to turn something down**
1 (a radio, the volume) **baisser** [1] quelque
chose
They won't turn the sound down. Ils ne
veulent pas baisser le son.
2 (an offer) **rejeter** [1]
• **to turn something off**
1 (a light, an oven, a TV, a radio) **éteindre** [60]
quelque chose
2 (a tap) **fermer** [1] quelque chose
• **to turn something on**
1 (a light, an oven, a TV, a radio) **allumer** [1]
quelque chose
2 (a tap) **ouvrir** [30] quelque chose
• **to turn out**
se terminer ⊘ [1]
The concert turned out well. Le concert
s'est bien terminé.
The holiday turned out badly. Les vacances
se sont mal terminées.
• **to turn over**
1 (by itself) **se retourner** ⊘ [1]
2 (a page, a steak) **tourner** [1]
• **to turn up**
arriver ⊘ [1]
They turned up an hour later. Ils sont
arrivés une heure plus tard.
• **to turn something up**
1 (heating, gas) **augmenter** [1] quelque chose
2 (a radio, the volume) **monter** [1]
Can you turn up the volume? Est-ce que tu
peux monter le son?

turn NOUN ▸ SEE **turn** VERB
1 (in games, on a rota) le **tour** MASC
It's your turn. C'est ton tour.
Whose turn is it? C'est à qui le tour?
We'll take turns. On le fera, chacun à son
tour.
It's Jane's turn to wash up. C'est à Jane de
faire la vaisselle.
to take turns doing something faire [10]
quelque chose à tour de rôle
Mum and Dad took turns driving. Ma mère
et mon père ont conduit à tour de rôle.
2 (in a road) le **virage** MASC
the next turn on the left la prochaine rue
à gauche

⊘ means the verb takes être to form the perfect

turning *NOUN*
le **virage** *MASC*
Take the third turning on the left. Prenez la troisième rue à gauche.

turnip *NOUN*
le **navet** *MASC*

turquoise *ADJECTIVE*
turquoise *MASC & FEM*

turtle *NOUN*
la **tortue marine**

TV *NOUN*
la **télé** *FEM*
I saw her on TV. Je l'ai vue à la télé.

tweezers *NOUN*
la **pince à épiler**

twelfth *ADJECTIVE*
1 **douzième** *MASC & FEM*
on the twelfth floor au douzième étage
2 *(in dates)* **the twelfth of May** le douze mai

twelve *NUMBER*
1 **douze**
Daniel's twelve. Daniel a douze ans.
2 **at twelve o'clock at night** à minuit
3 **at twelve noon** à midi

twentieth *ADJECTIVE*
1 **vingtième** *MASC & FEM*
2 *(in dates)* **the twentieth of August** le vingt août

twenty *NUMBER*
vingt
Marie's twenty. Marie a vingt ans.
twenty-one vingt-et-un
twenty-five vingt-cinq

twice *ADVERB*
deux fois
twice as many people deux fois plus de personnes
He eats twice as much as me. Il mange deux fois plus que moi.
It's twice as expensive here. C'est deux fois plus cher ici.

ℰ to **twin** *VERB* ▶ SEE **twin** *NOUN*
to be twinned with être [6] jumelé avec
York is twinned with Dijon. York est jumelée avec Dijon.

ℰ **twin** *NOUN* ▶ SEE **twin** *VERB*
le **jumeau** *MASC*, la **jumelle** *FEM*, *(PL* les **jumeaux)*
her twin sister sa sœur jumelle
Helen and Tim are twins. Helen et Tim sont jumeaux.
• **twin room**
la chambre à deux lits

• **twin town**
la ville jumelle

to **twist** *VERB*
tordre [3]
to twist your ankle se tordre ◎ [3] la cheville

two *NUMBER*
deux
Ben's two. Ben a deux ans.

to **type** *VERB* ▶ SEE **type** *NOUN*
taper [1]

type *NOUN* ▶ SEE **type** *VERB*
le **type** *MASC*
What type of computer is it? C'est quel type d'ordinateur?
She's not my type. Elle n'est pas mon genre.

typical *ADJECTIVE*
typique *MASC & FEM*

ℰ **tyre** *NOUN*
le **pneu** *MASC*
a flat tyre un pneu crevé

Uu

UFO *NOUN*
un **ovni** *MASC*

ℰ **ugly** *ADJECTIVE*
laid *MASC*, **laide** *FEM*

UK *NOUN*
(= United Kingdom) le **Royaume-Uni** *MASC*
They don't live in the UK. Ils n'habitent pas au Royaume-Uni.

WORD TIP Countries and regions in French take le, la or les.

ulcer *NOUN*
un **ulcère** *MASC*

Ulster *NOUN*
l'**Irlande du Nord** *FEM*

WORD TIP Countries and regions in French take le, la or les.

ℰ **umbrella** *NOUN*
le **parapluie** *MASC*

umpire *NOUN*
un **arbitre** *MASC*

UN *NOUN*
(= United Nations) l'**ONU** *FEM*
= Organisation des Nations Unies

ℰ indicates key words

unable ADJECTIVE
to be unable to do something ne pas
pouvoir [12] faire quelque chose
He's unable to come. Il ne peut pas venir.
I was unable to see him. Je n'ai pas pu le
voir.

unacceptable ADJECTIVE
inadmissible MASC & FEM
This is completely unacceptable. Ceci est
totalement inadmissible.

unanimous ADJECTIVE
unanime MASC & FEM

unattractive ADJECTIVE
(person, place) peu attrayant MASC, peu
attrayante FEM

unavoidable ADJECTIVE
inévitable MASC & FEM

unbearable ADJECTIVE
insupportable MASC & FEM
I find them unbearable. Je les trouve
insupportables.

unbelievable ADJECTIVE
incroyable MASC & FEM

uncertain ADJECTIVE
incertain MASC, incertaine FEM
to be uncertain whether ... ne pas être [6]
sûr que ...
I'm uncertain whether they're coming. Je
ne suis pas sûr qu'ils viennent.

unchanged ADJECTIVE
inchangé MASC, inchangée FEM

uncivilized ADJECTIVE
barbare MASC & FEM

ℰ **uncle** NOUN
un oncle MASC
my Uncle Bill mon oncle Bill

ℰ **uncomfortable** ADJECTIVE
1 (shoes, chair) inconfortable MASC & FEM
2 (journey, situation) pénible MASC & FEM
to feel uncomfortable se sentir ◎ [2] mal
à l'aise.
I'm feeling pretty uncomfortable. Je me
sens plutôt mal à l'aise.

uncommon ADJECTIVE
rare MASC & FEM

unconscious ADJECTIVE
sans connaissance
Tessa's still unconscious. Tessa est toujours
sans connaissance.

ℰ **under** PREPOSITION
1 (underneath) sous
Harry hid under the bed. Harry s'est caché

sous le lit.
Perhaps it's under there. C'est peut-être
là-dessous.
2 (less than) moins de
Tickets cost under £20. Les billets coûtent
moins de vingt livres.
It's free for children under five. C'est
gratuit pour les enfants de moins de cinq
ans.
It took under two hours to get there. Il a
fallu moins de deux heures pour y aller.

under-age ADJECTIVE
to be under-age être [6] mineur
Jane can't go. She's under-age. Jane ne
peut pas y aller. Elle est mineure.

underclothes PLURAL NOUN
les sous-vêtements MASC PL

undercooked ADJECTIVE
pas assez cuit MASC, pas assez cuite FEM

to **underestimate** VERB
sous-estimer [1]

underground ADJECTIVE ▸ SEE **underground**
NOUN
souterrain MASC, souterraine FEM
an underground carpark un parking
souterrain

ℰ **underground** NOUN ▸ SEE **underground**
ADJECTIVE
le métro MASC
I saw her on the underground. Je l'ai vue
dans le métro.
Shall we go by underground? On prend le
métro?

to **underline** VERB
souligner [1]
Underline all the adjectives. Soulignez tous
les adjectifs.

ℰ **underneath** ADVERB ▸ SEE **underneath**
PREPOSITION
dessous
Look underneath. Cherche dessous.
I was wearing a T-shirt underneath. Je
portais un tee-shirt dessous.

ℰ **underneath** PREPOSITION ▸ SEE **underneath**
ADVERB
sous
It's underneath these papers. C'est sous
ces papiers.

ℰ **underpants** PLURAL NOUN
le slip MASC
my underpants mon slip

underpass NOUN
1 (pedestrian) le passage souterrain
2 (for traffic) le passage inférieur

◎ means the verb takes être to form the perfect

𝒫 to **understand** VERB
comprendre [64]
Do you understand how it works? Est-ce que tu comprends comment ça marche?
I don't understand. Je ne comprends pas.
I couldn't understand what he was saying. Je n'ai pas compris ce qu'il disait.
They don't understand me. Ils ne me comprennent pas.

understandable ADJECTIVE
(instructions, language) compréhensible MASC & FEM
You're upset. That's understandable. Tu es contrarié. Ça se comprend.

understanding ADJECTIVE ▶ SEE **understanding** NOUN
compréhensif MASC, compréhensive FEM
He was very understanding. Il a été très compréhensif.

understanding NOUN ▶ SEE **understanding** ADJECTIVE
la **compréhension** FEM

undertaker NOUN
un **entrepreneur de pompes funèbres**
at the undertaker's aux pompes funèbres

underwear NOUN
les **sous-vêtements** MASC PL

to **undo** VERB
1 (a button, a tie) défaire [10]
2 (a parcel, a zip) ouvrir [30]

undone ADJECTIVE
to come undone se défaire ◉ [10]
Your button's come undone. Ton bouton s'est défait.

𝒫 to **undress** VERB
to get undressed se déshabiller ◉ [1]
I got undressed. Je me suis déshabillé (boy speaking), Je me suis déshabillée (girl speaking).

𝒫 **unemployed** ADJECTIVE ▶ SEE **unemployed** NOUN
au chômage
She's unemployed. Elle est au chômage.

𝒫 **unemployed** NOUN ▶ SEE **unemployed** ADJECTIVE
the unemployed les chômeurs MASC PL
benefits to help the unemployed des allocations pour les chômeurs

𝒫 **unemployment** NOUN
le **chômage** MASC

uneven ADJECTIVE
irrégulier MASC, irrégulière FEM

unexpected ADJECTIVE
imprévu MASC, imprévue FEM
an unexpected event un événement imprévu

unexpectedly ADVERB
(to happen, arrive) à l'improviste

unfair ADJECTIVE
injuste MASC & FEM
It's unfair to young people. C'est injuste pour les jeunes.
It's unfair of them to do that. Il est injuste qu'ils fassent ça.

unfashionable ADJECTIVE
démodé MASC, démodée FEM

to **unfasten** VERB
(a belt, a button) défaire [10]

unfit ADJECTIVE
to be unfit ne pas être [6] en forme
I'm terribly unfit. Je ne suis pas du tout en forme.

to **unfold** VERB
déplier [1]

unforgettable ADJECTIVE
inoubliable MASC & FEM
It was an unforgettable experience. Cela a été une expérience inoubliable.

𝒫 **unfortunate** ADJECTIVE
1 regrettable MASC & FEM
an unfortunate experience une expérience regrettable
2 (unlucky) malheureux MASC, malheureuse FEM
the unfortunate victims les victimes malheureuses

𝒫 **unfortunately** ADVERB
malheureusement
He's not here unfortunately. Il n'est pas là malheureusement.

unfriendly ADJECTIVE
pas très sympathique MASC & FEM
Some people are unfriendly. Certaines personnes ne sont pas très sympathiques.

unfurnished ADJECTIVE
non meublé MASC, non meublée FEM

ungrateful ADJECTIVE
ingrat MASC, ingrate FEM

𝒫 **unhappy** ADJECTIVE
malheureux MASC, malheureuse FEM

unhealthy ADJECTIVE
1 (person) maladif MASC, maladive FEM
2 (food) malsain MASC, malsaine FEM

𝒫 indicates key words

unhurt *ADJECTIVE*
   indemne *MASC & FEM*
   to escape unhurt from an accident sortir ◎
   [72] indemne d'un accident

♟ **uniform** *NOUN*
   un **uniforme** *MASC*
   She was in school uniform. Elle était en
   uniforme scolaire.
   They don't wear a uniform. Ils ne portent
   pas d'uniforme.

> ⓘ **UNIFORM**
>
> French pupils wear casual clothes to school as
> there is no school uniform.

uninhabited *ADJECTIVE*
   inhabité *MASC*, **inhabitée** *FEM*

union *NOUN*
   (a trade union) le **syndicat** *MASC*

Union Jack *NOUN*
   le **drapeau du Royaume-Uni**

♟ **unique** *ADJECTIVE*
   unique *MASC & FEM*

unit *NOUN*
1 *(for measuring, section in a book)* une **unité**
   FEM
   a unit of measurement une unité de
   mesure
2 *(for kitchen storage)* un **élément** *MASC*
3 *(a hospital department)* le **service** *MASC*
   the intensive care unit le service des soins
   intensifs

to unite *VERB*
   unir [2]

United Kingdom *NOUN*
   le **Royaume-Uni** *MASC*

> **WORD TIP** Countries and regions in French take
> le, la or les.

United Nations *NOUN*
   l'**Organisation des Nations Unies** *FEM*

United States (of America) *PLURAL NOUN*
   les **États-Unis** *MASC PL*
   in the United States aux États-Unis
   He's at college in the United States. Il est à
   l'université aux États-Unis.
   to the United States aux États-Unis
   Have you ever been to the United States?
   Est-ce que tu es jamais allé aux États-Unis?

> **WORD TIP** Countries and regions in French take
> le, la or les.

universe *NOUN*
   l'**univers** *MASC*

♟ **university** *NOUN*
   une **université** *FEM*
   She's at university in London. Elle est à
   l'université à Londres.
   to go to university aller ◎ [7] à l'université
   Do you want to go to university? Tu veux
   aller à l'université?
• **university education**
   la formation universitaire
• **university lecturer**
   le maître de conférences, la maîtresse de
   conférences
• **university professor**
   le professeur d'université, la professeure
   d'université
• **university town**
   la ville universitaire

unjust *ADJECTIVE*
   injuste *MASC & FEM*

unkind *ADJECTIVE*
   pas gentil *MASC*, **pas gentille** *FEM*
   He's unkind to animals. Il n'est pas gentil
   avec les animaux.

unknown *ADJECTIVE*
   inconnu *MASC*, **inconnue** *FEM*

♟ **unleaded petrol** *NOUN*
   l'**essence sans plomb** *FEM*

♟ **unless** *CONJUNCTION*
   unless ... ne ... à moins que ... ne ...
   I'm not going unless he phones. Je ne vais
   pas à moins qu'il ne téléphone.
   She won't know unless you tell her. Elle ne
   saura pas à moins que tu ne le lui dises.

unlike *PREPOSITION*
1 *(in contrast to)* **contrairement à**
   Unlike me, she hates dogs. Contrairement
   à moi, elle déteste les chiens.
2 *(uncharacteristic of)* **It's unlike her to
   be late.** Ce n'est pas son genre d'être en
   retard.

unlikely *ADJECTIVE*
   peu probable *MASC & FEM*
   It's unlikely. C'est peu probable.
   It's unlikely that we'll be going. Il est peu
   probable que nous y allions.

unlimited *ADJECTIVE*
   illimité *MASC*, **illimitée** *FEM*
   an unlimited choice un choix illimité

to unload *VERB*
   (a lorry, a ship, goods) **décharger** [52]

to unlock *VERB*
   ouvrir [30]
   The car's unlocked. La voiture est ouverte.

ϼ **unlucky** *ADJECTIVE*
1 *(person)* **to be unlucky** ne pas avoir [5] de chance
I was unlucky, it was shut. Je n'ai pas eu de chance, c'était fermé.
2 *(colour, number)* **to be unlucky** porter [1] malheur
Thirteen is an unlucky number. Le treize porte malheur.

unmarried *ADJECTIVE*
célibataire *MASC & FEM*

unnatural *ADJECTIVE*
anormal *MASC*, **anormale** *FEM*, **anormaux** *MASC PL*, **anormales** *FEM PL*

unnecessary *ADJECTIVE*
inutile *MASC & FEM*
It's unnecessary to book. Il est inutile de réserver.

to **unpack** *VERB*
défaire [10]
I unpacked my rucksack. J'ai défait mon sac à dos.
I'll just unpack and then I'll come down. Je vais juste défaire ma valise et puis je descendrai.

unpaid *ADJECTIVE*
1 *(bill)* **impayé** *MASC*, **impayée** *FEM*
2 *(work)* **non rémunéré** *MASC*, **non rémunérée** *FEM*

ϼ **unpleasant** *ADJECTIVE*
désagréable *MASC & FEM*
an unpleasant trip un voyage désagréable
to be unpleasant to somebody être [6] désagréable avec quelqu'un
The waiter was unpleasant to us. Le garçon a été désagréable avec nous.

to **unplug** *VERB*
(a computer, a TV, a kettle) **débrancher** [1]

unpopular *ADJECTIVE*
impopulaire *MASC & FEM*
to make yourself unpopular se rendre ◌ [3] impopulaire

unrealistic *ADJECTIVE*
peu réaliste *MASC & FEM*

unreasonable *ADJECTIVE*
pas raisonnable *MASC & FEM*
He's being really unreasonable. Il n'est vraiment pas raisonnable.

unrecognizable *ADJECTIVE*
méconnaissable *MASC & FEM*
You're unrecognizable in that costume. Tu es méconnaissable dans ce costume.

unreliable *ADJECTIVE*
1 *(information, computer, car)* **peu fiable** *MASC & FEM*
2 **She's unreliable.** On ne peut pas compter sur elle.

to **unroll** *VERB*
dérouler [1]

unsafe *ADJECTIVE*
(wiring, building) **dangereux** *MASC*, **dangereuse** *FEM*

unsatisfactory *ADJECTIVE*
peu satisfaisant *MASC*, **peu satisfaisante** *FEM*
an unsatisfactory result un résultat peu satisfaisant

to **unscrew** *VERB*
dévisser [1]

unshaven *ADJECTIVE*
pas rasé *MASC*, **pas rasée** *FEM*

unsuccessful *ADJECTIVE*
to be unsuccessful ne pas réussir [2]
I tried, but I was unsuccessful. J'ai essayé mais je n'ai pas réussi.
After a few unsuccessful attempts, I gave up. Après quelques essais vains, j'ai abandonné.

unsuitable *ADJECTIVE*
inapproprié *MASC*, **inappropriée** *FEM*

untidy *ADJECTIVE*
en désordre
The house is always untidy. La maison est toujours en désordre.

to **untie** *VERB*
(a knot, a lace) **défaire** [10]

ϼ **until** *PREPOSITION*
1 **jusqu'à**
until Monday jusqu'à lundi
He's on holiday until the tenth. Il est en vacances jusqu'au dix.
until now jusqu'à présent
I didn't know about it until now. Je n'étais pas au courant jusqu'à présent.
until then jusque-là
There was no electricity until then. Il n'y a pas eu d'électricité jusque-là.
2 **not until** pas avant
not until September pas avant septembre
It won't be finished until Friday. Ce ne sera pas fini avant vendredi.

unusual *ADJECTIVE*
peu commun *MASC*, **peu commune** *FEM*
You chose an unusual colour. Tu as choisi une couleur peu commune.
Storms are unusual in June. Les orages au

A
B
C
D
E
F
G
H
I
J
K
L
M
N
O
P
Q
R
S
T
U
V
W
X
Y
Z

ϼ indicates key words

mois de juin sont rares.
It's unusual for Matt to be absent. Il est rare que Matt soit absent.

unwilling *ADJECTIVE*
  to be unwilling to do something ne pas vouloir faire quelque chose
  He's unwilling to wait. Il ne veut pas attendre.

to **unwrap** *VERB*
  déballer [1]

up *PREPOSITION, ADVERB*
1 *(out of bed)* **to be up** être [6] levé
  Liz isn't up yet. Liz n'est pas encore levée.
  to get up se lever ◯ [50]
  I get up at seven. Je me lève à sept heures.
  We got up at six. Nous nous sommes levés à six heures.
2 *(not yet in bed)* **to be up late** se coucher ◯ [1] tard
  I was up late last night. Je me suis couché tard hier soir *(boy speaking)*, Je me suis couchée tard hier soir *(girl speaking)*.
3 *(higher up)* en haut
  up at the top of the house tout en haut de la maison
  Hands up! Haut les mains!
  up here ici
  It's up there. C'est là-haut.
  We went up the road. Nous avons remonté la rue.
  It's just up the street. C'est tout près.
  He's working up in Glasgow. Il travaille à Glasgow.
4 *(what's the matter?)* **What's up?** Qu'est-ce qui se passe?
  What's up with him? Qu'est-ce qu'il a?
5 **up to** jusqu'à
  up to here jusqu'ici
  You can invite up to fifty people. Tu peux inviter jusqu'à cinquante personnes.
6 **to come up to somebody** s'approcher [1] de quelqu'un
  She came up to me. Elle s'est approchée de moi.
7 **to be up to something** faire [10] quelque chose
  What's she up to? Qu'est-ce qu'elle fait?
8 **It's up to you to decide.** C'est à toi de décider.
  It's not up to me. Ce n'est pas à moi de décider.
9 *(finished, over)* **Time's up!** C'est l'heure!

to **update** *VERB* ▸ SEE **update** *NOUN*
1 *(information, timetables)* mettre [11] à jour
2 *(style, decoration)* moderniser [1]

update *NOUN* ▸ SEE **update** *VERB*
  la mise à jour

Here's an update on the delays. Voici une mise à jour des retards.

upheaval *NOUN*
  le bouleversement *MASC*

uphill *ADVERB*
  (path) en montée
  to walk uphill marcher [1] en montée
  The road goes uphill to the square. La route monte jusqu'à la place.

to **upload** *VERB*
  (a document, photos) mettre [11] en ligne

upright *ADJECTIVE, ADVERB*
  droit *MASC*, droite *FEM*
  Put it upright. Mets-le droit.
  Try to stand upright. Essaie de te tenir droit.

to **upset** *VERB* ▸ SEE **upset** *ADJECTIVE, NOUN*
  contrarier [1]
  You've upset your mother. Tu as contrarié ta mère.
  I was upset by it. Ça m'a contrarié.

upset *ADJECTIVE* ▸ SEE **upset** *NOUN, VERB*
  contrarié *MASC*, contrariée *FEM*
  He's upset. Il est contrarié.
  to get upset se vexer ◯ [1]
  They teased her and she got upset. Ils l'ont taquinée et elle s'est vexée.

upset *NOUN* ▸ SEE **upset** *ADJECTIVE, VERB*
  a stomach upset une indigestion

upside down *ADJECTIVE, ADVERB*
  à l'envers

upstairs *ADVERB*
  en haut
  Mum's upstairs. Maman est en haut.
  to go upstairs monter ◯ [1]
  He went upstairs to get a towel. Il est monté chercher une serviette.

up-to-date *ADJECTIVE*
1 *(clothes, equipment)* moderne *MASC & FEM*
2 *(information)* à jour
  The website's not up-to-date. Le site web n'est pas à jour.

upwards *ADVERB*
  (to look, point) vers le haut

urban *ADJECTIVE*
  urbain *MASC*, urbaine *FEM*

urgent *ADJECTIVE*
  urgent *MASC*, urgente *FEM*
  Is it urgent? C'est urgent?
  to be in urgent need of a doctor avoir [5] un besoin urgent d'un médecin

urgently *ADVERB*
  d'urgence

◯ means the verb takes être to form the perfect

She wants to see you urgently. Elle veut te voir d'urgence.

ℱ **us** PRONOUN
1 (as a direct and indirect object) **nous**
 She knows us. Elle nous connaît.
 They saw us. Ils nous ont vus.
 She hasn't spoken to us yet. Elle ne nous a pas encore parlé.
 Can you point out the post office to us? Pouvez-vous nous indiquer la poste?
 He gave us a cheque. Il nous a donné un chèque.
2 (in orders) **nous**
 Wait for us! Attendez-nous!
 Tell us the answer! Dis-nous la réponse!
 Don't tell us! Ne nous le dis pas!
3 (after prepositions like avec, sans) **nous**
 My gran lives with us. Ma grand-mère habite avec nous.
 They went off without us. Ils sont partis sans nous.
4 (in comparisons) **nous**
 They're older than us. Ils sont plus âgés que nous.
 They're luckier than us. Ils ont plus de chance que nous.

US NOUN
 les U.S.A. MASC PL

USA NOUN
 les U.S.A. MASC PL

WORD TIP Countries and regions in French take le, la or les.

ℱ to **use** VERB ▶ SEE **use** NOUN
 utiliser [1]
 We used the dictionary. Nous avons utilisé le dictionnaire.
 Use the information to fill in the gaps. Utilise les renseignements pour remplir les blancs.
 May I use the phone? Puis-je passer un coup de téléphone?
 to use something to do something se servir ◌ [71] de quelque chose pour faire quelque chose
 I used a knife to open the parcel. Je me suis servi d'un couteau pour ouvrir le paquet.
 What did they use to decorate the garden? Ils se sont servis de quoi pour décorer le jardin?
 to be used for doing something servir [71] à faire quelque chose
 It's used for cleaning the screen. Ça sert à nettoyer l'écran.
• to use something up
1 (food, shampoo, petrol) consommer [1] quelque chose

2 (money) dépenser [1] quelque chose
ℱ **use** NOUN ▶ SEE **use** VERB
1 l'**emploi** MASC
 the instructions for use le mode d'emploi
2 (pointless) It's no use. Ça ne sert à rien.
 it's no use doing ça ne sert à rien de faire
 It's no use phoning. Ça ne sert à rien de téléphoner.
 It's no use going on about it. Ça ne sert à rien d'insister.
3 to be of use servir [71]
 It might be of some use. Ça pourrait servir.

ℱ **used** ADJECTIVE
1 (car, book) d'**occasion**
 They want to buy a used car. Ils veulent acheter une voiture d'occasion.
2 to be used to something être [6] habitué à quelque chose
 She's used to life in France. Elle est habituée à la vie en France.
 I'm not used to the noise. Je ne suis pas habitué au bruit.
3 to be used to doing something avoir [5] l'habitude de faire quelque chose
 We're used to walking to school. Nous avons l'habitude d'aller à l'école à pied.
 I'm not used to eating in restaurants. Je n'ai pas l'habitude de manger au restaurant.
4 to get used to (doing) something s'habituer [1] à (faire) quelque chose
 I've got used to living here. Je me suis habitué à habiter ici.
 You'll get used to it! Tu t'y habitueras!

ℱ **used to** VERB
 She used to smoke. Elle fumait avant.
 They used to live in the country. Ils habitaient à la campagne avant.
 He used not to cycle to school. Il n'allait pas à l'école en vélo avant.

ℱ **useful** ADJECTIVE
 utile MASC & FEM
 a useful piece of information un renseignement utile
 to be useful for doing something être [6] utile pour faire quelque chose
 It's useful for storing plates. C'est utile pour ranger les assiettes.

ℱ **useless** ADJECTIVE
 nul MASC, nulle FEM
 This knife's useless. Ce couteau est nul.
 You're completely useless! Tu es complètement nul!
 I'm useless at art. Je suis nul en dessin.

user NOUN
 (of a computer, product, book) un

utilisateur *MASC*, une **utilisatrice** *FEM*
road users les usagers de la route

user-friendly *ADJECTIVE*
convivial *MASC*, **conviviale** *FEM*, **conviviaux** *MASC PL*, **conviviales** *FEM PL*

ℰ **usual** *ADJECTIVE*
habituel *MASC*, **habituelle** *FEM*
It's the usual problem. C'est le problème habituel.
as usual comme d'habitude
He was late as usual. Il était en retard comme d'habitude.
It's colder than usual. Il fait plus froid que d'habitude.

ℰ **usually** *ADVERB*
d'habitude
I usually leave at eight. D'habitude je pars à huit heures.

utensil *NOUN*
un **ustensile** *MASC*
kitchen utensils les ustensiles de cuisine

Vv

vacancy *NOUN*
1 *(in a hotel)* 'Vacancies' 'Chambres libres'
'No vacancies' 'Complet'
2 *(for employment)* **a job vacancy** un poste vacant

vacant *ADJECTIVE*
libre *MASC & FEM*

to **vaccinate** *VERB*
vacciner [1]

vaccination *NOUN*
la **vaccination** *FEM*

to **vacuum** *VERB* ▶ SEE **vacuum** *NOUN*
passer [1] l'aspirateur
to vacuum my room passer l'aspirateur dans ma chambre

vacuum *NOUN* ▶ SEE **vacuum** *VERB*
le **vide** *MASC*

vacuum cleaner *NOUN*
un **aspirateur**

vagina *NOUN*
le **vagin** *MASC*

vague *ADJECTIVE*
vague *MASC & FEM*

vaguely *ADVERB*
vaguement

vain *ADJECTIVE*
1 **vaniteux** *MASC*, **vaniteuse** *FEM*
2 **in vain** en vain
She tried in vain to wake him. Elle a essayé en vain de le réveiller.

valentine card *NOUN*
la **carte de Saint-Valentin**

Valentine's Day *NOUN*
la **Saint-Valentin** *FEM*

valid *ADJECTIVE*
valable *MASC & FEM*
This ticket's not valid at peak times. Ce billet n'est pas valable en période de pointe.

valley *NOUN*
la **vallée** *FEM*

valuable *ADJECTIVE*
1 *(jewellery, painting)* **de valeur**
some valuable jewels des bijoux de valeur
to be valuable avoir [5] de la valeur
That watch is very valuable. Cette montre a une grande valeur.
2 *(appreciated)* **précieux** *MASC*, **précieuse** *FEM*
He gave us some valuable information. Il nous a donné des renseignements précieux.

to **value** *VERB* ▶ SEE **value** *NOUN*
(some help, an opinion, friendship)
apprécier [1]

value *NOUN* ▶ SEE **value** *VERB*
la **valeur** *FEM*

van *NOUN*
1 *(small)* la **fourgonnette** *FEM*, la **camionnette** *FEM*
2 *(large)* le **fourgon** *MASC*, le **camion** *MASC*

vandal *NOUN*
le & la **vandale** *MASC & FEM*

vandalism *NOUN*
le **vandalisme** *MASC*

to **vandalize** *VERB*
vandaliser [1]

ℰ **vanilla** *NOUN*
la **vanille** *FEM*
a vanilla ice cream une glace à la vanille

to **vanish** *VERB*
disparaître [27]

variable *ADJECTIVE*
variable

variety *NOUN*
la **variété** *FEM*

ℰ **various** *ADJECTIVE*
plusieurs *MASC & FEM*
There are various ways of doing it. Il y a plusieurs façons de le faire.

⊜ means the verb takes être to form the perfect

We got letters from various people.
Nous avons reçu des lettres de plusieurs
personnes.

to **vary** VERB
varier [1]
It varies a lot. Ça varie beaucoup.
It's good to vary the tasks. Il est bien de
varier les tâches.

vase NOUN
le **vase** MASC

VAT NOUN
(= Value Added Tax) la **TVA** FEM
= Taxe à la valeur ajoutée

ᵖ **veal** NOUN
le **veau** MASC

vegan NOUN
le **végétalien** MASC, la **végétalienne** FEM

ᵖ **vegetable** NOUN
le **légume** MASC
vegetable soup la soupe aux légumes
You don't eat enough vegetables. Tu ne
manges pas assez de légumes.

ᵖ **vegetarian** NOUN, ADJECTIVE
le **végétarien** MASC, la **végétarienne** FEM
a vegetarian recipe une recette
végétarienne
He's vegetarian. Il est végétarien.

ᵖ **vehicle** NOUN
le **véhicule** MASC

vein NOUN
la **veine** FEM

velvet NOUN
le **velours** MASC

vending machine NOUN
le **distributeur automatique**

ventilated ADJECTIVE
aéré MASC, aérée FEM

ventilation NOUN
l'**aération** FEM

verb NOUN
(Grammar) le **verbe** MASC
a plural verb un verbe au pluriel

verdict NOUN
le **verdict** MASC

verge NOUN
1 (roadside) l'**accotement** MASC
2 **to be on the verge of doing something**
être [6] sur le point de faire quelque chose
I was on the verge of leaving. J'étais sur le
point de partir.

ᵖ **version** NOUN
la **version** FEM

versus PREPOSITION
contre
Arsenal versus St Étienne Arsenal contre
St Étienne

vertical ADJECTIVE
vertical MASC, verticale FEM, verticaux MASC
PL, verticales FEM PL

vertigo NOUN
le **vertige** MASC

ᵖ **very** ADVERB ▶ SEE **very** ADJECTIVE
très
a very funny film un film très drôle
You sang very well. Tu as très bien chanté.
They were driving very fast. Ils roulaient
très vite.
very much beaucoup
I'm enjoying myself very much. Je
m'amuse beaucoup.
You haven't changed very much. Tu n'as
pas beaucoup changé.
very little très peu
It costs very little. Ça coûte très peu.

very ADJECTIVE ▶ SEE **very** ADVERB
(the exact) **He found the very thing he was
looking for.** Il a trouvé exactement ce qu'il
cherchait.
The very person I need! Exactement la
personne qu'il me faut!

vest NOUN
le **maillot de corps**

vet NOUN
le & la **vétérinaire** MASC & FEM
She's a vet. Elle est vétérinaire.

via PREPOSITION
to go via somewhere passer [1] par
quelque part
We went via Dover. Nous sommes passés
par Douvres.

vicar NOUN
le **pasteur** MASC

vicious ADJECTIVE
1 (dog) méchant MASC, méchante FEM
The dog turned vicious. Le chien est
devenu méchant.
2 (attack) brutal MASC, brutale FEM, brutaux
MASC PL, brutales FEM PL

victim NOUN
la **victime** FEM

victory NOUN
la **victoire** FEM
a resounding victory une victoire écrasante

ρ to **video** VERB ▶ SEE **video** NOUN
(a programme, a film) enregistrer [1]

ρ **video** NOUN ▶ SEE **video** VERB
1 *(recorded video)* la **vidéo** FEM
We were watching a video. On regardait une vidéo.
I've got it on video. Je l'ai en vidéo.
2 *(video recorder)* le **magnétoscope** MASC
• **video game**
le **jeu vidéo** (PL les **jeux vidéo**)

ρ **view** NOUN
1 *(from a room)* la **vue** FEM
a room with a view of the lake une chambre avec vue sur le lac
You're blocking my view. Tu me bouches la vue.
I climbed to the top to get a better view. Je suis monté jusqu'en haut pour mieux voir.
2 *(opinion)* un **avis** MASC
in my view à mon avis
In your view, what does it mean? À ton avis, qu'est-ce que cela signifie?
from my point of view de mon point de vue

ρ **viewer** NOUN
(TV) le **téléspectateur** MASC, la **téléspectatrice** FEM
Several viewers complained. Plusieurs téléspectateurs se sont plaints.

viewpoint NOUN
le **point de vue**
other viewpoints d'autres points de vue

vigorous ADJECTIVE
vigoureux MASC, **vigoureuse** FEM

vile ADJECTIVE
abominable MASC & FEM
The food was vile. La nourriture était abominable.

villa NOUN
la **villa** FEM

ρ **village** NOUN
le **village** MASC
a fishing village un village de pêcheurs

villager NOUN
le **villageois** MASC, la **villageoise** FEM

vine NOUN
la **vigne** FEM

ρ **vinegar** NOUN
le **vinaigre** MASC

vineyard NOUN
le **vignoble** MASC

violence NOUN
la **violence** FEM

ρ **violent** ADJECTIVE
violent MASC, **violente** FEM
a violent storm une tempête violente
I don't like violent films. Je n'aime pas les films violents.

violin NOUN
le **violon** MASC
to play the violin jouer [1] du violon
Jo plays the violin. Jo joue du violon.

violinist NOUN
le & la **violoniste** MASC & FEM

virgin NOUN
la **vierge** FEM

Virgo NOUN
Vierge
Sophie's Virgo. Sophie est Vierge.

WORD TIP Signs of the zodiac do not take an article: un or une.

virtually ADVERB
pratiquement
Virtually everyone was there.
Pratiquement tout le monde était là.

virtual reality NOUN
la **réalité virtuelle**

virus NOUN
le **virus** MASC
I got a nasty virus. J'ai attrapé un sale virus.
anti-virus software un logiciel antivirus

visa NOUN
le **visa** MASC

visibility NOUN
la **visibilité** FEM
Visibility was poor. La visibilité était mauvaise.

visible ADJECTIVE
visible MASC & FEM

ρ to **visit** VERB ▶ SEE **visit** NOUN
1 *(a museum, a castle, a town)* visiter [1]
We visited the Louvre. On a visité le Musée du Louvre.
2 *(a person)* aller ⊙ [7] voir
We visited Auntie Pat at Christmas. Nous sommes allés voir tante Pat à Noël.
Come and visit us! Viens nous voir!
We're just visiting. Nous sommes seulement de passage.

ρ **visit** NOUN ▶ SEE **visit** VERB
1 *(by a friend, family, a VIP)* la **visite** FEM
an official visit une visite officielle
I really enjoyed your visit. Ta visite m'a fait vraiment plaisir.
2 *(to a house, museum, site)* la **visite** FEM
They organized a visit to the castle. On a

⊙ means the verb takes être to form the perfect

organisé une visite du château.
3 *(stay)* le **séjour** *MASC*
my last visit to France mon dernier séjour
en France

visitor *NOUN*
1 *(guest)* un **invité** *MASC*, une **invitée** *FEM*
We've got visitors tonight. On a des invités
ce soir.
2 *(tourist)* le **visiteur** *MASC*, la **visiteuse** *FEM*
It's a guide for visitors. C'est un guide pour
les visiteurs.

visual *ADJECTIVE*
visuel *MASC*, **visuelle** *FEM*

to **visualize** *VERB*
(a scene, a person) **s'imaginer** [1]
Try to visualize the scene. Essaie de
t'imaginer la scène.

vital *ADJECTIVE*
indispensable *MASC & FEM*
it's vital to do something il est
indispensable de faire quelque chose
It's vital to book. Il est indispensable de
réserver.

vitamin *NOUN*
la **vitamine** *FEM*

vivid *ADJECTIVE*
(colours) **vif** *MASC*, **vive** *FEM*
a poster in vivid colours une affiche aux
couleurs vives
to have a vivid imagination exagérer [1]
He has a slightly vivid imagination. Il
exagère un peu.

vocabulary *NOUN*
le **vocabulaire** *MASC*

vocational *ADJECTIVE*
professionnel *MASC*, **professionnelle** *FEM*
• **vocational education**
la formation professionnelle

vodka *NOUN*
le **vodka** *MASC*

ℓ **voice** *NOUN*
la **voix** *FEM*
Keep your voice down! Baisse ta voix!
Jasmine has a great voice. Jasmine a une
belle voix.
His voice is breaking. Sa voix mue.

voicemail *NOUN*
la **messagerie vocale** *FEM*

volcano *NOUN*
le **volcan** *MASC*

volleyball *NOUN*
le **volley-ball** *MASC*
to play volleyball jouer [1] au volley-ball

volume *NOUN*
le **volume** *MASC*
Could you turn down the volume? Est-ce
que tu peux baisser le volume?

voluntary *ADJECTIVE*
1 *(not compulsory)* **volontaire** *MASC & FEM*
2 **to do voluntary work** travailler [1]
bénévolement
I do voluntary work once a week. Je
travaille bénévolement une fois par
semaine.

volunteer *NOUN*
1 *(for a task)* le & la **volontaire** *MASC & FEM*
2 *(doing charity work)* le & la **bénévole** *MASC
& FEM*

ℓ to **vomit** *VERB*
vomir [2]

ℓ to **vote** *VERB* ▶ SEE **vote** *NOUN*
voter [1]
Marie always votes Green. Marie vote
toujours pour les Verts.
They voted against the changes. Ils ont
voté contre les changements.

ℓ **vote** *NOUN* ▶ SEE **vote** *VERB*
le **vote** *MASC*
She got 20 votes. Elle a obtenu 20 votes.

voucher *NOUN*
1 *(for a discount, special offer)* le **bon** *MASC*
2 *(for a gift)* le **chèque-cadeau**

vowel *NOUN*
(Grammar) la **voyelle** *FEM* *(the letters: a, e,
i, o, u)*

voyage *NOUN*
le **voyage** *MASC*
a voyage across the Atlantic un voyage à
travers l'Atlantique

vulgar *ADJECTIVE*
vulgaire *MASC & FEM*

Ww

waffle *NOUN*
la **gaufre** *FEM*

to **wag** *VERB*
remuer [1]

wage *NOUN*
le **salaire** *MASC*
a weekly wage of £250 un salaire
hebdomadaire de 250 livres

ℓ **waist** *NOUN*
la **taille** *FEM*

...surement
...e taille

... VERB ▸ SEE **wait** NOUN
...ndre [3]
...ey're waiting outside. Ils attendent
dehors.
I've been waiting for an hour. J'attends
depuis une heure.

2 to wait for somebody, something attendre
[3] quelqu'un, quelque chose
He's waiting for you. Il t'attend.
We're waiting for the train. Nous
attendons le train.

3 to keep somebody waiting faire [10]
attendre quelqu'un
The dentist kept me waiting. La dentiste
m'a fait attendre.

4 (showing impatience) I can't wait for the
holidays. J'attends les vacances avec
impatience.

wait NOUN ▸ SEE **wait** VERB
une **attente** FEM
an hour's wait une heure d'attente

ℓ **waiter** NOUN
le **serveur** MASC

waiting list NOUN
la **liste d'attente**

ℓ **waiting room** NOUN
la **salle d'attente**

ℓ **waitress** NOUN
la **serveuse** FEM

ℓ to **wake** VERB
1 (somebody) réveiller [1]
Jess woke me at six. Jess m'a réveillé à six
heures.

2 (to wake up) se réveiller ⊙ [1]
We woke at six. Nous nous sommes
réveillés à six heures.
Wake up! Réveille-toi!

ℓ **Wales** NOUN
le **pays de Galles**
in Wales au pays de Galles
to Wales au pays de Galles
We go to Wales every summer. On va au
pays de Galles tous les étés.

WORD TIP Countries and regions in French take
le, la or les.

ℓ to **walk** VERB ▸ SEE **walk** NOUN
1 (in general) marcher [1]
I like walking on sand. J'aime marcher sur
le sable.

2 (to go for a walk) se promener ⊙ [50]

We walked around the old town. Nous
nous sommes promenés dans la vieille ville.

3 (to go) aller ⊙ [7]
I'll walk to the station with you. J'irai avec
toi jusqu'à la gare.

4 (to go on foot) aller ⊙ [7] à pied
We can walk there easily. On peut y aller à
pied sans problème.

ℓ **walk** NOUN ▸ SEE **walk** VERB
1 la **promenade** FEM
It's five minutes' walk from here. C'est à
cinq minutes à pied d'ici.
I'm going to take the dog for a walk. Je
vais promener le chien.
to go for a walk faire [10] une promenade,
se promener ⊙ [50]
We went for a walk in the woods. Nous
avons fait une promenade dans la forêt.
They've just been for a walk. Ils sont sortis
se promener.

2 (stroll) le **tour** MASC

walking NOUN
(hiking) la **randonnée** FEM
We're going walking in Scotland. Nous
allons faire de la randonnée en Écosse.

walking distance NOUN
to be within walking distance être [6] à
quelques minutes à pied

walking stick NOUN
la **canne** FEM

ℓ **wall** NOUN
1 (of a house) le **mur** MASC
2 (of a city) la **muraille** FEM

ℓ **wallet** NOUN
le **portefeuille** MASC

wallpaper NOUN
le **papier peint**

walnut NOUN
la **noix** FEM (PL les **noix**)

to **wander** VERB
to wander around a place se balader ⊙ [1]
quelque part
We wandered around the town. On s'est
baladé en ville.

ℓ to **want** VERB
vouloir [14]
I want a watch for Christmas. Je veux une
montre pour Noël.
Do you want some coffee? Tu veux du café?
Who wants some ice cream? Qui veut de
la glace?
to want to do something vouloir faire
quelque chose

⊙ means the verb takes être to form the perfect

I want to go for a swim. Je veux aller me baigner.
What do you want to do? Qu'est-ce que tu veux faire?

war NOUN
la **guerre** FEM

ℓ **wardrobe** NOUN
1 (cupboard) une **armoire** FEM
2 (clothes) la **garde-robe** FEM

warehouse NOUN
un **entrepôt** MASC

ℓ to **warm** VERB ▸ SEE **warm** ADJECTIVE
(the plates, water) **chauffer** [1]
Warm the plates. Chauffez les assiettes.
• to **warm up**
1 (after feeling cold) se **réchauffer** ☁ [1]
2 (food) **réchauffer** [1]
3 (athletes) s'**échauffer** [1]

ℓ **warm** ADJECTIVE ▸ SEE **warm** VERB
1 (food, drink) **chaud** MASC, **chaude** FEM
a warm drink une boisson chaude
to keep something warm tenir [77] quelque chose au chaud
I'll keep your dinner warm. Je tiendrai ton dîner au chaud.
2 (weather, places) **to be warm** faire [10] chaud
It was warmer yesterday. Il faisait plus chaud hier.
It's warm in the kitchen. Il fait chaud dans la cuisine.
3 **to be warm** avoir [5] chaud
I'm warm. J'ai chaud.
4 (welcome) **chaleureux** MASC, **chaleureuse** FEM

warmth NOUN
la **chaleur** FEM

to **warn** VERB
1 (to inform) **prévenir** [81]
I'm warning you, don't do it. Je te préviens, ne le fais pas.
2 **to warn somebody not to do something** **conseiller** [1] à quelqu'un de ne pas faire quelque chose
Ruth warned me not to go. Ruth m'a conseillé de ne pas y aller.

warning NOUN
un **avertissement** MASC

wart NOUN
la **verrue** FEM

ℓ to **wash** VERB ▸ SEE **wash** NOUN
1 (clothes, car, floor) **laver** [4]
I've washed your jeans. J'ai lavé ton jean.
2 (yourself) se **laver** ☁ [4]

to wash your hands se laver les mains
I've washed my hands. Je me suis lavé les mains.
She's washing her hair. Elle se lave les cheveux.
3 **to wash the dishes** faire [10] la vaisselle
• **to wash up**
faire [10] la vaisselle

wash NOUN ▸ SEE **wash** VERB
1 **to give something a wash** laver [4] quelque chose
My jeans need a wash. Mon jean a besoin d'être lavé.
2 **to have a wash** se laver ☁ [4]

ℓ **washing** NOUN
1 (dirty) le **linge sale**
2 (clean) le **linge** MASC
• **washing machine**
la machine à laver
• **washing powder**
la lessive

ℓ **washing-up** NOUN
la **vaisselle** FEM
Are you going to do the washing-up? Tu vas faire la vaisselle?
• **washing-up liquid**
le liquide à vaisselle

wasp NOUN
la **guêpe** FEM

ℓ to **waste** VERB ▸ SEE **waste** NOUN
1 (food, money, paper) **gaspiller** [1]
2 (time) **perdre** [3]
You're wasting your time. Tu perds ton temps.

waste NOUN ▸ SEE **waste** VERB
1 (of food, money) le **gaspillage** MASC
It's a waste of money. C'est de l'argent gaspillé.
2 (of time) la **perte** FEM
a waste of time une perte de temps
3 (household, industrial) les **déchets** MASC PL
• **wastepaper basket**
la corbeille à papier

ℓ to **watch** VERB ▸ SEE **watch** NOUN
1 (to look at) **regarder** [1]
I like watching TV. J'aime regarder la télé.
2 (to keep a check on) **surveiller** [1]
You have to watch him. Il faut le surveiller.
3 (to be careful) **faire** [10] attention
Watch that step. Fais attention à cette marche.
Watch out! Attention!

ℓ **watch** NOUN ▸ SEE **watch** VERB
la **montre** FEM
My watch is fast. Ma montre avance.
My watch is slow. Ma montre retarde.

ℓ **indicates key words**

to water VERB ▶ SEE **water** NOUN
  (the plants) **arroser** [1]

♪ **water** NOUN ▶ SEE **water** VERB
  l'eau FEM
  a glass of water un verre d'eau

watercolours NOUN
  la **peinture pour aquarelle**

waterfall NOUN
  la **cascade** FEM

watering can NOUN
  un **arrosoir** MASC

watermelon NOUN
  la **pastèque** FEM

waterproof ADJECTIVE
  imperméable MASC & FEM

♪ **water-skiing** NOUN
  le **ski nautique**
  to go water-skiing faire [10] du ski
  nautique

to wave VERB ▶ SEE **wave** NOUN
1 (with your hand) **saluer** [1] de la main
  to wave at somebody saluer quelqu'un de
  la main
  They're waving at us. Ils nous saluent de
  la main.
2 (a flag, newspaper) **agiter** [1]

wave NOUN ▶ SEE **wave** VERB
1 (in the sea) la **vague** FEM
2 (with your hand) le **signe** MASC
  to give somebody a wave faire [10] signe à
  quelqu'un

wavy ADJECTIVE
  (hair) **ondulé** MASC, **ondulée** FEM

wax NOUN
  la **cire** FEM

♪ **way** NOUN
1 (route, road) le **chemin** MASC
  the way to town le chemin pour aller en
  ville
  We met Chris on the way. Nous avons
  rencontré Chris en route.
  I got a puncture on the way back. J'ai eu un
  pneu crevé sur le chemin de retour.
  I'm on my way. J'arrive. ▶ SEE **way in** ▶ SEE
  way out
2 (direction) la **direction** FEM
  Which way did they go? En quelle direction
  sont-ils partis?
  They went that way. Ils sont partis par là.
  Come this way. Venez par ici.
3 (manner) la **façon** FEM
  a way of speaking une façon de parler
  Is that the way to do it? Est-ce qu'on le fait
  comme ça?

  Do it this way. Fais-le comme ceci.
4 (in expressions) **Is it the right way up?** C'est
  à l'endroit?
  It's the wrong way round. C'est à l'envers.
  It's a long way. C'est loin.
  No way! Pas question!
  by the way à propos
• **way in**
  une **entrée**
• **way out**
  la **sortie**

♪ **we** PRONOUN
1 (as subject) **nous**
  We live in Cardiff. Nous habitons Cardiff.
  We're students. Nous sommes étudiants.
2 (informally) **on**
  We're going to the cinema tonight. On va
  au cinéma ce soir.

♪ **weak** ADJECTIVE
1 (not strong) **faible** MASC & FEM
  I feel weak. Je me sens faible.
2 (tea, coffee) **léger** MASC, **légère** FEM
  a cup of weak tea une tasse de thé léger

wealth NOUN
  la **fortune** FEM

wealthy ADJECTIVE
  riche MASC & FEM

weapon NOUN
  une **arme** FEM

♪ **to wear** VERB
1 (clothes, shoes, etc) **porter** [1]
  Tanya's wearing her new boots. Tanya
  porte ses nouvelles bottes.
2 (perfume, sun cream, jewellery) **mettre** [11]
  Are you wearing perfume? Est-ce que tu as
  mis du parfum?
  to wear make-up se maquiller ◎ [1]
• **to wear something out**
  (clothes, shoes) **user** [1] quelque chose

♪ **weather** NOUN
  le **temps** MASC
  What's the weather like? Quel temps
  fait-il?
  The weather here is terrible. Il fait un
  temps affreux ici.
  in fine weather quand il fait beau
  The weather was cold. Il faisait froid.

♪ **weather forecast** NOUN
  la **météo** FEM
  according to the weather forecast ... selon
  la météo ...

web NOUN
1 (spider's) la **toile** FEM
2 **the Web** le Web MASC

◎ means the verb takes être to form the perfect

- **webcam**
  le webcam
- **web designer**
  le concepteur de sites web, la conceptrice de sites web
- **website**
  le site web

> 🌐 **WEB**
>
> Lots of expressions linked to the Internet (Internet or le Net) are based on English: surfer le Net, un site web, un email, etc. When giving your email address, @ = arobase, dot = point.

ℓ **wedding** NOUN
le **mariage** MASC

ℓ **Wednesday** NOUN
le **mercredi** MASC
on Wednesday mercredi
last Wednesday mercredi dernier
next Wednesday mercredi prochain
every Wednesday tous les mercredis
on Wednesdays le mercredi
See you on Wednesday! À mercredi!
I saw Mike last Wednesday. J'ai vu Mike mercredi dernier.

> **WORD TIP** Months of the year and days of the week start with small letters in French.

weed NOUN
la **mauvaise herbe**

ℓ **week** NOUN
la **semaine** FEM
this week cette semaine
She came back last week. Elle est rentrée la semaine dernière.
I'm on holiday next week. Je pars en vacances la semaine prochaine.
I'll see you in two weeks' time. Je te vois dans deux semaines.

weekday NOUN
le **jour de semaine**
on weekdays en semaine

ℓ **weekend** NOUN
le **week-end**
last weekend le week-end dernier
next weekend le week-end prochain
at weekends les week-end
They're coming for the weekend. Ils vont passer le week-end chez nous.
I'll do it at the weekend. Je le ferai pendant le week-end.
Have a nice weekend! Bon week-end!

weekly ADVERB
une **fois par semaine**

ℓ to **weigh** VERB
1 (a suitcase, a person, ingredients) **peser** [50]

I weigh fifty kilos. Je pèse cinquante kilos.
How much do you weigh? Tu pèses combien?
2 **to weigh yourself** se peser ◉ [1]

ℓ **weight** NOUN
le **poids** MASC
to put on weight prendre [64] du poids
She's put on weight. Elle a pris du poids.
to lose weight perdre [3] du poids
Have you lost weight? Est-ce que tu as perdu du poids?
- **weightlifting**
  l'**haltérophilie** FEM
- **weight training**
  la **musculation**

weird ADJECTIVE
bizarre MASC & FEM

to **welcome** VERB ▶ SEE **welcome** ADJECTIVE, NOUN
accueillir [35]

ℓ **welcome** ADJECTIVE ▶ SEE **welcome** NOUN, VERB
bienvenu MASC, **bienvenue** FEM
'Thank you!' — **'You're welcome!'** 'Merci!' — 'De rien!'
Welcome to Chester! Bienvenue à Chester!

ℓ **welcome** NOUN ▶ SEE **welcome** ADJECTIVE, VERB
un **accueil** MASC
a warm welcome un accueil chaleureux

ℓ **well** ADVERB ▶ SEE **well** NOUN
1 (in general) **bien**
Henry played well. Henry a bien joué.
The operation went well. L'opération s'est bien passée.
Well done! Bravo!
2 (to say how you feel) **to feel well** se sentir ◉ [2] bien
I don't feel well. Je ne me sens pas bien.
I'm very well, thank you. Ça va très bien, merci.
3 **as well** aussi
Katie's coming as well. Katie vient aussi.
4 (to start talking) **alors**
Well, what's the problem? Alors, quel est le problème?
5 (to say you agree) **very well** très bien
Very well then, you can go. Très bien, tu peux y aller.
6 (when hesitating) (informal) **ben**
Well ... I'm not sure. Ben ... je ne suis pas sûr.

ℓ **well-behaved** ADJECTIVE
sage MASC & FEM

ℓ **well-done** ADJECTIVE
(steak) **bien cuit** MASC, **bien cuite** FEM

ℱ **well-dressed** ADJECTIVE
  bien habillé MASC, bien habillée FEM

wellington boot NOUN
  la botte en caoutchouc

well-known ADJECTIVE
  célèbre MASC & FEM

ℱ **well-off** ADJECTIVE
  aisé MASC, aisée FEM

well-paid ADJECTIVE
  bien payé MASC, bien payée FEM

ℱ **Welsh** ADJECTIVE ▶ SEE **Welsh** NOUN
1 gallois MASC, galloise FEM
  David is Welsh. David est gallois.
  Rhiannon is Welsh. Rhiannon est galloise.
2 (music, accent) gallois MASC, galloise FEM
  the Welsh team l'équipe galloise

  WORD TIP Adjectives never have capitals in
  French, even for nationality or regional origin.

ℱ **Welsh** NOUN ▶ SEE **Welsh** ADJECTIVE
1 (people) the Welsh les Gallois MASC PL
2 (language) le gallois MASC
  to speak Welsh parler [1] gallois
  to learn Welsh apprendre [64] le gallois

  WORD TIP Languages never have capitals in
  French.

ℱ **west** ADJECTIVE, ADVERB ▶ SEE **west** NOUN
  ouest INVARIABLE ADJECTIVE
  the west side of the city le côté ouest de
  la ville
  a west wind un vent d'ouest
  a town west of Paris une ville à l'ouest de
  Paris
  We're going west. Nous allons vers l'ouest.

  WORD TIP ouest never changes.

ℱ **west** NOUN ▶ SEE **west** ADJECTIVE, ADVERB
  l'ouest MASC
  in the west à l'ouest
  in the west of Ireland dans l'ouest de
  l'Irlande

ℱ **western** NOUN
  (film) le western MASC

West Indian ADJECTIVE ▶ SEE **West Indian** NOUN
  antillais MASC, antillaise FEM

West Indian NOUN ▶ SEE **West Indian** ADJECTIVE
  un Antillais MASC, une Antillaise FEM

West Indies PLURAL NOUN
  les Antilles FEM PL

ℱ **wet** ADJECTIVE
1 (damp) mouillé MASC, mouillée FEM
  The grass is wet. L'herbe est mouillée.
  My hair's wet. J'ai les cheveux mouillés.

to get wet se faire ☻ [10] mouiller
  We got wet. Nous nous sommes fait
  mouiller.
2 (weather) a wet day un jour de pluie
  in wet weather quand il pleut
3 (paint) frais MASC, fraîche FEM
• **wet suit**
  la combinaison de plongée

whale NOUN
  la baleine FEM

ℱ **what** DETERMINER, PRONOUN
1 (in questions: as object) qu'est-ce que, qu'
  (before a, e, i, o, u or silent h)
  What's she doing? Qu'est-ce qu'elle fait?
  What did you say? Qu'est-ce que tu as dit?
  What is it? Qu'est-ce que c'est?
  What's the matter? Qu'est-ce qu'il y a?
2 (in questions: as subject) qu'est-ce qui
  What's happening? Qu'est-ce qui se passe?
  What scared Joe? Qu'est-ce qui a fait peur
  à Joe?
3 (as object relative pronoun) ce que, qu'
  (before a, e, i, o, u or silent h)
  Show me what you bought. Montre-moi ce
  que tu as acheté.
  I'll tell him what we've done. Je vais lui dire
  ce qu'on a fait.
4 (as subject relative pronoun) ce qui
  She told me what had happened. Elle m'a
  dit ce qui était arrivé.
5 (with nouns in questions) quel MASC, quelle
  FEM
  What's your address? Quelle est ton
  adresse?
  What colour is it? C'est de quelle couleur?
  What make is it? C'est quelle marque?
6 (in exclamations) quel MASC, quelle FEM
  What a bore! Quelle barbe!
  What a strange idea! Quelle idée bizarre!
7 (when you don't hear, etc) What?
  Comment?

wheat NOUN
  le blé MASC

wheel NOUN
  la roue FEM
• **wheelchair**
  le fauteuil roulant

ℱ **when** ADVERB, CONJUNCTION
  quand
  When's your birthday? C'est quand, ton
  anniversaire?
  When is she arriving? Quand est-ce qu'elle
  arrive?
  It was raining when I went out. Il pleuvait
  quand je suis sorti.

☻ **means the verb takes être to form the perfect**

ℓ **where** *ADVERB, CONJUNCTION*
   où
   Where do you live? Tu habites où?
   Where are you going? Où vas-tu?
   I don't know where they live. Je ne sais pas où ils habitent.

whether *CONJUNCTION*
   si
   I don't know whether he's back or not. Je ne sais pas s'il est rentré ou non.

ℓ **which** *DETERMINER* ▸ SEE **which** *PRONOUN*
   quel *MASC*, **quelle** *FEM*
   Which lipstick did you buy? Quel rouge à lèvres as-tu acheté?
   Which jacket do you prefer? Quelle veste préfères-tu?

ℓ **which** *PRONOUN* ▸ SEE **which** *DETERMINER*
  1 *(which one)* **lequel** *MASC*, **laquelle** *FEM*
   'I saw your brother.' — 'Which one?' 'J'ai vu ton frère.' — 'Lequel?'
   'I saw your aunt.' — 'Which one?' 'J'ai vu ta tante.' — 'Laquelle?'
   Which of these jackets is yours? Laquelle de ces vestes est à toi?
  2 *(which ones)* **lesquels** *MASC PL*, **lesquelles** *FEM PL*
   'I borrowed some bowls.' — 'Which ones?' 'J'ai emprunté des bols.' — 'Lesquels?'
  3 *(as subject relative pronoun)* **qui**
   the lamp which is on the table la lampe qui est sur la table
  4 *(as object relative pronoun)* **que**, **qu'** *(before a, e, i, o, u or silent h)*
   the book which you borrowed from me le livre que tu m'as emprunté
   the books which you borrowed from me les livres que tu m'as empruntés

ℓ **while** *CONJUNCTION* ▸ SEE **while** *NOUN*
   pendant que
   You can watch TV while I finish my homework. Tu peux regarder la télé pendant que je finis mes devoirs.

ℓ **while** *NOUN* ▸ SEE **while** *CONJUNCTION*
   a while quelque temps
   a while ago il y a quelque temps.
   for a while pendant quelque temps
   in a little while dans peu de temps

to **whip** *VERB*
   fouetter [1]
   whipped cream la crème fouettée

whiskers *PLURAL NOUN*
   les **moustaches** *FEM PL*

whisky *NOUN*
   le **whisky** *MASC*

to **whisper** *VERB*
   chuchoter [1]

to **whistle** *VERB* ▸ SEE **whistle** *NOUN*
   siffler [1]

whistle *NOUN* ▸ SEE **whistle** *VERB*
   le **sifflet** *MASC*

ℓ **white** *NOUN* ▸ SEE **white** *ADJECTIVE*
   le **blanc** *MASC*

ℓ **white** *ADJECTIVE* ▸ SEE **white** *NOUN*
   blanc *MASC*, **blanche** *FEM*
   a white shirt une chemise blanche
   white wine le vin blanc
  • **whiteboard**
   le tableau blanc
  • **white coffee**
   le café au lait
  • **white-water rafting**
   le rafting en eau vive

ℓ **who** *PRONOUN*
  1 *(in questions)* **qui**
   Who is it? Qui est-ce?
   Who wants some chocolate? Qui veut du chocolat?
  2 *(as subject relative pronoun)* **qui**
   My friend who lives in Paris. Mon ami qui habite à Paris.
  3 *(as object relative pronoun)* **que**, **qu'** *(before a, e, i, o, u or silent h)*
   the friends who we invited les amis que nous avons invités, les amis qu'on a invités

ℓ **whole** *ADJECTIVE* ▸ SEE **whole** *NOUN*
   tout *MASC*, **toute** *FEM*
   the whole time tout le temps
   the whole family toute la famille
   the whole world le monde entier

whole *NOUN* ▸ SEE **whole** *ADJECTIVE*
   the whole of the cake le gâteau tout entier
   the whole of the class la classe tout entière
   for the whole of August pendant tout le mois d'août

ℓ **wholemeal bread** *NOUN*
   le **pain complet** *MASC*

whom *PRONOUN*
  1 **que**, **qu'** *(before a, e, i, o, u or silent h)*
   the person whom I saw la personne que j'ai vue
  2 *(after a preposition)* **qui**
   the person to whom I wrote la personne à qui j'ai écrit

whose *DETERMINER, PRONOUN*
  1 *(in questions)* **à qui**
   Whose is this jacket? À qui est cette veste?
   Whose shoes are these? À qui sont ces chaussures?
   Whose is it? À qui c'est?

ℓ *indicates key words*

I know whose it is. Je sais à qui c'est.
2 *(relative pronoun)* **dont**
the man whose car has been stolen le
monsieur dont la voiture a été volée
the ladies whose names I've forgotten les
dames dont j'ai oublié le nom

ℐ **why** ADVERB
pourquoi
Why are they always late? Pourquoi est-ce
qu'ils sont toujours en retard?
Why did she phone? Pourquoi a-t-elle
appelé?

wicked ADJECTIVE
1 *(witch, etc)* **méchant** MASC, **méchante** FEM
2 *(very good)* **génial** MASC, **géniale** FEM,
géniaux MASC PL, **géniales** FEM PL
(informal) **Wicked!** Génial!

ℐ **wide** ADJECTIVE ▸ SEE **wide** ADVERB
1 **large** MASC & FEM
a piece of paper 20 cm wide une feuille de
papier de vingt centimètres de large
The river is very wide. La rivière est très
large.
2 *(ocean, choice)* **vaste** MASC & FEM
a wide range of games une vaste gamme
de jeux

ℐ **wide** ADVERB ▸ SEE **wide** ADJECTIVE
1 **to be wide open** être [6] grand ouvert
2 **to be wide awake** être [6] complètement
éveillé

ℐ **widow** NOUN
la **veuve** FEM
She's a widow. Elle est veuve.

ℐ **widower** NOUN
le **veuf** MASC
He's a widower. Il est veuf.

width NOUN
la **largeur** FEM

ℐ **wife** NOUN
la **femme** FEM

wig NOUN
la **perruque** FEM

wild ADJECTIVE
1 *(animal, plant, landscape)* **sauvage** MASC
& FEM
2 *(idea, party, person)* **fou** MASC, **folle** FEM
**The crowd went wild when she came on
stage.** Le public s'est déchaînée quand elle
est entrée en scène.

wildlife NOUN
la **faune** FEM

will VERB
1 *(talking about the future)* **He will be glad to**

see you. Il sera content de te voir.
There won't be a problem. Il n'y aura pas
de problème.
I'll see you soon. Je te reverrai bientôt.
It won't rain. Il ne pleuvra pas.
2 *(talking about the immediate future)* **I'll
phone the doctor at once.** Je vais appeler le
docteur tout de suite.
What will you do? Qu'est-ce que tu vas
faire?
3 *(to make requests)* **Will you help me?** Est-ce
que tu peux m'aider?
4 *(to say somebody won't do something)*
He won't open the door. Il ne veut pas
ouvrir la porte.
She won't speak to me. Elle ne veut pas
me parler.

willing ADJECTIVE
to be willing to do something être [6] prêt
à faire quelque chose

willpower NOUN
la **volonté** FEM

ℐ **to win** VERB ▸ SEE **win** NOUN
gagner [1]
I won! J'ai gagné!
Rovers won by two goals. Rovers ont
gagné de deux buts.

to wind VERB ▸ SEE **wind** NOUN
1 *(a rope, a tape)* **enrouler** [1]
2 *(a clock)* **remonter** [1]
• **to wind something down**
(a car window) **baisser** [1]
• **to wind something up**
(a car window) **remonter** [1]

ℐ **wind** NOUN ▸ SEE **wind** VERB
le **vent** MASC

wind farm NOUN
la **ferme d'éoliennes**

ℐ **window** NOUN
1 *(in a building)* la **fenêtre** FEM
I was looking out of the window. Je
regardais par la fenêtre.
2 *(in a car, bus, train)* la **vitre** FEM

ℐ **windscreen** NOUN
le **pare-brise** MASC (PL les **pare-brise**)
• **windscreen wiper**
un **essuie-glace**

ℐ **windsurfing** NOUN
la **planche à voile**
We went windsurfing. Nous avons fait de
la planche à voile.

windy ADJECTIVE
1 **to be windy** avoir [5] du vent
It's windy today. Il y a du vent aujourd'hui.

⬤ **means the verb takes être to form the perfect**

2 *(place)* **venteux** *MASC*, **venteuse** *FEM*

_ℰ_**wine** *NOUN*
le **vin** *MASC*

wing *NOUN*
1 *(of a bird, plane)* une **aile** *FEM*
2 *(in sport)* un **ailier** *MASC*

winner *NOUN*
le **gagnant** *MASC*, la **gagnante** *FEM*

_ℰ_**winter** *NOUN*
l'**hiver** *MASC*
in winter en hiver
next winter l'hiver prochain
last winter l'hiver dernier
• **winter sports**
les sports d'hiver *MASC PL*

_ℰ_to **wipe** *VERB*
essuyer [41]
I'll wipe the table. Je vais essuyer la table.
to wipe your eyes s'essuyer [41] les yeux
to wipe your feet s'essuyer les pieds

wire *NOUN*
le **fil** *MASC*

wisdom *NOUN*
la **sagesse**
• **wisdom tooth**
la dent de sagesse

_ℰ_**wise** *ADJECTIVE*
sage *MASC & FEM*

to **wish** *VERB* ▸ SEE **wish** *NOUN*
si seulement …
I wish he were here. Si seulement il était
ici.
We wish we could go. Si seulement on
pouvait y aller.

wish *NOUN* ▸ SEE **wish** *VERB*
le **vœu** *MASC* (*PL* les **vœux**)
to make a wish faire [10] un vœu
Best wishes Meilleurs vœux

witch *NOUN*
la **sorcière** *FEM*

_ℰ_**with** *PREPOSITION*
1 *(in general)* **avec**
with James avec James
with me avec moi
I bought it with my pocket money. Je l'ai
acheté avec mon argent de poche.
Beat the eggs with a fork. Battez les œufs
avec une fourchette.
2 *(in descriptions)* **au, aux**
a girl with red hair une fille aux cheveux
roux
the boy with glasses le garçon aux lunettes
3 *(because of)* **de**
filled with water rempli d'eau

covered with mud couvert de boue

_ℰ_**without** *PREPOSITION*
sans
without Charlotte sans Charlotte
without you sans toi
without sugar sans sucre
without a sweater sans pull

witness *NOUN*
le **témoin** *MASC*

wizard *NOUN*
le **magicien** *MASC*

wolf *NOUN*
le **loup** *MASC*

_ℰ_**woman** *NOUN*
la **femme** *FEM*
a woman doctor une femme médecin

to **wonder** *VERB* ▸ SEE **wonder** *NOUN*
se demander ◌ [1]
I wonder why. Je me demande pourquoi.
I wonder where Jake is. Je me demande où
est Jake.

wonder *NOUN* ▸ SEE **wonder** *VERB*
la **merveille** *FEM*
No wonder you're tired. Ce n'est pas
étonnant si tu es fatigué.

wonderful *ADJECTIVE*
merveilleux *MASC*, **merveilleuse** *FEM*
a wonderful holiday des vacances
merveilleuses

_ℰ_**wood** *NOUN*
le **bois** *MASC*

wooden *ADJECTIVE*
en bois

_ℰ_**wool** *NOUN*
la **laine** *FEM*

woollen *ADJECTIVE*
en laine

_ℰ_**word** *NOUN*
1 le **mot** *MASC*
What's the French word for 'window'?
Comment dit-on 'window' en français?
Mum had a word with my teacher. Ma
mère a parlé avec mon prof.
2 *(of a song)* **the words** les paroles *FEM PL*
I've forgotten the words. J'ai oublié les
paroles.
• **word game**
le jeu de lettres

_ℰ_to **work** *VERB* ▸ SEE **work** *NOUN*
1 travailler [1]
She works in an office. Elle travaille dans
un bureau.
Leila works in advertising. Leila travaille

dans la publicité.
She works as a librarian. Elle travaille comme bibliothécaire.
2 *(to operate)* **se servir** ⓢ [71] **de**
Can you work the video? Est-ce que tu sais te servir du magnétoscope?
3 *(to function)* **marcher** [1]
The dishwasher's not working. Le lave-vaisselle ne marche pas.
• **to work out**
1 *(to exercise)* **s'entraîner** [1]
2 *(to succeed)* **marcher** [1]
• **to work something out**
1 *(the cost, a sum)* **calculer** [1] **quelque chose**
2 *(to find)* **trouver** [1] **quelque chose**
We'll work out how to get there. On va trouver un moyen d'y aller.
3 *(to understand)* **comprendre** [64] **quelque chose**
I'm trying to work out how he did it. J'essaie de comprendre comment il l'a fait.

ᵖ **work** NOUN ▸ SEE **work** VERB
le **travail** MASC *(PL les travaux)*
I've got some work to do. J'ai du travail à faire.
That was a good piece of work. C'était un bon travail.
Mum's at work. Maman est au travail.

workbook NOUN
le **cahier de travail** MASC

worked up ADJECTIVE
to get worked up **s'énerver** [1]

worker NOUN
1 *(in general)* le **travailleur** MASC, la **travailleuse** FEM
2 *(in a factory)* un **ouvrier** MASC, une **ouvrière** FEM

ᵖ **work experience** NOUN
to do work experience **faire** [10] **un stage**
I did two weeks' work experience in an office. J'ai fait un stage de deux semaines dans un bureau.

working-class ADJECTIVE
ouvrier MASC, **ouvrière** FEM

working conditions PLURAL NOUN
les **conditions de travail** FEM PLURAL

worksheet NOUN
la **fiche de travail** FEM

workstation NOUN
le **poste de travail** *(PL les postes de travail)*

world NOUN
le **monde** MASC
the best team in the world la meilleure équipe du monde

World Cup NOUN
the World Cup la Coupe du Monde

world war NOUN
la **guerre mondiale**
the Second World War la Seconde Guerre mondiale

worm NOUN
le **ver** MASC

worn out ADJECTIVE
1 *(person)* **épuisé** MASC, **épuisée** FEM
2 *(clothes, shoes)* **complètement usé** MASC, **complètement usée** FEM

ᵖ **worried** ADJECTIVE
inquiet MASC, **inquiète** FEM
She looks worried. Elle a l'air inquiète.
to be worried **s'inquiéter** [24]
They're worried. Ils s'inquiètent.
We're worried about Susan. Nous nous inquiétons pour Susan.

ᵖ **to worry** VERB
s'inquiéter [24]
Don't worry! Ne t'inquiète pas!
There's nothing to worry about. Il n'y a pas de quoi s'inquiéter.

ᵖ **worse** ADJECTIVE, ADVERB
1 *(showing worsening)* **pire**
even worse encore pire
to get worse **empirer** [1]
The weather's getting worse. Le temps empire.
2 *(in comparisons)* **He's worse at English than French.** Il est pire en anglais qu'en français.
You're worse than he is! Tu es pire que lui!
It's worse than before. C'est pire qu'avant.
3 *(less ill)* **to feel worse** **se sentir** ⓢ [58] **plus malade**
I feel worse. Je me sens plus malade.

worst ADJECTIVE, ADVERB
1 *(with nouns)* **the worst** le plus mauvais MASC, la plus mauvaise FEM
the worst day of my life la journée la plus mauvaise de ma vie
It's the worst film I've ever seen. C'est le film le plus mauvais que j'aie jamais vu.
if the worst comes to the worst au pire
2 *(with verbs)* **He plays the worst.** Il joue la plus mal.

worth ADJECTIVE
1 **to be worth something** **valoir** [80] **quelque chose**
How much is it worth? Ça vaut combien?
It's worth a lot of money. Ça vaut beaucoup d'argent.
2 **to be worth doing something** **valoir** [80] **la peine de faire quelque chose**

ⓢ **means the verb takes** être **to form the perfect**

It's worth doing it. Ça vaut la peine de le faire.

ℐ **would** VERB

1 (to say what you'd like) **I would like an omelette.** Je voudrais une omelette.
I'd like to go to the cinema. J'aimerais aller au cinéma.
That would be a good idea. Ce serait une bonne idée.
If we asked her, she would help us. Elle nous aiderait, si nous le lui demandions.

2 (to make offers and requests) **Would you like something to eat?** Voulez-vous quelque chose à manger?
Would you like to come too? Veux-tu venir aussi?
Would you give me a hand? Tu veux me donner un coup de main?

3 (to show refusal) **He wouldn't answer.** Il n'a pas voulu répondre.
The car wouldn't start. La voiture n'a pas voulu démarrer.

to **wound** VERB ▸ SEE **wound** NOUN
blesser [1]
seriously wounded grièvement blessé

wound NOUN ▸ SEE **wound** VERB
la **blessure** FEM

to **wrap** VERB
emballer [1]

wrapping paper NOUN
le **papier cadeau**

to **wreck** VERB
1 (a building, a car, a train) **détruire** [26]
2 (a plan, an occasion) **gâcher** [1]

wrestler NOUN
le **catcheur** MASC, la **catcheuse** FEM

wrestling NOUN
le **catch** MASC

wrist NOUN
le **poignet** MASC

ℐ to **write** VERB
écrire [38]
She's writing her essay. Elle est en train d'écrire sa rédaction.
to write somebody a letter écrire une lettre à quelqu'un
I'll write them a letter. Je leur écrirai une lettre.
to write to somebody écrire à quelqu'un
I wrote to Jean yesterday. J'ai écrit à Jean hier.
to write to each other s'écrire
We write to each other regularly. On s'écrit régulièrement.

• **to write something down**
noter [1] quelque chose

writer NOUN
un **écrivain** MASC

ℐ **wrong** ADJECTIVE
1 (not correct) **mauvais** MASC, **mauvaise** FEM
the wrong answer la mauvaise réponse
It's the wrong address. Ce n'est pas la bonne adresse.
to go the wrong way se tromper [1] de chemin
I went the wrong way. Je me suis trompé de chemin.
Did you take the wrong bus? Tu t'es trompé de bus?
You've got the wrong number. Vous vous êtes trompé de numéro.

2 (mistaken) **to be wrong** se tromper [1]
I was wrong. Je me suis trompé.
They were wrong. Ils se sont trompés.

3 (against the rules) **What's wrong?** Qu'est-ce qu'il y a?
There's nothing wrong. Il n'y a rien.

4 (false) **faux** MASC, **fausse** FEM
The information was wrong. Les renseignements étaient faux.

Xx

xerox® NOUN ▸ SEE **xerox®** VERB
la **photocopie** FEM

to **xerox®** VERB ▸ SEE **xerox®** NOUN
photocopier [1]

Xmas NOUN
Noël

ℐ **X-ray** NOUN ▸ SEE **X-ray** VERB
la **radio** FEM
I saw the X-rays. J'ai vu les radios.

to **X-ray** VERB ▸ SEE **X-ray** NOUN
faire [10] une radio de (part of the body)
They X-rayed her ankle. Ils ont fait une radio de sa cheville.

Yy

yacht NOUN
1 (sailing boat) le **voilier** MASC
2 (large luxury boat) le **yacht** MASC

to **yawn** VERB
bâiller [1]
I can't stop yawning. Je n'arrête pas de bâiller.

℗ **year** NOUN

1 un **an** MASC
six years ago il y a six ans
I've known them for almost two years. Je les connais depuis presque deux ans.

2 *(the whole period)* une **année** FEM
the whole year toute l'année
She spends part of the year in France. Elle passe une partie de l'année en France.
They lived in Moscow for years. Ils ont habité Moscou pendant des années.

3 *(in the school system)* **I'm in Year 9.** Je suis en quatrième.
I'm in Year 10. Je suis en troisième.

4 *(for someone's age)* un **an** MASC
a two-year-old child un enfant de deux ans
I'm fifteen years old. J'ai quinze ans.

WORD TIP Always use ans in French even when in English you say your age without 'years' e.g. **I'm fifteen.**

> **YEAR**
>
> French pupils start secondary school in la sixième (Year 7) and progress through la cinquième (Year 8), la quatrième (Year 9) to la troisième (Year 10). Then they change to a lycée for three years: la seconde, la première and la terminale.

yearly ADJECTIVE
annuel MASC, **annuelle** FEM
a yearly event un événement annuel

to **yell** VERB
hurler [1]
You don't have to yell. Tu n'es pas obligé de hurler.

℗ **yellow** ADJECTIVE

jaune MASC & FEM
She's wearing yellow socks. Elle porte des chaussettes jaunes.

℗ **yes** ADVERB

1 *(in general)* **oui**
Yes, I know. Oui, je sais.
'Is Sam in his room?' — 'Yes, he is.' 'Est-ce que Sam est dans sa chambre?' — 'Oui.'

2 *(when ne pas is used in a question)* **si**
'You don't want to go, do you?' — 'Yes, I do!' 'Tu ne veux pas y aller, n'est-ce pas?' — 'Mais si!'
'You haven't finished, have you?' — 'Yes, I have.' 'Tu n'as pas fini?' — 'Si si.'

℗ **yesterday** ADVERB

hier
yesterday morning hier matin
yesterday afternoon hier après-midi
the day before yesterday avant-hier
I saw her yesterday. Je l'ai vue hier.

℗ **yet** ADVERB

not yet pas encore
It's not ready yet. Ce n'est pas encore prêt.
I haven't finished yet. Je n'ai pas encore fini.

yoga NOUN
le yoga MASC

℗ **yoghurt** NOUN

le yaourt MASC
a banana yoghurt un yaourt à la banane

yolk NOUN
le jaune d'œuf (PL **les jaunes d'œuf**)

℗ **you** PRONOUN

1 *(informal form as a subject)* **tu**
You look happy. Tu as l'air content.
Do you want to go to the cinema? Tu veux aller au cinéma?

2 *(as an object)* **te**
I'll lend you my bike. Je te prêterai mon vélo.
I'll write to you. Je t'écrirai.
I've invited you. Je t'ai invité.

WORD TIP tu becomes t' before a a, e, i, o, u or silent h.

3 *(after prepositions like avec, sans)* **toi**
I'll go with you. J'irai avec toi.
Did they leave without you? Est-ce qu'ils sont partis sans toi?
I'm buying it for you. Je l'achète pour toi.

4 *(in comparisons)* **toi**
He's older than you. Il est plus âgé que toi.
She's not as nice as you. Elle n'est pas aussi sympa que toi.

5 *(polite form: singular & plural)* **vous**
You're very kind. Vous êtes très gentil.
Can you tell me where the station is, please? Est-ce que vous pouvez m'indiquer la gare, s'il vous plaît?
I can't help you, I'm sorry. Je ne peux pas vous aider, je suis désolé.
It's a present for you. C'est un cadeau pour vous.
They're older than you. Ils sont plus âgés que vous.

6 *(to more than one person)* **vous**
I'll invite you all! Je vous inviterai tous!
Are you coming? You too? Vous venez? Vous aussi?

℗ **young** ADJECTIVE

jeune MASC & FEM
a young woman une jeune femme
She's the youngest in the class. C'est elle la plus jeune de la classe.
Tim's younger than me. Tim est plus jeune que moi.
Hannah's two years younger than me.

⌂ means the verb takes être to form the perfect

Hannah a deux ans de moins que moi.
a young man un jeune
young people les jeunes

𝒫 **your** ADJECTIVE
1 (informal form: masc singular nouns) **ton**
   your father ton père
   your number ton numéro
2 (informal form: fem singular nouns) **ta**
   your sister ta sœur
   your skirt ta jupe
   What's your address? Quel est ton adresse?

> **WORD TIP** Use ton with nouns beginning with a, e, i, o, u or silent h.

3 (informal form: masc & fem plural nouns) **tes**
   your cousins tes cousins
   your friends tes amis
4 (formal form or to several people: masc & fem singular nouns) **votre**
   your garden votre jardin
   Thank you for your hospitality. Merci pour votre hospitalité.
5 (formal form or to several people: masc & fem plural nouns) **vos**
   your children vos enfants
   You can all bring your friends. Vous pouvez tous amener vos amis.

yours PRONOUN
1 (informal form: masc singular nouns) **le tien**
   My brother's younger than yours. Mon frère est plus jeune que le tien.
2 (informal form: fem singular nouns) **la tienne**
   I've got his address but not yours. J'ai son adresse mais pas la tienne.
3 (informal form: masc plural nouns) **les tiens**
   There are my books. Where are yours? Voilà mes livres. Où sont les tiens?
4 (informal form: fem plural nouns) **les tiennes**
   I don't like her photos, I prefer yours. Je n'aime pas ses photos, je préfère les tiennes.
5 (formal form or to several people: masc singular nouns) **le vôtre**
   My son is younger than yours. Mon fils est plus jeune que le vôtre.
6 (formal form or to several people: fem singular nouns) **la vôtre**
   My daughter is younger than yours. Ma fille est plus jeune que la vôtre.
7 (formal form or to several people: masc & fem plural nouns) **les vôtres**
   My children are younger than yours. Mes enfants sont plus jeunes que les vôtres.
8 (belonging to you: informal) **à toi**
   Is this pen yours? Est-ce que ce stylo est à toi?

9 (belonging to you: formal or with several people) **à vous**
   Is this car yours? Est-ce que cette voiture est à vous?
10 (in letter endings) **Yours, Cordialement.** (informal)
   Yours sincerely, Veuillez agréer l'expression de mes sentiments distingués. (formal)

𝒫 **yourself** PRONOUN
1 (in reflexive verbs: informal) **te**
   You'll hurt yourself. Tu vas te faire mal.
2 (in reflexive verbs: formal) **vous**
   Are you enjoying yourself? Est-ce que vous vous amusez?
3 (for emphasis: informal) **toi-même**
   Did you do it yourself? Est-ce que tu l'as fait toi-même?
4 (for emphasis: formal) **vous-même**
   You said it yourself. Vous l'avez dit vous-même.
5 **all by yourself** tout seul
   Amy, did you do it all by yourself? Amy, tu l'as fait toute seule?

yourselves PRONOUN
1 (in reflexive verbs) **vous**
   Help yourselves. Servez-vous.
   You can amuse yourselves. Vous pouvez vous amuser.
2 (for emphasis) **vous-mêmes**
   Did you do it yourselves? Est-ce que vous l'avez fait vous-mêmes?

youth NOUN
1 (being young) la **jeunesse** FEM
   He travelled a lot in his youth. Il a beaucoup voyagé dans sa jeunesse.
2 (young people) les **jeunes** MASC & FEM PL
   today's youth les jeunes d'aujourd'hui
3 (male teenager) le **jeune** MASC
   a group of youths un groupe de jeunes
• **youth club**
   le club de jeunes
• **youth culture**
   la culture des jeunes
• **youth hostel**
   une auberge de jeunesse (PL les **auberges de jeunesse**)
• **youth worker**
   un éducateur, une éducatrice

Yugoslavia NOUN
   la **Yougoslavie** FEM
   the former Yugoslavia l'ex-Yougoslavie

A B C D E F G H I J K L M N O P Q R S T U V W X Y Z

ENGLISH—FRENCH

Zz

zany ADJECTIVE
loufoque MASC & FEM

zebra NOUN
le zèbre MASC
• zebra crossing
le passage pour piétons

zero NOUN
le zéro MASC

to **zigzag** VERB
zigzaguer [1]

zip NOUN
la fermeture éclair®

zodiac NOUN
le zodiaque MASC
the signs of the zodiac les signes du
zodiaque

zone NOUN
la zone FEM
the Euro zone la zone euro

zoo NOUN
le zoo MASC

zoom lens NOUN
le zoom MASC

A
B
C
D
E
F
G
H
I
J
K
L
M
N
O
P
Q
R
S
T
U
V
W
X
Y
Z

⊙ **means the verb takes être to form the perfect**